The Celebrity Culture Reader

The Celebrity Culture Reader investigates the cultural implications of celebrity through a definitive collection of the best writing on this complex contemporary phenomenon.

The Celebrity Culture Reader is introduced and organized into the following thematic sections, each with an introduction by the editor:

- Celebrity and modernity: the historical pattern of celebrity
- The textual and the extra-textual dimensions of the public persona
- Ascribed celebrity: the transformed public sphere
- Transgression: scandal, notoriety and infamy
- Narcissism, fandom and the will to celebrity
- The celebrity industry: the management of fame.

From the new celebrity culture that has emerged from reality television and the Internet to the paparazzi-filled endgame of Princess Diana and the bizarre trials and tribulations of Michael Jackson, *The Celebrity Culture Reader* documents the significant role that celebrities occupy in contemporary culture.

Contributors: Francesco Alberoni; David L. Andrews; Frances Bonner; Daniel Boorstin; Leo Braudy; C. L. Cole; Rosemary Coombe; Richard de Cordova; Kathy Davis; Richard Dyer; Charles Fairchild; Neal Gabler; Joshua Gamson; David Giles; Lawrence Grossberg; Alison Hearn; Joke Hermes; Stephen Hinerman; Richard Johnson; Barry King; Elizabeth Arveda Kissling; John Langer; Leo Lowenthal; Catharine Lumby; P. David Marshall; Kembrew McLeod; Joe Moran; Momin Rahman; Chris Rojek; Richard Sennett; Jackie Stacey; Ernest Sternberg; John Street; Richard Tithecott; Graeme Turner; Max Weber; Jeffrey J. Williams.

P. David Marshall is Professor and Chair of the Department of Communication Studies at Northeastern University. He is the author of *Celebrity and Power* (1997) and *New Media Cultures* (2004), and the co-author of *Fame Games* (2000) and *Web Theory* (2003).

The
Celebrity
Culture
Reader

Edited by

P. David Marshall

Routledge
Taylor & Francis Group

NEW YORK AND LONDON

First published 2006
by Routledge
270 Madison Ave, New York, NY 10016

Simultaneously published
by Routledge
2 Park Square, Milton Park, Abingdon, Oxon OX14 4RN

Routledge is an imprint of the Taylor & Francis Group, an informa business

Typeset in Perpetua by
RefineCatch Limited, Bungay, Suffolk
Printed and bound in Great Britain by
The Cromwell Press, Trowbridge, Wiltshire

Library of Congress Cataloging-in-Publication Data
The celebrity culture reader / edited by P. David Marshall.
    p. cm.
    Includes bibliographical references and index.
    1. Civilization, Modern.   2. Popular culture.   3. Celebrities.   4. United States—
Civilization.   5. Popular culture—United States.   6. Celebrities—United States.
7. Fame—Social aspects—United States.
    CB358.C45 2006
    909.82—dc22   2006033283

British Library Cataloguing in Publication Data
A catalogue record for this book is available from the British Library

ISBN 10: 0–415–33791–7 (hbk)
ISBN 10: 0–415–33792–5 (pbk)

ISBN 13: 978–0–415–33791–5 (hbk)
ISBN 13: 978–0–415–33792–2 (pbk)

Contents

Acknowledgements

A book such as this has had many helping hands building its content over the years and I am not referring to the many pampered celebrities exposed to analysis as you leaf through the contents. There are many collaborators who helped me bind ideas and content into a completed and – I hope – coherent work. I would like to thank the editors at Routledge for their long and unflagging support for the project over the years – in particular Rebecca Barden, Natalie Foster, and Aileen Storry. Julene Knox worked very hard on getting the copyright permissions for many of the selections in the book.

As I developed my thinking about how to organize and develop the *Celebrity Culture Reader*, I have relied on some key people who have provided very useful guidance. Graeme Turner, Catharine Lumby, Rebecca Barden (again!), Louise McBryde, and Saeko Ishita immediately come to mind. I would also like to thank my colleagues at Northeastern University – most notably Joanne Morreale, Murray Forman, Alan Zaremba, and Vincent Rocchio – who have been very supportive and generous in their thoughts about celebrity culture as the book developed. I have also been assisted by Angela Chin and Meaghan Sinclair who have helped in the organization of the text. The following students have also aided the completion of the *Celebrity Culture Reader*: Jessica Volpy, William Danforth, Cristina Caldero, Karen Corson, and Sophia Bielenberg. I also want to mention that elements of this book also took shape in organizing the Persona series of panels for the Cultural Studies Association (US) conference in 2004, editing the 2004 *Fame* issue of the online journal *M/C*, and presenting at the Celebrity Culture conference in Ayr, Scotland in 2005: I want to thank the organizers and editors for those opportunities to trial ideas and hear others address the complexities of celebrity culture.

And I would like to thank my family for enduring another period of juggling schedules and an entity whose piecing together never was as simple as it originally appeared in my originally elegant outline. Louise, Hannah, Zak, and Erin – I hope you think that this outcome was worth your patience and help!

Permissions

Lowenthal, Leo (1961) "The Triumph of Mass Idols". *Literature, Popular Culture and Society*. Reproduced by kind permission of Susanne H. Lowenthal.

Dyer, Richard (1979) *Stars*. London: BFI 1979, 1990, pp. 38–65. Reproduced by permission of BFI Publishing.

Langer, John (1981) "Television's 'Personality System'." *Media, Culture & Society*, 4, © Sage Publications 1981. Reproduced by permission of Sage Publications Ltd.

Marshall, P. David (1997) *Celebrity and Power*. Minneapolis, Minn.: University of Minnesota Press. © 1997 by the Regents of the University of Minnesota. Reproduced with permission of the University of Minnesota Press.

Rahman, Momin (2004) "Is Straight the new Queer? David Beckham and the Dialectics of Celebrity". From *m/c- a journal of media and culture*. Online. <http://journal.media-culture.org.au/0411/15-rahman.php>. First published in the *Fame* issue of *M/C Journal* <http://journal.media-culture.org.au>), November 2004.

King, Barry (1991) "Articulating Stardom". In Christine Gledhill (ed.) *Stardom: Industry of Desire*. London: Routledge. Reproduced by kind permission of *Screen* and the author.

Stacey, Jackie (1994) "Feminine Fascinations: A Question of Identification". From Jackie Stacey, *Star Gazing: Hollywood Cinema and Female Spectatorship*, London: Routledge. Reproduced by kind permission of the publisher and author.

Fairchild, Charles (2004) "Australian Idol and the Attention Economy". From *m/c- a journal of media and culture*. Online. <http://journal.media-culture.org.au/0411/09-fairchild.php>. First published in the *Fame* issue of *M/C Journal* (<http://journal.media-culture.org.au>), November 2004.

Hermes, Joke (1995) "Reading Gossip Magazines: The Imagined Communities of 'Gossip' and 'Camp' ". In Hermes, Joke and Johnson, K. *Reading Women's Magazines: An Analysis of Everyday Media Use*. Cambridge: Polity Press, pp. 118–142. Reproduced by permission of Polity Press.

Marshall, P. David (2005) "Intimately Intertwined in the Most Public Way: Celebrity and Journalism". In Stuart Allen (ed.) *Journalism: Critical Issues*. Maidenhead: Open University Press, pp. 19–29.

Moran, Joe (2000) *Star Authors: Literary Celebrity in America*. London: Pluto Press, pp. 35–57. Reprinted by permission of Pluto Press.

Cole, C. L. and Andrews, David L. (2001) "America's New Son: Tiger Woods and America's Multiculturalism". In David L. Andrews and D.L. Jackson (eds) *Sport Stars: The Cultural Politics of Sporting Celebrity*. London: Routledge. Reproduced by kind permission of the publisher.

John Street (2003) "The Celebrity Politician: Political Style and Popular Culture". In John Corner and Dick Pels (eds) *Media and the Restyling of Politics*. London and Thousand Oaks, Calif.: Sage, pp. 85–98. Reprinted by permission of Sage Publications Ltd.

Jeffrey J. Williams (2001) "Name Recognition". *The Minnesota Review*, numbers 52–54, fall. Reproduced by kind permission of the editor of *The Minnesota Review*.

Rojek, Chris (2001) "Celebrity and Religion". In Chris Rojek, *Celebrity*. London: Reaktion Press, pp. 51–68. Reprinted by permission of Reaktion Books.

Sternberg, Ernest (1998) "Phantasmagoric Labor: The New Economies of Self-Presentation". In *Futures*. Vol. 30, No. 1, pp. 3–28. Reproduced by permission of Elsevier.

Tithecott, Richard (1997) *Of Men and Monsters*. Milwaukee, Wisc.: University of Wisconsin Press. © 1997. Reprinted by permission of The University of Wisconsin Press.

Heinerman, Stephen (1999) "(Don't) Leave Me Alone: Tabloid Narrative and the Michael Jackson Child-Abuse Scandal". In James Lull and Stephen Hinerman (eds) *Media Scandals*. New York: Columbia University Press. © 1999 Columbia University Press. Reprinted with permission of the publisher.

Giles, David (2000) *Illusions of Immortality: A Psychology of Fame and Celebrity*. New York: St. Martin's Press, Macmillan Press: London, pp. 33–53. Reproduced by permission of Palgrave Macmillan.

Turner, Graeme (2004) "Celebrity, the Tabloid and the Public Sphere". In Graeme Turner, *Understanding Celebrity*. Thousand Oaks, Calif.: Sage. © Sage Publications 2004. Reproduced by permission of Sage Publications Ltd and the author.

Marshall, P. David (1999) "The Celebrity Legacy of the Beatles". In Ian Inglis (ed.) *The Beatles, Popular Music and Society*. Basingstoke: Macmillan, pp. 163–175. Reproduced by permission of Palgrave Macmillan.

Johnson, Richard (1999) "Exemplary Differences: Mourning (and Not Mourning) a Princess". In A. Kear and D. L. Steinberg (eds) *Mourning Diana: Nation, Culture and the Performance of Grief*. London and New York: Routledge. Reproduced by permission of the publisher.

Lumby, Catharine (1999) "Vanishing Point." In Catharine Lumby, *Gotcha: Life in a Tabloid World*. Sydney: Allen & Unwin, pp. 68–98. Reproduced by permission of Allan & Unwin Book Publishers.

Kissling, Elizabeth Arveda (1993) "I Don't Have a Great Body, But I Play One on TV: The Celebrity Guide to Fitness and Weight Loss in the United States". *Women's Studies in Communication*, Vol. 18, 2, Fall. Reproduced by permission of the journal editor.

Davis, Kathy (1995) "Beauty and the Female Body". From Kathy Davis, *Reshaping The Female Body: The Dilemma of Cosmetic Surgery*. London: Routledge. © 1995. Reproduced by kind permission of the author and Routledge/Taylor & Francis, PLC.

Grossberg, Lawrence (1992) "Is There a Fan in the House? The Affective Sensibility of Fandom". In Lisa Lewis (ed.) *Adoring Audience: Fan Culture and Popular Media*. London: Routledge. Reproduced by kind permission of the author and publisher.

Hinerman, Stephen (1992) " 'I'll Be There with You': Fans, Fantasy and the Figure of Elvis". In Lisa Lewis (ed.) *Adoring Audience: Fan Culture and Popular Media*. London: Routledge. Reproduced by kind permission of the author and publisher.

Rojek, Chris (2004) "The Psychology of Achieved Celebrity". In *Sinatra*. Cambridge: Polity Press, pp. 102–6; 112–20. Reproduced by permission of Polity Press.

Hearn, Allison (2006) "John, a 20-year-old Boston Native . . ." In *International Journal of Media and Cultural Politics*. Vol. 2, Issue 2.

Introduction

A USEFUL WAY TO THEORIZE about celebrity is along two axes – surface and depth. Celebrity provides a surface through which contemporary culture produces significance and a depth of investment in particular identities, moments, and personalities.

Surface (in the guise of depth)

In 2001, long before the moment of September 11, I was asked to speak on CNN to answer the question haunting America: "Are we a celebrity-obsessed culture?" By the structure of the interview that included three others who were journalists from *Vanity Fair, Time Magazine* and *Vogue* I was positioned as the resident academic that would provide the historical and conceptual background about celebrity for the other guests.

"Professor Marshall – when did this all begin? – surely we haven't always been this focused on celebrities?" asked Greta Van Susteren, the host of *The Point*.

I meandered for my 15 seconds and tried to explain that though there is a longer history of celebrity it had intensified in recent years. They then went back to the funnier journalists who were able to talk gently around our celebrity world as a presage to the upcoming Academy Awards. The interview ended and I was chauffeured back to my Boston apartment, which was by far the most pleasant part of the experience. Although I had been interviewed by the media many times before this event, and have been many times subsequent to this, it was this particular interview that I have returned to for understanding celebrity culture. Part of its allure was my apparent failure in the American media system to play my role or, more accurately, to participate in the production of significance. On another level, I was intrigued how a news program found it comfortable to talk about celebrities but not really deal with their role in contemporary culture in a substantive way. The interview was classic surface without any depth. Even though the entire piece lasted almost 10 minutes it played celebrity rather than analyze its meaning. In fact, talking about celebrities on a news commentary program was exactly about not getting too serious. This was meant to be a fluff piece that bookended a week of high-school shootings and other intense social and political debates.

Depth (disguised as surface)

On March 11, 2005 the *New York Times*, on its front page and inner page follow-up story, reported the trial of Michael Jackson for kidnapping and pedophilia. This was by no means the first time the trial was part of the paper's news section, but its movement to the front page was prompted by the dramatic photo of Michael Jackson dressed in pajama pants and a suit jacket assisted by his father as he arrived danger-ously late for the day's proceedings. Apparently Jackson had fallen and hurt his back, which delayed his arrival; the judge gave Jackson an hour before his bail would be revoked. Jackson arrived 14 minutes past the hour deadline. The judge, at the end of the day's testimony, did not invoke his threat of putting Michael Jackson in jail for the rest of the trial.

All news outlets have covered the minutiae of Jackson's trial. Court TV employed actors to reenact the day's proceedings. The trial has provided lurid testimony from the boys who have accused Michael Jackson of the crimes as well as classic moments for depicting the ethereal Jackson. The detail of coverage is both normal and extra-ordinary. Like other celebrity trials, from Robert Blake and Winona Ryder to O. J. Simpson and Sean (Puff Daddy/P. Diddy) Coombs, the Jackson days in court have been subjected to the greatest amount of scrutiny from the papers to the magazines, from the talk shows and news channels to the comedy chat shows and entertainment. Surrounding the event was speculation upon speculation, but ultimately at its very centre was some discussion of what has brought Michael Jackson such intense cover-age. Whether it was the television coverage of the "dangling baby" moment (where Jackson held his infant child over a hotel balcony) or whether it was further supportive evidence of molestation in his Neverland ranch, Jackson's individuality was micro-scopically examined. Can the celebrity be above the law, above morality, or do these trials ritualistically provide the cultural circumscription of Jackson's alleged idio-syncrasies? The in-depth coverage makes the original claim to fame – where Jackson was the self-proclaimed King of Pop – recede into a pivotal back-story narrative. Jackson's fame has become increasingly organized around his abnormalities and less about his qualities as a performer or an artist.

This depth of coverage is significant in a number of ways. Celebrities are part of a very elaborate media economy which is connected to audiences and value. When there is saturation coverage as we have seen in the case of Jackson – but also that which defined the coverage of the death of Pope John Paul II in 2005 and, in turn, was reminiscent of the death of Diana in 1997 – it is a recognition of cultural value.

The major media industries are constantly looking for elements that interpellate their increasingly dispersed audiences. Jackson as a persona is believed to capture that level of connection to an audience that transcends categories such as musical taste to something larger and more significant. The television industry thus allows Jackson to enter as a news category that is transcendent – once again as we have seen with Diana and Pope John Paul II – and thus Jackson is used as a powerful brand identity that is deployed by television networks, magazines, and newspapers. Celebrities and celebrity events of this order, then, are unifying forces in terms of coverage which work to make media momentarily resemble each other to produce a cultural moment. Celebrities thus *interpellate or hail* national and international audiences in the way only presidents, royalty, and prime ministers can hope to achieve. The saturation coverage, which appears to be unique to the individual persona, is in fact serialized into a pattern where the dispersed media industries occasionally agree on a particular event/personality.

Second, the saturation coverage of the Jackson trial also reveals the place of celebrities in a key trope of contemporary culture: The source of the self and identity. Celebrities serve as the lingua franca of identity and, in some cases, identity politics in the contemporary scene. The invasive lenses of television and magazine paparazzi provide us with what appears to be the minutiae of celebrity lives. In that pervasive coverage or potential coverage, the media produce a "reality-effect" which is alluring if not intoxicating to an audience: It appears that we are discovering the "real" star, in Richard Dyer's terminology (Dyer 1979), every time we see a glimpse of the star out of their constructed world in sport, film, television, or popular music. Jackson, through his trial, has exited his managed space and moved into the differently mediated space that produces this reality-effect. It is an exegesis that rivals theology: we are offered the chance to see what Jackson is *really* like, an identity revealed the way theologians and fundamentalist Christians might believe that God's desires and intentions are uncovered through the biblical scriptures – the images and scenes are there for the audience to work on and interpret what is uncovered through the day's events. As much as the audience-watch via the media is an elaborate exegesis of the celebrity, it also resonates with notions of identity that have emerged from a century of psychoanalytical inquiry. The "texts" that surround the celebrity are the source material for determining what is exhibited and what is repressed by the individual celebrity. The audience member becomes the analyst from the images, interviews, biographies, and actual productions they have been involved with in making sense of the star.

Identity, individuality, and the self are explored through these readings of celebrities. In some instances the texts are sensational in their subject matter and challenge our norms of behavior, as Michael Jackson has done in his 2005 trial and acquittal. Magazines work to uncover the salacious rumors and use paparazzi to reveal the unguarded self. In other instances, magazines and entertainment media reports are designed to present the celebrity in the most positive light in fawning interviews that are highly structured by the star and his/her management. In either case, the audience continues to interpret the meaning of the celebrity in a grand narrative on the dimensions of individuality and identity in contemporary culture where comparisons between the self and the celebrity are continuously made and cultural norms are supported, altered, or dismantled.

Making sense of celebrity culture: Oddly central to contemporary experience

The boundaries of this elaborate discourse on and about celebrities are very permeable precisely because celebrities articulate identity and individuality. Individuality represents one of the essential components in the structure of consumer culture as well as the aspirational qualities of democratic culture. Celebrities are hyper-versions that express the potential and possibilities of the individual under the rubrics of capitalist democracy (Marshall 1997).

Yet within those layers of texts and discourses about celebrity, there is also a clear and loudly hailed sentiment that our attention to celebrity is misguided. Although following celebrities does not carry the censorious weight that watching pornography sustains, it nonetheless is seen as drawing us away from more serious forms of news and events. At supermarket checkout counters, the covers of the various tabloids and magazines with their celebrity exposés draw our often furtive glances to determine the latest scandal, marriage, or promotional profile. Actually buying a celebrity-oriented magazine could be classed as a guilty pleasure that may be seen as betraying a lack of seriousness.

Nonetheless, the most mainstream news media more than cater to our desires to see the celebrated. In the summer of 2005, as much as the war in Iraq, the threatening potential of North Korea, the nomination of Supreme Court justices, the gulag of Guantanamo Bay, the bombings in the London Underground and the G8 summit were some of the major stories, they vied for coverage with the transformed Tom Cruise and his declarations of love and marriage to Katie Holmes, Angelina Jolie's and Brad Pitt's new romance at the cost of a marriage to Jennifer Aniston, Colin Farrell's sex video, and Live8's efforts to use music celebrity to encourage the G8 to focus on African aid and globalization.

One could argue that these political and celebrity spheres are quite discontinuous; in other words, both media producers and readers separate real political news from celebrity material. Perhaps the focus on celebrity is a form of escape from the pressing issues of the day, in the way that film was often analyzed as escapist during the twentieth century's Great Depression and World War II. However, this form of analysis leads one to overlook how celebrity represents an intensifying and proliferating discourse over the course of the twentieth century, one that not only populates entertainment magazines, but is also an essential component of the production of newspapers, newsmagazines, web-based news sites and blogs, television news, and television entertainment channels (which are sometimes devoted entirely to celebrity coverage). It has also become clear that celebrity style of coverage and presentation is very much a component of contemporary politics. Bill Clinton's intern sex scandal paralleled those of Hollywood in the late 1990s and served to link the political to the entertainment discourses on the individual. The 2005 Live8, organized by Bob

Geldolf with participation from key popular music figures such as Bono of U2, also acknowledged the continuity between the political and the entertainment spheres.

This blending and blurring of what constitutes celebrity and entertainment and what constitutes politics and news identifies not only the significant depth of investment in meaning that individuals such as Michael Jackson might engender in the culture, but also how news itself has shifted its focus, shifted its organization of issues and concerns to a new kinds of political discourse. Celebrity coverage thus could be described as an intricate feminization of the news, where soft news becomes more central to the news experience and new social and political issues emerge from its often scandalous content. Celebrity coverage also identifies the way that contemporary culture uses the individual to focus attention: Celebrity becomes the lens through which we understand a variety of issues, disciplines, and concerns. Nature, science, and wildlife are translated through the gonzo celebrity crocodile hunter Steve Irwin, the chastising David Suzuki, or the exuberant David Attenborough. Network television news anchors, although less powerful than 20 years ago, become celebrity journalists and are positioned to provide a familiar channel for understanding the day's events. Even the legal profession has its celebrity lawyers who, like Johnnie Cochrane, handle the most high-profile cases or, like Alan Dershowitz, are media icons representing legal opinion on television programs.

As the celebration and elevation of individuals into the media system has expanded, there has been a correlated support industry that has grown rapidly to manage these public entities. Politicians are now surrounded by support staff who are working on all the elements of administering their public presentation. In the 2004 American presidential election, there were teams of assistants who coached and advised the party candidates as they prepared for their televised debates. In Massachusetts, the Governor Mitt Romney has an "operations" staff of fourteen to handle the logistics of media events and public appearances for the telegenic and presidential-hopeful governor in 2008.

Historically, the entertainment industry has always had a large staff handling the public image of their stars. Hollywood's film industry in the mid-century "studio" era not only handled fan mail, but also managed the public appearances of their stars. In the breakdown of the studio system where stars operated as free agents, new layers of representation have been placed on the industry. Most major film stars work with a coterie of support – from their agents to their managers and publicists. These forms of publicity are placed along with the industry's publicity and promotion staff for particular films. At times, the organization of publicity for a major star is an orchestration of the film studio; at other times it is done by the celebrity's own team. Tom Cruise's apparent change in personality and accessibility in 2004 has been attributed to his change in publicists. Long-time Cruise publicist Pat Kingsley was replaced by Cruise's older sister Lee Anne DeVette, and what has transpired is what *Advertising Age* described as a "publicity glasnost"(Creamer and Ives, 2005). Cruise is no longer tightly controlled but has allowed himself to appear everywhere with much more verve and, for some, bizarre and inexplicable behavior.

Celebrities like Cruise are treated by the larger media industry as brands to sell and market films, television programs, and magazines. Branding public identity is a clear translation of a personality into a commodity that is brokered and exchanged throughout the extended entertainment industry. The celebrity brand can be used for all sorts of purposes: Celebrities can be deployed for political support either for candidates (as Ben Affleck did for John Kerry's 2004 presidential bid) or issues (as we have seen in the Live8 attempts to shift public sentiment around poverty in Africa). Companies regularly attempt to link their products with particular celebrities. Michael Jackson's 1980s branding with Pepsi was designed to provide a synergy between cola and youth culture. Indeed, an entire agency called Marketing Evaluations is devoted to determining the relative value of celebrities for advertisers to deploy in their campaigns. One of its sub-departments is determining the relative value of dead celebrities: *Forbes Magazine* lists twenty-two dead celebrities as earning more than 5 million dollars in 2004, with Elvis still having an income of 40 million dollars (Heinemann 2005). Celebrity identity, then, is a form of intellectual property that is sometimes regularly updated or sustained over decades, if not centuries.

From an industrial as much as a cultural vantage point, celebrities are integral for understanding the contemporary moment. As phenomena, celebrities intersect with a remarkable array of political, cultural, and economic activities to a threshold point that it is worth identifying the operation of a *celebrity culture* embedded in national and transnational cultures. They serve as channels through which even the concept of globalization can be understood: Celebrities are entities that often internationalize entertainment, generalize expansively an expression of individuality and often presage the movement of other goods and services from continent to continent and nation to nation. Whether it is via sports celebrities such as Michael Jordan, Tiger Woods, or David Beckham, or entertainment celebrities such as Tom Cruise, Jennifer Lopez, or Jim Carrey, there is a massive movement of information, services, and goods that support the internationalization of personalities. Celebrity culture could be thought of as emblematic of a new form of ideological colonization in an era ostensibly post-colonial. Celebrities serve as embodiments of desires that are universalized as much as they mutate the organization of desires in particular cultures. Celebrity as culture can be seen as a particular lens through which we can investigate and understand contemporary culture. Celebrity culture produces a layer of discourse that allows us to explore the articulation of identity, individuality, value, and norms within particular cultures, as well as the movement of these articulations between cultures.

In this book, I have collected a diverse but interconnected group of writings that both identify and analyze celebrity culture. The approaches taken are drawn from different disciplines and have netted distinct readings of the phenomenon. There have been a few guiding principles in organizing this collection of readings. One of these is that when celebrity is explored directly, it is understood as a phenomenon that is specifically beyond stardom in its focus on the extra-textual dimensions of celebritydom. *The Celebrity Culture Reader* thus is a study of the interplay between the performance (the textual), which could be playing sports, singing at a concert, or acting in a film or television role, and the performance of everyday life (the extra-textual) of the public personality. These two layers produce the public personality and are dependent on a media system that reports their actions.

Grouping the various writings on celebrity could have been via particular media form or genre. However, this form of organization would have led to a great deal of repetition and would have overlooked the obvious pattern in celebrity that they transcend media and genre as they perform in their everyday lives. Moreover, celebrity culture relies on a particular reading of the public and the public sphere that is dependent on media and genres but is not defined by their practices. The structure of the book thus provides different paths through celebrity culture that generate some distinctive insights. I must admit that the very complexity of celebrity culture – its ubiquity and its ricocheting intersection with many professions and a multiplicity of practices – sometimes frustrated the attempts to edit "order" into its study. What the book attempts to do is provide refractions through the crystalline celebrity culture. The metaphor of the refracted paths through a crystal best describes the way that celebrity culture relies on media to transparently convey meanings but recognizes that the production of the meaning of celebrity is altered by these mediated representations and by the various audiences' interpretations of these images and texts.

I have divided the book into parts which each highlight some aspect of celebrity culture. Each of these parts opens with an introduction that provides a working vignette on its themes and contents. The book moves from Part One, which deals with the historical and classical analyses of celebrity texts to Part Two's study of the extra-textual nature of celebrity and then on to Part Three, which explores the extensions of the category of the celebrity into wider domains of contemporary public life. Part Four elaborates on the extra-textual nature of celebrity through a group of readings that address the notorious, the infamous, and the scandalous, tropes of celebrity gossip that both encircles its culture and invites the participation of the audience. The penultimate part addresses the audience and its narcissism in articles that deal with the "will to celebrity" that pervades the contemporary moment. The final part focuses on various studies of the industry that produces the celebrity and the myriad texts that support it as a system. What follows is a greater elaboration on the themes of each of the book's parts and a discussion of the authors and various articles contained therein.

Part One: Celebrity and modernity: The historical pattern of celebrity

The collection begins by providing a theoretical and historical road map to the emerging significance of celebrity culture. The section resonates with debating the relationship between the public and the persona and it works through this debate via some of the classical essays in the related fields that have informed reading celebrity. Richard Sennett's article positions the public in the persona in a short excerpt from his Habermasian doppelgänger *Fall of Public Man*. Habermas's contribution to understanding celebrity can be summarized in his distinction between representative public and public representativeness where there is the transformation from monarchical structures of representation into something connected to the bourgeois democratic public sphere (Habermas 1991: 5–15). Sennett's work, in its study of the nineteenth century and this particular transformation of staged public representation, betrays the reality that however much celebrity is wedded to democratic capitalism, it existed in some form since antiquity. Our own selective tradition of personalities, our perpetual elevation of some individuals to be visually identified and hailed above others, has ensured some individuals a celebrated past and present. Braudy's monumental work on fame, *Frenzy of Renown*, generated an intriguing study of Alexander the Great which helps our study of celebrity culture to at least claim nominally that it understands this longer dance of celebrity culture – albeit differently constituted.

Without necessarily using the terminology, the other articles in the opening part expand on the "modern" subjectivity that imbues the construction of the celebrity. Identity is at the core of celebrity culture, a culture that has expanded discursively and materially over the past century hand in hand with Freudian psychoanalysis's interpretation of the individual, the expansion in psychology, Jungian psychotherapy, and the equally important massive growth of the self-help publishing industry. From these discourses of self-analysis – or what Charles Taylor might describe as the sources of the self – we have the ingredients for the particular relationship between the individual and the hyper-individual (celebrity) in contemporary culture (Taylor 1989). Max Weber's elaborate study of the birth of bureaucracy contained in *Economy and Society* provides the most detailed excursus on charisma and the institutionalization of representative power as well as the way that charisma shifts our thinking from the rational to the irrational. Daniel J. Boorstin, from his classic text *The Image*, helps us to read the public personality from the proto-McLuhan perspective where media forms shift our constellation of influences and cultural significance. Contemporaneous to Boorstin's efforts, it must be remembered, were the iconic celebrity art installations of Andy Warhol, who quietly intoned the essence of the democratic ideology of fame and celebrity: "In the future everyone will be famous for 15 minutes," where the media spectacle which anoints the significance of the individual momentarily with its audio and visual gaze and its broadcasting dissemination. Leo Lowenthal, a sociologist with mid-twentieth-century roots firmly entwined with the Frankfurt School, isolates on a shift in twentieth-century journalism from celebrations of the exploitations of the captains of industry in America to the expanding entertainment industries. The triumph of mass idols exemplifies an approach to popular culture championed by key critical figures such as Theodor Adorno and Max Horkheimer: Mass culture serves to blind and deafen the masses through its forms of entertainment and its production of "pseudo-individuality" represented through its star system. Francesco Alberoni's sociological reading of the odd dyad of celebrity – the powerless – elite uncovers the instability of the celebrity system along with its persistent allure.

The field of film studies has perhaps provided the most concerted effort to make sense of the contemporary celebrity. As an industry, there is little question that film expanded the extra-textual dimension of the film star in the early part of the twentieth century. Richard de Cordova's absolutely seminal work on the transformation of the picture personality into the star outlines these discursive constructions that allowed the star to exit the screen and become public personality that ultimately became foundational to the film industry itself. Part One concludes with Richard Dyer's work on stardom in the 1970s and 1980s, which isolates beautifully on the extra-textual nature of stars as they become discursive enigmas for their audiences where the search for the authentic and real version of the screen image becomes a Sisyphean narrative of contemporary culture.

Part Two: The textual and extra-textual dimensions of the public persona

The study of celebrity is historically layered and it parallels the emergence and legitimation of others areas of intellectual inquiry. Film, for instance, gained a certain legitimacy of investigation in the 1950s and 1960s that led to a consideration of its star system, but also, perhaps more significantly of their directors as auteurs. Literary analysis had an even longer history through the biographical analysis of the author to help explain the significance of the text – a kind of exegetical move that celebrated the formation of original work. Other dimensions of popular culture – that is, in this instance, areas differentiated from film, classical and serious music, literature, and theatre that lacked the connection to what Bourdieu described as cultural capital (Bourdieu 1984) and allowed for their distinctive class-based value – were less closely analyzed until the 1970s and 1980s. To make sense of celebrity culture demanded a particular reading of the popular that was against the grain of any mid-twentieth-century mass culture critique of contemporary society. A particular convergence of intellectual inquiry emerged from the 1960s that actually made it possible to investigate the peculiar constitution of the celebrity. Via cultural studies and to a lesser degree French structuralist and post-structuralist thought, the popular became an object of study that revealed the structure of everyday life and the formation of political and cultural struggles. Cultural studies demanded a leveling of the textual terrain that produced our culture and gave entry into what Williams referred to as the "structure of feeling" for any cultural moment (Williams 1965: 64–88). This demanded a study of the proliferation of "texts" beyond their origins to investigate their transformation and use by audiences and cultural groups. Culture was made and remade through its uses and its rearticulation and a cultural studies inquiry needed to work from the text outwards to the many texts produced around the text. Blended into this mix was an Althusserian-inspired Gramsci-inflected Marxist approach to the organization of a culture economy, where cultural change was not entirely determined by the economic base and ideas (what we can read as cultural activity) could transform the culture. In terms of analysis, what is implied here is in fact the need to recognize the power of the economic system to determine culture *at the same time* as the possibility (however weak this is) that ideas may emerge that are used for different ends from this system. To make sense of celebrity culture inevitably leads us to a study of how an extended industry helps construct the celebrity as a text – what we could call the cultural economy of celebrity production – as well as how audiences transform, reform, and remake these texts and meanings.

The second section of the collection concentrates on how the celebrity is reliant on many texts in its movement through contemporary culture. To make sense of a celebrity, then, is not simply a study of the primary text – what perhaps a simple film-studies analysis of John Wayne and his roles in films produces is an overcoded star text – but rather the magazine profiles, the television interviews, the presentation of premieres, the many unplanned photos and stories about the celebrity's personal lives that populate the mediascape along with the fans' work on the celebrity and how they have re-presented the famed. Out of this combination of the presented textual and the extra-textual one can make sense of the celebrity and highly constructed subjectivity. For instance, John Langer's 1981 article isolates on how television is much less a cultural economy of producing stars but rather more about producing "personalities" which fit into the familial structure of television viewing. Langer's work is a particular political economy of celebrity and how it is structured into the exigencies of both production and, more particularly, reception of television. Working from a different perspective in this section is Barry King's elucidating piece on "Articulating Stardom" while still dealing with economic models of production works out how the individual star is a text that organizes production. I have included a chapter from my own book, *Celebrity and Power*, that tries to capture the intertextual duality that is required to comprehend the operation of celebrity in contemporary culture. Through a close study of New Kids on the Block (NKOTB), a pop group of the late 1980s and early 1990s, I work through the intricate production pattern that is fundamental to the music industry's production of stardom. To make sense of NKOTB requires a close study of industry efforts to construct their personas, other industry efforts to constrain their meaning as inauthentic pop music, and the core audience's close affective investment in their personas and their music. Charles Fairchild, in his brief study of the television program *Australian Idol*, makes us understand the public relations economic model that is organizing this televisual presentation of fame and how this model migrates through contemporary culture. Momin Rahman in his work on David Beckham makes it clear that audiences matter in the construction and rearticulation of fame and celebrity as Beckham's persona weaves between straight and queer for a new form of cultural capital.

Forms of identification by audiences translate the presented cultural economy of celebrities into quite different variations. Jackie Stacey's fascinating study of the varied connections fans have to film stars of the 1930s and 1940s allows us entry into the extra-textual dimensions of celebrity. Joke Hermes' foundational study of how women's magazines are used permits us to understand how both celebrity gossip and image differentiate readers and fans. In all, the various essays in this section engage with the contradictions of the text as much as the contradictions of the economic structure of the celebrity's identity. The audience is ultimately at the center of the economic and cultural power of the celebrity, and the textual and extra-textual dimensions of celebrity express the reach for that power and the expression of how that power is articulated through a multitude of contemporary issues including those concerned with identity, gender, and sexuality.

Part Three: Ascribed celebrity: The transformed public sphere

A common journalistic critique of celebrity culture is one filled with lament. Here the journalist invokes something Thomas Carlyle expressed 150 years ago: where have all the heroes gone (Carlyle 1969)? Indeed, one of the peculiar moments post-9/11 in the United States was a belief that hero-worship had finally returned through the efforts of the firefighters and police in rescuing survivors from the inferno of the Twin Towers collapse. Emerging from this sobering moment was also a hope that this was the end of celebrity and a new seriousness would take hold in the new millennium. Within a few months, the celebrity apparatus in all its various media forms and venues continued – 9/11 was just an extended hiccup that temporarily transformed the news cycle and how celebrity news was addressed. The firefighting heroes did not in the end transform the celebrity system: They were incorporated where possible into its virile juggernaut.

If there is one truism that emerges from celebrity culture it is that the sensibility has expanded outwards from entertainment culture to envelop many other dimensions of contemporary life. Part Three of the reader tries to deal with these extensions of the celebrity apparatus. It begins with an essay I wrote on the closely wedded histories of journalism and celebrity. Joe Moran addresses the widespread development of literary celebrity, something that certainly was present in the nineteenth century but has grown with celebrity culture in the twentieth century. Sport is perhaps the transitional cultural activity in its mediated form that moves between the idea of the hero and the celebrity. Authors Cole and Andrews work through the meaning of Tiger Woods in the context of a new multiculturalism. Politics and celebrity seem natural bedfellows, and John Street's essay on the celebrity politician investigates the play of style in contemporary politics that replicates the personas of popular culture icons. And it is perhaps chilling for an academic to read Jeffrey J. Williams' study of the academic star system as the celebrity system is deeply embedded into the university systems of higher education. Chris Rojek provides an intriguing look at the links in meaning systems between religion and celebrity. Ernest Sternberg's reading of the changing ways of public self-presentation provides an indication of how the desire for fame and recognition are part of any culture that has invested in a system of celebrity in constituting individual value.

Part Four: Transgression: Scandal, notoriety and infamy

Celebrities are performative texts: They act out. When celebrities are tightly controlled by a stringent publicity apparatus, the public persona resonates with their established roles. A kind of stereotype – a typecast – emerges that replicates their roles in sport, television, or popular music. But celebrities are fundamentally extratextual: They exit the screen or stage and become the object of the gaze of the camera as mediated onlooker. An industry of professional voyeurs – known as paparazzi – stakes out the celebrity scenes which populate the globe. Their intention is to reveal the hidden in order to show the truth about our celebrated personalities. Along with celebrity journalists, paparazzi uncover the transgressions from type that allow for the flow of gossip about celebrities by their fans. All in all, these elaborate documents on celebrities are in essence discourses on individuality in contemporary culture. Scandal represents a kind of rupture that allows a communal realization that celebrities are fabrications that have literally emerged from the populace and could easily return to these roots. The construction of scandal is often a morality tale presented for wide debate and expansive parasocial gossip. Scandal represents a site where there is some kind of contestation over meaning and significance and the audience is drawn into forming conclusions about identities and actions that coalesce around issues. The scandals of celebrity culture very often elucidate the feminist adage that "the personal is political."

The readings in this section move from the infamous, where a study of the serial killer is investigated by Richard Tithecott, to the tragic, where two articles by Richard Johnson and Catharine Lumby address the meaning and significance of the death of Princess Diana in 1997. Sandwiched between these ends are articles that trace the production of scandal, from Graeme Turner's study of tabloid culture to Stephen Hinerman's deciphering of the now scandalous persona of Michael Jackson. David Giles's psychological reading of stardom and scandal isolates well on their meaning in contemporary culture. And, although their career was chequered with scandalous moments, there is also a study I wrote on the Beatles that establishes the value of transgression by celebrities to build their sense of autonomy from the entertainment apparatus that constructs stars and celebrities.

Section Five: Narcissism, fandom and the will to celebrity

Celebrity is an elaborate discourse on individuality. Via the representations of celebrities, individuals take their cues as to what is significant and what is at the very least in fashion and temporarily valued. Hairstyles, such as Kevin Costner's Caesar moment in the mid-1990s (depicted in the film *The Bodyguard*), Farrah Fawcett's layered waves of the 1970s, or the bounteous hair of Julia Louis-Dreyfus of *Seinfeld* fame, become models for emulation. Similarly, as major fashion designers understand and the general entertainment industry regularly complicitly develops, celebrities' choices in clothing also allow for a wider general adoption. It is not that these styles necessarily begin with the celebrity; rather, it is their appropriation that makes them migrate out of subcultural or perhaps haute-couture choices into a wider consumer and popular culture. Russell Crowe's wearing of a sarong moved the dress style into a cultural moment at the end of the millennium. Mariah Carey's relatively early adoption of low-slung hip-hugger jeans allowed for the style to move through female youth culture rapidly thereafter from 2000–4. Body piercing and tattooing have had similar recent historical trajectories that have depended on their expansive reach into popular culture via key public personas and their overt displays captured in various mediated poses. Perhaps Madonna's adoption of underwear as outerwear (1984 onwards) has to be considered the quintessential regularization of a fashion into wider popular acceptance.

As celebrities perform individuality in their various guises, they are expressions of hyper-versions of possible transformations that anyone in consumer culture could achieve. Popular music has been the home of a variety of stage presences, both before David Bowie but much more expansively since his 1970s Ziggy Stardust moment that express this desire to be looked at in their grandiose gestures of difference and distinction. David Lee Roth's various striped spandex pants (1982–6) expresses one version of the excessive quality of the performer's presentation of self. Celebrities are constructed to be looked at and in that internalization of the gaze – a kind of contemporary mirror-effect where the culture reflects back the value of the celebrity's image in a cybernetic feedback loop – there is a cultural acceptance of a form of narcissism. The look of the fashion/magazine cover model is imbued with self-knowledge of how they are to be looked at by the viewer: the hold of the head, the intensity of the eye contact, and the expression formulated by the mouth all work to produce a sexual allure that is perhaps overcoded. The recent film *Zoolander* (2004) captures the comic quality of the overcoded "look" of fashion that depends on the internalization of the gaze now pervasive through contemporary culture.

The selections in this section deal with this intensified reconstruction of the gaze where the audience often internalizes the narcissistic outward look of the celebrities. Elizabeth Arveda Kissling's early work on the transformation of the body beautiful via the vehicle of the celebrity self-help fitness "movement" begins this exploration. In conjunction with Kathy Davis's prescient work on cosmetic surgery, one can see the will to celebrity articulated with the desire to transform the body into representational idealized conceptualizations.

Fanaticism has been studied in the context of social and political movements; but in rich detail the fanaticism of devotion to the icons of popular culture has cultivated an ever-growing research and literature. One can think of the fascinating work of Henry Jenkins as being at the center of understanding the relationship between fan and television program (see Jenkins 1992). Lawrence Grossberg's article here theorizes the constitution of the fan and its play through personality and affect. Stephen Hinerman's reading of Elvis fans exemplifies the peculiar and particular form of love and devotion that envelopes fans' lives as they connect to their icons. Chris Rojek's fascinating reading of what he calls "achieved celebrity" in some ways finishes the cybernetic loop of connection between fan and public persona. Sinatra's internalization produces a certain psychological trope that organizes his public self.

The fan is constructed in a dialogical relationship to the celebrity and star. Although fan clubs identify the value of the social solidarity that is part of fan culture, the fan/star is a dyad that replicates and reinforces the centrality of the mythic romantic love in the organization of contemporary identity and individuality. The final two articles in this section deal with the inversing of the inequality in the love dyad. The audience, with its desire for the love that comes from fame, works very hard to become part of the circuit of fame. This desire we can call the will to celebrity: In a sense it is the logical extension of the democratic quality that is at the ideological core of the celebrity. The democratization of fame and celebrity has expanded partly through the new media technologies. Alison Hearn's critique of reality television discusses the way in which the individual, through her/his elevation into the televisual text, makes their ordinary/extraordinary life fit into the celebrity commodity structure. My article deals explicitly with how new media are altering the organization of celebrity culture both in its presentation and in the pervasive efforts by new media users to be validated by being seen, heard, or noticed in and through the cacophony and plenitude of images and texts.

Part Six: The celebrity industry: The management of fame

The concluding part of the book is an excursus on how this celebrity culture can be thought of as an industry. As developed in the previous section, there is a dyad operating between the celebrity and the audience that is connected through some kind of affective power I have linked at its extreme to romantic love. The media is instrumental in producing this powerful connection through the distribution of a family of familiar celebrity images that operate as the icons of any cultural moment. An industry surrounds this distribution through developing, organizing, explaining, evaluating, calibrating, controlling, and capitalizing on personas to help make them into valued celebrities.

I have called this elaborate organizing structure an apparatus or a system in order to capture the massive amount of resources that are devoted to its management (Marshall 1997: 185–99). The celebrity industry is not a small entity. It is at the very center of a host of media industries. The mass-market magazine industry in particular is highly organized, through its focus (via covers and content) on the appeal of celebrities. Television, with its wide variety of programming, regularly markets the content of its shows through their star vehicles through the use of the talk show and gossip program and the regular diet of entertainment news. Indeed, much of the flow of channels such as E! is organized around celebrities and their backstories, as the now long-running *True Hollywood Stories* underlines. Film promotion relies on the publicity tours of their stars and in some cases the scandals that they can produce in their public roles in order to create a positive buzz around the release of any major studio film.

Although the celebrity apparatus operates at the hub of the entertainment industry, its management structure is designed to be unorganized and ethereal. This structure of management is to maintain the appearance that audience desires are determining the shape of the public world of celebrities and it is partially true that there is a form of audience power that determines success; however, it is also true that there are managers in place to first position potential celebrities and then capitalize on their public presence as efficiently as possible. In the same way as the trading on the stock exchanges appears frenzied, chaotic, and random, it betrays the highly methodical way in which capital operates and expands. Celebrities are commodities with present values and future values – like stocks – that are traded upon by an elaborate intersecting and interlocking entertainment industry.

The first two articles of this section establish the yin and the yang of the celebrity industry. Kembrew McLeod's work establishes the emerging structure of property rights that are connected to public identity. Neal Gabler, in contrast, in his study of Walter Winchell describes how gossip and background about public individuals help determine their futures – the press's intimate involvement in constructing the personality is elemental to the wider cultural industries both historically and in the contemporary scene.

Joshua Gamson's early 1990s work has been seminal in understanding the machinations behind the actions of stars and the production of cultural moments by audiences and different entertainment industries, and I have included one of his key chapters from his book *Claims to Fame*. Rosemary Coombe extends our thinking by providing the most sophisticated reading of the branding of the individual as a form of intellectual property that has helped advance our understanding of the personality as commodity and the cultural implications of these attempts to protect and instantiate these forms of property. To complete the section, I have excerpted a chapter from the co-authored study by Graeme Turner, Frances Bonner and myself on the Australian celebrity industry, which details the interlinking world of managers, impresarios, publicists, public relations specialists, and agents that feed the celebrity industry, and guide its personal charges into public personas that are branded for use in a variety of venues and exhibitions.

How to read and make sense of *The Celebrity Culture Reader*

The research on celebrity is expanding rapidly. This collection serves as a guide to some of the best work that has been conducted on this complicated area and will certainly help students and researchers to work in interesting directions into the future. Celebrity, as I have argued, has the appearance of both surface and depth, and it is this combination of both appearance/reality and surface/depth that makes celebrity such a powerful way to comprehend contemporary culture. Like other aspects of popular culture, it is difficult to live within its midst, enjoy its offerings and critically analyze it as a phenomenon. This reader is, at the very least, a path to engage with celebrity culture in a challenging way. It demands of the student a familiarity with a variety of disciplines and subdisciplines as they intersect with the production of public personalities. To use this book effectively sometimes implies also gaining a familiarity with media and communication, cultural studies, film studies, literary studies, political science, sociology and anthropology, political economy, and legal studies, to name some of the prime sites where the authors included in this reader find their original intellectual homes.

The book certainly does not need to be read sequentially; but I think that each of the sections works as a unit that is best appreciated when read collectively where the call and response of arguments and positions can be engaged with by the reader. I have attempted to launch each part via a short introduction-vignette to provide the fuel for understanding the section's thematic debate(s) – essentially a simple and short guide to how the articles intersect. The conclusion which follows Part Six is designed to discuss where research and thinking should advance in the future based on what has been deciphered about celebrity culture as developed in this reader. And from here, it is your turn.

PART ONE

Celebrity and modernity
The historical pattern of celebrity

Introduction to part one

■ P. David Marshall

IN ORDER FOR CELEBRITY to "work," there has to be some commonality of experience. Celebrity requires a knowledge and para-intimacy of individuals that depends on sophisticated communication networks that connect the people to the "thronged." And it relies on somehow making a group of people significant and interesting enough that disconnected people follow their exploits and lives. Perhaps the origins for this extension of the public individual are through political processes and how power was represented and articulated over geographical spaces. Sovereigns and sovereignty depend on a representational regime that helps to establish legitimacy – a kind of working hegemony that is reinforced often by a commanding military force and presence. Perhaps this extension of personal influence emerged with the expansion via certain individuals of particular religious movements. Charismatic leaders of religious cults may have been the early purveyors of celebrity culture, where ideas moved through these individuals and their prophets who relayed stories of their unusual power and influence over the many.

As much as these early patterns of personal influence resemble contemporary patterns of connection that we associate with celebrities, it needs to be added that celebrity culture depends on conceptualizations of individuality and self-transformation that are very much linked with the Renaissance and what has been called modernity. Celebrity is a modern phenomenon in the sense that it depends on an audience that understands and celebrates the malleability of identity and primacy of the individual. Along with the promises of consumer culture and democratic engagement, celebrities provide a new representational regime of individuality. What we understand as entertainment – the songs, stories, images that are conveyed to us through different cultural forms and technologies – has moved to the ideological center of our culture in their capacity to express both temporary moments of transformation, transcendence, and individuality. Celebrity culture elaborates and unravels entertainment further through moving the discourse of the individual from the imaginary to the "real" for the audience of modernity.

The history of celebrity culture, then, is a history of how individuality and exception are articulated and explained. It involves understanding the will to fame, the ethereal notion of charisma, the representation of individuality in entertainment industries, and the implications of a mediated world that provides the connecting fibres of a modern culture. The selections chosen for this section engage these foundational elements of celebrity culture.

Chapter 1

Richard Sennett

MAN AS ACTOR

T HERE IS A FINAL question to ask about the public realm of the 18th Century. What kind of man inhabited it? The people of the time gave a clear answer to this question: he was an actor, a performer. But what is a public actor? How, say, is he different from a father? It is a question of identity, and identity is a useful but abused word. In the sense Erik Erikson gave it, an identity is the meeting point between who a person wants to be and what the world allows him to be. Neither circumstance nor desire alone, it is one's place in a landscape formed by the intersections of circumstance and desire. The image, two centuries ago, of public man as an actor was a very definite identity; precisely because it was so forthrightly declared, it serves in retrospect a valuable purpose. It is a point of reference; against it, as the material and ideological conditions of public life grow confused, fragmented, and finally blank after the fall of the *ancien régime*, man's sense of himself in public can be charted.

Public man as an actor: the image, however evocative, is incomplete, because standing behind it, giving it substance, is a more basic idea. This is the concept of expression as the presentation of emotion, and from this comes the actor's identity: the public actor is the man who presents emotions.

Expression as the presentation of emotion is really a general principle which includes such practices as the speech signs [. . .]. Suppose one person tells another about his father's dying days in the hospital. Today the sheer recounting of all the details would be enough to arouse the other person's pity. Strong impressions minutely described are for us identical with expression. But imagine a situation or society in which the sheer reporting of these details of suffering would not signify to another person. The man recounting these moments could not merely relive them, but had to mold them, selecting some details to emphasize, suppressing others, even falsifying his report, in order to fit it into a form or fit a pattern which his listener understood to be what dying was about. Under these conditions the speaker wants to present to his hearer the death so organized in its details that it fits the picture as an event which arouses pity. Similarly, "pity" is not different depending on what death one hears about; pity exists as an independent emotion, rather than varying with and, therefore, depending upon each experience of it.

This theory of expression is incompatible with the idea of *individual* personality as expressive. If the sheer recital of what I've seen, felt, experienced, without any filtering or shaping or falsifying of my experience to fit it to a standard, if this were expressive, then "pity" in my life can hardly be expressive in the same way to you as your own sense of pity, derived from different experience. In the representation of emotion, when I tell you about my particular feelings as they appear to me, there is no expressive work to be done, "just living." No shaping of gesture or tidying of the scene makes it more expressive; just the reverse, because, once shaped to fit into a general pattern the experience would seem less "authentic." Equally, the principle of representation of emotion is asocial, for in not having the same report of pity to make, people do not have a common sense of pity to share as a social bond.

By contrast, under a system of expression as the presentation of emotion, the man in public has an identity as an actor – an enactor, if you like – and this identity involves him and others in a social bond. Expression as a presentation of emotion is the actor's job – if for the moment we take that word in a very broad sense; his identity is based on making expression as presentation work. When a culture shifts from believing in presentation of emotion to representation of it, so that individual experiences reported accurately come to seem expressive, then the public man loses a function, and so an identity. As he loses a meaningful identity, expression itself becomes less and less social.

I apologize for compressing this theory so, but it will be helpful at the outset to know how much underlies the idea of public man as actor. Indeed, a sense of these logical connections is necessary to understand the very peculiar terms in which man as actor was spoken of by people who inhabited the public world of the *ancien régime* capitals. There were three major voices.

The first was the most common voice to be heard among the cosmopolites of the time: if we inhabit a *theatrum mundi*, and have become like actors, then a new, happier morality is upon us. The second was the more probing one of writers like Diderot, who explored acting in relation to public life and in relation to nature. The third was the singular voice of Rousseau. Rousseau's was the greatest theory of the time about the bridge between cosmopolitan life and theater, and a strong condemnation of it. Analyst and critic, he was also prophet, predicting that the public order would succumb to a life based on authentic intimate feeling and political repression combined. Of this new condition – so much like our present-day condition – he approved. Yet he was also a bad prophet, for he believed that the new order would come through the fall of the city and the resurgence of the small town. His ideas are a touchstone to exploring how this public world has come to be lost in modern urban culture, a culture replacing the expressive life and identity of the public man with a new life, more personal, more authentic, and, all things considered, emptier.

The common-sense view of man as actor

By the opening of Book Seven of *Tom Jones*, the young man's adventures have become centered in London. It is at this point that Fielding presents a little essay called "A Comparison Between the World and the Stage." He begins as follows:

> The world hath been often compared to the theatre . . . this thought hath been carried so far, and become so general, that some words proper to the theatre, and which were, at first, metaphorically applied to the world, are now indiscriminately and literally spoken of both: thus stage and scene are by common use grown as familiar to us, when we speak of life in general, as when we confine ourselves to dramatic performances. . . .

Fielding is apologetic in tone a little later on; of course his readers know that the stage and the street are realms that "literally" translate into each other; he is talking in clichés and he excuses himself. He just wants to remind his dear readers that the mixture of dramatics and ordinary life is real, is no fancy "metaphor" as it was in the Restoration.[1]

"The world as a stage" was indeed an old cliché dressed up in new ways by the mid-18th Century. We have observed that one of the classic functions of the *theatrum mundi* imagery was to detach human nature from social action, by separating actor from act. In the common-sense view of man as actor, personally you were no longer indictable as a bad man for committing a bad act; you just needed to change your behavior. Man as actor bears a lighter moral yoke than either Puritan or devout Catholic: he is not born into sin, he enters into it if he happens to play an evil part.

Fielding himself put it well. In his essay he argued that "a single bad act no more constitutes a villain in life than a single bad part on the stage," and that indeed, as the realms of city and theater have become intermixed, the analogy becomes a literal truth. The character of acts and the character of actors are separate, so that a man of the world "can censure an imperfection, or even a vice, without rage against the guilty party." Further, there is no clear way to tell who men are in the great city, so the emphasis must be entirely upon what they do. Does a man harm others? Then, in the fashion of Garrick, the problem before him is to change his roles. And why should he not reform, since no appearance, no role, is fixed in the great city by necessity or by knowledge others have of one's past?[2]

If, in general, man as actor relieved himself of the burdens of innate sin by divorcing his nature from his acts, 18th Century common sense concluded that he thus could enjoy himself more. Tied in public neither to the realm of nature nor to the Christian duties of the soul, his playfulness and pleasure in the company of others could be released. This is why writings of the time so often allied images of man as actor to cosmopolitan life; their version of *theatrum mundi* did not refer to the relations between man and the gods or to dark pessimism about the meaning of human life, as did the Renaissance Platonists on the one hand and the Elizabethan dramatists on the other. There is a marvelous *Persian Letter* of Montesquieu's, in which his hero, wandering into the Comédie Française one night, cannot distinguish who's on stage and who's supposed to be watching; everyone is parading, posing, having a good time.

Amusement, cynical toleration, pleasure in the company of one's fellows, these were the tones of feeling contained in the everyday notion of man as an actor.

But there were those who understood that the prevalent clichés of man as actor depended, in their very sense of sociability, on a deeper and unspoken idea of expression. Greatest of these was Diderot, whose *Paradox of Acting* connected acting to a more general psychological theory.

Diderot's paradox of acting

Diderot summed up what he called the paradox of acting quite simply:

> Do not people talk in society of a man being a great actor? They do not mean by that that he feels, but that he excels in simulating, though he feels nothing . . .

Diderot was the first great theorist of acting as a secular activity. Most 16th and 17th Century French theories of acting correlated how an actor performed with the contents of what he or she performed. The truth of the lines spoken had some relationship to how well the actor could speak. Thus it was possible to subsume the idea of acting under the rubric of rhetoric, and to talk of rhetoric in relation to morals and religion. In this formula the priest became the greatest possible rhetorician because the lines he spoke were absolute truth. No good Christian would dream, of course, of directly comparing priest and actor, but the reason lay precisely in the fact that the priest's rhetoric was innately superior to anything possible on the stage, because he was speaking divine truth.[3]

Diderot broke this connection between acting, rhetoric, and the substance of the text. In his *Paradox* he created a theory of drama divorced from ritual; he was the first to conceive of performing as an art form in and of itself, without reference to what was to be performed. The "signs" of the performance were not for Diderot the "signs" of the text. I put this less clearly than Diderot. He writes:

> If the actor were full, really full, of feeling, how could he play the same part twice running with the same spirit and success? Full of fire at the first performance, he would be worn out and cold as marble at the third.[4]

An actor who believes in his own tears, who governs his performance according to his sentiments, who has no distance from the emotions he projects, cannot act consistently. An actor must not respond to the substance of the text to act it, nor is his art governed by the substance of the text. We know, for instance, that a great actor in a bad play can still give a great performance. The reason lies in the very nature of performed expression: without some work on the emotions to be conveyed, without the exercise of judgment or calculation in showing them, an expression cannot be performed more than once.[5]

The theory Diderot propounds concerns more than the tricks of stagecraft; it addresses itself to the superiority of artifice over nature in expressing an emotion. Diderot puts a question:

Have you ever thought on the difference between the tears raised by a
tragedy of real life and those raised by a touching narrative?

He answers by saying that tears of real life are immediate and direct, while the tears
brought on by art must be produced consciously, by degrees. But while the natural
world may therefore seem superior to the world of the actor, it is in fact much more
vulnerable and liable to accident. Think of a woman weeping, Diderot says, who has
some minor disfigurement which takes your attention away from her woe, or whose
accent you find difficult to understand, and so you are diverted, or who shows you her
grief at a moment when you are unprepared to receive it. In all these ways the world
where people react directly and spontaneously to each other is a world where expression is often perverted; the more natural the expression between two people, the less
reliably expressive they will be.[6]

At best, in the world where sympathy and natural feeling govern, if there is an
exact representation of an emotion it can happen only once.[7]

Diderot then asks how an expression can be presented more than once, and in
answering it he defines the idea of a conventional sign. A feeling can be conveyed more
than once when a person, having ceased to "suffer it," and now at a distance studying
it, comes to define its essential form. This essence is a subtraction of the accidental: if
by chance a rigid posture appears to detract from the scene of a woman expressing
sorrow over an absent husband, then the rigid posture is replaced by a stoop. If
declaiming loudly occasionally draws attention to the volume of the voice rather than
the words spoken, the voice is taught to stay lower. By such studies, the essential
character of an emotion is established. In the process of arriving at these signs, an
actor has ceased to feel the emotion as the audience to whom he conveys these
emotions will feel them. He does not stop feeling: Diderot is often falsely interpreted
that way; rather the actor's feelings about the gesture have become different from the
feelings the gesture will arouse in the audience.[8]

Gestures of this sort are the only way expressions can be stable, the only way they
endure. The purpose of a gesture is to defeat the deformation of time:

You are talking to me of a passing moment in Nature. I am talking to you
of a work of Art, planned and composed – a work which is built up by
degrees, and which lasts.

Repeatability is the very essence of a sign.[9]

Diderot's model of a great actor was the Englishman David Garrick. He met
Garrick in the winter of 1764–65; in a passage from the *Paradox*, Diderot describes the
impression Garrick made on him:

Garrick will put his head between two folding doors, and in the course of
five or six seconds his expression will change successively from wild
delight to temperate pleasure, from this to tranquility, from tranquility to
surprise, from surprise to blank astonishment, from that to sorrow, from
sorrow to the air of one overwhelmed, from that to fright, from fright to
horror, from horror to despair, and thence he will go up again to the point

from which he started. *Can his soul have experienced all these feelings, and played this kind of scale in concert with his face?*[10]

A cliché of Diderot criticism has it that Diderot set Art against Nature, that the power of an actor like David Garrick was seen to be great to the degree that it was unnatural, almost monstrous. This simple opposition won't do. Diderot believed that all the study of the actor was directed at finding the essential forms which govern the natural world; the actor distills these forms out. By withdrawing his own feelings from the material, he has acquired the power to be conscious of what form is inherent in the realm of natural feeling. Because the performer builds on nature, he can communicate with people who remain in that chaotic state. By finding forms of expression which are repeatable, he brings a momentary sense of order into their own perceptions. The communication is not a sharing of this sign. One person must become master of – and distant from – the feeling to which another will submit. Embedded in the notion of a sustained, repeatable expression, therefore, is the idea of inequality.

This potentially friendly relationship between art and nature in Diderot's theory is important in analyzing performing offstage. Diderot meant to encompass more than the activities of a very few geniuses like Garrick. He meant to use them as models for other expressive social transactions. Social acts which are innately expressive are those which can be repeated. Repeatable social acts are those in which the actor has put a distance between his own personality and the speech or bodily dress he shows to others. Appearances at a distance from self are subject to calculation, and the person making the appearance can change his speech or bodily dress depending on the circumstances in which he is placed. Diderot's is the rationale of such signs as the elaborate, impersonal compliment, repeatable almost indiscriminately to others, an explanation of why such a sign should have continued to give pleasure. The compliment has a life of its own, a form independent of the particular speaker and his particular hearer. It signifies of itself. So does the *pouf au sentiment*; so does the face patch. The impersonality of successful speech between the classes has the same rationale: to the degree that it is purposely elaborate, a world unto itself, a form signifying apart from the circumstances of speaker and audience, it is expressive. In sum, from successful acting Diderot moves to a theory of emotion as presentation. The feelings an actor arouses have form and therefore meaning in themselves, just as a mathematical formula has meaning of its own no matter who writes it. For this expression to occur, men must behave unnaturally, and search for what convention, what formula can be repeated, time after time.

Diderot's ideas in retrospect appear as an intellectual underpinning for the public life of his era. But in no direct sense can Diderot be read as a spokesman for his fellow Parisians; his text, finally finished in 1778, did not appear in print until 1830. In the 1750's there were writers on the theater who explicitly rejected views like Diderot's and instead followed an emphasis on natural sympathies. Indeed, the *Paradox* was itself a response to a well-known treatise of 1747, *Le Comédien*, by Remond de Sainte-Albine, quickly translated into English by John Hill, then translated back into French by Sticotti in 1769 – the version Diderot read. *Le Comédien* argued sentiment, and thus the soul of the actor, to be the source of the actor's power; if he were a cold soul, he would be an indifferent actor. But the views Diderot espoused were popular in the 1750's, if less cogently argued. Diderot was anticipated by Ricoboni's *L'Art du Théâtre*;

by Grimm's writing on the theater; later, in the *Encyclopédie*, they were codified in an article on Declamation by Marmontel.[11]

It was in the 1750's that the argument theater historians call the war between Sentiment and Calculation first took form. A charming and most unbelievable instance of it is recorded a few years later, in which the two great actresses of Diderot's time, Madame Clairon and Madame Dumesnil, meet at the Théâtre Boule-Rouge. Madame Clairon was in Diderot's eyes the female Garrick; Madame Dumesnil was to him an actress of middling talent because she depended on her own feelings. The two actresses began debating the question of sensibility versus calculation in creating a role. Madame Dumesnil declared, "I was full of my part, I felt it, I yielded myself up to it." To which Madame Clairon replied abruptly, "I have never understood how one could do without calculation." The actor Dugazon jumped in: "[It is not] our object to know whether dramatic art exists . . . but whether in this art fiction or reality is to dominate." Madame Clairon: "Fiction"; Madame Dumesnil: "Reality."[12]

For all the pleasing triviality in which this argument could end up, the most important aspect of it was an assumption both sides shared. From the writing of Remond de Sainte-Albine and Riccoboni in the 1750's to Diderot, and then on into the 19th Century in the reflections of such actors as Coquelin, Diderot's basic premise was accepted by all. This was the independence of the activity of performing – its independence from the text. The war between sentiment and calculation concerns what the actor feels, not the correctness of those feelings in terms of the correctness of the words he or she had to speak. How can you be moved by my eloquence, Bishop Bossuet asked his congregation in a famous sermon of the 17th Century, and not thereby be moved to confess your sins to God? Eighty years later, it was possible to discuss Bossuet's qualities as a great speaker, perhaps hotly arguing how much he was in control, how much he was subject to the fire he heaped upon his parishioners, without troubling oneself too much with the proposition that, if he was a great speaker, one ought to be more devout. Both sides in Diderot's time secularized the phenomenon of performing, cut it loose from external indexes of truth. Diderot's arguments extended the secular idea to its logical conclusion as a theory of expression: if performing was an activity which has meaning independent of the particular text, then it also must have a meaning independent of the particular performer, his private sentiments, his passing moods.

The completion of this idea of secular performing lay in Rousseau's linking of it to the city.

Rousseau's indictment of the city as theater

Oddly, the greatest writer on, the most constant student of, urban public life was a man who hated it. Jean-Jacques Rousseau believed cosmopolitanism was no high stage of civility, but a monstrous growth. More than any other of his contemporaries, Rousseau investigated the great city thoroughly, as though dissecting a cancer. Paris was his main concern, but the theatrical qualities of life in Paris he believed to be spreading to all the capitals of Europe. Rousseau must be read as more than a reporter of his times, more than a moral commentator. In castigating the mixture of stage and street life, he arrived at the first complete and probing theory of the modern city as an expressive milieu.

Rousseau was the first writer to depict the city as a secular society. He was the first to show that this secularism arose out of a particular kind of city – the cosmopolitan capital; that is, he was the first to envision discontinuities in "urban" experience, and thus to arrive at a theory of cosmopolitanism. He was the first to link the public codes of belief in the cosmopolis to basic psychological experiences like trust and play; the first to relate the psychology of cities to a psychology of creativity. And all this, so insightful, so probing, was directed toward a terrible end; from his anatomy of the great city, Rousseau concluded that mankind could achieve psychologically authentic relationships – the opposite of cosmopolitanism – only by imposing on itself political tyranny. And of this tyranny he approved.

The circumstances under which Rousseau came to write down his theory give some clues to what he wrote. Sometime between 1755 and 1757 the French philosopher d'Alembert wrote an article for the *Encyclopédie* on the city of Geneva. D'Alembert noted that there were no theaters in the city. Given the Calvinist traditions of Geneva, this did not much surprise d'Alembert; he knew the Genevans feared "the taste for adornment, dissipation, and libertinism which the actors' troops disseminate among the young." But as an outsider he saw no reason why this strict and ascetic city could not tolerate a theater; in fact, he thought a theater could do the citizens some good. "A finesse of tact; a delicacy of sentiment," he wrote, "is very difficult to acquire without the help of theatrical performances."[13]

D'Alembert's sentiments were much like Fielding's: the theater has lessons of behavior for ordinary life. These sentiments roused Rousseau, a citizen of Geneva, who had passed some years in Paris; in 1758 he published the *Letter to M. d'Alembert*. This letter is a reply to much more than d'Alembert intended to say. To justify political censorship of the drama, Rousseau had to show that d'Alembert's values were those of a cosmopolitan; he then had to show that the spread of cosmopolitan values to a small town would destroy its religion and that as a result people, in learning how to behave with the "delicacy of sentiment" of actors, would cease having a deep and honest inner life.[14]

All of Rousseau's opposites – cosmopolitan, small town; acting, authenticity; liberty, just tyranny – come from a theory of corruption, the corruption of *moeurs*. *Moeurs* can be rendered in modern English as a cross of manners, morals, and beliefs. Eighteenth Century writers use the word in a sense that terms like "value orientation," "role definition," and the rest of the sociological lexicon cannot encompass; *moeurs* concern the complete manner, the style a person possesses.[15]

Moeurs are corrupted, Rousseau maintains, when people form a style that transcends work, family, and civic duty. To step outside the context of functional survival, to think of pleasures that do not contribute to begetting and maintaining life – this is corruption. One way to read Rousseau is that he identified corruption with what we think of as abundance.[16]

How easy is it to corrupt a man or woman? At the opening of the *Letter*, Rousseau claims it is hard: "A father, a son, a husband, and a citizen have such cherished duties to fulfill that they are left nothing to give to boredom." But then Rousseau amends himself immediately, for clearly the enemy – frivolous pleasure, foreign amusement, idle gossip in cafés – is everywhere. The habit of work can be undone by "discontent with oneself, the burden of idleness, the neglect of simple and natural tastes." In other words, man is in rather constant danger of corruption.[17]

The historian Johan Huizinga defines play as a release from the economic, by which he means activity which transcends the world of daily necessity, of survival duties and tasks. Play in this sense is Rousseau's enemy. Play corrupts.[18]

Play takes place in at least a temporary condition of leisure. The Protestant relationship between leisure and vice is that when men have no necessary duties pressing on them, they give way to their natural passions, which are evil. The sloth, the glutton, the seducer, and the libertine are natural man, revealed by his or her play. Such was Calvin's idea, and Geneva was organized by him to give man no rest, and therefore no chance for sin.

Calvin's idea of the small city as a perfect theocracy was straightforward. Here was an economically viable environment, a physical place offering protection in time of war, still small enough to permit constant surveillance of the populace. From a religious point of view, the advantage of the small city is that it is the most secure political tool to repress man's natural baseness. Rousseau struggled to view mankind as naturally good and yet view the political control as legitimate; therefore his view of the relationship of *moeurs* to the small city is more complicated than Calvin's.

What would happen, he asked, if people were freed of the rigidities of small-city life? What would happen if men and women possessed genuine leisure? Freedom from the duties of survival would mean that men and women had more chance for social interactions – for visits in cafés, walks on promenades, and the like. Sociability is the fruit of leisure. The more people interact, however, the more they become dependent on one another. Thus the forms of sociability we have called public Rousseau thought of as social relations of mutual dependence. In the *Letter*, the mutual dependence of people, cut loose from bonds of necessity, is portrayed as terrifying.

People come to depend on others for a sense of self. One manipulates one's appearance in the eyes of others so as to win their approval, and thus feel good about oneself. Lionel Trilling has summarized Rousseau's argument in the *Letter* in this way:

> . . . the spectator contracts by infection the characteristic disease of the actor, the attenuation of selfhood that results from impersonation . . . by engaging in impersonation at all the actor diminishes his own existence as a person.[19]

In a state of leisure, men and women develop the *moeurs* of actors. The seriousness of losing independence is masked because people are at play: they experience pleasure in losing themselves. In Rousseau's words,

> . . . the principal object is to please; and, provided that the people enjoy themselves, this object is sufficiently attained.[20]

It is no accident that Rousseau entered the lists when a theater was proposed for his city. The theater, rather than licentious books or pictures, is a dangerous art form because it promotes the vices of men and women who do not have to struggle to survive. It is the agent of loss of self.

Now enters the capital, cosmopolitan city: its public culture is the realm where this loss of self occurs.

All cities are places with large numbers of people living closely packed together, a central market or markets, and the division of labor carried to a high degree. These conditions ought to influence the *moeurs* of people in all cities. For the small city, Rousseau believes, the influence is direct.[21] The small city is a place which brings to fruition all the virtues of good, decent people struggling to survive. By contrast, in London or Paris, economics, family background, and other material conditions have an indirect influence on styles of life; they directly influence the *volonté*, the will, of city men. *Moeurs* then result from what this will desires.[22]

Why make this distinction? For two reasons. First, by inserting this middle term, Rousseau gets to talk about the large city in special moral terms. He gets beyond modern liberal formulas of bad urban behavior as the result of bad social conditions – with the noble soul of the offender waiting in the wings for liberation. Large cities matter to Rousseau because they corrupt the very center of a human being, corrupt his or her will.

Second, the very complexity of social and economic relations in the great city means you cannot tell what kind of man you are dealing with in any given situation by knowing what work he does, how many children he supports – in short, by how he survives. The very complexity of social relations in the city makes reading character from material conditions difficult. Equally, the economic nature of a cosmopolitan center is to accumulate what would now be called "surplus capital." It is the place where rich men enjoy their fortunes through leisure activities and poor men imitate them; the very concentration of capital means a few people have genuine leisure and many people out of envy become "idle" – that is, sacrifice their material interests for the sake of having a leisure "style."

The great city Rousseau thus perceived as an environment wherein you cannot tell what kind of man a stranger is in a given situation by finding out how he survives. The situations, indeed, in which you are likely to meet him are those in which you are not meeting for some functional purpose, but meeting in the context of nonfunctional socializing, of social interaction for its own sake. And on this insight he imposes his analysis of the nature of leisured play. For in a state of leisure, people interact more and more for the sheer pleasure of contact; the more they interact outside the strictures of necessity, the more they become actors. But actors of a very special sort:

> In a big city, full of scheming, idle people without religion or principle, whose imagination, depraved by sloth, inactivity, the love of pleasure, and great needs, engenders only monsters and inspires only crimes; in a big city, where *moeurs* and honor are nothing because each easily hiding his conduct from the public eye, shows himself only by his reputation . . .[23]

Reputation – being known, being recognized, being singled out. In a big city this pursuit of fame becomes an end in itself; the means are all the impostures, conventions, and manners which people are so free to toy at in the cosmopolis. And yet these means lead inexorably to the end, for when one has no fixed "place" in a society, dictated by the state which in turn is but the instrument of a Higher Power, then one makes up a place for oneself by manipulating one's appearance. Because playacting is corrupt, all one wants to get from playing with one's appearance is applause. For Rousseau, the cosmopolis, in turn, destroys the believability of religion, because one can make up one's own place, one's own identity, rather than submit to the indentity the Higher Power has assigned one. The pursuit of reputation replaces the pursuit of virtue.

There are many Rousseaus, because many of the works Rousseau wrote contradict each other or possess divergent points of view. The Rousseau of *Émile* is not exactly the Rousseau of the *Letter* as concerns these ideas of play, reputation, and religion. The Rousseau of the *Confessions* is a man who has partially broken free of the strictures of the *Letter*. The *Letter* is an extreme position, argued to its logical conclusion.[24]

Nonetheless, throughout Rousseau's work this accusation of cosmopolitan public life recurs. From *Julie:*

> Just as clocks are ordinarily wound up to go only twenty-four hours at a time, so these people have to go into society every night to learn what they're going to think the next day.[25]

And here is another extraordinary passage from the same novel in which, Ernst Cassirer comments, "nothing is 'invented'; every word is drawn from Rousseau's own experience" of Paris:

> People meet me full of friendship; they show me a thousand civilities; they render me services of all sorts. But that is precisely what I am complaining of. How can you become immediately the friend of a man whom you have never seen before? The true human interest, the plain and noble effusion of an honest soul – these speak a language far different from the insincere demonstrations of politeness (and the false appearances) which the customs of the great world demand.[26]

The great city is a theater. Its scenario is principally the search for reputations. All city men become artists of a particular kind: actors. In acting out a public life, they lose contact with natural virtue. The artist and the great city are in harmony, and the result is a moral disaster.[27]

But some questions should be asked at this point. Paris is a theater, a society of men and women posing to one another. But poses sometimes heal deformities of nature or the wounds of circumstance. Rousseau tells us the pursuit of reputation is rife in cities. So what, if men are spurred to produce great things in hopes of being praised? In *Émile* there is a scornful passage in which Rousseau speaks of role playing in the great city as a means for people to forget their often humble origins, but, on the scale of sins, this would hardly seem to rank with rape or murder.

Rousseau's critique of the city seems headed, from a brilliant beginning, to a vulgar end – the celebration of the simple, truthful yokel. Rousseau saves his argument from banality by suddenly and dramatically within the text changing its terms.

Rousseau began with the paradigm of virtue/work, vice/leisure. Obviously the big city bustles; it has an electric energy which the sleepy everyday round of home, work, church, home can scarcely have had in Geneva. In the middle of the *Letter*, a new scale of action is introduced: frenetic coming and going, actions without meaning characterize the great city, because without the pressures of survival, man spins crazily. In the small city, action proceeds at a slower pace; this permits leisure to reflect on the true nature of one's actions and self.[28]

Rousseau makes this sudden shift because now he can show the effect of a city on the general pattern of human expression. Truly creative expression is done by the man in search of a true self; he expresses this discovery in words, music, and pictures. The works of art are like reports of a psychological inquest. Art of the great city, which starts with an interdependent set of social relations, produces fictions and stylizations of self. These conventions exist on their own; they have no relation to personal character. Rousseau detests the presentation of emotions on these terms; he wants a more inward-turning probe of character. Here is part of Rousseau's contrast between presentation and representation:

> . . . true genius . . . knows not the path of honors and fortune nor dreams of seeking it; it compares itself to no one; all its resources are within itself.[29]

Rousseau has performed a sleight of hand: expression will be determined by how honest – *honnête* – a man is, and honesty is defined by how unique he or she is. Honesty for the Calvinist is making an inventory of how-I-have-sinned-today; for Rousseau it is losing a consciousness of how one appears to the world at large.[30]

Thus arises a marvelous paradox. What's wrong with the actor is that he or she, sensitive to insult and to praise, moves in a world in which there exist definitions of good and bad, virtue and vice. Similarly, the trouble with the great city is that there is *too much* community. The values of the community, whatever they are, count for too much, because people try to win reputation from others by acting out these values. The small town has better values, survival virtues, but by the end of the *Letter* Rousseau has developed a second virtue of the small town. It permits more isolation, it permits people to ignore the community's standards and search out their own hearts to "see whatever there is, just to see." Here is Rousseau's summation of the small town:

> . . . more original spirits, more inventive industry, more really new things are found there because the people are less imitative; having few models each draws more from himself and puts more of his own in everything he does.[31]

Censorship of an art, the theater, is therefore justified, for the same reason that thought reform is justified. Indeed, if the theater flourishes, the legislation of morality cannot. In a city like Geneva, the theater could seduce people into having models for behavior. In Geneva, in the midst of political tyranny, men should become creatively unique. In a large city, censorship is useless; what plays are produced is less important than the fact that plays are produced at all. The actor on the stage becomes the model of what every Parisian aspires to achieve in private life.[32]

Rousseau's prophecies

These are the outlines of a great, and frightening, argument about public life. Its very contradictions are a part of that greatness, contradictions which have dogged all those who followed in Rousseau's wake. Political tyranny and the search for individual authenticity go hand in hand. That is the essence of Rousseau's prophecy, and it has been fulfilled. By contrast, when men pose to win fame, accommodate others, or even to be kind, each appears to end up having no soul of his own. That also has become modern belief.

But Rousseau was also a very bad prophet of modern times. Perhaps the most revealing error is seen by comparing his theory with the behavior of Wilkes and the Wilkesites. The Wilkesites, the first mass movement of the 18th Century city, of all shades of rank from wealthy merchant to penniless hackboy, overturned the dramatics of the *ancien régime* metropolis in a manner Rousseau did not dream of. For him, destruction of convention would occur only as the environment in which men lived became more controlled. For them, the destruction would develop only as their freedom from control expanded. Rousseau could imagine the end of public life only in a small town — that is, he could imagine an alternative to the metropolis, but not its historical growth. Coherence, political control, a perfect fit of tyranny with the needs of the natural man: this was his vision. It was a retreat into a past, a mythical past at that, a withdrawal from the great city. But the forces within that city which were overturning the principles of appearance of the *ancien régime* were directed to contrary ends, to the achievement of a lack of constraint, a liberty within the great city. This boundary-less liberty men hoped to understand through the symbolization of personal experience.

Notes

1   Henry Fielding. *Tom Jones* (London: Penguin, 1966; first published 1749), p. 299.
2   *Ibid.*, p. 302.
3   Lee Strasberg, "An Introduction to Diderot," in Denis Diderot, *The Paradox of Acting*, trans. W. H. Pollack (New York: Hill & Wang, 1957), p. x; Arthur M. Wilson, *Diderot* (New York: Oxford University Press, 1972), pp. 414–16; Felix Vexler, *Studies in Diderot's Esthetic Naturalism* (New York: Ph.D. thesis, Columbia University, 1922).
4   Diderot, *Paradox*, p. 14.
5   *Ibid.*, pp. 15, 24.
6   Quotation from *ibid.*, p. 20; *ibid.*, p. 23.
7   *Ibid.*, p. 25.
8   *Ibid.*, pp. 15 ff.
9   Quotation from *ibid.*, p. 25.
10   *Ibid.*, pp. 32–33, italics added.
11   T. Cole and H. Chinoy, *Actors on Acting* (rev. ed.; New York: Crown, 1970), pp. 160–61.
12   Diderot, *op. cit.*, pp. 52 ff.; K. Mantzius, *A History of Theatrical Art in Ancient and Modern Times* (London: Duckworth & Co., 1903–21), V, 277–78.
13   The dating is established as follows: D'Alembert prepared the article after a visit to Voltaire at his estate outside Geneva; Voltaire had moved to the estate in 1755; the article was slated to appear in 1757; and Rousseau's response to it appeared in 1758. Rousseau, *Politics and the Arts: The Letter to M. d'Alembert*, trans. A. Bloom (Ithaca: Cornell University Press, 1968), p. xv. The title *Politics and the Arts* is an

English title for the English translation of the *Letter*; hereafter it will be referred to by the correct title: *Letter to M. d'Alembert*; quotation from d'Alembert, quoted in *ibid.*, p. 4.

14   There are grounds for believing that in so closely rebutting d'Alembert's description of moral and religious life in Geneva, Rousseau was also arguing with himself about the value of a militant ascetic religion for a city. See Ernst Cassirer, *The Question of Jean Jacques Rousseau*, trans. and edited by Peter Gay (New York: Columbia University Press, 1954), pp. 73–76, for Rousseau's religious thought.

15   See "Translator's Notes," in Rousseau, *op. cit.*, p. 149, note 3.

16   *Ibid.*, pp. xxx, 16.

17   *Ibid.*, p. 16.

18   Johan Huizinga, *Homo Ludens* (Boston: Beacon, 1955), pp. 1, 6, 8–9.

19   Lionel Trilling, *Sincerity and Authenticity* (Cambridge, Mass.: Harvard University Press, 1972), p. 64.

20   Rousseau, *op. cit.*, p. 18.

21   This is precisely the point of view of d'Alembert's article. The treatment of religion in the last five paragraphs is a good example, reprinted as an appendix to Rousseau, *op. cit.*, pp. 147–48.

22   *Ibid.*, p. 58.

23   *Ibid.*, pp. 58–59.

24   Not all the instruction in *Émile* is purposive, nor are the incidents of the *Confessions* recorded in terms of a central formal plan based on "utility."

25   Quoted in English translation in M. Berman, *The Politics of Authenticity* (New York: Atheneum, 1970), p. 116.

26   Cassirer, *Question*, p. 43; Rousseau, quoted in *ibid.*

27   Berman, *op. cit.*, pp. 114–15; the idea of reputation as an achieved meaning begins, as Berman points out, with Montesquieu; Rousseau gives the image a new, more negative meaning.

28   Rousseau, *op. cit.*, pp. 59–61.

29   *Ibid.*, p. 60.

30   *Ibid.*

31   *Ibid.*

32   *Ibid.*, pp. 65–75.

Chapter 2

Leo Braudy

THE LONGING OF ALEXANDER

... [W]hen a man compoundeth the image of his own person, with the image of the actions of an other man; as when, a man imagins himselfe a *Hercules*, or an *Alexander*, (which happeneth often to them that are much taken with reading of Romants) it is a compound imagination, and properly but a Fiction of the mind. . . . The *vain-glory* which consisteth in the feigning or supposing of abilities in our selves, which we know are not, is most incident to young men, and nourished by the Histories, or Fictions of Gallant Persons; and is corrected often times by Age, and Employment.

—THOMAS HOBBES, *Leviathan*

IN THE BEGINNINGS, AS we can decipher them from the tumbled temples and the half-eroded inscriptions, fame meant a grandeur almost totally separate from ordinary human nature. In Egypt particularly evolved the extraordinary exaltation of a single man, the pharaoh, the ultimate ruler whose giant image gazed down at his subjects through the centuries. In their tombs, like those of the earliest emperors of China, were the objects and images of their power, including the bones of servants and the statues of retainers – testimony to the future of the greatness that once was. In civilizations with a god-king, especially those that used a written language primarily for religious, astronomical, and mercantile computation, rulers often took the same name as their predecessor because the role of leader was much more important than the individual who occupied it. He became greater not by asserting his personal characteristics but by fitting into the eternal role as fully as possible. For king or general, priest or artist, the preexisting name shored up the weak and kept in check the strong.

But the true history of fame begins, not with the grandly repeated names of Egypt or Persia or China or Yucatán, but with a self-naming that steps out of the bounds of dynasty, beyond even the stature of the Egyptian god-king, and into a status simultaneously unique and yet suffused with the atmosphere of human possibility. Like so many other aspects of Western culture, such a fame receives its first clear definition in the Greece of the fifth and fourth centuries B.C. For many centuries there had been established traditions of celebrating the heroes of the past by shrines and cults. But with the rise of Athens as the center of Greek culture came the casting of the oral epics of the *Iliad* and the *Odyssey* into written form, followed by the grand fifth-century flowering of drama and philosophy, when the scattered images of the heroic drew together into a prolonged cultural mediation on the meaning of heroism. We do not know who Homer was or where and when he lived, although it was certainly hundreds of years after the events and people he depicts. But his works (if indeed he wrote both the *Iliad* and the *Odyssey*) embody the importance to the Greeks of the pursuit of an honor that will allow a man to live beyond death, as Hector says in the *Iliad*, "immortal, ageless all my days, and reverenced like Athena and Apollo" (198).[1] Such honor, which can be achieved only in war, frees its possessor from human time. Thus although the greatest heroes lived in ages long before the present, their memory remains. Set in a war the Greeks won, the *Iliad* is yet in great part a lament for a lost civilization of great men and women composed for the descendants of those who had destroyed them, assimilated them, or driven them out – as if an American of European descent would in the twenty-third century write an epic celebrating the heroic world of the American Indians. True heroism is ever receding. Even in the *Iliad* the ancient Nestor speaks of the great men who *used* to be around, so diminished does he consider heroism to be in the present.

The Greek word "hero" in Homer's works generally means "gentleman" or "noble," and his concept of heroism accordingly contains a strong element of class status and class obligation. But since only the future can know if the hero has achieved perfect glory, the present too often judges stature by material possessions, especially the booty captured in war. The plot of the *Iliad* therefore begins when Agamemnon, the military leader of the Greek expedition against Troy, uses the power of his position to force Achilles to give up the prize that his personal honor demands. As Aristotle would later imply in his *Politics*, the actions and temperament necessary for heroic fame may be opposed to those that make a good citizen. For most of the *Iliad*, Achilles sits passively in his tent, disdaining a glory that has been polluted by the greed of Agamemnon. Through this heroic conflict, Homer explores the division between the hero's loyalty to a social order and his aspiration to an honor sanctioned only by his ancestors and the gods. Achilles is capable of transcending the values of his society by a vision of the absolute honor beyond even life itself. But he also wants it to be clear that he is the greatest hero of the Greeks. If Agamemnon cannot accommodate Achilles' need for personal honor, then Achilles, until the death of his best friend Patroclus, will submit neither to Agamemnon's will nor to the social goal of winning the war against the Trojans.

Clearly, such choices, embedded in their greatest poem of war, were vexing to Homeric and post-Homeric society. The *Odyssey*, through its emphasis on the testing of Odysseus not in battle but in travel and adventure, turns away from the two time-honored places of heroic assertion – where one was born and where one fights – to explore instead the possibility that heroism may flourish better outside the pre-ordained world of social hierarchy and military rituals. The values of the *Odyssey* are instead values of movement, and even at the end of the poem, Odysseus is destined to leave for yet another adventure. In the *Odyssey*, when Odysseus is a leader and has an official troop of men with him, he generally gets them and himself into trouble. Only by the end of the poem, after he has wandered back to his home disguised as a beggar, has he been through enough alone to win his wife and his house back from the brash young suitors who had collected there. As the terms of the poem imply, even though heroic action often has a social dimension, its roots are best anchored by a private, even a domestic, sense of self. Odysseus, who is caught in the framework of Agamemnon's power and Homer's story, not only navigates through his world disguised and alone, but also himself tells a good deal of the story of the *Odyssey* to an eager audience.

In the *Iliad* competing warriors bellowed their own names and the names of their fathers and grandfathers. In the *Odyssey* this penchant for heroic publicity is explicitly criticized, for Odysseus has discovered that the echo of one's name in the world is not always a soothing sound. In Book IX, alone and virtually naked, he has been thrown by the sea on the shores of Phaiakia. Nausikaä, the king's daughter, has found him and brought him to her father's court where, after hearing a minstrel sing of Odysseus at Troy, he decides to reveal himself and tell his own story of what happened since. First, he tells them his name and then briefly recounts his voyages until he arrived at the land of the Cyclopes, a race of giants with one eye, who live isolated from each other in caves. Exploring the island, he and his men come on a Cyclops who captures and begins eating them two at a time. Recovering from his shock, Odysseus devises a plan. First, he offers the Cyclops wine and, when asked his name, gives a word close to the Greek for "nobody." After the Cyclops is drunk and falls asleep, Odysseus puts out his one eye with a flaming and sharpened stake of olive wood. Raging, the Cyclops calls to his neighbors that "nobody" has injured him. They leave and, says Odysseus, "I was filled with laughter / to see how like a charm the name deceived them" (169). Escaping the cave with his men, Odysseus boards his ship. But although the Cyclops is hurling huge rocks at the sound of his voice and his men warn him against taunting the monster, Odysseus cannot resist shouting his real name across the water:

> Kyklops,
> if ever mortal man inquire
> how you were put to shame and blinded, tell him
> Odysseus, raider of cities, took your eye:
> Laertes' son, whose home's on Ithaka! (172)[2]

Whereupon the Cyclops, whose name we have already learned is Polyphemus, calls upon the god of the sea, Poseidon, to prevent Odysseus from reaching home again until many years have passed and all his companions are gone. In effect Odysseus's need to brag of his exploits, to tell his name to the Cyclops, has forced him into the twenty-years' wandering that makes up the *Odyssey*. And returning his name to him, with a prayer that Poseidon bring him despair and pain is the Cyclops Polyphemus, whose name in Greek means "many fames" – for Odysseus, at least one too many.

The Homeric analysis of the place of heroic assertion in a world more complex than that of the battlefield stands directly behind the career of the man the Romans called "Alexander the Great." For the worldwide scale of his grappling with the problem of fame and his constant awareness of the relation between accomplishment and publicity, Alexander deserves to be called the first famous person. Nothing was ever enough for him. Like Achilles, he wanted fame through battle and conquest. But like Odysseus, he was constantly on the move, impelled by an urge to see and do more than any Macedonian or Greek ever had before. In an ancient world where so many rulers were amassing wealth and land, defeating armies, and killing enemies, Alexander remained in the world's imagination, not just for the quantity of his achievements, but for what was immaterial about them, the unspecifiable spiritual greed that constantly seeks new challenges. To many of his early historians his urges were almost mystical, welling from his inmost being. Arrian, a Roman military governor who wrote five hundred years later but is still our best general source for Alexander's career, called the urge *pothos* (longing), one of the Greek terms for sexual desire. Whenever Alexander does what Arrian cannot explain, he says it is due to his longing – to cross a river, to climb a mountain, to see the wagon of Midas at Gordium. *Pothos* is a cause of action that is entirely within Alexander, an endless desire to strive with no specific goal. In his short life of thirty-three years, Alexander constantly posed, fulfilled, and then went far beyond a series of new roles and new challenges until he himself was the only standard by which he could be measured. At the head of his army, his eyes forever on the horizon, he stood self-sufficient but never self-satisfied.[3] Unlike the time- and role-bound rulers of the more ancient civilizations, who believed that their greatest achievement was to come into accord with the rhythms of dynastic history, he sought to be beyond time, to be superior to calendars, in essence to be remembered not for his place in an eternal descent but for himself.

To reshape the nature of fame in a society as hierarchical as Alexander's, one must first step away from stability. Plutarch among others recounts the story that when Alexander was in Corinth, long before he started his war against Persia, he went to visit the philosopher Diogenes and found him sitting under a tree. Leaving his military escort, Alexander went up to Diogenes and asked what he could do for him. Stay out of the way, Diogenes said, you're blocking the sun. The soldiers were horrified, expecting an outburst of Alexander's already famous anger. But Alexander just laughed and remarked that if he were not Alexander, he would like to be Diogenes. The visionary ruler and the philosophic recluse were equal in their desire for what was absent, equal in their separation from society, and therefore equal in their fame. The story recalls as well another favorite account of an incident in the youth of Alexander, when he tamed the great horse Bucephalus by turning its face toward the sun so it wouldn't be frightened of his shadow. One could either bask in the sun or become its rival. If Alexander could not stay out of the sun, he might strive instead to become the sun to others. All his visual representations take something from the iconography of Helios, the sun god. Like Diogenes, the philosopher who rejected the corruption of human society to live outside of it, Alexander was bent on defying any order that he had not created himself.

Many of Alexander's actions, particularly in his early career, seem to spring from a feeling of tenuous legitimacy that he transforms into a drive for superhuman achievement. Born in 356 B.C., Alexander grew up under the protection of his mother Olympias, a passionate worshiper of Dionysus, who in later years even committed murder to further her son's interests. Philip, Alexander's father, had made himself king of Macedonia at twenty-three, three years before Alexander's birth. As a hostage in Thebes some years before, Philip had acquired both a respect for Greek culture and a desire to make it his own. Thus a succession of tutors for the young Alexander significantly included Aristotle who, although he had already made a reputation in Athens, was born hardly thirty miles away from the Macedonian royal city of Pella. While Alexander grew up, Philip unified Macedonia internally and modernized the army beyond any in the ancient world. Forging a series of military alliances and capturing several crucial gold mines that allowed him to mint coins rivaled in value only by those from Athens, Philip began to extend his influence into Greece. Finally, in the summer of 338, with the important help of a cavalry charge led by the eighteen-year-old Alexander, he defeated a coalition of Greek city-states at Chaeronea and started to lay the groundwork for an attack against the Persian Empire, which had almost defeated Greece more than a hundred years earlier and was still a subversive force in Greek politics. But before Philip's plans could get much further than pre-liminary organization, he was murdered during the wedding of his daughter, a wedding that featured the appearance of Philip's image as the thirteenth among the twelve Olympian gods.

Aristotle thought that the murder of Philip was purely a private matter. But although it has never been proved that Alexander had anything to do with it, there is some reason to suspect the hand of Olympias. Two years before, Philip had taken another wife, Cleopatra, the niece of one of his generals, whereupon both Olympias and Alexander went into exile. Alexander was soon recalled to the court, but Olympias stayed behind in her native Epirus. Whatever the facts of Philip's assassination, a year or so later, when Alexander was away, Olympias had both Cleopatra and her infant son murdered. In this haze of intrigue Alexander moved swiftly to justify his inheritance, putting down a revolt in Thessaly and taking over Philip's leadership of the war against Persia. Of all Greece, only the Thebans resisted his rule, forming an army with the help of Persian bribes while Alexander was battling tribes to the north. Alexander speedily returned and, with some Greek allies, razed Thebes to the ground, divided its territory among the loyal states, and sold most of its men, women, and children as slaves. There would be no more armed resistance from within Greece until after his death. His home base now secure, in the spring of 334 B.C. Alexander crossed the Hellespont to invade the Persian Empire. Even in death, he would never return.

Since Agamemnon, a thousand years before, Alexander was the first Greek to lead an army against Asia. With self-conscious restaging, he went out of his way to lift anchor at Elaeus, the same place where, according to tradition, Agamemnon's fleet set sail to conquer Troy. Elaeus was not necessarily the best embarkation point, and the now-quiet town of Troy was hardly a strategic objective in the war against Persia. But the gesture meant something both to the army Alexander led and to Alexander himself. Not only would the Persian war be a revenge for Persian attacks against Greece, it would also justify the men of the present as heroic inheritors of Homeric grandeur. The Greeks of Alexander's day were hardly the Greeks of the *Iliad*. The families of most had vanished. But the royal house of Epirus still claimed Achilles as its ancestor, and, through Olympias, Alexander was considered his direct descendant. As war leader of all Greece, he therefore combined the blood of Achilles and the author-ity of Agamemnon, the hero and the leader. In contrast with the melancholic nostalgia of the *Iliad* for a lost race of heroes, Alexander's claim of connection with the past could make the present at least equal and perhaps superior to its greatness. Heavily conscious of his role as inheritor, Alexander at Elaeus also sacrificed at the tomb of the first Greek to be killed in the war with Troy. Landing on the other side, Alexander immediately went to the site of Troy, where he laid a wreath on the tomb of Achilles; he sent his lifelong friend Hephaestion to do the same at the grave of Patroclus, the friend of Achilles. Then, taking up a shield said to be that of Achilles, Alexander replaced it in the shrine with his own, which would be there for the edification of Roman tourists hundreds of years later. The Homeric holy war against the Persians had begun.[4]

Xerxes, the Persian king who had launched the war against Greece more than a century before Alexander's birth, had called it revenge for the Trojan War. Within hardly a month of landing at Troy, Alexander had returned the favor, winning a major battle at the Granicus River and beginning a series of sieges that effectively liberated the predominantly Greek cities of Asia Minor from Persian sovereignty. But simple repayment for past injuries did not seem to be Alexander's goal. Within just over a year he had won another major victory, at Issus in the northeastern end of the Mediterranean, and extended his control over all of Asia Minor, inciting the Persian Empire to take enough notice to make a peace offer – which was quickly refused.

Between the battle of the Granicus and the battle of Issus, Alexander was in winter quarters at a city named Gordium, the capital of Phrygia, whose most cele-brated ancient king was Midas of the golden touch. One day Alexander, who was always interested in the heroic legends of the lands he was passing through, went to the acropolis of Gordium to see the ancient wagon on which Midas had ridden when, otherwise unknown, he was designated king by an oracle. Midas's father had tied the yoke of the wagon to the pole by an intricate knot whose ends could not be seen, the Gordian knot. Like the Arthurian sword in the stone, it was a test that only the true king could pass: Whoever united the knot would rule Persia. Riding on a crest of military success, Alexander was equal to the symbolic challenge as well. Either by slashing it apart with his sword or (depending on the story) pulling out the linchpin that held yoke and pole together, Alexander cut the Gordian knot. By stepping outside the traditional terms of the puzzle, Alexander had created a new solution. It was a scene that immediately became proverbial, propelling him once again beyond the usual triumphs of kings and conquerors into the realm of the imagination.

After Gordium and the victory at Issus, Alexander charged around the eastern end of the Mediterranean, accepting the submission of Phoenicia and conquering such fortress cities as Tyre and Gaza. Buoyed by these victories, he defeated Egypt easily and, hardly two years after leaving Greece, was crowned pharaoh at Memphis. To the political and military power Alexander was wresting from the great Persian Empire, he had added the Egyptian authority of the god-king. The next spring, after founding Alexandria, he cemented his new status by journeying to Siwah, an oracle in the middle of the Libyan desert noted throughout the Greek world for its truth telling. The oracle was dedicated to Ammon, a supreme god who, as Ra the sun god, was also father of the pharaohs and had been identified by the Greeks with Zeus. According to one account of Alexander's visit to Siwah, the head priest greeted him as the son of Ammon/Zeus; according to another, it was the priest's faulty Greek that made it seem such a greeting; according to a third, it was merely politically motivated flattery. In any case, after the greeting, Alexander had a private audience with the priest, although nothing of what passed between them has come down to us. Supposedly,

Alexander wrote to his mother Olympias that he would tell her the oracle's secret message on his return to Greece. But, of course, he never did.[5]

Six hundred years later St. Augustine wrote that Alexander at Siwah had learned that the pagan gods were originally men. But surely Alexander's own exploits were teaching him that already. Later that same year he won the final battle over the Persian king, Darius; sacked the Persian capital of Persepolis; and set off for the East in pursuit of a fleeing Darius, whom he later found murdered by Persian officials in hopes of reward from the new conqueror. With Darius dead and Alexander's army in possession of all the richest and most powerful cities of the Persian Empire, it might seem that Alexander's mission was complete. But he was not out to conquer an empire but to conquer a world. Becoming pharaoh had added a crucial element of grandeur no Greek ruler had ever had. But the journey to Siwah emphasized Alexander's search for an unprecedented importance that belonged not to his power or his authority but to himself. Further and further toward the East he led his army, through present-day Iran and Afghanistan, north to Samarkand in Russia, and south to invade India. To commemorate his progress across Asia, he founded some eighteen cities named after himself as well as one named for his horse and another for his dog. It was an empire with a nomad king, and midway between the Aral Sea and the borders of China, he built Alexandria Eschate – Alexandria the Farthest, forty-five hundred miles from Macedonia.

Philip had also been a city builder, and Alexander had followed his father's example by founding Alexandropolis when he was about fifteen, during a military campaign. But the cities Alexander founded in the course of building his empire were less garrison towns than cultural beachheads. Like Achilles, he wanted to win the battles of personal honor and family prestige. Like Odysseus, he also wanted the submission of strange peoples in strange lands, where no Greek ever walked before. An Achilles in prowess and authority, he wanted also to be an Odysseus in movement and sensibility, a hero to be honored not because of his inheritance but because of himself. Unlike the Greeks, whose geographically mountainous and divided land set the stage for constant internal wrangling, unlike the Macedonians, whose domination was most secure over the plains but stopped uncomfortably at the foothills, Alexander considered the subduing of more and more geography as part of his achievement. Along the way he occasionally sent new information back to Aristotle to correct his former tutor's insular geopolitics. Three hundred years later, in the odd combination of competitiveness and respect that characterizes the Roman attitude toward Alexander, Livy writes that Alexander would never have conquered Italy because of Italy's mountains and forests. But if he had known of their existence, they would only have whetted his appetite. Plutarch recounts that a sculptor once suggested that Alexander commission him to carve Mt. Athos in northern Greece into his likeness. But Alexander replied that the Caucasus Mountains, the Tanaïs River, and the Caspian Sea would be monuments enough.

After his campaigns in India Alexander stops advancing toward the rising sun: practically because mutinies were developing among his weary soldiers and symbolically (perhaps) because a voyage down the Indus to the Arabian Sea had convinced him that he had finally reached the Great Ocean that surrounds the world. Marching back through the deserts of southern Pakistan and Iran while he sent his fleet through the Persian Gulf, Alexander returned to Persepolis and the other seats of Persian power.

For the first time in his career a grand consolidation seemed to be in order, and the Persian model was infectious. He had long abandoned his early practice of appointing men from his own train to rule conquered areas and now generally kept the previous ruler as an underling. Similarly, he began to adopt *proskynesis*, the act of obeisance in Persian court ritual, and for a time maintained two separate courts, one Greek and one Persian. To the extent that he had a program for the nations he conquered, however, it was far more cultural than political. What has been called his "policy of fusion" aimed to bring Greeks, Macedonians, and Persians together into one grand culture whose presiding genius was Greek, nowhere more spectacularly than in the mass marriages celebrated between ten thousand Macedonian men and ten thousand Persian women at Susa after Alexander's return from the East. Among the marriage celebrants at Susa was Alexander's close friend Hephaestion, who ten years before had joined him in the ritual tribute to Achilles and Patroclus at Troy. Not long after the Susa marriages, Hephaestion was dead and Alexander decreed for him honors and funeral games that easily surpassed those given for Patroclus by Achilles in the last book of the *Iliad*. Within the next year Alexander himself was dead of a fever, eleven years after he had set sail to conquer the Persian Empire in the name of Greece.

The Homeric pattern

> No wonder that Alexander carried the Iliad with him on his expeditions in a precious casket. The written word is the choicest of relics. It is something at once more intimate with us and more universal than any work of art. It is the work of art nearest to life itself.
>
> <div align="right">HENRY DAVID THOREAU, <i>Walden</i></div>

To the extent that Alexander sought fame for his own achievement rather than for his predetermined place in society, he could create Alexander the Great from Alexander III of Macedonia by two means: achievements beyond those of the past and achievements unheard of in the past. In recounting his extraordinary career, it hardly seems useful to separate the Alexander he created from the Alexander he became to others, or even from the Alexander he was to himself. Such distinctions assume that inner nature is more "real" than the social self and that a "true" explanation of Alexander would root his actions in adolescent fantasies of power (although his were hardly fantasies) or his personal and family history. But since Alexander was so overwhelmingly successful by the standards of his society and many societies to come, it is worth asking how that success might have been constructed. Instead of separating Alexander into the strands of his mother's passion, his father's military talent, and his tutor's teachings, we might focus on how Alexander brought those influences together uniquely into himself. For Alexander, as for all who live a life in public, the crucial question is less who he *was* than who he was *like*, how he explained himself to his own times and therefore how he wanted to be seen. Only then might we know in part how he saw himself. Throughout his career his achievements are inextricably tied to the way he understood the actions and characters of the heroes and gods he admired and emulated. So intertwined are his actions with the publicity that surrounds and shapes them that Alexander becomes the first clear example of the great man whose desire to excel puts earthly opponents a lowly second to the challenges posed by the heroes of the past, by the gods, and finally by his own nature.

I have used the contrast between Achilles and Odysseus to define Alexander's goals because he himself consciously exploited a genealogy of heroic fame that stretched back to the heroes of the *Iliad* and the *Odyssey*. Plutarch called the *Iliad* and the *Odyssey* Alexander's "equipment," as essential to his triumphs as his soldiers and more conventional weapons. On all his campaigns, it is said, he carried with him a copy of the *Iliad* especially annotated for him by Aristotle, and it was Aristotle's nephew Callisthenes who calculated for Alexander that it was exactly a thousand years to the month between the attack on Troy sung by Homer and the one embarked on against Persia by Alexander. Certainly, many other ancient rulers claimed descent from such semihistorical, semimythological figures. But Alexander invoked them as precedents by which he could convince others of not only his debt, but also his difference. His friendship with Hephaestion, for example, may have been modeled on that of Achilles for Patroclus, but it surpassed its model in intensity and glory. With the career of Alexander, the urge to fame begins to rely less on inheritance than on the willingness to assert that one deserves it as a member of a psychological tribe, with more affinities between each other than with any actual blood relatives, ancestors, or descendants.

Alexander's "program" was for fame as well as for achievement, and he succeeded beyond previous aspirants in part because he was raised in a society that had become self-conscious of its own inherited values. As a natural synthesizer, constantly assimilating and organizing meaning for his own purposes, Alexander illustrates that the monarchical personality is always a premediated construction. The only difference is in the quality and understanding of the builder. Many of the stories about Alexander indicate his special talent for transforming himself into the stuff of symbol and myth, and in the Macedonian society of his youth he found ready materials in a pervasive standard of Homeric heroism more intense even than that of Greece. In fact Macedonian society of the fourth century was much closer than Greek society to the world of the *Iliad* — with its proud nobles, its king the first among equals, and its constant need for a military defense against marauding tribes. Yet Macedonia also had a strong royal tradition of supporting Greek culture. It was in Pella under King Archelaus, fifty years or more before the time of Alexander, that Euripides wrote *The Bacchae*, with its tale of the fatal combat between the rationalist city-ruler Pentheus and the inspired followers of Dionysus, ancestor of the Macedonian kings. Alexander, a great reader and quoter of Euripides (as were most educated Macedonians), hardly needed his mother's example as a Dionysiac to reject the example of this boy-king who had only reason and order to protect himself. The artistic culture of Macedonia, although often sneered at by the Greeks, was in Alexander's time a rich heritage. Even before Archelaus, the Macedonian kings of the fifth century B.C. had welcomed Greek artists and artisans, philosophers and thinkers, to their courts — often when they were in flight from their native cities for political reasons. Alexander I brought Pindar, Perdiccas II invited Hippocrates, and Archelaus had his palace decorated by Zeuxis and even extended an invitation to Socrates in the midst of his trial.

Alexander's Macedonian heritage therefore included both a warrior aristocracy that valued the social forms embodied in the *Iliad* as well as a sophisticated culture that was often the product of artists unhonored in their native cities. His friend and early historian Onesicritus, would call him a "philosopher in arms," and Plutarch praised him as the greatest of philosophers although he wrote nothing. But I want to stress the strongly "bookish" way Alexander viewed himself and his world — a bookishness that was for him inseparable from realization in action. The honoring of the unknown soldier, invented by the British after World War One, depends on a modern army and a mass society. For the Greeks there is no such thing as an anonymous hero. Words and writing preserve the greatness of the past, and once that greatness has been described, it can be surpassed. The poems that celebrate fame and honor are handbooks of heroism for the future. To act historically, to make a figure in history, one must first stand apart and decide what history is. "Bookish" in our time implies a retreat from the world. But books for Alexander helped codify a world whose standards he first perfected and later transcended. Born in the middle of the fourth century B.C., Alexander is the true inheritor of fifth-century Greek literature — the drama of Aeschylus, Sophocles, and Euripides; the history of Herodotus and Thucydides; the newly written-down *Iliad* and *Odyssey* — because he understands how it allows a stepping back from mythology and the tales of heroes and thereby a new consciousness of how those stories might be reenacted and improved. Not long before, the Olympian family of twelve supreme gods had coalesced from the innumerable local gods and goddesses of Greece. Taking advantage of this new ecumenism of Greek religion, Alexander made himself the heir of almost all of its most outstanding figures.

In the restless search for achievement that took him beyond the boundaries of the known world, Alexander was also pressing beyond the traditional definitions of royal character. As familiar to Alexander as the works of Homer and the dramatists were the prescriptions for the good ruler in the writings of philosophers like Plato and his own teacher Aristotle. But until the biographies of Alexander that began to appear shortly after his death, there were few efforts to recount a king's life — or the life of any man. Power was not quite reason enough, unless an individual — like Cyrus in Xenophon's *Cyropaedia* or Pericles in Thucydides' *History of the Peloponnesian War* — might help define the ideal of the good leader. But the interest in Alexander is as much an interest in the mystery of his personality as it is an effort to detail his political and military abilities. Aristotle in the *Politics* had allowed a supreme leader to exist only if the *arete* (the perfectly expressed virtue) of that leader is the summation of all the individual *arete* of the community. Thus the *arete* of the great individual is inclusive and absorptive, a kind of ultimate in nonprofessionalism. But the self-deception of rulers was also a major theme in fifth-century drama: If, like Oedipus or Pentheus, you don't know who you are, the trappings of public power will fall from you and you will end in disgrace or death. With such tutors of ideal and failure, Alexander realized the need to control the way he is perceived, making himself into someone to be talked about, interpreted, puzzled over, so that the mystery of his meaning would be as endless as his empire.

The tragedy of Oedipus is his unawareness of his ancestors, even his father and mother. But Alexander constantly manipulates his heroic background, even to the extent of superseding his parents with their famous forebears. By birth Alexander could call not only on Achilles as an ancestor, but also on Dionysus, Perseus, and Hercules — all heroic adventurers in whom the line between god and man was uncertainly drawn. The great dramatists of the fifth century had filled Greek places with their history and myths, not as vaguely remembered stories but as immediate, dramatic, and coherent events. Hercules especially was an attractive forebear (and one also emphasized by Philip), since he was the prime example in Greek mythology of the human being who by his own efforts became like a god.[6] Hercules was a man of action, a transcendent strongman whose twelve labors – in Greek *athloi* – placed him beyond the early attacks by Greek writers on the honors athletes received as opposed to thinkers. *Athloi* was also the word for the contests at the Olympian and Pythian games in which all the cities of Greece participated. The poet Pindar, a Theban of the previous century, had risen to fame on the basis of his poems in celebration of the winners. In a world where the calendar was usually determined by local priests or civic officials, the games represented the only division of time that was recognized across Greece, and in his odes Pindar celebrated the athletic hero by situating him in a national and familial mythology that was firmly anchored in the geography of a specific time and place.

When Thebes rebelled shortly after Alexander ascended the throne, he quickly destroyed the city and sold its citizens into slavery, exempting only the house and the descendants of Pindar. The action was telling, for Thebes was not only where his father Philip had been held hostage as a teenager, it was also the traditional birthplace of Hercules, not incidentally the founder of the Macedonian royal family. Thus Alexander combines cultural and military conquest by honoring the writer, the celebrator of heroes, while defeating the mythic protector of the rebellious city and progenitor of his own royal line. Alexander later restores the temple of Artemis, built long before by Croesus, and rebuilds the crumbling tomb of Cyrus the Great, honoring the great figures of the recent past. But the mythic gods and heroes are another matter. Alexander's relationship to these forerunners is like that of the *Odyssey* to the *Iliad*, the traveling Odysseus to the static Achilles. Turning away from an identity supplied by social order, Alexander opportunistically forges his name in a self-consciously staged combat with the past. Even much later, during his campaigns in India, when he hears of a citadel on an enormous rock that even Hercules could not conquer, he immediately lays siege to it and is the first to get to the top. In his respect for Pindar and his effort to supersede Hercules, Alexander defines this early moment of his public career in analogy to the situation of the competing athlete: Beyond your prowess, beyond your talent, can you also bear being looked at, praised if you win, but ignored or execrated if you lose? On his coins the features of Hercules and Helios gradually grow to resemble Alexander's – with his touseled hair, distracted gaze, and head slightly cocked to hear something more. Shortly after his death, Ptolemy I – Alexander's general and founder of a dynasty of Greek-speaking Egyptian rulers that ended three centuries later with Cleopatra – issued coins showing the head of Alexander, crowned with the skin of the Nemean lion, trophy of the first labor of Hercules. They were among the first coins to depict realistically an actual human being.[7]

In the *Odyssey*, Odysseus is most often likened to Hercules. But Alexander may also have been attracted to the Odysseus whom Homer compares three times to a poet. The final stage in Alexander's creation of his legend will involve becoming his own audience, combining both Pindar and those he praises. In contrast with the Platonic inclination to judge all by a philosophically determined ideal, Alexander's career displays a conviction that literature and story, the human record of the past, contain the basic standards against which behavior and character should be measured. The same historical consciousness sets Alexander against Aristotle's more practical ethics as well. Praise and blame, the monitors of Aristotelian behavior, are hardly appropriate ways to judge the hero who exists not in the context of a present society so much as in the timeless community of others like himself. Arrian, Alexander's Romanized Greek historian, recounts that Alexander at the grave of Achilles lamented that he himself had no Homer to celebrate his memory. This loss Arrian says he will supply with his book. But despite Arrian's bold claims to rescue Alexander from unjustified oblivion some five hundred years after he lived, in actuality there were at least six accounts of Alexander written by contemporaries as well as many later works. In order to present himself as the transcendent hero, Alexander clearly knew that he not only had to act heroically, but also had to make sure his actions were set properly into the records of time. To such awareness of the sanction of history, Pindar and Hercules may stand as godparents, for only recently had a universal calendar been generally accepted in Greece. Before, such local models as the succession of Spartan kings or Argive priestesses had been used. But by the time of Alexander the prime model had become the years of the Olympic games, and a crucial member of Alexander's Persian expedition was Aristotle's nephew Callisthenes, previously known for helping his uncle compile an authentic list of the winners of the Pythian games, now Alexander's official historian.

Empires have risen through the military and political ability of powerful kings only to vanish, leaving behind crumbling monuments and the dust of a few anecdotes. But Alexander's urge was for cultural and imaginative domination as well. Callisthenes' specific audience was the people of the Greek city-states, whom Alexander hoped to convince that he was the legitimate heir of the Iliadic heroes and the true standard-bearer of Greek culture. Accordingly, Callisthenes' particular role as historian-press agent was to note the indications of divine favor shown to Alexander in his quest and to underline the parallels between Alexander's actions and those of past (especially Homeric) heroes. With the first great victories in Asia Minor, Alexander also began to employ visual artists to depict him (and three hundred years later Horace would complain that Alexander had much better taste in visual artists than in poets). Of the artists, only Apelles the painter, Lysippus the sculptor, and Pyrgoteles the gem carver were allowed to depict Alexander from life; the others had to be contented with imitating their patterns.[8] By bringing the deeds of the Homeric heroes to life, Alexander gains a power over the minds of men as much as over their bodies, their land, or their gold. Plutarch praises Alexander highly for his support of the arts, while Arrian's Alexander is preeminently the great tactician and military strategist. But both appreciate Alexander's awareness of himself as an actor, a performer in public, who required art and language to preserve what he had done.

Kings have always been performers, but Alexander introduces the possibility that the king might be his own playwright and stage manager as well. Ancient historians concentrate so much on the battles fought by the great men of the past because there the premediated will is clear. Only in their anecdotal reporting of strange episodes in the hero's life do they touch on why he has been remembered when so many great generals have been forgotten. Through his strategic abilities, his unparalleled development of siege machinery, and the decisive quality of the army he inherited from Philip, Alexander simultaneously helped to undermine the self-approval of the fighting soldier – so important to the Homeric conception of personal honor in war – even as he gave that sense of honor back by lavishly rewarding the heroic acts of individuals and units. He himself was the source of honor in his followers, their human intermediary with the standards of the heroic world. As all our sources attest, Alexander, unlike the Persian Great King and the Egyptian pharaoh, could maintain a closeness to his soldiers and companions – eating, drinking, being wounded – even while he was being worshiped elsewhere as a god or a god-hero. Absorbing precedents as rapidly as he absorbed land, Alexander therefore remains the earliest example of that paradoxical fame in which the spiritual authority of the hero is yet a model for a support of ordinary human nature.

Beyond the horizon

Through the medium of the publicist-historian Callisthenes, Alexander had broadcast the story of his triumphs in terms that were understandable to a Greek world brought up on Homer. But in the next phase of his career that analogy is superseded. Previously, Alexander could be considered a hero who accomplishes things that anyone could do if they had only the opportunity, the power, the foresight, and the daring; afterward he becomes the hero who escapes even such grand categories in his constant urge to do things impossible, outsized, and unprecedented. In this new phase of his career, which begins after the first swift defeats of the Persian forces, Alexander's cutting of the Gordian knot is an emblematic incident. By refusing to untie the Gordian knot and slashing it apart instead (the most dramatic possiblity), Alexander presents himself as someone free from the endless puzzles posed to men by the past. Unlike Oedipus, who has the wit to figure out the answer to the riddle of the sphinx but does not understand his own history, Alexander creates a new history for himself. Instead of unweaving the intricate knot, he swiftly and decisively makes its intricacy irrelevant to his solution. Alexander knew that cutting the Gordian knot would fulfill a prophecy of a conqueror come to Persia. But the act shows how Alexander both used and stepped beyond mere prophecy, first acquiescing in the usual ways of determining whom the gods favor, then creating his own portents. From the evidence of the story of the Gordian knot, as from so many other actions, we glimpse in Alexander a man who had an incredible sensitivity to the symbolic possibilities of his own personality. If there is premeditation in Alexander's construction of himself, it is not that of intrigue and plot. He defined boundaries in order to go beyond them, cutting the Gordian knot of past expectations of how problems should be solved and kings behave.

The victories after Gordium and the submission of Egypt to Alexander's power confirmed his assurance. Receiving the title of pharaoh had an important impact on Alexander's idea of his fame, just as triumphant visits to Egypt would later strongly affect Julius and Augustus Caesar, Marc Antony, and Napoleon. The Persians had created the first real world empire. But of all the rulers of the Middle East, the pharaohs had most elaborately and self-consciously kept the records of their dynasties and promulgated a national cult of their adoration. No more would Alexander's triumphs be sufficiently described in terms of the athletic labors of Hercules, the contests celebrated by Pindar, or even the martial prowess of the heroes of the *Iliad*. The fame of the athlete or of the soldier can be by extension a celebration as well of human nature, even that of the man drinking beer while he watches football on television. But in Egypt Alexander passes beyond the stages of athletic and military fame as celebrated by Pindar and Homer to enter a realm in which fame comes, not from the way one extends human nature, but from the way one goes beyond human nature – the realm of the man-god.

After being named pharaoh and founding Alexandria in the Nile Delta, the journey to the celebrated oracle of Siwah seems an almost compulsory next step for Alexander. Arrian notes that there was a tradition that the oracle had been consulted by both Hercules and Perseus, whom the Greeks considered to be the progenitor of the Persians, half of whose empire Alexander now controlled. As I've mentioned, we don't know with any accuracy what happened at Siwah. But the uncharacteristic secrecy of Alexander's meeting with the priest may itself be part of the publicity. Plutarch, like other later opponents of the Roman emperor cult, tries to exonerate Alexander from the charge of actually believing that he was the son of a god by saying that the assertion was made purely for policy, "to keep other men under obedience by the opinion conceived of his god-head" (North translation, 1286). But it is hardly necessary to make such a distinction. Not only does the ambiguity preserve the suggestion of divinity (always a vexed question for the historians of Alexander), but it also clearly implies Alexander's new effort to appear totally uncaused and uncreated by any earthly will but his own. Unlike the Homeric heroes, who went into battle as laden with their genealogy as with their armor, Alexander sought a self-motivation that could be sanctioned only by a direct relation to the gods. Previously, during his campaigns in Asia Minor, he had accepted his adoption by Ada, queen of Caria, in order to affirm his power over a nation otherwise uninterested in Greek politics or culture. Through the Siwah oracle's connection with the most high gods of Greece and Egypt, he had put himself up for adoption again, in a much more decisive way. The standards of the *Iliad* and the *Odyssey*, where gods intervened in the affairs of men, had been left behind for the possibility that god and man might meet on earth, in the person of Alexander.

After Siwah the atmosphere of Alexander's fame contains the new element of aloneness, his separation from mere mortals. More and more he saw in himself the intersection and mediation of disparate heroic, mythological, and national traditions. Conversely, if he could mediate those traditions, rule those territories, and be the living expression of those gods and heroes, then his own nature was coherent. Many later historians have denied that Alexander was a self-conscious Hellenizer. But he certainly made Greece and especially Greek literature the touchstone of value for an entire world, even to the extent that caused the historian Jacob Burckhardt to remark that if Alexander had not existed, we wouldn't know or care about the Greeks. Much as he had defined himself and his mission in accordance with the standards of Greek culture, so did he have to replicate that culture as he marched forward, in order that his achievement could be properly appreciated. But if the Greek polis now existed for him at all, it was not a geographical or a historical city, but a psychic one. In the Libyan desert Alexander's only competitor was the sun, until the oracle revealed how the sun – as Zeus, Ammon, or Ra – was his father. The journey toward the East and India is therefore also a journey toward the sun, as Alexander virtually established the tradition of a ruler's identification with the sun (perhaps once again superseding Odysseus, who had only stolen the Sun's cattle). Four hundred years later, in an effort to claim for themselves a large chunk of Alexander's former empire, Antony and Cleopatra would name their twin children Alexander Helios and Cleopatra Selene, Alexander the Sun and Cleopatra the Moon. As we shall see, by then the gesture had become a hollow repetition. But, for Alexander it was the necessary next phase in his sense of himself and the perception of himself he wished to give others. Lysippus, his official sculptor, blamed Apelles, the official painter, for now depicting Alexander with a thunderbolt in his hand rather than a spear. But the secret of Siwah made such a change in iconography almost compulsory.

Until Siwah, Alexander was self-consciously fitting himself into a tradition that in the process he was helping to define. After the oracle, and especially after the defeat and death of Darius, he begins to forge a tradition of his own, consciously or unconsciously dispensing with all who in any way might lay claim to having caused him to come into being. In the eyes of his ancient historians, his career falls into two parts. The second, although more triumphant, is marked with greater personal excesses, elaborate anecdotes about his drinking (a Macedonian tribute to Dionysus unappreciated by sober historians), and his frequent uncontrollable rages, which Plutarch calls the worst of passions because they are antisocial. In fact it does seem that a social control Alexander exercised over himself earlier in his career has, at least selectively, disappeared. Whether the oracle of Siwah confirmed his belief that the most high gods of Greece and Egypt were his real, his spiritual, or his symbolic fathers, no one can tell. But almost immediately following on the final defeat of the Persian forces and the discovery that Darius had been murdered, Alexander, through premeditation or chance or accident, rids himself of several crucial earthly rivals and progenitors: by the execution of Philotas, head of his elite corps of Companions; the execution of Parmenio, father of Philotas and head general of Alexander's army; the accidental murder of his cavalry commander Cleitus, who had saved his life at the battle of Granicus and whose sister had been his wet nurse; and finally the arrest and execution of Callisthenes, his historian and propagandist.

The pattern seems clear. In one way or another all four had asserted that they were either rivals to Alexander, antagonists of his new view of empire, or creators of his success. Two of the men, Parmenio and Cleitus, were his father's age and had been party to Philip's plans for the revenge attack on Persia. The two others, Philotas and Callisthenes, were closer to Alexander's age, yet loyal to his past preceptors. In addition all four were extremely hostile to Alexander's increasing effort to bring Macedonia and Persia together culturally as well as militarily. Cleitus especially had denounced Alexander's adoption of a modified Persian court dress and his new practice of maintaining two courts, Macedonian and Persian. Philotas had bragged that all of Alexander's military victories were due to him. Parmenio could easily have been thought to have encouraged his son's claim and in any case had been Philip's general as well. Cleitus, whom Alexander killed in a fit of drunken rage he deeply regretted, had the difficult honor of having saved Alexander's life and boasted of it; he also accused Alexander of having turned his back on his Greek and Macedonian heritage to enforce the "servile" ways of Persians toward their king.

Finally, after these military and political rivals, Callisthenes, the man of words, was accused of treason in his turn. The propagandist of Alexander's heroic grandeur, Callisthenes was also a nay-sayer to his divinity and had refused to perform the new court ritual of *proskynesis*. In the way of unreflective teachers, he was cut down by a power he helped to create. Appropriately enough, he was accused of instigating an assassination plot among Alexander's young pages, who were his pupils. Thus begins that conflict between rulers and writers that will become even more intense at Rome:

the sharp and easily crossed distinction between the writers who support the great man and those who attack him; the king-politician's well-founded suspicion that all writers, whether now friends or enemies, believe that their work is innately superior to the conquering of lands and peoples. Some four hundred years later, the example of Callisthenes echoes ominously in the writings of the philosopher-politician Seneca. Once tutor to Nero and virtual coruler of the empire, Seneca had been forced into retirement, and soon was to commit suicide for complicity in a plot to assassinate the emperor:

> The murder of Callisthenes is the ever-lasting crime of Alexander, which no virtue, no success in war, will redeem . . . Whenever it is said, "He conquered everything all the way to the Ocean and even made an attack on the Ocean itself with ships unknown to that water; and he extended his empire from a corner of Thrace to the farthest boundaries of the East," it will be said: "But he killed Callisthenes." Although he went beyond all the achievements in antiquity of generals and kings, of the things which he did nothing will be as great as his crime (193–95).

We have two traditions of what happened to Callisthenes: one that he was executed immediately; the other that he was carried around by the army in a cage until he died, fat and worm-ridden. Whatever its historical accuracy, it is the carnival-show revenge that accords symbolically with Alexander's new sense of himself. In the long battle between philosophers and politicians, his farcical exhibition of Callisthenes has the blooming mockery of a man who had decided to become his own historian. The Greek world of agonistic, one-on-one achievement – achievement through emulation and competition – was now irrelevant to his constantly recharted horizons and his constant movement beyond each succeeding set of limits. Instead of affording him a place to rest, each achievement impelled Alexander forward. Only a mutiny in his own army finally forced him to turn back. Callisthenes had compared Alexander's triumphs with those of myth and legend. But after surpassing Dionysus in India, Alexander was writing a history without analogy or parallel, his unending desire to assimilate the whole world to himself thwarted only by rebellions within. Fitting each newfound image of heroic power into the mosaic of his nature, Alexander made the past work for him, proclaiming by his career that those who would last through time would only be those who refused to be bound by time. He had been to Athens perhaps only once. But through Callisthenes he sent reports of his triumphs back to an Athens that was born from his own definition of its meaning rather than from the sordid realities of fourth-century Greek politics. A few years after the death of Callisthenes and only a year before his own death at thirty-three, Alexander asked for and received the status of a god in Athens. But on his deathbed, according to stories put out among his troops, he expressed a wish to be buried at Siwah.

The heritage of Alexander

> . . . [T]he noblest deeds do not always show men's virtues and vices, but oftentimes a light occasion, a word, or some sport makes men's natural dispositions and manners appear more plain than the famous battles won wherein are slain ten thousand men, or the great armies or cities won by siege and assault.
>
> PLUTARCH, "Alexander"

Alexander, like many of the surpassingly famous through history, was an individual who challenged basic assumptions about the way individuals intersect with their times and their societies. As the greatest figures often do, Alexander had appeared at a crucial juncture in history, when older definitions of both public and private behavior were breaking down. Somehow he had managed to synthesize elements of character and action that then and later struck many as a tissue of disparities and contradictions. In the course of his career he became simultaneously more abstract (as the Persian Great King) and more individual (as the unprecedented Alexander). Newly spun fantasies about his life still had tremendous popularity into the Middle Ages, when some authors postulated that he was at once god and demon. Even now historians continue to ask the ancient questions about his character: How could he build cities and yet murder a friend in a fit of anger, conquer the world's greatest empire and yet get drunk with his companions, assert that he was the son of a god and yet be wounded and even joke about the inconsistency?

Talent, of course, had much to do with Alexander's victories. But it was a talent thrust forward by an enormous desire to achieve and an endless longing to fulfill itself. His policies of resettlement, the founding of cities the separation of civic from military power, and cultural fusion between Greeks, Macedonians, and Persians under the aegis of Greek language and culture created a new definition of what it meant to rule. In his wake Greek culture flowed daily, even permeating areas, such as Cappodocia in the center of the old Persian Empire, where Greek politics and arms had not.

Alexander's material achievements were unparalleled. But what supplied the inner force for those achievements as well as for the legend of Alexander was his special attitude toward himself. At the extreme eastern limit of his conquests, Alexander raised an altar to the twelve members of the Olympian family. Sometime before this, in yet another example of his unceasing exercises in comparative mythology, he had decided that by occupying and passing beyond the city of Nysa, he had now superseded Dionysus ("the god from Nysa") and the city's traditional founder. In this double inheritance of divinity – the official Olympians and the outsider Dionysus – may be some clue to the kind of renown he sought. In the Greek tradition Zeus was the head of the Olympian family and thereby the ruler of the heavens and the earth as well.

As W. K. C. Guthrie and others have pointed out, the Greeks viewed Zeus as somewhat on the order of the universal god of the monotheists, a supreme heavenly power who could potentially be likened to a supreme power on earth. But to this divine political power Alexander added the more personal politics of Dionysus, whose divinity enters into the worshiper. In the Olympian ritual, the god is *worshiped*, while in the Dionysian, the god (in his animal form) is *consumed*. Thus there are two

Alexanders. In the later iconography of his sculptured image – a flowing mane of hair, head twisted toward the left, eyes turned toward the sky – Alexander resembles an enraptured Dionysiac or an inspired poet. But in his conquests and his empire, he inclines more to Zeus and the other sun gods, who stand at the top of all earthly and divine hierarchies, furnishing the pattern for divine rule in Western Europe from the Romans down to the Stuarts of England and the Bourbons of France.

In his time Alexander was alone. But that void of competitors was destined to become more crowded, if only because his career was now available as a guide. Whether their goals were to conquer the world through arms, through art, or through spirit, in some sense he had first shown the way. After his death, his myth, like his empire, was dispersed in a myriad of directions. From his generals arose a new generation of hero/god/kings, the Successors, who fought for shares in the sprawling empire. Of these, the most successful was Ptolemy of Egypt. With Alexander as his preceptor, he seems to have learned best how to gather to himself the traditions of another culture. Appropriately enough, it was Ptolemy who diverted the funeral cortege of Alexander on its way to Macedonia and brought it instead to Alexandria, where it could be viewed in uncorrupted conditions three centuries later: first by Julius Caesar after his defeat of Pompey at the battle of Pharsalus; and then by Caesar's heir, Octavian (later Augustus), after his defeat of Antony and Cleopatra. Like Alexander, Ptolemy put himself up for adoption, and his later policies of encouraging science, agriculture, and learning in Egypt imply that as Alexander's general he had also learned the lessons of cultural commingling along with those of military and political conquest. Ruling with Alexander's mythic sanction, Ptolemy also became one of his earliest historians and laid the groundwork for the great library of Alexandria, the center of Greek learning and intellectual activity for the whole Mediterranean world. And the hero-emulating Alexander may have been pleased with the irony that Zenodotos, the first head of the great Library of Alexandria, published a Homeric glossary, collated manuscripts of the *Iliad* and the *Odyssey*, and, in tribute to the Greek alphabet, divided the two poems for the first time into the twenty-four books by which we now know them.

Alexander's example seems to have had a strong influence on political and national aspirations as well. In one of the most striking cases, Chandragupta, an Indian prince who had visited Alexander's camp on the Hydaspes, went on to found the Mauryan dynasty. His grandson Asoka extended the rule of this first great Indian empire to nearly all of India and Afghanistan. After his conquests, he renounced violence and converted to Buddhism. In the great expansion of religious building that followed, monumental column sculpture began to appear in a religion previously marked by an antagonism or indifference to representational imagery. Buddha himself would not be depicted for some centuries to come. But it is intriguing to note that one prime source of that later visual imagery is Gandhāra, a center of Buddhist studies in what is now northern Pakistan, which was ruled by Greek generals until the first century A.D. On the heads of these Buddhas is a characteristic topknot that some have traced from Indian precedents and others from the Macedonian war helmet, while their faces definitely resemble those of Apollo or Hermes. Thus although the image itself has predominantly Indian roots, the urge to such imagery owes some debt to the forces set into motion by Alexander. As Heinrich Zimmer writes, "the concept of the Buddha [was imbued] with the strong personal character of a victorious spiritual individual. . . . The cosmic savior was humanized in the manner of a semidivine Greek hero" (I, 345).[9]

Who could say that the career of Alexander did not have a philosophical effect as well? On the news of his death, Aristotle fled from Athens and died a year later. Not long after, another philosopher came to Athens: Zeno, the founder of Stoicism — a philosophy that would find its largest audience among the Romans who accepted Augustus's empire. So too returned to Greece a member of Alexander's train in Asia named Pyrrho, who founded the school of sceptical philosophy that asserted no knowledge was definite. But perhaps most intriguing of all the intellectual fallout from the career of Alexander was the work of Euhemerus, who served under Cassander, a longtime antagonist of Alexander.

After Alexander's death Cassander had asserted his rule over Greece by murdering Alexander's wife, his son, and his mother Olympias. Euhemerus, however, may have understood the lesson of Alexander's career better than the man who thought he could extinguish the fame of Alexander with his own. His most influential work, known to us only through fragments and an epitome by Eusebius, is a philosophical novel in which Euhemerus travels to an imaginary island where he learns from inscriptions that the gods – especially the high gods Uranus, Cronus, and Zeus – were in fact human kings about whom myths and stories collected. The idea had been around before, but never so forcefully presented, and it caught men's imaginations. Hardly a century after Alexander's death, Ennius, the first great Roman writer, wrote his own version of Euhemerus's novel, including the Roman Jupiter as well among the gods who had been kings.

With the establishment of the Ptolemaic dynasty and the Library of Alexandria, something of the institutional had come into the boundary-bursting world of Alexander's achievements. In the West it is Alexander-Zeus rather than Alexander-Dionysus who boasts the most descendants. At Rome his ever-expansive *pothos* and his dream of cultural fusion appear as a thirst for domination, ultimately transformed into a consolidation of administrative and military power under one supreme ruler, the Roman emperor. Alexander could still build in empty spaces. But by three centuries later the world was already getting more populated and the opportunities for uniqueness more restricted. What happens when there turns out to be too many Alexanders? In the fame society of Rome, as well as in the Renaissance, men were particularly intrigued by a late-blooming anecdote in which a young man named Herostratus, on the day of Alexander's birth, burns down the Temple of Diana at Ephesus so that he can be as famous as the newborn king's son: If the goal was only fame, then any extreme act, even violence and destruction, might do. Or, as the Renaissance writers often phrased it, we know the name Herostratus, but the names of the temple's architects are lost.

Notes

1   As Bruno Snell points out in *The Discovery of Mind*, the Homeric phrase "imperishable fame" (*kleas afthiton*) agrees with Indo-European poetic diction and is thus both a conceptual and linguistic inheritance from one of the roots of the world language system (164).

2   Similarly, the lure of the song of the Sirens (*Odyssey*, XII) is their flattery of Odysseus as the hero of Troy: "the temptation is to know your ultimate reputation before you are dead" (Vermeule, 203). In effect this has already happened to Odysseus when, in the court of Alkinoös, a minstrel sings the Troy story and Odysseus secretly weeps. When this happens a second time and his weeping is noticed by the king, the stage is set for the revelation of his name and the telling of his story.

3   For the connection of *pothos* with *eros* rather than with mere desire (*himeros*), see Vermeule, 145–78.

4   According to Plutarch, Alexander also wanted to play the lyre of Achilles, perhaps as Achilles himself is playing it when, as Homer describes it, he receives Odysseus and others into his tent on their embassy to persuade him to return to the battle.

5   The different versions are recounted in Plutarch's biography of Alexander, which was written not long before Arrian's. See any edition of the *Lives of the Noble Greeks and Romans*. It is most conveniently available in Ian Scott-Kilvert's Penguin translation, Plutarch, *The Age of Alexander* (1973), 283–84. (Scott-Kilvert's Penguin translations rearrange the "parallel lives" intended by Plutarch into a more chronological sequence.)

6   According to myths reflected in Sophocles's *Trachiniae* (and later moralized by Isocrates), after the human body of Hercules was burned in the funeral pyre on Mt. Ida, his divine part ascended to heaven.

7   Athletes were probably the earliest heroes to be praised formally by their contemporaries. The Olympic and other periodic sport competitions in ancient Greece furnished a chance to see the traits of a warrior's individual valor displayed before an audience, with a proper subordination to rules that are the equivalent of an internalized personal virtue. The games in this sense spiritualize war, and the athlete is a transcendent warrior.

8   Renaissance painters were especially attracted to a story that Alexander had magnanimously given up his mistress Campaspe to Apelles, who had fallen in love with her while doing her portrait. None of the earliest sources contain the story, but it clearly appealed to the newly self-conscious Renaissance painters as a paradigm of the relationship between the great painter and the great patron.

9   In the early ages of Buddhism, before the introduction of Buddhist representational imagery, the *stūpa* or burial mound was one of the sole places for acts of veneration. Alexander commemorated the death of Bucephalus in Gandhāra by founding the town of Bucephala along the Hydaspes, and in nearby Rawalpindi there is an ancient *stūpa* locally venerated as the tomb of Bucephalus (Bamm, 55).

In Greece itself, as fifth-century dramatic literature had brought the myths into a more direct relationship with their audience, so portraiture in the same period was also becoming much more realistic. Even when it was idealized, it was based on living models rather than on traditional rules for the appearance of a god. The extent to which Alexander's actual features appeared on coins in his lifetime is arguable. But his example was influential, and it soon became common for local rulers in various parts of his former empire to impress some version of their faces on their money. Alexander's impact on Buddhist conceptions of authority, while still debated, are at least more uplifting, for his iconography introduces the possibility that visualization might enhance rather than diminish greatness.

Chapter 3

Max Weber

THE SOCIOLOGY OF CHARISMATIC AUTHORITY

The general character of charisma

BUREAUCRATIC AND PATRIARCHAL STRUCTURES are antagonistic in many ways, yet they have in common a most important peculiarity: permanence. In this respect they are both institutions of daily routine. Patriarchal power especially is rooted in the provisioning of recurrent and normal needs of the workaday life. Patriarchal authority thus has its original locus in the economy, that is, in those branches of the economy that can be satisfied by means of normal routine. The patriarch is the 'natural leader' of the daily routine. And in this respect, the bureaucratic structure is only the counter-image of patriarchalism transposed into rationality. As a permanent structure with a system of rational rules, bureaucracy is fashioned to meet calculable and recurrent needs by means of a normal routine.

The provisioning of all demands that go beyond those of everyday routine has had, in principle, an entirely heterogeneous, namely, a *charismatic*, foundation; the further back we look in history, the more we find this to be the case. This means that the 'natural' leaders – in times of psychic, physical, economic, ethical, religious, political distress – have been neither officeholders nor incumbents of an 'occupation' in the present sense of the word, that is, men who have acquired expert knowledge and who serve for remuneration. The natural leaders in distress have been holders of specific gifts of the body and spirit; and these gifts have been believed to be supernatural, not accessible to everybody. The concept of 'charisma' is here used in a completely 'value-neutral' sense.

The capacity of the Irish culture hero, Cuchulain, or of the Homeric Achilles for heroic frenzy is a manic seizure, just as is that of the Arabian berserk who bites his shield like a mad dog – biting around until he darts off in raving bloodthirstiness. For a long time it has been maintained that the seizure of the berserk is artificially produced through acute poisoning. In Byzantium, a number of 'blond beasts,' disposed to such seizures, were kept about, just as war elephants were formerly kept. Shamanist ecstasy is linked to constitutional epilepsy, the possession and the testing of which represents charismatic qualification. Hence neither is 'edifying' to our minds. They are just as little edifying to us as is the kind of 'revelation,' for instance, of the Sacred Book of the Mormons, which, at least from an evaluative standpoint, perhaps would have to be called a 'hoax.' But sociology is not concerned with such questions. In the faith of their followers, the chief of the Mormons has proved himself to be charismatically qualified, as have 'heroes' and 'sorcerers.' All of them have practiced their arts and ruled by virtue of this gift (charisma) and, where the idea of God has already been clearly conceived, by virtue of the divine mission lying therein. This holds for doctors and prophets, just as for judges and military leaders, or for leaders of big hunting expeditions.

It is to his credit that Rudolf Sohm brought out the sociological peculiarity of this category of domination-structure for a historically important special case, namely, the historical development of the authority of the early Christian church. Sohm performed this task with logical consistency, and hence, by necessity, he was one-sided from a purely historical point of view. In principle, however, the very same state of affairs recurs universally, although often it is most clearly developed in the field of religion.

In contrast to any kind of bureaucratic organization of offices, the charismatic structure knows nothing of a form or of an ordered procedure of appointment or dismissal. It knows no regulated 'career,' 'advancement,' 'salary,' or regulated and expert training of the holder of charisma or of his aids. It knows no agency of control or appeal, no local bailiwicks or exclusive functional jurisdictions; nor does it embrace permanent institutions like our bureaucratic 'departments,' which are independent of persons and of purely personal charisma.

Charisma knows only inner determination and inner restraint. The holder of charisma seizes the task that is adequate for him and demands obedience and a following by virtue of his mission. His success determines whether he finds them. His charismatic claim breaks down if his mission is not recognized by those to whom he feels he has been sent. If they recognize him, he is their master – so long as he knows how to maintain recognition through 'proving' himself. But he does not derive his 'right' from their will, in the manner of an election. Rather, the reverse holds: it is the *duty* of those to whom he addresses his mission to recognize him as their charismatically qualified leader.

In Chinese theory, the emperor's prerogatives are made dependent upon the recognition of the people. But this does not mean recognition of the sovereignty of the people any more than did the prophet's necessity of getting recognition from the believers in the early Christian community. The Chinese theory, rather, characterizes the charismatic nature of the *monarch's position*, which adheres to his *personal* qualification and to his *proved* worth.

Charisma can be, and of course regularly is, qualitatively particularized. This is an internal rather than an external affair, and results in the qualitative barrier of the charisma holder's mission and power. In meaning and in content the mission may be addressed to a group of men who are delimited locally, ethnically, socially, politically, occupationally, or in some other way. If the mission is thus addressed to a limited group of men, as is the rule, it finds its limits within their circle.

In its economic sub-structure, as in everything else, charismatic domination is the very opposite of bureaucratic domination. If bureaucratic domination depends upon regular income, and hence at least *a potiori* on a money economy and money taxes, charisma lives in, though not off, this world. This has to be properly understood. Frequently charisma quite deliberately shuns the possession of money and of pecuniary income *per se*, as did Saint Francis and many of his like; but this is of course not the rule. Even a pirate genius may exercise a 'charismatic' domination, in the value-neutral sense intended here. Charismatic political heroes seek booty and, above all, gold. But charisma, and this is decisive, always rejects as undignified any pecuniary gain that is methodical and rational. In general, charisma rejects all rational economic conduct.

The sharp contrast between charisma and any 'patriarchal' structure that rests upon the ordered base of the 'household' lies in this rejection of rational economic conduct. In its 'pure' form, charisma is never a source of private gain for its holders in the sense of economic exploitation by the making of a deal. Nor is it a source of income in the form of pecuniary compensation, and just as little does it involve an orderly taxation for the material requirements of its mission. If the mission is one of peace, individual patrons provide the necessary means for charismatic structures; or those to whom the charisma is addressed provide honorific gifts, donations, or other voluntary contributions. In the case of charismatic warrior heroes, booty represents one of the ends as well as the material means of the mission. 'Pure' charisma is contrary to all patriarchal domination (in the sense of the term used here). It is the opposite of all ordered economy. It is the very force that disregards economy. This also holds, indeed precisely, where the charismatic leader is after the acquisition of goods, as is the case with the charismatic warrior hero. Charisma can do this because by its very nature it is not an 'institutional' and permanent structure, but rather, where its 'pure' type is at work, it is the very opposite of the institutionally permanent.

In order to do justice to their mission, the holders of charisma, the master as well as his disciples and followers, must stand outside the ties of this world, outside of routine occupations, as well as outside the routine obligations of family life. The statutes of the Jesuit order preclude the acceptance of church offices; the members of orders are forbidden to own property or, according to the original rule of St. Francis, the order as such is forbidden to do so. The priest and the knight of an order have to live in celibacy, and numerous holders of a prophetic or artistic charisma are actually single. All this is indicative of the unavoidable separation from this world of those who partake ('κλῆρος') of charisma. In these respects, the economic conditions of participation in charisma may have an (apparently) antagonistic appearance, depending upon the type of charisma — artistic or religious, for instance — and the way of life flowing from its meaning. Modern charismatic movements of artistic origin represent 'independents without gainful employment' (in everyday language, rentiers). Normally such persons are the best qualified to follow a charismatic leader. This is just as logically consistent as was the medieval friar's vow of poverty, which demanded the very opposite.

Foundations and instability of charismatic authority

By its very nature, the existence of charismatic authority is specifically unstable. The holder may forego his charisma; he may feel 'forsaken by his God,' as Jesus did on the cross; he may prove to his followers that 'virtue is gone out of him.' It is then that his mission is extinguished, and hope waits and searches for a new holder of charisma. The charismatic holder is deserted by his following, however, (only) because pure charisma does not known any 'legitimacy' other than that flowing from personal strength, that is, one which is constantly being proved. The charismatic hero does not deduce his authority from codes and statutes, as is the case with the jurisdiction of office; nor does he deduce his authority from traditional custom or feudal vows of faith, as is the case with patrimonial power.

The charismatic leader gains and maintains authority solely by proving his strength in life. If he wants to be a prophet, he must perform miracles; if he wants to be a war lord, he must perform heroic deeds. Above all, however, his divine mission must 'prove' itself in that those who faithfully surrender to him must fare well. If they do not fare well, he is obviously not the master sent by the gods.

This very serious meaning of genuine charisma evidently stands in radical contrast to the convenient pretensions of present rulers to a 'divine right of kings,' with its reference to the 'inscrutable' will of the Lord, 'to whom alone the monarch is responsible.' The genuinely charismatic ruler is responsible precisely to those whom he rules. He is responsible for but one thing, that he personally and actually be the God-willed master.

During these last decades we have witnessed how the Chinese monarch impeaches himself before all the people because of his sins and insufficiencies if his administration does not succeed in warding off some distress from the governed, whether it is inundations or unsuccessful wars. Thus does a ruler whose power, even in vestiges and theoretically, is genuinely charismatic deport himself. And if even this penitence does not reconcile the deities, the charismatic emperor faces dispossession and death, which often enough is consummated as a propitiatory sacrifice.

Meng-tse's (Mencius') thesis is that the people's voice is 'God's voice' (according to him the *only* way in which God speaks!) has a very specific meaning: if the people cease to recognize the ruler, it is expressly stated that he simply becomes a private citizen; and if he then wishes to be more, he becomes a usurper deserving of punishment. The state of affairs that corresponds to these phrases, which sound highly revolutionary, recurs under primitive conditions without any such pathos. The charismatic character adheres to almost all primitive authorities with the exception of domestic power in the narrowest sense, and the chieftain is often enough simply deserted if success does not remain faithful to him.

The subjects may extend a more active or passive 'recognition' to the personal mission of the charismatic master. His power rests upon this purely factual recognition and springs from faithful devotion. It is devotion to the extraordinary and unheard-of, to what is strange to all rule and tradition and which therefore is viewed as divine. It is a devotion born of distress and enthusiasm.

Genuine charismatic domination therefore knows of no abstract legal codes and statutes and of no 'formal' way of adjudication. Its 'objective' law emanates concretely from the highly personal experience of heavenly grace and from the god-like strength of the hero. Charismatic domination means a rejection of all ties to any external order in favor of the exclusive glorification of the genuine mentality of the prophet and hero. Hence, its attitude is revolutionary and transvalues everything; it makes a soverign break with all traditional or rational norms: 'It is written, but I say unto you.'

The specifically charismatic form of settling disputes is by way of the prophet's revelation, by way of the oracle, or by way of 'Solomonic' arbitration by a charismatically qualified sage. This arbitration is determined by means of strictly concrete and individual evaluations, which, however, claim absolute validity. Here lies the proper locus of 'Kadi-justice' in the proverbial – not the historical – sense of the phrase. In its actual historical appearance the jurisdiction of the Islamic Kadi is, of course, bound to sacred tradition and is often a highly formalistic interpretation.

Only where these intellectual tools fail does jurisdiction rise to an unfettered individual act valuing the particular case; but then it does indeed. Genuinely charismatic justice always acts in this manner. In its pure form it is the polar opposite of formal and traditional bonds, and it is just as free in the face of the sanctity of tradition as it is in the face of any rationalist deductions from abstract concepts.

This is not the place to discuss how the reference to the *aegum et bonum* in the Roman administration of justice and the original meaning of English 'equity' are related to charismatic justice in general and to the theocratic Kadi-justice of Islamism in particular.[1] Both the *aegum et bonum* and 'equity' are partly the products of a strongly rationalized administration of justice and partly the product of abstract conceptions of natural law. In any case the *ex bona fide* contains a reference to the 'mores' of business life and thus retains just as little of a genuine irrational justice as does, for instance, the German judge's 'free discretion.'

Any kind of ordeal as a means of evidence is, of course, a derivative of charismatic justice. But the ordeal displaces the personal authority of the holder of charisma by a mechanism of rules for formally ascertaining the divine will. This falls in the sphere of the 'routinization' of charisma, with which we shall deal below.

Charismatic kingship

In the evolution of political charisma, kingship represents a particularly important case in the historical development of the charismatic legitimization of institutions. The king is everywhere primarily a war lord, and kingship evolves from charismatic heroism.

In the form it displays in the history of civilized peoples, kingship is not the oldest evolutionary form of 'political' domination. By 'political' domination is meant a power that reaches beyond and which is, in principle, distinct from domestic authority. It is distinct because, in the first place, it is not devoted to leading the peaceful struggle of man with nature; it is, rather, devoted to leading in the violent conflict of one human community with another.

The predecessors of kingship were the holders of all those charismatic powers that guaranteed to remedy extraordinary external and internal distress, or guaranteed the success of extraordinary ventures. The chieftain of early history, the predecessor of kingship, is still a dual figure. On the one hand, he is the patriarchal head of the family or sib, and on the other, he is the charismatic leader of the hunt and war, the sorcerer, the rainmaker, the medicine man – and thus the priest and the doctor – and finally, the arbiter. Often, yet not always, such charismatic functions are split into as many special holders of charisma. Rather frequently the chieftain of the hunt and of war stands beside the chieftain of peace, who has essentially economic functions. In contrast to the latter, the chieftain of war acquires his charisma by proving his heroism to a voluntary following in successful raids leading to victory and booty. Even the royal Assyrian inscriptions enumerate booties of the hunt and cedars from Lebanon – dragged along for building purposes – alongside figures on the slain enemies and the size of the walls of conquered cities, which are covered with skins peeled off the enemies.

The charismatic position (among primitives) is thus acquired without regard to position in the sibs or domestic communities and without any rules whatsoever. This dualism of charisma and everyday routine is very frequently found among the American Indians, for instance, among the Confederacy of the Iroquois, as well as in Africa and elsewhere.

Where war and the big game hunt are absent, the charismatic chieftain – the 'war lord' as we wish to call him, in contrast to the chieftain of peace – is absent as well. In peacetime, especially if elemental calamities, particularly drought and diseases, are frequent, a charismatic sorcerer may have an essentially similar power in his hands. He is a priestly lord. The charisma of the war lord may or may not be unstable in nature according to whether or not he proves himself and whether or not there is any need for a war lord. He becomes a permanent figure when warfare becomes a chronic state of affairs. It is a mere terminological question whether one wishes to let kingship, and with it the state, begin only when strangers are affiliated with and integrated into the community as subjects. For our purposes it will be expedient to continue delimiting the term 'state' far more narrowly.

The existence of the war lord as a regular figure certainly does not depend upon a tribal rule over subjects of other tribes or upon individual slaves. His existence depends solely upon a chronic state of war and upon a comprehensive organization set for warfare. On the other hand, the development of kingship into a regular royal administration does emerge only at the stage when a following of royal professional warriors rules over the working or paying masses; at least, that is often the case. The forceful subjection of strange tribes, however, is not an absolutely indispensable link in this development. Internal class stratification may bring about the very same social differentation: the charismatic following of warriors develops into a ruling caste. But in every case, princely power and those groups having interests vested in it – that is, the war lord's following – strive for legitimacy as soon as the rule has become stable. They crave for a characteristic which would define the charismatically qualified ruler.[2]

THE NATURE OF CHARISMATIC
AUTHORITY AND ITS ROUTINIZATION

Charismatic authority

THE TERM "CHARISMA" WILL be applied to a certain quality of an individual personality by virtue of which he is set apart from ordinary men and treated as endowed with supernatural, superhuman, or at least specifically exceptional powers or qualities. These are such as are not accessible to the ordinary person, but are regarded as of divine origin or as exemplary, and on the basis of them the individual concerned is treated as a leader. In primitive circumstances this peculiar kind of deference is paid to prophets, to people with a reputation for therapeutic or legal wisdom, to leaders in the hunt, and heroes in war. It is very often thought of as resting on magical powers. How the quality in question would be ultimately judged from any ethical, aesthetic, or other such point of view is naturally entirely indifferent for purposes of definition. What is alone important is how the individual is actually regarded by those subject to charismatic authority, by his "followers" or "disciples."

For present purposes it will be necessary to treat a variety of different types as being endowed with charisma in this sense. It includes the state of a "berserker" whose spells of maniac passion have, apparently wrongly, sometimes been attributed to the use of drugs. In Medieval Byzantium a group of people endowed with this type of charismatic war-like passion were maintained as a kind of weapon. It includes the "shaman," the kind of magician who in the pure type is subject to epileptoid seizures as a means of falling into trances. Another type is that of Joseph Smith, the founder of Mormonism, who, however, cannot be classified in this way with absolute certainty since there is a possibility that he was a very sophisticated type of deliberate swindler. Finally it includes the type of intellectual, such as Kurt Eisner,[3] who is carried away with his own demagogic success. Sociological analysis, which must abstain from value judgments, will treat all these on the same level as the men who, according to conventional judgments are the "greatest" heroes, prophets and saviours.

It is recognition on the part of those subject to authority which is decisive for the validity of charisma. This is freely given and guaranteed by what is held to be a "sign" or proof,[4] originally always a miracle, and consists in devotion to the corresponding revelation, hero worship, or absolute trust in the leader. But where charisma is genuine, it is not this which is the basis of the claim to legitimacy. This basis lies rather in the conception that it is the *duty* of those who have been called to a charismatic mission to recognize its quality and to act accordingly. Psychologically this "recognition" is a matter of complete personal devotion to the possessor of the quality, arising out of enthusiasm, or of despair and hope.

No prophet has ever regarded his quality as dependent on the attitudes of the masses toward him. No elective king or military leader has ever treated those who have resisted him or tried to ignore him otherwise than as delinquent in duty. Failure to take part in a military expedition under such leader, even though recruitment is formally voluntary, has universally been met with disdain.

If proof of his charismatic qualification fails him for long, the leader endowed with charisma tends to think his god or his magical or heroic powers have deserted him. If he is for long unsuccessful, above all if his leadership fails to benefit his followers, it is likely that his charismatic authority will disappear. This is the genuine charismatic meaning of the "gift of grace."[5]

Even the old Germanic kings were sometimes rejected with scorn. Similar phenomena are very common among so-called "primitive" peoples. In China the charismatic quality of the monarch, which was transmitted unchanged by heredity, was upheld so rigidly that any misfortune whatever, not only defeats in war, but drought, floods, or astronomical phenomena which were considered unlucky, forced him to do public penance and might even force his abdication. If such things occurred, it was a sign that he did not possess the requisite charismatic virtue, he was thus not a legitimate "Son of Heaven."

The corporate group which is subject to charismatic authority is based on an emotional form of communal relationship.[6] The administrative staff of a charismatic leader does not consist of "officials"; at least its members are not technically trained. It is not chosen on the basis of social privilege nor from the point of view of domestic or personal dependency. It is rather chosen in terms of the charismatic qualities of its members. The prophet has his disciples; the warlord his selected henchmen; the leader, generally, his followers. There is no such thing as "appointment" or "dismissal," no career, no promotion. There is only a "call" at the instance of the leader on the basis of the charismatic qualification of those he summons. There is no hierarchy; the leader merely intervenes in general or in individual cases when he considers the members of his staff inadequate to a task with which they have been entrusted. There is no such thing as a definite sphere of authority and of competence, and no appropriation of official powers on the basis of social privileges. There may, however, be territorial or functional limits to charismatic powers and and to the individual's "mission." There is no such thing as a salary or a benefice. Disciples or followers tend to live primarily in a communistic relationship with their leader on means which have been provided by voluntary gift. There are no established administrative organs. In their place are agents who have been provided with charismatic authority by their chief or who possess charisma of their own. There is no system of formal rules, of abstract legal principles, and hence no process of judicial decision oriented to them. But equally there is no legal wisdom oriented to judicial precedent. Formally concrete judgments are newly created from case to case and are originally regarded as divine judgments and revelations. From a substantive point of view, every charismatic authority would have to subscribe to the proposition, "It is written . . ., but I say unto you, . . ."[7] The genuine prophet, like the genuine military leader and every true leader in this sense, preaches, creates, or demands *new* obligations. In the pure type of charisma, these are imposed on the authority of revelation by oracles, or of the leader's own will, and are recognized by the members of the religious, military, or party group, because they come from such a source. Recognition is a duty. When such an authority comes into conflict with the competing authority of another who also claims charismatic sanction, the only recourse is to some kind of a contest, by magical means or even an actual physical battle of the leaders. In principle only one side can be in the right in such a conflict; the other must be guilty of a wrong which has to be expiated.

Charismatic authority is thus specifically outside the realm of every-day routine and the profane sphere.[8] In this respect, it is sharply opposed both to rational, and particularly bureaucratic, authority, and to traditional authority, whether in its patriarchal, patrimonial, or any other form. Both rational and traditional authority are specifically forms of every-day routine control of action; while the charismatic type is the direct antithesis of this. Bureaucratic authority is specifically rational in the sense of being bound to intellectually analysable rules; while charismatic authority is specifically irrational in the sense of being foreign to all rules. Traditional authority is bound to the precedents handed down from the past and to this extent is also oriented to rules. Within the sphere of its claims, charismatic authority repudiates the past, and is in this sense a specifically revolutionary force. It recognizes no appropriation of positions of power by virtue of the possession of property, either on the part of a chief or of socially privileged groups. The only basis of legitimacy for it is personal charisma, so long as it is proved; that is, as long as it receives recognition and is able to satisfy the followers or disciples. But this lasts only so long as the belief in its charismatic inspiration remains.

The above is scarcely in need of further discussion. What has been said applies to the position of authority of such elected monarchs as Napoleon, with his use of the plebiscite. It applies to the "rule of genius," which has elevated people of humble origin to thrones and high military commands, just as much as it applies to religious prophets or war heroes.

Pure charisma is specifically foreign to economic considerations. Whenever it appears, it constitutes a "call" in the most emphatic sense of the word, a "mission" or a "spiritual duty." In the pure type, it disdains and repudiates economic exploitation of the gifts of grace as a source of income, though, to be sure, this often remains more an ideal than a fact. It is not that charisma always means the renunciation of property or even of acquisition, as under certain circumstances prophets and their disciples do. The heroic warrior and his followers actively seek "booty"; the elective ruler or the charismatic party leader requires the material means of power. The former in addition requires a brilliant display of his authority to bolster his prestige. What is despised, so long as the genuinely charismatic type is adhered to, is traditional or rational every-day economizing, the attainment of a regular income by continuous economic activity devoted to this end. Support by gifts, sometimes on a grand scale involving foundations, even by bribery and grand-scale honoraria, or by begging, constitute the strictly voluntary type of support. On the other hand, "booty," or coercion, whether by force or by other means, is the other typical form of charismatic provision for needs. From the point of view of rational economic activity, charisma is a typical anti-economic force. It repudiates any sort of involvement in the every-day routine world. It can only tolerate, with an attitude of complete emotional indifference, irregular, unsystematic, acquisitive acts. In that it relieves the recipient of economic concerns, dependence on property income can be the economic basis of a charismatic mode of life for some groups; but that is not usually acceptable for the normal charismatic "revolutionary."

The fact that incumbency of church office has been forbidden to the Jesuits is a rationalized application of this principle of discipleship. The fact that all the "virtuosi" of asceticism, the mendicant orders, and fighters for a faith belong in this category, is quite clear. Almost all prophets have been supported by voluntary gifts. The well-known saying of St. Paul, "If a man does not work, neither shall he eat," was directed against the swarm of charismatic missionaries. It obviously has nothing to do with a positive valuation of economic activity for its own sake, but only lays it down as a duty of each individual somehow to provide for his own support. This because he realized that the purely charismatic parable of the lilies of the field was not capable of literal application, but at best "taking no thought for the morrow" could be hoped for. On the other hand, in such a case as primarily an artistic type of charismatic discipleship, it is conceivable that insulation from economic struggle should mean limitation of those who were really eligible to the "economically independent"; that is, to persons living on income from property. This has been true of the circle of Stefan George, at least in its primary intentions.

In traditionally stereotyped periods, charisma is the greatest revolutionary force. The equally revolutionary force of "reason" works from without by altering the situations of action, and hence its problems, finally in this way changing men's attitudes toward them; or it intellectualizes the individual. Charisma, on the other hand, may involve a subjective or internal reorientation born out of suffering, conflicts, or enthusiasm. It may then result in a radical alteration of the central system of attitudes and directions of action with a completely new orientation of all attitudes toward the different problems and structures of the "world."[9] In pre-rationalistic periods, tradition and charisma between them have almost exhausted the whole of the orientation of action.

The routinization of charisma

In its pure form charismatic authority has a character specifically foreign to every-day routine structures. The social relationships directly involved are strictly personal, based on the validity and practice of charismatic personal qualities. If this is not to remain a purely transitory phenomenon, but to take on the character of a permanent relationship forming a stable community of disciples or a band of followers or a party organization or any sort of political or hierocratic organization, it is necessary for the character of charismatic authority to become radically changed. Indeed, in its pure form charismatic authority may be said to exist only in the process of originating. It cannot remain stable, but becomes either traditionalized or rationalized, or a combination of both.

The following are the principal motives underlying this transformation: (a) The ideal and also the material interests of the followers in the continuation and the continual reactivation of the community, (b) the still stronger ideal and also stronger material interests of the members of the administrative staff, the disciples or other followers of the charismatic leader in continuing their relationship. Not only this, but they have an interest in continuing it in such a way that both from an ideal and a material point of view, their own status is put on a stable every-day basis. This means, above all, making it possible to participate in normal family relationships or at least to enjoy a secure social position in place of the kind of discipleship which is cut off from ordinary worldly connexions, notably in the family and in economic relationships.

These interests generally become conspicuously evident with the disappearance of the personal charismatic leader and with the problem of succession, which inevitably arises. The way in which this problem is met, if it is met at all and the charismatic group continues to exist, is of crucial importance for the character of the subsequent social relationships. The following are the principal possible types of solution:—

(a) The search for a new charismatic leader on the basis of criteria of the qualities which will fit him for the position of authority. This is to be found in a relatively pure type in the process of choice of a new Dalai Lama. It consists in the search for a child with characteristics which are interpreted to mean that he is a reincarnation of the Buddha. This is very similar to the choice of the new Bull of Apis.

In this case the legitimacy of the new charismatic leader is bound to certain distinguishing characteristics; thus, to rules with respect to which a tradition arises. The result is a process of traditionalization in favour of which the purely personal character of leadership is eliminated.

(b) By revelation manifested in oracles, lots, divine judgments or other techniques of selection. In this case the legitimacy of the new leader is dependent on the legitimacy of the technique of his selection. This involves a form of legalization. It is said that at times the *Schofetim* of Israel had this character. Saul is said to have been chosen by the old war oracle.

(c) By the designation on the part of the original charismatic leader of his own successor and his recognition on the part of the followers. This is a very common form. Originally, the Roman magistracies were filled entirely in this way. The system survived most clearly into later times in the appointment of "dictators" and in the institution of the "interrex." In this case legitimacy is acquired through the act of designation.

(d) Designation of a successor by the charismatically qualified administrative staff and his recognition by the community. In its typical form this process should quite definitely not be interpreted as "election" or "nomination" or anything of the sort. It is not a matter of free selection, but of one which is strictly bound to objective duty. It is not to be determined merely by majority vote, but is a question of arriving at the correct designation, the designation of the right person who is truly endowed with charisma. It is quite possible that the minority and not the majority should be right in such a case. Unanimity is often required. It is obligatory to acknowledge a mistake and persistence in error is a serious offence. Making a wrong choice is a genuine wrong requiring expiation. Originally it was a magical offence.

Nevertheless, in such a case it is easy for legitimacy to take on the character of an acquired right which is justified by standards of the correctness of the process by which the position was acquired, for the most part, by its having been acquired in accordance with certain formalities, such as coronation. This was the original meaning of the coronation of bishops and kings in the Western World by the clergy or the nobility with the "consent" of the community. There are numerous analogous phenomena all over the world. The fact that this is the origin of the modern conception of "election" raises problems which will have to be gone into later.

(e) By the conception that charisma is a quality transmitted by heredity; thus that it is participated in by the kinsmen of its bearer, particularly by his closest relatives. This is the case of hereditary charisma. The order of hereditary succession in such a case need not be the same as that which is in force for appropriated rights, but may differ from it. It is also sometimes necessary to select the proper heir within the kinship group by some of the methods just spoken of; thus in certain Negro states brothers have had to fight for the succession. In China succession had to take place in such a way that the relation of the living group to the ancestral spirits was not disturbed. The rule either of seniority or of designation by the followers has been very common in the Orient. Hence, in the house of Osman, it has been obligatory to eliminate all other possible candidates.

Only in Medieval Europe and in Japan universally, elsewhere only sporadically, has the principle of primogeniture, as governing the inheritance of authority, become clearly established. This has greatly facilitated the consolidation of political groups in that it has eliminated struggle between a plurality of candidates from the same charismatic family.

In the case of hereditary charisma, recognition is no longer paid to the charismatic qualities of the individual, but to the legitimacy of the position he has acquired by hereditary succession. This may lead in the direction either of traditionalization or of legalization. The concept of "divine right" is fundamentally altered and now comes to mean authority by virtue of a personal right which is not dependent on the recognition of those subject to authority. Personal charisma may be totally absent. Hereditary monarchy is a conspicuous illustration. In Asia there have been very numerous hereditary priesthoods; also, frequently, the hereditary charisma of kinship groups has been treated as a criterion of social rank and of eligibility for fiefs and benefices.

(f) The concept that charisma may be transmitted by ritual means from one bearer to another or may be created in a new person. The concept was originally magical. It involves a dissociation of charisma from a particular individual, making it an objective, transferable entity. In particular, it may become the charisma of office. In this case the belief in legitimacy is no longer directed to the individual, but to the acquired qualities and to the effectiveness of the ritual acts. The most important example is the transmission of priestly charisma by anointing, consecration, or the laying on of hands; and of royal authority, by anointing and by coronation. The *character indelibilis* thus acquired means that the charismatic qualities and powers of the office are emancipated from the personal qualities of the priest. For precisely this reason, this has, from the Donatist and the Montanist heresies down to the Puritan revolution, been the subject of continual conflicts. The "hireling" of the Quakers is the preacher endowed with the charisma of office.

Concomitant with the routinization of charisma with a view to insuring adequate succession, go the interests in its routinization on the part of the administrative staff. It is only in the initial stages and so long as the charismatic leader acts in a way which is completely outside every-day social organization, that it is possible for his followers to live communistically in a community of faith and enthusiasm, on gifts, "booty," or sporadic acquisition. Only the members of the small group of enthusiastic disciples and followers are prepared to devote their lives purely idealistically to their call. The great majority of disciples and followers will in the long run "make their living" out of their "calling" in a material sense as well. Indeed, this must be the case if the movement is not to disintegrate.

Hence, the routinization of charisma also takes the form of the appropriation of powers of control and of economic advantages by the followers or disciples, and of regulation of the recruitment of these groups. This process of traditionalization or of legalization, according to whether rational legislation is involved or not, may take any one of a number of typical forms.

The original basis of recruitment is personal charisma. With routinization, the followers or disciples may set up norms for recruitment, in particular involving training or tests of eligibility. Charisma can only be "awakened" and "tested"; it cannot be "learned" or "taught." All types of magical asceticism, as practiced by magicians and heroes, and all novitiates, belong in this category. These are means of closing the group which constitutes the administrative staff.[10]

Only the proved novice is allowed to exercise authority. A genuine charismatic leader is in a position to oppose this type of prerequisite for membership. His successor is not, at least if he is chosen by the administrative staff. This type is illustrated by the magical and warrior asceticism of the "men's house" with initiation ceremonies and age groups. An individual who has not successfully gone through the initiation, remains a "woman"; that is, is excluded from the charismatic group.

It is easy for charismatic norms to be transformed into those defining a traditional social status on a hereditary charismatic basis. If the leader is chosen on a hereditary basis, it is very easy for hereditary charisma to govern the selection of the administrative staff and even, perhaps, those followers without any position of authority. The term "familistic state"[11] will be applied when a political body is organized strictly and completely in terms of this principle of hereditary charisma. In such a case, all appropriation of governing powers, of fiefs, benefices, and all sorts of economic advantages follow the same pattern. The result is that all powers and advantages of all sorts become traditionalized. The heads of families, who are traditional gerontocrats or patriarchs without personal charismatic legitimacy, regulate the exercise of these powers which cannot be taken away from their family. It is not the type of position he occupies which determines the rank of a man or of his family, but rather the hereditary charismatic rank of his family determines the position he will occupy. Japan, before the development of bureaucracy, was organized in this way. The same was undoubtedly true of China as well where, before the rationalization which took place in the territorial states, authority was in the hands of the "old families." Other types of examples are furnished by the caste system in India, and by Russia before the *Mjestnitschestvo* was introduced. Indeed, all hereditary social classes with established privileges belong in the same category.

The administrative staff may seek and achieve the creation and appropriation of individual positions and the corresponding economic advantages for its members. In that case, according to whether the tendency is to traditionalization or legalization, there will develop (a) benefices, (b) offices, or (c) fiefs. In the first case a praebendal organization will result; in the second, patrimonialism or bureaucracy; in the third, feudalism. These become appropriated in the place of the type of provision from gifts or booty without settled relation to the every-day economic structure.

Case (a), benefices, may consist in rights to the proceeds of begging, to payments in kind, or to the proceeds of money taxes, or finally, to the proceeds of fees. Any one of these may result from the regulation of provision by free gifts or by "booty" in terms of a rational organization of finance. Regularized begging is found in Buddhism; benefices in kind, in the Chinese and Japanese "rice rents"; support by money taxation has been the rule in all the rationalized conquering states. The last case is common everywhere, especially on the part of priests and judges and, in India, even the military authorities.

Case (b), the transformation of the charismatic mission into an office, may have more of a patrimonial or more of a bureaucratic character. The former is much the more common; the latter is found principally in Mediterranean Antiquity and in the modern Western world. Elsewhere it is exceptional.

In case (c), only land may be appropriated as a fief, whereas the position as such retains its originally charismatic character. On the other hand, powers and authority may be fully appropriated as fiefs. It is difficult to distinguish the two cases. It is, however, rare that orientation to the charismatic character of the position disappears entirely; it did not do so in the Middle Ages.

For charisma to be transformed into a permanent routine structure, it is necessary that its anti-economic character should be altered. It must be adapted to some form of fiscal organization to provide for the needs of the group and hence to the economic conditions necessary for raising taxes and contributions. When a charismatic movement develops in the direction of praebendal provision, the "laity" become differentiated from the "clergy"; that is, the participating members of the charismatic administrative staff which has now become routinized. These are the priests of the developing "church." Correspondingly, in a developing political body the vassals, the holders of benefices, or officials are differentiated from the "tax payers." The former, instead of being the "followers" of the leader, become state officials or appointed party officials. This process is very conspicuous in Buddhism and in the Hindu sects. The same is true in all the states resulting from conquest which have become rationalized to form permanent structures; also of parties and other movements which have originally had a purely charismatic character. With the process of routinization the charismatic group tends to develop into one of the forms of every-day authority, particularly the patrimonial form in its decentralized variant or the bureaucratic. Its original peculiarities are apt to be retained in the charismatic standards of honour attendant on the social status acquired by heredity or the holding of office. This applies to all who participate in the process of appropriation, the chief himself and the members of his staff. It is thus a matter of the type of prestige enjoyed by ruling groups. A hereditary monarch by "divine right" is not a simple patrimonial chief, patriarch, or sheik; a vassal is not a mere household retainer or official. Further details must be deferred to the analysis of social stratification.

As a rule the process of routinization is not free of conflict. In the early stages personal claims on the charisma of the chief are not easily forgotten and the conflict between the charisma of office or of hereditary status with personal charisma is a typical process in many historical situations. . . .

The transformation of charisma in an anti-authoritarian direction

A charismatic principle which originally was primarily directed to the legitimization of authority may be subject to interpretation or development in an anti-authoritarian direction. This is true because the validity of charismatic authority rests entirely on recognition by those subject to it, conditioned as this is by "proof" of its genuineness. This is true in spite of the fact that this recognition of a charismatically qualified, and hence legitimate, person is treated as a duty. When the organization of the corporate group undergoes a process of progressive rationalization, it is readily possible that, instead of recognition being treated as a consequence of legitimacy, it is treated as the basis of legitimacy. Legitimacy, that is, becomes "democratic." Thus, for instance, designation of a successor by an administrative staff may be treated as "election" in advance; while designation by the predecessor is "nomination"; whereas the recognition by the group becomes the true "election." The leader whose legitimacy rested on his personal charisma then becomes leader by the grace of those who follow him since the latter are formally free to elect and elevate to power as they please and even to depose. For the loss of charisma and its proof involves the loss of genuine legitimacy. The chief now becomes the freely elected leader.

Correspondingly, the recognition of charismatic decrees and judicial decisions on the part of the community shifts to the doctrine that the group has a right to enact, recognize or repeal laws, according to their own free will, both in general and for an individual case. Under genuinely charismatic authority, on the other hand, it is, to be sure, true that conflicts over the correct law may actually be decided by a vote of the group. But this takes place under the pressure of the feeling that there can be only *one* correct decision and it is a matter of duty to arrive at this. The most important transitional type, is the legitimization of authority by plebiscite. The commonest examples are to be found in the party leaders of the modern state. But it is always present in cases where the chief feels himself to be acting on behalf of the masses and where his recognition is based on this. Both the Napoleons are classical examples, in spite of the fact that legitimization by plebiscite took place only after the seizure of power by force. In the case of the second Napoleon, it was confirmed on this basis after a severe loss of prestige. Regardless of how its real value as an expression of the popular will may be regarded, the plebiscite has been formally the specific means of establishing the legitimacy of authority on the basis of the free confidence of those subject to authority, even though it be only formal or possibly a fiction.

Once the elective principle has been applied to the chief by a process of reinterpretation of charisma, it may be extended to the administrative staff. Elective officials whose legitimacy is derived from the confidence of those subject to their authority and to recall if confidence ceases to exist, are typical of certain types of democracies, for instance, the United States. They are not "bureaucratic" types. Because they have an independent source of legitimacy, they are not strongly integrated in a hierarchical order. To a large extent their "promotion" is not influenced by their superiors and, correspondingly, their functions are not controlled. There are analogies in other cases where several charismatic structures, which are qualitatively heterogeneous, exist side by side, as in the relations of the Dalai Lama and the Taschi Lama. An administrative structure organized in this way is, from a technical point of view, a greatly inferior "instrument of precision" as compared with the bureaucratic type consisting of appointed officials.

The use of the plebiscite as a means of legitimizing leadership on a democratic basis is the most conspicuous type in which democracy is combined with an important role of leadership. In its fundamental significance it is a type of charismatic authority in which the authoritarian element is concealed, because the traditional position of the leader is held to be dependent on the will of those over whom he exercises authority and to be legitimized only by this will. In actual fact the leader, in this case the demagogue, is able to influence action by virtue of the devotion and trust his political followers have in him personally. In the first instance his power is only a power over those recruited to his following, but in case, with their aid, he is able to attain positions of wider authority it may extend to the political group as a whole. The type is best illustrated by the "dictators" who have emerged in the revolutions of the ancient world and of modern times. Examples are: the Greek Aisymnetes and the tyrants and demagogues; in Rome the Gracchi and their successors; in the Italian city states the *Capitani del popolo*; and certain types of political leaders in the German cities such as emerged in the democratic dictatorship of Zürich. In modern states the best examples are the dictatorship of Cromwell, and the leaders of the French Revolution and of the First and Second Empire. Wherever attempts have been made to legitimize this kind of exercise of power legitimacy has been sought in recognition by the sovereign people through a plebiscite. The leader's personal administrative staff is recruited in a charismatic form usually from able people of humble origin. In Cromwell's case, religious qualifications were taken into account. In that of Robespierre along with personal dependability also certain "ethical" qualities. Napoleon was concerned only with personal ability and adaptability to the needs of his imperial "rule of genius."

At the height of revolutionary dictatorship the position of a member of the administrative staff tends to be that of a person entrusted with a specific *ad hoc* task subject to recall. This was true of the role of the agents of the "Committee of Public Safety." When a certain kind of communal "dictators" have been swept into power by the reform movements in American cities the tendency has been to grant them freedom to appoint their own staff. Thus both traditional legitimacy and formal legality tend to be equally ignored by the revolutionary dictator. The tendency of patriarchal authorities, in the administration of justice and in their other functions, has been to act in accordance with substantive ideas of justice, with utilitarian considerations and in terms of reasons of state. These tendencies are paralleled by the revolutionary tribunals and by the substantive postulates of justice of the radical democracy of Antiquity and of modern socialism. The process of routinization or revolutionary charisma then brings with it changes similar to those brought about by the corresponding process in other respects. Thus the development of a professional army in England is derived from the principle of free choice in the participation in religious struggles in the days of Cromwell. Similarly, the French system of administration by prefects is derived from the charismatic administration of the revolutionary democratic dictatorship.

The introduction of elected officials always involves a radical alteration in the position of the charismatic leader. He becomes the "servant" of those under his authority. There is no place for such a type in a technically rational bureaucratic organization. He is not appointed by his superiors and the possibility of promotion is not dependent on their judgment. On the contrary, his position is derived from the favour of the persons whose action he controls. Hence he is likely to be little interested in the prompt and strict observance of discipline which would be likely to win the favour of superiors. The tendency is rather for electoral positions to become autocephalous spheres of authority. It is in general not possible to attain a high level of technical administrative efficiency with an elected staff of officials. This is illustrated by a comparison of the elected officials in the individual states in the United States with the appointed officials of the Federal Government. It is similarly shown by comparing the elected communal officials with the administration of the reform mayors with their own appointed staffs. It is necessary to distinguish the type of democracy where positions of authority are legitimized by plebiscite from that which attempts to dispense with leadership altogether. The latter type is characterized by the attempt to reduce to a minimum the control of some men over others.

It is characteristic of the democracy which makes room for leadership[12] that there should in general be a highly emotional type of devotion to and trust in the leader. This accounts for a tendency to favour the type of individual who is most spectacular, who promises the most, or who employs the most effective propaganda measures in the competition for leadership. This is a natural basis for the utopian component which is found in all revolutions. It also indicates the limitations on the level of rationality which, in the modern world, this type of administration can attain. Even in America it has not *always* come up to expectations.

Notes

1   Frederick II of Prussia.
2   The manuscript breaks off here (German Editor).
3   The leader of the communistic experiment in Bavaria in 1919.
4   *Bewährung*.
5   *Gottesgnadentum*.
6   Weber uses the term *Gemeinde*, which is not directly translatable.
7   Something contrary to what was written, as Jesus said in opposition to the Scribes and Pharisees.
8   Weber used the antithesis of *Charisma* and *Alltag* in two senses. On the one hand, of the extraordinary and temporary as opposed to the every-day and routine; on the other hand, the sacred as opposed to the profane.
9   Weber here uses *Welt* in quotation quotation marks, indicating that it refers to its meaning in what is primarily a religious context. It is the sphere of "worldly" things and interests as distinguished from transcendental religious interests.
10   On the charismatic type of education, see *Theory of Social and Economic Organization*, chap. iv.
11   *Geschlechterstaat*.
12   *Führerdemokratic*.

Chapter 4

Daniel J. Boorstin

FROM HERO TO CELEBRITY
The human pseudo-event

"He's the greatest!"

ANONYMOUS (BECOMING UNANIMOUS)

IN THE LAST HALF century we have misled ourselves, not only about how much novelty the world contains, but about men themselves, and how much greatness can be found among them. One of the oldest of man's visions was the flash of divinity in the great man. He seemed to appear for reasons men could not understand, and the secret of his greatness was God's secret. His generation thanked God for him as for the rain, for the Grand Canyon or the Matterhorn, or for being saved from wreck at sea.

Since the Graphic Revolution, however, much of our thinking about human greatness has changed. Two centuries ago when a great man appeared, people looked for God's purpose in him; today we look for his press agent. Shakespeare, in the familiar lines, divided great men into three classes: those born great, those who achieved greatness, and those who had greatness thrust upon them. It never occurred to him to mention those who hired public relations experts and press secretaries to make themselves look great. Now it is hard even to remember the time when the "Hall of Fame" was only a metaphor, whose inhabitants were selected by the inscrutable processes of history instead of by an *ad hoc* committee appointed to select the best-known names from the media.

The root of our problem, the social source of these exaggerated expectations, is in our novel power to make men famous. Of course, there never was a time when "fame" was precisely the same thing as "greatness." But, until very recently, famous men and great men were pretty nearly the same group. "Fame," wrote Milton, "is the spur the clear spirit doth raise. . . . Fame is no plant that grows on mortal soil." A man's name was not apt to become a household word unless he exemplified greatness in some way or other. He might be a Napoleon, great in power, a J. P. Morgan, great in wealth, a St. Francis, great in virtue, or a Bluebeard, great in evil. To become known to a whole people a man usually had to be something of a hero: as the dictionary tells us, a man "admired for his courage, nobility, or exploits." The war hero was the prototype, because the battle tested character and offered a stage for daring deeds.

Before the Graphic Revolution, the slow, the "natural," way of becoming well known was the usual way. Of course, there were a few men like the Pharaohs and Augustus and the Shah Jahan, who built monuments in their own day to advertise themselves to posterity. But a monument to command the admiration of a whole people was not quickly built. Thus great men, like famous men, came into a nation's consciousness only slowly. The processes by which their fame was made were as mysterious as those by which God ruled the generations. The past became the natural habitat of great men. The universal lament of aging men in all epochs, then, is that greatness has become obsolete.

So it has been commonly believed, in the words of Genesis, that "there were giants in the earth in those days"—in the days before the Flood. Each successive age has believed that heroes – great men – dwelt mostly before its own time. Thomas Carlyle, in his classic *Heroes, Hero-Worship, and the Heroic in History* (1841), lamented that Napoleon was "our last great man!" Arthur M. Schlesinger, Jr., at the age of 40, has noted with alarm in our day (1958) that while "great men seemed to dominate our lives and shape our destiny" when he was young, "Today no one bestrides our narrow world like a colossus; we have no giants. . . ." This traditional belief in the decline of greatness has expressed the simple social fact that greatness has been equated with fame, and fame could not be made overnight.

Within the last century, and especially since about 1900, we seem to have discovered the processes by which fame is manufactured. Now, at least in the United States, a man's name can become a household word overnight. The Graphic Revolution suddenly gave us, among other things, the means of fabricating well-knownness. Discovering that we (the television watchers, the movie goers, radio listeners, and newspaper and magazine readers) and our servants (the television, movie, and radio producers, newspaper and magazine editors, and ad writers) can so quickly and so effectively give a man "fame," we have willingly been misled into believing that fame – well-knownness – is still a hallmark of greatness. Our power to fill our minds with more and more "big names" has increased our demand for Big Names and our willingness to confuse the Big Name with the Big Man. Again mistaking our powers for our necessities, we have filled our world with artificial fame.

Of course we do not like to believe that our admiration is focused on a largely synthetic product. Having manufactured our celebrities, having willy-nilly made them our cynosures – the guiding stars of our interest – we are tempted to believe that they are not synthetic at all, that they are somehow still God-made heroes who now abound with a marvelous modern prodigality.

The folklore of Great Men survives. We still believe, with Sydney Smith, who wrote in the early nineteenth century, that "Great men hallow a whole people, and lift up all who live in their time." We still agree with Carlyle that "No sadder proof can be given by a man of his own littleness than disbelief in great men. . . . Does not every true man feel that he is himself made higher by doing reverence to that which is really above him?" We still are told from the pulpit, from Congress, from television screen and editorial page, that the lives of great men "all remind us, we can make our lives sublime." Even in our twentieth-century age of doubt, when morality itself has been in ill repute, we have desperately held on to our belief in human greatness. For human models are more vivid and more persuasive than explicit moral commands. Cynics and intellectuals, too, are quicker to doubt moral theories than to question the greatness of their heroes. Agnostics and atheists may deny God, but they are slow to deny divinity to the great agnostics and atheists.

While the folklore of hero-worship, the zestful search for heroes, and the pleasure in reverence for heroes remain, the heroes themselves dissolve. The household names, the famous men, who populate our consciousness are with few exceptions not heroes at all, but an artificial new product – a product of the Graphic Revolution in response to our exaggerated expectations. The more readily we make them and the more numerous they become, the less are they worthy of our admiration. We can fabricate fame, we can at will (though usually at considerable expense) make a man or woman well known; but we cannot make him great. We can make a celebrity, but we can never make a hero. In a now-almost-forgotten sense, all heroes are self-made.

Celebrity-worship and hero-worship should not be confused. Yet we confuse them every day, and by doing so we come dangerously close to depriving ourselves of all real models. We lose sight of the men and women who do not simply seem great because they are famous but who are famous because they are great. We come closer and closer to degrading all fame into notoriety.

In the last half century the old heroic human mold has been broken. A new mold has been made. We have actually demanded that this mold be made, so that marketable human models – modern "heroes" – could be mass-produced, to satisfy the market, and without any hitches. The qualities which now commonly make a man or woman into a "nationally advertised" brand are in fact a new category of human emptiness. Our new mold is shaped not of the stuff of our familiar morality, nor even of the old familiar reality. How has this happened?

I

THE TRADITIONAL heroic type included figures as diverse as Moses, Ulysses, Aeneas, Jesus, Caesar, Mohammed, Joan of Arc, Shakespeare, Washington, Napoleon, and Lincoln. For our purposes it is sufficient to define a hero as a human figure – real or imaginary or both – who has shown greatness in some achievement. He is a man or woman of great deeds.

Of course, many such figures remain. But if we took a census of the names which populate the national consciousness – of all those who mysteriously dwell at the same time in the minds of all, or nearly all Americans – we would now find the truly heroic figures in the old-fashioned mold to be a smaller proportion than ever before. There are many reasons for this.

In the first place, of course, our democratic beliefs and our new scientific insights into human behaviour have nibbled away at the heroes we have inherited from the past. Belief in the power of the common people to govern themselves, which has brought with it a passion for human equality, has carried a distrust, or at least a suspicion of individual heroic greatness. A democratic people are understandably wary of finding too much virtue in their leaders, or of attributing too much of their success to their leaders. In the twentieth century the rise of Mussoliniism, Hitlerism, Stalinism, and of totalitarianism in general, has dramatized the perils of any people's credulity in the power of the Great Leader. We have even come erroneously to believe that because tyranny in our time has flourished in the name of the Duce, the Führer, the omniscient, all-virtuous Commissar, or the Dictatorship of the Proletariat, democracy must therefore survive without Great Leaders.

Yet, long before Hitler or Stalin, the cult of the individual hero carried with it contempt for democracy. Hero-worship, from Plato to Carlyle, was often a dogma of anti-democracy. Aristocracy, even in the mild and decadent form in which it survives in Great Britain today, is naturally more favorable to belief in heroes. If one is accustomed to a Royal Family, a Queen, and a House of Lords, one is less apt to feel himself debased by bending the knee before any embodiment of human greatness. Most forms of government depend on a belief in a divine spark possessed by a favored few; but American democracy is embarrassed in the charismatic presence. We fear the man on horseback, the demigod, or the dictator. And if we have had fewer Great Men than have other peoples, it is perhaps because we have wanted, or would allow ourselves to have, fewer. Our most admired national heroes – Franklin, Washington, and Lincoln – are generally supposed to possess the "common touch." We revere them, not because they possess charisma, divine favor, a grace or talent granted them by God, but because they embody popular virtues. We admire them, not because they reveal God, but because they reveal and elevate ourselves.

While these democratic ideas have been arising, and while popular government has flourished in the United States, the growth of the social sciences has given us additional reasons to be sophisticated about the hero and to doubt his essential greatness. We now look on the hero as a common phenomenon of all societies. We learn, as Lord Raglan, a recent president of the Royal Anthropological Institute, pointed out in *The Hero* (1936), that "tradition is never historical." Having examined a number of well-known heroes of tradition, he concludes that "there is no justification for believing that any of these heroes were real persons, or that any of the stories of their exploits had any historical foundation. . . . these heroes, if they were genuinely heroes of tradition, were originally not men but gods . . . the stories were accounts not of fact but of ritual – that is, myths." Or we learn from Joseph Campbell's *The Hero with a Thousand Faces* (1949) that all heroes – Oriental and Occidental, modern, ancient, and primitive – are the multiform expression of "truths disguised for us under the figures of religion and mythology." Following Freud, Campbell explains all heroes as embodiments of a great "monomyth." There are always the stages of (1) separation or departure, (2) trials and victories of initiation, and finally, (3) return and re-integration with society. Nowadays it matters little whether we see the hero exemplifying a universal falsehood or a universal truth. In either case we now stand outside ourselves. We see greatness as an illusion; or, if it does exist, we suspect we know its secret. We look with knowing disillusionment on our admiration for historical figures who used to embody greatness.

Just as the Bible is now widely viewed in enlightened churches and synagogues as a composite document of outmoded folk beliefs, which can nevertheless be appreciated for its "spiritual inspiration" and "literary value" – so with the folk hero. He is no longer naively seen as our champion. We have become self-conscious about our admiration for all models of human greatness. We know that somehow they were not what they seem. They simply illustrate the laws of social illusion.

The rise of "scientific" critical history and its handmaid, critical biography, has had the same effect. In Japan, by contrast, the divine virtue of the Emperors has been preserved by declaring them off-limits for the critical biographer. Even the Meiji Emperor – the "Enlightened" Emperor, founder of modern Japan, who kept detailed journals and left materials to delight a Western biographer – remains unportrayed in an accurate critical account. In the United States until the twentieth century it was usual for biographies of public figures to be written by their admirers. These works were commonly literary memorials, tokens of friendship, of family devotion, or of political piety. This was true even of the better biographies. It was Henry Cabot Lodge, Sr., who wrote the biography of Alexander Hamilton, Albert J. Beveridge who wrote the life of John Marshall, Douglas Southall Freeman who enshrined Robert E. Lee, and Carl Sandburg who wrote a monument to Lincoln. This has ceased to be the rule. Nor is this due only to the new schools of debunking biography (represented by Van Wyck Brooks' *Mark Twain* (1920) and *Henry James* (1925), W. E. Woodward's *George Washington* (1926) and *General Grant* (1928)) which grew in the jaundiced 'twenties. The appearance of American history as a recognized learned specialty in the early twentieth century has produced a new flood of biographical works which are only rarely inspired by personal admiration. Instead they are often merely professional exercises; scholars ply their tools and the chips fall where they may. We have thus learned a great deal more about our national heroes than earlier generations cared to know.

Meanwhile, the influence of Karl Marx, the rise of economic determinism, a growing knowledge of economic and social history, and an increased emphasis on social forces have made the individual leader seem less crucial. The Pilgrim Fathers, we now are told, were simply representatives of the restless, upheaving middle classes; their ideas expressed the rising "Protestant Ethic," which was the true prophet of modern capitalism. The Founding Fathers of the Constitution, Charles A. Beard and others have pointed out, were little more than spokesmen of certain property interests. Andrew Jackson became only one of many possible expressions of a rising West. The Frontier itself became the hero instead of the men. "Isms," "forces," and "classes" have spelled the death of the hero in our historical literature.

Under the hot glare of psychology and sociology the heroes' heroic qualities have been dissolved into a blur of environmental influences and internal maladjustments. For example, Charles Sumner (1811–1874), the aggressive abolitionist Senator from Massachusetts, who was beaten over the head with a cane by Representative Preston S. Brooks of South Carolina, had long been a hero of the abolitionists, a martyr for the Northern cause. From the excellent scholarly biography by David Donald in 1960, Sumner emerges with barely a shred of nobility. He becomes a refugee from an unhappy youth. His ambition now seems to have stemmed from his early insecurity as the son of an illegitimate father, a half-outcast from Cambridge society. His principles in his later years (and his refusal to sit in the Senate for many months after his beating) no longer express a true Crusader's passion. Henry Wadsworth Longfellow once eulogized Sumner:

> So when a great man dies,
> For years beyond our ken,

The light he leaves behind him lies
Upon the paths of men.

But now, in David Donald's technical phrase, Sumner's conduct in his late years becomes a "post-traumatic syndrome."

In these middle decades of the twentieth century the hero has almost disappeared from our fiction as well. The central figure in any serious book is more likely to be a victim. In the plays of Tennessee Williams and Arthur Miller, in the novels of Ernest Hemingway, William Faulkner, and John O'Hara, the leading roles are played by men who suffer from circumstances. Even the novelist's imagination is now staggered by the effort to conjure up human greatness.

Today every American, child or adult, encounters a vastly larger number of names, faces, and voices than at any earlier period or in any other country. Newspapers, magazines, second-class mail, books, radio, television, telephone, phonograph records – these and other vehicles confront us with thousands of names, people, or fragments of people. In our always more overpopulated consciousness, the hero every year becomes less significant. Not only does the newspaper or magazine reader or television watcher see the face and hear the voice of his President and the President's wife and family; he also sees the faces and hears the voices of his cabinet members, undersecretaries, Senators, Congressmen, and of their wives and children as well. Improvements in public education, with the always increasing emphasis on recent events, dilute the consciousness. The titanic figure is now only one of thousands. This is ever more true as we secure a smaller proportion of our information from books. The hero, like the spontaneous event, gets lost in the congested traffic of pseudo-events.

II

THE HEROES of the past, then, are dissolved before our eyes or buried from our view. Except perhaps in wartime, we find it hard to produce new heroes to replace the old.

We have made peculiar difficulties for ourselves by our fantastic rate of progress in science, technology, and the social sciences. The great deeds of our time are now accomplished on *unintelligible frontiers*. When heroism appeared as it once did mostly on the battlefield or in personal combat, everybody could understand the heroic act. The claim of the martyr or the Bluebeard to our admiration or horror was easy enough to grasp. When the dramatic accomplishment was an incandescent lamp, a steam engine, a telegraph, or an automobile, everybody could understand what the great man had accomplished. This is no longer true. The heroic thrusts now occur in the laboratory, among cyclotrons and betatrons, whose very names are popular symbols of scientific mystery. Even the most dramatic, best-publicized adventures into space are on the edges of our comprehension. There are still, of course, rare exceptions – a Dr. Albert Schweitzer or a Dr. Tom Dooley – whose heroism is intelligible. But these only illustrate that intelligible heroism now occurs almost exclusively on the field of sainthood or martyrdom. There no progress has been made for millennia. In the great areas of human progress, in science, technology, and the social sciences, our brave twentieth-century innovators work in the twilight just beyond our understanding. This has obviously always been true to some extent; the work of profound thinkers has seldom been more than half-intelligible to the lay public. But never so much as today.

Despite the best efforts of ingenious and conscientious science reporters (now a profession all their own) our inventors and discoverers remain in the penumbra. With every decade popular education falls farther behind technology. Sir Isaac Newton's *Principia Mathematica* was popularized "for ladies and gentlemen" who glimpsed the crude gist of his ideas. But how many "popular" lecturers – even so crudely – have explained Einstein's theory of relativity? Nowadays our interest lies primarily in the mystery of the new findings. Fantastic possibilities engage our imagination without taxing our understanding. We acclaim the flights of Yuri Gagarin and Alan Shepard without quite grasping what they mean.

Not only in science are the frontiers less intelligible. Perhaps most worshipers in Florence could grasp the beauty of a painting by Cimabue or Giotto. How many New Yorkers today can understand a Jackson Pollock or a Rothko?

Our idolized writers are esoteric. How many can find their way in Joyce's *Ulysses* or *Finnegans Wake?* Our most honored literati are only half-intelligible to nearly all the educated community. How many understand a T. S. Eliot, a William Faulkner, a St. John Perse, a Quasimodo? Our great artists battle on a landscape we cannot chart, with weapons we do not comprehend, against adversaries we find unreal. How can we make them our heroes?

As collaborative work increases in science, literature, and social sciences, we find it ever harder to isolate the individual hero for our admiration. The first nuclear chain reaction (which made the atom bomb and atomic power possible) was the product of a huge organization dispersed over the country. Who was the hero of the enterprise? Einstein, without whose theoretical boldness it would not have been conceivable? Or General Grove? Or Enrico Fermi? The social scientists' research enterprises have also become projects. *An American Dilemma*, the monumental study of the Negro and American democracy that was sponsored by the Carnegie Corporation, was the combined product of dozens of individual and collaborative studies. Gunnar Myrdal, director of the project and principal author of the book, played much the same role that the chairman of the board of directors does in a large corporation. The written works which reach the largest number of people in the United States today – adver-tisements and political speeches – are generally assumed to be collaborative work. The candidate making an eloquent campaign speech is admired for his administrative ingenuity in collecting a good team of speech writers. We cannot read books by our public figures, even their autobiographies and most private memoirs, without being haunted by their ghost writers.

In the United States we have, in a word, witnessed the decline of the "folk" and the rise of the "mass." The usually illiterate folk, while unself-conscious, was creative in its own special ways. Its characteristic products were the spoken word, the gesture, the song: folklore, folk dance, folk song. The folk expressed itself. Its products are still gathered by scholars, antiquarians, and patriots; it was a voice. But the mass, in our world of mass media and mass circulation, is the target and not the arrow. It is the ear and not the voice. The mass is what others aim to reach – by print, photograph, image, and sound. While the folk created heroes, the mass can only look and listen for them. It is waiting to be shown and to be told. Our society, to which the Soviet notion of "the masses" is so irrelevant, still is governed by our own idea of the mass. The folk had a universe of its own creation, its own world of giants and dwarfs, magicians and witches. The mass lives in the very different fantasy world of pseudo-events. The words and images which reach the mass disenchant big names in the very process of conjuring them up.

III

OUR AGE has produced a new kind of eminence. This is as characteristic of our culture and our century as was the divinity of Greek gods in the sixth century B.C. or the chivalry of knights and courtly lovers in the middle ages. It has not yet driven heroism, sainthood, or martyrdom completely out of our consciousness. But with every decade it overshadows them more. All older forms of greatness now survive only in the shadow of this new form. This new kind of eminence is "celebrity."

The word "celebrity" (from the Latin *celebritas* for "multitude" or "fame" and *celeber* meaning "frequented," "populous," or "famous") originally meant not a person but a condition — as the Oxford English Dictionary says, "the condition of being much talked about; famousness, notoriety." In this sense its use dates from at least the early seventeenth century. Even then it had a weaker meaning than "fame" or "renown." Matthew Arnold, for example, remarked in the nineteenth century that while the philosopher Spinoza's followers had "celebrity," Spinoza himself had "fame."

For us, however, "celebrity" means primarily a person — "a person of celebrity." This usage of the word significantly dates from the early years of the Graphic Revolution, the first example being about 1850. Emerson spoke of "the celebrities of wealth and fashion" (1848). Now American dictionaries define a celebrity as "a famous or well-publicized person."

The celebrity in the distinctive modern sense could not have existed in any earlier age, or in America before the Graphic Revolution. *The celebrity is a person who is known for his well-knownness.*

His qualities — or rather his lack of qualities — illustrate our peculiar problems. He is neither good nor bad, great nor petty. He is the human pseudo-event. He has been fabricated on purpose to satisfy our exaggerated expectations of human greatness. He is morally neutral. The product of no conspiracy, of no group promoting vice or emptiness, he is made by honest, industrious men of high professional ethics doing their job, "informing" and educating us. He is made by all of us who willingly read about him, who like to see him on television, who buy recordings of his voice, and talk about him to our friends. His relation to morality and even to reality is highly ambiguous. He is like the woman *in* an Elinor Glyn novel who describes another by saying, "She is like a figure in an Elinor Glyn novel."

The massive *Celebrity Register* (1959), compiled by Earl Blackwell and Cleveland Amory, now gives us a well-documented definition of the word, illustrated by over 2,200 biographies. "We think we have a better yardstick than the *Social Register*, or *Who's Who*, or any such book," they explain. "Our point is that it is impossible to be accurate in listing a man's social standing — even if anyone cared; and it's impossible to list accurately the success or value of men; but you *can* judge a man as a celebrity — all you have to do is weigh his press clippings." The *Celebrity Register*'s alphabetical order shows Mortimer Adler followed by Polly Adler, the Dalai Lama listed beside TV comedienne Dagmar, Dwight Eisenhower preceding Anita Ekberg, ex-President Herbert Hoover following ex-torch singer Libby Holman, Pope John XXIII coming after Mr. John the hat designer, and Bertrand Russell followed by Jane Russell. They are all celebrities. The well-knownness which they have in common overshadows everything else.

The advertising world has proved the market appeal of celebrities. In trade jargon celebrities are "big names." Endorsement advertising not only uses celebrities; it helps make them. Anything that makes a well-known name still better known automatically raises its status as a celebrity. The old practice, well established before the nineteenth century, of declaring the prestige of a product by the phrase "By Appointment to His Majesty" was, of course, a kind of use of the testimonial endorsement. But the King was in fact a great person, one of illustrious lineage and with impressive actual and symbolic powers. The King was not a venal endorser, and he was likely to use only superior products. He was not a mere celebrity. For the test of celebrity is nothing more than well-knownness.

Studies of biographies in popular magazines suggest that editors, and supposedly also readers, of such magazines not long ago shifted their attention away from the old-fashioned hero. From the person known for some serious achievement, they have turned their biographical interests to the new-fashioned celebrity. Of the subjects of biographical articles appearing in the *Saturday Evening Post* and the now-defunct *Collier's* in five sample years between 1901 and 1914, 74 per cent came from politics, business, and the professions. But after about 1922 well over half of them came from the world of entertainment. Even among the entertainers an ever decreasing proportion has come from the serious arts – literature, fine arts, music, dance, and theater. An ever increasing proportion (in recent years nearly all) comes from the fields of light entertainment, sports, and the night club circuit. In the earlier period, say before World War I, the larger group included figures like the President of the United States, a Senator, a State Governor, the Secretary of the Treasury, the banker J. P. Morgan, the railroad magnate James J. Hill, a pioneer in aviation, the inventor of the torpedo, a Negro educator, an immigrant scientist, an opera singer, a famous poet, and a popular fiction writer. By the 1940's the larger group included figures like the boxer Jack Johnson, Clark Gable, Bobby Jones, the movie actresses Brenda Joyce and Brenda Marshall, William Powell, the woman matador Conchita Cintron, the night club entertainer Adelaide Moffett, and the gorilla Toto. Some analysts say the shift is primarily the sign of a new focus of popular attention away from production and toward consumption. But this is oversubtle.

A simpler explanation is that the machinery of information has brought into being a new substitute for the hero, who is the celebrity, and whose main characteristic is his well-knownness. In the democracy of pseudo-events, anyone can become a celebrity, if only he can get into the news and stay there. Figures from the world of entertainment and sports are most apt to be well known. If they are successful enough, they actually overshadow the real figures they portray. George Arliss overshadowed Disraeli, Vivian Leigh overshadowed Scarlett O'Hara, Fess Parker overshadowed Davy Crockett. Since their stock in trade is their well-knownness, they are most apt to have energetic press agents keeping them in the public eye.

It is hardly surprising then that magazine and newspaper readers no longer find the lives of their heroes instructive. Popular biographies can offer very little in the way of solid information. For the subjects are themselves mere figments of the media. If their lives are empty of drama or achievement, it is only as we might have expected, for they are not known for drama or achievement. They are celebrities. Their chief claim to fame is their fame itself. They are notorious for their notoriety. If this is puzzling or fantastic, if it is mere tautology, it is no more puzzling or fantastic or tautologous than much of the rest of our experience. Our experience tends more and more to become tautology – needless repetition of the same in different words and images. Perhaps what ails us is not so much a vice as a "nothingness." The vacuum of our experience is actually made emptier by our anxious straining with mechanical devices to fill it artificially. What is remarkable is not only that we manage to fill experience with so much emptiness, but that we manage to give the emptiness such appealing variety.

We can hear ourselves straining. "He's the greatest!" Our descriptions of celebrities overflow with superlatives. In popular magazine biographies we learn that a Dr. Brinkley is the "best-advertised doctor in the United States"; an actor is the "luckiest man in the movies today"; a Ringling is "not only the greatest, but the first real showman in the Ringling family"; a general is "one of the best mathematicians this side of Einstein"; a columnist has "one of the strangest of courtships"; a statesman has "the world's most exciting job"; a sportsman is "the loudest and by all odds the most abusive"; a newsman is "one of the most consistently resentful men in the country"; a certain ex-King's mistress is "one of the unhappiest women that ever lived." But, despite the "supercolossal" on the label, the contents are very ordinary. The lives of celebrities which we like to read, as Leo Lowenthal remarks, are a mere catalogue of "hardships" and "breaks." These men and women are "the proved specimens of the average."

No longer external sources which fill us with purpose, these new-model "heroes" are receptacles into which we pour our own purposelessness. They are nothing but ourselves seen in a magnifying mirror. Therefore the lives of entertainer-celebrities cannot extend our horizon. Celebrities populate our horizon with men and women we already know. Or, as an advertisement for the *Celebrity Register* cogently puts it, celebrities are "the 'names' who, once made by news, now make news by themselves." Celebrity is made by simple familiarity, induced and re-enforced by public means. The celebrity therefore is the perfect embodiment of tautology: the most familiar is the most familiar.

IV

THE HERO was distinguished by his achievement; the celebrity by his image or trade-mark. The hero created himself; the celebrity is created by the media. The hero was a big man; the celebrity is a big name.

Formerly, a public man needed a *private* secretary for a barrier between himself and the public. Nowadays he has a *press* secretary, to keep him properly in the public eye. Before the Graphic Revolution (and still in countries which have not undergone that revolution) it was a mark of solid distinction in a man or a family to keep out of the news. A lady of aristocratic pretensions was supposed to get her name in the papers only three times: when she was born, when she married, and when she died. Now the families who are Society are by definition those always appearing in the papers. The man of truly heroic stature was once supposed to be marked by scorn for publicity. He quietly relied on the power of his character or his achievement.

In the South, where the media developed more slowly than elsewhere in the country, where cities appeared later, and where life was dominated by rural ways, the celebrity grew more slowly. The old-fashioned hero was romanticized. In this as in many other ways, the Confederate General Robert E. Lee was one of the last surviving American models of the older type. Among his many admirable qualities, Southern compatriots admired none more than his retirement from public view. He had the reputation for never having given a newspaper interview. He steadfastly refused to write his memoirs. "I should be trading on the blood of my men," he said. General George C. Marshall (1880–1959) is a more recent and more anachronistic example. He, too, shunned publicity and refused to write his memoirs, even while other generals were serializing theirs in the newspapers. But by his time, few people any longer considered this reticence a virtue. His old-fashioned unwillingness to enter the publicity arena finally left him a victim of the slanders of Senator Joseph McCarthy and others.

The hero was born of time: his gestation required at least a generation. As the saying went, he had "stood the test of time." A maker of tradition, he was himself made by tradition. He grew over the generations as people found new virtues in him and attributed to him new exploits. Receding into the misty past he became more, and not less, heroic. It was not necessary that his face or figure have a sharp, well-delineated outline, nor that his life be footnoted. Of course there could not have been any photographs of him, and often there was not even a likeness. Men of the last century were more heroic than those of today; men of antiquity were still more heroic; and those of pre-history became demigods. The hero was always somehow ranked among the ancients.

The celebrity, on the contrary, is always a contemporary. The hero is made by folklore, sacred texts, and history books, but the celebrity is the creature of gossip, of public opinion, of magazines, newspapers, and the ephemeral images of movie and television screen. The passage of time, which creates and establishes the hero, destroys the celebrity. One is made, the other unmade, by repetition. The celebrity is born in the daily papers and never loses the mark of his fleeting origin.

The very agency which first makes the celebrity in the long run inevitably destroys him. He will be destroyed, as he was made, by publicity. The newspapers make him, and they unmake him – not by murder but by suffocation or starvation. No one is more forgotten than the last generation's celebrity. This fact explains the newspaper feature "Whatever Became Of . . .?" which amuses us by accounts of the present obscurity of former celebrities. One can always get a laugh by referring knowingly to the once-household names which have lost their celebrity in the last few decades: Mae Bush, William S. Hart, Clara Bow. A woman reveals her age by the celebrities she knows.

There is not even any tragedy in the celebrity's fall, for he is a man returned to his proper anonymous station. The tragic hero, in Aristotle's familiar definition, was a man fallen from great estate, a great man with a tragic flaw. He had somehow become the victim of his own greatness. Yesterday's celebrity, however, is a commonplace man who has been fitted back into his proper commonplaceness not by any fault of his own, but by time itself.

The dead hero becomes immortal. He becomes more vital with the passage of time. The celebrity even in his lifetime becomes passé: he passes out of the picture. The white glare of publicity, which first gave him his specious brilliance, soon melts him away. This was so even when the only vehicles of publicity were the magazine and the newspaper. Still more now with our vivid round-the-clock media, with radio and television. Now when it is possible, by bringing their voices and images daily into our living rooms, to make celebrities more quickly than ever before, they die more quickly than ever. This has been widely recognized by entertainment celebrities and politicians. President Franklin Delano Roosevelt was careful to space out his fireside chats so the citizenry would not tire of him. Some comedians (for example, Jackie Gleason in the mid-1950's) have found that when they have weekly programs they reap quick and remunerative notoriety, but that they soon wear out their images. To extend their celebrity-lives, they offer their images more sparingly – once a month or once every two months instead of once a week.

There is a subtler difference between the personality of the hero and that of the celebrity. The figures in each of the two classes become assimilated to one another, but in two rather different ways. Heroes standing for greatness in the traditional mold tend to become colorless and cliché. The greatest heroes have the least distinctiveness of face or figure. We may show our reverence for them, as we do for God, by giving them beards. Yet we find it hard to imagine that Moses or Jesus could have had other special facial characteristics. The hero while being thus idealized and generalized loses his individuality. The fact that George Washington is not a vivid personality actually helps him serve as the heroic Father of Our Country. Perhaps Emerson meant just this when he said that finally every great hero becomes a great bore. To be a great hero is actually to become lifeless; to become a face on a coin or a postage stamp. It is to become a Gilbert Stuart's Washington. Contemporaries, however, and the celebrities made of them, suffer from idiosyncrasy. They are too vivid, too individual to be polished into a symmetrical Greek statue. The Graphic Revolution, with its klieg lights on face and figure, makes the images of different men more distinctive. This itself disqualifies them from becoming heroes or demigods.

While heroes are assimilated to one another by the great simple virtues of their character, celebrities are differentiated mainly by trivia of personality. To be known for your personality actually proves you a celebrity. Thus a synonym for "a celebrity" is "a personality." Entertainers, then, are best qualified to become celebrities because they are skilled in the marginal differentiation of their personalities. They succeed by skillfully distinguishing themselves from others essentially like them. They do this by minutiae of grimace, gesture, language, and voice. We identify Jimmy ("Schnozzola") Durante by his nose, Bob Hope by his fixed smile, Jack Benny by his stinginess, Jack Paar by his rudeness, Jackie Gleason by his waddle, Imogene Coca by her bangs.

With the mushroom-fertility of all pseudo-events, celebrities tend to breed more celebrities. They help make and celebrate and publicize one another. Being known primarily for their well-knownness, celebrities intensify their celebrity images simply by becoming widely known for relations among themselves. By a kind of symbiosis, celebrities live off one another. One becomes better known by being the habitual butt of another's jokes, by being another's paramour or ex-wife, by being the subject of another's gossip, or even by being ignored by another celebrity. Elizabeth Taylor's celebrity appeal has consisted less perhaps in her own talents as an actress than in her connections with other celebrities – Nick Hilton, Mike Todd, and Eddie Fisher. Arthur Miller, the playwright, became a "real" celebrity by his marriage to Marilyn Monroe. When we talk or read or write about celebrities, our emphasis on their marital relations and sexual habits, on their tastes in smoking, drinking, dress, sports cars, and interior decoration is our desperate effort to distinguish among the indistinguishable. How can those commonplace people like us (who, by the grace of the media, happened to become celebrities) be made to seem more interesting or bolder than we are?

V

As OTHER PSEUDO-EVENTS in our day tend to overshadow spontaneous events, so celebrities (who are human pseudo-events) tend to overshadow heroes. They are more up-to-date, more nationally advertised, and more apt to have press agents. And there are far more of them. Celebrities die quickly but they are still more quickly replaced. Every year we experience a larger number than the year before.

Just as real events tend to be cast in the mold of pseudo-events, so in our society heroes survive by acquiring the qualities of celebrities. The best-publicized seems the most authentic experience. If someone does a heroic deed in our time, all the machinery of public information – press, pulpit, radio, and television – soon transform him into a celebrity. If they cannot succeed in this, the would-be hero disappears from public view.

A dramatic, a tragic, example is the career of Charles A. Lindbergh. He performed singlehanded one of the heroic deeds of this century. His deed was heroic in the best epic mold. But he became degraded into a celebrity. He then ceased to symbolize the virtues to which his heroic deed gave him a proper claim. He became filled with emptiness; then he disappeared from view. How did this happen?

On May 21, 1927, Charles A. Lindbergh made the first nonstop solo flight from Roosevelt Field, New York, to Le Bourget Air Field, Paris, in a monoplane, "The Spirit of St. Louis." This was plainly a heroic deed in the classic sense; it was a deed of valor – alone against the elements. In a dreary, unheroic decade Lindbergh's flight was a lightning flash of individual courage. Except for the fact of his flight, Lindbergh was a commonplace person. Twenty-five years old at the time, he had been born in Detroit and raised in Minnesota. He was not a great inventor or a leader of men. He was not extraordinarily intelligent, eloquent, or ingenious. Like many another young man in those years, he had a fanatical love of flying. The air was his element. There he showed superlative skill and extraordinary courage – even to foolhardiness.

He was an authentic hero. Yet this was not enough. Or perhaps it was too much. For he was destined to be made into a mere celebrity; and he was to be the American celebrity par excellence. His rise and fall as a hero, his tribulations, his transformation, and his rise and decline as a celebrity are beautifully told in Kenneth S. Davis' biography.

Lindbergh himself had not failed to predict that his exploit would put him in the news. Before leaving New York he had sold to *The New York Times* the exclusive story of his flight. A supposedly naive and diffident boy, on his arrival in Paris he was confronted by a crowd of newspaper reporters at a press conference in Ambassador

Myron T. Herrick's residence. But he would not give out any statement until he had clearance from the *Times* representative. He had actually subscribed to a newspaper clipping service, the clippings to be sent to his mother, who was then teaching school in Minnesota. With uncanny foresight, however, he had limited his subscriptions to clippings to the value of $50. (This did not prevent the company, doubtless seeking publicity as well as money, from suing him for not paying them for clippings beyond the specified amount.) Otherwise he might have had to spend the rest of his life earning the money to pay for clippings about himself.

Lindbergh's newspaper success was unprecedented. The morning after his flight *The New York Times*, a model of journalistic sobriety, gave him the whole of its first five pages, except for a few ads on page five. Other papers gave as much or more. Radio commentators talked of him by the hour. But there was not much hard news available. The flight was a relatively simple operation, lasting only thirty-three and a half hours. Lindbergh had told reporters in Paris just about all there was to tell. During his twenty-five years he had led a relatively uneventful life. He had few quirks of face, of figure, or of personality; little was known about his character. Some young women called him "tall and handsome," but his physical averageness was striking. He was the boy next door. To tell about this young man on the day after his flight, the nation's newspapers used 25,000 tons of newsprint more than usual. In many places sales were two to five times normal, and might have been higher if the presses could have turned out more papers.

When Lindbergh returned to New York on June 13, 1927, *The New York Times* gave its first sixteen pages the next morning almost exclusively to news about him. At the testimonial dinner in Lindbergh's honor at the Hotel Commodore (reputed to be the largest for an individual "in modern history") Charles Evans Hughes, former Secretary of State, and about to become Chief Justice of the United States, delivered an extravagant eulogy. With unwitting precision he characterized the American hero-turned-celebrity: "We measure heroes as we do ships, by their displacement. Colonel Lindbergh has displaced everything."

Lindbergh was by now the biggest human pseudo-event of modern times. His achievement, actually because it had been accomplished so neatly and with such spectacular simplicity, offered little spontaneous news. The biggest news about Lindbergh was that he was such big news. Pseudo-events multiplied in more than the usual geometric progression, for Lindbergh's well-knownness was so sudden and so overwhelming. It was easy to make stories about what a big celebrity he was; how this youth, unknown a few days before, was now a household word; how he was received by Presidents and Kings and Bishops. There was little else one could say about him. Lindbergh's singularly impressive heroic deed was soon far overshadowed by his even more impressive publicity. If well-knownness made a celebrity, here was the greatest. Of course it was remarkable to fly the ocean by oneself, but far more remarkable thus to dominate the news. His stature as hero was nothing compared with his stature as celebrity. All the more because it had happened, literally, overnight.

A large proportion of the news soon consisted of stories of how Lindbergh reacted to the "news" and to the publicity about himself. People focused their admiration on how admirably Lindbergh responded to publicity, how gracefully he accepted his role of celebrity. "Quickie" biographies appeared. These were little more than digests of newspaper accounts of the publicity jags during Lindbergh's ceremonial visits to the capitals of Europe and the United States. This was the celebrity after-life of the heroic Lindbergh. This was the tautology of celebrity.

During the next few years Lindbergh stayed in the public eye and remained a celebrity primarily because of two events. One was his marriage on May 27, 1929, to the cultivated and pretty Anne Morrow, daughter of Dwight Morrow, a Morgan partner, then Ambassador to Mexico. Now it was "The Lone Eagle and His Mate." As a newlywed he was more than ever attractive raw material for news. The maudlin pseudo-events of romance were added to all the rest. His newsworthiness was revived. There was no escape. Undaunted newsmen, thwarted in efforts to secure interviews and lacking solid facts, now made columns of copy from Lindbergh's efforts to keep out of the news! Some newspapermen, lacking other material for speculation, cynically suggested that Lindbergh's attempts to dodge reporters were motivated by a devious plan to increase his news-interest. When Lindbergh said he would co-operate with sober, respectable papers, but not with others, those left out pyramided his rebuffs into more news than his own statements would have made.

The second event which kept Lindbergh alive as a celebrity was the kidnaping of his infant son. This occurred at his new country house at Hopewell, New Jersey, on the night of March 1, 1932. For almost five years "Lindbergh" had been an empty receptacle into which news makers had poured their concoctions — saccharine, maudlin, legendary, slanderous, adulatory, or only fantastic. Now, when all other news-making possibilities seemed exhausted, his family was physically consumed. There was a good story in it. Here was "blood sacrifice," as Kenneth S. Davis calls it, to the gods of publicity. Since the case was never fully solved, despite the execution of the supposed kidnaper, no one can know whether the child would have been returned unharmed if the press and the public had behaved differently. But the press (with the collaboration of the bungling police) who had unwittingly destroyed real clues, then garnered and publicized innumerable false clues, and did nothing solid to help. They exploited Lindbergh's personal catastrophe with more than their usual energy.

In its way the kidnapping of Lindbergh's son was as spectacular as Lindbergh's transatlantic flight. In neither case was there much hard news, but this did not prevent the filling of newspaper columns. City editors now gave orders for no space limit on the kidnaping story. "I can't think of any story that would compare with it," observed the general news manager of the United Press, "unless America should enter a war." Hearst's INS photo service assigned its whole staff. They chartered two ambulances which, with sirens screaming, shuttled between Hopewell and New York City carrying photographic equipment out to the Lindbergh estate, and on the way back to the city served as mobile darkrooms in which pictures were developed and printed for delivery on arrival. For on-the-spot reporting at Hopewell, INS had an additional five men with three automobiles. United Press had six men and three cars; the Associated Press had four men, two women, and four cars. By midnight of March 1 the New York *Daily News* had nine reporters at Hopewell, and three more arrived the next day; the New York *American* had a dozen (including William Randolph Hearst, Jr., the paper's president); the New York *Herald Tribune*, four; the New York *World-Telegram, The New York Times*, and the Philadelphia *Ledger*, each about ten. This was only a beginning.

The next day the press agreed to Lindbergh's request to stay off the Hopewell grounds in order to encourage the kidnaper to return the child. The torrent of news did not stop. Within twenty-four hours INS sent over its wires 50,000 words (enough to fill a small volume) about the crime, 30,000 words the following day, and for some time thereafter 10,000 or more words a day. The Associated Press and United Press served their subscribers just as well. Many papers gave the story the whole of the front page, plus inside carry-overs, for a full week. There were virtually no new facts available. Still the news poured forth – pseudo-events by the score – clues, rumors, local color features, and what the trade calls "think" pieces.

Soon there was almost nothing more to be done journalistically with the crime itself. There was little more to be reported, invented, or conjectured. Interest then focused on a number of sub-dramas created largely by newsmen themselves. These were stories about how the original event was being reported, about the mix-up among the different police that had entered the case, and about who would or should be Lindbergh's spokesman to the press world and his go-between with the kidnaper. Much news interest still centered on what a big story all the news added up to, and on how Mr. and Mrs. Lindbergh reacted to the publicity.

At this point the prohibition era crime celebrities came into the picture. "Salvy" Spitale and Irving Bitz, New York speakeasy owners, briefly held the spotlight. They had been suggested by Morris Rosner, who, because he had underworld connections, soon became a kind of personal secretary to the Lindberghs. Spitale and Bitz earned headlines for their effort to make contact with the kidnapers, then suspected to be either the notorious Purple Gang of Detroit or Al Capone's mob in Chicago. The two go-betweens became big names, until Spitale bowed out, appropriately enough, at a press conference. There he explained: "If it was someone I knew, I'll be God-damned if I wouldn't name him. I been in touch all around, and I come to the conclusion that this one was pulled by an independent." Al Capone himself, more a celebrity than ever, since he was about to begin a Federal prison term for income-tax evasion, increased his own newsworthiness by trying to lend a hand. In an interview with the "serious" columnist Arthur Brisbane of the Hearst papers, Capone offered $10,000 for information leading to the recovery of the child unharmed and to the capture of the kidnapers. It was even hinted that to free Capone might help recover the child.

The case itself produced a spate of new celebrities, whose significance no one quite understood but whose newsworthiness itself made them important. These included Colonel H. Norman Schwarzkopf, commander of the New Jersey State Police; Harry Wolf, Chief of Police in Hopewell; Betty Gow, the baby's nurse; Colonel Breckenridge, Lindbergh's personal counsel; Dr. J. F. ("Jafsie") Condon, a retired Bronx schoolteacher who was a volunteer go-between (he offered to add to the ransom money his own $1,000 life savings "so a loving mother may again have her child and Colonel Lindbergh may know that the American people are grateful for the honor bestowed on them by his pluck and daring"); John Hughes Curtis, a half-demented Norfolk, Virginia, boat-builder who pretended to reach the kidnapers; Gaston B. Means (author of *The Strange Death of President Harding*), later convicted of swindling Mrs. Evalyn Walsh McLean out of $104,000 by posing as a negotiator with the kidnapers; Violet Sharpe, a waitress in the Morrow home, who married the Morrow butler and who had had a date with a young man not her husband on the night of the kidnaping (she committed suicide on threat of being questioned by the police); and countless others.

Only a few years later the spotlight was turned off Lindbergh as suddenly as it had been turned on him. *The New York Times Index* — a thick volume published yearly which lists all references to a given subject in the pages of the newspaper during the previous twelve months — records this fact with statistical precision. Each volume of the index for the years 1927 to 1940 contains several columns of fine print merely itemizing the different news stories which referred to Lindbergh. The 1941 volume shows over three columns of such listings. Then suddenly the news stream dries up, first to a mere trickle, then to nothing at all. The total listings for all seventeen years from 1942 through 1958 amount to less than two columns — only about half that found in the single year 1941. In 1951 and 1958 there was not even a single mention of Lindbergh. In 1957 when the movie *The Spirit of St. Louis*, starring James Stewart, was released, it did poorly at the box office. A poll of the preview audiences showed that few viewers under forty years of age knew about Lindbergh.

A *New Yorker* cartoon gave the gist of the matter. A father and his young son are leaving a movie house where they have just seen *The Spirit of St. Louis*. "If everyone thought what he did was so marvelous," the boy asks his father, "how come he never got famous?"

The hero thus died a celebrity's sudden death. In his fourteen years he had already long outlasted the celebrity's usual life span. An incidental explanation of this quick demise of Charles A. Lindbergh was his response to the pressure to be "all-around." Democratic faith was not satisfied that its hero be only a dauntless flier. He had to become a scientist, an outspoken citizen, and a leader of men. His celebrity status unfortunately had persuaded him to become a public spokesman. When Lindbergh gave in to these temptations, he offended. But his offenses (unlike those, for example, of Al Capone and his henchmen, who used to be applauded when they took their seats in a ball park) were not in themselves dramatic or newsworthy enough to create a new notoriety. His pronouncements were dull, petulant, and vicious. He acquired a reputation as a pro-Nazi and a crude racist; he accepted a decoration from Hitler. Very soon the celebrity was being uncelebrated. The "Lindbergh Beacon" atop a Chicago skyscraper was renamed the "Palmolive Beacon," and high in the Colorado Rockies "Lindbergh Peak" was rechristened the noncommittal, "Lone Eagle Peak."

VI

SINCE THE GRAPHIC REVOLUTION, the celebrity overshadows the hero by the same relentless law which gives other kinds of pseudo-events an overshadowing power. When a man appears as hero and/or celebrity, his role as celebrity obscures and is apt to destroy his role as hero. The reasons, too, are those which tend to make all pseudo-events predominate. In the creation of a celebrity somebody always has an interest — newsmen needing stories, press agents paid to make celebrities, and the celebrity himself. But dead heroes have no such interest in their publicity, nor can they hire agents to keep them in the public eye. Celebrities, because they are made to order, can be made to please, comfort, fascinate, and flatter us. They can be produced and displaced in rapid succession.

The people once felt themselves made by their heroes. "The idol," said James Russell Lowell, "is the measure of the worshiper." Celebrities are made by the people.

The hero stood for outside standards. The celebrity is a tautology. We still try to make our celebrities stand in for the heroes we no longer have, or for those who have been pushed out of our view. We forget that celebrities are known primarily for their well-knownness. And we imitate them as if they were cast in the mold of greatness. Yet the celebrity is usually nothing greater than a more-publicized version of us. In imitating him, in trying to dress like him, talk like him, look like him, think like him, we are simply imitating ourselves. In the words of the Psalmist, "They that make them are like unto them; so is everyone that trusteth in them." By imitating a tautology, we ourselves become a tautology: standing for what we stand for, reaching to become more emphatically what we already are. When we praise our famous men we pretend to look out the window of history. We do not like to confess that we are looking into a mirror. We look for models, and we see our own image.

Inevitably, most of our few remaining heroes hold our attention by being recast in the celebrity mold. We try to become chummy, gossipy, and friendly with our heroes. In the process we make them affable and flattering to us. Jesus, we are told from the pulpit, was "no sissy, but a regular fellow." Andrew Jackson was a "great guy." Instead of inventing heroic exploits for our heroes, we invent commonplaces about them (for example, in the successful juvenile series "The Childhood of Famous Americans"). It is commonplaces, and not exploits, which make them celebrities.

Our very efforts to debunk celebrities, to prove (whether by critical journalistic biographies or by vulgar "confidential" magazines) that they are unworthy of our admiration, are like efforts to get "behind the scenes" in the making of other pseudo-events. They are self-defeating. They increase our interest in the fabrication. As much publicity yardage can be created one way as another. Of course most true celebrities have press agents. And these press agents sometimes themselves become celebrities. The hat, the rabbit, and the magician are all equally news. It is twice as newsworthy that a charlatan can become a success. His charlatanry makes him even more of a personality. A celebrity's private news-making apparatus, far from disillusioning us, simply proves him authentic and fully equipped. We are reassured then that we are not mistaking a nobody for a somebody.

It is not surprising that the word "hero" has itself become a slang term of cynical reproach. Critics of the American Legion call it "The Heroes' Union." What better way of deflating or irritating a self-important person than by calling him "Our Hero"? The very word belongs, we think, in the world of pre-literate societies, of comic strip supermen, or of William Steig's Small Fry.

In America today heroes, like fairy tales, are seldom for sophisticated adults. But we multiply our Oscars and Emmies, our awards for the Father of the Year, our crowns for Mrs. America and Miss Photoflash. We have our Hall of Fame for Great Americans, our Agricultural Hall of Fame, our Baseball Hall of Fame, our Rose Bowl Hall of Fame. We strain to reassure ourselves that we admire the admirable and honor the meritorious. But in the very act of straining we confuse and distract ourselves. At first reluctantly, then with fascination, we observe the politicking behind every prize and the shenanigans in front of every effort to enshrine a celebrity or to enthrone a Queen for a Day. Despite our best intentions, our contrivance to provide substitute heroes finally produces nothing but celebrities. To publicize is to expose.

With our unprecedented power to magnify the images and popularize the virtues of heroes, our machinery only multiplies and enlarges the shadows of ourselves.

Somehow we cannot make ourselves so uncritical that we reverence or respect (however much we may be interested in) the reflected images of our own emptiness. We continue surreptitiously to wonder whether greatness is not a naturally scarce commodity, whether it can ever really be synthesized. Perhaps, then, our ancestors were right in connecting the very idea of human greatness with belief in a God. Perhaps man cannot make himself. Perhaps heroes are born and not made.

Among the ironic frustrations of our age, none is more tantalizing than these efforts of ours to satisfy our extravagant expectations of human greatness. Vainly do we make scores of artificial celebrities grow where nature planted only a single hero. As soon as a hero begins to be sung about today, he evaporates into a celebrity. "No man can be a hero to his valet" – or, Carlyle might have added, "to his *Time* reporter." In our world of big names, curiously, our true heroes tend to be anonymous. In this life of illusion and quasi-illusion, the person with solid virtues who can be admired for something more substantial than his well-knownness often proves to be the unsung hero: the teacher, the nurse, the mother, the honest cop, the hard worker at lonely, under-paid, unglamorous, unpublicized jobs. Topsy-turvily, these can remain heroes precisely because they remain unsung. *Their* virtues are not the product of our effort to fill our void. Their very anonymity protects them from the flashy ephemeral celebrity life. They alone have the mysterious power to deny our mania for more greatness than there is in the world.

Chapter 5

Richard de Cordova

THE DISCOURSE ON ACTING

MOVING PICTURES EXISTED FOR over a decade before anything resembling a star system appeared. Although personalities from other fields (particularly politics) were presented in documentary "views" from a very early date, they were not in any strict sense of the term movie stars. The basis of their notoriety lay elsewhere. One can cite, as an example, the series of five films Edison copyrighted in 1899 documenting Admiral Dewey's role in the Spanish-American War (largely the parade upon his return). Although the cinema certainly capitalized upon Dewey's notoriety, it had neither a direct role in creating it nor the means to control it. The fame of personalities such as Dewey was caught up in a circulation of events exterior to the cinema as an institution.

The cinema's function in relation to these personalities was, in a sense, merely to represent them. Dewey, McKinley, Roosevelt, and Prince Henry were the raw material in what was principally a new form of photojournalism. This cannot be said of stars such as Florence Lawrence and Mary Pickford, who emerged out of an explicitly fictional mode of film production. The spectator did not pay to see a record of Mary Pickford's movements, but paid, rather, to see her activity in the enunciation of a fiction.

There was thus no simple continuity between the intermittent representations of these famous figures and the star as such. Nor did these representations in any clear way mark out the conditions for the emergence of the star. In fact, one cannot locate the incipience of the star system in the industry's practices prior to 1907.

Of course the question this raises is why the cinema did not have a star system before this date. The theater, vaudeville, and professional sports all banked on the ability of name performers to attract an audience. The theater had, in fact, based its popularity on star performers through much, if not most, of the nineteenth century. According to Benjamin McArthur, a theatrical star system had begun to gain momentum in America with George Frederick Cook's 1810 tour. By the 1870s, certainly, a star system dominated American theater. Star-centered combination tours were driving local stock companies out of business, and "matinee idols" such as Harry Montague (and later Kyle Bellew and Maurice Barrymore) were being hounded by hundreds of ardent female fans. In the 1880s and 1890s, Charles Frohman achieved unparalleled success as a theatrical producer by using the expanding press and the techniques of modern advertising to make stars out of Maude Adams, Ethel Barrymore, May Robson, and William Faversham. By the end of the century the theatrical star system was operating at full force.[1]

It might seem natural then that the cinema—from the beginning—would have adopted a similar strategy. But it is a mistake to assume that this presented itself as an option for the early leaders of the industry. Given the nature of the industry at the time and the early film's status as discourse, the movie star, as it would later develop, was in a very real sense unthinkable. Between 1898 and 1906 the film industry depended wholly upon such institutions as vaudeville and amusement parks as its means of exhibition. Moving pictures had a relatively restricted role in vaudeville. They were not incorporated into it as a means of mechanically reproducing the labor of star acts (so that those acts could appear in a number of theaters at once, in absentia). Although Edison's early films did present snippets of vaudeville acts and playlets, they did not catch hold in any profound way; they were soon superseded when documentary views of exterior objects and events proved more interesting. These topical genres, which dominated film production during this period, had, at best, an oblique relation to that part of the vaudeville commodity that depended upon name performers. Moving pictures were a replacement for certain vaudeville acts only in a broad, structural sense: they occupied a particular slot in the show (that which had been typically occupied by other visually oriented acts, such as pantomime spectacle, puppetry, and tableaux vivants) and fit into a tradition of entertainment that melded scientific gadgetry and visual novelty.[2] They did not replace live acts by transferring them to the screen.

Thus, owners of vaudeville houses did not see in the reproducibility of moving pictures a kind of Benjaminian solution to the increasing demand and competition for live acts. Their interest in the kinetoscope was more immediate. They saw it as a genuine novelty that, for a time at least, would attract a crowd. At first, the novelty of the cinema followed from its capacity to represent iconic movement of any kind. The kinetoscope appeared as the most sophisticated version of a long line of nineteenth-century devices, whose purpose was to do precisely this. It is not clear how long this novelty propelled interest in the cinema. Robert C. Allen argues that by 1897 "moving picture acts based their appeal less on the cinema's ability to render highly iconic representations and more on the subject matter which was represented." The system of genre that emerged and predominated film production during these years attests to this. Genres such as the documentary, travel film, newsreel, and sports film (which together accounted for 86.9 percent of production) were both characterized and differentiated by their reference to a particular field of objects and events.[3]

Still one cannot dismiss the continuing effectivity of the novelty of the technological base. The trick film (which gained popularity around 1901), although it recalled certain traditions of stage magic, depended wholly on the magical qualities of the cinematic apparatus for its effect. Even the topical film, to the extent that it represented extraordinary events, focused a good measure of attention onto the ability of the machine to "capture" them.

The question here is not whether spectators paid to see "content" or whether they paid to see the marvelous workings of the machine – they obviously paid to see both. The kinetoscope held the spectators' attention between these poles in a kind of "economy." What is important to note is that this economy precluded the kind of attention that would be the precondition for the emergence of the star – that is, an attention to the human labor involved in the production of film. Eric Smoodin has convincingly argued that early journalistic discourse of the time characterized film as a product independent of human labor.[4] What he calls a "reification of the apparatus" is clear in the titles of articles such as "Moving Pictures and the Machines Which Create Them" and "Revelations of the Camera." Such articles posited the apparatus as the singular site of textual productivity.

Thus, the enunciative position that the vaudeville performer occupied on stage was not replicated in the enunciative system of film. The activity behind a particular representation was relegated to the workings of the machine, not to the "creative" labor of humans. The kind of emphasis that would permit the emergence of the star system was impossible under these conditions.

A number of sweeping changes began to take place in the industry after 1905. The first and most important of the changes was undoubtedly the emergence of the nickelodeon as the dominant means of film exhibition. For the first time the cinema had its own exhibition outlet. This prompted a certain reorganization of the relation between production, distribution, and exhibition. As Robert C. Allen has pointed out,

> The use of films in vaudeville did not require a division of the industry into distinct production, distribution and exhibition units. In fact, it favored the collapsing of these functions into the "operator," who, with his projector, became the self-contained vaudeville act. It was not until American cinema achieved industrial autonomy with the advent of store-front movie theaters that a clear separation of functions became the dominant mode of industrial organization, and film entered its early industrial phase.[5]

One can see in the formation of the Motion Picture Patents Company in 1908 (and in fact in the earlier alliance between the Edison licensees and the Film Service Association) an attempt by the manufacturers to regularize the relations between production, distribution, and exhibition. It is, of course, no accident that this attempt at "industrial reform" was designed to form a monopoly and secure enormous profits for the producers. The Patents Trust later argued that its actions had been beneficial in that it had organized a set of chaotic practices that were hindering the expansion of the industry. And there is no doubt some truth to this.

The nickelodeon boom brought with it an exponential rise in the demand for moving pictures – a demand that the industry, as it was structured at the time, could not efficiently supply. There had been few nickelodeons prior to 1905 but by 1907 there were, by the most conservative estimates, at least 2,500. Each of these nickelodeons needed new films on a regular basis. So, a more systematic means of getting films into distribution channels and into the theaters was in order. And of course the production process itself had to be accelerated substantially. Some of the most significant changes that took place during these years stemmed from the manufacturers' attempts to meet the rising demand for films. They built more studios, set up property departments, and formed stock companies. In short, they instituted more factorylike methods to assure a regular, adequate flow of films.

Crucial to this move toward more rationalized production practices was the shift toward fictional film production. This shift began around 1902, but reached an important point of consolidation in the years 1907 and 1908. Robert C. Allen has argued that "between 1907 and 1908 a dramatic change occurred in American Motion Picture Production. In one year narrative forms of cinema (comedy and dramatic) all but eclipsed documentary forms in volume of production." Even more remarkably, the percentage of dramatic production increased from 17 to 66 percent in 1908. Allen's figures come from a consideration of copyrighted titles during those years. Charles Musser has demonstrated, by looking at the amount of footage distributed (fiction films were longer and more prints of each film were distributed), that the economics of the industry had turned toward fiction somewhat earlier, certainly by 1904.[6] But he notes the uneven development that existed between filmmaking, which "remained a cottage industry," and exhibition, "which had become a form of mass production." It is in 1907 and 1908 that film production caught up, instituting a mode of fictional filmmaking (Musser refers to it, in quotation marks, as the " 'Griffith mode' ") based on standardization, narrative efficiency, and maximization of profits. For Bordwell, Staiger, and Thompson, it is during these years that the primitive cinema began to give way to a mode of filmmaking that would lead to a standardized, classical style. As films lengthened, more complex narratives began to be constructed around the psychological traits of characters, and a mode of editing and shot distance emerged that stressed, beyond all else, the linearity of the narrative and the characters' goals in propelling it forward. D. W. Griffith's work at Biograph, which began in late 1908, offers the clearest and most familiar evidence of this new mode.[7]

Allen argues that this shift toward fictional production was at least in part the industry's attempt to gain control over the production situation. Prior to this shift, when topical genres dominated production, the popularity of moving pictures depended all too much upon events the industry had no control over – wars, disasters, coronations, etc. The fictional film lent itself to a more rationalized set of procedures. Production could be centralized and a rough but more efficient division of labor put in place. More important, the availability of good subjects would be a matter of imagining them, rather than finding them in the world. By focusing on fictional production the industry changed the status of film as a commodity in such a way that it could assert a greater degree of control over its defining features as a commodity. Events exterior to the cinema would no longer have such a profound and potentially devastating effect on the popularity of moving pictures. Films would be differentiated from one another by factors largely internal to, and within the control of, the cinema as an institution.

Of course, as long as the supply of films from producers was sporadic and the demand great, the problem of product differentiation fell most pointedly on the shoulders of the exhibitors. By 1907 the incredible proliferation of nickelodeons had saturated the market for moving pictures in most urban areas, causing increased competition among exhibitors for a limited number of customers. In such cases, the individual nickelodeon's success became dependent upon the extent to which it could differentiate the service it offered from that of its competitors.

Such differentiation could be effected in three ways. First of all, the physical setting of the nickelodeon could be upgraded. Exhibitors discovered that the crowded, dusty storefront (the stereotypical nickelodeon) could not compete with more comfortable, opulent moving picture theaters. The latter were not only more attractive to regular nickelodeon customers, but they also drew in a more upscale audience that perhaps enjoyed moving pictures in vaudeville but (because of class divisions) had been left out of the initial nickelodeon boom.[8]

Second, vaudeville acts could be introduced back into moving picture presentations. This happened increasingly after 1907 and culminated in small-time vaudeville, which interspersed film and vaudeville acts in larger capacity theaters. The theater was one aspect of this scheme, but exhibitors could also attract customers with the quality of their live acts.

Finally, exhibitors could attempt to offer either more frequent program changes or better films than their competitors. Unfortunately, this strategy involved factors over which the exhibitor typically had very little control. A regular flow of films was often very difficult to come by. Furthermore, the manufacturers were not putting out a product that was designed to give the exhibitor leverage in this increasingly competitive situation. This is not to say that all of the films were bad or that all were the same. The point is that the shift toward fictional film production did not automatically bring with it a system of product differentiation commensurate with the needs of the exhibitors.

It should be noted that the labor involved in moving pictures – to the extent that it was emphasized – appeared at the level of exhibition. In the early days of the cinematograph the moving picture "act" consisted not only of the film but of the projectionist as well, and lecturers often accompanied films with commentary throughout this period. Thus, a live entertainer, much in the tradition of vaudeville, held an intermediary position between the audience and the film. With the star system, we see a shift of attention away from this performance at the level of exhibition and toward the labor that began to manifest itself at the level of production – that is, the performance of those who appeared in films.

It is in this context that one must view the earliest appearance of the discourse on acting. Around 1907 a number of articles began to appear that placed into the foreground the role of human labor in the production of film. This should not be viewed as a demystification of the means of production but rather as the regulated appearance of a certain kind of knowledge. This knowledge entered into a struggle destined to resituate the site of textual productivity for the spectator away from the work of the apparatus itself. A number of potential "sites of productivity" were involved in this struggle – the manufacturer, the cinematographer (or director), and the photoplaywright, but of course it was the actor/star that finally became central in this regard.

In May of 1907 a series of articles began to appear in *Moving Picture World* entitled "How the Cinematographer Works and Some of His Difficulties." These articles offered a general account of the labor involved in producing films and focused a large measure of attention on the labor of those who appeared in films. The first installment began,

> Should you ever seek the source of the moving pictures of the vaudeville theater, you will learn that the comic, the tragic, the fantastic, the mystic scenes so swiftly enacted in photographic pantomime are not real but

feigned. You will find that the kinetoscopic world is much like the dramatic, that it has its actors and actresses, its playwrights and stage directors, its theatrical machinery, its wings, its properties, its lights, its tricks, its make-ups, its costumes, its entrances and its exits.[9]

In exposing the creative labor at the "source" of the moving picture, the article makes a direct appeal to a theatrical model. The reader is told that those who appear on screen are actors and is to assume, it seems, that their activity is acting. This, however, becomes somewhat problematic if we believe the definition of the "picture performer" given in the next installment of the series:

> Those who make a business out of posing for the kinetoscope are called 'picture performers' and many a hard knock they have to take. Practically all of them are professional stage people, and while performing on Broadway at night they pick up a few dollars day times in a moving picture studio. In a variety show, therefore, it sometimes happens that the same tumblers who a moment ago were turning handsprings and somersaults in real life, again appear in such roles as the traditional "Rube" and the "green goods man," but only in a phantom form upon the pictured screen.[10]

We can see something of a retreat from a theatrical model in this passage. Although the article claims that the performers are professional stage people, the example that follows seems to indicate that their stage is that of vaudeville, not theater. Acting is not mentioned here. Those who occupy the "traditional roles" are not actors, but tumblers.

It is not difficult to understand why the labor involved in the production of film would be symbolized through a comparison with the vaudeville act. The moving picture industry retained strong institutional ties to vaudeville, even though the nickelodeon was strongly challenging vaudeville as the dominant outlet of exhibition. As the quotation indicates, moving pictures had typically appeared alongside live vaudeville acts. It seems quite logical that the activity of the "picture performer" would, from the start, be set within the tradition of performance that characterized vaudeville.

However, it was a discourse on acting and therefore a theatrical model that would, over the next couple of years, define and determine the enunciative status of those who appeared in films. The above passage demonstrates, among other things, the equivocation with which this discourse was put forward. One notes a certain tentativeness in the symbolization of the performer's labor in terms of acting in much of the writing of the period. Acting was a profession associated with the legitimate stage, and the contention that people acted in films was neither immediately apparent nor altogether unproblematic. As we shall see later, the "film actor" emerged in a particularly contradictory field of discourses and traditions of entertainment.

"How the Cinematographer Works and Some of His Difficulties" appeared as an initiatory attempt to define and situate the work of those involved in the production of moving pictures. In particular, these articles (and others like them that began to appear in the last half of 1907) worked to constitute the "picture performer" or "film actor" as a subject of discourse. In so doing, they precipitated a significant shift in the enunciative status of film. Much of the knowledge that emerged about the picture performer in these early articles proceeded through a highly conventionalized form of narrative. The same type of stories appear again and again in explanations of the performer's work. All of the stories were predicated on the distinction drawn in the previous passage between the "phantom form on the screen" and the real performer and, more generally, between the filmic and profilmic.[11] The real performer's role in the profilmic event was the subject of all of these stories.

Note, for instance, this description of the filming of a bank robbery scene:

> In the most realistic way, the "robbers" broke into the bank, held up the cashier, shot a guard "dead" who attempted to come to the rescue, grabbed up a large bundle of money, and made their escape. Thus far all went well. The thieves were running down the street with the police in pursuit, just as the picture had been planned, when an undertaker, aroused by the racket, looked out of his shop. One glance sufficed to tell him that the time had come at last when he might become a hero. The "robbers" were heading toward him, and, leaping into the middle of the sidewalk, he aimed a revolver at the foremost fugitive with the threat: "Stop, thief, or I'll blow your brains out."[12]

The undertaker apprehended both of the bandits and refused to release them until he was convinced, by the head of the bank, that the robbery was staged.

Another story is prefaced by the following claim: "It may sometimes be said that the picture performer becomes so engrossed in his work that he forgets that he is simply shamming."[13] What follows is a story about the filming of a scene in which the hero must rescue a drowning girl. A crowd of bystanders who thought the girl was really drowning jumped into the lake to rescue her. The hero seemed to forget it was all an act, and – not to be outdone by his competition – raced to rescue the girl.

Both of these stories play upon a confusion between the filmic, the profilmic, and the real, but they do so primarily as a way of making distinctions between the three. The possibility of these distinctions was a necessary condition for the emergence of the picture performer. First of all, this emergence depended upon a knowledge of the performer's existence outside of the narrative of the film itself. By introducing the contingency of the profilmic event into what is otherwise a simple retelling of the (planned) narrative of the film, these stories differentiate the profilmic from the filmic and ascribe the former a relatively distinct status. Another narrative is set forth (separable from that of the film) that takes as its subject the performer's part in the production of film. These stories not only distinguish the profilmic from the filmic, they also, more obviously perhaps, distinguish the profilmic from the real. In straightening the two out the performer – and the reader – must confront the fictional status of that which is photographed by the camera.

The attention to the fictiveness of the scenes enacted in moving pictures had a direct bearing on the status of those who appeared in films, because it worked to establish the filmed body as a site of fictional production. It would be wrong to suggest that the body had not supported fictional material prior to 1907 because much evidence exists to the contrary. However, many of the early articles that described the work of those who appeared in films (such as "How the Cinematographer Works and Some of His Difficulties") were clearly under the sway of – or at least struggling with – a quite different, more established conception of the filmed body.

This conception was rooted in a photographic tradition and is manifested most clearly in the use of the verb *pose* in many of these early articles. In photography the pose is, in a sense, the limit of the body's complicity with the act of representation. The photograph may be posed or unposed, but it is not, within dominant practice at least, anything else. The verb *pose* may have described fairly unproblematically the nature of the activity of those who were represented in the topical, "documentary" films that dominated production prior to 1907. But it did not adequately account for the activity of those who appeared in dramatic or comedic films, because the pose does not usually carry connotations of a fictional production. The posed body is admittedly a highly conventionalized one; as Barthes has noted, in posing one transforms oneself in advance into an image.[14] Yet it is only in the context of the tension between the conventionality of the pose and the existence of a more spontaneous bodily identity that the "truth" of the pose is typically called into question. The more fundamental belief that the photograph represents something real remains undisputed. The fact that a picture is posed does not therefore necessarily lead to the conclusion that it is less real, that it is fictional or faked.

The shift in the status of the filmed body after 1907 was built precisely on this conclusion, however. Although the photographic conception of the body retained a kind of currency, it could not unproblematically accommodate the activity of those who were engaged in the presentation of a fiction. From 1907 we can see a kind of struggle between a photographic conception of the body and a theatrical one – between posing and acting. The ascendancy of the latter followed in part because it could account for the body as the site of a fictional production.

A correlation obviously exists between the consolidation of fictional filmmaking in 1907 and 1908 and the emergence of the discourse on acting. How is this correlation to be understood? Was the discourse on acting caused by this shift in production or vice versa? One must guard against these overly simple views to stress the complexity of the interaction between these two levels.

The fictional film existed long before the notion that people acted in films. As we have seen, the discourse on acting only appeared at the point at which the fiction film became the dominant, standardized product of the manufacturers. I have argued that the increasing dominance of the fictional film rendered the photographic conception of the body ("posing," "modeling") problematic and called for a model that could account for the body as a site of a fictional production. The theatrical model – and "acting" – met this requirement (as did other designations such as "faking" and, more ambiguously, "performing"). Insofar as it did, the discourse on acting can be seen as a response to the shift in film production. However, it would be a mistake to assume that the discourse on acting was simply a descriptive response. Although "acting" could account for the fictional status of the filmed body, in other respects it was an inappropriate description of the activity of those who appeared in films between 1907 and 1909. The moving pictures of the time generally provided little evidence to support acting's associations with art, expression, and interiority.

In fact, much writing of this period implicitly called into question the descriptive capacity of the discourse on acting: "the repertoire actor has discovered a new use for his talents. He is now a moving picture. That is, he now poses for moving pictures. By lying down, rolling over and jumping in front of the camera he is able to earn in three days a sum equal to a week's salary at his former industry."[15] Although the writer acknowledges that actors appear in films he must, for obvious reasons, stop short of claiming that their activity is acting. "Lying down, rolling over and jumping" are not what one thinks of when one thinks of an acting performance. Yet it was this kind of broad action (however parodically it is portrayed here) that characterized most of the films of the day.

For this reason, writers often made the claim that people acted in films with a marked degree of irony or irresolution. The word *actor* (and *artist*), for instance, usually appeared in quotation marks in these early articles. Note the following description of the making of a fiction film: "A man skilled at the business will impersonate the miserable husband in the case and a vaudeville actress temporarily out of work will play the role of the wife. Having secured permission of the city authorities to have a lot of sham disorder in the streets, the head man sends out photographers and 'actors.' "[16] The quotation marks allow the writer to assert that actors appear in films while acknowledging the problematic status of that assertion – and in fact making a joke out of it.

A similar tack is taken by Walter Prichard Eaton in "The Canned Drama." Eaton begins by describing an encounter with a professional actor friend who had turned to moving picture work. Yet, later in the article, Eaton parodies the contention that professional actors appear in films by distinguishing between two horses on a movie set. The horse that had cooperated with the director was apparently a professional actor while the more recalcitrant one was "merely an amateur."[17]

The tentative, contradictory treatment that film acting received in much of this early writing was prompted by the disjunction between the aesthetic pretensions of the discourse on acting and the types of films being produced at the time. It should be clear that the discourse on acting did not emerge simply because people acted in films. There was obviously some uncertainty about *what* people did in moving pictures. The discourse on acting worked against rather contradictory evidence to assert and establish the "fact" that people acted in films. It therefore had an active role in the changes taking place in the production and reception of moving pictures; it was not merely an effect or a reflection of those changes.

In fact, it was not until well after the discourse on acting emerged that films began to appear that fully supported and gave credence to the claim that people acted in films. The most famous and influential of these films were the French Films D'Art distributed by the Pathé Company. The films were offered by reviewers as proof that the art of acting could be translated to the screen:

> The greatest improvement at present (and there is still plenty of room for more) is along the line of dramatic structure and significant acting. Does it sound silly to talk thus pedantically, in the language of dramatic criticism, about moving pictures? If you will watch a poor American picture unroll blinkingly, and then a good French one, you will feel that it is not silly after all.

> With reference to the Pathé Film D'Art, "The Return of Ulysses," to which I referred last week, it is interesting to point out that the story was written by Jules Lemaitre, of the Academie Francaise, and the principal characters are taken by Mme. Bartet, MM. Albert Lambert, Lelauny and

Paul Mounet, all of the Comedie Francaise, Paris. This is equivalent to David Belasco and his Stuyvesant company doing the work for the Edison Company. Again I say, American Manufacturers please note![18]

The artistic pretensions of the discourse on acting were clearly borne out by these films. The Films D'Art were a series of films produced in a Neuilly studio by a production group of the same name and controlled and distributed by Pathé. Although the group began making films in 1908 their early efforts were not released in the United States until 1909. A certain amount of American publicity accompanied their production, however, and therefore preceded their release here. A French correspondent for *Variety*, reporting in July 1908, announced that some of France's greatest playwrights were "writing versions of the best works for famous actors to play – before the camera." As an example he noted that Hugenot, "the latest member of our great national stage," was appearing before the camera in *Blanchette* under the direction of Germier. Elsewhere it was rumored that Bernhardt, Duse, and "other great actresses of the day" were performing their greatest theatrical successes on film for Pathé.[19]

The first Film D'Art released in America, in February 1909, was entitled *Incriminating Evidence*. The *New York Dramatic Mirror* reacted to it this way: "It promises to be the most important dramatic subject ever issued by any company. It is acted by Severin, the great French pantomimist, who has proven one of the vaudeville sensations of the year in America. He is assisted in the film by his own company." The second American release (which had actually been the first produced) was *The Assassination of the Duke de Guise*. The names of the famous actors who appeared in the films were given a great deal of prominence in reviews and publicity, as they had been for the Severin picture: "The story was written for Pathe Freres by M. Henri Levedan of the Academie Francaise, and the chief parts were played by Mlle. Robinne and Mssrs. Lebargy and Albert Lambert of the Comedie Francaise." The *Dramatic Mirror* immediately hailed the film as "one of the few masterpieces of motion picture production."[20]

The Film D'Art series continued, apparently in monthly releases, with such films as *The Tower of Nesle* from the novel by Dumas (September 1909), *Drink* from *L'Assomoir* by Zola (October 1909), *Rigoletto* from Verdi's opera (November 1909), and *La Grande Breteche* from the novel by Balzac (December 1909).[21] The publicity surrounding the first three of these films did not call any special attention to specific actors. It made more general claims about the artfulness of these films. For instance, we are told that *The Tower of Nesle* is "enacted by the leading exponents of dramatic art," and that *Drink* is the "greatest picture ever produced." The ads that appeared for *La Grande Breteche* made similar claims, but they also stressed the cast – Phillipe Garnier of the Comédie Française, André Calamettes of the Gymanase, and Mlle. Sergine of L'Odéon.[22]

It should be noted that Pathé released other prestige pictures during this time which were not technically part of the Film D'Art series. *Her Dramatic Career*, for instance, received the same kind of publicity as *La Grande Breteche*, a month before the latter's release. And one reviewer judged an earlier effort, *The Hand* (from February of 1909), to be in the same class as the initial Films D'Art.[23] The Films D'Art were the most visible examples of a more general interest Pathé had in "high-class" productions.

Early Film D'Art releases of 1910 presented Mlle. Victoria Lepanto in *Carmen* and *The Lady with the Camelias*. Although Lepanto received more publicity than any actor who had previously appeared in Films D'Art, nothing was said to imply that she had a theatrical background. This marks a significant departure from earlier practice and takes us into the province of the picture personality. The Film D'Art's supreme contribution to the contention that people acted in films probably did not come until 1912 with the release of a filmed version of *Camille* starring Sarah Bernhardt. Bernhardt's entry into moving pictures had been long awaited. Her capitulation was seen as "a milestone in the evolution of the moving picture."[24] The world's greatest and most famous actress (by many accounts at least) had become a photoplayer, thus blurring – for an instant at least – all distinctions between the moving picture and the legitimate theater.

Camille was not different from the initial efforts of the Film D'Art in kind so much as degree. Bernhardt's name was a household word while those of Robinne and Lebargy were not. "Bernhardt" had attained the status of a popular symbol, the name itself signifying the art of great acting. The producers certainly took this into account when they paid Bernhardt a reported $30,000 to appear before the camera. The promoters of *Camille* (as well as those who promoted *Queen Elizabeth*, Bernhardt's next film) capitalized on it with an intensive publicity campaign, and the many journalists who had an interest in advancing the aesthetic legitimacy of the cinema used it to make some of their most zealous claims. *Camille* apparently succeeded. According to the publicity for the film and an attendant article in *Moving Picture News* the film was the "fastest seller ever offered States Rights buyers."[25]

The theatrical model, which had been taken up somewhat awkwardly by the discourse on acting in discussions of other films, was fully embodied by the Film D'Art. The comparisons between the theater and moving pictures were quite appropriate here. The Films D'Art, after all, were moving pictures of theatrical plays. Because of this, it probably seemed natural (as well as expedient) to emphasize the performance of the actors involved and publicize their names. Plays were promoted and consumed in this way. The enunciative position that the theatrical actor assumed in the theater was reproduced in these films. The notion of the film actor emerged through its association with this established tradition.

The Films D'Art have a prominent place in this history not because they were the first films of their kind (though this is arguable), but because they were the most visible, the most regularly released, and the most influential. Writers quite commonly held the films up to the public and to the American producers as the foremost examples of film art. For many they represented the future of the moving picture industry – that ideal point at which the theater and the cinema would seamlessly merge to elevate the tastes of the masses to an appreciation of theatrical art. This future was not realized of course; the cinema would not become "filmed theater." Nevertheless, the Film D'Art had a significant impact on the course the cinema took during these years.

Developments in American production paralleled the "advances" of the Film D'Art. Manufacturers began to release prestige pictures – adaptations of famous literary and dramatic works – as early as 1907. Kalem released a version of *Ben Hur* in late 1907 that later became famous in connection with a copyright decision regarding adaptations. By March of 1908 Selig had produced versions of *The Count of Monte Cristo*, *Dr. Jekyll and Mr. Hyde*, and *Rip Van Winkle*, and Vitagraph released *The Story of Treasure Island* and *Francesca da Rimini*. Vitagraph, in fact, was the company that most vigorously pursued a policy of producing "artful" adaptations on a regular basis. At least five adaptations of plays by Shakespeare were produced by Vitagraph in 1908.[26] The manufacturers in presenting these adaptations attempted to both exploit the already constituted fame of these titles and establish the aesthetic legitimacy of moving pictures. The films worked toward this latter end by taking up a theatrical model and giving support to the discourse on acting. One does not, after all, "pose" the role of Macbeth. The very existence of some of these films gave credence to the contention that people acted in films.

Reviews of these films often noted the acting and discussed its quality. "The leading role and character part executed by the man who plays the double life of Dr. Jekyll – at times Mr. Hyde – is so convincing that no greater display of ability to fulfill this role could be shown by any actor. . . . Throughout the performance the scenes are as realistic as in any theater." "The acting of the principal characters in Richard III is all that can be desired, the only blemish being in the battle where the smiles on the faces of the actors are ill-timed."[27] One expects such references to acting in reviews today, but they were exceptional at the time.

Vitagraph's activities in prestige production accelerated in 1909. In February, a version of *Virginius* appeared that was "said to be" (by the promoters no doubt) "another step higher in the excellent work of the Vitagraph players." Ads for the film stressed that it was "elaborately staged, gorgeously costumed, superbly acted." This became the slogan for Vitagraph's prestige pictures, which soon appeared under the designation "High Art" films. Another name, *Film de Luxe*, was given to a number of films (among them a series of five films derived from Hugo's *Les Misérables*).[28] These designations clearly associated Vitagraph's quality productions with the type of film bearing the name *Film D'Art*.

There was, however, at least one significant difference between a Film D'Art such as *Incriminating Evidence* (released in February 1909) and the Vitagraph films (such as *Virginius*) released around the same time. The latter did not exploit the names of actors. We do not see an effort on the part of American producers to adopt this strategy until the middle of 1909. Vitagraph's move in this direction came in May, with a High Art production of *Oliver Twist*. An ad in the *New York Dramatic Mirror* announced that Miss Elita Proctor Otis appeared in the film "as Nancy Sykes, the role which this eminent actress has made famous throughout the world."[29] The ad displayed Otis's name prominently, in bold-face type the same size as that used for the title.

This did not, by any means, become standard practice for Vitagraph. In fact, most of the High Art films that followed *Oliver Twist* were not marketed in this way (though there was a continued emphasis on the superb acting in the films). One can argue that this was because truly famous actors were not appearing in the films. Yet the company claimed that they were, and – without naming names – they continued to use this as a selling point:

> Several notable productions of the Shakespeare drama have been made by the Vitagraph and these have excited unstinted praise from the dramatic commentators, but *The Twelfth Night* is to be the best of all and the most elaborate preparations are being made . . . A Shakespearean player of country-wide fame is one of the Vitagraph producers, and he has been

given absolutely a free hand in the selection of special players. If the Vitagraph could announce the cast of characters on the sheet you would be astonished at the display of familiar names.[30]

Although the Edison Company had produced adaptations previously (a 1903 version of *Uncle Tom's Cabin*, for instance) they do not seem to have had a strong role in the high-class-film movement until the latter half of 1909, when they produced a version of *The Prince and the Pauper* with Miss Cecil Spooner:

> Miss Cecil Spooner was especially employed to enact the difficult role of Tom Canty, the pauper boy, and Edward, the boy prince of Wales in Mark Twain's celebrated story, *The Prince and the Pauper*. Graceful, effective and polished as an actress, her finished art has contributed much to the beauty and strength of this notable silent drama.
>
> We hope to employ others as well-known [as Spooner] in the near future and meantime we are building up our own force with care and discrimination.
>
> We intend from time to time (as we have in the past) to put out especially high class pictures, based on familiar themes or plots of well-known playwrights and literary producers, with actors of known reputation. And these special pictures, sold as they will be at the same price will, we believe, commend themselves strongly to the trade as an indication of what the Edison Company is willing to do to advance the interests of the business.[31]

The earlier high-class films mentioned here may have been produced, but they were not accompanied by a comparable amount of publicity. And they certainly were not part of a regular policy of manufacturing and promoting films with well-known actors.

In September 1909, *Moving Picture World* published a cast list of the Edison film *Ethel's Luncheon*. None of the cast members were famous. The list itself served to stress the "fact" that the film contained actors, and that it should be received much as a play would be received. But the Edison Company's great coup was the engagement of the French pantomimist Pilar-Morin in September of 1909. Pilar-Morin was known in America, having toured successfully as a special attraction in Vaudeville. Her first film with the Edison Company was *Comedy and Tragedy*. An article in the *Edison Kinetogram* (later reproduced in *Moving Picture World*) authored by Pilar-Morin and entitled "The Value of Silent Drama; or Pantomime in Acting" accompanied its release.[32] In it, Pilar-Morin argues that the art of pantomime is at the base of all great drama, thus effacing the differences not only between pantomime and legitimate theater, but also between pantomime (itself a respected cultural form) and moving pictures. She ends by praising the great advances of the Edison Company in "elevating the art of moving pictures" and in "securing well-known artists and actors."

There is every reason to believe that Cecil Spooner and Elita Proctor Otis's appearances in film were, at the time, designed as one-shot ventures. Edison obviously engaged Pilar-Morin on a more long-term basis. Although she only appeared in special releases, she became in effect the star member of the Edison stock company. After *Comedy and Tragedy* she appeared in at least six other films: *The Japanese Peach Boy,*

Carmen, The Cigarette Maker of Seville, The Piece of Lace, From Tyranny to Liberty, and *The Key of Life*.

These films were released at the time picture personalities were beginning to achieve fame for their work in moving pictures. Pilar-Morin has a transitional and somewhat ambiguous status in this history. On the one hand she clearly fits into the tradition of Severin and Proctor — actors whose appearance in moving pictures traded upon their fame as actors outside of moving pictures. It is in this sense that she was such a central figure in articulating the discourse on acting. However, on the other hand, she was promoted through an intense publicity campaign that not only pointed to the fact that an accomplished actor was appearing in films, but also attempted to establish her identity across a number of films as something that was marketable. She became a personality:

> Mlle. Pilar-Morin has come at the psychological moment, or, it may also be put, she is a happy accident — very gifted, very optimistic and very earnest. Curiosity as to the personalities of leading artists connected with the opera and the stage is becoming duplicated in the moving picture field, where, in the last few months, the renowned and the favorite performers have become familiar to the 7,000,000 public of the United States. The most renowned of them all, who easily takes pride of place in virtue of her record and her transcendental ability is Mme. Pilar-Morin.[33]

Later in this article Pilar-Morin's notion that the silent drama is "the expression of one's personality in one's acting" is voiced. As we shall see in the next chapter it is this notion that characterized the kind of knowledge that emerged to create the picture personality. It can be argued, in fact, that throughout 1910 Pilar-Morin functioned for the Edison Company in much the same way (though probably not as successfully) as Florence Lawrence and Florence Turner did for Imp and Vitagraph. The notable difference is that Lawrence and Turner never had any previous fame as actors outside of moving pictures.

The Biograph Company's activities during this time should be noted. Biograph did produce a number of theatrical and literary adaptations between 1907 and 1910.[34] It did not, however, publicize the names of its actors, whether famous or not. In this respect, it can be said that Biograph refrained from participating fully in the strategy pursued by Vitagraph and Edison. Yet the Biograph films did strongly emphasize acting and did therefore support the discourse on acting, even if it did so with somewhat less fanfare. A review of *The Better Way* in August 1909 stated that the film's "good acting is the point."[35] And, as we shall see in a moment, *The Better Way* was later held up as an example of a film with pure acting. Even as early as May 1909 the *New York Dramatic Mirror* could claim:

> The progress that is being made by American film manufacturers along the lines of higher dramatic art in picture pantomime is probably best illustrated by the results that have been accomplished by the Biograph Company. It is no reflection on the other American manufacturers and the great improvement they are all making to assert that the Biograph Company at present is producing a better general average of dramatic pantomime than

any other company in America. If we except Pathe Freres, this claim for the Biograph may be extended to include the world.[36]

The rising emphasis on a theatrical model of "fine acting" during this period culminated in the formation of the Famous Players Film Company in 1912. Adolph Zukor set up the company specifically with the intent of presenting great theatrical actors in prestigious roles. The company would be more exclusively identified with this kind of prestige production than the other American companies, which only produced them intermittently. Zukor entered into an agreement with Daniel Frohman, a respected manager of theatrical actors, and Charles Frohman, a powerful producer on Broadway, to assure a steady stream of talent and material and, no doubt, to give his venture the stamp of respectability. Although Mary Pickford soon became Famous Players's biggest star (of course by this time she could be billed as a great actress, having conquered Broadway), and the company's reliance on the theater eventually weakened, during its early years it presented such renowned legitimate actors as Sarah Bernhardt, Mrs. Fiske, Jack Barrymore, and James K. Hackett.[37] These efforts further supported the idea that actors appeared in films and in fact exploited the public's desire to see identifiable figures acting on the screen.

As noted earlier, though, this desire was not a natural one; it had a specific history and had in fact been solicited in the years following 1907. Previous histories of the star system have largely ignored the appearance and elaboration of the discourse on acting. This chapter has traced the early history of this discourse and argued that it was through this discourse that the idea of the film actor was constituted. Around 1907 attention began to be focused away from the projectionist and the mechanical capabilities of the apparatus and toward the human labor involved in the production of film. Specifically, attention was turned to those who appeared in films, and their activity began to be characterized, after a theatrical model, as acting. In effect, a system of enunciation was put in place that featured the actor as subject. This institutionalized a mode of reception in which the spectator regarded the actor as the primary source of aesthetic effect. It is the identity of the actor as subject that would be elaborated as the star system developed.

It is clear that the symbolic work that established the actor as subject is closely linked to a specific economic strategy. The status of film as enunciation clearly changed through the discourse on acting; but it can also be said that the actor changed the status of film as commodity. The discourse on acting emerged at a time of a rapid expansion of the film industry. Companies were faced with the need to rationalize production and produce a larger and more predictable supply of films. The move toward fictional production and the formation of stock companies can be seen as a response to this need. The companies were faced with another problem within this environment – how to differentiate any of their films from the hundreds of other films on the market. Their company name and the genre of the particular film accomplished this to a degree, but not to the degree or with the force that the presence of an actor would. Films with actors could be differentiated from films without actors, and, as the presence of actors became accepted as the norm, particular actors (their identities) could be differentiated from other actors. Product differentiation quite typically follows a semiotic scheme in which differences in meaning become differences in value in an economic exchange. The discourse on acting began to put in place a system of product differentiation that would be based on the identity of the subject within an institutionalized system of enunciation.

Notes

1   See Benjamin McArthur, *Actors and American Culture, 1880–1920* (Philadelphia: Temple University Press, 1984), and David Carroll, *The Matinee Idols* (London: Peter Owen, 1972).

2   See Robert C. Allen, *Vaudeville and Film 1895–1915: A Study in Media Interaction* (New York: Arno Press, 1980). My discussion of the industry prior to 1907 owes a great deal to Allen's analysis.

3   Ibid., pp. 127, 128.

4   Eric Smoodin, "Attitudes of the American Printed Medium toward the Cinema: 1894–1908," unpublished paper, University of California, Los Angeles, 1979.

5   Allen, p. 105.

6   Ibid., pp. 212, 213; Charles Musser, "Another Look at the 'Chaser Theory,'" *Studies in Visual Communication* 10, no. 4 (Fall 1984): 24–44.

7   Charles Musser, "The Nickelodeon Era Begins: Establishing the Framework for Hollywood's Mode of Representation," *Framework* 22–23 (Autumn 1983): 4; David Bordwell, Janet Staiger, and Kristin Thompson, *The Classical Hollywood Cinema: Film Style and Mode of Production to 1960* (New York: Columbia University Press, 1985); On Griffith and Biograph see Tom Gunning's important work, *D. W. Griffith and the Origins of American Narrative Film: The Early Years at Biograph* (Urbana: University of Illinois Press, 1991).

8   See Allen, *Vaudeville and Film 1895–1915*, pp. 192–260.

9   "How the Cinematographer Works and Some of His Difficulties," *Moving Picture World*, May 18, 1907, p. 165.

10   Ibid., June 8, 1907, p. 212.

11   The events and actions that appear on screen are, in terms of this distinction, filmic. The profilmic designates the existence of those events (whether staged or unstaged) in real time and space before the camera. See Etienne Souriau, *L'univers filmique* (Paris: Flammarion, 1953).

12   "How the Cinematographer Works," *Moving Picture World*, May 18, 1907, p. 166.

13   Ibid., June 8, 1907, p. 21.

14   Roland Barthes, *Camera Lucida*, trans. Richard Howard (New York: Hill and Wang, 1981), pp. 10–15.

15   *Moving Picture World*, Oct. 21, 1907, p. 453.

16   Ibid., Aug. 29, 1908, p. 94.

17   Walter Prichard Eaton, "The Canned Drama," *American Magazine* 68 (Sept. 1909), pp. 493–500.

18   Ibid., p. 499; *Moving Picture World*, Mar. 20, 1909, p. 326.

19   *Variety*, July 7, 1908, p. 11; *Moving Picture World*, Sept. 5, 1908, p. 177.

20   *New York Dramatic Mirror*, Feb. 27, 1909, pp. 18, 13.

21   *Moving Picture World*, Sept. 25, 1909, p. 426; Oct. 23, 1909, p. 557; Nov. 13, 1909, p. 671; Dec. 4, 1909, p. 789.

22   Ibid., Oct. 23, 1909, p. 557; Dec. 4, 1909, p. 789.

23   Ibid., Nov. 13, 1909, p. 671; *New York Dramatic Mirror*, Feb. 27, 1909, p. 13.

24   *Moving Picture World*, Feb. 26, 1910, p. 294; Feb. 17, 1912, p. 596; see also *New York Times*, Sept. 15, 1911, p. 9.

25   The figure of $30,000 was of course part of the publicity and, as with all such figures, must be taken with a degree of suspicion; *Moving Picture News*, Mar. 16, 1912, p. 1089; see also *Moving Picture World*, Mar. 9, 1912, p. 874.

26   *Moving Picture World*, Feb. 1, 1908, p. 70; Mar. 7, 1908, p. 194; May 2, 1908, p. 406; Mar. 7, 1908, p. 195; Feb. 8, 1908, p. 103; Apr. 25, 1908, p. 374; Oct. 3, 1908, p. 25; Jan. 2, 1909, p. 21. For a broader account of the issues raised by the Vitagraph "quality" films, see Roberta Pearson and William Uricchio's forthcoming book, *Invisible Viewers, Inaudible Voices: Intertextuality and Reception in the Early Cinema* (Princeton, N.J.: Princeton University Press).

27   *Moving Picture World*, Mar. 7, 1908, p. 194; Oct. 3, 1908, p. 253.

28   *New York Dramatic Mirror*, Feb. 6, 1909, p. 19, 18; see, for instance, *Moving Picture World*, June 19, 1909, p. 862, and July 17, 1909, p. 79; Aug. 7, 1909, p. 184.

29   *New York Dramatic Mirror*, May 1, 1909, p. 43.

30   *Moving Picture World*, Aug. 14, 1909, p. 64.

31   *The Edison Kinetogram*, Aug. 1, 1909, p. 14, and *Moving Picture World*, Aug. 28, 1909, p. 277.

32   *The Edison Kinetogram*, Sept. 15, 1909, p. 3; Nov. 15, 1909, pp. 12–13; *Moving Picture World*, Nov. 13, 1909, p. 682.

33   *Moving Picture World*, Jan. 22, 1910, p. 204.

34   See Tom Gunning, "D. W. Griffith and the Narrator-System: Narrative Structure and Industry Organization in Biograph Films, 1908–1909" (Ph.D. diss., New York University, 1986), pp. 342–50.

35   *Moving Picture World*, Aug. 21, 1909, p. 253.

36   *New York Dramatic Mirror*, May 1, 1909, p. 34.

37   *Moving Picture World*, Jan. 11, 1913, p. 123; Aug. 23, 1913, pp. 854–55; July 11, 1914, p. 186; *Moving Picture News*, Aug. 2, 1913, p. 12; Jan. 17, 1914, p. 34.

Chapter 6

Francesco Alberoni

THE POWERLESS 'ELITE'
Theory and sociological research on the phenomenon of the stars[1]

Francesco Alberoni, 'L'Élite irresponsable; théorie et recherche sociologique sur *le divismo*', *Ikon*, vol. 12–40/1, 1962, pp. 45–62.

This Reading is presented in this volume in a new translation by Denis McQuail.

General conditions for the existence of the phenomenon

IN EVERY SOCIETY ARE to be found persons who, in the eyes of other members of the collectivity, are especially remarkable and who attract universal attention. This applies most often to the king and nobles, to priests, prophets and men of power, although often in very diverse ways and in varying degrees. In general it is a question of persons who hold power (political, economic or religious) – that is to say, of persons whose decisions have an influence on the present and future fortunes of the society which they direct. This rule holds true even in modern western society. However, besides these persons, one finds others, *whose institutional power is very limited or non-existent, but whose doings and way of life arouse a considerable and sometimes even a maximum degree of interest*. This interest is not related to the consequences which the activities and decisions of these particular individuals (stars, idols, '*divi*') can have on the lives and future expectations of members of the society. They belong to another sphere of evaluation.

The existence, at the heart of a society, of two categories of persons whose behaviour is an object of great attention, is accompanied effectively by a difference *in orientations and in criteria of evaluation*. Because the holders of power are 'evaluated' almost exclusively according to the direct or indirect consequences of their activities for the attainment of societal goals and for the organization of the community, with them it is a question of a specific criterion of evaluation. With the second group, a more complex system, which we are going to analyse in the course of the present research, is involved.

Such a separation stems from the fact that decision-making activities which concern the collectivity (power) are made up of autonomous and specific social roles: these activities, engaged in by persons who hold institutionally established positions have their effects in a real sphere of decision and are subject to forms and criteria of evaluation which are fixed in advance. At a given stage of social development, it follows that an impersonal evaluation of activities of collective interest is possible. The preliminary conditions for a situation of this type comprise the establishment of a state of law and of an efficient bureaucracy.

A phenomenon like 'stardom' does not exist unless certain systems of action are institutionally considered as *unimportant from a political point of view*. In other words 'stars' exist in that measure to which their activities are not mainly evaluated according to the consequences which they involve for the collectivity. There is a social mechanism of separation which, put schematically, holds that the 'stars' do not occupy *institutional positions of power*. One may note that this situation could not, in theory, hold in a marxist social system where every member of a social group has a function for the collectivity and is responsible for the consequences of his action. It could, however, hold in these circumstances in respect of persons who, living outside the system and belonging to the capitalist world, have no power over the system itself. In this sense, 'stardom' does not so much presuppose a pluralism of evaluation or culture, as the existence of autonomous centres of power, whether private or not, which are institutionally guaranteed against the intervention of the State.

These conditions hold today in the western world, just as they did in Greece and above all in imperial Rome (it does not seem that 'stardom' in the true sense of the term existed in the Egypt of the Pharaohs – a fact which can be explained without inconsistency with earlier remarks: in this particular case the governing bureaucracy did not permit the existence of autonomous centres of private power, governed and guaranteed by public power).

Besides these two conditions which we have indicated, we can mention several others: the degree of structuring of the social system; the growth in size of societies; the increase in economics wealth; social mobility.

As far as the *structuring* of the social system is concerned, what we have already said has implied this. The separation out of specific principles of evaluation, important for the growing institutional cadres of decision-making power, cannot help but produce a complex structure in a society.

As to the size of the social system, we observe that in public–star relationships, each individual member of the public knows the star, but the star does not know any individuals. The star views the public as a collectivity. This does not mean that personal relationships between the star and other actors cannot exist, but that it is not these personal relationships which characterize the phenomenon. For a relationship of this kind to be set up, one must presuppose a large number of spectators and the existence of certain specific social mechanisms. Even if the star is perceived in his or her individuality, the spectators cannot be perceived in theirs. This situation is best exemplified in a large-scale society, with a high level of interdependence, at the core of which and by virtue of its very large size, only a small number of persons can provide a point of reference for all. In a more restricted community, the same process would be possible, bearing in mind the existence of those institutional barriers of the type which separate the king, or certain priests or nobles. In this case, the phenomenon would be something other than 'stardom', since for the latter there is no institutional barrier. On the contrary, the obstacle arises in most cases either because observation of the person concerned cannot be direct or because of the sheer number of aspirants to such a type of relationship. We can see that the relationship between star and public lacks an element which we would label 'mutuality'.

An increase of economic wealth is a third basic condition. In effect, only an income above subsistence level allows the mobilization of interests and attention which gives rise to the phenomenon of stardom. Nevertheless, one must be cautious in establishing a correlation between these two orders of phenomena. On the one hand, the rise in income above subsistence level is always the fruit of an economic and structural transformation of society – a point which connects with the two earlier conditions – on the other hand, we can find the phenomenon of 'stars' at very low levels of income and economic development (football-players in South America; cinema actors in India). One might even wonder whether the phenomenon in its most accentuated form is not peculiar to societies which are socially and economically under developed.

Social mobility, which is dependent on the transformation of the system, is also a fundamental condition for enabling one to have admiration, rather than envy, for the star.

Stardom and charisma

We will use the word 'stars' and 'stardom' with a rather wider meaning than common usage allows, especially in Italy.[2] Following Panzini's definition (1963, p. 202), one would understand by this word the phenomenon by which a certain individual attracts, in the eyes of many others, an unconditional admiration and interest. The cry of the crowd to the victorious champion 'you are a god' provides a typical example. The champion is credited with capacities superior to those of all other men, and thus with super-human qualities. Weber defined this situation as *charismatic* (1968, vol. 1, p. 241). He writes

> By charisma we mean a quality regarded as extraordinary and attributed to a person. . . . The latter is believed to be endowed with powers and properties which are supernatural and superhuman, or at least exceptional even where accessible to others; or again as sent by God, or as if adorned with exemplary value and thus worthy to be a leader.

We can, first of all, ask ourselves what the relevance of this example is in assessing the phenomenon of stardom as we have presented it. Are the stars truly gods in the literal meaning of the word, or rather charismatic figures?

According to Max Weber, charisma leads to a power relationship by virtue of the fact that the possessor of charisma is perceived as a leader or chief (thus producing an internalized feeling of obligation); under his leadership, those who submit derive benefits which constitute proof of charisma. In the definition of 'stardom' we have made it clear that the star is not endowed with authoritative power and that his decisions are not collectively felt to have any influence on the life and the future of members of the collectivity. How is it that the charismatic element of 'stardom' does not get transformed into a power relationship? The explanation must be sought in the mechanisms which, in a highly structured society, give rise to the specificity of social roles. Whoever occupies a social position is appraised according to the specific content of the function which characterizes this position (see Parsons, 1949). In the case of a multiple classification, the specificity of the function and of the evaluation does not disappear (see Alberoni, 1960, pp. 37–42).

In other words, a bank employee is judged in the light of specific criteria which relate to the kind of work he does. If at the same time he is a member of some association, the kind of normative qualities required of him in the second system and the evaluative criteria used in relation to it, are not only specific, but often will not relate to the former. It is exactly this independence of social roles which, in modern societies, leads to conflicts between the roles themselves. Thus the bank employee or the unattached person who rejoices at the victory of his sporting hero and who calls out 'you are a god' does not cease to be a bank employee or a private citizen in order to follow his idol and share in his idol's charisma. The behaviour in which charisma is expressed is in reality behaviour in a particular role, while the behaviour of the spectator is defined by exclusion from this role and by the retention of his ordinary roles. The spectator is present at, shares in, but does not act. The manifestation of charisma which concerns us presupposes, therefore, a stable social structure – that is, a system of pre-established and internalized roles, of such a kind that the sharing in charisma does not result in the restructuring of habitual systems of action. In this way, the charisma is highly specific.

The racing cyclist who is a demi-god in the eyes of his enthusiastic admirer does not necessarily show competence in other fields. The specificity of charisma should be understood as a specificity relating to one class of actions, all requiring the same kind of skill. This is why a great racing cyclist can also be a great athlete. Specialization lies at the heart of any particular field. Besides, a champion's superiority in fields different from his speciality, but within the same category, can furnish confirmation of his true charismatic nature. It would be very interesting to make an empirical study of the size of this area of generalization, in terms of conscious and unconscious expectations. Nevertheless, there exist institutional limits to such generalizations: political activity is one example.

By contrast, in a society where there is no complexity of social structures, nor mechanisms for separating out social roles, charisma tends to become generalized. This is one of the reasons why stardom does not exist in small-scale societies. The exceptional man raises himself to a charismatic level and becomes a hero. He thus acquires over the community a power which, at the same time, exposes him to aggressively violent reactions on the part of his opponents and to the envy of those who are less adept than he. Change occurs within two limiting points: either the hero is overthrown by envy and aggression, or he succeeds over his enemies and his power is institutionalized. Neither case would be expected in large-scale societies with a high level of structuring. In such cases, charisma is not generalized, the star does not acquire power and as a result is not exposed to envy or aggression. The sharp separation between roles which prevents the stars from acquiring an institutionalized position of power in a highly structured society is the social system's protection mechanism against the menace of generalized charisma. The separation of roles in this respect offers much stronger guarantees than does simply specificity of roles. In the case of multiple allocation, the specification of roles is only efficacious up to the point where the corresponding modes of evaluation are deeply internalized. If the specificity of evaluation were strongly internalized, the star would be able to occupy a power position because he or she would be evaluated quite differently as a holder of power than as artist, football champion, etc. But if the internalization is shallow, there is always the danger in this situation that charisma will become generalized. The great actor, the great athlete, the personage known to all, sympathetic, attractive – all these could be raised to power, not independently of the fact of their being actors, cyclists or well-known figures, but precisely because they are such. This would occur especially in countries where the structuring is still weak and where specific and rational modes of evaluation are little internalized.

(We have recently seen a case of a country choosing as parliamentary deputies football players who were victorious in a world championship. In Italy we have had the candidature of Bartali in parliamentary elections. Elia Kazan, in his film 'Face in the Crowd' shows a situation in which a very gifted singer becomes a charismatic leader and, supported by unscrupulous politicians, finds himself on the point of attaining power.)

The mechanism by which social roles are sharply separated seems therefore to have the function of a defence against the generalization of charisma. In the light of these considerations one may assume that the condition of sharp separation of roles will lose its importance along with a greater internalization of specific modes of evaluation.

The 'stars' as an elite

In any society which is socially stratified, normal methods for the study of stratification always enable us to identify a more exalted social stratum which has sharply different characteristics from other social strata. A primary feature of this difference is the existence, amongst members of this particular stratum, of a higher degree of interaction than is found between members of other strata.

A second feature derives from the fact that in this group, competition, and often very active competition, always takes place with a high regard for the rules and mores of the group, thus ensuring that the decisions of members of the 'elite' do not have too sudden and sharp repercussions on the non-privileged.

The third feature is a certain degree of isolation, compared with other strata and groups. In general this is a question of ensuring a degree of secrecy for the activities of competition and cooperation, since these might not accord with the those of the non-privileged. The reduction in what we will call observability has the effect of enabling those who hold power to follow strategies for conserving it, and sometimes constitutes a means for preserving privilege. In contrast, an increase in observability is often an expression of the diminution of power. All of which comes back to the point that a power elite can never be exposed to a high degree of observability. In any case, the forms and the nature of observability, as far as the holders of institutional power are concerned, are institutionally established (in democracy in very liberal measure); this characteristic, which is most important, is respected even when there is a high degree of observability. In the case of the stars, on the contrary, observability is practically unlimited.

The highest degree of observability in a power elite is to be found in aristocratic or monarchic states whose legitimacy is securely founded on popular consent, and in popular democracies. The king, court and nobles are objects of valuation in varied ways, including, amongst other things, that type of valuation reserved for 'stars'. In this case the situation is very close to that of very small communities. This is facilitated by the lack of influence which observability has on power, attributable in turn to the particular criteria which affect selection for, and participation in, the elite (for example the requirement of membership of certain noble families).

Charismatic totalitarianism accords with this situation only superficially. In fact the chief or leader parades a total observability, even of his private life, which is presented as exemplary. But the behaviours truly deserving attention (as far as power is concerned) are kept carefully hidden and removed from all control. The observability of the charismatic leader is carefully foreseen and manipulated. Its purpose is to guarantee that only those evaluative orientations conducive to the exercise of power itself and favourable to it, will be set working.

On the other hand, in the democracy typical of industrial societies, there develop specific traditional evaluative orientations towards the power elite. It is, in general, a question of highly specific evaluations, from which are eliminated all elements which are not functionally important. Other evaluative orientations are no longer directed towards elites, but towards 'significant others' whose observability is not institutionally limited, that is to say the 'stars'. By comparison the observability of the latter is thus very heightened, and the evaluative orientations very complex.

One must, nevertheless, admit that the specificity of evaluations concerning persons who occupy institutionalized positions of power in a democracy can vary in degree. In long-established and well-consolidated democracies, where the internalization of the values of the social system is deepest, observability is greater and more diffused. This probably stems from the fact that the danger represented by the generalization of charisma is least; the institutionalized rules coincide in greater measure with the mores of the community. The limitation of evaluations within highly specific limits here loses its importance. In England, or in the United States, politicians are evaluated (in a greater measure than in Italy, for example) with regard to activities which are not strictly or specifically political. The President of the United States, in order to be elected, must present a total image of his private life, of his relations with the community, etc., something which is inconceivable in a democracy of recent origin, menaced by the generalization of charisma. The mode of behaviour in the community becomes the object of evaluation in order to demonstrate the adherence of the candidate to the mores of the society, mores which constitute the fundamental basis of evaluation internalized from the political system. The President will become a symbol for the nation, an ideal model for universal reference; he crystallizes in himself many of the characteristics belonging to stardom. Hence a necessity for an *a priori* evaluation of his manner of life and of his capacities in office. The latter is possible when the values inspired by the political system are widely shared and deeply internalized. A very slight deviation can then rapidly provoke the condemnation of the person, whatever may be his institutional power position. The case is very different if this internalization does not exist. Satisfaction can easily transform itself into admiration, qualities into superhuman properties, superiority into charisma, and admiration into devotion.

In democracies of recent date, where the process of consolidation of democratic institutions is under way, where the progressive change of the system is leading towards industrial rationalization, a specific evaluation should be interpreted either as a latent function or as an anticipatory manifestation of socialization, ensuring that the evolution of the system remains in accord with the model of rationalization. One would predict that when a deeper internalization of democratic values occurs and of specific and rational modes of evaluation, there will appear, in this type of social system, forms of values which are more general, while still retaining a specific character.

We can say that the stars are, like the power elite, an object of reference for the community, but of a different kind. It seems to us useful to stress that a good many of these stars appear in the eyes of the public as being in close interaction and making up a true elite which occupies a central place (although without power) in a community of an industrialized kind. They constitute a genuine core of the community, and although deprived of any fixed or stable location, they do at least partially congregate as a group in certain privileged places.[3]

If we were to choose any list whatsoever of people of this kind, based on a sampling of weekly magazines, we would soon find that the majority has been or is effectively in interaction. We are here concerned with a world of entertainment, related to everyday society by reason of business or profession, or because they frequent the same fashionable places, the same receptions, etc.

In the eyes of the public, this commonality probably seems higher than it really is, either by reason of the false impression of proximity suggested by television shows, or through the juxtaposition of photographic evidence with press articles, or because of the care which is taken to present to the public friendly and cooperative forms of interaction and to soften hostile and competitive forms. The members of this elite thus appear, contrary to fact, as being potentially in interaction. (It would be interesting to study how this type of relationship is perceived by the public and what sort of constellations, especially of a spatial kind, they imagine to exist).

One can say that the stars form a social group with very fluid and uncertain limits. The group is not structured, but it shows certain centres of interaction which sometimes take on the character of sub-group or sub-community: for example, the community group of the Via Veneto in Rome, the Frank Sinatra clan, etc. Those who make up a lower group (the fringe constituted by those who, in the eyes of the public, interact only occasionally with the group, like certain writers, painters or fashionable thinkers) do not, however, exhaust the totality of these personages who are 'significant', *although lacking in power or authority*. The protagonists in national scandals (as Brusadelli or Giuffre in Italy), those accused of famous crimes like Giuliano, are not part of this elite: participants in televised competitions or television plays enter it in a rather fleeting manner. One knows of people who have become famous as a result of an exceptional exploit like Lindberg or Gagarin who can enter into interaction with the core we have spoken of, but who often remain completely separate from it, or, in contrast, can even belong marginally to the elite of power as did Gagarin. Even when they lack interactive relationships with the community core, or when they are institutionally excluded from it, these people (even the criminals) are nevertheless potential members of it in the eyes of the public.

Evaluation of modes of conduct in the community

We have said that the stars are those members of the community whom *all* can evaluate, love or criticize. They are the chosen objects of collective gossip, the channels of which are the mass media of communication.

To fulfil such a social function, they must be observable to people of all degrees. In a small-scale community, observability is very much heightened, and the tension which accompanies observability is very great, but there also exist specific mechanisms for reducing observability and for preserving an area of privacy. All members of the social groups are subject to continual observation and other members of the group evaluate their behaviour (often by means of gossip) in order to:

1. Decide whether, according to group values and rules, their morality or character is deviant.
2. Compare performance with expectation.
3. Verify culturally established predictions and expectations, based on earlier behaviour and the pressures exerted by the milieu.
4. Assess the influence of their behaviour on the community (for instance, the effect of their example on morals).

    The result is to encompass behaviour in a system of value-norms and procedure-results, which is predetermined but also in a continual, if rather slow, state of revision. Each behaviour is, therefore, a matter to be experienced by the collectivity and the result serves to test the systems of expectation (normative or not) of the group under consideration.

5. One other source of tension associated with observability lies in its direct correspondence with conscious or unconscious desires or impulses (voyeurism, release of aggression, love, etc.);
6. There is, finally, one class of evaluations from which several advantages might be expected in connection with interactive relations. In this case observation is useful to an individual to the extent that the behaviour is particularly instrumental for him.

This is notably the case when the behaviour concerned has an economic bearing, more generally it is true of the behaviour of persons who have some power in relation to the observer. We should bear in mind that in a small village each inhabitant has a certain power in relation to every other and, as a result, that this last mentioned component is always present and linked inextricably to others. The greater the power possessed by one person, the greater is the interest of the others in increasing his observability. An increase in observability signifies, in effect, an increase in the possibilities of predicting the actions of the other, and therefore means for the observer an increase in his own possibilities for action.

As the community increases in size, direct interactions lose their importance and observability diminishes. The large city guarantees to its members a weak degree of observability or a high degree of anomie. On this account it is impossible to examine collectively the behaviour of all the members of a populous community, in the light of the principles of evaluation which we have noted. This evaluation is reserved by each member for those with whom he is in direct interaction and for those particularly 'significant' personages.

In particular, as far as the evaluative orientation of the sixth type is concerned, it can apply to persons with whom the subject is in interaction (members of his family, friends, acquaintances, rivals, etc.) and persons who hold power in the community (the power elite). Orientations of types 1, 2, 3, and 5 are, in a large-scale community, directed towards the stars, while orientations of types 4 and 6 are specifically directed towards the power elite. We can note that, even when limited to evaluations of types 1, 2, 3, and 5, there is a profound difference between the gossip which goes on in small villages and that which applies to the stars. The former is more critical, aggressive, scandalous than the latter. The majority of the stars chooses freely, or at least accepts its collective role, and the group to which they belong retains a sufficient degree of stability. These two conditions would not be realizable if the aggressive and competitive components which develop in community life were free to attach to them.

One other interesting fact is that the stars are not objects of envy. Further, the elite of the stars is not in general perceived as a privileged class; their very existence is not regarded as a clear and brutal witness to social injustice.

The lack of slander, of envy and of class demands – these are the phenomena between which one can see a correlation, but which, from a sociological point of view, are not necessarily linked.

In general, scandal occurs without those who are its object being considered as a privileged group. It consists essentially in sharing with someone else the knowledge and reprobation of some moral act of another known to both, and in deriving a satisfaction from the condemnation which compensates for a personal aggressiveness in relation to the person who is the object of scandal. Such a satisfaction exists when, in a small community, the shared condemnation effectively harms the intended person; from this condemnation issue collective punitive acts (sanctions). The fact that such a condemnation is made according to shared standards of evaluation avoids, on the other hand, any feelings of guilt which might be provoked by the consciousness of personal aggression. The unconscious aggression which is the driving force of the action is transformed in this manner into 'moral disdain'. From the point of view of the community, this process functions as a mechanism for assessing all behaviour according to the values and rules of the group. This mechanism presupposes the existence of rigorous principles of evaluation and the possibility of an effective prejudice against the deviant person (sanction), and moreover the existence of prior motives of aggressiveness. In relation to the stars these three conditions exist only in very small measure.

The shared principles of evaluation which are present in a modern industrial society are less integrated and less rigorous than those of a small community, by reason especially of the continuous transformation which an industrial society undergoes. The possibilities of effective prejudice against a deviant person are very few. Only by collective acquiescence could it be achieved, and the latter, in the absence of a direct interaction between the members of a social group, is limited to the means of mass communication, and as a result finds itself in large measure controlled by the elite with which it is concerned. As for the existence of an aggressiveness which can be transformed into 'moral disdain' this is equally very weak, as we will have occasion to see in speaking of envy.

Actions are not only evaluated in the light of the values and rules of the group, but also according to the results which are expected; their efficacy is also evaluated. A large part of scandal fulfils the important social function of assessing the correspondence between normal behaviour and the success achieved in the realization of certain ends. As a result of this, one can anticipate the results of all behaviour in terms of its efficiency. In scandal such a process of prediction has a sharply pessimistic character, because negative and inefficient consequences are foreseen and desired for nearly all actions which are capable of modifying the status of an actor in the community. This is to be understood according to the degree to which any modification of status is reprehensible in a stable society.

This negative prediction has, by its collective character, according to Thomas's theorem, the effect of increasing the probability that things will turn out as expected. Moreover, the verification of results contrary to expectations (or desires) sets into motion an interpretive mechanism of the following kind: since the actor could not, by conforming to common models of behaviour arrive at this result, this must signify: (a) that the actor has behaved randomly, and it does not follow that next time the same result would be produced; (b) or that he has acted dishonestly, that is to say that he has not conformed to the 'rules of the game', to the established modes of behaviour (even if we do not know exactly how).

His behaviour is then examined afresh from a critical point of view, in order to discover the proof of the deviation from the values and norms. It is in the implicit and basic acceptance that behaviour according to rule cannot modify the status of the member of a group and, correlatively, that an alteration of status must mean that he has not behaved morally that we find one of the most basic signs of the lack of evolution in a system.

The testing of efficiency in such a system has for its main function the guaranteeing of its static character. In contrast, the verification of efficiency in an industrial society has a totally different function, because in this system it is acknowledged that the individual status or the social structure can be modified.

Those behaviours which can result in modification can be classified as either conformist with, or different from, or neutral in respect of social norms. In other words, men can be considered as virtuous, neutral or dishonest. Hence the possibility of conflict when these are behaviours which differ from the norm yet are not the most likely to assure success. While in a traditional society successes which are attained by deviant means are rejected, in an industrial society, on the other hand, a selection is effected to assure maximum success consistent with respect for the norms. The criterion of efficiency in this type of society becomes a principle of evaluation and acts as a principle of rationalization of behaviour. In a community of this kind, predictions about the outcomes of any behaviour are no longer required to be pessimistic, and the attained success is not considered to imply a social fault.

The fact that in a static society any aspiration towards a modification of status is resented as a failing signifies that such a modification is regarded as socially dangerous. The acquisition by someone of any new advantage takes on the implication of harm done to others.

We thus arrive at a discussion of envy. In envy an acquisition of some kind, or an advantage obtained by a person, is considered by some other person as an injustice. The roots of envy, as psychologists have demonstrated, lie in infancy. In most cases it is the *transfer* from competitive infantile situations concerning a frustrated love object, which is internalized to allow its exclusive possession. An analogous mechanism can be found in static societies. Competition for some good in limited supply (like land) develops on the supposition that acquisition of one part of the good by an individual automatically implies the potential deprivation of all other individuals.[4] This mechanism tends to disappear in an economic system in which goods are capable of accumulation without limit by means of rationally controlled individual and collective action (following the principle of efficiency). In such a reference system, any action which is revealed as efficient for attaining an end is judged as likely not to diminish but to increase the probability that other individuals can attain the same result. In place of the mechanism of envy there is released the mechanism of admiration.

A powerful component of stardom is the admiration for the success achieved by the stars. Gina Lollobrigida, Sophia Loren, Marilyn Monroe bear witness, by their existence, to the large possibilities for social mobility. From the point of view of communal orientations of evaluation, the problem is to demonstrate that such a great improvement of status has been obtained not by illicit means but thanks to meritorious conduct and to exceptional or charismatic qualities. A major part of 'gossip' about stars performs this function. It is evident that this interpretation depends on the existence of a certain degree of social distance between the star and the public, so as to permit only an indirect or partial confrontation between the one and the other. This can be verified without difficulty when information is provided by the more remote means of communication, and in particular by mass communication. This absence of direct interaction is often felt by the public as a limitation, a hindrance to full and entire knowledge of the stars. But this last aspiration, if it were satisfied, would lead to a complete development of a moral critique and the freeing of components of aggression and envy which exist all the time, but under control. These components would threaten the existence even of the stars.

Let us conclude this point with a last observation. We have noted in passing, and it has been verified in our experimental research, that the moral evaluation of the stars is more 'indulgent' than that reserved by the public for those who are socially nearer to them. This shows itself particularly in the case of small communities where social control is rigorous and where the contrast is very obvious between this control and the tolerance shown towards the stars. This phenomenon can be explained in part by the absence of those aggressive components which underlie slander and envy, and in equal part by social distance. On the basis of previously stated considerations, we can understand the reasons for this fact in sociological terms. Amongst the modes of evaluation already discussed, the fourth type has, in small communities, a very great importance where the evaluation aims to test the consequences of a way of acting for the community (the influence of example on morals). Moral vigilance and negative evaluation equally function to protect the community against the threat represented by the example of deviant behaviour which goes unpunished. In the case of stars, this category of evaluation loses its importance because they are not judged institutionally responsible for the results of their actions on the community. In small communities, there is an awareness of the potentially scandalous and corrupting character of their behaviour, but there is no possibility of applying sanctions. In the more generalized community, the separation of roles has such an important function that it makes this danger pass to a second level. As a result, a strong component of moral evaluation disappears or is attenuated. At the psychological level, this reduction is achieved by a relative evaluation: in effect each person judges, not in relation to the standards of his own community, but in relation to those of the stars (elite) who serve as a reference group. A big gap between the rules of the community of membership and those of the reference group requires continual recourse to a mechanism of separation between 'us' and our community and 'them' and their community. This can lead to an opposition between the reference group and the community of membership. We will see how strong are the critico-aggressive components which are then released.

Action within the community and action on the part of the community

Taken together, these factors which we have illustrated strongly reduce the aggressive and competitive components which develop in action in a community. However, they do not suffice to explain why the elite of stars is not considered as a privileged class, witness to the injustice of the social system. Their wealth, the manner of life they lead, constitute evident affronts to egalitarian ideals. The most commonly given explanations of this phenomenon appeal on the one hand to the mechanisms of the 'star system' and on the other to the 'narcotizing illusion'.

In the former case, one observes that stardom is the product of an important publicity organization which is useful to the entertainment industry. Thanks to the media of communication, the public are presented with the image of the person who has most chance of attracting attention and sympathy, of exciting human warmth or curiosity. The whole life of the stars is thus astutely orchestrated and arranged, so that nothing is left to chance. This type of explanation suffers from a certain naiveté. It is simplistic and naive to think that a phenomenon like stardom can be the intentional result of artful manoevres. Publicity agents, by their actions, do no more than facilitate and direct into a chosen path, a phenomenon which is an expression of the society as a whole. They are no more than part of the social mechanism which they are supposed to create.

Moreover, this thesis is contradicted by the history of stardom. In the early days film producers were opposed to the development of the system which nevertheless became established; and it was only after the event that they came to favour it, realizing that they could exploit it to their own ends, rather than find themselves crushed by opposing it. Furthermore, one cannot say that the star system has tended to cover up the wealth of the stars, their luxury, or their extraordinary earnings, in order to stress their social merits and their social function, etc. The star system has never, indeed, sought to legitimate the position of the stars on any other basis than their personality, their private life, their friends, their intimate tragedies and their eccentricities. Without any doubt it has attenuated the competitive elements of their ways of acting in the community, and has proclaimed the existence of amicable relations between such and such amongst them, and between them and the public. That could have contributed, marginally, to the avoidance of any growth of class resentment, but it certainly would not have been possible so to act if resentment of this kind was clearly manifested.

The theory of the 'narcotizing illusion' sees in the star system a cultural product of the economic power elite, having as its object to supply the masses with an escape into fantasy and an illusion of mobility, in such a way as to prevent their taking stock of their real condition as exploited masses. Against this theory, which has achieved considerable success, there is the fact that the star system has prospered, and prospered in nearly all countries and at all social levels – even amongst groups which adopt a marxist perspective. Interest in stars can be found through the whole range of the political keyboard, without any distinction. It would be interesting to make a closer study of the changing attitude of the press, and especially of the communist press, towards the stars. Immediately after the war (until about 1950) the stars were criticized or condemned. Subsequently they, and their way of life, were given a warm welcome. Many amongst them were men of the left who had never in their lives sought to become stars and who, on the contrary, had even denounced the phenomenon. The stars are proclaimed as such by the collectivity. It is not they themselves who impose themselves on the latter by a power acquired independently of the collectivity. This does not stem only from the fact that the stars are an open elite. Things would not be different if the stars were self-perpetuating, and if what is the case for some individuals like, for example, Greta Garbo and Clark Gable, were a universal rule. What counts is the fact that their *status* is always potentially revocable: by the public. The star system thus never creates the star, but it proposes the candidate for 'election', and helps to retain the favour of the 'electors'. Certainly those who activate the star system have an ascendancy of power which they hold over the public, but that is precisely why it is towards them and not towards the stars, that there can and does form some class resentment. In the eyes of the public, the producer is someone of quite a different order from the star whom he launches. Even when he enters into the elite of the stars he always remains an ambivalent figure, and the public forgets his power only when his personal affairs, as also his way of acting in the community, assume an autonomous interest.[5]

We can now appreciate a last and interesting phenomenon peculiar to stardom. Although most stars are not dispersed, but grouped together, the evaluative orientation is not directed towards the group. It is almost always the individual and not the group, that is, the ways of acting within the community and not the community itself, which become the object of evaluation. It can turn out that the community itself becomes an object of evaluation, but in this case the framework changes completely and the critical-aggressive components of which we have spoken are released.

In this case, the elite of the stars, instead of becoming the centre of the community as a whole, is detached from it and is differentiated as a distinct and privileged community, an expression of organized social forces and, as a result a holder of power. In such a case the star no longer belongs to the wider community, that is to say to ours, but to an opposed community.

The innumerable denunciations of the moral poverty and the corruption of Hollywood, together with marxist critiques, or again films like *La Dolce Vita*, tend towards the production of a frame of meaning of this kind. But this restructuring does not persist and tends quickly to dissolve. It gives way, on the whole, to an evaluation of each individual and his influence on the community. That is why men can scorn and condemn the morals of Hollywood, the way of life of the Via Veneto and of criminal circles, and continue meanwhile to be touched by the vicissitudes which affect Carla Gravina and Sacha Distel, to admire Lana Turner, to express sympathy for Frank Sinatra and to respect the memory of Clark Gable.

Meaning and perspectives of stardom

In the light of the foregoing considerations, stardom appears as a phenomenon appropriate to a certain moment in the development of industrial societies, in which it fulfils certain variable functions which depend on the socio-political configuration of the society. Stardom carries a time dimension, which enables us to make a dynamic study of it.

The development of industry, the rise in population, urbanization, the increasing interdependence of the economic system and the appearance of the means of mass communication all tend to break down traditional social relationships. Society becomes differentiated and develops associations and organizations which are impersonal, rational and variable, controlled by a limited number of men who possess particular qualities and who monopolize the instruments of control. The information which, transmitted by the traditional channels of communication, sufficed in more limited communities to provide the coordinates of orientation in the heart of the general system, rapidly became insufficient because of the increasing complexity of the latter, because of its novelty and variability. The political organization of the whole society and of the state is largely controlled by new strata and by classes under formation; in addition the society and the state become rationalized according to the model of economic arrangements. The system presents a new structure formed from an articulated assemblage of positions defined in universalist ways, to which correspond specific roles, which are themselves universal, neutral and subject to the criteria of efficiency. The culture ceases to be a collection of pre-ordained solutions to recurring problems; it is differentiated in two directions. On the one hand it becomes a science capable of obtaining results wished for by means of procedures open to theoretical deduction; on the other hand the culture depends on a large area of consensus concerning the implicit meaning of given situations or about the possibility of attaining certain ends and realizing certain values. In this process the horizon of the community widens. The symbols of power of the community constitute the emotional centre of the social system as a whole. Sometimes one might see the emergence of national fascism, sometimes, when conflict between classes occurs in the absence of a dominant class, the community is identified with the class.

In such a case the community sees itself in those individuals who have symbolic value, and who at the same time occupy positions of symbolic power. They are the charismatic leaders who interpret new and former values of the whole community; on this basis they give unity to the experiences and expectations of members of the community, while creating the consensus which permits the whole process to go forward. In other countries with a democratic tradition, representative institutions are modified so as to welcome and meet the new demands which continually arise.

In those countries (an example is provided by Italy before the rise of fascism) the daily demands for orientation of community life (met in the small community by relations of neighbourhood, by gossip, by the exercise of applied morals, etc.) begin to be met at the level of a more general community life. The media of mass communication begin to present to the public persons who belong to the extended community and who become an object of interest, identification and collective evaluation. With the progress of visual information persons of the entertainment world begin, to an increasing degree, to make their mark. Their lives, their social relationships, become an object of identification or a projection of the needs of the mass of the population, a benchmark for positive or negative evaluation, the chance to have experience in the domain of the morally possible, and a living testimony to the possibility of achieving a rise in personal status. Thanks to a collective consensus, their capacity and their skill readily acquire a charismatic dimension. However, the generalization of charisma is impeded by the simultaneous articulation of the structuring in the form of specific roles. Correspondingly, a preponderance is established of modes of evaluation which are impersonal, neutral and specific. On the other hand, since the danger of charisma exists in a much higher degree where the internalization of new evaluative orientations is shallowest (that is to say that it exists especially when the process of nation-forming is at its beginning) one also sees appearing mechanisms for the rigorous separation of roles. For this reason one must posit a more or less sharp distinction between the elite of power and the elite of stars. This mechanism of separation acquires a particular importance in countries which, after an experience of charismatic power, becomes democratic again (like Italy) at the moment when the process of economic development and rationalization is unleashed.

We are witnessing a rigorous separation of roles. Alongside a political class considered as responsible for the results of its decisions on the collectivity, there develops an elite of politically irresponsible stars, whose whole way of life and personal relationships excite interest, and whose influence on morals is profound. Members of small isolated communities which make up the large general community meet and discover the stars before they come across political men for whom they retain feelings of distrust and incomprehension. It is television in particular, which by its violation of the intimacy of family life introduces figures representative of the community into each isolated group and contributes to the development of consciousness of common belonging. The fact of taking part in this experience makes the psychic domain more isomorphic and constitutes, as a result, a condition which facilitates reciprocal comprehension (mutuality) and hence social interaction.

Our account has been concerned with progress towards a particularly interesting stage of transition, where a society is both rationalized and democratic, where the manifestations of charisma are henceforth under control, where the mythic forms of stardom tend to disappear and where regard for the wider society is strong and has already lost the implication of a euphoric participation in its 'power', although it has not yet become a responsible participation. How should this phenomenon be projected into the future? It is difficult to predict future developments, but it is at least very probable that the stars will continue to exist, both as privileged members of the wider community and as an object of reference for members of the latter. This might follow from the great extension of the wider community which only allows a few members to be a collective object of reference; or it could be so because, in a society under transition, there is always some insufficiency in the culture and consequently a need for a collective consensus about the new implications of reality and new solutions to be found to the problems of family, neighbourhood, of production and consumption, etc.

The progressive increase in interdependence in industrial society ought to lead us to take account of the responsibilities of all public personages, with rather more rigour than one finds in practice. We have seen that the stars are not held institutionally responsible for the consequences of their own actions on the community, since this responsibility rests uniquely on those men who occupy positions of institutional power. A decrease in the sharp separation of social roles and in their specificity can create the necessary conditions for opening to evaluation the 'private' life of the stars as well as of men engaged in politics, according to the consequences which their actions have for the collectivity.

Other likely changes can be foreseen if the tension of aspirations is reduced: this might create, or add to, the chances for individuals to satisfy personal ambition while at the same time supporting the institutional mechanisms provided by the society.

Notes

1   Extract from research conducted for the Institute of Sociology of the Catholic University of Milan, with financial help from UNESCO.

2   In French, the word '*divismō*' has been retained as a concept, and 'divi', in the plural as a related term; but the word 'vedette' has usually been used instead of the singular 'divo'.

    Translator's note: In this English translation, 'divi' has been rendered as 'stars'; similarly, the key term 'divismo', for which there is no English synonym, has been translated usually as 'stardom', and occasionally as 'star system' or 'phenomenon of the stars' (as in the title). It is hoped that the context fully conveys the intended meaning of these related concepts.

3   These are the star 'communities', as in Hollywood, or the Via Veneto, Rome, and all other places where the fashionable set meet. The most frequent occasions are for film premières, festivals, exhibitions, cruises, receptions and presentations of literary and artistic prizes, etc.

4   Alberoni (1961, pp. 69–80). This phenomenon is well described in Banfield (1961).

5   What we have just said is of great sociological interest, since we can establish in the same way that class resentment and the experience of injustice do not depend on the fact of contrasting inequalities with egalitarian ideals, but that they depend essentially on the fact that one perceives the existence of an autonomous illegitimate power underpinning the inequality. If the autonomous power goes by default (as in stardom) class resentment and the experience of injustice are consequently lacking.

Chapter 7

Leo Lowenthal

THE TRIUMPH OF MASS IDOLS

THE FOLLOWING STUDY IS concerned with the content analysis of biographies. This literary topic had inundated the book market for the three decades previous to the writing of this article in 1943, and had for some time been a regular feature of popular magazines. Surprisingly enough, not very much attention had been paid to this phenomenon, none whatever to biographies appearing in magazines, and little to those published in book form.[1]

It started before the first World War, but the main onrush came shortly afterwards. The popular biography was one of the most conspicuous newcomers in the realm of print since the introduction of the short story. The circulation of books by Emil Ludwig,[2] André Maurois, Lytton Strachey, and Stefan Zweig, reached a figure in the millions, and with each new publication, the number of languages into which they were translated grew. Even if it were only a passing literary fad, one would still have to explain why this fashion has had such longevity and is more and more becoming a regular feature in the most diversified media of publications.

Who's Who, once known as a title of a specialized dictionary for editors and advertisers, has nowadays become the outspoken or implied question of innumerable popular contexts. The interest in individuals has become a kind of mass gossip. The majority of weeklies and monthlies, and mass dailies too, publish at least one life story or a fragment of one in each issue; theater programs present abridged biographies of all the actors; the more sophisticated periodicals, such as *The New Republic* or *Harper's*, offer short accounts of the main intellectual achievements of their contributors; and a glance into the popular corners of the book trade, including drug store counters, will invariably fall on biographies. All this forces the conclusion that there must be a social need seeking gratification by this type of literature.

One way to find out would be to study the readers' reactions, to explore by means of various interviewing techniques what they are looking for, what they think about the biographical jungle. But it seems to be rather premature to collect and to evaluate such solicited response until more is known about the content structure itself.

As an experiment in content analysis, a year's publication of *The Saturday Evening Post* (*SEP*) and of *Collier's* for the period from April 1940 to March 1941 was covered. It should not be inferred that the results as presented here are without much change applicable to all other magazines which present general and diversified topics. From a few selections taken from less widely circulated and more expensive magazines, ranging from *The New Yorker* to the dollar-a-copy *Fortune*, it seems very likely that the biographies presented there differ in their average content structure and therefore in their social and psychological implications from the lower-priced popular periodicals. The difference in contents corresponds to a difference in readership.

It is regrettable that a complete investigation could not be made for the most recent material, but samples taken at random from magazines under investigation showed that no basic change in the selection or content structure has occurred since this country's entry into World War II.

I   Biographers' idols

Before entering into a discussion of our material we shall briefly look into the fate of the biographical feature during the past decades.

Production – yesterday

Biographical sections have not always been a standing feature in these periodicals. If we turn back the pages we find distinct differences in the number of articles as well as in the selection of people treated.

Table 7.1 gives a survey of the professional distribution of the "heroes" biographies between 1901 and 1941.[3]

This table indicates clearly a tremendous increase in biographies as time goes on. The average figure of biographies in 1941 is almost four times as high as at the beginning of the century. The biography has nowadays become a regular weekly feature. Just to illustrate how relatively small the number of biographies was forty years ago: in fifty-two issues of the *SEP* of 1901–02 we find altogether twenty-one biographies as compared with not less than fifty-seven in 1940–41. The smallness of the earlier figure in comparison to the present day is emphasized by the fact that nonfictional contributions at that time far outnumbered the fictional material. A fair average of distribution in the past would be about three fictional and eight nonfictional contributions; today we never find more than twice as many nonfictional contributions and in the majority of cases even fewer.

We put the subjects of the biographies in three groups: the spheres of political life, of business and professions, and of entertainment (the latter in the broadest sense of the word). Looking at our table we find for the time before World War I very high interest in political figures and an almost equal distribution of business and professional men, on the one hand, and of entertainers on the other. This picture changes completely after the war. The figures from political life have been cut by 40 per cent.

Table 7.1 Distribution of biographies according to professions in *The Saturday Evening Post* and *Collier's* for selected years between 1901 and 1941

	1901–1914 (5 sample yrs.)		1922–1930 (6 sample yrs.)		1930–1934 (4 years)		1940–1941 (1 year)	
	No.	%	No.	%	No.	%	No.	%
Political life	81	46	112	28	95	31	31	25
Business and Professional	49	28	72	18	42	14	25	20
Entertainment	47	26	211	54	169	55	69	55
Total Number	177	100	395	100	306	100	125	100
Yearly average of biographies	36		66		77		125	

This numerical relation seems to be rather constant from 1922 up to the present day. If we re-formulate our professional distribution by leaving out the figures from political life we see even more clearly the considerable decrease of people from the serious and important professions and a corresponding increase of entertainers. The social impact of this change comes to the fore strikingly if we analyze the composition of the entertainers. This can be seen from Table 7.2.

While at the beginning of the century three quarters of the entertainers were serious artists and writers, we find that this class of people is reduced by half twenty years later and tends to disappear almost completely at present.

As an instance of the selection of biographies typical of the first decade of the century, it is notable that out of the twenty-one biographies of the *SEP* – 1901–02, eleven came from the political sphere, seven from the business and professions, and three from entertainment and sport. The people in the political group are numerically prominent until before Election Day in the various years: candidates for high office, i.e., the president or senators; the secretary of the treasury; an eminent state governor. In the business world we are introduced to J. P. Morgan, the banker; his partner, George W. Perkins; James J. Hill, the railroad president. In the professions, we find one of the pioneers in aviation; the inventor of the torpedo; a famous Negro educator; an immigrant scientist. Among the entertainers there is an opera singer, Emma Clavé; a poet, Eugene Field; a popular fiction writer F. Marion Crawford.

If we look at such a selection of people we find that it represents a fair cross-section of socially important occupations. Still, in 1922 the picture is more similar to the professional distribution quoted above than to the one which is characteristic of the present day magazines. If we take, for example, *Collier's* of 1922, we find in a total of twenty biographies only two entertainers, but eight business and professional men and ten politicians. Leaving out the latter ones, we find among others: Clarence C. Little, the progressive President of the University of Maine; Leonard P. Ayres, the very outspoken Vice-President of the Cleveland Trust Company; Director-General of the United States Railroad Administration, James C. Davis; President of the New York Central Railroad, A. H. Smith; and the City Planner, John Nolen. From the entertainment field, we have a short résumé of the stage comedian, Joe Cook (incidentally, by Franklin P. Adams), and an autobiographical sketch by Charlie Chaplin.

Table 7.2 Proportion of biographies of entertainers from the realms of serious arts[a] in *SEP* and *Collier's* for selected years between 1901–1941

(In per cent of total biographies of entertainers in each period)

Period	Proportion entertainers from serious arts	Total no. entertainers
1901–1914 (5 sample yrs.)	77	47
1922–1930 (6 sample yrs.)	38	211
1930–1934 (4 yrs.)	29	169
1940–1941 (1 yr.)	9	69

[a] This group includes literature, fine arts, music, dance, theater.

We might say that a large proportion of the heroes in both samples are idols of production, that they stem from the productive life, from industry, business, and natural sciences. There is not a single hero from the world of sports and the few artists and entertainers either do not belong to the sphere of cheap or mass entertainment or represent a serious attitude toward their art as in the case of Chaplin. (We have omitted from our discussion and our figures a number of very short biographical features which amounted to little more than anecdotes. These were published fairly regularly by the *SEP* until the late twenties under the headings "Unknown Captains of Industry," "Wall Street Men," sometimes called "Bulls and Bears," "Who's Who and Why," "Workingman's Wife," "Literary Folk.") The first quarter of the century cherishes biography in terms of an open-minded liberal society which really wants to know something about its own leading figures on the decisive social, commercial, and cultural fronts. Even in the late twenties, when jazz composers and the sports people are admitted to the inner circle of biographical heroes, their biographies are written almost exclusively to supplement the reader's knowledge of the technical requirements and accomplishments of their respective fields.[4] These people, then, are treated as an embellishment of the national scene, not yet as something that in itself represents a special phenomenon which demands almost undivided attention.

We should like to quote from two stories which seem to be characteristic of this past epoch. In a sketch of Theodore Roosevelt, the following comment is made in connection with the assassination of McKinley:

> We, who give such chances of success to all that it is possible for a young man to go as a laborer into the steel business and before he has reached his mature prime become, through his own industry and talent, the president of a vast steel association — we, who make this possible as no country has ever made it possible, have been stabbed in the back by anarchy.[5]

This unbroken confidence in the opportunities open to every individual serves as the *leitmotiv* of the biographies. To a very great extent they are to be looked upon as examples of success which can be imitated. These life stories are really intended to be educational models. They are written — at least ideologically — for someone who the next day may try to emulate the man whom he has just envied.

A biography seems to be the means by which an average person is able to reconcile his interest in the important trends of history and in the personal lives of other people. In the past, and especially before the first World War, popular biography lived in an optimistic atmosphere where understanding of historical processes and interest in successful people seemed to integrate pleasantly into one harmonious endeavor.

> We know now that the men of trade and commerce and finance are the real builders of freedom, science, and art — and we watch them and study them accordingly. . . . Of course, Mr. Perkins is a "self-made man." Who that has ever made a career was not?[6]

This may be taken as a classical formulation for a period of "rugged individualism" in which there is neither the time nor the desire to stimulate a closer interest in the organizers and organization of leisure time, but what is characterized by eagerness and confidence that the social ladder may be scaled on a mass basis.

Here and there we find a casual remark on the function of biographies in models for individual imitation. "In 1890 a book appeared entitled *Acres of Diamonds*, by Russell H. Conwell. This book dealt especially with the problems of attaining success in life. The author attempted to encourage the reader by giving examples of the struggles and triumphs of noted successful men and women. This pattern of encouraging the reader by citing examples of great men has continued, and in recent years a number of books have appeared in which most of the content dealt with case histories of noted individuals. Some psychologists have suggested that interest in autobiographies and biographies has arisen in part from the attempts of the readers to compare their own lives with those about whom they read, and thus to seek encouragement from the evidence of the struggles of successful people."[7]

Helen M. Hughes in her suggestive study has not avoided the tendency to settle the problem of biographies by rather simplified psychological formulae. By quoting generously O'Neill, Bernard MacFadden, and André Maurois, she points to the differences of the more commemorative and eulogistic elements in earlier biographies and the "anxious groping for certainty of people who live in times of rapid change," which is supposed to be connected with the present interest in biography.

Consumption – today

When we turn to our present-day sample we face an assortment of people which is both qualitatively and quantitatively removed from the standards of the past.

Only two decades ago people from the realm of entertainment played a very negligible role in the biographical material. They form now, numerically, the first group. While we have not found a single figure from the world of sports in our earlier samples given above, we find them now close to the top of favorite selections. The proportion of people from political life and from business and professions, both representing the "serious side," has declined from 74 to 45 per cent of the total.

Let us examine the group of people representing non-political aspects of life. Sixty-nine are from the world of entertainment and sport; twenty-five from that which we called before the "serious side." Almost half of the twenty-five belong to some kind of communications professions: there are ten newspapermen and radio commentators. Of the remaining fifteen business and professional people, there are a pair of munitions traders, Athanasiades (118)[8] and Juan March (134); Dr. Brinkley (3), a quack doctor; and Mr. Angas (20), judged by many as a dubious financial expert; Pittsburgh Phil (23), a horse race gambler in the "grand style"; Mrs. D'Arcy Grant (25), a woman sailor, and Jo Carstairs (54), the owner of an island resort; the Varian brothers (52), inventors of gadgets, and Mr. Taylor (167), an inventor of fool-proof sports devices; Howard Johnson (37), a roadside restaurant genius; Jinx Falkenburg (137), at that time a professional model; and finally, Dr. Peabody (29), a retired rector of a swanky society prep school.

The "serious" people are not so serious after all. In fact there are only nine who might be looked upon as rather important or characteristic figures of the industrial, commercial, or professional activities, and six of these are newspapermen or radio commentators.

We called the heroes of the past "idols of production": we feel entitled to call the present-day magazine heroes "idols of consumption." Indeed, almost every one of them is directly, or indirectly, related to the sphere of leisure time: either he does not belong to vocations which serve society's basic needs (e.g., the heroes of the world of entertainment and sport), or he amounts, more or less, to a caricature of a socially productive agent. If we add to the group of the sixty-nine people from the entertainment and sports world the ten newspaper and radio men, the professional model, the inventor of sports devices, the quack doctor, the horse race gambler, the inventors of gadgets, the owner of the island resort, and the restaurant chain owner, we see eightyseven of all ninety-four non-political heroes directly active in the consumers' world.

Of the eight figures who cannot exactly be classified as connected with consumption, not more than three – namely, the automobile producer, Sloan; the engineer and industrialist, Stout; and the air line czar, Smith – are important or characteristic functionaries in the world of production. The two armament magnates, the female freight boat skipper, the prep school head, and the doubtful market prophet remind us of the standardized protagonists in mystery novels and related fictional merchandise: people with a more or less normal and typical personal and vocational background who would bore us to death if we did not discover that behind the "average" front lurks a "human interest" situation.

By substituting such a classification according to spheres of activity for the cruder one according to professions, we are now prepared to present the vocational stratifications of our heroes in a new form. It is shown in Table 7.3 for the *SEP* and *Collier's* of 1940–1941.

If a student in some very distant future should use popular magazines of 1941 as a source of information as to what figures the American public looked to in the first stages of the greatest crisis since the birth of the Union, he would come to a grotesque result. While the industrial and professional endeavors are geared to a maximum of speed and efficiency, the idols of the masses are not, as they were in the past, the leading names in the battle of production, but the headliners of the movies, the ball parks, and the night clubs. While we found that around 1900 and even around 1920 the vocational distribution of magazine heroes was a rather accurate reflection of the

Table 7.3 The heroes and their spheres

	Number of stories	*Per cent*
Sphere of production	3	2
Sphere of consumption	91	73
Entertainers and sports figures	69	55
Newspaper and radio figures	10	8
Agents of consumers' goods	5	4
Topics of light fiction	7	6
Sphere of politics	31	25
Total	125	100

nation's living trends, we observe that today the hero-selection corresponds to needs quite different from those of genuine information. They seem to lead to a dream world of the masses who no longer are capable of willing to conceive of biographies primarily as a means of orientation and education. They receive information not about the agents and methods of social production but about the agents and methods of social and individual consumption. During the leisure in which they read, they read almost exclusively about people who are directly, or indirectly, providing for the reader's leisure time. The vocational set-up of the dramatis personae is organized as if the social production process were either completely exterminated or tacitly understood, and needed no further interpretation. Instead, the leisure time period seems to be the new social riddle on which extensive reading and studying has to be done.

The human incorporation of all the social agencies taking care of society as a unity of consumers represents a literary type which is turned out as a standardized article, marketed by a tremendous business, and consumed by another mass institution, the nation's magazine reading public. Thus biography lives as a mass element among the other elements of mass literature.

It will be very important to check how far the war situation confirmed, changed, or even reversed the trend. A few casual observations may be mentioned.

The *New York Times* "Magazine" on July 12, 1942, published an article "Wallace Warns Against 'New Isolationism.'" The Vice-President of the United States is photographed playing tennis. The caption for the picture reads "Mr. Wallace's Serve." This picture and its caption are a very revealing symbol. The word "serve" does not refer to social usefulness, but to a feature in the vice-president's private life.

This remark can be supplemented by quoting a few issues of the *SEP* and *Collier's*, picked at random from their publications during the summer of 1942. While everywhere else in this study we have limited ourselves to the analysis of strictly biographical contributions, we should like, by quoting some of the topics of the entire issues which we have chosen for this year, to emphasize the over-all importance of the spheres of consumption. Not only has the selection of heroes for biographies not changed since America's active participation in the war, but many other of the non-fictional articles are also still concerned with consumers' interests.

Of the ten non-fictional articles in the *SEP*, August 8, 1942, five are connected with the consumers' world: a serial on Hollywood agents; a report on a hometown circus; a report on roadside restaurants; an analysis of women as book readers; and an essay on the horse and buggy. In an issue one week later, August 15, 1942, there is a report on the International Correspondence School; the continuation of the serial on the Hollywood agents; and a biography on the radio idol, Kate Smith. Or let us look at *Collier's*, which as a whole, devotes a much higher percentage of articles to war topics than the *SEP*. Out of nine articles in the issue of July 4, 1942, five belong to the consumers' world. There is again one on the horse and buggy, another one on a baseball hero, a third one on an Army comedian, a fourth one on a Broadway producer, and finally, one on budget buffets. Three weeks later, on July 25, out of ten articles, again five belong to the same category.

In other words, out of thirty-seven articles found in four issues of two leading popular magazines during the present crisis, not less than seventeen treat the gustatory and entertainment features of the average citizen. Much of the fare presented to the reading public during the times immediately preceding the war and during the war itself was almost completely divorced from important social issues.

Our discovery of a common professional physiognomy in all of these portraits encouraged us to guess that what is true of the selection of people will also be true of the selection of what is said about these people. This hypothesis has been quite justified, as we propose to demonstrate in the following pages. Our content analysis not only revealed impressive regularities in the occurrence, omission, and treatment of certain topics, but also showed that those regularities may be interpreted in terms of the very same category of consumption which was the key to the selection of the biographical subjects. Consumption is a thread running through every aspect of these stories. The characteristics which we have observed in the literary style of the author in his presentation of personal relations, of professions and personalities, can all be integrated around the concept of the consumer.

For classification of the stories' contents, we decided on a four-fold scheme. First there are what one might call the sociological aspects of the man: his relations to other people, the pattern of his daily life, his relation to the world in which he lives. Second, his psychology: what the nature of his development has been and the structure of his personality. Third, his history: what his encounter with the world has been like – the object world which he has mastered or failed to master. Fourth, the evaluation of these data which the author more or less consciously conveys by his choice of language. Granted that this scheme is somewhat arbitrary, we think that our division of subject matter has resulted in a fairly efficient worksheet, especially when we consider the backward state of content analysis of this type.

We proceeded to collect all the passages in the 125 stories pertaining to our four categories. It is not intended here to analyze the 2,400 quotations exhaustively, but merely to present a few observations or hypotheses which their study suggested to us and which we hope may be stimulating to further research in content analysis. As we studied our stories, we looked almost in vain for such vital subjects as the man's relations to politics or to social problems in general. Our category of sociology reduces itself to the *private lives* of the heroes. Similarly, our category of psychology was found to contain mainly a static image of a human being to whom a number of things happen, culminating in a success which seems to be none of his doing. This whole section becomes merged with our category of history which is primarily concerned with success data, too, and then takes on the characters of a catalogue of "*just facts*." When we survey the material on how authors evaluate their subjects, what stands out most clearly is the biographers' preoccupation with justifying their hero by means of undiscriminating *superlatives* while still interpreting him in terms which bring him as close as possible to the level of the average man.

II   Private lives

The reader may have noticed in public conveyances a poster called "Private Lives" depicting the peculiarities of more or less famous people in the world of science, sports, business, and politics. The title of this feature is a fitting symbol for all our biographies. It would be an overstatement, but not too far from the truth, to say that these stories are exclusively reports on the heroes' private lives. While it once was rather contemptible to give much room to the private affairs and habits of public figures this topic is now the focus of interest. The reason for viewing this as an overstatement is in a way surprising: we learn something, although not very much, about the man's professional career and its requirements, but we are kept very uninformed about important segments of his private life.

Inheritance and parents – friends and teachers

The personal relations of our heroes, on which we are enlightened, are, as a whole, limited to two groups, the parents and the friends. Both groups are taken in a specific sense: the parents comprising other older relations or forebears of former generations, the friends being more or less limited to people who were valuable in the hero's career. In more than half of the stories the father or the mother or the general family background is at least mentioned. Clark Gable's "stubborn determination" seems derived from his "Pennsylvania Dutch ancestors" (6); the very efficient State Department official, Mrs. Shipley, is the "daughter of a Methodist minister" (8); Senator Taft is a "middle-of-the-roader like his father" besides being "an aristocrat by birth and training" (101). We are let in a little bit on the family situation of Brenda Joyce because "somewhere there was a break-up between mamma and papa" (110). The general pattern of the parental home, however, is more on the Joan Carroll side, where we find the "young, quietly dignified mother . . . the successful engineer father . . . a star scout brother six years her senior" (143); we hear in a very sympathetic way about the old Fadimans, "the father a struggling Russian immigrant and pharmacist, the mother a nurse" (47); we learn a good deal about ancestors as in the case of Clark Gable cited above. Of the Secretary of Labor, Frances Perkins, we are told that her "forebears had settled all over New England between 1630–1680" (22); the female freighter skipper, D'Arcy Grant, has "an ancestral mixture of strong-headed swash-buckling Irish and pioneer Americans" (25); Raymond Gram Swing is the "heir of a severe New England tradition" (42); the Varian brothers have "Celtic blood" (52); in the woman matador, Conchita Cintron, we find "Spanish, Connecticut Irish, and Chilean elements" (116).

The curious fact here is not that the authors mention parentage, but that they have so much to say about it and so little to say about other human relations. It is a good deal as if the author wants to impress on the reader that his hero, to a very considerable extent, must be understood in terms of his biological and regional inheritance. It is a kind of primitive Darwinian concept of social facts: the tendency to place the burden of explanation and of responsibility on the shoulders of the past generations. The individual himself appears as a mere product of his past.

The element of passivity is also found in the second most frequently mentioned group of personal relationships: friends and teachers. Let us look again into some of the material. We hear that the woman diplomat, Mrs Harriman, was made "Minister to Norway because of her many powerful and loyal friends" (14); of the friendship between the hard-hit restaurateur, Johnson, and his wealthy doctor-friend (37); the movie actress Brenda Marshall, was somehow saved in her career "by the friendship if a script girl" (161); Senator Byrnes got a good start because "a disillusioned old

Charlestonian . . . showed him the ropes" (18) while Miss Perkins is " 'protected' by her personal secretary . . . (who) worships her" (22).

There is very rarely an episode which shows our heroes as active partner of friendship. In most cases their friends are their helpers. Very often they are teachers who later on become friends. Perhaps it is stretching a point to say that a vulgarian Darwinism is supplemented at this point by a vulgarian distortion of the "milieu" theory; the hero is a product of ancestry and friendship. But even if this may be somewhat exaggerated, it nevertheless helps to clarify the point, namely, that the hero appears in his human relationship as the one who takes, not as the one who gives.

We can supplement this statement by going back to our remark that decisive human relationships, and even those which are decisive for private lives, are missing. The whole sphere of the relations with the opposite sex is almost entirely missing. This is indeed a very strange phenomenon. We should assume that the predilection for such people as actors and actresses from stage and screen, night club entertainers, and so forth, would be tied up with a special curiosity in such people's love affairs, but this is not the case at all. The realm of love, passion, even marriage, seem worth mentioning only in terms of vital statistics. It is quite a lot to be informed that Dorothy Thompson "got tangled up in love"; very soon Lewis "asked point blank whether she would marry him" (9); Senator Byrnes "married the charming wife who still watches over him" (18); the industrial tycoon Sloan, remarks, "Mrs. Sloan and I were married that summer . . . she was of Roxbury, Mass." (24); Mrs. Peabody married the rector "at the close of the school's first year" (29). We are told about Raymond Gram Swing only that he was married twice (42); as far as Lyons', the baseball player's, bachelor situation goes we hear that he "almost married his campus sweetheart" (53); while his colleague, Rizzuto, is "not even going steady" (57). In the high life of politics we are glad to know that Ambassador Lothian "gets on well with women" (115); and that Thomas Dewey is "a man's man, but women go for him" (117); we are briefly informed that Chris Martin "married, raised a family" (121); and that "one girl was sufficiently impressed to marry" Michael Todd, the producer, at the tender age of seventeen (131).

These statements of fact, in a matter of fact way, as, for instance, the mention of a marriage or a divorce, is all that we hear of that side of human relations which we were used to look upon as the most important ones. If we again imagine that these popular biographies should at a very distant historical moment serve as the sole source of information, the historian of the future would almost be forced to the conclusion that in our times the institution of marriage, and most certainly the phenomena of sexual passions, had become a very negligible factor. It seems that the fifth-rate role to which these phenomena are relegated fits very well with the emphasis on parentage and friendship. Love and passion require generosity, a display of productive mental and emotional forces which are neither primarily explained nor restrained by inheritance and advice.

A rather amusing observation: we found that the eyes of the hero were mentioned in almost one-third of the stories. It is quite surprising that of all possible physiognomic and bodily features just this one should be so very popular. We take delight in the baseball umpire Bill Klem's "bright blue eyes," in his "even supernaturally good eyes" (104); or in the "modest brown eyes" of General Weygand (107). Miss Cintron, the matador, is "blue-eyed" (116); the night club singer, Moffett, has "very bright blue eyes" (119).

We are not quite certain how to explain our biographers' bodily preferences. The eyes are commonly spoken of as "the windows of the soul." Perhaps it gratified the more inarticulate reader if the authors let him try to understand the heroes in the same language in which he believes he understands his neighbor's soul. It is just another example of a cliché served up in lieu of a genuine attempt at psychological insight.

Home and social life – hobbies and food preferences

The heroes, as we have seen, stem predominantly from the sphere of consumption and organized leisure time. It is fascinating to see how in the course of the presentation the producers and agents of consumer goods change into their own customers. Personal habits, from smoking to poker playing, from stamp collecting to cocktail parties, are faithfully noted in between 30 and 40 per cent of all stories under investigation. In fact, as soon as it comes to habits, pleasures, and distractions after and outside of working hours, the magazine biographer turns out to be just a snoopy reporter.

The politicians seem to be an especially ascetic lot – Taft "doesn't smoke" (101); neither does General Weygand (107); the former British Ambassador, Lothian, "hasn't taken a drink in twenty-five years" (115). There is also the movie actor, Chris Martin, who "doesn't smoke cigars or cigarettes" (121); the German Field Marshal Milch whose "big black Brazilian cigars are his favored addiction" (146). To quote some of the favorite habits or dishes of the crowd: Dorothy Thompson is all out for "making Viennese dishes" while her "pet hates . . . are bungled broth and clumsily buttered tea bread" (9). We are invited to rejoice in Art Fletcher's "excellent digestion" (7). We hope that Major Angas is equally fortunate, for: "Eating well is his secondary career"; he is "perpetually hungry" (20). The circus magnate, North, also seems to have a highly developed sense for food and what goes with it: "His cud-cutters for a three-pound steak are a Martini, a Manhattan, and a beer, in that invariable order, tamped down with a hatful of radishes" (26).

As for the innocent hobbies of our heroes: Art Fletcher likes "the early evening movies" and also "to drive about the country" (7); Senator Byrnes finds recreation in "telling of the long saltily humorous anecdotes which all Southerners love" (18). The pitcher, Paige, is "an expert dancer and singer (19); Westbrook Pegler "plays poker" (28); and his special pet foe, Mayor Hague, also "likes gambling" (36); his colleague, the London *Times* correspondent, Sir Willmott Lewis, also "plays poker" (49), while Swing takes to badminton (42). More on the serious side is Greer Garson who "reads a great deal and studies the theater every minute she is free" (113). The hobby of golf unites Senator Taft (101), the fascist, Muti (114), the "Blondie" cartoonist, Chic Young (165), the baseball player, Lyons (53), and Ambassador Lothian (115).

We are furthermore told who likes to be "the life of the party," and who does not; and also how the daily routine in the apartment or private house is fixed. The Fletchers, for instance, "retire early and rise early" (7); while Hank Greenberg "lives modestly with his parents" but also "likes nightclubs, bright lights, and pretty girls" (56). We hear of the actress Stickney's charming "town house" (145), of the "fifteen rooms and five baths and the private elevator to the street" of political Boss Flynn (138); of the way to which the ballet director Balanchine is "snugly installed in an elaborate Long Island home, and a sleek New York apartment" (152).

As to social gatherings: Nancy Hamilton's parties "aren't glittering at all but they are fun" (103). The newspaperman, Silliman Evans, "has introduced the Texas-size of large scale outdoor entertainment" (39); while his colleague, Clifton Fadiman, has "very little social life, seldom goes to dinner parties" (47). His habits seem related to those of the private island queen Jo Carstairs: ". . . A few friends of long standing make up one of the world's shortest guest lists" (54).

And so it goes, through over two hundred quotations, changing a study in social relations into consumers' research. It is neither a world of "doers" or a world of "doing" for which the biographical curiosity of a mass public is evoked. The whole trend goes toward acceptance: the biological and educational heritage; the helpful friends and teachers; the physical protection of the house, and the physiological one of eating and drinking; the security of social standing and prestige, through social entertaining; the complete resting of mind and work-wise energy through the gamut of hobbies. Here we come very close to decisive trends to which the modern individual seems subjected. He appears no longer as a center of outwardly bound energies and actions; as an inexhaustible reservoir of initiative and enterprise; no longer as an integral unity on whose work and efficiency might depend not only his kin's future and happiness, but at the same time, mankind's progress in general. Instead of the "givers" we are faced with the "takers." These new heroes represent a craving for having and taking things for granted. They seem to stand for a phantasmagoria of world-wide social security; for an attitude which asks for no more than to be served with the things needed for reproduction and recreation; for an attitude which has lost any primary interest in how to invent, shape, or apply the tools leading to such purposes of mass satisfaction.

We cannot avoid getting something of a distorted picture of society if we look at it exclusively through the personal lives of a few individuals. But in the past an effort was made to show the link between the hero and the nation's recent history. As one of those earlier biographers, D. G. Phillips, put it:

> Each era, conscious of the mighty works that could be wrought, conscious that we are all under sentence of speedy death, eagerly seeks out the younger man, the obscure man. It has need of all powers and all talents. Especially of the talents for creating, organizing, and directing.[9]

Today the emphasis is on the routine functions of nourishment and leisure time and not on "the talents for creating, organizing, and directing." The real battlefield of history recedes from view or becomes a stock backdrop while society disintegrates into an amorphous crowd of consumers. Greer Garson and Mahatma Gandhi meet on common ground: the one "likes potatoes and stew and never tires of a breakfast of porridge and haddock" (113); the other's "evening meal is simple – a few dates, a little rice, goat's milk" (124); Hilter and Chris Martin "don't smoke . . ."(121).

III   Just facts

Phillips' comments made on Pierpont Morgan's "Right Hand" about sixty years ago may serve as a transition from the sociology of our heroes to their psychology. With its emphasis on the independence and leadership awaiting the exercise of personal initiative, it expresses the ideal character type of private capitalism.

There are at least two elements in this quotation, the presence of which characterizes the psychological concept of former biographies, and the absence of which is very meaningful for the present situation: development and solitude.

"The young, obscure man" has something of the heritage, however trivial in this case, of the personality as it was conceived during the rise of the middle-class culture: the individual as a totality of potentialities, men as moral, and emotional, which have to be developed in a given social framework. Development, as the essence of human life, was connected with the idea that the individual has to find himself in the soliloquy of the mind. Human existence seemed to be made up of the loneliness of the creature and his emergence into the outer world by displaying his own gifts. Our quantization is one of the late forms of this concept: the self-developing and fighting individual with all the chances in the world for creation and conquest.

Souls without history

In an essay on present-day man, Max Horkheimer states: "Development has ceased to exist."[10] His remarks on the immediate transition from childhood to adult life, his observation that "the child is grown up as soon as he can walk, and the grown-up in principle always remains the same,"[11] sounds as if they were a comment on our biographical heroes. Among our questions we have a collection of passages which try to tie up the childhood of the hero with his later life. Almost every second story brings some report of the road from childhood to maturity. Does this not seem to contradict the general remark, is this not a variation of the classical concept of the emergent personality? Before answering, let us examine a few representative passages. At the age of twelve "wrestling . . . was the answer to my problem," says the wrestler, Allman (13). The king of horse race betting, Pittsburgh Phil "began betting when he was fourteen – on his own game chickens" (23). To the inventor, Stout, it is remarked: "Wherever his family lived, he would rig up a crude shop and try to make things"(41). At twelve, the future actor Ezra Stone, ran a kid's radio program "directing the actors and paying them off at the end of the week" (108). For the Ringling-Barnum head, J.R. North: "a real circus was his toy" (26). The future film star, Greer Garson "wanted to be an acress from the time she could walk" (113). The nightclub singer Hildegarde's parents "weren't surprised when Hildegarde, aged eighteen months, hummed a whole aria of an opera they had carried her to" (135).

Childhood appears neither as prehistory and key to the character of the individual nor as a stage of transition to the growth and formation of the abundant diversity of an adult. Childhood is nothing but a midget edition, a predated publication of a man's profession and career. A man is an actor, a doctor, a dancer, an entrepreneur, and he always was. He was not born the tender and unknown potentiality of a human life, of an intellectual, mental emotional creativeness, effective for himself and for society, rather he came into the world and stayed in it, rubber stamped with and for a certain function. The individual has become a trademark.

In more than a third of the stories an attempt at a "theory of success" seems to be made but no magic formula is offered which an average individual might follow for his own good. The bulk of the answers consists of more or less trivial suggestions that the key may be found in "instinct" of other vague qualities. The golf player, Bobby Jones, "must have been born with the deep love for the game" (11). As to the Senator: "Leadership is Byrnes' real genius" (18). Pittsburgh Phil was "a good horse player by instinct" (23). The businessman, Durand N. Briscoe, seemed to have an instinct for promotion and speculation" (24). The achievements of the football coach, Kendrigan, are a mystery even to him: "how he did it he never figured" (50). The airline tycoon, Cyrus R. Smith, may count on "an unerring gambler's instinct" (51). This key formula of instinct is supplemented by a collection of almost tautological truisms: The fascist, Muti, "loves his danger highly spiced" (114). The sociable ambassador, Lothian, "likes newspapermen" (115). Howard Johnson knows what makes a restaurant successful: "A man that is properly supervised never goes haywire" (37). And as far as Clark Gable's success is concerned (and this could be applied to all the 125), "The answer . . . is personality" (6).

We venture to interpret this pseudo-psychology of success as another aspect of the timeless and passive image of modern man. Just as childhood is an abbreviation of the adult's professional career, so is the explanation of this career nothing but an abstract, rather inarticulate, reiteration that a career is a career and a success is a success.

The psychological atmosphere breathes behaviorism on a very primitive level. Childhood as well as that vague realm of instincts represents, so to speak, the bio-logical background from which a variety of human qualities emerge. It is a psychology which shows no need of asking why and, precisely in the same sense in which we tried to show it for sociology, testifies to the transformation from the worship of a spon-taneous personality to the adoration of an existence shaped and molded by outside forces. These people live in a limbo of children and victims. The way leads to what we are inclined to call "a command psychology" because people are not conceived as the responsible agents of their fate in all phases of their lives, but as the bearers of certain useful or not so useful character traits which are pasted on them like decorations or stigmas of shame.

There are a few traits which seem to have some bearing on a man's ability to manipulate his environment. We mean the columnist who is a "spotlight stealer" (9); the playwright and actress who never overlooks "good spots for herself" (103); the producer who is "his own ballyhoo artist" (131). We mean the baseball manager who is "chemically opposed to being on the sucker end of a ball game" (2); the smart night club star who sees "no point in disclosing that King Gustave's favorite singer had been born over the father's delicatessen store" (135); the actress who has real "talent for meeting people" (103); the person who shows up "at the right place at the right time" (109); who is a "great man in flying, handshaking and backslapping trips" (21).

The majority of such attitudes are likely to evoke a slyly understanding smile on the part of the observer and reader. These are the "sure-fire" tricks on the road to success, a little doubtful, but not too bad; these are the equipment of the shrewd man and the smart woman. But these psychological gadgets exhaust the list of qualities pertaining to creative and productive abilities. They generate an atmosphere of pseudo-creativeness in an attempt to convince us that a man has contributed his personal, individual share in the general cause of progress. "Something new has been added," insists the advertisement, but beware of inquiring too closely into the nature of the novelty. Thus, the good-natured statements of a certain lack of meticulous innocence on the road to success, become for the sociological interpreter's sad revelation of a lack of originality in productive strength.

This is brought out even more clearly when we turn to the presentation of the actual history of success. Here success is not even attributed to some happy instinct— it merely happens. Success has lost the seductive charm which once seemed to be a promise and a prize for everybody who was strong, clever, flexible, sober enough to try. It has become a rigid matter on which we look with awe or envy as we look at the priceless pictures in our galleries or the fabulous palaces of the rich. The success of our heroes in consumption is in itself goods of consumption. It does not serve as an instigator for more activity, it is introduced as something we have to accept just like the food and drink and the parties; it is nourishment for curiosity and entertainment.

The mythology of success in the biographies consists of two elements: hardship and breaks. The troubles and difficulties with which the road to success is paved are discussed in the form of stereotypes. Over and over again we hear that the going is rough and hard. The baseball umpire goes "the long, rough road up to that night of triumph" (104); the lightweight champion "came up the hard way" (123); a Senator knew in his youth the "long hours of hard work" (149); and the ballet director "worked hard (152). In identical words we hear that the baseball manager (2) and the great film star (6) "came up the hard way." The "hard way" it was for Dorothy Thompson (9) and for Billy Rose (43). We are reminded of official military communiques, reporting a defeat or stalemate in a matter-of-fact tone, rather than descriptions of life processes.

The same applies to the reverse side of hardship: to the so-called breaks. All our stories refer to successes and it is fair enough that somehow we must be informed when and how the failures stopped. Here the tendency to commute life data into facts to be accepted rather than understood becomes intensified. Usually, the beginning of the peak is merely stated as an event: A high civil servant was "fortunate in her first assignment" (8); a cartoonist merely gets a "telegram offering him a job on the paper" which later leads to his fame (34); a columnist "bursts into certain popularity" (42); an actor "got a break" (112); another "got the job and it turned out well" (121); for a middleweight champion "the turning point of his career had arrived" (142). If any explanation is offered at all, we are told that the turn occurred in some freakish way: the night club singer gets started by "a king's whim" (135); Clark Gable's appointment as a timekeeper with a telephone company appears as the turning point in his career (6); a baseball player goes on a fishing trip, loses his old job and thereby gets another one which leads to his success (133a).

These episodes of repetition and freakishness seem to demonstrate that there is no longer a social pattern for the way up. Success has become an accidental and irrational event. The dangers of competition were tied up with the idea of definite chances and there was a sound balance between ambition and possibilities. Appropriately enough, our heroes are almost without ambition, a tacit admission that those dangers of the past have been replaced by the cruelties of the present. It is cruel, indeed, that the ridiculous game of chance should open the doors to success for a handful, while all the others who were not present when it happened are failures. The "facts" of a career are a reflection of the lack of spontaneity. Behind the amusing, fortuitous episode lurks a terrible truth.

The spectacle of success, hardships, and accidents is attended in the biographies by an assortment of numbers and figures which purport to bestow glamour and exactness to the narration. The ideal language of modern biographies seems to belong to the scientific mentality which sees its ideal in the transformation from quality into quantity. Life's riddle is solved if caught in a numeric constellation. The majority of figures refer to income, to which may be added relatively few data on capital. Other figures pertain to the spectators of a ball game, to the budget of a city, or to the votes of an election.

Hardships and breaks are standard articles for the reader. They are just a better brand of what everyone uses. The outstanding has become the proved specimen of the average. By impressing on the reading masses the idols of our civilization, any criticism or even reasoning about the validity of such standards is suppressed. As a social scientist the biographer represents a pitiless, almost sadistic trend in science, for he demonstrates the recurring nature of such phenomena as hardships and breaks, but he does not attempt to reveal the laws of such recurrence. For him knowledge is not the source of power but merely the key to adjustment.

Catalogue of adjustment

When we turn to a study of the approval and disapproval which our authors attach to the various character traits they describe, we find a striking and simple pattern.

In tone the catalogue of these traits, like the mythology of success, resembles a digest of military orders of the day: brusque laudations and reprimands. There is no room for nuances or ambiguity. In content it is on a very simple level and the criterion of approval or disapproval is also very simple. The yardstick is social adjustment. Once we realize the subconscious and conscious opinions of present-day society on what an adjusted person should and should not be, we are thoroughly familiar with the evaluation of character traits and their owners. The yardstick has three scales: behaviour toward material tasks; behavior toward fellow men; and behavior in relation to one's own emotions. The one who is efficient scores in the first sphere; the one who is sociable, in the second; and the one who is always restrained in the third.

In a separate study of all passages mentioning character traits, we found that of a total of seventy-six quotations referring to a hero's commendable behavior toward "things to be done," not fewer than seventy, or over 30 per cent, mentioned competence, efficiency, and energy; the remaining few referred to ambition. The majority read: "very capable" (154); "no sacrifice of time, effort, or my own convenience was too great" (24); "an inordinately hard worker" (48); "was never fired for inefficiency" (167); "thorough and accurate" (16); "being idle is her idea of complete torture" (140).

Out of a total of forty-eight quotations mentioning commendable behavior in relation to people, all forty-eight quote "co-operation," "sociability," and "good sportsmanship." There is a constant repetition of such adjectives as "co-operative," "generous," and "sociable." A baseball manager is "easy to meet, sociable, unsparing in his time with interviewers" (27). The "sociable" Chief of the Passport Division (8); the Secretary of Laber "a delightful hostess" (22); the Republican candidate for the president with his "liking for and interest in people" (133); the matador, "genuine, friendly, hospitable" (116); a smart actress, "amiable and friendly" (140) – they all belong to one big happy family which knows no limits in being pleasant and agreeable to each other. Like Don James, the barker for sideshows, they all seem to have "hearts so huge and overflowing" (127).

The number of quotations pertaining to disapproved character traits is very small, but conspicuous among them are criticisms of the unrestrained expression of emotion. It is virtually horrible that one of our baseball heroes "is no man for a jest when losing a game" (53); that a movie actress "cannot bear to be teased" (105); or that our Secretary of Labor's "public relations are unfortunate" (22). Unrestrained behavior traits like being "irritating and harsh" (32), "swift, often furious testiness" (117), being "unbalanced" (56), or even possessing a "somewhat difficult personality" (117) are really most unpleasant. Such faults can be tolerated only if they are exceptional like the man who "for once got his feelings beyond control" (23).

The catalogue of normalcy leaves no room for individuality. This catalogue levels human behavior by the rejection of emotional eruptions; the bad marks given to the poor "joiners" and the temperamental people; the complete lack of creative and passionate behavior among the commendable qualities. The absence of love and passion in our catalogue of human relations finds its counterpart in this catalogue of human qualities. It is a world of dependency. The social implications of such atmosphere seem to be considerable because in their social status the majority of our heroes are either their "own boss" or they have climbed to such a high step in the social ladder that whole worlds separate them from the average employee. Yet the few "big ones" do not differ basically from the many little ones. They demonstrate, taken as a group, not the exception, but the typical cross-section of the socio-psychological condition of modern society.

The foregoing examples from our catalogue of character traits should make clear why we emphasize the double feature of the absence of development and solitude. The average man is never alone and never wants to be alone. His social and his psychological birth is the community, the masses. His human destiny seems to be a life of continuous adjustment: adjustment to the world through efficiency and industriousness; and adjustment to people by exhibiting amiable and sociable qualities and by repressing all other traits. There is no religious or philosophical framework according to which the character traits are classified and evaluated. The concepts of good and bad, of kindness and sin, of truth and falsehood, or sacrifice and selfishness, of love and hate are not the beacons which illuminate our human landscape. The character image on which an affirmative judgment is passed in the biographies is that of a well-trained employee from a well-disciplined lower middle-class family. Our people could occupy an imaginary world of technocracy; everybody seems to reflect a rigid code of flexible qualities: the rigid and mechanized set-up of a variety of useful mechanical institutions. Behind the polished mask of training and adjustment lurks the concept of a human robot who, without having done anything himself, moves just such parts and in just such directions as the makers wished him to do.

Formerly it was only the sick who needed handling because it was known that their symptoms were similar to many others. Now everyone is reduced to the same dependency. The pride of being an individual with his own very personal ways and interests becomes the stigma of abnormality. Interest in the consumption of others is an expression of lack of interest in genuine consumption. The detailed character description is dominated by the same acceptance and passivity which came to the foreground in the concept of souls without development.

IV   Language

Superlatives

Our analysis would not be complete without some discussion of our stories' language which has several characteristic features. The most obvious one is the superlative.[12] Once we are made aware of this stylistic device, it cannot be overlooked. The heroes themselves, their accomplishments and experiences, their friends and acquaintances, are characterized as unique beings and events. The superlative gives a good conscience to the biographer – in applying a rhetorical gadget, he achieves the transformation of the average into the extraordinary. Mr. Muti is "the toughest Fascist of them all" (114) Dr. Brinkley is the "best advertised doctor in the United States" (3); our hero is the "luckiest man in the movies today" (121); another is "not only the greatest, but the first real showman in the Ringling family" (26). There is a general who is "one of the best mathematicians this side of Einstein" (107). There is a columnist with "one of the strangest of courtships" (2) another statesman with "the world's most exciting job" (144). There are also the downward-pointed superlatives. Some sportsman was once "the loudest and by all odds the most abusive of the lot" (2); a newspaper man is "one of the most consistently resentful men in the country" (28); another person is "one of the unhappiest women that ever lived" (154).

As if the biographer had to convince himself and his public that he is really selling an excellent human specimen, he sometimes is not satisfied with the ratio of one superlative per sentence but has to pack a lot of them into a single passage. Pittsburgh Phil is "the most famous and the most feared horse player in America" (23). The German Labor Front is "the best led, most enlightened and most powerful labor organization in Europe" (21). The producer, Lorentz, "demands the best writing, the best music are the best technical equipment available" (126). The baseball manager, Clark Griffith, "was the most colorful star on the most colorful team in baseball" (2). Tilden is ". . . the greatest tennis player in the world and the greater guy in the world" (111).

This wholesale distribution of highest ratings defeats its own purpose. Everything is presented as something unique, unheard of, outstanding. That nothing is unique, unheard of, outstanding. Totality of the superlative means totality of the mediocre. It levels the presentation of human life to the presentation of merchandise. The most vivacious girl corresponds to the best tooth paste, the highest endurance in sportsmanship corresponds to the most efficient vitamins; the unique performance of the politician corresponds to the unsurpassed efficiency of the automobile. There is a pre-established harmony between the objects of mass production in the advertising columns and the objects of biography in the editorial comment. The language of promotion has replaced the language of evaluation. Only the price tag is missing.

The superlative pushes the reader between two extremes. He is graciously attempting to become conversant with people who are paragons of human accomplishment. He may be proud that to a great extent these wonderful people do nothing but entertain him. He has, at least in his leisure time, the best crowd at his fingertips. But there is no road left to him for an identification with the great, or for an attempt to emulate their success. Thus the superlative, like the story of success itself, brings out the absence of those educational features and other optimistic implications which were characteristic of biographies during the era of liberalism. What on first sight seems to be the rather harmless atmosphere of entertainment and consumption is, on closer examination, revealed as a reign of psychic terror, where the masses have to realize the pettiness and insignificance of their everyday life. The already weakened consciousness of being an individual is struck another heavy blow by the pseudo-individualizing forces of the superlative. Advertisement and terror, invitation to entertainment, and summons to humility form their unity in the world of superlatives. The biographer performs the functions of a side show barker for living attractions and of a preacher of human insignificance.

High and low language

The use of the superlative is reinforced by frequent references to an assortment of mythical and historical associations, in order, it would seem, to confer pseudo-sanctity and pseudo-safety to the futile affairs of modern mass culture. Clark Gable does not just make a career – he lives the "Gable saga" (6), and the movie actress, Joyce, experiences at least a "little saga" (110). "Historic" is the word for Ilka Chase (140) as well as for Hildegarde (135). What happens to the softball player Novikoff is "fabulous" (158); the fate of the actress Morison is "history" (162); of the movie producer Wallis (166) as well as of the baseball player Allen (45) "a miracle"; the baseball manager Griffith experiences "baseball destiny," he accomplishes "a historic piece of strategy" (2). Greek mythology is a favorite; Clark Gable lives in "Olympian regions" (6); the passport administrator Shipley (8) as well as the gadget inventor Taylor (167) have an "Herculean task"; the producer Todd called an "Archon" (131) and our Taylor "Orpheus" (167). Of course Christianity and the middle ages have to help Dorothy Thompson "like a knight with a righteous sword" (9); the Nazi Ley is the "Jacob of German labor" with "labor itself the Esau" (21). Vice-President Wallace is "Joseph, a dreamer of dreams" (38); Casals is a "good Samaritan" (106). There are no limits. Ruth Hussey sometimes "looked a bit like a Buddha" (151); the showman Rose like a "priest of Osiris" (43). And so it goes on with myths, legends, sagas, destinies, miracles.[13] And yet, in the same breath which bestows the blessings of venerable symbols on our heroes, they and we are brought together on the easy level of slang and colloquial speech. McCutcheon, the cartoonist, might be called the "king" of his island possession, but we hear that "kingship is a safe investment" (1); Fletcher, who made history, is also "the soul – or the heel – of honesty" (7); Swing, called "an apostle," has also "radio's best bedside manner" (42). When Taft's father was president the "crown of Roosevelt I fitted him like a five and ten toupee" (101). There is a boxer who finds it "good business to be brave" (12); there is "gossip a dime a gross" (23); there is talk of a "personal blitzkrieg" (29); of "votes enough to elect a bee to a beehive" (109); of the "moguls of celluloid" (13) of "that genius business" (152). The historizing hymns of praise and transfiguration correspond to movie "palaces" and the sport "stadiums." It is a colossal façade, a "make-believe ballroom," as one radio station announces its swing program. Behind the façade of language there rules, just as behind the architectural outside make-up, a versatility of techniques, gadgets, and trucks, for which nothing is too expensive or too cheap that may serve the purpose of entertaining or being entertained.

These substitutes and successors of creative production require a language which substitutes for elucidating, revealing, stimulating words a linguistic confusion that strives to produce the illusion of rooted tradition and all around alertness. Thus this new literary phenomenon complies with the highest artistic criteria: inner, necessary, inseparable connection between form and content, between expression and the expressed – in short, a linguistic creation which will not permit an anatomic clear-cut separation between words and their intentions! These biographies as a literary species are "true."

Especially for you

The pseudo-individualization of the heroes corresponds to the pseudo-individualization of the readers. Although the selection of heroes and what is reported about them are as thoroughly standardized as the language of these reports, there is the superlative functioning as the specifying agent for the chosen hero and there is also, as crown and conclusion, the direct speech as the bearer of a personal message to the reader. Affably or condescendingly, everyone is personally invited to attend the spectacle of an outstanding life. Individual meets individual; the biographer takes care of the introduction.

Coach Fletcher and his wife "can be reached only by telegram provided you know the address" (7). Should you happen to be a Brenda Joyce fan: "If you come at the right time, you will see her second-hand car" (110). Watching our election campaign: "If Hull and Mr. Taft are the candidates, your emotion will not be fired, nor will your sleep be disturbed by them" (109). For those interested in film stars: "Let's sit down with Bill Powell and listen to his story" (112); "perhaps, girls, you would like to know how Clark Gable got that way" (6). Reporting McCutcheon's acquisition of an island, the author teases the reader: "so, you want to be a king" (1). For the car owner: "You can't help seeing Johnson's restaurants if you drive along main highways" (37). There is the London *Times* representative Sir Wilmott Lewis: "Meet him on Pennsylvania Avenue. He will stop and talk to you as if you were a five hundred audience" (49). Umpire Klem "knows the multitudinous rules of baseball better than you know the alphabet" (104). Let there be no mistake: the night club singer Moffett "went to the very best schools, my dear" (119). But let's not neglect her colleague Hildegarde: "If you haven't heard her or seen her, don't stand there – go, do something about it" (135). Casals' biographer is a little less imperative: "Meet the blond bowman from Spain" (106). Dependability is the word for Miss Fitzgerald: ". . . you can bank on her for the truth" (105).

The direct apostrophe is similar in function to the superlative: it creates elation and humiliation. The reader, besides being admitted to the intimate details of the hero's habits in eating, spending, playing, has the pleasure of personal contact. There is nothing of the measured distance and veneration which a reader in the classics in biography had to observe before the statesman of the past, or the poet or the scientist. The aristocracy of a gallery of isolated bearers of unusual achievements seems to be replaced by a democratic meeting which requires no special honors and genuflection before the great.

But the ease of admission is not devoid of menacing features. The "You" means not only the friendly gesture of introduction but also the admonishing, calling voice of a superior agency, proclaiming that one has to observe, has to comply. The language of directness betrays the total coverage planned by all modern institutions of mass communication. "Especially for You" means all of you.

V   The reader

Magazine biographies have undergone a process of expansion as well as of atrophy. They have become a standard institution in magazines which count their audience by the millions. It is significant that in the middle of World War II *The Saturday Evening Post* and *Collier's* were able to double their sales price without incurring any serious setback in circulation. But the scope of this expanding world of biographies narrowed down to the highly specialized field of entertainment. If we ask again what social need they serve, we might find the answer in this combination of quantitative increase and qualitative deterioration.

An hypothesis on the pseudo-educational and pseudo-scientific functions of the popular biography can be formulated as follows: the task of the social scientist is, in very broad terms, the clarification of the hidden processes and inter-connections of social phenomena. The average reader who, like an earnest and independent student, is not satisfied with a mere conglomeration of facts or concepts, but wants to know what it is all about, seems to gain insight from these biographies, and an understanding of the human or social secret of the historical process. But this is only a trick, because these individuals whose lives he studies are neither characteristic of this process, nor are they presented in such a way that they appear in the full light of it. A rather satisfactory understanding of the reader is possible if we look upon the biography as an agent of make-believe adult education. A certain social prestige, the roots of which are planted during one's school days, constantly drives one toward higher values in life, and specifically, toward more complete knowledge. But these biographies corrupt the educational conscience by delivering goods which bear an educational trademark but which are not the genuine article.

The important role of familiarity in all phenomena of mass culture cannot be sufficiently emphasized. People derive a great deal of satisfaction from the continual repetition of familiar patterns. There are but a very limited number of plots and problems which are repeated over and over again in successful movies and short stories; even the so-called exciting moments in sports events are to a great extent very much alike. Everyone knows that he will hear more or less the same type of story and the same type of music as soon as he turns on the radio. But there has never been any rebellion against this fact; there has never been a psychologist who could have said that boredom characterized the faces of the masses when they participate in the routine pleasures. Perhaps, since the average working day follows a routine which often does not show any change during a life-time, the routine and repetition characteristics of leisure-time activities serve as a kind of justification and glorification of the working day. They appear in the guise of beauty and pleasure when they rule not only during the average day, but also in the average late afternoon and evening. In our biographies, the horizon is not extended to the realm of the unknown, but is instead painted with the figures of the known. We have already seen the movie actor performing on the screen and we have seen the cartoons of the competent newspaperman; we have heard what the radio commentator has to say and have noted the talents of boxers and baseball players. The biographies repeat what we have always known.

André Maurois has made a wrong prophecy:

> We shall come once more into periods of social and religious certainty in which few intimate biographies will be written and *panegyrics* will take their place. Subsequently we shall again reach a period of doubt and despair in which biographies will reappear as a source of confidence and reassurance.[14]

The reader who obviously cherishes the duplication of being entertained with the life stories of his entertainers must have an irrepressible urge to get something in his mind which he can really hold fast and fully understand. It has been said of reading interests that: "In general, so long as the things of fundamental importance are not presenting one with problems, one scarcely attends to them in any way."[15] This remark has an ironical connotation for our biographies, for it can hardly be said that "things of importance" are not presenting us with problems today. Yet they are scarcely attended to unless we would admit that our heroes' parents, their likes and dislikes in eating and playing and, in the majority of cases, even their professions were important data during the initial stages of the second World War. But the distance between what an average individual may do and the forces and powers that determine his life and death has become so unbridgeable that identification with normalcy, even with Philistine boredom becomes a readily grasped empire of refuge and escape. It is some comfort for the little man who has become expelled from the Horatio Alger dream, who despairs of penetrating the thicket of grand strategy in politics and business, to see his heroes as a lot of guys who like or dislike highballs, cigarettes, tomato juice, golf, and social gatherings – just like himself. He knows how to converse in the sphere of consumption and here he can make no mistakes. By narrowing his focus of attention, he can experience the gratification of being confirmed in his own pleasures and discomforts by participating in the pleasures and discomforts of the great. The large confusing issues in the political and economic realm and the antagonisms and controversies in the social realm – all these are submerged in the experience of being at one with the lofty and great in the sphere of consumption.

Appendix

Differences between The Saturday Evening Post and Collier's

If we study the professional distribution for the two magazines separately we find the following result.

Table 7.4 Distribution of biographical subjects by occupation in *The Saturday Evening Post* and *Collier's* from April 1940–April 1941

Occupation of subjects	Saturday Evening Post		Collier's	
	No.	*%*	*No.*	*%*
Politics	16	28	15	22
Business and professions	20	35	5	7
Entertainment, sports	20	37	49	71
Total	56	100	69	100

This table shows a considerable difference between *The Saturday Evening Post* and *Collier's* in the occupational distribution of heroes. There are far more "serious" people and far fewer entertainers in *The Saturday Evening Post*. This corresponds to a difference in the audiences of the two magazines.[16] Surveys have shown that the average *Saturday Evening Post* reader is older, wealthier, and more attached to his home and more interested in social and economic problems than the average reader of *Collier's*.

However, the difference between the two magazines becomes negligible (see Table 7.5) when we re-classify the heroes according to the spheres of politics, production, and consumption. For our purpose this is a more meaningful classification. As the two magazines are rather alike under this classification we felt justified in treating them together in the main text.

We give below the list of the biographies from *The Saturday Evening Post* and *Collier's* appearing in the issues between April 1940 and 1941.

Table 7.5 Comparison of *The Saturday Evening Post* and *Collier's* heroes according to general spheres of activity

Spheres	Saturday Evening Post 1940–1941		Collier's 1940–1941	
	No.	*%*	*No.*	*%*
Politics	16	28	15	22
Production	3	5	..	..
Consumption	37	67	54	78
Total	56	100	69	100

LIST OF BIOGRAPHIES USED

The Saturday Evening Post

Date	"Hero"	Profession	No.
4–6–40	John T. McCutcheon	Cartoonist	1
4–13, 20–40	Clark Griffith	Baseball manager	2
4–20–40	John R. Brinkley	Physician	3
5–4–40	Robert Taft	Senator	4
5–4–40	Jack Johnson	Boxer	5
5–4–40	Clark Gable	Movie actor	6
5–11–40	Art Fletcher	Baseball coach	7
5–11–40	Mrs. Shipley	Chief, Passport Division, State Department	8
5–18, 25–40	Dorothy Thompson	Columnist	9
5–25–40	Richard A. Ballinger	Former Secretary of Interior	10
6–8–40	Bobby Jones	Golfer	11
6–22–40	Bob Donovan et al.	Boxers	12
6–22–40	Bob Allman	Wrestler	13
6–22–40	Daisy Harriman	Ambassador	14
7–6–40	Oche Tone	Slovenian immigrant	15
7–13–40	Ullstein Corp.	Publishing house	16
7–20–40	Hitler	Fuehrer of Third Reich	17
7–20–40	Jimmy Byrnes	Senator	18
7–27–40	Satchel Paige	Baseball pitcher	19
7–27–40	Angas	Investment counselor	20
7–27–40	Dr. Robert Ley	Head of the German Labor Front	21
7–27–40	Frances Perkins	Secretary of Labour	22
8–3, 10, 17–40 8–17, 24–40	Pittsburgh Phil	Professional gambler (horses)	23
9–14, 21, 28–40	Alfred P. Sloan, Jr.	Businessman	24
8–17–40	D'Arcy Grant	Woman sailor	25
8–24–40	John Ringling North	President of Ringling-Barnum & Bailey shows	26
9–14–40	Bill McKechnie	Baseball manager	27
9–14–40	Westbrook Pegler	Columnist	28
9–14–40	Endicott Peabody	Rector of Groton	29
10–5, 12, 19, 26–40, 11–9, 16, 30–40	William Rogers	Actor	31
10–12–40	James C. Petrillo	Pres. Am. Fed. Musicians	32
10–12–40	Louis McHenry Howe	Presidential secretary	33
10–19–40	Jay Norwood Darling	Cartoonist	34
10–19–40	Sidney Hillman	Labor leader	35
10–26–40	Frank Hague	Mayor of Jersey City	36
11–2–40	Howard Johnson	Owner of a restaurant chain	37
11–2–40	Henry Wallace	Vice-President	38
11–23–40	Silliman Evans	Newspaperman	39
11–30–40	Jesse H. Jones	Secretary of Commerce	40
12–7–40	William B. Stout	Inventor	41
12–13–40	Raymond Gram Swing	Radio Commentator	42
12–21–40	Billy Rose	Showman	43
12–28–40	Charles A. Lindbergh	Aviator, etc.	44
12–28–40	Bobby Allen	Basketball player	45

The Saturday Evening Post

Date	"Hero"	Profession	No.
1–4–41	Mrs. E. K. Hoyt and Toto	Gorilla owner and ward	46
1–11–41	Clifton Fadiman	Book and radio critic	47
1–18–41	Sam Rayburn	Speaker, House of Representatives	48
1–15–41	Sir Willmott Lewis	London *Times* Emissary to United States	49
2–1–41	J. H. Kendrigan	Football coach	50
?–1–41	Cyrus R. Smith	Pres. Amer. Airlines	51
2–8–41	Varian Brothers	Inventors	52
2–15–41	Theodore A. Lyons	Baseball player	53
2–22–41	Jo Carstairs	Island proprietress	54
3–8, 15–41	Preston Sturges	Movie director and writer	55
3–15–41	Hank Greenberg	Baseball player	56
3–22–41	Phil Rizzuto	Baseball player	57

Collier's

Date	"Hero"	Profession	No.
4–6–40	Robert A. Taft	Senator	101
4–13–40	Mme. Chao Wu-Tang	Chinese Partisan Chief	102
4–13–40	Nancy Hamilton	Playwright, actress	103
4–13–40	Bill Klem	Baseball umpire	104
4–20–40	Geraldine Fitzgerald	Movie actress	105
4–20–40	Pablo Casals	Cellist	106
4–27–40	General Weygand	General	107
4–27–40	Ezra Stone	Stage, radio and screen actor	108
5–4–40	Cordell Hull	Secretary of State	109
5–4–40	Brenda Joyce	Movie actress	110
5–4–40	Bill Tilden	Tennis champion	111
5–11–40	William Powell	Movie actor	112
5–18–40	Greer Garson	Movie actress	113
5–25–40	Ettore Muti	Fascist politician	114
5–25–40	Philip Kerr, Marquess of Lothian	British Ambassador	115
5–25–40	Conchita Cintron	Woman matador	116
6–8–40	Thomas Dewey	Politician	117
6–8–40	Athanasiades	Munitions merchant	118
6–15–40	Adelaide Moffett	Night club entertainer	119
6–22–40	Dutch Leonard	Baseball player	120
6–11–40	Chris Martin	Movie actor	121
6–29–40	Gene Tierney	Movie actress	122
7–20–40	Lew Jenkins	Lightweight champion	123
7–20–40	Mahatma Gandhi	Indian political leader	124
7–27–40	Jean Arthur	Movie actress	125
8–3–40	Pare Lorentz	Movie producer	126
8–10–40	Don James	Sideshow barker	127
8–24–40	Larry Adler	Harmonica player	128
8–31–40	Ernest Bevin	British Minister of Labor	129
9–7–40	Helen Bernhard	Tennis player	130
9–7–40	Mike Todd	Producer – show business	131
9–14–40	Ingrid Bergman	Movie actress	132

The Saturday Evening Post

Date	"Hero"	Profession	No.
9—21—40	Wendell Willkie	Politician	133
9—28—40	Walters and Derringer	Baseball players	133
10—5—40	Juan March	Industrialist	134
10—5—40	Hildegarde	Night club singer	135
10—12—40	Jack Grain	Football player	136
10—12—40	Jinx Falkenburg	Advertising model	137
10—12—40	Eddie Flynn	Democratic Nat'l Chairman	138
10—19—40	John Latouche	Writer	139
10—26—40	Ilka Chase	Actress: movie, radio, film	140
11—2—40	Winston Churchill	British Prime Minister	141
11—2—40	Ken Overlin	Middleweight champion	142
11—9—40	Joan Carroll	Child movie actress	143
11—9—40	Lord Woolton	Britain's Minister of Food	144
11—16—40	Dorothy Stickney	Actress – theater	145
11—30—40	Field Marshal Erhard Milch	Organizer of German air force	146
11—30—40	Barbara Ham	Musical writer – college girl	147
12—7—40	Martha Scott	Movie actress	148
12—7—40	Joseph H. Ball	Senator	149
12—14—40	"Schnitz"	Producer – jitterbug leader	150
12—21—40	Ruth Hussey	Movie actress	151
12—28—40	George Balanchine	Ballet director	152
1—4—41	Billy Soose	Boxing champion	153
1—4—41	Carol and Magda Lupescu	Ex-King of Roumania and paramour	154
1—4—41	Annie Laurie Williams	Hollywood literary agent	155
1—11—41	Katherine Dunham	Dancer	156
1—18—41	Dorothy Comingore	Actress: theatre and films	157
1—25—41	Lou Novikoff	Softball player	158
2—1—41	Zivic Brothers	Boxers	159
2—8—41	Three young actresses in "Charley's Aunt"	Actresses	160
2—15—41	Brenda Marshall	Movie actress	161
2—24—41	Patricia Morison	Movie actress	162
3—1—41	Marilyn Shaw	National ski champion	163
3—15—41	Cliff Thompson	Hockey coach	164
3—15—41	Chic Young	Comic strip cartoonist	165
3—15—41	Hal Wallis	Movie producer	166
3—29—41	James Taylor	Inventor of gadgets	167
3—29—41	Bob Riskin	Scenario writer	168

Notes

The first published version of this chapter appeared as "Biographies in Popular Magazines" in *Radio Research: 1942–1943*, edited by Paul F. Lazarsfeld and Frank Stanton (New York: Duell, Sloan and Pearce, 1944).

1   Cf. Edward H. O'Neill, *A History of American Biography* (Philadelphia: University of Pennsylvania Press, 1935). His remarks on pp. 179ff. on the period since 1919 as the "most prolific one in American history for biographical writing," are quoted by Helen McGill Hughes, *News and the Human Interest Story* (Chicago: University of Chicago Press, 1940), p. 285f, copyright 1940 by the University of Chicago. The book by William S. Gray and Ruth Munroe, *The Reading Interests and Habits of Adults* (New York: The Macmillan Company, 1930), which analyzes readers' figures for books and magazines, does not even introduce the category of biographies in its tables on the contents of magazines, and applies it only once for books in a sample analysis of readers in Hyde Park, Chicago. The only comment the authors have to offer is: "There is some tendency to prefer biographies and poetry, especially in moderate doses to other types of reading except fiction" (p. 154). Finally, I want to quote as a witness in this case of scientific negligence, Donald A. Stouffer, *The Art of Biography in Eighteenth Century England* (Princeton, N. J.: Princeton University Press, 1941), who in his excellent and very thorough study says: "Biography as a branch of literature has been too long neglected" (p. 3).

2   Up to the spring of 1939, 3.1 million copies of his books were sold: 1.2 million in Germany, 1.1 million in the U.S., 0.8 million elsewhere. Cf. Emil Ludwig, *Traduction des oeuvres* (Moscia, 1939), p. 2.

3   For the collection of data prior to 1940 the writer is indebted to Miss Mariam Wexner.

4   See, for instance, the *SEP*, September 19, 1925, where the auto-racer, Barney Oldfield, tells a reporter details of his racing experiences and of the mechanics of racing and automobiles; September 26, 1925, in which the vaudeville actress, Elsie Janis, comments on her imitation acts and also gives details of her techniques. The same holds true for the biography of the band leader, Sousa, in the *SEP*, October 31, 1925, and of the radio announcer, Graham McNamee, May 1, 1926; after a few remarks about his own life and career, McNamee goes on to discuss the technical aspects of radio and his experiences in radio with famous people.

5   *The Saturday Evening Post*, October 12, 1901.

6   *The Saturday Evening Post*, June 28, 1902.

7   Mandel Sherman, "Book Selection and Self Therapy" in *The Practice of Book Selection*, ed. Louis R. Wilson (Chicago: University of Chicago Press, 1939), p. 172. Copyright 1940 by the University of Chicago.

8   The figures in parentheses refer to the bibliography of stories studied; see Appendix to this chapter. Figures 1 to 57 refer to the *SEP* and figures 101 to 168 refer to *Collier's*. On the difference between the *SEP* and *Collier's*, see Appendix, Tables 7.4 and 7.5.

9   D. G. Phillips, "The Right Hand to Pierpont Morgan," *The Saturday Evening Post*, June 28, 1902.

10   Max Horkheimer, "The End of Reason" in *Studies in Philosophy and Social Science*. Vol. IX (1941), No. 3, p. 381.

11   *Ibid*.

12   A study by this writer on popular German biographies in book form shows that they also are characterized by the use of superlatives. These books by Emil Ludwig, Stefan Zweig, and others are on a different intellectual level, yet it seems probable that similar sociological implications hold for them as for magazine biographies. See, Leo Lowenthal "Die biographische Mode" in *Sociologica*, Frankfurt a.M.: Europäische Verlagsanstal 1955, pp. 363–86.

13   Helen McGill Hughes, *op. cit.*, p. 183, is aware of the fact that the association of "classical" names has a stimulating effect on what she calls "the city demos": "Stated in terms of his popular literature, the mind of modern man lives in the present. And as the present changes, so his news is voluminous and rapidly succeeded by more news. But what fascinates him is the news story – the true story – even though it may duplicate *Bluebeard* or *Romeo and Juliet* so exactly that the headline tells the news just by mentioning the familiar names. The human interest of the common man in the modern world will and does, ensnare him into reading folktales or even the classics, dull and unreal as he finds them in themselves, if they are paraphrased as the careers of twentieth century Electras, Macbeths and Moll Flanders, for he is pre-occupied with the things that depart from the expected and make news."

14   André Maurois, *Aspects of Biography* (New York: Appleton-Century-Crofts, Inc., 1939), p. 203. Copyright 1929, D. Appleton & Co.

15   Franklin Bobbitt, "Major Fields of Human Concern," quoted in Gray and Munroe, *op. cit.*, p. 47.

16   *A Qualitative Study of Magazines: Who Reads Them and Why.* McCall Corporation, October, 1939.

Chapter 8

Richard Dyer

STARS AS IMAGES

LOOKING AT STARS AS a social phenomenon indicates that, no matter where one chooses to put the emphasis in terms of the stars' place in the production-consumption dialectic of the cinema, that place can still only be fully understood ideologically. The questions, 'Why stardom?' and 'Why such-and-such a star?', have to be answered in terms of ideology – ideology being, as it were, the terms in which the production-consumption dialectic is articulated.

With stars, the 'terms' involved are essentially images. By 'image' here I do not understand an exclusively visual sign, but rather a complex configuration of visual, verbal and aural signs. This configuration may constitute the general image of stardom or of a particular star. It is manifest not only in films but in all kinds of media text.

As suggested [. . .], star images function crucially in relation to contradictions within and between ideologies, which they seek variously to 'manage' or resolve. In exceptional cases, it has been argued that certain stars, far from managing contradictions, either expose them or embody an alternative or oppositional ideological position (itself usually contradictory) to dominant ideology. The 'subversiveness' of these stars can be seen in terms of 'radical intervention' (not necessarily conscious) on the part of themselves or others who have used the potential meanings of their image – the struggles of Mae West, Greta Garbo, Bette Davis and Barbra Streisand over representation (expressed as a demand for 'decent parts for women') would clearly suggest them as interventionists. However, the question of subversion need not be conceptualised in this way. One can think of it simply as a clash of codes, quite possibly fortuitous, in which the very clash or else the intensity with which the alternative/oppositional code is realised result in 'subversion' (or, at any rate, make reading them 'subversively' possible or legitimate). The discussion of images in this part looks at examples of stars and ideological contradiction, both in terms of how they are grounded in such contradictions and how they 'manage' or 'subvert' them.

1 Stars as stars

In this first section I want to look briefly at some of the characteristics of the overall image of stardom. This general image forms a background to the more specific analyses of particular stars in sections 2 and 3.

Stardom is an image of the way stars live. For the most part, this generalised life-style is the assumed backdrop for the specific personality of the star and the details and events of his or her life. As it combines the spectacular with the everyday, the special with the ordinary, and is seen as an articulation of basic American/Western values, there is no conflict here between the general life-style and the particularities of the star. In certain cases, however, the relationship between the two may be ambivalent or problematic. Marilyn Monroe's aspiration to the condition of stardom and her unhappiness on attaining it are part of the pathetic/tragic side of her image. Much of the early publicity surrounding Marlon Brando concerns his unshaven, unkempt appearance and his unruly behaviour at parties, matters that signified a rejection of the general life-style of stardom. Jane Fonda has sought in recent years to negotiate stardom politically – that is, to maintain a certain level of star glamour in order to connect with the predominant culture of working people while at the same time gaining credibility for her progressive views by living in an ordinary house in an ordinary working-class neighbourhood.

I have illustrated this section chiefly from *The Talkies, Hollywood and the Great Fan Magazines* and *Photoplay Treasury*[1]. As these all cover much the same period (the twenties to the forties), the image that emerges is essentially that of Hollywood's classic period. It might be useful to compare this with contemporary film magazines (e.g. *Photoplay, ABC Film Review, Modern Screen, Films and Filming*) to see where the different emphases lie – e.g. fashion seems less important now than sex, there is perhaps more interest in films as such, the 'dream' of stardom is more jaded and sour. (The emphases also differ, of course, from one publication to another.)

The general image of stardom can be seen as a version of the American dream, organised around the themes of consumption, success and ordinariness. Throughout, however, there is an undertow that, as it were, 'sours' the dream. In addition, love, marriage and sex are constants of the image.

Consumption

The way stars lived is one element in the 'fabulousness' of Hollywood. One can approach this in different ways.

i) An anatomy of the life style

A list of the recurrent features of that life style would include, to begin with, swimming pools, large houses, sumptuous costumes, limousines, parties, etc. Let us look at the connotations of one of those features, fashion.

For instance what meanings are packed into the recurrent image of women stars as leaders of fashion? If we look at the article 'See These Latest Chanel Styles in

Gloria's Picture', the fact that the designer is Chanel links Gloria Swanson to the world of *haute couture*, with its connotations of high society, European 'taste' and exclusiveness. A certain inwardness with the idiosyncrasies of couturiers is assumed on the part of the reader by a remark like 'Who but Chanel would add [wing-like draperies] to a black velvet evening gown?' Equally, the expensiveness of the materials used is stressed (satin, fur, jewels), while the designs themselves are examples of 'conspicuous consumption' (see below), with their yards of material and awkward hanging pieces that would make any form of industry (including, be it noted in passing, the activity of acting) impossible. Finally, all of this promotes the notion of woman as spectacle, a theme that is even more insistent in other articles such as 'Motoring Beauty Hints' and 'How I keep my figure' (by Betty Grable) (*Photoplay Treasury* pp. 132–4 & 286–7), and 'Beauty "Tips" from the Beautiful – Little things that add to the good looks of the stars could add, also, to your own attractions'.[2] As these last examples show, however, fashion and notions of beauty (charm/glamour/sex-appeal, etc.) were also to be shared by star and fan. In this context, the 'exclusiveness' of the *haute couture* connection was problematic, and in fact there is increasing emphasis over the years in the fan magazines on the idea of Hollywood itself as the arbiter of fashion. (The ascendancy was finally achieved by America's being cut off from Paris styles during World War II.) This is indicated by the article 'Hollywood snubs Paris. Movie capital is self-reliant as a style center. Designer [Travis Banton] no longer looks to "shabby" Paris for ideas'. (*The Talkies* pp.192–3, 347) In this article, the fact of Paris as a leader of fashion is rejected with the implication that America and/or democracy can do just as well. At the same time, the notion of 'taste' as an absolute value is still asserted, without any recognition of the relativity of the term or its provenance, in the discourse of fashion; namely, Paris . . .

One could similarly explore the associations and contradictions of other image clusters – sport, dances, architecture (of the stars' homes), and so on.

ii) Conspicuous consumption

Thorstein Veblen made the notion of conspicuous consumption central to his *Theory of the Leisure Class*. Conspicuous consumption is the way by which the wealthy display the fact that they are wealthy. It displays not only the fact that they have wealth in the scale on which they consume and their access to the canons of taste and fashion, but also the fact that they do not have to work. Women are crucial in this process – a man may have to work, but his wife must not. It is she who carries in her consumption patterns the signs of his wealth. Fashion is one example of this – access to the canons of taste, wearing clothes made of expensive materials in exclusive designs, designs that clearly made work impossible and are even, in the pursuit of this aim, debilitating for the wearer, as they squeeze, shape, mis-shape and constrict her body. Equally, activities such as sport or the arts are not pursued for health or enlightenment but for the sake of displaying the leisure time and money at one's disposal. Thus a man's athletic body may be much admired, but only on condition that it has been acquired through sports not labour.

These themes emerge very clearly in an analysis of the fan magazines: 'Hollywood at Play' and 'Stars off the Set', for instance,[3] the latter showing how a star's non-working life is presented as consisting in sports and hobbies. What is suppressed, or only fleetingly acknowledged, in these articles is that making films is work, that films are produced. An interestingly self-conscious play on this occurs in the article. 'Those Awful Factories' with a spread of pictures of stars 'at work' in their sumptuous studio dressing rooms. Even on the shop-floor, stars are not shown working, that is, making films. (Note also the delineation of sex roles by decor.)

iii) Idols of consumption

Leo Lowenthal in his study of biographies in popular magazines noted a marked shift in emphasis between 1901 and 1941. In the earlier period the biographies' subjects were 'idols of production' — people interesting because they achieved something in the world, made their own way, worked their way to the top, were useful to society: bankers, politicians, artists, inventors, businessmen. In the intervening years however there is a shift to 'idols of consumption'. Of 'present-day magazine heroes':

> . . . almost every one . . . is directly, or indirectly, related to the sphere of leisure time: either he does not belong to vocations which serve society's basic needs (e.g. the heroes of the world of entertainment and sport), or he amounts, more or less, to a caricature of a socially productive agent. (p.115)

Contemporary heroes 'stem predominantly from the sphere of consumption and organised leisure time' (p.121) (i.e. they are entertainers or sportspeople), and equally their 'private' lives are lives of consumption. So '. . . in the course of the presentation the producers and agents of consumer goods change into their own customers'. (ibid.)

Although Veblen's account of the way in which leisure, dress, consumption patterns, etc. bespeak wealth is useful in the analysis of the image of stardom, Lowenthal's model perhaps comes closer to the social significance of all this consumption. For whereas with Veblen conspicuous consumption preserves the leisure class as a distinctive class, with Lowenthal the stars become models of consumption for everyone in a consumer society. They may spend more than the average person, but nonetheless they can be, on a smaller scale, imitated. Their fashions are to be copied, their fads followed, their sports pursued, their hobbies taken up. Heroes, in Lowenthal's words, are 'a lot of guys [sic] who like or dislike highballs, cigarettes, tomato juice, golf and social gatherings . . .' (p.135) We may note that many economists (e.g. Galbraith, Baran and Sweezy) consider that during the twentieth century capitalism has shifted decisively from an economy based on production to one based on consumption – that the 'problem' for capitalism is not how to produce enough for the market but how to sell the amount produced in excess of immediate market demand.[4] A connection between this and the growth of 'idols of consumption' irresistably suggests itself, the idols expressing in ideological form the economic imperatives of society – though the neatness of the connection should perhaps also make us wary.

Success

Albert McLean in his study of vaudeville, *American Vaudeville as Ritual*, has shown how this form was built around the myth of success. The cinema derived the star system from this theatre, and with it the emphasis on the star as a symbol of success.

The general meaning of the myth of success is that American society is sufficiently open for anyone to get to the top, regardless of rank. As Daniel Boorstin puts it:

> The film-star legend of the accidentally discovered soda-fountain girl who was quickly elevated to stardom soon took its place alongside the log-cabin-to-White-House legend as a leitmotif of American democratic folk-lore.
>
> (*The Image*, p.162)

The myth of success is grounded in the belief that the class system, the old-boy network, does not apply to America. However, one of the myth's ambiguities is whether success is possible for anyone, regardless of talent or application. Particularly as developed in the star system, the success myth tries to orchestrate several contradictory elements: (i) that ordinariness is the hallmark of the star; (ii) that the system rewards talent and 'specialness'; (iii) that luck, 'breaks', which may happen to anyone typify the career of the star; and (iv) that hard work and professionalism are necessary for stardom. Some stars reconcile all four elements, while with others only some aspects are emphasised. Stardom as a whole holds all four things to be true.

The Jolson Story *as a paradigm of the myth of success*

The Hollywood 'biopic' illustrates in its charting of a star's rise to fame these contradictory cornerstones of the success myth. *The Jolson Story* is paradigmatic, managing to hold together all four elements: (i) Jolson is just an ordinary guy from an ordinary Jewish family – he has no 'connections', no wealth; (ii) Jolson has an exceptionally beautiful voice, which captivates audiences (e.g. in the early scene where he is attending a vaudeville matinée, singing along in the audience, but so beautifully that everyone else stops to listen); (iii) it is just lucky that when a fellow artiste is too drunk to perform, Jolson goes on in his stead on the very night that two leading impresarios happen to be in the theatre; (iv) Jolson is a dedicated professional, always inventing new aspects to his act, taking on the challenge of movies, etc. What is suppressed in the film is the activity of the machinery of impresarios, agents, producers, backers – the 'business' of show business. Jolson never gets to be active in that sphere, he is as it were carried up through the machinery. Interestingly, even films *about* producers, such as *The Great Ziegfeld*, suppress examination of this.

The myth of success also suggests that success is worth having – in the form of conspicuous consumption. Barry King[5] has suggested that the stars imply that not only success but *money* is worth having, that the stars 'are models of rapid social mobility through salary'. What they earn (not class connections, breeding, education or 'artistic' achievement) gives them access to the world of good living, to that part of the élite that C. Wright Mills in *The Power Elite* calls 'cafe society'. Thus, argues King, the stars as successes can be seen as affirming 'in fantasised form' wage earning, selling one's labour power on the market, as a worthwhile goal in life.

Ordinariness – are stars 'different'?

One of the problems in coming to grips with the phenomenon of stardom is the extreme ambiguity/contradiction, already touched on, concerning the stars-as-ordinary and the star-as-special. Are they just like you or me, or do consumption and success transform them into (or reflect) something different?

Violette Morin suggests that in the case of superstars ('Les Olympiens', the title of her article), they are believed to be different *in kind* from other people. She sees this as stemming from the way stars are treated as superlatives. Stars are always the most something-or-other in the world – the most beautiful, the most expensive, the most sexy. But because stars are 'dissolved' into this superlative, are indistinguishable from it, they *become* superlative, hence they seem to be of a different order of being, a different 'ontological category'. Their image becomes gradually generalised, so that from being, say, the most beautiful they become simply 'the greatest'.

One of Morin's examples is Elizabeth Taylor, and the points she makes about her are similar to those made by Alexander Walker in his chapter on Taylor in *Sex in the Movies*. Whereas other stars may stand for types of people, Taylor stands for the type 'star' – the most expensive, the most beautiful, and the most married and divorced, being in the world. Her love life plus her sheer expensiveness are what make her interesting, not her similarity to you or me.

Walker does not claim that Taylor is typical of all stars, and it is not clear how wide Morin would define her category of 'Olympien'. I am myself not persuaded that a belief in the ontological difference of the stars is at all widespread. Even the case of Taylor seems to me suspect, for it does not take into account the way in which her love life may be paradigmatic of the problems of heterosexual monogamy (see below), nor does it deal with, for instance, the 'common-ness' of her playing in *Cleopatra* or her particular success when playing 'bitch' roles.

The paradox of the extravagant life-style and success of the stars being perceived as ordinary may be explained in several ways:

i)   Stars can be seen as ordinary people who live more expensively than the rest of us but are not essentially transformed by this.
ii)   The wealth and success of the stars can be seen as serving to isolate certain human qualities (the qualities they stand for), without the representation of those qualities being muddied by material considerations or problems.

Both (i) and (ii) fit with notions that human attributes exist independently of material circumstances. Stars may serve to legitimate such notions.

iii) Stars represent what are taken to be people typical of this society; yet the types of people we assume characterise our society may nevertheless be singularly absent from our actual day-to-day experience of society; the specialness of stars may be then that they are the only ones around who are ordinary! (This is another way of conceptualising the charisma model.)

The dream soured

Consumption and success, with their intimations of attendant values such as democracy, the open society, the value of the common/ordinary person, are the key notes of the image of stardom, but it would be wrong I think to ignore elements that run counter to this. Through the star system, failures of the dream are also represented.

Both consumption and success are from time to time shown to be wanting. Consumption can be characterised as wastefulness and decadence, while success may be short-lived or a psychological burden. The fan magazines carried articles such as 'The Tragedy of 15,000 Extras' (about people who don't get lucky breaks – 'Struggling to win a place in the cinema sun, they must put behind them forever their dreams of screen success'), 'They, Too, Were Stars' (about big stars who have declined into obscurity), 'Tragic Mansions' (about the superstitions that have grown up around the dwellings that stand as 'monuments of shattered careers') and 'The Price They Pay for Fame' ('In Hollywood, Health, Friends, Beauty, even Life Itself, are Sacrificed on the Altar of Terrible Ambition'; see *Hollywood and the Great Fan Magazines*, pp.94–5).[6] These are all from the thirties. The themes of decadence, sexual licence and wanton extravagance emerged more strongly in the fifties and sixties, not only in fan magazines and the press but also in novels and even films set in Hollywood (e.g. *Valley of the Dolls*). Yet even the 'Tragic Mansions' article is sub-headed 'the strange story of heartbreak houses in heartbreak town', implying that the idea of tragedy and suffering being endemic to Hollywood was commonplace. These perspectives, and much else of the image of Hollywood stardom, come across in this extract from the semi-pornographic pulp novel *Naked in Hollywood* by Bob Lucas. Carla is on her way to Hollywood, in the company of a second-rate agent named Herb:

> Carla could not recall the precise moment she decided she would become a star. As she grew older it seemed that the dream was born in her. She had no illusions about developing into a great actress. It was the glamour, the make-believe, the beauty, the adulation that were the increments of stardom that bedazzled her. She knew more about Hollywood – that part of it *she* was interested in – than Herb could ever tell her.
>
> The heart-shaped swimming pools, the Rolls Royces, the estates, the mink and ermine, Scotch and champagne – all this she knew as intimately as if she had created the Technicolor paradise where dwelt the screen gods and goddesses.
>
> Rita, Eva, Liz and Marilyn; Rock, Tab, Rip and Frankie – their real names, their broken romances and artistic triumphs, even their pet peeves and favourite foods were part of the movieland lore Carla had crammed into her brain. Books, fan magazines and newspaper columns were the source of her knowledge. Now she was headed for the promised land and had not the slightest doubt that one day in the not too distant future she would join the ranks of the immortals.

> Hollywood — it can break your heart, rip out your guts, Herb had
> warned. Carla was not impressed. To become a star, she was prepared to
> trade her immortal soul.

The recognition of Hollywood as a destroyer was perhaps most forcibly expressed by the deaths of Marilyn Monroe and Judy Garland, whose ruined lives and possible suicides were laid at the door of Hollywood's souless search for profits. Latterly, Monroe has also come to symbolise the exploitation of woman as spectacle in film.

Love

A central theme in all the fan magazines is love. This is achieved partly by the suppression of film-making as work and partly by the over-riding sense of a world in which material problems have been settled and all that is left is relationships. These relationships are invariably heterosexual emotional/erotic ones — 'love' — and the magazines carry the implication that these are the only kinds of relationship of any interest to anyone — not relationships of, for instance, work, friendship, political comradeship or, surprisingly enough, parents and children. (Births are featured, it is true, but seldom the developing relationship of a star and her/his child.) One can see this as diverting mass attention away from such areas, as indeed it does, although it is also worth remembering that the majority of the audience was (and still is) placed within the structures and expectations of heterosexual relationships. What is interesting about the fan magazines is that, despite Edgar Morin's views in *The Stars*, love is often not so much celebrated as agonised over.

   Morin sees the essence of the myth of stardom as love. Love, that is, intense heterosexual passion, he sees as forming the substance of writing about the stars, carrying with it the implication that life is about love. This has various manifestations, notably the obsession with physical beauty and youth (caught in the paradoxical pair of cliches that 'the heart is ageless' because it is 'always twenty', p.175) and the magic of the kiss:

> The kiss is not only the key technique of love-making, nor the cinematic
> substitute for intercourse forbidden by censorship: it is the triumphant
> symbol of the role of the face and the soul in twentieth century love. The
> kiss is of a piece with the eroticism of the face, both unknown in ancient
> times and still unknown in certain civilisations. The kiss is not only the
> discovery of a new tactile voluptuousness. It brings to life unconscious
> myths which identify the breath from one's mouth with the soul; it thus
> symbolises a communication or symbiosis of souls. The kiss is not only the
> piquancy in all Western films. It is the profound expression of a complex
> of love which eroticises the soul and mystifies the body. (p. 179)

Love then ceases to be a question of physical and practical relations and becomes a metaphysical experience.

   Certainly this notion of love is promoted by films and by articles in the fan magazines, but what emerges far more strongly from an examination of the latter is a concern with the *problems* of love. Articles with titles like the following predominate: 'The Inside Story of Joan's Divorce' (Joan Bennett) (pp.30–1), 'What's the Matter with Lombard? Is it true that her marriage to Clark Gable is responsible for Carole's recent unprecedented behaviour?' (pp. 56–7, 181–2), 'Tarzan Seeks a Divorce' (pp. 106–7, 196), 'Why is Bette Living without her Husband – after Six Compatible Years?' (pp. 110–2, 198–9), and 'This Year's Love Market' (dealing with 'the marital mergers and tangles, the Blessed and not so Blessed Events of the past year') (pp. 114–5, 199–200; all quotes from *Hollywood and the Great Fan Magazines*). Frequently the attempt is made to blame Hollywood itself for the endless round of marriages, divorces, quarrels, etc. In 'What's Wrong with Hollywood Love?' (ibid., pp. 60–2, 183–4) it is suggested that romance cannot flourish under the glare of publicity ('real love thrives on romantic secrecy', (p.61). 'The High Price of Screen Love-Making', about the effect of on-screen romance on off-screen relationships, observes:

> Be reasonable. If you spent a day in Ronald Colman's arms, could you forget it? Or, if you are a man, and you had spent eight hours clasping and unclasping, kissing and un-kissing Marlene Dietrich – would you forget it? Could you go home to your sweet, thoughtful, kind loving mate and swear to yourself that such days had made no impression on you!
>
> (*Photoplay Treasury*, pp. 200–1)

However, putting the blame on Hollywood seems to be a way of disguising the fact that what these articles are really doing is endlessly raking over the problems posed by notions of romance and passion within the institution of compulsory heterosexual monogamy. Thus in addition to the display of romantic-marital agony and the putting-the-blame-on-Hollywood pieces, there are also those that draw a 'lesson' from Hollywood romances – whether it be the value of endurance and suffering ('Don't be Afraid of a Broken Heart' by Olivia de Havilland, *Hollywood and the Great Fan Magazines*, pp. 148–9) or tips on keeping a marriage together (e.g. 'How to Stay Married to a Movie Star – or to Anybody for that matter', *Photoplay Treasury*, pp. 134–7 – here the connection with the readers' own problems is made explicit). And the divorce stories themselves also carry messages as to what a proper marriage really consists in, what a woman and a man's correct role and essential needs are. Thus we learn that Joan Bennett '. . . knew fame and wealth and popularity. She had a beautiful home. She had a husband who was brilliant, fascinating, devoted. She had every outward reason to be happy. But always, despite all that she said in her interviews and tried to believe herself, something was missing from her happiness. In her heart of hearts, she did not have the love that every woman lives to have.' (*Hollywood and Great Fan Magazines*, p. 177). Bette Davis' marriage to Harmon Nelson is breaking up because:

> It's asking a lot of a man to expect him to be the lesser half of a marital partnership indefinitely – the lesser in income, the lesser in prestige. No matter how much a man loves his wife, it's almost too much to expect him to be happy in the role of just-a-husband, in which people confuse him with just-a-gigolo, say he's living on her salary, and call him by her name with a 'Mr.' attached.
>
> (ibid., p.112)

2 Stars as types

Despite the extravagant life-style of the stars, elements such as the rags-to-riches motif and romance as an enactment of the problems of heterosexual monogamy suggest that what is important about the stars, especially in their particularity, is their typicality or representativeness. Stars, in other words, relate to the social types of a society.

The notion of social type

The notion of a type – or rather a social type – has been developed by O.E. Klapp, and its ideological functioning is discussed [. . .]. Here we are concerned with what social types are.

In *Heroes, Villains and Fools*, Klapp defines a social type as 'a collective norm of role behaviour formed and used by the group: an idealized concept of how people are expected to be or to act'. (p.11) It is a shared, recognisable, easily-grasped image of how people are in society (with collective approval or disapproval built into it).

On the basis of this Klapp proceeds to provide a typology of the prevalent social types in America, and he frequently provides stars' names to illustrate the different social types. Thus under 'heroes of social acceptability', he lists Will Rogers, Sophie Tucker and Perry Como, and under 'snobs' he lists Grace Kelly, Elizabeth Taylor, Ingrid Bergman, Zsa Zsa Gabor, Katharine Hepburn, Garbo and Davis. (A star may of course be listed under several different, even contradictory categories, reflecting both the ambiguity of their image and the differences in audience attitudes – thus Monroe for instance is used as an example of 'love queen' and 'simpleton', while Liberace is a 'charmer', a 'dude', a 'deformed fool' and a 'prude'.) The star both fulfills/ incarnates the type and, by virtue of her/his idiosyncrasies, individuates it. (Critics committed to individualism as a philosophy or tenet of common sense tend to speak of the star's individuation of a type as 'transcendance'.)

There are problems with Klapp's work. Firstly, he does not explore the sources of social types, seeing them simply as 'collective representations'. He sees social types as positive and useful, as opposed to stereotypes, which are wrong and harmful because they deal with people 'outside of one's cultural world' – yet he never examines just who is within and without the 'cultural world'. That is, he never examines the possibility that the cultural world articulated by social types may represent the hegemony of one section of society over another. Yet it is clear from his typology that if you are not white, middle-class, heterosexual and male you are not going to fit 'the cultural world' too well – women only fit uneasily, whilst blacks, gays and even the working-class hardly fit at all. (I have discussed this in *Gays and Film*.) Secondly, one does rather wonder where his categories come from, how he arrived at them. There is no discussion of methodology in his writings.

Nevertheless, despite all this, one can I think *use* Klapp's typology as a description of prevalent social types, providing one conceptualises this ideologically (i.e. he is describing the type system subscribed to by the dominant groups in society) and of course allows for modifications and additions since he wrote.

Three prevalent social types as defined by Klapp are the Good Joe, the Tough Guy, and the Pin-up.

i) The good Joe

Klapp takes the 'good Joe' or 'good fellow' as 'the central theme of the American ethos'. He is

> . . . friendly and easy going; he fits in and likes people; he never sets himself above others but goes along with the majority; he is a good sport – but also a he-man who won't let anyone push him around where basic rights are concerned. (p.108)

He is characterised by

> . . . dislike of bullies, snobs, authoritarians, and stuffed shirts; sympathy for the underdog; and liking for the good Joe or regular fellow who, for all his rough-and-ready air wouldn't try to dominate anybody, not even his wife. (ibid.)

and is to be distinguished from squares, sissies and eggheads. Star examples are Perry Como, Bing Crosby, Lucille Ball, Will Rogers, Pat Boone, Eddie Cantor, Bob Hope and William Holden.

> Failure to understand the good Joe complex I believe is a major source of the misunderstanding of Americans by non-Americans. (p.109)

Klapp is right to pinpoint the good Joe as the central American social type, although we should ask questions as to what it also suppresses or conceals, at what cost this good Joeism is achieved. Although Klapp maintains that women can be good Joes, his description excludes this (women cannot be he-men, do not have wives . . .); and the implicit, taken-for-granted maleness of the type is reinforced by its opposition to sissies. Equally the opposition to eggheads can also be (as Klapp does hint) a resistance to any attempt to think outside of dominant beliefs and the status quo.

John Wayne as a good Joe

Although John Wayne is many things besides being a good Joe, a useful way of studying his image and the good Joe complex is to analyse his films in terms of the way his easy-going, self-contained, male stance is affirmed by (a) differentiating him from other characters (including women, villains and other men who don't 'fit' – see the Hawks Westerns with Wayne for an examination of how a man (or a woman) 'fits' and how he or she does not) and (b) dissolving ideological tensions in the 'unanswerable' good Joe normalcy of his presence (e.g. war films such as The Sands of Iwo Jima and The Green Berets). It needs to be added, of course, that not all Wayne's roles would meet this analysis, because of, for example, casting against type, villainous inversions, self-reflexive roles, etc., and that there are aspects of his image – his awkwardness with women, his 'hawkish' political stance – that relate ambivalently to it. They may undermine his good Joe-ism – but equally the latter may justify the former.

ii) The tough guy

This type is discussed by Klapp in his examination of 'the deterioration of the hero'. Klapp's examples are Mike Hammer, Ernest Hemingway and Little Caesar, but he could have supplemented this with film star examples such as James Cagney, James Bond/Sean Connery or Clint Eastwood. What concerns Klapp about this type is not its existence, but its ambivalence. A disapproved type of violence, aggressivity, callousness and brutality would serve a useful function, so 'it is as hero, not villain, that the tough guy is a problem'. (p.149) The tough guy embodies many values that can make him a hero:

> . . . he is like a champ (you have to hand it to him, he licks the others). So long as this is so he has the almost universal appeal of the one who can't be beat. Since he usually fights others as tough as himself, he has a kind of fairness (whereas we should have little trouble rallying against a bully). Another thing that confuses the issues is that sometimes the only one who can beat him is another tough guy . . . Tough guys often display loyalty to some limited ideal such as bravery or the 'gang code', which also makes it possible to sympathize with them. Finally, they may symbolize fundamental status needs, such as proving oneself or the common man struggling with bare knuckles to make good. (p.150)

As a result he confuses the boundaries between good and bad behaviour, presses the anti-social into the service of the social and vice versa. In this instance, the type does not indicate collective approval, disapproval or ridicule, but confusion and ambiguity. Klapp's point is to bemoan the 'corruption of the hero', the collapsing of moral and social categories. I would tend to see it more in terms of the tough guy working through contradictions in the male role, which are disguised in more traditional types (cowboys, swashbucklers, war heroes). This is in some measure born out by Patrick McGilligan's study of James Cagney (*Cagney – The Actor as Auteur*).

McGilligan on Cagney

He sees Cagney as embodying both the positive and the negative connotations of toughness:

> At worst, Cagney presents the liberal guise of fascist instincts: the drive to be on top, to go solo, to dominate women, to buy one hundred suits, to succeed – the competitive, individualist, capitalist ethic. At best, he represents an optimistic faith in circumstances, hope in the future, a gritty refusal to be dominated in any situation and a stubborn resistance to accepted social standards and *mores* that is exemplary. (p.181)

What makes McGilligan's account useful is that he moves beyond this statement of an ambiguity or contradiction (which is where Klapp basically would leave it) to make connections with specific other aspects of cultural meaning and to explore the ideological complications these connections bring with them. Thus he links Cagney's toughness to notions of the working-class and masculinity. The link with the working-class is present equally in the early film roles, the biographies' stress on Cagney's New York East Side Irish background and in his known championing of 'radical' causes. Yet, as McGilligan show, this working-class toughness — always problematic for middle-class and/or feminist socialists — was easily pressed into the service of right-wing themes in the later films, so that by the time of *One, Two, Three* (1961) '. . . all the characteristics of the younger Cagney [are] put to the service of the older Cagney persona — patriotic, rightist and complacent' (p.192). The link between toughness and maleness is yet more ambiguous. Cagney was, says McGilligan, 'outrageously masculine in his every action'. As a result his relations with women are problematic. It is not so much the question of violence (the grapefruit in Mae Clarke's face in *The Public Enemy* — the only caress gesture in his repertoire, a gentle prod from a clenched fist), as the notion that 'Only a woman who is tough [tough like Cagney/tough like a man] is a fitting mate for the male Cagney' (p.169). In his career only Joan Blondell and Ann Sheridan really come up to this, forming with Cagney examples of the equal heterosexual couple that Molly Haskell admires (on Cagney in particular see her 'Partners in Crime and Conversion' in *The Village Voice*, Dec. 7, 1972). Quite how one assesses these instances (cf. the Hawksian woman's masculinisation) — as images of equality or as an inability to conceive the feminine — I will leave for now. A further aspect of the link of tough guy/Cagney with maleness is the role of the mother. As McGilligan suggests, Cagney's closeness (on screen) to his mother is important because it 'exonerated the nastier actions of the Cagney character'; at the same time, the almost fanatical devotion of the two has an implicit neurosis, so that films in which it is emphasised, such as *Sinner's Holiday, The Public Enemy* and *White Heat* 'show the perversion of the close American family (perhaps unintentionally), not how wonderful such a family is' (p.109). McGilligan's study is an example of the way that, by following through the chains of association of a star's incarnation of a social types, some of the contradictions elided in that type can be explored.

iii) The pin-up

As already mentioned, Klapp's typology is noticeably short on women. He points out that, because 'It is still a man's world when it comes to handing out the medals' (p.97), there are particularly few women hero types, resulting in the dilemma of modern woman's 'loss of identity' (p.98). (He does not get very far in asking why this should be so — but he did observe it at a time when few other writers were doing so.) It is interesting to note that when he does propose a predominantly female type, it is one that exists primarily in media representation — the pin-up. (He could perhaps have used the term 'glamour girl'.)

Although he does include some men in his list of synonyms of the pin-up, the emphasis is on women:

Such a model of bodily perfection need be neither a great lover nor a social lion. Photogenic perfection is enough. It may be surprising to say that a pin-up need not be unusual even in looks (many people have complained of the monotony of American cheesecake and Hollywood beauty). Fashion, cosmetology, and hair styling actually increase the resemblance of pin-up types. (p.39)

One might say, with heroes like that, who needs villains and fools? As a social model, the pin-up promotes surface appearance and depersonalisation, woman as sexual spectacle and sex object.

The pin-up is an important part of the way a star's image is built up, but we should not confuse this with the pin-up as a social type. All the stars we are concentrating on in this study, men as well as women, have had pin-up photographs taken and used, but of these only Monroe and Fonda were 'pin-ups'. They conformed, in their pin-up photos, to the conventions described by Thomas B. Hess in 'Pin-up and Icon':

By the 1940s, the pin-up image was defined with canonical strictness. First of all, there was the 'pin-up girl' herself. She had to be the healthy, American, cheerleader type – button-nosed, wide-eyed, long-legged, ample hips and breasts, and above all with the open, friendly smile that discloses perfect, even, white teeth. Then there is her costume and pose. These must be inviting but not seducing; affectionate but not passionate, revealing by suggestion while concealing in fact. The legs are carefully posed so that not too much of the inner thigh is shown; the navel is covered and so are most of the breasts except for the famous millimeters of 'cleavage'. The body is evident beneath the costume, but not its details – the bulges of nipples or of the *mons veneris* are scrupulously hidden. There is a dialectical pressure at work, between the voyeuristic public which wants to see more and more, and that same public which, in its social function, supports codes and laws that ban any such revelations. Caught between these two forces, the image tends towards an almost Byzantine rigidity, and assumes some of the symbolizing force of an icon. The pin-up girl and the Virgin in Majesty both are instantly legible visual images of the comforting and commonplace which is also ideal, and thus unattainable. (p.227)

Much of the sexual charge of the image is carried by symbolism of various kinds. Hess sees this as produced by censorship and puritanism, forbidding any more direct representation of sexuality. A reading of this following Laura Mulvey's analysis in 'Visual Pleasure and Narrative Cinema' would, on the other hand, put a different emphasis – the pin-up as woman represents the possiblility of castration for the male viewer (as do all women for him); to avoid this, a substitute phallus is provided in the form of sexual symbols (including of various obviously phallic kinds) or fetishes. Unless one chooses to accept that all fetishism is to be explained in terms of phallic substitution, I am not sure how far I would go along with this. Sexual imagery may be fetishistic simply in the sense of being a heightening of erotic/sensual surfaces (fur, leather, satin, etc. being 'more like skin than skin'); at the same time it also links the woman to other images of power and wealth (e.g. fur, etc., as expensive fabrics; frequent linkage to Art, *haute couture*, leisure, etc.). She may thus be seen as an example of wealth (which the viewer in his fantasy possesses), or as being something that can be obtained through wealth.

In terms of films, the pin-up typing of Monroe and Fonda can be analysed in terms of their visual presentation, how they are kept (or not) within the conventions described above, how the association of images pointed to in the last paragraph is developed. Mulvey also indicates a further aspect for analysis. She suggests that one of the aesthetic consequences of woman as spectacle in film is a tension in films centred on glamorous women stars between the narrative (we want to know what happens next) and the spectacle (we want to stop and look at the woman – Mulvey assumes that the only audience position is constituted in terms of male heterosexuality). It is worth examining a film like *Gentlemen Prefer Blondes* or *Barbarella* to see how far this is true, and how they 'manage' this tension.

Alternative or subversive types

Most types discussed by Klapp, and indeed most stars discussed as social types, are seen as representing dominant values in society, by affirming what those values are in the 'hero' types (including as those values are relatively appropriate to men and women) and by denouncing other values in the villain and fool types. Klapp argues, however, that there may also be other types that express discontent with or rejection of dominant values. These types will also be grounded in a normative world-view, but as an alternative to the dominant one.

Klapp calls these other types 'anomic types', and his basic examples are 'beat' heroes and 'square' villains and fools. The concept of 'anomie' was developed in sociological theory deriving from Durkheim. Unlike alienation, a term with which it is often confused, anomie is not seen as stemming from inequalities and struggles between social groups (classes, genders, races, minorities). To put the difference between the concepts crudely, we may say that people are said to feel 'anomic' because they do not fit in with prevailing norms and/or because they see the latter's pointlessness, whereas people are said to feel 'alienated' because the goals of society and the norms which carry them are the goals and norms of groups other than those to which the people in question belong. You feel anomic because you are outside society in general; you feel alienated because you are outside the ruling groups in society. From a Marxist perspective, then, Klapp's notion of 'anomic types' is problematic because it is based on the notion of anomie and hence is reducible to an inescapable, quasi-metaphysical *Angst* that does not challenge existing power relations in society. At the same time, the notion of types alternative, or in opposition, to types incarnating dominant values is suggestive and worth pursuing. What we have to examine is whether these types are anomic or alienated, in the senses just defined, and to ask whether these represent real challenges to the *status quo* and the dominant ideology or are simply 'holidays' from it.

i) The rebel

The type that springs most readily to mind in this context is 'the rebel'. In her article 'The Rebel Hero', a brief survey of this type, Sheila Whitaker lists John Garfield, Montgomery Clift, Marlon Brando, James Dean, Albert Finney, Paul Newman, Steve McQueen and Jane Fonda as representative of the rebel hero. She stresses different relations of rebellion – the immigrant (Garfield), the rebel against his own class (Clift), generation gap rebels (Brando, Dean), the anti-hero (Newman, McQueen, Finney) and the politically conscious rebel (Fonda). The question with these stars is – to what extent do they really embody oppositional views (and in what terms)?

We can break this question into two parts:–

a)   Are they informed by concepts of anomie or alienation? (I do not mean to imply that they or those responsible for their image were students of sociology; but sociological concepts like anomie and alienation can be seen as theoretical abstractions of widely-known beliefs and understandings – the common sense and political practice of society throw up the theoretical constructs of sociology which enable us to see that sense and that practice with greater clarity.) Are they grounded in material categories or in a generalised *Angst*? The answer does not seem to be clear cut. Immigration and youth are material categories, and one can see Finney and Fonda as embodying working-class and women's situations respectively. However, not all the rebels Whitaker lists can be seen in similar terms, nor is it clear that the rebellion of those who can is actually cast in terms of that material situation. Are Garfield's films *about* the oppression of immigrants? Is Finney in *Saturday Night and Sunday Morning* a rebel against the middle class? Brando, Dean and Fonda do expressly articulate the situation of youth and women, and could be said to be 'alienated' rebels to that degree;

b)   Do these stars, in expressing rebellion, heavily promote it or recuperate it? In answering this question, we would do as well to remember that in terms of 'effect' we do not really know whether Garfield *et al.* made people more rebellious or not. What we can examine is the degree to which the image points to the legitimacy of rebellion or its inadequacy. In general, I would suggest it does the latter, because of the characteristics of the *type* to which the stars belong and because of the film *narratives* in which they are placed. *The type itself* is problematic because firstly, most of the heroes are either actually anomic or largely so (see above), so that in the case of those that are not, the alienated/materialist elements are liable to be subsumed under anomie. (Garfield, Finney, Fonda are not rebelling as immigrant, worker, woman respectively, but because they don't 'fit' even amongst immigrants, workers and women.) Secondly, the heavy emphasis on youth in the type carries with it the notion of the 'passing phase', the 'inevitable', 'natural' rebellion (often shored up with garbled notions of the Oedipus complex). Youth is the ideal material term on which to displace social discontent, since young people always get older (and 'grow up'). Thus the rebellion of Garfield, Finney or Fonda can be seen as symptomatic of their youth rather than anything else. This process of displacement reflects that analysed in *Resistance through Rituals*,[7] whereby press reaction to youth movements of the fifties and sixties is shown to have consistently avoided recognising these movements as class-specific. Thirdly, the type is very little connected to the basic structures of society. Class really only has relevance in the case of Finney. Most of the heroes are male in very traditional ways (often enforced by generic associations from the Western and the thriller), though I would agree with Jack Babuscio that Clift and Dean, who were both gay, did something to launch a non-macho image of a man.[8] Fourthly, inarticulacy (a symptom of anomie) is the defining characteristic of the type, and it inhibits him/her from any analysis of his/her situation. (Fonda is, of course, the exception to the last two points. It may be that I am wrong to follow Whitaker's inclusion of her alongside Garfield *et al*. It may be that the cinematic rebel type is defined by being male and inarticulate, and that Fonda is a different type altogether. At the same time, many of the other points that can be made about the 'rebelliousness' of the rebel type do seem applicable to her attempt to embody radical attitudes.) The *narratives* of the films in which these stars appeared tend to recuperate rather than promote the rebellion they embody. This is partly due to the way in which they tend to develop the problem of the hero as an individual, quasi-psychological problem. The fault is liable to be located in her or him and not in the society in which she or he lives (e.g. *The Wild One, Klute*). When there is some suggestion that the problem lies outside the hero, then this problem is often defined as the failure of some persons in her or his world to live up to traditional concepts and dominant values. James Dean's two 'youth' films, *Rebel Without A Cause* and *East of Eden*, seem to me to indicate that the character played by Dean has problems that are not only his psychological hang-up but in the family situation in which he lives. This does not mean, however, that the films are critical of the family as an institution, but rather of the failure of the parents of the Dean character to fulfill adequately their familial roles. In *Rebel* he has too weak a father, in *Eden* too charismatic a mother. In other words, the rebellion against family is recuperated because it is against an inadequate family rather than the family as a social institution.

ii) The independent woman

Perhaps one of the reasons for the almost implacable recuperation of the rebel type is that she or he is too obviously oppositional to social values. A more covert example is the independent woman type (or series of types) embodied by Davis, Katharine Hepburn, Barbara Stanwyck, Rosalind Russell, Joan Crawford and others during the thirties and forties. Do these stars represent a more complete alternative or opposition to dominant values?

Molly Haskell on the superfemale and the superwoman

In *From Reverence to Rape*, Molly Haskell suggests a distinction within these stars between the superfemale and the superwoman. (The same star may be both types at different points in her career.) The superfemale is:

> . . . a woman who, while exceedingly 'feminine' and flirtatious, is too
> ambitious and intelligent for the docile role society has decreed she play.
> . . . She remains within traditional society, but having no worthwhile
> project for her creative energies, turns them onto the only available
> material – the people around her – with demonic results. (p.214)

The chief example of this category is Bette Davis, particularly in *Of Human Bondage, Jezebel, The Little Foxes, Dangerous, Dark Victory* and *Mr. Skeffington*. The superwoman is:

> . . . a woman who, like the superfemale, has a high degree of intelli-
> gence or imagination, but instead of exploiting her femininity, adopts
> male characteristics in order to enjoy male prerogatives, or merely to
> survive. (ibid.)

The chief examples here are Joan Crawford as Vienna (in *Johnny Guitar*) and Katharine Hepburn.

This is a suggestive distinction, although it could do with some working-up to be made more directly usable. Is it just a question of the difference between roles within and without the domestic arena? Are there characteristic narrative patterns that structure the representation of the two types? What is the relationship between the star as a total image and the specific character constructed in given films? Are the types carried by physical features, iconography of dress and gesture, modes of performance? These are genuine questions, not disguised attacks on Haskell's distinction. Answering them would be a way of clarifying the distinction and how it operates.

There is a second order of problems with the distinction, and that is how the superfemale or the superwoman actually embodies a radical alternative/opposition to prevalent female types. The 'superfemale' seems inevitably to be shown as demonic in her actions, and it is hard to distinguish her too firmly from other 'strong', 'magnetic' types such as the 'bitch' (Davis), the *femme fatale*, and the intellectual/ aristocratic type (Hepburn), all of which strongly discount the value of female strength and intelligence. At most, the superfemale type seems capable of articulating the damage done when a person of great capacities is confined to a demeaning or over-restricted world.

The superwoman on the other hand raises a more complex set of problems. What exactly is going on when a female character 'adopts male characteristics'? There are perhaps two ways of understanding this.

On the one hand, one can recognise that 'characteristics' of personality are not gender-specific (there is nothing innately male about aggressiveness or innately female about gentleness), but that, for whatever historical-cultural reasons, certain characteristics are associated with one gender rather than the other and that, as a consequence, individual women and men have a great deal invested (in terms of their identities as women and men) in preserving the association between such-and-such a character-istic and one gender or the other. This means that attempts to alter this, to cross gender barriers, to adopt the characteristics associated with the opposite sex, is a matter of negotiation, of working out a way of doing this which both frees people from the constrictions of gender-roles and yet does not utterly damage their self-identities. This seems to be the kind of process that Haskell admires in, especially, Katharine Hepburn. In her relationship with Spencer Tracy, 'Tracy can be humiliated and still rebound without (too much) loss of ego. Hepburn occasionally can defer to him and still not lose her identity'. (p.230) More generally, Hepburn's superwoman:

> . . . is able to achieve her ends in a man's world, to insist on her intelli-
> gence, to insist on using it, and yet be able to 'dwindle', like Millamant in
> The Way of the World, 'into marriage', but only after an equal bargain has
> been struck of conditions mutually agreed on. (p.230)

As Claire Johnston has pointed out, the emphasis in Haskell on 'reconciliation between men and women . . . flexibility of role playing, "love" and camaraderie' ignores 'the question of the nuclear family [that] has been central to the feminist critique of patriarchal culture' (Screen vol.16 no.3 p.121), and treats the problem simply as people deciding to relate better to each other rather than analysing what prevents this, where the roles come from. However, perhaps as a model of how relationships between the sexes might be conducted (a practical ideal rather than a romantic one), as a 'utopian' expression (telling us where we want to get to, rather than how to get there), the negotiated adoption of 'male characteristics' celebrated by Haskell could be acceptable as an alternative/oppositional statement. As she herself develops it, however, there are I think two further problems. One is that the women seem to have to do all the running, make all the moves (including most of the concessions); it might be worth examining one of the Tracy-Hepburn films to see how far Tracy is prepared to adopt 'female characteristics'. The second is that there is a strain of anti-gayness in her writing, which suggests that the ideal relationship between women and men is also the ideal human relationship – in other words, Haskell is heterosexually normative (or heterosexist).

On the other hand, some recent feminist theory suggests that in a patriarchal culture there is no such thing as 'the female', only the non-male.[9] That is to say that films are unable to conceive of, or to cope with, anything that is female, which means in effect that the only way a woman can be accepted as a person (except as a demeaned, and still ultimately threatening, sexual object) is for her to become 'non-male'; that is to say without gender. Although Haskell herself does not work within these terms, some of her accounts of the superwoman stars do support it. Thus the relationship between Joan Blondell and James Cagney in Blonde Crazy is based on:

> . . . the unspoken understanding that a woman is every bit the 'gentle-
> man' – or nongentleman – as a man is and can match him in wits and guts
> and maybe even surpass him. (p.130)

and she quotes a very revealing piece of dialogue from the Rosalind Russell film Take A Letter, Darling, in which Robert Benchley, her boss, complains that her competitors – all men – don't understand her –

'They don't know the difference between a woman and a . . .'
'A what?' Russell asks.
'I don't know,' Benchley replies, 'there's no name for you.'

The Hawks women that Haskell admires are accepted into the male group, as soon as they cease to be womanly – Jean Arthur in *Only Angels Have Wings* is a striking case in point. What seems to me to be happening in the narrative of these films is that there is a contempt for female characteristics yet an obligation to have woman characters. This problem is resolved in the person of the woman who becomes a man (almost). What one thinks about this procedure depends upon one's politics, and in particular whether one does despise female characteristics or whether one sees them as, certainly, oppressed and not, potentially anyway, gender specific, yet still nonetheless representing real strengths and values that form the basis and power of the women's movement.

Narrative and the independent woman

The 'independence' of the stars under consideration here is expressed both in the characters they play and in what was reported about them in magazines (e.g. Davis's fight with Warner Brothers over her contract. Hepburn's intellectual background, Crawford's struggle to the top from a background of poverty). Do the narratives of the films they appear in legitimate and promote this image, or undermine it?

The endings of the films usually involve a 'climb-down' on the part of the star. As Elizabeth Dalton observes, in a survey of Warner Brothers' films about working women:

> A woman could be resourceful, intelligent, even cynical, for 59 minutes but in the last two, she would realise that it was love and marriage that she really wanted.
>
> ('Women at Work: Warners in the Thirties', p.17)

This dénouement may also involve punishment and humiliation for the star – not only at the hands of the male character(s), but at the hands of the film itself. In *His Girl Friday*, when Rosalind Russell corners the sheriff who wants to avoid her questions, she is filmed in a way that makes her look comic, not resourceful. *Mildred Pierce* blames Mildred/Crawford for the death of her youngest daughter; despite the fact that the latter is in the care of her father at the time, the film manages to put the blame onto Mildred/Crawford for her independence. Though there are exceptions to the rule, the narratives do not appear to legitimise independence.

Haskell, however, has argued that, in a sense, these endings do not matter. What we remember is the independence not the climb-down or the humiliation:

> We see the June bride played by Bette Davis surrender her independence at the altar; the actress played by Margaret Sullavan in *The Moon's Our Home* submit to the straitjacket in which Henry Fonda enfolds and symbolically subjugates her; Katharine Hepburn's Alice Adams achieve her highest ambitions in the arms of Fred MacMurray; Rosalind Russell as an

advertising executive in *Take A Letter, Darling* find happiness in the same arms; Joan Crawford as the head of a trucking firm in *They All Kissed The Bride* go weak at the knees at the sight of labor leader played by Melvyn Douglas. And yet we remember Bette Davis not as the blushing bride but as the aggressive reporter and sometime-bitch; Margaret Sullavan leading Fonda on a wild-goose chase through the backwoods of Vermont; Katharine Hepburn standing on the 'secretarial stairway' to independence; Rosalind Russell giving MacMurray the eye as her prospective secretary; and Joan Crawford looking about as wobbly as the Statue of Liberty. (pp.3–4)

Of course, we cannot know what 'we' – the audience in general – remember, but I think one could argue that in terms of emphasis, weighting within the film, perform-ance, *mise en scène*, etc., the independence elements are stronger, more vivid, than the climb-down resolutions. Two observations support this. One, unlike the rebels, the narratives do not seem invariably to point to inadequacies in the psychology of either the independent woman stars or the people of their immediate environment to explain, and explain away, their independence. Two, because we are dealing with stars, and not just fictional characters, the specific details of what happens in the plot of the film may matter less than the 'personality' that the film as a whole reveals – the star phenomenon emphasises the kind-of-person the star is rather than the specific circumstances of particular roles.

Marjorie Rosen in *Popcorn Venus* argues that the narratives of the independent woman films always show the star's independence and intelligence in the service of men. It is men who define the social goals and norms; it is to get a man, or for love of a man, that the star acts as she does:

> It's unfortunate that Hollywood could not visualize a woman of mental acumen unless she was fixing up a mess her man/boss had made, covering a scoop to prove herself to a man, or deftly forging a life of dishonesty. (p.147)

It's hard to say how true this really is. Many of the films are about the star's independence *threatening* her relationship with the man she loves, but the pattern suggested by Rosen may also operate, thus effectively denying the woman's independ-ence any autonomy. *Now, Voyager* might be a case in point – the narrative details Davis's liberation from the dowdy spinster role imposed on her, yet it is a man, a psychiatrist (Claude Rains), who 'gives' her the 'means' to be free, and a man (Paul Henreid) who provides her with her ultimate project in life, namely, his daughter. Whilst this element is certainly there, it does not – in my opinion – totally undermine the progressive elements in the film. It is just one of the contradictions of the film, and I suspect this narrative aspect, when it is there, often largely acts as a contradiction of rather than an utter denial of 'independence'.

Extraordinary women

As Molly Haskell herself has pointed out, the independent women stars are often signalled as being exceptional or extraordinary women. Dietrich, Hepburn, Rosalind

Russell, Davis all have strong upper-class, intellectual or, in the case of Dietrich, exotic associations which make them 'exceptions to the rule, the aristocrats of their sex' (p.160). Haskell argues this 'weakens their political value'. I am not myself so sure of this. All stars are in one way or another exceptional, just as they are all ordinary. The un-extraordinary 'girl next door' types like June Allyson, Doris Day, Betty Grable are no less characteristic of the star phenomenon than are extraordinary types like Hepburn *et al*. It's worth remembering too that other independent women stars – Barbara Stanwyck, Ann Sheridan, Claire Trevor – do not carry upper-class or intellectual associations.

Sexual ambiguity and role playing

Many of the stars in the independent woman category were characterised by sexual ambiguity in their appearance and presentation. This can be an aspect of their physical attributes – the broad shoulders of Joan Crawford and Greta Garbo, Katharine Hepburn's height, the 'tough' face of Barbara Stanwyck, Bette Davis's strutting walk – which, in the case of Crawford, could also be exaggerated by the way she was dressed. It can also be a play on costume, sequences of cross-dressing such as:

> Dietrich in white tie and tails, Garbo as the lesbian Queen Christina (although with 'cover' romance), Eleanor Powell in top hat and tails for her tap numbers, and Katharine Hepburn as the Peter Pan-like Sylvia Scarlett; all introduced tantalizing notes of sexual ambiguity that became permanent accretions to their screen identities.
>
> (Haskell, p.132)

This could of course be seen as another instance of cinema being unable to cope with the female and so presenting splendid women as men. However, recent discussion of the cinema in relation to homosexuality has suggested a different emphasis.

Janet Meyer and Caroline Sheldon see these stars as an oblique expression of lesbianism:

> The qualities they projected of being inscrutable to the men in the films and aloof, passionate, direct, could not be missed. They are all strong, tough and yet genuinely tender. In short, though rarely permitted to hint it, they are lesbians.
>
> (Janet Meyer, 'Dyke goes to the Movies', p.37)

Sheldon suggests in *Gays and Film* that if we understand lesbianism, not necessarily in purely sexual terms, but in terms of 'woman-identification', then these stars are lesbian. They are 'women who define themselves in their own terms', '. . . playing parts in which they are comparatively independent of domestic expectations and of men'. Meyer and Sheldon are working within a lesbian feminist political perspective, that will not be acceptable to many (including many feminists), but their emphasis is a useful corrective to Haskell's heterosexist assumptions. Both recognise that lesbianism (in the erotic sense) may be used in film for the titillation of heterosexual men, but the sense of aloofness, 'otherness', and non-domesticity combined with sometimes quite overtly erotic relationships with women could be seen as subversive of the heterosexual male's pleasure at being titillated.

Jack Babuscio and I have suggested a different emphasis to this, whereby the cross-dressing and play on sexual roles can be seen as a way of heightening the fact that the sex roles are *only* roles and not innate or instinctual personal features. This can be seen as part of the phenomenon of camp in the cinema:

> Camp, by focusing on the outward appearances of role, implies that roles and, in particular, sex roles are superficial – a matter of style . . . Finding stars camp is not to mock them . . . It is more a way of poking fun at the whole cosmology of restrictive sex roles and sexual identifications which our society uses to oppress its women and repress its men – including those on screen.
>
> (Jack Babuscio, *Gays and Film*, pp.44, 46)[10]

In this respect then, independent-woman type stars make explicit the life-as-theatre metaphor which underpins the star phenomenon. This can be seen especially in the work of Bette Davis. Davis is one of the most 'mannered' of the independent women – or any other – stars, yet being mannered effectively foregrounds manners as a social code. With most stars, their particular manner is seen as a spontaneous emanation of the personality; but Davis is hard to treat in the same way since her manner is so obviously 'put on'. In certain films – *Jezebel, The Little Foxes, Dark Victory, Now, Voyager, All About Eve* – this sense of the artifice of social performance meshes with notions of social expectations and requirements, of women and/or of class. (Cf. the discussion [. . .] below of her performance in *The Little Foxes*. Another similar instance is Barbra Streisand. I have discussed the possibly subversive effect of her performance in *The Way We Were* in *Movie* no. 22.)

Notes

1   Barbara Gelman (ed.), *Photoplay Treasury*; Richard Griffith (ed.), *The Talkies*; Martin Levin (ed.), *Hollywood and the Great Fan Magazines*.

2   *Film Pictorial*, September 30, 1933; reprinted by Peter Way Ltd. in 1972 as part of the series 'Great Newspapers Reprinted'.

3   *The Talkies*, pp.106–7, 302–4.

4   Solutions to the production of surplus include the expansion of overseas markets and war, but also the stimulation of home consumption through advertising, product differentiation, etc., all leading to an emphasis on consumption, hence the tag, 'the consumer society'. See J.K. Galbraith, *The Consumer Society* and Paul Baran and Paul Sweezy, *Monopoly Capital*.

5   See note 1 to Part One concerning King's work.

6   *The Talkies*, pp.136–7, 331; *The Talkies*, pp.140–142, 337; *Photoplay Treasury*, pp.144–7, *Hollywood and the Great Fan Magazines*, pp.94–6.

7   In Tony Jefferson *et al.* (eds.), *Resistance through Rituals*, originally published as *Working Papers in Cultural Studies* 7/8.

8   See Jack Babuscio, 'Screen Gays' in *Gay News* nos. 79 (Dean) and 104 (Clift).
9   The *locus classicus* of the view that 'culture is male' is Simone de Beauvoir: *The Second Sex*. For a discussion of more recent, psycho-analytically oriented theorisations, see Elizabeth Cowie, 'Woman as Sign', *m/f* no.1.
10 See also Richard Dyer, 'It's being so camp as keeps us going', *Body Politic* (Toronto) no. 36, pp.11–13.

PART TWO

The textual and the extra-textual dimensions of the public persona

Introduction to part two

■ P. David Marshall

I MAGINE THREE DIMENSIONS: One dimension – "storyworld" – is contained within a narrative. It has characters who act in a certain way within the framework of the story. Storyworld is enhanced by having actors play these characters, and these renditions are recorded both to be seen by more people and repeatedly.

The second dimension – "Realworld" – has stories and tales about the actors who play their parts in Storyworld. In Realworld, the actors may talk about their roles in Storyworld or they may talk about their own lives. These stories are not as contained as Storyworld and can expand outwards in unpredictable ways; but these renditions are recorded similarly to Storyworld to be seen by more people and repeatedly.

The third dimension – "Audienceworld" – is the place for the interpretation of Storyworld and Realworld. It is filled with the people that are targeted by Storyworld and Realworld. Audienceworld may generate interpretations of the meaning of particular characters or it may try to interpret the meaning of the actors playing characters and roles. Audienceworld actually works to link Storyworld and Realworld together. Although some in Audienceworld record new stories, they are not seen very widely.

Celebrity culture produces chains of signification which cross these various dimensions and activities. The meaning of a celebrity is a combination of some primary texts such as a film, secondary texts such as interviews and paparazzi photos, and tertiary audience work on the meaning of these various texts. Layers and layers of texts thus are piled onto the meaning of the individual celebrity that operate like sediments. Some of these texts, when acted upon by audiences and industries, serve to "fossilize" or instantiate the celebrity into a particular type or character; and others work to modify the mold or at least allow for the transformation of the dominant meaning of the public individual.

Readings in this section flesh out the cultural and technological apparatuses that both connect these textual dimensions of the celebrity and essentialize their activities and meanings.

Chapter 9

John Langer

TELEVISION'S 'PERSONALITY SYSTEM'

I BEGIN WITH A question: What is the significance of the fact that whereas the cinema established a 'star system', television has not? There are stars of stage screen *and* television, but no stars of television alone. Instead we encounter what television calls its 'personalities'—those individuals constituted more or less exclusively for and by television, who make regular appearances as news readers, moderators, hosts, compères or characters, and those individuals who exist outside of television in their own right, but are recruited *into* television at various strategic junctures as resource material – politicians, celebrities, experts or 'ordinary people . . . made strangely important' (Monaco, 1978: 7). This question is not asked innocently. First, it assumes that television, along with other institutional agencies of the superstructure, displays 'a systematic tendency . . . to reproduce the ideological field of a society in such a way as to reproduce also its structure of domination' (Hall, 1977: 346). This is achieved by television's ability to construct social knowledge selectively, to establish classifying schemes which 'actively rule in and rule out certain realities', and integrate these definitions of reality into a consensual order 'in which the direct and naked intervention of the real unities (of class, power, exploitation and interest) are forever held somewhat at bay' (Hall, 1977: 340–342). Second, in order to understand television's place in ideology it has to be seen in terms of the way it produces its 'symbolic goods'. We can only understand what television *means* ideologically by finding out *how* it means and by analyzing the way in which this works. What television 'says' is merely what it claims to say – the window on the world, the live broadcast, the direct satellite report, balance, impartiality – are part of television's claim that it is simply a transparent medium for the message behind it. The production of television messages, however, cannot be accomplished without the intervention or mediation of certain codes, conventions, operational rules or structures of usage. Events on their own cannot 'mean'. They must be 'made intelligible', transformed into symbolic discourses for television's purposes. It is this process of what Hall describes as 'encoding' – selecting codes which give meaning to events – which allows television to perform its ideological work. Universalized and naturalized, these codes become the currency of common sense, appearing to be the only forms of intelligibility available, the only field of possible meanings from which to choose, both for audience *and* for those who make television programmes.

> That they contain premises, that these premises embody dominant def-initions of the situation, and represent or refract the existing structures of power, wealth and domination, hence that they structure every event they signify and accent them in a manner which reproduces the given ideo-logical structures – this process has become unconscious even for the encoders.
>
> (Hall, 1977: 344)

Third, for television to perform its ideological work effectively and to provide it with 'the least inhibited passage', the 'sense' by which television constructs its symbolic goods needs to 'win consent' in the audience to its 'preferred readings'. This does not mean in terms of some 'biased' presentation, or capturing audiences through success-ful programming, but by the very *legitimacy* of the encoding practices themselves. Hence, the day to day professional working principles used to put together television programmes – the structure of everyday practices of encoding – also come to struc-ture the way the audience will receive and 'decode' television's messages. As Hall points out, at the phenomenal level these practices 'seem to amount to recipes and tags which can be integrated within the notion of what constitutes *good* television' (Hall, 1976: 246–252). 'Good television' can be characterized by the way it presents itself for watching: it is smooth, rapid, close to 'reality', transparent as a medium, straightforward, balanced, not overly rhetorical or deeply committed, on-going, polite, visually dramatic and full of incident. 'Good television' also personalizes whenever it can, rarely using a concept or idea without attaching it to or transforming it through the 'category of the individual'. As a result, 'good television' is television that embodies and articulates a world of 'personalities' who thoroughly penetrate and organize its viewing agendas, or enter television by being on those agendas. It is with this 'personaliaty system', which television celebrates and orchestrates as one of its 'preferred codes', and through which it sustains some of its ideological work, that the rest of this article will be concerned.

Two qualifications are presented. First, the forms of television need to be recog-nized as a 'complex unity', heterogeneous and multi-faceted, with a vast range of codes simultaneously making up the totality of television output, some working in contradiction to others. Therefore, any attempt to delineate television's personality system does not necessarily imply a blanket, totally schematized process of encoding which holds in all cases. Like television's reproduction of the ideological field in dominance, the television personality system must be referred to only as a 'systematic tendency'. Nonetheless, this systematic tendency can be read symptomatically as a way of entering critical discussion of television's place in ideology. Second, the dis-tinction which will be made between 'fiction'/'dramatic' forms of television and 'actuality'/'factual'/'non-fiction' forms of television is purely arbitrary and used only for analytic purposes. It has been relatively well established in a variety of instances that those forms of television purported to be most closely aligned with the 'real world' – news, sports, documentaries – are consistently structured in terms which are generally regarded as representative of traditional dramatic forms. In one basic sense, all television is 'a fiction' (see, for example, Epstein, 1973; McArthur, 1978; Buscombe, 1976).

A brief glance at any current television programme guide will give some indication of the pervasiveness of the personality system. Virtually every television form has incorporated within its structure some aspect of this system. Those television genres which can be crudely classified as non-fiction, actuality forms – news, current affairs, talk shows, variety, game and quiz shows to name just a few of the dominant and historically well-established of these forms – are all significantly structured in and around various manifestations of the television personality. Each of these genres is developed and organized around a central persona or sometimes personae – the news 'reader', the current affairs 'anchorman', the talk show 'host', the variety programme 'headliner', the quiz show 'master of ceremonies' – each of whom appears to be essential to the programme's unfolding action, pace and thematic directions, as well as providing his/her 'on-air personality' as a crucial aspect of the programme's televisual identity. Television's traditional fiction forms – the cop show, the situation comedy, the soap opera, the mini series – are similarly structured around personalities, not 'real' personalities as in the case of actuality television, but central 'characters' through whom the narrative is generated. It is not surprising then to find that so many of television's fictional forms take as titles the names of their leading characters – *McCloud, Columbo, Perry Mason, Rhoda, The Brady Bunch* are only a small sample from the endlessly repeated variations of this theme. McArthur makes a similar point in relation to television's historical drama series, where history is above all else the dramatic construction of historical 'personages' articulated as 'personalities', and once again the titles of the programmes are reflective of this structure: *Edward the Seventh, Jenny, Elizabeth R, Elenor Marx, The Six Wives of Henry the Eighth* (McArthur, 1978).

Advertising on television employs the same formulation. Recommendations for products become the function of particular personalities who are then inexorably bonded to that product and its brand name. In some cases these personalities are constituted specifically for television – thus the manicurist 'Madge' as named personality is synonomous with a particular brand of dishwashing liquid. In other instances, individuals situated in some external sphere of influence as celebrities are incorporated into television advertising as 'personalities'. Once incorporated, they lend their celebrityhood to products so that the product is interchangeable with it – one is a sign of the other. The world of sport and show business are rich quarries for this kind of personality coding in television. Even 'already made films', discrete cultural objects in their own right, are reshaped within the boundaries of the personality system each time television's film formats are structured around the ubiquitous 'host'. No longer is it just a matter of 'watching a movie on TV'. One watches with an ever-watchful host, who guides us through the viewing situation pointing out the film's highlights and delights and who, depending on his or her particular time slot, may make up to five appearances a week – for example, the midday movie matinée, a regularly hosted event on most television channels in Australia.

Star system and personality system as paradigms

In order to locate and define the personality system as it is coded into television it may be useful to look at what might be seen as its paradigmatic counterpart and historical antecedent in the cinema – the star system. It has been argued that the star system experienced and finally fell victim to the 'embourgeoisement of the cinematic imagination', which eventually saw the transformation of stars from 'gods and goddesses, heroes, models' – embodiments of ideal ways of behaving to 'identification figures, embodiment of typical ways of behaving' (Dyer, 1979: 24). According to Morin, this process was inextricably bound up with cinema's 'search for realism', which was marked by certain technical innovations (the introduction during the 1930s, the psychologization of cinema's protagonists and paradoxically, the 'dogma' of the happy ending. 'Realism, psychologism, the "happy ending" . . . reveal precisely the bourgeois transformation of this imagination' (Morin, in Dyer, 1979: 25)

> Chance and occult possession are replaced by psychological motivation. Bourgeois individualism cannot take the death of the hero, hence the insistence on the happy ending. So stars become more usual in appearance, more 'psychologically' credible in personality, more individuated in image.
>
> (Dyer, 1979: 25)

Stars became less directly the filmic representatives of particular 'virtues' or 'essences'. The cinematic archetype – the vamp, the good girl, the gentleman, the clown, the innocent, the landlord – gave way to more individuated social types. Psychological realism and the motivational credibility of screen characters were accompanied by the desire of audiences to know the stars that played these characters 'as people', to have access to their 'real' lives, to what they were 'really' like; in short, to know their 'personalities' – hence the proliferation of the fan magazines and the publicity machine which became crucial to the star system as an image maker. Lowenthal traces a similar process at work during the first half of the century in the expansion of biographical stories in popular magazines, where he finds a significant shift away from what he calls the 'idols of production' who serve primarily as 'educational models' to be 'looked upon as examples of success which can be imitated' (Lowenthal, 1961: 113) toward the 'idols of consumption' who provide a 'readily grasped empire', merely confirming 'identification with normalcy' (ibid.: 135). Analyzing the stories over time, he discovers that 'while it once was rather contemptible to give much room to the private affairs and habits of public figures, the topic is now the focus of interest' (ibid.: 119). Parentage, personal relationships, friendships, domesticity, sociability, hobbies and culinary proclivities abound as the thematic structures through which the heroes and celebrities of magazine biography are revealed in their 'private lives', not so very different a format, so it seems, from that used in the fan magazine for the star system.

This 'intimate vision' with its attendant 'obsession with persons' – one of the most pervasive conditions characterizing social life under modern capitalism (Sennett, 1974) – seriously eroded the 'divine' status of the star system, but it did not succeed in doing this completely. As Morin points out, the star does not cease to be special, but now combines 'the exceptional with the ordinary, the ideal with the everyday' (Morin in Dyer, 1979: 25). The 'magic' of the silver screen still lingers, even if this is only in terms of a collective but very powerful folk memory of Hollywood 'as it used to be'. It is left to television's personality system to take up this process of embourgeoisement and move it forward, considerably advancing the 'intimate vision' to the point where what is presented on television is precisely that which is 'the ordinary', where 'the everyday' has superseded and supplanted 'the exceptional', where 'the exceptional' is the exception rather than the rule.

In some respects what might be termed the classical paradigm of the star system, before its subjugation to the 'reign of intimacy', can be situated in direct opposition to the personality system manifest in television. It is this opposition which begins to articulate some of the terms of each system. Whereas the star presenting the cinematic universe as 'larger than life', the personality system is cultivated almost exclusively as 'part of life', whereas the star system always has the ability to place distance between itself and its audiences through its insistence on 'the exceptional', the personality system works directly to construct and foreground intimacy and immediacy; whereas contact with stars is unrelentingly sporadic and uncertain, contact with television personalities has regularity and predictability; whereas stars are always playing 'parts' emphasizing their identity as 'stars' as much – perhaps even more than – the characters they play, television personalities 'play' themselves, whereas stars emanate as idealizations or archetypal expressions, to be contemplated, revered, desired and even blatantly imitated, stubbornly standing outside the realms of the familiar and the routinized, personalities are distinguished for their representativeness, their typicality, their 'will to ordinariness', to be accepted, normalized, experienced as *familiar*.

Media contexts

If television is indeed an apparatus for the production of symbolic goods which are made intelligible by a process of encoding, how then is the personality system 'arranged' within the television discourse, and what operations are at work which preclude the formation of a star system? To begin with what at first glance seems most obvious: watching television by and large, as a socially constructed act, takes place, to use a phrase adopted frequently and fondly by television's practitioners, 'in the comfort of one's own home', very much embedded within the intimate setting that circumscribes the routines of everday life; watching film, however, except of course those on television, leads away from the home, elsewhere into an unfamiliar 'exceptional' setting not directly connected with the network of intimacies which make up everyday life. Television is always 'there', routinely encountered and ready for use whenever the television experience is required. Cinema watching, on the other hand, needs to be pre-arranged, calculated and attended to. The intimacy of domestic life has to be set aside in order to participate in the 'special' experience of the cinema. In fact this is one of the major ways in which film as a leisure activity is promoted in advertising – 'give yourself a break, go to a movie', 'go for a night out and be entertained'. The television image is 'close', occupying a relatively restricted space within the field of vision (Heath and Skirrow, 1977: 54), in a sense positioning the spectator to take a 'closer look'. It can be acted on and manipulated in the moment of transmission – turned on, off, fine tuned or switched for alternative images. Because of its proximity to the ebb and flow of every day life it can be received casually, with the potential to become the focus for social participation during the viewing situation itself. The film screen image, in contrast, hovers over and above the spectator massively imposing itself upon the visual field. By not being subject to control or modification at the time of its reception, it remains 'distant, inaccessible and fascinatingly fixed' (Heath and Skirrow, 1977: 54). Once the film begins, even if one goes with a group of people to the theatre, the conditions of viewing are constituted by anonymity – the nexus of screen image and spectator alone, silent and in the dark, the possibility of social participation ruled out until the film is over.

Like the world, television never stops, is more or less continuous (Heath and Skirrow, 1977: 54). Its reality runs a parallel course to the reality of everyday life itself, can be tuned in or out at will, and can be 'met' virtually at any one point in time. Television's 'flow' is contemporaneous with the flow of life. So, not only is television 'always already available', there will always be something to watch immediately, as soon as the set warms up. Television's 'communicationality' is not constrained by time or scheduling. Certainly there are programmes organized around particular time slots within the continuous flow, but if one programme is missed, there will always be another one to take its place. As Heath and Skirrow explain, 'the role of the image is to be present' (ibid.: 56). Cinema, on the other band, is more institutionally grounded within temporal operations – it requires active attention to its delineation in time. Unlike just sitting down to 'watch television', 'going to the movies' generally means going on time, 'getting there for the credits', 'not wanting to miss the beginning', 'staying to the end'.

At this point it becomes clear that those apparently 'natural' taken-for-granted arrangements which differentially structure viewing in relation to film and television are also working to inscribe and reproduce an entire cluster of terms – distance/intimacy, ordinary/extraordinary, familiar/exceptional, immediate/remote – as they pertain to the star/personality systems, and this occurs even before the set is switched on or the film is rolling through the projector gate. The act of television watching is found in the intimate and familiar terrain of everyday life where we receive television's own 'intimacies' and 'familiarities' brought to us through its personalities. This correspondence between the intimacy structure of television watching and the way in which intimacy is structured through the personality system forms one of the major conditions through which television negotiates effectively to win the consent of audiences and to render invisible its ideological work.

The regular and the episodic

If one of television's central characteristics is the 'experience of flow', another is its ritual regularity, its tendency 'toward an idea that it is capable of reproduction'. (Alvarado and Buscombe, in Eaton, 1978/79: 68). Within the sequential flow of television there are moments carved out and arranged into particular cyclical, repeatable televisual occurrences which give the flow its shape and substance. Television programming, in the main, operates in terms of 'seasons' – the series, for example, if initiated, usually runs for a number of consecutive episodes normally scheduled at the same time on the same day each week, although these schedules may be altered in response to poor ratings. If a series is deemed successful – winning ratings, capturing audiences and landing sponsors – there is every chance that it will re-appear for the next season. On this basis a series can be sustained for several years in a row. This has, in fact, been common practice with genres like the police drama, the situation comedy, or the late-night talk show. Other programmes are not necessarily subject to seasonality – the news cycle, for example, is one which recurs each day, and possibly several times a day on a single channel all through the year. These cycles of repetition provide a forum for the regular appearance of the personality – the newsreader, the talk show host, the lead actor in a cop show – around which the programme is organized. As a result, these cyclical repetitions tend to play a part in television's structure of intimacy and immediacy. Each repeated appearance, even though it may not elicit 'personal data' – as in the case of the very formal demeanor of the newsreader – nonetheless tends to build what is perceived to be a knowable and known 'television self'. This television self, increasingly authenticated with each regular appearance, coheres into the form of a 'genuine' personality. Finally, the very appearance itself becomes a mark of knowledge about that personality.

This, of course, is quite different from the appearance of a star in a film, which occurs perhaps twice in a year at best. The star's appearance occurs as an eventful arrival, often heralded ahead of time in press and industry releases, not to be repeated in that same context again, except perhaps in a sequel. Even there, however, the event is discrete and unique. It needs to be caught in its singularity, and if it is repeated, it always emerges full blown in its originally fixed form. Access to stars through their films must be deferred over long periods of time: it is episodic and ephemeral, coming only once in a while. In between appearances, time can be spent re-viewing their earlier films or reading fan magazines in an attempt to rekindle the 'aura', or other stars can be taken up and appreciated. There is none of this capriciousness or uncertainty where the television personality is concerned. He or she reliably appears over and over again, week after week, even year after year, providing the coherent fixed point of regularity within the overall flow of television. By never becoming overly routinized and familiar the star system can maintain its remoteness and unattainability, whereas the personality system, crucially embedded within televison's cyclical rituals can much more readily facilitate a sense of familiarity and accessibility.

Identity

Television personalities also become anchoring points within the internal world that each programme uniquely establishes in and for itself. They exist as more or less stable 'identities' within the flow of events, situations or narratives which are presented in a particular programme at any given point in its cycle of repetition. For example, despite the panoramic flow of news stories which constitute any single early evening news broadcast, it is always the newsreader who remains the constant, unfaltering and coherent indentity, who 'carries on regardless'. The world changes, but the television personality stays the same. In the case of the news, one of the conventionalized marks of this coherent stable identity which persists despite a world of flux and change, is the way the news reader is framed by the camera. The head and shoulders dominate, appearing balanced and central in glistening, unwavering focus – like the authoritative carriage of a portrait – which looks at us with calm deliberation. The 'real' world, where stories come from, is, in contrast, often skewed, off balance, with shaky camera work done in the heat of the newsworthy moment. The 'real' world may be unstable and unbalanced, but the world of the television news personality who *explains* that world to us is not.

The establishment of the television personality as a coherent identity is also the occasion for coherence to be imparted to what is potentially a diverse and seemingly chaotic universe of events. Newsreaders, then, not only function as coherent identities in the flow of events, but they act as the principle instrument for classifying and unifying these events into some kind of acknowledged order. The newsreader is responsible for giving events meaning, placing them in referential contexts and provid-ing appropriate clues to their significance in 'the scheme of things', functioning as 'a very definite ethical figure (giving) unity to what is essentially a very disjointed format' (Mills, 1980). Similar encoding procedures work to build the personality system across a whole range of non-fiction/actuality forms of television – essentially the same principles appear to be at work in current affairs, talk shows, variety shows, documentaries and so on.

Once again, the persistent tendency of television to feature the name of its personalities in the programme titles appears in relation of its 'factual' forms – *The Don Lane Show, The Mike Walsh Show, Shirl's Neighbourhood, Simon Townsend's Wonder World, Parkinson in Australia, Whicker's World* – confirming right from the outset the critical centrality of the television personality's identity within the television flow and within the programme's own structure. The title proclaims unequivocally that this is *their* show, *their* vehicle where we can reliably and repeatedly encounter them, no matter what else might happen along the way, either inside the show itself or before and after it. If a programme is designated in strictly generic terms like 'the early evening news' (which may in fact be a way of signalling the journalistic ideology of objectivity/ neutrality; the news 'belongs' to no one), there are often elaborate efforts made through advertising to distinguish the programme as an entity from its counterparts on other channels by infusing it with some kind of identity linked to the newsreader of the news reading 'team' thus Channel 9's news is presented to us by 'the men with experience', Channel 10's is centred around a dynamic young team whose compatibil-ity 'only comes along once in a while' and Channel 7's news is read by 'a man who knows what he is talking about'.[1]

The significance of the television personality's star identity seems to have its parallels in television's fictional or dramatic forms as well, although it operates in a more complex fashion. Many shows demand some sort of narrative progression across the series in the interests of dramatic realism, where a character or characters develop through and by means of a number of experiences from week to week or season to season (Eaton, 1978/79: 69). In the situation comedy *All in the Family*, for example, the narrative develops from an initial 'situation' – Archie, Edith, their daughter Gloria and her husband Mike are living together in the same house and Archie is working in a factory. In the course of several seasons Archie takes up a new vocation, becoming the proprietor of a local bar, and Mike and Gloria have a child and move to California, hence out of the series. However, despite definite temporal developments – which tend to be unusual unless a programme has been running for several years – 'the idea of the series' itself always prevails. The temporal development of the situation comedy, or any other series, never occurs at the expense of the cycles of repetition. According to Eaton, nothing is allowed to happen in the narrative to radically alter or complicate the character or the situation. Events from the 'outside' are permitted entry into the 'situation', but these events have to be dealt with and then expelled so that the characters remain coherent and stable within this problematic (ibid.: 70). For example, Edith has a major menopausal trauma which begins, develops and is conveniently resolved all in the space of one episode, never to be referred to again, leaving her intact and basically unaltered as a character. Similarly, Starsky, one of the hip young plain-clothes police officers in the series *Starsky and Hutch* falls in love with a dedicated social worker who subsequently gets shot and dies as a result of a vendetta set up by one of Starsky's old enemies. Again, the narrative's events emerge, develop and get resolved entirely within a single discrete episode, never to surface again, and Starsky emerges from this apparently traumatic occurrence unscarred as a character, as evidenced by his performance in the next cycle of action the following week. As in the case of television's non-fictional forms, the world of television drama changes, but the television personality stays the same: once a character, always a character. Two viewings establish this fact, the first to locate the distinctive 'qualities' of the television character, the second to confirm them. From then on, it is more or less 'known' that this is the way these characters will behave, with seemingly little variation. The humour in a situation comedy like *All in the Family* comes in part not from the element of surprise or novelty, but from anticipating when Archie will 'do something funny' the way he did it the week before. These ritualized routines come to represent his identifiable, reliable features as a 'personality'. Each episode one waits for Archie to call Mike a 'meathead', Edith a 'dingbat', get confused over large words, tell someone to get out of his chair, roll his eyes in exasperation or make a racist remark. These become the foibles to look forward to each week, which create the 'timeless-nowness of television situations' (Eaton, 1978/79: 70) and which help to sustain a sense of familiarity and intimacy.

Of course this kind of anticipated repetition happens with stars as well. If one goes to see a western with John Wayne in it, one expects to see him as the laconic man of few words who ties his horse to the hitching post with idiosyncratic flair and will always be good with his fists as well as a gun. What is important, however, is that in the cinema these attributes are seen to reside in the *star* as performer, whereas in television they reside in the *character* being constructed. The character in a film is, in a special sense, the vehicle for the star to perform on. Dyer explains that

> stars are known as performers because what is interesting about them is not the character they have constructed . . . but rather the business of constructing/performing/being . . . a 'character'.
>
> (Dyer, 1979: 24)

The star's presence in a film is one of the major ways by which films are 'read' by audiences. One speaks of 'a John Wayne film' or a 'film with John Wayne in it', rarely remembering the name of the character that John Wayne actually played. The star absorbs the identity of the film character, taking it over as his/her own, so that finally it vanishes completely. The process seems to operate in reverse in relation to television personalities. Who, for example, recalls that Archie Bunker is really the actor Carroll O'Connor, or Starsky is played by Michael Glaser. In television fiction it is the characters themselves that maintain a high public profile and are retained as memorable identities. The actors who 'play' them are virtually invisible and anonymous. What is remembered in television is not the name of the performer, but the name of the recurrent character or personality in the series.

Notable exceptions to this process are shows like *The Jimmy Stewart Show, The Tony Randall Show* or *The Doris Day Show* where individuals who exist as 'stars' outside of television become incorporated into it on a regular basis, usually as protagonists in a series. Like stars in films, these appropriated stars essentially absorb the character they play, so that what is remembered, for example, is Lucille Ball rather than the character she performs in her series. Nonetheless, the 'idea of the series' itself powerfully structures the stars within a cycle of repetition so that, if they are a part of a series for long enough, they finally move from a film past which has been constructed around their status as 'stars' to a television present which is constructed around television's tendency to produce personalities. Thus, over time, distant and inaccessible Lucille Ball becomes familiar and predictable 'Lucy'.

Finally, it might be noted that in the cinema, because identity and characteristic attributes are lodged with the star rather than in any part which he or she plays, moving from film to film and from character to character causes few problems. However, these transitions are less smooth for the television personality. An actor going from one long-running series where identity is well established to a new series in order to 'play' a new character may encounter reluctant acceptance from the television audience. Any straightforward 'reading' of the new programme is complicated by the lingering residue of the earlier show's 'personality'. Hence, Raymond Burr as Chief Inspector Ironside can never become fully autonomous from Raymond Burr as Perry Mason; the television personality can never be extricated from past television lives. This may account for television's frequent use of the 'spin-off', which is usually explained in terms of 'programme popularity'. When a satellite character from one series ends up as the central personality/title character in another show – *Lou Grant* and *Rhoda* from *The Mary Tyler Moore Show*, *Maude* from *All in the Family*, and *Laverne and Shirley* from *Happy Days* – the consistency of character identity is preserved, the actor stays invisible, and the discomfort of an incongruous 'reading' is avoided.

Disclosure: talk shows, interviews, talking heads

If television's personality system is inflicted through a vision of intimacy, what better way to promote this vision than to set aside certain places within the flow of television where intimacy itself can be both the form and substance of programming. These places are usually filled by the ubiquitous talk shows, but they are also taken by the more idiosyncratic programmes such as *This is Your Life*. These programmes have no direct equivalent in relation to the star system, except perhaps the fan magazine or the gossip column with their anxious concern to locate the 'real person' assumed to lurk behind the star image. This search for intimacy, however, is never carried on within the film object as such, but is always arranged around it at a secondary level, whereas television has been able to incorporate it directly into itself as a routine part of its discourse. In the context of the talk show's carefully orchestrated informality, with its illusion of lounge-room casualness and leisurely pace, the host and guest engage in 'chat'. During the course of this chat, with suitable questions and tactful encouragement from the host, the guest is predictably 'drawn in' to making certain 'personal' disclosures, revealing aspects of what may be generally regarded as the private self – in fact, becoming incorporated into television's personality system by disclosing for the purposes of television, one's 'personality'.

Talk shows, however, are rarely just 'about' intimate talk between guest and host. Chat has its price. A tacit exchange of 'goods' takes place around which the talk show is structured – guests can 'be themselves' with the stipulation that time is allocated for the promotion of their latest enterprise. Thus, the talk serves as an advertising forum for any number of commodities or services which guests happen to be involved with at the time of their appearance. Nonetheless, if certain products, concerts, or books, and when and where to obtain them, get mentioned along the way, their overt status as commodities is always posed as secondary to congenial talk and public offerings of personal anecdotes. What prevails in the end is not the talk show's diluted huckster-ism and commercial 'hype', but its capacity to provide a special setting for personal disclosure where guests appear to be showing us their 'real' selves, where they can discuss how they 'feel' and reflect on their private lives with impunity. If these guests are among the ranks of the great and powerful, or are well known celebrities, which is most frequently the case, this is the place where the cares and burdens of high office or public life can momentarily be set aside, where we can see them as they 'really are', which in the end after all, as these programmes set out to illustrate, is just like us, 'ordinary folks'.

Whatever else they might represent, structurally talk shows are really just extended interviews which appear to allow guests 'to speak for themselves'. As one of the major codes used to organize talk on television, the interview has been naturalized across a variety of television's actuality forms. The news, current affairs, sports and documentaries regularly recruit individuals who exist outside of television, but whose appearances are constituted primarily in terms of an interview situation where they can be seen in a scene speaking for themselves (Heath and Skirrow, 1977: 46). Apart from the literal contents of talk, another level of meaning operates within the structure of the interview. Simply put, what is important is not so much what you actually say, but the fact that you can be seen saying it *for yourself*. The very act of speaking for oneself is a type of disclosure. Talking for yourself and being 'caught' and recorded doing so individuates you, makes you a personality whether you are the Prime Minister or last week's national lottery winner. The key strategy in terms of disclosure in the talk show interview, for example, is the fact that we see the personal confession or revelation taking place *before our very eyes*. The actual scene/seen of disclosure is *there* for us to know and to judge. As Barthes points out, 'pictures . . . are more imperative than writing, they impose meaning at one stroke, without analysing or diluting it' (Barthes, 1973: 130). The interview in a fan magazine may have as much and possibly even more personal detail than the television talk show interview, but the 'personal' is not intimately and immediately 'present' in the same way. When the subject of the interview is framed by the camera as a 'talking head', through a relatively close-up shot of the face, which television convention usually insists on, the disclosure effect becomes doubly articulated, generating an even more compelling sense of the intimate and the immediate. Special psychological significance is widely claimed for the close-up, since it is this kind of shot, out of the repertoire of all possible shots, which is thought to provide the optimal conditions for the disclosure of the 'most subjective and individual of human manifestations'. To Balazs, for example, the close-up acts to reveal the 'language of the face' in which reside 'the hidden mainsprings of the unique personality' (Balazs, in Dyer, 1979: 16–17). Thus speaking for oneself on television also means speaking through the language of facial expression, and together these two encoding operations work toward producing the personality system and saturating it with a sense of intimacy.

It needs to be carefully noted, however, that neither in the instance of the interview nor the close-up is television merely operating as a transparent medium through which the personality may be glimpsed as it is disclosed in speech or appearance. The reading of facial expressions is derived from several complex interlocking sets of artistic, social and textual conventions: personality on television does not just 'appear' unrestrained in close-up (Dyer, 1979: 17). Similarly, individuals seen in television interviews do *not* in fact 'speak for themselves', but are thoroughly situated and organized in terms specific to television itself, which always reconstitutes them in relation to their 'reality-for-the-programme' (Brunsdon and Morley, 1978: 61). Nonetheless, it is the powerful interplay of these encoding procedures was well as their persistent regularity which, in the end, give the sustained *impression* of intimacy so important for television's personality system.

Direct address

Totally unlike classical narrative cinema, television utilizes direct address. In the cinema the spectator 'looks' from a position not unlike the voyeur wherein the film text remains distant and fixed, the object of the look but never looking back, never acknowledging openly the presence of the spectator. There are some exceptions to the rule – a film like *Tom Jones* where the protagonist halts the narrative by addressing the audience directly with his reflections, Groucho Marx turning to the camera with a quick aside, the final shot of *The Lacemaker* – but these are rare. Television, on the other hand, has conventionalized and universalized the form of direct address where the viewer is spoken to and looked at directly, engaged in what is potentially an intimate, interactive scene. Direct address is generally reserved for the regular representatives of television – television personalities who exist as those stable identities within the flow: newsreaders, moderators, hosts and so on – and penetrates, at some point, into virtually every television genre, except the pure narrative fiction. Sometimes direct address is handed over to others not specifically located as regular television personalities: celebrities who speak directly to us in commercials about the virtues of breakfast cereals, life insurance policies or alcoholic beverages; singers and comedians who look directly at us as they perform or tell jokes; politicians 'addressing the nation'.

Danziger writes that in interactive contexts eye contact and physical proximity combine to produce and express high 'levels of intimacy' (Danziger, 1976: 65). Given that the viewing structure of television is one of closeness – the 'little box in the corner', an accessible part of everyday life – and given the propensity of television toward the use of direct address, which includes by definition 'eye contact' with the spectator as part of its operating mode, it comes as no surprise to find that the television personality is so firmly structured within a vision of intimacy. Through direct address, television personalities appear actively to be taking their viewers 'into account'. The spectator becomes the constant focus of television's attention. Unlike the cinema, which remains uncompromisingly distant and aloof, television comes to us 'here and now', directly 'for me' (Heath and Skirrow, 1977: 54). The direct gaze of the television personality is the literal inscription of television's own intimate vision. Simultaneously, direct address summons the viewer – 'looking at another', explains Danzinger, 'is another way of calling him' (ibid.: 66). The spectator is positioned to engage with the television personality with equivalent directness and intimacy.

Reproducing the ideological field

This brief overview of some of the elements that constitute the star and personality systems in a relational opposition is relevant to the general discussion of television in the production and reproduction of 'the repertoire of dominant ideologies'. By foregrounding its own personalities as well as the personalities of those recruited from outside as part of its programming agendas, the 'lived realities' that television represents come to be understood 'not by reference to certain structural arrangements or social processes, but either as the work of individuals or through their effects on individuals' (Chibnall, 1977: 27). The category of the individual constituted as television personality overwhelmingly becomes the 'central structuring category' for almost all of television's actuality and fictional forms. The effect of structuring television around personalities suggests that the world, first and foremost, is constructed through the actions of individuals behaving as free agents rather than by the complex relations among classes, institutions, and interest groups. Focus on personalities systematically encourages an obsessive absorption in motivation and feeling in which the real categories of political and social life are constantly transmuted into psychological terms. The locus and structure of action in the world is significantly shifted out of the public domain and into the region of the private. The television personality, to paraphrase Sennett, has entirely reversed Fielding's dictum that praise or censure should apply to actions rather than actor's: what matters for television 'is not what you have done, but how you feel about it' as a person (Sennett, 1974: 263); and the more you can be seen in a scene talking about and/or 'living out' these feelings, the closer your chances are of fulfilling television's criteria of intimacy and immediacy and hence of being judged as 'good television'. This ideology of personalization resonates out to the spectator as well, so that finally the range of possible decoding procedures necessary 'to get the message' and to win audience consent is fixed principally in terms of questions about personal authenticity: how 'real' and 'genuine' are these personalities performing in the public arena. The intimacy structure of viewing as well as the rhetorical structure of intimacy within programming works to maintain this 'reading'.

Television, both in its conception of programming and in its social setting suggests that there is a reduction of distance between itself and the viewer, that both television personalities and viewers exist within a common universe of experience, a kind of community of like minds where television is merely an extension of everyday life. By reducing this distance and creating what might be seen as a pseudo-gemeinschaft television ostensibly reduces *social* distance between those who appear and those who watch. By implication, the social distance between all those who watch together is reduced as well. If, for example, we all have 'contact' with the Prime Minister during his address to the nation or during a press conference, in what sense can we say that we are unequal, or have unequal access, particularly when he is taking us into account 'personally' by speaking to us directly. In overtly stratified societies, contact with the powerful is made only by those at the top – only certain privileged individuals have the 'ear of the king'; television ostensibly allows *everyone* into the presence of the power-ful. By diminishing the sense of social distance, television reduces the sense of power as well. The powerful appear as mere personalities, just like you or me, beamed electronically into the comfort of our own living rooms, to talk and reveal themselves to us personally and intimately. In traditional societies the underlings, the dominated groups, sought to enter the presence of those in power: king and chiefs 'held audi-ences', and their constituency came along accordingly. Television's structure of intim-acy reverses this situation, creating the illusion that the powerful are in fact seeking an audience with us – they come to us through television, amiable, accessible, and in spite of everything just a familiar 'part of life'. Thus the bourgeoisie as a social class 'disappears . . . in passing from reality to representation' (Barthes, 1973: 138). Through the personality system its position in relation to the 'real' structure of domination and subordination is systematically absorbed and represented in terms of that pervasive, on-going televisual universe of 'momentary disclosure of the self'. By appearing to reduce distance through intimacy the personality system operates to mask the gap between the powerful and the powerless, ensuring that the real unities of power, class, prestige and interest can continue relatively intact and unexamined.

Because personalities are embedded in television's cycles of repetition, becoming over time both intimate and familiar, they also may come to be defined as trustworthy and credible sources of knowledge and experience. The very repetition of their appearances week after week supports the authority of their wisdom. The way that they are seen to make sense of the world and to contextualize events – whether in 'factual' or 'fictional' forms – begins to take on a certain truthfulness and even a certain infallibility. The longer they remain within television, the more likely their judgements, pronouncements, and behaviour will be accorded some kind of serious attention. Television personalities become 'guarantors of truth'. The illusion of tele-vision, then, is not only that it presents itself as a 'window on the world' but the truth of that view is doubly authenticated by those who show it to us. Hence, if 'Brian told me', it must be so.[2] In this sense, the intimacy that operates through the personality system turns into a gentle yet pervasive form of paternalism where viewers, meta-phorically speaking, are taken by the hand and carefully guided through the daunting, potentially chaotic complexities of life with the assurance that there will always be someone there to advise them, someone 'who stands in . . . and makes the compli-cated plain, simple and straight' (Hall, 1976: 251) and, in the face of adversity or confusion, can set the world right.

Finally, in some respects television personalities can be seen to operate like totems, around which viewers can be arranged and differentiated from one another. Thus the unities of class are fragmented and cut across by totemic attachments – what unifies and differentiates people then is not their position in the social and political structures, but their totemic allegiance to a particular television personality. Hence, the question of the social context and structural arrangements of television production and consumption is re-posed in terms of personal likes and dislikes. Just as there is a plurality of personalities offered up on television so too there is a plurality of responses to these personalities. Rather than defining audiences in terms of their structural relation to television, the fostering of totemic attachments constitutes viewers as 'individuals' in a world where choice appears a real possibility: viewers, as individual free agents can choose what to watch and not to watch, what personalities to like or not. If one television personality is unappealing, there is always another one to choose. What the viewer *cannot* choose, however, is a completely different way by which television might be constructed and organized, in which the personality system might be altered, or even excluded entirely.

Notes

1   These examples are specific to the Australian context, but given the generality of television's encoding procedures, it could be estimated that little variation would occur in relation to any other national situation. See, for example, J. Tunstall (1977) and H. I. Schiller (1969).

2   This was a slogan used by a Melbourne television channel in an influential advertising campaign for its evening news. The campaign aimed at suggesting that viewers need to go no further than this particular newsreader to be 'in the know' about events of the day. The ad was organized around a jingle which contained a question and answer: How did you know that there was a strike, a major political speech, a reduction in taxes etc.? Brian told me, that's how I know.

Chapter 10

P. David Marshall

THE MEANINGS OF THE POPULAR MUSIC CELEBRITY
The construction of distinctive authenticity

THE TRANSFORMATIONS THAT HAVE taken place in popular music in the twentieth century can be attributed to a number of factors, including the use of new technologies, changes in the size of performance venues, the growth of the recording industry, and the segmentation of the mass market. Discursively, all of these factors have been modalized around concepts of authenticity. At the center of these debates concerning the authentic nature of the music is the popular music performer; how he or she expresses the emotionality of the music and his or her own inner emotions, feelings, and personality and how faithful the performer is to the intentions of the musical score are all part of how the individual performer is determined to be authentic. What follows is an examination of the genealogy of the popular music celebrity and how the focus on the star has shaped debates concerning the authentic quality of popular music. Like the movie industry, the popular music industry has become located primarily in the United States. Aside from a few deviations, the following discussion of the industry-celebrity relationship in popular music is concerned with American popular music.

The industrial construction of the popular music star

The development of celebrity status in the production of popular music is closely connected with the mass reproduction of songs. In the nineteenth and early twentieth centuries, sheet music production and distribution were the economic heart of the music industry. Performers in music halls and vaudeville theaters became the principal means of expanding the market for particular compositions beyond regional boundaries and interests. As vehicles for the promotion of songs, song performers were very important for the music publishing companies. At the same time, poor material—that is, unpopular songs—could hurt singers' performance careers. In the construction of the sheet music commodity, the singing star was simultaneously developed. Above the illustration on the cover page of most sheet music productions, the name of the performer would vie in size with the name of the song. In this way, the buying public was able to link song with singing star. Million-selling song sheets were not uncommon in the late nineteenth and early twentieth centuries. In fact, between 1900 and 1910, one hundred song sheets sold a million copies each and therefore occupied the very center of the music industry.[1] The audience for popular songs was composed primarily of the middle class, among whom a popular pastime was to sing the pieces with piano accompaniment in their own living rooms. The arrangements were quite simple, so that the singing and playing could be handled by a large amateur population.

Essentially, there were two overlapping markets for song production: the stage performance and the song publication. The performer, working with elaborate orchestration and arrangement, created the professional version of the song – the official text. At the turn of the century, the nascent recording industry built on the reproduction of these official texts of music and song. To establish a recording's authenticity, the most famous performer associated with the song would be enlisted to sing it. Thus, the recording industry used the system of stars established by the music publishing business for its foundation.

The industry, centered in New York City, rapidly developed a division of labor in order to maintain a level of production that could satisfy the primary market of song sheets and the secondary market of records. This entailed the employment of what were called "tunesmiths" to manufacture new songs for performers and publication. It was critical to the organization of the industry that these composers were employees, because the principal means of revenue/profit accumulation for the industry was the copyright, which was held by the music publishing company. This gave the company, not the individual, the recording and publishing rights to any song produced by its employees for fifty years. The tunesmiths themselves were usually paid a flat rate per song. For example, Charles Graham, the writer of a popular song of 1891, "The Picture That Is Turned Towards the Wall," received about fifteen dollars for that work.[2] The writers of Tin Pan Alley remained relatively anonymous for the first two decades of the twentieth century. Songs were identified either by their titles or by the names of the star performers associated with them – also employees of the recording industry.

The other critical transformation of musical culture that the music industry fostered was the active generalization of regional differences. The tunesmiths were often involved in the appropriation of regional folk music – which was intimately connected to particular communities' systems of meaning – and the homogenization of its appeal. David Buxton connects this transformation to the industrialization and urbanization of American culture and the new social needs that emerged as people were divorced from these regional contexts. The songs produced maintained an abstract stylistic connection to regional folk music, but were new in their appeal to persons living and working in the cities. The types of songs produced could be said to contain traces of social memories of regions; these traces, from an array of sources, were now used to construct differences and variety in popular song production.[3] The repetition of an uncopyrighted folk song generated no capital; variations in the composition and lyrics of folk songs allowed for the application of copyright and the generation of capital. As many authors have attested, one of the key sources for appropriation (because it was free) was antebellum black American music.[4] This appropriation of black musical style into the mass production of popular music established one of the dominant strains of contemporary popular music.

Singers of the late nineteenth and early twentieth centuries were part of this process of generalization for the mass market of regional styles. Buxton describes most vaudeville and music hall singers as local celebrities.[5] They left their home areas to perform in other communities and presented musical styles that were not of the regions in which they performed. Thus, their market reach was somewhat limited. Buxton uses the example of the transformation of country music to detail the changes many performers underwent to appeal to the developing mass market. The original country musicians who recorded in the 1920s were older part-time musicians who had achieved a certain celebrity status within their region playing a particular style of music. Performers like Fiddlin' John Carson and Charlie Oaks were well into their fifties when they first recorded. According to Buxton, record sales and radio play fostered the attribution of distinctive regional style to the personal style of the recording artist. The recording artist, because of the consumption demands of an audience whose use of the music was less connected to the cultural significance of a particular regional musical style and more connected to a general capitalist culture and leisure, quickly depleted his or her traditional repertoire of songs. Because of this different relationship to the music, which had been abstracted from its regional source, the recording artist became the center for production of new songs in a similar style. By the 1940s, a performer's musical style became a resource upon which he or she would draw to construct new melodies and thus new "personalizations." The incorporation of regional style had been completed through the development of the versatile country music artist.[6]

The technology of the popular music celebrity

Through the use of the technologies of reproduction and distribution, the possibility of a fundamentally different relationship of the audience to the pleasures of popular music and their stars became manifest. The breakdown of difference on the basis of region became reconstituted in the urban setting in terms of tastes, likes, and dislikes. New conceptions of authenticity had to be developed in popular music that integrated this new relationship to musical style.

The technology of reproduction problematizes the concept of authenticity. In the development of the popular music celebrity, the recording technology has worked to authenticate the particular and individual performance, partly through the progressive perfection of sound recording and sound reproduction technology. However, the construction of the technological reproduction of songs has also changed the meaning of the live and in-person performance of concerts. The music industry, through its stars, has constructed two sometimes contradictory levels of the "real" and authentic. The recording has become the true representation of the music; the concert has become the faithful reproduction of the "authentic" recorded music.[7] It has become a common experience of concert audiences to sense the inadequacies of the live performance in comparison with the recorded music they associate with the performer. Studio technology and studio sound, with its twenty-four-track editing capability, cannot be matched by the indeterminate acoustics of the concert hall/stadium, the fallibility of performers, and the inability to produce all of the same recorded sounds within less controlled environments. In some instances, the stars of the concert no longer actually sing or perform; instead they lip-synch and dance to the reproduced sounds of their records in front of the audience.[8] I shall return to the new meanings of the live concert in a subsequent part of this chapter. What I want to deal with specifically here are the different meanings and experiences that are offered by the technology in the production and consumption of records, and how these have constructed the types of celebrity figures that have emerged in popular music in the twentieth century.

First of all, as I have mentioned above, recordings tend to sanctify particular performers' renditions of particular songs. A song, in essence, becomes a sign of the performer. It has been quite common, therefore, for popular music celebrities to "possess" signature tunes. Roy Rogers's "Happy Trails," Sinatra's comeback "My Way," Judy Garland's "Over the Rainbow," and Paul Robeson's "Old Man River" are all examples of songs and performers that are inseparable.

The same focus on the correct or original version of a song by a particular star changes the uses made of music by the audience. With song sheets, the audience was involved in their own reproduction of the work. With records, the use of music became oriented toward an audience of listeners, not amateur performers. The record professionalized the means of musical production through its coding of orchestration and the performer's singing, codes that far surpassed the capacity of the amateur piano player and singer. To hear a particular song in the home increasingly meant listening to it, either on a record or on the radio.

The domestic nature of the technology of reception worked in the reorientation of the perception of the popular music performance and performer. Within their own living rooms, listeners could enjoy the very best and most popular singers and performances. The record player privatized the technology of exhibition. Moreover, the activity of listening permitted the investment of personal experiences into the meaning of the music to a greater degree than did concert performances. In the privatized world of consumption, the listener, by purchasing a record, could sense his or her personal possession of the song and performer. Though distanced through technological apparatuses, performer and audience were brought closer together by the audience's listening to recorded music, thus domesticating entertainment and the performance of the popular music star.

In successive technological inventions, the private and personal activity of listening has been privileged. The development of the 45 rpm record and record player in the 1950s was a way to increase the sales of smaller format, more portable machines for the rapidly expanding youth market. Middle-class teenagers could potentially have their own record players and singles record collections in their own rooms. Similarly, transistor radios could be produced cheaply in compact, lightweight sizes for personalized uses.[9] Popular music, through the portable transistor radio, became an integral part of a variety of leisure pursuits. Transistor technology was embraced particularly by youth in their attempts to construct distinctive social spaces. Finally, consumer acceptance in the early 1980s of the Sony Walkman, the entirely personalized stereo radio and tape player, articulated the ultimate privileging of private listening practices. With headphones, the Walkman listener isolated his or her pleasure in a manner that the radio speaker never achieved. The tape player also allowed for the personal programming of taste; the listener, with complete portability, was also independent of radio stations' programming styles. All of these technological innovations have served to personalize the relationship between the musical artist and the listening public.

Technology and performance

In terms of the technology of musical production, one can identify a trend that has also been configured around the privileging of the personal and the individual. This movement can be seen in the changes in popular music performing styles that resulted from the integration of electronic recording and the use of the microphone.

The first performer to sell in excess of a million records was the opera star Enrico Caruso, in 1901.[10] Caruso possessed the technical perfection of the voice – at least as it was understood in the aesthetics of classical music. In contrast, popular music singers of the past thirty-five years have eschewed the classical perfection of the voice in favor of expressing the emotionality and personality of the voice. The other model of the professional vocalist from the early recording era of popular music – equally rejected by most contemporary performers – was the music hall and vaudeville star. Like the opera singer, the popular singer was able to project his or her voice to the very back of the concert hall. Al Jolson epitomized this early-twentieth-century style of singing, where the power of the voice – its depth and range – qualified the singer for star status. However, the invention of the microphone made the need for such large, full voices less central in popular music. Al Jolson, with his half-singing/half-talking, minstrel/vaudeville style, never adapted to the microphone. Rudy Vallee, the mega-phone star, was the first to work comfortably with the microphone in expressing the new possibilities of intimacy that it allowed. Bing Crosby, along with a host of other singers known as crooners, managed to use the microphone as if he were singing quietly to one other person.[11] The relaxed nature of the crooning style became dominant on 1930s radio shows hosted by the leaders of various big bands of the swing era. This movement to intimacy and personal style complemented the development of the receiving technology of popular music. Since the crooners, vocalists have continued to experiment with the "grain of the voice," the texture of vocal style that can express intimacy, individuality, and a range of emotions.[12]

Popular music's performance codes

Performance also emerged from the structure of the popular music industry. With specific people employed as composers – the tunesmiths of Tin Pan Alley – there was a complementary network of stars to interpret those songs. The division of labor between stars and the relatively anonymous songwriters was further accentuated by the major Hollywood studios' purchase of the principal music publishing houses of New York during the 1930s. The movie musical, which served as a promotional vehicle for the introduction of film sound, also aided in the construction of identifiable images and personalities connected to the popular songs that were heard on the radio. The emphasis on the vocalist was in sharp contrast to the big band/swing era's emphasis on the band leader. In retrospect, it is surprising to learn that Crosby, the most famous of the crooners, was relegated to the back row of Paul Whiteman's orchestra and, like other vocalists of the early swing era, was treated like any other musician with an instrument to play.[13] Film and radio exposure gradually changed the orientation of the music industry toward the star vocalist.

In sharp contrast to the construction of the star vocalist in mainstream popular music, the black popular music tradition of the twentieth century presented the model of the singer-songwriter. But within black blues and jazz, there was a gender division in place from the 1920s to the 1940s that articulated the acceptability of black female performers singing for white audiences and the inacceptability, in most clubs, of black male performers singing for white audiences. Bessie Smith, the renowned female blues singer of the 1920s, was a veritable star. In contrast, black male blues performers such as Blind Lemon Jefferson and Robert Johnson performed and played in relative obscurity, even though their music formed the basis of much of the blues repertoire of singers like Bessie Smith. It was impossible for these musicians to become included in the culture industry's starmaking machinery.

The integration of this other contrasting tradition in the production of popular music into the mainstream of the industry is connected to two labor and copyright disputes that took place in the early 1940s. First of all, the American Society of Composers, Authors and Publishers (ASCAP), an organization that represented composers and publishers and collected royalties for the use of songs on radio and by performers, demanded a 200 percent increase in royalty rates in 1941.[14] The radio networks refused to pay the increase and subsequently organized Broadcast Music Incorporated (BMI), their own copyright organization, and started to play records that were not under ASCAP's jurisdiction. This led to the use of non-Tin Pan Alley songs, which generally meant country and western and blues music. In 1942, a musicians' union strike meant that once again radio was without the records it had relied upon for its shows for the previous decade. The radio networks turned to the only non-unionized musical worker – the vocalist. According to Buxton, this led to further reliance on vocal stars in popular music and a decline in the influence of the big bands.[15] The temporary dependence on marginal musical sources by radio, combined with the fostered maturation of the solo singing star, permitted the development and acceptance of the performance style of the rock and roll of the 1950s.

Several writers consider the singer Johnnie Ray to be the transitional figure in the development of the contemporary popular music performance style.[16] Ray freely acknowledged that he was not a very good singer; rather, he could be characterized as an expressionist. He integrated the body and sexuality in his often tearful pleas to his audience; his movement was described by one music critic as "writhing" in torment. He gesticulated wildly with his arms, unlike the controlled, virtually unmoving professionalism of Sinatra, whose only bodily gesture of individuality was the snapping of his fingers. Ray often punctuated the finish of a song by falling dramatically to his knees as he caressed the microphone. Elvis Presley's characteristic roll of the hips and snarl carried on the tradition of expressing individuality in performance through the public codes of sexual gesture. The stance of the male rocker, the guitar as phallic symbol, and the energy and vitality of stage movement and acrobatics have all become codes of rock performance. The rock performance style emerged out of the confluence of black performance style with the need to express the sincerity of personality and individuality of the performer/star.

The rhetoric of performance

Although the integration of sexuality and expressivity into the performer's style identifies a break with some of the past traditions of twentieth-century musical representation, there is also a continuity of form in performance. The mode of address, unlike in the play or the film, is constructed to be direct. Whether on record or in concert, the vocalist includes the audience in this address. In the love song, the address is quite direct; the audience replaces the lost or newfound love. In the blues song, the address is often one of lament; it remains a story directed at the audience, as if it were another individual in the conversation. Indeed, structured into the blues song is the call and response between guitar and vocals. It is quite common for blues audiences to "respond" in simple affirmations, as if engaged in conversation. The directness of the address of the musical performer has always constructed the relationship between performer and audience at a very personal level. Classical and professional performance codes attempt to distance the singer from the content of the music. In the attempt to express the emotions of the musical and lyrical content of the song, the contemporary popular music performer has worked to authenticate his or her performance through acknowledgment of the direct nature of the address. The personal sentiments expressed in the song's lyrics are freely exposed in action and voice. Audience participation and response are encouraged in the concert setting during the performance of most songs. In this way, a ritualized dialogue is maintained between performer and audience.

There also exists a rhetorical dialogic relationship between the concert performance and the recording. Audience members' use of the concert is mediated by their prior use of the records. In the production of popular music, most of the music performed in concert has appeared in recordings prior to the concert appearance. The concert is used by the band or performer and the recording company as a method of promoting the record commodity; it sustains interest in the product beyond its release date in the popular press, in trade papers, and with fans.[17] The concert is therefore not an introduction to the music for the fans, but a form of ritualized authentication of pleasure and meaning of the records through a "lived" experience; it heightens the significance of the records and the pop star. The fan is demonstrating his or her solidarity with the artist's message and with the rest of the audience. The concert, then, becomes much more a display and expression by the audience member of a personal commitment to and a celebration of the performer than an appreciation of the performer's skill and technique in performing live.

Youth and the construction of the contemporary popular music star

Central to the construction of the popular music star of the past forty years is the capacity for its sign to express the difference and significance of youth. It has been argued, by Simon Frith and others, that in the postwar years the teenager became a kind of categorization that broke with the usual form of differentiation on the basis of class.[18] Youth was one of the ways in which categories of consumption could redefine the social world, and therefore it became a useful passageway for the elaboration of a new consumer subjectivity. The potential youth market in most Western societies grew enormously after World War II. In England, teenage disposable income grew by 100 percent between 1938 and 1958; similarly, in the United States, teenagers' average weekly revenue grew from $2.50 to $10 a week.[19] Without the weight of family obligation, teens could devote their income completely to the construction of a style of leisure consumption. The cues for the construction of a distinctive style were drawn from the movies and popular music, which began servicing the social needs of this new market.

Several authors have interpreted the new divisions in society created by the development of a separate and distinct youth culture in terms of the way the dominant culture viewed the transformation as a threat.[20] The 1950s have been construed as a period of moral panic, when the dominant culture considered the new ethics, the new focus on sexuality, and the emphasis on leisure, entertainment, and pleasure as assaults on the traditional values of hard work and just reward. Teenage films of the period oscillated between depicting the pleasures of the new morality and the dangers of excess. Popular music – specifically rock and roll – stars represented the incarnation of excess, decadence, and pleasure without connection to morality. For parental culture, according to this interpretation, rock and roll stars presented the emulatory material for the corruption of their teenagers. A clear-cut generational opposition is at the center of the moral panics hypothesis, which asserts that the progressive forces of change aligned squarely with youth and its representatives in popular music, and the disciplining nature of the dominant culture was articulated through the category of parents. Popular music, then, became a kind of battleground of ideal representations to include youth. On one side, black performers like Little Richard and – more dangerously, because their turf was the racial and economic center of American culture – white performers like Elvis Presley and Jerry Lee Lewis, who had integrated black performance styles, represented the out-of-control nature of teenage lifestyle. On the other side, the disciplined singing and performing style of performers like Pat Boone, who reinterpreted rock and roll with larger orchestrations and less sexually suggestive lyrics, represented the acceptable form of youth culture for parents and the dominant morality.

What needs to be integrated into the moral panics hypothesis, which continues in various forms to be at the center of the study of contemporary popular music, is the fact that the oppositional structure between parents and youth has been fostered by elements of the dominant culture itself. The 1950s, therefore, represent not only the clear distinctiveness of a youth culture, but a clear-cut emergence of a market segment for the circulation of goods and services. The new threat of youth is the integration of a consumption ethic into the general culture. The clash between a production and consumption ethos, openly displayed in the 1950s and 1960s, is configured through a generational conflict. Implicit in the structuring of a conflict in generational terms is its ultimate resolution through the succession of one generation by the next. Thus, consumption in the succeeding generation can be seen as a positive form of constructing one's social identity. The division of the social world into patterns of consumption generally configured around the concepts of style and lifestyle has become naturalized and is no longer in opposition to a morality of work and production. The oppositional structure of the 1950s and 1960s was reconfigured by the 1970s and 1980s into stylistic differentiation. In terms of the market, the differentiation is labeled market fragmentation or segmentation.

Popular music and its celebrities have operated at the nucleus of the production of stylistic differentiation through consumption and leisure. The presentation of the star, his or her musical roots, style of dress, manner of speech, and public display of sexuality are all significant markers for the structuring and differentiating of youth culture. In the 1960s, differentiations of style were modalized around the display of authenticity as a rupture from the performing styles of past generations. The largest and most enduring transformation took the form of a move toward performers' writing their own material and the related celebration of the singer-songwriter. In this way, new artists appeared to the audience to control their own destinies and thereby directly shaped the entire recording industry to reflect specific aspirations and desires. Top stars demanded and received "artistic freedom" partly through the opportunity to produce their own records and partly through the financial rewards of large royalties and record sales that allowed them to experiment. The star's cultural power depended on a very close affinity with a specific and loyal audience. The star, then, was actively engaged in the construction and differentiation of audience groups, in terms of style and taste, and in authenticating their elevated position. The popular music star, more than other forms of celebrity, had to be a virtual member of his or her own audience in order to sustain his or her influence and authenticity, and the commitment of the fan.

In the 1960s, some performers constructed their authenticity around naturalness and the rejection of performance codes. Folk performers such as Joan Baez eschewed the concept of spectacle in dress and appearance to be more closely affiliated with the audience. Barefoot, without makeup, and wearing simple clothes, Baez would sing with only the accompaniment of an acoustic guitar. The stylistic configuration she portrayed was emulated by a generation of women. Rock performers like the Rolling Stones built their authenticity on their musical and lyrical roots. Their musical and performance style of overt sexuality was built on black rhythm and blues. Bob Dylan's authenticity depended on a literary aesthetic code of the genius creator.

Innovation and transformation in the popular music celebrity

A recurring technique for establishing authenticity in popular music performance is the breaking of codes and the creation of new or transformed codes of style. *Style* may indicate, for example, a different musical code, a new form of dance, or an altered way of dress. The new style is invariably drawn from a particular audience group or subculture and is then rearticulated by the popular music performer. Style represents a statement of difference as well as a statement of solidarity with the particular audience. A change in style indicates a reassertion by the performer of his or her own authenticity. Any style eventually loses its power to represent difference, as the marketplace continuously appropriates the idiosyncrasies of codes of style for commodity innovation. Thus, the popular music performer is also continuously appropriating new representations of individuality through style.

There are two implications connected to the instability of the codes of style of popular music. First, popular musical style is defined through collectivities. The subcultural and marginal origins for the appropriation of style demand an affinity with the meaning and significance of the subcultural style on the part of the popular performer. It is also relevant that popular music is collective in nature; the dominant structure in rock music is not the individual performer, but the band. A band may have a leader or key figure who comes to represent the band publicly, but the band's name usually is more widely known than are the names of any of the individual players. Collective forms of identity, then, are central to contemporary popular music. The individual star may emerge from this emphasis on collective identity, but in distancing him – or herself from the band, the individual draws on codes of performance that are more connected to the conceptions of the singing star of the 1930s and 1940s.

Second, popular music's attempts to break and remake codes bring the form into closer alignment with movements in modern art than with other culture industries. The popular musician's play with style can also be thought of in aesthetic terms. Moreover, many of the British popular music groups of the 1960s and 1970s were formed in the art schools opened in the 1950s.[21] Artistic movements such as avant-gardism, dadaism, impressionism, abstract art, surrealism, and, most significant, pop art have entered into popular music partly in the form of album covers and partly in terms of the claims and pretensions of practice that musicians have maintained in their pose as popular artists. A number of romantic connotations of the nineteenth- and twentieth-century artist have been integrated into the posturings and styles of the contemporary popular music celebrity. The pallor of the rock star recalls the consumptive starving artist or the genius whose body has been ravaged by excess and drugs. The litheness and thin frame recall the youthfulness of the romantic poets, who, like the near mythic Thomas Chatterton, died before they were thirty.[22] The experiential lifestyle refers to a number of artistic movements that have emerged out of the twentieth century. The anarchy and nihilism graphically depicted, for example, by the Who's ritualistic destruction of their instruments, hearkens back to the dadaists. The bohemian lifestyle that surfaced in many European cities in the nineteenth century has served as fecund ground on which to construct the pop star's public presence.[23] Finally, the ultimate play with the pretensions of artistic posture are articulated in the music videos produced to embellish the image of the popular group. Videos are often filled with surrealism; they represent avant-garde filmmaking that serves to associate the popular star with the style and romantic connotations of the innovative artist.

Summary

The celebrity of popular music is constructed from elements quite different from those that make up the film celebrity. These elements are related to the technology of production and reception, the form of address that is peculiar to the singing of a song, the industrial and commodity configuration of the musical product, and the audience's collective and individual relationship to the music and performer. Fundamental to the construction of the popular music celebrity is the conveyance of both commitment and difference. *Commitment* in this context refers to the audience's close and intimate relationship to the pop star as well as the way in which the artist conveys his or her authenticity in representing the audience. In some cases, authenticity is displayed through emotional sincerity: the performer's direct and personal address in the song is further individualized through the private forms of reception. This kind of personal relationship between performer and audience describes the more classical construction of the popular music star to emerge in the twentieth century. In other cases, authenticity is expressed through the performer's communication of solidarity with an audience. The focus in these instances is on the creation and maintenance of codes of difference and particularity by both audience and performer.

The development of this second discourse on authenticity in popular music coincides roughly with the emergence of rock music. Within rock music, the appeal to authenticity has been developed by industry, artist, and audience into the formation of taste cultures, where the expression of a particular consumption style becomes more central to the public presentation of identity. As discussed above, popular music has been at the interstices of the formation of a new consumer subjectivity. Its active work in construction of new collectivities and new social categories on the basis of lifestyle and taste has bestowed on its representatives – its celebrities – social power. Occasionally, the social power that has congealed in popular music has facilitated the organization of social movements opposed to the general organization of the social structure. In a sense, the configuration of power in popular music identifies an elemental risk in the organization of new social identities in consumer capitalism. Differentiation and innovation to create distinction are fundamental parts of commodity production; however, they necessitate an active play with the meanings and social needs that are embodied in the commodity for the consumer. The popular music celebrity represents the continuous reorganization of consumer subjectivities into collective forms of identity.

In the following section, I present an analysis of the group New Kids on the Block in terms of the way the celebrity signs of the group and its members have emerged in the public sphere from the organization of the popular music industry. The discourses of authenticity, commitment, and difference operate in the formation of any popular music group, and the following hermeneutic reveals the particular manner in which these discourses operate in the formation and success of New Kids on the Block.

The construction of a "phenomenon": New Kids on the Block

An integral part of the lexicon of the popular music industry and its forms of self-promotion is the concept of the "phenomenon." Because of the 90 percent failure rate of recordings manufactured to generate profit, the industry is organized toward "hitting."[24] The 10 percent of records that actually generate earnings not only subsidize the failures but also account for the substantial profits of the entire industry. Thus, in actual fact, very few of the recordings made generate most of the revenues. As a result, the industry appears to be disorganized; it seems to be incapable of determining with any consistency which records and acts are going to sell well and which acts are going to be financial losses. The industry attempts to solve this problem in three principal ways: by issuing compilations of recordings that have previously sold well ("greatest hits" records); by concentrating on production, distribution, and promotion of established acts (e.g., the Rolling Stones are what is often called a "bankable" act); and by intensely promoting specific new acts with costly videos, tour support, and advertisements.

The popular music industry is often described as volatile and unpredictable. The product the industry deals with is, possibly more than other cultural products, in the domain of affect and outside of the realm of reason and the rational. Music and the uses of music are very much connected to the emotive side of human existence. The recording industry is constantly trying to tap this emotive side through the production of music. In a sense, it is attempting to contain feelings so that, at least temporarily, they can be defined by singers or songs.

The "phenomenon" in popular music is the recording act that has somehow captured a massive audience. In the language of the industry, these phenomena are out of the industry's control. The term *phenomenon*, which was used to describe the Beatles in a previous era and New Kids on the Block in the late 1980s and early 1990s, borrows from the manner in which nature is described: much like a hurricane or a tornado, the popular music phenomenon is a naturally occurring event that appears to be unpredictable in time, place, or force. It "hits" with incredible power and, if strong enough, may "hit" more than once. A rash of sales statistics chart the power of the phenomenon: in 1989, New Kids on the Block sold more than fourteen million records in North America, composed of ten charted albums and singles; their album *Hangin' Tough* was the second best-selling album of that year; in terms of concerts, the group made $73.8 million in ticket sales in 1990, which places them second in all-time concert tour revenues.[25] *People*'s cover story on New Kids revels in the language of powerful nature: "The Kids are riding the crest of the most frenzied pop-music phenomenon since Beatlemania."[26] Integrated with this force-of-nature conception of popular music's construction of the relationship between the audience and the cultural product is the language of warfare. New musical groups "explode onto the scene," and a recent surge in the popularity of dance music was called an "explosion." In the 1960s, the plethora of successful British bands in North America was described as an "invasion." Following the punk "invasion" of the 1970s, there was the "new wave," which in its terminology successfully blends militaristic language with another metaphor from the forces of nature.

This use of natural phenomenon/battlefield terminology by the popular music press and the industry itself has developed over time into a shorthand method of trying to describe the irrationality that is central to the way the industry operates. As well, descriptions of popular music changes and transformations, often referred to in previous decades as "crazes," have functioned as central metaphors in the discourse of cultural change itself, of a culture in constant transformation and upheaval. It is a discourse that, through its emphasis on unpredictability coupled with the inevitability of change, reshapes people's actions into reactions to these various phenomena. The invasive discourse that surrounds popular music is constructed to encourage us to be caught up in the wave of sentiment that affirms the significance of the latest phenomenon. In that affirmation and acceptance of the new musical sound and group, we collectively are encouraged to let the sentiment of the last phenomenon dissipate into history. With New Kids on the Block, the mainstream press explains that the "fever" they have created has "reached delirium status."[27]

The framing of popular music discourse in the language of spontaneous and explosive phenomenal change is also constructed to emphasize the cultural products' close relationship to the audience. What is being underlined is that the audience is determining the style of music, the types of personalities elevated to superstar status, and the timing of change and transformation. The industry becomes in this construction merely a way of channeling the popular will. As it is explained in one of myriad biographies that have accompanied New Kids' emergence, the group's popularity may be accounted for by the fact that "they care about their fans so much."[28] Popular music phenomena such as the New Kids on the Block are pure expressions of popular will, which is represented as pure sentiment.

To describe the nature of these phenomena of popular music, which are organized around personalities and groups, is thus a very difficult process. They are packaged in a discourse of change and are intimately tied to the way in which cultural change is articulated in postwar American society in particular and Western society in general. This discourse of change is elemental in their formation in the culture and elemental in their construction of power. As well, they house formations of collective sentiment and feeling; in other words, they are defined to a degree by the audience that, through a specific array of cultural products, feels connected to the phenomenon. In embodying a form of collectivity, the popular music phenomenon represents the modern crowd in all its irrationality and emotionality. To extend logically from this, the popular music industry, in its perpetual construction of new phenomena, is an apparatus that tries to organize and focus the crowd's intensity into recognizable forms and products of consumption. The industry is an apparatus for the congealing of emotions and sentiments into recognizable sounds, images, and personalities that work to maintain the intensity of emotion. When the emotional intensity dissipates, the industry works to construct new forms of intense sentiments around new images, sounds, and personalities. In many senses, the popular music industry works to manage the contemporary crowd and, in fact, to organize its irrationality.

The established structure

The industry, in its massaging of public tastes, has developed certain patterns or structures in how new popular music celebrities are presented. What appears to be new and is presented as new and different to a large degree is organized around these structures of representation. Thus, New Kids on the Block, in terms of marketing positioning, style of promotion, and industry support, had certain precursors. The group was also positioned by the industry in clear opposition to and distinction from other forms of music and celebrity images. This form of distinction and opposition is also a well-trodden path; apart from differences that emerge from musical style and the contingency and lived experience of the group's core audience, New Kids on the Block followed this structure.

First of all, central to the identity and position of New Kids on the Block was the youth of the group's members. Within popular music, minor differences in age can be constructed as crucially significant. The emergence of any new star is often organized to present his or her youthfulness in contradistinction to established acts. New stars represent the vitality of their music. They also are constructed as a form of initiation for new music buyers. The bulk of the record-buying public is roughly between the ages of sixteen and thirty-two, and is overwhelmingly male.[29] As discussed above, the music industry is involved in the servicing of a youth market that first arose with the growth in disposable income among youth in North America following the

Second World War. Since the 1950s, popular music stars have represented the same age (and generally the same sex) as the central record-buying demographic. However, there have always been some pop stars who have been marketed to appeal to a demographic much younger and more female than the central record-buying public. New Kids on the Block was a group that was positioned to appeal to the neophyte consumer of popular music.

If one looks at the history of pop stars who have been marketed and positioned in the role of "teen idol," it becomes readily apparent that though all are musical performers, music has often been less central to these individuals' profitability as celebrities than have other products. Marketing of the teen idol generally focuses on the image, which is circulated in a number of formats that go beyond the musical product: posters, animated television series, Barbie-sized look-alike dolls, comic and photobiographical books, fanzines, clothing, and lunch pail designs, to name a few of the more visible and successful examples. The intense focus on the image has often been the line of demarcation between male and female audiences, preteen and young adult audiences, and, in terms of musical categories, pop and rock.[30] The teen idol is structured to appeal to the preteen and young teen female pop audience member and children in general. Teen idols are generally scorned by older music buyers as inauthentic and fabricated. For the younger record-buying market, the teen idol is the conduit for the move from the toy market of childhood into the market of youth. Teen idols are positioned as transitional icons for the youthful audience that will ultimately form the future mainstay of recording industry sales. It is because of this transitional quality that teen idols are commodified in forms and images that are relatively non-threatening to this young audience and to the ancillary market of parents. Indeed, the teen idol is himself generally managed and chaperoned as an entirely dependent being throughout his entire career as a teen idol (which is invariably brief). In this way, the teen idol never appears to be autonomous and therefore is never threatening as an adult; he remains, as long as he is popular, perpetually childlike and dependent. The teen idol's image is similarly controlled and works to reinforce his lack of full independence.

The structure I have outlined concerning the teen idol that emerges from popular music varies somewhat with each incarnation. One can see that often the organization of the popular music star centers on the individual's relative autonomy. The less autonomous and independent the star, the more he is structured purely as teen idol. In the 1950s and 1960s, Elvis Presley surfaced as a popular music star of enormous influence and market appeal. However, unlike "pure" teen idols of the same era, Presley cultivated a clearly sexualized image, which constructed a code of independence, adulthood, and autonomy in his celebrity sign. In contrast, stars like Fabian, Frankie Avalon, and, to a degree, Pat Boone represented nonthreatening types of personalities that were constructed to present a harmless form of sexuality. Their predominant musical form was the ballad; Presley's original claim to fame was his raucous treatment of rock and roll songs.[31]

The question that arises from this delineation of type with the larger structural type of teen idol is, Why do these differentiations exist? The teen idol's image is structured to be ambiguous, particularly with reference to rebellion and sexuality. What must be remembered is that the teen idol is a transitional commodity that must in some instances appeal to parents' sensibilities as well as represent the youth culture and its spirit of difference and sometime opposition to parent culture. For example, there is an ambiguous quality in most teen idols' representation of sexuality. First, there is the clear structural division between predominantly male performer and young female audience. The male performer, though more often than not a young adult and therefore somewhat older than the younger female audience, is constructed not to be an adult. In terms of image, the obvious signs of puberty are underplayed, so that the male performer is seen as a "representationally removed" image of maleness. The male teen idol is overcoded to have a baby face, on which the absence of facial hair is significant in its articulation of nonmasculinity. The Beatles' bobbed long hair, lack of seriousness, and clean, hairless faces when they became famous can be seen as once again a play with sexuality, as they represented maleness and nonmasculinity simultaneously to their young female audience. Similarly, teen idol pop stars of the 1970s, such as David Cassidy, Leif Garrett, and Shaun Cassidy, possessed these same qualities of prepubescent maleness; they were physically slight and possessed boyish looks and wore hairstyles that resembled the predominant feminized fashion of the period.[32] Serious transgressions of these ambiguous codes of nonmasculinity/masculinity would remove the teen idol from the circulation of commodities aimed at this transitional market.

New Kids on the Block built on these patterns of the teen idol music star. The industry operates as the cultural memory of what is effective in this construction of the transitional commodity. The Beatles, the Monkees, the Jackson Five, the Osmonds, and the Bay City Rollers provided the structural framework for the development of the concept of New Kids. It is interesting to see that most types of commodities that were associated with New Kids had been previously tested and marketed for these precursors. Like the Beatles, New Kids had their own Saturday-morning animated television series. The animated series also indicated that these musical groups were positioned to entertain children, and, when defined as commodities, they moved between toy products and promotional products of the recording industry. Their level of rebellion, then, was somewhat muted. The marketing of New Kids produced a plethora of products aimed at school-age children. Folders for school notes, lunch pails, T-shirts, dolls (which came in several sizes and materials), concert videos, television shows, games, and comic books made New Kids into a sign that served to sell a host of commodities beyond their music. The group also expended into new techniques for reaching specific audience groups. For example, in 1989, 100,000 fans were calling a 900 number each week to hear their favorite New Kid reveal a "secret."[33] A sales estimate for the 1990 New Kids line of merchandise was put at $400 million. Over and above this figure were concert earnings and video and record sales.[34] From 1989 to 1992, New Kids were constantly on the covers of preteen magazines in the magazines' efforts to ensure high sales. Their ubiquity through their attachment to a host of commodities made New Kids the most financially successful pop group ever.[35]

Partly because of this ubiquity, and partly because of New Kids members' appeal as clear pop stars, the popular music press has generally considered the group to be the epitome of inauthenticity.[36] Teen idols are therefore significant not only in terms of their core audience, they are also extremely relevant in establishing the authenticity of other forms of music and performers in the music industry. New Kids on the Block established the domain of the authentic in their obvious commerciality, their overt appeal to children, their studied and controlled rebellion, and their generally nonthreatening masculinity. These qualities provided the binarism that operates throughout the music industry between pop music and rock music, between the banal and the serious. New Kids were declared a contrivance and a marketing scam, the ultimate example of pop music's commercialism and superficiality.

New Kids' emergence does provide virtually all of the appropriate markers to indicate that they were a marketing invention that had been fabricated to be teen idols. There is a subtle distinction being made here. In popular music that is usually called rock, the audience is believed to be independent and therefore able to discern what is good music from bad or contrived music. The performers are likewise independent thinkers and creators. In contrast, the audience of groups like New Kids is considered to be manipulated, duped by marketers and promoters. It is for this reason New Kids appealed only to children; anyone else would have recognized the marketing scheme and identified the inauthentic nature of the group. Like their principal audience, this argument goes, New Kids themselves were controlled and managed by a team of marketers and coaches.

The verity of most of these claims is borne out in any study of the group's formation. But what is missing in such an analysis is that New Kids itself was used as a foil for the legitimation of other forms of music that appear to be less contrived and, in comparison with New Kids, less commercial. In the entire field of popular music and popular music meanings, these comparisons are useful to define the various markets and market fragments that use music to define their social identities.

Briefly, here is the now overcoded story of the emergence of New Kids from the position of a discourse of authenticity. Maurice Starr, a moderately successful singer-songwriter and former member of the group the Johnson Brothers, had by the 1980s begun developing and managing popular singing groups. In the early 1980s, he had conceived and developed a young black group called the New Edition. In the popular press, the New Edition was immediately compared with the Jackson Five of the late 1960s and early 1970s. Songs were organized around the lead vocals of the youngest member of the group, whose voice had not deepened. Starr composed and produced virtually all of the New Edition's songs, managed their promotional tours, and helped choreograph their stage shows; the members of the group were purely performers. The group was moderately successful. In the mid-1980s, Starr, in association with Boston talent manager Mary Alford, attempted to produce a similar group with white boys.[37] He scoured the racially mixed Boston inner-city schools for white performers who had some interest in black dance and rap music. Starr held auditions for six months before he constructed the right blend of personalities. From that search, he chose the members of New Kids on the Block (originally called Nynuk). The average age of the performers at the beginning, in 1985, was about fifteen. The youngest, Joey, sang lead vocals for the first recordings in a high soprano voice. Once again, Starr wrote and produced all of the group's original songs. He also developed the group's highly choreographed concert show. New Kids on the Block, much as the Monkees were originally nonplayers in the 1960s, did not play instruments, and occasionally in their performances they used taped vocals so that they could continue their choreographed dance routines without interruption. However, the use of taped segments in their programs led to a steady stream of criticism in the press and from some parents of fans, who claimed either that they were too manufactured or that they were not really the singers.[38] After an initial album that did poorly, their three follow-up albums all sold multiplatinum.[39] The group toured for months on end, hence their appropriated slogan, "the hardest working act in show business."

As is evidenced by this standard history of New Kids, which has been reproduced in magazine profiles, fanzines, and books, they possessed all of the qualities of illegitimacy: they didn't write their own songs; they didn't play their own instruments; they were chosen in a talent search and didn't develop independent of the music industry apparatus; they made a great deal of money; they appealed to preteens; and they were managed very carefully. All of these truths about New Kids underline their illegitimacy in rock music. Their emergence, then, was more clearly in line with the show business origins of singing stars like Frank Sinatra and – to a lesser degree – Elvis Presley than groups like the Beatles, the Rolling Stones, or R.E.M. What makes them doubly cursed is that they had the appearance of being a group that had come together on its own, when in fact its origins were highly planned. The irony of the entire discourse of authenticity that envelops rock and popular music is that it is dependent on the existence of such examples for the maintenance of the mainstream of what rock means for other audiences. New Kids on the Block operated as a highly successful scapegoat that maintained an equally fabricated sense of purity of the authentic in other examples of popular music.[40]

Building difference: music celebrities embodying subcultures

In the construction of social identities among youth, music figures prominently. Likes and dislikes are represented through one's musical taste, which betrays a series of connected tastes. A celebrity who arises from the popular music industry is thus positioned by both the industry and the audience to represent aspects of difference and differentiation. It is a system of celebrities, where each celebrity sign is partially constructed in opposition to, in contradistinction to, or in relation with other popular music celebrities. New Kids on the Block, much like other groups, established a close rapport with their audience through differentiation from other performers. They made their public identities valuable social markers for their audience. Although not entirely synonymous, the fans of New Kids constructed a series of codes based on these celebrity figures that resembled the structures of meaning of a subculture. The level of commitment to New Kids, the level of what is often called fanatical support, determined the level of understanding of the various codes and histories. This loyalty to and solidarity with New Kids among their fans was expressed in a number of ways, most prominent among which were buying their records and videos, knowing the words to all of their songs, attending their concerts, collecting their images in posters and magazines,[41] buying "officially" produced and authorized New Kids paraphernalia, knowing the "personalities" of all members of the group, and defending their music and its integrity from attackers. The depth of a fan's commitment to New Kids could be determined by how well she knew the codes.

Although I have generally spoken of the image as being the key variant in the meaning of New Kids, this image must be contextualized in terms of the kind of music they performed, because the music establishes a clear form of delineation of audience groups. The full meaning of music is difficult to conceptualize. It is embedded with the affective associations of the listener, which makes any reading of its meaning a game of searching for commonalities in idiosyncratic decoding. Nevertheless, music does have social contexts worked into its rhythms, its musical notation, in the words and phrases and topics that are part of any group's repertoire.[42] New Kids drew principally from three sources: dance music, which has part of its origins in the Motown sound; Western love ballads; and rap/hip-hop music. Each of these origins had a great deal of significance to the sound and meaning of New Kids.

New Kids' use of dance music indicated that they were not attempting to appeal to some intellectualized aesthetic. This is music for the movement of the body. In their concerts, the performance was very much focused on dance and movement. The group moved often in unison through a song, in the tradition of black groups of the 1960s such as the Temptations and the Four Tops. No doubt this expression of black dance music had been orchestrated to a large degree by their songwriter and manager, Maurice Starr. The use of young white boys to work through music that arose in African American culture has been a common technique of the entertainment industry of the twentieth century, and New Kids furthered this tradition. Like Elvis, the Beatles, the Rolling Stones, and the Bee Gees, New Kids used this resource to extend the reach of a certain type of music to a suburban American and youthful population. In the biographical details that appeared in the teen magazines, biographies, and various interviews New Kids members gave, there was an emphasis on their intimate connection to black culture or the music of the street, as they often referred to it.[43] Their Boston accents were identified in *People* as "coming from the wrong side of the tracks." Donnie Wahlberg, the recognized leader of the group, has said that he thought of his music as being like basketball, because it kept him away from the dangers of the street. There was a degree of celebration of working-class roots that allowed for the public representation that they came to this form of music honestly: once again, the discourse of authenticity is articulated in the meanings of any popular music celebrity. Four of the five members of New Kids went to the same elementary school, and their humble beginnings as children of large, poor Irish Catholic families reinforced their legitimate right to sing music of the street.

The incongruity between their black dance style and song construction and their white American looks was also used to discredit the New Kids. The group was used to articulate various sentiments about the realm of the authentic and the inauthentic. New Kids' complete commodification buttressed the rock discourse of musical rip-off and sellout of black musical culture. Moreover, their virtual lack of involvement in the writing of their songs made them vulnerable to accusations of the same kind of rip-off that Chappell and Garafalo have chronicled concerning black performers in the 1950s.[44] The vociferousness of the attack on their credibility served not only to galvanize some fragments of youth culture and popular music criticism against them, but to construct a siege mentality among their fans and the ancillary teen press that supported them. The intensity of the discourse of authenticity worked to establish much clearer uses of popular celebrities for the articulation of social identities and distinctions.

The second source of New Kids' music presented a different line of demarcation for the use of audiences. The popular ballad, which formed one of the three sources of musical style in their recorded and concert performances, follows in the tradition of the Broadway and movie musical love song and is firmly ensconced in Western

European popular music. It identifies a line of demarcation in terms of the principal audience's gender.

Susan McClary has done some work on the way in which music is defined as masculine or feminine that is relevant to the current discussion.[45] *Feminine ending* is a term used in music criticism to describe a weak or softened conclusion to part of a composition. Principally, the term has been used in a negative sense. Although McClary begins her discussion with an exploration of the way patriarchy inflects the meanings of classical musical texts, she adapts it successfully to the organization of popular music in her treatment of Madonna and Laurie Anderson.[46] Similar readings can be made of the love ballad, although with much greater emphasis on its social uses than on its textual configuration. The feminized popular musical text has been constructed as the love song, which, in its softened sound, its entreating (male) voice, and its romantic construction of love, works to construct a female listener. Paralleling the development of the romance novel and the soap opera, the female listener has embraced the love song text in a proprietary way. The New Kids' core audience of young adolescent and preadolescent girls took the love song and not only incorporated its general message into their own lives and everyday experiences, but also constructed a close connection to the artists themselves. The bedroom shrines of New Kids images that many female fans created indicate that the celebrity figure himself has been thought of directly as a romantic possibility. In their choice and performance of these love songs, New Kids on the Block were playing within these social constructions of a feminized text. The love song was a willful acknowledgment of their own fans and a way in which to "talk" to their fans' fantasies directly.

Implicit in the relationship between female fan and the boys of New Kids on the Block was the play with proximity and distance. The love song, in its direct appeal to another individual, is an intimate declaration and an indication that the fan is hearing the personal and private realm of the singer. Popular music works quite specifically in the affective realm, where sentiments and feelings are conveyed. In this sense, the New Kids love song broke down the distance between the pop star and the individual audience member at the very least in the level of fantasy for the audience member. Simultaneously, the emotion and intimacy that the song expressed was being conveyed to thousands, if not millions, of other core audience fans. The subjective experiences that developed from listening to the love song, although not identical among all the fans, would be correlative in the play with the fantasy of intimacy and the reality of distance. For the young female fan, the distance from the personal maintains the pop icon as a nonthreatening personality. The sexual innuendo is real at the emotive level but perfectly impossible at the level of the real. It is this wonderful combination of the feeling of intimacy and the structure of distance that makes the teen idol so powerfully appealing at the level of fantasy.

New Kids members typically presented themselves as personally open and intimate while objectively distant and unknown, except through their images and sounds. The bedroom shrine discussed above articulates the way in which intimacy was connected between the images of the teen idols and the private world of the fan's bedroom. The music, then, was coordinated with the various other sources of information the fan could collect about the members of the group. One of these, a glossy photo album of the band members peppered with their commentary on their feelings, provides the typical play between accessibility to the group members' intimate world and the impossibility of fully entering that world. In this publication, various "bedroom" pictures are juxtaposed beside performance images in the thirty-page section devoted to each member. Superimposed on an image of a performing, shirtless Jordan surrounded by fans' hands trying to reach out and touch him is the question, "How do you feel about all the girls reaching out to touch you at shows?" His reply maintains the possibility of his fans' possessing him: "If I know they can't reach me I love it. I feel in control of the situation, but sometimes times I'd like to get attacked. It seems like it'd be fun."[47] The anchoring text for an "intimate" photo of Jonathan in a terry bathrobe invites the audience to complete the romantic sentiment in fantasy: "I think romance is very sweet. I don't think there's too much of it out there these days. Men try to be too macho."[48]

Whereas the love song was central to the maintenance and organization of the New Kids audience, its construction as a feminized and preadolescent discourse also served to delegitimate the group in the eyes of others. Heavy metal music, which, it could be argued, is a celebration of the masculine text and is talked about in masculinized terms of power and hardness, operated as the antithesis to much of New Kids music. Rock music in general also functions as a masculinized discourse that in its self-criticism often tries to purge the feminized love song from the lexicon of what constitutes good popular music. Derogatory terms such as *bubblegum* and *teenybopper music* are used to separate the female-constructed popular music audience from the mainstream of male rock culture.

What surfaces from this type of audience differentiation is the kind of identification that is central to each audience group. With New Kids there was an emphasis on what I would call a *completing* identification: the audience did not identify with the group members directly, but rather in relational terms. The performers were male and the audience primarily female, and thus the normative discourse that underplayed this organization was heterosexuality, which in this construction was played out at the level of a fantasy of intimacy. In contrast, the heavy metal performer, the punk rocker, and the thrash metal idol work to construct an emulating identification with audience members. These kinds of performers are predominantly male, and their primary audience is also predominantly male. The performance is meant to empower, so that audience members see themselves as if they were the performers. In a sense, both forms of identification are the invocations of a normative discourse of patriarchy. The relational completion form of identification proffered by New Kids established that social power is derived from the male figure; the emulative form of identification establishes, first, the bond between the male audience and the male performer and, second, that empowerment flows along these gender lines.

A different layer of meaning was constructed through New Kids' use of another musical/cultural source that was simultaneously built on their relational form of identification with their fans. Through the adoption and adaptation of rap music and hip-hop into their performance, New Kids on the Block established a connotational connection. The general social context connected to this type of music – that is, urban street culture and black ghetto culture – provided two principal meanings for the construction of the celebrity signs of New Kids on the Block: authenticity and contemporaneity.

With the use of black urban forms of music and dance, the New Kids underlined their own humble origins and thus their own claim to a discourse of the authentic.

As well, the musical form connected a social text of populism and nonelitism to the members' positions as public personalities. Drawing on the conventions of current street music was a way of connecting to the audience and indicating that there were no barriers to the music and meanings they conveyed through song and dance.

Second, rap music provided a social context of currency and contemporaneity. To position New Kids as in fact something unique to their cultural moment and thereby distance their constructed sign from previous popular music idols, the new currency of musical expression ensured their status as a contemporary phenomenon. In this way, New Kids and popular music have continued to fill the role of constructing a discourse of change and transformation. And each new phenomenon represents a celebration of change itself. Not only does this celebration of change aid in the circulation of new commodities connected to new social constructions of signs, it also works to reconstruct peripheral cultural phenomena as economically valuable forms of innovation for the mainstream of a cultural industry. Thus, New Kids' sign operated as a signal of the successful integration of popular cultural forms previously marginalized as now aesthetically manipulable cultural commodities.

The meaning of the group

On one level, New Kids operated as a cohesive moniker for public identity. As with other popular music groups, New Kids on the Block was a brand name for a commodity. Although there were five members in the group, there was a concerted effort to maintain the cohesiveness and solidarity of the group behind the group's name. The name stood for their distinctive sound and, by implication, a particular audience. Maintaining consistency around the name ensured a degree of brand loyalty among music consumers. Thus, one of the meanings of the group identity was to organize the popular music market.

On another level, group identity for New Kids grafted them onto a tradition of rock music. At least in the romantic connotations, the musical group is a collective, where the various interests of each band member contribute to the musical sound. As mentioned in the analysis of popular music formations above, the group identity also represents a democratic solidarity among the artists and ultimately the fans. New Kids, even though the group was orchestrated in its formation by a manager, connected itself to this collective spirit of rock music. Instead of an emphasis on the individual, group identity became paramount.

New Kids, however, operated under another tradition that often works in contradistinction to the meaning of the group: that of the highly individualized and mediated teen idol or pop star. In fan literature and printed interviews, the members of the group were presented as possessing individual though very typecast personalities. There was Joey, the youngest member, chosen for his youth, to attract younger audience members.[49] Jordan represented the leading boy-man and was constructed as the best-looking member of the group. Donnie, who frequently appeared in the tabloid press – in 1991 for alleged arson – was constructed as the rebel. Jonathan was the quiet introvert, and Danny represented the more mature masculine personality. Photographs and texts reaffirmed and reinforced these constructed categories for the play of relations with their fans. For example, Danny was frequently depicted as a bodybuilder, thereby evoking a connotation of hypermasculinity. In contrast, Joey was desexualized; in at least one book (and in a network TV special) he was represented as a young performer in the mold of Frank Sinatra, and with the image of Sinatra as pop icon, Joey established his own image as something that predated and circumvented the overt sexuality of the entire history of rock music.[50] In sum, what was constructed was a series of rather simplistic caricatures of boy-types that could be reread and distinguished for use by their predominantly young female audience. Extensive personal information about each New Kid was presented to help audience members choose their favorites. In making the choice of a favorite, the female fan played with the conception of a greater intimacy and empathy with that particular member. The meaning of the constructed heterogeneous group, then, was not only to establish a brand name and a connection to the romantic tradition of popular music, but also to construct a series of celebrity signs within the group that allowed for fans to play with the notion of a more personal attachment to one of the members.[51]

Conclusion: dissipation of celebrity status

More than any other form of celebrity, the popular music celebrity, and in particular the celebrity who emerges from the adulation of a preteen or young teen female audience, demonstrates the rapidity of dissipation of the power and influence of a public personality. The reason for part of this dissipation is the way in which the popular music industry has helped to construct itself as a symbol of change and transformation. Thus, each new popular music star represents virtually simultaneously the moment of innovation and the moment of replacement. In popular music's reconstruction of a youth culture, the succession of apparent new images and sounds constitutes the representation of change that is often used by the culture at large as a representation of the vitality of the entire culture.

To explain the particularly rapid dissipation of teen idols, one needs to consider the way in which the audience has been constructed by the various cultural industries. As mentioned above, the audience of the teen idol is considered to be irrational, in a frenzy of devotion to the idol. The fan's relationship to the teen idol can be thought of as built on an incredible level of emotional intensity. Thus, the economic power of the pop star is configured around affect. However, the challenge of affective power is that it is very difficult to maintain; it is by its very nature subject to dissipation. Because the recording industry has organized itself around the momentary capturing of expansive affective power, it is also organized around losing the ability of any given commodity to produce that affective power. The industry's solution to its own construction of successive waves of affect is to produce new commodities that allow for the containing of collective affect. The pop music celebrity, then, is the convertible personality who can capture youth's affective intensity.

What we can conclude about New Kids on the Block is that they achieved through the industry the status of a powerfully affective commodity. Their sales worldwide of albums alone were truly staggering and indicate the economic clout they wielded. However, we can also conclude that New Kids on the Block's power as a commodity has dissipated. The group has been succeeded by new so-called phenomena that maintain the discourse of change that is at the center of the popular music industry and the culture in general. Indeed, by all indications the performer known as Vanilla Ice led many fans of New Kids to pull down their shrines, although he has now disappeared from public consciousness. For a moment, several of the characters from the television series *Beverly Hills 90210* overflowed the preteen magazines, while New Kids occupied only the mail-order pages. In 1994, New Kids attempted a reincarnation as a young adult group with varying degrees of facial hair, more hip-hop music, and extensive writing and producing credits on their music to indicate their new autonomy; however, their new album, *Face the Music*, and their new image disappeared rather quickly from the charts and were virtually shunned both by radio stations fearful of stigma and by music magazines aware of the ever-present backlash to the group's seen-to-be-illegitimate success.[52] The succession of the play with affect continues with the young and temporarily loyal female fan as it migrates to cluster around new identities produced by the entertainment industries.

Notes

1   David Buxton, *Le Rock: star système et société de consommation* (Grenoble: La Pensée Sauvage, 1985), 30.

2   John Shepherd, *Tin Pan Alley* (London: Routledge, 1982), 9.

3   Buxton, *Le Rock*, chs. 1–2.

4   See Steve Chappell and R. Garafalo, *Rock 'n' Roll Is Here to Pay: The History and Politics of the Music Industry* (Chicago: Nelson-Hall, 1977). Also see Le Roi Jones [Imamu Amiri Baraka], *The Blues People* (New York: Morrow, 1963) (reissued, Edinburgh: Payback, 1995).

5   Buxton, *Le Rock*, 27.

6   Ibid., 27–29.

7   Simon Frith has recounted: "A couple of years ago I went to see Al Green in concert in the Royal Albert Hall in London. At one point he left the stage (and his microphone) and walked through the audience, still singing. As he passed me I realized that this was the first time, in 30 years as a pop fan, that I'd heard a star's 'natural' voice!" Simon Frith, "The Industrialization of Popular Music," in James Lull (ed.), *Popular Music and Communication* (Newbury Park, Calif.: Sage, 1987), 53.

8   The rapid expansion of karaoke bars in North America and Europe represents the blending of the authentic background track with the personal for the representation of performance. It is an active positioning of a cultural practice in the interstices between the authentic (and the public) and the private (and the personal). A recent example of this revelation of inauthenticity was the confession of the two young men who performed as Milli Vanilli that they did not sing their songs on record or at concerts. They were purely actors of the songs and lip-synchers. The confession resulted in the duo's being stripped of two Grammy Awards. Likewise, the group New Kids on the Block was accused on many occasions of using a great deal of prerecorded vocals and music in their programs.

9   Simon Frith, *Sound Effects: Youth, Leisure and the Politics of Rock 'n' Roll* (New York: Pantheon, 1983), 113.

10 Buxton, *Le Rock*, 26.

11 Shepherd, *Tin Pan Alley*, 103–5.

12 Roland Barthes, "The Grain of the Voice," in *Image-Music-Text* (New York: Hill & Wang, 1977), 179–89.

13 Buxton, *Le Rock*, 33.

14 Shepherd, *Tin Pan Alley*, 97.

15 Buxton, *Le Rock*, 37.

16 See in particular ibid., 64–68; Shepherd, *Tin Pan Alley*, 135–38; and Richard Middleton's discussion of subjectivity in *Studying Popular Music* (Buckingham: Open University Press, 1990), 266.

17 It is generally acknowledged that most concert tours are money-losing ventures. Thus, in recent years, many rock bands undertaking major tours have done so with the sponsorship of beer or soft drink corporations, in order to defray expenses.

18 Frith, *Sound Effects*, 182–94.

19 Buxton, *Le Rock*, 71.

20 See in particular the development of British subcultural studies: Stanley Cohen, *Folk Devils and Moral Panics* (London: McGibbon & Kee, 1972); Stuart Hall and Tony Jefferson (eds.), *Resistance through Rituals: Youth Subcultures in Post-War Britain* (London: Routledge, 1990); Dick Hebdige, *Subculture: The Meaning of Style* (New York: Methuen, 1979).

21 See Simon Frith and Howard Horne, *Art into Pop* (London: Methuen, 1987), ch. 2.

22 Chatterton, who attempted to create a long-lost poet named Rowley from a previous century, committed suicide at the age of seventeen in the late eighteenth century when his faked discovery and his faked poet gained no attention. What makes this otherwise insignificant event one of resonance is how Chatterton's life (and death) was celebrated and relived by nineteenth-century romantic poets like Wordsworth, Byron, Keats, and even a young Coleridge. See Leo Braudy, *The Frenzy of Renown: Fame and Its History* (New York: Oxford University Press, 1986), 421–25.

23 See Robert Pattison, *The Triumph of Vulgarity: Rock Music in the Mirror of Romanticism* (New York: Oxford University Press, 1987). Pattison maintains that rock music epitomizes a contemporary version of romantic pantheism.

24 Frith, *Sound Effects*, 147. In fact, this statistic on the success of records roughly parallels the success rate for the introduction of any new consumer product.

25 Paul Grein, "New Kids Have Blockbuster Year," *Billboard*, December 23, 1989, 10; "New Kids Top Tour List," *Variety*, December 13, 1990, 52. Most of these statistics do not indicate international sales of New Kids records. Comparable levels of sales and success were recorded in the United Kingdom, Canada, Australia (to a lesser degree), Japan, and Europe. For example, see International Charts, *Billboard*, December 16, 1989, 66. Other indications of the group's "phenomenal" status include the fact that the release of their 1990 album *Step by Step* established a first-day sales record. Also, New Kids released a series of videos to coincide with their albums. Their first two music video releases became the first music videos to have sales of more than one million copies. See Ed Christman, "New Kids' *Step by Step* Sells by Leaps and Bounds," *Billboard*, June 16, 1990, 6, 92.

26 Steve Dougherty, "The Heartthrobs of America," *People*, August 13, 1990, 78.

27 Ibid.

28 Grace Catalano, *New Kids on the Block* (New York: Bantam, 1989), 5.

29 This is also the rough demographic of the audience for MTV and Much-music, two video music channels in North America. Particularly the teenage demographic

is seen to be an extremely valuable commodity to "capture": the value of this audience for advertisers is one of the principal motivations for the development of these specialty channels focusing on youth culture.

30   Frith develops the significance of the distinctions between pop and rock in *Sound Effects*, 27–38.

31   In his third and final appearance on *The Ed Sullivan Show* in 1957, Presley's sexually provocative hip gyrations were not shown; only his upper body was televised. After his first two appearances on the program, in which his entire body was visible to the viewing audience, public furor resulted in the decision to photograph him only in close-up when he next appeared. His full image was thought to be too dangerous to be left uncensored for young female audience members. Alex McNeil, *Total Television: A Comprehensive Guide to Programming from 1948 to the Present*, 3rd ed. (New York: Penguin, 1991), 226–27.

32   David Cassidy, in the tradition of the early 1970s, had shoulder-length extremely straight hair; Leif Garrett, a mid-1970s teen idol, had flowing locks in the style of Farrah Fawcett; Shaun Cassidy, emblematic of the boy-man, had characteristic dimples and baby face.

33   Catalano, *New Kids on the Block*, 4.

34   Dougherty, "The Heartthrobs of America."

35   A 1990 advertising insert in *Billboard* estimated the various revenues New Kids had amassed from the spring of 1989 to December 1990. Merchandising revenue dwarfed all the other categories: $400 million of a total of $861,373,000 of earnings were derived from merchandising agreements. By comparison, the group's record sales totaled $143.8 million domestically and concerts totaled $120 million. The ad also identified the products New Kids images were connected with: "posters, t-shirts, hats, banners, buttons (the regular concert fare) . . . . then the merchandise diversified – postcards, poster books, jewelry, baseball-type trading cards, sleeping bags, bed sheets, poster puzzles, beach towels, watches, jackets, cups, laundry bags, balloons, boxer shorts, pajamas, water bottles, rainwear, umbrellas, gloves, scarves, mittens, shower curtains, sunglasses, sunglass cords, lunchboxes, mirrors, slippers, paper tattoos, belts, socks, sweater, storage trunks, bedspreads, and of course, Hasbro Inc.'s two lines of dolls – one in concert clothes with stage set available, and one in street clothes." Karen Schlossberg, "Merchandising: The Amazing Business of Defining, Controlling and Marketing an Image Explosion" (in an advertising supplement), *Billboard*, December 15, 1990, NK-22, 32, 34. The ad supplement itself was an interesting phenomenon. It indicated, through a series of congratulatory inserts, the number of companies that had been involved in the New Kids' success.

36   Typical of such reportage is D. Wild, "Puberty to Platinum," *Rolling Stone*, November 2, 1989, 15–17. Even more typical is the general overlooking of the band in many music publications, including *Creem*.

37   Catalano, *New Kids on the Block*, 16.

38   This controversy plagued New Kids' claims to legitimacy or "authenticity." The latest claim, made in early 1992, is that they in fact did not sing major parts of their albums. So, in this latest variation not only is their authenticity of performance challenged, but their authenticity in the "official" records of their music is put under suspicion.

39   The original album, after the success of their second album, also went platinum (i.e., had sales of more than one million).

40   The age of listeners attracted to New Kids was quickly seen as a "problem" for radio programmers throughout North America. For example, Mike Edwards, a programmer for a Buffalo, New York, station, explained that "some of our research has shown burn on the New Kids and that the perception of playing too much of New Kids can be a negative for you. We have to be very cautious." Other programmers indicated that by April 1991 stations were getting a lot of hate calls about the group. Many stations chose not to play the group except during certain early evening hours. Their fear was that they were losing an older listening demographic, a demographic much more lucrative to their advertising clientele than six- to ten-year-olds. Sean Ross and Thom Duffy, "Radio Gridlock on New Kids' Block?" *Billboard*, April 28, 1990, 4, 74.

41   The female preteen magazine has a heavily overcoded structure. Operating as fantasy magazines organized around male adolescent stars, *Tiger Beat, Bop, Teen Machine, Superteen*, and others build each of their segments around full-page or two-page photo spreads of these individual stars. Thus, from 1988 to 1991, the members of New Kids on the Block individually were repeatedly the subjects of these photo features. The utility of the magazines is as sources of these one- or two-page photos for decoration of the bedroom. The magazines must reorganize themselves constantly so that the images presented are in concert with the newest stars of television, film, and popular music. In order to do so, they sponsor a plethora of contests and polls interspersed with profiles of idols. The contests represent an essential marketing technique for a magazine industry that must continually re-present fantasy materials for the preteen female audience.

42   See John Shepherd, *Music as Social Text* (Cambridge: Polity, 1991).

43   Indeed, Starr's choices of the five members had a great deal to do with their familiarity with black street culture and break dancing. For instance, Donnie's claims to fame were his dance imitations of Michael Jackson and the bravado to engage in spontaneous rap performances in the local park. Jordan and Danny were part of rival break-dance groups who would practice and perform their moves in downtown Boston every Saturday well before they became New Kids members — white kids engaged in what was an essentially black youth activity. As Danny's fellow break-dancer and friend David Harris described it: "We would select a suitable store and start break-dancing on it, with cushions in our hats . . . We'd perform for half an hour or so then move on to another store. By lunchtime, we'd have earned around forty dollars, which wasn't bad for thirteen and fourteen year olds." Robin McGibbon, *New Kids on the Block: The Whole Story by Their Friends* (New York: Avon, 1990), 16.

44   See Chappell and Garafalo, *Rock 'n' Roll Is Here to Pay*.

45   Susan McClary, *Feminine Endings: Music, Gender, and Sexuality* (Minneapolis: University of Minnesota Press, 1991).

46   Ibid., chs. 6–7.

47   Lynn Goldsmith, *New Kids* (New York: Rizzoli/Eastman Kodak, 1990), n.p.

48   Ibid.

49   For example, one teen magazine feature about Joe McIntyre was titled "Get Cozy with Joey," *Superteen*, February 1992, 20.

50   Goldsmith, *New Kids*.

51   According to their lawyer, Barry Rosenthal, an integral part of the marketing of New Kids was to construct them as five individuals who "have their own set of fans. Our concept was to make these kids bigger than the group so they cannot be

replaced. Fan appeal to the kids as individuals was the insurance that we did for our clients." Advertising insert, *Billboard*, December 15, 1990, NK-32, 33.

52   In addition, they changed their name to just the initials NKOTB, and the first single from the album, the raunchy "Dirty Dawg," was released on a white label. Even Columbia's publicity listed the group in anagram fashion as BONK-T. They dropped their Svengali, Maurice Starr, and took on other producers who allowed them greater control to return to the musical roots they love. See Craig Rosen, "Columbia, NKOTB 'Face the Music' with New Album," *Billboard*, January 15, 1994, 10.

Chapter 11

Momin Rahman

IS STRAIGHT THE NEW QUEER?
David Beckham and the dialectics of celebrity

> He is, surely, the only heterosexual male in the country who could get away with being photographed half-naked and smothered in baby oil for *GQ* and still come over as an icon of masculinity.
>
> (*GQ* October 2002. Article on Beckham as *GQ's* Sportsman of the Year, 264)

Indeed.

Let us tear our thoughts away from the image of David basted in oil and consider the extract as one of innumerable examples of the media fascination with Beckham. Given his penetration in Europe, Asia, Latin America and Africa, we can take as self-evident that Beckham is a quantifiably significant figure in contemporary global popular culture. By any measure of celebrity and any taxonomy of fame (Turner 15–23), Beckham qualifies as a striking example. He has inevitably appeared in a number of recent academic publications as an exemplar of celebrity and sports culture (Whannel, Turner, Cashmore and Parker) and, more notably in Cashmore's book, as the focus of a social biography (*Beckham*).

In his book *Understanding Celebrity*, Turner provides a comprehensive overview of the vast literature which has developed on issues of celebrity and fame, painting a broad picture of concerns divided between the significance of the apparent explosion in celebrity 'culture' and the focus on celebrities themselves.

Within the literature on the social significance of celebrity culture, we can discern two key themes. First, celebrity culture is a manifestation of globalised commodity consumerism in advanced capitalism and second, its social function as a system of meanings and values which is supplanting traditional resources for self and social identities in late modern culture, including structures such as class, gender/sexuality, ethnicity and nationality. Whilst the authors mentioned above both draw on and contribute to these arguments, their focus remains broad, citing Beckham as a key manifestation of the complex interdependence between globalised sports and media industries, and transformations in gender and consumption. For example, although Cashmore's book is solidly researched on the impact of media finance on football and has a sound argument on the significance of consumerism, he is prone to generalisations about the transformations in masculinity and celebrity culture which he suggests are central to understanding Beckham's significance.

Turner suggests that there needs to be more focused empirical work on the specific construction of celebrity since 'modern celebrity . . . is a product of media representation: understanding it demands close attention to the representational repertoires and patterns employed in this discursive regime' (8). This is how this short piece offers a contribution to the literature – drawing on a qualitative analysis of articles on Beckham, my discussion focuses on the meanings of Beckham's celebrity and whether they can tell us something about the way the culture of fame operates.

I have drawn selectively from my data, but a fuller discussion of both the data and grounded theory methodology can be found in a previous article (Rahman). Out of the six categories of meaning established through the grounded theory procedures used in the study, my contention is that masculinity is a core nexus in 'cultural circuitry' (Hall) – making the stories relevant, understandable, and often controversial. Moreover, the accompanying photo spreads often create a tension with the text, emphasising dissonant/controversial images which testifies to a dynamic of respect/ridicule in the representations.

To be more precise, there is a construction of deference to Beckham's professional status and to the Beckham family as the premier celebrity unit in the UK. Deference to and respect for their status is evident not only in those magazines which have paid for the privilege of access, but also the more gossip orientated celebrity weeklies such as *Heat* (18–24 May: 6–8): 'those lucky enough to be asked to join David and Victoria enjoyed one the most extravagant soirees in recent memory. The sheer scale of the £350000 shindig was stunning, even by the standards of Celebville's most extravagant couple'.

Coupled with this respect is a sense of ridicule, often in discrete publications, but also within the same magazine and even sometimes the same article. Ridicule undercuts the celebrity credentials of extravagance and glamour with an implication of tackiness and vulgarity, and this gentle undercurrent becomes stronger when linked to Beckham's fashion icon status:

> We've supported David through the highlights and lowlights of his various haircuts: the streaked curtains, the skinhead and his travis bickle style mohican. But this latest look is a 'do too far' – more village idiot than international style icon . . .
>
> (*Heat* 13–19 April: 24–5)

This dynamic of respect/ridicule relies heavily on another dynamic; that of queer/normative invocation and recuperation. It is not only his fashion icon status being ridiculed here but also his status as a heterosexual masculine icon:

People say you're vain. Do you think so?
You can see why people might think you're a bit of a big girl's blouse,
because you have manicures, sunbeds and bleach your hair.
You're also one of the few footballers to become a gay icon.
                    (*Marie Claire* June 2002: cover of Beckham, and 69–76)

His gender/sexuality is anchored in hetero-family/masculine status but is somewhat dissonant in terms of vanity/grooming and gay icon status. 'Queerying' Beckham
is not just a technique of ridicule (how very old fashioned that would be!) but also a
deliberate destabilisation of ontological anchors which induces a sense of dissonance:

An example from *Heat* (20–26 July 2002) has the cover byline 'Phwoar! Another
new look for Becks' with a trail for a story on pages 18–20 which has a photograph of
Beckham with his nail varnish highlighted and the text:

> David sported a new blonde barnet and a fitted black suit, and despite the
> controversy caused by his pink nail varnish he still managed to look macho
> and absolutely beautiful.

This demonstrates some feminisation of Beckham but is counterbalanced by the
very masculine anchor of 'macho'. There is a recognition that the highlighted ambiguity
in gender coding is potentially disruptive or controversial and hence it is recuperated
– 'he still managed to look macho'. *GQ* from June 2002 repeats the play on gender and
sexuality, with a cover photo of Beckham lying down, bare torso but in a suit and hat,
with one hand showing a ring and nail varnish, and the other in the waistband of his
trousers. Inside, on pages 142–55, there follow seven full pages of photos and an
interview conducted by David Furnish, a family friend of the Beckhams but also Elton
John's partner and so one of the most visible gay men in celebrity culture. However,
rather than any danger of queering by association, the presence of Furnish seems only
to enhance the mega-celebrity and hetero status, since he is careful to sound all the
right notes of family, football and fatherhood in his questions in the text. Rather, it is
the photospread which induces the queerness in this example, with four of Beckham's
naked torso in baby oil, of which one is him in unbuttoned cut-off denim shorts on a
weights bench – very retro 1970s gay.

In his history of male sports celebrities, Whannel suggests that Beckham is an
exceptional figure, both because he is one of the few footballers in the UK to achieve
full celebrity status, but also because he transgresses the discipline and work ethic
associated with sporting bodies, indulging himself through conspicuous and narcissistic consumption (212). Whannel notes Beckham's emergence during the development of a men's style press in the UK, documented thoroughly in Nixon's study
of men's magazines, which provides an account of the historical moment from
1984–1990 which saw the emergence of 'new man' imagery. Drawing on Mort's
contention that this is the first period which showed men being sexualised – a
representational strategy previously applied only to women – Nixon concurs with
Mort that this moment marks the beginning of men being addressed as a specific
gender. However, these images of Beckham push at the boundaries of 'new man'
constructions and 'respectable' images of sporting bodies, suggesting that the deliberate, indelicate and delicious sexualisation of Beckham's body derives its power

from the 'danger' this presents to sporting masculinity as well as simply heterosexual masculinity. Thus we need 'family, fatherhood' *and* 'football' to anchor the 'queer' Beckham.

Given these and more recent images (*Vanity Fair* cover in July 2004, for example), we might be tempted to agree with Cashmore and Parker and Whannel that Beckham is indeed a 'postmodern' or 'hybrid' celebrity, appearing singularly able to float free of context and to signify many different meanings to many different groups. But the brief examples of the queer/normative dynamic presented here suggest that this is too glib an answer, precisely because there seems to be an explicit recognition of this dynamic: the editor of *GQ* says of Beckham that 'he is in touch with his feminine side, but he is so obviously heterosexual that he can afford to be' (*Hot Stars* 2–8 Nov. 2002: 36–9). The deliberate induction of dissonance suggests a reflexivity about the constructedness of these representations; a knowing indication that queerying Beckham's masculinity is not the reality of Beckham, but rather that the queerying is perhaps a hyper reality as Baudrillard might have it. Beckham does not float 'free': dialectical signs are precisely mapped onto him. Dyer argues that film stars could be read as signs for specific versions of individuality, but crucially, that these signs reflect the dominant ideological constructions of class, ethnicity and gender/sexuality. In one example, he demonstrates how the sexually transgressive and potentially lesbian elements of Jane Fonda's star persona are recuperated through the emphasis on her nationality and ethnicity, her 'all-Americanness' (81). Similarly, Beckham's queerness is deliberately deployed as a sign, to be neutralised by heterosexual signs, thus recuperating the ideological dominance of a heteronormative culture.

Beckham's masculinity can be read as a 'sign', divorced from traditional referents and remarked into a queer sign, specifically to promote consumption through the heady mix of respected status and apparently exciting transgression as a key aspect of this status. But this is a simulation, not indicating any 'real' queering of either the subject, or indeed of the assumed audience who have to make sense of the sign. Rather, the potential to remark Beckham as 'queer' seems to indicate that whilst heterosexual masculinity can be a sign, so perhaps too does queer itself become a sign, similarly divorced from its traditional referents. The 'reality' is thus simulated through pre-determined codes of representation, and one such code seems to be that gender transgression is culturally significant. Dialectical signs are mapped onto a reality/hyper reality dynamic, with queerness presented knowingly as the hyper real – after all, the reality is that Beckham is 'so obviously heterosexual . . .'

It is possible to argue that the dynamics at work in making these representations effective can be understood as dialectical since there are opposing momentums at work in the construction of celebrity and fame. The respect/ridicule dynamic demonstrates that constructions of celebrity cannot be uncritically deferential. The gentle and knowing ridicule is a collusion between the media (tors) and the audience: an indication that this relationship is the true romance of celebrity culture rather than that between fans and icons. And why should this be so? Precisely because the media needs to continue to feed the desires of the audience but there is no guarantee that the desire will continue when an icon's star wanes – unless of course, watching the decline is as much part of the romance as building the respect. Marshall argues that celebrity legitimises the individuality central to the lock between consumer capitalism and liberal democracy and the respect/ridicule dynamic exemplifies this function. The necessary continuation of consumption produces a dialectical dynamic, wherein both respect and ridicule exist to permit easy shifts in *emphasis* whilst maintaining the *attention* on the celebrity, which promotes continued consumption. Beckham's own demonisation and rehabilitation in the wake of France 98 testifies convincingly to the necessity for continuity of producing items for consumption, no matter what the spin. Furthermore, the recent scandals over alleged infidelities has generated a production spike in the amount of images and words produced, whilst this time, not directly attacking Beckham.

The queer constructions of Beckham amplify respect/ridicule along a specific dimension, supplying a dialectic of its own. The modes of meaning surrounding Beckham do indicate a shift in the possible effective constructions of masculinity, with the incorporation of a feminised interest in fashion (hairstyles, nail varnish, presentation in general) and the affirmation of gay icon/object of desire. It is in these constructions of dissonance that the de-essentialising of masculinity occurs, which may be the productive moment of disruption for those receiving the images and texts, and incorporating them into their own meaning systems around Beckham, footballers, masculinities, heteronormativity. The fact that these queer moments are possible may be testament enough to Beckham's social significance; he is in the right place at the right time (with the right body and profession) to be our cultural lightning conductor for contemporary anxieties around gender/sexuality.

However, the dialectic of queering Beckham has a synthesis which suggests that the route into queerness is not as important as the route out. These are only fleeting materialisations of the queer David Beckham — flashes of fleshy dissonance glimpsed briefly before the recuperation into the heterosexual subject, coded by footie, family and fatherhood. The newer dissonant properties of masculinity are literally contextualised within ideological codes of heterosexuality. The evident theatricalisation and appropriation may appear to signal a productive route into queerness — from heterosexual to queer (the pink nail varnish, the oiled fashion shoots, the gay gym denim cut offs shot), but what if it is actually working in reverse? What if the cultural effectivity is achieved by appropriating and theatricalising from gay/transgender to heterosexual? — de-essentialising 'queer' for productive dissonance and amusement, but safe in the knowledge that there is a secure and policed route out of 'queerness' — the encoded red carpet of heterosexual masculinity.

The possibilities of a queer visibility are thus denied through the recuperative effects of the dialectics at work. The ridiculing of his gender transgressions may be necessarily gentle, in order to walk the tightrope of respect/ridicule, but they nonetheless assume that transgressions are problematic. Furthermore, the reality/hyper reality dynamic deploys queer as a 'sign' precisely in order to effect a recuperation of a normative version of 'reality'. It seems that the weight of a predominantly heteronormative culture reinforces the dialectics in celebrity culture, making the unproblematic visibility of queer subjects improbable. After all, in these examples — focused one on the world's premier celebrities — 'queer' itself is not actually cool — it seems that only the simulation of queer is cool. Within contemporary fame, perhaps straight is really the new queer?

Chapter 12

Barry King

ARTICULATING STARDOM

Despite the early interest shown by the Prague School, the role of the actor as re-presenter of signs has barely been examined.[1] The writing on the semiotics of acting looks very undernourished when contrasted with the literature of adulation, anecdote and reminiscence that has colonised the discussion of this aspect of the performing arts. Thus one of the main purposes of this article is to focus attention on the categories and variables that I take to be essential to the development of a semiotics of acting in film and, by extension, television. My second purpose underlies the first: I want to suggest that the kinds of variables I identify enable us to organise the materials on film acting available to us into an account that, if developed, will provide a means of reconciling a "political economy" approach to, especially, stardom in the mainstream (Hollywood) cinema and the theorisation of the role of the star in terms of film as an interplay of representation and identification.

More generally speaking, the style of argument advanced here—which I would identify as a cultural materialist one[2]—aims to specify a reconciliation between the sorts of determinations that arise from economic organisation in the traditional sense of that term and the determinations that are immanent to the process of signification *per se*. Those persuaded of the absolute autonomy of the "text" are certain to find this line of argument unappealing. On the other hand, those who take the far more cogent position that the textual production of meaning is relatively autonomous will find in what follows an attempt to isolate a specific, albeit importance instance, of the subordination of the textual production of meaning to factors of economic and social control.[3] The manner in which this occurs, that is, the manner in which textual autonomy is articulated, is what I will attempt to show. But the crux of my argument is that stardom is a strategy of performance that is an adaptive response to the limits and pressures exerted upon acting as a discursive practice in the mainstream cinema.

To pursue this argument it is necessary to show how stardom develops as a response to the interaction of three areas of discursive practice which I shall term economies – systems of control that mobilise discursive resources in order to achieve specifiable effects. These are: the cultural economy of the human body as a sign; the economy of signification in film; and the economy of the labour market for actors. Broadly, while I think that, in the last instance, it is the mediation of the labour market for actors that sets the limits of variation in the other fields of practice – and hence the hegemonic form of acting as stardom – these latter practices present recurrently possibilities and contradictions on the boundaries of and within the hegemonic practice. In other words, stardom, a response to the labour market for actors, determines the consequences of the other processes that I identify.[4] At the outset, it is desirable to emphasise that what follows does not constitute an analysis of a given performance nor, indeed, does it constitute a theory of performance *per se*, rather it seeks to theorise the fundamental constraints on acting as a discursive practice in film (and television) that produces a particular kind or mode of performance strategy – a strategy that must continually negotiate a way through the forcefield of other practices.

But before addressing these latter points directly, it is necessary to explore the relationship between stage and screen acting in some detail, since it is my reading of this relationship that conditions the treatment that follows.

Stage and screen

The view that stage acting provides a yardstick against which to evaluate acting on screen is widespread among actors, even among those whose main professional activities have been confined to the screen. A common argument is that the stage is an actor's medium, in the sense that it is on the stage that the actor is best placed to realise his or her "creative intentions" in character portrayal.[5] While such assertions may be seen, as does Bourdieu, as conditioned by the desire to be publicly associated with an elite institution – the "Stage," its "Great" tradition, etc. – or, alternatively, as an attempt to align acting with professions that sustain the claim to autonomy more effectively with the public at large and clients in particular, it is necessary to recognise that certain empirical features of the work situation of the actor tend to confirm the general direction, if not the elitist texture, of such a judgement.[6]

Two recurrent themes can be identified. First, that "good" acting is based on some concept of intentionality, or even authorship. It is taken for granted that the participation of the actor(s) in the process of signification should be an outcome of the deployment of a conscious and constitutive control at the point of performance. Such constitutive control is not necessarily inconsistent with the taking of *direction*, emanating from considerations of signification at the level of the total, usually narrative, performed text, of which the actor's performance, even if a leading player, is "merely" a subtext. But it does imply that interventions into the subtext of the actor's performance, even if emanating from positions that are extra-discursive, should be left to the actor to articulate *within* the discursive practices of acting. It is more or less uniformly held that film (or video) presents a latent and readily actualised threat to this requirement, whereas theatre does not. Secondly, it is regularly assumed that theatre as a medium, because it entails "live" performance before an audience and because the duration of the performance is the performance *per se* rather than the provision of materials editable downwards into a performance given elsewhere, requires of the actor a more sustained exercise of skills and commitment than is the case where an editable medium is used. A recent representation of the "loss" of quality and commitment entailed in shifting from stage to screen is given by Sam Shephard:

> There's a certain voyeurism about the camera. With a live audience in the theatre, an actor has to meet total physical and emotional demands, while in a film you can use little pieces of yourself and that's construed as acting.[7]

Faced with the empirical fact of a preference for stagework over screen among actors whose occupational standing is high, the problem for a constructive analysis is to steer a path between uncritical acceptance or rejection of the datum of preferences as a mere *parti pris* and the allure of an essentialist appreciation of the media in question. Such a datum of preference, echoing Bourdieu again, is arbitrary but not gratuitous. It expresses a reaction and an adaptation within the discursive practices of acting to the organisational realities of working in the mainstream theatre and cinema. To uncover these constraints in full implies either the existence of a well-developed political economy of acting, with the delineation of its historical phases and contexts of development or a programmatic statement of what such an analysis would cover. The absence of the former and the redirection of effort implied by the latter renders such an undertaking impractical in the confines of this article. Nevertheless from an immanent perspective, it is possible to identify the operation of variables that impose a certain strategic cast on contemporary acting. One is, therefore, required to read in the actors' preference for the stage a situational logic that entails a more serious assessment than matters of status-hunger would imply.

In the first place, the discursive practice of acting, in Britain and the USA at least, is deeply implicated in the project of intentionality or the actor as a particular kind of "knowing" subject which needs to be correctly assessed. The most concrete evidence of this implication relates to the role of practice in the training of actors, or for that matter, performers in general.[8] The regime of exercises that constitute an actor's training, while certainly increasing his or her adaptability in respect of casting for specialised skills like juggling, dancing and so on, are nevertheless intended to increase the conscious mastery of the actor over verbal, gestural and postural behaviour. The objective of the control installed through practice is to reduce behaviours like these to a state of automaticity so that they are summonable at will in relation to consciously formulated expressive purpose. In a similar way, versatility of accent, posture, walk and other markers of difference, is *intended* to enable the actor to "naturalise" such exogenous behaviours (or possibly, some elements of own behaviour to be used consciously in performance) as his or her own for the duration of performance in order to be convincing "in character."[9] At its extreme, the prioritisation of intentionality – the intention, in this case, to communicate some "truth" about the interior reality of the character – has a Cartesian ring about it: the maximisation of conscious control over acquired dispositions, inherited characteristics (the utopia of make-up) and their conventionalised meanings in the culture at large. Taken to its extreme, and to the extent that actors, like any other occupational group, have an interest in excluding untrained entrants, such an extreme has a pragmatic value, such a project leads to the requirement that:

> . . . [the] actor must be able to be true to any conceivable character, making all actions believable and spontaneous.[10]

More routinely, such a project leads to the norm of impersonation. This states that in playing any character, the "real" personality of the actor should disappear into the part or, conversely, that if the range of the actor is limited to parts consonant with his or her personality then this constitutes "poor" acting. This latter, negatively valued converse, I shall refer to, hereafter, as personification. A number of points can be made about impersonation: for example, it seems to transcend acting styles – Method and Broadway/repertoire styles tending to propose different strategies of realisation of the same objective[11] – and it serves to grade positively the standing of the actor among peers. But probably the key theoretical issue relates to the concept of authorship implicit in such a project.

As Foucault has argued, the concept of "Author" can be seen as a principle of coherence, governing the identification, organisation, circulation and reception of texts, rather than as verbal marker denoting a discrete historical identity that unfolds transparently through the text. In this regard, he writes of the "author function" rather than the "author."[12] One of the key thrusts to Foucault's argument is to highlight the various ways in which the romantic conception of the author – as a unified subject purposively unfolding his or her interiority before a reader, a parallel coherence in the sphere of reception – constitutes a denial of intertextuality. Does the concept of impersonation, in fact, constitute a performance variant of the myth of the author?

My answer to this is, basically, no. To put it bluntly, so long as the contribution of the actor (or for that matter any other functionary in the process of collective production) disappears into character, then the performance text – or more strictly the text created by the ensemble of performances – can be assigned a unitary, global author. Notwithstanding this fact, the romantic myth of the author has readily and voraciously fastened itself to the world of performance by a facile, but plausible extension of the literary conception of the author to that field.[13]

The objective of performance is the re-presentation of a text through the activation of its various parts – in acting usually a narrative realised through its characters or in music the realisation of the score through the execution of its instrumental parts and so on. The relationship between the execution of the "parts" and the ultimating "text" may be more or less specified by the nominal author through a system of notation, but the intrinsic relationship between the script or score is inter-textual: it is only through the performance – in reality, an ensemble of performances – that the "text" is fully realised, yet each performance constitutes a specific text in itself, more or less a version or a token of the notated or written text and implicated in the discourse of the past, present and future versions of the text. Thus it is meaningful, if finally misleading, to speak of Shakespeare's Hamlet in relation to Olivier's or Gielgud's Hamlet and so on.[14] The notion of the author as opposed to author-function is clearly, if mistakenly operative in such formulations in the sense that it is the leading actor's name that is used (especially when he assumes a directorial role) to indicate a specific realisation or re-presentation of the text, but neither the text nor its version constitute a definitive "work" or vision transhistorically foreclosed around the intentions of the author. For actors, intentionality is doubly articulated: the actor deals with a part which is only a moment of the totality of the performances given by other actors (or other participants, a one-man show is never produced by just one individual) and that totality is itself, as already indicated, intrinsically intertextual. The actor's intention to portray a specific character in a specific way may seem at first sight, and in the case of a leading actor is often so represented, to correspond to authorship conceived as the creative principle of the fixed, delimited text. But the process of character representation through impersonation entails that the actor should strive to obliterate his or her sense of identity in order to become a signifier for the intentionality inscribed in character. Such obliteration returns the project of intentionality to the level of the narrative itself which is usually "authored" reductively in terms of the director's or playwright's "vision," rather than as a meaning emergent from a collective act of representation.[15] The full participation of the actor in the narrative as character thereby depends upon the suppression of the literary conception of the author.

The other aspect of intertextuality relates to the fact that the actor as a private individual is already constituted as a sign within the host culture, insofar as his or her behavioural and physical attributes have been read and will be read as cues to personality. The placing of the actor on stage or screen certainly intensifies this inferential process and for the purposes of a single casting may re-enforce characterisation. But overall the range of characters an actor may attempt is limited by the emphasis, rather than de-emphasis on the given-ness of her or his physical and behavioural attributes. Once again, impersonation "frees" the actor for a range of parts insofar as it suppresses what in non-actors would be regarded as the authenticating markers of their personality.

These considerations point towards the conclusion that the norm of impersonation, apart from its presence as an empirical regularity in the orientation of professional actors, serves as the basic instrument of the construction of difference in acting, an instrument that renders intelligible the programme of control inscribed in the regime of practice and training that many actors undergo. Certainly attempts to define what acting is, whether on stage or screen, that are chary of defining impersonation as a norm of evaluation have a tautological quality. Both Richard Dyer, in his discussion of John Wayne, and John Ellis, probably more so, given his deployment of the terms under- and overacting, suffer from this fault since the terms of the contrasts they seek to advance are never established: any attempt to pronounce on screen behaviour evidently requires the specification of the terms of variation.[16]

The impact of the technology of film on impersonation constitutes the final aspect of the situational logic that underpins the often unanalysed preference for stage over screen. Put in its bluntest form, there is a widespread belief among actors and other commentators that film as a medium regularly if not necessarily entails a deskilling process, in the sense of rendering the skills of the actor obsolete or of entailing dilution – the substitution of the untrained actor for the trained. As Edgar Morin put it:

> The cinema does not merely de-theatricalise the actor's performance. It tends to atrophy it.[17]

While it's absurd to conclude as Morin does that acting in film requires no skills whatsoever, it is important to identify the transformations in the practices of acting that film technology, as routinely deployed in the mainstream cinema, entails. The impact of film on acting rests ultimately on the sheer variety of codes that can be mobilised in order to fabricate the movement (through the imaginary time and space of the diegesis) of the narrative.[18] At the level of the immediate concerns of the actor, the formative capacities of film threaten to disrupt the project of constructing, from actor-located processes of signification, a psychologically consistent character. As is well known, the construction of character in film, as opposed to stage, is not usually a linear temporal process. The behaviour of the character, a supposedly coherent subject unfolding within the place and time set by the narrative, is very often constituted out of minute quanta of behaviour, repetitiously delivered (takes). Such quanta, necessary because of contractual or locational economies, are dramatically discontinuous in terms of the chronology of character and plot, e.g. the actor as character must play to a character he has never seen or act out the aftermath of an affair that has yet to be enacted. Equally, a given quantum of performance, itself a mere fraction of an action, may be greatly inflected by camera position, omitted altogether, cut and reduced, resited through editing and so on.[19] Alternatively, though interrelatedly, the formative capacity of film, particularly its capacity as a medium for what Metz calls cosmorphism – sequences in which only inanimate objects appear – and the substitution of such objects for the actor as a signifier, can readily displace the actor from the action, so that inanimate or non-human animate objects signify states of emotion formally within the capacity of the actor(s) to project.[20]

The basis of such a complaint is consistent with a psychologistic conception of character "as a more or less complex and unified network of psychological and social traits; that is as a distinct personality" which is counterposed to the actantial view of character as a function within the narrative as found in semiological analysis.[21] This is undeniably the case, but it is equally the case that in mainstream forms of drama and video/film production the predominance of naturalistic conventions means that any disagreement between an actor's conception of character *vis-à-vis* the director, who may be regarded as the custodian of the actantial level of the narrative, turns around interpretation *within* a naturalistic characterology. One may with Brecht deplore the stereotypical and regressive consequences of this theatrical formation:

> Parts are allotted wrongly and thoughtlessly. As if all cooks were fat, all peasants phlegmatic, all statesmen, stately. As if all who love and loved were beautiful. As if all good speakers had a fine voice.[22]

But it confronts actors as a fact of employment and constitutes the prevalent characterological direction given to impersonation.[23]

With these qualifications in view, it is important to recognise that film technology as routinely deployed confronts the actor with an effect which may be broadly identified as de-skilling. This is not to imply that acting in film does not entail the use of skills. A movement from stage to screen, in a literal sense involves re-skilling – though conversely the kinds of skills acquired by stage training are not easily mastered by those only experienced in film work.[24] Rather the notion of skill does not rest on some simplistic conception of a fixed technical content so much as the question of whether such content, at whatever level of complexity, is monopolisable by a specific set of workers. And whether in this context – a politics or frontier of control – the technology is implemented in a way that enhances or undermines the control of the contending parties of employees and employers.[25]

Viewed in this light, it is clear enough that the routinised practices in the mainstream cinema tend to shift the frontier of control away from the actor towards the director or, where this is not the same person, those empowered to render the final cut. Equally it is no small matter for professional standing and employment chances that the formative capacities of film (or video) can be used to compensate for a low level of technical ability as an actor, enabling untrained actors to produce convincing on-screen performances.[26] Under such circumstances a preference for the theatre is not surprising. The requirement of unaided projection and the necessity of repeat performances before a "live" audience virtually eliminates this threat in the theatre. So, too, it is in the theatre that actors have the greatest degree of direct control over the signifying direction and grain of their performance – even if this control is only unevenly realised in practice.[27]

Again, this preference is materially reinforced by the historical priority of the stage and by the fact that where acting is taught in drama schools and colleges, such teaching has a stage bias, for obvious reasons of cost, but also because the demands of stage acting can be scaled down whereas film acting techniques cannot be readily scaled up.[28]

The issue of essentialism

The drift of these remarks is towards what I would term a qualified technological determinism. In general my view of technology is that it always represents a complex of potential uses, but that the social relationships of production in which it is embedded tend to prioritise particular forms of use and patterns of technological application over others. At the level of appearances such uses and applications may appear as "givens" or as "essences," but the apparent essence of the technology resides ultimately within the historically specific relations of production (use and application) in which the technology is embedded. It is possible to speak, therefore, of a situational technological essentialism.

Bearing this in mind, it would be a mistake to see the foregoing as resting on the view that film is necessarily restrictive and impoverishing and theatre necessarily liberative and enriching of the actor's efforts. Such a proposition only needs spelling out for it to collapse into indefensibility. To be explicit, the implementation of the formative capacities of film and video, a desirable if complex factor of its use – its ability to construct an integral diegesis and narrative irrespective of the duration and priority of the pro-filmic events it records – does not necessarily mean that acting in film is "bad" acting. A more precise formulation is that the effects of characterisation achievable by the cumulative process of the actor's performance on stage are only sustained in film and television if measures are taken to compensate for the atomising effects of normal usage. Where such measures – e.g. rehearsals or collective decision-making – are absent, self-referential compensations arise such as playing to the camera, assumption of producer or director's role on the part of leading players and stardom. Such remedies, particularly the latter, may be individually successful, but they clearly leave the question of collective involvement unresolved.[29]

On the other hand, the fact that in the theatre the actor maintains a direct, unmediated control over the pacing and behavioural architecture of his or her performance does not guarantee that actors have control over the total effect of the performance. Once again, it is the social relationship between the director and cast that is determinative. Thus, for example, the work of director-producers like Craig or Appia, particularly the former who wanted to rid the stage of actors, and the organisation of theatre companies in nineteenth-century Europe left the vector of control firmly in the hands of the director-producer and prioritised *mise-en-scène* over performance.[30] Equally, in the contemporary debate surrounding Simon Callow's manifesto for an actor's theatre,[31] it is clear that the relationship between the director and actors is crucial. Ian McKellen puts it well:

> When actors are allowed to function as complete people-of-the-theatre, expressing positive views of their own work and the work of the director, they mature as individuals and as a unit. When they are primarily employees, selected as the last pieces in some jigsaw plan originating in the mind of their director-manager, the audience (and the critic) may still approve of the result. But what a waste of potential.[32]

The Callow-McKellen position and the debate it inspired identifies very clearly that it is the social relations of theatrical production – the social deployment of theatre's formative capacities, one might say – that determine the texture and level of the actors' participation in the production of signs in the theatre. In itself Callow's claim for actors' control has a regressive, elitist, ring about it – the actor-writer nexus is merely to depose the director-writer nexus as a better arrangement for retrieving the "essential" meaning of the text, a theatrical variant of historicism. But this particular nuance acknowledged, the substantive point that the theatre (and film/video) is a collective activity in which no discrete input should be prioritised over and against the process of collective decision making, and that actors are an important element in this process, the public face of it as it were, is defensible. Certainly a more radical variant of the actor in command argument can be identified in the writings of Jerzy Grotowski. Grotowski argues that the actor is the centre of the theatre *per se*, not merely the centre of the performance. On the basis of the plausible contention that scenery, make-up and costumery are common to stage, cinema and television, and in any case, better realised by film and video, Grotowski's "poor" theatre relies centrally on the architecture of the actor's body, voice and gesture to constitute the process of representation.[33]

What such arguments demonstrate, of course, is an untheorised assumption that the maximisation of the actor's control over the detail of his or her performance necessarily leads to an aesthetic enhancement of the totality of the text. There is certainly no *a priori* warrant for such a conclusion. For one thing, the aesthetics of performance are insufficiently developed to support it and for another, such a radical re-centring of film or video on the actor would limit the known capacities of the medium to a mere transcription of theatrical performance. Again, in the analysis of specific film texts – the only level at which it might be possible to distinguish the specific contribution of the actor to characterisation – it is by no means clear where the actor's contribution, as opposed to the director's, cinematographer's, editor's or other actors' contributions, begins and ends.[34]

Having provided a qualified defence of impersonation, particularly to rescue it as a usable category from those, some of whom are actors, who would use it to mask a raw preference for stage over screen, I want to take a few steps towards the understanding of stardom as a particular variant of performance in film – a variant that is, I would contend, only comprehensible as an interaction, with varying situational outcomes, of the three economies signalled at the outset of this article.

The cultural economy of the human body

Performance or representational arts, whether these occur in a theatrical, cinematic or televisual context, necessarily bear a relationship to the diversity of signs distributed in the culture at large. Music itself, of course, in performance is brought into such a relationship by the behaviour of the performers. Such activities are governed by specific sub-codes of representation that allow the production of signs which are understood by the performers and audience alike to bear a conventional relationship to everyday life. The exact nature of the relationship between the representation regime within the theatre and the world outside has been historically variable, but in the West, at least since the late nineteenth century, the theatre and subsequently film and television have been dominated by naturalism. Naturalism may be defined as that mode of theatrical representation that enters a strong claim that the external aspects of the individual, his or her utterances, behaviour and appearance in everyday settings, give a privileged access to personal and collective realities.[35] The representational regime of naturalism has been much analyzed, notably by Brecht in his polemic against Aristotelian drama or the theatre of empathy, and I do not intend to take these issues up here.[36] What interests me specifically is what naturalism implies in terms of acting.

If we take the familiar contrast between naturalism and more formalistic regimes of theatrical representation in which symbolic as opposed to iconic or indexical signs predominate, such as the Chinese classical or the Japanese Noh theatres, then the implications of naturalism become clear. (C. S. Peirce defines a symbol as signifying by convention, an icon by resemblance and an index by physical connection.) Under a naturalistic system all signs deployed in performance lay claim (however spurious) to be motivated – to be a mimesis of the extratheatrical, extra-cinematic and so on. This mimetic relationship can be seen as a constraint on the autonomy of sign production since the subcoding of resemblance is constantly referred back to the iconic or indexical actuality of the signified – or, rather, what in such a system can be construed as the same, the perception by the audience of verisimilitude. In non-naturalistic theatre, however, the regime of signification creates its own signified(s) as it were self-consciously by the deployment of highly conventionalised systems and subcodes of reference – the audience not expecting verisimilitude (in the naturalistic sense) but an internal consistency in the relationship between signifiers and signified. Since even naturalistic regimes have their own specific sub-codes, the difference here is between a covert and overt use of signs and codes of representation and the gearing of the relationship between the signifier(s) and signified(s) as more or less conventional, more or less motivated.[37]

In a theatrical tradition permeated with naturalism, and the American theatre is particularly notable for this development, the actor confronts problems in character-isation that relate to his or her being as a general cultural object rather than a theatrical object.[38] Thus it is correct to say that the actor is a re-presenter of signs in that he or she activates or deactivates via impersonation those aspects of the general cultural markers that he or she bears as a private individual for character portrayal.[39] The nub of these problems stems from the fact that if the theatre is to "mirror" the street, the street is already populated with signs. So that the actor as a member of the host culture – with a given hair colour, body shape, repertoire of gestures, registers of speech, accent, dialect and so on – always pre-signifies meaning. Such a relationship creates difficulties for the process of impersonation which are well-known. Firstly, there is the pre-performance selection process of type-casting, which has a persistent ten-dency towards self-fulfilment – only actors who look the part get the part.[40] This relationship, which ties the actor as it were to biological and social destiny, is com-pounded by another in performance – the process of semioticisation: the fact that anything appearing in the frame of the proscenium arch or of the camera is by that fact invested with meaning. The difficulty here lies in the suppression of those elements of the actor's appearance and behaviour that are *not intended to mean* at the level of the characterisation.[41]

By contrast, in a theatrical regime where the gearing between off-stage codes and onstage sub-codes is low or conventional and is consciously understood to be so by actors and audience alike, the physical qualities of the actor, as supposed charactero-logical markers, provide a weaker constraint on casting. The application of make-up, dress and mannerisms do not require a literal defence, either iconically or indexically. Obviously enough, these differences are only a matter of degree, since as Eco has pointed out, even iconic sign-functions rely on conventions.[42] But it is still the case that naturalism offers a constraint not found in more canonical systems – systems where the distance between stage/screen are formally coded. Hence Brecht's criticism of casting cited earlier.

Finally, while it is useful to present the relationship between naturalistic regimes and the process of impersonation as in a state of contradiction, this should be seen as a problem within the discourse of naturalism. Indeed, it seems likely that impersonation has evolved out of the dominance of naturalism anyway. For although the problem of appearing convincingly as someone else is common to acting *tout court*, the notion that a great actor disappears into character without trace is clearly a reinforcement of this species of illusionism. On the other hand, naturalism does allow the possibility that "poor" actors judged by such criteria can turn in convincing performances in which habits and genes outweigh the skills of acting as currently taught.

The economy of signification in film

As pointed out above, film (and video) can reduce the actor's control over perform-ance. On *a priori* grounds one cannot say that this is necessarily a bad thing, aesthetically speaking; much will depend on what the original performance was and how it is edited. But this empirical question aside, the maximisation of the formative capacities of film have been represented so far as arising mainly from the social relations of film production in the mainstream cinema. There remains the question of the features of film as a medium and how these provide, as it were, a semiotic "conduit" for the implementation of social decisions and objectives related to control. To understand these features it is necessary to identify the point of engagement of the actor with the narrative through his or her engagement with character. As Stephen Heath has pointed out, the terms "character" and "actor" are ambiguous because they cover what are a whole series of positionalities in relation to the narrative. For example, following Greimas' *Sémantique structurale*, Stephen Heath discusses actants, or units of narrative grammar, that are neither specific narrative events nor characters, but structural oppositions that recur and, through their punctual recurrence, constitute and resolve the narrative as a total act. *Actants* can, therefore, be distinguished from *actors* which in this sense, to use Heath's phrase, "are the units of discursive realization of a particular narrative" and "animated entities . . . susceptible of individuation."[43] The relationship between actant and actor is a variable one. One actor may synthesise more than one actant and, vice-versa, a number of actors may constitute one actant. Equally, it is possible to identify characters that are not actors, that have only a diegetic status as "colour."

Whatever the status of the applicability of literary models to the discourse of film, the distinction between units of meaning within the forcefield of the narrative, as it were, and the global units of narrativity is important to preserve. This more or less articulates the sort of contrast I have identified in relation to the place of the actor as a performer and the film as an edited text. As Heath points out, his analysis of the film as system perforce must leave on one side the development of individuation as "character" or, in other words, the close analysis of the actors' work in the construction of a psychologically consistent "animated entity." But along with other writers in the area he observes that the actor is not a "mere" entity animated by the flow of the narrative but a concrete person or actor-person. In short, there is in film a potential for increased individuation which in mainstream cinema has been epitomised by the star.

In Heath's exposition a series of distinctions are made, which are useful in framing the exposition given here:

(a)   Agent – approximately equivalent to actor in Greimas' sense, which undertakes or effects an action with narrative consequence. An anthropomorphic, cosmomorphic or zoomorphic entity which may or may not appear on screen.

(b)   Character – a subset of an agent, a personage with a more or less realised personality or psychological unity. All characters are agents but not vice-versa.

(c)   Person – the actor in the occupational sense as a physical/behavioural presence, the figurant of agent and character.

(d)   Image – the moment of stardom "since the star is exactly the conversion of the body, of the person, into the luminous sense of its film image." The image constitutes the temporary triumph or excess of the spectacle centred on the person over the narrative centred on the character, with its problematic representation of imaginary coherence.

(e)   Figure – the immanent possibility of the disturbance/disarticulation of the
      imaginary coherence generated by the confluence of character, person and
      image.[44]

For purposes of explaining the immediate interaction between actor and medium,
the variables that have a direct, as opposed to contextual, pertinence are *character,
person* and *image*. At the same time it is necessary to modify Heath's specifications to
emphasise how they represent levels of anthropomorphic meaning that are variously
integrated within the norm of impersonation. An obvious modification is to allow for
extension of the term *image* to cover both filmic and extrafilmic or cinematic processes
of representation and their interaction. Heath's brief specification suffers from a
paradoxical mixture of over-valuation and under-valuation. In the first place, it has
long been recognised that to any actor's appearance and behaviour before camera, film
adds its own enhancement, producing effects that while originating in the apparatus
nevertheless appear to be part of the "natural" physical and behavioural properties of
the actor.[45] Such a process of enhancement, whether by omission – the gauzing out of
wrinkles in close-up, "best side" shots and so on – or by addition – low angle
enhancement of stature, lighting and so on – does not merely affect stars, though these
are obviously the epitomising benefactors of such processes, *but actors in general*. The
element of over-valuation stems from the fact that the image on screen is itself,
especially in the case of the star, usually reinforced by extra-discursive practices, or
more exactly the interaction of filmic and non-filmic discourses.[46] Two of these can be
mentioned here. Firstly, actors tend to develop or are expected to develop a "personality" for purposes of public interaction, which indicates that they are actors and
suggests to potential employers that they are interesting and energetic people. This
seems to be particularly true of Hollywood:

> Another New Yorker, an actor I'll call Kevin, was having a hard time in
> Los Angeles. The agents, the scriptwriters and producers don't quite get
> him. He played a major role in a Broadway hit, one that moreover had
> intellectual pretensions, but this success doesn't translate into cinemese.
> . . . Shy, reserved and a bit scholarly, Kevin has trouble radiating "person-
> ality" during an interview (no one in Hollywood gets a chance to audition,
> that is to *act*; one must already *be* the part during the face-to-face meeting
> in an office). Worse, the personality he is (rather than the one he might
> but can't assume) somehow doesn't go with his looks.[47]

It is important, therefore, to distinguish the extent to which an actor assumes or
needs to assume a valid personality for employment purposes, including in this the
entire paraphernalia of body maintenance, grooming and so forth. Secondly it is also
the case, always with stars, that the image on screen is already contextualised by the
circulation of biographical and personal anecdotal materials that frame their appearances on and off-screen. Against this John Ellis has argued that the screen performance
necessarily provides the moment of completion of the fan's engagement with the
image of the star. While it is useful, nearly commonplace, to emphasise as others have
done that the image of the star does not merely subsist, as Heath implies, at the level
of the visual image, it is by no means clear that the animated image should be seen as

the terminal point of the fan's engagement. One might with parallel plausibility suggest that the incompleteness of the cinematic experience – its presence *but* absence – leads to the phenomena of fetishistic requests and collection of indexical materials – autographs, stills, locks of hair, clothing and so on. Likewise still photography can be seen as expressing the fetishistic desire to tear the star from the submerging pull of the diegesis and narrative, the better to contemplate the image without the depersonalising intrusion of the narrative, its slippery movement through space and time.[48] One can go further than this and suggest, as studies of Ingrid Bergman and Doris Day have shown, that it is the extra filmic discourse that has the greatest impact on the public's knowledge of the star, contradicting the evidence of what can be seen at the point(s) of performance.[49]

While these considerations have yet to be adequately theorised, it is safe to say that in the case of stars (or stars to be) it is the extra-filmic discourse(s) that precedes and supersedes the mobilisation of the image-making capacities of film and to a large extent conditions the (mis-) reading of what is seen. In this connection, Richard Dyer's term "star image" is useful, since as his analysis shows many of the devices used to privilege the presence of stars in films equally enter into the construction of character. The moment of the star image is, in fact, the moment of a proprietorial claim to such effects as though they were a property of the star as a person, a claim which subsists not primarily in what is represented on screen, but in the subsidiary literature where the image is rendered as a "real life" property of its bearer, the actor as star.

Dyer, on the other hand, in his discussion of stars as signs deploys a global opposition between character, "a constructed personage in film," and personality as "the set of traits and characteristics with which film endows [characters]." This definition, which in respect of his analysis is reader-centred, nevertheless includes audience foreknowledge, name, appearance and dress, decor and setting – codes which are not specific to film – alongside codes which are, so that his specification remains ambiguous in respect of the interweaving of the filmic and non-filmic that Heath's specifications, at least partially, preserve.[50]

In order to preserve what is useful in these specifications for an analysis of acting I suggest the following modifications. The term *character* is adequate as it stands. The term *person* should be taken to include an understanding that the physical presence of the actor is already coded in the general sense of having the socially recognised attributes of an individual in the host culture (however problematic this "fix" may be), a "personality," and in the specific sense that this "personality" is adapted to the exigencies of acting. In either case, I assume conformity is a condition of success. Likewise, the term *image* should be restricted to the visual impact of the film "system" on the actor's "personality" off screen, so that the coherence of the actor's image on screen is clearly identified as a technologically based construction. Finally, I would introduce the term *persona* to cover what Heath calls "the conversion of the body, of the person, into the luminous sense of its film image."[51] The reason for this should be apparent, but it is because what Heath terms *image* is in the case of stardom (or its intentional project) an articulation of person and image as I have redefined them. The persona, in other words, is the intersection of cinematic and filmic discursive practices in an effort to realise a coherent subjectivity.

With these background points in mind, I want now to indicate two specifically filmic processes that provide what I referred to earlier as the semiotic conduit through which social decisions affecting the standing of personae or stars are infiltrated into the filmic system. These are hypersemiotisation and the displacement of interiority. By the former, I mean to indicate the intensification of the process observed in theatre. The use of close shooting in the cinema invests great meaning in the actor as a signifying mass, involving in the process of signification parts of the actor's body, such as the eyes, mouth and so forth. This means, in effect, that the actor can signify merely because he or she has automatic or physiologically given qualities, e.g. lip shape and movement, facial mass and habitual expressions.[52] Under such circumstances, imper-sonation becomes the ever more refined control of fine as opposed to gross bodily behaviour. The problem here is that as one increases the scale of observation, the range of behaviours approach the uncontrollable or, conversely, mere passivity will signify. The scale of observation has conventional limits. Thus the close-up commonly goes no closer than the face, with more radical variation limited by the canons of naturalism. The face itself, which is posed in point-of-view cutting as the centre of the look as the authenticating moment of the character, is usually presented without ostensible make-up. That is to say, make-up is constructed in such a way as to obliterate its own occurrence and where possible the minimally retouched features of the actor provide the basis of the significatory play of depth of shot, focus, lighting and so on.[53] Such a *conventional* system for rendering apparently *motivated* signs seems a logical con-sequence of naturalism and to a large extent it clearly is. But it impacts with economic criteria, as evidenced by Jack Warner's exasperation at having paid Paul Muni so much for a performance in *Juarez* in which the star was unrecognisable.

For the actor committed to impersonation in such circumstances, the gross details of physical endowment pose severe problems since they are very often unalterable.[54] Generally speaking, the actor cannot be moved out of the naturalistic personality implications of his or her physique, however stereotypical or factually wrong these are. Ernest Borgnine can be made into a better looking Ernest Borgnine, not another Robert Redford. On the other hand, if the physical endowment of the actor *means* already and if there is an over-supply of actors of every type, there are few grounds, to potential employers, for radical interventions into the "facts of nature." Actors may as well content themselves with emphasising the socially recognised attributes of their type and employers select from the types so presented accordingly. The star would provide an exception to these observations in part, but such exceptions really demon-strate, in the time-honoured fashion, the presence of the rule: unless the actor has been selected for stardom or is through ageing in danger of falling out of type, radical interventions are not indicated.

In fact, the predominant tendency is for the norm of impersonation to be abandoned at the level of casting in favour of a strategy of selection based on personification – let the actor be selected by physical type anyway and let these physical attributes mean in and of themselves. In other words, the actor becomes the most rudimentary form of the sign, the ostensive sign in which the substance of the signifier is the substance of the signified: the actor is the person, has the personality, his or her appearance suggests s/he is, notwithstanding the fact that this construction relies on a first order conventionality in the culture which the actor re-presents and, sometimes, redefines.[55] Such a form of type-casting is to be found in its most pro-nounced and literal form in the film (and television) industry and, to a lesser degree, in the theatre.

Thus, the ideal young leading man should be aged between 19–25 years, at least 5 feet 10 inches tall but not over 6 feet 2 inches, well proportioned physically, handsome, rugged or interesting looking, have all his own teeth and hair. The ideal ingenue should be aged between 18–25, 5 feet 3 inches to 5 feet 7 inches tall, possess a well-proportioned body and an exceptionally beautiful and interesting face.[56] Obviously enough, few if any actors meet all these requirements, but this does not remove their pertinence as the criteria of selection. Again, while it might be objected that these specifications are hardly precise at the logical level, they are situationally very precise indeed. Casting directors may not be able to articulate "ruggedness" with any precision, but they know it when they see it, which is probably the most absolute form of constraint – intuitive appreciation. Again, it is certainly the case that types change in the long term, but this does not eliminate their effectiveness in the short term. For the majority of actors the short term is all there is.

Given the selection of actors by type – a factor as we shall see advanced by labour market pressures – there follows the fact of type-casting as a serial phenomenon: actors are limited to a particular kind of character for their working life – what might be called the Elisha Cook Jr. syndrome – or, at least, will be so unless vigorous efforts are made to overcome type. Just as importantly, though, actors become committed in their on and off screen life to personification in the hope that by stabilising the relationship between person and image on screen they may seem to be the proprietors of a marketable persona. Robert De Niro is an interesting case in this regard, since he appears, paradoxically, to combine to a stunning level of virtuosity the capacity for impersonation with a drive, role by role, to transform himself physically into the substance of the signified, e.g. Jake La Motta in *Raging Bull*. In fact, De Niro's approach to acting is entirely consistent with an effort to adapt impersonation to the control relationships and techniques implied in film work. On the one hand:

> With a play you've got that one performance that night, but if you're doing a movie it's piece by piece. You can do maybe ten takes – one or two could be exceptional – you've got the chance to get it right. I never tire of doing takes.

On the other:

> The main thing is the script. . . . Then I have to get to know the director . . . because it's so much work – you can be stuck with someone for six months and it's an absolute nightmare. You've got to know that you're on the same track: you can disagree, you can try it your way, their way, ultimately they edit it and it's their film. . . .[57]

In other words, the advantages of takes are premised on the social relations of production. Clearly De Niro's commitment to Method acting gives a particular direction to his efforts to research the background and seek out real-life models for the characters he portrays. But it is at least consistent with the atomising effects of film on character portrayal that there is such a radicalising displacement towards the "real" in order to get an authenticating sense of character outside the process of filming. The emphasis on the script points towards a similar form of monitoring device to control portrayal of character "in pieces" and the physical transformation of the self seems the last step in the mimetic grasp of the extra-cinematic real.

The tendency for film to transform the actor into an ostensive sign, its problematic insertion into the norm of impersonation, is enhanced by the second process, the displacement of interiority. It is generally accepted that film poses limits on the representation of interiority, inclining towards behaviourism, showing the "surface of things." For this reason Brecht, for example, saw film as smashing the introspective psychology of the bourgeois novel and refusing ideology.[58] Such a view was clearly over-optimistic, for the mainstream cinema has developed a range of devices that reconstitute the interior space of the character, but the basic point remains: films tend to re-site the signification of interiority, away from the actor and onto the mechanism. Richard Dyer has ably catalogued these effects elsewhere[59] and I do not intend to pursue them here, but this process of displacement underlies and produces the image. This means that the process of character portrayal in film, whether angled towards impersonation or personification, takes on a quasi-automatic form in which the actor's performance in part originates in his or her behaviour and in part in the action of the filmic apparatus, including in the latter lighting and camera deployment. In other words, the projection of interiority becomes less and less the provenance of the actor and more and more a property emerging from directorial or editorial decision. Under such circumstances, a potential politics of the persona emerges insofar as the bargaining power of the actor, or more emphatically, the star, is materially affected by the *degree* of his or her reliance on the apparatus (the image), as opposed to self-located resources (the person) in the construction of persona. Consequently it is plausible to speak of high and low autonomy stars to compare, for instance, Bette Davis's use of acting skills to broaden her range of characterisations, with Joan Crawford's singular pre-*Mildred Pierce* persona.[60] Similarly, the established policy of building stars from inexperienced players under the studio system, can be seen to contain an element of fabricating subordination among potential stars.

The twinned processes of hyper-semioticisation and displacement of interiority lead to a paradoxical situation: while film increases the centrality of the actor in the process of signification, the formative capacity of the medium can equally confine the actor more and more to being a bearer of effects that he or she does not or cannot originate.

The economy of the labour market for actors

The effects so far identified at the level of film have a latent status, or rather would have were it not for the effects of the labour market on actors seeking continuous and stable employment. The broad features of the labour market for actors in film and television are well known and have remained unchanged for decades. Wherever and whenever we look there is a large oversupply of actors, as measured by membership in the appropriate union. Thus in 1979 roughly 90% of Hollywood's Screen Actors Guild membership of 23,000 earned less than a living wage and among the membership of Equity in the UK, 70% of members are unemployed in any one year.[61] Again, of those actors who do find work, there is a marked disparity between the earnings of leading players and stars, who are able to negotiate personal contracts and the majority of actors who earn at or slightly above the basic rate set by collective agreements; the magnitude of difference being in excess of fifty times, sometimes a hundred.

The ramifications of these circumstances could be explored further, but the chief point for my consideration here is that under such circumstances criteria of selection based on *discontinuous* as opposed to *continuous* variables are likely to predominate as a solution to the problem of oversupply. By *continuous* variables I mean criteria based on skills which are necessarily, albeit unevenly, distributed among the collective of actors as part of the effect of the operation of drama schools and the like. One would certainly want to qualify these criteria in terms of a distinction between kinds of performers – e.g., specialists in a particular skill, like juggling, singing and so on, who are termed "performers" *and* actors *and* celebrities – but all of these crowding into the market with union cards do not drastically after the overall picture.

By *discontinuous* variables I mean criteria based on the assessment of physical and psychological traits, that are accidentally combined or acquired by the individual as a member of the host culture. Such traits are susceptible to ordering on a continuous scale – degrees of blondeness, bust size, muscularity, height, etc. – but their combination in the individual, even when signifying a class of attributes, is nonetheless a uniquely formed index, a property of the actor as a person or an ostensive sign of some of the values of the host culture. The emphasis on such discontinuous variables represents a rational response to the situation of over-supply. Actors of any level of ability (or even with no particular ability) compete with others who are equally well qualified. Obviously enough the very fuzziness of casting, its anticipatory nature and the fact that a character is, after all, before embodiment merely a set of notations for a performance, is an additional factor here. But as a result, competition for parts, *given the operation of naturalistic conventions*, leads to an emphasis on what is unique to the actor, displacing emphasis from what an actor can do *qua* actor onto what the actor *qua* person or biographical entity is. In this manner, what Robert Brady calls a personal monopoly is constructed.[62]

In film, the construction of a personal monopoly rests on shifting the emphasis in performance towards personification, but such a shift takes the radical form of carrying the implications of the actor's persona into everyday life. Thus actors seeking to obtain stardom will begin to conduct themselves in public as though there is an unmediated existential connection between their person and their image. Another way to put this is to say that the persona is in itself a character, but one that transcends placement or containment in a particular narrative (or in the case of the vehicle subordinates the narrative to the spectacle of the persona) and exists in cinematic rather than filmic time and space.[63] Indeed, the persona, buttressed by the discursive practices of publicity, hagiography and by regimes of cosmetic alteration and treatment, is relatively durable and if sedimented in public awareness will tend to survive discrepant casting and performances.

For actors of limited or average ability, investing their energies in the cultivation of a persona represents something within their control and a means of competing with actors who have ability in impersonation. Indeed, in the studio system impersonatory skills were assigned a lower value compared to the cultivation of personae.[64] In contemporary times, the tendency towards personification may have increased with the advent of advertising as a field of employment, which combines naturalism with the sedulous cultivation of personal charm as an ingredient in the sales pitch.[65] On the other hand, the self-referentiality of Method acting – the so-called personal expressive realism of Brando, for example – rather than representing the triumph of the actor as impersonator can be seen as a successful adaptation of impersonation to the pressures of personification, deploying impersonation to refer back to the person of the actor, the consistent entity underlying each of his or her roles.[66] The possible relationship between film acting styles and economic realities would be worth exploring in this light.

The tendency towards the formation of personae as a monopoly strategy should not be taken as unproblematic, however. As hinted earlier such processes have a hegemonic texture. The norm of impersonation maintains a powerful presence in Hollywood, for example, for a number of reasons. It is and can be seen as an integral value central to the practice of acting itself. Again, even under the most automatised conditions of production, there remains a need for actors who can 'effortlessly' produce performances in character – hence the remark that character actors are a 'brassiere for the star, literally holding him or her up.'[67] Nor is the adhesion to such a norm surprising, given that it provides an avenue of accomplishment for actors who do not fit into prevailing stereotypes. Accordingly, alongside the star system, the realm of the ostensive sign *par excellence*, one finds the operation of a hierarchy of character actors, whose professional reputation, length of careers and durability of earnings may outpace that of more transitory stars. Such a hierarchy provides, as it were, its own counterstars, individuals like Robert Duvall, for example, whose claims to eminence rest squarely on their impersonatory skills and character playing. On the other hand, one of the decisive and recurrent effects of casting is that a given character type will sediment itself into the actor's personality so that the line between character and persona becomes blurred or, at least, requires extreme vigilance:

> I find that the character of JR keeps taking me over in real life. Not that
> I get that mean, I hope, but I do find the Texas accent drifting in and out.
> People I meet really want me to be JR, so it's hard to disappoint them.
> – Larry Hagman.[68]

Finally, it is necessary to qualify the view that personification arises *solely* out of the actor's adaptation to his or her conditions of employment. Such conditions are products in turn of the interests of monopoly capital operating in the sphere of cultural production. The ramifications are complex, but basically personification serves the purposes of containing competition amongst the tele-film cartel companies by representing the star's contribution as resting on his or her private properties as a person. In such a manner, a specific production can be valorised by "values" that are not distributed throughout the field of production as a whole – such as technical expertise, for example. The exploitation of the latter, as the latest wave of special effects pictures shows, tends to escalate costs enormously. Equally, the centrality of personae (stars) as an index of value provides a form of control – shifting or even threatening to shift, signifiers from the actor to the apparatus – over the detail of performance in favour of those who have control over the text. The readiness of actors to function as ostensive signs can be seen as a defensive strategy: by accepting the loss of autonomy (either real or merely latent) entailed in the transfer of signification from the actor to the camera, with its offscreen constraints arising from stardom as a way of life, the actor paradoxically increases the reliance of the apparatus on his or her presence as a unique object or, more precisely, a behavioural commodity. The contra-dictory pressures, the paradoxes of identification that are induced by the shifts between personification and impersonation rather than some diffuse notion of a fit between stardom and capitalism, as advanced, for example, by Edgar Morin, provides the basic configuration of stardom in mainstream cinema.

Provisional conclusions

Stardom as it emerges from these considerations is a particular articulation of the relationship between the actor and role, which from the perspective of the narrative prioritises the spectacular. In terms of the theorisation of the "look," it is clear that stardom provides a confirmation of cinematic fetishism. As Metz puts it:

> The fetish is the cinema in its *physical* state. A fetish is always material: insofar as one can make up for it by the power of the symbolic alone one is precisely no longer a fetishist.[69]

Evidently the star is one, an important one, indeed, of the ways in which the cinema, or strictly the filmic part of the cinematic, is reduced to the state of things – of stills, magazines, books of adulation that float about the act of cinematic narration.

But one of the problems raised by the analysis here is the question of whether or not fetishistic looking – a variant of the fundamentally voyeuristic mode of looking promoted by what John Ellis calls cinematic narration – requires for its prioritisation extra-filmic, economic, pressures. Does not the prioritised incursion of the fetishistic look, a part of the experience of looking in the cinema to be sure, require explanation through extra-filmic variables? Does not the literature of stardom provide a framework and a warrant for such a reading of the symbolic which is not "there" at the level of the spectatorial experience itself? Obviously such questions need further analysis.

Secondly, the non-disappearance of the actor into character threatens (and, indeed, in the case of the vehicle, achieves) the conversion of the text into a signifier for the personal "expressive" reality, no less of a representation, of the key player or players. Richard Dyer has counterposed this "opening out" as a challenge to the ideological work of the narrative, in that the persona of the star tends to subvert the value implications of the narrative, particularly in the area of gender identity.[70] The potential contradiction between the discourse of stardom and the narrative is in my view real and the analysis here can be taken as extending our knowledge of the situational determinants. The view of stardom as demystificatory is another matter, depending in Dyer's case on the view that the "personal is political" – a formulation that seems to forget that it is the relationship between the personal and collective representations that is the space of the political.[71] More to the point, such a view of stardom elides the fact that the persona of the star is a collective representation that presents/re-presents itself as the private expressivity of a unique individual. Mirror-ing, and taking to a new level of concreteness, the romantic notion of the author, the view of the star as the centre of cinematic meaning carries no less of a charge than these parallel constructions. Indeed, the apparent immediacy of stardom as a discourse argues for its efficacy as a demonstration of the primacy of the individual over collective relationships. More could be said on this, but the articulation of the star as a sign in the discourse of acting, rather than the impact of stardom in the audience sphere, has been my concern here.

Finally, I would like to point to the question of stardom and television. It has long been recognised, as Marshall McLuhan pointed out in *Understanding Media*, that leading players on television tend to be "taken" in character by the public in face-to-face encounters. (Ironside not Raymond Burr was McLuhan's example, Captain Kirk not William Shatner can be ours). It would be necessary to analyse further the sorts of factors, notably the duration and repeats of a single series, that underpin this difference. But it is equally the case with the TV series (e.g. *Dynasty* and Joan Collins) that the familiar shading off towards a persona is more or less parallel to what is observed in the cinema. Certainly in Hollywood both Joan Collins and Clint Eastwood are stars for purposes of publicity, agentry and so forth. At the level of the medium itself (though the advent of High Definition Television may render this contrast redundant) it seems probable that the visual qualities of the film image – its clarity, its spatially mobile setting, its alternation between long and close shots – and the relative impoverishment of these features in television has a pertinence for the development of the persona. While television is a close-up medium, its visual qualities do not add "luminosity" to the person of the star. In any case, character in television tends to be a trans-narrational entity, so that playing in character does not conflict with personification. The "fight to be oneself" on screen, as it were, encounters no resistance from the text and hence does not move so intensively towards it. Obviously these matters are speculative and require further elaboration, as does the question of the size of the image, the condition of its reception and so on.[72] The foregoing analysis is offered as a way into these considerations.

Notes

1   A recent discussion can be found in Keir Elam, *The Semiotics of Theatre and Drama*, London, Methuen, 1980. In what follows I will assume for purposes of simplification the perspective of a single film actor (male or female). I wish to acknowledge the useful criticisms of the *Screen* editorial collective, particularly Andrew Higson, of an earlier draft of this paper.

2   Cf. Raymond Williams, *Culture*, London, Fontana, 1981, p. 29ff.

3   See, for example, Paul Corrigan and Derek Sayer, "Hindess and Hirst: a Critical Review," *Socialist Register 1981* and Franco Rossi-Landi, "Sign Systems and Social Reproduction," *Ideology and Consciousness*, no 3, 1978.

4   Cf. Erik Wright, *Class, Crisis and the State*, London, New Left Books, 1978, pp. 15–29.

5   See the accounts in Lillian and Helen Ross, *The Player: The Profile of an Art*, New York, Simon and Schuster, 1962 and Ivan Butler, *The Making of Feature Films: a Guide*, London, Penguin, 1961. For a recent statement see Tony Booth's remarks in "All Actors Should be Working Class," *Marxism Today*, October, 1984.

6   Pierre Bourdieu, "Intellectual Field and Creative Project" in MFD Young (ed.), *Knowledge and Control*, London, Collier-Macmillan, 1971.

7   Quoted in the *Sunday Times Magazine*, August 26, 1984, p. 16.

8   Cf. J. Bensman and R. Lillenfield, *Craft and Consciousness*, Wiley Interscience, 1973.

9   Peter Barkworth, *About Acting*, London, Secker and Warburg, 1980, p. 13.

10   D. Mixon, "A Theory of Actors," *Journal for the Theory of Social Behaviour*, March, 1983, vol. 13 no. 1.

11   Cf. Richard Dyer, *Stars*, London, British Film Institute, 1979, p. 158. By psychological identification or behavioural imitation, respectively.

12   Michel Foucault, "What is an Author?," *Screen*, Spring 1979, vol. 20 no. 1, pp. 13–33.

13   For a recent example of this incursion see Hal Hinson, "Some Notes on Method Actors," *Sight and Sound*, Summer 1984, p. 200 ff.

14   Cf. Richard Wollheim, *Art and its Objects*, London, Pelican, 1978, p. 90 ff.

15   The complaint that actors attempt to make any role convincing, regardless of the consequences of making e.g. Eva Peron, Lovable, has its origins in this displacement of intentionality.

16   Richard Dyer, op cit, p. 165. Though Dyer stresses that his account has nothing to do with evaluation, it clearly does. See also John Ellis, *Visible Fictions*, London, Routledge and Kegan Paul, 1982, p. 104 ff.

17   Edgar Morin, *The Stars*, New York, Grove Press, 1960, p. 144; and on skill, on p. 152.

18   Cf. Bill Nichols, *Ideology and Image*, Bloomington, Indiana University Press, 1981, p. 82.

19   Bruce Dern has suggested, implausibly, that the actor may overcome the problem of arbitrary editorial control, given the centrality of the character he plays, by making each take the same. See J. Kalter, *Actors on Acting*, Oaktree Press, 1979, p. 192, and James Mason's remarks in Ivan Butler, op cit.

20   The classic statement is A. Knox, "Acting and Behaving," in R. Dyer MacCann (ed.), *Film: a Montage of Theories*, Dutton, New York, 1966.

21   Keir Elam, op cit, p. 131 ff.

22   Bertolt Brecht, *The Messingkauf Dialogues* (trans. John Willett), London, Eyre Methuen, 1971, p. 87.

23   Richard Dyer, op cit, p. 119 ff has some very astute remarks on this point, i.e. that the rejection of naturalism does not necessarily imply a "deconstructive" approach to character.

24   Cf. Jack Lemmon's remarks on Tony Curtis in W. Hyland and R. Hatnes, *How to Make It in Hollywood*, Nelson-Hall, 1975.

25   See David Harvey, *The Limits to Capital*, Blackwell, 1982, p. 109 and p. 119. For a general discussion, see Paul Thompson, *The Nature of Work*, London, Macmillan, 1983.

26   Rod Steiger makes this point in Ross and Ross, op cit, p. 278.

27   The use of "live" audiences on television would have to be assessed carefully in this regard. Such performances are usually edited for transmission.

28   See P. K. Manning and H. L. Hearn, "Student Actresses and their Artistry," *Social Forces*, XLVII, 1969 and A. K. Peters, "Acting and Aspiring Actresses in Hollywood," Ph.D. Thesis, UCLA 1971.

29   V. I. Pudovkin, *Film Technique and Film Acting*, (Mayflower edition, 1958) was one of the first to recognise the impact of editing on the actor's motivation and to propose the necessity of involving the actor in the total process of production.

30   See M. Hays, "Theatre and Mass Culture: the Case of the Director," *New German*

Critique, 29, Summer 1983 and M. Gorelik, *New Theatres for Old*, Octagon Books, 1975 p. 23 ff.

31   Simon Callow; *Being an Actor*, London, Methuen, 1983.

32   *Guardian*, May 4, 1984.

33   Jerzy Grotowski, *Towards a Poor Theatre*, London, Methuen, 1975.

34   Cf. Robin Wood, "Acting Up," *Film Comment*, vol. 12 no. 2, 1976.

35   See Raymond Williams, *The Long Revolution*, London, Penguin, 1971, p. 271–299 and M. Gorelik, op cit, p. 47 ff.

36   A. Hozier, "Brecht's Epic Form: the Actor as Narrator," *Red Letters* no. 14.

37   For these reasons Brecht admired the Chinese theatre and saw it as enshrining the "A-effect." See John Willett (ed), *Brecht on Theatre*, London, Eyre Methuen, 1977, p. 136 ff.

38   On the dominance of naturalism in the U.S. theatre, see G. B. Wilson, *A History of American Acting*, Bloomington, Indiana University Press, 1966.

39   See Richard Sennett, *The Fall of Public Man*, Cambridge University Press, 1974, especially Chapter 6, for the history of the relationship between the theatre and the street.

40   J. Turow, "Casting for TV parts: the Anatomy of Social Typing," *Journal of Communication*, 28, 1978, pp. 19–24.

41   Cf. Jonathan Miller cited in Elam, op cit, p. 77. Erving Goffman's distinction between signs given and signs given off is important here. See his *The Presentation of the Self in Everyday Life*, London, Penguin, 1971, p. 14.

42   See Umberto Eco, *A Theory of Semiotics*, Bloomington, Indiana University Press, 1976, p. 199.

43   Stephen Heath, "Film and System: Terms of Analysis," Part II, *Screen*, Summer 1975, vol. 16 no. 2, especially pp. 101–107.

44   Stephen Heath, op cit, pp. 104–5.

45   Cf. I. Pichel, "Character, Personality and Image: a Note on Screen Acting," *Hollywood Quarterly*, 1946, pp. 25–29.

46   "In other words, a film is significant only insofar as it mobilises one discourse to produce effects in another"—Sue Clayton and Jonathan Curling, "On Author-ship," *Screen* Spring 1979, vol. 20 no. 1, p. 41. A more extensive treatment of the occupational determinants of stardom, from the side of the cinematic as opposed to the filmic, can be found in Barry King, *The Hollywood Star System*, Ph.D. thesis, University of London, 1984.

47   Edmund White, *States of Desire*, London, Andre Deutsch, 1980, pp. 3–4.

48   John Ellis, op cit, p. 94. But compare his acknowledgement on p. 99 that the film performance is closer to a "pure voyeurism" than the fetishistic circulation of subsidiary materials. For a catalogue of the requests received in Hollywood see L. Handel, *Hollywood Looks at its Audience*, Arno Press, 1976.

49   Richard Dyer, "Four Films of Lana Turner," *Movie* 25, pp. 30–52; J. Damico, "Ingrid from Lorraine to Stromboli," *Journal of Popular Film*, vol. 4 no. 1, 1975, pp. 2–19; and Jane Clarke and Diana Simmonds (eds), *Move over Misconception*, London, British Film Institute Dossier no. 4, 1980.

50   Richard Dyer, *Stars*, op cit, p. 100 ff.

51   Stephen Heath, op cit, p. 105.

52   Cf. D. Thomson, "The Look on the Actor's Face," *Sight and Sound* vol. 46 no. 4, 1976. Bela Balazs' *Theory of Film* is the locus classicus of this view.

53   See P. Stallings and H. Mandelbaum, *Flesh and Fantasy*, St. Martin's Press, 1978.

54   Though there are examples of anticipatory cosmetic alteration. Joan Crawford's career provides some classic examples.

55   See Umberto Eco, "Semiotics of Theatrical Performance," *The Drama Review* 21, 1976, p. 111.

56   See N. Blanchard, *How to Break into Movies*, New York, Doubleday, 1978, p. 41 ff; J. Selznick, "The Talent Hunters," *American Film*, Dec.–Jan. 1979, p. 60; and L. G. Yoaken, "Casting," *Film Quarterly*, 1958, p. 36.

57   Transcript of Guardian Lecture, reprinted in *Three Sixty°*: British Film Institute News, May 1985, pp. 10–11.

58   John Willet (ed), *Brecht on Theatre*, op cit, p. 48.

59   Richard Dyer, *Stars*, op cit.

60   See Barry King, op cit.

61   See Jeremy Tunstall and David Walker, *Media Made in California*, Oxford University Press, 1981, p. 78. If only actors, as opposed to other performers, are taken into account employment is at 80%. See John Lahr, *New Society*, December 20, 1984 pp. 468–469.

62   Robert Brady, "The Problem of Monopoly," in Gordon Watkins (ed), *The Motion Picture Industry*, Annals of the American Academy of Political and Social Science, November 1947, vol. 254, pp. 125–136.

63   Cf. Christian Metz, *Psychoanalysis and Cinema*, London, Macmillan, 1982, p. 67.

64   H. Powdermaker, *Hollywood: The Dream Factory*, New York, Little, Brown and Co, 1950, p. 206.

65   Employment in advertising is not only an alternative to "straight" acting but can be very lucrative if syndicated.

66   Roland Barthes, *Image-Music-Text*, (Stephen Heath, ed), London, Fontana, 1977, p. 75.

67   H. Powdermaker, op cit, p. 210.

68   Quoted in the *Sunday Times Magazine*, August 26, 1984.

69   Christian Metz, op cit, p. 75.

70   Richard Dyer, *Stars*, op cit, p. 23.

71   Marshall Colman, *Continuous Excursions*, London, Pluto Press, 1982, p. 10 ff.

72   Cf. John Langer, "Television's Personality System," *Media, Culture and Society*, vol. 3 no. 4, 1981, pp. 351–365; and David Lusted, "The Glut of the Personality," in Len Masterman (ed), *Television Mythologies*, London, Comedia, 1985, pp. 73–81.

Chapter 13

Jackie Stacey

FEMININE FASCINATIONS
A question of identification?

I talked to friends and colleagues, mainly about their [favourite stars']
style, hair-dos etc., and to family about their singing and acting. I preferred stars with whom I could identify as being like women in everyday
life – but I also enjoyed it when their lives became more exciting than
everyday. . . .

    I liked to be able to identify with them, but again, I preferred them to
have more charm and ability than I did.

(Anon)

I don't think I consciously thought of myself *looking like* any particular star
– it was more the semi-magical transformation of screen identification! I
adored Ava Gardner's dark magnetism, but knew I wasn't like that.

(M. Palin)

BOTH THESE STATEMENTS CAPTURE well the complexity of the pleasures
of cinematic identification. They raise questions about the relationship between
stars and spectators and the processes of the formation of feminine identities through
cinematic modes of address.

    In the first statement, the respondent comments on the enjoyment in the recogni-
tion of familiar aspects of everyday life, and yet also describes the possible fantasy
of something better. Similarity between self and star is combined with the memory of
a pleasure in a more successful femininity: 'more charm and ability'. In the second
example, the star is adored, but the spectator recognises the impossibility of being
like her ideal. Despite the recognition of the fixity of their differences, however,
the spectator remembers 'the semi-magical transformation of screen identification',
suggesting that her own identity is indeed transformed through processes of spectatorship. Thus, whilst recognising the difference between herself and her favourite

Hollywood star, the fixity of the difference is open to temporary fluidity, and yet there is a conscious knowledge that the difference will indeed be reimposed after the magic of Hollywood wears off. Both these examples introduce the contradictions of similarity and difference, recognition and separateness which characterise the relationship of female spectators to their star ideals.

Many respondents described their pleasures in Hollywood stars in terms of 'identification': this term was used in numerous ways to refer to a whole range of spectator/star relations. As these two examples demonstrate, what is meant by such a term is complex and difficult to put into words: hence, the description of the process as 'semi-magical'. The difficulty of representing the feelings remembered in relation to Hollywood cinema is expressed here through a common characterisation of Hollywood itself: both are described as magical. This highlights well the problems of pinpointing the exact processes at stake for spectators in cinematic identification.

One way to think about 'identification' in this context is in terms of the negotiation between self and other, which some have argued characterises all 'object relations' (Benjamin, 1990). At the centre of this negotiation between spectators and their star ideals is the recognition of similarities and differences.

> I preferred stars to be unlike women in everyday life. The stars gave us a lift, took us away from everyday life, from worrying about how to make our meat ration go further, and going stockingless to save some coupons. . . . I preferred female stars who were like me in some way because I could imagine what I would do if I were in a position that happened to them on the screen.
>
> (Vera Barford)

> Because I had auburn hair in my younger days and I related to stars with red hair (dreaming only) I had one thing in common with a movie star . . . but I preferred stars unlike me because you wanted to see stars different from everyday people – it made life more interesting, so it was easy to believe you were in some way like a star and yet you only wanted to be 'in' the movie whilst in the cinema.
>
> (Audrey Westgarth)

> I preferred stars who were like me in some way – I liked to think I was like them – but in fact I was very tall, thin, shy and gangly. So the answer should really be no!
>
> (Anon)

These examples are typical of the contradictory feelings spectators have in relation to Hollywood stars: on the one hand, they value difference for taking them into a world in which their desires could potentially be fulfilled; on the other, they value similarity for enabling them to recognise qualities they already have.

The match or mismatch between self and ideal is constantly reassessed by female spectators. In the first example, the star is appreciated for providing light relief from the burdens and material deprivation of life in 1940s Britain: the spectator's situation is temporarily forgotten as she fills her imagination with the fictional life of the star. Women going 'stockingless' is a striking contrast to images of Hollywood glamour in which the stockinged leg has almost become an icon of desirability; the shot which moves up the female star's leg from ankle towards thigh is a favourite convention within Hollywood to introduce the desirable protagonist. Yet at the same time, this respondent also preferred stars like her in some way so she could imagine herself in their position and decide what she would do if she were. Thus the processes here involve the negotiation between self and other, but also between self and an imaginary self which temporarily merges with the fictionalised feminine subject to test out new possibilities. The recognition of a potential self in the fictionalised situation, based on some similarity between star and spectator, is operating simultaneously with a desire to maintain the difference between self and ideal.

In the second example, the recognition of similarity between spectator and star takes a more concrete form in the common feature of auburn hair: typically the identification is made through similarity of physical appearance. Yet the respondent represents this relation to her favourite stars as 'dreaming only': it is thus only an imaginary point of identification that belongs to the realm of dreams. However, this respondent also expresses contradictory feelings about her star ideals: she prefers them both like and unlike herself. As well as recognising a common feature between herself and Hollywood stars with red hair, she also enjoys the differences between self and idealised other. Indeed, it is this gap between the film star and everyday people that produces the self-transformation to become more like the star. Thus the difference provides the space for the production of a fantasy self more like the ideal, and yet simultaneously the gap is closed as that new fantasy self is produced. This temporary self-transformation is written about as a process that the spectator realises will end as the film does. In this case there is enough difference to affirm the subject, desired self and idealised image: thus self and other are simultaneously held apart and merging in a complex process of recognition based on similarity and difference.

The third example further highlights the complexity of this interplay between spectator and star: the respondent shifts from asserting that she prefers stars like herself to the reluctant realisation that perhaps this connection remains at the level of desire, and thus admits – 'the answer should really be no!' She describes herself, again in terms of physical appearance, in derogatory terms (tall, thin, shy and gangly) to contrast herself with the ideals in which she mistakenly recognised herself. In other words, her desire would be to recognise herself in these ideal feminine images, and yet, upon reflection, she recognises that the gap is too great. However, the preference is stated clearly at the beginning, suggesting that some recognition of similarity did, nevertheless, characterise the spectator/star relationship in this case. Again the subject and the idealised image produce a contradictory set of negotiations of identities in which similarity and difference between spectator and star are continuously reassesed.

Indeed, what comes across most forcefully from the analysis of spectators' memories of Hollywood discussed in this chapter is the diversity and complexity of processes involved in what might be referred to as 'identification'. Existing theories of cinematic identification have attempted to analyse this 'magical' process. However, in the light of my research, I shall argue that they fail to account for the complexity and diversity of meanings at stake. Specifically, the dominance of psychoanalytic accounts of identification within feminist film criticism has led to the exploration of universal patterns of unconscious processes, ignoring the particularities of forms of cinematic identification, and, indeed, its meaning to cinema spectators. In this chapter some key aspects of these existing theories of identification are reassessed in the light of female spectators' accounts of their relationships to Hollywood stars in 1940s and 1950s Britain.

Theorising cinematic identification

In film studies generally, the term 'identification' has been widely used to suggest a rather amorphous set of cultural processes. Drawing on literary analysis, identification has often loosely meant sympathising or engaging with a character. It has also been understood to suggest something analogous to the idea of 'point of view', watching and following the film from a character's point of view. This involves not only *visual* point of view, constructed by type of shot, editing sequences and so on, but also *narrative* point of view, produced through the sharing of knowledge, sympathy or moral values with the protagonist (Perkins, 1972). Identification has thus been used as a kind of commonsense term within some film and literary studies, referring to a set of cultural processes which describe different kinds of connections between spectators/readers and fictional others.

The main body of work on cinematic identification, however, has drawn upon Freudian and Lacanian psychoanalysis. The feminist analysis of the pleasures of the cinema for female spectators has been largely based on a particular reworking of psychoanalytic theories of identification. It is with this work that I shall take issue, arguing against some of its premises and conclusions.

Within psychoanalytic theory, 'identification' has been seen as the key mechanism for the production of identities. Freud analysed the unconscious mechanisms through which the self is constituted in relation to external objects. In her paper 'Identification and the star: a refusal of difference', Anne Friedberg draws upon Freud's theory of identification as follows:

> First identification is the original form of emotional tie with an object; secondly, in a regressive way it becomes a substitute for a libidinal object-tie, as it were by means of introjection of the object into the ego; and thirdly, it may arise with any new perception of a common quality shared with some other person who is not an object of sexual instinct. The more important this common quality is, the more successful may this partial identification become, and it may thus represent the beginning of a new tie.
>
> (Freud, 1921, quoted in Friedberg, 1982: 48)

The role of vision in identification has always been part of the Freudian formulation; the emphasis on the significance of the moment of the *sight* of sexual difference in the constitution of feminine and masculine identities, for example. For Freud this relationship, between self and ideal other, could be understood within his third example of the narcissist's love objects: 'what he himself [*sic*] would like to be' (Merck, 1987: 6).

Freud argued that it was women who were particularly prone to narcissism. Within this framework, narcissism is often a derogatory term, used to suggest a self-love which has yet to mature and be directed outwards towards an external object. Indeed, in commonsense usage narcissism typically has taken on connotations of feminine self-indulgence and vanity.

Lacanian theory could be said to have rescued narcissim from its derogatory connotations. The 'specular role of identification' has taken centre stage, most particularly in Lacan's theories of the mirror phase, through which subjects are constituted through a specular misrecognition of an other. According to Lacan, it is a necessary stage in the development of the human subject. The process is summed up succinctly by Elizabeth Wright thus:

> the child looks in the mirror and is delighted by several qualities of its own image simultaneously. Whereas before it experienced itself as a shapeless mass, it now gains a sense of wholeness, an ideal completeness, and this all without effort. This gratifying experience of a mirror image is a metaphorical parallel of an unbroken union between inner and outer, a perfect control that assures immediate satisfaction of desire.
>
> (Wright, 1984: 108)

Since all subjects are fascinated by their ideal reflected back to them during the pre-oedipal formation of subjectivity, narcissism is seen to be a necessary part of the development of all subjectivities. As Mandy Merck has pointed out: 'Freud's opposition of ego and object love neglects "the fundamental narcissistic nature of all object relations", if they begin with the child's fascination with its own image in the Lacanian mirror' (Merck, 1987: 6, quoting Penley, 1985).

However, it is important not to lose the gender specificity of such psychic processes which becomes clear when they are analysed within particular social domains. Whilst narcissism may indeed be part of the psychic formations of subjectivity generally, the cultural construction of femininity in terms of physical appearance and 'to be looked-at-ness' shapes the meanings of such narcissistic object relations for female spectators. The early attachment to an ideal image of the self has a different significance in relation to masculinity and femininity, since the latter is so centrally defined in terms of being an image in this culture. Indeed, narcissism takes on a particular social and historical meaning for women in a culture dominated by the endless circulation of idealised visual images of femininity. The relationship between self, ideal self and idealised image of femininity has specific meanings in the female spectator/star relationship.

These models of identification employed within psychoanalysis to explore the developments of unconscious identities have been adopted by some film theorists, such as Christian Metz (1975). Here early psychic processes are seen as analogous to cinematic identification. As Friedberg outlines:

> Primary identification as Metz describes it (as distinct from Freud's 'original and emotional tie') means a spectator who identifies with the camera and projector, and like the child positioned in front of the mirror, constructs an imaginary notion of wholeness, of a unified body. . . .

> Secondary identification is with an actor, character or star . . . any body becomes an opportunity for an identificatory investment, a possible suit for the substitution/misrecognition of self.
>
> (Friedberg, 1982: 50)

Psychoanalytic film theorists have thus developed a complex analysis of cinematic identification, based on an analogy between the construction of individual identities in infancy in relation to others, and the process of watching a film on a screen.

Following Laura Mulvey's original attack on the visual pleasure of narrative cinema, much feminist work on the process of identification is still marked by a suspicion of any kind of feminine role model, heroine or image of identification. Mulvey's films (such as *Amy!*, 1980), as well as her influential theoretical work, have advocated a rejection of the conventions of popular representations, not simply for the images of femininity constructed, but also for the processes of identification offered to the cinema spectator. 'Identification' itself has been seen as a cultural process complicit with the reproduction of dominant culture by reinforcing patriarchal forms of identity. Anne Friedberg sums up what feminists have seen as the problematic functions of identification thus:

> Identification can only be made through recognition, and all recognition is itself an implict confirmation of an existing form. The institutional sanction of stars as ego ideals also operates to establish normative figures. Identification enforces a collapse of the subject onto the normative demand for sameness, which, under patriarchy, is always male.
>
> (Friedberg, 1982: 53)

Identification of any kind is thus criticised for reproducing *sameness*, *fixity* and the *confirmation of existing identities*.

In her contribution to the *Camera Obscura* retrospective on female spectatorship, Jacqueline Rose affirms these criticisms:

> it was not possible to ask cinema for a positive identification for women, unless at the expense of rendering invisible once again – and this I had thought had been the crucial contribution of film theory in the 1970s – the psychic economy of cinematic process which had generated that image and on which in turn it had seemed so heavily to rely. If I was interested in criticizing a too monolithic image of Hollywood – the idea, for example, that all narrative film effectively ended in some type of oedipal resolution for the man, or that his look was the controlling gaze of the film – it was not in order to insert women as positivity (image on the screen, or spectator off-screen), but because I read this fundamental visual economy of cinema as always prey to its own dissolution.
>
> (Rose, 1989: 275)

This relegation of 'woman' to the position of negativity, absence or lack is typical of the Lacanian framework in which 'woman' can have no positive place in the symbolic order of patriarchy. As Linda Williams argues: 'Lacan's description of castration and female "lack" – though it offered an eloquent statement of the nullity of woman within the symbolic structure – was beginning to seem such an overstatement of the problem as to become a problem itself' (Williams, 1989: 335). Within a Lacanian framework, then, women's pleasure in Hollywood cinema, either through identification with the female protagonist, or otherwise, can only be conceived of as a sign of their complicity with their oppression under patriarchy. Identification, both as a psychic and as a cinematic process, is criticised for fixing the meaning of sexual difference within a patriarchal symbolic order in which femininity functions as the 'other' to the masculine subject of desire.

It is easy to understand the rejection, and indeed condemnation, of cinematic identification within such a framework. However, identification is conceptualised here as a singular and rigid process which fixes the spectator as the subject of the filmic discourse. Although Rose's argument rests on the assumed fragility of the visual economy of patriarchal cinema, it assumes identification itself to be a process with little fluidity of meaning or flexibility for the female spectator. The only pleasure for the female spectator can be that of masochism in her identification with her place as object in the patriarchal order. Within such a reading, the Hollywood cinema is seen as 'a powerful ideological tool, the spectator its gullible victim' (Greig, 1987: 40).

Identification has been seen as the feminine counterpoint to masculine desire in feminist criticisms of popular narrative cinema. The visual economy and narrative trajectory of Hollywood cinema, it has been argued, are typically organised around the masculine desire of the protagonist and the spectator. Feminists have found little space for feminine desire within Hollywood cinema, except the desire to be a passive object of masculine desire. Female desire in the context of cinematic spectatorship, then, has generally been discussed in terms of passivity (taking pleasure in being desired), or masochism (desire to submit to the punishing will of the masculine subject). Both these readings of female desire, whilst highlighting the dominant construction of sexual 'complementarity' in which the man expresses his desire and woman is the object of it, come too close to reinforcing women's place as passive victims of patriarchal culture for comfort.

Through a more flexible model of cinematic spectatorship, based on a notion of fantasy elaborated by Laplanche and Pontalis (1968), Cowie (1984) has attempted to move beyond the rigidities of such problems within feminist film criticism. In her analysis Cowie explores the multiple identifications offered to the spectator by a film text and the interchangeability of different subject positions for the spectator. Cowie's model of spectatorship, it has been argued, is one in which the spectator has 'a relative autonomy' from the text and, rather than being positioned mechanistically to identify or not, the spectator is provided with 'a series of possible entries and identifications with characters according to their different roles and functions within a network of character relations' (Greig, 1987: 40). Identification for the female spectator might therefore be conceptualised as something less rigid and less easily dismissed as colluding with the dominant patriarchal order.

Thus, rather than being constrained by the negative construction of feminine identification discussed above, female spectators, like male spectators, are able to make multiple identifications across gender boundaries. As a result, the feminine spectator may or may not be a woman, or only women; or, as Constance Penley puts it, the emphasis on fantasy highlights the great range and diversity of identificatory positions in film, and how those positions can be taken up by either the man or the woman watching the film. While there are 'masculine' and 'feminine' positions in fantasy, men and women, respectively, do not have to assume those positions according to their assigned genders.

(Penley, 1984: 256)

However, such a model of identification and spectatorship would seem to make the task of the feminist critic a redundant one, since this reading of fantasy as the location of sexually undifferentiated, multiple subject positionings suggests that the gender of characters and spectators might cease to be of significance. There is no acknowledgement here of the relationship between 'the social' and 'the psychic'.

Thus, a general problem with psychoanalytic work on cinematic identification is highlighted, namely that the relationship between the unconscious workings of film texts and the identities of actual female spectators in the cinema remains of little or no significance. As Gaylyn Studlar has argued, an engagement with actual cinema spectators' responses may unsettle some of the neater psychoanalytic formulations prevalent within feminist film theory:

> The attempt to analyze gendered spectatorship and the representation of women in film has encouraged generalizing claims centered around the notion of a hypothetical, ideal spectator 'constructed' by coercive textual mechanisms. . . .
>
> If for no other reason than for its theoretically well-behaved nature, the textually constructed spectator is methodologically attractive. Actual spectators' responses are much more unruly, but they obviously demand attention in the debate over spectatorship. . . . I am concerned . . . that feminist film theory is reluctant to mediate theory through the response of real (i.e., nonacademic) spectators.
>
> (Studlar, 1989: 302–3)

My analysis of cinematic identification is based on female spectators' accounts of Hollywood stars. It is therefore necessarily working on a broader level than the psychoanalytic accounts that concentrate primarily on the unconscious processes at stake in identification. Psychoanalytic theory may seem to be the obvious starting point for a consideration of the processes of identification, since it does offer some account of the meaning and significance of these processes. However, as I shall go on to demonstrate, these psychoanalytic theories of identification used within film criticism have led to very narrow conceptualisations of *cinematic* identification, which have ignored the broader meanings of spectator/star relations and indeed have led to some overly pessimistic conclusions about the pleasures of popular cinema.

What, then, does identification mean to female spectators? How might we conceptualise cinematic identification, not solely as analogous to early psychic developments, but as a cultural process with social meanings beyond the cinema? In classifying the material I received from female spectators it was hard to pinpoint a single process and name it 'identification'. Instead I found that these accounts forced me to reflect upon the meaning of such a concept. 'Identification' seemed to include forms of feminine desire, rather than being strictly constituted as their opposite. When women wrote of their love and adoration of a particular star this was in fact a form of identification: because of such devotion to some stars, there remains a kind of bond with favourites. In addition, 'identification' seemed to involve many diverse, if overlapping, processes which could usefully be separated out for the purpose of analysis. Thus, rather than finding a single and fixable process which could be labelled 'identification', I was confronted with a whole range of connections between female spectators and their ideals on the screen. This necessitated moving beyond the narrower psychoanalytic conceptualisations of identification and rethinking its diverse meanings within an understanding of the social context of the cinema.

A broader framework for conceptualising audience–star relations has been developed by Andrew Tudor. Reworking Leo Handel's audience study (Handel, 1950), Tudor maps out a useful set of possible relations between stars and their audiences within a more sociological framework (see Table 13.1). The model suggests a helpful distinction between the audience–star relations which take place in the cinema itself (context specific) and those which take place outside the cinematic context (diffuse). It also distinguishes between particularly intense connections between star and audience (high) and less intense involvements (low). 'Emotional affinity' refers to a loose attachment to the star, what Tudor calls 'standard involvement' (Tudor, 1974: 80). 'Imitation', primarily found among young members of the audience, involves the audience using film stars as role models for clothes, hairstyles or behaviour. 'Projection' is used to describe processes whereby the audiences' identities become bound up with those of their favourite stars outside the cinema context. Finally, 'self-identification' describes the intense pleasure of taking on the identity of the star whilst watching the film.

However, in the light of my research, this model remains overly schematic and in need of further elaboration. It ignores the ways in which the 'range of identifications' and 'range of consequences' may vary according to gender: do women develop a particularly strong attachment to their star ideals, and if so, why and under what circumstances? Furthermore, what is the relationship between imitation and projection and do these take on a particular significance at different times and in different contexts? Nevertheless, Tudor's model does provide a useful starting point here, since it introduces the argument that audience–star relations involve a diverse set of practices whose meanings extend beyond the cinema itself.

Table 13.1 Types of audience–star relation

	Intensity of involvement	Range of consequences	
Range of star-individual identification	High	Context specific Self-identification	Diffuse Projection
	Low	Emotional affinity	Imitation (of physical and simple behavioural characteristics)

Source: Tudor, 1974: 80.

In the exploration of cinematic identification which follows I examine the multiplicity of processes connecting female spectators to female Hollywood stars. Respondents' memories of Hollywood stars are analysed in relation to the question of what cinematic 'identification' signified to spectators. The categories of spectatorship around which the following sections are organised are thus not psychoanalytic categories (though they may overlap with them considerably), but rather categories through which spectators articulated the pleasures offered by female Hollywood stars in the 1940s and 1950s. In taking spectators' accounts, rather than film texts, as the basis for this exploration, I am clearly focusing on conscious memories, rather than unconscious processes. Indeed, it could be argued that my challenge to the psychoanalytic models is limited by such a focus. However, as we shall see, taking spectators' memories as the material for an exploration of cinematic identification does not exclude the psychic dimensions of such processes, since fantasy is central to these memories, but rather it necessitates a broader analysis which does not exclude conscious practices and spectators' activities.

The first section addresses processes of identification that involve fantasies about the relationship between the identity of the star and the identity of the spectator. On the whole, these forms of identification relate to the cinematic context; in other words, they are processes that take place during the actual viewing of a film. The second section examines forms of recognition that involve practice as well as fantasy, in that spectators actually transform some aspect of their identity as a result of their relationship to their favourite star. These practices extend beyond the cinema itself and thus spectatorship is considered in relation to the construction of feminine identities more generally.

The distinction between fantasy and practice employed here aims to differentiate between the processes of spectatorship that do not involve the spectator in activities or self-transformations in a physical way, and those that do. In other words, the fantasies are processes that only take place in the spectator's private imagination, and may not be evident to others, whereas the practices, which are obviously fantasies as well, involve activities that are perceivable to others, and indeed often rely on the participation of others. Although this is a problematic dichotomy in some ways, some distinction between these different processes of spectatorship is necessary, especially in order to highlight the ways in which the latter categories have been ignored within theories of spectatorship in film studies.

Cinematic identificatory fantasies

In the first group of categories of spectatorship, 'devotion', 'adoration' and 'worship', the star is at the centre and the spectator only included in so far as she facilitates the construction of the star's image and identity. These memories, then, make little reference to the relationship between self-image and Hollywood ideal and focus instead upon the wonder the spectator remembers feeling in relation to the star.

Devotion

> I wanted to write and tell you of my devotion to my favourite star Doris
> Day. I thought she was fantastic, and joined her fan club, collected all the
> photos and info I could. I saw *Calamity Jane* 45 times in a fortnight and still
> watch all her films avidly. My sisters all thought I was mad going silly on a
> woman, but I just thought she was wonderful, they were mad about Elvis,
> but my devotion was to Doris Day.
>
> (Veronica Millen)

The passion for female stars expressed by spectators is striking in its intensity: it is
difficult to see *Calamity Jane* (1953, David Butler) forty-five times in a fortnight! In this
example, the adoration of female fan for female star is commented upon in contrast to
her sisters' attachments to Elvis, the epitome of smouldering heterosexual masculinity. They disregarded her love for her favourite female star which did not fit into the
conventional heterosexual model. Her sisters describe her devotion as 'going silly on a
woman', suggesting an important attachment to her favourite star, but denigrating it
as immature and lacking the seriousness of adult, heterosexual love. Another way to
describe such an attachment, which again has had rather dismissive connotations, is in
terms of a crush: 'Then stars had far more mystique and . . . one tended to look up to
them and yours truly was still at the age of "crushes" ' (Jo Keen). Here the respondent
draws attention to her age, indicating that 'crushes' belong to adolescence or school-
girl years, where adoration of feminine ideals is more acceptable.[1] Numerous memories of favourite female stars included accounts of such devotion. In this example, the
contrast to heterosexual devotion is made by the spectator herself, but the homoerotic
connotations of such attachments are left implicit.

Adoration

Such feelings, however, continued into adulthood for many female spectators, though
there may have been an intensification of attachment to feminine ideals at the time of
transition into adulthood; as the following respondent says this was 'no passing fancy'.
Her elucidation of her adoration for Deanna Durbin is worth quoting at length to
capture the narrative elements of the description:

> In the late 1930s, when I was about nine or ten, I began to be aware of a
> young girl's face appearing in magazines and newspapers. I was fascinated.
> The large eyes, the full mouth, sometimes the wonderful smile, showing
> the slightly prominent but perfect teeth. I feel rather irritated that I do not
> recall the moment when I realised that the face belonged to a very lovely
> singing voice beginning to be heard on the radio record programmes.
>   The face and the voice belonged to Deanna Durbin. . . .
>   In 1940 at the age of twelve, I was evacuated from my house in South
> London to Looe in Cornwall, and it was there that I was taken to the
> pictures for a special treat. There at last I saw her. The film, a sequel to her
> first, was *Three Smart Girls Grow Up*. The effect she had upon me can only

be described as electrifying. I had never felt such a surge of admiration and adoration before.

Even if Deanna had not possessed her beautiful soprano voice, I believe that she would still have been a favourite of mine. But the singing was of course the reason for such adoration. . . . When she sang the most simple melody it became so beautiful and moving that it moved me to tears.

My feeling for her was no passing fancy. The love was to last a lifetime. Over the next few years, we watched as Deanna grew into a stunningly lovely woman. Her voice matured and completely fulfilled its earlier promise, and we eagerly awaited every film. To the four hundred or so members of 'the Deanna Durbin Society', she remains the loveliest Hollywood film star of all time. She keeps in touch with us. Our meetings and our newsletter bring us all such a great deal of pleasure.

I feel it quite extraordinary that Deanna can inspire such devotion, as it is now forty years since she made a film or any kind of public appearance.

I must just add that the members of our society seem to be about equal in number male and female. I think perhaps that it would be considered a bit of a giggle today, if a large number of women confessed to feeling love for a girl. Nobody seemed to question it then. Just in case; I have been married since 1948! Have two sons and a daughter, one grandchild.

(Patricia Robinson)

Deanna Durbin is introduced here within the discourse of romance. The memory of the first 'meeting', or rather 'sighting', is retold within the structure of a romantic narrative whose sequence of events culminates in the moment of seeing her favourite star on the cinema screen. Its structure is built around a series of gaps, enigmas or absences which is typical of the romance narrative (see Stacey, 1990). The story begins with her fascination with an anonymous female face, the details of which are easily reconjured. Then a beautiful singing voice is heard on the radio. In a forgotten moment the beauty of the face and of the singing voice of this Hollywood star are coupled to produce a tantalising combination for the young female spectator. This lost moment interrupts the smooth flow of the narrative and draws attention to the processes of recollection at work. The memory of the star's face is crystal clear, but a magical moment of realisation is frustratingly lost in the past. Its loss, however, foregrounds its importance to this respondent and it thus becomes a 'treasured moment' (rather than a treasured memory) by its absence. This lost moment of realisation is the only (apparent) missing link in the story, and yet its absence becomes part of the narrative structure.

It is only at this point in the narrative that the repondent introduces her favourite star by name – Deanna Durbin – and yet the picture continues to remain incomplete since the moving image of this Hollywood star on the cinema screen remained out of reach. The anticipation of finally seeing the star on screen is recreated through the gradual build up to the moment when 'there at last I saw her': the picture is thus completed – face, voice, name and, finally, the 'real thing'. Magazines and radio could only offer partial pleasures, preliminaries to the excitement of the moment of seeing her on screen. Only the cinema could offer that combination of 'reality' and intimacy which gave a sense of meeting the star of your dreams. Far from being the closure of this narrative, however, this moment signifies the beginning of a lifetime's devotion to Deanna Durbin.

This recreation of the step-by-step movement towards the moment of seeing Deanna Durbin offers a structure for the articulation of increasingly intense feelings for the star. At the beginning of the story the respondent describes herself as being 'aware of a young girl's face' when she first saw it in magazines; she then becomes 'fascinated' by her, and finally, on seeing Deanna on screen she recalls: 'the effect she had upon me can only be described as electrifying'. This rhetorical device – 'can only be described as' – draws attention to the singularity of the experience. Indeed, she had 'never felt such a surge of admiration and adoration before'. The use of the words 'electrifying' and 'surge' suggest the peculiar intensity and indeed conjure up a sense of the immediate physicality of such emotions, which, in their newness and unfamiliarity, took this young female spectator by surprise. These feelings of 'adoration', 'admiration', and, indeed, 'love', were, we are told, to last a lifetime. The strength of feeling is conveyed in the repetition of words such as 'adoration' and 'devotion'; and the significance of that first moment is reinforced by the continuing membership of Deanna's fan club, fifty years later, given as evidence confirming the intensity and durability of the devotion. Thus the memory is not only structured like a romantic narrative but is also characterised by its use of romantic language.

This respondent conveys a certain amount of surprise herself at the strength of her feelings for Deanna. Interspersed with the story of her devotion are indications of self-reflection about the reasons for her attachment and even some unease about how it might be interpreted. At one point it is Deanna's voice which is given as the reason for such devotion, and yet even without it 'she would still have been a favourite'. 'Feeling love for a girl' is remembered as being all right in the 1940s, clearly suggesting a contrast with today's interpretations of such feelings.

The anxiety about the possibility of homoerotic connotations is here expressed through the respondent's heterosexual identity and confirmed by her marital status and reproductive roles. Heterosexuality is thus invoked to protect against any interpretations, including those which have clearly occurred to this respondent, of such love of another female as containing homoerotic pleasures. The rigid boundary between heterosexuality and homosexuality as two mutually exclusive identities is thus reaffirmed, despite the strength of adoration and love 'for a girl' expressed in this respondent's story. The homoeroticism of such romantic recreations is nevertheless striking in this narrative of 'love at first sight'.

Worship

The feelings of love and adoration towards stars are often represented through the discourse of religious worship in which stars become goddesses and no longer belong to our world:

> Film stars . . . seemed very special people, glamorous, handsome and way above us ordinary mortals.
>
> (June Thomas)

Rita Hayworth . . . she was just the personification of beauty, glamour and sophistication to me and to thousands of others. Self-assured, wore gorgeous clothes beautifully, danced gloriously and her musicals were an absolute delight. She just seemed out of this world!

(Mary Marshall)

They were screen goddesses – stars way up in the star studded galaxy, far removed from the ordinary hum-drum lives of us, the cinema-going fans.

(Dawn Hellmann)

These respondents emphasise the difference between themselves and their ideals by representing stars as 'out of this world' and 'way up in another galaxy' and thus located at a vast spatial distance from the cinema spectator.

The language of religious love is drawn upon to convey the significance of the attachment to favourite stars. This combined with a 'love at first sight' story in which the sequencing of the anonymous star, the film and finally the star's name replicate the conventions of romance narratives referred to above (see section on adoration):

I'll never forget the first time I saw her, it was in *My Gal Sal* in 1942, and her name was Rita Hayworth. I couldn't take my eyes off her, she was the most perfect woman I had ever seen. The old cliché 'screen goddess' was used about many stars, but those are truly the only words that define that divine creature. . . . I was stunned and amazed that any human being could be that lovely.

(Violet Holland)

Stars were fabulous creatures to be worshipped from afar, every film of one's favourite gobbled up as soon as it came out.

(Pauline Kemp)

These statements represent the star as something different and unattainable. Religious signifiers here indicate the special status and meaning of the stars, as well as suggesting the intensity of the devotion felt by the spectator. They also reinforce the 'otherness' of the stars who are not considered part of the mortal world of the spectator. The last example, however, does introduce the star into the mortal world by a metaphor of ingestion reminiscent of the act of communion.

Worship of stars as goddesses involves a denial of self found in some forms of religious devotion. The spectator is only present in these quotes as a worshipper, or through her adoration of the star. There is little reference to the identity of the spectator or suggestion of closing the gap between star and fan by becoming more like the star; these are simply declarations of appreciation from afar. The boundaries between self and ideal are quite fixed and stable in these examples, and the emphasis is very strongly on the ideal rather than the spectator. Even in the last statement, where the self is implicit in that the star is to be gobbled up, the star nonetheless remains the subject of the sentence.

In these first three categories, then, spectators articulated their attachments to their favourite stars within the language of love, adoration and worship. The 'identification' here is not a question of similarity with the star, indeed the identity of the spectator remains absent from the equation. Thus, we might ask whether they are in fact forms of cinematic 'identification'. I have included them here because they are forms of spectator/star relations which recurred in accounts of Hollywood cinema of this time and they seemed to me to be representing something rarely considered within theories of identification, yet not entirely separable from it. These memories of Hollywood idols are not straightforward articulations of desire for, or desire to be, the love object. Rather they express something else, somewhere in between: an intense, often homoerotic bond between idol and worshipper.

In the next group of categories of cinematic identificatory fantasies, the relationship between the star's image and the spectator's identity can be seen as rather more fluid and relational. Instead of the rather static division between mortals and goddesses characteristic of the pleasures expressed in the sections above, here it is the imagined transformation of self which produces the cinematic pleasure. The spectator takes pleasure in escaping into the world of Hollywood favourites, and indeed in taking on the star's identity. This section overlaps considerably with my analysis of escapism in the last chapter. It is repeated here since its absence in either chapter would have left too large a gap. Indeed, the overlap could be seen to be indicative of the important connections between escapism and identification.

Transcendence

Many women wrote of the pleasure in imagining themselves taking on the roles and identities of the stars whilst in the cinema:

> An ultra glamorous star was an awesome sight for us gangly girls. A sight to behold forever in our minds. During these spectacular musicals we were transported to a fantasy land where we were the screen movie queens.
>
> (Gwyneth Jones)

> It made no difference to me if the film was ushered in by a spangled globe, the Liberty Lady or that roaring lion, I was no longer in my seat but right up there fleeing for my life from chasing gangsters, skimming effortlessly over silver ice, or singing high and sweet like a lark. . . . No secret agent served their country more bravely, and no one tilled the earth more diligently.
>
> (Dawn Hellmann)

The movement from spectator to star identity in these examples is more fluid than in the previous categories, and this fluidity provides the opportunity for the well-known pleasure of the cinema, 'losing oneself' in the film [. . .]: 'no matter how bad things were around you, you could lose yourself even for one moment in time' (Betty Cunningham); 'Growing up was difficult (even in those days); the films were where I could sit and lose myself and imagine it was me up there and they usually had happy endings too! I suppose they were really the "Mills and Boon" of the age for us girls' (Anon).

This temporary loss of self in an ideal other is reflected upon here as being akin to the pleasures of contemporary romance fiction for women. In retrospect, this respondent suggests she now sees how Hollywood 'really' functioned which she sums up with the gloss 'Mills and Boon' — typically considered to be 'dope for the dopes'.[2] This kind of 'put down', often accompanied by a kind of embarrassment about the escapist pleasure of cultural forms such as romances, soaps and Hollywood, emerged occasionally when respondents began to reflect upon their enjoyment of Hollywood cinema. However, the point here is not to deny that Hollywood is escapist, but rather, as I argued in the previous chapter, to analyse the processes of escapism in relation to Hollywood cinema in wartime and postwar Britain.

In contrast to the distinction between self and ideal maintained in the processes of spectatorship discussed above, in this version the spectator's identity merges with the star in the film, or the character she is portraying: 'I always put myself in the heroine's place' (Anon). The pleasure this fantasy transformation offers is frequently associated with particular stars:

> my favourite was Bette Davis. Her films always held me in thrall, always dramatic, the sort of film with a real good story that one could lose oneself in.
>
> (Mrs G. Adams)

> In the 40s it was Betty Grable for me, I loved musicals — she was so bubbly, so full of life it took you out of yourself, you could bury yourself in her parts.
>
> (Betty Cunningham)

> Joan Crawford could evoke such pathos, and suffer such martydom . . . making you live each part.
>
> (Marie Burgess)

It is the intensity, here of narrative, personality and emotion respectively, which spectators remember as bonding them to their favourite stars. Another respondent writes of 'getting high' on Hollywood stars:

> I was enraptured by any star who appeared in a Hollywood musical. I was completely lost — it wasn't Ginger Rogers dancing with Fred Astaire, it was me. My going to the movies in the forties and fifties was akin to the high young people get now by doing drugs.
>
> (Kay Barker)

There is a striking intimacy between spectator and star in these moments of intense feelings. Some respondents remembered particular moments in films in which they had become one with the star and had shared her emotions:

> Jennifer Jones made a great impression in *Duel in the Sun* — her sheer beauty — her voice — magnetic eyes and the merest trembling of her chin could convey so much feeling and emotion. I'll never forget the last crawl towards Gregory Peck over the rocks. I was with her every inch of the way and my heart was bursting to reach him.
>
> (Yvonne Oliver)

Processes of spectatorial identification are articulated in relation to both similarity and difference between self and ideal. Some respondents imagined themselves as their ideals because of some similarity with the star with whom they identified. For example:

> [My favourite star was] Dorothy Lamour (I don't want to be big headed, but my mother thought I looked like her). . . . The stars in the 1940s and 1950s were really beautiful and at that time I suppose we felt we were the characters we were watching.
>
> (Mrs P. Malcolmson)

Others clearly found that the difference facilitated their shift in identity. For example, one respondent remembers:

> I preferred stars who were unlike everyday women because I went to the cinema to escape into a world of fantasy, wealth, and, above all, glamour. I preferred those unlike me because I could put myself in their place for a short while and become everything I wasn't — beautiful, desirable and popular with the opposite sex.
>
> (Elizabeth Rogers)

In many cases these processes of identification involve a complex interplay of similarity and difference as this example demonstrates:

> If they were like women in everyday life, one could associate oneself with them in their film parts. On the other hand, if they were sometimes unlike real life it did one good to fantasize and think of oneself in such a situation. . . . One could enter into the situation more easily and lose oneself in it — a form of escapism I suppose.
>
> (Anon)

The pleasures of becoming part of the fantasy world on the screen thus take many different forms. However, all these examples demonstrate the importance of the pleasure of shifting identity during the film screening. What is remembered here, albeit in a variety of ways, is the temporary loss of self and the adoption of a star persona, especially in terms of sharing emotional intensity with the star. Thus the boundary between self and ideal is not fixed in these examples, since there is a temporary fantasy self which takes over, and yet the star's identity is still primary here. In other words, the forms of identification articulated here involve a one-way movement towards the star, with little mention of the spectator, except by way of poor comparison (such as 'the gangly girls', see p. 266). The boundary between the self and ideal is therefore relatively stable, being crossed during the film viewing in terms of the spectator entering her fantasy world and becoming her fantasy self, but this temporary, one-way movement leaves the spectator's own identity apparently unchanged by the process.

Aspiration and inspiration

In this next section, the processes analysed involve the spectator's identity more centrally. Here the star's identity is written about more in relation to the desire for transformation of the spectator's identity. The discourses through which the star is remembered, then, are ones which centre on the feminine identity of the spectators, as opposed to the other way around, as in the previous sections.

In some examples the relationship between star and spectator is articulated through the recognition of an immutable difference between star and spectator:

> Hollywood stars in the roles they depicted were all the things we'd have liked to have been, wearing glamorous clothes and jewels we had no chance of acquiring and doing so many wonderful things we knew we would never have the nerve to do – even given the opportunity . . . Bette Davis was the epitome of what we would like to be, but knew we never could!
>
> (Norah Turner)

Yet here the desire to move across that difference and become more like the star is expressed, even if this is accompanied by the impossibility of its fulfilment (see Stacey, 1987a). The distance between the spectator and her ideal produces a kind of longing which offers fantasies of transformed identities. 'The cinema took you into the realm of fantasy and what you as a person would like to be and do' (Anon).

These desires to become more like the stars occur on several levels. Many of them are predictably articulated through the discourse of glamour. Stars offer ideals of feminine appearance:

> I finally kept with Joan Crawford – every typist's dream of how they'd like to look.
>
> (May Ross)

> And of course her [Betty Grable's] clothes – how could a young girl not want to look like that?
>
> (Sheila Wright)

> Joan Bennett – not so much for her acting, I can't even remember her films. I just thought she was gorgeous. The star I would most like to look like.
>
> (Joyce Lewis)

We liked to think we were like them, but of course, we couldn't match any of the female stars for looks or clothes. It was nice to have them as role models though!

(Valerie Channell)

Not surprisingly, stars serve a normative function to the extent that they are often read as role models, contributing to the construction of the ideals of feminine attractiveness circulating in the culture at that time. Stars were variously referred to as 'role models', 'someone to emulate' and 'the epitome of what every woman should be'. Spectators often felt 'unattractive', 'dowdy', 'plump' and 'gangly' by comparison. Stars are remembered through a discourse of feminine glamour in which ideals of feminine appearance (slim, white, young and even-featured) were established and in comparison to which many spectators felt inadequate.

Successful physical attractiveness also signifies successful romantic conclusions:

Although I wished to look like a different star each week depending on what film I saw, I think my favourite was Rita Hayworth, I always imagined if I could look like her I could toss my red hair into the wind . . . and meet the man of my dreams.

(Rene Arter)

Furthermore, glamour is linked to wealth and property, as the following example demonstrates:

my enjoyment of going to the pictures was my way of imagining myself one day going somewhere equally lovely and being able to wear lovely gowns and meet a rich handsome man and have a big house with servants, especially when I had seen a colour film!

(Jean Forshaw)

Thus Hollywood stars function as role models encouraging desire for feminine 'attractiveness', attachment to a man and possession of property (and even servants!). This encouraged traditional forms of aspiration among women whose lives were very unlike anything they saw on the Hollywood screen.

However, star glamour was understood not only in terms of appearance, but also as signifying confidence, sophistication and self-assurance, which were perceived by female spectators as desirable and inspirational:

Maureen O'Hara seemed to me, a teenager, the type of person I would have liked to be as she was the complete opposite of me. Her fiery beauty and nature, and the way she handled situations in her films were magical to me. The same applies to Marilyn Monroe. I was a shorthand typist-cum-secretary; life was rather run of the mill, the lifestyles they portrayed were something we could only dream about.

(Brenda Blackman)

What is interesting here is that it is not only the 'beauty' which was admired, but also 'the way she handled situations', suggesting a kind of ability and confidence in the world which the spectator herself felt she lacked:

> I liked seeing strong, capable and independent types of female characters mostly because I wished to be like them.
>
> (Joan Clifford)

> Likening myself to women who portrayed characters I would have liked to have been or had the courage to have been.
>
> (Mrs P. McDonald)

> I think I admired the ones I would like to have been like and considered myself uninteresting, being quiet and shy.
>
> (Anon)

Thus the courage, confidence and independence of feminine stars is aspired to by spectators who saw themselves as unable to enjoy such admirable qualities.

Some female stars, such as Bette Davis, Joan Crawford and Katharine Hepburn, were frequently referred to as representing images of power and confidence. These were frequent favourites because they offered spectators fantasies of power outside their own experience:

> We liked stars who were most different to ourselves and Katharine Hepburn, with her self-assured romps through any situation, was one of them. We were youngsters at the time, and were anything but self confident, and totally lacking in sophistication, so, naturally, Bette Davis took the other pedestal. She could be a real 'bitch', without turning a hair, and quelled her leading men with a raised eyebrow and a sneer at the corners of her mouth.
>
> (Norah Turner)

> Bette Davis . . . was great, I loved how she walked across the room in her films, she seemed to have a lot of confidence and she had a look of her own, as I think a lot of female stars had at that time.
>
> (Anon)

Powerful female stars often played characters in punishing patriarchal narratives, where the woman is either killed off, or married, or both, but these spectators do not seem to select this aspect of their films to write about. Instead, the qualities of confidence and power are remembered as offering female spectators the pleasure of participation in qualities they themselves lacked and desired.

Again, the age difference between the star and the younger fans is central here, and stars provide ideals of femininity for adolescent women in the audience who are preoccupied with attaining adult femininity:

> Doris Day . . . seemed to epitomise the kind of person, who with luck, I as a child could aspire to be.
>
> (Betty Cole)

> I favoured stars I could identify with – romantic, adventurous, glamorous, strong minded – all the things I hoped to become 'when I grew up'.
>
> (M. Palin)

Thus female stars represented not only ideals of feminine glamour in terms of appearance, but also a mature femininity which was a source of fascination to younger spectators. Stars were envied for their confidence and their capabilities in the fictional worlds of Hollywood cinema.

These examples demonstrate not simply the desire to overcome the gap between spectator and star, but a fantasy of possible movement between the two identities, from the spectator to the star:

> I preferred stars who were unlike women I knew. They were better dressed and looked much more attractive. They gave me the ambition to do more for myself.
>
> (Anon)

Hollywood stars can thus be seen as offering more than simple role models of sexual attractiveness (though clearly they offered this too!). However, they were also remembered as offering female spectators a source of fantasy of a more powerful and confident self:

> I think everyone needs an inspiration or aspiration. Some of the stars I liked because they were down to earth, but they usually became something quite different in their films, making one feel that the unattainable could be reached.
>
> (Marie Burgess)

So far, then, I have discussed processes of spectatorship which involve negotiating the difference between the star and the spectator in various ways. These all overlap to some extent, but what can be seen clearly is that these processes of spectatorship involve distinct relations between self and ideal. First, the processes of spectatorship which involved the denial of self in favour of praising the screen goddesses were analysed. Second, there was a discussion of those relations involving the loss of self in the fantasy world of the star ideal and thus the merging of self with ideal. In the final section, the desire to transform the self and become more like the ideal were explored. Thus, the early examples in which the difference between the star and the spectator remained fixed, and was itself a source of pleasure, contrast increasingly with those in which the boundary between self and ideal is more fluid and relational. This boundary dissolves further in the following sections, in which aspects of the star's identity are taken on by the spectator in a variety of practices that take place outside the cinematic context.

Extra-cinematic identificatory practices

In this section, the processes of spectatorship that concern what I shall call 'identificatory practices' are discussed. I have called these 'extra-cinematic' to indicate that they relate to forms of identification that take place outside the cinematic context. These processes also involve the spectators engaging in some kind of practice of transformation of the self to becomes more like the star they admire, or to involve others in the recognition of their similarity with the star. This transformation does not only take place at the level of fantasy, but also involves activities in which the star becomes part of discourses of the spectator's identity outside the cinema. This is not to suggest that practices do not involve fantasies, or that fantasies cannot be seen as practices, but rather to distinguish between those categories of spectatorship that involve the spectator in some kind of social practice outside the cinema, and those in the previous section, which remained within the spectator's imagination during the viewing of a film. These examples provide the opportunity to explore the meaning of stars for spectators in their everyday lives beyond the spectatorial fantasies of the viewing situation. This is an area of film reception which has been largely ignored within film studies in the past.

Pretending

> [T]here was a massive open-cast coal site just at the tip of our estate – there were nine of us girls – and we would go to the site after school, and play on the mounds of soil removed from the site. The mounds were known to us as 'Beverly Hills' and we all had lots of fun there. Each of us had our own spot where the soil was made into a round – and that was our mansion. We played there for hours – visiting one mansion after another and each being our own favourite film star.
>
> (Mary E. Wilson)

Here the familiar childhood games of make-believe are played out through an imaginary transformation of a physical place into the Hollywood residence, constantly written about in film magazines at that time, called 'Beverly Hills'. Many young spectators would have seen pictures of stars' mansions in magazines such as *Picturegoer*, which most of these respondents read frequently; it regularly featured articles about particular stars' mansions, showing interiors, gardens, swimming pools and so on. The wealth of Beverly Hills, the affluent world of Hollywood stars, contrasts here especially strikingly with the image of the open-cast coal site next to this respondent's housing estate.

The adaptation of their physical surroundings enables each girl to take on a different identity of a Hollywood star. This game of pretending to be famous film stars visiting each other's mansions was clearly a favourite one – 'we played there for hours' – and indeed proved to be a treasured memory of lasting significance for these women who continued to call each other by their Hollywood names some fifty years later: 'it was such fun and your letter brought back all these things – I've had such a laugh about them. I often bump into Betty Grable in Morpeth – I'll mention your letter to her next time I see her' (Mary E. Wilson).

The durability of the significance of particular stars is very striking. Again, fifty years later another spectator remembers the significance of Loretta Young, whom she used to pretend to be in childhood games, despite having only ever seen her in one film:

> Loretta Young was probably the first star that I was aware of. I think it was her hair that I remember most – very long and glossy with a heavy fringe over her forehead. I always wanted hair like that! I also remember wishing that she could be my mother. (My real mother was very nice, I hasten to add.) Childhood games were often played using film star's names. I was always Loretta Young. . . . I probably only saw Loretta Young in one film – but she must have made a lasting impression on me because when I think of '40s films, she's the first person that comes to mind.
>
> (Molly Frost)

Stars' names prompted an obvious source of recognition between self and ideal. A number of respondents wrote of their connection to particular stars because of sharing their name:

> I really loved the pictures, they were my life, I used to pretend I was related to Betty Grable because my name was Betty, and I used to get quite upset when the other children didn't believe me.
>
> (Betty Cunningham)

> Esther Williams would fascinate me always. This was only vanity on my part. I was quite a good swimmer in those long ago days. I belonged to a swimming club and the young men there used to call me 'Esther'.
>
> (Audrey Lay)

Pretending to be particular film stars involves an imaginary practice, but one where the spectator involved knows that it is a game. This is rather different from the processes of entering a fantasy world or taking on a fantasy self in the cinema discussed above, whereby the spectator feels completely absorbed in the star's world and which thus involves a temporary collapsing of the self into the star identity, discussed in the section on 'transcendence'. The first example given above is also different in that it involves a physical as well as an imaginary transformation. Furthermore, pretending does not simply involve the privatised imagination of individual spectators, as in the processes which take place in the cinematic context, but also involves the participation of other spectators in the collective fantasy games. It thus becomes a social practice in so far as the stars are given meanings through activities with others outside the cinema. This kind of representation of the relationship between star and fan is based more on similarity than difference, since the fan takes on the identity of the star in a temporary game of make-believe, and the difference between them is made invisible, despite the recognition of the whole process as one of pretending.

Resembling

The connection between the spectator and the star established through childhood games of pretending to be one's favourite star is also remembered as a consequence of shared physical appearance. There are numerous points of recognition of similarities between the spectator and the star. These are not based on pretending to be something one is not, but rather selecting something which establishes a link between the star and the self based on a pre-existing part of the spectator's identity which bears a resemblance to the star. This does not neccesarily involve any kind of transformation, but rather a highlighting of star qualities in the individual spectator. In some cases, a general physical resemblance connected spectator and star:

> I have *many many times*, both then and since, been told that I could be Bette Davis' double – I never argued. And I can assure you, I do not look like her now!
>
> (Mary May)

Clearly being taken to resemble a Hollywood star by other people was perceived as flattering and complimentary ('I never argued'), but in some cases the resemblance with Bette Davis was perceived as more threatening:

> Bette Davis – her eyes were fabulous and the way she walked arrogantly. . . . I have dark eyes, those days I had very large dark eyebrows . . . and my Dad used to say . . . 'Don't you roll those Bette Davis eyes at me young lady. . . .' Now Doris Day, that's a different thing – we share the same birthday.
>
> (Patricia Ogden)

Bette Davis was of course known for the use of her eyes as part of her performance style: they signified intensity and passion at key moments of dramatic tension in the narrative.[3] Her star image was also associated with confidence and power. Thus the significance of particular features, such as 'Bette Davis eyes', seems to exceed physical likeness, to suggest a certain kind of femininity, in this case a rebellious one which represented a challenge to the father's authority.

The perceived personality types of Hollywood stars were also a point of connection for some spectators:

> Monroe appealed to me deeply and desperately, little girl lost with the body of a desirable woman. She lit up the screen with her performances, the glamour, her movements were so exciting. Watching her made me feel she was in some way lonely and vulnerable, she was my cult figure, I felt like me, she was running away from herself.
>
> (Betty Cruse)

Here the spectator recognises aspects of herself – vulnerability and fear – in Marilyn Monroe, despite her glamour and the excitement of her performance. Thus resemblance involves connecting to a favourite star through the name, looks or personality of the spectator.

Imitating

Unlike the above process of recognising a resemblance to a star, which involves select-ing an already existing common quality with the star, many respondents wrote about imitating their favourite star. This is different from the fantasy of becoming the star whilst viewing a film, or even expressing the desire to become more like the star generally, since it involves an actual imitation of a star or of her particular character-istics in a particular film. In other words, this identificatory practice involves a form of pretending or play-acting, and yet it is also different from pretending, since pretend-ing is represented as a process involving the whole star persona, whereas imitation is used here to indicate a partial taking on of some aspect of a star's identity.

Several respondents gave examples of imitating the singing and dancing of favourite stars after the film performance:

> My favourite female star was Betty Grable. The songs she sang in the film, I would try to remember, I would sing and dance all the way home.
>
> (Pam Gray)

> My favourite star was Deanna Durbin. I absolutely adored her voice when she sang it was like an angel's; and so was her face, she was such a sweet girl and her acting too was always so appealing. I've often tried to sing like her, but of course couldn't ever reach her top notes.
>
> (May Nuckley)

The singing and dancing associated with Hollywood cinema in the 1940s and 1950s also offered a sense of community. A favourite cinema experience from the 1940s is remembered as:

> in a village cinema, a group of teenagers, we filled a row. Lena Horne sang 'Paper Doll' and our row of seats rocked. We sang all the way home.
>
> (Jean Barrett)

Groups of friends were frequently remembered as recreating Hollywood scenarios:

> Deanna Durbin had such a beautiful voice. I too loved to sing and my friends and I used to put on shows singing her songs.
>
> (June Thomas)

> We used to go home and do concerts based on the songs and dances we had seen in the films, and one of my friends had an auntie who was a mine of information on the words of songs from films.
>
> (Jean Forshaw)

> The films we saw made us sing and sometimes act our way home on the bus.
>
> (June Thomas)

These performances often involved others in the judgement of success or failure of the imitation:

> I adored Judy Garland. She was just a couple of years older than me. Her face and her voice were pure magic to me. I saw almost every one of her films from the early days, right to the end of her life. I always longed to meet her, but of course knew I never would. I would even try to sing like her, thought I could, but the family thought different!
>
> (Anon)

The imitation of stars was not limited to singing and dancing, but was clearly a pleasure in terms of replicating gestures, speech and star personalities:

> I had my favourites of course. . . . One week I would tigerishly pace about like Joan Crawford, another week I tried speaking in the staccato tones of Bette Davis and puffing a cigarette at the same time.
>
> (Dawn Hellmann)

The types of stars who were most frequently imitated in terms of posture, movement and gesture tended to be those associated with the more 'confident', 'powerful' feminine identities, such as Bette Davis and Joan Crawford:

> I remember seeing Bette Davis, and, as nobody had cars then, strutting home a mile and a half flashing my eyes pretending I was Bette, lovely days, and for the next few days, using the same movements around the office until everyone got sick . . . until my next good film came out.
>
> (Patricia Ogden)

Copying

Although imitation and copying are very closely linked as practices, I want to use them here differently to distinguish between audiences *imitating* behaviour and activities, and *copying* appearances. As the attempted replication of appearance, then, *copying* relates back to the desire to look like stars discussed above. However, it is not simply expressed as an unfulfillable desire or pleasurable fantasy, as in the earlier examples; it is also a practice which transforms the spectators' physical appearance.

Copying is the most common form of cinematic recognition outside the cinema. Perhaps this is not surprising given the centrality of physical appearance to femininity in general in this culture, and to female Hollywood stars in particular. Here individualised fantasies become practices aimed at the transformation of the spectator's own identity:

> I was a very keen fan of Bette Davis and can remember seeing her in *Dark Victory*. . . . That film had such an impact on me. I can remember coming home and looking in the mirror fanatically trying to comb my

hair so that I could look like her. I idolised her . . . thought she was a wonderful actress.

(Vera Carter)

This process involves an intersection of self and other, subject and object. The impact of the film on the spectator caused her to desire to resemble the ideal physically. In front of a reflection of herself, the spectator attempts to close the gap between her own image and her ideal image, by trying to produce a new image, more like her ideal. In this instance, her hair is the focus of this desired transformation.

Indeed, hairstyle is one of the most frequently recurring aspects of the star's appearance which the spectators try to copy:

My friends and I would try and copy the hair styles of the stars, sometimes we got it right, and other times we just gave up, as we hadn't the looks of the stars or the money to dress the way they did.

(Anon)

Now Doris Day . . . I was told many times around that I looked like her, so I had my hair cut in a D.A. style. . . . Jane Wyman was a favourite at one stage and I had my hair cut like hers, it was called a tulip. . . . Now Marilyn Monroe was younger and by this time I had changed my image, my hair was almost white blonde and longer and I copied her hairsyle, as people said I looked like her.

(Patricia Ogden)

These forms of copying involve some kind of self-transformation to produce an appearance similar to that of Hollywood stars. Some spectators clearly have a stronger feeling of their success than others: the first example includes a sense of defeat whilst the last seems to be able to achieve several desired likenesses, especially bearing in mind that this respondent is the one who had 'Bette Davis eyes'! The difference, then, between the star and the spectator is transformable into similarity through the typical work of femininity: the production of oneself simultaneously as subject and object in accordance with cultural ideals of femininity.

Copying the hairstyles of famous film stars can be seen as a form of cultural production and consumption. It involves the production of a new self-image through the pleasure taken in a star image. Many examples of copying intersect with the consumption of commodities other than the Hollywood star image. The construction of women as cinema spectators overlaps here with their construction as consumers.

I have separated hairstyles from other aspects of this process, since changing hairstyles does not necessarily involve the actual purchasing of other products to transform the identity of the spectator, although bleach and so on may have been bought. The purchasing of items such as clothing and cosmetics in relation to particular stars brings into particularly sharp focus the relationship between the cinema industries and other forms of capitalist industry. [. . . A] few examples are given here, since copying is such a central identificatory practice.

Stars are consumable feminine images which female spectators then reproduce through other forms of consumption:

and I bought clothes like hers (Doris Day) . . . dresses, soft wool, no sleeves, but short jackets, boxey type little hats, half hats we used to call them and low heeled court shoes to match your outfit, kitten heels they were called. . . . as people said I looked like her (Marilyn Monroe). I even bought a suit after seeing her in *Niagara*.

(Patricia Ogden)

Stars are thus identified with particular commodities which are part of the reproduction of feminine identities. The female spectators in these examples produce particular images of femininity which remind them of their favourite stars. In so doing, they produce a new feminine identity, one which combines an aspect of the star with their own appearance. This is different from imitation, which is more of a temporary reproduction of a particular kind of behaviour which resembles the star. It transforms the spectator's previous appearance, and in doing so offers the spectator the pleasure of close association with her ideal.

As teenagers and young girls we did not have the vast variety of clothing and choices of make-up that is available today, so hairstyles and make-up were studied with great interest and copied . . . I seem to remember buying a small booklet by Max Factor with pictures of the stars, M.G.M. mostly, with all the details of their make-up and how to apply it.

(Anon)

Their make-up was faultless and their fashion of the forties platform shoes, half hats with rows of curls showing at the back under the hat. . . . We used to call the shoes 'Carmen Miranda' shoes. . . . I felt like a film star using Lux Toilet soap, advertised as the stars' soap.

(Vera Barford)

Through the use of cosmetic products, then, as well as through the purchasing and use of clothing, spectators take on a part of the star's identity and make it part of their own. The self and the ideal combine to produce another feminine identity, closer to the ideal. This is the direct opposite of the process of identification I began with in the first section, in which the spectator's own identity remained relatively marginal to the description of the pleasure taken in female Hollywood stars. In this final process, the star becomes more marginal and is only relevant in so far as the star identity relates to the spectator's own identity. As has been noted by other commentators, these latter practices demonstrate the importance of understanding Hollywood stars and their audiences in relation to other cultural industries of the 1940s and 1950s.[4]

Conclusion: rethinking cinematic identification[5]

Having outlined the different forms of identification in spectator/star relations, it is now important to reconsider some of the earlier models of identification and spectatorship in the light of this research. First, the *diversity* of the processes of identification and desire evident in these examples is striking. Within psychoanalytic film theory, the multiplicity of its formations in relation to the cinema have been ignored. The idea of a singular process of identification, so often assumed in psychoanalytic film theory, is unsatisfactory, and indeed reductive in the light of the range of processes discussed above.

Besides categorising the many different kinds of identification in the relationships between spectators and stars, I have drawn attention to the broad distinction between two different forms of identification: *identificatory fantasies* and *identificatory practices*. As I have stressed this is not to suggest that the practices do not also involve fantasies, or that fantasies cannot also be considered as practices. The analytic distinction has been used here to highlight the fact that identifications do not take place exclusively within the imagination, but also occur at the level of cultural activity. It is thus important to extend our understanding of cinematic identification, previously analysed solely at the level of fantasy, to include the practices documented by these spectators, in order to understand the different forms of overlap between stars' and spectators' identities.

Another significant distinction is that between *cinematic identification*, which refers to the viewing experience, and *extra-cinematic identification*, referring to the use of stars' identities in a different cultural time and space. So far, film studies have, not surprisingly, been concerned with the former. However, the importance of these extra-cinematic forms of identification to these female spectators came across very forcefully in their accounts of their relationship to Hollywood stars. Not only was this one of the most written-about aspects of the relationship between stars and spectators, but the pleasure and force of feeling with which they recalled the details of the significance of stars in this context was also striking.

All the above forms of identification relate to a final distinction which I have used to frame the sequence of the quotations: identification based on difference and identification based on similarity. The early categories of identification concern processes where the differences between the star and the spectator produce the sources of pleasure and fascination. The representations of these processes tended to emphasise the presence of the star and de-emphasise the identity of the spectator. The later categories concern processes where the similarity between stars and spectators, or at least the possibility of closing the gap produced by the differences, is the source of pleasure expressed. In these examples the reproduction of the spectators' identities tended to be the focus of the commentary. Thus identifications do not merely involve processes based on similarity, but also involve the productive recognition of differences between femininities.

Indeed, the processes of identification articulated most strongly in terms of difference seem to be those relating more directly to the cinematic context where the image of the star is still present on the screen. The processes, and practices, which involve reproducing similarity seem to be those extra-cinematic identifications which take place in the spectator's more familiar domestic context, where the star's identity is selectively reworked and incorporated into the spectator's new identity. Even in these cases, identification involves not simply the passive reproduction of existing femininities, but rather an active engagement and production of changing identities.

The assumption behind much of the psychoanalytic work discussed earlier is that identification fixes identities: 'identification can only be made through recognition, and all recognition is itself an implicit confirmation of existing form' (Friedberg, 1982: 53). Many of the examples I have discussed contradict this assumption and demonstrate not only the diversity of existing forms, but also that identification involves the production of desired identities, rather than simply the confirmation of existing ones. Many forms of identification involve processes of transformation and production of new identities, combining the spectator's existing identity with her desired identity and her reading of the star's identity.

Furthermore, Friedberg's critique is symptomatic of the psychoanalytic attack on identity itself typical of some feminist film theory. Any cultural process which is productive of identities is seen as confirming the fixed place of the subject within discourse and thus reinforcing dominant culture; it further offers the subject the pleasure of illusory unity, it is claimed. The implied corollary of this is the claim that cultural forms which fragment and deny identity are necessarily radical and transgressive of bourgeois, patriarchal norms. However, this research challenges the assumption that identification is necessarily problematic because it offers the spectator the illusory pleasure of unified subjectivity. The identifications represented in these examples speak as much about partial recognitions and fragmented replications as they do about the misrecognition of a unified subjectivity in an ego ideal on the screen. Thus, the cultural consumption of Hollywood stars does not necessarily fix identities, destroy differences and confirm sameness.

Identificatory and ideal love

One of the central arguments in this analysis of cinematic identification is that there is a complexity of relationships between stars and spectators, between self images and screen images, and between identification and desire, which cannot be accounted for within many of the existing frameworks of feminist film theory. In much of this work there is a misplaced assumption that 'desire' in the cinema can be straightforwardly conceptualised within the psychoanalytic model of 'erotic object choice' and, as such, is necessarily the opposite to 'identification'. Within this framework, 'desire' involves wanting to 'have' and identification involves wanting to 'be'.

What I hope to have shown in this chapter [. . .], is that the spectator/star relationship significantly concerns forms of *intimacy between femininities*. These forms of intimacy are not direct articulations of 'erotic object choice'; nevertheless, there is an obvious homoeroticism to some of the spectator/star relationships discussed here. The 'love' and 'devotion' which are expressed repeatedly by these respondents do not suggest an overt lesbian desire, but neither can they be described as mere expressions of 'identification' devoid of erotic pleasure. The intensity and the intimacy found in these memories repeatedly strike the reader as signifying more than simply 'the desire to become'. Instead they involve some forms of homoerotic pleasure in which the boundary between self and ideal produces an endless source of fascination. So much feminist film criticism has focused on sexual *difference* as the key cinematic signifier,

ignoring the importance of differences between femininities to the meaning of popular cinema for female spectators. Within existing theories of spectatorship there are
few possible ways of understanding these forms of fascination between femininities in
the cinematic context.

In the final section of this chapter, then, I shall suggest some new directions
for the theorisation of these forms of female spectatorship by drawing on Jessica
Benjamin's theory of 'identificatory and ideal love' (1990). This needs to be situated
briefly before I go on to discuss its relevance to the spectator/star relationship. Using
object relations theory,[6] Benjamin develops an argument about identity formation in
which she seeks to combine what she calls the 'intrapsychic' — 'the inner world
of fantasy, wish, anxiety and defense; of bodily symbols and images whose connections defy the ordinary rules of logic and language' — with the 'intersubjective' —
the 'capacities which emerge in the interaction between self and other' (Benjamin,
1990: 20).

Central to the intersubjective theory of identity formation proposed by Benjamin
is the concept of *recognition*. The need for recognition, based in early infancy, continues
to inform self-perception throughout adult life. Benjamin's theory of recognition
extends beyond the pre-oedipal phase of the Lacanian mirror stage, and differs from it
further in its emphasis on the exchange between self and external other, rather than
the internal (self and imagined self, or self and internalised other) structures of the
individual psyche:

> Recognition . . . appears in so many guises that it is seldom grasped as one
> overarching concept. There are any number of near-synonyms for it: to
> recognise is to affirm, acknowledge, know, accept, understand, empathize,
> appreciate, see, identify with, find familiar, love.
>
> (Benjamin, 1990: 12)

Within the concept of recognition Benjamin includes many of the pleasures of spectatorship described by my respondents; identification here is one of the many forms of
recognition at work in the constitution of the subject in relation to others involved
in the social and cultural processes of cinematic spectatorship.[7]

The relationship between stars and spectators involves many of the processes of
recognition which Benjamin analyses in her work. In particular, Benjamin introduces
the concepts of 'identificatory love' and 'ideal love' which involve the relationship
between the self and its ideal. In separating from the mother, the first bond, the child
develops an attachment to the father, or rather to the ideal of the father:

> The boy's identificatory love for the father, his wish to be recognised
> as like him, is the erotic engine behind separation. The boy is in love with
> his ideal, and through his ideal he begins to see himself as a subject of
> desire. Through this homoerotic love, he creates his masculine identity
> and maintains his narcissism in the face of helplessness.
>
> (Benjamin, 1990: 106)

What Benjamin calls identificatory love is the prototype for ideal love, being in love
with one's ideal, and underlying both, she argues, is the need for recognition. Ideal

love refers to 'a love in which the person seeks to find in the other an ideal image of himself' (Benjamin, 1990: 107). What is crucial here is that the homoeroticism of the self/ideal relationship is central to the processes of identity formation.

Unfortunately, a similar analysis of the place of homoeroticism in the girl's identificatory and ideal love in the development of her feminine identity remains somewhat absent from Benjamin's model. Instead, Benjamin focuses on the father/daughter relationship and offers an account of the girl's desire for identification as thwarted by difference and typically resulting in 'submission' to an ideal in defeated envy and feelings of failure.[8]

If we focus on the development of femininity in relation to the ideals explored in this chapter, however, then a parallel analysis can usefully be developed. These spectator/star relationships all concern the interplay between self and ideal. Such an interplay involves forms of 'identificatory' and 'ideal' love. The spectator in many cases may be described as being 'in love with' her screen ideal. The homoeroticism of such attachments comes across clearly; indeed, it is commented upon by one of the respondents recollecting the intensity of her past passions when she realises how this might appear in a contemporary light.[9] The love of the ideal, then, may express a desire to become more like that ideal, but this does not exclude the homoerotic pleasures of a love for that ideal. Thus, forms of identificatory and ideal love in the spectator/star relationship can be seen to articulate homoerotic desires.

This kind of claim suggests the need to rethink the concept of narcissism. If all object relations contain a form of narcissism (Merck, 1987), then narcissistic love is not to be dismissed as a mere form of reflective self-appreciation. Not only can it be argued that narcissism is part of all object relations, but, furthermore, that narcissism can also be seen as a type of object choice itself. Merle Storr demonstrates how, even within psychoanalytic terms, narcissism does not lack an object choice, but rather is seen as one of the two types of sexual object choice, the other being 'anaclitic' (Storr, 1992). However, as Storr goes on to argue, homoerotic desire between women requires a complete rethinking of these psychoanalytic distinctions. After a thorough assessment of the ways in which psychoanalytic theory has failed to account for same-sex desire between women, Storr criticises psychoanalysis for trying to define it 'in terms of the anaclitic/narcissistic divide at all . . . since it is both, and yet at the same time not really either' (Storr, 1992: 17).

Recognising oneself as different from, yet also as similar to, a feminine ideal other produces the pleasure between femininities which has been referred to as the 'intimacy which is knowledge' (Frith, 1989). Thus, the self and ideal are not collapsed into one, in a narcissistic self-love, but rather there is 'enough difference to create the feeling of reality [so] that a degree of imperfection "ratifies" the existence of the world' (Benjamin, 1990: 47). This difference produces a distance which is desirable both as something to overcome and as something to maintain. [. . . T]he relationship of star and spectator to similarity and difference changes significantly depending on the specific temporal and spatial locations. However, across this specification, the continual negotiation of self and ideal involves the mediation of similarity and difference across the multiple meanings of cinematic desire and identification.

Cinematic identificatory fantasies and practices do indeed contain forms of desire, thus demanding a deconstruction of this dichotomy. Can processes of spectatorship such as those discussed within the categories of 'devotion' and 'adoration', for example, really be dismissed as devoid of desire? My argument is that cinematic 'identification' does include some forms of desire. However, I am not suggesting the de-eroticisation of 'desire', but rather the eroticisation of some forms of 'identification'.[10] By this I do not mean to suggest that there is never any distinction between desire and identification. Clearly the two processes may be usefully seen as distinct in certain contexts. Rather, my argument is that the insistence upon the rigid dichotomy between these two processes within feminist film criticism has made it very difficult to conceptualise the complexity of spectator/star relationships. My analysis of these respondents' accounts of the cinema introduces processes of spectatorship which require a rethinking of the conceptualisation of 'identification' as completely extricable from erotic desire. Whilst desire and identification may be separate processes in some instances, then, in others, such as the attachment of female spectators to their female star ideals, identification may involve erotic pleasure. Indeed, it is precisely in same-sex relations that the distinction between desire and identification may blur most easily and, moreover, it might be suggested that therein lies their particular appeal.[11]

Notes

1   See Daniel Miller (1987) for an analysis of material culture and consumption.
2   For an analysis of the relationship between cinema and other cultural industries, see Angela Partington (1991).
3   The connection between shopping and matinées at the cinema for women is also represented within films: see for example *Brief Encounter* (1945, David Lean) in which the weekly shopping trip of the female protagonist, 'Laura' (Celia Johnson), is routinely combined with a matinée screening.
4   See Foucault (1971 and 1979) for his analysis of the ways in which the forms of subjectivity produced by discourse have also been forms of subjection and control. For a discussion of the relevance of his work to feminism, see Diamond and Quinby (1988).
5   See Chapter 4 for a discussion of the problems with Bourdieu's analysis of the pleasures of consumption in terms of gender.
6   'The intimacy which is knowledge' is a phrase borrowed from Gill Frith's study of female friendship in literature, originally formulated in Virginia Woolf's *To the Lighthouse* (see Frith, 1989).
7   See Marx (1976) on commodity fetishism, and Freud's 'Fetishism' (1963).
8   Much psychoanalytic theory has restricted analysis of desire to that produced by sexual difference and has ignored questions of same-sex desire, reading it within a rigidly dichotomous framework of sexual difference. See Merle Storr (1992), Valerie Traub (1991) and the discussion at the end of Chapter 5.
9   According to Lacan, the mirror phase necessitates the fundamental division between subject and object in all subjectivities (see Lacan, 1977); the argument made here, however, depends upon a consideration of the historical and gendered specificity of such a division.
10 The celebration of pleasure in popular culture is frequently criticised as a naive populism which has been identified with certain tendencies in cultural studies.

11   Janet Thumin is at present studying the gendered discourses of broadcasting
     programming in 1950s Britain. For an analysis of the gendered cinema audience at
     this time see Thumin (1991 and 1992).

Chapter 14

Charles Fairchild

AUSTRALIAN IDOL AND THE ATTENTION ECONOMY

THE ELABORATE CROSS-MEDIA spectacle, *Australian Idol*, ostensibly lays bare the process of creating a pop star. Yet with so much made visible, much is rendered opaque. Specifically, *Idol* is defined by the use of carefully-tuned strategies of publicity and promotion that create, shape and reshape a series of 'authentic celebrities' – pop stars whose emergence is sanctified through a seemingly open process of public ratification. Yet, *Idol's* main actor is the music industry itself which uses contestants as vehicles for crafting intimate, long-term relationships with consumers. Through an analysis of the process through which various contestants in *Australian Idol* are promoted and sold, it becomes clear that these populist icons are emblematic of an industry reinventing itself in a media environment that presents remarkable challenges and surprising opportunities.

Curiously, the debates, strategies and motivations of the public relations industry have received little sustained attention in popular music studies. While much has been written about the contradictions between the rhetoric of rebellion and the complicated realities of corporate success (Frank; Negus), less has been written about the evolution of specific kinds of publicity and the strategies that shape their use in the music industry. This is surprising given the foundational role of public relations strategies within the culture industries generally and the music industry in particular. Specifically, what Turner et al. define as 'the promotional culture' is central to the production and marketing of mainstream popular music. The 'Idol' phenomenon offers a rich opportunity to examine how the mainstream of the popular music industry uses distinct and novel marketing strategies in the face of declining sales of compact discs, an advertising environment that is extraordinarily crowded with all manner of competing messages, a steady rate of trade in digital song files and ever more effective competition from video games and DVDs. The 'Idol' phenomenon has proved to be a bundle of highly successful strategies for making money from popular music. Selling CDs seems to be almost ancillary to the phenomenon, acting as only one profit centre among many. Indeed, we can track the progress and deployment of specific strategies for shaping the creation of what has become a series of musical celebrities from the start of the first series of *Australian Idol* through a continuous process of strategic publicity.

The attention economy

It has been somewhat hysterically estimated that the average resident of Sydney might be presented with around 3000 commercial messages a day (Lee). It is this kind of communication environment that makes account planners go weak in the knees in both paralysing anxiety and genuine excitement. Many have taken to paying people to go to bars, cafes and clubs to talk up the relative merits of a product to complete strangers in the guise of casual conversation. Similarly, commercial buskers have recently appeared on City Trains to proclaim the virtues of the wares they've been contracted to hawk. One can imagine 'Cockles and Mussels' has been updated as 'MP3 Players and Really Cool Footwear.' These phenomena are variously referred to as 'viral,' 'tipping point,' 'word of mouth' or 'whisper' marketing (Gladwell; Godin; Henry; Lee; Rosen). Regardless of what you call it, the problem inspiring these promotional chats and arias is the same: advertisers can no longer count on getting and holding our attention. As Davenport and Beck, Brody and even Nobel Prize winning economist Herbert Simon have noted, the more taxed public attention gets, the more valuable it becomes. By most industry accounts, the attention economy is an established reality. It represents a significant shift of emphasis away from traditional methods of reaching consumers, instead inspiring new thinking about how to create lasting, flexible and evolving relationships with target audiences. The attention economy is a complicated and often contradictory response to a media environment that appears less and less reliable and to consumers whose behaviour is often poorly understood, even mysterious (Elliott and Jankel-Elliott).

This challenging backdrop, however, is only the beginning for a seemingly beleaguered music industry. Wherever one looks, from the rise of the very real threat of global piracy to the expansion of the video game industry to mobile phones and hand held players to increasing amounts of money spent on DVDs and ring tones, selling CDs has become almost a sideline. The main event is the profitable use and reuse of the industry's vast stores of intellectual property through all manner of media, most which didn't exist ten years ago. Indeed, the *Idol* phenomenon shows us how the music industry has been incorporating its jealously-guarded intellectual property and familiar modes of industrial self-presentation into existing media environments to build long-term relationships with consumers through television, radio, DVDs, CDs, the internet and mobile phones. Further, *Idol's* producers have supplemented more traditional models of communication by taking direct and explicit account of how and where audiences use a wide variety of media. The broad range of opportunities to participate in *Idol* is central to its success. It demonstrates a willingness on the part of producers to accept the necessity of bending somewhat to the audience's existing and evolving uses of the media. In short, they are simply not all that fussy about how participation actually happens so long as it does. Producers allow for many kinds of participation in order to constantly offer more specific and more active levels of involvement. 'Idol' has transformed consumer relationships within the music industry by coaxing into being ever more intimate, active and reciprocal relationships over the course of the context by encouraging increasingly specific acts by consumers to complete a continual series of transactions.

The use and reuse of celebrity

In many quarters, *Australian Idol* has become a byword for bullshit. The competition seems rigged and the contestants are not seen as 'real' musicians in large part because their experience appears to be so transparent and so transparently commercial. As the mythology of the music industry has traditionally had it, deserving pop stars are established as celebrities through what is a more or less a linear progression. Early success is based on a carefully constructed sense of authentic cultural production. Credibility is established through a series of contestable affiliations to ostensibly organic music cultures, earned through artistic development and the hard slog of touring and practice (see Maxwell 118). The fraught possibilities of mainstream success continually beckon to 'real' musicians as they either 'crossover' or remain independent all the while trying to preserve some elusive measure of public honesty. As this mythology was implicitly unavailable to the producers of *Idol*, a different kind of authenticity had to be constructed. Instead of a 'battles of the bands' (read: brands) contest, *Idol* producers chose to present 'unbranded' aspirants ("Sydney Audition"). These hopefuls are presented as appealingly ambitious or merely optimistic individuals with varying degrees of talent. Those truly blessed, not only with talent but the drive to work it into saleable shape, would be carefully chosen from the multitude and offered an opportunity to make the most of their inherent yet unformed ability. Thus, their authenticity was assumed to be an implicit, inchoate presence, requiring the guiding hand of insiders to reach full flower. Through the facilitation of competition and direction provided in the form of knowledgeable music industry veterans who never tire of giving stern admonitions to indifferent performers who do not take full advantage of the opportunity presented to them, contestants are asked to prove themselves through an extended period of intense self-presentation and recreation. The lengthy televised, but tightly-edited auditions, complete with extensive commentary and the occasional gnashing of teeth on the part of the panel of experts and rejected contestants, demonstrate to us the earnest intent of those involved.

Importantly, the authenticity of those proceeding through the contest is never firmly established, but has to be continually and strategically re-established. Each weighty choice of repertoire, wardrobe and performance style can only break them; each successful performance only raises the stakes. This tense maintenance of status as a deserving celebrity runs in tandem with the increasingly attentive and reciprocal relationship between the producers and the audience. The relationship begins with what has proved to be a compelling first act. Thousands of 'ordinary' Australians line up outside venues throughout the country, many sleeping in car parks and on footpaths, practising, singing and performing for the mobile camera crews. We are presented with their youthful vigour in all its varied guises. We cannot help but be convinced of the worth of those who survive such a process.

The chosen few who are told with a flourish 'You're going to Sydney' are then faced with what appears to be a daunting challenge, to establish themselves in short order as a performer with the X factor' (*Australian Idol* 14 July 2004). A fine voice and interesting look must be supplemented with those intangible qualities that result in wide public appeal. Yet these qualities are only made available to the public and the performer because of the contest itself. When the public is eventually asked to participate directly, it is to both produce and ratify exactly these ambiguous attributes. More than this, contestants need our help just to survive. Their celebrity is almost shockingly unstable, more fleeting than its surrounding rhetoric and context might suggest and under constant, expected threat. From round to round, favourites can easily become also rans – wild cards who limp out of one round, but storm through the next. The drama can only be heightened, securing our interest by requiring our input. As any advertiser can tell you, an effective campaign must end in action on our part. Through text message and phone voting as well as extensive 'fan management' through internet chat rooms and bulletin boards (see Stahl 228; http://au.messages.yahoo.com/australianidol/), our channelled 'viral' participation both shapes and completes the meanings of the contest. These active and often inventive relationships (http://au.australianidol.yahoo.com/fancentral/) allow the eventual *Idol* to claim the credibility the means of their success otherwise renders suspect and these activities appear to consummate the relationship.

However, the relationship continues well beyond the gala final. In a fascinating re-narration of the first series of *Australian Idol*, *Australian Idol: The Winner's Story* aired on the Friday following the final night of the contest. The story of the newly crowned Idol, Guy Sebastian, was presented in an hour long program that showed his home life, his life as a voice teacher in the Adelaide suburbs and his subsequent journey to stardom. The clips depicting his life prior to *Idol* were of ambiguous vintage, cleverly silent on the exact date of production; somehow they were not quite in the past or the future, but floated in some eternal in-between. When his *Australian Idol* experience was chronicled, after the second commercial break, we were allowed to see an intimate portrait of an anxious contestant transformed into 'Your Australian Idol.' There could be no doubt of the virtue of Sebastian's struggles, nor of his well-earned victory. 'New' footage began with the sudden sensation reluctantly commenting on other contestants at the original Adelaide cattle call at the prompting of the mobile camera crew and ended with his teary-eyed mother exultant at the final decision as she stood in the front row at the Opera House. Further, not only is the entire run of the first series dramatically recounted in documentary format on the *Australian Idol: Greatest Moments* DVD, framed by Sebastian's humble triumph, so are the stories of each member of the Final 12 and the paths they took through the contest. These reiterations serve to reinforce not only Sebastian's status, but the status of the program itself. They confirm the benevolent success of the industry it so dutifully profiles. We are taken behind the curtain, allowed to see the machinery of stardom grind inevitably to a conclusion, knowing we will be allowed back again when the time is right.

Whereas *Idol* is routinely pilloried for its crass commercialism, it remains an unavoidable success. Viewers keep tuning in, advertisers still clamour to sponsor all aspects of the production and the CDs keep selling. Most importantly, the music industry has a showcase for its own operations. The structures of feeling it exists to produce take on a kind of subtle explicitness that ensures their perpetuation. Within an industry faced with threats perceived to be foundational, the creators of *Idol* have produced an audacious and arrogant spectacle. They have made a profitable virtue out of an economic necessity. The expensive and unpredictable process of finding and nurturing new talent has not only been made more reliable, but *Idol* has shown that it can actually turn a profit. The brand of celebrity produced by *Idol* possesses no mere sheen of populist approval, but embodies that more valuable commodity: popular attention, however reluctant or enthusiastic it may be.

Chapter 15

Joke Hermes

READING GOSSIP MAGAZINES
The imagined communities of 'gossip' and 'camp'

About gossip magazines

PRINTED GOSSIP HAS A long history in the form of cheap populist newspapers and broadsheets (an example is the yellow press, popular at the turn of this century; see Kobre, 1964) but also in, for example, biographies (see Meyer Spacks, 1986). Contemporary gossip magazines such as the Dutch *Privé* and *Story* or the British *Chat* and *Hello!* do not have such long histories. The Dutch gossip magazines were launched in the mid seventies, to cater for a group of female readers, who – according to publishers' market research – were not reading the women's magazines then published. The popular domestic weeklies had become more serious (partly, I assume, because of second-wave feminism) and were writing less than before about film stars, celebrities and royalty. Surprising publishers and critics alike, there turned out to be quite a large market for magazines that did (see Bardoel and Vasterman, 1977). In Britain *Chat* and *Hello!* were introduced a decade later. They too appear to be commercially successful. All these magazines print practical advice, horoscopes and so on, alongside articles about celebrities, stars, TV personalities and royalty. Articles are mainly made up of pictures accompanied by a little text and suggestive headlines. The royalty magazines concentrate on royal families around the world.

In order to elucidate the kind of gossip that is printed in the magazines my informants talk about, it is helpful to distinguish between three different varieties of gossip in gossip magazines: malicious gossip and scandal, friendly stories about celebrities (usually with a focus on babies) and stories about royalty. Most of the gossip magazines reader I spoke to have a preference for me of these three areas. The British magazine *Majesty* and the Dutch magazine *Vorsten* (Sovereigns) differ slightly from other gossip magazines in their more expensive look; they are also older. They write about the trials and tribulations of royal families, most of whom have lost their empires. Kings of dubious East European countries that have not existed since the

First World War abound. Magazines like the British *Chat* and the Dutch *Story* are friendlier and more focused on celebrities having babies than a magazine like *Hello!* or the Dutch magazines *Weekend* and *Privé*. Or, as Eduard Spaans, one of my informants, said:

> *Story* is more baby-oriented, full of Vanessas [Vanessa is a Dutch singer][1] who have babies, and it is sillier and on a smaller-scale. (. . .) While *Privé* is bent on scandals, really. Abortions, Sonja Barends' [chat-show host] wrinkles hugely enlarged. *Story* would never do that. [Would they have stories about very young girls having children?] That would never be in *Story*, or they would immediately have a Mother Mary, or a convent who takes care of the girl, they'd have a happy ending. It always ends more or less well. No drug-addicted artists in *Story* who die. They do have the funeral, but not as closely photographed. In *Privé* they have funerals, including the very last tear [and close-ups of the grieving] widow. (. . .). [On dramatic occasions] *Privé* will have pictures of everyone who was moved, while *Story* would write: 'They had a singer and it was nice.'

Gossip has a bad reputation. It is considered a typical women's pastime and is often taken to be highly malicious talk about persons who are not present. Academic sources underline that gossip creates in-groups and out-groups and that it is a social menace. Anthropologists have presented many examples of gossip's dire consequences. Marlene de Vries, for example, researched gossip in the Turkish migrant community in the Netherlands. She suggests defining gossip as 'talking in an informal manner, with a certain satisfaction, about third persons who are not present in a more or less unfavourable vein; conveying to others a perhaps exaggerated version of specific unfavourable things one feels one knows about someone' (1990: 48). Her main conclusion is that gossip serves as an informal control of young women, especially as regards going out and seeing Dutch men, which makes it virtually impossible for them to do so, out of fear of having their entire family ostracized. Gossip thus serves to tie the Dutch Turkish community together and to discipline young women.

Gossip does not always have the consequences it has for the young Turkish women in the research of de Vries. I find the reputation of gossip somewhat harsh and one-sided. Gossip can also be a highly pleasurable experience for those involved in it and it does not necessarily influence other people's lives and choices. Patricia Meyer Spacks (1986) has taken up the cause of gossip, based on her own experience and on extensive literary research. She defines gossip as a continuum. Her description is so apt and altogether complete that I will quote it at length, to show how gossiping and reading gossip magazines may be a pleasurable, intimate pastime rather than a force of social control:

> At one extreme, gossip manifests itself as distilled malice. It plays with reputations, circulating truths and half-truths and falsehoods about the activities, sometimes about the motives and feelings, of others. Often it serves serious (possibly unconscious) purposes for the gossipers, whose manipulations of reputation can further political or social ambitions by damaging competitors or enemies, gratify envy and rage by diminishing

another, generate an immediately satisfying sense of power, although the talkers acknowledge no such intent . . . More common is gossip issuing not from purposeful malice but . . . from lack of thought, the kind of gossip accurately characterized as 'idle talk.' It derives from unconsidered desire to say something without having to ponder too deeply. Without purposeful intent, gossipers bandy words and anecdotes about other people, thus protecting themselves from serious engagement with one another . . .

At the opposite end of the continuum lies the gossip I call 'serious', which exists only as a function of intimacy. It takes place in private, at leisure, in a context of trust, usually among no more than two or three people. Its participants use talk about others to reflect about themselves, to express wonder and uncertainty and to locate certainties, to enlarge their knowledge of one another. Such gossip may use the stuff of scandal, but its purposes bear little on the world beyond the talkers except inasmuch as that world impinges on them. It provides a resource for the subordinated (anyone can talk; with a trusted listener, anyone can say anything), a crucial means of self-expression, a crucial form of solidarity.

(1986: 4–5)

Reading gossip magazines may be a form of 'serious gossip'; it may serve to enlarge the reader's private world, and to create moral community. In this chapter I shall argue that printed gossip, like oral gossip, may serve (unconscious) needs for the reader. Reading gossip magazines may involve building fictions that are comparable to the intimacy and the stories that spoken gossip spins. In the case of both spoken and printed gossip a sense of community may be established. While spoken gossip is built on learning about the other speaker through what she or he says about 'third persons who are not present', written gossip tends to create closeness or familiar faces in a wider world by helping the reader to bring celebrities into her or his circle of family, friends and acquaintances and by inviting readers to share in a moral universe that is at times petty, and at times rich.

During the first set of interviews it became clear that many readers regard gossip magazines as women's magazines. I would have thought them to be a genre in their own right, but it is true that gossip magazines, like women's magazines, write about people's emotions. Excluding the royalty magazines, most of them have a problem page, a medical advice section, a crossword. Some of them have recipes. But, as in the case of the feminist magazines, gossip magazines' resemblance to women's magazines in some respects makes the differences in other respects stand out strongly. Gossip magazines write about famous people rather than about anonymous women and men who could be 'living next door'. When those who read the subgenre talk about gossip magazines, the difference between gossip and women's magazines becomes even more pronounced. Gossip magazines inspire strong feelings, as much among those who would not define themselves as readers as among those who do. The quotations in this chapter come from both kinds of readers. They are considerably longer than the quotations about other women's magazines, which faithfully reflects the time readers took to talk about gossip magazines as compared with the time they took to talk about, for example, domestic weeklies. A second important difference between gossip magazines and other magazines with regard to how they are read and talked about concerns how gossip magazines become meaningful. The repertoires I found point not so much to fantasies of perfect selves, as was the case with traditional and with feminist magazines, as to 'imagined' communities, to use Benedict Anderson's (1983) term.

This chapter roughly divides styles of reading and talking about gossip magazines into two categories: serious reading and camp reading. This is the unintended result of the fact that in my search for readers I happened upon two widely divergent groups that enjoyed gossip magazines. The larger group consists mainly of women, who speak more or less seriously about gossip magazines. The other group consists mainly of gay men, who never seem to speak seriously about gossip magazines (nor about other popular media genres). Some of the men were found when searching for male readers of women's magazines in general, and some of them were on the list of names a research bureau I hired to find respondents came up with after a computer-aided telephone search. One, Eduard Spaans, was interviewed with the clearly stated goal of finding more information about reading gossip magazines, 'camp' and the gay community. First I shall turn to 'serious reading', describe the pleasure readers in general derive from these magazines, and then explore whether any specific repertoires were used to talk about gossip magazines and, if so, what they were like. I shall then turn to 'unserious reading of gossip magazines', discuss irony and camp as strategies that readers may employ, to then show how gossip magazines have an important role in gay subculture. Ten women are quoted at some length in this chapter and four men. Brief quotations from another four women are also included.

'Serious' reading of gossip magazines

The pleasure of reading gossip magazines

Generally speaking, reading gossip magazines is very much like reading traditional women's magazines: it is pleasant to look at pictures, to read photo captions, the more so because the pictures are of people we are familiar with through television. Some of the women's magazine readers introduced in the previous chapters, who would not define themselves as gossip readers, do occasionally read gossip magazines (Jeanne Rousset and Mrs Dobbel) and enjoy their unpretentious, undemanding stories. Others are fascinated, but express puzzlement at their fascination or defend their taste for this low-valued genre by making it clear that they are aware of this low status and that they are not taken in by the magazines and what they write (Joan Becker).

> Every now and then [I read] *Story* and *Privé*. (. . .) I don't know what I find in them, but I read them at my hairdresser's. (. . .) That kind of thing, when you have to wait, or something, and then it's lovely. I'll flick through them and read small bits and pieces . . . Usually it's more looking at pictures and the captions [than reading].
>
> (Jeanne Rousset)

> *Story* and *Weekend*, that's looking at pictures. [When the collection of magazines comes] usually *Story* is the first I pick up, 'cause it is nice to leaf

through, you don't have to really read it. (. . .) It's looking at pictures, I
don't get anything out of it.

(Mrs Dobbel)

My mother reads herself silly with that *Privé* and *Weekend*. (. . .) When I
visit her, I dive into her magazine basket and I'll look for them. With a lot
of scepticism. (. . .) I really hate those magazines, but I have to look
through them. Not that I believe them.

(Joan Becker)

They are stupid stories, but you are curious. You buy it. (. . .) When you
see them on the counter, you think, 'I won't buy it, I won't.' But when
you get home from work, have a cup of coffee, and there's something to
browse through . . . you buy it.

(Marion Gerards)

Apart from describing the simple pleasure of browsing through these magazines
or stressing critical distance, however, gossip magazine readers would often also
enthusiastically describe the different forms their attachments to the genre take. An
important aspect of the pleasure in gossip magazine reading, for example, is to feel
involved with the stars and celebrities the magazines write about.

Things on the front page, well, I want to read that. When a couple breaks
up, and it turns out to be not true . . . you thought so, but you do want
to check.

(Tina Poorter)

When I read about Mies [Bouwman, a chat-show host] and I see her
swollen face . . . That happened to me too, when I had that medication.
(. . .) If *Story* wrote about strangers, you wouldn't be interested.

(Christine Klein)

I do want to know who has been married and who is going to divorce.

(Joan Becker)

[They are called gossip magazines] because they are about famous people.
[Domestic weeklies] are also about people, but they aren't well-known.
These are all really well known, from television; it's twice as interesting to
know something about them or to read about them.

(Ina Dammers)

Reflecting on what my respondents told me, there appear to be different kinds of
pleasure involved in reading gossip magazines. The pleasure of reading about celebrities is a pleasure both of vicariously enjoying the world of glitter and glamour and of
gaining a 'secret', inside knowledge that may confer an imaginary sense of power over
the rich and powerful. Then there is the pleasure of extending your family by including the stars, as well as a kind of pleasure that is akin to the pleasure of puzzle solving.

Since some of these pleasures have been described in relation to other popular genres, I shall briefly turn to work on soap opera, before returning to my readers.[2]

Maarten Reesink (1990), speaking from a dual perspective as student of popular culture and as gossip magazine aficionado, likened reading *Privé* to watching soap opera. Just as the soap opera viewer follows the ups and downs of a large cast of characters through highly diverse plots, reading a gossip magazine engages one in the lives, or 'plots', of the rich and famous. Gossip magazines appear to offer the pleasure of fiction in the guise of journalism, reminiscent of how Kim Schrøder (1988) typified what makes watching the prime-time soap opera *Dynasty* worthwhile and pleasurable. Schrøder proposes that part of the fun of watching the series is to be engaged in a 'fictional jigsaw puzzle, constantly on the look-out for new pieces, imagining what they look like, tentatively fitting them into gaps in the narrative structure or character relations and experiencing triumphant gratification [when one] succeeds' (1988: 63). *Dynasty* viewers forecast how relations between characters will develop. Part of the fun of reading gossip magazines, likewise, is to ferret out the extent of truth in what the magazines write about stars, princes and television personalities, and to put together who is involved with or pregnant by or breaking up with whom.

Defending one's credentials

That reading gossip magazines involves (or may involve) intellectual exercise in hypothesizing about relationships, based on a trained intuition, is not a generally accepted view. As a rule reading gossip magazines is condemned as a silly waste of time, something that mindless women engage in. The alleged untruth of most of what is written is one of the grounds on which reading gossip magazines is criticized. Although the gossip magazine readers I spoke to did not mind sharing their enthusiasm and ideas about the genre with me, they also told me that they, in turn, were critical of the fact that reading gossip magazines is not approved of. They suspected many people who condemn them of hypocrisy and suggested that those who say they happened to have seen a copy at their hairdresser's read them secretly at home. They also made clear that they were certainly not the silly women gossip magazine readers are made out to be. Christine Klein, quoted below, has just sarcastically remarked that all those people who disapproved of gossip magazines tend to grab them, first thing, when they come to visit her. Moreover, they appear to be well informed about the trials and tribulations of the stars, one of her favourite topics for talk and speculation. She herself holds the view that a practised reader may learn much from careful reading about the stars she feels connected to and will be able to tell true from false information, for example by comparing the information in different magazines.

> Gossip or not, there is always a kernel of truth. When they write, 'Martine is divorcing her husband' [Martine Bijl is a Dutch singer and performer], she'll leave, that's for sure, but how? . . . Then you search, the other magazines write slightly different things . . . People are so negative about that. If I want to talk about something, I talk about Martine Bijl. That is what I like.
>
> (Christine Klein)

They do print a few lies, but you still read it. You see these people often on television and you know a little bit more about them. You know it is a lie sometimes, but you do read it . . . Gerard Joling [popular singer] is supposed to be gay. It is hard to believe that.

(Solema Tillie)

You don't have to believe everything, but I do like to read them. (. . .) I often think, they add a little to it, to make a good story. But [since it is about these well-known people] I always think some of it must be true.

(Ina Dammers)

When I tell my husband about something I've read, he says, 'you read it in *Privé*, didn't you? I don't understand why you believe all that.' Well, there are things that I don't believe.

(Tina Poorter)

Tina Poorter occasionally disputes the gossip magazines' interpretation and comes up with her own. So does Solema Tillie.

Part of it is true, but I don't know. (. . .) They write quite a lot now about [a celebrity whose name could not be transcribed.] But they say she has been partying all night. They say it without thinking. You don't know how they [famous people] live; she could be having a miserable time she is only human. Yeah, what do I care whether she parties all night? They don't have to write about that for me, I won't read it anyway. They [famous people] have their lousy times too. Those bags under her eyes don't have to come from just partying. (. . .) I think they simply like to write filth about a person like her. Sometime I think it is just to drag a person through the mud. I hate it when people say things about me that aren't true at all. That is why I don't believe everything.

(Tina Poorter)

What Rob de Nijs [popular singer] did, with that girl, he saved her from becoming a prostitute. [Apparently de Nijs brought a South Asian girl to the Netherlands and made a video with her.] I don't think they were lovers. (. . .) They rescued that girl from poverty and gave her a few nice days here. I really like that.

(Solema Tillie)

The extended family repertoire

The pleasures of reading gossip magazines – the soap opera like pleasure of puzzling over what is 'really' happening in the lives of the celebrities the magazines write about, vicariously enjoying the world of the rich, gaining a sense of secret power, a scandalized sense of outrage, or simply of things happening – are reported on and legitimated through two main repertoires: the extended family repertoire and the repertoire of melodrama. The extended family repertoire has been referred to above.

On an imaginary level it helps readers to live in a larger world than in real life – a world that is governed by emotional ties, that may be shaken by divorces and so on, but that is never seriously threatened. Sociological realities such as high divorce rates, broken families, children who leave home hardly ever to be seen again are temporarily softened.

Tania Modleski (1984) has put forward a similar argument about soap opera based on an analysis of soap opera's narrative structure. Whatever may happen to the enormous cast of characters who are all lead characters (though from time to time less prominently so), they tend to come back to the family, the hospital or small village in which the story is set. Modleski claims that it is reassuring for viewers to see that, whatever happens, families do not fall apart. Gossip magazines hold the same kind of attraction, even though the extended family in question is more loosely structured than the fictional families in soap operas. Tina Poorter likes to read about artists she has been following for years. Joan Becker said, 'I want to know who has been married and who is going to divorce'. Christine Klein professed her deep and personal liking for Martine Bijl (a performer) and Mies Bouwman (a TV-show host). Solema Tillie spoke of the artists she likes to read about with much feeling and in great detail. Like some of the others, she stresses that she feels she knows these artists because she sees them on television. In point of fact, some of those she mentioned have not been on television for a long time, though over the years they seem to have become heroes of Dutch popular culture. Given all the years of bits of information, one might well feel one knows these people and address them by name.

The extended family repertoire is a relatively simple and straightforward repertoire. It engenders a highly personal form of address in which solidarity and connectedness resound. In the interviews the extended family repertoire tended to be mixed with a disapproval that was clearly savoured, with a sense of outrage and a wish to reset the societal power balance, if only through the pleasure of knowing things about the high and mighty, with a relish for misery and tragedy. These I consider traces of another, much more complex repertoire, which has been called the repertoire of melodrama because of its exaggeration and revelry in states of great emotion. Tina Poorter used the extended family repertoire when she said she liked to read about how 'Gert and Hermien [singers who midway in their career "saw the Lord" and changed their repertoire, and now, it seems, have changed back again] are doing, haven't heard from them for years. They had such difficult times', as if these singers were acquaintances she would like to have a good chat with. But Tina Poorter also enjoyed 'a bit of sensation', and used the repertoire of melodrama (see below) to give an example of other stories she likes, such as a celebrity drinking outrageously heavily, something she claims she did not hear about among her friends and acquaintances. Joan Becker, who did not consider herself a gossip reader, mixed the two repertoires when she explained that she wants to know 'who has been married and who is going to divorce'. She loves and loathes the stars as well as the magazines.

The repertoire of melodrama

Some readers hardly used the extended family repertoire at all. Dot Groeniers, for example, emphasized that she enjoyed it when the rich and famous were put in their place by their share of misery and unhappiness: 'I like [it] when things go really badly for those [people]' (full quotation below). She predominantly used the repertoire of melodrama, which focuses on misery, drama, sentimentalism, sensation and paying for daring to rise above other people or for being filthy rich. Melodrama is associated with a fascination for misery, sorrow, heartbreak and so on. As an art form it consists of 'a sensational dramatic piece with crude appeals to the emotions and usually a happy ending', according to the eighth edition of *The Concise Oxford Dictionary*. The joy, for readers or spectators, is to wallow in the sorrow and misery of others, rather than in one's own. Life is a vale of tears. Life in the repertoire of melodrama becomes grotesquely magnified.

Whereas the extended family repertoire is centred around a certain kind of content (a usually benevolent interest in a cast of well-known people and how they are doing) and does not evaluate, measure or condemn, the repertoire of melodrama is as outspoken in its indignation as in its sentimentality. It questions what makes life worthwhile, though normally not by rational reasoning, but by emotional appeal or outrage. Thus, the repertoire of melodrama may provide solace for individual readers. The misery of others may either make them feel better about their own lives or allow them to have a good cry over frustrations and sorrow they choose not to analyse more closely. Elizabeth Veenstra cried her eyes out over a story of a seriously ill child that dies. There is a certain satisfaction in being able to do so, to experience a deep sense that the world is not just, not only to the child and its parents but, of course, also to you yourself. The sense of injustice that is at the heart of the repertoire of melodrama also points at a more collective sense of social inequality. To enjoy it when things go badly for 'rich and famous people' is a way of imagining cosmic (rather than political) justice taking its toll, it is a moral stance.

To illustrate the repertoire of melodrama, first a quotation is offered about how 'enjoying the misery of others' can be a way of displacing injustice we feel we have suffered.

> I noticed that when I was in a rotten mood, I wasn't reading those magazines for cheerful subjects and I thought, you want to read about others having an even worse time than you're having. [For] they mainly write about misery. [Later during the group interview Tina Poorter remarked that when you read about the woes of others, your own troubles do not seem so bad.] That's what I mean, that comfort, when I read about other people's trouble, I think, I am not doing all that badly. I'm doing fine, really.
>
> (Martha Steenman)

The melodrama of the repertoire of melodrama can be found as much in the subjects it deals with (emotions of the stars over divorces, heartbreak and dead children or, to the irritation of readers, dead pets) as in the suggestion that the speakers have a hard life themselves. 'I'm not all that badly off' was never said smugly. Rather, it was meant to denote constraint in not complaining about one's life. Interestingly, in the group interview with Tina Poorter, Martha Steenman and Marion Gerards this constraint fell away. While they announced ritually that they did not mean to complain, they all talked at length about hardships in their lives: divorce, illnesses and loneliness. The sphere of melodrama, conjured up by talking about gossip magazines, stretched to envelop the personal lives of the three speakers. For a change, they were interviewed, they held centre stage, and they used the codes of the genre in the way it had meaning for them. Melodrama was as prominent in Marion Gerards's story about her lonely life as a sailor's wife as it was prominent in what Tina Poorter said about her mother (who had to have psychiatric help after a period of loneliness and the breaking up of a relationship) or about the partners of gay celebrities. The drama, sensation, misery and wretchedness readers talked about often concerned not their own lives, but the lives of people they knew. The quotations below attest to the *frisson*, the commiseration and the indignation that reading about other people's misery may give.

> You wouldn't usually hear about it. I mean, I wouldn't. You read some-
> times about someone who's given to drink. That wouldn't happen around
> here. That's why it's nice to read. It's sensation, really. (. . .) They have
> these stories about artists. Not the kind of thing that would happen in my
> daily life. (. . .) And they had this piece about Jos Brink [gay performer
> and television personality] and André van Duin [humorist, also gay], about
> their partners who they had to keep in the background. And that Jos Brink
> came out and when he went to a party, someone else would come with
> her husband (. . .) and his boyfriend would have to keep out of the way in
> those ballrooms . . . It's the kind of thing that gets you thinking . . . that
> those people had really difficult times.
>
> (Tina Poorter)

> I really read [instead of browse in *Story*], I like that . . . All that happens in
> those [circles]. (. . .) People like that don't live in this village. (. . .) They
> just have nice stories about those stars. (. . .) I really think I'm not doing
> that badly when I read some of those things, divorces and so on. That is
> what I read, what I like, when things go really badly for those [people] . . .
> It's nice to read because you wouldn't hear about it otherwise. (. . .) I like
> *Weekend* for their real life stories about girls of twelve years old who have
> babies, or girls of nine years old. A child has a child, they then write.
>
> (Dot Groeniers)

> . . . and the misery. You often think for those people, on television or
> wherever, that life is all roses. When you see them, they are always looking
> so fine, but it gets you thinking they may be unhappy in some other way.
> (. . .) Their lives aren't as easy as you might think. Maybe because of the
> kind of circles they live in. This one is carrying on with that one, and that
> one is carrying on with that one. Then I think, but that's not right. They
> have a totally different kind of life.
>
> (Ina Dammers)

In what Ina Dammers and Tina Poorter say there is more than just the thrill of partaking in sorrow, or seeking sensation, there is also a strong moral feeling. Their basic moral assumption seems to be that all people are equal and that all have their crosses to bear, their portion of grief to deal with. Obviously such moral assumptions are closely linked to how those who are not rich or well-to-do, experience social inequality. Money does not set one free of sorrow, nor ought it to bestow privileges. Like Ina Dammers, both Tina Poorter and Christine Klein criticized the fact that apparently those who are very rich, or have much social prestige, may live above laws of morality. Christine Klein felt very strongly about the corrupting powers of money. 'We stayed honest,' she says, 'because we didn't have any money.' Her other strong claim is, 'Money can't buy happiness'. Happiness, friendship and her close-knit family are her riches.

> I have had an awfully rich life. Very rich. I have been ill a lot, but I can say that I've always had a load of fun too. (. . .) Money is the problem. Money is the biggest evil in society. You need it, I know, you need money. But when you have too much, you start spending it, children get spoiled. I have known poverty, real poverty; because I was ill, you know. Back then, you couldn't just go to hospital, we had to pay. (. . .) Money is the biggest dirt that exists. (. . .) Friendship is the richest thing one has. Like my youngest son, who was born and brought up here, he still goes on holiday with a friend [he was at school with] for three weeks every year. And my other son still sees his first friend. And my daughter is still friends with a girl from the house we lived in before this one. They live in Australia now and have invited her over. Those are friendships. I have friends myself whom I met fifty years ago.
>
> (Christine Klein)

Christine Klein has a sharp eye for social inequality and for the different rules on behaviour that apply. She is very much aware that whereas a film actress might wear funny hats, she would not be able to do so, because 'the whole street would be in an uproar'. Her strong belief in friendship and having fun is an alternative system for evaluating what life is worth. Tina Poorter is more conventional in the moral systems she recognizes. She mixes a need for 'a bit of sensation', or, as Patricia Meyer Spacks (1986) would say, 'the living breath of event', with a firm belief that all women and men are equal, and with 'the good citizen's' outcry: they are spending my tax money!

> [Those soccer players] they're young, they earn a lot, they do what they like. They live [in Italy] and they come to Amsterdam to go out. What that must cost! (. . .) But they are all ordinary people for me. You do find that out. You thought some of them were really special, I used to think that, but they are all ordinary people, just like us. Beatrix, the queen, or a minister, they are all just like us. (. . .) They have their fiascos. On the one hand you think, they earn a lot and they can do everything they want to do, because you read about that. And you start to think about it and you think, they are close to the fire. They have jaunts abroad. They have to go to do this or that, but they turn it into a junket . . . I get angry at that: why do they need to do that? It's my tax money they're spending.
>
> (Tina Poorter)

The (moral) community of gossip

In their own ways the extended family repertoire and the repertoire of melodrama betoken a wish for and a forging of community, a quality that, I would argue, is inherent in all gossip. The extended family repertoire in its friendly manner simply draws a wide circle of people into a person's private life by discussing them intimately. On an imaginary level, this creates a form of community. Going by hints and sometimes open remarks made by the readers I spoke to they also use the extended family repertoire in conversations with friends. Christine Klein finds talking about her favourite stars a comfortable way of spending her time with other people. Gossip draws speakers together in their sharing and evaluation of 'news' about 'third persons who are not present'.

The repertoire of melodrama creates community in a different manner. This repertoire comes into play when readers are indignant, when they are shocked or deeply moved and wish to evaluate explicitly what they have heard. By either reading gossip or talking about what they have read with friends they appeal to and thus construe shared standards of morality (with an imagined community of other gossip readers, or with other readers who are present in the flesh) that alternate between disapproval and understanding. Gossip brings together by creating an intimate common world in which private standards of morality apply to what is and what is not acceptable behaviour. It is about basic human values and emotions, about the fact that, in the end, all human beings are equal, whether they are rich or poor, whether they live in the glittery world of showbusiness or whether they only read about it. Going by the two repertoires I found, reading gossip magazines revolves not around fantasies of perfect selves but around fantasies of belonging: to an extended family or to a moral community. Moreover, in interpreting the gossip magazine text readers use and validate their own personal knowledge and experiences. Solema Tillie (a proud mother and grandmother), for example, drew upon her own experiences to challenge what was written about the Dutch queen mother Juliana:

> In Surinam I used to read a lot. I remember reading about when that girl Christina [the Dutch royal princess] had a bad eye, and her mother [then Queen Juliana] had gone to see a clairvoyant. And I read that there was a scandal about that in the Netherlands. The woman worked in the palace or Queen Juliana had her called in (. . .) And I wondered whether that girl couldn't be operated on for her eye. Maybe a doctor had said that that was impossible and that's why her mother went on. Even if you are a queen, it is about your child. When you hear that someone may help, you'll try. Whatever you are, whatever title you have, you'll try. She is a mother. She didn't think, I am the queen, she thought, I am going to try and see if it works. (. . .) When it concerns the health of your child, even if someone is fooling you, that's not what you think of, you'll always try. [The 'clairvoyant' was a kind of faith healer called Greet Hofmans. She was thought to inspire communist ideas in the Queen, which at the height of the Cold War, at the end of the fifties, gave rise to a huge political scandal.]

'Unserious' gossip reading: irony and camp

Stereotypically, women are thought of as gossipers, whereas men are not. A close second, as far as stereotypes are concerned, are gay men. And, indeed, although I did not initially set out to find gay gossip magazine readers, a first interview with a male reader about gossip magazines strongly suggested that reading gossip magazines for him was part of an 'act', a playful way of showing off and playing with other people's cultural values and judgements – the kind of act, in fact, that some gay men like to use in confusing others and enjoy among themselves, often labelled as 'camp'. All four male gossip readers who were interviewed to some extent used irony or camp when talking about women's magazines. Only one of them (Eduard Spaans, the last to be interviewed) was asked with the explicit goal of talking about the relationship between gossip magazines, camp and the gay community. Before I go on to explore how gossip magazines relate to yet another kind of imagined community (the camp fantasy world of appearances and superficiality, of living a public image rather than a life), let me explain about camp and the difference between camp and irony.

Camp and irony

Camp is notoriously hard to define and, according to some, 'in appalling taste – because camp defined no longer is' (Schiff, 1984: 65). Camp is mainly to be found in the male homosexual community. Camp mocks existing standards and perverts them by turning them upside down. It is camp, for example, to make a top ten of 'the worst films that have ever been made' and to flirt with knowing them back to front. 'To perceive Camp in objects', according to Susan Sontag, 'is to understand Being-as-Playing-a-Role. It is the farthest extension, in sensibility, of the metaphor of life as theater' ([1984] 1982: 109). Camp divides the world between those who are 'in the know', *cognoscenti*, and those who are not by offering those who are in the know a different, supplementary set of standards (p. 114).

　　Andrew Ross (1989) takes a slightly different and somewhat exalted but interesting view of camp. Ross sees all culture as a product of power relations. Camp, in particular, he sees as containing 'an explicit commentary on feats of survival in a world dominated by the taste interests, and definitions of others' (1989: 144). Camp is not a fixed category. Rather, in the words of Thomas Hess, it 'exists in the smirk of the beholder' (quoted in Ross, 1989: 145). Camp, according to Ross, involves 'a celebration, on the part of cognoscenti, of the alienation, distance, and incongruity reflected in the process by which hitherto unexpected value can be located in some obscure or exorbitant product' (1989: 146). Quoting Mark Booth, he goes on to say that: 'far from being a "fugitive" or "ineffable" sensibility, camp belongs to the history of the "self-presentation" of arriviste groups. Because of their marginality, and lack of inherited cultural capital, these groups parody their subordinate or uncertain social status in a self-mocking abdication of any pretentions to power' (p. 146).

　　There is a difference between camp and irony. The first concerns, for example, gay readers of gossip magazines, who aggressively flaunt their 'bad taste', their 'being different' to the world. Ross would call them the marginal camp intellectuals, who 'express [their] impotence as the dominated faction of a ruling bloc at the same time as [they] distance [themselves] from the conventional morality and taste of the ascendant middle-class' (1989: 146–7). Irony, on the other hand, is parody rather than outright subversion on the part of groups outside the homosexual community. It is a much more defensive stance on the part of those with enough cultural capital to feel sure that they will distinguish themselves as 'cultured' by admitting that they feel critical about the system of taste and the exclusiveness of high culture.

Whereas camp is a means by which to immerse oneself in low taste, to enjoy thoroughly 'the bad taste of yesterday', as a friend says, irony is a way of distancing oneself from low culture, of laughing it away, as it were. Joppe Boodt (1992), one of my co-interviewers, concentrated on male readers of women's magazines (including gossip magazines) and found that among them there are two dominant ways of talking about women's magazines, one serious and involved, the other ironic. Irony, he argues, following Bourdieu (1980), is a highly effective way of distinguishing oneself. Irony is a means of detaching oneself from what one reads (or watches on television). Irony indirectly confirms cultural competence. One shows one has knowledge of what is and what is not Culture or Art by commenting on one's occasional bouts of bad taste. Irony suggests not only duplicitous knowledge, but also that since one knows how bad it is, one is surely inoculated against it. Cultural competence, according to Bourdieu (1980), is the result of class background and education. Boodt found that education was, in fact, a fitting explanation for the difference between the two groups of men (the involved and serious readers versus the ironic and detached readers) he found among our respondents.

> The seven respondents with a university education all thought *Privé* amusing, they were not irritated by the magazine. The other men [with lower-level education] stressed that they found both the content and the journalistic method employed by the gossip magazines objectionable. The same mechanism was found for other magazines. The men who did not have much education did not use irony when they occasionally read magazines they did not particularly appreciate (*Cosmopolitan*, for example). They got angry when they talked about them, they were not at all amused.
>
> (Boodt, 1992: 10)

To talk seriously about gossip magazines is to argue that it is legitimate to want to know how one's favourite stars are doing, the low cultural status of the genre notwithstanding. To speak of reading gossip magazines ironically is to underline that occasional indulgence in low culture is legitimate for the cultured. Camp, though, dismisses out of hand the question of the legitimacy of enjoying low culture. Camp talk makes fun of the magazines, and of the stars and celebrities the magazines write about and about the speaker as reader. Camp is to 'adore *and* to jeer, to be sucked in *and* then to pull back in derision' (Schiff, 1984: 65, my italic). Serious reading may be intent on ferreting out the particles of truth that articles must be based on. Camp reading is not interested in whether or not what is written is 'true'; life is a farce, a comedy of manners, which is nowhere more clear than in gossip magazines.

Camp is not strictly confined to the gay community. Some women (regardless of their sexual orientation) sport the same affected tone. Generally speaking, however, irony and camp were less important in the interviews with women. Comparing all women with all men, it would seem to be the case that women tend to talk more seriously and more respectfully about women's magazines and gossip magazines. To some extent women with more education tended to be more distanced from and more ironic about what they read, a difference in cultural capital that has also been found by other researchers (see, for example, Gray, 1992).

Fun and exaggeration

Irony and camp are alike in that both use and parody available repertoires to talk about gossip magazines. Frederik Paulsen alluded to the extended family repertoire during a group interview with Ingrid Meertens, his partner, and Marga Koster, a friend. In the middle of a discussion about a cover story about black women in *Marie Claire*, a glossy that had just been published in a Dutch version, and about the level and critical potential of such stories, Frederik felt the need to confess, a broad grin on his face: 'I have to say, on the other hand, that I was sailing with friends and what did we buy? *Panorama, Story* and *Privé* and we had a wonderful time reading that in the sun. [Everybody laughs.] I could pretend to be better than I am, but I really loved that. And I'll think, whatever happened to Hans van der Togt [a newsreader]? Really blissful.' Lies Machielse, who does not and never did read women's magazines, employed the same strategy when we happened on the subject of gossip magazines: 'Well, *Privé* I find delightful, too. [This was said in a slightly mocking tone of voice.] All that dirty gossip about royal families, I really love it. And then that awful van der Meyden [editor-in-chief of *Privé* and a national celebrity and television personality himself], that piece of scum, I like that [page of his in a right-wing daily] too. I would never buy [*Privé*]. I see it on the counter when I'm buying cigarettes: Willem-Alexander [Dutch crown prince] with a beautiful lass'. Joan Becker (a self-trained secretary) made fun of her fascination for gossip magazines (and also criticized them for their unethical methods), Christine Klein (who is seventy-four), crossing over from serious reading, used both the extended family repertoire and the repertoire of melodrama when she character-ized *Story* and *Privé* as 'tasty garbage': 'There is no real sorrow in those two [maga-zines], you have to take them with a pinch of salt. (. . .) [Later on in the interview, laughing] Ahh, Ron Brandsteder [good-looking chat-show host], well, I'm too old for him.'

Irony, I agree with Boodt, in general seems to be the weapon of the 'cultural capitalist'. It is not always perfectly clear whether one is dealing with irony, with unwitting forms of camp or with simply making fun. To make such distinctions based on the few quotations above would be risky. Suffice it to say that reading gossip magazines, for all readers, is to some degree shot through with reser-vations about their truthfulness, with the fun of speculation and with the pleasure of gaining 'forbidden' knowledge, both in the sense of scandal and in the sense of partaking in low and almost illegitimate culture. When reading seriously we may experience the added pleasure of moral indignation and an equally moral sense of connectedness, while reading ironically bars others from questioning our taste: we can enjoy what is deemed 'bad' without enabling others to hold us responsible for what we read.

Camp comments occasionally surface in interviews that are otherwise serious and/or ironic in tone. True camp sensibility that extended far beyond gossip magazines, however, seems to be so much a part of specific communities that it is very different in style (though not so much in content) from other ways of talking about gossip magazines. Camp turns reading gossip magazines (and, I would imagine, gossip itself) into a performative art. In doing so camp, like irony, poaches the extended family repertoire and the repertoire of melodrama. The interview with Charles Vlaming provided examples:

> Which one do I get first? Do I really have to answer completely honestly? [Yes, you do.] *Privé*. [He laughs.] I enjoy gossip immensely, I really like to read that. *Privé* is really aggressive, so that is the one I get first. (. . .) I'll look over what subjects they have and then I start to leaf through it. I wouldn't be looking for a specific part, you'll get there anyhow. I'll read like: 'Ooh, she has adopted three children again' [parodying woman's voice]. (. . .) [Which parts do you think are 'tastiest'?] Hmmmm, the misery, the misery. Especially the misery that you know is absolutely untrue. It sounds funny, you know; a friend of a star or a well-known acquaintance of that star said something and you think, aha, that kind of story. People with unhappy marriages . . . We make fun of it at the sports centre, 'Have you read . . .?' You know? Like that, as if you yourself know her. They become your acquaintances. Like: 'I told her that she shouldn't . . .' That kind of thing. We make it into a game.
>
> (Charles Vlaming)

Charles easily extended his camp style of reading to the domestic weeklies *Margriet* and *Libelle* which he also talked about quite seriously in terms of learning, using the repertoire of connected knowing:

> I do read the problem page. [For the problems or for the answers?] For both, really. The problems people see themselves confronted with! And then, really, those answers, I split my sides laughing about those. Really! For example, a woman writes her life story and it is very, very sad [sad tone of voice]. And she is answered, 'Come on, girl' and 'Do let us know how you are doing.' And I'll think, oh, my God!

The contact with other people at the sport centre where Charles Vlaming works for a few hours per week and where he trains bears all the hallmarks of a small community that enjoys camp games. Others find similar enjoyments in the gay community. That was made clear particularly by Eduard Spaans, who is quoted at length below.

Camp and the gay community

In constructing a common frame of reference regarding taste among a relatively small group of insiders camp creates community. It 'offers a subversive response to mainstream culture, and provides both ingroup solidarity and an opportunity to express distance from and disdain for the roles most gay people play most of the time' (Gross, 1989: 143). Although all community, ultimately, is imagined (Anderson, 1983) and exists as a notion and a loyalty among those who feel they belong to it, the kind of community camp creates is closer than most forms of community. One might speak of a subculture, in the sense that camp functions 'to win, or at least contest "cultural space" for [its] members; [it] also generate[s] and confirm[s] important modes of both collective and individual identity and orientation towards the dominant values of wider social and cultural order' (O'Sullivan et al., 1983: 231). Camp not only creates community in its imagined sense, it also creates community in a more material, subcultural sense through play-acting in clubs, for instance. Debby Olders told me about a gay disco she regularly visited where a group of other guests organized contests in replaying episodes from the prime-time soap opera *Dynasty*.[3] From the following quotations from the interview with Eduard Spaans it will become evident that for him a particular kind of parodying investment in gossip magazines is very much part of interaction in the gay community in Amsterdam.

Eduard Spaans says that he enjoys gossip magazines because they are all bluff and pretension. Part of the fun is that others, apparently, are fooled by the magazines. His involvement with the gossip press started as a joke:

> I was in London some time ago and they have all these posters and postcards of the British royal family, really garish, on every street corner, really shameless, and I took four of them home, bought them with money that was left over or something. We had a noticeboard in the corridor and people saw that and started sending me cards. Now no one sends me normal postcards any more, I only get royal families. And I get magazines (. . .) those French magazines on dynasties that have long ceased to be dynasties. That is very funny to read. They keep saying 'Roi de France' and who knows who else is in those magazines. (. . .) Maybe the Bourbons are still kings of France. One that hasn't been decapitated. And there are still several houses who claim the throne and so on. I don't know, they are very busy playing that game. (. . .) It is funny because it is really silly. (. . .) It's funny. A dynasty . . . it is no more than a function now, nothing much else. They haven't got much to show for it. And what makes it extra funny is all the brouhaha that is made about them. It is so interesting because there is nothing that is really interesting. They blow it up out of all proportion and that is amusing. (. . .) I read gossip to see how other people are fooled and how they fall for it too.

Eduard Spaans and Frank Stevens, who is also gay, both share their pleasure in the make-believe world of gossip and royalty magazines and television programmes with others.

> A friend of mine works in a library as a typing goat – that is what he calls himself – but he says he always has to explain to people at his workplace that *Glamourland* [a televised version of a gossip magazine] is persiflage. And it is fun to talk about that with him.

> (Eduard Spaans)

Frank Stevens, a teacher, and a colleague of his like to embarrass others by flaunting what outside the codes of camp is seen as bad taste.

> I have noticed that you can really shock [others by talking about royalty magazines]. And then I do it on purpose, of course. 'Ha, the new *Vorsten* [Sovereigns] has arrived.' People react furiously. When I say in the staff-room, 'I had such a good time reading *Vorsten* yesterday', [they say] 'Do you read that? Ridiculous', like that. Well, then I put on an even stronger act. Although I do enjoy it genuinely. (. . .) It is my kind of romanticism, I think. [I have heard the royal family is really an object of interest in gay circles?] Oh, yes, that's true. I have a gay colleague and we share this interest, so we always take time to talk about the new *Vorsten*. He doesn't subscribe – he is too stingy – but his old mother has a subscription, so we discuss what was in the latest issue.

To embarrass others, to shock them and provoke them into showing their dis-approval of what you happen to like, in my experience, is one of the favourite ploys of the gay scene towards the outside world. Reading gossip magazines is made into a provoking and noticeable mark of difference as well as a sign of 'membership' (that extends to those outside the gay scene who are also 'in the know'), apart from being something to enjoy genuinely. To prize what are considered worthless cultural objects and prove that what is deemed valueless by dominant culture is a matter of rules and conventions rather than inherent value is also a means of protesting against the con-tinuing ostracization of homosexuality. Camp is as much a political weapon as it is cultural enjoyment. Of the objects camp chooses to cherish the most favoured are actresses and singers past their prime, bad films and the transparent pretensions of gossip journalism, and kings and queens whose titles, if not their countries, are wholly imaginary. A part of camp is serious and based on real drama, which it recognizes but also relativizes. Camp enacts the pain of playing a role that does not suit, of trying to be who you are not. Camp is the at times bitter mockery of having to try to be someone you are not. It is laughing at one's own expense and at all those who cannot distinguish the fiction from facts, the blatant untruth from real sorrow and real suffering.

This interpretation is more political and dramatic than the reports of readers were. It is borne out, however, by the work of Sontag and Ross and by informal inquiry among friends. All agree that gossip is very much part of the male homosexual community, in printed and oral forms, as is a sense of (melo)drama. Eduard Spaans enthusiastically changed from the status of respondent to that of an informer in the true gossip sense and confirmed the status of gossip in the gay community:

> I used to see a lot of Paul de Leeuw [gay cabaret artist] and people often asked me, 'Is it true that . . .?' They doubt it a little, but they believe it too. [What did they write about Paul de Leeuw?] Well, they recently had a ridiculous piece about him, saying that he wanted to have children with a girlfriend. [They wrote that] he lived with a boyfriend and they even gave the boyfriend a name. And it was a boy he had had an affair with, but three years ago, and they suggested that they were living together. And he wanted to have children and raise them with this boyfriend. How all these

people related to one another, they left out of the story. Was that woman supposed to give birth to that child and then give it up? But the funny thing was that there were all sorts of real, true things in that story. That he was going to act in *Les Miserables* and that he was going to go to New York. That is really scary. They had spiced the story with things that seemed to give it truth content. (. . .)

I know a guy, well, not really, that man [name of journalist] who gets taken to court all the time. He is gay too. You know, he writes about the royal family . . . Maybe Paul was drunk and got talking with one of those guys. [It really is a gossip circuit, isn't it, the gay world?] That's true. Because all those gossip journalists are gay too.

Eduard Spaans is not a walking caricature. He gossips, he laughs about gossiping and gossip magazines, is awed by the frightening mixture of half-truths the magazines print, but he also feels everyone, including gossip readers of any kind, deserves respect: 'My mother is in a nursing home at the moment and she hates it that all those women don't have anything else to do but [to read gossip magazines], and she condemns that a bit. She doesn't respect them or that they might want to have their own kind of pleasure'.

Community, solidarity, criticism

Whereas the repertoires that are used to make other genres of women's magazines meaningful stress dreams of perfection, control and mastery, the repertoires that are used to make gossip magazines meaningful seem to do something completely different. In so far as the repertoire of melodrama and the extended family repertoire betray specific fantasies or dreams, they are fantasies of belonging, of imagined communities. In a more direct sense, gossip magazines have a special place in communities that are held together by a shared camp sensibility, which can be read as a form of protest against prevailing norms and values. In fact, the discussion of camp reading of gossip magazines has made clear that 'serious gossip reading' and 'camp gossip reading' are not so very different from each other. Both recognize and confirm the realness of drama and sorrow as part of the everyday. Camp talk uses the same repertoires serious gossip readers use, though in a more exaggerated and parodying fashion.

Generally speaking, printed gossip is not all that different, then, from oral gossip. It serves an unconscious need to belong and it also serves a need to address social inequality, whether through creating moral standards or by challenging 'good taste'. Like serious, intimate oral gossip, printed gossip is a resource for the subordinated: it can be a means of self-expression and solidarity (the male homosexual community and camp); it can be a means of sharing judgement of an unequal society as well as a source of sentimental enjoyment and thus the confirmation of what is usually considered 'low taste' as a taste culture in its own right. 'Low taste' is, of course, an aesthetic criterion that precludes the possibility of recognizing that everyday experience could have any value whatsoever.

Gossip magazines have even lower status than other women's magazine genres. Marie Stemerdink defended her reading of gossip magazines to her daughters: 'The children don't like it, but I cull from them what I want to know.' Tina Poorter manoeuvred around a critical husband. Naturally, readers themselves were critical of the magazines too. Criticism of their journalistic methods and their highly suggestive style of writing was often expressed by informants. Eduard Spaans, Solema Tillie and Frederik Paulsen all qualified their enjoyment of the magazines (however incidentally in Frederik Paulsen's case) by criticizing how gossip magazines dig around in other people's lives. I suspect their complaint is partly sincere and partly evidence of their added enjoyment of what is deemed to be scandalous and absolutely not done. Others, such as Pam Gradanus and Ina Dammers, were critical of the pretensions of gossip magazines. For readers criticism of the magazines often appears to go hand in hand with enjoying them. Mona Brooks made fun of gossip magazines with Natacha Cuellar and Tina Smart, and they shared their embarrassment about their mothers who read them:

Natacha: I mean it [*Hello*] has got lots and lots of pictures, but it's articles about pictures, you know, absolute rubbish. I mean, like the second son of this Jew, someone you've never heard of, couldn't give a damn about anyway. You know, how he went on holiday to Portugal . . .

Mona: My mum reads the one that talks about, you know, TV personalities . . . Nasty things you hear about them – she holds them against them for the rest of their lives . . . I think it's *Chat* she reads.

Becky: My mum does that. She points out . . . whoever went with who, you know.

Referring to the music magazines, which also carry much gossip and personal information about celebrities and which she still likes (though less than when she was a teenager), Mona said. 'You get a buzz from it somehow, I don't know why. You feel more alive'.

Notes

1   The plural is used by the speaker to rob the singer of all individuality, the implication being that as an artist she is exchangeable.

2   The pleasures American readers take in supermarket tabloids are remarkably similar to those my interviewees took in European gossip magazines. For a highly interesting discussion and analysis of this gossip magazine related genre see Bird, 1992.

3   Schiff (1984) describes the same phenomenon for the New York gay community, in which D&D – Dinner and *Dynasty* – was at that time also a fixture of social life. *Dynasty*'s creator, Esther Shapiro, allegedly knew of 'a coven of BBD&O executives who re-enact *Dynasty* scripts every week, over champagne and caviar' (in Schiff, 1984: 64). I should like to thank Kim Schrøder for sending me this article.

PART THREE

Ascribed celebrity

The transformed public sphere

Introduction to part three

■ P. David Marshall

A T THE HEART OF celebrity culture is the anxiety that there is nothing of value there. Indeed some authors argue directly that the definition of celebrity is exactly the surplus value of a public personality (Schmidt 2005). Daniel J. Boorstin similarly defines the falseness of media/celebrity culture in the context of the pseudo-event. Famous for being famous thus represents the ultimate recursive loop in contemporary popular culture, where the celebrated individual has no meritorious reason for being acclaimed. Fame itself has no intrinsic merit.

Rather than debate the relative emptiness of fame and celebrity, it is probably more useful to investigate its production as a proliferating practice/discourse that has certain tropes and particular ways to convey value in contemporary culture. Celebrity culture is a way in which the public world is depicted. The representation of public events has a certain structure and style. Red carpets are rolled out for film premieres as they are for visiting heads of state. Media scrums gather at these events to capture the moment and to both produce and ascertain what is significant and alluring about particular personalities. Audiences are drawn to these produced moments of significance and engage in another round of interpretation of value. Bodies and body-types are adjudicated; relational connections are debated; speeches and responses are dissected for their capacity to reveal the fabricated aura and possibly break down the distinctions it constructs.

Merit or no merit, there has been a migration of this structure of the celebration of the individual beyond entertainment and into many other domains. The reading selections in this section identify this shifted public sphere – where the public sphere is a representation of the famed and acclaimed that serves as the focal point for discussion and debate among the populace. Merit and fame become twinned and intertwined in a variety of professions and activities. Celebrity culture has migrated from its media home into other dimensions of contemporary culture.

Chapter 16

P. David Marshall

INTIMATELY INTERTWINED IN THE MOST PUBLIC WAY
Celebrity and journalism

Aᴸᴛʜᴏᴜɢʜ ᴛʜᴇ ᴄᴇʟᴇʙʀɪᴛʏ ᴀɴᴅ journalism have been twinned for most of the past 200 years, their intertwining has regularly betrayed the less noble side of journalistic practice. Both journalism and celebrity articulate a changing public sphere and a different constitution of engagement and significance by any nation's citizenry. That transformation of significance has been linked to the emergence of democratic polities and political debate; the transformation has also been aligned with the emergence of an elaborate entertainment industry and the panoply of information that fuels its cultural forms. This chapter investigates the way that journalism and celebrity intersect and how their alliance has produced very specific forms of presentation and writing practices that have become not only standard in the features section of newspapers but populate the organization of information throughout the news.

To begin this investigation, it must be understood that celebrity-inspired journalism has become so routinized in papers that its origins are no longer easily identifiable. For example, a 13 May 2004 *New York Times* article (Bumiller 2004) on Donald Rumsfeld, the Secretary of Defence in President Bush's administration was designed as a 'profile' of the man during a particularly vigorous scandal over abuse and atrocities committed by Americans on their Iraqi prisoners. The headline 'Stolid Rumsfeld Soldiers on, But Weighs Ability to Serve' encapsulates the tone of the article: discerning the state of mind and psychological condition of a man under siege. Thus we learn the personal details of his daily life including that he 'spent last Sunday in the backyard of his elegant Washington home, poring over documents piled 10 inches high in his lap'. And that the visiting friend indicated 'that at least he was sitting outside – it was a beautiful day. That's a good thing if you are under a lot of pressure'. The article continues to provide personal background details about the man: that he had the president and his wife Laura Bush (along with Alan Greenspan) over to dinner at his home 'in the graceful, old-world Kalorama section of Washington' on the day the scandal broke and that 'everyone appeared relaxed in each other's company'; that 'despite Mr. Rumsfeld's ferocious exterior, he is a principled man' who with his wife regularly visited wounded soldiers on Sundays and stopped by three times a week to visit a high school friend, 'who was dying of brain cancer' even though at the time Rumsfeld was preoccupied with the war in Afghanistan. We also discover he is a relentless worker and finds 'stability in his normal workaholic routine'. The investigative element to the story was whether Rumsfeld would resign; but the kinds of information generated were classically derived from celebrity journalistic practice of finding out what the famous person is *really* like. Although the story is in the front section of the newspaper surrounded by other sobering articles about the occupation in Iraq, the Rumsfeld profile stylistically resembled what one would regularly find in the features section of the newspaper. In contemporary newswriting and presentation these delineations are no longer in play. To actually produce such an article, the reporter has to ensure access to the various sources. As a result, what sometimes emerges from celebrity journalism is a further convergence with the practices of public relations and promotion. In this particular instance, the author, Elisabeth Bumiller, had to build some sort of trust with friends of Rumsfeld to obtain the personal details and to gain these sources' consent to speak publicly about him. The building of trust ensured that the story would take on a more positive reading of Rumsfeld. The result: a story that crosses between a fluff personality profile and the underlying story of possible resignation.

Origins

Why this kind of reportage on the personality of the famous emerged in the nineteenth century along with the development of mass circulation newspapers is intriguing. The celebrity as a social category developed from a number of changes in the political and cultural landscape in the late eighteenth and early nineteenth centuries. First among them is a shift in participation in what has later been described as the public sphere. The concept of the celebrity articulates a distinct engagement by the famous individual with the public that is differentiated from the way royalty and significant leaders of the Church may have represented themselves. Celebrity is an acknowledgement of the public's power – indeed, the celebrity is in many ways the embodiment of the collective power of an invested audience in a particular person (Marshall 1997). Thus, the way to understand the emergence of the celebrity in the nineteenth century is its close affinity with democracy and the new forms of power it expressed. Images of heads of state may have been statically and ceremoniously replicated in coinage and other representations of power but with the expansion of democratic power a new kind of public identity developed that was dependent on the emerging power of the crowd and the masses. The celebrity embodied that contradiction of being individually elevated and thus relatively unique, but dependent on a new system of 'democratically inspired' value that was derived from popular audiences.

Journalism, although born from the origins of business reporting as much as political tracts and proclamations, has had a similar history in its association with the development of democracy. The expansion of newspapers and other print publications was partially dependent on a different organization of power. Combined with the expanded political enfranchisement and general literacy in the nineteenth century, the newspaper transformed into the key site for information and popular debate about political issues in countries such as the US, France and UK. With the shift to a mass subscriber base for income and profits (through selling space to advertisers interested in reaching this wider audience), some newspapers in these countries at least symbolically came to represent the interests and desires of the populace. American newspaper magnates of the late nineteenth century such as Joseph Pulitzer and William Randolph Hearst built their empires on a brand of news story that acknowledged a wider proportion of the population and attempted to cater to what was believed to be their interests and desires. Typically called yellow journalism, reporters developed stories that were both sensational and closer to the everyday lives of this new urban readership. Profiles of celebrated individuals emerged alongside the development of what were perceived to be more salacious stories and muckraking to discover scandal. These profiles of famous people over the course of the nineteenth century began to change from carefully choreographed studies of public moments involving these people to revelations about their private lives and how that intersected with their public lives. As Charles Ponce de Leon's work has revealed, celebrity journalism changed, from the nineteenth to the twentieth century, from reporters piecing together stories from people who knew famous people to direct interviews with famous people in their private homes (Ponce de Leon 2002).

There were a number of reasons for the emergence and expansion of celebrity journalism from the nineteenth century into the twentieth century. First of all, the stories articulated a celebration of individuality that intersected with the ideologies of the self that had been advancing since the renaissance. Celebrities represented heightened examples of individual achievement and transformation and thereby challenged the rigidity of class-based societies by presenting the potential to transcend these categories.

The kind of individuality that celebrities embodied also intersected with the expansion of consumer capitalism enabling the populace to use consumption as a means of self-actualization and transformation. Consumer culture, through advertisements, department stores and the actual expanded range of products and services, presented a diverse array of possibilities for modern individuals to make themselves anew. Celebrities provided a refracted form of knowledge of the modern self that became another resource in the developing choices of consumer culture.

Celebrity journalism also worked to fulfil other rising apparent needs of contemporary culture. Emile Durkheim used the term 'anomie' to describe the isolating condition of urban social life that was ubiquitous (Durkheim 1964). In the mid-twentieth century David Reisman coined the term and title 'the lonely crowd' to express a similar sense of distance in mass society (Reisman 1950). The processes of industrialization, the migration of workforces to cities and internationally to new centres of manufacturing, and the general sense of disconnection and dislocation that had enveloped the architecture and organization of cities, helped create a sense of both anonymity and alienation. Profiles of celebrities provided a constellation of recognizable and familiar people who filled the gap and provided points of commonality for people to reconnect both with celebrities and with each other. Instead of a discourse that highlighted the distance and aura of the celebrity, celebrity journalism worked to make the famous more real and worked to provide a greater intimacy with their everyday lives. Celebrities, via these journalistic profiles, became better known for their ordinariness along with their extraordinariness as these stories worked to connect individually with the mass audience. Audiences in turn would have a degree of 'affective investment' (Marshall 1997) in particular celebrities because of the amount of personal background that was provided about them in newspapers and magazines.

As much as celebrity journalism appeared to be fulfilling a particular need in the cultural fabric of contemporary life, it was also clearly an instrument of the various political and cultural industries. Tom Mole's study of the emergence of literary celebrities is particularly revealing of some of the changed conditions that were connected to the mass production of cultural commodities. Mole's study found that as writing became less anonymous (anonymous attribution had been standard in the eighteenth century) publishers became more focused on differentiating their lists from others'. The most effective way to ensure the distinctiveness of a publisher's list was to invest in making the authors more visible and in many senses more real to the audience. Thus Byron was not only a literary figure; he was known for his personal life and became a widely known popular figure who had a clearly developed public persona. Mole also links this transformation to the need to connect to the newly distanced mass audience. The personal connection brought the material to life more by providing the massive reading public with the author's background (Mole 2004).

In the development of the mass circulation newspaper, owners and journalists alike were also developing techniques and discourses that pulled often disparate audiences together. In the US, the newspapers worked very hard at making stories that appealed across class and ethnic lines. Entertainment reporting over many decades gradually served as one of the principal sites for such a crossover. More popular arts were featured and reviewed by newspapers to appeal to the working class and their leisure interests; at the same time, this reportage on vaudeville and cinema worked to legitimize the 'artistic' merit of these newer cultural forms and thereby made them more acceptable as sources of stories for the middle class. Celebrity profiles of film actors and musical stars eventually were stories that transcended clear class differences quite acceptably by the 1920s and 1930s (Ponce de Leon 2002, 206–40).

In the wider dimensions of cultural activity, celebrity journalism functioned as a technique for simplifying the representational dimension of the public sphere. It helped focus attention on particular individuals above others and provided a constellation of the famous for the public's attention. In the US, this kind of construction was closely connected with the emergence of national markets and national politics. In the mid-nineteenth century P. T. Barnum, the ultimate huckster, tried to ensure that profiles of his individual stars, such as Jenny Lind, were in the local papers before his travelling show arrived in a particular community. He discovered that these background pieces added to the star quality and attracted the public to his events. Through this advanced publicity, national markets for entertainment were developed and buttressed by the press who also realized the value in creating celebrated individuals for the selling of their papers and magazines.

The subjective quality of celebrity journalism:
its connection with press agentry and publicity

One of the most important reasons for studying celebrity journalism is that it often illustrates the particular dependencies journalistic practice has on its sources and what is considered news value. Celebrity status simplifies the determination of news value precisely because the level of fame of the person *a priori* establishes its newsworthiness. Whereas other news events may not produce the same effect of attracting readers, celebrity guarantees a certain high level of interest.

Parallel professions to journalism developed in the nineteenth century and flourished in the twentieth century to organize, contain and foster this interest in particular personalities. Press agentry was generally seen as the practice of ensuring the appearance of individuals and events in the newspaper in the most favourable light. P. T. Barnum's work in this area was seen to be seminal. Much like advertising, press agentry was involved in puffery and exaggeration of the significance of a particular event or personality for its greater impact on the public. Press agents were thus employed in the expanding entertainment industries both by individuals and corporations. A large element of their positions in Hollywood from the 1920s onwards in fact involved maintaining correspondence relationships with fans on behalf of the star. Public relations – as it was formulated in the early twentieth century – was established as a more legitimate profession in clear contradistinction to the practices of the press agent. Working on behalf of corporations and individuals, public relations specialists were expert at producing copy that resembled the manner that journalists would formulate for newspapers. The press release, as common for companies trying to control a potentially negative event as they were for entertainers and politicians trying to provide advance publicity about their respective tours, was the invention of public relations, which has been instrumental in shifting the balance of editorial content of newspapers throughout the twentieth century.

In certain areas of journalistic coverage, the work of press agentry, publicity and promotion became normalized into the structure of stories. Entertainment journalism, like other forms of journalism, has had to adapt to the cycle of news and events of its particular industry and 'beat'. Film releases, music releases, or the opening of a particular play or concert tour has demanded a certain close relationship with the press for mutual success. Publicity and promotion departments have been expert at controlling access to the stars for such releases. Thus, the press junket has become standard for the interview of movie stars in advance of the release of the film. With promotion predating the film, the junket might be in an on-location setting. As a film is released internationally, the stars may be part of the film's local premiere and the interviews are organized around such an event. Along with the critical review, most major films are twinned with this form of advance publicity where a feature interview of one of the stars appears in newspapers and on principal television networks. The elaborate press kit provides background information for the journalists to complete their story. With more expensive productions, an 'electronic' press kit is provided: clips of the film are compiled along with an 'interview' with the star that can be used by local stations with the local interviewer asking the stock questions provided.

The development of the official and authentic story

The system of publicity is designed to provide an insider's role for the journalist. Through general cooperation between the entertainment industry and the journalist, it is tacitly agreed that having 'contact' with the star ensures a positive spin in the story. The system has produced what have now become standard structures and motifs for the celebrity profile or feature interview in a large newspaper or mainstream magazine that can be summarized in series as follows:

A.   The meeting of journalist and star in either domestic setting or café.
B.   The description of the casual dress and demeanour of the star.
C.   The discussion of their current work – which is essentially the anchor for why the story is newsworthy.
D.   The revelation of something that is against the grain of what is generally perceived to be the star's persona – something that is anecdotal but is revealing of the star's true nature.

(Adapted from G. Baum, 1998)

This pattern has developed since the mid-1920s. It is a structure that is non-threatening, generally flattering and a celebration of the idiosyncratic self. Celebrity profiles possess, then, a combination of the reporter's obsequiousness around the creativity and uniqueness of the individual and an effort to reveal something that is normally hidden, to uncover the 'true self' (Dyer 1979) of the celebrity.

The magazine industry has perhaps relied on the celebrity profile to a greater degree than newspapers. The magazine cover and the cover story function as the principal advertising mechanisms for magazine sales. Choosing a particular celebrity as the cover image, then, is as much a marketing strategy for the magazine as a news event. Thus, there have been moments where a particular celebrity has blanketed the covers of a wide range of magazines. At the time of the release of *Titanic* in 1997, it was difficult to find a magazine that did not have a cover image of Leonardo di Caprio: his image graced the covers of teen, news, gossip, entertainment and women's magazines. Being on the cover of many magazines was not a source of income for the star; rather it often meant some sort of editorial control of the content (Turner *et al.* 2000). Some of the most famous celebrity covers – for example, the naked and pregnant body-painted image of Demi Moore on the cover of *Vanity Fair* in 1991 – have been designed to help reposition a star's persona as much as to make a publicity flashpoint for the magazine.

Certain magazines have based their principal editorial content on celebrities. Andy Warhol's *Interview* was simply an oversized magazine devoted to fawning and often vacuous discussions with famous people. Historically, pictorial magazines such as *Life* and *Look* have organized their content periodically around profiles of celebrity figures. More recently, the American *People* magazine was built from the 'People' section of *Time* magazine and became a separate publication in 1974. It was designed to be a showcase for celebrities to give their side of any story. Exclusive interviews have been used by the Australian *People* franchise, *Who*, to not only sell magazines but also to ensure that the magazine's writers would have access to the private and domestic life of the celebrity (Turner *et al.* 2000: 132–5). The exclusive interview is also a way to ensure news values for the particular magazine; exclusive interviews are often the way in which a celebrity attempts to counteract bad press coverage around a scandal.

Exclusivity of a celebrity profile can become a bidding war as well as a source of some tension and rivalry among magazines and television networks in each national market. For instance, *OK!* magazine won exclusive rights to publish official photographs of the wedding of Michael Douglas and Catherine Zeta-Jones in 2000 for $1.6 million. Three days before the publication of the wedding by *OK!*, *Hello*, a competitor, had published some unauthorized paparazzi wedding photos. Douglas, Zeta-Jones and *OK!* sued successfully for damages and won a very modest legal fees settlement. Exclusive interviews of Michael Jackson or O. J. Simpson have been hotly contested in the American market among the major television networks and, when landed, they are often located in the flagship newsmagazine programmes for each network. Indeed, journalistic careers have been built through the journalist's capacity to allow famous personalities to speak on their programmes. In the US, Barbara Walters became a celebrity profiler and interviewer during and after a successful career as a television journalist and anchorwoman. David Frost and Clive James have built similar television careers as interviewers of the famed and infamous in the UK. Oprah Winfrey, in her occasional move from afternoon talk show host to prime time, became the interviewer of choice of Michael Jackson and Michael Jordan in the 1990s. In the United States, Katie Couric and Diane Sawyer have continued this tradition of providing a sympathetic platform for celebrities to address their massive audiences.

Scandal, celebrity and news reporting

Where official versions of stories have made journalistic practice veer closely to the role of publicists and public relations, reporting celebrity scandals places journalists in adversarial roles with regard to the entertainment publicity machines. The American-based *National Enquirer* had a reputation for its stories of aliens and other hard-to-believe accounts of human freaks along with photos of celebrities caught in clearly unsanctioned, private moments. Nonetheless, its relentless pursuit of the O. J. Simpson murder investigation netted some tangible evidence that linked Simpson to the murder of his ex-wife and her boyfriend. What was more remarkable was that other newspapers and magazines reported the findings of the *National Enquirer* and for a short period in the mid-1990s, the supermarket tabloid had achieved a new version of the journalistic high ground. Without the usual restrictions that have limited the muckraking of other established press institutions, the *National Enquirer* not only led with discovered facts in the O. J. Simpson case – it has also been the first to reveal Jesse Jackson's love child. Its greatest claims to fame are the series of celebrity images, whether it is an unflattering picture of Elizabeth Taylor or a clearly disturbed photo of Whitney Houston, that have populated its four decades of 'reporting'. There is no question that the fall of any celebrity is a major news story. Although this may be the primary content of tabloids, it has become an element of the most highbrow of newspapers. Treading the fine line between scandal and official story are the television programmes, which have spawned another layer of celebrity journalism. *Entertainment Tonight*, which began as a syndicated early evening nightly programme in the 1980s, has become the standard in the American television industry for reporting both gossip and officially sanctioned information about stars and their current projects. Variations of *Entertainment Tonight* have appeared in many countries throughout the world. Modelled on the evening newscast, it presents the entertainment news as standard news fare – with the added dimension of greater amounts of smiling by the news anchors.

Celebrity scandal has the potential to transform news values quite dramatically. Certainly the O. J. Simpson murder trial became front-page news beyond all proportion to what would be perceived as normal news values. The death of Diana, Princess of Wales, allegedly as a result of a car chase with paparazzi, generated an overwhelming amount of coverage in all media forms and dwarfed any other news event for weeks. Michael Jackson's arrest and trial connected with the alleged sexual assault of minors has similarly produced an inordinate amount of news coverage. From blanket coverage of Jackson's arrest to speculative reporting on his changing support and defence team, Jackson's latest scandal has maintained a media circus that allows some journalists to work full time on the story. When particular scandals with this kind of potency emerge they bleed from the entertainment sections of the newspapers towards the front pages. Celebrities have become focal points for the discussion of a wide range of issues and concerns. In a peculiarly contemporary way, celebrities, via journalistic reportage, have become the effective conduit for discourses about the personal: celebrities have become the discursive talking points for the political dimensions of a host of formerly private and personal concerns.

The all-encompassing celebrity system: journalist as celebrity

As much as journalists present the ideal profile of chronicler, which maintains a certain neutrality from their subjects, it is clear that journalism itself has become part of the celebrity system in its own power hierarchies. Throughout the latter half of the twentieth century, bylines have been increasingly used in newspapers and magazines (with perhaps *The Economist* one of the few exceptions in the English language). This practice has intensified the identification of the individual journalist and a celebration of particularly successful journalists. Similarly, from the emergence of television in the 1950s, there has been a cultivation of the broadcast news star. Walter Cronkite, anchor for more than two decades of the *CBS Evening News*, became a news star and remains an iconic figure of celebrity status in television journalism. Geraldo Rivera, an American talk-show host and confrontational journalist has become well known in the US more as a celebrity than for his journalistic expertise. In urban markets throughout the US, the local news anchor has developed lesser versions of the star quality of Cronkite. In print, journalists strive to move from the simple byline to columnist status. As a columnist, the journalist becomes more equal to the celebrated individuals that he or she may cover in politics, entertainment or sport.

This general transmogrification of journalist into celebrity has pushed certain individuals towards fabrication of their stories. It was discovered in 2004 that the *US Today's* star reporter, Jack Kelley, built part of his 20-year reputation on spectacular stories and images that were works of fiction built on coached informants who were not even present at the news events covered. Similarly, in 2003 the *New York Times* dealt with Jayson Blair's efforts at constructing fictional news stories in an effort to build his reputation. Perhaps one could link these developments to the new celebrity status of the Internet muckraker Matt Drudge and his *Drudge Report* as the related phenomenon of an industry that relies on celebrity status as much as politics and entertainment.

Conclusion

It is difficult to separate the histories of journalism and the emergence of the contemporary celebrity system. Journalism has been instrumental in proselytizing a new public sphere and celebrities have been a foundational means and method for the expansion of key elements of that new public sphere. In that convergence, journalism has expanded its 'coverage' of entertainment and sports by developing features on personalities. It has also used techniques developed in writing about entertainment stars for its coverage of the famed and notorious in politics and many other domains. The coverage of entertainment has expanded massively and has become a major component of information and news reporting in all media. With the celebrity reporting that has accompanied this expansion of coverage, there has been a naturalization and normalization of the close connection between the sources of information and journalistic practice; in other words, celebrity journalism is one of the key locations for the convergence of publicity, promotion and journalism in terms of the generated editorial content. Celebrity journalism has also been instrumental in the exploration of a different form of cultural politics that is an investigation of the self, the private and the intimate. Through celebrity profiles, the investigation of scandals in all their sordid details and the psychotherapeutic ramblings published in celebrity interviews, celebrity journalism is the location for the exploration of the 'politics of the personal' in our transformed and shifting public sphere.

Chapter 17

Joe Moran

THE REIGN OF HYPE
The contemporary star system

THE LAST FEW DECADES have seen the proliferation of an extraordinary range of activities aimed at publicizing and promoting American authors. This chapter investigates some of these activities by exploring the specifically contemporary aspects of the literary 'star system'. It begins by looking at the implications for literary celebrity of recent changes in the media industries, specifically book publishing's absorption into a global entertainment and information industry under the control of a handful of large conglomerates. It goes on to explore how the commercial imperatives of major publishers are complicated by the continuing importance of cultural capital in the literary marketplace, and considers finally how this negotiation between pure profit making and 'higher' cultural values has produced intense debates and conflicted meanings around literary celebrity in contemporary culture. I want to argue that the contemporary star system, far from being a closed shop populated by mutual log-rollers and backscratchers and number-crunching accountants, is an evolving organism which is not immune to intense self-scrutiny and soul-searching about its more malign aspects.

The mediagenic author

There is now an unprecedented series of opportunities for authors to receive public attention in the US, and many of these new opportunities can be linked to shifts in the economics of literary production – what one observer has described as

> the unrestrained reign of hype, with its seemingly irresistible attraction for opportunistic and big-money writers, and its eerie capacity for luring and ensnaring unwary artists and for turning them, often against their better judgment, into travelling salesmen and TV pitchmen.[1]

The recent transformation of the publishing industry from a large number of family-run houses to a small number of major publishers owned by giant, multimedia parent companies has completely transformed the nature of authorship and publishing in America and, increasingly, throughout the world. Although outside interests have been involved in American publishing since the 1960s, with companies like CBS, ITT and RCA leading the way, the mergers which took place in the 1980s and 1990s brought all the major trade book publishers into the hands of large, transnational communications conglomerates with holdings and interests in many other, usually more profitable, areas of the mass media. As a parallel phenomenon occurring steadily since about 1960, these major publishers have also been purchasing small or medium-sized independent houses, so that there are now few areas of book publishing which do not, either directly or indirectly, come under the control of seven main conglomerates: Bertelsmann, Pearson, Viacom, Rupert Murdoch's News Corporation, Time Warner, Hearst and Holtzbrinck. These large corporations have made more venture capital available to publishers, thus solving the perennial cash-flow problems of the small independently owned houses while also increasing the pressure for commercial success, so that sophisticated forms of book publicity have been developed to market books more effectively.

In order to appreciate the impact of conglomeration in this area, it is worth stressing that, until recently, book promotion was widely viewed as one of the most inefficient areas of the industry. Lewis Coser, Charles Kadushin and Walter Powell, in a definitive 1982 survey of book publishing, pointed to the erratic and unresearched nature of book marketing, particularly within what publishers generally regarded as the unpredictable area of trade books.[2] Jacques Barzun, in a 1984 Library of Congress colloquium, similarly claimed that 'if cornflakes were sold like books, nobody would eat breakfast'.[3] This inefficiency was partly a product of the widespread belief that books were all distinct products and therefore unmarketable anyway, but it was also due to the survival within many houses of the genteel image of the 'gentleman publisher', working for the love of literature rather than mere financial gain. While the publishing industry became progressively more commercially astute throughout this century, it also became more strenuous in its efforts to professionalize itself, producing a hierarchy which sealed off the most prestigious areas of publishing from its commercial aspects. Publishers, as James L.W. West III argues, 'gained dignity and status by removing themselves from the inkstains of the printshop, the blue pencil of the editor, and the cashbox of the bookseller'.[4] In this urbane, old-boy network, a publisher like Alfred Knopf could say that he preferred not to publish any author whom he would not want to invite to dinner.[5] This attitude encouraged a lack of coordination in the marketing of books, particularly since responsibilities for public relations, advertising, sales and distribution were often located in separate departments, and made book publicity, as one of the elements in the chain closest to the consumer, a low status area of responsibility. Publicists, who were predominantly female, were often referred to disparagingly by insiders as the 'airline stewardesses' of the industry.[6]

In the last two decades, however, the status and significance of these departments within publishing houses has steadily risen. Publishers have also realized the cheapness and effectiveness of forms of publicity which concentrate on the author — magazine and newspaper features and television and radio appearances — over paid advertising.

For example, a ten-city author tour costs about the same as, and reaches considerably more prospective customers than, a full-page advertisement in the *New York Times Book Review*.[7] Among these forms of cheap publicity, the superiority of television over newspapers and magazines as a book marketing tool has also long been recognized. As long ago as 1981, Thomas Whiteside described an appearance by an author on a major talk show as 'one of the biggest promotional prizes around for any publisher', second only to being selected by the Book-of-the-Month Club.[8] In recognition of this clear relationship between book sales and personal television appearances, the major publishers are even beginning to introduce authors on to direct-mail advertisements – usually 'infomercials' in talk-show format – and home shopping television channels like QVC, on which viewers can phone to order copies by credit card.

The large number of recent novels written by (or, more usually, ghost-written for) celebrities such as Ivana Trump, William Shatner, Martina Navratilova and Joan Collins suggests the increasing importance of the recognizable, media-friendly personality as a kind of brand name with which to sell the literary product.[9] A variation on this theme is the bestselling author producing work from beyond the grave – after the death of Alistair MacLean in 1987, for example, HarperCollins decided to perpetuate his bankable name by turning some of his old story ideas into novels, for which task they chose an unknown, first-time author with the suspiciously similar name of Alastair MacNeill. (After a court ruling in 1991, though, the publishers were forced to make MacLean's name smaller than MacNeill's on the book jacket.) Some publishers can be influenced by the attractiveness or screen presence of an author in deciding whether or not to accept a book for publication. The *New York Times* has reported cases of authors being sent to speech tutors and image consultants by publishers, and of literary agents providing publishers with dummy videotapes of their clients along with book proposals, acceptance or rejection of the manuscript sometimes hinging on the author's performance.[10]

These still seem to be isolated cases, however, if only because the publishing industry produces too many books to vet all its authors this closely. As Richard Schickel has shown, the modern phenomenon of celebrity developed in early American cinema partly because the popular demand for personalities, unlike the demand for particular plotlines or genres, was relatively stable. As films became more costly and studios needed to take out loans in order to make them, 'star names came to lead the list of collateral that bankers looked upon with favour when their assistance was sought'.[11] The involvement of a particular star can still decide whether a film project goes ahead because of his or her ability to 'open' a movie – to guarantee that audiences will go and see it in the crucial first few weeks of release. The fact that the book publishing industry does not require such a large initial investment as a Hollywood film, however, encourages the speculative overproduction of books. About 80 per cent of the titles produced every year are commercial failures, a ratio which would quickly bankrupt a Hollywood studio or television network. Because the initial cost of publishing a book is quite small, however, a house usually requires only one 'blockbuster' in a season to counterbalance all its other losses, and it is this kind of work which therefore receives the biggest promotional effort. Sales representatives decide in marketing meetings which few books among a publisher's many titles get 'the full treatment – the six-figure print run, the lavish book jacket, the pressure on the news media, the 10-city tour, the television interviews, the advertisements, the four-color posters and bookstore displays'. In these meetings, they may well be influenced by extra-literary factors – especially since, to aid them in their decision making, they are often sent not only proof copies of the books but also videotapes on which editors and authors pitch the book to them.[12] Publishers will therefore only make serious efforts to publicize a small percentage of their list, and the gap between the so-called 'leads' and the 'midlist' (the books with modest advances and modest sales) is becoming wider.

While supporters of the conglomeration of the industry often maintain that the blockbusters help to subsidize the loss-making books, and it is certainly true that the ratio of books produced to those which actually make a profit is extremely high, this argument does not take account of the headstart given to a small number of books by the hugely varying sums spent on book publicity. As Whiteside explains this growing disparity in the publishing industry: 'If you are not in show business, you are really off-Broadway.'[13] The increasingly large advances paid out to star-name authors also help to encourage this inequality, because publishers naturally spend more on promoting these authors in order to recoup their initial outlay. In addition, since the largest of these advances are often reported in the press, they can function by themselves as an important source of publicity. Many publishers admit that even bestselling authors are not always expected to earn back their huge advances, which are used as a way of obtaining free publicity not only for the author but for the publishing house.[14]

The opportunities this creates for the book publishing industry to decide which authors are noticed and read by consumers are given added significance by the influence of the parent companies. All the major conglomerates involved in American book publishing have extensive additional interests in newspapers and magazines, satellite and cable television stations, CD-Roms and on-line services and, in some instances, movie, video and music production and distribution. The real significance of these conglomerates lies in the increased opportunities they afford for cross-subsidization between different strata of the same company. As Joseph Turow suggests, the critical change in the communications industries in the 1980s was that 'conglomeration was now seen as a way to link media holdings actively in the interest of greater profits'. The term commonly used to describe this kind of cooperation is *synergy*, which denotes 'the coordination of parts of a company so that the whole actually turns out to be worth more than the sum of its parts acting alone'.[15]

There is clearly great potential for synergy in the area of book publicity, which involves selling books through other mass media – magazines, newspapers, television and radio – often owned by the same parent company. Possible (although unverified) examples of such cooperation are the cover story on Scott Turow which *Time* magazine published in June 1990, at the same time as its corporate sibling Warner Books distributed *Presumed Innocent* in paperback and Warner Brothers released the film version of the same book, or the extensive profile of the then unknown Donna Tartt in the September 1992 edition of *Vanity Fair* which, like Tartt's publisher, Knopf (an imprint within Random House), was owned by Newhouse. Such profiles and interviews are prearranged long before books are subjected to press reviews or appear in bookstores, the intention being to bypass the normal critical responses which books receive, either in print media or through word of mouth, by pitching the book directly at the individual consumer.

There is also evidence that publishers have used their corporate muscle to influence the process of book reviewing, which can function as a powerful intermediary between reader and author. The complaint that commercial considerations, and in particular the power of the parent companies, can affect the production and placement of book reviews in other media has been made since the late 1960s.[16] As the synergetic interconnections between books and other kinds of media become greater, this accusation – that book reviews are inextricably linked to the process of book promotion – is likely to become even more insistent. Before Newhouse sold Random House to Bertelsmann in March 1998, for example, one independent publisher suggested that Random House had 'cornered the review space' in Newhouse-owned magazines such as the *New Yorker, Vanity Fair* and *Vogue*.[17] There is no suggestion that the influence of the parent company is in any way altering the content of the reviews, but since most books are wholly ignored by book reviewers, even bad reviews can be good publicity. Of the 8,000 books sent to the *New York Times Book Review* every year, for instance, only about 2,500 receive even a mention and only a fraction receive a full review.[18] A review on the front page of this magazine, for many years a site of 'unparalleled positional power',[19] can virtually guarantee a book's commercial success, regardless of the review's content.

The conglomerates, in other words, have put pressure on publishers to create the largest possible readership for a small number of books, by pushing commercially successful authors on to mainstream television and other media. There is thus a danger that media interest will only be generated for the kinds of authors who have a chance of making the bestsellers lists, leaving the majority of them to manage with little publicity other than press releases. Frank Rich, in a recent *New York Times* op-ed piece bemoaning the star system in publishing, puts it more forcefully when he writes that 'these days, even *Moby Dick* might not be enough to get Melville booked on *Good Morning America*'.[20] These trends have been reinforced by the growth of large book chains like Barnes and Noble and Borders, which are forming increasingly close ties with publishers, and which aim similarly to foster and promote a small number of bestselling authors by giving them particular attention through book signings and 'dumpbins' (special displays for prioritized books).[21]

The relatively concealed nature of these processes makes them even more effective in controlling the cultural marketplace. Richard Dyer, in a study of Hollywood stardom, distinguishes between two ways in which studios market films – *promotion*, or paid advertising, and *publicity*, or profiles and interviews with the stars of the film in the media – and suggests that the public tends to see the latter as less consciously manipulated by the studio and therefore more authentic.[22] The marketing strategies outlined above come under the definition of publicity rather than promotion: cover stories, book reviews and talk show appearances by authors are presented not simply as public relations exercises but as (to some extent at least) spontaneously generated by popular interest in these authors. Journalists and television interviewers thus serve, with varying degrees of willingness or unwillingness, as conduits for astutely controlled publicity.

The increasing power of publishers in this context has led George Garrett, among many others, to suggest that 'the great corruption . . . of the last half of the century has been the attempt on the part of the publishers to *create* (by fiat as much as fact) its own gallery of stars and master artists'.[23] These lavish promotional campaigns, which give an unfair advantage to certain authors in the quest for public recognition, point to a wider pattern in the media industries in general, in which the response of consumers is stabilized and standardized through the 'name recognition' of certain prominent figures. The increasing importance of book publicity in promoting authors as 'personalities' is therefore a symptom of the continuing integration of literary production into the entertainment industry, making authors and books part of the cultural pervasiveness of celebrity as a market mechanism of monopoly capitalism – the celebrity in this case being 'anyone whose name and fame have been built up to the point where reference to them, via mention, mediatized representation or live appearance, can serve as a promotional booster in itself'.[24] In this context, stardom becomes wholly self-fulfilling: the visibility of the author's celebrity name is used to bankroll products, making it harder for unknown or first-time authors and their work to gain recognition.

These developments appear to point to the ascendancy, in Bourdieu's terms, of the large-scale field of cultural production, a market in which 'success goes to success' and 'announcing a print run contributes to making a bestseller'.[25] In fact, Bourdieu's most recent work reveals a change in emphasis from his earlier accounts of literary production by critiquing what he sees as the 'regressions to heteronomy' of the cultural field, resulting from the 'increasingly greater interpenetration between the world of art and the world of money'. According to Bourdieu, this is threatening to undermine the traditional division between avant-garde and commercial production which has been in place since the mid-nineteenth century. He argues that 'the holders of cultural capital may always "regress" . . . the claim of autonomy which is inscribed in the very existence of the field of cultural production must reckon with obstacles and powers which are ceaselessly renewed'. The transformation of the American publishing scene in the last few decades would seem to support Bourdieu's concerns about the triumph of the 'doxosophes' – the media-oriented, heteronomous produc-ers who seek to manoeuvre their way into the restricted field and challenge its traditional autonomy and independence.[26]

The trade in cultural capital

While these developments in conglomerate-owned publishing are highly significant, however, they are only one aspect of the highly diversified environment in which books are marketed and consumed in the US. It is worth stressing, perhaps, that people have been criticizing the American publishing industry for many of these same flaws – trend-chasing, bestseller-fixation, excessive hype, rampant commercialism – for at least a century, if not longer. These criticisms have often originated from within the industry itself: as long ago as 1905, the publisher Henry Holt commented in an essay in the *Atlantic Monthly* that his profession was 'as crazy about advertising as the Dutch ever were about tulips'.[27] As Ken Worpole writes, 'the complaint – that publishers ignore new writing, preferring to play safe with a stock-list of general titles – dates back almost to Caxton'.[28] In fact, book publishing has proved remarkably adaptable to these commercial pressures, remaining one of the few areas of the mass media where market values have not triumphed wholesale – there are still many editors committed to 'literary' fiction even within commercially minded publishing houses, as is shown by the survival and growth of prestigious imprints such as Scribner's and Flamingo within corporate-owned publishers like Simon and Schuster and HarperCollins. The familiar argument that media conglomeration produces the triumph of short-term profit over artistic merit is thus qualified by the peculiar status of book publishing within the culture industries.

More important, perhaps, literary celebrity is not simply an effect of the increasingly promotional nature of the publishing industry – the cultural field is characterized by a perpetual conflict between internal demands and external pressures, and celebrity authors continue to ply their trade in the middle ground between cultural kudos and commercial success. Indeed, this middle ground has flourished in recent years as cultural and economic capital have become increasingly interchangeable in progressively diverse and stratified capitalist societies like the US. This has been most evident in the 1980s and 1990s in the growth of 'serious' literature as a marketable commodity, the product of a whole series of economic and cultural factors. Jason Epstein's founding of Anchor Books in 1953 initiated a 'quality paperback' revolution in the US, in which publishers exploited the low risk, more prolonged shelf life and higher returns of quality paperbacks as compared with their massmarket counterparts. (A similar development had already taken place in Britain, after the creation of Penguin Books in 1935.)

The pace of this revolution was stepped up in the 1980s, a key event being the establishment of Random House's innovative *Vintage Contemporaries* series by Gary Fisketjon in 1984, which attempted to combine commercial clout with literary prestige by marketing a stable of new and semi-established authors such as Raymond Carver, Jay McInerney and Thomas McGuane. The highly successful positioning of this series 'at the center of the crossroads of culture and commerce',[29] in Stephanie Girard's words, has since been duplicated by many other publishing houses. These new conditions have put pressure on 'literary' authors, even publicity-shy ones like Don DeLillo, Cormac McCarthy and William Gaddis, to do some promotional work by at least submitting to print interviews. 'These days', as the *New York Times* puts it, 'the most ardent apostles for art roll up their sleeves, hold their noses against the meretriciousness of the marketplace and practice a little economic determinism'.[30]

The current situation in American publishing is particularly difficult to unravel because its macro-tendencies have been accompanied by micro-tendencies. In other words, while collectivization within the industry promotes the vigorous marketing of books to as wide a readership as possible, American media have also militated against this trend by diversifying and demassifying as a product of technological and sociological change, as evidenced by the growth of interactive multimedia, so-called 'narrowcasting' on cable and satellite channels and 'niche' market magazines. In particular, more specialized magazines have proliferated and thrived in recent years because of their attraction to potential advertisers (due to the clearly defined nature and relative affluence of their readerships), and their increasingly cheap production costs. The long-term decline in circulation of popular, general interest 'consensus' magazines like *Time* and *Life* has been accompanied, therefore, by the emergence of a huge range of publications interested in writing about 'serious' authors. These range from the highbrow *Paris Review* (which has run a prestigious series of 'Writers at Work' interviews since 1953), to tabloidy outlets like *People*, to glossies like *Esquire* and *Vanity Fair*. With its annual 'Hall of Fame' ('the thirty-five people who made the year') and combination of elaborate photo spreads and higher gossip, this latter magazine has been extremely influential in bringing some of the elements of entertainment celebrity into the sphere of high culture – as David Wyatt says, it 'gives off heat precisely by confounding the distinction between copy and ad [and] trades openly on the irresistible habit of validating taste by confirming it through the visibility – the celebrity – of authors'.[31] *Vanity Fair's* approach has been contagious – the previously staid *New Yorker* broke its long-held rule against combining text with photographs in the mid-1980s, and introduced a much more gossipy, celebrity-friendly element to its pages after Tina Brown (previously at *Vanity Fair*) became editor in 1992. Newspapers such as the *New York Times* and *Washington Post*, meanwhile, have also expanded their arts, books and culture pages in recent years to incorporate author interviews, profiles and other similar features.

The willingness of both the book industry and other print media to exploit the potential of literary prizes is another factor which points to the interconnectedness of cultural and economic capital in the creation of contemporary literary fame. (Indeed, book publishers have directly sponsored and even been involved in the judging of prizes like the National Book Awards and the ABBY, the American Booksellers' Book of the Year.) These prizes help to create a kind of 'major league' of literary heavyweights by stimulating sales and inspiring media coverage, while also appealing to the existence of higher values which surpass mere commercial considerations. This direct negotiation between commercial and cultural worth is often at the root of the controversies surrounding the awards, particularly the suspicion that they provide only a veneer of intellectual and aesthetic authority, rubber-stamping bestselling success and ignoring innovative, challenging authors – a suspicion reinforced in 1974 when the Pulitzer committee rejected the judges' recommendation for the fiction prize, Thomas Pynchon's *Gravity's Rainbow*, and gave no award. But the way that publishers invest heavily in the prestige attaching to such prizes makes it clear that they are far from only being concerned uncomplicatedly with the 'bottom line'.

Their penchant for list-making is further evidence of this: Random House's recent roll-call of the hundred 'best' novels of the twentieth century, compiled with the help of authors such as Gore Vidal, A.S. Byatt and William Styron, was clearly both a successful publicity-grabbing exercise (it received wide newspaper coverage) and an attempt to claim the cultural high ground. The continued growth of literary festivals where readers can meet famous authors – such as the Arizona and Los Angeles Times Book Festivals, and the Miami Book Fair, begun in 1983 and still the largest, attracting hundreds of authors and over 400,000 people – also attests to this interlocked relationship between literature and the market. As one festival organizer puts it, these events are 'mongrels – part commerce, part art, part street fair', including book 'plugs' and signings as well as weightier lectures and panels. Clearly their main function from the publisher's viewpoint is to promote books, but the people who attend them have a variety of more elevated motives – as one author-participant, Allan Gurganus, says, they are indicative of 'a kind of righteous remnant, of people looking for some kind of spiritual existence apart from the sand-paper of the culture'.[32]

The major impetus behind the interdependent relationship between cultural and economic capital in contemporary American culture has, however, been the increased clout of the academy – one of the prime symbols and disseminators of cultural capital in capitalist societies – and its institutional sponsorship of authors. The huge growth of college bookstores after the Second World War, stimulated by a rise in enrolment on the back of the GI Bill and then the Baby Boom, has made universities a large and significant factor within the broader literary marketplace. Indeed, as Philip Fisher says, the success of the quality paperback revolution in the United States has largely been a product of the commercial success of college course texts.[33] In an era of mass education, there is a constant demand for new authors as raw material for undergraduate courses, doctoral theses, critical monographs and articles in journals like *Modern Fiction Studies, Contemporary Literature* and *Critique*. More generally, the postwar rise in college enrolment has greatly enlarged the educated reading public who are interested in buying work by new authors.

Just as important, universities have also been involved in more direct forms of sponsorship of authors through the setting up of creative writing courses and workshops, which are largely a postwar phenomenon and have mushroomed particularly over the last 20 years. The first and most celebrated writer's programme, at the University of Iowa, now stands, according to the *New York Times*, 'unshakably in the mainstream of our literary life'.[34] Although the work produced out of some of these courses is destined never to reach beyond the readerships for university quarterlies, little magazines and small-press publications, the more prestigious of them are far from being an ivory tower, a haven from the corrupted world of commerce – they are designed to feed organically into the marketplace, producing professional authors who will be of interest to mainstream magazines, agents and major publishers. It is striking, in fact, how many of the most successful literary celebrities of the last 25 years are products of writers' workshops – Raymond Carver, Jay McInerney and John Irving, to name only a few.

Perhaps the most telling indication of the influence of the universities in American cultural life is the fact that tenured academics have often become mainstream celebrities themselves: critics such as Edward Said, Harold Bloom and Camille Paglia are recognized media figures and even occasionally make the bestsellers lists in the US. Paglia is perhaps the best example of this crossover success – she has transformed herself into a media celebrity by appearing on MTV, television talk shows and both writing for and being profiled in popular magazines like *Wired, Harper's* and *Penthouse*. Her own account of the cultural resonance of female film and pop stars – most famously her claiming of Madonna as a feminist icon – has clearly contributed to her own celebrity, as has her talent for producing punchy soundbites which make their way regularly into newspapers' 'quotes of the week'. She has also developed a particularly distinctive, aggressively self-promoting public image, posing in extravagant attire on the covers of magazines and including cartoon caricatures of herself in her books.[35] Celebrities like Paglia are often controversial figures within the academy, criticized for pandering to base commercial tastes and reproducing the conservative politics of the mass media. bell hooks, for example, has suggested that Paglia's books are 'bought not for their ideas but because the hype surrounding the author entices', and accuses her and other media feminists like Katie Roiphe and Naomi Wolf of being white, privileged women presuming to speak for women in general in an 'opportunistic bid for stardom', and producing 'revamped patriarchal logic passing for "new feminism" that the mass media hypes, and that sexist men and women cheer'.[36] Paglia, meanwhile, has attacked academic critical theory, particularly the work of Jacques Lacan and Michel Foucault, and what she calls the 'PC feminism' formulated within university humanities departments.[37] Allan Bloom is another example of an academic who has achieved bestseller status (with *The Closing of the American Mind* in 1987) and a considerable degree of media attention – but not generally professional approval – by vehemently criticizing current paradigms in the humanities.

'The new mediocracy'

The phenomenon of intellectual celebrity is not, of course, unique to the United States. The peculiar status of intellectuals in French society, for example, has helped to produce a whole group of celebrity thinkers (the most famous being Bernard-Henri Lévy), who appear as frequent guests on late-night television chat shows. The most influential of these shows was Bernard Pivot's book review programme, *Apostrophes*, which ran between 1975 and 1990 and had a huge effect on the public prominence and book sales of leading intellectuals.[38] The power of television to make or break intellectual reputations in France has led Godfrey Hodgson, among others, to suggest that it is a country in which '40 mediacrats have the power of life and death over 40,000 authors'.[39] The debate in France about the role of these intellectuals offers a useful way into a discussion not only about the celebritization of academics in the US but also, more generally, the complicated mediation between cultural and economic capital I have been discussing above.

Régis Debray first criticized these developments in France in the late 1970s, deploring the way in which his country's intellectuals had forged an alliance with 'the new mediocracy'.[40] (In fact, though, the French tradition of denouncing intellectuals as 'sellouts' and traitors to their calling dates at least as far back as Julien Benda's 1927 *La Trahison des Clercs*.[41]) According to Debray, the wholesale appropriation of intellectual production by the media has produced 'an Americanized intelligentsia in Europeanized France [which] puts the emphasis on smiles, good teeth, nice hair and the adolescent stupidity known as petulance'. Debray suggests that intellectuals have been corrupted by the broadening of their constituency beyond the narrow confines of their own peer group. He argues that

> by extending the reception area, the mass media have reduced the sources of intellectual legitimacy, surrounding the professional intelligentsia, the classic source of legitimacy, with wider concentric circle that are less demanding and therefore more easily won over . . . The mass media have broken down the closure of the traditional intelligentsia together with its evaluative norms and its scale of values.[42]

One of Bourdieu's most polemical works to date, *On Television and Journalism*, is also an attack on French media intellectuals (although, like Debray's book, it mentions none of them by name). Bourdieu note witheringly that

> television rewards a certain number of *fast-thinkers* who offer cultural 'fast food' – predigested and prethought culture . . . Like the Trojan horse, [such intellectuals] introduce heteronomous agents into autonomous worlds. Supported by external forces, these agents are accorded an authority they cannot get from their peers.[43]

In fact, these comments on the usurpation of intellectual life by the journalistic field form part of Bourdieu's overall criticisms of any kind of culture which attempts to bridge the distinction between high and mass culture, what he calls the 'partial revolutions in the hierarchies' created by 'the new cultural intermediaries' who 'have invented a whole series of genre half-way between legitimate culture and mass production'. He defines' 'a culture moyenne', or middlebrow culture (typified by such culture phenomena as literary prizes, 'light' classical music and intellectual talk shows) as an 'imposture' which relies on the 'complicity of the consumers'. The kind of culture, according to Bourdieu, simply exploits the inferiority complex of an aspirant petit bourgeoisie which 'bows, just in case, to everything which looks as if it might be culture', a knee-jerk reaction which he defines as a 'cultural allodoxia, that is, all the mistaken identifications and false recognitions which betray the gap between acknowledgement and knowledge'.[44] As David Swartz points out, there is a tension in Bourdieu's work between the unmasking of the provisional nature of cultural hierarchies in his 'field' theory, and a much more prescriptive view of how intellectuals and authors should critically engage with society and culture,[45] and these comments seem to belong to this latter aspect of his work.

American cultural critics have tended to follow Bourdieu's approach in arguing that the new cultural conditions in the US represent the appropriation of high culture by mass consumption – a 'dumbing down' rather than a 'wising up'. As early as the mid-1970s, Richard Ohmann argued that a diverse network of academic and journalistic book critics, literary prize committees, editors, book publicists, metropolitan book buyers and authors now constituted 'a cultural establishment, inseparable from the market, both influencing and influenced by it', creating a literature produced and received within what he called 'a nearly closed circle of marketing and consumption, the simultaneous exploitation and creation of taste, familiar to anyone who has examined marketplace culture under monopoly capitalism'.[46] In particular, the close link between university writing courses and the broader marketplace has been condemned for promoting only certain kinds of books and authors, creating a kind of invisible screening process for contemporary fiction and poetry. Donald Morton and Mas'ud Zavarzadeh, in an article which seeks to expose the cultural politics of the fiction workshop, argue that writer's courses are 'colonized by the mass media. Cultural representations that sell in the marketplace, such as realist fiction, dominate university humanities programs.'[47] Charles Newman also points to this cosily interdependent relationship when he states that

> insofar as literature ever provided a social frame of reference, it has been obliterated by the two growth industries of the Post-Modern era – the democratized academy and the mass entertainment industry. The academy absorbs literature as a subsidiary, a paper acquisition in which assets are not redeployed but only displayed more attractively on a newly consolidated balance sheet.[48]

One of the most sustained critiques of this new situation is made by John Aldridge in his book, *Talents and Technicians*, an attack on 'assembly-line fiction', exemplified for him by such celebrity authors as Raymond Carver, Ann Beattie,

Bobbie Ann Mason, Louise Erdrich, Lorrie Moore, Jay McInerney and Bret Easton Ellis. Aldridge argues that 'such reputations as [these writers] have acquired are mainly the products of book reviews, literary gossip, and publishers' advertising and have scarcely come under examination or been ratified by serious criticism'. He sees them as a by-product of the commodification of the book business, which is now run by 'merchants operating a vast corporate enterprise engaged in the mass manufacture and promotion of books', and, echoing Boorstin's well-used phrase, claims that they 'have become familiar names mostly for being familiar names'. However, Aldridge then goes on to examine the connection between book publishing and other areas of the mass media and a new cultural establishment originating out of the universities, suggesting that this new breed of authors 'belong[s] to the first generation in American history . . . ever to be created almost exclusively through formal academic instruction in creative writing'. The writers' workshops, he argues, produce not authentic literary talents but 'clonal fabrications' of authors, whose appeal is precisely that they are standardized and safe – there is thus an almost perfect fit between the authors churned out by a process of academic accreditation and the broader demands of the marketplace.[49] To summarize: the argument in all these accounts is that various overlapping spheres or institutions – journalism, book publishing, academia – have been able to function as a kind of self-contained literary establishment helping to determine which authors receive the most public attention in contemporary American culture.

The problem with these accounts is that they suppose the existence of a 'pure' form of literary and intellectual production without the corrupting influences of money or the craving for prestige. Aldridge, for example, posits a highly romanticized vision of the 'real writer' who has been displaced by the processes he describes, someone who 'becomes a witness and an incurable isolate, doing his work alone and in secret, and being in the end not only fully aware of his otherness but coming to coddle and cultivate it'.[50] In this sense, his critique is broadly similar to the jeremiads against celebrity by Boorstin and others [. . .], in its assumption of a prelapsarian state in which major figures rise to prominence 'naturally'. Debray's unexamined notion of 'intellectual legitimacy' similarly seems to assume that literary and intellectual expression can be mediated transparently, and that when intellectuals themselves control the means of mediation, this transparency is achieved. Even Bourdieu – despite the overall emphasis in his work on the relational nature of different fields, and on the 'interestedness' of all forms of cultural production, whether obviously commercial or not – ultimately nails his cultural elitism to the mast. As R.M. Shusterman puts it: 'Bourdieu rigorously exposes the hidden economy and veiled interests of the so-called disinterested aesthetic of high culture but nonetheless remains too enchanted by the myth he demystifies to acknowledge the existence of any legitimate popular aesthetic.'[51] All these critics, then, implicitly support a dubious notion of authors or intellectuals as ethereal, detached individuals, which overlooks the kinds of capital, either economic or cultural, at stake in all forms of cultural production – the fact that writers who disseminate their ideas to a public, however narrowly defined, have always been at least partly concerned with presenting themselves competitively.

A promotional culture

It is true that there have been significant changes in the American cultural landscape in recent years, partly as a consequence of the trends to which Aldridge and others refer. The range and diversity of authors who achieve fame in contemporary culture, however, shows that American literary culture is too complex and contradictory to allow for the formation of a sealed-off cultural establishment, conspiratorially determining the rise and fall of literary reputations. In fact, the highly specific celebrity constructions of 40 or 50 years ago — notably the white, male, representatively 'American' author championed by *Time* and *Life* and epitomized in figures like Hemingway and Faulkner — have been increasingly challenged, allowing many different kinds of authors, including the less obviously 'mainstream', to be marketed as public personalities. To give one example, the celebritization of African-American women authors like Toni Morrison shows how questions of simple market appeal can merge with broader social, cultural and racially inflected issues in the construction of celebrity authorship. Morrison's transformation over the last 20 years into what the *New York Times* calls 'the nearest thing America has to a national novelist'[52] has been supported by a wide range of phenomena. Her name was clearly established by critical discussion of her work within the academy: the increasing marketability of black women authors as a whole, in fact, has been greatly stimulated by the movements towards canon revision in American universities since the 1960s. Morrison and other authors have thus benefited greatly from the growth in black studies, multicultural studies and women's studies courses (the latter being particularly receptive to black writers), as well as their integration into more general literature courses.[53]

In more recent years, however, Morrison's celebrity has been significantly reinforced by two events outside the academy — the huge media interest surrounding her Nobel Prize success in 1993 (after she had already received a series of smaller, national prizes like the Pulitzer and the National Book Award), and her promotion on Oprah's Book Club, a monthly part of Oprah Winfrey's talk show. The effects of *Oprah* on book sales were first recognized in 1993, when 250,000 extra copies of Robert James Waller's *The Bridges of Madison County* were sold after it was featured on the show. Oprah's Book Club, established soon afterwards, was one of the most important innovations in book promotion in the 1990s. Winfrey focuses on one book a month — with a bias towards black and/or women authors, who make up a large part of her audience — and every volume featured so far has gone on to make the bestsellers lists. Morrison's *Song of Solomon* became a bestseller 19 years after its first publication, as did her more recent novel, *Paradise* — a much more complex, technically innovative text which would not normally be expected to appeal to so wide a readership.

Unlike many [. . .] other celebrities [. . .], Morrison has largely welcomed her own fame and bestsellerdom, and that of other black women authors such as Terry McMillan and Alice Walker, as a way of opening up literature to wider readerships and challenging established canons. She took part in the hour-long *Oprah* special on *Paradise*, leading a study group of 20 viewers in a discussion of the novel, and says approvingly: 'Oprah uses her show to promote books to the kind of people who might be intimidated by bookshops, the people I want to reach and am keen to address.'[54] Morrison has also used her celebrity to speak out on race and gender issues

provoked by such events as the Clarence Thomas–Anita Hill hearings of 1991 and the
O.J. Simpson trial of 1995. In particular, she has sought to challenge the dominant
representations of mainstream media on these issues, dedicating herself to the task of
'representing one's own race to, or in spite of, a race of readers that understands itself
to be "universal" or race-free'.[55]

Morrison's fame – both in the way it has been constructed and the way she has
sought to use it as a model of public, socially engaged authorship – shows that recent
changes in the cultural marketplace have, at least in some cases, allowed different
literary traditions to reach new audiences and previously marginalized authors to
achieve fame and success. Morrison's celebrity has been accompanied by the new
prominence of black public intellectuals like Cornel West, Henry Louis Gates, Jr and
Michael Eric Dyson, who have written for general interest magazines and newspapers
in debates over such issues as the Rodney King riots, 'political correctness' and canon
revision. This has spilled over into bestselling books (West's *Race Matters* made the
New York Times bestsellers list in 1993 and he received lengthy profiles in both *Time* and
Newsweek as a consequence) and television appearances (Dyson has guested on talk
shows such as *Today, Good Morning America* and *Oprah*).

Aside from these shifts in contemporary canon formation, there is another
problem with the conspiratorial model put forward by Aldridge and others – the
sheer complexity of the way that literary celebrity circulates in contemporary culture,
the fact that it amounts to much more than the cumulative effect of the promotional
strategies of publishing companies and other institutions. In this context, Andrew
Wernick employs the useful term 'promotional culture' to describe the increasing
consolidation of a system of competitive exchange in ostensibly non-commercial
institutions – by which he means the permeation of the *logic* of the marketplace into
all areas of cultural life rather than the straightforward co-opting of culture into
commodity production. Wernick, for example, outlines a number of key stages in 'the
promotional constitution of the authorial name': first, the name of an individual
author is assigned to a work (a relatively recent innovation, as Michel Foucault also
points out in his essay, 'What is an Author?'); second, the author's name enters the
business of authorship and publishing, where it can be used to sell a recognized
product in a competitive marketplace; finally, this promotional name becomes
detached from the book or other product it sells, and starts to circulate separately,
becoming part of 'the vast discourse constituted by promotion as a whole'.[56]

Wernick is suggesting that, although there are direct ways in which authors can be
promoted as part of the marketing strategies of publishers and other media, the
general dissemination of different forms of publicity in contemporary culture makes
it increasingly difficult to distinguish these from other means by which the author's
name can circulate. This is a general pattern in celebrity culture as a whole: the
'imaged name' of the celebrity represents 'a banked and transferable store of promotional capital', useful in many different contexts. According to Wernick, this is what
distinguishes contemporary celebrity from older types of fame – not so much its
'mediatized artificiality' (as Boorstin might argue) but the fact that it is 'freefloating'.
The celebrity is not just the product of promotional strategies, then, but is part of
'the vortex of promotional signs . . . a great, swirling stream of signifiers whose only
meaning, in the end, is the circulatory process which it anticipates, represents and
impels'.[57]

I want to argue that the intertextuality of celebrity – the fact that it is, as Richard de Cordova points out, a discursive as well as a narrowly economic phenomenon[58] – makes the star a site of considerable ambivalence and contestation. A number of critics have examined this intertextuality through recent controversies surrounding copyright law, created by the simultaneous growth of trademark rights to protect celebrities and a more nebulous and less controllable sphere of publicity.[59] These controversies emerge from the fact that more and more institutions are seeking to market the celebrity for profit (either for economic or cultural capital), and using trademark law to protect the unauthorized appropriation of his or her 'image', at the same time as they are also losing control over that image as it disseminates inexorably through many different media. These tensions – between the exchange value of celebrity and its status as a site for disputed cultural meanings – mean that it functions as 'an ambiguous sign in contemporary culture that inscribes within and between its various forms a tension of signification'.[60] In other words, celebrity works through its own contradictions, critiquing and commenting on the tenuousness of its claims to single people out for special attention.

This allows the celebrity to function at the centre of debates about what constitutes an individual, and specifically an exceptional individual, in contemporary society, clustering around polarities such as depth and surface, authenticity and superficiality, cultural capital and commercial value. One example of this is the entertainment media's schizophrenic attitude to the stars – the same publications which publish *Hello*-style, uncritical profiles of celebrities will also frequently complain that celebrity as a whole is a shallow and trivial phenomenon, accompanying this with a debunking of stars for their inflated salaries, huge entourages, on-set tantrums and extravagant lifestyles. Similarly, although publishers and other institutions may attempt to sponsor particular authors over others, this process is not uncontested: there are countless articles in newspapers and magazines deploring the barrage of hype, the way that overrated star authors can deprive the humble foot-soldiers of attention and sales. In one sense, then, the critical comments of Aldridge and others about literary celebrity feed back into the phenomenon, reinforcing the familiar notion of celebrities as contentious figures.

In addition to this, literary celebrities are particularly controversial figures within celebrity culture as a whole because of their position at the centre of an ongoing battle about the relationship between art and money in contemporary culture. Bourdieu may argue in the comments quoted above that the balance has shifted towards the large-scale field in recent years, but one of the defining characteristics of the cultural field is still this 'chiastic structure' in the distribution of cultural and economic capital, based on the perpetual contest between two competing principles of legitimacy: autonomy and heteronomy.[61] Bourdieu's seminal work on the 'field' – as opposed to his later protests about the triumph of heteronomy – is valuable here because it recognizes the contested nature of literary production, showing the importance of border positions between different fields as a source of struggle and change. As a structuralist, Bourdieu concedes that the field of cultural production does function as a star system, in which 'what "makes reputations" is not . . . this or that influential person, this or that institution, review, magazine, academy, coterie, dealer or publisher . . . it is the field of production, understood as a system of objective relations between agents or institutions.'[62] However, he suggests that this system (as with the structure of other fields) is constantly open to negotiation and debate by individual and collective agents within the field. These debates are particularly fiercely fought in the cultural field because one of its chief characteristics is its 'weak degree of institutionalization', which means that the various positions it offers are diverse, constantly changing and always up for grabs.[63] The cultural field is also unstable because (like celebrity itself) it is constituted symbolically as well as materially, and is therefore always liable to be altered by the discourses and debates produced by the agents within it.

The role of author-recluses in celebrity culture – where the authors' apparent distance from celebrity seems to contribute to their fame – is perhaps the most obvious example of this symbolic struggle between the restricted and large-scale fields. As Philip Stevick has written:

> A substantial number of figures from the age of electronic media . . . have been famous in ways that owe nothing to television . . . it is the supreme paradox of literary fame in our century that, insofar as writers have elected to act out such marginality, they have become more central; as they have acted out such alienation, they have become integrated and embraced; and as they have acted out a kind of cultural nihilism, their culture has made them famous.[64]

The most celebrated of these recluses, of course, are J.D. Salinger and Thomas Pynchon. Salinger has given no interviews since the mid-1950s, has not published any new work since 1965, and has banned all blurbs and dustjacket photographs on the covers of his four published books, fiercely resisting any other kind of reprinting or commercial exploitation of his work. (In 1986, he took Ian Hamilton and Random House to the Supreme Court to prevent the publication of a biography which used quotations from some of his private letters.) Pynchon, while continuing to publish at longish intervals, has proved similarly elusive: there are only two widely available photographs of him and he never appears in public (he sent a stand-up comic to receive his National Book Award for *Gravity's Rainbow* in 1974). The rarity of these authors' appearances in print seems to be particularly valued in contemporary culture. The news that Salinger was to publish a short novella with a tiny Virginian publisher, Orchises Press – even though it was only a reprint of his last published story, which appeared in the *New Yorker* in 1965 – merited front-page coverage in many newspapers in January 1997.

This kind of mystique surrounds not simply authors who are never seen, but even authors who, for a variety of reasons, do not publish for long periods. Harold Brodkey's novel, *The Runaway Soul*, had a celebrated 27-year gestation period (sustained by lucrative contracts with several publishing houses) which provoked a considerable amount of media interest – the *New York Times* and the *Washington Post* both ran front-page headlines at various times reporting (mistakenly, as it turned out) that the novel was nearly finished.[65] The book, when eventually published in 1991, was an inevitable anti-climax and garnered mostly poor reviews – one critic wrote that 'death would have been a smarter career move'.[66] Truman Capote's *Answered Prayers*, which was never finished and appeared only in shortened form three years after his death, also had a very long and well-publicized incubation period. This kind of figure has become a familiar element in mainstream celebrity culture – a recent episode of *Frasier*, for example, has the eponymous radio shrink and his brother, Niles, pursuing a reclusive and rarely published author, T.H. Houghton, around the bars of Seattle, pouncing on a beermat doodle which they wrongly believe has been drawn by him, and then stealing the manuscript of his long-awaited book.

Of course, it is possible to argue that these cultural phenomena provide an indication of the all-consuming nature of the culture of celebrity, its ability to incorporate diverse and apparently unassimilable elements to its own ends. There were certainly those who argued that authors like Brodkey and Capote were inverting the terms of celebrity for their own self-promoting purposes; some saw Brodkey, in particular, as 'an amusing fraud, whose celebrity in Manhattan literary circles was a classic case of the emperor's clothes'.[67] Brodkey did prove adept at publicizing himself in various ways, telling interviewers that *The Runaway Soul* was 'too brilliant', and that he had been the inspiration for both the character of Satan in John Updike's *The Witches of Eastwick* and the Sean Connery role in the film *Indiana Jones and the Last Crusade*.[68] However, this does not explain the *peculiar* fascination with such authors in celebrity culture, which would seem to run counter to the perpetual impulse towards commodity production in monopoly capitalism. Although Brodkey's publishers, for example, were clearly able to use the publicity surrounding the book's non-appearance as a marketing strategy, the celebrity industry would not normally be able to sanction such underproduction – no Hollywood star, for example, could afford not to make films for so long without dropping off the A-list.

The appeal of such authors, then, rests primarily in the ability of celebrity to critique itself from within. As Ron Rosenbaum puts it:

> Their varieties of reticence and concealment and self-effacement cumulatively constitute a provocative dissent from the culture of self-promotion that has swept contemporary publishing, a reproof to the roaring 'white noise' . . . of the publicity-industrial complex that dominates contemporary celebrity culture.[69]

Of course, the fact that Rosenbaum's comments come in a long *Esquire* profile of Salinger – one of many to follow the author to his home in Cornish, New Hampshire and make a vain attempt to contact him by leaving a message in his mailbox – shows the extent to which this particular brand of dissent has become implicated in what it condemns. Author-recluses are thus particularly indicative of a tension (evident to a lesser degree in other kinds of literary celebrity) between what Walter Benjamin refers to as 'cult value' and 'exhibition value' – in other words, between the uniqueness and particularity of art and culture, and its reproducibility to as wide an audience as possible.[70] They represent a kind of routinization, for the purposes of the celebrity industry, of the high-culture ideal of the artist as authentic, individual genius, and of what Bourdieu calls 'the autonomous principle . . . which leads its most radical defenders to make of temporal failure a sign of election and of success a sign of compromise with the times'.[71]

These examples show that conflicts about the meaning and purpose of literary celebrity – whether they are discussions about the commercialization of literature and the ubiquity of the publicity machine, or the attempts by authors like Salinger and

Pynchon to extricate themselves from that machine – are part of the whole fabric of literary fame itself. The contemporary literary star system is still a system, then, but one with considerable internal dissonance and fluidity, which makes it difficult to view celebrity authors as simply the product of publishers' and media hype. As Jennifer Wicke puts it in a different context, 'celebrity visibility per se should not be automatically associated with corruption or selling out – our mass-cultural tag sale took place long ago. The logic of celebrity construction is complex, rich and historically specific.'[72] This is not to say that the unequal wielding of power and influence is not significant in literary reputation making: it is clear that there are vast disparities in the prominence (or lack of prominence) achieved by contemporary authors which have little to do with differences in talent, ambition or cultural relevance. Some of the processes analysed above raise important questions about the relationship between culture and the marketplace in advanced capitalist societies and the way in which certain authors can, almost imperceptibly, achieve a disproportionate share of commercial and critical attention. What I am suggesting, though, is that the market will not triumph in a straightforward, mechanical way, because cultural capital plays such a pivotal role in the construction of literary celebrity, with often surprising consequences not caught by simple oppositions between markets and cultures. Above all, the contemporary literary star system attests to the persistence of the notion, in spite of the changes to the cultural marketplace outlined above, of the world of art and culture as what Bourdieu describes as 'a sacred island systematically and ostentatiously opposed to the profane world of production, a sanctuary for gratuitous, disinterested activity in a universe given over to money and self-interest'.[73]

Notes

1   Thomas Whiteside, *The Blockbuster Complex: Conglomerates, Show Business and Book Publishing* (Middletown, CT: Wesleyan University Press, 1981), p. 192.

2   Lewis A. Coser, Charles Kadushin and Walter Powell, *Books: The Culture and Commerce of Book Publishing* (New York: Basic Books, 1982), pp. 202–5.

3   M.P. Levin, 'The Marketing of Books – A National Priority for the Eighties', *Library Trends*, vol. 33, no. 2 (1984): 199.

4   West, *American Authors and the Literary Marketplace*, p. 17.

5   Quoted in Ted Solataroff, 'The Literary-Industrial Complex', *New Republic*, 8 June 1987, p. 28.

6   Coser et al., *Books*, pp. 206, 158.

7   C. Anthony, 'Beating the Drum for Books', *Publishers' Weekly*, 30 November 1992, p. 27.

8   Whiteside, *The Blockbuster Complex*, p. 34.

9   Random House's court battle with Joan Collins in February 1996, in which the publishers unsuccessfully sued Collins for the return of $1.2 million as part of a two-book contract after receiving manuscripts which they deemed unpublishable, was portrayed in the press as a blow for the celebrity novel but actually illustrated the ways in which big-name authors are treated differently by publishers. The contract had only stipulated the submission of two 'complete' novel manuscripts, with no caveat about the quality of the work received, an unusual arrangement which would not have been signed with a non-celebrity.

10   Edwin McDowell, 'Coaches Help Authors to Talk Well to Sell Well', *New York Times*, 2 March 1988.

11   Richard Schickel, *His Picture in the Papers: A Speculation on Celebrity in America, Based on the Life of Douglas Fairbanks, Sr.* (New York: Charterhouse, 1973), p. 27; see also deCordova, *Picture Personalities*, p. 46.

12   Michael Norman, 'A Book in Search of a Buzz: The Marketing of a First Novel', *New York Times Book Review*, 30 January 1994.

13   Whiteside, *The Blockbuster Complex*, p. 198.

14   James B. Twitchell, *Carnival Culture: The Trashing of Taste in America* (New York: Columbia University Press, 1992), p. 100.

15   Joseph Turow, 'The Organizational Underpinnings of Contemporary Media Conglomerates', *Communication Research*, vol. 19, no. 6 (1992): 688, 683.

16   See, for example, Richard Ohmann, *Politics of Letters* (Middletown, CT: Wesleyan University Press, 1987), pp. 72, 75; Richard Kostelanetz, *The End of Intelligent Writing: Literary Politics in America* (New York: Sheed and Ward, 1974), p. 64.

17   Joanna Coles, '$$$$$$$$$$$ That's Publishing!', *Guardian*, 30 April 1993.

18   Michael Norman, 'Reader by Reader and Town by Town, a New Novelist Builds a Following', *New York Times Book Review*, 6 February 1994.

19   Kostelanetz, *The End of Intelligent Writing*, p. 91.

20   Frank Rich, 'Star of the Month Club', *New York Times*, 23 March 1997.

21   Doreen Carvajal, 'Book Chains' New Role: Soothsayers for Publishers', *New York Times*, 12 August 1997.

22   Richard Dyer, *Stars* (London: BFI, 2nd edn 1998), pp. 60–1.

23   George Garrett, ' "Once More Unto the Breach, Dear Friends, Once More": The Publishing Scene and American Literary Art', *Review of Contemporary Fiction*, vol. 8, no. 3 (Fall 1988): 15.

24   Andrew Wernick, *Promotional Culture: Advertising, Ideology and Symbolic Expression* (London: Sage, 1991), p. 106.

25   Bourdieu, *The Rules of Art*, p. 147.

26   Ibid., pp. 367, 343–7.

27   Quoted in James Surowiecki, 'The Publisher's Curse', *New York Times Magazine*, 31 May 1998.

28   Worpole, *Reading By Numbers*, p. 16.

29   Stephanie Girard, ' "Standing at the Corner of Walk and Don't Walk": Vintage Contemporaries, *Bright Lights, Big City*, and the Problems of Betweenness', *American Literature*, vol. 68, no. 1 (March 1996): 161.

30   Norman, 'A Book in Search of a Buzz'.

31   David Wyatt, *Out of the Sixties: Storytelling and the Vietnam Generation* (Cambridge: Cambridge University Press, 1993), p. 51.

32   Peter Applebome, 'Festivals Booming Amid Publishing Gloom', *New York Times*, 7 April 1998.

33   Philip Fisher, 'Introduction: The New American Studies', in idem (ed.), *The New American Studies: Essays from Representations* (Berkeley, CA: University of California Press, 1991), p. ix.

34   Maureen Howard, 'Can Writing Be Taught at Iowa?', *New York Times Magazine*, 25 May 1986.

35   For example, Paglia posed for *Vanity Fair* in 1992, in her own words, 'in full vamp drag, with fake red nails and my arms around the bulging biceps of two

black bodyguards'. See Camille Paglia, 'Downfall of a Glittering Star', *Observer*, 12 July 1998.

36 bell hooks, *Outlaw Culture: Resisting Representations* (New York: Routledge, 1994), pp. 83, 92, 88. For other negative critiques of Paglia, see Sandra M. Gilbert, 'Freaked Out: Camille Paglia's *Sexual Personae*', *Kenyon Review*, vol. 14, no. 1 (1992): 158–64, and Jennifer Wicke, 'Celebrity Material: Materialist Feminism and the Culture of Celebrity', *South Atlantic Quarterly*, vol. 93, no. 4 (Fall 1994): 754–6.

37 See Camille Paglia, 'Junk Bonds and Corporate Raiders: Academe in the Hour of the Wolf', in idem, *Sex, Art, and American Culture: Essays* (New York: Vintage, 1992), pp. 170–248, and 'The M.I.T. Lecture: Crisis in the American Universities', in ibid., pp. 249–98.

38 Pierre Bourdieu, *On Television and Journalism*, tr. Priscilla Parkhurst Ferguson (London: Pluto Press, 1996), p. 93.

39 Godfrey Hodgson, 'A Backsliding, Backscratching Elite', *British Journalism Review*, vol. 9, no. 2 (1998): 71.

40 Régis Debray, *Teachers, Writers, Celebrities: The Intellectuals of Modern France*, tr. David Macey (London: New Left Books, 1981), p. 1.

41 Benda himself had bitter experience of the corruptions of literary politics: he was deprived of the Prix Goncourt, France's most prestigious literary prize, in 1912 because of his vocal support for Dreyfus.

42 Debray, *Teachers, Writers, Celebrities*, pp. 165, 81.

43 Bourdieu, *On Television*, pp. 29, 59.

44 Bourdieu, *Distinction*, pp. 323–26.

45 David Swartz, *Culture and Power: The Sociology of Pierre Bourdieu* (Chicago, IL: University of Chicago Press, 1997), p. 222.

46 Ohmann, *Politics of Letters*, pp. 75, 71.

47 Donald Morton and Mas'ud Zavarzadeh, 'The Cultural Politics of the Fiction Workshop', *Cultural Critique*, vol. 11 (Winter 1988–89): 169.

48 Newman, *The Post-Modern Aura*, p. 131.

49 John W. Aldridge, *Talents and Technicians: Literary Chic and the New Assembly-Line Fiction* (New York: Charles Scribner's Sons, 1992), pp. xii, 7, 9, 15, 28.

50 Ibid., pp. 28–9.

51 R.M. Shusterman, *Pragmatic Aesthetics* (Oxford: Blackwell, 1992), p. 172, cited in Bridget Fowler, *Pierre Bourdieu and Cultural Theory: Critical Investigations* (London: Sage, 1997), p. 152.

52 Cited in Jason Cowley, 'Writing is My Work, But Not My Job', *The Times*, 5 May 1998.

53 See Edwin McDowell, 'Black Writers Gain Audiences and Visibility in Publishing', *New York Times*, 12 February 1991.

54 Cowley, 'Writing is My Work'.

55 Toni Morrison, *Playing in the Dark: Whiteness and the Literary Imagination* (Cambridge, MA: Harvard University Press, 1992), p. xii; see also Toni Morrison, 'The Official Story: Dead Man Golfing', in Toni Morrison and Claudia Brodsky Lacour (eds), *Birth of a Nation'hood: Gaze, Script, and Spectacle in the O.J. Simpson Case* (London: Vintage, 1997), pp. vii–xxviii.

56 Andrew Wernick, 'Authorship and the Supplement of Promotion', in Maurice Biriotti and Nicola Miller (eds), *What is an Author?* (Manchester: Manchester University Press, 1993), pp. 92–6.

57   Wernick, *Promotional Culture*, pp. 109, 121.

58   deCordova, *Picture Personalities*, p. 11.

59   See, for example, Jane M. Gaines, *Contested Culture: The Image, The Voice, and The Law* (London: BFI, 1992), Rosemary J. Coombe, 'The Celebrity Image and Cultural Identity: Publicity Rights and the Subaltern Politics of Gender', *Discourse*, vol. 14, no. 3 (1992): 59–87, and George M. Armstrong, Jr, 'The Reification of Celebrity: Persona as Property', *Louisiana Law Review*, vol. 51, no. 3 (1991): 443–68.

60   Marshall, *Celebrity and Power*, p. x.

61   Bourdieu, *Distinction*, p. 122.

62   Bourdieu, *The Field of Cultural Production*, p. 78.

63   Bourdieu, *The Rules of Art*, pp. 383, 256.

64   Philip Stevick, 'The World and the Writer: A Speculation on Fame', *South Atlantic Quarterly*, vol. 85, no. 3 (1986): 251.

65   James Wood, 'Literary Calculations', *Guardian*, 29 January 1996.

66   Quoted in Michael Arditti, 'A Stylist in Search of a Style', *Independent*, 18 December 1998.

67   'Obituary: Harold Brodkey', *The Times*, 29 January 1996.

68   Julian Loose, 'The Great, Brave Journey: Harold Brodkey', *Sunday Times*, 27 March 1994.

69   Ron Rosenbaum, 'The Man in the Glass House', *Independent on Sunday*, 7 September 1997.

70   Walter Benjamin, 'The Work of Art in the Age of Mechanical Reproduction', in idem, *Illuminations*, ed. Hannah Arendt, tr. Harry Zohn (London: Fontana, 1973), pp. 226–7.

71   Bourdieu, *The Rules of Art*, pp. 216–17.

72   Wicke, 'Celebrity Material', 757.

73   Pierre Bourdieu, *Outline of a Theory of Practice*, tr. Richard Nice (Cambridge: Cambridge University Press, 1977), p. 197.

Chapter 18

C. L. Cole and David L. Andrews

AMERICA'S NEW SON
Tiger Woods and America's multiculturalism[1]

Oprah Winfrey:	Well, you don't have to know what a birdie or bogey is to love my guest today. You don't need to understand par. You don't even have to like golf, because Tiger Woods transcends golf. He is magical and he's mesmerizing. He's just what our world needs right now, don't you think?
Audience:	(*In unison*) Yeah!
Oprah Winfrey:	Whoo! Whoo! I call him America's son.

(*Oprah Winfrey Show*, April 24, 1997)

Introduction

TYPICAL OF HER INSPIRING insights that resonate with mainstream sensibilities, and which have made her the most influential woman in American entertainment today, Oprah Winfrey's declaration extends the euphoric public consensus evidently reached over Tiger Woods (the show was taped soon after Woods' victory at the 1997 US Masters). Winfrey's proclamation enlists elements embedded in popular discourses – particularly elements encoded through and aligned with race, family, and nation – that facilitated and framed Woods' march into the American consciousness. Invoking the national familial bond, Winfrey identifies Woods as an "antidote" to the anxieties weighing down America ("the world") at the end of the century. Although the anxieties remain unnamed, Woods enters a context defined by the regular fanning of apprehensions about and celebrations of America's multicultural racial future: racially-coded celebrations which deny social problems and promote the idea that America has achieved its multicultural ideal. At the same time, racially thematized crises related to sexuality, family, crime, welfare, and moral depravity, normalize the policing and punishment of already vulnerable populations. This dynamic is encoded and enacted in the rhetoric of color-blindness which guides, for example, the argument that America no longer needs race-conscious affirmative action programs. Ironically, contemporary debates about the role of race and ethnicity in public policy declare the importance of not being classified by race while panics regularly surface over the ever impending demotion of the white population from the statistical majority.

Woods, an appointed symbol of national multiracial hybridity, is an element in the stabilizing "narrative of continuity" (Jeffords, 1993) that furnishes Oprah's American audience with a reassuring sense of self. After all, the virtuous Woods was born in a contemporary America defined by affirmations of color-blindness and the close association of, even slippage between, America and the world. The universalism invoked by Winfrey's extended valorization of America's new *son* directs attention to an imagined international – national future – present. In that imagination and in an era of global restructuring, America has assigned itself a privileged and superior moral position.

We contend that Winfrey's rhetorical question and directive, "He's just what our world needs right now, don't you think?", reference dominant ways of thinking about nation, race, and progress which govern American popular cultural politics. Thus, we seek to investigate how the narrative around Woods participates in normalizing and routinizing these ways of thinking. In particular, we consider the relations among a prominent reactionary sensibility and politics (as they are regularly expressed in the related logics of anti-affirmative action and white victim masculinity) and the facilitation of a multinational (upwardly mobile) sporting figure as the prototypical future–present American. In order to begin to "make sense" of the duplicitous optimism invested in the national icon Tiger Woods, we build on Lauren Berlant's (1996) analysis of the state of American citizenship in the last decades of the twentieth century.

Facing America's future

Berlant argues that the contemporary formation of American citizenship pivots around heteronormativity, personal acts, and a national intimacy generated through the mass media. Within this conjuncture, a new sexual politics (expressed and authorized most virulently through the *hyper*mythologized American family) now regularly trades places with and suppresses the experience of economic and political injustice. Moreover, the mass media – with the exception of a slew of populist products aligned with the new moral politics – replaces and demonizes any semblance of public debate and activism.

Central to Berlant's explanation of the new citizenship is the invention and promotion of a series of *new* "faces of America": computer-generated, racially hybridized, *feminine* representations of a future, post-white, American populace. Such simulations have appeared on the covers of *Time* and *Mirabella*, and have even shaped the latest rendition of the Betty Crocker brand embodiment. As Berlant depicts it, these cybergenetic visions of the future, multiracial American citizenry are constituted by an amalgam of racially hybridized phenotypes (skin tone, facial structure, hair, etc.). Such simulations, Berlant argues, are imagined to be civic and commercial solutions to the "problems of immigration, multiculturalism, sexuality, gender, and (trans)national identity that haunt the U.S. in the present tense" (1996, p. 398).

Like Berlant, we contend that despite their progressive appearance, such representations of America's racial future are aligned with a regressive racial politics. This racial politics is embedded in a national familial politics that, by our view, has accompanied and is inseparable from, the crisis of white masculinity (for the campaign to strengthen white masculine privilege routinely escalates the rhetoric of family values). In its most recent version, a prominent masculinity is figured around the popular belief that white men (the future minority) are the new persecuted majority. Moreover, in post-civil rights America, minuscule advances made by women and people of color are imagined as the impediments to white men's access to the means of making their own destinies. In other words, women and people of color are perceived as *the* restraints on white men's realization of the American way of life. In the white male victim imaginary, the American Dream itself has been extinguished . . . for white men.

Enter Eldrick "Tiger" Woods, characterized as "a breath of fresh air." Indeed, Wood's cultural significance is inseparable from the figures (explicit and implicit) over and against which he is defined. Woods, a critic for *Business Week* explains, is a breath of fresh air for an American public "tired of trash-talking, spit-hurling, head-butting sports millionaires" (Stodghill, 1997, p. 32). Although race is not explicitly mentioned, Stodghill's reference is clearly to African American professional basketball players who are routinely depicted in the popular media as selfish, insufferable, and morally reprehensible. Woods' cultural significance is further implicated in the politics of post-national familial multiculturalism and mediated intimacy that govern ways of thinking about America's future citizenry:

> But times are changing. Interracial marriage and reproduction are on the upswing, and a new generation of post-1960s multiracial children is demanding recognition, not in the margins of society but as a mainstream of their own . . . To get a glimpse of its future, look at Eldrick "Tiger" Woods, the golf prodigy. His mother, from Thailand, is half Thai, a quarter Chinese, and a quarter white. His father is half black, a quarter Chinese and a quarter American Indian.
>
> (Page, 1996, pp. 284–5)

It is our contention that Tiger Woods is an extraordinary exemplar of the new American logic. That is, Woods is the masculine extension of the already familiar hybridized American [feminine] face invested in white American culture. As such, he is the latest (but perhaps the first masculinized) rendition of the American supericon: a commercial emblem who makes visible and concrete late modern America's narrative of itself as a post-historical nation of immigrants. Woods thus embodies the imagined ideal of being and *becoming* American which, in its contemporary form, requires proper familial affiliations and becoming the global-American. As a figure embedded in and who renders multiple national narratives comprehensible, it is no wonder Woods appears to be a "universally celebrated" example of "America's son" – the "new commercial stereotype advertising the future of national culture" (Berlant, 1996, p. 417).

In this chapter, our preliminary discussion of the unfolding Tiger Woods phenomenon, we seek to clarify some of the dynamics governing the national euphoria inscribed on Woods. Here, we offer a critical–contextually based reading of the promotional discourses (primarily, but not exclusively, those emanating from Nike Inc.) which contributed to the fabrication of Tiger Woods as a national crisis resolving, *new face* of America. We concentrate on a period defined by his joining the PGA Tour (August 1996) and his winning the US Masters in April 1997. We contend that the commercialized multicultural masculinity advanced through and around Woods is the latest in America's imagined realization of its ideals (agency, equality, responsibility, and freedom) and its imagined transformed sense of national self (America has become the world that came to it). Indeed, we argue that the representation of national ideals through the global multiculturalism inscribed on Woods tacitly extends optimistic ways of thinking about the nation (the post-Cold War resurgence of American nationalism) which are constitutive of racism directed at America's non-white populations in general, and the African American population in particular. The multicultural future-present embodied by Tiger Woods is deeply implicated in expressions related to America's declared color-blindness and white male as victim fantasies.

Nike's national *Moment in the Making*

According to the "origin stories" which ostensibly document Woods' rise to national prominence, the American public has long recognized Tiger Woods' exceptionalism. Numerous video-clips of the child-Tiger's accomplishments are sutured together and recirculated to provide evidence of an America collectively anticipating a sporting, cultural, and economic phenomenon in the making. We (the American populace) watch America watching a precocious (in terms of ability) and atypical (in terms of racial difference) child-golfer drawing the attention of the "human interest" popular media. Clips featuring the child-Tiger from television programs such as *The Mike Douglas Show, That's Incredible*, and *Eye on L.A.* are recast in ways that position each as a snapshot in the national family album. Images of a playful freedom embodied by the young Woods are accompanied by clips of a comically-impressed Bob Hope, James Stewart, and Mike Douglas. Such images evoke sentimental feelings as they suggest that we have caught a glimpse of the national record of America's white patriarchs previewing and approving the figure of the nation's future.

National intimacy was encoded and enacted through these recontextualized media clips of the child-Woods. Through the trite machinations of the American popular media, Tiger Woods was positioned and confirmed as America's son. Relatedly, Woods' personal achievements were easily translated into national accomplishments. Recollections of his ground-breaking successes on the golf course (most notably winning his first tournament at the age of eight, an unprecedented three US Junior National Championships, three straight US Amateur Tournaments, and appearing in the 1992 Nissan Los Angeles Open as a high school sophomore) corroborate the fantasy of a conflict-free and color-blind America.

Stirred by the aftermath of his record breaking third consecutive victory at the US Amateur Championship and media speculation over his decision to leave the amateur ranks during August of 1996, Woods' popular presence reached a new intensity.

Indeed, Woods' immediate future became a focal point of media, and therefore, national attention. His announced decision to enter the PGA Tour was greeted with much enthusiasm by Tim Finchem, the PGA Tour commissioner. Finchem, speaking on ABC's *Nightline* (September 2 1996), defined the characteristics that made Woods a welcome addition into the professional fold:

> I just think that there are three major elements to Tiger Woods. One is his, his, the level of his competitive skills he has demonstrated time and time again. Secondly, he is from a multi-racial ethnic background which makes him unique. And, third is, he has exhibited the poise, and the integrity, and the image, of the kind of players who have performed well on the PGA Tour. And that is the package, and it's a very marketable package.

Finchem's *very marketable package* was taken up, in much the same vein, by the expectant titans of the American sport industry. Mark McCormack's International Management Group (IMG) had so aggressively courted the 15-year-old Woods that they offered his father, Earl Woods, a paid position as "talent scout" for the American Junior Golf Association (whose tournaments his son was then dominating). Upon turning professional, Woods *officially* signed with IMG. He also signed a $40 million five-year sponsorship deal with Nike, which expected that Woods' racial difference *and* prodigious talent would "revolutionize" the public's relation to golf. That is, Nike anticipated that Woods, as a multi-market endorser, would resuscitate their stagnant golf division and, in so doing, significantly bolster the company's overall profits. The success of America's latest revolution, orchestrated around Woods' body and style, would be measured in terms of the diversification and expansion of the market for golf-related products and services both within the United States and abroad.

On Wednesday August 28, 1996; two days after Tiger turned professional and on the eve of the Greater Milwaukee Open, Woods held his first press conference as a PGA Tour player. At the microphone, a seemingly sheepish Woods intoned, "I guess, hello world." The familiar global address simultaneously insinuated the decline of national boundaries and trumpeted the significance of Nike's latest worldly American citizen. The *faux* spontaneity of this carefully scripted sound-byte was made evident when, the next day, Nike launched a print and television advertising campaign featuring Woods, entitled "Hello World." Despite a chain of events intimating Nike's swift and creative response to a national moment in the making, the national moment in the making, was, no doubt, an example of the sort of strategic marketing that placed Nike at the vanguard of contemporary promotional culture (Wernick, 1991).

The "Hello World" television campaign introduced Woods (as he was apparently introducing himself to "the world at large" [Allen, 1996, p. 11C]), by interspersing, and overlaying, the following text between and upon images of his early golfing exploits and recent successes at US Amateur championships:

> Hello world.
> I shot in the 70s when I was 8.
> I shot in the 60s when I was 12.

I won the US Junior Amateur when I was 15.
Hello world.
I played in the Nissan Open when I was 16.
Hello world.
I won the US Amateur when I was 18.
I played in the Masters when I was 19.
I am the only man to win three consecutive US Amateur titles.
Hello world.
There are still courses in the US I am not allowed to play because of the
    color of my skin.
Hello world.
I've heard I am not ready for you.
Are you ready for me?

Wood's recitation was accompanied by an emotive musical score, whose pseudo-African tones and timbre added to the dramatic – and the familiarly exotic – content of the visual narrative.

As Nike's "Hello World" advertisement reinforced a familiar aesthetic, it seemingly presented a challenge to America by disrupting and violating America's unwritten racist ("no national critique, particularly in terms of racism or sexism") code. By highlighting Woods' energy, skill, and earned successes, and then deliberately confronting America with a "racial dilemma," America's ideals of color-blindness and proper citizenship were – at least apparently – frankly violated and questioned. Moreover, while previous annotations to the burgeoning Woods phenomenon exploited his difference in ways that maintained a non-threatening ambiguity concerning his *precise* racial identity, the "Hello World" campaign flouted such American racial propriety by "determining" his African Americanness. According to Henry Yu, a professor of history and Asian American studies at UCLA, the "Hello World" campaign was evidence of Nike's attempt to *African Americanize* Woods: "To Nike (*at least at this juncture*), he was African American" (Yu, 1996, p. 4M, italics added).

Race carding and white victim masculinity

The abundance of popular counters to the "Hello World" campaign intimate the force accrued by America's color-blind credo and codification of citizenship – the suppression of the specter of racial politics – over the last two decades. Reactionary critiques habitually invoked the rhetoric of "the race card" which had been exceptionally promoted and legitimated through the media's coverage of the O.J. Simpson trial (Higginbotham *et al.*, 1997). As one critic neatly summarized the accusation: "In Tiger's case, the race card was quickly slapped on the table. Dealt face-up and from the bottom of the commercial deck" (Spousta, 1996, p. 1C).

The race card is a primary and explicit expression of the regulatory logic that governs discourses around race in the USA. As an accusatory category, it implies that the introduction of racial divisions is inappropriate and unfair. Moreover, it implies that consciousness of race is itself an obstacle to racial equality. Drawing attention to restrictions based on the color of Woods' skin violates, according to anti-affirmative action logic, America's unquestioned obedience to the doctrines of individualism and meritocracy.

At least from one available point of view, then, "Hello World" relies on the strategy of race carding. From this point of view, it is an expression of the imagined victimization of white males. Other criticisms of the campaign are also symptomatic of this barely submerged anxious white masculinity. That Woods' destiny was not shaped by his talent alone was a popular, repeated, and revealing response:

> It is funny how it works. Part of Woods' appeal is his race. If he were just another blond-haired, blue-eyed golfer, he wouldn't be this overnight marketing phenomenon. He would be just another blond-haired haired, blue-eyed golfer struggling to finish in the top 125 in earnings to gain exempt status on the PGA Tour.
>
> (Knott, 1996, p. B1)

In his comments about Nike's promotional strategy, noted sports journalist John Feinstein expressed familiar anti-affirmative action rhetoric as he named race as the key dimension of his extraordinary marketability. For Feinstein, Woods was:

> the great black hope for golf . . . The fact that Nike is marketing him as a black player, not just as a talented player, but as a black player, tells you that all this money that's being thrown in his direction has as much to do with the color of his skin and his ability to be a role model as it does with his golf.
>
> (*Nightline*, September 2, 1996)

While such expressions of resentment are entangled in contemporary white male identity, blame was not directed at Woods. Instead, racial consciousness was seen to be an outgrowth of Nike's opportunistic politics. For example, Spousta names Nike, not Woods, as the player of the race card:

> if any of that made you feel uncomfortable, don't squirm too much . . . Truth is, Woods never portrayed himself as our social conscious until Nike pushed him across that line . . . But it's the message that makes you wince, not the messenger, and we should embrace and celebrate Tiger as a person and a player. Watching him develop into a champion should be a great adventure for fans of any color.
>
> (Spousta, 1996, p. 1C)

And, in one of the most revealing moments of displacement, *Advertising Age*'s Rance Crain admonished Nike for Woods' "militant, almost angry stance" (1997, p. 13).

The theme of Nike's mismanagement of Woods' identity is a rhetorical mechanism that sidesteps critical reflection on national racial politics. In addition, it makes Woods a casualty of Nike, and in so doing, disavows the possibility of Woods' political assertiveness. This proclamation of political "lack" locates the virtue of his personal acts through terms which designate Woods as apolitical. By extension, his apolitical, even pre-political classification is crucial to his capacity to signify personal and national "goodness." As Woods is articulated as innocent, pure, virtuous, and victimized, the possibility for multiple consumer desires and identifications are created and mobilized:

> The ad agency argues that Woods approved the ad. Woods, 20, might be mature beyond his years, but he still is 20 and perhaps somewhat naive in the ways of the world . . . Woods has never been inclined to use his influence as a bully pulpit on the issue of race and golf. He disdains the notion that he is the great black hope. He has never expressed a desire to be the best black golfer in history, only the best golfer in history . . . The world not only is at Woods' feet, it is on his side. Why would Nike see fit to embroil him in a senseless, needless controversy that threatens to turn some against him, from day one of his career?
>
> (Strege, 1996, p. D10)

In response, Nike reclaimed the critics' charges and announced that it had intentionally fashioned a highly charged advertisement. Jim Small, Nike's director of public relations, embraced the controversy by depicting the conflict as indicative of Nike's success: "The very fact that it made people so uncomfortable shows it did what it was intended to. We hit the nail on the head" (quoted in Custred, 1996, p. 27). But the popular investment in Woods, despite the controversy surrounding the advertisement, suggests that the "Hello World" campaign did not significantly discomfort national consumers. Instead, Nike and Tiger Woods were united in the pursuit of another of America's favorite pastimes – the hailing of American consumers through, what paraphrasing Cornell West (1988) might be called, pragmatic symbols (symbols through which America tells stories about itself).

Although the "Hello World" campaign identified and named racism, it did so through the familiar and acceptable terms of social criticism. Capitalizing on narratives already in place – and particularly narratives that America loves to consume through sport – Woods' entry into professional golf was cast as an event of national magnitude. Consumer identification was invited and secured by cloaking Woods in a swathe of overtly patriotic sentiment: he was vaunted as an emblem of racial progress, a righter of wrongs à la foundational figures such as Jackie Robinson and Arthur Ashe. Indeed, the extraordinary proliferation of allusions to Jackie Robinson surrounding Tiger underscores the sort of pleasures promised to American consumers. Thus, the "Hello World" campaign announced itself as America's quintessential tantalizing tale of racial progress: one that combined race, sport, masculinity, national healing, and proper citizenship. As Woods and Nike crossed the final sporting frontier (a remote sector of a frontier typically conflated with the American way of life and the American Dream), consumers, hailed as compassionate, informed citizens, were invited to recollect mediated national-ethical moments of the past and to participate in a national-familial-ethical moment of the present.

In this way, Tiger Woods became the latest version of a commercialized raced masculinity implicated in political backlash while certifying national transformation, progress, and equality (see Andrews, 1996; Cole, 1996). One commentator pointedly captured the conservative "some of my best friends . . ." orientation of Tiger Woods' enthusiastic appropriation by the hearts and minds of the American establishment:

the core constituency of golf, those "members only" who have managed to make the country club, after the church, the most segregated institution in America, think Tiger will get people off their backs. How can you call golf racist now, you liberal jogger, just look who we invited to tee?

(Lipsyte, 1996, p. 11)

Woods, like Colin Powell, Michael Jordan, and Oprah Winfrey, was thus used by the populist defenders of core American values and ideologies (i.e. those cultural producers operating within the ratings-driven media- and poll-driven centrist politics), as self-evident proof of the existence of a color-blind meritocracy. So, in a time of increasing racial polarization along social and economic lines (cf. Kelley, 1997; Wilson, 1997), Tiger Woods emerged as a popular icon from whom the American populace could derive a sense of intimacy, pride, and reassurance.

To the extent that Woods was perceived to be an activist, it was clearly a nationally sanctioned activism linked to media, family, and consumption. In this case, a familiar dramatic and heroic narrative – in and through which consumers could participate – was fabricated against the backdrop of an exceptional experience. In a national context ostensibly already devoid of racism, Woods and Nike had identified a local and temporary situation of racial discrimination in the private and protected elite space of golf. Moreover, its already given and expeditious resolution to make golf the place of the people (all people, regardless of race or sex, now seemingly had the right to participate in the multiple consumption practices surrounding golf) would be mediated "live." *Under the guise* of public debate and intervention, America's self-congratulatory mood was affirmed. Rather than encouraging critical thought about contemporary national politics and the complexity of racism, the "Hello World" campaign relied on and reproduced a mediated-patriotism. Ironically, racial discrimination, formulated as a holdover from another time, was used to reauthorize the nation's view of itself as beyond race.

America's post-historical *everyman*

During the Fall of 1996, the media coverage of Tiger Woods reached extraordinary proportions following his victories at the 1996 Las Vegas Invitational and 1996 Walt Disney World/Oldsmobile Classic tournaments. As much as they were interested in his exploits on the golf course, the popular media were obsessively concerned with documenting, and thereby advancing, the "Tigermania" seemingly sweeping the nation. Paradoxically, Tigermania was represented through the dramatically increased viewing and attendance figures for tournaments and blanket media coverage incited by the popular media (Potter, 1997; Stevens and Winheld, 1996; Williams, 1996).

Nike, in a moment symptomatic of the expansion of Woods' celebrity-citizenship, debuted their second Tiger Woods commercial. Nike's Tiger Woods Mk II was revealed to an expectant prime time American public during coverage of IMG's made-for-TV "Skin's Game", which ran on the ABC network over the Thanksgiving Day 1996 weekend. Nike undermined any sparks from the "Hello World" backlash as it capitalized on Woods' accruing cultural capital as the unequivocal embodiment of America's future multicultural citizenry. Capitulating to dominant cultural norms and values in a more banal – and therefore – even more powerful way, Nike contributed to the fabrication of Woods as the latest version of the *new* face of America.

Woods' apparently re-engineered racial image was facilitated via a television commercial entitled "I am Tiger Woods." The 60-second commercial's visual, a mixture of black and white and color images with still, slow, and full motion footage, was accompanied by a musical soundtrack incorporating an understated mix of drum beats and chorus harmonies. The result was a somewhat pious celebration of that which Tiger Woods had come to represent. This process of deification centered on a cast of racially diverse and geographically dispersed children (on golf courses and distinctly urban settings), who collectively embodied Nike's vision of Tiger Woods' essential heterogeneity. Moreover, they signified, by inference, the future American populace.

Borrowing the "I am . . ." strategy previously adopted in both Stanley Kubrick's *Spartacus* (1960), and more recently Spike Lee's *Malcolm X* (1992), each strategic child representative proclaimed, with varying degrees of solemnity, "I am Tiger Woods." The golfing Woods is periodically glimpsed as young males and females possessing characteristics stereotypically associated with African Americans, Asian Americans, or European Americans offer invocations of "I am Tiger Woods." The commercial ends with slow motion footage of Woods hitting a drive down the center of a tree-lined fairway. As he reaches the apex of his follow through, "I am Tiger Woods" in white text appears in the bottom center of the frame, followed by Nike's international – national sign, the obligatory swoosh.

Less than three months earlier, the "Hello World" campaign had enabled, despite its immediate displacement, the possibility of reading Woods as an outspoken racial insurgent. Now, Woods was clearly re-articulated into a multicultural figure who, like his young imitators, was framed as the pre-political and post-historical embodied manifestation of contemporary racial politics. Moreover, a significant change is claimed for the golf world: not only have we witnessed an immediate change in personnel but, golf's future will include a significantly different cast of characters. Indeed, through what Yu (1996) depicts as a shift away from Nike's African Americanized representation, Woods, Yu argues, was conclusively cast as "a multicultural godsend to the sport of golf" (ibid., p. 4M). Under the sign of multiculturalism and in America's golfing future, everyone will be included.

It was the emotive appeal of this post-historical multiculturalism that situates Oprah Winfrey's anointing of Woods as "America's son":

Oprah Winfrey:	Can we get this straight? What do you call yourself? Do you call yourself African American? I know you are – your – father's half black, quarter Chinese, quarter American Indian; your mother's half Thai, quarter Chinese and quarter white. So you are – that's why you are America's son.
Tiger Woods:	Yes.
Oprah Winfrey:	You are America's son.

(Oprah Winfrey Show, April 24, 1997)

With Oprah's designation and the ascending understanding of Woods and the nation as multicultural hybrids in the background, Woods lends authenticity to the imaginary moment by listing his multicultural qualifications. Conjuring up America's fantasy continuum (marked by a past in which the world had come to America and a present in which America had become the world), Woods locates himself:

Tiger Woods:	Yeah. I guess two things . . . is that I guess now that I'm on the Ryder Cup team, which – we get to go over and play in Europe in September – that I won't be representing the United States: I'll be representing the United Nations . . . which is a little different . . . a little funny thing is, growing up, I came up with this name. I'm a Cablinasian: Ca, Caucasian; bl, black; in, Indian; Asian – Cablinasian.
Oprah Winfrey:	That's what you call yourself?
Tiger Woods:	Yeah.

(Oprah Winfrey Show, April 24, 1997)

Woods, denying any particular allegiance, appeals to a mythic globalization and declares himself a citizen of the world. While he and the apparently complex identity he claims appear to work against the discourse of nationalism, both are very much part of it. Not only does his refined multi-racial category suggest that identity is a factual representation of genetic and cultural heritage, but it, paradoxically, reinforces the notion of the abstract person (detached from time and place) and imagines identity as voluntary (like the identity implanted in the multicultural new face of America). This is not to say that Woods is not implicated in globalization. Indeed, Woods *is* part of the international community, he *is* embedded in multiple connections to multiple places. However, those connections are economic and political, not the innocent invention of a child "growing up." National interests are naturalized through mechanisms that imagine larger global loyalties and current and familiar racial categories obsolete. Like the feminine cultural hybrids manufactured by *Time, Mirabella*, and Betty Crocker, Woods seemingly provides morally sufficient answers to the cultural, economic, and political crises afflicting the contemporary United States and its position in global capitalism.

Affirmative culture in 1990s America

In this chapter, we have introduced the salient and remarkable assertions about identity, community, and culture made in the name of America through Tiger Woods. Indeed, Woods signifies a post-national order, suggests a transnational coalition of sorts, and is imagined as a global-national antidote. In the USA, a global organic community (an organic community that links the local, national, and global) is visualized through thoroughly nationalist terms. Most distinctively, at the level of nation, Woods is coded as a multicultural sign of color-blindness.

Proclamation of the nation's venture to be color-blind, as Judith Butler explains, "is still to be related to race in a mode of blindness. In other words, race does not fall away from view, it becomes produced as the absent object that structures permissible discourse" (1998, p. 156). Keeping the productive dimensions of discursive constraints in mind, we conclude by underscoring the contradictory effects of the national multicultural myth advertised through Woods. We review how disavowals of racism, apparently principled claims of inclusivity, and declarations of color-blindness, organize the regulatory discourses about race and nation, as they are encoded and enacted around a national event called "Tigermania."

America's responses to Nike's "Hello World" campaign, as we have argued, rely on and reactivate the logic guiding opponents of racial consciousness and affirmative action. Anti-affirmative action sentiment, particularly as it has become entwined with demands for color-blindness, was most recently reinvigorated during the mid-1990s as the media focused national attention on the Board of Regents of the University of California. The UC Regents were among the first to repeal their affirmative action program. Despite the perceptible distance (geographically and conceptually) between public affirmative action debates and America's celebration of Woods, Woods' intelligibility is deeply embedded in the commonplace values expressed in and through opposition to affirmative action. Thus, Woods is a crucial transfer point in the network of resistance to affirmative action. These dynamics are illustrated in the ambivalent representations of Woods as he repeatedly is designated a racial sign of America's radical racial transformation.

As the "Hello World" campaign identified racism as a contemporary problem, the issue of racism was quickly translated into a problem of race consciousness. Evaluated through the restrictions on post-civil rights discourse, the problem was redefined in terms of *how* the category was introduced. By associating Woods with a racial category, Nike is deemed an agent of victimization. According to neo-liberal and conservative post-civil rights logic, Woods is the victim of an ill-conceived marketing strategy which denies him his deserved transcendent position.

Moreover, a logic of reverse discrimination is expressed in another of the popular responses to Woods: "It is funny how it works. Part of Woods' appeal is his race. If he were just another blond-haired, blue-eyed golfer . . . he would be just another blond-haired, blue-eyed golfer struggling" (Knott, 1996, p. B1). Such a reactive comment is symptomatic of the historical moment in which white men claim to be unfairly burdened by history. In particular, white male athletes are introduced as the new class of victims who suffer because race (rather than merit and accomplishment) determines value and marketability. Racial preference, presumed to be and presented as a violation of America's moral model (the transcendent figure who bears no marks of history is the effect of the moral model), is advanced as a fundamental issue.

"The national moment in the making" narrative (exemplified by the invitation to consumers to participate by watching "live" as Woods breaks through what is presumably the final racial barrier) seemingly departs from and intervenes in anti-affirmative action sentiments. Yet, both anti-affirmative action arguments and the national moment in the making narrative draw on the same celebrated morals that are the core of national culture. The isolation technique, which reduces racial discrimination in terms of time and space, is crucial to the event's national consumer appeal. Moreover, the already-in-place "hero," a hero encoded as an antidote to an outdated race discrimination that can be fathomed only because it exists in the "remote and elite" golf world, enhances its marketability. National intimacy is further secured as America imagines itself anticipating this hero's arrival for more than a decade. Thus, "the national moment in the making" that consumers experience is not simply a celebration of Tiger's personal accomplishments, but of America's accomplished abolition of golf's elitism. Both the technique of isolation and the mediation of the event establish a national intimacy that allows consumer-citizens to take part in this intimate national event.

Relatedly, Tiger is codified through terms that deny and inscribe, in ways that are specifically anti-African American, racialized Othering. Indeed, the precise terms of opposition through which Tiger is interpreted as "a breath of fresh air" (Stodghill, 1997, p. 32) are telling. The phrase easily recalls the now familiar demonizing representations of generations of African American NBA players whose diverse infractions are routinely translated into a criminalized contempt for authority. And, more often than not, those infractions are taken up as a sign of a collective irresponsible sexuality and consumption. Woods, in this case, is offered as a carefully hued multiracial *response* to what is widely considered to be the primary *source* of the dissolution of the familial and – by extension – the national core culture: the regularly pathologized African American population (cf. Reeves and Campbell, 1994; Scott, 1997; Smith, 1994).

Given the prominence of reproduction and family in the contemporary national politics of intimacy, the declaration of Woods as America's new son is telling. Again, in a historical moment in which African American athletes are routinely characterized as engaging in non-familial sexual relations, Woods is represented as the embodiment of normal, immigrant-familial America. Like the other simulated multicultural figures discussed by Berlant, Woods' very existence sanctions the "disinvestment in many contexts of African-American life in the present tense," and points to a "new citizenship-form that will ensure the political future of the core national culture" (Berlant, 1996, p. 424).

Woods, America's *multicultural* son, is a seductive element in a national image archive figured on the paradoxical claims about the nation. While African American basketball players are regularly charged with violating national core values, Woods has become revered for his cultural heritage and cultural literacy. Aware that earlier promotional incarnations of Tiger Woods' persona had created media and popular interest but not the desired level of commodity consumption, Nike sought to appeal to the "classic" golfer (i.e. middle class and white) whose high levels of disposable income bolstered the golf economy. So, Nike's Tiger Woods strategizing sought to evoke a brand image that was "more Armani than Gap" (Meyers, 1998, p. 2B). This involved the use of more conservative designs and materials for the Tiger Woods apparel collection and, more crucially, it signalled a distinct change in the way Woods was represented within Nike advertising campaigns. This shift is exemplified in the deeply reverential "I am lucky" Nike advertising campaign which followed the "I am Tiger Woods" commercial: "Hogan [Ben Hogan] knows, Snead [Sam Snead] knows, Jack [Jack Nicklaus] knows. I am lucky. Everything I have I owe to golf, and for that I am lucky." This appeal to Woods' position among the litany of golfing greats was indicative of the "revamping" of the "Woods brand" (ibid., p. 1B), in that it highlighted and mobilized another dimension of contemporary cultural dynamics and larger political concerns in America. Its rhetoric, a conservative appeal to tradition, draws a connection between Woods and those who came before him, thus furnishing Woods with a reassuring sporting and national cultural lineage. Unlike popular reactions to rank-and-file NBA players, Woods was thus codified as a multicultural agent who restores virtue to, as he is designated an extension of, America's sporting tradition.

Woods' iconic national sporting pedigree was subsequently underscored by his superlative displays during the 1999 and 2000 PGA seasons. In 1999 Woods won eleven events, including the US PGA Championship (his second major title) to finish top of golf's world rankings and the PGA money list. Even these stellar achievements were surpassed in the 2000 season when Woods won the US Open, the British Open, and the US PGA Championship (three of golf's four major championships), and a total of nine PGA tour events. In the wake of his domination of golf, Woods – everybody's favorite multicultural American – has been rendered a cultural phenomenon, distinguished by his ability to stimulate popular interest (as measured by either the number of spectators at events or television audience ratings figures) rather than incite critical reflection. So this potentially progressive cultural figure has effectively been neutered by the forces of corporate capitalism, such that presently:

> Most of us don't need him to be a savior or a hero or a role model. We simply want the spectacle: Tiger gliding down the fairway, Tiger hitting rainmaker drives, Tiger pummeling his opponents and then putting his arm around them, Tiger hugging his mom. If he turns and winks back at us every once in a while, that will be enough.
>
> (Ratnesar, 2000, p. 66)

The popular spectacle that Tiger Woods has become was evidently enough for Nike which, in September 2000, signed him to a new five-year endorsement contract worth $100 million: Nike effectively paying this exorbitant sum in order to augment their – somewhat faltering – brand identity through a continued association with a suitably benign, yet engaging, face of America's future citizenry that is Tiger Woods.

In the end, this national–multicultural icon's agency is figured through his squeaky clean image, his enormous smile, and his ability (in terms of cultural work) to reproduce the permissible discourse of nation and race. America's Tigermania is, finally, a celebration of cultural literacy, of a national myth, projected onto and relayed through Woods, that reinvigorates, rather than contests, white cultural prestige. Threats of cultural miscegenation, interference with the myth's facile reproduction, are displaced onto racial identities now declared outdated. Thus, the narrative of continuity, Woods' place within the genealogy of white male golfers and his location in the lineage of black athletes, work to enhance what it means to be an "American" in a global-moment, which translates, in the last instance, into augmenting white culture. It is in this sense that Woods is America's new model entrepreneur and citizen.

Note

1   This chapter is a revised and updated version of an article that appeared as Cole and Andrews (2000).

Chapter 19

John Street

THE CELEBRITY POLITICIAN
Political style and popular culture

Arlette Laguiller, candidate for extreme left Lutte Ouvrière (Worker's Struggle) and surprise third favourite [in the 2002 French Presidential campaign], has a team of media finesse merchants who are driving political journalists crazy. *Le Monde*'s Caroline Monnot rails against the Trotskyists: 'Lutte Ouvrière is borrowing the tactics from movie stars' agents. Accreditations have to be applied for, there are waiting lists and you only get three timed questions with the star. It's as though you were interviewing Julia Roberts or Andie MacDowell.' (Stuart Jeffries, 'How the French lost their cleavage', The *Guardian*, 14 April 2002)

THIS REPORT ON THE 2002 French Presidential contest suggests that politicians – even those on the far left – now act like film stars. It prompts a question that this chapter tries to answer: do we gain anything in our understanding of modern politics and of modern political communications by making this comparison between politics and show-business? In a world in which pop stars increasingly are portrayed as, or behave like, politicians does it make equal sense to think of politicians as pop or film stars? When Bono, lead singer of the rock band U2 and tireless campaigner for an end to third world debt, is granted an audience with the Pope or is invited to spend time with the US President in the White House, it certainly *seems* as if the worlds of politics and popular culture are almost inseparable.

Over half a century ago, the economist Joseph Schumpeter wrote *Capitalism, Socialism and Democracy* (1976; first published 1943) in which he drew a different analogy. He focused on the similarity between the world of commerce and the world of politics. Just as the business person dealt in oil, he suggested, so the politician dealt in votes. Both were governed by the operation of the market, by the law of supply and demand. Success in business and success in politics were just a matter of producing a product that customers wanted. Competition ensured that the best won.

Were he alive to survey the modern world, Schumpeter might feel a certain pride or vindication in the way that his insight has become the norm of political practice. Parties and politicians use the language of, and experts in, market research. Policies are advertised and citizens targeted; parties are branded and politicians hone their image. As if to confirm the wisdom of Schumpeter's argument, political scientists now devote considerable time and energy to the ideas and practices of political marketing (see Scammell (1999), for an overview of the field).

But before we slip too easily into the embrace of this conventional wisdom, it is important to look carefully at both the argument that underlies it and the implications of it. The two are connected by a concern about democracy. Familiarly, the development of political marketing has been the focus of complaints about the trivialisation of politics (the substitution of the substantial by the superficial), by the spread of cynicism (politics as appearance and presentation), and by the failure of accountability (the management of news/political coverage) (for example, Franklin, 1994; Hart, 1999; Meyrowitz, 1986). Paradoxically, though, the intellectual move that Schumpeter made, and which involved the comparison between business and politics, was inspired by a desire to *rescue* democracy and to give it a firmer grounding in a world in which its rhetoric and many of its practices had been systematically abused by the great dictators of the twentieth century.

What I want to do in this chapter is, first, to look more closely at the intellectual heritage provided by Schumpeter and others who belong to the 'economic theories of democracy' school, to draw attention to the assumptions (about both politics generally and democracy in particular) that are incorporated within the analogy between politics and business and which help ground 'political marketing'. Second, I want to turn to the way in which the notion of political marketing is being used to make sense of modern political communications – and the limits to this approach. While the notion of marketing does provide an insight into the strategies and practices of political agents, it also obscures other aspects. Finally, the chapter ends by drawing out some of the neglected aspects of modern forms of political communication. Put simply, rather than seeing political communication as a branch or application of commercial marketing, we should see it as a branch of a rather different business: show-business. Here the currency is celebrity and fame, and the products are stars and performances. Politicians' concern with how they look and sound, the techniques of self-projection/promotion that they use, and the associations they exploit, might be best understood as analogous with the practices of popular culture. The thought is that understanding politicians as 'celebrities' or 'stars' calls for a different story to be told about what is going on than that which draws on the traditional marketing model. Pushed to its extreme, this argument suggests not just that politics is *like* a soap opera, but that it *is* a soap opera. If this is the case, the way politics is understood and analysed is changed too. Sting, Bono and Warren Beatty cease to be isolated cases of politically ambitious or engaged stars; instead they become political role models (and the 'art' of politics takes on a new meaning). When Schumpeter wrote *Capitalism, Socialism and Democracy*, he was doing more than introducing a simile; he was not just saying that the two realms – politics and the market – were like each other. He was offering an analogy; our understanding of how firms and markets operate could help us understand how politicians and politics operate. This chapter adopts a similar stance by asking whether politicians do, in fact, act like stars or artists.

Selling policies, buying power

The idea that politics is 'marketed', with pointers to the accompanying political marketing literature, has become a conventional wisdom of much contemporary comment. Whether as the source of complaint or innovation, it is suggested that we need to understand political communication as 'marketing'. But in the rush to embrace this idea, there has been relatively little attention paid to the assumptions and theories that animate it. These, I have noted above, can be found in a particular school of thought. Much of the thinking about what modern politicians do and how they must be understood derives, explicitly or implicitly, from what have become known as economic theories of democracy. In the 1940s and 1950s, writers like Schumpeter and Anthony Downs (1957) argued that politics could (and should) be understood through the insights generated from within economics. Their arguments added force to the ideas that Max Weber (1991; first published 1919) had voiced in his essay 'Politics as a Vocation'. In doing this, the economic theorists created the intellectual basis for viewing politics as a form of marketing.

What is a politician? Schumpeter's answer is that it is someone who seeks power, and who achieves it by 'selling' the public a product that it wants and/or that it rates above alternative products. Schumpeter's argument derives from his rejection of 'classical democracy', by which he means a system intended to realise some notion of the 'common good' (1976: 250). For Schumpeter, democracy cannot involve the imposition of something that is 'believed' to be good, but which the people 'do not actually want – even though they may be expected to like it when they experience its results' (1976: 237). Undemocratic means cannot be justified by 'democratic' ends, and democracy must be defined, insists Schumpeter (1976: 242) as a 'method'. Democracy is a system for *reaching* decisions and has nothing to say about the decisions themselves. Democracy is an instrument, not an end.

In asking what method is appropriate, he rejects the idea that it can be based on the 'will of the people'. Not only is he sceptical about whether the people do indeed possess a 'will' (i.e. not just a 'indeterminate bundle of vague impulses loosely playing about given slogans and mistaken impressions' (1976: 253)), but even if they do have independent and rational thoughts, the aggregation of these would not necessarily result in coherent policy choices (1976: 254). This scepticism has subsequently been reinforced by Arrow's Impossibility Theorem, which demonstrates that there is no logically consistent method of aggregating preferences. Schumpeter himself makes this case, not via formal logic, but by reference to human nature. He argues that there are two conflicting forces at work. First, there is the capacity for people to be manipulated. He is drawing here on Gustav Le Bon and the idea of 'crowd psychology'. When gathered together, people are easily worked into 'a state of excitement' in which 'primitive impulses', 'infantilisms and criminal propensities' replace 'moral restraints and civilised modes of thinking' (1976: 257). The agglomeration of people deprives them of their capacity to reflect rationally. They become a 'rabble', and this is the case whether or not they are 'physically gathered together'; it applies equally to 'newspaper readers' and 'radio audiences' (1976: 257).

The counter-force to which Schumpeter refers is people's capacity to develop rational expertise in relation to matters of direct relevance to them. While people may be seduced by the messages of advertisers, repeated experience of the products advertised teaches consumers about their actual worth. Direct experience of things 'which are familiar to him [the voter] independently of what his newspaper tells him' will be more likely to induce 'definiteness and rationality in thought and action' (1976: 259). As he famously remarks: 'The picture of the prettiest girl that ever lived will in the long run prove powerless to maintain the sales of a bad cigarette' (1976: 263). Applying this logic to politics, Schumpeter argues that local politicians and local politics are more likely to be judged rationally than national ones, and at the national level, it is those issues that directly affect citizens that will receive rational attention. This is not a matter of intelligence versus stupidity, but of rationality and experience (1976: 260–1). Equally, without the equivalent of the 'bad cigarette' test, political decisions lack the 'rationalising influence of personal experience' (1976: 263).

Out of these arguments emerges Schumpeter's revised form of democracy in which the decision making is allocated to others, not the 'people'. The latter are confined to the role of deciding between competing decision-makers (1976: 270–3). Leaders compete for votes in the same way that business people compete for customers.

Subsequent application of economic theory to politics reached similar, if not identical, conclusions. Downs (1957), for example, drew attention to the impact of imperfect information on political behaviour in a democracy. In a situation where the views of voters are not immediately transparent to parties, and party policy is unclear to voters, each has to incur costs in finding out such information. Such costs have to be weighed against the benefits of the vote cast. And given that no single vote is likely to be decisive, the incentives for voters to be informed are weak. In such circumstances, it pays parties to produce information in easily (i.e. in relatively cost-less) forms. 'Ideology', by this logic, is less an indicator of political principle, and more a 'brand', a device for identifying the general character of the party. Once again, the idea and the practice of marketing and commerce are placed at the heart of the democratic process.

What is important to note, however, is that Schumpeter and Downs are both concerned with showing how democracy develops (or needs) a form of politics that is analogous to business practice. This argument is based on two important assumptions: the first is about what is meant by democracy (the competitive struggle for power, decided by the popular vote), and the second is the motivation of agents within democracy (as actors operating with bounded-rationality). These assumptions give weight to the notion of marketing as a legitimate and appropriate form of political practice, which establishes the connection between the world of commodities and the world of politics.

Schumpeter and Downs might be seen as explaining the emergence of political marketing. They are offering reasons for rational actors to adopt a marketing approach. But my concern here is not so much with the explanatory power of their theories, but rather with the way their view of politics as a form of marketing is prevalent throughout the discussion of politics. The language of marketing shapes accounts of politics generally, and is not confined to a particular aspect of political life, namely political communications and electioneering.

What started with Schumpeter and Downs as a set of reflections on the development of modern democracy has become a political practice. Or at least, it is now interpreted as such. Political marketing is treated as a fact of life, and the point is (for politicians) to use it better and (for political scientists) to understand it better. It seems that much understanding of contemporary politics implicitly and explicitly works with the insights produced by Schumpeter and Downs, not just in the emergence and application of rational choice theory (for example, McLean, 1987), but in the political science and sociology of voting behaviour. The dealignment thesis of Ivor Crewe and Bo Sarlvik (1983) suggested that voters choose between parties on the basis of policy preferences, like consumers in a market. Just as Anthony Heath and his colleagues (1991) explained the Labour Party's electoral defeats in the 1980s in terms of their failure to offer a credible product to their natural constituency.

The way political marketing, and the assumptions it incorporates, is being integrated within political science is best illustrated by Jennifer Lees-Marshment (2001) who talks of the 'marriage' of marketing and political science (see also Scammell, 1999). She argues that political science should not just recognise that politics is marketed, but that it should draw on the approaches and literature generated within the study and practice of marketing.

She notes the ways in which political science already thinks in terms of marketing in accounting for the behaviour of parties, but she goes on to argue that 'marketing' is not one thing. She distinguishes, for instance, between different marketing orientations: product-oriented, sales-oriented, and market-oriented (2001: 695). She also draws attention to the different dimensions of marketing – product, pricing, promotion and place (the 4Ps) (2001: 695). The particular orientations of a party affect its behaviour. A product-oriented party is to be seen as one in which its ideas (its 'product') take precedence over all else, and will not be sacrificed or modified, whatever their electoral consequences. Whereas a sales-oriented party aims to persuade. It uses 'the latest advertising and communication techniques to persuade voters that it is right'(2001: 696). With each orientation a different marketing mix – a different balance of the 4Ps – is adopted. Lees-Marshment contends that her differentiated approach better explains the behaviour of parties (2001: 709). In other words, in understanding the kind of business parties are in, and the marketing strategy they adopt, we can explain their behaviour. Political marketing does not just *describe* an aspect of party practice; it *explains* how parties operate.

But while the marketing analogy, and Lees-Marshment's refinement of it, may help us to understand a key dimension to the character of modern political communications, there is a danger that it may obscure other, equally important dimensions. Marketing – or the way marketing is discussed in the political science literature – tends to think in terms of products and brands. The point is that this understanding is not simply the product of objective, innocent observation. Rather, it is a consequence of an economic approach to politics (incorporating a particular account of economics) that necessarily casts politics in terms in terms of goods and markets. But what if the business of politics is not commercial business (i.e. selling oil) so much as show-business (selling people and performances)? What if politics is not understood as purely instrumental, but expressive, as a cultural relationship rather than a market one? It is this thought that I want to pursue in the next part of this chapter.

Selling performances, buying reputations

The idea of politics as a particular form of marketing belongs to a distinct tradition, one, as I have suggested, that can take sustenance from Schumpeter's claims about modern democracy. But there is another element to Schumpeter's argument, one that is implicated in his argument for democratic elitism, but which gets lost in the discussion of marketing. This is the capacity for the people to act 'irrationally', to become a 'rabble', to be manipulated. These are the responses that Schumpeter wants to guard against and that cause him to be critical of 'classical' notions of democracy. But such responses cannot be eliminated, merely curbed. Indeed, we might argue that they are still present in the ways in which people are invited to judge between competing politicians or party brands. We are responding to the images, rather than to actions or experiences. This suggests that politics is about more than the instrumental means for achieving prior ends. Politics, in F.R. Ankersmit's (1996) distinction, is about aesthetics, rather than ethics; it celebrates and depends on the gap between representative and represented, and it is about the imagined bridging of this gap.

Although there are important insights to be garnered from the study of political marketing and the approach to political communications derived from it, it does not provide a complete or adequate picture. There are two (related) criticisms to be made. First, economic theories of democracy, and the logic with which they invest political marketing, derive from a particular account of political rationality. Politics is driven by instrumentality, with rational action being viewed as the mechanistic matching of means and ends. This is to privilege, though, one version of rationality and politics, one which is committed to what Habermas (1971) once described as the scientisation of politics. The application of marketing to politics follows the same logic as did the application of 'science' to management (Braverman, 1974). What critics of this process have argued is that there is another rationality available that is premised, not on instrumentality, but on expressivity based around the recognition and realisation of some concept of the 'good life' (Fay, 1975; Hargeaves-Heap, 1989; Sandel, 1996).

The second criticism of the emphasis on political communication as marketing and politics as consumption is that this entails an ideological perspective, rather than hard-headed realism. Political marketing does not emerge simply from the 'realities' of modern politics, but rather it is a discourse that shapes or constitutes those realities. Schumpeter's 'irrational' citizen is not an insurmountable fact of life but the product of a political order that makes rational engagement (as defined by Schumpeter) impossible. If these criticisms are valid, then the question arises as to how political communication should better be understood?

One answer is to adopt a better analogy. This is the strategy suggested by David Marshall (1997) who argues that we need to incorporate into our account of politics the 'irrationality' of the emotions that inspire political life. We find this 'irrationality', suggests Marshall, in the world of entertainment, and the relationship established between celebrities and their audience. Political parties and politicians are not mere instruments. They *represent*, and this means more than offering a conduit for prior preferences. They have instead to give expression to inchoate thoughts and feelings. As Marshall writes (1997: 203): 'In politics, a leader must somehow embody the sentiments of the party, the people, and the state. In the realm of entertainment, a

celebrity must somehow embody the sentiments of an audience.' These two imperatives draw, suggests Marshall, from similar sources. The linkage is provided by the fact
that both sets of relationships (politician-people, celebrity-audience) are built around
the 'affective function' (1997: 204). This refers to the emotive response that is
generated by these relationships – the feelings and meanings that constitute them and
motivate the actions that follow from them. The rational calculations of Downsian or
Schumpeterian citizens would not generate the required response, any more than
'need' explains why people buy particular cars, records or clothes.

Marshall argues that the construction of politicians *as celebrities* has to be understood as part of this process of filling out political rationality. The business of political
communication is about turning politicians into celebrities in order to organise the
sentiments they want to represent. Spin doctors are the equivalent of PR people in
film and record companies, managing the image of, and access to, their stars. Celebrity
status is a matter of managing access and output. It is about deciding on what interviews, with whom, when and managing the supply to coincide with the release of the
latest record/policy initiative. Managing access is also about insuring that it reaches
its target audience – *Smash Hits* or *NME* or *The Face; Today* or David Frost or Des
O'Connor. And just like pop stars and football clubs, parties have their own merchandising. The Labour Party sells merchandise coffee mugs, T-shirts and cuff-links
branded with its logo. Sometimes they even use the same support personnel. It was
reported, for instance, that Ann Widdecombe, the prominent Conservative politician,
hired a former manager of Shaun Ryder's group Black Grape as her House of Com-
mons' secretary (*The Independent*, 17.11.2000). Politicians may be commodities, just
like pop and film stars are commodities, but the way they are sold does not fit into the
pattern set by consumer goods. Instead, they belong to the field of cultural goods,
which are significantly different in kind and character from other consumer products.
Their value lies in their meaning as texts, rather than their use as commodities.
Marshall writes (1997: 214): 'The political leader, in terms of function and as a form
of political legitimation, is constructed in a manner that resembles other public
personalities that have emerged from a variety of cultural activities . . . Entertainment
celebrities, like political leaders, work to establish a form of cultural hegemony.'

By focusing on politicians as celebrities, rather than as traditional commodities,
our account of political communication can be enriched in a way that enables us to
make sense of, and accord prominence to, what might otherwise appear trivial and
irrelevant (from a traditional political perspective). A politician's dress sense, for
instance, may be read politically. Maria Pia Pozzato (2001: 292) describes how a previously anonymous Italian politician 'repositioned' himself in the political realm
through his choice of dress and venue. He was, Pozzato reports, 'increasingly seen at
social events in smart evening dress – or, at the opposite extreme, in shorts, a fishing
hat and gumboots while pottering about the olive trees at his country home.'

In the UK, *The Mirror* revealed (6.6.2001) that Tony Blair wears Calvin Klein
underpants. On the front page, it reported: 'Tony Blair has let his guard slip – and
revealed that he wears the world's trendiest underpants.' Chancellor Gerhard
Schröder, it was announced (*The Observer*, 7.4.2002) was taking action to prevent the
German media from discussing whether or not he dyes his hair. The point here is not
whether indeed the Chancellor is going grey, but that it matters what people think
about his hair.

Marshall's analogy between the world of politics and celebrities, just as Schumpeter's between dealing in oil and votes, is revealing of the processes at work. But although Marshall supplements and extends Schumpeter's insight, he still leaves some questions unanswered. Marshall says, for instance, relatively little about the politicians themselves, about how they differ in the way they play out their 'celebrity' status. Marshall's focus, like Schumpeter's, is on the structural dimensions of the process, and so says little about the individuals who occupy their roles as celebrities. For this, I want to suggest, we need a new analogy, one that takes yet more seriously the link between politics and culture. This means seeing politicians as 'artists' or 'performers', or in David Hesmondhalgh's (2002: 5) more neutral language 'symbol creators'. We cannot hope to understand the ways in which political communication works (or fails to work) without acknowledging the activities of a key intermediary. Just as cultural life cannot be understood simply in terms of the industry and the audience, so political life cannot be understood in terms of system and citizens. In focusing on politicians, and in thinking of them as 'symbol creators', the focus is shifted from commodities and marketing to art and style.

By way of illustration, consider how Simonetta Falasca-Zamponi (1997) analyses and accounts for the rise of Mussolini in Italy in the 1920s. Where Schumpeter's answer to the question 'what is a politician?' is someone who trades in votes the same way that business people deal in oil, Falasca-Zamponi's answer is that a politician is an 'artist' (1997: 7) and that the people are their 'work of art'.

This argument derives from a general assumption about the way political reality is produced through narrative: 'we make sense of our experience by telling stories that draw upon a common stock of knowledge, a cultural tradition that is inter-subjectively shared' (1997: 3). These narratives are not simply expressions of a pre-existing social world; they constitute that world: they 'produce power while representing it' (1997: 3). One way in which narratives come to constitute political reality is by giving an identity to the 'people'. The suggestion is that who 'we' are is created via, among other things, the rhetoric of those who seek political power. This is not marketing as selling to an established market or 'demographic'; this is about *creating* an identity (that may subsequently be exploited by marketing strategies). Creating an identity depends on the use of the symbols and devices of poetry, song, processions and the like. This is exactly what the early Fascists did to create an emotional response and identity in the people that served the Fascist cause. Hence, Falasca-Zamponi's discussion of how Mussolini worked with the 'conception of the "masses" as a passive material for the leader-artist to carve', but that this 'was counterposed by his belief in people's active, symbolic participation in politics' (1997: 7–8). Mussolini himself is quoted as saying: 'That politics is an art there is no doubt . . . In order to give wise laws to a people it is also necessary to be something of an artist' (quoted in Falasca-Zamponi, 1997: 15). As Falasca-Zamponi explains: 'Guided by an aesthetic, desensitized approach to politics, Mussolini conceived the world as a canvas upon which to create a work of art' (1997: 13). Falasca-Zamponi not only argues that Fascism has to be understood as an artistic project by which the people are fashioned, but also that this fashioning has a particular character because of who is doing it.

Central to this process of fashioning the people is giving them 'style'. Again Falasca-Zamponi quotes Mussolini himself: 'Democracy has deprived people's lives of "style". Fascism brings back "style" in people's lives . . .' (1997: 26). The point was to create a sense of what it was to be an 'Italian', but this was not simply encoded in the language of political ideology, but rather within a way of being, a 'structure of feelings' (in Raymond Williams' formulation).

This argument is not exclusive to the peculiarities of Fascism. Pozzato, writing of contemporary European politics, claims that style is fundamental to what is being communicated. The person responsible for 'branding' François Mitterrand in the 1980s admitted that 'However brilliant a candidate, he cannot allow himself to neglect his image' (Pozzato, 2001: 288). Pozzato (2001: 295) goes on to observe that 'The political star is liked, much in the way that singers or actors are liked.' They both deal in 'authenticity'.

The cultural approach to politics generates ideas that are similar to those generated by the economic approach in that they are about image and emotional responses, but there are also important differences too. The economic approach talks of *products*, while the cultural approach offers *performances*. And in doing so it invites a different literature and approach. While Lees-Marshment's attempt to marry marketing and politics is entirely appropriate to the former, it has little to say about the latter. The question becomes, then, how we might make sense of, and assess, political performance.

Performing politics

If political communication is to be understood as a work of art or a performance, the issue is: what kind of art, what kind of performance? Who or what are politicians trying to be and say? There is clearly not one answer to these questions. First, there is a general distinction to be made between the kind of performance, and associated aesthetics, required by different political ideologies. The populism of Fascism, and its particular evocation of the 'people', is different from the democratic elitism of representative politics. And within democratic politics, political communication is performed through different dress codes and lifestyle choices as much as by political ideology or policy decisions. Second, it will also matter what the context is and who is being addressed. Performing grief at the death of a member of the Royal Family involves a different set of criteria to performing to a party conference, which is, in turn, different to the performance given in an interview (which will vary depending on whether it is for a chat show or a current affairs programme). These aspects have a strongly political character: they represent competing notions of the people and establish a variety of relations to them. They also have a cultural dimension. The way they are performed is dependent upon generic conventions deriving from the cultural resources upon which they draw. When political leaders appear on chat shows, they have a clear political agenda (they may want to be seen as 'human', as 'like us'), but the way they convey their 'human-ness' and the 'us' they address are defined through the generic conventions of the chat show – the anecdotes, the jokes, the banter with the host, etc. Cristina Giorgetti (2001: 279) makes this point in relation to styles of dress: 'Clothing has always been a vehicle of political communication in societies where conflicting ideologies exist. Having to live with, and be compared with, political opponents generates the need to diversify one's language and proclaim – through posture, gesture, rhetorical style and clothing – the validity of one's own proposals.' What is being created in these performances is political capital, the resources by which politicians are enabled to act. As with any profession, politicians have to acquire appropriate skills. Traditionally, these have been learnt via activism within political parties or other cognate careers. Whatever their apprenticeship, skills of political performance are essential to their armoury. It was, therefore, to be expected perhaps that, in Britain, the Royal Academy of Dramatic Art, the country's leading drama school, was reported (*Today*, BBC Radio 4, 5.3.2002) to be training local councillors in performance skills ('If you don't breathe', one tutor advised, 'neither can your audience'). Skills of performance are skills in self-presentation, in style. Style matters to politics, just as it does to other cultural forms. But if style is an important component of political performance, how should it be understood and analysed?

Within cultural studies, it is widely assumed that style is significant. The very idea of cultural studies is premised on claims about the centrality of style. But what cultural studies has represented, at least when it first emerged in the 1960s and 1970s, was that style was 'political'. For Dick Hebdige, Paul Willis and other members of the Birmingham Centre for Contemporary Culture Studies, style was political, even when it appeared to have no direct connection to the conventional political realm (see Gelder and Thornton (1989), for a good overview). Dress codes and musical tastes, among other things, gave form to political attitudes and ideas. These claims were focused on the subcultures of punk, skinheads, bikers and their ilk, who, it was suggested, challenged the hegemonic conventions of the dominant order. While cultural studies was subject to criticism, its critics, for the most part, did not attack the underlying assumption that style was politically significant. If anything, they tended to confirm this assumption. Their criticism focused as much on the Birmingham CCCS's tendency to privilege the radical politics of subcultures, ignoring the politics of other cultures, and even to overlook the conventional politics of the subcultures (i.e. their attitude to, and treatment of, women, for example). Despite the prominence of the style-as-political approach within cultural studies, it remained confined to that discipline (and to sociology). Political studies have, for the most part, ignored it. The exception to this general rule is to be found in work on new social movements (NSM), where cultural forms and practices have been incorporated into accounts of NSM politics (see Eyerman and Jamison, 1998; Martin, 2002). But if traditional politics are to be understood as a form of popular culture in their dependence on style and performance, then the methods and concerns of cultural studies need also to be applied to traditional politics.

Cool politics

By way of illustration, let us consider one particular stylistic convention that is deployed by representative politicians. One, but by no means the only, way in which politicians try to present themselves is as 'cool'. This is not just a matter of being popular, but of being popular in a particular way. They want to be stylish in the way that stars of popular culture are stylishly cool. We need only to think of Tony Blair with Bono or Noel Gallagher or with a Fender Stratocaster.

The reasons politicians want these associations derives from the general cultural value placed on cool, and the notion of 'authenticity' associated with it. 'Cool' represents being in charge *and* in touch. Dick Pountain and David Robins (2000: 9) quote Norman Mailer's definition of cool: 'to be cool, to be in control of a situation because you have swung where the Square has not . . .'. This sense of being in charge and in touch chimes with criteria that define someone as authentically representative.

But while the notion of 'cool' links to the discourses of representation, the idea itself derives from popular culture, and is dependent on the meanings that it acquires from this field. As a result, political aspirations to coolness cannot be guaranteed to succeed. First, as Dick Pountain and David Robins (2000) illustrate, the historical roots of 'cool' can be found in opposition to the very authority that politicians seek. 'Cool' has entailed challenging authority (think of James Dean or Marlon Brando). Second, contemporary notions of 'cool' have typically been associated with indifference to, or transcendence of, politics (think of John Travolta in *Pulp Fiction*). Pountain and Robins (2000: 26) locate 'cool' in persons, not things, and define it as displaying 'three core personality traits, namely narcissism, ironic detachment and hedonism.' Each would seem to capture exactly what politicians are not, indeed what they cannot afford to be. 'Cool is never directly political, and politics, almost by definition, can never be Cool,' write Pountain and Robins (2000: 171): 'To get anywhere in politics you need to care passionately about something, whether it is a cause or merely the achievement of personal power, and you need to sacrifice present pleasures to the long and tedious process of campaigning and party organisation.' And while it may be that some politicians can be deemed 'cool' (for example, J.F. Kennedy), most are not, and all – including Kennedy – inevitably enact policies that are deemed 'uncool'. Despite New Labour's associations with 'cool' (as in the use of the slogan 'Cool Britannia'), their attitudes belie the adjective (Pountain and Robins, 2000: 174–5). This tension between the 'cool' and the 'political' works in reverse. It represents one of the obstacles faced by stars of popular culture when they try to engage with conventional politics.

'Coolness' is just one of the possible aspects of contemporary political style. It has been used here to illustrate a facet of political communication that might otherwise be missed if the focus were exclusively on marketing and economistic accounts of political relations. Many other forms of self-representation – as caring and compassionate, as tough and decisive – could be treated in the same way. The point is to analyse them through the repertoire and conventions of the popular culture upon which they draw and through which they are articulated.

Conclusion

In discussing the way certain styles translate into politics, it does not follow that style is all that matters. Rather, it draws attention to one important dimension of political communication. Nor should it be concluded that, by focusing on style, we are dealing with the product of individual 'genius' or 'inadequacy'. The style is part of a process, just as is marketing and branding. Styles are manufactured too, but in analysing this process we need to appreciate the appropriate analogy – not commerce but celebrity, not business but show-business. Too much attention on the marketing model will cause us to lose sight of the aesthetics of politics. In focusing on the style in which politics is represented, we need to go beyond mere description of the gestures and images. We need to assess them, to think about them as *performances* and to apply a critical language appropriate to this. In what and how successfully do Bono or Blair evoke feelings and passions that are acted upon? These are questions about the politics of popular culture itself.

What I have been trying to do is to reveal another analogy to political communication, one not drawn from commerce but from entertainment. This analogy, like Schumpeter's, is intended to reveal the actual nature of a relationship, not just to find a metaphor. To see politics as coterminus with popular culture is not to assume automatically that it is diminished, any more than associations with marketing necessarily diminish it. The point is to use this approach to discover the appropriate critical language with which to analyse it. Just as there are good and bad performances in popular culture, so there are good or bad political performances. Just as cultural critics assess cultural performance in terms of its fidelity to democratic ideals, so political performances may be assessed on similar lines. Disillusionment with politics has, by this account, less to do with some inevitable social trend or structural change, and instead has more to do with the performances given by politicians. Just as Schumpeter's competing parties may lose elections because they fail to win customers in the (political) market place, so competing politicians may also lose because they fail to evoke symbols and styles that their audience responds to.

Chapter 20

Jeffrey J. Williams

ACADEMOSTARS
Name recognition

I have written a number of books and articles, and I have achieved that limited kind of fame whereby certain people in academe know my name and my work.

—A literary scholar in his memoir

Academy babylon

I F, A S A K I N D of academic Rorschach test, one were given a list of names – say, Stanley Fish, Homi Bhabha, Andrew Ross, and Judith Butler – what would be the first thing to come to mind? Most likely the academic star system, specifically in literary and cultural studies. By now, the star system has become a naturalized feature of the academic landscape, something that everyone, from deans and provosts to grad students, is aware of, and it is generally acknowledged to be one of the more striking epiphenomenon in academic life over the past twenty years. It arose, according to the standard account, in conjunction with the growth of the "Small World" conference circuit and the advent of literary theory, and elevated to center stage an order of academic celebrities – Derrida, Fish, Spivak, et al. appearing in auditoriums near you in the 1980s, and Bhabha, Butler, Ross, and others in a slightly younger generation gaining leading roles from the 1990s on. It also seems that academic stars have broken through to larger public audiences, occasionally appearing on TV and in other mass media, with some of the trappings of popular celebrity, most notably profiles and photo-ops in the *New York Times Magazine*, the *New Yorker*, and elsewhere.[1]

Yet, while widely acknowledged, the star system has incurred mostly troubled reactions. On the milder end of the spectrum, it is taken as a version of gossip and thus dismissed, sometimes with amusement and sometimes with irritation, as superficial. Under more serious consideration, it is seen as a popular cultural phenomenon imported to the academic sphere, and then criticized as a foreign or specious measure imposed on scholarly work. Most extremely, it is viewed as evidence of venal influences encroaching on the presumably purer academic realm, and condemned as one further sign of the decline of the academy and contemporary intellectuals therein. Overall, the star system is seen as a rarefied phenomenon applying to the academic rich and famous, separate from the normal and more staid careers and practices of work-a-day academics.

For instance, Andrew Ross comments that "the phenomenon of academic celebrity in some respects [i]s an extension of the genre of academic gossip, which is a culture unto itself – this extraordinary phenomenon whereby high-powered intellectuals spend a lot of their downtime trading scurrilous and detailed rumors about far-away colleagues" (84). That is, Ross sees the star system as an unsurprising and even normal part of academic culture, although he locates it as peripheral, a function of "downtime" rather than work time. Still, while he frames his remark as an imperturbable observation of the state of the profession, for him it takes a negative cast – scurrilous rather than frivolous, or simply an exchange of information.

Less imperturbably, Judith Butler declares that "it's unfortunate that this sort of culture emerges" (MacFarquhar 7). Responding to *Lingua franca*'s coverage of the fanzine, *Judy*, devoted to her, Butler objects that "It draws attention away from my work and puts it on my person" (7). Like Ross, Butler separates the question of celebrity from work, but rather than seeing it as a normal part of academic life, criticizes it as a categorical error or confusion with popular culture, wrongly taking "academia to be a kind of star culture" (7). Similarly though more somberly, Peter Brooks deems the advent of star culture "regrettable." Like Butler, Brooks indicts the influence of popular culture, although he broadens the charge to include the general ethos of postmodernism, diagnosing the recent trend of autobiographical criticism as an "academic version of the postmodern replacement of personhood by celebrity – as if one did not really exist until celebrated in *People* magazine" (520).

Taking a step further, the most severe responses find the star system not simply to be a case of mistaken identity but to reflect the insidious seepage of capitalism into the sacrosanct environs of the academy, thus revealing a fundamental corruption. Perhaps the most prominent display of this appeared in a 1997 front-page article in *The New York Times*, which ominously declared "Scholars Fear that 'Star' System May Undermine their Mission." This charge carries a moralistic tone, denouncing academics as yielding to a mortal flaw, enamored with (if not actually achieving) fame or money, and taps into a long tradition of assuming a monastic model for academic work, counterposed against business and prescribing that academics should deny worldly concerns like salary and prestige.[2]

The consensus, in short, seems to abnegate the star system – as a distraction, a mistake, or a fall. Still, if it is so wrongheaded, why has it so readily been adapted to academic culture? Rather than seeing it only in terms of popular culture, how is its instantiation in the academy distinctive? What does it say about our institutional channels that legitimate or delegimate work, and that confer or deny prestige? Given its currency among administrators as well as scholars, what productive purposes does it serve? What kind of legitimation does it present, and what relation to public culture does it project? How does it differ from earlier modes of legitimation and of career? Besides its dangers, what kind of rewards does it pose?

In this essay, I will argue that the star system is not trivial or peripheral but central to the current construction of professionalism; that it is not simply a misguided aping of popular culture external to academic work but that it functions primarily internally and with a specificity to academic life; and that it is not a corruption but represents a different historical model of career, and code of academic evaluation, negotiating among incommensurate practices in the research university. Further, the vista of stardom does not only apply to a small group of superstars, with their picture on the cover of the *Times Magazine*, but goes all the way down, incorporating grad students through senior professors. In general, I argue that the star system is in a certain sense indigenous to academic modes, in what I will call "name recognition," which provides a shorthand for our extant system of distinction. Name recognition registers naturalized attitudes and affects which make us desiring participants in that hierarchy and professional economy, as well as projects our symbolic relation to a public sphere. That it taps into the affective life of our profession is in fact probably what makes it such a fraught topic.

Profession of fame

Thinking about stars gravitates toward the model of Hollywood. This appeals to a certain common sense, as Hollywood supplies much of the colloquial rubric through which we talk about celebrity. And it appeals to a broad historical sense, as theatre and then film originated and institutionalized a formal star system in the early twentieth century, which seems to permeate the zeitgeist of modern culture. It also appeals to a certain scholarly sense, as there is a prodigious body of commentary on the history of film stars, the studio apparatuses that invented and mobilized the star formula, and their audiences, in well known books such as Richard Dyer's *Stars*, Richard deCordova's *Picture Personalities*, and Joshua Gamson's *Claims to Fame*. These sometimes extend to other cultural spheres, such as television and rock 'n' roll, but they are generally seen as offshoots of the film star system. If one were to research "stardom" in any library database, the overwhelming result would be the film system.

But the Hollywood model, I believe, generates many of the problems and misconceptions in thinking about the academic star system. It is usually framed as a homology, the academic following its template. Literalized, this frame prompts common dismissals that go something like this: no academic has the popular fame of, say, Leonardo DiCaprio or Nicole Kidman, nor has yet been featured in a bio-pic on the E!-channel, so it is ridiculous or deluded to think there is really an academic star system. Or, in a more cynical version, academics are wannabes aping movie stars. But this homology is obviously misguided: when we say someone is a famous eighteenth-century scholar, or a star in his or her field, we are not mistaking him or her for Brad Pitt or Julia Roberts. While there is a vague way in which the Hollywood image inflects contemporary life, fame – or celebrity or stardom – largely means something different in an academic context, and is defined not primarily by reference to larger culture but within the specific parameters of the academic field.[3] Part of the problem might simply be semantic, but the deeper problem is the default homology that elides the differences and distinctive attributes of the academic system.

A more general problem broached by the Hollywood model is the relation of the popular and the academic. For Butler and Brooks, the academic system derives from "star culture" – Hollywood writ large – but the problem lies not in its failing the homology; rather, they bemoan its success, casting celebrity as an illicit, foreign intrusion of the popular upon the academic. That is, they rely on a rigid opposition between the two spheres, enacting a kind of professional surveillance. However, this opposition is insupportable, not only because of its obvious resort to a binary that begs deconstruction, but because in practice the academic is permeable and continually negotiates a relation with the popular, in curriculum, in the lived experience of teachers and students, and in the roles that universities play in community and corporate life.[4] One might even say that academic culture is a kind of popular culture, given that, according to current statistics, 70% of the U.S. population has attended college at some point. This relation is a two-way street, the academic impacting the popular as well, in language (for instance, a TV commentator recently referring to US policies as "USocentrism," or the permeation of postmodern terminology, like the verb "deconstruct"), in conceptual analysis (academic experts as a staple of news commentary), in corporate structures (it is not an accident that Microsoft calls their plant a "campus"), and in the popular imaginary (as evidenced by movies and TV shows, like *Felicity* or *The Education of Max Bickford*, and on and on). My point is not that the academic star system is indeed cognate with the popular system, but that it turns on a quintessentially professionalist negotiation between the academic and the popular. Hollywood is the negative imaginary to be shunned rather than emulated, which asserts a special status for the academic, not to deny its popular relevance but to assure a higher public seriousness.

That she relies on this blunt opposition is particularly surprising for Butler, given her otherwise vigilant undoing of binaristic thinking, her advocacy of cultural studies, and her celebration of popular phenomena like crossdressing and film like *Paris Is Burning*. In fact, one could see the star system precisely as an instantiation, in her famous formulation, of performativity in the academic sphere. Performativity, for her, combines both the linguistic sense of the effectivity of speech acts with the sense of theatricality. When Butler uses theatricality, it is not as a homology with Broadway shows; rather, it is a broad figure that describes the fundamental process that creates identity (rather than deriving from an essence, or even from a cultural construction that is "internalized" and expressed; instead, it is embodied and acted out).[5] Analogously, one could see the current academic use of celebrity, like theatricality, as a broad descriptive figure, and the star system as a performative signification process that embodies professional identity through extant practices and acts.

In her own case, it seems flatly inaccurate for Butler to claim that she does not have a species of celebrity – certainly more so than most academics – or, more to the point, that her celebrity is irrelevant to her work, as it speaks to her position in the professional field, her getting a hearing, being read, cited, discussed, imitated, and so on within that field. This is not to say that Butler is being disingenuous in disclaiming the star system; rather, her disavowal exemplifies the priority of professionalist logic. Butler's response performs a classic move of professional control by setting a boundary that projects a putative outside as illegitimate, thereby reassuring the legitimacy of the inside. Her polemic is not motivated against popular culture per se (it would be difficult to see her adhering to a Frankfurt School position), but to control the dissemination of her work. That's the real stake for her, and the heart of her anxiety. Her disavowal of the star system reassures the professional seriousness of her work.

In this light, rather than seeing the star system as an incursion of the outside into professional terrain, a more telling way to see it is as working from the inside out, as an issue (in both senses) of professionalism and our profession's self-image. In the standard sociological view, to gain legitimacy professions define themselves as producing and solely possessing specialized knowledges, separate from common, popular knowledges. The worth of academic work depends on its distinction from the popular and everyday (hence the protectionist tenor of Butler's and Brooks's responses). This explains a good deal of the ambivalence toward if not disdain of the star system, or more exactly the colloquialization it potentially threatens. Further, professions also claim a disinterest in the pursuit of higher, more altruistic goals – the preservation of culture, or the pursuit of humanistic knowledge, or critical analysis in literary studies. This again explains some of the ambivalence toward the star system, which carries the taint of self-interest, gaining fame, power, or money for academics. Butler distances herself not only from the popular but from the charge of such an interest, asserting the putatively disinterested category of her work separate from that of her person.

However, at the same time that they assert a separate status, to gain legitimacy professions also claim a relevance to the larger world and the fulfillment of a public need. Thus they play out a tension between contradictory poles, a dilemma that Bruce Robbins underscores in *Secular Vocations*, where he teases out the constitutive ambivalence of professional intellectual life, negotiating between vocation and the world. The star system represents one contemporary version of the negotiation between vocation and the world. Most rebuttals of it express the vocational or protectionist side of professionalism, but ignore its converse, worldly aspect. Against the common academic anxiety of ineffectuality, especially in the humanities, the star system heightens the sense of the academic realm as one of influence, acclaim, and relevance, projecting a species of public effect (even if only symbolic, as publicity), at the same time that protestations stave off charges that it brooks the banal popular and venal interest.[6] Affirming the vista of worldly import, it thus serves a productive professional function, which helps explain why charges of its illegitimacy do not dispel it.

Further, in possessing special knowledge professions garner monopoly control on the dispensation of their presumably needed services. While asserting an altruistic motivation, this monopoly also gains prestige and higher salaries for accredited members, thus serving the interest of professionals. (Though humanities professors are not paid as well as doctors or business professors, it is worth remembering that we are paid significantly more than school teachers, not to mention the secretaries and maintenance workers at universities, who might also be said to serve a public need, essential to keep universities running, but without professional status.) In this light, the star system expresses the professionalist logic of prestige, garnering a tangible (if not always remunerative) reward. Butler's "work," after all, is not exempt from this interest, and has obviously accrued prestige for her. One way to see the star system in the humanities, where it seems most pronounced, is as a compensation for lesser paid humanists in the form of prestige, as well as a compensatory gesture of humanists to assure the status of the humanities in the contest of faculties, particularly the applied sciences and other practical disciplines where status more directly stems from grants and funding.[7]

Displacing the centrality of the Hollywood model, in *Celebrity and Power: Fame in Contemporary Culture* P. David Marshall examines the varied, largely self-defined and autonomous systems of celebrity across contemporary life, not only in film and television but in politics and other spheres. Marshall suggests how this might extend to other realms, such as lawyering or journalism – or professing literature or physics. Each system orgainzes its own "identifiable and categorizable audience group," which projects its symbolic representatives, or stars (6ff.). The celebrity draws his or her power not from culture at large but from his or her particular audience. Marshall specifies that celebrities are "elevated individuals" who make sense of the incongruities of their audience's social worlds, largely without power and agency, and project a species of symbolic power, articulating their audience's desires for agency.

Adapting Marshall, in my view the academic star system is largely autonomous and self-contained, with a specific genealogy, operation, and function within our profession, and which articulates the desires and projects the symbolic power of its academic audience. To emphasize its difference from other extant forms of celebrity, I've used the term "academostars" to connote its specificity of operation within the academic institution.[8] Even if Stanley Fish occasionally appears on *The O'Reilly Factor*, the star system primarily serves an intra-professional rather than an extra-professional function, and the power that accrues from being an academostar takes place for the most part within the academic sphere, not the public sphere.[9] The star system records our internal system of distinction, elevating certain individuals who bear symbolic power, which fulfills a desire for (and psychic reward of) greater agency, while the vast majority of us sit at our desks and grade a stack of freshman comp or lit survey papers, and furtively watch the clock during office hours.

Despite eschewals of "star culture," on its own terms academic culture *is* a fame culture. In a certain sense, it is indigenously a charismatic culture, insofar as teaching structurally elevates particular individuals, in Marshall's phrase. One might speculate that this charismatic dimension also stems from the religious basis of U.S. colleges, which through the nineteenth century largely served evangelical missions.[10] (The relation of preaching and teaching or lecturing, and its residual effect, poses an interesting question.[11]) In the twentieth century, American colleges evolved secular missions, in curriculum and eventually, after World War II, centering on research.[12] At present, the charismatic function primarily occurs through research rather than teaching, or more precisely professional fame accrues almost entirely through "scholarly" rather than pedagogical reputation. The overriding professional criterion, which is structurally mandated and naturalized through tenure and promotion requirements, is in fact fame-based: to develop a "national" or "international reputation" in research, or a kind of name recognition. Not a household name, but a professional name, formally recognized and regulated through peer review, among other intra-professional devices. If celebrity is the broad figure marking the star system, research is the structural vehicle, and peer review and other practices the mechanisms.

Role models

A corollary assumption stemming from the Hollywood model is that the academic star system only applies to top headliners – to "high-powered academics," in Ross's phrase, or to leading lights of theory in David Shumway's view, or to those who appear in major media. Shumway's "Star System in Literary Studies," the first concerted exposition of the phenomenon, avoids both the disdain for popular culture and the schematic homology with the Hollywood system, but places a great deal of weight on certain kinds of stars – theory superstars – and their photo spreads, particularly the 1986 *New York Times Magazine* feature on the Yale School, "The Tyranny of the Yale Critics" (Campbell), replete with full-page shots of Harold Bloom, Geoffrey Hartman, Hillis Miller, and especially Jacques Derrida in a glam pose. While the *Times Magazine* features seemingly mark a new public visibility of academics, in my view the star system applies through the field, not only to rarefied superstars and not only to progenitors of theory, and the measure of stardom is not primarily public renown but academic renown.[13]

The star system goes all the way down, incorporating eminent theorists and other literary scholars to graduate students, forming a dominant model of attainment. There are various declensions or quantum levels of stardom, ranging from who is the star of one's department; of a specialization within a subfield (the star of 18th c. French furniture, as I heard a colleague called, which makes one wonder how many other people are in the field); of a subfield or figure (say, thirteenth-century lyric or Twain); of a field or area (Victorian lit); of a genre (the novel); of a critical movement (giving it its namebrand, like the new historicism or queer theory); of a discipline (Greenblatt or Fish in literature); or of academic-intellectual life (Cornel West, Butler). One also recognizes and measures who is a rising or competing star in each of these domains, who is an orbiting star, or who is a receding star. At the other end of the spectrum, one aspires to be the star of one's graduate program, or of the job pool in a particular field. Hiring committees, especially at research universities, look for potential stars.

It is not only an acknowledged system of relative measure or status, but an informal discursive register threaded through the profession. It is something that most of us talk about, at conferences, on the phone, in departmental hallways, and the other locales of our work. As one of Andrew Ross's interviewers adds to his comments about celebrity gossip, "Even not so famous or high-powered intellectuals do that," and, as I would add, the rumors aren't necessarily scurrilous, and often about professional rather than private matters, like jobs, book contracts, and talks, as well as timely, well-taken, or outrageous arguments in books and articles. Despite its low repute, professional gossip binds academic practitioners with a kind of communicative glue, so that people can talk across fields, specializations, ranks, and hierarchies.

In short, the star system is not a rarefied or foreign phenomenon, but provides a central index of professional accomplishment and success, and informs the imagination, construction, and affect of all our professional careers, with or without stardom. To put this another way, it forms a kind of professional imaginary, of present-day academic career, expectations, and rewards, which hails and incorporates us. Its effect is not just symbolic, but has material consequence, since the perception of one's standing as a star influences hiring, tenure and promotion decisions, later job offers and raises, as well as opportunities to publish, to speak at conferences, and the like.

This system is historically notable and distinct. To make a broad surmise, the previous system was largely traditional, seniority-governed, campus-centered, and patrilineal – whose student you were and what school you went to, whereby rewards were garnered by being a faithful member of that lineage or limited by not being in it, and what campus you eventually taught on and what position you held there. This system is perhaps best exemplified by the nearly extinct festschrift, which celebrates (literally feting) the master teacher, to whom literal or figurative students express fidelity and homage. The senior professor, in other words, was the celebrity and constituted the apex of career, and embodied traditional authority. As Gerald Graff tells it in *Professing Literature*, before World War II "the senior professor virtually owned his field, including the right to monopolize its graduate seminars and upper-division courses, direct its dissertations, and control its junior appointments – though this paternalism at least carried the responsibility when the time came of getting one's students jobs, as a later, more democratized system has not" (142). This system was regulated by what Graff calls "baronial arrangements," perpetuated by senior and enforced upon junior professors; as Graff paraphrases its logic, "older professors tended to feel that if *they* had to work their way up in this system, why should not others as well" (142).

Not that this system has entirely disappeared, but the current system represents a different criterion of authority, of individual prestige and name recognition over position in a lineage, and a different model of career, of the original individual over the tradition-adhering professor. In a certain sense stardom claims no lineage (whose student was Andrew Ross? Judith Butler? Cornel West?), invoking the image of the transcendent individual. The star system employs a different court of "legitimating bodies," in Pierre Bourdieu's phrase, answering to a professional audience at large over a campus audience or lineal fidelity. Rather than the accretionary husbandry of a cumulative tradition, the primary criterion is to "advance a field," as readers' reports are asked to attest and many dustjacket blurbs somewhat hyperbolically claim, or even more successfully, "to create a new field," which one can do through one widely recognized book or a set of influential essays (for instance, initially in the cases of Gayatri Spivak and Homi Bhabha).

The abandonment of traditional authority and the ensuing stress on the individual generate some of the more serious criticisms of the star system. For instance, David Shumway finally ajudges its loss of traditional criteria (like "soundness") and community to threaten our public legitimation. However, as Bruce Robbins points out in "Celeb-Reliance," we should have no nostalgia for the previous community, more commonly called "the old boys' network." Whatever its problems, the star system represents a more democratic model (based on equal opportunity to accrue individual merit), less beholden to inherited privilege than the patrilineal one.[14] As Robbins argues, "By supplying an alternative method for distributing cultural capital, the celebrity cult has served (among its other functions) to open up . . . professional circles," and poses more opportunity for social mobility.[15] Presumably anyone, no matter what school you came from or where you teach, can attain status; status derives directly from work (though specifically work defined as research). This is not to celebrate the utopian promise of the star system, but merely to distinguish its meritocratic aspect. The problem finally is not with the displacement of the patrilineal system, but that mobility is not available to more people.

Perhaps the best figure to illustrate the hinge between the patrilineal and the star model is Paul de Man, arguably the most important American critic of the 1970s and early 1980s. In the *New York Times Magazine* feature on the Yale Critics taken as emblematizing the star system, the one person conspicuously absent (and unmentioned by Shumway) is de Man. De Man did have substantial notoriety – there are precious few literary critics who have front-page *New York Times* obituaries (followed four years later by a front-page story on the discovery of the wartime writings). Though he might have been absorbed into the star system at the time of his death in 1983 (or posthumously), I would place him more in the line of an earlier generation, like Lionel Trilling or Cleanth Brooks or Northrop Frye, who all achieved a degree of eminence and public notoriety, but whose casting was decidedly different from contemporary stars and was as much pedagogical as scholarly.[16] This suggests that the star system is not contingent on the rise of theory per se (surely Frye was an avatar of theory[17]), but generational, as de Man, born in 1919, was a member of the World War II generation, whereas later figures, like Stanley Fish or Derrida, born in the 1930s, were of the generation who came of professional age in the 1960s, during the expansion of the research university, and yet more contemporary figures, like Ross, Butler, etc., affiliated with the project of cultural studies, came of professional age during the 1980s.

De Man was embedded in the patrilineal system, studying at Harvard with Reuben Brower, a leading New Critic, to whom he pays warm homage in "Return to Philology." In that essay, he attributes his method of deconstructive reading not to Derrida or other expected influences, but precisely to Brower, for whom he served as a teaching assistant in the late 1950s in a general education course, "The Interpretation of Literature." As he puts it, "My own awareness of the critical, even subversive, power of literary instruction does not stem from philosophical allegiances but from [that] very specific teaching experience" (23). De Man's model of career turns on his training at Harvard and this pedagogical emphasis. From Harvard he was plugged into the Ivy network, attaining appointments at Cornell and later Yale on the basis of very little scholarly publication. His model was decidedly non-starlike by contemporary standards, as he published little before he was fifty. His primary influence was within those networks, as a teacher and lecturer, and initially only as an occasional writer (his "Rhetoric of Temporality" famously circulated in typescript for years before it saw print in *Blindness and Insight*, his first book, published in 1971 when he was 52).

In a famous aside in "The Resistance to Theory," de Man sternly rebukes charisma; he distinguishes true pedagogy – for him, untying the knots of language – from performance, dismissing personality-driven teaching with the quip that "analogies between teaching and various aspects of show business . . . are more often than not excuses for having abdicated the task" (4). But de Man could be claimed as the most charismatic teacher of his generation, and of the theoretical project in American literary study. In *Cultural Capital*, John Guillory convincingly argues that de Man instantiated bureaucratic charisma, attaining his influence through institutionally routinizable practices and through a powerful transference of desire of his students. To put this another way, de Man had substantial fame, but he attained it through the traditional channels of the patrilineal system and effected it pedagogically, through his many students in that system. De Man carried out his most enduring influence precisely through his long list of loyal students and followers.[18] One way to read the fate of deconstruction is that his students adhered to the patrilineal model, remaining faithful to his injunction in "Semiology and Rhetoric" that "This will in fact be the task of literary criticism in the coming years" (17). Notable exceptions are Gayatri Spivak and Eve Kosofsky Sedgwick. Their distinctive difference is their swerve from that lineage, forging the innovative research programs of postcolonial feminist criticism and gay studies and queer theory, now recognized under their names.

Back story

This offers some explanation of the academic habitus of the star system, as well as the shifting model of career it represents, I hope relocating discussion of it to professionalism rather than Hollywood. To look at a somewhat different range of questions, why did it come about in the past twenty-five years? What historical factors did it respond to? While there are many contingent factors – David Shumway stresses the growth of the conference circuit, featuring keynote speakers to draw an audience, and the advent of glamorous speculative pursuits like theory in the place of staid scholarship – in my view the most decisive influence has been the rise and the ensuing protocols of the research university.[19]

To rehearse a familiar history, the period after World War II witnessed the exponential growth of established U.S. universities and the founding of many new state universities. Both private and public universities were seeded with a massive infusion of government and foundation money to perform research directly and indirectly for industry, military, and other governmental services.[20] Before World War II, the federal government contracted with independent labs for research, and there was far less state funding for such ends.[21] But after the war, as R.C. Lewontin shows in "The Cold War and the Transformation of the Academy," the cost of research was massively socialized "in the face of American antistate ideology" through the unprecedented continuation of a war economy in peace time (10). This was driven ideologically by the specter of the Cold War, as well as enabled by the emergence of the liberal, welfare state initiated with the New Deal. A corollary effect was the opening of higher education to returning G.I.s from classes previously excluded, and then their baby boomer children.

This expansion caused considerable change in the idea and the practices of the university. Before the war, universities were suspicious of government mandates and much more guardedly accepted external funds, but afterwards, and following upon funding shortages during the Great Depression, universities changed their policies, readily drawing on federal and other sources.[22] In turn they adopted a research rationale, which progressively gained prominence over teaching, as their official modus operandi. Teaching of course did not disappear, but became integrated with (if not subordinate to) the goals of the research university, particularly in the vast expansion of graduate education.

This likewise transformed the professional bearing of faculty. By 1970, as Jencks and Riesman observe in *The Academic Revolution*, the predominant rationale of faculty became research rather than teaching. And the profession at large became the adjudicator of value, over the individual campus – and over senior professors on that campus. As Lawrence Veysey, the author of the standard *Emergence of the American University*, recounts, "The 1950s brought about a great elevation of the research-centered ideal in American higher education, carrying it far beyond its initial peak of influence in the 1890s [upon the introduction of the German model, most famously at Johns Hopkins]. For the first time, research chairs became fairly common, at least toward the top of the academic system. Some would go so far as to say that this change ushered in an entirely new era because it meant that leading professors no longer had to bid for students in order to gain prestige" (17), instead bidding for it and gaining it through research.

These changes precipitated a decentering of traditional authority and measures of value among the plethora of universities, within disciplines in the new "multiversity," in Clark Kerr's apt phrase, and among faculty. The growth and multiplication, particularly of state universities, disrupted established rankings, and funding protocols generated a competition among universities. The measure of value became "prestige," accumulated through faculty and their individual standing in research more so than from traditional standing and teaching reputation.[23] The fledgling University of California at Irvine might have the most highly ranked program in literary theory, assessed by the research reputations of their roster of critics, not Harvard, the school of Emerson, Thoreau, and T.S. Eliot. Prestige provided a kind of exhange rate to negotiate the disparity of institutions, calculated each year in the administrative grail of rankings like those in the *U.S. New and World Report*.

Within the loose aggregate of the multiversity, no longer unified under the auspices of the liberal arts, departments burgeoned, and divided into and spun off multiple subfields and specialized areas. This disrupted traditional disciplinary authority.[24] In literary studies, with increasing specialization and the death of the generalist, it became ever more difficult to adjudicate among different fields and areas. A modernist might little understand, not to mention evaluate, what a medievalist did. Whereas an earlier scholar like Cleanth Brooks was conversant across a wide breadth of the discipline, and his scholarship spanned from the British roots of American South dialects to Shakespeare's plays to Keats's poems to Faulkner's novels, in the multiversity literary scholars rarely attain expertise beyond one field or subfield, and their merit is assessed autonomously by those within their particular areas.

For faculty, the influx of funding freed professors from teaching (both in increased opportunities for leave time and in a precipitous drop in course loads, from a common 4-4 to the now standard 2-2 in literature departments) to pursue research. Further, faculty was drawn from a wider and more diverse array of institutional channels, not only from the traditional prep school-Ivy circuit — from Wisconsin or Stony Brook or Santa Barbara, as well as from Yale. This complicated traditional measures of status, less attached to traditional pedigree or institutional affiliation and more based on an abstract professional merit. Although pedigree was not inconsequential, the primary measure of standing was in individual research assessed through a national system of peer review.

The star system is an outgrowth of these changes, which emerged through the 1960s though probably were not fully naturalized until the late 1970s. It arises from the stress on research and the resulting drive for individual professional reputation over local campus service, and it responds to the ethos of competition for prestige among institutions and among faculty. It fulfills a need for a measure of value across divergent fields and disciplines, providing a lexicon to translate judgments of incommensurate practices. We might not have any idea what the Romanticist down the hall or across the quad does, but we can recognize, by familiar tokens such as an oft-cited Oxford book or prestigious speaking engagements, that she is a rising star. By extension, the star system fulfills a need for universities, providing data in the calculus of rankings, as well as offering a certain marquee value, for a university to boast of the most famous faculty and hence program in Romanticism.

That stardom is an abstract measure of value generates some of the more gnawing suspicions of it. Not readily quantifiable, it seems amorphous; abstracted from scholarly work, it seems chimerical and groundless. Shumway, for instance, compares it unfavorably to the traditional value of "soundness," which purports a more concrete measure of merit. But, like any other currency, the discourse of stardom provides a way to translate the relative value of essentially incommensurate things, fields, and practices, and a way to negotiate values across disparate institutions. "Soundness," after all, is a value contingently defined within its institutional field, as speculative originality is now. Bruce Robbins rather soundly debunks the shibboleth of merit, turning the question instead to its underlying social roots: "Dig deep enough into any instance of merit, and you can always dissolve it back into social determinants, factors like family and friends, lovers and mentors, identities, interests, and institutions that advanced some and disadvantaged others" ("Celeb-Reliance"). The problem with the star system, or any system of distinction, lies not in a loss of standards, but in the institutional channels that control access and opportunity to gain merit and distinction.

Name recognition

Alongside its institutional and professional functions, in my view a significant reason for the entrenchment of the star system is also its affective function, in particular in what I have called name recognition. This other dimension offers some account of why it has taken hold, not just as an answer to the conditions of the research university, but for us, particularly as literary scholars. This might be considered part of the domain of professionalism, but shifts focus from the objective system to the subjective process through which we become present-day academics. It speaks to what Raymond Williams calls the "structure of feeling" of our profession, and the lived experience of working in it. That this broaches the realm of "professional feeling" makes it somewhat amorphous, but it is nonetheless tangible and speaks to our professional reward structure.

There is a common form of academic disgruntlement and complaint, especially in the impractical humanities, that we do not get paid much, at least compared to other professions requiring advanced degrees and against which we might compare ourselves (not secondary school teachers, but lawyers and doctors, who we might have gone to school with or live next door to). And money, as any American knows, is a concrete measure of the public recognition of a profession, or of the success of that profession's projecting a needed public service and garnering a monopoly on dispensing it. To add insult to injury, it does not seem that professors, especially in the humanities, have the kind of god-like status of, say, surgeons; typical public images run from being out of touch with the real world (one's head in the clouds, or ivory tower) or prissy grammar-correcting pedants (as in the clichéd cocktail party comment, upon learning that you are an English professor, "I had better watch my grammar"), to small-minded denizens of vipers' nests (the Kissinger quip that "the stakes are so small") or drunken lechs (the poetic professor).

So, what do we do it for? There are of course many reasons, sometimes idiosyncratic and sometimes contradictory, sometimes altruistic and sometimes by default. While we might be hard-pressed to conceive of our rewards (and I think it would be worthwhile to make a grammar of our reward system, to understand what we are legitimating when we defend this profession), one significant reward is name recognition. Indeed one's name might be known across America and even over the expanse of the world (as a Cambridge brochure proudly tells its authors, despite their normally limited print runs), if only in databases and libraries, and to the people who use them. In the alienated, anonymous world we live in, one can attain a degree of fame.[25]

Lennard Davis gives one testimony to this professional feeling in the epilogue to his memoir, *My Sense of Silence*, from which I take my epigraph: "I have written a number of books and articles, and I have achieved that limited kind of fame whereby certain people in academe know my name and my work" (145). (Davis was first known for his work in the history of the novel, though more recently he has moved to a higher level of recognition as one of the creators of the new field of disability studies.) He says this not as braggadocio, but as a sober assessment of his life in answer to the question, "How many of my life's achievements have resulted from my having working-class deaf parents, and how much has been accomplished despite that circumstance?" As Davis characterizes it, professional fame carries entirely positive connotations: it is not shameful but something worth seeking; not brazenly popular but professionally legitimate; not specious or groundless but derived from work (books and articles, not teaching); not frivolous or inappropriate but earned and meritorious; and not inconsequential but a tangible and gratifying reward. That his fame is limited to the professional realm is not a deficit, but in fact represents the successful fulfillment of his career. Further, it symbolizes his class rise, justly deserved through work. In a professionalist way, he finds the fame or name recognition he has attained to confirm his success, rather than money. That name recognition is symbolic does not cheapen its reward; still, it is not only a psychic gratification, but represents the accrual of cultural capital, which has material effect in garnering social privilege (his salary upon moving to the University of Illinois-Chicago has reportedly moved into the six-figure zone).

Though "name recognition," like stardom, has a colloquial currency, it takes a form specific to academics ("that limited kind of fame whereby certain people in academe know my name and my work"), especially in the humanities where the rewards are primarily symbolic rather than monetary (not only compared to other professions, but other disciplines, like business or engineering). It is perhaps even more pronounced in literary studies and disciplines like philosophy where the focus is precisely on language, writing, and the history of thought, and on the circulation of writers' names and works in that history. The form it takes is *citationality*. Indeed, "citation," as Cary Nelson remarks, "is somewhat like academia's version of applause" (39). Although the representation of academics in popular visual media (like the *New York Times* features) has drawn most attention, in my view the primary motor of academic fame is not (popular) visuality but (academic) citationality, which is professionally mandated, and specific, distinctive, and indigenous to academic culture.

Name recognition – or other cognate terms like "national reputation" – is difficult to measure in any exact way (though people count citations in the *Arts and Humanities Citation Index*, and such computations are used in tenure and promotion decisions), but it is embedded in professional practices in several ways. First, the protocol of citations in scholarship. A typical article of normal criticism – that is, the vast body of criticism that appears not only in *Critical Inquiry* but in common journals, such as *Studies in the Literary Imagination*, or *Studies in the Novel*, or *Victorian Poetry*, begins, as one is taught in grad school, with a litany of previous scholarship. What is this for? The standard disciplinary explanation is that citations have a logical function, serving as premises to be proven and elaborated, or to be disproven or qualified. That is, they act as building blocks in the accretion of disciplinary knowledge.

Probably more frequently, citations serve a rhetorical purpose. Typically, they invoke authority to assure a professional purchase. As Anthony Grafton reasons in his offbeat study, *Footnotes*, "Long lists of earlier books and articles . . . supposedly prove the solidity of the author's research by rendering an account of the sources used. In fact, however, only the relatively few readers who have trawled their nets through the same archival waters can identify the catch in any given set of notes with ease and expertise. For most readers, footnotes play a different role. In a modern, impersonal society, in which individuals must rely for vital services on others whom they do not know, credentials perform what used to be the function of guild membership or personal recommendations: they give legitimacy" (7).

Alternatively, citations function rhetorically to provide a starting point, similar to what Grafton calls a "traditional poet's prayer." As he puts it, "All over the modern historical world, articles begin with an industialized civilization's equivalent to the ancient invocation of the Muse" (7). Probably more often, however, citations work in a less celebratory way as set-ups, "the obligatory pat on the back before the stab in the entrails" as Jane Tompkins puts it (124), showing how previous critics are wrong (in Richard Levin's phrase, "My theme can lick your theme," or in Tompkins's, "fighting words") to thereby launch one's argument. This also serves a professional purpose, attributing and validating a need for yet another piece of criticism – that will likewise be displaced in similar fashion, but will have earned, as one hears people say, a cv line.

However, a significant alterior function is as memorial homage. Though they might serve logical and rhetorical purposes, citations also function to reinforce the code of name recognition. Rather than invoking the Muse, they beckon the system of professional recognition – recognizing others presumably with the hope that one will also be recognized. The ritual intoning of names – even if in disagreement – might be seen as a kind of memorial narrative, familiar in the Bible, *Beowulf*, or other instances of the oral formulaic tradition (see Opland). Citations work to spur the repetition, memorialization, and sacralization of those they name. Even if you've written an obscure article on Goldsmith's journalism in eighteenth-century England, your name appears in the Goldsmith litany in perpetuity, or at least for a few years, to be cited as by other Goldsmithians, perhaps as well as by those writing on, say, the public sphere and coffeehouse culture. This reward structure is enforced by professional protocol, mandated by normal practices such as readers' reports which ask, "Does the author deal adequately with relevant scholarship?" Indeed, one would be irresponsible or unscholarly *not* to cite other scholars, and one's writing would be deemed unpublishable in scholarly venues.

Besides the common mode of citation in notes and quotations, name recognition also occurs through terms and phrases. There is a litany of signature "terms and concepts" that any academic practitioner, if competent and up on scholarship, can be expected to identify. For instance, given the following list – hybridity, national culture, logocentrism, no consequences, crossdressing, technoculture – what names would you attach to them? Graduate education reproduces this kind of knowledge, tacitly circulating the relevant names. Although most evident in signature terms, this mode of citation applies through fields and subfields, as when an essay employs the familiar device, "In x's phrase . . .," not necessarily referring to a disciplinary star. The competition for professional position, in a significant way, rests on the competition for the currency of one's words. It rests not only on the logical efficacy of one's arguments, or the depth of one's historical knowledge, but on being credited with and thereby claiming ownership of the terms and phrases that capture the attention of other academics – through their speculative originality, rather than their traditional bearing – in turn accruing fame to one's name.

Another form of citation, marking the apex of name recognition, is in the adjectification of one's name – Butlerian,[26] Derridean, Bhabhaesque. This is sometimes employed as a shorthand, in a brief mention, although more often it designates a general frame of thinking and terminology, when a figure is considered to have a kind of copyright on a critical model. It signals the most thoroughgoing kind of citation, imitation, whereby a scholar applies, say, Butler's views of the body to a reading of a literary text like *Jane Eyre*. This is especially common in graduate education, where a student might conduct a Berlantian study of state's rights and regional literature, and declares his or her theoretical imprimatur in the first chapter of the dissertation. Imitation testifies to a certain victory in the competition for prestige, enacted within the academic field.

Outside of publication, another channel of name recognition occurs in conversation and gossip. (The Oscar Wilde principle of name recognition: "The only thing worse than being talked about is not being talked about.") I do not mean gossip in the sense of who is fucking whom (although that might not be irrelevant to our professional social system and levels of prestige), but in the sense of the scorecard of reputation that we are probably all aware of – who you should read, who's dispensable, who's the most important name in the field of x, in the new field of y, and so on. This mode takes place at conferences, over academic dinners, in hallways – any time, as the saying goes, two academics get together. Though fleeting compared to the durability of citation in writing, this kind of name recognition permeates the lived experience of our professional habitus.

In the protocol and practice of citation, name recognition might be said to be indigenous to academic life. It is a form that we have naturalized and internalized, or in Butler's frame, that we embody and perform, not only by striving for it ourselves, but by recognizing and circulating other names, and the work attached to them. And it is a form that finds its elaboration in the current star system, which in this sense is not an imposition on sacrosanct professional folds but an expression of indigenous professional feeling. In my surmise, most work on professionalism deals with its structural and historical features, rather than with its peculiar but formative production of affect. But it is affect – our hopes, anxieties, aspirations, fears, desires, resentments – that makes us do what we do and act as the professionals we are. Alongside a grammar of rewards, it might be worthwhile to make a grammar of affect in order to understand our professional lives.

Notes

1   See Timothy Spurgin's "The *Times Magazine* and Academic Megastars".

2   In a well-known review of the landmark *Cultural Studies* volume, Laurie Langbauer charges that the volume itself (published and heavily promoted by Routledge) demonstrates the corrupting influence of marketing in the anti-capitalist realm of cultural studies. The smoking gun for Langbauer was Routledge's featuring the volume's cavalcade of stars in its advertising. This generally follows an Adornian condemnation of mass culture; a less sophisticated but more traditional version, evidenced in the *New York Times*, adopts a more Christian frame which condemns the venal influence of money in the temple of the academy. The *Times* story makes a particular point of a professor making a "perfectly reasonable salary of $42,000"; while not a bad salary compared to many Americans, I doubt many of the *Times* readers who are professionals in New York would consider it a livable salary. For a more dispassionate exposition of the Adornian line, see Arnowitz, "Critic as Star."

3   Leo Braudy's *The Frenzy of Renown* conducts a wide-ranging survey of the history of fame, and its permutations of celebrity and stardom; this suggests that the more relevant context might not be the film system, but the larger cultural history of notoriety. It also suggests that, while participating in that lineage, the academic system is a specific (if minor) moment in the permutations of fame.

4   See Jennifer Wicke's discussion of Butler in "Celebrity Material," where she likewise criticizes the "rigid line between unsullied intellectual thought and the corruption of the marketplace" (771) and "the recourse to a pure academicism to protect theory from celebrity culture" (772). She concludes, "The academy, including empyrean intellectual thought, is permeable to celebrity, colonized by it and colonizers of it in return" (772). While I agree with this view of the permeability of the academic, I differ from Wicke in locating the primary import of celebrity within the profession; her focus is the current apotheosis of certain feminists in major media, and thus the uses – and positive potential – of popular celebrity for feminism.

5   See the famous closing section of *Gender Trouble*, as well as the retrospective preface of the second edition, where she discusses the blending of the linguistic and theatrical senses of performativity.

6   The recent bruiting of the figure of the *academic* public intellectual, according to the *New York Times* reborn in the 1990s, is a related answer to the same professionalist call for public effect. See note 9.

7   Though other disciplines no doubt have their own star systems, it is remarkable that the figures featured in the *New York Times* (as Spurgin details), as well as the *Chronicle of Higher Education*, are so frequently humanists.

8   I confess, perhaps unfortunately, as the word became another bit of evidence in the *New York Times* article.

9   Though the figure of the public intellectual seems to counter this, for the most part it currently designates an academic figure who sometimes publishes in mainstream journalistic media, not one who has power in public policy. That is, his or her transcendence of the academic primarily accrues power within the academic, answering the desire for agency of the academic.

10   As Gerald Graff notes, in the nineteenth century the "typical American college was a quasimonastic institution where 'the preparation of individuals for Christian leadership and the ministry,' as one college president put it, was considered a more important goal than the advancement of knowledge" (20). I mention this particularly because, in my surmise, most work on the university, like Bill Readings's well-known *University in Ruins*, locates the idea of the university on the secular basis of reason or national culture. Though these no doubt were competing goals, most current accounts do not adequately address this historical genealogy of the American college. It is an open question how much residual effect it has, but the humanities are still often cast as fulfilling a spiritual role (for instance, in the current reclamation of "beauty"), counterposed against the sciences.

11   Shumway stresses the movie star-like personae of theorists in their public lectures, but this dimension has received little attention. One might think of, for instance, Cornel West's lectures, in ministerial cadences; or even Derrida's, in a kind of sacred reading that demands sustained attention. Robbins, offering one corrective to Shumway's account, argues that the popular lecture circuit in the nineteenth century instantiated a kind of celebrity. That lecture circuit had its roots in preaching.

12   As Lawrence Veysey recounts, the post-1950s research university "ushered in an entirely new era because it meant that leading professors no longer had to bid for students in order to gain prestige" (17), instead gaining it through research.

13   If one employs the measure of popular notoriety, as Shumway does, how new it really is remains doubtful; for one instance, Jacques Barzun appeared on the cover of *Time* in 1956, advertising a lead article on American (mostly New York) intellectuals also including Trilling. However, although I disagree in terms, I agree overall with Shumway's pinpointing the rise of the star system in the past few decades – as an outgrowth of the research university and its internal protocols.

14   Graff, in the passage quoted above, notes that the patrilineal system might be superior to the democratic one in enjoining the responsibility of senior professors toward their lieges; however, it is debatable whether contemporary professors are any less responsible in boosting their students, and, again, that responsibility was self-selecting, nice if you were deemed a fair-haired boy, but not so nice otherwise.

15   In *The Frenzy of Renown*, Braudy makes this general surmise: "Since the eighteenth century, the imagery of fame has been more connected with social mobility than inherited position" (595). Sharon O'Dair also focuses on mobility, but sees the star system as a cause of inequity; in contrast, I see it perhaps as an expression, but not the cause. See Cary Nelson's corrective of complaints about salary disparities in "Superstars."

16   Put another way, a significant goal of the scholarly was pedagogical. This is especially clear in the case of Brooks and in the program of the New Critics, notably in Brooks's and Warren's popular series of textbooks such as *An Approach to Literature, Understanding Poetry*, and *Understanding Fiction*. Trilling and Frye were famous as teachers, and Trilling was instrumental in developing the Great Books

course at Columbia and has a number of evocations of teaching in his criticism (such as the essay, "On the Teaching of Modern Literature").

17   In Lentricchia's well-known account, Frye is the decisive figure inaugurating theory. Grant Webster locates what he calls "The Age of the Theorists" even earlier, beginning in 1949 with the work of René Wellek and Murray Krieger.

18   Many of whom contributed to one of the last festschrifts, *Reading de Man Reading*. With the exception of contemporaries like Hartman (but not Hillis Miller), its other contributors faithfully carry out the demanian project. *Yale French Studies* also published a well-known memorial issue, "The Lesson of Paul de Man," with over twenty contributors. On de Man's students, as well as the issue of generations, see my "Posttheory Generation."

19   Shumway does also cite disciplinary changes stemming from research protocols (92, 94). However, he stresses events like conferences because of his belief in the centrality of visuality and performance – paralleling to a degree the construction of popular stardom. As I discuss in the next section, I believe the primary motor of the academic system is citationality, not visuality, which is distinctive to academic life.

20   Roger Geiger's *Research and Relevant Knowledge: American Research Universities since World War II*, among other sources, details this history at length.

21   See Menand's comments in this issue.

22   See Lowen's study of Stanford in *Creating the Cold War University* on the mistrust of outside funding, the effect of the Depression, and the precipitous change this represented.

23   The economists Charles A. Goldman, Susan M. Gates, and Dominic J. Brewer address this shift in *In Pursuit of Prestige*, where they measure prestige in direct correlation with the amount of federal research funding. This probably holds most in the sciences or disciplines like economics or business, but the relation is more indirect, especially for the humanities, which benefited from "indirect costs" spread over the university. See Lewontin on the limits of the disparity between the sciences and the humanities (30–31).

24   See Louis Menand's extremely informative "The Demise of Disciplinary Authority," which also tells the story of the impact of the rise of professionalism and the research university on literary studies, although Menand's focus is the impasse of literary studies after it has deconstructed its disciplinary grounds.

25   As Braudy remarks, "In its root sense, 'fame' means to be talked about, and the talk of fame has always been widespread" (608).

26   Wicke offers this anecdote: "Henry Abelove told me that, as he left the movie theater after seeing *The Crying Game*, he heard one young spectator say to another in admiration of the film, 'How Butlerian!' " (773). Also see Stanley Fish's interview in this issue, where he adds the variant of the first name test.

Chapter 21

Chris Rojek

CELEBRITY AND RELIGION

C ELEBRITY WORSHIP IS REGULARLY condemned in public as idolatry, which carries connotations of slavery, false consciousness and 'the Devil's work'. More prosaically, it is bracketed with triviality and superficiality. Certainly, relationships between fans and celebrities frequently involve unusually high levels of non-reciprocal emotional dependence, in which fans project intensely positive feelings onto the celebrity. The obsessed fan participates in imaginary relations of intimacy with the celebrity. In extreme cases these relations may be a substitute for the real relations of marriage, family and work. For example, Fred and Judy Vermorel,[1] who interviewed many fans in order to question them about the reasons and motives behind their devotion, reported that Joanne, a middle-aged Barry Manilow fan with three children, admitted that when she made love with her husband she imagined him to be Barry. She compared her devotion to Barry with religious experience, in as much as it provided a grounded, affirming quality to her life. Other respondents declared that they regularly engaged in mind-voyaging or mild fantasy-work with the celebrity as the precious other. That is, streams-of-identity thought that imaginatively projected them into the experience of the celebrity to whom they found themselves attracted. High levels of identification are reflected in the wardrobe, vocabulary and leisure practice of such fans. In rare cases they undergo cosmetic surgery to acquire a simulacrum of the celebrity's public face. More generally, the celebrity is an imaginary resource to turn to in the midst of life's hardships or triumphs, to gain solace from, to beseech for wisdom and joy. Piquantly, one ventures that hatred is never far from the surface of adulation because the fan's desire for consummation is doomed to fail.

For fans like Joanne, the emotions aroused by the celebrity do not belong to the levels of trivial or superficial experience. Nor do they belong to the categories of slavery or false consciousness, as some Structuralist accounts suggest. On the contrary, these fans seek validation in imaginary relationships with the celebrity to whom they are attached in order to compensate for feelings of invalidation and incompleteness elsewhere in their lives. It is as if the celebrity provides a path into genuine meaningful experience, and the routine order of domesticity and work is the domain of inauthenticity.

The term 'para-social interaction' is used to refer to relations of intimacy constructed through the mass-media rather than direct experience and face-to-face meetings. This is a form of second-order intimacy, since it derives from representations of the person rather than actual physical contact. None the less, in societies in which as many as 50 per cent of the population confess to sub-clinical feelings of isolation and loneliness, para-social interaction is a significant aspect of the search for recognition and belonging. Celebrities offer peculiarly powerful affirmations of belonging, recognition and meaning in the midst of the lives of their audiences, lives that may otherwise be poignantly experienced as under-performing, anti-climactic or sub-clinically depressing. A peculiar tension in celebrity culture is that the physical and social remoteness of the celebrity is compensated for by the glut of mass-media information, including fanzines, press stories, TV documentaries, interviews, newsletters and biographies, which personalize the celebrity, turning a distant figure from a stranger into a significant other. The tension has inescapable parallels with religious worship, and these are reinforced by the attribution by fans of magical or extraordinary powers to the celebrity. Celebrities are thought to possess God-like qualities by some fans, while others – experiencing the power of the celebrity to arouse deep emotions – recognize the spirit of the shaman.

Shamanism and celebrity

Anthropological studies of comparative religion and shamanism demonstrate that all cultures possess rites, myths, divine forms, sacred and venerated objects, symbols, consecrated men and sacred places. Each category is attached to a distinctive morphology that organizes experience and bestows sacred or extraordinary meaning on certain types of conduct and experience. It is reasonable to think of these morphologies as establishing principles of inclusion and exclusion. Indeed, all religious systems are ultimately founded on these principles. In secular society, the sacred loses its connotation with organized religious belief and becomes attached to mass-media celebrities who become objects of cult worship. Magic is often associated with celebrities, and powers of healing and second sight are frequently attributed to them. Rock concerts can generate ecstasy and swooning in the audience, which is comparable to some rites of magic.

In order to contextualize the link between shamanism and celebrity, which will be substantiated later, it is necessary to say a little more about the nature of the sacred and the history of magic. At the outset, one should be aware that there is huge diversity in the content of sacred morphologies. Yet they also share significant common structural features. These are generally expressed as the manifestation of the sacred in a material fragment of the universe. This manifestation may either be personalized, in the form of a particular human being, or depersonalized, in the form of a physical object or cultural artefact, such as a river, a rock formation or a stone circle. In either case, it is the focus of intense, and occasionally over-powering, feelings of recognition, awe and wonder.

Keith Thomas's detailed account of the history of magic in England traces a long decline from the high point in the Middle Ages, when ecstatic and healing powers were widely attributed to sorcerers, witches and wizards.[2] Urban-industrial development and the rise of science combined to prune back these folk beliefs. However, neither the Puritan nor Scientific Revolutions succeeded in completely uprooting them. The popularity of Spiritualist and New Age beliefs today reveals the strength of the sentiment of anti-scientism and the persistence of folk beliefs in magic and the sacred. If organized religion has declined, it is counterbalanced by the tenacity of strong spiritualist beliefs in Nature and the indivisible struggle in the world between good and evil.

According to the anthropologist Mircea Eliade, nearly all religions posit the existence of sky gods or celestial beings.[3] Human experience is typically divided into three realms: sky, earth and underworld. Men and women are of the earth, but their lives are invested with heightened meaning by the journeys – offered through religious rites and ceremonies – to the sky or the underworld. Most religions can be structurally reduced to a combination of rites and ceremonies of ascent and descent. Journeys above and below are associated with ecstatic experience.

To some extent, this form of ecstasy can be explained as a function, per se, of transgression – that is, conscious desire and behaviour that breaks moral and social conventions. Transgression is a universal characteristic of human culture. It is a source of anxiety and curiosity, prohibition and pleasure. The journey to the sky or underworld is inherently transgressive, because it involves entering realms that are seldom visible in earthly life. By penetrating the veil of prohibitions, religious rites and ceremonies, individuals satisfy their curiosity and experience ecstasy. The journey has a different purpose. Entry to the underworld allows contact with the dead, who, theoretically, possess all knowledge. The journey to the sky brings one closer to the eternal knowledge of the divinities that rule the earth. The journeys provide one with knowledge that cannot be gained by earthly delving or reflection. The underworld is a realm of past knowledge that can illuminate the conditions of the present.

Shamans, sorcerers and medicine men are distinguished by extraordinary qualities. All have been singled out by the spirits, either by virtue of bloodline, or by dint of stigmata. The stigmata may be physical, such as ugliness and deformity, or neuropsychological, such as a nervous disorder or neurological disability. Shamans, sorcerers and medicine men are believed to possess what, in the Melanesian belief system, is called *mana* – the mysterious, active power that belongs to some living people, and which is shared by the souls of the dead and all spirits. *Mana* enables individuals to conduct rites of worship that assist journeys to sky and underworld.

Ascension rites typically involve a sacrifice, usually of an animal. The sacrifice frees the soul of the slaughtered being and the shaman accompanies the soul on its journey to the sky. Ascension rites also usually involve physical acts of climbing – up mountains, for example, or trees. Rites of descent require the shaman to become like the dead, generally through fasting or symbolic burial, which reveals the sub-frame of the body, but also by forms of self-mutilation, such as burning or cutting.

Religious rites typically involve the wearing of masks that announce the incarnation of a spirit (ancestor, mythical animal or god). The shamanic seance is constructed around spectacle and the interruption of patterned routine. Magical feats, such as rope- and fire-tricks, the consumption of drugs and alcohol, and the relaxation of conventional mores of dress and deportment, disrupt the collective sense of earthly order. In Eliade's words:

> The exhibition of magical feats reveals another world – the fabulous world of the gods and magicians, the world in which *everything seems possible*, where the dead return to life and the living die only to live again, where one can disappear and reappear instantaneously, where the 'laws of nature' are abolished, and a certain superhuman 'freedom' is exemplified and made dazzlingly *present* . . . the shamanic 'miracles' not only confirm and reinforce the patterns of the traditional religion, they also stimulate and feed the imagination, demolish the barriers between dream and present reality, open windows upon worlds, inhabited by the gods, the dead, and the spirits.[4]

The shamanic spectacle is associated with revelation and rebirth. The ostensible purpose of the spectacle is to achieve social reintegration. The shaman stands out in the tribe as a figure who possesses the capacity for transgression. This is because the shaman possesses the power to conjure different collective intensities of being that, through the metaphor and experience of the ecstatic journey, admit transcendence.

Religion, collective effervescence and celebrity

Might we postulate a connection between celebrity culture and religion? After all, in his classical study of religion, Emile Durkheim, anticipating later anthropological findings, proposed that the religious ceremony both consecrates the sacred belief system of the community and provides an outlet for 'collective effervescence'.[5] The latter condition refers to a state of popular excitement, frenzy, even ecstasy. Durkheim argued that the growth of moral individualism is bound to reduce the significance of organized religion. However, since social equilibrium demands structured breaks from routine, the state must assume responsibility for organizing a series of regular secular holidays in which collective effervescence can be released and the bonds of collective life reaffirmed.

Durkheim's prediction about the decline in popularity of organized religion has proved to be accurate. However, his proposition that state policy should increase the number of secular holidays never came to pass. To be sure, secular holidays increased in the twentieth century, but they rarely adopted the programmatic form of organized collective effervescence. With notable exceptions, such as New Year's Eve celebrations, Bastille Day, Mardi Gras and so forth, days off have tended to be interpreted as time spent with partners and kids, rather than as opportunities for remaking a moral life with others.

The secularization thesis usefully draws attention to the deregulation and de-institutionalization of religion. However, it exaggerates the degree to which religion has been replaced by science and legal-rational systems of thought. Religious belief has certainly been partly restructured around nature and culture. For example, spectator sports, the animal rights campaign and various ecological movements clearly arouse intense collective effervescence that has religious qualities. That is, they replicate clear principles of inclusion and exclusion, they are faithful to transcendent spiritual beliefs and principles, and they identify sacred and profane values. There appears, then, to have been substantial convergence between religion and consumer culture. For our purposes, the decisive question is the degree of convergence.

Neal Gabler posits a 'moral equivalence' between the dedication to God and the worship of celebrity.[6] In doing so, he suggests that celebrity culture is secular society's rejoinder to the decline of religion and magic. Celebrity culture is now ubiquitous, and establishes the main scripts, presentational props, conversational codes and other source materials through which cultural relations are constructed. Gabler's account suggests not so much a convergence between consumer culture and religion as a one-way takeover, in which commodities and celebrity culture emerge as the lynchpins of belonging, recognition and spiritual life. Does this view stand up?

Theologians submit that religion is our 'ultimate concern'. By this is meant that religion addresses the fundamental questions of being in the world. Even if traditional organized religion declines, these questions do not disappear. Since the 1960s, the revival of Spiritualism and New Age cultism suggests that these questions remain prominent in culture. But the growing significance of celebrity culture as, so to speak, the backcloth of routine existence reinforces the proposition that, as it were, 'post-God' celebrity is now one of the mainstays of organizing recognition and belonging in secular society.

Celebrity reliquaries and death rites

There are many striking parallels between religious belief and practice and celebrity cultures that reinforce the hypothesis that considerable partial convergence between religion and celebrity has occurred. In secular society fans build their own reliquaries of celebrity culture. Always, the organizing principle behind the reliquary, from the standpoint of the fan, is to diminish the distance between the fan and the celebrity. From Hollywood's earliest days there are reports of fans requesting film stars' soap, a chewed piece of gum, cigarette butts, lipstick tissues and even a blade of grass from a star's lawn. One wonders how many unrecorded incidents there are of individuals sifting through celebrity dustbins in search of a discarded accessory of fame.

Anthropologists observe that ancestor worship and cults organized around the dead are prominent features of shamanism in Asia and Africa. Relics of the dead often form a part of rites of initiation and worship. The Melanesians believe that a dead man's bone possesses *mana* because the spirit inheres in the bone. They also believe that the excretions of the shaman are receptacles of power because they externalize embodied *mana*. Christians also believe that the blood, sweat, hair and semen of the saints possess healing powers. The preservation of relics from the bodies and possessions of the saints is a common feature of religious practice.

In secular society, celebrity reliquaries range from items from public sales of Andy Warhol's collection of junk to Jacqueline Kennedy's possessions and Princess Diana's dresses. All fetched astounding prices. Swatch watches collected by Warhol that cost $40 were sold for thousands of dollars. President Kennedy's golf clubs were sold for $772,500 (858 times Sotheby's estimate); $453,500 was paid for his rocking-chair, which Sotheby's estimated would be sold for $3,000–5,000.

Fans covet autographs and signed photographs of celebrities, preferably delivered with a 'personal' message to the fan. The Hard Rock Café chain displays rock memorabilia and rotates them between branches. Celebrity artefacts like automobiles, clothes, shoes, beds and guitars are prized. Indeed, celebrity homes are often preserved as shrines, or when they are put on the open market, value is added to the price because of the association with celebrity. Visits to Graceland, Elvis Presley's Tennessee home, are regarded by fans as analogous to the Christian pilgrimage. The number of visitors per annum is remarkable: 750,000, a figure that comfortably eclipses the visitor total for The White House. The homes of George Washington, Thomas Jefferson, Abraham Lincoln and Eva Peron have similar iconic status. If only cranks see Elvis as a holy figure, the belief in his capacity for reincarnation is amazingly widespread among his fans. Elvis died in 1977, yet sightings of him occur regularly. An entire sub-genre of celebrity literature is devoted to the proposition that his death was merely a staged event.

Cemeteries that contain the remains of celebrities are also popular tourist attractions, just as cathedrals housing the graves of saints were once popular places of pilgrimage. Père Lachaise in Paris, Highgate in London, the Hollywood and Westwood cemeteries in Los Angeles, are among the most popular destinations. Highgate now even charges an entry fee. Paying to visit the graves of George Eliot, Ralph Richardson and Karl Marx in Highgate cemetery may prove that death provides no obstacle to the commodification of the celebrity. But it is eclipsed by the product innovation now available at the Hollywood Memorial Cemetery in Los Angeles. Colloquially known as the Valhalla of Hollywood, it is the final resting place of Rudolph Valentino, Tyrone Power, Cecil B. DeMille, Douglas Fairbanks, Nelson Eddy, Bugsy Siegel, Peter Lorre, John Huston, Mel Blanc, Peter Finch and several other stellar Hollywood *habitués*. Facing bankruptcy at the end of the 1990s, the site was taken over, rebranded as 'Forever Hollywood'; and marketed as the Valhalla of the stars. Budget internment in the 60-acre site currently costs $637, which includes a specially made video of the deceased that is replayed on a big screen during the ceremony, incorporating highlights from home videos. For executive interment, in the vicinity of a Hollywood star grave, prices currently fetch as much as $5,000. The move has transformed the finances of Forever Hollywood. The number of funerals has increased twenty-fold since the marketing campaign began.

Forever Hollywood offers the fan the ultimate *kitsch* experience – becoming a posthumous neighbour of the celebrity in afterlife. The desire to be joined to a celebrity, even in death, further underlines the peculiar seduction of celebrity culture. At the death of a celebrity, it is quite common for fans to carry away flowers and message tags from wreaths and even handfuls of burial earth as relics. The headstones of James Dean, Dylan Thomas, Sylvia Plath, Buddy Holly and Jim Morrison have all been stolen.

Even grave-robbing plays a part in celebrity culture. In 1876 the shimmering cultic significance of Abraham Lincoln for the American nation resulted in a bizarre attempt to steal his body from its resting place in the Oak Ridge Cemetery at Springfield, Illinois. A gang hatched a conspiracy to use the body as ransom to persuade the state of Illinois to release an imprisoned criminal. The plan was foiled. However, fears that the grave-robbers might strike again persuaded the authorities to remove the casket from the sarcophagus and secrete it in a place of greater safety. For eleven years tourists who came to pay their respects at Lincoln's grave gazed at what was actually an empty tomb, thus perhaps unwittingly illustrating a central insight into the true nature of celebrity, namely that façade is crucial. In 1886 Lincoln's body was re-interred in a new grave. However, when its monument was found to be settling unevenly, the casket was again shifted. Robert Lincoln, the President's son, determined that state officials and grave-robbers would never cause his father's body to be moved again. He had seen a new device, used in the burial of the Chicago tycoon George M. Pullman, a steel cage erected around the coffin and filled with cement. In 1901 Lincoln was reburied, this time in a canopy of cement and steel.

Strangely, the bizarre movements of Lincoln's corpse are not without comparison in celebrity culture. In 1978 the body of Charlie Chaplin was snatched from Vevey cemetery in Switzerland and, in an unusual case of celebrity 'posthumous kidnapping', a ransom of 600,000 Swiss francs was demanded. The police eventually captured the conspirators and recovered the body.

In Christian religion, bread and wine symbolize Christ's body. Consuming them in communion symbolizes the sharing of Christ's body in this world, and is honoured as confirmation in the reality of the supreme creator. In celebrity culture the scattering of ashes is a similar, albeit secularized, rite of sharing. The scattering of Bill Shankly's ashes on the turf of Anfield, home of Liverpool Football Club, symbolized both Shankly's godlike status among fans and a sense of continuity with the values and success associated with his management. Scattering the ashes of sports celebrities around a stadium with which they have strong associations is now relatively common.

Interestingly, celebrity bears no moral connection with moral elevation. Notoriety is an equivalent source of public fascination. For example, members of the families of Jeffrey Dahmer's victims planned to auction the serial killer's instruments of torture and divide the proceeds. Although their plan was thwarted, public interest in owning the artefacts was considerable. In Britain, similar controversy was aroused by plans to sell 25 Cromwell Street, Gloucester. This was the so-called 'house of horror' in which the serial killers Fred and Rosemary West tortured and murdered their victims. The controversy turned on commercial interests that aspired to memorialize the site as a 'museum' to caution the public against the infernal wiles of transgression. The local council eventually decided to demolish the house. Disposal arrangements for the bricks, timber and mortar were shrouded in secrecy so as to deter ghoulish souvenir hunters.

The St Thomas effect

The expression 'doubting Thomas' derives from the biblical story of St Thomas. When Christ appeared to the Apostles after the Resurrection, it was Thomas who vehemently doubted his presence until he touched the wounds of crucifixion on Christ's body. The term *St Thomas effect* refers to the compulsion to authenticate a desired object by travelling to it, touching it and photographing it. Fans manifest the St Thomas effect in stalking and mobbing celebrities and in obsessively constructing celebrity reliquaries. The imaginary relation of intimacy with the celebrity translates into the overwhelming wish to touch the celebrity, or possess celebrity heirlooms or other discarded items. The intensity of desire aroused in the St Thomas effect may result in the suspension of self-control, which can place both fan and celebrity at personal risk.

For example, in July 2000, Karen Burke, a 19-year-old student, was put on probation for harassing the feminist writer and celebrity Germaine Greer. The court was told that Burke was infatuated with Dr Greer, and wanted to adopt her as a 'spiritual mother figure'. She engaged in peripatetic correspondence with Greer, which terminated when Greer decided that Burke was possibly in need of psychiatric help. Burke developed intense feelings of dependency and travelled to Greer's house, where she was graciously accommodated in the summerhouse. The next day Greer drove Burke to Cambridge to catch a train. Within 48 hours Burke returned to the house, and Greer rang the police to have her removed. The following day Burke returned again. When Greer became alarmed and threatened to call the police, Burke pinioned her, crying 'Mummy, Mummy don't do that!' For about two hours a struggle ensued, in the course of which both Greer and Burke were hurt. The incident ended when friends – whom the writer had arranged to meet – arrived at the house and found Burke screaming and clinging to Greer's legs. The incident must have been extremely distressing for both parties. But it illustrates how the imaginary relation that a fan has with a celebrity can sometimes escalate, from the wish to authenticate the desired object, to an overpowering determination to establish the truth of their presence, to authenticate them by grabbing them or holding on to them.

The passionate concern of many fans to authenticate celebrity artefacts is perhaps in direct proportion to the abstract desire that the fan nurtures to possess the celebrity. Celebrities are elusive and inaccessible. In contrast, celebrity artefacts can be possessed and cherished. However, the artefact is only worth having if its relationship to the celebrity can be verified. If a relationship with the personification of abstract desire cannot be consummated, the inanimate artefact at least enables the fan to savour proximate possession of the celebrity.

Celebrity and death

The pilgrims who flock to Graceland, the burial place and former home of Elvis Presley, do not so much honour a dead God as proclaim the presence of a living secular one in popular culture. Many fans believe that Elvis faked his death so as to retire from the intrusions of celebrity culture. Even those who accept his death as a literal fact regard him as a living cultural presence.

Conversely, the death of John Lennon is not disputed, either by fans or the mass-media. Even so, he remains a superhuman, inspirational figure for millions. Lennon was certainly conscious of the extraordinary power of celebrity in popular culture. His comment in the 1960s – that The Beatles were more popular than Jesus Christ – drew outrage in the press and led to public burnings of Beatles records by some religious groups in America. However, it was arguably true. Like religion, Beatles music in the 1960s seemed to communicate the incommunicable.

Lennon clearly found it difficult to cope with fame. His lyric in *The Ballad of John & Yoko* – that 'the way things are going they're gonna crucify me' – suggests he was suffering from a Christ complex. Certainly, the ill-thought-out interventions into politics during the 1970s suggested that he was consciously trying to save the world.

Was not Lennon's journey from working-class Liverpool to celestial stardom in the 1960s and '70s a parallel of Christ's journey from the wayside inn's manger to become the 'light of the world'? And did not Lennon's assassination in 1980, at the hands of a deranged fan, echo Christ's death on the cross? For some people, the spiritual comparisons are unmistakable. Against this, if Lennon sometimes presented himself as a messiah-like figure, his sense of the absurdity of celebrity and his irreverence nearly always deflated this public 'face'. While Lennon's ability to engender collective effervescence in audiences is legendary, his worldliness was never an issue. Figuratively speaking, Lennon may have transported audiences to sky and underworld, but he was emphatically of the earth.

Stalkers

The long police hunt to find the killer of the BBC TV presenter Jill Dando, murdered in 1999, uncovered 180 men who harboured unnatural fixations on her. The police pursued two theories in their line of enquiry. First, that Dando's role as a presenter of the popular TV show *Crimewatch*, inspired a contract killing from a professional hitman. Second, that she was a victim of a crazed stalker. When a reward for information failed to generate information from the Underworld, the police concluded that they were probably looking for a lone stalker.

The psychological profile that the police constructed suggested that the man they were seeking was either divorced or lived alone. They suspected that he tried to contact Dando by letter, fax, phone or email but either failed to reach her, or was rebuffed. They found evidence of attempts to get details of her electricity, gas, water and telephone bills. If this was the work of one man, the police speculated, it was reasonable to assume that, driven by frustration, anger or jealousy, he began to plot his revenge.

As Dando's wedding approached, his obsession with her increased. A glamorous photograph of her on the cover of the *Radio Times* may have sparked his decision to kill her. Witness accounts suggest that he travelled to her house and probably loitered around the premises on three or four occasions on different days before shooting her in the back of the head on her doorstep. The psychological profile eventually resulted in the police arresting and charging a local man, Barry George, with the murder in May 2000. He was convicted at the Old Bailey in July 2001.

The notion that para-social interaction is fundamental in engendering and reproducing celebrity culture is well established. Celebrities are often said to exert a magnetic attraction over fans. However, this magnetism typically operates through the organized mobilization of fantasy and desire. Essential to the concept of para-social interaction is that the relationship is at bottom imaginary. The overwhelming majority of celebrities and fans do not actually know one another or engage in face-to-face interaction. In addition, celebrities maintain a distinction between the celebrity public face and the veridical self. But occasionally, the magnetic attraction of the public face erodes the distinction. In such cases celebrities may experience the mortification of the veridical self and fans may foster obsessional-compulsive neurosis.

This type of neurosis may perpetuate fantasies of seducing or possessing celebrities. The fan who suffers from obsessional-compulsive neurosis is incapable of mentally recognizing the staged reciprocity between celebrities and audiences in public set-tings, and instead imagines that this reciprocity is validated in the relationship between the celebrity and the fan. It matters not that the relationship is basically imaginary, because its effects in organizing the emotions and lifestyle of the fan are real.

Symptoms of obsessional-compulsive neurosis in fans include devouring news data on celebrities, creating scrapbooks and files, finding out the addresses of celebrity homes from the internet, loitering near such premises, generating unsolicited and unwelcome letters, telephone calls, electronic mail, graffiti, and, in some cases, engag-ing in physical and sexual assaults. From the standpoint of the fan, the organization of his or her habitual life course around the imagined routines and public responsibilities of the celebrity, merely confirms the reality of the reciprocity between the fan and the celebrity. However, this reciprocity is founded on abstract desire and depends on imaginary relations appearing to be tenable.

Stalking is one of the most extreme manifestations of this behaviour. Indeed stalking may be defined as the development of an obsessional-compulsive neurosis in respect of a celebrity, which results in intrusive shadowing and/or harassment. It is often associated with abandonment, rejection and feelings of low self-esteem. Interest-ingly, stalking is not confined to celebrity culture. The UK Parliament passed the Protection from Harassment Act in 1997 so as to protect the privacy of individuals from non-reciprocated, intrusive interest from others. In 1998, no less than 2,221 people were convicted of stalking under the terms of the Act. By 1994, 48 US states had passed anti-stalking legislation, and nearly 200,000 reports were investigated. Ordinary people experience harassment from stalkers. But the high public profile of celebrities, and the peculiar imaginary nature of para-social desire and recognition, make celebrities the stalkers' prime target.

The mass-media has awarded a high profile to cases of celebrity stalking in recent years. Famous cases include Monica Seles, stabbed by Gunther Parche, who had a long history of obsession with Steffi Graf. Madonna, who was stalked for five years by Robert Dewey Hoskins, who threatened to 'slice her from ear to ear'. Helena Bonham-Carter, who was stalked for six years by Andrew Farquharson. Michael J. Fox, who received 5,000 letters, usually filled with rabbit droppings, from one fan. Klaus Wagner, who trailed Princess Diana to protect her from a 'Satan conspiracy' sup-posedly conducted against her by the Queen. Brooke Shields who was stalked by Ronald Bailey for fifteen years, which resulted in a court order in September 2000 to keep away from her for at least a decade, or go to prison. Ulrika Jonsson, who was bombarded with obscene phone calls and nude photos by Peter Casey, who threw himself under a train after police questioning. And Lady Helen Taylor, who was stalked by Simon Reynolds, who eventually killed himself.

The search for fame is often an unambiguous motive in stalking. Mick Abram, who stabbed former Beatle George Harrison on 30 December 1999, boasted on Christmas Eve to his ex-partner that 'I am going to be famous'. Abram, a former heroin addict, was reported to suffer from a deep-seated paranoid psychosis that turned into an obsession with The Beatles, and particularly Harrison, whom Abram believed was a witch.

Stalking brutally underlines the power of celebrity to arouse deep, irrational emotions. In the psychology of the stalker, unconsummated desire is distorted into an overpowering wish to achieve consummation or recognition. This wish may be irrational, but it is generally premeditated and establishes itself as the ultimate end of conduct. Stalkers regard celebrities as magical figures or demons, and stalking as a way of communing with magic. By executing the celebrity, the stalker either validates his or her superior power or eliminates from the world the magic that has turned into a cause of irritation and distress. Abram's purpose in seeking to murder Harrison was to save the world from what he took to be a demonic force.

Shamanism in rock and film culture

The connection between shamanism and popular music goes back to the birth of the Blues, which, in the Southern states of the USA was known as 'the Devil's music'. The murder of the Delta blues-man Robert Johnson in 1938, poisoned by drinking strychnine from an unsealed bottle of whisky, created a shamanic hero of the Blues, virtually overnight. In the 1940s and '50s the stereotype was taken over by jazz musicians like Charlie Parker, Miles Davis and John Coltrane, whose playing and transgressive lifestyles were yoked, in the public imagination, by supernatural powers. Coltrane must be the only celebrity to have a church founded in his name: St John's African Orthodox Church in San Francisco. In their best work Coltrane and Davis achieved a purity of expression that was indeed religious in its intensity. Yet precisely because it carried the capacity to transport audiences away from earthly cares, it was associated with possession and magic, thus reinforcing the links with shamanism and the devil.

But, arguably, it was not until the emergence of rock in the 1960s that the twinning of the shaman with certain types of charismatic musical personality became uniform. Jimi Hendrix, Jim Morrison, Mick Jagger, Lou Reed, Iggy Pop, Marc Bolan and David Bowie consciously presented themselves as shamanic figures. Bowie invented the part of the alien rock messiah 'Ziggy Stardust'. As with Pete Townshend's earlier creation of the eponymous youth messiah in *Tommy* (1968); it was never exactly clear what Ziggy Stardust's sacred mission involved, or who he was interested in saving. The content of religious convictions did not matter. Rather it was the state of collective effervescence that these characters induced that was the main lever of their cultural power.

Shamanism is a potent source of fantasy and self-delusion. Alan Parker's film *The Wall* (1982) emphasized the thin line between rock shamanism and Fascism. The concentration on image, might and moral certainty occurs in both genres. In 1976 David Bowie outraged the media and many of his fans by apparently greeting them with a Nazi salute when he arrived at Victoria railway station from the Continent. The press publicised his comment made to a Swedish reporter that 'Britain could benefit from a Fascist leader'. Not surprisingly, Bowie later recanted, and explained his flirtation with Nazism as a by-product of physical and psychological exhaustion. However, the mythologizing aspects of Nazism, notably the passionate concern with regeneration and the search for new order, has strong overtones with the myths of finding spiritual wholeness and emotional integration through worshipping the *Übermensch*, the prototypal celebrity in Nietzsche's philosphy.

However, in this regard, the fate of the hated statue of Stalin that stood at Letna Plain overlooking the Vltava river in Prague is perhaps instructive. Unveiled at the peak of Communist power in 1955, the 14,000-ton, 98-feet-high granite statue was the largest figure of Stalin ever erected. Khruschev denounced Stalin in the following year, leaving the Czech Communist Party with a prominent and embarrassing white elephant. The monument was eventually blown up in 1962, but the plinth remained as a reminder to the Czech public of *temps perdu*. In 1996 it was occupied by a ten-metre-high inflatable replica of Michael Jackson, who was passing through the city on his latest world tour, which, one may ruefully note, was called 'History'.

The rock shaman produces excitement and mass hysteria rather than religious salvation. The ability to act as a conducting rod of mass desire, and to precipitate semi-orgiastic emotions in the crowd, are the most obvious features of this form of shamanic power. When an attempt is made to articulate or codify creeds, it usually falls flat. Coltrane boiled down his religious conviction into two words: 'live right'. The message of The Beatles was equally attractive yet just as tenuous: 'All you need is love'. The efforts by later rock shamans, such as Michael Jackson, Marvin Gaye, Kurt Cobain, Michael Hutchence, Bono and Liam Gallagher, to express a creed of living, are confused and often embarrassing. 'All you need is love' is a truism, but one that obviously glosses over many difficulties and inconsistencies.

Perhaps one reason for the significance attributed to these simplistic celebrity philosophies is that they are generally presented to an audience that is peculiarly impressionable. Typically, rock shamans address youth cultures. For people who are consciously seeking role models that contrast with the models of family life, passionate convictions, delivered with sincerity and glamour, have a strong resonance. In societies where rates of divorce are high, and where the future of the nuclear family is in doubt, celebrities are notable 'significant others' in the public management of emotions. Because youths are the immediate 'victims' of divorce and marital troubles, the impact of celebrity culture is likely to be particularly strong on them.

However, it is a mistake to limit this impact to the status of youth. Judy Garland's iconic status in gay culture partly derived from her ability to cope with disapproval, rejection and marginalization. The enduring celebrity of Marilyn Monroe derives from her projection of vulnerability as a mode of communication with her audience. Monroe enables audiences of all ages to escape the category of their private worries and troubles by identifying with her highly public personal difficulties.

Yet it is undoubtedly in youth culture that the category of celebrity possesses deepest force. This is one reason why the method of rock celebrity presentation is usually intensely sexual. As cultural icons they adopt the public face of a sexual object. Because their mass appeal depends on presenting themselves as constantly available, their stage dress and presentation coaxes crowds to want them, especially in the sexual sense. The fantasies born as youths listen to a CD or tape in their parents' home or in a bedsit are part of the energy used in the stage perform-ance, which presents the performer as someone who apparently lives without taboos. 'Jesus died for somebody else's sins, but not mine', declared Patti Smith in the 1975 album *Horses*.

The absence of guilt and taboos are also prominent motifs in Hollywood celebrity culture. The shaman figure in Hollywood is typically associated with amoral and dangerous influence. Rudolph Valentino in the Jazz Age symbolized the threat that male American audiences professed in the face of 'erotic outsiders'. For females, Valentino was an object of desire precisely because his body and behaviour refused to comply with ethnocentric masculine stereotypes. For males, he was condemned as an indolent foreigner whose public face concealed the genetic inferiority attributed to all such immigrants.

Moral panics about the amoral attitude of Hollywood on sexual questions in the 1920s were replaced in the 1930s with fears about the influence of violence in gangster films. Movies like *Doorway to Hell* and *Little Caesar* (both 1930), *Scarface* (1931) and *Public Enemy* (1932) were criticized for glorifying violence. Actors associated with gangster roles, such as Edward G. Robinson, Paul Muni, George Raft and James Cagney, were vilified for playing parts that taught audiences that crime does pay. The gangster movies seemed to comment directly on the perceived American lust for money, and the invalidation of American males in repressing their desires. Robinson's mobster, Rico Bandello in *Little Caesar*, is evidently a psychopath, but the film is ambiguous about others who, unlike Rico, simply accept their lot as jobsworths and stable family men. They will never have Rico's wealth, or experience his unbridled aggression. They must rein in and disguise their desires and thus, the film suggests, they cannot, like Rico, ultimately be true to themselves.

In the 1950s, Elvis Presley, James Dean and Marlon Brando symbolized the lust for money and violated stereotypes of masculine invalidation in other ways. They were obviously profligate with money; they prioritized self-expression over conformity, and they placed hedonism above responsibility. In the eyes of the moral majority, unlike Valentino who symbolized 'foreignness', they were 'the enemy within' – the youthful, ingrate inheritors of the sacrifices made by the adults of Eisenhower's generation who had defeated Hitler and Tojo in the Second World War. Their *insouciance* was an affront to the work ethic that demanded relentless endeavour in the workplace and sobriety at home.

David Riesman captured the state of public anxiety that existed in the early 1950s with his famous distinction between 'inner' and 'other' directed personalities.[7] Inner-directed personalities are the archetype of pioneering stock, who rely on the Bible, the example of their parents and their own efforts and energies to construct a tenable moral framework and make their way in the world. Other-directed types abandon internalized moral systems in favour of the fashions and fads of the mass-media. It was the seductive role model that Presley, Dean and Brando presented to impressionable, other-directed types that so perplexed the moral majority in the 1950s. Riesman was troubled with the fear that Western society had already exchanged the principle that work is the central life interest for an addiction to consumption as the end of life. Further, the Hollywood stars expressed this metamorphosis in highly conspicuous and morally dangerous ways.

The exiled Frankfurt School theorist Leo Lowenthal had already anticipated an historical dimension to this thesis. He argued that, in the 1920s and '30s, American popular culture exchanged its respect for figures of industry and administration, such as Thomas Edison and Teddy Roosevelt, for the adulation of show business idols, such as Charlie Chaplin, James Cagney, Al Jolson, Clara Bow, Theda Bara and Mae West. For Lowenthal, the entertainment celebrity was now the most desired object in popular culture, leaving the traditional role models of industrial society – the inventor, the teacher and the public official – stranded.

For the moral majority in 1950s America, Hollywood celebrity was a deeply ambivalent construct. The wealth, freedom and popularity of stars fulfilled the American dream. Hollywood celebrities were self-made individuals who achieved their wealth and power by their talents and industry. This was in stark contrast with the inherited wealth of the lazy, self-approving European aristocracy or the children of the American *nouveaux riches* that the economist Thorstein Veblen had rebuked in his attack on the perils of conspicuous consumption. Conversely, Hollywood celebrity was also regarded as the worm in the bud of the American dream. Stars worked, but unlike other Americans, they seemed to enjoy their work. They were paid, but by the standards of Middle America, they received a king's ransom for their labour. Moreover, in the highly public reporting of the sex lives of Hollywood celebrities, Middle America sat goggle-eyed at the freedom from moral restraint and public censure enjoyed by the celebritariat.

Hollywood film directors have exploited the popular association between celebrity and superhuman powers. Oliver Stone's film *The Doors* (1991) was built on the premise that, as a child, Jim Morrison's spirit was possessed by the spirit of an Amer-Indian shaman. For Stone, nothing but *mana* could explain Morrison's uncanny ability to encourage audiences to shed inhibitions and be carried outside themselves.

Inviting Hollywood celebrities to play the role of the Devil and take the audience on a journey into the Underworld is also a theme in American film. In recent years, Robert De Niro (*Angel Heart*, 1986), Jack Nicholson (*The Witches of Eastwick*, 1987) and Al Pacino (*The Devil's Advocate*, 1997) have played the Devil, while Brad Pitt has played Death (*Meet Joe Black*, 1999). The choice of these actors is revealing. Each of them has claim to be regarded as a shamanic emblem for their generation. In a variety of films in the 1970s and '80s, De Niro and Pacino played rebels, anti-heroes, outsiders and romantic misfits who symbolized the rebellious and misplaced sense of identity in large sections of the audience. Jack Nicholson broke through to mainstream audiences with *Easy Rider* (1969), a *succès de scandale* in Hollywood, not only for its controversial content but for its enormous box-office appeal too, which briefly created independent film-making as a sunrise industry. Brad Pitt in *Fight Club* (1998) played the ultimate shamanic figure by representing the id (Dionysus) to Edward Norton's ego (Apollo).

Celebrity ceremonies of ascent

Celebrity culture is secular. Because the roots of secular society lie in Christianity, many of the symbols of success and failure in celebrity draw on myths and rites of religious ascent and descent.

Celebrity culture is not organized around a system of ecumenical values that link this-worldly conduct to salvation. Nor should one underestimate the complexity of modalities of celebrity culture, each with its specific beliefs, myths, rites and symbols. The variety and diversity of celebrity culture is a constant barrier to meaningful generalization. Yet, without wishing to minimize these analytical problems, honour and notoriety are, very often, prominent features of the celebrity status economy, and money is typically the currency in which honour and notoriety are measured.

The rise of celebrity culture is, indeed, intimately connected with the rise of a money economy and the growth of populations concentrated in urban-industrial locations. It is partly a product of the world of the stranger, wherein the individual is uprooted from family and community and relocated in the anonymous city, in which social relations are often glancing, episodic and unstable. Just as the Puritan in the seventeenth century looked to Christ for comfort and inspiration, fans today, like Joanne mentioned at the beginning of this chapter, seek out celebrities to anchor or support personal life. The dominant motive here is not salvation. Fans are attracted to celebrities for a variety of reasons, with sexual attraction, admiration of unique personal values and mass-media acclaim being prominent. Hardly any believe that celebrities can 'save' them in an orthodox religious or quasi-religious sense. But most find comfort, glamour or excitement in attaching themselves to a celebrity. Through this attachment a sense of glamorous difference is enunciated.

In a money economy the shaman's belief in the supreme being above and the underworld below is diminished, as is the Christian belief in God and the Devil. Yet if the religious division between earth, sky and underworld is mitigated, consciousness of material success and failure is accentuated. Celebrity culture has developed a variety of ceremonies of ascent and descent to symbolize honorific status and the loss of it. The central ascension beliefs and rites are organized around three themes: elevation, magic and immortality.

Elevation refers to the social and cultural processes involved in raising the celebrity above the public. Elevation is literally achieved in Hollywood celebrity because the magnified screen and billboard images are raised above the eye-level of cinema-goers. The wealth and luxury of celebrities are staple, and instantly recognized, symbols of success in market society.

Further evidence of elevation is found in the ubiquity of celebrity biographies in popular culture. Popular, mass-circulation magazines like *Hello* and *OK* are largely devoted to glossy photo-journalism, documenting the marriages, houses, holidays, divorces, births, medical operations, and deaths of celebrities. The TV talk show, such as *Parkinson, Larry King Live, The Late Show with David Letterman* and the *Jay Leno Show*, enhances the image of celebrities as figures of significance by affording them the opportunity to present a variation on the public face in, so to speak, 'out of role' contexts.

The TV talk show was invented in America in 1950, when Jerry Lester started hosting a five-nights-a-week show called *Broadway Open House*. However, the form was defined by Johnny Carson, a former stand-up comedian turned host. Carson first presented *The Tonight Show* in 1962. Most commentators agree that he dominated the medium until his retirement in 1993. Carson cultivated the talk show as a vehicle for celebrity indiscretion and revelation. His invention of the role of the talk-show host was a continuation of the close-up technique, by purporting to offer audiences more intimate, out-of-face encounters, with celebrities. (D. W. Griffith, who directed the first full-length feature film, *Birth of a Nation*, in 1915 is generally regarded to have invented the close-up shot, which enabled audiences to see not only the faces of stars but the portrayal of emotions too, thus intensifying the intimacy between the audience and the star.) The set design of *The Tonight Show* conveyed the impression that the studio was an extension of Carson's own home. By identifying the set with domesticity, *The Tonight Show* established the chat show as a relaxed and friendly after dinner tête-à-tête rather than a public confrontation. Later generations of talk shows copied the format by using carpets, rugs, flowers in vases, sofas, easy chairs and *trompe l'œil* background windows to convey a sense of reassuring domesticity.

Elevation is a perpetual feature of the honorific status of celebrity. Generally, it is geared to market requirements. Thus, when Tom Cruise, Tom Hanks, Britney Spears, Janet Jackson, John Grisham or Will Self has a new film, album or book to plug, they become the subject of a media saturation campaign by the companies selling the product. A common technique in marketing campaigns is to require the celebrity to participate in out-of-face encounters with chat-show hosts. Plugging a product on TV is more effective if celebrities use the occasion to open up, and reveal personality layers that are hidden from the screen persona. However, celebrity interviews are only effective if the essential role distance between the celebrity and the audience is maintained. Celebrities may slip out of role in chat show interviews so as to appear more human. But if they do so continuously they neutralize the charisma on which their status as exalted and extraordinary figures depends.

Celebrity power depends on immediate public recognition. As we shall see, celebrities often feel hunted by the devouring public. The silent film star Clara Bow complained, 'When they stare at me, I get the creeps.' Harrison Ford attested that 'I'm very uncomfortable when people stare at me.'[8] Without wishing to minimize the sincerity of these sentiments, we should place them in the context of celebrity motivation. Instant public acclaim is part of the appeal of being a celebrity. Along with the wealth and the flexible lifestyle, it is one of the reasons why achieved celebrity is sought after with such deliberate and often frenzied ardour.

Magic, the second theme, is invoked by the shaman, who partly asserts and reinforces his power through the performance of various tricks and undertakings. Celebrities cultivate the same practice. Hollywood celebrities are able to perform magical feats on celluloid. Action-movie stars like John Wayne, Robert Mitchum, Harrison Ford, Bruce Willis, Mel Gibson and Pierce Brosnan are frequently required to perform remarkable and magical feats on screen. Sports celebrities like David Beckham, Romario, Ronaldo, Wayne Gretsky, Brian Lara, Kapil Dev, Mark McGwire, Conchita Martinez, Venus Williams, Tiger Woods and Anna Kournikova are expected to do the same thing in the sports arena.

Edgar Morin contends that there is a spillover effect between the role incarnated by an actor in a performance and the public perception of the actor. 'From their union', he writes, 'is born a composite creature who participates in both, envelops them both: the star'.[9] It is this spillover effect that contributes to the public perception of the celebrity as a magical, cultural colossus. Part of the appeal of the Planet Hollywood restaurant chain is the idea that diners have access to major celebrity investors, notably Bruce Willis, Demi Moore, Sylvester Stallone and Arnold Schwarzenegger. The restaurants display celebrity artefacts, and the celebrities make scheduled live appearances. Planet Hollywood memorabilia and star appearances are calculated with mathematical precision to give the illusion of proximity to celebrity. Yet face-to-face encounters are so rare as to belong to the realm of exotica. Bodyguards, publicists and 'impression managers' constitute key elements in the celebrity retinue that manage the presentation of the celebrity face to the public. Public appearances of celebrities are not always accompanied with a roll of drums, although, interestingly, heavy drumbeats are often used in shamanic rites to summon spirits. However, public appearances of celebrities are generally staged events in which publicists, bodyguards and public relations staff announce and manage contact between the celebrity and fans. The celebrity retinue enhances the aura of magic that surrounds the celebrity.

Their pomp and mass announces to the public that a figure of significance has descended to – so to speak – break bread with them.

As for *immortality*, the third theme, in secular society the honorific status conferred on certain celebrities outlasts physical death. Madame Tussaud imported her wax museum from France into England in 1802. It consisted of a collection of celebrity manikins. It was of huge interest to audiences that had never seen photographs of the great celebrities and notorious criminals of the day. It supplemented the engravings of famous personages widely coveted in the eighteenth century. Celebrity immortality is obviously more readily achieved in the era of mass communications, since film footage and sound recordings preserve the celebrity in the public sphere. Mass communication preserves the cultural capital of celebrities and increases their chances of becoming immortal in the public sphere. Graham McCann, pondering the immortality of Marilyn Monroe, notes the central paradox of celebrity immortality: 'Monroe is now everywhere yet nowhere: her image is on walls, in movies, in books – all after-images, obscuring the fact of her permanent absence.'[10]

Descent and falling

Celebrities take themselves and their fans higher. They are the ambassadors of the celestial sphere. But they can also descend to the underworld, and drag their fans down with them. Hitler is arguably the twentieth century's principal example of celebrity ascent and descent. His astonishing rise to power was, at first, internationally acclaimed as an example of a strong leader presiding over the rebirth of a nation. Millions of Germans developed passionate, deep, not to say irrational feelings of devotion towards him and genuinely regarded him to be their real Führer, i.e., their 'leader'. However, as the true extent of his intrigue, callousness and brutality became exposed, he was turned into a global pariah. Some even regarded him as the incarnation of the Anti-Christ. As the vanity of his military ambitions was revealed, by crushing defeats on the Russian Front, by the persistence of the British and the Resistance movements on the Continent, and by America's entry into the war, he literally became unhinged. Before his suicide in the command bunker in Berlin he raved against the German people for their cowardice and issued instructions for a scorched-earth policy to spoil the fruits of victory for the Allies. The unutterable disgrace of his genocidal practices became a millennial standard of inhumanity, which post-Nazi Germany has failed to erase entirely.

Descent and falling are twinned with ascent and rising. Elevation is, in itself, a source of envy as well as approval. Celebrities acquire so much honorific status and wealth that their downfall becomes a matter of public speculation and, on occasion, is even desired. Sometimes this provokes conspiracy. Orson Welles based a female character in *Citizen Kane* (1941) on the mistress of the media tycoon William Randolph Hearst. Indeed, the demonic figure of Kane himself is widely believed to be based on Hearst. The tycoon's revenge was to conduct an unstinting campaign against Welles and the film in the mass-media. Welles even alleged that Hearst planted an under-age girl in his hotel bedroom. A scandal was only averted by a tip-off to Welles from the police. Hearst certainly damaged Welles's reputation, and contributed to his later difficulties in gaining finance to develop his film work. Similarly, public disquiet about

Charlie Chaplin's private life and media reports of his apparent sympathy with Communism resulted in him being barred from McCarthyite America. The mass-media who build up celebrities are often unable to resist engineering their downfall.

Celebrities, however, also collude in bringing about their own descent. The inventories of alcoholism, drug addiction, mania and depression constructed by Kenneth Anger, Gary Herman and Dave Thompson of celebrities in film and rock support the commonsense intuition that constantly being in the public eye produces psychological difficulties and trauma. The public face estranges the veridical self and results in fears of personal disappearance or annihilation. Public appearances become associated with self-denial, or confirm, in the sight of the celebrity, that the veridical self has been destroyed. The public face becomes a living tomb of staged personality. Addictive, maniacal and obsessive behaviour are the corollaries of chronic feelings of helplessness and inauthenticity. Celebrities often feel both personally unworthy after receiving public adulation and out of control of their own careers. Celebrities suffer an abnormally high incidence of mania, schizophrenia, paranoia and psychopathic behaviour.

Descent is established by routines of behaviour that centre on the mortification of the body. Thus, celebrities may become anorexic or balloon in weight, develop phobias about being in public places, succumb to narcotic addiction or engage in public displays of drunkenness. The mortification of the body brings the celebrity down to earth. In cases of suicide and attempted suicide, it literally seeks to bury the body under the earth. Outwardly, suicide is a destructive act, but inwardly it offers the celebrity permanent refuge from a rapacious public.

The theme of mortification in the rites surrounding celebrity descent seems to take three general forms: scourging, disintegration and redemption. *Scourging* refers to a process of status-stripping in which the honorific status of the celebrity is systematically degraded. It has two forms: *auto-degradation*, in which the primary exponent of status-stripping is the celebrity, and *exo-degradation*, in which external parties, usually situated in the mass-media, are the architects of the status-stripping process. In general the ceremonies surrounding both forms interrelate and are mutually reinforcing.

The celebrated 1960s soccer star George Best was arguably the greatest player of his generation. However, the media and fan expectations of producing a world-class performance every week resulted in gambling and drink problems. After Manchester United won the European Cup in 1968, Best felt strongly that aging players in the team should be replaced. When the manager, Matt Busby, proved reluctant to buy new stars, Best became disenchanted. This reinforced his alcohol dependence and alienated him from other members of the team, and eventually from the manager too. Best became prone to temper tantrums and unpredictable behaviour. Gradually, he became a liability to the team and in his late twenties decided to retire from soccer. Best blamed himself for not being able to withstand the pressures of soccer stardom, but he was also condemned by the media for squandering his gifts.

The snooker player Alex 'Hurricane' Higgins was the victim of similar pressures. He dealt with the strain of trying to please his fans with magical skills every time he played by developing a dependence on alcohol. His playing became increasingly erratic and his public outbursts were frequently savage.

James Fox, the star of *The Servant* (1963), *The Chase* (1966) and *Performance* (1970), is another example of a celebrity who became prey to addictive, self-destructive behaviour. He despaired of the superficial values of Hollywood and became oppressed by what he saw as the inadequacy of his public face. Fox abandoned acting for ten years. He joined a religious sect and became involved in community work. It was not until the early 1980s that he returned to the screen.

Lena Zavaroni, the British child star, died from anorexia in adulthood. Margaux Hemingway and Princess Diana suffered from bulimia. Media speculation about apparent dramatic weight loss has surrounded Calista Flockhart and Portia de Rossi of *Ally McBeal*, Jennifer Aniston of *Friends* and Victoria Beckham of The Spice Girls. Richey Edwards of the Manic Street Preachers engaged in self-mutilation, suffered from depression and alcohol problems, and in 1995 abruptly vanished and is presumed dead. Sid Vicious and Kurt Cobain displayed erratic drug-related behaviour, seemed unable to cope with fame, and both committed suicide, one by a heroin overdose, the other by means of a bullet to the head. Elizabeth Taylor, Elvis Presley, Marlon Brando, Roseanne Barr, Elton John and Oprah Winfrey fought highly public battles with their weight.

Examples of celebrity auto- and exo-degradation could be endlessly added. The point that needs to be re-emphasized here is that status-stripping ceremonies are typically focused on the body. The mortification of idealized masculine and feminine celebrity constructions centres on the scourging of the body, which includes ripping, cutting, shedding, flailing and, conversely, overeating, addiction, agoraphobia and claustrophobia.

In extreme cases, scourging results in a status-stripping vortex – *disintegration* – that leads the celebrity to conclude that nothing can be salvaged, because nothing remains in the veridical self which is recognized as trustworthy or worth saving. The resultant erosion of the veridical self undermines the individual's sense of security. Where this results in clinical or sub-clinical depression it may culminate in suicide. The wounded self aims to both protect itself from residual erosion and offer a sacrifice to the public. Celebrity suicide often springs from feelings of contempt or hatred for the mass-media and fans. George Sanders, the character actor, killed himself by taking a drug overdose in 1972. His suicide note read 'Dear World: I am leaving because I am bored: I am leaving you with your worries in this sweet cesspool'. Kurt Cobain's suicide in 1994 followed drug problems and well-publicized complaints of feeling hounded by the public and the paparazzi. Marianne Faithfull's attempted suicide in 1969 followed Brian Jones's apparent death by misadventure in the same year. In her autobiography she sifts through her motives. In part, she reasons, taking a drug overdose was an act of revenge on other members of The Rolling Stones and the mass-media, whom she regarded as over-complacent about Jones's death. Faithfull identified with Jones, and she believed his death to have been a 'sacrifice'. Because the sacrifice failed to change the attitudes and behaviour of the group, the media and the fans, she decided that she must go one step further and really shock everyone. Her close identification with Jones – she refers to him as her 'twin' – is typical evidence of the veridical self's feelings of mortification or disappearance. According to her:

> From the age of seventeen until fairly recently, my life had been the life of a sleepwalker . . . Managers, star-spotters, the press, the public. What they see in you might be who you really are, or it might be somebody else entirely. It doesn't matter; part of you falls asleep. The image with which

you are imprinted is so indelible that it has the power to hypnotize you and those close to you . . . In the struggle for my own direction, I began pushing everybody away, constantly saying: 'No, no, no' – to people, to situations and eventually to life itself. I am not this, I am not that, I am not the other. I always thought there was something wrong with me for not being happy with what I've got . . . But sometimes it didn't feel like my life, it was as if I was living somebody else's.[11]

This section of Faithfull's memoir takes the form of a confession. Her suicide attempt was not cathartic. She did not abandon heroin use and, for a time, lived on the streets. However, in recognizing the factors involved in the gestation of her own personal disintegration, she identifies a surface in which it is possible to imagine personal reintegration. There is no abandonment of the public face, because wearing a 'front' is the inescapable condition of celebrity. At the same time, through public confession, she acknowledges a vulnerability that helps her to mediate her face in public without suffering from clinical or sub-clinical self-estrangement.

Paula Yates, the so-called 'Princess of Punk', died in September 2000, aged 40. The press reported that the police found empty vodka bottles, prescription drugs and heroin at her bedside, but no suicide note. In Britain, Yates was the Punk Era's trademark mediagenic female reveller in outrage and publicity. Originally famous for being the celetoid girlfriend of Bob Geldof, Yates posed naked at the Reform Club for *Penthouse*, and published a book of photographs called *Rock Stars in their Underpants*. Eventually, she married Geldof and had three daughters with him. She also became a TV presenter. First she co-presented Channel 4's flagship '80s music show, *The Tube*. Later she worked as an interviewer for the *Big Breakfast* show, where her forté was to interview celebrities from a bed. One fateful interviewee was the INXS singer Michael Hutchence.

Yates cultivated a dizzy, voluptuous, flirtatious public image. This was temporarily softened in the mid-1980s when Geldof's Live Aid campaign to relieve Third World hunger projected her in the role of a co-humanitarian, and also by her proselytizing role as a celebrity mother. However, perhaps because of this, the media portrayed her affair with Michael Hutchence in 1995 as a scandal. Yates was used to being cast as an amoral wild child, but now she suffered the additional media taunt of being vilified as an irresponsible mother. Geldof won custody of the children, but eventually agreed to share the responsibility with Yates. In 1996 Hutchence and Yates became the parents of their own child, Heavenly Hiranni Tiger Lily. A year later, Hutchence died in bizarre circumstances. He was found hanging from a belt in a Sydney hotel room. Yates's despair seemed to be all consuming. Her behaviour became increasingly erratic and volatile. She was treated for depression and fought an acrimonious custody battle over Tiger Lily with Hutchence's parents. She fiercely rejected the coroner's verdict that Hutchence's death was suicide. She insisted that it was a case of auto-erotic asphyxiation when a sexual game went tragically wrong.

In 1997 public revelations that her true father was Hughie Greene, the quiz show host of the 1960s and '70s, and not, as she believed, Jess Yates, a presenter of religious broadcasting, contributed to her fractured sense of self. Yates's public face was denigrated and publicly humiliated. Vilified by the media for leaving Geldof, she was assailed by the public judgement that Hutchence had killed himself and hence,

deliberately abandoned her. Now DNA tests questioned the authenticity of her veridical self. Bereft of a sense of origins and sundered from her lover in painful and
ambiguous circumstances, her veridical self became increasingly embattled. In 1998
she was admitted to a psychiatric hospital, and two weeks later apparently tried to
hang herself. She embarked on a series of well-publicized relationships, one with an
ex-heroin addict who later sold his story to the newspapers. In 1999 she tried to
relaunch her career by presenting *An Evening with Jerry Springer*, which flopped. *The
Guardian*'s obituary (18 September 2000) listed her death as 'apparent suicide' (a
premature, censorious judgement that was later refuted by the coroner's report), and
concluded that 'She loved the spotlight, and her fame by association. Anonymity never
suited her. She was vulgar, irrepressible and eccentric, and in many ways, represented
all that is silly and vacuous about modern celebrity.'

The public confession is the medium through which the celebrity renegotiates a
public face, following the acknowledgement of states of disintegration or near disintegration. Thus, Anthony Hopkins has regularly been interviewed about his fight against
alcoholism and his Alcoholics Anonymous membership. Keith Richards is open about
his former heroin addiction. Jim Bakker and Jimmy Lee Swaggart, the televangelists,
both admitted extra-marital affairs and asked forgiveness from their tele-congregations.
Swaggart, who confessed to consorting with a prostitute, begged for absolution on
live TV from his wife, from his son, from the pastors and missionaries of his denomin-
ation and from his global followers. At the end of his public confession he turned to
God: 'I have sinned against you, my Lord, and I would ask that your precious blood
would wash and cleanse every stain until it is in the seas of God's forgetfulness, never
to be remembered against me any more.' Bill Clinton also eventually, and after several
public denials, confessed, in a TV broadcast to the nation, no less, that he did, despite
all his previous denials, have sexual relations with Monica Lewinsky.

Celebrity homosexuality has a long history of being vigorously denied.
Montgomery Clift, Terence Rattigan, Noel Coward, J. Edgar Hoover, John Gielgud
and James Dean were all highly reticent about their sexuality. Liberace sued *The Daily
Mirror* in 1956 for describing him as a 'sniggering snuggling, scent-impregnated,
quivering, fruit-flavoured, mincing heap of mother love'. Not unreasonably, Liberace
claimed that the description imputed homosexuality. However he refuted the claim
that he was a homosexual. Liberace remained in the closet until his death in 1987 from
an AIDS-related illness, when he was posthumously outed by a coroner who insisted
on an autopsy.

An interesting variant of the disintegration/confession nexus that has become quite
prominent in recent years is the presentation of celebrity illness. Until quite recently,
the presentation of serious, life-threatening celebrity illness was masked from the
public. Physical disintegration following cancer, Alzheimer's disease or AIDS was
hushed up until after death, or until the truth could no longer be disguised. The
announcement that Ronald Reagan had Alzheimer's was delayed until his symptoms
had made him a virtual recluse. The news that Michel Foucault, Ian Charleston,
Anthony Perkins, Robert Fraser and Rudolf Nureyev had AIDS was only made public
after their deaths. Rock Hudson, Freddie Mercury and Robert Mapplethorpe with-
held the news that they were suffering from the illness until they were at death's door.
This contrasts with other celebrities who were highly public about their condition.
Derek Jarman, Oscar Moore, Kenny Everett, Magic Johnson, Holly Johnson and Harold

Brodsky were very open about their HIV status. Indeed, Jarman became something of a crusader for raising public awareness about AIDS and combating hypocrisy about gay lifestyle. Similarly, Frank Zappa announced that he was suffering from cancer early on in his illness. The playwright Dennis Potter agreed to a famous British TV interview with Melvyn Bragg in which he announced that he was suffering from terminal cancer, and spoke movingly about the illness and his imminent death. The journalists Ruth Picardie, Martyn Harris and John Diamond all became national celebrities in the UK when they began to write newspaper columns about their own terminal cancer. Diamond's column in *The Times* left him with the unwelcome sobriquet of 'Mr Celebrity Cancer'.

This type of celebrity disintegration and confession does not derive from auto- or exo-degradation. Interestingly, and chillingly, Diamond revealed that he received emails and letters accusing him of being a narcissist in devoting a newspaper column to his illness and a class enemy in 'whingeing *ad infinitum*' about cancer of the tongue and throat while ignoring the 'true face of low-income disease'. But this form of exo-degradation in which diagnosis of class guilt, character weakness or personality defect is an element in the aetiology of the illness, is a negligible feature in the disintegration–confession nexus. Being open about celebrity terminal illness presents the celebrity in an out-of-face relationship with the public and ultimately reveals the resilience of the veridical self. The disintegration of the body produces a new surface on which the self coheres and continues in a different kind of dialogue with the public.

Redemption

Auto- and exo-degradation ceremonies traumatize the relationship between celebrities and their fans because they reveal a schism between the public face and the veridical self. Celebrities who openly show contempt for their fans and expose the public face as a mask run the risk of cultural disinvestment by the public. Both O.J. Simpson's murder trial and Gary Glitter's prison sentence for downloading child pornography from the internet had a devastating effect on their relationships with the public. So far, their attempts to repair the shattered chains of attraction by public interviews and confessions have failed.

Promiscuity in sexual relations, addiction to alcohol and narcotics or conspicuous consumption also degrades the idealized image of the celebrity in the eyes of the public. Fatty Arbuckle's career as a film comedian was destroyed in the early 1920s after he was tried for the manslaughter of the starlet Virginia Rappe. Arbuckle was acquitted, but he never escaped the taint of sexual perversity in connection with Rappe's death. Despite professing his innocence and trying to return to the screen, he was never again accepted by the public.

Louise Brooks, the scintillating silent star of *Pandora's Box* and *Diary of a Lost Girl* (both 1929), acquired the reputation for sexual libertinism, which resulted in the collapse of her career. Interestingly, Brooks was rediscovered by the English critic Kenneth Tynan in the 1970s living in obscurity and poverty. His profile revived public interest in her, both as a neglected icon of the 1920s and as a feminist heroine who had been punished for her sexual independence.

In 1994 Michael Jackson paid an undisclosed sum, believed to be over $25 million, to prevent the allegation that he sexually molested a thirteen-year-old boy being brought to trial. In interviews Jackson complained that he had been the victim of police intimidation and denied all charges. However, his position as the supreme idol of his day was seriously damaged.

But as the live TV broadcasts made by Jimmy Swaggart and Bill Clinton demonstrate, confession can indeed produce redemption. Redemption is the ritualized attempt by a fallen celebrity to re-acquire positive celebrity status through confession and the request for public absolution. In admitting to battles with alcoholism, Elizabeth Taylor, Richard Burton, Paul Merson, Tony Adams, Alex 'Hurricane' Higgins and George Best counterposed their idealized status with the public face of vulnerability. They appealed for compassion from the public rather than blind worship.

Redemption bids carry no guarantee of success. Political commentators usually agree that Clinton's confession and request for forgiveness over the Lewinsky affair hobbled his claim to be the moral leader of the nation. Curiously, for a nation that sets such outward store on cultural probity, Clinton's revelations did not fatally damage his position. His leadership of the longest bull market in postwar history deflected much of the criticism. He left the office of President in 2001 with the highest public approval ratings on record. Then again, he never regained the reputation of a 'Teflon President', one able to withstand moral taint. Clinton was branded as an amoral leader, an iconic status that fittingly summed up the hypocrisy and empty meretriciousness of the 1990s.

The fallen celebrity may never regain the former level of elevation in the public sphere. But confession can produce a more nuanced relationship with the public, in which frailty and vulnerability are recognized as the condition of embodiment, common to celebrity and fan alike. A sort of democracy is established between the celebrity and the fan on the basis of common embodiment, and the vulnerability that is the corollary of embodiment.

Redemption processes involve the active complicity of the audience. For fans are requested either to grant forgiveness in respect of personality weaknesses or negative behaviour that contrasts with the idealized image of the celebrity, or acknowledge the vulnerability and weakness of celebrity.

When Robert Downey Jnr was sentenced for drugs offences in 1999, an internet vigil was established. The 'To Know Him is To Love Him' website was run by 'lovers, friends and supporters' of the actor, and consisted of poems, letters and messages designed to keep him in the public eye. Downey claimed to have renounced drugs when he was released from the California State Penitentiary at Corcoran in August 2000. His drug use, and the prison sentence, made him a scandalous figure in Hollywood. However, his fan base remained substantially intact, thus increasing his chances of getting back into films. The point re-emphasizes the socially constructed character of celebrity. Redemption involves representational negotiation to restore the diminished cultural capital of the celebrity. In Downey's case, public sympathy was orchestrated by the website and a profile in *Vanity Fair* in which he expressed penitence. But the redemption script is high risk, since it acknowledges personality defects and depends on avoiding slipping back into the pattern of behaviour that provoked the public censure and punishment.

The cult of distraction

Celebrities are part of the culture of distraction today. Society requires distraction so as to deflect consciousness from both the fact of structured inequality and the meaninglessness of existence following the death of God. Religion provides a solution to the problem of structured inequality in this life by promising eternal salvation to true believers. With the death of God, and the decline of the Church, the sacramental props in the quest for salvation have been undermined. Celebrity and spectacle fill the vacuum. They contribute to the cult of distraction that valorizes the superficial, the gaudy, the domination of commodity culture. The cult of distraction is therefore designed to mask the disintegration of culture. Commodity culture is unable to produce integrated culture, because it brands each commodity as momentarily distinctive and ultimately replaceable. Likewise, celebrity culture cannot produce transcendent value because any gesture towards transcendence is ultimately co-opted by commodification.

Celebrity culture is a culture of faux ecstasy, since the passions if generates derive from staged authenticity rather than genuine forms of recognition and belonging. Materialism, and the revolt against materialism, are the only possible responses. Neither is capable of engendering the unifying beliefs and practices relative to sacred things that are essential to religious belief. The cult of distraction, then, is both a means of concealing the meaninglessness of modern life and of reinforcing the power of commodity culture. Celebrity provides monumental images of elevation and magic. The psychological consequence of this is to enjoin us to adjust to our material circumstances and forget that life has no meaning. We adjust either by adopting the celebrity as a role model or colluding with the inference that the masses are obviously inferior to the gilded minority that occupy the pantheon of celebrity since they have not 'made it'. In each case there is a strong tendency to adopt celebrity style as a way of deflecting attention from the deeper, perhaps insoluble, questions about the proper content of life. On this account, celebrity culture produces an aestheticized reading of life that obscures material reality and, in particular, questions of social inequality and ethical justice.

The dichotomy concerning whether to regard celebrity culture as an energizing force or a stupefying one recurs throughout the literature. Arguably, it is a misleading dichotomy, leading to profitless debate. In every case, the social impact generated by a particular celebrity is a matter for empirical analysis. For example, it is not in serious dispute that Princess Diana's involvement in the landmines campaign dramatically raised public awareness of the issue and mobilized resources. Whether this outcome was the accomplishment of an essentially meretricious and self-serving personality is beside the point. The campaign helped to relieve suffering, and this relief could not have been accomplished so readily by other available means.

Celebrity placement and endorsement

Celebrities can indeed change things and fill us with powerful inclinations and cravings. This is one reason why celebrity endorsement is a sought-after feature in the market-place, and corporations will pay large sums to acquire it. The Nike advertising campaigns featuring Michael Jordan, Spike Lee and Bo Johnson in the late 1980s and early '90s dramatically increased sales. The Nike campaign slogan – *'just do it'* – entered popular culture as a catch-phrase. In these examples, the economic and publicity effect of celebrity involvement can be measured quite precisely. What is less clear are the psychological, emotional and cultural motives that make people respond to celebrity campaigning and endorsement. Do we buy Nike because we desire to be associated with the physical prowess and power of Michael Jordan? Or do we have confidence in his personal veracity as a self-made athlete? Is Jordan's endorsement popular because he is a symbol of material success, with a bank balance most of us would envy? Or is the attraction more to do with Jordan's lifestyle, which is built around leisure and sport, whereas for most of the audience leisure and sport are available only *after* work? Was Jordan's playful, relaxed style a factor in suggesting that the Nike product is fun? His appeal in the Nike ads is probably a mixture of all these things.

Commodity placement operates on the principle that the public recognition of the celebrity as an admirable or desirable cultural presence can be transferred onto the commodity in a commercial or ad. The cultural impact of placement depends on the condensation of associations in the consciousness of spectators around an overwhelming image that the celebrity confers positive value. The Coors and Hershey advertising campaigns of the 1980s used retro Pop culture to advertise their product. Images of Neil Armstrong on the moon, Elvis Presley, Marilyn Monroe and Sugar Ray Leonard were presented as 'American Originals'. The re-mythologizing of American Pop culture was used as the lever to mythologize the commodity. In the late 1990s, Apple used billboard images of John Lennon and Yoko Ono, Gandhi, Orson Welles, Alfred Hitchcock, Albert Einstein and other celebrity mavericks in the 'Think Different' campaign to suggest the unique cachet conferred by possessing an Apple computer.

The examples illustrate the complexity of the relationship between mass desire and celebrity status. We are drawn to celebrities for a variety of reasons. These can only be concretely established through empirical investigation. At the level of theory, it might be hypothesized, *inter alia*, that celebrities provide us with heroic role models in an age of mass standardization and predictability. They are idealized sexual objects who present an intense sexuality that is designed to attract us but, at the same time, to withhold consummation. They express human vulnerability and frailty that engages our sympathy and respect, and which also, perhaps, sets a standard of physical and mental decomposition that exerts a cautionary influence in the management of emotions in daily life. They are symbols of material success, and in flaunting the prodigious surplus given to them they are, at one and the same time, magnets of desire, envy and disapproval. In addition, notoriety allows society to present disturbing and general social tendencies as the dislocated, anti-social behaviour of folk demons. Mass murderers like Timothy McVeigh and serial killers like Fred and Rosemary West and Harold Shipman are presented by the mass-media as isolated figures in a macabre theatre of horror. Arguably, their notorious celebrity distracts us from facing the eternal questions concerning life, death and the meaning of existence. By distracting us from the terror of realizing that existence is ultimately meaningless, it might be argued that celebrities perform a significant therapeutic function in contemporary culture. However, because this function is not typically organized or planned in any rigorous or binding way, it is more plausible to regard it as a by-product of a wider cult of materialism in which the purpose of distraction is to accumulate value for the celebrity. The idea that celebrity culture is a means of cultural displacement, in which the loneliness of existence is compensated for by the illusion of recognition and belonging, is certainly at the heart of Structuralist readings that equate celebrity culture with social control and economic exploitation. But do these readings adequately explain the extraordinary prodigality of celebrity culture in contemporary society?

The prodigality of celebrity culture

The shaman in tribal society is either a singular figure or part of a small group defined by ancestral bloodline or bio-cultural stigmata. His role is constrained by inherited beliefs and rituals and his influence is culturally synchronized to become pre-eminent in relation to cyclical or ceremonial requirements. At feast-time, war, birth, mourning and burial, the shaman's power is ascendant. At other times it is an understated, immanent element in the life of the tribe.

In contrast, celebrities are relatively profuse in modern society, and their presence is ubiquitous. It is not merely a question of the manifold ranks of celebrity relating to sport, music, art, film, literature, humanitarianism, politics and the other institutions of modern culture. Within these ranks, upward and downward mobility is a continuous characteristic of the status hierarchy to which celebrity watchers, and the general public, are perpetually attuned. In addition, the mass-media supply a diet of celetoids and celeactors to the public. The very prodigality of celebrity culture in contemporary society suggests an absence.

It might be thought, as Structuralists do, that the cause of this absence is materialism. The desire for wealth creates an overheated culture in which celebrities are constructed as commodities for economic accumulation. The celebrity race is very obviously bound up with the desire for wealth. But material explanations alone cannot explain the prodigality of celebrity in modern culture. After all, celebrity performers do not stop performing after they become millionaires. Michael Caine, Sean Connery, Jack Nicholson, Clint Eastwood, Tina Turner, Joni Mitchell, Barry White, Eric Clapton, Keith Richards, Elton John, Mick Jagger and Neil Young are sufficiently rich never to have to work again. Greed alone is not a sufficient motive to explain their readiness to devote much of their fifties and beyond to performing. Yet while they may now pace themselves more carefully, they do not retire from the screen or stage. Public acclaim answers to a deep psychological need in all of us for recognition. Acclaim carries the sensual pleasure of being acknowledged as an object of desire and approval.

Despite external appearances, celebrities are perhaps among the most insecure people in our midst. Their appeal is certainly a measure of our own insecurity. The original condition of being in the world is openness. This is the cause of our vulnerability and our desire to impose control. Being in the world is always socially interconnected. Hence there is an inherent tension between being and society, for we can never be entirely comfortable in a world where the satisfaction of our desires depends on others, and where the principles of scarcity and human vulnerability pattern our actions and responses. The sociological attempt to integrate being and society around ideology or hegemony is inadequate, for it presents a one-dimensional view of openness in which, for example, being is understood as the reflection of corporate power, the culture industry, capital, the state, patriarchy, money culture or an equivalent directing agency. On this reading, a significant function of celebrity is to enable us to manage vulnerability and cope with the fact of our own mortality.

Certainly the dilemma of vulnerability and immortality is accentuated in 'post-God' societies. The death of God is the original end of the unifying recognition that we live under one ideological system. Henceforward, the differentiation of taste and the pluralization of culture become more pronounced in the public sphere. In the absence of a unifying deity, some people search for cult figures to give life new meaning. From the particularity of a cultural position, universal claims are often made. It is unsatisfactory to view celebrities only as objects of control and manipulation. They are also symbols of belonging and recognition that distract us in positive ways from the terrifying meaninglessness of life in a post-God world. Our desire for distraction makes us peculiarly vulnerable to shamanism.

Both Charles Manson and Jim Jones exerted hypnotic power over their disciples. Manson was the ringleader behind the murders of Sharon Tate and other celebrities in Hollywood in 1969. Jones was the eponymous head of Jonestown, a religious community in Guyana, who ordered his flock of 913 to commit 'revolutionary suicide' in 1978. More recently, David Koresh was the inspirational leader at the centre of the Waco massacre. Shoko Asahara was the figurehead of the Aum Shinrikyo ('Supreme Truth') movement in Japan, who was found guilty of unleashing sarin nerve gas on Matsumoto city in 1994, killing seven people and injuring 144 others and in the Tokyo subway system in 1995, killing twelve and injuring thousands. In 2000, at the Ugandan settlements of Rugazi, Buhunga, Roshojwa and Kanungu, the remains of over 900 people were exhumed. The dead were recovered from the headquarters of the 'Movement for the Restoration of the Ten Commandments of God'. They were the victims of a sect headed by Joseph Kibwetere, Father Dominic Kataribabo and a former prostitute Credonia Mwerinde. The millennarian 'Movement' predicted the end of the world on the last day of the twentieth century. The sect members were prophesized to be rescued by 'a chariot of fire sent by the Lord'. When the prophecy failed, the congregation grew restive, and Mwerinde postponed the date of deliverance until March. At the time of writing, the subsequent pattern of events remains unclear. Newspaper reports suggest that 400 of the followers may have been executed, and a further 550 immolated themselves at the behest of their leaders.

The success of televangelism in the USA is further evidence of the persistence of religious belief. However, without seeking to mitigate the significance of evangelicals, fundamentalists and pentecostals in American culture and economy, their public profile exaggerates their power. Their prominence is a symptom of the relative decline of the mainstream churches. The theatricality and emotionalism of Jimmy Swaggart and Pat Robertson draws on the folk tradition of evangelism in America. But televangelism is also an extension of the mass-media, and employs the basic devices of elevation and magic that are integral to celebrity culture.

Celebrity culture is inherently inflationary. For the impetus is always on being bigger and brighter. Organized religion has itself succumbed to this tendency. By 1995 Pope John Paul II had canonized 276 saints and beatified 768 people. This is more than all the other twentieth-century popes combined. Jean Paul II's world tours, with the ritual kissing of the soil on alighting from his aircraft, and the staged authenticity of mass rallies and live TV links, clearly borrow many of the ceremonies and devices refined by Hollywood and the rock industry for the presentation of celebrity to the public.

Celebrity culture is no substitute for religion. Rather, it is the milieu in which religious recognition and belonging are now enacted. That this milieu has adapted ceremonies of ascent and descent that were prefigured in religion is beside the point. The ubiquity of the milieu is the real issue. Today perhaps only the family rivals celebrity culture in providing the scripts, prompts and supporting equipment of 'impression management' for the presentation of self in public life. Indeed, a good deal of evidence, notably the high rate of divorce and the rising number of single-person households, suggests that the family is in decline, while celebrity culture seems to be triumphantly ascendant.

The desire to be recognized as special or unique is perhaps an inevitable feature of cultures built around the ethic of individualism. The overwhelming desire for ordinary people to be validated as stars is, arguably, part of the modern psychopathology of everyday life, and is significant only in the age of celebrity culture. For example, Jennifer Ringley, an otherwise 'ordinary' person, has constructed a website that consists of scenes from her daily life – eating, reading, talking to friends and sleeping. Her sex life is not shown. In 1998 her site was receiving over 500,000 hits daily.

Some years ago Christopher Lasch argued that the 'cult of narcissism' permeates contemporary culture.[12] The narcissistic personality lives in a condition dominated by self-absorption, in which psychic and social relevance is focused on the practices and wants of the self rather than on the state of society. Narcissism is associated with the hyper-inflation of the ordinary. The musings and experiences of a housewife, an office worker, a student – ordinary people – are invested with cosmic significance. Lasch had in mind the spread of popular psychology and psychic self-help programmes in the late 1960s and '70s.

Ringley's website is an extension of the cult of narcissism. It presupposes not only that a mass audience will find the monotonous, predictable existence of an ordinary person interesting, but that regularly following this routine produces social cohesion. To begin with, spectators are perhaps drawn to the site for voyeuristic reasons. It offers a keyhole into the private existence of someone else. But voyeurism is an insufficient reason to explain the longevity and popularity of the site. In addition the website offers repeated opportunities for identification and recognition. By entering the site regularly, spectators establish a routine in their own lives that is the basis for filling the void of loneliness.

In this chapter I have questioned whether celebrity culture has replaced religion as the focus of recognition and belonging. I submit that the rites of ascent and descent that were originally developed in primitive religion have been taken over and recast by celebrity culture. This is not, however, a one-way process. Organized religion has borrowed some of the forms and styles of retailing and mass communication perfected in the organization of celebrity in public life. Disneyland has been used as a stage for religious recruitment, and Pope John Paul II has turned some aspects of the papal dispensation of sainthood into an Oscar ceremony. I have also submitted that convergence is not total. Organized religion remains committed to producing a general view of social and spiritual order. Celebrity culture motivates intense emotions of identification and devotion, but it is basically a fragmented, unstable culture that is unable to sustain an encompassing, grounded view of social and spiritual order. None the less, some elements of celebrity culture do have a sacred significance for spectators. To the extent that organized religion has declined in the West, celebrity culture has emerged as one of the replacement strategies that promote new orders of meaning and solidarity. As such, notwithstanding the role that some celebrities have played in destabilizing order, celebrity culture is a significant institution in the normative achievement of social integration.

Notes

1   See F. Vermorel & J. Vermorel, *Starlust* (London, 1985).
2   Keith Thomas, *Religion and the Decline of Magic* (London, 1971).
3   M. Eliade, *Shamanism* (London, 1964).
4   Eliade, *Shamanism* p. 511.
5   E. Durkheim, *The Elementary Forms of Religious Life* (New York, 1915).
6   In N. Gabler, *Life: The Movie* (New York, 1998).
7   D. Riesman, *The Lonely Crown* (New York, 1950).
8   Cited in J. Fowles, *Starstruck* (Washington, DC, 1992), p. 192.
9   E. Morin, *The Stars* (New York, 1960), pp. 38–9.
10   G. McCann, *Marilyn Monroe* (London, 1996), p. 199.
11   M. Faithfull, *Faithfull* (London, 1994), p. 191.
12   In C. Lasch, *The Culture of Narcissism* (London, 1980).

Chapter 22

Ernest Sternberg

PHANTASMAGORIC LABOR
The new economics of self-presentation

IT HAS BECOME COMMON wisdom that we are entering or have entered the information era. This is a time when production depends upon computing and scientific reasoning, knowledge and rational calculation underlie wealth, and society comes to be dominated by an educated elite.[1] I will contend, however, that the pre-eminent economic phenomenon of our times is quite different: the driving force in the new economy is not information but image.[2] We are entering a phantasmagoric capitalism, driven by the economic capacity to load products, including both objects and persons, with evocative meaning.

We can observe the rise of this new capitalism in numerous products, ranging from consumer icons like automobiles and clothes, to the commercial and residential sanctuaries that make up the landscape, to the pilgrimage sites frequented by tourists.[3] In this article I explore only once facet of the new economy, its labor market, in which workers and managers raise their value through calculated self-presentation, using techniques originally meant for the making of celebrities.[4] The result is labor-value dependent not on bits, bytes and expertise, but on tidbits, sound bites and notoriety. This article traces the Anglo-American history of self-presentation in labor markets, from the renaissance through romantic and modernist labor, up to the phantasmagoric style. As we shall see, this is a style in which labor has become intimate and personal: sellers of labor have learned from the celebrity world how to adapt persona to the requisites of the market.

Phantasmagoric medicine

We will begin our study of phantasmagoric labor by taking a look at health care, a field still mired in the traditional routines of twentieth-century medicine. Hospitals are only now becoming aware – says an article in *Healthcare Forum* – that "Service is always performance." Health care executives are starting to appreciate "what is perhaps the most important factor in the long-term success of a hospital: its face to the customer." They can learn from successful retail establishments, where "Employees know that everything in the store, including themselves, is directed toward one end: creating a person-enhancing performance for the customer." After all, the article continues, health is not just about feeling well but "feeling good". Most hospitals still release patients discombobulated by long waits and exotic procedures, but increasingly, "Feeling good is one of those intangibles that we now recognize as important in healing and health." Hospital workers themselves are essential in conveying this good feeling. Workers must be initially screened or later trained to help the hospital project a consistent image, so that, even in brief exchanges, they can "form a relationship" with the client.[5]

The authors, one of whom is a well-known management researcher, do not go into more detail, but if we supplement the article with many others on image making in business, we can draw clear lessons. All levels of workers from orderlies to executives help shape the facility's caring image, and should foster that image through their personal conduct. The organization's face workers – those making direct face to face contact with patients – should especially personify the virtues associated with healing, such as those of caring, hygiene and expertise. The executive has the double responsibility to direct her employees' performances and to control her own demeanor in front of subordinates, colleagues, and the hospital's external overseers and benefactors.

This phantasmagoric labor is now performed in industry after industry. At one Manhattan clothing retailer, where the interior expresses leisurely gentility, the employees' confirm the theme through their colorful clothes, engaging banter and a penchant for carefree hugging. At another store, this one purposefully minimalist and muted, the personnel are austere, tall and somber-suited.[6] Recognizing that workers are part of the product, some restaurants are quite deliberate in their theatrical preparation. They train waiters for table-side performances, hire out-of-work actors when available, and hold auditions instead of interviews.[7] On airlines, the flight attendant's requisite attribute is the smile, which is part of the service itself; when professionally performed and nimbly adapted to changing situations on board, the smiling countenance conveys welcome upon boarding, confidence that the plane is airworthy, reassurance about timeliness and an invitation to return.[8]

Performance having become essential, the job interview takes on added importance, conveying not only the aspirant's formal skills, but also his or her ability to perform properly for colleagues and clients. Of course the applicant must make a good impression through attire, speech, manner, grooming and posture, but what's critical is that these effectively portray the persona that is to be put forward. For a future in the corporation, she would do well to show competence, exude authority and inspire trust, but also to suggest friendly colleaguality. The applicant who is anxious can turn to acting coaches and image consultants for good advice.

To calm stage fright, summon the right emotion by remembering a past victory or joy. Uncertain of what persona to put forward, create a character as an actor does from a script, by imagining the role – the ideal executive or perfect candidate – and walking, talking, acting and dressing as he would. Rehearse in front of friends, make your entrance, project your voice and maintain stage presence. After all, "A job interview is really an audition in which you're being asked to improvise a role", while guessing the expectations for the part.[9]

On the job, the self-presentational challenge varies by the performer's status and ambition. One hoping only to provide a well defined service, say retail service, need not convey a well-rounded persona, but only stereotyped bites of persona. Borrowing from the field of iconography – the study of the meanings of images – I will call this kind of self-presentation a *personification*: a human figure whose gesture, body position, costume and surrounding objects refer to a concept, usually a human virtue or failing, like Love, Faith, Truth, Veracity, Melancholy, Good Fortune and Greed.[10] Variously according to business setting, contemporary work performers must accomplish the iconographic task of personifying their virtue. Through physiognomy, costume, bearing, gesture and word, they personify Initiative, Approachability, Submissiveness, Trustworthiness or other qualities, as appropriate to the context. In this phantasmagoric labor market, the orderly, the nurse assistant, the waiter and the flight attendant have bits parts, expressing the same virtue over and over again to a procession of anonymous customers.

The executive, by contrast, must master the larger corporate drama, which she partly directs, but which she also acts in. Since many people are routinely befuddled, Confidence and Decisiveness are particular assets. At the business meeting, the executive (or the up-and-comer) must control the well-known business attributes of posture, eye contact, speech and handshake to personify Self-confidence above all,[11] but the executive cannot rest there. Well aware of organizational intrigue, she must monitor the audience and tactically adapt her performance to promote herself, ingratiate and intimidate, as the occasion may call for.[12] The executive must also shift roles during the course of the day, now acting as a confidante, showing compassion to a valued colleague who is facing troubles; next as a disciplinarian, reprimanding a poorly performing employee; then as a tolerant superior, patiently unraveling employee problems in a meeting; and finally as the company's eloquent promoter of new plans and new products. Each role requires attention to scene, timing, support cast and audience.[13]

At every economic level, the ability to present oneself has become a critical economic asset. As mere skills and credentials have become pervasive, and the world's pool of labor can claim to have ever more productive efficiency, mere workaday ability – what I have to offer through my commodified labor power – becomes an insufficient market asset. Aspiring for advancement and success, or merely for a job, I must still demonstrate formal capabilities like efficiency, credentials or technical skills, but I must also figuratively express merit through the images I convey to my evaluators. I must seek to heighten my value on labor markets through work *performance* through the expressive labor of the persona.

Mere stage tricks like a power wardrobe and assertive gaze are, however, no longer enough for business success. Within any industry, corporation or profession, the aspirant reaches the economic apex when she becomes a celebrity, a human icon. Now colleagues cite her name with awe or jealousy when she is not present; subordinates show deference as a matter of course; her ideas are respected by the very fact that they arose from her; even to meet her is an honor; and all long to hire her, work with her, and gain her counsel, were she only available. Now lifted above the usual competitive anonymity, the performer can use her hard-won iconicity to assert advantages over competitors and to command for her services a market premium.

To explain what it takes to arrive at these heights of the phantasmagoric labor market, run-of-the-mill success manuals will not do. So I will look to the more profound work of composition that goes into the making of the media celebrity, but first we must make our way through some potentially confusing ideas. We must particularly steer clear of the truisms that firms are interested in the worker's true skills, such that I am talking about little more than marginal enhancement, a kind of window dressing; and, contradictorily, that all human conduct is thoroughly theatrical, so that what I have to say is obviously true and nothing new. Making my way between these viewpoints, I will hold that labor has indeed always been performed, but performed in keeping with the stylistic possibilities of the time and culture. Having undergone a stylistic evolution, labor is now performed in the phantasmagoric style.

Drama and the renaissance of the self

To speak of self-presentation as a kind of drama is already old hat in some circles. In the years since the publication in 1959 of Erving Goffman's *The Presentation of Self in Everyday Life*,[14] the 'dramaturgical approach' has turned into a small but lively genre of the social sciences, complete with studies of labor negotiators, imprisoned felons, surgical room personnel, con artists, and numerous other common and uncommon social performers.[15] Like the iconographic ideas that I propose here, dramaturgy in the understanding of conduct is more than a metaphor: a person who rehearses and then acts out a role in a job interview is literally – not metaphorically – putting on a dramatic performance. Dramaturgy can even be defined as "the study of how human beings accomplish meaning in their lives"[16] and Goffman's work can be seen as the search for a language by which to make sense of the human capability to express meaning. Iconography differs from dramaturgy mainly in that it encompasses all the arts, not just theater, and provides a general language by which to examine objects as well as performances. Both kinds of inquiry look to the humanities for the language by which to comprehend the production of meaning.

I also want to keep some distance between what I have to say here and the dramaturgical approach. Firstly, writers in the dramaturgical genre seem to hold that human conduct is ahistorically and universally theatrical.[17] Goffman's book explains self-presentation through anecdotes about matters as diverse as Mandarin rituals in late imperial China, domestic banter in the Shetland islands, and the behavior of baseball umpires in America. The ahistorical mode fits the theory that there is nothing new under the sun. After all, in the years around 1600, the signboard over the entrance to the Globe Theater bore the Latin inscription meaning "All the World is a Theater", and as one of the theater's better known playwrights put it, "All the world's a stage, And all the men and women merely players."[18] If conduct is universally and ahistorically theatrical, then perhaps there is no particular merit to what is my claim – that there is something different about self-presentation now, at the beginning of the twenty-first century.

Secondly, Goffman (and other writers that I know who have been influenced by him) treats performances as social rituals, seemingly never tiring of the running joke that we are not as rational as we think. Self-presentation is treated as ritual even when it is practiced by shoe clerks or funeral home operators, who seem to be using dramaturgic tactics quite consciously for business purposes. I would say, however, that when the shoe clerk clearly has something to gain by attuning his behavior to the expectations of the audience, then he is not simply acting out a ritual but making expressive choices in response to economic constraints. He chooses his personification, say that of Courtesy, Solicitousness or Friendship, specifically to move the customer. This is not ritual but thematic calculation, drawing on the sample of cultural referents that he has at his disposal.

Since I will argue that contemporary markets generate a much more determined shaping of the persona for business purposes, I have to show that human conduct is neither ritualized nor ahistorically given. Indeed, a quote from Shakespeare does not clinch the ahistorical argument. To reconstruct why this is, we should recall that in the Europe of the Renaissance, though men and women could increasingly contend with alternative modes of thought drawn from ancient classics, natural history and humanism, their lives were still preordained. Labor was still immersed in ties to family, trade, status and religion. Through the sixteenth century, sumptuary laws in hundreds of European towns still required each man's and woman's dress to reflect ascribed rank and place. Renaissance Venice, Florence and Milan set many precedents for modern commerce, but they were not free markets for the vast majority of their citizens. Leonardo da Vinci did not sell his talents on the market; he pursued his callings by declaring loyalty to successive patrons, who thereby gained the right not merely to employ him but to govern him.[19]

In sixteenth- and seventeenth-century England, including the American Colonies, labor was still a social as well as economic commitment. The master usually had jurisdiction over the worker and exclusive rights to his energies, subject to shared moral constraints. The worker's violation of the master's will was almost universally punishable by imprisonment. Depending on jurisdiction, masters could recover runaway servants (the seventeenth-century English word 'servant' covers a broader range of workers than it would in later centuries), subject them to additional servitude, administer corporate punishment and prohibit their marriage without consent.[20] The worker, servant or tradesman could be well aware of the ironies and injustices of his fate, but was still caught between an emerging sense of freedom and a lingering servitude; he sees no choice but to adhere to his status and place.

As the renaissance progressed, there was increasing intellectual room for skepticism, humor and ironic distance from one's worldly lot, though little room to violate inherited constraints. It was for this reason that pretense and disguise are such common renaissance motifs — but they are explicitly understood as violations. In Shakespearean drama, when a character takes on a role that is not properly his, he does so to escape danger, gain an inheritance or engage in a romance, and this violation of the character's ascribed place typically becomes an occasion for humor or tragedy.[21] Apart from farce and tragedy, characters stick to ascribed roles. Travel narratives, personal reflections and even pornography were still dim and unfocused, as if authors were merely vehicles for the expression of their rank, status and nationality.

It was only in the eighteenth century, as the renaissance ended, that autobiography graduated from confessions and defenses of one's public character, to intimate self-reflection.[22] Until then, "All the world's a stage" only because men and women must play their assigned roles in each of their seven different ages or suffer the dramatic consequences, and not because they can wilfully compose their self-presentations for personal advantage.

Romantic labor

By the second part of the eighteenth century, a new sense of individual self-identity abounds in the autobiography, novel and travel narrative, and in individualistic philosophy and liberal political economy. Where individuals once understood their own soul as part of universal divinity, they now increasingly prized their autonomy. They saw significance in the particularities of their own life course, wanted to explore their own feelings and the depths of consciousness, and valued the creative imagination.[23] It is more than a coincidence that it was in this period, the late eighteenth and early nineteenth centuries, as romantic concepts of the self spread through Europe and North America, that free labor also came on the scene. The historic transformation that created the free market in which labor could be bought and sold was also the one in which the autonomous, rationally disengaged self appeared in human history; and they reinforced each other's rise. Indeed, the new romantic mode of self-presentation spread from the elite to the general population during the same century that most of the workforce had to explicitly sell its labors on the market.

Romantic self-presentation and free labor converge revealingly in nineteenth-century America's self-help manuals. In these days before formal business education, these books (along with newspaper articles and lectures) were the primary means by which business people acquired their concepts of business conduct. Irving Wylie writes that, by the second half of the century, these books had a common line. Repetitively and almost uniformly they tout depth of character as the fount of success.[24]

Of the inner faculties that the manuals recommended, the most important were industry, perseverance and moral uprightness, not to mention punctuality, reliability, loyalty, obedience and humility.[25] These moral requisites applied to the master as well as the worker. Prominent men frequently recalled in their own youth, and continued to express through their own conduct, the character traits they advocated to the young. William Astor put in more hours than his employees; Andrew Carnegie required his partners to prove their frugality through savings; New York merchant Arthur Tappan forbade his employees from going to the theater; Russell Sage never drank liquor; some disdained the habit of reclining in easy chairs.[26] Masters and workers made their way in the market through the power of character.

How did one obtain these faculties? It helped to submit to one's God-given vocation, something one discovered and cultivated through personal effort. It also helped to have white race, male gender, Anglo descent, upright stature and respectable physiognomy; and it was especially good to have been a country boy, raised far from the city's saloons and gambling dens, and made hale, strapping and diligent by farm work and fresh air.[27] But these starting endowments did not take the man far. He still had to slog up the ladder of success through the power of his inner faculties, and those faculties had to become manifest – had to be recognized – to gain market value. Therefore, the romantic era's aspirant to success already performed a labor of the personality, the hard labor or exhibiting the industry, perseverance and sobriety that would bring his strength of character to his evaluators' attentions.

Modernist labor

To begin a look at twentieth-century modernist labor, let's consider 'Schmidt', Frederick W. Taylor's pseudonym for a laborer he met at the Bethlehem Iron Company in Pennsylvania in 1899. In an anecdote in Taylor's *Principles of Scientific Management*, Schmidt epitomizes the 'first class' laborer. He is a determined and independent individual (he is unmoved by fellow workers' opposition to piecework methods that Taylor introduced) who has the vigor and stamina to load ever more pig iron onto railway cars, in response to the differential wage incentives that Taylor had designed for that very purpose – to increase Schmidt's and his fellow workers' output.[28] Schmidt stands as the epitome of modern, commodified labor: atomized and individualistic, valued for the output he can generate, and responsive to quantitative incentives.[29] In diametrical contrast to Schmidt stood the scientific manager, someone whom Taylor conceived to be much like himself, someone with the brains, technical education and scientific understanding to make the systems that lead Schmidt to increase his output.

Though Taylor's specific advice was rarely implemented in pure form, Taylorism as a set of assumptions about work and the workplace has hung like a specter over twentieth-century labor and management, dominating academic education in business,[30] and setting the prejudices of generations of business students. Let's consider some of the assumptions. Unlike the romantic laborer, who works to express inner diligence and persistence, the modern worker works because he knows he can increase his income by increasing output. The manager, who is himself an employee, is uninterested in his moral standing vis-a-vis subordinates: his job is to design or maintain the system of incentives that make the worker do his work efficiently. Inherited concepts of obligation and vocation must crumble in the face of the overarching significance of output. Work is a literal, unambiguous and measurable activity taking place in a disenchanted setting, in which work roles are minutely subdivided, and all is coordinated by an impersonal hierarchy. Managers design and maintain the organizational system; workers function within it. Workers like Schmidt obey a management engineer like Taylor not out of archaic notions of loyalty, but because of self-interest: their submission to orders and incentives increases output, enriches the company and stabilizes society, to workers' and managers' mutual benefit.

As the modernist era progresses, however, the modernist assumptions never grasp the meaningfulness of the workplace, since the workplace is, after all, constructed as such; it is meaningfully made into a world of streamlined calculation. Since products and production methods frequently change, output is often a poor or unworkable indicator of personal effort. Workers learn they would better signify efficiency through rapidity in body movement and alacrity in speech, even if – out of sight of management – they subvert the production line or curse the manager. Managers themselves have to express in dress and demeanor the streamlined, replicable, unidimensional, emotionally detached and no-nonsense character associated with modern efficiency. Invented by nineteenth-century English dandies, and adopted in that century as a mode of male self-expression in commercial exchange,[31] the suit and necktie evolve by the twentieth century into a regularized sign of personal adherence to the bureaucratic setting.

Business modernism reaches its apex in the quantitative and algorithmic techniques developed in the 1950s and 1960s. Useful enough in delimited operations like truck scheduling and inventory keeping, they are hopelessly impractical in the management of the firm. Yet in those same two decades, operations research, quantitative models and fiscal analyses acquire such high prestige that even the manager who recognizes their inadequacies has to speak the technocratic lingo, for fear that he would be faulted for lacking modern sensibilities.[32] Ultimately the high modernist organization, and the labor of self-presentation that goes with it, succumbs to the rise of new organizations in which decisions are dominated by charismatic judgment and work by dramatic performance.

The phantasmagoric workplace

By the late twentieth century, the products of the modernist firm were available in surfeit. A plain commodity like Schmidt's pig iron was producible in abundance, so there was little profit in making just a little more of it or making it just a little more efficiently. The modernist concept of the firm as a set of rationalized operations reached its apex in efforts at the cybernetic systematization of the firm – just when rationalist assumptions about the purposes of the firm were becoming less tenable. Consumers were already less swayed by the conventionalized practicalities of stream-lined, replicable goods meant for the mass market. Rather they sought, and firms increasingly offered, goods distinguished by their capacity to deliver experiential content, like security, home life, sensuality and exoticism. Product meanings would have to be produced, composed, presented, distributed, phased out and redesigned, ever more quickly. Modernist commodity production now descended to capitalism's lower tier, while the capitalist vanguard shifted to the phantasmagoric style.

Businesses would now focus their energies on product iconicity. Bereft of the rational algorithms that had once guided them, businesses would both have to stage the dramatic reality on which the organization's viability depended, and to engage in the uncertain, creative, iconographic work of making products meaningful. As nineteenth-century romanticist *masters* were replaced by modern *managers*, these managers were themselves superseded by a new breed of *executives*, ones who could direct this creative work of product presentation.

In this new day, the executive no longer relies on modernist assumptions about a systematic reality manageable through science. Rather he cultivates the flair and charisma through which to execute decisions even in the absence of rationalist managerial criteria that could justify them. At the heights of the corporate firmament, the executive must exhibit the poise, persona and reputation that lend credence to his decisiveness. Though the executive often favors the assertiveness vaguely associated with the prominent entrepreneurs of the romantic era, he does not really claim or want the inner characteristics that the romantics touted, but rather – consistently with phantasmagoric values – puts on the pose of the Entrepreneur as a facet of the executive persona. Indeed, the capacity for calculated posing is now a routine requirement of the job. The executive has to master the arts of producing, directing, and acting in dramatic reality, thereby to earn the celebrity salary that both verifies and reinforces his glittering status.

The new firm must reward iconographic capabilities in the workforce. Whether the firm sells services, or packaged vegetables, or residences, workers must have the iconographic capability to heighten product value. Workers must act out their persona on the job. Aspirants to promotion and success must demonstrate their merit on labor markets and administrative hierarchies through the evocativeness of their self-presentations.

Unlike Taylor's engineered workplace, this phantasmagoric setting provides no clear standards or quantitative indicators of labor performance – except for one. In a world of rapid change and shifting meanings, a world in which rational principles are lacking and requisite skills are unclear, notoriety and recognition serve as proxy indicators of personal ability. In phantasmagoric capitalism, an aspirant for promotion and success would best prove his image-making capability through his actual notoriety.

Daniel Boorstin's definition of a celebrity as "a person who is known for his well-knownness"[33] now gains a specific economic logic: since each person advances through the demonstrated effectiveness of the persona, each person must prove his good repute. Therefore, in every industry and line of business, each of us must learn from celebrities, those human icons whose successes in presenting the persona are verified through their renown. Achieving celebrity is no small task. Following the path that celebrities themselves have taken, we must engage in the hard labor of the persona.

Composing the persona

Having learned from celebrities, we know that ordinary clothing, forgettable faces, hapless behavior and indistinct personalities command little market interest. Performers gain market value by mobilizing demeanor and conduct so they reference a realm of meaning that consumers find evocative. Since this may seem mysterious, we can gain some conceptual guidance from the field of iconography, which studies the meanings of images, including images of persons. In renaissance iconography, 'personification' is a human figure that gains heightened meaning by referencing any of the well-known realms of renaissance knowledge, like biblical stories, lives of the saints, Greek and Roman myths, and findings of natural history. An informed contemporary could guess that an image of a naked woman holding a mirror and compass and resting her left foot on a book held some figurative meaning (she may personify Prudence), and would know that a hovering Cupid was not to be taken literally as an avian infant. In the two centuries since the end of the renaissance, romanticism and modernism sought to fashion new and solid foundations for knowledge, while suppressing such figurative meaning. But now market forces have exuberantly reasserted figurative meaning, with consequences for all products, including labor.

Whereas – in our schematic review of modernism – the modernist worker merely had to perform a Schmidt or a Taylor, his successor in this new era must enter into a much more elaborate work of personal composition. To be sure, the labor performer can rarely afford the personality technicians that celebrities count on, such as agents, publicists, PR firms, personal managers, personal promoters, press

secretaries, spin doctors, spokespersons, advance men, speech writers, image consultants, therapists and personal groomers, including assorted costumers, cosmeticians,
cosmetic surgeons, voice coaches and hair-stylists. Despite this practical constraint,
the personal work of self-making offers much creative latitude. It requires complex
and subtle work of iconographic composition. The aspirant should begin by positioning the *personified* concepts she wants to present, and then selecting the *attributes* and
allegories through which she manifests them to the audience.

Personification

In the work of personification, choices are vast; but only a few will effectively serve
the market. To correctly select her virtue, the performer has to position herself with
respect to the audience.[34] This is not a simple matter, since there are multiple audiences: the target audience of clients and superiors, prop audiences selected in order to
impress the target audience, as well as a number of public audiences, which may be of
lesser interest. Having selected the target audience, the aspirant should try to understand its desires, and present herself as the personified fulfillment of those desires,
while keeping this incipient personification distinct from others that are already in
circulation and serve the same target audience.[35]

The aspiring star should, therefore, purposefully scan and comprehend those
phantasmagoric realms – movies, news events, street cultures, religious traditions,
histories – that provide to her target audience evocative meaning. Not at all a matter of
inscrutable instinct, this is work of deliberate cultural investigation. It is accomplished
through strenuous regimes of TV watching, going to movies, keeping in touch with
contacts, checking out web pages, attending parties and testing ideas in front of people
('focus groups') all in the rigorous search to understand the personal qualities that
move the audience.

Once immersed in the cultural realms that situate personal meanings, the performer can begin to make an informed choice of personifications. In general, political
aspirants can profit from Competence and Caring, along with qualities of being
Hard-working, Sincere and Confident. Aspiring business leaders also benefit from
Assertiveness, Decisiveness and Dynamism. A measure of Gravitas can only help,[36] but
excess Maturity may backfire, unless the person also exhibits Youthfulness and Vigor.
Some occupations require Artistry, so they tolerate Spontaneousness. Others prefer
Dependability and Responsibility, though they may frown on Submissiveness. Being
Unassuming and Likeable have their place, but the ambitious should not carry them to
excess. Face workers can often stress Considerateness and Solicitousness, spicing them
up with some Sexiness for good measure.

In some settings, as in retail facework, the performer need only exhibit one rote
virtue, since the audience is never present for long enough to think of the behavior as
excessively stereotyped. Higher-ranking jobs often require more complex personas,
so their assembly requires more compositional forethought. The effective persona
should be distinct from competing personas; should be well-rounded, with multiple
traits; should maintain consistency over time, though some personal evolution is
allowed; and – since romanticist concepts are still with us – should exhibit interiority,
meaning that it should appear to reflect the person's inner thoughts and feelings.[37]

Some charm, wit and pertinent knowledge can be learned even by those with little previous track record, and it may be possible to hide a bad trait, like a distant manner, short temper or tendency to vacillate in a crisis.[38] It is, however, usually unwise to invent personified virtues from scratch, especially the more demanding ones. Performers should avoid trying to express Honesty, if that is something for which they have demonstrated little previous competence, much less should they try to make a full persona for which they have had no prior inclination. Some do try the 'whole Pygmalion thing', but it is not normally to be recommended.[39] Performers are most persuasive playing a virtue they have come to master through its exercise and cultivation.

Even if the performer does feel comfortable with, say, Honesty as a personal asset, her iconographic task has only begun, since she still has to bring Honesty to its dramatic realization. Once a personified virtue (or set of virtues assembled into a persona) has been positioned for a target audience, the question is how to dramatize it. How, asks politician's consultant Brendan Bruce, "can conviction, optimism, determination or honesty be communicated? Most difficult of all, how can caring and competence be brought alive?" Margaret Thatcher's image makers "accurately identified her strengths: courage, conviction, and vision, then single-mindedly underlined them."[40] They had to bring such traits to dramatic realization through the careful selection of attributes and preparation of allegories.

Attribute

A technical term in the field of iconography, 'attribute' refers to the objects, clothes, body positions and accessories that reveal qualities of character, as a lily represents the bearer's purity, a crown shows the wearer's royal station, and a lion's hide shows the possessor's heroism.[41] The personal iconographer faces the creative task of selecting, making or modifying the attributes that will effectively signify the desired personification.

Clothes and cosmetics are the easiest place to begin. Chosen with a little care, they express dignity or informality, intensity or casualness, rebellion or propriety, liberality or conservatism, fashionableness or insouciance. Dark suits with pinstripes are said to make the man more authoritative, light brown suits make him approachable, impeccably shined shoes make him punctilious.[42] While bureaucratic performances are best kept fairly grave, retail face work is often profitably enhanced with a touch of the sensuous. Female workers can enliven the most routine commercial transaction with perfume, dress and cosmetically flushed cheeks that can be taken subliminally as signals of arousal. In Hollywood, actresses have even been known to keep their nipples erect with little rubber bands over them.[43] For men, however, overt signs of arousal are normally to be discouraged.

Voice is another vital attribute, but is tough to manage. Wishing to express confidence, the speaker should control a rising inflection, since it is often taken as a sign of inner doubt. At moments when she mentions a problem, she should avoid a sudden lowering of pitch, since it could be taken as tentativeness. Excessive nasality, such as that caused by sinuses, makes the speaker inexpressive and indistinct. Those wishing to have a more authoritative tone should particularly lengthen their pauses and slow their breathing. The speaker may well wish to confide to the audience, but this is especially difficult in broadcast media, not because confiding to a broadcast audience is seen as a contradiction in terms, but because slight mistakes in voice control can ruin the confidential tone and make the speaker sound strident or annoyed. For additional effect, the speaker may cultivate a foreign accent or regional dialect, and since deep voices still signify masculine authority and confidence, high pitched speakers can be coached, as Margaret Thatcher was, to lower pitch through vocal exercises.[44]

Movement, gesture, body position and eye contact can confirm or undermine the intended effect. Already upon her entrance, the performer's brisk gait suggests vigor and determination, but sunken chest and hunched shoulders signify her defensiveness; the performer is advised to imagine that a string is lifting her head, straightening the vertebrae, or to imagine that she is showing off a medal or pendant on the chest. She should note, however, that even assertiveness can be overplayed; a jaw jutting too far forward can seem not just assertive but combative. Now sitting down, the performer would seem stiff and nervous is she perches at the chair's edge, so a basic but effective move is to center the pelvis on the chair. Now in the midst of the conversation, she would best lean forward to the interlocutor to express intense interest.[45] She should avoid nervous movements like touching her mouth and nose, since these can be taken as signs of insecurity, or worse, of deception. Remembering that rapid eye fluctuations suggest shiftiness, while lack of eye contact may indicate insecurity, the good performer works on the direct gaze, which she can avoid turning into a stare by focusing on the bridge of the interlocutor's nose. But caution is called for if the performance is televised, since the same gaze that looks Steadfast when performed in person may seem Hostile when it comes through the television screen directly at the viewer.[46]

Since the face itself does so much to convey personal attributes, the most thorough performers have profited from advances in facial modification. The most remarkable achievement came after World War I, when army physicians sought to treat soldiers with severe facial wounds. They found that when incisions were made in front of the ear and under the cheeks, the facial skin peeled back easily, after which it could be redraped over the skull to better effect.[47] Giving renewed meaning to the word 'persona', their discovery – the face lift – demonstrated that the face is in itself a mask. Since then, the menu of cosmetic options has considerably expanded, so that it now includes eyelid surgery, ear surgery, cosmetic dentistry, breast augmentation, hair implantation and rhinoplasty, better known as the nose job. For the rest of the body, liposuction is available to sculpt the fat in buttocks, thighs, tummy and knees. Therefore, along with clothes, adornment, voice and movement, the face and body themselves are the attributes through which personification is expressed.

How do cosmetic technicians know what is better? For persons with apparent facial anomalies, the modernist standard appears to be a modal face roughly assembled from composites of the person's ethnic backgrounds. But for those with more or less standard faces, the cultural justification for a nose made less pointy or ear made less jutting is quite obscure. Perhaps the main cultural source is inherited popular stereotype, much of it formalized by nineteenth-century physiognomists. Their physiognomic manuals would explain that certain patterns of forehead wrinkles indicate intelligence, a downturned nose shows heartlessness or ill-humor, a pointed chin is a sign of craftiness, black eyes show intensity of passion, curly hair indicates a quick temper, and eyebrows are variously artistic, imaginative, shrewd or practical.[48] If these physiognomic ideas persist today, they do so, probably not because of secret readings by cosmetic surgeons, but because depictions of persons in novels, television and cinema have perpetuated physiognomic ideas.

But the media themselves have evolved. As they seek to move the audience, they test the new celebrities, new plots, new situations and new personas through which personal attributes like face acquire meaning. Indeed, attributes like the face depend for their meaning on the movies, news events and live performances in which they have recently been manifested. Perhaps the business performer wants to be brusk, or rugged, or cosmopolitan, or stylish, or commanding. She still needs to discover which attribute generates that effect. To make an effective choice (one that fulfills market demand), the performer must be aware of how recent celebrities have already used the attribute in support of their own personifications. The point is not to imitate, but to emulate: to use clothes, gait, voice and facial features as effectively as celebrities have. As opposed to the romantic physiognomy, or the modernist standardized face, the phantasmagoric face is a shifting composite of recent celebrities.

Allegory

In the field of iconography, an allegory is an event or situation that illustrates an abstract concept.[49] Though allegory has been in low repute in western art and literature since the end of the renaissance, it is in effect making a comeback in economic life, with celebrities leading the way. Sylvester Stallone displays his art collection to visiting reporters. The star performers and director of a movie are photographed bowling together after a day's shooting. One politician of elite background concludes a meeting with a highly visible lunch in a low-class eatery, and later leaves his limousine to mingle with the crowd; another displays his wife and children near the podium and makes available photographs from his military service. Still another celebrity (it could be a politician or entertainer) conspicuously maintains a box seat at Los Angeles Lakers games. Margaret Thatcher is photographed pulling a tiny dog on a beach.[50]

Now let's consider the meanings. The *Rambo* movies notwithstanding, Stallone is shown after all to be a person of refinement. The stars who go bowling reveal that they do get along with each other after work hours, at a pastime every American can understand. The politician variously demonstrates that he is a man of the people, loves his family and perhaps is even heroic. The celebrity attending the Los Angeles Lakers game shows he likes things that ordinary people can identify with, and Thatcher reveals that, besides being a severe executive, she appreciates small cuddly things.

The celebrities do not literally say 'we are sociable' or 'we are ordinary like you'; instead they go bowling. The bowling event is allegorical in the strict sense of the word: like the cheap-restaurant event and the dog-walking event, it figuratively refers to a personified virtue. Since pure fabrications are unnecessarily risky, each event dramatizes some real – no matter how tenuously real – event in the person's real life.[51] Stallone does really have an art collection. The star members do go bowling together, though only for as long as the photographer is there. One or another presidential or prime-ministerial candidate does eat in a cheap restaurant and have records of his military service. Thatcher did walk on the beach with the dog, which her advisers had borrowed for the occasion.

Though such dramatization is often thought to occur through the media, it does not have to. One can allegorically express one's virtues even through real events, like real restaurants one eats in or real dogs one walks, whether one is photographed or not. Indeed, since reputation spreads through recounted incidents and snippets of gossip, dramatized events in life are not very different from the media news bites that are so often derided. In media drama and in living drama, the shared requirement is that one be observed and remembered.

Note also that each event conveys fragments of the intended persona. Celebrity-watching scholar Joshua Gamson calls them 'tidbits', which come in two kinds, fluff and dirt, these being tidbits with respectively positive and negative valences. The celebrity and her retinue strive to generate fluff while suppressing or controlling dirt.[52] If particular outcomes are wanted, like job offers, the flow of fluff is itself organized into a coherent 'pitch'. Otherwise, celebrity makers try to manage the flow of tidbits to enhance and maintain a long-term persona.

Lacking the entourage and media coverage, ordinary strivers are hampered in their ambition, but not excessively so. Workers, entrepreneurs and aspiring business executives must all generate the impressions that sustain their credibility, and the examples in the beginning of this article do not exhaust the ways.

An additional way is through the management of personal lifestyle with a view to target audiences.[53] Properly displayed, children, status possessions, sports, musical avocations and volunteer activity can express personified virtues like family commitment, exclusive taste, healthful vigor, personal refinement and social conscience. Another way is through acquaintances, contacts, recommenders and endorsers. When properly cultivated, they can more or less reliably generate the flows of tidbits that affirm one's chosen personifications. And there is still another way – to mobilize job experiences and professional accomplishments. As in the phenomenon of the resume, past jobs and past clients are displayed for their capacity to signify Competence, Mastery, Follow-through, Responsibility and other virtues. Therefore, work experiences must be selectively chosen and work background carefully edited for their allegorical power. It is through such methods that performers raise their value on the phantasmagoric labor market.

The new economic man

As I have argued in the preceding pages, the labor of self-presentation has undergone a market-driven evolution. Relying in part on Kenneth Gergen's book *The Saturated Self*[54] I have identified the earlier styles of self-presentation as romantic and modernist. Despite their differences, these styles had in common the notion of the essential self – the self that serves as a template against which demeanor and conduct could be judged. In the new period we are entering, which Gergen and a number of other writers call 'postmodern', the old certainties are in question. As we shape persona for advancement and profit, has the essential self – or the belief in the essential self – disappeared?

There is much room for angst, since the premeditated composition of the persona contradicts cherished beliefs about the inner self. Those who write about image making must inevitably grapple with the contradiction between these inherited beliefs and the new forces of personal modification. To many authors, prototypically Daniel Boorstin, the moral response is uncompromising: we must stick with the hard distinction between the reality and artifice, self and image, and substance and surface, and decry the incessant spread of inauthenticity and illusion.[55]

Even the success literature that teaches how to put on images for personal advantage cannot relieve the moral tensions. One advisor on impression management in organizations says on one page "Carefully choose a desired image and present yourself accordingly", but adds on the next page "Be yourself", and "never try to be something you're not" (not least because "People will see through the facade").[56] In effect, this author takes the easiest course, which is to advocate premeditated image making without admitting any threat to received notions of the self. A less facile alternative is the outright cynicism found in a recent wave of success books. Partly in reaction to the mid-century's therapeutic get-along-and-make-friends success literature, these books show the way to *Winning through Intimidation* and *Power! How to Get It, How to Use It*. The books admit that image manipulation violates received values, but are eminently willing to violate them, on the practical grounds that being a nice guy doesn't work.[57] So, faced with the dilemmas of self-presentation, the writers either decry pretense and artifice, or try to slip out of the moral contradiction, or descent into an amoral cynicism.

The very fact that authors must contend with the moral dilemma reveals that romantic and modernist conceptions of the self still persist. Most of us are still drawn to the image of the man of integrity: the rugged individual who says what he means, who puts on no pretenses, who is straight and uncompromising. In times when inward depth is in question, a deep and unhurried voice, upright stature, furrowed brow, grey-streaked hair, unhesitant manner and firm opinions signify the inner essences for which audiences still yearn. In some circumstances, a record of military service and a biography that includes at least some personal struggle, along with occasional horseback riding and outdoor barbecues, can enhance the effect.

But yearn as we might, romantic essences cannot be revived. When horseback riding and past work history are premeditatedly allegorical events, they compromise their claim to revealing inner character. The man's deep tan, lumbering gait, towering stature and unhurried voice might reflect tanning machines, acting classes, growth hormones and vocal exercises. Or if the roughened hands were really obtained through outdoor living, they were roughened during leisurely weekends from superfluous wood chopping. With genetic testing, prenatal intervention, hormone treatments and lifelong cosmetic modifications, the last vestiges of the natural face may soon disappear. No matter how sincerely cultivated, the performer's frontier demeanor necessarily reflects mediated (media conveyed) notions of the rugged individual, and therefore necessarily violates the romanticist ideal to which it aspires.

We cannot rescue enough of the romantic ideal even to call this deceit, since audiences themselves expect their stars to perform. The celebrity-viewing audience is often well prepared with the jaundiced attitude that Joshua Gamson calls "audience sneer". Should the performer make the self-mocking admission that he is actually performing, viewers are likely to be left quite unshaken. But the performer need not always go so far, since on most occasions the viewers will be disinclined to reflect on the performer's deliberate calculation and prefer simply to enjoy the show. One of Gamson's celebrity-making respondents compares the celebrity viewers to the consumers who eat the carefully packaged hamburger at the fast-food outlet. They know the cow had to be killed and frozen and ground, but they do not necessarily need to be reminded of it.[58] Calculated image-making is not clearly deceitful in part because the audience itself desires the images.

So, perhaps we have as Kenneth Gergen and other writers believe, reached a time in which "the very concept of personal essences is thrown into doubt. Selves as possessors of real and identifiable characteristics – such as rationality, emotion, inspiration and will – are dismantled."[59] To Gergen, postmodern persons must contend with the construction of the self, leaving them in a condition of 'multiphrenia', a splitting of the self to form what he and others variously call the relational self, saturated self, mutable self or protean self.[60] If the self only arose for the first time in history in the renaissance, perhaps it is waning once again, soon to disappear.

Having gone along this far with the postmodernist arguments, I would rather now step back, since we must distinguish the *self* on the one hand and *styles of self-presentation* on the other. Throughout history, men and women have depended on their social world in constructing the self, constructing it with reference to concepts and themes characteristic of the times. So, in the nineteenth century the aspirant for business eminence had to construct the self with reference to the romantic notions of the time, just as much as today's aspiring executive does with phantasmagoric referencing; only the styles of self-expression differ. The self is a construct to be sure, but it is nonetheless each person's inalienable and precious resource.

The phantasmagoric world does not and cannot possibly eliminate the self. Rather, it spreads a new style of self-expression and self-denotation, *style* to be understood in the strong sense of the word, as the coherent set of referential realms – the stock of cultural referents – through which we make sense of the world. All styles, from the renaissance through the romantic, modernist and phantasmagoric, are imperfect and distorting, yet they provide the stylistic vocabulary through which each person can construct and present the self. The self is still a private resource; contemporary market actors just have new and broader stylistic opportunities by which to exploit it for economic benefit.

Even more than in the past, the economy rewards dynamic self-command: the executive capacity to downsize unwanted character, and nimbly adapt to changing markets. Indeed, the self persists. What comes to seem fallacious is the notion of the self as a genuine, innate, original, unmediated fount of personality. But while self-presentation can no longer be a *genuine* excrescence of an original self, it can be quite *authentic*. The persona can be esthetically appraised for its authenticity. How well do its constituent personifications relate to each in terms of coherence, contrast and complementarity? Does the person more or less honestly reveal, to those who are interested, the fact of its premeditated construction? Does the self-presentation lead to the beholders' debasement and exploitation, or otherwise to their insight and personal growth? Is it plodding and crudely self-serving, or eloquent and inspiring, developing both the presenter and the beholder?

Let's consider as an illustration the dilemmas faced by a gentle and caring delivery-room nurse, whom I will call Chuck. Chuck intently cares for his patients, but since caring is both a skilled and expressive performance, he must also dramatically enact the caring, though his six-foot-three height and red beard are in explicit nonconformity with attributes stereotypically associated with caring. With some dedication, practice and humor, Chuck manages an authentic health care performance, without making any claims that infant care is his innate calling. If authenticity is possible in Chuck's performance of his job, perhaps it also is for other composers of the persona, despite the limits imposed by the market. Like the renaissance painters who produced remarkably illuminating portraits, even though they were commissioned by egotistical and artless patrons, the phantasmagoric nurse can have the stylistic wherewithal to produce an authentic performance, despite the economic constraints.

Because he saves his creative effort for authenticity, Chuck compromises his potential rise to stardom. To truly advance his value on the market, the ambitious performer must be willing to calculatedly adapt persona to the desires of the audience. Quite to the contrary of the theoreticians of a postmodern, fractured self, the aspirant to phantasmagoric stardom must be far more realistic than the normal run of human beings. Like the marketers of politicians and entertainment celebrities, he cannot afford to be under any illusion about the images he constructs. He must have heightened iconographic capability – a superior cultural insight into the symbols, ideas, personifications and themes that move the audience. Ready to shape persona in consonance with market forces, he must have a hard and rigorous command of self.

The romantic era's rugged individual – the entrepreneurial inventor – expressed his calling through faculties of industry, perseverance and sobriety, and through them, set a moral example for others' betterment. The modernist period's economic man – the corporate functionary – sacrificed family calm and emotional need for income and efficiency, thereby serving society through his productivity. Now in the phantasmagoric era, the new economic man is epitomized by the celebrity cosmetic surgeon. Through self-presentations that build his own celebrity, he not only profits himself but prescribes the facelifts and antidepressants that also serve society, palliating fear, restoring confidence and making patients feel good, in their anxious rush to produce persona for the market.

Acknowledgement

The author thanks the Rollo May Center of the Saybrook Institute, San Francisco, for supporting his research on humanistic approaches to the study of the economy.

Notes

1   Classic works include Bell, D., *The Coming of Post-Industrial Society: A Venture in Social Forecasting*. Basic Books, New York, 1976; and McHale, J., *The Changing Information Environment*. Paul Elek, London, 1976. More recent works include Robins, K. (ed.), *Understanding Information: Business. Technology and Geography*. Belhaven, London, 1992. Among many recent articles in this vein, see Kenney, M., The role of information, knowledge and value in the late 20th century. *Futures*, 1996, **28**(8), 695–708.

2   This new age of images is presented alongside seven other contemporary trans-formations in Sternberg, E., Transformations: The eight new ages of capitalism. *Futures*, 1993, **25**, 1019–1040.

3   These realms of phantasgmagoric capitalism are explored in Sternberg, E., A case of iconographic competition: The building industry and the postmodern land-scape. *Journal of Urban Design*, 1996, **1**(2), 145–163; and Sternberg, E., The iconography of the tourism experience. *Annals of Tourism Research*, 1997, **24**(4), 951–969.

4   Compare this view of the future of work to that of Applebaum, H., Work and its future. *Futures*, 1992, **24**, 336–350.

5   Kanter, R. M. and Esty, K., Face to the customer: what customers can learn from the world's greatest department store. *Healthcare Forum* Sept./Oct. 1985, pp. 26–28. Quotations are taken from each of the article's three pages. For more in the same vein, see John, J., A dramaturgical view of the health care encounter. *European Journal of Marketing*, 1996, **30**(9), 60–74.

6   Gladwell, M., The science of shopping. *New Yorker*, 4 November 1996, 66–75, especially p. 74.

7   Gardner, K. and Wood, R. C., Theatricality in food service. *International Journal of Hospitality Management*, 1991, **10**(3), 267–278.

8   Hochschild, A. R., *The Managed Heart: The Commercialization of Feeling*. University of California Press, Berkeley, CA, 1983, pp. 4–5.

9   See Furse, J., Playing the part. *Executive Female*, May/June 1989, 25–27; the quote is from p. 27. Also Russell, A., Fine tuning your corporate image. *Black Enterprise*, May 1992, 72–28; this article says there are nearly 1000 image consulting firms in the US.

10   Van Straten, R., *An Introduction to Iconography*, (tr. Patricia de Man). Gordon and Breach, Yverdon, Switzerland, 1993, chapter 2.

11   Personal image manuals, like Bixler, S., *Professional Presence*, G.P. Putnam's Sons, New York, 1991, generally stress control and confidence.

12   Gardner, W. L., III, Lessons in organizational dramaturgy: The art of impression management. *Organizational Dynamics* Summer 1992, 33–46.

13   Freeburn, R. D., The actor manager. *Executive Development*, 1994, 7(2), 22–23. Also Kelly, I., The corporate theater of action. *Business Horizons*, January-February 1996, 67–74.

14   Goffman, E., *The Presentation of Self in Everyday Life*. Doubleday-Anchor, Garden City, New York, 1959.

15   For a useful compilation of major writings, see Brissett, D. and Edgeley, C. (eds.), *Life as Theater: A Dramaturgical Sourcebook*, 2nd edn. Aldine de Gruyter, New York, 1990.

16   Brissett, D. and Edgeley, C., The dramaturgical perspective. In *Life as Theater*, eds. Brissett and Edgeley, p. 2.

17   The extreme position is found in Evreinoff, N., The never ending show. In *Life as Theater*, eds. Brissett and Edgeley, pp. 419–423.

18   *As You Like It* II. vii. 149–150.

19   Aries, P. and Duby, G. (eds.) *A History of Private Life*. Vol. II (tr. Goldhammer A.). Belknap Press of Harvard University Press, Boston, MA, 1987. Some writers have gone as far as to say that medieval Europe was a world without self or without individuality, but I agree with Anthony Giddens' assessment that that view is an exaggeration: that we should not look for the historical origins of the self, *per se*,

but for the emergence of modern elements of the self. See Giddens. A., *Modernity and Self-Identity: Self and Society in the Late Modern Age*. Stanford University Press, Stanford, CA, 1991, pp. 74–80.

20   Steinfeld, R. J., *The Invention of Free Labor: The Employment Relation in English and American Law and Culture, 1350–1870*. University of North Carolina Press, Chapel Hill, NC. 1991, pp. 3–14.

21   Lyons, J. O., *The Invention of the Self: The Hinge of Consciousness in the Eighteenth Century*. Southern Illinois University Press, Carbondale, IL, 1978. He discusses meanings of disguise in renaissance and early romantic literature on pp. 13, 15, 83, 214 and elsewhere.

22   Lyons, *The Invention of the Self*.

23   I am relying here particularly on Taylor, C., *Sources of the Self*. Harvard University Press, Cambridge, MA, 1989, especially Part IV.

24   Wylie, I. G., *The Self-Made Man in America: The Myth of Rags to Riches*. Free Press, New York, 1954.

25   *Ibid* chapter 3.

26   *Ibid* pp. 42–48.

27   *Ibid* p. 2.

28   Nelson, D., *Frederick W. Taylor and the Rise of Scientific Management*. The University of Wisconsin Press, Madison, WI, 1980, pp. 94 and 171–172.

29   Taylor's anecdote appears in *The Principles of Scientific Management*. Harper and Brothers, New York, 1911, p. 59.

30   Nelson, D., Scientific management and the workplace, 1920–1935. In *Masters to Managers: Historical and Comparative Perspectives on American Employers*, ed. S. M. Jacoby. Columbia University Press, New York, 1991, pp. 74–89.

31   Finkelstein, J., *The Fashioned Self*. Polity Press, Cambridge, UK, 1991, chapter 4.

32   Levitt, T., A heretical view of management science. *Fortune*, Dec. 18, 1978, 50–52; Ackoff, R. L., The future of operational research is past. *Journal of the Operational Research Society*. 1979, **30**, 93–104; Sternberg, E., Incremental vs methodological policy making in the liberal state. *Administration and Society*, 1989, **21**(1), 54–77, esp. pp. 68–72.

33   Boorstin, D. J., *The Image: A Guide to Pseudo-Events in America*. Vintage Books, New York, 1987 [1962]. p. 57. Italics in the original.

34   Bruce, B., *Images of Power: How the Image Makers Shape Our Leaders*. Kogan Page, London, 1992, puts positioning at the center of image making (p. 87).

35   See Gamson, J., *Claims to Fame: Celebrity in Contemporary America*. University of California Press, Berkeley, CA, 1994, pp. 111–113 and 66ff.

36   On gravitas in leaders, see Bruce, *Images of Power*, 174. Also see Rein, I. J., Kotler, P. and Stoller, M. S., *High Visibility*. Dodd, Mead and Company, New York, 1987.

37   Dyer, R., *Stars*. British Film Institute Educational Advisory Service, London, 1979, pp. 104–108, cited in Rein, Kotler, and Stoller, *High Visibility*, p. 206.

38   Bruce, *op cit*, reference 34, pp. 73–74.

39   Gamson, *op cit*, reference 35, p. 74.

40   Bruce, *op cit*, reference 34, pp. 73 and 76.

41   Van Straten, *op cit*, reference 10, pp. 48–51.

42   Rein, Kotler and Stoller, *High Visibility*, pp. 218–223; Bruce, *Images of Power*, pp. 52–58.

43   Gamson, *op cit*, reference 35, p. 73.

44   Bruce, *op cit*, reference 34, pp. 58–62.

45   Furse, *op cit*, reference 9, pp. 26–27.

46   Bruce, *op cit*, reference 34, p. 50.

47   See Finkelstein, *op cit*, reference 31, chapter 3.

48   *Ibid*, pp. 26–39 and 92–95.

49   See Van Straten, *op cit*, reference 10, p. 37.

50   The anecdotes are from Gamson, *Claims to Fame*, pp. 74–78; Bruce, *Images of Power*, pp. 62–73.

51   In *Images of Power*, p. 40, Bruce writes that "Lies are unnecessary (one can always say nothing) and are invariably found out." The others commentators on celebrity-making largely agree. Rein, Kotler, and Stoller, in *High Visibility*, pp. 146–152, use the term 'dramatic reality' to describe these kinds of stories.

52   Gamson, *op cit*, reference 35, pp. 88–91 and 75–78.

53   See Giddens, *Modernity and Self-Identity*, p. 81.

54   Gergen, K. J., *The Saturated Self: Dilemmas of Identity in Contemporary Life*, Basic Books, New York, 1991.

55   These are underlying assumptions in Boorstin, *The Image*; Fwen, S., *All Consuming Images: The Politics of Style in Contemporary Culture*. Basic Books, New York, 1989, p. 271, and many other works.

56   Gardner, Lessons in Organizational Dramaturgy, pp. 44–45. This is in effect Brendan Bruce's position in *Images of Power*.

57   Biggart, Rationality, Meaning, and Self-management, p. 304. The cited books are Korda, M., *Power! How to Get it. How to Use It*. Random House, New York, 1975; and Ringer, R. J., *Winning through intimidation*. Fawcett, Connecticut, 1973.

58   Gamson, *op cit*, reference 35, pp. 49–54 and 123.

59   Gergen, *op cit*, reference 54, p. 7.

60   Gergen, *op cit*, reference 54, p. 73; also Lifton, R. J., *The Protean Self: Human Resilience in an Age of Fragmentation*. Basic Books, New York, 1993.

PART FOUR

Transgression
Scandal, notoriety and infamy

Introduction to part four

■ P. David Marshall

MUCH HAS BEEN WRITTEN about how news is selected. Somewhere in the elaborate ideological gatekeeping mechanisms, there is some designation that the extraordinary is newsworthy. Defining extraordinary moves us quickly into another round of interpretation as to what constitutes news.

Scandal produces news. For the already famous, it maintains a presence in the popular media, albeit a presence imbued with potentially negative connotations. A scandal can work to make us think of a particular celebrity differently and allow them to slide out of the straitjacket of an industry-defined identity: It can be thought of as a transgression to build autonomy in an industry. Child stars sometimes allow scandals to break away from a controlled identity into something that could be characterized at the very least as not childlike. Established stars can refocus attention on their extracurricular activities to enliven a fading career.

Scandals also produce new celebrities – the notorious and the infamous – where criminal investigations sometimes lead to saturation media coverage of the crime, the defendant, and their lifestyle.

And scandal advances political and cultural debates. Issues of divorce, privacy, paternity, fidelity, abuse, addiction, and theft are elaborated through celebrity missteps and paparazzi oversteps. Through celebrity stories via the gossip generated, the political and cultural boundaries of individuality are played out and debated in contemporary culture. The key figures perform in these new terrains of debate outside of their normally more highly structured and defined roles.

Richard Tithecott

INVESTIGATING THE SERIAL KILLER
The seeking of origins

The serial killer and the idea of the individual

The human and social sciences have accustomed us to see the figure of
Man behind every social event, just as Christianity taught us to see the
Eye of the Lord looking down upon us. Such forms of knowledge project
an image of reality, at the expense of reality itself. They talk figures and
icons and signs, but fail to perceive forces and flows.

> (Mark Seem, "Introduction," in Deleuze and Guattari, xx)

They go for your mind in prison today—where before, it was all
physical suffering.

> (Abbot 20)

"17 Killed, and a Life Is Searched for Clues" says the headline of a *New York Times*
article on Dahmer (4 August 1991: A1). Even following the serial killer's capture,
arrest, and conviction, policing proceeds unabated. It is not conviction which brings
the illusion of closure, only that which we really seek: origins of the story of *his*
violence, origins which we figure as belonging solely to the individual, to *a* life. Our
discourse of detection continues by reconstructing the history of the individual serial
killer as a case, as something to be solved, as something whose center begins (and
usually ends) in the unspeakable. Like Victor Frankenstein, we build a monster, only to
peel back the skin and see what's inside. And sometimes we do it in a manner which
makes distinguishing ourselves from those under study not always an easy task: "We
shall attempt a dissection with surgical precision" (Leyton 31) is Elliott Leyton's pep
talk to the readers of *Compulsive Killers*, before mentioning in the main body of the
text, in his discussion of the descendants of the most infamous surgeon of them all,
Jack the Ripper, the number of medical titles attached to the names of the nineteenth

century's serial murderers ("Dr. William Palmer, Dr. Thomas Cream, Dr. Marcel Petiot, and many others").

In the *New Republic* Lincoln Caplan notes that "it's fashionable to argue that Americans now take less responsibility for their actions than they once did. Insanity defendants are sometimes portrayed as emblematic of the trend, because they are seen as seeking an undeserved dodge" (30 March 1992: 20). Perhaps in response to the common perception of the criminal too ready to blame society for the crime, the 1980s and early 1990s have seen a questioning of the existence of society itself, a renaissance of the individual at the expense of society to the extent that the self is perceived as the only or at least the main form of reality. It is a renaissance important to the FBI's construction of monstrosity. In a climate of respect for "the individual," that "individual" is also the means by which estrangement proceeds. Violence in the name of sex is perceived as originating in the body of an individual instead of indicating misogyny. An unquestioning distinction is made between the individual and the social context, and the latter fades from view.

For Simone de Beauvoir, Sade is "quite right in cutting through sophisms and exposing the inconsistencies of a society that protects the very things it condemns, and which, though permitting debauchery, often punishes the debauchee" (Beauvoir 67). Like *In Cold Blood's* Officer Dewey, who finds it difficult to understand "how two individuals could reach the same degree of rage, the kind of psychopathic rage it took to commit such a crime" (82), and who fails to consider the possibility that such a "meaningless" crime could be shared, communal, social, we see only individual rage; we see monsters but are blind to monstrosity. We might *think* social groups, but we *see* individuals. For Don Davis, "Many people killing many other people is one thing . . . one person killing many people can be terrifying" (Davis 1991, 167). An edition of ABC's *Day One* opens with the screen filled with a close-up of Jeffrey Dahmer's eye and a voice-over telling us, "His name has come to mean simply murder" (18 April 1993). From what can begin as a shock to the social consciousness, giving voice to meanings of our shared world which have gone without saying, the representation of the serial killer can evolve into the loading of all that unspeakableness onto *a* name, *a* body. Figured as acultural, isolated from a cultural context, the serial killer is the spectacle whose brilliance dazzles us. Focused on him, we fail to see beyond.

Wondering "whether an individualism in which the self has become the main form of reality can really be sustained," the authors of *Habits of the Heart* argue that "philosophical defenders of modern individualism have frequently presumed a social and cultural context for the individual that their theories cannot justify" (Bellah et al. 143). Their main concern is that individualism "may have grown cancerous – that it may be destroying those social integuments that Tocqueville saw as moderating its more destructive potentialities, that it may be threatening the survival of freedom itself" (vii). Philosophical defense of individualism – a defense which more often than not perceives the conflict as being between illusory abstraction and tangible manliness – is redundant in an age whose currency is personalities. On an episode of *Geraldo* entitled "Jeffrey Dahmer: Diary of a Monster," the host highlights our separation of personalities from social and political issues: "The conduct of the Milwaukee Police Department in this case, as you all know, is under intense scrutiny right now. Was it the fact that they thought this was a gay thing that made them so disinterested? Was it because most of the victims were minority people? What was it that caused them to essentially downplay or ignore these cries for help? . . . Our story, though, is not that story. Our story is the human aspect of this, and coming up, you'll meet more people whose lives were touched by Jeffrey Dahmer" (*Geraldo*, 12 September 1991). The "human story" we mostly hear is one which is celebrated as transcending less tangible "social questions." It is a story in which lives "touch" and which is given the quality of being "more real." While Dahmer's goal is, according to Masters, to make "depersonalized person[s]" (Masters 1993, 97) of his victims – and perhaps a depersonalized person of himself – his "success" brings to him the reality of "personality," one which, as a former classmate of Dahmer's suggests, can matter above all else: "I'm not surprised he made it to the cover of *People* magazine – in some way he was living up to [his home town's] high expectations" (Martha Schmidt, *Day One*, ABC, 18 April 1993).

Making "personality" more real, more relevant (as compared to the unreality, the abstraction, or the trivialization of those spaces without "personal reference") is the FBI's "personality profile." FBI officers list "age, race, employment, grooming habits, level of education, arrest and military history (if any), pastimes, marital status, socio-economic status, type of residence and home environment, with whom he is residing" (*House* 35) as some of the characteristics upon which they particularly focus in assembling profiles of uncaught serial killers. The personality profile may indicate a change in the direction of law enforcement, away from the policing of a particular act and towards a particular type of person. Already the authority of the personality profile is such that it gives the police unprecedented powers of entry: "Profiling concepts have been used in search warrants in several instances where we have done a profile, and that has been used as part of the search warrant, part of the probable cause to search a particular individual or search an individual's property" (*House* 10–11). And it is also the means by which the police extend their influence beyond law enforcement and into the justice system: "We sometimes assist in the development of prosecutive strategies of the district attorneys. Pre-sentence, parole, and commutation opinions based on data base research – we have assisted in counseling Governors and in counseling other individuals who are dealing with the issue of parole and commutation of a particular individual who is incarcerated for a serial violent crime. We have testified in pre-sentence hearings" (*House* 11).

"What, after all, is crime or the criminal but the exercise of the power of the state to control certain behaviors or people believed to have a certain criminal identity within particular historical circumstances?" asks Stephen Pfohl (Pfohl 33). Cynics like Pfohl might argue that the FBI's personality profile, misused, or used to its full advantage, can be instrumental in the production and reinforcement of criminal stereotypes, that is, the connecting of personal characteristics to criminal behavior. Of course the potential dangers of policing based on the assembling of statistics are that common knowledge of the "likely" characteristics of, in this case, a serial killer can lead to a common belief that the relationship between those characteristics and behavior is causal. The personality profile can be the basis for what amounts to a legal inscription of personal abnormality (as well as, of course, normality). Having figured serial killing as a parasitical disease afflicting our social body, or as an evil which manifests itself only in individuals, that is, having safeguarded the idea of our normality, we may feel exonerated and safe in aiming to eradicate all things that our serial killer "represents." And when this mood is accompanied by a way of seeing our world as made up of only individual bodies, we may feel comfortable about selecting individual "characteristics" or "lifestyles" as targets of eradication. Dreams of the cleansing of humanity feed on the belief in a causal relation between individual characteristics and behavior. The extent to which the FBI's increased powers of surveillance over "deviant" individuals are perceived as justified depends on how entrenched the idea of policing as purifying has become in our common psyche. As well as being an aid to detective work, and supposedly a way of improving the efficiency of the police,[1] the personality profile can also be a useful tool in the policing of values and in the policing of and construction of criminal "types."

While we fail to see beyond personality, beyond individual types, Dahmer, we tell ourselves, takes his self a little too far away from the rest of us. His putative *selfishness*, his inability to relate to others socially (enabling him to regard them as objects, things) corresponds with psychology's definitions of psychopathy. According to a *New York Times* article headlined "Brain Defect Tied to Utter Amorality of the Psychopath" (7 July 1987: C1–2), "the term refers to someone with . . . the apparent incapacity to feel compassion or the pangs of conscience". Despite the headline's focus on the possible biological cause of or relation to psychopathy (a possibility pursued with much vigor in the case of Dahmer, with teams of psychiatrists and psychologists searching for genetic disorders, neurological impairments, and biochemical imbalances), many of those quoted in the article figure psychopathy as something which does not so much originate in the psychopath but rather circulates socially. It is noted, for example, that the "detachment may be partly due to problems in moral and intellectual development that can be dealt with through behavioral treatment" (C1). It is also suggested that in recent years psychopathy seems to be on the rise – an observation which if accurate is less likely to be explained by neurological changes than by social change. Later in the article, criminologist José Sanchez is quoted as follows: "The young criminal you see today is more detached from his victim, more ready to hurt or kill . . . The lack of empathy for their victims among young criminals is just one symptom of a problem that afflicts the whole society. The general stance of the psychopath is more common these days; the sense that I am responsible for the well-being of others is on the wane" (C2). And Robert Hare, psychologist, notes that if the official psychiatric diagnosis of psychopathy is used, 50 percent of prisoners fit the definition; but he and other psychiatrists argue that "the diagnostic criteria focus too much on criminal misbehavior – because they were developed through the study of psychopaths who got caught – and too little on the underlying personality problems" (C2).

Also challenging the idea that serial killing results from individual pathology are the many cases in which murders are committed by two or more offenders. Philip Jenkins suggests that "group serial homicide" may "account for 10 or 20 percent of all serial murder cases" (Jenkins 1990). As Freud – who, in *Civilization and Its Discontents*, contemplates the problem of diagnosing whole civilizations as neurotic without the aid of a comparative context (Freud 1953b, 141–142) – might remark, we should be wary of diagnosing psychopaths within what can appear to be a context made up in part by psychopathy. If he could observe us now, existing in a world described by Christopher Lasch in *Culture of Narcissism* as one of radical individualism engendering a narcissistic preoccupation with the self, he might also consider us presumptuous for allowing the burden of proof in an insanity trial (as is the case in Wisconsin law) to fall on the defense.

If the ability to estrange with the use of psychopathy is made difficult by a context of social psychopathy, the idea of evil helps us out (once again) by giving momentum to our individualizing procedures. The confession we want to hear is one in which the crime originates wholly with the confessee. Judith Halberstam notes that our common perception of evil is that it "resides in specific bodies, particular psyches. Monstrosity as the bodily manifestation of evil makes evil into a local effect, not generalizable across a society or culture" (Halberstam 37). With our condemnation of Dahmer as evil, we say, simply, *he happened:* there is no need to explain the crime, to speculate about context, only to deal with him, the criminal. Unlike insanity, a concept which requires continual rewriting and substantiation, evil has a relatively unchanging history, a history of going without saying, and is something which, as we search a serial killer's life for clues, can lead us to the safety of silence instead of the risk of further explication.

While we, with religious zeal, can condemn Dahmer as evil, we have no time for the idea that evil forces took possession of him, that evil has an external source. It is an irony of which Dahmer is apparently aware: "Is it possible to be influenced by spirit beings? I know that sounds like an easy way to cop out and say that I couldn't help myself, but from all that the Bible says, there are forces that have a direct or indirect influence on people's behavior" (quoted in Masters 1993, 112). Evil is a concept of which only the prosecution can make use. When Dennis Nilsen was tried in 1983, the jury, split on the question of Nilsen's legal insanity, sought help from the judge, who consequently declared that "a mind can be evil without being abnormal" (quoted in Masters 1991, 269). While a judge can be taken seriously (at least by the jury) in condemning Dennis Nilsen, for example, as evil, and while the notion of evil functions for society as a whole as a means of condemnation, a defendant's references to such notions generally are rejected.

Halberstam argues that "modernity has eliminated the comfort of monsters because we have seen, in Nazi Germany and elsewhere, that evil works often as a system, it works through institutions as a *banal* (meaning 'common to all') mechanism" (Halberstam 37). But our current preoccupation with individualizing by use of the term *evil*, with creating monsters and ignoring monstrosity, indicates our notalgia for the premodern, for the comfort that those old monsters offered us. Individualization and our serial killer construction are interdependent, naturalize each other, give each other meaning. Threatened by an unknown of unidentified, violent individuals, and respectful of policing powers of surveillance, we argue the need for "the assignment to each individual of his 'true' name, his 'true' place, his 'true' body, his 'true' disease" (Foucault 1979, 198). In the process, we fail to provide a cultural context which may enable us to identify normative expectations which both our heroes and our monsters fulfill.

"Are you raising a Jeffrey Dahmer?"

She continued to suffer from long bouts of nausea; but now, a more serious form of rigidity developed, one which none of the doctors who saw her was ever able to diagnose exactly. At times, her legs would lock tightly in place, and her whole body would grow rigid and begin to tremble. Her jaw would jerk to the right and take on a similarly frightening rigidity. During these strange seizures, her eyes would bulge like a frightened animal, and she would begin to salivate, literally frothing at the mouth.

> (Lionel Dahmer describing his then wife, Joyce, carrying Jeffrey:
> Dahmer 33–34)

Phone-in caller: We certainly haven't heard much about Jeffrey Dahmer's parents. Can you tell me if you see any connection between his upbringing and the crimes he's committed?

Mr. Boyle (Dahmer's attorney): My job would have been a lot easier if I had found that there were some problems with his upbringing. The opposite was true.

> *Larry King Live*, 17 February 1992)

The idea of the family does not contradict individualism but complements it. Bellah et al. describe a culture in which "the family is the core of the private sphere, whose aim is not to link individuals to the public world but to avoid it as far as possible" (112). They suggest that "the tendency of our individualism to dispose each citizen to isolate himself from the mass of his fellows and withdraw into the circle of family and friends, that so worried Tocqueville, indeed seems to be coming true (112). In the late twentieth century, families are individuated, not *extended*, and the idea of "family," like that of "individual," is constructed, and indeed celebrated, as an "asocial" entity. *Family values* – a controversial phrase in the politics of the nineties – are presented as the panacea to social ills by their making redundant the need for society and its institutions altogether.

If the crimes of a serial killer cannot be neatly and completely figured as originating in the criminal's individual identity, his family can function by mopping up the remaining meaning, leaving the rest of us untainted. "Clues to a Dark Nurturing Ground for One Serial Killer" (that strange, redundant "one" indicative of an out-of-control desire to individualize?) reads the headline of a *New York Times* article (7 August 1991, A8) which figures Dahmer as growing up in a self-contained plant-pot of an existence called "family." The struggle between the acknowledgment of and the denial of a relation between society and Dahmer's actions is played out in an edition of *Oprah* entitled "Are you Raising a Jeffrey Dahmer?" (4 September 1991). In response to the suggestion by one of Dahmer's classmates that Dahmer's actions may have been related to cultural homophobia and racism, an audience member says, "I think that's up to his family to take care of that, and the people that are around him when he's growing up. That's not the whole society in general." The classmate's assertion that "families don't exist in a vacuum" has little meaning in the world in which the mythical serial killer exists, one composed only of family units, dysfunctional family units, and individuals lacking an assigned familial role. For Larry King an obvious question to ask Dahmer's attorney is whether "the victims' families show any anger towards [Dahmer's] parents" (*Larry King Live*, 17 February 1992). An answer came two years later when the parents of Steven Hicks, Dahmer's first victim, sued Dahmer's parents, alleging that their negligence contributed to the death of their son (*People Weekly*, 28 March 1994). And if there is no family to blame, the neighbors will do. Dahmer's neighbors complain of hate-mail, threatening phone-calls, shootings from passers-by, and bomb threats (Dvorchak and Holewa 238).

Foucault notes that homicidal mania was abandoned shortly before 1870, and one reason was "the idea of degeneration" (1978, 11), which made it no longer necessary "to make a distinction between the great monstrous and mysterious crimes which could be ascribed to the incomprehensible violence of *insanity* and minor delinquency" (11). In consequence there existed "a psychiatric and criminological continuum" which provided "a causal analysis for all kinds of conduct, whether delinquent or not, and whatever their degree of criminality" and which also "permitted one to pose questions in medical terms at any level of the penal scale" (12). A comparable continuum is described by the Behavioral Science Unit, allowing the potential for being a serial killer to be identified in childhood. The connection between a "dysfunctional" family background and the phenomenon of serial killing is described in the House of Representatives' hearing on serial killing. After noting that "certainly our society is more mobile. We are hearing, and perhaps we are just now discovering these instances of child abuse, the type of chaotic childhood that you are talking about. We have more working parents today and latch key kids and all that goes with it," Chair English asks his FBI guests, "Does that, on a per capita basis, lead you to believe – the FBI to believe – that we will see more of this phenomenon as these young people grow up and mature?" To this question of whether there is a continuum between "working parents" (presumably he means working mothers), "latch key kids" (and "all that goes with it"), and serial killing, the FBI responded positively: "I think very well we will" (*House* 53). And the continuum of which the serial killer is a part also apparently includes "peeping Tom." "Is there a pattern to at least give some hope of identifying these individuals in the future? In other words, do they go from, say, being a peeping Tom to assault, to rape, to murder? Is there a pattern that fits in there in which we can predict that this person is a likely candidate to be a serial murderer?" asks English. Again responding positively, FBI Officer Douglas talks of the need to identify "these young children at school age years" (*House* 54).

In the hearing, a constant theme is the physical, social, and economic mobility of the serial killer, a mobility which makes him difficult to identify. It is a stable familial role which especially gives an individual meaning, renders him visible, *immobile*. In answer to English's question, "Is there some key that would indicate – that would trigger this type of phenomenon?" (*House* 53), Officer Douglas replies, "That's a very good question . . . In our research with serial murderers, we found that, for example, the backgrounds, without exception, everyone had a chaotic early childhood, a lot of mobility, a lot of transientness in their family, abusive parents, absent parents . . ." (53). Stallybrass and White refer to Henry Mayhew's definition of nomads as possessing habits which are not "domestic" and who "transgress all settled boundaries of 'home' . . . simultaneously map[ping] out the areas which lie beyond cleanliness" (Stallybrass and White 129). They see his definition as "a demonized version of what Bakhtin later defined as the grotesque" (128). Notwithstanding evidence which suggests that "among perpetrators of homicide, almost 60 percent are relatively close to their victims in the sense of being spouses, family, or acquaintances" (Jenkins 1994, 46), our policing discourses describe a world divided between families and nonfamilies, fixity and transientness, noncriminality and criminality, meaning and nonmeaning, cleanliness and dirt – oppositions which are frequently conflated.

Conflating several is Anne E. Schwartz: "The state of Wisconsin, specifically Milwaukee, has become a welfare magnet, since neighboring states have drastically cut their welfare benefits. In 1991, Milwaukee's record year for homicides, police say the victims and perpetrators are not local but from Illinois, Michigan, and Indiana. They flock to Wisconsin because of our lucrative welfare benefits" (176). The image Schwartz presents is a twentieth-century version of Mayhew's. After quoting Mayhew who refers to "pregnant and pestilential diseases, and whither all the outcasts of the metropolitan population seem to be drawn," Stallybrass and White remark, "That last phrase is troubling, implying that the 'filthy' are *drawn* to the filth" (132). Schwartz conflates the poor with transiency and criminality and figures them, like Mayhew, as beings who unconsciously are drawn to, attracted to, flock to things and places which satisfy their animalistic urges. And as Stallybrass and White note, once such meta- phoric relations have been established, they can be reversed: if transients or, in the case of particular representations of Dahmer, failed transsexuals (or indeed most other embodiments of transgression) *are* criminals, then criminals *are* those who lack fixity in the way which is perceived by, among others, English and Douglas.

We identify a link between "abnormal family" backgrounds and serial killers, and we conclude that the link is causal. To come to that conclusion, we ignore other possibilities. When we spot "abnormalities" in serial killers' family backgrounds we, like Douglas, seem to forget the majority who come from what we would consider normal family backgrounds, and we find it easy to ignore Westley Allan Dodd's remark that "I was never abused. I was never sexually abused. I was never physically abused. I wasn't neglected. The family had plenty of money, owned our own house, two cars, a trailer. I had a happy childhood" (quoted on CNN's *Murder by Numbers*). We ignore the majority of those who suffer child abuse and never go on to commit crimes such as Dahmer's, and we ignore the possibility that "victims of abuse are just as likely, if not more likely, to grow up and become ruthless businessmen and victimize unsuspecting consumers for pleasure – not just for profit – as they are to grow up to become serial killers" (James Alan Fox, quoted in Schwartz 145). We prefer not to consider the possibility that the causal link we identify can prove troublesome to certain individuals of whom society expects the worst. In Sonya Friedman's previously mentioned show, "The Criminal Mind" (*Sonya Live*, 1 March 1993) – possessors of criminal minds being, according to Friedman, "career criminals" who start "very young" – one of the show's guests describes the pressure exerted by a society that expects those from violent homes to become violent adults, those who were abused as children to become adult abusers. Lorenzo Carcaterra, whose book describes growing up in a violent and abusive home dominated by a father who had murdered his first wife, calls the idea of "the cycle of violence" an "unfair burden" and says, "One of the reasons I wrote the book is people who grow up like I did are labeled that [potentially criminal], that we're going to do that, we're going to repeat that." We ignore the possibility that with the reduced demand for reproduction in the context of consumer capitalism, a decreasing need for kinship in a more mobile society, and the declining importance of gender roles in the division of labor – all factors which helped natural- ize the idea of the traditional family – the "collapse of traditional values . . . [is] in a sense the result of the very success of the capitalist societies these value systems had helped engender" (Altman 1982, 90–91). Fetishizing detection and surveillance, we largely disregard such possibilities and prefer to channel our energies into "identifying these young children," a decision based on the conclusion that "we will see more of this phenomenon [of serial killing] as these young people grow up and mature" (*House* 53).

Births and origins go together naturally enough, and when we trace the origins of a particular serial killer, we can find ourselves dwelling on the image of the newborn with its mother. If we find no familial trauma, our stories can begin and end with this image. "So many of us wanted to believe that something had traumatized little Jeffrey Dahmer, otherwise we must believe that some people simply give birth to monsters," writes Ann E. Schwartz (39). She would have rested a little easier if she had watched an episode of *Inside Edition* in which Jeffrey's father and stepmother, Shari, told the interviewer that his natural mother, Joyce, took medication for her bouts of anxiety depression while she was pregnant with Jeffrey. In their books on Dahmer, Norris and Brian Masters both dwell on Joyce's mothering of little Jeff. Norris's account suggests that Jeffrey suffered from a condition caused by his mother's medication (prescribed to alleviate the most "feminine" of ailments, anxiety depression). He also notes that Joyce was "a very 'hyper' person" (Norris 1992, 62) – another "feminine trait" according to patriarchal myth? Masters remarks on Joyce's decision not to breast-feed and, while mentioning that "thousands of mothers in the Western world decline to feed their offspring at the breast," admonishes the mother who "may not reflect that by denying her breast to the infant she is placing self before benevolence." Masters concludes that the lack of breast-milk can explain Dahmer's sense of loss throughout his life.

While Jeffrey's biological mother takes most of the hits, Shari fails to escape being connected with the actions of her stepson. When Geraldo asks someone introduced as a "friend of the Dahmer family" whether Shari is "a wicked stepmother," the friend replies that she "is the epitome" of one (*Geraldo*, September 12, 1991). Although on the same show claims are made that Dahmer was molested by his father when he was eight years old,[2] it is our monster's mothers or stepmothers who usually receive the most attention. Typical of the attention given to Dahmer's origins (and typical, perhaps, of small-town America's desire to connect itself with national concerns, however tenuous or befouled the link may be) is a front-page headline of the *Chippewa Herald Telegram* (25 July 1991): "Mother of Accused Mass Murderer Lived Here."

As we read *In Cold Blood*, struggling to identify the meaning of the killer's acts, we can find ourselves interrogating the killers in the manner of Detective Church, insisting that they "tell us something about [their] family background" (Capote 217). Once there, in that mysterious origin of life's meaning, we tend to give a disproportionate amount of attention to the mother and not much to the father (at least, not his presence). The mother of Church's interviewee is quoted as saying, "People are looking at me and thinking, Well, she must be to blame somehow. The way I raised Dick. Maybe I did do something wrong" (Capote 287). The dysfunctional family unit is largely figured as a place lacking the father. With patriarchy absent, matriarchy rules, and the results are perceived as monstrous: "Serial killers are almost invariably found to have experienced environmental problems in their early years. In many cases they stem from a broken home in which the parents are divorced or separated, a home with a weak or absent father-figure and dominant female, sometimes a home-life marked by a lack of consistent discipline" (Wilson and Seaman 40). With the family figured as the originator of the meaning of our lives, the amount of structure in our lives depends on the type of family from which we come. And we have come to expect that to defy the law of the father is to disperse meaning, that matriarchally produced narrative is inevitably chaotic. Like Dahmer, whose life, in the words of Oprah Winfrey, "spun out of control" (*Oprah*, 4 September 1991), the individual growing up in a female-dominated family (Dahmer lived with his grandmother after his parents were divorced) is commonly perceived as an unpredictable figure whose actions appear motiveless.

A woman who knew much about both narrative and monsters is Mary Shelley. In her introduction to the 1831 edition of *Frankenstein*, she tells us of her agreeing to her publisher's request for an account of "the origin of the story." Making an analogy between text and monster, she ends her introduction by bidding her "hideous progeny go forth and prosper." But Shelley, weary of people asking her how "she came to think of and to dilate upon so very hideous an idea," might tell us not to locate the *truth* of a monster in his mother, not to figure mothers as the origins of their sons' stories, and thus not to add to the anxiety of the mothers of our monsters, or potential mothers-to-be like Anne E. Schwartz, whose nightmare is to give birth to something akin to what she writes about: "I wondered if I would give birth to a two-headed child someday, to serve as a constant memory of the biggest story of my life" (Schwartz 15).

Do we fathers or potential fathers-to-be feel anxious about the possibility of fathering a monster? According to common wisdom, if we do, it should be because of our absence, not our active participation. While Lionel Dahmer feels guilty for not spending enough time with his son, masculinity's involvement in the "creation" of Jeffrey is represented negatively, as a "good" force not implemented. From the perspective which sees men as the originators of structure, of a sense of place, of visibility, the serial killer, the archetypal purveyor of meaninglessness, can only be the product of femaleness. The struggle between our law enforcers and the serial killer is represented as the struggle between the law of the father and the disorder of the mother, between post-Oedipal language spoken by the police and heard nightly on crime shows, and pre-Oedipal language spoken by the killers, by "mummy's boys" who never grew up to be real men. Our policing discourses, implied to be and valorized as masculine, conflict with feminine discourse, discourse lacking motive and logic.

We perceive this conflict as pertinent to the case of Dahmer. With homosexuality associated with the feminine, those little men, those mummy's boys – like "the homosexual mass murderer" Dean Corll, who "had become a mother's boy" (Wilson and Seaman 271) because of his father's being out of town – are people we like to figure as naturally tending towards homosexuality and criminality, or rather a criminality inscribed with homosexuality, or homosexuality inscribed with criminality. Possible links between the serial killer and patriarchy and masculinity are effaced by our tendency to originate his story in terms either of his individual asocial being or his dysfunctional family, a family deemed dysfunctional by the absence of the father and the presence of the mother. Within this apparatus, detection of the serial killer becomes the detection of all that is perceived as weakening the structure built in obedience to the laws of the father; investigation and policing of ideas about the individual and the family are naturalized; and the dependency of the meaning of those ideas upon ideas of mainstream society and culture is negated.

With the psychiatric profession being commonly perceived as failing in its (fatherly) duties of punishing the suspect, the FBI has stepped in to carry out those duties as an extrajudicial element in the penal system and to naturalize the metaphor "child as potential criminal" by its figuration of serial killing as originating in preadulthood. In the process, the prevention of serial killing is restricted to the policing of childhood, an activity which is instrumental in the *construction* of our idea of childhood, that is, it is a space to be policed. Discussing *The Silence of the Lambs*, Elizabeth Young argues that the success of Clarice's "coming-of-age as an FBI agent means that she is now fully trained to enforce the power of the state through modes of invasion, surveillance, entrapment, discipline and punishment that not only parallel but literalize, as Foucault's work helps to remind us, the operative modes of psychoanalysis itself. This plot development, in other words, twins psychoanalysis, the metaphoric FBI of the psyche, with the FBI, that literal enactment of psychoanalysis" (Young 25). In locating the origins of serial killing in childhood, our policing discourses (those that we speak as fluently as the FBI) reenact the simultaneous construction of and investigation of the space with which psychoanalysis has been especially preoccupied. However, we are happy also to reverse the metaphor's terms (criminal as child), to regard the relationship between police and criminal as one of father to child, a move which can help to normalize the inscription of all us who are not part of the "law enforcement community" as children/potential criminals, and to normalize the idea of members of that "community" as apolitical patriarchs. The stories we tell about serial killing have the effect of sustaining the mystique of patriarchal/police power, and indicate a "childish" trust, a "childish" respect for that power.

Notes

1   The FBI sees the personality profile as a "cost-effective way and a more efficient way to reduce . . . investigative man-hours" (*House* 10) – important qualities to advertise, no doubt, when one is attempting to secure increased federal jurisdiction.
2   A notation in Dahmer's probation files refers to a statement by his father, suggesting that Jeffrey was abused by a neighbor's boy. Dahmer has denied being abused by anyone (see Dvorchak and Holewa 35).

Chapter 24

Stephen Hinerman

(DON'T) LEAVE ME ALONE
Tabloid narrative and the Michael Jackson child-abuse scandal

Michael is not of this world.

Brooke Shields, 1993.

IN THE VIDEO OF Michael Jackson's song "Leave Me Alone," the world, in the form of the body of the singer, is turned into a giant amusement park/sideshow, populated by animals, cameras, phones, and, most of all, the presence of tabloids. By employing what Andrew Goodwin has termed his image of "fantastic other-worldliness" (1992: 112), Jackson then becomes a modern space traveller who is seen gliding through this display. As he moves past numerous computer-enhanced images, the viewer sees references to children, to the fantastic, and, most interesting of all – within the images of tabloid newspapers – to many of Jackson's own reported "scandals," from buying the Elephant Man's bones to a fascination with Liz Taylor and plastic surgery.

Michael Jackson and scandal – the two appear to be locked in an eternal equation, one that Jackson himself seems to acknowledge. As the video tells the story, the hounded Jackson, afloat and singing in his spaceship, is able not only to laugh at his tabloid public image as it passes by his window, but to transcend the whole contro-versy. Jackson proceeds through his public body as (apparently) effortlessly as he can sing, proving that, however much he is attacked, he can always triumph through the power of pop song and superstardom.

The actual "source" song for the video is almost forgotten in the blur of color and movement the video images provide, and viewers could be forgiven if, watching the video, they came away only remembering the song for its driving drumbeat and the swooping Jackson voice.[1] A closer hearing of the song apart from its video representation reveals that – lyrically, at least – the song *seems* to be (and its references are, one suspects, purposely vague) about a personal betrayal, the story of someone who has been loaned or has taken money and been granted other favors, only to then ask for "more" once too often. This "subject" is never represented in the video, because it probably would be the last story Jackson wished to tell. For someone with a career (and a life) grounded in carefully calculated business moves, Jackson has always been careful to hide such machinations from the public eye.[2] But there is another reason that the images chosen for the video make perfect sense: it had become impossible by the time of the video to view Michael Jackson outside of his relationship to the tabloids.[3]

In 1993, that impossibility threatened to overwhelm everything else about Jackson's career, his life, his music, and his commercial endeavors. In the early fall of that year, the young son of a southern California doctor accused Jackson of sexual abuse. In the ensuing five months, the Jackson child-abuse case became the main story of the tabloid industry, and the resulting scandal became topic A on the list of stories Americans were talking about. It soon became clear that Michael Jackson could no longer navigate above these accusations the way he did in his video universe, floating above the rumors incorporated into "Leave Me Alone." And whereas at the end of that video, a Gulliver-like Jackson tears himself free from the Lilliputian tabloid universe, this scandal threatened to reduce the self-proclaimed "King of Pop" to a social outcast.

An out-of-court settlement finally took the story out of the mainstream of public consciousness. But looking back at the tabloid coverage of Jackson and the accusations, a number of questions remain. Why did the scandal capture the public imagination so completely? What is it about Jackson that made the allegations so plausible and yet so shocking? And what does the scandal itself tell us about the nature of stardom, the tabloid press, and news in the postmodern media environment?

This chapter addresses these questions. First, I will discuss the theoretical litera- ture which analyzes how stardom functions in the tabloid universe. Next, I will show how the specific Jackson star image had been articulated in the press up to 1993, looking at it through three stages of development. Finally, I will examine coverage of the Jackson sex scandal in tabloid television and newspaper accounts from the fall of 1993, illustrating how the constellation of images in place previous to the scandal was disrupted by the scandal reports, and how the resulting tabloid coverage gives us insight into the nature of modern scandal and its relationship to stardom in general.

Stardom and the tabloids

It is virtually impossible to discuss the nature of media stardom today without taking into account both scandal and the tabloid press. Tabloid television shows and news- papers are pervasive, often featuring narratives of stars as their primary focus. These media outlets display for their audience the private lives of stars, their public adven- tures, and their shocking secrets. As a primary star of the 1980s and 1990s, who appears to have more than his share of secrets and enigmas, Michael Jackson has always been a tabloid favorite.

Yet what it is it about the nature of stardom and the role and function of tabloids that shapes the narratives of scandals like that of Jackson and his accuser? To answer this question, it is necessary to understand how stardom operates today in the context of its audience, and how the tabloid press uses this "image system" on behalf of its readers.[4]

Since the development of the film star, everyone from gossip columnists to academic scholars has attempted to understand the relationship between stars and audiences.[5] Reasons for the mere establishment of such a relationship, at least on a superficial level, seem obvious. Modern stardom is partly about the circulation of popular, recognizable image systems. Insofar as many of these circulating systems are film or video, one way that stars are made in the twentieth century is through consistent patterns of visualization constructed in various (often analogous) narrative settings, which are then repeated until recognized by audiences as being associated with a particular star. In addition, certain verbal descriptors attach to the stars of pop culture. Written accounts of those stars will often employ these predictable descriptors.

Out of this process, stars accrue particular sets of meanings for audiences. Audiences look at the star's skill level or talent, performances, look, and personality, and from these factors stars take on symbolic meaning for their publics. Given the specific culture of the star and the audience, these meanings can vary and mutate, but in all cases, the image systems of stars always say something about cultural values and attitudes. Audiences develop relationships with stars who simultaneously reflect and help construct their cultural practices. At this fundamental level, Richard Dyer notes that stars repeat, reproduce, reconcile, and even displace and compensate audience values within particular cultural formations (1979: 30).

Examples of this process are numerous. If one looks, for instance, at the image of John Wayne, the American actor, it is clear that from the film *Stagecoach* on his visual image as a tall, solitary cowboy is repeated over numerous movie texts. This image soon becomes one with the actor, and verbal descriptors like "brave," "courageous," and "American" soon attach to Wayne. When these meanings are taken into the everyday politics of a country, Wayne's impact on American values and the way they are seen in his own country and in much of the rest of the world is undeniable. Indeed, Wayne is soon seen to "stand for" something unique to the American psyche, a moral code that moves quickly from reflection to action on behalf of mainstream values. That John Wayne managed to avoid any hint of scandal during his life meant that these values remained unchallenged until certain outside political events of the 1960s made Wayne a figure of symbolic contestation.

It is in the narrative of scandal that this relationship between stardom and cultural values is most apparent. If we take as our starting place that the media scandal is a narrative of a disruption, where a particular set of acts is seen to violate the moral boundaries of a culture, then stars, with their uniquely telling cultural signifiers, are likely candidates for morality tales. Such tales tell us about a culture's moral constraints and its moral values.

Authenticity and morality

To give an example of how this process unfolds, various tabloids reported at one time that Tim Allen, the star of an American hit television series, *Home Improvement*, had been imprisoned as a young man on drug charges. The reasons that this event may be termed a scandal seem obvious. First, imprisonment on drug charges for any person is seen by most as constituting "immoral behavior" in America. Second, Allen has certain specific meanings for his audience related to his role on the program. His image as the "everyman family person" clearly contradicts his drug use and imprisonment. No doubt, a scandal narrative was ripe for tabloid television and newspapers. But what saved Allen from a protracted and even more damaging scandal was that the arrest took place before his star had risen, allowing audiences to attribute his indiscretion to "youthful living." The scandal, therefore, was soon gone from the airwaves, and faded quickly in the public mind.

Why do audiences in cases such as this assume that the roles played on television or film – and the values of that character – are in any way related to those of "real life?" Why do audience members perceive stars of fictional programs as indicators of the real world's moral or immoral behavior? The reason is simple: *for audiences, modern stardom entails a belief in the ideology of authenticity*.

With roots in the Enlightenment view of "man" (often gender-specified), the notion of authenticity derives from the idea that a person is an integrated individual with inner and outer selves, public and private "personalities," which may or may not overlap.[6] Dyer suggests that all modern stardom "reproduces the overriding ideology of the person in contemporary society" by its use of the concept of authenticity (1986: 14). According to Dyer, stars are clearly seen by audiences as "individuals," persons with identity and consciousness, with public roles and private lives. This not only allows for identification to take place in the audiences' relationship to the star; it also allows the star to carry over the effects of previous work and notoriety into new projects, as audiences desire to view the relatively stable person behind the new public persona.

Indeed, the notion of authenticity appears inseparable from that of stardom. Audiences see stars as persons who are at once their roles in public and at the same time (to varying degrees) separate from those roles in private. For instance, in the midst of the *Dirty Harry* films, Clint Eastwood was seen by his fans not as a gun-toting vigilante, but as an actor in a role. Yet Eastwood's assumed "private authentic self" – a tough and uncompromising male figure – brought a certain depth to the character, while the part further defined for audiences who Eastwood "might really be." As Dyer notes (1986), some stars are valued due to the high correspondence between their public and private roles; some are valued in the way their star turns are so "unlike" their "real selves." But all stars operate in this nexus of authenticity.

The public/private conception of authenticity introduces the notion of morality, which is key in scandal narratives, into stardom. Stars are seen by audiences to act out of private sets of values, which may or may not impinge upon their public image. It is this moral center that all stars (indeed, all post-Enlightenment individuals) are supposed to have. The moral center should dictate public choices and, therefore, public images. Thus, a scandal can occur when a star's existing public image system, one which has been circulated and repeated, and which bears a connection to a particular cultural formation, is disrupted by some "immoral" private action at odds with both cultural norms and the star's image. Suddenly, the "authentic" star, with a cultivated public and private image, is thrown into crisis. For example, in the case of Hugh Grant, the public image drawn from roles played in movies (of the reserved, shy Englishman) was put into crisis by private behavior at odds with the image (paying for sex on the streets of Los Angeles). That this private act also violated normative behavior created a sense of scandal among the public. This certainly could account for the numerous women who were heard to ask, "Why would a man that handsome – and a star – have to pay for it?" Or, to look at another example, one may see a similar process at work in the case of the Olympic skater Nancy Kerrigan, whose public image throughout the early stages of the Tonya Harding skating scandal was that of the quiet, pretty victim. We can observe how this image was disrupted when members of the media overheard her make slurs on Disney characters ("That stupid Mickey Mouse"), revealing a private self at odds both with a public image and with cultural practices of respect. In the case of both Grant and Kerrigan, the public became confused as to who the authentic, real star was. Was it the private person who seemed to be so disrespectful or the public person who seemed so good and innocent? In many ways, narrativization of the crisis – the media scandal – was an attempt to address this confusion so that audiences could resolve the seeming contradiction. In this sense then, scandals can begin a process of restoring a star's authenticity, at least within certain cultural boundaries.

Returning to the career of Michael Jackson, and in light of this discussion over authenticity, we see that a series of image systems has been developed to write about him. These categories help writers and audiences to link up the "past" Michael Jackson with the current one, and they assume that there is an individual linking various projects, an identity ("Michael Jackson") which has a private constancy from which creative work springs. These images allow fans to stay loyal to Jackson while helping them more easily negotiate new information about his life and work. However, when information arises about a private Jackson that is at odds with the public image and normative moral codes, a crisis occurs.

The role of tabloids

When scandal emerges in the public life of a star, tabloids quickly enter the process. They have often been instrumental in cementing a star's image system, and are crucial institutions for explaining the seeming contradiction which the scandal reveals in the authentic star.

The presence of the tabloid has been well documented.[7] In relation to scandal and stardom, tabloids have specific roles and functions which shape the resulting narrative. These arise from how tabloid journalism becomes, for readers, an authoritative source on events in the star's life. It does this by promising the reader access to the private world of the star, thereby playing upon the public/private dichotomy of authenticity. The reader is offered a look at the "real, authentic" star away from the public work he or she does. Then, when a scandalous private act exposes a gap between the public and private images of a star, the tabloid, by showing the reader something a star does privately that impinges upon the public image, and by granting some answer as to what the truth of this scandal was, becomes a kind of guarantor of public morality. The tabloid passes judgment on the star by standing in for the reader. Tabloid tales thus "set out to teach moral lessons by exposing worthy and unworthy actions" (Connell 1992: 77).

It is important to note that for tabloids to fulfill their function in covering star scandals (and sometimes in restoring star images), there must be a "truth" to be discovered. When tabloids use their authority to uncover private secrets, those secrets must be there in the first place. In this sense, as we will soon see, the Jackson child-abuse scandal presented a troubling situation for tabloid reporting, for it has been next to impossible to fix the sexual "truth" of the Jackson private life, and therefore to find out who the "real" Michael Jackson is.

I will now seek to identify and explain the image system of Michael Jackson as he operated in and through the popular press. This will allow us to see the star as he appeared to be on the eve of the child-abuse scandal, and will help illustrate how the narrativization of that scandal in fact drew upon descriptors of Jackson previously in place.

Michael Jackson as a star

If one examines the coverage of Michael Jackson in the mainstream press from 1970 to 1993, it becomes clear that his image system goes through three fairly distinct stages. These are not absolutely demarcated, of course, but they are general ways in which Jackson has been talked about during those years. Stage 1, beginning in 1970, presents Jackson as a particularly talented member of his family. Stage 2, which begins in 1983 and goes through 1985, presents Jackson as a solo artist and "Peter Pan" figure. Commentators speak about him as if he were some strange combination of child and man, white and black, woman and man, sexual and asexual creature. Finally, by 1987, stage 3 begins. Now, Jackson becomes even more "eccentric" and begins to appear associated with strange incidents and whims, behavior that causes him to be labeled as a tabloid favorite. As the eccentricity becomes more pronounced, Jackson now becomes described as "weird."[8] In the course of these stages, Jackson's sexuality, age, race, and gender are of increasing interest and debate. By the time of the child-abuse scandal in 1993, Jackson's image is firmly set in the public mind, and it is that image system which the scandal disrupts and displaces.

Examining these three stages, we see that in 1970 the mainstream press showed little interest in the Jackson family or Michael in particular. But *Ebony* did offer an initial portrait of the family that singles out Michael and establishes themes that reappear later in discussions of his image. Not surprisingly, the major aspect of Jackson it noted was his showmanship. It states that Michael Jackson is a "singer and dancer with bold and innovative showmanship astounding in one so young[.] Michael is viewed by many as being a potential equivalent to Sammy Davis Jr. and James Brown" (Robinson 1970: 152). Here, the article has done what must be done with all new stars: it places them in the context of stardom existing at the time, contextualizing the Jackson talent in light of a tradition that helps readers interpret the new style. So, Jackson is compared to earlier performers but shown to be somehow "new" and "innovative."

Interestingly enough, Jackson's personality is ignored in the *Ebony* piece. But the family as a whole is commented upon, in much the same language as will later be used to describe Michael. Because the Jackson Five are still children, they must take "limited and well-chaperoned trips to nearby parks and the like, but little else. This, coupled with the demands of school, rehearsal, recording sessions . . . and appearances means that the Jackson Five, for all their celebrity, enjoy a lot less fun than the average teenager" (Robinson 1970: 153). Here, an important theme appears: because

Jackson began his career as a child, his development as a person was not "normal," giving rise to his status as "unique," "not average," and "special." That these categories also are those inevitably linked to stardom only makes his later ascension easier to explain.

In 1980, Michael Jackson recorded his *Off the Wall* album, but it was in 1983, with the release of *Thriller*, that the finally agreed to be profiled and interviewed apart from his family. And it was here that his image began to take on further attributes. In the period between 1983 and 1985, Jackson was increasingly written about as an androgynous figure who on the one hand was childlike (shy, gentle, and innocent), but on the other was a man who operated in the adult world of record production and sales. A whole series of uncertain dichotomies was posited as to who Jackson might "really be": a man or a child; a sexual or asexual being; a hetero- or homosexual; a man who was white in some ways but black in others.[9] In addition, a series of image systems was seemingly placed outside any debate – that Jackson is a superstar who is affectionate with children, and a harmless innocent who is adored by millions.

Jackson's shy and childlike nature was clearly seen as an outgrowth of a life in show business. In an interview in *Rolling Stone* in 1983, Gerri Hershey wrote that Jackson appears to be "excruciatingly shy . . . [one who] guards his private life with an almost obsessive caution 'just like an hemophiliac who can't afford to be scratched in any way'. [The analogy is his]" (1983: 11). Director Steven Spielberg compared Jackson to the fictional film character ET, noting that Jackson is "an emotional child star" (Hershey 1983: 13).

The idea that a 24-year-old, multi-talented, multi-platinum performer could still be seen as a "child star" was common in articles written in the mid-1980s. *Newsweek* labeled him "the Peter Pan of pop" (one suspects Jackson himself of responsibility for the label) and spoke about his childlike love of a pet llama named Louis and a boa constrictor named Muscles. Clearly, this Peter Pan was a puzzle even Disney couldn't figure out, a grown man with the soul of an animal-loving child:

> Despite his showy style, Michael Jackson remains something of an enigma. Onstage in one of his sequined jump suits, he's a flamboyant picture of grace, a sleek jaguar ready to pounce. In photographs he's a creature of sweet sensuality, beguiling, angelic, androgynous. In person, though, he's quiet and reserved, a gangling young man of cagey reticence, with a childlike aura of wonder.
>
> (Miller 1983: 52)

Such contradictions are reinforced when producer Quincy Jones calls him a "truth machine. He's got the balance between the wisdom of a 60 year old and the enthusiasm of a child" (Miller 1983: 53). In a logical extension of the problems of 1970, *Newsweek* concluded, "Here is a black giant who sacrificed his childhood to become a pop idol, a demigod detached from his fellow men, now sealed in a transparent bubble – a lonely prophet of salvation through the miracle of his own childlike, playful, life-giving music" (Miller 1983: 54). Already then, Jackson's image was piling on contradictions, from child to man, one in control but playful, possessor of pure wisdom and pure innocence. That all of this could be attributed to an unusual upbringing may or may not be as important as the Peter-Pan-like curio into which he was developing.

Rumors of strange behavior began to add to the image fascination. In 1984, *People Magazine* reported on the visit of Jackson to the Reagan White House, where, expecting to see just a few children, Jackson was surprised by some seventy-five adults, causing the singer to retreat into the men's room off the presidential library (Why Michael hid out . . . 1984: 75). And the one-sequined glove, worn during the visit, became an object of fascination for the world. *People*, in an issue later that year, featured the glove in a full-page photograph where it looked like nothing less than a Hollywood version of the Turin Shroud (Arrington 1984: 98). Indeed, Michael Jackson was becoming a royal figure, but still a creature who could only be described in contradistinctive adjectives. *McCalls* weighed in with precisely this judgment, calling Jackson, in a summation of the contradictions of his image during this period:

> part man, part child; part lover; part son; black with almost Caucasian features; urban, streetwise, trendy-slick *and* ethereal, pixielike, other-worldly; a fantastically polished professional who's as shy as the darting fawn he in fact resembles; a man, yes, but – with his dreamy, high voice, his facial hairlessness and sheer prettiness – so boldly possessed of the female as to seem androgynous.
>
> (Weller 1984: 40)

As *McCalls* notes, Jackson's sexuality was also a matter of speculation. *Parade Magazine* wondered if Jackson was taking hormones to keep his voice girlish (reported in Miller 1983: 69). *Newsweek* also addressed questions of Jackson's virility, reporting that one journalist met Jackson at his home and found his hand to be "like a cloud." Indeed, speculation reached such a peak that in 1984 *Discover* magazine asked psychologist Carin Rubenstein to address the question of what it means when young people become worshippers of "an androgynous admirer of Peter Pan." The conclusion was that, "In a society obsessed with sex, there could be worse role models for young people" (Rubenstein 1984: 70). By 1984, then, much of the Jackson image repertoire that was later involved in the child-abuse scandal was already in place. These images were elaborated in the next round of Jackson publicity, in 1987, when his behavior was seen to become even stranger and speculation abounded as to just how "weird" Jackson really was.[10]

The flurry of publicity that surrounded Jackson in 1987 seemed predicated upon the release of his third solo album, *Bad*. But when the 1987 stories began, it was as if the contradictions laid out in the early 1980s had grown progressively more strange. In 1987, *Rolling Stone* noted the increased fascination with the star:

> For the past three years, Michael Jackson has been conspicuous mainly by his absence, and fans have made do with odd tidbits of info gleaned from tabloids. Less has been known about his artistic endeavors than about his attempts to purchase the remains of the Elephant Man, to marry Elizabeth Taylor, to levitate himself and to prolong his life through hyperbaric treatment.
>
> (Good news . . . 1987: 11)

A Davitt Sigerson record review in *Rolling Stone* (1987: 87) later that year began not by discussing the new album, but by reciting his recent scandal history:

> Michael Jackson is a man. Agreed, he is a young man, emotional age about thirteen, with a young man's interest in cars, girls, scary movies and gossip. But adolescent stardom, Jehovah's Witness wackiness and unadulterated genius have kept this faux-porcelain elephant man more childlike than any oxygen-tank sleeping device ever could.

A *People* article that same year addressed this concern directly, asking the question: "Is Michael weird or what?" While conceding that Jackson "beggars description," the article then proceeds to describe him anyway, as both creative and normal – Quincy Jones is quoted as saying Michael is "one of the most normal people I've ever met" – and eccentric and strange (Durkee 1987: 87). In terms of the latter, visual evidence is offered, from a record of his plastic surgeries with accompanying photos of the changing face, to his oxygen chamber photograph, to snapshots of his being accompanied by young boys more and more frequently.[11]

For our purposes, what makes Jackson a particularly interesting figure during this time is the confusion over who the "real" Michael Jackson was. It is as if the modernist conception of the human, a person with a stable and consistent private center, is now foreign to much of Jackson's image system. Certainly, he is seen as innocent and giving in his love of children, and childlike himself, but even these descriptions are hedged in press accounts. Allusions remain to a calculation and skill in Jackson that only a full adult could possess. In a very real sense, the Michael Jackson pictured from 1987 to the first half of 1993 was still a star in the making, fascinating precisely because he seemed so far from other stars in the way his multiple private and public selves consistently assumed and displaced identities. That this very confusion over identities gathered around those mirrored by the larger society where his stardom had such great meaning (i.e. around gender, race, sexuality) meant that Jackson not only was a great performer, but represented classic fissures of modern culture and society.

Therefore, when the child-abuse scandal hit, the image of Jackson as a mass of contradictions clustering around age, race, sexuality, and gender had clearly solidified, as had specific questions about his behavior. So while pictures of Jackson in the company of young boys were seen as evidence of his childlike quality in 1987, six years later those same pictures were to be offered as evidence for quite another set of image markers.

Tabloid coverage of the scandal

The allegations that Michael Jackson had sex with young boys seemed tailor-made for tabloid scandal coverage. It was a clear case of the secret, private actions of a star which lay at odds with public morality. And if the tabloids, with their function as fearless organs of "truth" on behalf of their audiences, could only discover the reality behind these allegations, then moral judgments could readily be offered by them as to the star's behavior.

Yet Jackson's image was not like many stars'. Authenticity assumes a certain consistency of personality. While many stars are seen to have "wild" or "crazy" private sides, they are usually perceived as consistent in that craziness by much of the public. Madonna, for instance, could have a baby out of wedlock, but few of the public were likely surprised by that feat. Her image system allowed such behavior to be consistent with her previous actions. She may be wild, but you can count on her being wild.

Jackson was anything but a clear figure. What was the "truth" about Michael Jackson? Was he gay, straight, sexual, asexual, a child or a man? For all of the talk of who the "real" Michael Jackson might be, it was the child-abuse scandal that was seen as able to finally provide a clear set of answers. It was clear that Jackson could be a child molester. He was, after all, weird, unusual, and of indeterminate sexuality, and his fondness for the company of young boys was well documented. It was equally possible that he was simply a strange, childlike man who enjoyed the company of those pre-adolescents. If the allegations were true, then Jackson seemed to be (in private, at least) a very sexual, not innocent man who preferred the company of young boys to women or girls. However, if the allegations were the result of an opportunistic Hollywood social power play or a money-making scam, then the possibility remained that Jackson was a true innocent – a child in an honest-to-goodness never-never land of platonic playfulness.

The intrigue of the scandal was that the Jackson image, in all its complexity, rendered either answer equally plausible. It was up to the tabloids to uncover which truth was the more likely one, thereby restoring Jackson's image to acceptable cultural moral practices, at least in the sense that a majority of Americans might use the term, or banishing him into the netherlands of an especially "sinful" world. This search is clearly the driving force behind the narrative of the Michael Jackson child-abuse scandal.

The "truth" of scandal

Establishing the "real truth" of the scandal is clearly what both TV and print tabloids attempt to do when such a story breaks. First, they report the "news," informing the audience of allegations that have been made. Next, they draw upon the previously circulating star image system as a way of suggesting the truth of what might have really happened in private, "behind closed doors." The tabloids look for authoritative answers. If they find few, they may pose a series of "what-if" questions. They can then search out spokespeople, insiders, and confidants, continuing to reveal secrets about the "real" star.

The problem is that what happened behind those doors in the Michael Jackson case remains, even today, a matter of speculation. Without the ability to establish truth with specific evidence, the tabloids could act as neither authoritative voices nor guarantors of morality. Therefore, their coverage of the scandal became a series of fluctuations, of speculations and competing claims given equal coverage. Finally, in an air of confusion, the scandal simply died, unresolved.

Let me offer a few brief examples of how this process actually unfolded. Early in the scandal, less than two weeks after the abuse investigation began by the Los Angeles Police Department, the tabloid TV show *A Current Affair* broadcast an episode appropriately entitled: "Michael Jackson: The curtain closes"[12] (*Current Affair*, 1993a). This show began with a review of the Jackson image system, as host Maureen O'Doyle stated, "Michael Jackson was everything we wanted him to be – the ultimate entertainer . . . at once a grown-up whose music pulsated with sensuality; yet the eternal kid, whose greatest joy was having the other kids visit the home he calls Neverland Ranch." The narrator, over "exclusive" grainy footage of Jackson and a young boy at play in a closed-down amusement park, then amplified upon this image system, noting that Jackson is seen in the tape "being Michael – rich, eccentric and a child at heart." In the following few minutes, Jackson was also described as "definitely our Peter Pan," "remind[ing] us of the child we all have inside," and as an "icon of eternal youth."

In this sense, the program is simply drawing upon previously articulated sets of Jackson characteristics. Yet the allegations threatened to disrupt this series of opposi- tions. As the show notes, there may be more to the image than we know (the "image we take at face value," according to the program, may not be all there is). The narration then comments that, in the video of Jackson playing with the young boy, the visuals "sum up the image" of Michael Jackson:

> [He is] a millionaire idol with the quirky but willful energy to rent an entire amusement park for the night just so he and another kid could play. It may be indulgent, it may be eccentric, it may be weird, but it's a rare glimpse of pure Michael Jackson – the childlike joy that is catching and yet for those who would make Michael Jackson a target, it's a convenient circumstance.

These observations are fascinating on at least two levels. First, notice the degree to which the "real" Jackson is still presented as a child ("just so he and *another* kid"), yet entertains the possibility that the private Jackson is an adult who knows more than he lets on. Yet, without firm evidence to move the image from one side of the opposition to the other, the tabloid story hedges its bets. The tapes of Jackson and the young boy playing are said to give ammunition to "those who would make Michael Jackson a target." The show clearly distances itself from these people, yet, by showing the tape and discussing Jackson's "eccentric" behavior, it at least leaves open the possibility of his guilt. It is clear *A Current Affair* wants to have it both ways, presenting a wonderful, childlike Michael as his fans see him yet hinting that Michael might be an adult criminal.

Tabloid newspapers at the time show a similar ambivalence. The *Globe* of September 7 used an earlier interview of Jackson to paint him as admitting to "prefer- [ring] the company of children to adults." He is secretive, a man "who guards his privacy like a king guards his gold" (Tragic . . . 1993: 8). Therefore, his prior image as a child whose true, private personality is unknown is employed to suggest that the charges might be valid. Indeed, in this sense, Jackson's image certainly appears to make the charges plausible.

In order to get at the "truth" of the charges, the paper then recounted the results of an investigation by a "top psychologist," Marvin Fredman, who relates that Jackson's unusual love for the company of children revealed "he's still a little boy trapped in a man's body. Because he couldn't bond with his tyrannical father, his emotional development was stunted" (Why I prefer . . . 1993: 9). Still, even with this insight, the paper utimately refused to "fix the truth" of what really happened, and made no definitive judgment as to guilt or innocence.

This ambivalent coverage continues, and is perhaps best summed up in a graphic which appears first in the *Globe* on September 14 (Michael's fatal . . . 1993: 2). In a small box, two pictures of Jackson are featured side by side. In one, Jackson appears to be looking up while his hands are folded as if in prayer in front of his face. In the second, a darker, more sinister Jackson glares out behind heavy make-up. The caption is carried on the top and bottom of the picture in the words: "Peter Pan/or pervert?" This graphic will appear in much of the *Globe* coverage which follows in the coming months, and it is this question which cannot be answered in the remaining five months of tabloid coverage of the scandal.

By December, reports increasingly turn to "insider accounts" to uncover a possible "truth" to the allegations. A *National Enquirer* report of December 14 carries allegations by Jackson's former chef, Johnny Ciao, who states he saw Michael emerge from his "secret playroom" where he had been with young boys "in only his underwear" (Michael Jackson's weekends . . . 1993: 26). Yet the real activity that took place in that playroom remains a matter of speculation. Tabloid television shows offered much the same material, as a plethora of former Jackson employees came forward with their stories. *Hard Copy*, on December 14 (1993a), revealed the allegations of former Jackson maid Blanca Francia, who is presented as "the one person he trusted inside his home . . . inside his bedroom" (therefore promising, at last, the true account). Francia states she saw Jackson "naked" with other young boys, and the show states that "her painful secret" is all the more valid because she is more than an "eyewitness," she is the "mother of a son." The next day, Francia returned to *Hard Copy* (1993b) to reveal Jackson's private nickname for his playful games with young boys ("rubba"), and the day after that, she revealed Jackson's "secret hideaway," where she "witnessed very private behavior" of Jackson and young boys. But since Francia never actually witnessed abusive acts with the young boys in question, her account too is unable to establish a definitive truth about the scandal or about who the "real" Michael Jackson is.

The search for the "truth" to the scandal continued unabated, even after Jackson himself delivered a televised denial from his Neverland Ranch on December 22. A December 23 broadcast of *A Current Affair* (1993b) offered voice analyst Steven Lamb, who analyzed a soundtrack of Jackson's Neverland denial. According to Lamb, Jackson is "not totally innocent" of the charges. The question as to whether or not he is "totally guilty" is left unanswered.

Throughout the scandal narrative, then, the tabloids attempt to uncover the secrets that take place behind the closed doors and curtains of Michael Jackson's life. But the absence of agreement as to the "authentic" Michael Jackson – which turned out to be more a series of ambiguous contradictions than a coherent personality – make such a truth difficult to come by. One side of Jackson could have been guilty and another could just as easily have been innocent.

Therefore, the normal authoritative function of the tabloid press was reduced in this scandal to presenting a series of competing claims, driven only by new witnesses and promises of further glimpses into the family secrets which awaited a public trial for final certainty. But no trial was forthcoming, for the charges were settled out of court by Jackson and the boy's family. It is interesting to note that even the statement by Jackson's manager, Sandy Gallin (reported by the *Star* on February 8, 1994) relies upon the established image system of Jackson to attempt to absolve him of guilt: "Michael's innocent, open, childlike relationships with children may appear to be bizarre to adults in our society who cannot conceive of any relationship without some sexual connotations. This is not any kind of reflection on Michael's character. Rather, it's a symptom of the sexual phobias of our society" (How Michael Jackson plotted . . . 1994: 5).

So, five months after the scandal began, Michael Jackson was still, according to his management "innocent," "open," and "child-like." Some members of the public clearly agree with the assessment, some do not. But one still has the sense that the "real" Michael Jackson remains shrouded in mystery, just as enigmatic as always. Only one fact is beyond controversy: he remains always a star who cannot be left alone.

Conclusion

The Michael Jackson child-abuse scandal is, for all intents and purposes, over.[13] Yet it still gives us a fascinating look at the media scandal generally, and how it operates in the world of stardom. Michael Jackson had become a series of image descriptors, many of which were contradictory in nature. These contradictions may have made him, along with his voice, dancing, and other talents, a "larger-than-life" star. Yet these contradictions were also tailor-made for the kind of scandal in which Jackson found himself. One could always pick and choose which Michael Jackson was the authentic one, and the scandal gave audiences the chance to take sides. Jackson was the perfect polysemic figure, in that anyone's interpretation could never be completely wrong.

The tabloids attempted to close the argument by acting on behalf of its audience to uncover the truth. But what happened or did not happen in the secret rooms of Neverland Ranch never saw a public "final truth" reached in a courtroom. The Michael Jackson sex scandal became a narrative without an ending. The story had begun with a mass of contradictions already in place, and its middle contained a mass of "maybe/ maybe not" allegations. While this certainly frustrated the tabloid press, which had hounded Jackson for months looking for answers, it did have one positive benefit for the industry. It gave the tabloids a high-profile, ongoing subject. Even if they were ultimately unable to find a truth, the Jackson story gave them a profitable, lengthy narrative to focus on. The "Did he or didn't he?" question did not have to be answered so much as asked – and asked, and asked, and asked. The Michael Jackson scandal as it appeared in the tabloids was about the telling of a story that was never quite finished, about making promises that were never quite kept, and about giving its audiences something enduring to talk about. Whether or not the real Michael Jackson was ever uncovered, this scandal narrative sold lots of papers and brought in plenty of rating points.

In the end, the authentic Michael Jackson remains ambiguous. He is painted as a mirror, one who simply reflects the world rather than creates it. Perhaps this is where postmodern stardom is ultimately most comfortable, where the "authentic" star is whatever the audience is – devoid of motive, drive, or desire independent of that contained within the fans. In this sense, keeping one's image system a mass of contradictions which appear unresolvable is more than just a way to avoid getting caught in a career-ending scandal, it is the ultimate in postmodern marketing. There are always "halls of mirrors" for the mass-mediated, postmodern star to be reflected in; if one mirror shatters, the star can always point to the "real me, over there," in another reflection, one that could itself shatter at any moment. We sometimes speak of criminals staying "one step ahead of the law." What Michael Jackson has shown is that for public figures, it is best to always stay one step ahead of having a singular authentic identity. In this sense, Jackson is perhaps only the most spectacular example of postmodern stardom, a classification that now includes others whose contradictory and ever-changing image systems seem to allow them to escape the handcuffs of moral judgment, a line-up including, some would argue, figures as far afield as Bill Clinton and O.J. Simpson.

Of course, this was never the intention of Michael Jackson's image making, and while he has survived the child-abuse scandal, unbroken if not unbent, the threat it posed to his career and to his freedom was very real. In his early video, Jackson's cries of "leave me alone" clearly are muted; the last thing a star, particularly one like Jackson, desires is to be left alone by the publicity machine or by the public. But one should not forget that the cries he uttered on December 22, 1993 – his apologia broadcast from Neverland Ranch in the midst of scandal – were real. They sounded so desperate because Michael Jackson knew, better than anyone else, what was at stake in the outcome.[14] For as the scandal played out, it quickly became, for Jackson, a tale about the struggle over the one thing he knows he needs to remain a star: control over his own image. That this most important element of his life, his career, and his marketing began to slip from his control to that of the media and the public must have been the scariest thought of all.

Notes

1   I wish the reader to keep in mind a caveat here. Jackson is, above all, an extraordinary singer, and it is as a singer and melodist that he reaches people in the first instance. And if it were not for that first instance, I feel the tabloid coverage would be unnecessary. It is because he has the voice and stage actions, i.e. talent, that Jackson is tabloid fodder, not the other way around. When Kobina Mercer says, "It is the voice which lies at the heart of [Jackson's] appeal," he is cutting to the heart of the matter (1993: 93).

2   This becomes readily apparent when one reviews the remarkable correlation between articles on Jackson and Jackson's own efforts to promote a new product, be it album or tour. Jackson often literally vanishes from public view in the years between these projects. Then, when the merchandizing is underway, he emerges in a wide range of popular press reports, all of which seem to comment on his recent "reclusive" absence. The interesting aspect of this is that the logical explanation for his absence (that Jackson is consciously controlling his image proliferation in order to maximize sales when a product is new and available) is somehow effaced, replaced by the "mysterious" tendency of Jackson to appear and disappear. This not only illustrates just how much the business side of pop culture is hidden from public view; it also says something about the image of Jackson as innocent or childlike, which would seemingly preclude him from being in conscious control of his own marketing.

3   While a precise definition of what constitutes a tabloid is difficult to come by (generally, it is one of those things one knows when one sees it), I will argue that the item is known by the characteristics suggested by Bird. For her, tabloid publications and shows are heavy on "human-interest" stories and gossip, usually with a "sensational twist," told "graphically," visually intensive, with stereotyped prose or narration. See Bird (1992: 8) for more discussion of what defines a tabloid.

4   For a full discussion of "image systems," see Lull (1995: 9–21). I use "image system" in much the same way here. I am particularly concerned with how such systems are employed to "encourage audience acceptance and circulation of . . . dominant themes" (Lull 1995: 9).

5   See Bowser (1994: 103–20).

6   See Hamilton, who notes that the idea of the individual from the Enlightenment embodies "the concept that the individual is the starting point for all knowledge and action . . . Society is thus the sum or product of the thought and action of a large numbers of individuals" (1992: 22).

7   See Bird (1992).

8   It should be noted that, in stardom today, there is "weird" and there is "weird!" It certainly is an asset at times to be seen as eccentric. Yet to violate commonly-agreed-upon moral standards (such as a ban on child molestation) moves the star beyond eccentricity and weirdness into the reprehensible.

9   These characteristics not only stood in opposition to one another; they often defined themselves in dynamic relationship to other characteristics, while the very classification categories changed as often as Jackson's own skin color.

10 Characteristically, Jackson "disappeared" from public view from 1984 to 1987. The best explanation – as I noted above – is that he had no new product to merchandize.

11 While it is outside our emphasis here, the image of Jackson as a shrewd business-man also begins to appear at this time, as does his image as a philanthropist (Gold 1988). The fact that a number of pieces with the same theme appear in the same year may not be coincidental – Jackson, after all, does employ press agents. Indeed, one of these accounts, that Jackson slept in a special chamber to preserve his youth, was, it is claimed, given to the tabloids by Jackson himself. According to an editor of the *National Enquirer*, Jackson furnished Polaroids to the tabloid picturing him lying inside the machine. When he was informed that these were not of publishable quality, Jackson went back into the chamber and had the series reshot so the tabloid could feature them (*Frontline* 1994). This makes it ironic, to say the least, when the video of "Leave Me Alone" presents a tabloid picturing Jackson in the machine as some kind of threat to Jackson. Such irony is now, no doubt, just another kind of postmodern pop currency.

12 Images of curtains, pulled back by the authoritative narrators to reveal secrets, are common in the coverage of tabloid scandals.

13 As I write in early 1997, Jackson has married his dermatologist's assistant. It is his second marriage, following his divorce from the daughter of Elvis Presley, Lisa Marie Presley. The couple has just made Jackson a father, and the child has been named Prince. While the cynical among Jackson watchers may wonder if this event merely forecasts an upcoming record release or tour, it is interesting to note that the pregnancy and birth cannot be viewed by the press (and public) apart from the earlier scandal, which has exhibited real staying power in the discourse about Michael Jackson.

14   The question as to the scandal's effect upon Michael Jackson's record sales remains a point of debate. In an interview aired in late November, 1996, on the American music channel VH-1, Jackson denied published reports that his record sales were down and urged fans to "believe me" and not the media and tabloids. The levels of irony in this defense are multiple, but it is interesting to see that here, at least, Jackson seems to indicate that there is a "me" stable enough for fans to believe in.

Chapter 25

David Giles

THE QUEST FOR FAME

WHAT IS IT ABOUT fame that has made it so attractive to people throughout history? What drove Alexander the Great, Cicero, P. T. Barnum and Ronnie Kray to emulate their idols, establish their names in the history books and gain the worldly recognition of the present time? In this chapter I consider a variety of factors that might contribute to the individual desire to be famous. Some of these are established psychological theories applied to the subject of fame, while others are more speculative.

It is not known at the present time how prevalent the desire for fame might be in the general population. It could of course be that everyone harbours an intense wish to be famous but only a few realize that goal. It is more likely that a small subset of the population is inflamed with such a desire, and a substantial proportion of this set have their wishes granted. But there is no one-to-one correspondence between the desire for fame and its attainment, because so much fame is unwanted (Louise Woodward, for instance), and there are noted cases where the thirst for fame is unquenched (the poet Chatterton, for instance).

What is seldom clear is the nature of the relationship between the desire for fame and its attainment. All the evidence we possess for such a relationship are the retrospective accounts by famous people of how they came to be famous, and these may be of dubious accuracy. Hindsight can reinterpret an all-consuming thirst for fame at all costs into a spiritual or philanthropic mission; alternatively there may be some prestige value in claiming that fame was achieved systematically. Moreover, talk of wanting fame has declined in the twentieth century, since fame has acquired a vulgarity through the perceived low value of modern celebrity. If fame is represented by Maureen from *Driving School*, or a TV weather presenter, then it is a pretty poor ambition to own up to when you have a genuine talent for sport or music or writing. The myth of the 'gift' allows us to cling on to the belief that we will, eventually, be recognized and awarded for our innate potential, without having to seek out cheap and nasty publicity. Nevertheless, the pursuit of fame for its own sake has not completely died out.

Wanting it now: the case of Morrissey

During the mid-1980s one figure managed to dominate the pages of the weekly British pop papers: (Steven) Morrissey, eccentric singer with Manchester band the Smiths, who was the answer to the editors' prayers – an interviewee who would pour out his heart to anyone with a cassette recorder, throw in outrageous comments at the drop of a hat, and whose band were consistently producing music worthy of press attention.

Morrissey (he rarely used his first name) deserves a place in history simply for trying so hard to be famous, and achieving his aim in the end. As a teenager, he became an obsessive pop fan, endlessly compiling lists and critiques alone in his bedroom; on leaving school, he hung around on the fringes of the Manchester music scene, sang in bands, wrote reviews for music papers and even compiled a book on US glam rockers The New York Dolls (it was eventually published and sold over 3000 copies). Like so many famous figures of the past – from Alexander to Byron to Ronnie Kray – Morrissey was a *fan* above all else.

By the age of 18, he was becoming increasingly hungry for fame, and a scribbled note from this period reads: 'I'm sick of being the undiscovered genius, I want fame NOW not when I'm dead.'[1] But it was not for another six years that this hunger would be satisfied, when he and fellow Mancunian musician Johnny Marr put together the Smiths and had a string of hit singles and LPs, attracting massive media coverage before splitting up in 1987. Morrissey embarked immediately upon a solo career, enjoying acclaim for a while, and continued to release records up to the end of the century, albeit with comparatively limited success.

Unlike most of his peers Morrissey was never reticent about the source of his career ambitions; as he admitted in a later interview: 'I always had a religious obsession with fame. I always thought being famous was the only thing worth doing in human life, and anything else was just perfunctory.'[2] This is a significant revelation, since it harks back to the myth of the 'gift' while at the same time suggesting that, irrespective of whether or not Morrissey perceived himself as possessing talent, he nevertheless demanded fame for its own sake. Any mode of expression – writing, singing, criticism – would do as a vehicle.

Similar stories? Blur singer Damon Albarn:

> When I was at school, I never had any interest in pop music . . . I was just on this big 'this-is-what's-gonna-happen' thing. I guess it's quite insane to say, from the age of 11, 'I know I'm gonna be great!' But that's what I did. People just laughed at me.
>
> (*Melody Maker*, 6 April 1991).

It seems that, for some famous people at least, the desire for fame is something of which they are aware from an early age. To return to the question posed earlier: is the desire for fame something many harbour, which some achieve and others not? Or are those with early ambitions for fame in some way 'destined' for it? Certainly Morrissey felt that this was the case: 'I always knew something, shall we say, *peculiar* was going to happen.'³ Alternatively, fame may seem predestined because of some unusual feature of one's childhood; for example, the television presenter and model Rachel Williams:

> Since I was 10, I felt like I was headed for being in the public eye. I don't know where that comes from. My height. It probably has something to do with that. I always stood out.
>
> (The *Guardian*, 1 September 1996).

The desire for fame in any guise has strong historical traditions. A clear parallel with Morrissey is the French writer Jean-Jacques Rousseau. As mentioned in the previous chapter, Rousseau ushered in a new era of fame, where the emphasis was on the inner qualities of the individual rather than one's self-presentation in society. If the self is the 'gift' one has to present to the world, then its form of expression is arbitrary: so Rousseau, like Morrissey, flitted from one domain to another – from Venetian politics to Parisian music – before settling down to become a man of letters. Morrissey's career was the reverse, beginning in solitude but ending in high visibility. Unlike Rousseau, however, and unlike some of his more tragic peers, he saw no paradox between being both a private individual and a public centre of attention.

Explanations from psychological research

What can psychological theory say about the desire to be famous? An important source here is the work of D. Keith Simonton, an American researcher who has published over 100 articles on the psychology of historical figures and theories of creativity and genius. Simonton describes his approach as the psychology of history, and his methods, along with painstaking archival research, involve some fearsome statistical analyses of historical material. In his book *Greatness: Who Makes History and Why*⁴, he outlines a variety of theories that try to answer the question, which I will attempt to summarize here, along with other assorted theories and findings.

Biological inheritance: do genes play a part?

The study of 'bloodlines' linking famous individuals through their family trees was conducted as long ago as 1869 by Francis Galton, who identified a number of striking trails through various families, most notably the Bachs of Germany, who produced well over 20 musicians. He also argued that the more famous the individual, the greater the likelihood that he or she would have famous relatives.

Galton was thoroughly committed to the notion that genetic endowment is the major factor influencing human behaviour, later founding the eugenics movement (which attempted to block the spread of 'bad genes' through the population through social control). Some of his ideas have become fashionable again through the science of behavioural genetics, which seeks biological explanations for human behaviour. Much of the geneticists' evidence rests on the much-publicized cases of separated identical twins exhibiting remarkably similar behaviours in later life; indeed the Krays' biographer alludes to some of this work in attempting to account for the criminality of the twins.[5]

Quite apart from the absurd notion that 'criminality' is a universal, internal quality of an individual, the (identical) Kray twins are all the counter-evidence one needs to disprove the theory of biological inheritance. Inseparable from birth, sharing both the same genetic make-up and the same environment, we should expect them to demonstrate patterns of behaviour that are markedly similar. However, in his twenties Ronnie was diagnosed as having paranoid schizophrenia (argued by some to be an inherited disorder), and practised homosexuality throughout his civil life (likewise claimed to be genetically determined[6]), while Reggie showed no signs of *clinical* psychopathology and was also heterosexual.[7]

What about the blood lines of famous families? One flaw in Galton's research is that he failed to compare the inheritance of 'greatness' with the inheritance of any other similar traits. His fundamental error, though, is to assume that, like criminality, 'greatness' is a definable, universal human attribute that can account solely for success in the arts, sciences and other entirely *cultural* pursuits. He may as well have searched for bloodlines that predicted the inheritance of *toilet cleaning* as an occupation, and would undoubtedly have found similar patterns. It seems hardly surprising that there is a huge correlation between the career choices of parents and offspring.

As Simonton puts it: 'We should probably treat all psychobiological theories [of inherited greatness] with scepticism'.[8]

Psychodynamic explanations and the sublimation of the sexual instinct

Perhaps Freudian theory can shed some light on the psychological origins of fame. Freud never wrote about fame directly, although it is alluded to in his work on creativity, in which he argued that creative artists were primarily motivated by the desire for fame (along with wealth and romantic love). John Gedo, a practising psychoanalyst with a special interest in artists, claims that none of his clients have acknowledged the desire for fame and fortune as the primary motivating force behind their careers, and argues that there are much easier ways of obtaining the good life than struggling for artistic recognition.[9] This may be true in today's culture of instant stardom. John Milton was never in any doubt, however: '*Fame* is the spur that the clear spirit doth raise . . . to scorn delights and live laborious days' (*Lycidas*, lines 70–2).[10]

Where Freudian theory may be at its most persuasive is in his later work, notably *Civilization and its Discontents*, where he develops the theory of 'sublimation': essentially, all human cultural activity is the 'sublimation of the sexual instinct' – to put it simply, we invented culture as a way of keeping our minds off sex. Why should we have chosen to do this? Freud takes in rather a lot of complicated explanations involving taboos and incest avoidance which have since been successfully challenged by anthropological research. It is also important to remember, as Julian Jaynes[11] has pointed out, that civilization needed the right physical conditions to flourish, never mind cultural tools such as written language and basic architectural principles. However I don't think we need to seek a more complicated explanation than the fact that culture has made it possible for us to attain the illusion of immortality. Why should so many great artists, writers and composers have been happy to settle for posterity rather than instant fame? Before the contraction of the globe into the mass media 'village', people could not expect to achieve fame in their lifetime, yet they were not deterred in their quest by this minor detail.

Personality factors: does fame require a special kind of person?

Earlier I described how people such as Morrissey and Damon Albarn appear to have had a strong sense of destiny at an early age. Could it be that fame is, to some extent, self-determined? Perhaps the likes of Rousseau flitted from vocation to vocation because something in their personality forever drove them in the direction of greatness? It seems unlikely; but perhaps there are certain characteristics common to those who achieve fame.

Simonton reports the findings of a number of studies employing variations on the Thematic Apperception Test (TAT), a widely used nomothetic test of personality, in which people are shown a series of 20 ambiguous pictures of human actors and are required to compose a story for each picture including 'before' and 'after' material. The psychologist then codes the responses according to a number of selected criteria, notably, power and 'affiliation' (the need for love or companionship).[12]

In one study a variant of the TAT method was used to analyse the inaugural addresses of American presidents. Truman and Kennedy emerged as the most power-hungry, while Kennedy and Nixon scored highest on the affiliation measure (Roosevelt and Garfield were the lowest scorers). In general, high power-hungry scores were good predictors of the presidents' likelihood to engage in military conflict, while high affiliation scores predicted a tendency towards nepotism, notably the appointment of close friends or relatives to cabinet positions. Similar findings were achieved with analyses of the announcement speeches of presidential candidates and with analyses of Soviet politicians.

Simonton devotes a whole chapter of his book to the retrospective analysis of personality and its importance in determining greatness. He concludes that the personality characteristics most likely to produce fame are the drive to succeed (exemplified by the 'type A' pattern of behaviour), and the tendency to take risks (necessary for breaking new cultural and intellectual ground). Nothing startling there; elsewhere, his attempt to apply traits derived from psychometric tests to historical figures is rather more *descriptive* than predictive.

Once again, Braudy has the last word. While many great careers appear to have been masterpieces of long-term planning, he suggests that perhaps the most essential characteristic necessary for fame is a sensitivity to situation – the ability to improvise when planning fails.

> It may be in the nature of those who achieve the greatest fame that they can do both, subsuming the standards of the past and showing their insufficiency, yet at the same time responding in a spontaneous and instinctive way to the crisis of the moment, doing naturally and immediately what is necessary.[13]

Developmental factors

Simonton identifies three factors relating to family background that might contribute to the realization of 'greatness'. The least convincing of these is *early mental stimulation*, the argument being that a positive nurturant environment is a significant spur to future achievement, and that a 'love of learning' may be instilled in relatively affluent homes. This may be true, but like the role of schooling in producing greatness, when these variables are partialled out it is almost certain to be *social class* that emerges as the determining factor. It could be argued that affluent family backgrounds instil a more future-oriented time perspective in their children than do poor families, but this factor might only explain ambition in general, of which 'greatness' is only a small subset.

A counter-argument is that greatness may have been inspired by some *adversity* in early life. A general impoverishment of environment may be said to constitute 'adversity', but this theory relates specifically to some single trauma that leaves behind a scar and an urge to succeed in order to overcome the distress. Simonton estimates that well over half of a large sample of eminent historical figures lost a parent before the age of 30, and that nearly a third of all winners of the Nobel Prize for Literature lost a parent in childhood. Whether these compare with the average life expectancies of the periods covered is not disclosed. It has to be said that, even if early parental death *could* be found to predict later success, it is not a finding that parents would like their children to get wind of!

The most intriguing of the developmental theories suggested by Simonton is that of *birth order*. From a purely individualist (or genetic) perspective, this seems as haphazard a factor as the position of the stars at birth, or whether the month had an 'r' in it. But birth order has a major impact on the socialization of the child; if Freud was right, and infancy is a period during which one's essential character can be cast in stone, then the first-born has a special environment in which s/he is the absolute centre of attention and forms a unique parental bond: 'If a man has been his mother's undisputed darling he retains throughout life the triumphant feeling, the confidence in success, which not seldom brings actual success along with it'.[14]

The evidence for this theory looks quite promising: throughout history there has rarely been more than one sibling who achieves prominence, a trend that persists through to modern-day celebrities. Moreover, Simonton argues, first-borns do appear to have a higher success rate. Similar evidence was produced by Galton, apparently without it occurring to him that the heredity theory should surely predict a random distribution of greatness according to birth order. Adler later added a further, more plausible explanation: the first-born child desires fame and success because s/he needs to claw back the indulgent attention s/he received before the arrival of siblings.[15] This does not, of course, explain the success of only children. Simonton produces some evidence to suggest that later-born children who attain fame are more likely to be revolutionary figures or creative writers. But the net is cast so wide at this point that the argument starts to look somewhat tenuous.

Outsiders

Another explanation for 'greatness' suggested by Simonton is that it may reflect the desire for success in a culture within which one feels estranged. For example Cicero, an outsider in the context of Rome, was driven by his desire for personal glory rather than the glory of Rome. To Cicero we can add the (statistically) unexpectedly high number of Jewish Nobel Prize winners and, in more recent times still, the over-representation of Afro-Caribbeans and African-Americans in specific fields such as sport and pop music in Europe and America. Why should this be? It is possible that the intermingling of cultural backgrounds produces a fertile creative environment:

> Persons who have been uprooted from traditional culture, or who have been thoroughly exposed to two or more cultures, seem to have an advantage in the range of hypotheses they are apt to consider, and through this means, in the frequency of creative innovation.[16]

Another suggestion is that 'outsiders' within a culture may be driven to seek fame, particularly people who feel marginalized for reasons of sexuality. Simonton lists a large number of historical 'greats' who practised homosexuality, and there is little doubt that, in the fields of art and entertainment, the proportion of gay *men* in particular vastly exceeds that which would be predicted by the incidence of homo-sexuality within the general population. Simonton accounts for this in terms of 'unconventional life styles',[17] citing many examples of famous people who remained unmarried, and those who could never marry happily (like Bertrand Russell, who married four times). He explains this in terms of the 'autonomy' of the creative individual, which drives them to obsessive involvement in their work, leaving little time for romance, or even bringing up a family.

An alternative explanation for the high incidence of homosexuality in the arts and entertainment industries is that the prospect of everlasting fame through success in these areas may be a preferable alternative to preserving one's DNA through bio-logical reproduction. But why not in other areas inviting fame and 'greatness'? The answer could be that, in more conservative domains, such as politics and sport, great pressure is exerted on individuals to conform to dominant norms and be seen with opposite-sex partners; political leaders are nearly always married by the time they come to power, and sportsmen and women frequently marry at an early stage in their careers.[18] The more individualistic domains of art and entertainment place fewer pressures on sexual conformity. I will return to this theme later in the chapter.

Genius and madness

Some of the most popular stereotypes of creative pioneers through the ages have been the portrayal of the 'mad scientist', the individual whose brilliance is such that s/he cannot relate to ordinary people, and of the 'tortured artist' whose creative flights of fancy are indistinguishable from his or her bouts of melancholy or mania. Cicero himself described the thirst for fame (*gloriae cupiditas*) as a 'disease'.[19] Could it be that the neurological preconditions for genius are closely related to those for psychopathology?

Simonton lists a huge number of creative geniuses who appear to have suffered from some form of psychiatric disorder. Some of these are very well documented, for example Schumann's manic depression, where his 'manic' phases enabled him to compose his best work, and van Gogh's depression which resulted in suicide. Alongside these, he also lists a number of famous individuals who have had psychologically disturbed relatives, suggesting that genius and madness can 'run' together in the same family.

Of course, one of the problems of investigating psychopathology across history is that we are having to rely on archival material to supply retrospective diagnoses of disorders which have only been identified in the last 100 years. It is easy to look through the biographical details of a famous individual and spot eccentricities which might indicate schizophrenia, or obsessive-compulsive disorder. It is quite another thing to diagnose mental illness in a modern clinical context. There are relatively few cases of historical figures seeking treatment for psychological disorders (although this may be due largely to different attitudes towards mental health across historical periods); however, we know that Rachmaninov visited a hypnotherapist, leading him to compose his most famous works (the second symphony and second piano concerto), and we also know that Hemingway underwent electro-convulsive therapy. A more recent study looked at eminent British poets, and discovered that half had either been prescribed drugs or given hospital treatment in order to cope with depressive disorders.[20]

What are we to make of this large body of evidence? A clue may lie in the solitary nature of artistic pursuits: poets, composers and painters seem to be the most frequently troubled by their private cognitions, but then they are alone with them for most of the time. More gregarious pursuits, such as acting and music, seem to have lower rates of psychopathology, and where it does occur, perhaps it is related more to the experience of fame than to any innate characteristics.

Rather than inspiring artists to creative heights, might not psychological disturbance be more likely to hamper their ambitions? Indeed, as Gedo points out, 'current psychopathology is very likely to *interfere* with creativity', citing the example of the sixteenth-century Florentine painter Jacopo da Pontormo, who, when commissioned to paint frescos for a chapel, was found to spend so much time 'lost in private cogitation . . . that through an entire day he might fail to make a single mark on the painting'.[21] In today's time-pressured society, it seems highly unlikely that a seriously psychologically disturbed individual would get very far in his or her chosen career. Correspondingly, as Simonton suggests, had psychoactive drug treatments been available in past centuries, we may have lost some of the great masterpieces of history!

Other theories accounting for the desire for fame

Simonton's research, however thorough, is restricted to explanations for 'greatness' as opposed to the desire for fame itself; in many respects, it can only account for the fame of those who succeed in obtaining it. He also, by his own admission as a psychohistorian, has concentrated on famous individuals of the past; there is a wealth of research potential for anyone interested in the psychological characteristics of modern-day celebrities. In the remainder of this chapter I shall outline a number of alternative theories which might account for why so many people desire fame.

Generativity: the urge to live on

The theory of generativity derives from the work of the American lifespan psychologist Erikson, whose 'eight ages of man' includes a seventh stage, in middle adulthood, which is characterized by a struggle between 'establishing and guiding the next generation', and the indulgence of self in the here and now. The former impulse is described as *generativity*.[22]

What forms might generativity take? A variety of possibilities have been suggested, from professional and voluntary work through to community and leisure activities.[23] At a reductionist level, generativity is little more than the urge to reproduce biologically, to live on through one's children; the Eriksonian model suggests that child-rearing is a subset of a more general desire to invest in the next generation, a kind of altruistic desire for the future well-being of the species.

Where does fame fit into all this? It could be argued that fame is another way of preserving one's identity for future generations. One possibility is that this is a way of defying death, and that the basic human desire for immortality can be realized in a symbolic sense.[24] John Kotre argues that cultural immortality is more likely to be desired in the post-reproductive stage – in other words, in later life.[25] In either case, the authors envisage cultural generativity as taking place at a much later stage than is the case with the vast majority of famous individuals. It may be that altruistic or philanthropic fame tends to occur later in life; however the theory of generativity does not by itself account for the desire for fame that appears as early as childhood. Viewed from an evolutionary perspective, however, Erikson's theory might, along with Freud's theory of sublimation, serve as a possible insight into how culture and the desire for symbolic immortality emerged.

Discourses of success

Leo Braudy has written of the 'inescapable imagery by which one lives life' that is produced by famous individuals' accounts of their upbringing.[26] Narrative psychology is a field which investigates the kind of life stories produced by individuals; researchers are not necessarily interested in the truthfulness of these accounts, but in the way that we use stories to construct meaning for our lives, and a sense of destiny.

The power of language as a tool for shaping our behaviour is the concern of many modern psychologists who study the way that 'discourse' (which can include anything from everyday conversation to symbol systems operating in society at large) works not only to create 'reality' but also to structure society by producing 'subjectivity', power relations, the 'right' to speak, and so on.[27]

How might the discourses of fame have contributed to the desire for fame through history? The deeds of Alexander, in emulating the gods, helped to create what Braudy calls a 'vocabulary' of fame which can be 'reproduced and defined by others'.[28] By bringing heroic deeds within the scope of human beings, he acted as a role model, fashioning a 'text' that could be rewritten by future generations. As history progresses, a proliferation of 'fame texts' emerge, covering different ways of being famous (from Chaucer to Capone) and different outlets of expression (from writing to performance). One only needs to look at the way in which famous individuals from Byron through to Ronnie Kray and Morrissey absorbed themselves in the legendary exploits of their idols to see how powerfully these texts can influence an individual's outlook.

Some of the discourses surrounding fame have become a permanent feature of the overall text of 'making a famous life' – most notably, Alexander's heavenward gaze, reproduced by countless twentieth-century celebrities in publicity shots. Other images, such as the tortured artist or poet in his or her solitary garret, have been carried over into pop music and are still present in the discourse of even the most public, performance-oriented celebrities. The myth of the 'gift', referred to previously, is one of the most successful of modern discourses.

How might these discourses work in producing a desire for fame? Clearly not in any direct way; they are just 'ways of talking' that float through society. Where they may influence behaviour is through the promotion of a value system constructed in numerous magazine and television features whereby recognition, financial success and achievement are represented as the positive goals of the dominant culture.[29] The term 'V.I.P.' to signify a celebrity is a typical device, elevating an individual above the general mass of humanity; depictions of the 'good life' in celebrity magazines is another, constructing the hide-away home and the happy nuclear family as the Holy Grail of human existence. Another discourse, that of the 'ordinary', or 'girl/boy-next-door' celebrity is closely related, presenting fame as a means of attaining a dream home and happy family for the most humble reader or viewer. It has been argued that such discourses may play an essential role in consumer society's manipulation of celebrity to maintain the image of democracy.[30]

At the same time, however, there are a significant number of discourses of fame emerging whose theme is the damage that fame can do to an individual – disillusionment, loneliness, persecution by obsessive fans and stalkers. Given these counter-discourses, why is fame still sought by so many? Perhaps the positive aspects of fame appeal to something that is more deep-rooted than the fanciful notion that we can emulate our heroes.

Fame is sexy

Given the popularity of fame through history, and the tempting possibilities dangled before us in the mass media, what are the most appealing aspects of fame? What is it that really stokes the fire in the belly of ambition? In this next section I shall return briefly to the arguments of biological determinists and geneticists.

Joshua Gamson describes an (unreported) exchange between a journalist and a film star who, when asked why he got into acting, replied 'because there were a lot of pretty girls I wanted to fuck'.[31] A traditional sociobiological argument might go something like this: most of life (human or otherwise) is spent attempting to reproduce our DNA. That is the only identifiable purpose in life, and so most human activity needs to be interpreted in this light.[32] The attractions of fame are blindingly obvious: we crave fame because fame makes us popular, and brings us into contact with lots of people to make babies with. Quantity spawns quality, so both men and women stand to benefit from the reproductive advantage of being famous.

There is another huge advantage fame gives us in that respect; like power and wealth in general, it enables us in effect to transcend our inherited biological characteristics and compensate for any shortcomings in that department. We might be dealt a rotten pack of biological cards – physically ugly, endowed with a physique hopelessly inadequate for reproduction or attracting sexually receptive partners – and yet, by mixing with the famous and the beautiful we get to join their exclusive club with all the benefits of membership. Both Boswell and Rousseau admitted that the motivating feature of fame was for them the opportunities it opened up for meeting women.

If that were the case, how come so many celebrities *are* physically attractive? Why do they need the added advantage that fame brings them? One could argue that, in the period before this century – before the birth of celebrity – people were inspired to pursue an artistic career or a political quest as a means of becoming famous and transcending their lack of looks (there are suggestions, for example, that Byron sought fame to compensate for his club foot; however, as Braudy suggests, these may derive from a twentieth-century tendency to overrate the role played by bodily perfection in public life). Today, with visual media operating as the principal vehicles for publicity, being beautiful has become a *criterion* for fame, not a disincentive. *Fame has evolved into a superficial cultural pursuit that is of little benefit to most of the people who attain it.*

The 'gene pool' argument is unconvincing because it ignores the tremendous efforts individuals make to attain fame, their attempts to preserve it when threatened, and their willingness to endure the heavy costs of fame simply to remain in the limelight. And what of the desire for posterity, so strong in the precelebrity age? Many of us are still content with simply 'going down in history', regardless of fame's worldly attractions. Fame as a sexual strategy cannot, for example, explain why a financially and emotionally troubled hotelier should spend three months learning to fly in order to stage a high-profile suicide, as happened recently on the south coast of England. The pilot, Terry Brand, left a letter declaring: 'My full intention in learning to fly was to move on in one dramatic moment.'[33]

Fame and homosexuality

At this point I return to the theory introduced earlier, in an attempt to account for the over-representation (compared with the general population) of homosexuality in the arts and entertainments. Sociobiological explanations in general tend to fall apart once homosexuality is introduced into the equation (if ever there was a recessive gene it would be the hypothesised 'gay gene', and there are no signs of homosexuality's demise just yet!). Rather more convincing in this case is Erikson's theory of generativity, which allows for the possibility that human beings can achieve a sense of investment in the next generation through culture rather than biological reproduction.

But, you might argue, what about today's self-indulgent performances? How might, say, the fame of a supermodel or a DJ have any possible benefit for future generations? For the answer, I will have to invoke the notion of the 'selfish gene'[34] and argue that it is not enough simply to view culture as a rather nice philanthropic alternative to making babies. It may just as easily be a thoroughly self-indulgent alternative to biological reproduction, since the whole point of reproduction is the preservation of one's DNA. If we have no intention to reproduce biologically (and

I am *assuming* here that this is true of most homosexual individuals[35]) then we must find some other way of preserving some essence of self.

Is there any historical evidence for this, apart from the mere prevalence of homosexuality in the arts? There is a very interesting passage in Chaucer's *The House of Fame* which, if my interpretation is correct, suggests that fame has always had a special appeal for a homosexual population. As the nine groups line up to appeal for the goddess Fame's approval, there is one group who have a curious request. They say they haven't really done very much, and are not popular with women (indeed, detested by them). And yet, they desire fame so that it can appear as if 'wommen loven us for wod' (like mad):

> Thogh we may not the body have
> Of wymmen, yet, so God you save,
> Leet men gliwe on us the name!
> Sufficeth that we han the fame.
> (lines 1759–62)

In this passage they appear to be requesting fame for its own sake (read *gliwe* as 'stick'). But the interesting point is that they state explicitly that they are not interested in women's bodies; interested, that is, in having sex with them. For what other reasons should they wish to have the adoration of women? It does seem that the group Chaucer is describing here, although rather unflatteringly because they haven't actually achieved anything of note, is a homosexual group who desire fame for no other reason than the sake of posterity.

It may be that homosexuality is not the only reason for us to embrace fame as symbolic reproduction. There are historical cases of childless individuals who have craved fame as compensation for not being able to reproduce, such as Elizabeth I, who took great pains to ensure that her official portrait followed strict guidelines, drawing heavily on imagery associated with the Virgin Mary, or even John Lord Lumley, an early art collector of no note until all three of his children died, and he set about creating his own legend accordingly.[36] Again, I must emphasize that these are isolated cases. A thorough investigation would be of considerable interest.

Symbolic immortality

One of the features of the history of fame, as Braudy notes, is its apparent inverse relationship with the concept of the afterlife in any given culture. The societies of Ancient Egypt and Rome had gods but their idea of an afterlife was not strong. Reincarnation was popular, but the prospect of returning as a dung beetle has limited appeal compared with the Christian image of eternal salvation. Therefore it is not surprising to find the desire for fame flourishing in these earlier cultures, while it was certainly less popular during Medieval times when the Church had such a strong influence on Western society. More recently, the decline of religious faith in the West is in sharp contrast with the meteoric rise of celebrity culture.

There is a long literary tradition of presenting fame as immortality, from Virgil ('I too may . . . fly in victory on the lips of men') through to the lyrics of Irene Cara's song: 'Fame! I want to live forever!' Horace wrote that 'a great part of me will live beyond death', and Ovid echoed the sentiment. Later on, Dante's contemporary Petrarch wrote of 'another life' that could be gained through fame. By the eighteenth century, with the decline in importance attached to the afterlife, the clamour for fame in one's lifetime was so loud that theologians took it as evidence for the existence of the immortal soul – even though it would seem to imply precisely the opposite.

Being famous for eternity is one thing: what about the instant fame of the moment? It appears that, as history unfolds, technological development has given us an increasing number of ways that we can achieve immortality – words, pictures, records, video. It is worth considering the origins of these technologies, because historically we can see that, intentionally or not, they have always been treated as forms of reproduction of the self. The reproduction of the human face in visual art, for instance, has been a source of controversy over the last two millennia. In Roman times, the appearance of the emperor's face on coins and sculptured busts of famous individuals were the earliest attempts to capture the human form. An important honour in Rome was the *ius imaginis* – the right to have one's face preserved for ever.[37]

With the rise of the Church, however, there was increasing concern about the visualization of the human form. Reproduction is God's business, they argued, and only images of Jesus (and later the saints) were appropriate – hence the huge trade in icons in Eastern Europe in the first few centuries AD. Later on, such practices were outlawed by the 'iconoclasts' on grounds of blasphemy. Henry VIII's destruction of religious images in sixteenth-century Britain coincided with the rise of portraiture, promoted partly by Henry himself. Initially, the only reproductions of human faces had been engravings, but now portraits and illustrations became immensely popular. Not only were they a means of reproducing oneself, but the reproduction could be tailored to present your best side – hence Henry's, and later Elizabeth I's incessant interest in achieving complete control over their portraits, reflecting the later concern of celebrities and their publicity photos.

Photographs as replicators

The invention of the camera was a major step in the reproduction of self. Even more than a portrait, a photograph was an unarguable verification of an individual's existence. We can go further than that. Each time we are photographed, it could be argued, *we reproduce.* This may seem a rather far-fetched analogy, but this is partly because we have become so familiar with photography that we take it for granted; so many people in Western society own a camera, and we see so many photographs every day (it is almost impossible to avoid seeing at least one photographic image each day, from a billboard poster or a shop window) that it is hard to imagine life without them. Once again, it is necessary to adopt a strict historical perspective in order to appreciate the significance of photography in terms of human evolution.

This point was not lost on the early pioneers of photography, or on the social commentators of the time. Daguerre, the inventor of the photographic process, described it as 'a chemical and physical process which gives nature the ability to reproduce herself.' Meanwhile, the *Leipzig City Advertiser* of 1837, in the tradition of the early Church, denounced the reproduction of the human face in film as sacrilegious: 'The very desire to do so is blasphemy. Man is created in the image of God and God's image cannot be captured by any human machine.'[38] It was acceptable for an artist to attempt it 'in a moment of solemnity', but 'never by means of a mechanical aid' (overlooking the technicality that a paintbrush might be considered a mechanical aid).

Suddenly, it seemed, the possibility of replicating ourselves without biologically reproducing was becoming a possibility; given the limitations of the concept, it could be said that photography was the first step on the road to human cloning.

Television as a better replicator

Compared with the crude reproductive capability of daguerro-type portraits, the invention of the cine-camera was a huge step towards the perfect reproduction of the human form. Now the arguments around the validity of representation no longer applied; although the recording of one's voice and one's visual image are coded pieces of information, the reproductions are so lifelike that we have little option but to treat them as such. This phenomenon is described by postmodernists as *simulacrum* – 'a state of such near perfect replication that the difference between the original and the copy becomes almost impossible to spot'.[39]

With the advent of television, there were simulacra of human beings everywhere. The early film industry had already placed film stars in a compromising position. Now the famous were becoming the property of the public. For half an hour you could have Tony Hancock in your living room – and not just a visual representation of Tony Hancock, either – a walking, talking, (almost) three-dimensional representation of him, which sufficiently convinces you that it *is* Tony Hancock that you interact with him as though he were *there*.[40]

Again, put yourself in the shoes of the famous female recording artist. Shortly after your harrowing experience with the paparazzi, you are summoned to the studio by your record company (from the Los Angeles apartment you now rent) who insist that your contract requires you to make a second LP. The company urges you to release a particular song as a single ahead of the LP's release to act as a 'trailer' for it and, more importantly, as an opportunity for a burst of publicity work.

Your single is released and your press office arranges over 100 interviews for you, although you soon whittle this down to around half, spaced over a fortnight. You are booked into a plush hotel for most of them, although some take place elsewhere (such as television studios). In the week prior to the release of your single, you are being replicated furiously. Dozens of newspapers and glossy, full-colour magazines carry photographs of you along with the interview (and occasionally to accompany a news item about the release of your single). The video, for a start, receives heavy 'rotation' on specialist TV channels and several plays on terrestrial TV. You appear on a number of television shows to perform the song, and give a number of interviews. To gain maximum mileage out of you, a couple of shows, such as Saturday morning kids' TV, manage to persuade you to take part in some lowbrow slapstick comedy. The record is on the playlist at BBC radio and most commercial stations. Then the single is released, sells tens of thousands of copies, and provokes another week or two of saturation media coverage.

Think: each time someone plays your record, every time a radio is switched on while your song is being played, has you stroll into their living room via the television set, you are *there*. How many appearances have *you* made in a week? Probably hundreds of thousands of copies of *you* are floating around Great Britain (not to mention the rest of the world, where you will replicate yourself at a later date).

No wonder so many of us want to be famous.

Conclusion

In this chapter, the historical perspective has been broadened to include an evolutionary perspective as well. The focus in general has been on the desire to be famous, which is clearly something that obsesses many of us, occasionally to a dangerous degree. I have considered arguments that there may indeed be something special about the 'special people' we celebrate – that the answer may lie in their personality or even in their genes. Alternatively I have considered social constructionist explanations for fame's appeal and the reproduction of seductive discourses through the media. However these approaches seem inadequate to account fully for the long-standing and desperate desire for fame. My main argument in this chapter is that technological developments over time have enabled us to reproduce ourselves in a way that mimics the replication of DNA. I have argued that the progressive invention of better and better replicating devices, culminating in television and video, have opened up opportunities for individuals to reproduce themselves on a phenomenal scale, thus providing an evolutionary rationale for the obsessive pursuit of fame (albeit at a cultural, rather than biological, level).

Notes

1   Rogan, J. (1992) *Morrissey and Marr: The Severed Alliance*. London: Omnibus, p. 92.
2   Reynolds, S. (1990) *Blissed out: The Raptures of Rock*. London: Serpent's Tail, p. 25.
3   Ibid, p. 25.
4   Simonton, D. K. (1994) *Greatness: Who Makes History and Why*. New York: Guilford Press.
5   Pearson, J. (1995) *The Profession of Violence: The Rise and Fall of the Kray Twins* (4th edition). London: HarperCollins.
6   Claims to have identified the genetic basis of homosexuality have generated more media publicity than the research findings have perhaps warranted. Nevertheless, one leading US biologist (Simon LeVay) has been quoted in *Newsweek* (24 February 1992) as saying that he would 'give up a scientific career altogether' if unsuccessful in his attempt to demonstrate inherited differences in neurological structure between homosexual and heterosexual men (so much for scientific research starting out from the position of the null hypothesis!).
7   The Krays, of course, are a 'single case' from which it would be unfair to generalise; for a thorough tarring-and-feathering of identical twin research, see Rose, S.,

Lewontin, R. C. and Kamin, L. J. (1984) *Not in our Genes: Biology, Ideology and Human Nature*. London: Penguin.

8   Simonton, *Greatness*, p. 35.

9   Gedo, J. E. (1996) *The Artist and the Emotional World*. New York: Columbia University Press.

10   Milton, J. (1989) *Paradise Lost*, trans. C. Ricks, London: Penguin.

11   Jaynes, J. (1976) *The Origin of Consciousness in the Breakdown of the Bicameral Mind*. London: Penguin.

12   Simonton, *Greatness*.

13   Braudy, L. (1997) *The Frenzy of Renown: Fame and its History* (2nd edition). New York: Vintage Books, p. 84.

14   Cited in Clark, R. W. (1980) *Freud*. New York: Random House, p. 19.

15   Adler, A. (1938) *Social Interest* (J. Linton and R. Vaughan, trans.). London: Faber & Faber.

16   Campbell, D. T. (1960) 'Blind variation and selective retention in creative thought as in other knowledge processes'. *Psychological Review*, 67, pp. 380–400 (quoted in Simonton, *Greatness*., p. 166).

17   Simonton, *Greatness*., p. 170.

18   However, it should be noted that during 1998 a number of British government ministers were 'outed' as homosexual.

19   Cicero, M. T. (45 BC, 1943). 'Tusculan disputations'. In J. E. King (trans.) *Cicero in twenty-eight volumes, No. 18*. London: William Heinemann.

20   Jamison, K. R. (1989) 'Mood disorders and patterns of creativity in British writers and artists'. *Psychiatry*, 52, pp. 125–34.

21   Gedo, *The Artist and the Emotional World*, pp. 96–97.

22   Erikson, E. H. (1950) *Childhood and Society*. New York: Norton.

23   McAdams, D. P. and de St. Aubin, E. (1992) 'A theory of generativity and its assessment through self-report, behavioral acts, and narrative themes in autobiography'. *Journal of Personality and Social Psychology*, 62, pp. 1003–15.

24   See McAdams, D. P. (1985) *Power, Intimacy and the Life Story: Personological Inquiries into Identity*. New York: Guilford Press.

25   Kotre, J. (1996) *Outliving the Self: How We Live on in Future Generations*. New York: Norton.

26   Braudy, *The Frenzy of Renown*, p. 223.

27   The best writing on this topic can be found in Parker, I. (1992) *Discourse Dynamics: Critical Analysis for Social and Individual Psychology*. London: Routledge; and Edwards, D. (1996) *Discourse and Cognition*. London: Sage.

28   Braudy, *The Frenzy of Renown*, p. 55.

29   Sandeen, C. (1997) 'Success defined by television: The value system promoted by *PM* magazine'. *Critical Studies in Mass Communication*, 14, pp. 77–105.

30   Marshall, P. D. (1997) *Celebrity and Power: Fame in Contemporary Cultur*. Minneapolis: University of Minnesota Press.

31   Gamson, J. (1994) *Claims to Fame Celebrity in Contemporary America*, Berkeley, CA: University of California Press, p. 88.

32   'Evolutionary psychology' has become a popular branch of the discipline, inspired by advances in genetics. Nobody has written about genetics better, or more influentially, than the zoologist Richard Dawkins (*The Selfish Gene*, Oxford University Press 1976/1989). Dawkins is ambivalent about the influence of 'genes' on human behaviour – indeed, he claims that 'we, alone on earth, are able to rebel

against the tyranny of the selfish replicator' (ibid., p. 202). Others are less guarded, notably the biologist Robin Baker, whose *Sperm Wars* (1996) is, I think, a spectacularly misguided effort to apply the principles of animal behaviour to human sexual activity.

33   *Western Daily News*, 24 December 1997.

34   Dawkins, *The Selfish Gene*. Dawkins coined the term 'selfish gene' to counter arguments by earlier biologists that the 'unit' of natural selection might be family relatedness or even the species as a whole. Ultimately, Dawkins argues, all acts of apparent self-sacrifice can be interpreted as beneficial to the individual – therefore it would seem more likely that, rather than perpetuating a family line, reproduction is primarily geared to replicating one's own DNA as faithfully as possible. An objection to the term *selfish* might be that the attribution of selfishness to bits of DNA is at best anthropomorphic; at worst, liable to create unwarranted, and potentially dangerous, assumptions about animal (and human) behaviour.

35   I have attempted, wherever possible, to avoid using the term 'homosexuals' to denote a class of individuals. Michel Foucault argued (*The History of Sexuality*, Vol. 1, Penguin, 1981) that the term 'homosexual' used, prior to the Victorian era, to refer to a sexual practice rather than a class of person ('The sodomite had been a temporary aberration; the homosexual was now a species'). This is not linguistic pedantry; sexuality is, of course, a complex and elusive matter! If I refer to 'homosexuals' or 'homosexual individuals', then, I am referring to people whose dominant and preferred mode of sexual congress is with individuals of the same gender.

36   Braudy, *The Frenzy of Renown*.

37   Braudy, ibid.

38   Both this, and the earlier Daguerre comment, quoted in Tagg, J. (1988) *The Burden of Representation: Essays on Photographies and Histories*. Basingstoke: Macmillan, p. 41.

39   Harvey, D. (1990) *The Condition of Postmodernity*. Cambridge, MA: Blackwell, p. 289.

40   A form of interaction which has been called 'parasocial interaction' [. . .].

Chapter 26

Graeme Turner

CELEBRITY, THE TABLOID AND THE DEMOCRATIC PUBLIC SPHERE

Introduction

THE INFLUENCE OF CELEBRITY has been especially pronounced on certain kinds of media product. In television, it has become an increasingly significant component of news and current affairs programming. It is fundamental to the format of network talk shows such as *Oprah* and an increasingly important objective for guests appearing on talk and confession shows such as *Jerry Springer*, *Trisha* and *Ricki Lake* as well as reality TV game-show hybrids like *Big Brother*. The internet is littered with celebrity pictorial sites, ranging from the official and the anodyne to the mischievous and scandalous and finally to the pornographic. In the print media, celebrity journalism has completely dominated the tabloid newspaper market in the UK, as well as the 'supermarket tabloids' such as the *National Enquirer* and the *Globe* in the US. It has also dramatically reinvented the mass market women's magazine. In the US, the UK, Europe, Australia and Canada (at least), since the late 1980s, such magazines have revised their editorial mixes in response to falling circulation and the competition from the new local celebrity weeklies and the international glossy monthlies. While still retaining their traditional interest in fashion, domestic advice and 'beauty', the mass market women's magazines have progressively increased their focus on 'celebrity culture' (Gough-Yates, 2003: 136).

Cultural and media studies accounts of these developments have attempted to interpret the social and political implications of the increasing interest in celebrity. The spectrum of views is wide. On the one hand there are those who regard this trend as a lamentable example of the dumbing-down of the public sphere, as 'proper' news is replaced by gossip (see Langer, 1998). On the other hand, there are those who welcome the mass media's emancipation from its obsession with the public, the institutional and the masculine (see Lumby, 1997). Those who take this latter view regard what is now routinely described as the 'tabloidisation' of the public sphere as providing an opportunity for some democratisation of media access; as new, hitherto marginalised and often usefully undisciplined voices are being heard. In this chapter, I want to first review the establishment of celebrity in the area most conventionally regarded as the heartland of this form of media content: mass market magazines. I will then address the broader 'tabloidisation' debate – the arguments between those who perceive a democratic potential in current media developments and those who don't – before looking at the application of this debate to the production of celebrity.

Celebrity, mass market magazines and the tabloids

The key provocation to the late 1980s to early 1990s change in the content of the mass market women's magazines, according to Anna Gough-Yates' (2003) account of the British market, was the competition from the celebrity weeklies. In many other markets, the threat may not have been quite as direct, but the outcomes were similar as even the market leaders revised their editorial mix towards a much greater proportion of celebrity stories. In Holland, in fact, the trend began much earlier, with the 'gossip magazine' developing into a distinct genre incorporating practical advice and horoscopes alongside articles about celebrities, television stars and royalty during the 1970s (Hermes, 1995: 119). There, and elsewhere, while the traditional components of the mass market women's magazine may have remained in place – the beauty hints, the fashion, the horoscopes, the advice columns and so on – they lost their prominence among the screamers on the front cover to the latest gossip from national television and Hollywood. Increasingly, too, the mass market women's magazines took on the need to represent their own cultural identities in a more aggressive and coherent fashion; an attempt to construct 'the personality' of the magazine as well as the identity of the readers (Gough-Yates, 2003: 20). Such a strategy certainly helped the women's magazines to modernise and survive: in Australia, it took them to new heights of circulation for almost a decade. It also helped the modernisation of mass market magazines for young girls: *Dolly* and *Sugar*, for example, are thoroughly dependent upon celebrity content today. However, the incorporation of this strategy into these sectors of the magazine market could not hold off the development of what became a new genre of mass-market magazine, the celebrity gossip and news weekly.

There is now a whole segment of the market devoted to these magazines and, while much of their content is in fact local (national sports or television stars, for instance, or Euro-trash royals for *Hello!* and its parent, *Hola!*), they have a major international presence as well. *Hello!* and *OK!* are ubiquitous in news outlets around the western world as are the more downmarket US variants such as *Us* and the *National Enquirer*. In the large markets such as the UK and the US there is quite a spectrum available. At one end we have the sleazy nudie magazines that come and go, bearing names like *Celebrity Flesh*; their content is primarily nude or topless paparazzi shots and production or video capture stills from screen performances. Slightly above them in the market (but much more stable commercially) come the shock and sensation weeklies such as the *Star* or the *National Enquirer*. Similar to these, but slightly less scandalous in their news values, are the gossip news weeklies such as *Who* (Australia), *People* (USA) or *Now* (UK), where the stories come with an occasional coating of scepticism and the photos can be used to set celebrities up as objects of ridicule as well as admiration. In this lower end of the market, the magazine's commercial alignment with the interests of the publicity industries varies considerably. A weekly such as the *National Enquirer* has only a limited dependence on celebrity gossip but the gossip it does print tends to be scandalous, salacious and potentially damaging for its subjects. By no means does all of its news involve celebrities, however, and at various times it will deal with (and, as the O.J. Simpson case revealed, sometimes even break) major political stories. Most crucially, though, the *National Enquirer* (perhaps surprisingly) prides itself on its accuracy and this clearly limits the extent to which it could ever be fully incorporated into the publicity agenda of the major agencies (see Bird, 2002). With *Now*, however, and the American version of *People*, despite their trade in paparazzi images and constant excitement over minor celebrity scandals, there is some commercial alignment between their news items and the promotional needs of the major entertainment industry organisations.

These industrial links are even more evident in the central sector of the crowded UK celebrity magazine market where the market leaders *OK*, *Heat* and *Hello!* (among many others) woo their readers by offering positive pictures and gossip features about celebrities. While the *National Enquirer* may not care to enter into ongoing relationships with the publicity industry, *Hello!* and *OK* certainly do. These magazines deal with almost nothing but celebrity[1] and thus they must be tightly articulated to the industry and its promotional needs if they want a reliable supply of pictures and stories. As result, *Hello!* publishes uniformly appreciative features about celebrities' new marriages/houses/babies, recoveries from tragedy/divorce/career setbacks – clearly in collaboration with the celebrities concerned. *OK* is slightly less respectful of the celebrities it promotes, adopting a more populist and cheeky tone in its journalism, but none the less the magazine presents an overwhelmingly friendly view of the celebrities' lives to the reader. Both are highly respectable magazines. (*Hello!* is particularly so, going for glamour rather than sex, giving any whiff of scandal a fairly wide berth, and peppering its pages with respectful coverage of the activities of obscure Euro-royals.) Both share a curiously parochial and middle class perspective (Conboy, 2002: 149) and despite their international circulation they are a world away from the chic cosmopolitanism of the American glossies.

In recent years, these two magazines have been upstaged by a new competitor, the slightly trashier *Heat*. *Heat* is cheekier, less sophisticated and more news-oriented (that is, gossip) rather than feature-oriented (that is, staged promotions). It does not go in for the classic *Hello!* multi-page photo-spread on the celebrity at home – and so it does not carry so many signs of commercial collaboration with the celebrity industry – but its treatment of the celebrity is still very positive and sympathetic. The cover price is lower and its target market younger and less middle-class;[2] with a contemporary music-mag look, it has more street credibility than either competitor. The precise significance of its circulation figures at the time I researched them (2002) were in some dispute, but there was no doubt that *Heat* was taking readers from both of its competitors. Some indication of the concern this engendered was revealed when *OK* launched a spoiler campaign by including a *Heat* look-alike (called *Hot Stars*) as a giveaway with each issue of *OK*; *Hot Stars* shamelessly mimicked *Heat*'s layout, format and overall look.

To complete the spectrum I have been sketching out, there are probably two more layers. First, is the international movie/television magazine typified by *Premiere*, which exists solely to promote the industry's latest productions, with interviews, reviews, previews and so on. Given their relation to the industry, this is not the place to find the cheeky, the sceptical or anything that might threaten the commercial success of the projects it promotes. In terms of circulation, this is not a large sector of the market, it has to be said, and could be classified as belonging to the 'special interests' section of the magazine market. More commercially important is what I would regard as the final layer: the top end of the market – the international (or probably more accurately, the 'glocal'[3]) quality glossy, ranging from, say, *FHM* to *Vanity Fair*. While these magazines may observe more independent editorial policies than the movie magazines, it is important to note how thoroughly the transnational entertainment and media industries coordinate their interests with those of the high quality international glossies. We have already referred to Toby Young's account of his experience of working for *Vanity Fair* in New York, where he expressed alarm at how much power the entertainment industry agents and publicists enjoyed in determining what would be published about their clients in the magazine. His experiences would seem indicative of the broader relationship between such magazines and the celebrity industry. In fact, it would seem that the commercialisation of this relationship is deepening. Upmarket international magazines dealing with fashion, consumption, the arts, style, and other popular cultural topics (such as *Vanity Fair*, *Harpers Bazaar* and *Vogue*), have accorded celebrity news and features an ever more prominent position in their editorial mix. Stories on Nicole Kidman or Kylie Minogue are as likely to appear at this end of the market as they are to turn up in *Heat* or *People* – and they will likely be almost as anodyne and commercially helpful there as they would be in *OK*. It is important to emphasise this fact because criticisms of the effect of the promotion of celebrities upon the contemporary practice of journalism often assume that this is at its most active at the 'tabloid' end of the print media. My research on mass market magazines would suggest the reverse; that the alignment of the commercial interests of the magazine and the celebrity is at its most seamless at the higher end of the market.

Nevertheless, to assume that it is all the tabloids' fault would be an understandable error to make in the circumstances. There is, after all, significant convergence between the editorial content in certain sectors of the magazine market and the mainstream newspaper market. This is especially the case in the UK, where the tabloid newspapers (the so-called 'red-tops') long ago hitched their wagon to the popular appetite for celebrity stories. Indeed, Bromley and Cushion quote the editor of the *Mirror* in London saying that he thought the future of newspapers lay in *Big Brother* until September 11 (temporarily) revived his readers' interest in news (2002: 166). Certainly, the British tabloids have almost categorically redefined what qualifies for them as news, so that tabloid news is now utterly personalised and dominated by the actions of well-known people – politicians, public officials, sportsmen and women, celebrities, soon-to-be celebrities and wannabe celebrities. (The broadsheets' weekend colour supplements are devoted, to news background and lifestyle features, but the *Mirror* and the *Express* devote their weekend colour supplements entirely to celebrities.) Celebrity gossip achieves front-page status regularly and the whole sector has been influenced by the *News of the World*'s dogged pioneering of what has since been called 'bonk journalism' (that is, 'who's doing it with whom'). This mode of journalism is deliberately salacious and careless of its effect on the persons concerned. Celebrities are clearly fair game. At one point, the *News of the World* was offering a prize of £3,000 to any reader who could provide them with their personal 'account of adulterous sex with a reasonably well known personality' (Horrie and Nathan, 1999: 57).

As such strategies would lead you to expect, these papers have a highly fraught relationship to the celebrity industry. From one point of view, they are simply predators, keen to exploit any item of scandalous news to the full and at whatever cost to those concerned. From another point of view, their commercial power makes them almost irresistable as the quickest route to the public. They pitch so tirelessly to the consumer of celebrity that they offer an extraordinary commercial opportunity to anyone who can use them successfully. Consequently, the tabloids deal with the celebrity industries through a see-sawing pattern of scandalous exposures and negotiated exclusives – at one point threatening the professional survival of the celebrities they expose, and at another point contracting to provide them with unparalleled personal visibility. Little wonder that their mode of representation routinely works over the ambiguous territory between admiration and derision.

The 'tabloidisation' debate

This brings us to the issue of what is called the 'tabloidisation' of the media – the critical domain within which the production of celebrity is most often discussed. As a phenomenon, 'tabloidisation'[4] is most definitively located in sections of the British daily press, but the term has been extended to refer to a broad range of television formats as well. In the US it includes muck-raking current affairs programs such as *A Current Affair*, 'reality TV' programmes such as *Cops* and afternoon talk-confession shows such as *Oprah* and *Ricki Lake*. By its critics, the process of tabloidisation is usually considered to sacrifice information for entertainment, accuracy for sensation and to employ tactics of representation which entrap and exploit its subjects (the hidden camera, the reconstruction, the surprise talk-show guests). What are considered to be among its constitutive discourses range from the explicitly playful or self-conscious (the staged family conflicts, for instance set up in *Ricki Lake*), to the self-important but bogus *gravitas* of the journalist exposing an issue of 'public interest' (a politician's sex life, for instance). In practice, however, tabloidisation seems continually to expand as a category; it moves beyond the description of a particular kind of journalism to become a portmanteau description for what is regarded as the trivialisation of media content in general. As a term that accurately describes media formats and content, it is far too baggy, imprecise and value-laden to be useful as an analytic concept, in my view. However, it is a widely accepted label for a set of established debates about contemporary shifts in media content, production and consumption. As such, the production of celebrity through the media can be seen to fall under its ambit. I want to keep using the term tabloidisation in what follows, then, as a convenient means of labelling those concerns that are conventionally collected under it.

Concern about tabloidisation is a routine topic for media commentators and pundits of all political persuasions. Customarily, tabloidisation is framed as a broad-based cultural movement, mostly visible in certain media forms, which is made possible by the increasing commercialisation of modern life and a corresponding decline in 'traditional values'. While this would suggest that the concept of tabloidisation expresses a conservative hostility to popular culture as a domain, it must be said that it also generates concern on the political left and among many with a professional interest in the media and popular culture. Todd Gitlin, for example, criticises the 'trivialisation of public affairs, the usurpation of public discourse by soap opera, the apparent breakdown of mechanisms for forming a public will and making it effective'. For him, 'trivialisation – infotainment and the like – works against the principled right and left alike' (1997: 35). His concern is echoed by the doyen of American communications scholars, James Carey:

> In recent years, journalism has been sold, to a significant degree, to the entertainment and information industries which market commodities globally that are central to the world economy of the twenty-first century. This condition cannot be allowed to persist . . . The reform of journalism will only occur when the news organisations are disengaged from the global entertainment industries that increasingly contain them.
>
> (2002: 89)

The angry tone of Carey's piece indicates there is a moral or political dimension to his critique: it is not merely motivated by concern at shifts in the formal attributes of contemporary journalism. This is characteristic of critiques of tabloidisation (see Saltzman, 1999, for instance).

Alternative views have in turn attacked the moralistic nature of criticisms such as those outlined above, as well as their origin in elite conceptions of the public sphere. Ian Connell was severe on what he saw as the snobbery behind the criticism of tabloid journalism and rejected the accusation that such journalism diverted us from more important political and social issues. Indeed, he argued that the tabloid's personalisation of news actually provided a more effective means of demonstrating the importance of the political:

> Contrary to what has often been claimed about the tabloid press, they are every bit as preoccupied with social differences and the tensions which arise from them as serious journalists or for that matter academic sociologists. The focus on personality and privilege is one of the ways in which these differences and tensions are represented as concrete and recognizable rather than as remote, abstract categories.
>
> (1992: 82)

It would have to be admitted that many of the concerns expressed about the influence of tabloidisation are grounded in a conventional and longstanding hostility to popular culture itself. Cultural studies has a rich tradition of revealing and challenging such a position. John Hartley's *Popular Reality* (1996) repeatedly attacks the class- and gender-based binarism that places information against entertainment, hard news against soft news, the public sphere against private lifestyles and public service media against the commercial media. As Hartley says, such binarism has a long history as 'the common sense' of the media industry and among policy-makers, but that 'doesn't make it any the less prejudicial as a mental map of modern media':

> Not only do such binaries reinforce a systematic bias against popular, screen and commercial media, but they also tend to reinforce other prejudices, principally the one which considers many of the [denigrated terms in the opposition] as 'women's issues', with the (silent but inescapable) implication that serious politics and the public sphere is men's stuff.
>
> (1996: 27)

One of the key locations for what might be regarded as a moral panic about tabloidisation, and a location most directly associated with 'women's stuff', is the daytime television talk show. While some might condemn its 'Oprahfication' of America (see Shattuc, 1997: 86), others 'champion daytime talk shows as a new public sphere or a counter public sphere' (ibid.: 93). Far from stripping politics from the public arena, these are 'highly popular programs that depend on social topics and the participation of average citizens' (ibid.: 86). It is the access of such citizens to public debate that is so important in accounts of the television talk show; crucially, these are people who have not hitherto enjoyed access to the television audience and whose voices have been silenced or ignored. As a result, Jane Shattuc claims that certain power structures are challenged by this form of television:

> The shows not only promote conversation but do away with the distance between audience and stage. They do not depend on the power of expertise or bourgeois education. They elicit common sense and everyday experience as the mark of truth. They confound the distinction between the public and the private.
>
> (1997: 93)

Shattuc does not make excessively liberatory claims for this form of entertainment. Ultimately, she concedes, these shows are neither intrinsically progressive nor intrinsically regressive. However, in their capacity to replicate the operation of the town meeting – the model she uses to explain their politics and their human dynamics – they offer a mode of participation that is implicitly democratic (ibid.: 94). It is this implicitly democratic function I want to turn to next, more directly in relation to the construction of celebrity through the media.

'Democratainment'

[. . .] the proliferation of opportunities for fame has been seen by some as a fundamentally liberatory development for the media in modern societies. The rise to media prominence of ordinary people such as the contestants in *Big Brother* or the stars of the webcam sites can be described as a new form of freedom. Leo Braudy directly compares modern celebrity with the forms of prominence or visibility that preceded it:

> [T]he longing for old standards of 'true' fame reflect a feeling of loss and nostalgia for a mythical world where communal support for achievement could flourish. But in such societies that did exist, it was always only

certain social groups who had an exclusive right to call the tunes of glory, and other visual and verbal media were in the hands of a few.

(1986: 585)

The older patterns of class and privilege have thus lost their power, he argues, and in its place is a new media democracy, where ordinary people now have greater access to media representation.

Furthermore, the consumers of celebrity are now able to play a part in the production of cultural visibility. According to Charles Leadbetter (2000), Princess Diana was 'created in part by her consumers': 'she was jointly owned by the people who consumed her image, the readers of *Hello!* magazine, the media and Diana herself' (2000: 25). Such an image is not employed in the unproblematic way assumed by the myths of earlier versions of 'true' fame. Instead, Gary Whannel suggests, public figures of 'spectacular celebritydom seem precisely to offer' their audiences 'modes of public exchange in which moral and political positionalities can be rehearsed' (2002: 214).

The most developed version of this kind of position is found in John Hartley's work, particularly in his *Uses of Television* (1999). Here Hartley presents an optimistic account of the popular media as it increasingly informs the construction of cultural identities through its performance of 'transmodern teaching': 'using "domestic discourses" to teach vast, unknowable, "lay" audiences modes of "citizenship" and knowledge based on culture and identity within a virtualized community of unparalleled size and diversity' (1999: 41).

That such a pedagogic practice should occur largely through the provision of entertainment is no impediment to its productive capacity. Breaking decisively with the paternalistic model of media provision identified with Reithian regimes of public broadcasting, the newly heterogeneous commercial media sphere offers the possibility of 'DIY citizenship': the construction of cultural identity through the operation of motivated media consumption. The DIY citizen has a multiplicity of choices available – identities through which they might construct their own. Hartley calls this process 'semiotic self-determination'. Informed by Hartley's principled rejection of elitist assumptions that might allocate aesthetic or moral values to particular media forms or genres of content, this is the world of 'democratainment'. There, the process of selection and choice in media consumption structurally replicates the choices available to the free citizen in a democratic society. The evidence for such a possibility is found, with characteristic but pleasing perversity, precisely in the tabloidised forms so pilloried by other media commentators: television talk shows, fashion magazines and the semiotic furniture of suburbia.[5]

It seems widely accepted in media and cultural studies that the more dispersed possibilities of production and distribution in the contemporary media – and not only through new technologies such as the internet – do imply the potential to achieve a 'different, less unequal vision of the mediated public sphere' (Couldry, 2003: 140) than seemed possible even a decade ago. Such a position is consistent with Braudy's (1986) much earlier description of the proliferation of celebrity and the disarticulation of fame from achievement as an intrinsically democratising force. More recently, it is also consistent with the defence of television talk shows, which argues that these formats have brought new, previously marginalised, voices into the public sphere

(Lumby, 1997; Masciarotte, 1991). This new diversity, in turn, argues Chris Rojek, results in the 'recognition and celebration of lifestyles, beliefs and forms of life previously unrecognised or repressed' (2001: 191). Hence, there is a significant line of argument which suggests that, far from constituting an 'unrecognised threat to liberal democracy' (Schickel, 1985: 311), the media formats in question are a democratising force. And from one point of view, this would seem entirely self-evident. The celebrity offered to contestants through reality TV, contestants defined for us by their ordinariness, would certainly seem to constitute a more democratic phenomenon than a celebrity based on social, economic, religious or cultural hierarchies.

Frances Bonner, however, argues that there are limits to how 'ordinary' such people can be and thus to what extent we can see the spread of reality TV in particular as part of a democratising process. Even in TV's representation of the ordinary, there must be hierarchies. She points out that the contestants on game shows, reality TV and so on are exceptional in specific ways: television seeks those who can 'project a personality on television' and therefore some 'are more usefully ordinary than others' (2003: 53). Like a number of writers (for instance, Couldry, 2003), she reminds us that such shows employ a process of selection that has produced a particular, and motivated, construction of ordinariness for us to watch. It is in television's interest to mask and disavow this process. In its place, Bonner suggests (after Robert Stam) that television serves its 'inbuilt need to flatter the audience', by suggesting through the representation of ordinariness that they, too, belong on television. However, in fact, 'the people who appear ordinary on television' are 'just a little better looking, a little more articulate, a little luckier' (2003: 97) than the 'ordinary' we experience away from television.

Television's construction of the 'ordinary' is itself a category worth examining. Nick Couldry takes this next step in reference to *Popstars*:

> The ordinariness of these shows' contestants has a double significance in ritual terms: first, their 'ordinariness' confirms the 'reality' of what is shown (once their early performance strategies have, we assume, been stripped away by the continuous presence of the camera) and, second, that 'ordinariness' is the status from which the contestants compete to escape into another ritually distinct category, celebrity . . . [this is] special, higher than the ordinary world.
>
> (2003: 107)

Couldry argues that there are in fact two kinds of people – 'media people' (those who are visible through the media) and 'ordinary people' – and that the distinction is hierarchical. The great value of celebrity is that it enables the 'ordinary' person to make the transition to being a 'media' person: that this is seen as an achievement – or a spectacular ritual in Couldry's terms – only reinforces the hierarchical structure which separates media people from ordinary people:

> So, in *Big Brother* and elsewhere, media rituals which seem to affirm the shared significance of an individual's transition to celebrity in fact entrench further the working division between 'media people' and 'ordinary people'. Heavily ritualised processes such as media events which

seem to affirm the shared significance of media institutions' picture of the world in fact insist upon the hierarchy of that picture over any possible other.

(2003: 143)

Such arguments would suggest that the mere presence of the ordinary – a presence that has undeniably increased and is now firmly entrenched in programming formats on television – cannot be taken at face value.

Similarly, there are those who insist that the proliferation of social, gendered and ethnicised identities in the media generally cannot be seen as a democratising force, if only because of the larger ideological frame within which they are contained. Dovey claims that displays of deviance, such as those we might witness in a day-time talk show, 'actually serve to reinforce social norms by the individual pathologis-ing of the speaker by the judging audience' (2002: 13), while Conboy argues that the characteristic action of the tabloid media in general is to 'close down into reaction' rather than open up 'into contestation' (2002: 149). It is possible to argue, on the other hand, that the relentlessness of this process has weakened signifi-cantly over the last couple of decades and that the trends Hartley notices would constitute convincing evidence of the declining recalcitrance of these mechanisms of control and containment.

In his discussion of Hartley's *Uses of Television*, Couldry makes what seems to me a more telling criticism of the limits of the democratainment thesis. He acknowledges the justice of Hartley's proposition that the contemporary media, 'in its dispersed, and often ironic, form', sustain 'a public space in which the terms of public and private discourse are open to negotiation beyond formal political control' (Couldry, 2003: 18). That much, at least, seems to be conceded as a fair and reasonable account of the political possibilities released by the current configuration of the contemporary media, and it operates as a solid rebuttal to most aspects of the tabloidisation thesis. However, Couldry poses a fundamental question to Hartley, which defers the question about the effectivity of the DIY consumer by redirecting the debate towards the symbolic economy of the media itself. Hartley never addresses, Couldry says, the 'implications' for the democratainment thesis 'of the massive concentration of symbolic power in media institutions':

How does this affect our interpretation of the social 'uses' of television? Unless we rely on the jaded rhetoric of market liberalism, we can know nothing about the actual impacts, positive or negative, of contemporary media without considering, for example, the uneven symbolic landscape in which popular talk shows address their viewers and also their participants.

(2003: 18)

It's a familiar debate within cultural studies, of course, issues of agency and determination recirculate continually. But it also reminds us of another familiar debate – between cultural studies and political economy – in that it insists the discussion of processes of consumption must first consider the conditions of production that determined what choices are actually on offer in the first place.

The final qualification I want to raise in relation to democratainment is the connection it implies between the proliferation of celebrity, the widening of access, and the liberation of 'the ordinary', with the principles of democracy. I have argued this question in more detail elsewhere (Turner, 2001), but the simple version can be put quite briefly. Those who argue that the last decade or so has witnessed the opening up of media access to women, to people of colour and to a wider array of class positions, are certainly right. However, this is more correctly seen as a demotic, rather than a democratic, development. There is no necessary connection between demographic changes in the pattern of access to media representation and a democratic politics. At the empirical level, for every Oprah Winfrey, there is a Rush Limbaugh. At the structural level, no-one has yet even attempted to properly argue such a connection – it has simply been assumed. Or more correctly, there is a degree of theoretical slippage as the notion of semiotic self-determination mutates into a more explicitly political version of self-determination. Diversity, it would seem, must be intrinsically democratic.

The demotic turn

Thus far I have been emphasising the pervasiveness of the influence of celebrity throughout the media, as well as the proliferation of the production of celebrity throughout the various media industries. To some extent, this is a story of the convergence of market strategies – with television, print and the Internet, in particular, all milking the market opportunities available to them through the production, distribution and marketing of celebrity in one form or another. However, the multiplication of outlets, of formats and of the numbers of people subject to the discursive processes of 'celebrification', suggests a competing narrative: that of the opportunity of celebrity spreading beyond elites of one kind or another and into the expectations of the population in general. In conjunction with what seems like a widening of opportunity in this area, there is the proliferation of new sites of media production as well as the consolidation of non-traditional systems of delivery for media content – from cable television to mobile telephony. Both have encouraged optimism about possible changes to the current concentration of ownership for major media forms. DIY production technologies are springing up to service DIY consumer-citizens, it would seem. As a result, it is not surprising that cultural studies researchers should suggest that increased powers of self-determination are now in the hands of media consumers – hence the democratic political possibilities read into the 'demotic turn'.

That there is a demotic turn seems to me beyond dispute. The media discourses used to represent 'ordinariness' edge closer every day to the lived experience of 'the ordinary'. Ordinary people have never been more visible in the media, nor have their own utterances ever been reproduced with the faithfulness, respect and accuracy they are today (Couldry, 2003: 102). The talk and confession genre of television delivers us raw, inflamed and spectacular performances of the ordinary every afternoon, while game shows spend millions trying to reproduce it. What constitutes the ordinary in the media, too, has been opened up dramatically to offer us multiple versions of class, gender, sexuality and ethnicity. At the same time, the range of media material now available for ordinary individuals to consume, assimilate and use is probably unparalleled. But the objective of this explosion of the ordinary does seem to me, as Couldry suggests and at least to some extent, an attempt to turn the representation of the ordinary into a kind of media ritual. What informs this is not what I would regard as the positive byproducts – the openness, the accessibility, the diversity, the recognition of marginalised citizens' rights to media representation. Rather, what motivates the media's mining of the ordinary seems to be its capacity to generate the performance of endless and unmotivated diversity for its own sake. If this judgement is warranted, then the 'democratic' part of the 'democratainment' neologism is an accidental consequence of the 'entertainment' part and its least convincing component. It is important to remember that celebrity remains an hierarchical and exclusive phenomenon, no matter how much it proliferates. It is in the interests of those who operate this hierarchy in the contemporary context, however, to disavow its exclusivity; maybe what we are watching in the demotic turn is the celebrity industries' improved capacity to do this convincingly through the media.

For the individual celebrity, it might be possible to argue that, in the end, more opportunities are still more opportunities. Ordinary people can wind up on *Big Brother* or a network soap opera, just by the luck of the draw, and that possibility does have its liberatory dimension. One would want to move, though, to the examination of specific cases to think about what actually occurs. In the work that Frances Bonner, David Marshall and I did on celebrity in Australia, we found that the less connected the achievement of celebrity was to some training, performance background or the like – in fact, the more arbitrary it was – the less equipped the person concerned was to handle the inevitable discovery that their fame had nothing to do with them and that it could disappear overnight. The housemates on *Big Brother*, by and large, will not generate careers in the public eye; the young soap stars on *Neighbours*, by and large, will drift out of the industry as they are unable to find roles in anything more rewarding than regional British Christmas pantomimes. In such a situation, we felt, a key issue was the level of responsibility accepted by the promotions and publicity personnel who represented these celebrities and who traded their commodity status while it had value. Many of those personnel shared that view and expressed concern about the destructive cycle of discovery, exploitation and disposal that was fundamental to the way their industries used the individual star.

The reason for such a cycle is the pursuit of profit by large internationalised media conglomerates who, despite the demotic turn in representation and consumption, still control the symbolic economy. Notwithstanding the webcam girls, the trading of music on the internet, the availability of digital production technologies in all kinds of media forms, this is still in the same hands it has always been. It might be seductive to think of the internet as an alternative, counter-public sphere and in many ways its chaotic contents would support such a view. But, it is still a system that is dominated by white, middle class, American men and increasingly integrated into the major corporate structures of the traditional media conglomerates.

What does seem new, however – what Hartley's DIY citizenship also alludes to – is that we seem to be witnessing a new process of identity formation as media content mutates. Celebrity is playing an increasingly important role in this mutation as well as, I would argue, in these new modes of production of cultural identity. As it plays this role, celebrity itself begins to mutate: from being an elite and magical condition to being an almost reasonable expectation from everyday life. Certainly, the consumption of celebrity has become a part of everyday life in the twenty-first century, and so it is not surprising if it now turns up as part of young people's life plans. It is important to understand this shift.

In most respects my personal sympathies lie with the more optimistic and populist accounts of shifts in popular culture; when one sees who is presenting the more conservative case, it makes one suspect the interests it might serve. However, it is important to recognise that it is easy to overstate the democratic potential of the new media systems and formats. Reality TV has presented us with some interesting moments in media performance and the spectacle of 'everyday life', no matter how it is produced, can make for some compelling television. However, the industrial cycle of use and disposal mentioned above does seem to have radically accelerated in response to the demand created by new media forms. This suggests the activity of a process of increased commodification rather than enhanced political enfranchisement. As David Marshall demonstrates in such detail in *Celebrity and Power*, the interests served are first of all those of capital.

That said, it is all too easy to slide into a moralising political critique of the forms of celebrity, of the artificiality of the cultural status it appears to confer and of the media forms that carry its related products. To do this, I absolutely accept, would be to greatly underestimate the complexity of these forms and products as well as the varied cultural and social functions they might perform. Further, it would divert us from discussing what I would regard as the more important and interesting aspects of the modern phenomenon of celebrity. It is not the perceived triviality of the talk show or the celebrity magazine, nor even the extraordinary range of media forms the production of celebrity has adopted, that attracts *my* central interest. Rather it is the fact that celebrity now occupies an increasingly significant role in the process through which we construct our cultural identities.

Notes

1   Like many of the celebrity weeklies, *Hello!* retains remnants of the traditional women's magazine: beauty hints, recipes and fashion.

2   *Hello!* is particularly interesting in this regard. Far more respectable than any of its counterparts in the US, for instance, it offers an attractive reader demographic to advertisers. According to its website, it is the only mass circulation women's magazine (that is the category into which the circulation survey places it, and indeed 80 per cent of its readers are women) with nearly one-third of its readers falling into the upmarket AB demographic.

3   This is the increasingly accepted way of describing a global media product that conforms to a branded international format, but is localised in terms of its specific content. So the various national editions of *FHM* or *Vogue* may represent the franchising of the brand but each may contain substantially different editorial content from the other.

4   The discussion of tabloidisation in this section draws heavily upon Turner (1999) where some of these arguments were first developed and where some of the complications unable to be integrated into this account are discussed at greater length.

5   The ordinary person who becomes a celebrity is perhaps the epitome of what can be achieved through this semiotic self-determination (although this is achieved through gaining access to the processes of production rather than merely those of consumption).

Chapter 27

P. David Marshall

THE CELEBRITY LEGACY OF
THE BEATLES

T HERE ARE PECULIAR CONTEMPORARY moments that recall the celebrated past of the Beatles and which reinforce the belief that their influence continues and is vibrantly part of the present. Oasis is probably the most popular band regularly to acknowledge its debts to the Beatles and the Lennon–McCartney songwriting successes. In a similar vein, the New Zealand–Australian band Crowded House was often linked to the Beatles' pop sensibility in its approach to songmaking and its sartorial presence. But more than just adopting and adapting the foundations of a musical style, succeeding generations of musicians and singers have also built upon the public display of self that was a part of the various incarnations of the Beatles – both as a group and as individuals. The popular music industry has in many ways routinized the moments of public display that are part of the Beatles' mythology and has made them representative of youth and contemporary musical culture. This chapter seeks to understand the legacy of the Beatles as celebrity forms for contemporary culture. It is an investigation of the routinization of the pleasures of personality that have become models for the organization of popular music and popular culture.

To start this process it is important to define what I mean by celebrity and, more specifically, how I understand its meaning to intersect with popular music and its discourses. Celebrity is not pure construction, whereby an industry can manufacture a consumable personality; neither is celebrity a total expression of popular will, through which a public determines who is to be elevated into some level of stardom. Celebrity, as I have argued elsewhere (Marshall 1997), is a complex text that contains the tension *between* these two formulations. Moreover, somewhere within the proliferating discourses that define a public personality is the living and breathing individual who makes the projections and constructions that much more complex. Celebrity is not like a film character where there is a limited and original text. It is a presentation of the self for public consumption which accomodates something private and personal. In fact, *revelation* of the private and the personal is the central narrative-like pattern of the ways in which celebrities are viewed by the public. Scandalous disclosures that draw attention to the individual focus media attention and audience attention on what is normally concealed. So, when we hear about another punch-up involving Liam Gallagher, we have one more story that reveals something about the person, and which connects Oasis to a long rock lineage of notorious moments of illegality. Celebrities provide a topic for continuous discussions about the individual and the meaning of individuality in contemporary culture, about the location of the line between public and private, and about the significance of their actions for an audience. Celebrities are sites for the play of identification and identity; the celebrity is producing an identity which forms patterns of identification for audiences and publics.

The popular music celebrity is a particular incarnation of this celebrity system and the Beatles have been instrumental in shaping its construction. Several key elements of celebrity in popular music have been associated with the group's emergence, and it is that relationship which needs to be explored.

In postwar years, popular music has expressed and maintained a clear connection with an emerging youth culture. The marketing to youth, the development of the teenager as a demographic category, and the demarcation of distinctive youth technologies and spaces — from the transistor radio and the jukebox to dancehalls and cars — have all been part of a celebrated differentiation of experience for postwar youth. According to Frith (1983) the teenager is as much a marketing invention as a member of an authentic youth group. Within British culture, as the observations of Hebdige (1988) have suggested, youth became conflated with transformations in class formations through the celebration of the egalitarian spirit in the popular music and culture of the USA during that same postwar era.

The Beatles intervened in this process of the definition of youth-as-marketing segment in a number of interesting ways. Their accents identified them from Liverpool and from the state, rather than the public (that is, private), school system. Accents provide spatial and class co-ordinates within British culture; but the Beatles transcended these co-ordinates to represent something beyond class, something particularly modern that in its transcendence articulated a celebrated status of freedom — a freedom *from something*. In the tradition of postwar British youth, the 'freedom from' seemed to be conveyed through a connection to the black rhythm and blues culture of the United States, which gave its appropriation into British rock and roll a form of double signification: simultaneously, the celebration of something American (specifically in its focus on individual expression) and the celebration of a marginalized part of American culture (which provided the groundwork for the general tonality of rebellion). But this appropriation was without the political and cultural baggage — the very semiotic weight — of a sharply race-divided American society. When transposed into the British cultural mix, with its own residues of class and conflict, the Beatles' style expressed difference, change, and the potential for renewal. Youth, through its public expression in the Beatles, represented a break from the past and a celebration of the future. Although part of the emergence of a teenage marketing category, which might at first seem to be superficial, the Beatles' exuberant power and cultural influence stretched these marketing boundaries into a wider emotive celebration of the renewal of modernity in the 1960s.

I want to concentrate on how the Beatles were a part of the manufacture of the modern public self that has been essential to the maintenance of the myths of modernity.

As a cultural phenomenon the Beatles helped to produce persistent patterns with which we interpret public personalities, dialectical tensions that express the inherent instability of public personae, and more specifically the modes of interpretation that we employ to read and make sense of popular music performers. To unravel the connections between the Beatles and our continuing interpretation of celebrities, I have grouped the analysis under specific themes: the formation of affect and connection; the tension between authenticity and fabrication; the expression of individuality.

The formation of affect and connection

The emotive outpouring that accompanied the emergence of the Beatles has become the litmus test of cultural significance for most succeeding popular cultural phenomena. The Leonardo DiCaprio moment following *Titanic*'s 1997 release, when adolescent girls and young women returned to see the movie countless times, is in direct lineage with what came to be known as Beatlemania. In a similar manner the pop group Hanson – three brothers aged 11 to 17 – created frenzies of fans at shopping malls throughout North America during 1997 and 1998.

The key connection between these popular cultural moments is that they describe a form of investment that goes beyond the individual into a collective experience. The Beatles, particularly in their international tours of 1964, attracted remarkable crowds, some of which resulted from a combination of promotional strategies and the actions of dedicated fans. It is freely acknowledged that the promoters of Beatles paraphernalia gave a dollar and a t-shirt to each person who came to JFK Airport to greet the arrival of the Beatles in New York in February 1964 (Burrows 1996: 77). Through heavy promotion on radio stations and saturation news coverage, the group's arrival became the equivalent of a major international event. However, between hyperbole and the actual activities of 1964, the Beatles did manage to attract fans whose emotional commitment was undeniable. While at many of their concerts, the level of screaming made it difficult to hear the music, in fact, the music seemed relatively unimportant to the fans; it was ambient to the experience of proximity to their idols.

The Beatles succeeded in producing a peculiarly modern phenomenon that has become routinized and institutionalized in the reproduction of popular music since those early tours. They produced the popular music crowd. The group's concert at New York's Shea Stadium on 15 August 1965, which was attended by more than 55 000 fans, established a standard and scale of emotional connection which succeeding generations of popular music fans have sought to duplicate through the ritual attendance of performances at football and baseball stadia. Despite the physical distance from the performers, the Beatles' legacy was that the moment of the crowd was ultimately more significant. It was a form of solidarity with the performing group. The relationship between recorded music and the live concert consequently fell into a recognizable pattern in the promotion of popular music, in which it was not essential for the music to match the recording quality, since the concert was designed to be a collective experience of support and a moment of declaration that rivalled in devotion the most emotionally charged evangelical tent crusades (indeed, the US evangelist Billy Graham's stadium revivals of the 1950s could be seen as a direct precursor to the popular music concert industry).

Hysteria, the central metaphor in descriptions of what the Beatles created on their first US tour, has been utilized since nineteenth century crowd theorists tried to articulate the transformation of the individual to some form of group behaviour. Around the turn of the century, the accompanying loss of self was held responsible for the creation of a being of lesser intelligence (Le Bon 1960). Often, crowd behaviour was linked to the feminine, in a way similar to the manner in which Huyssen (1986: 44–62) has linked mass consumer culture to the feminine. In the nineteenth-century versions of this argument, there is a clear misogynistic reading of the crowd. Nevertheless, the idea that hysteria was linked to weakness in the female constitution carried on as a cultural connotation from early psychological investigations via crowd theorists like Le Bon and Gabriele Tarde through to the twentieth-century emergence of social psychology. The production of hysteria has enveloped the development of modern advertising as it worked through the process of connecting with the consumer – mass behaviour as fundamentally irrational or, in social psychological terms, appealing to prepotent motivations of the individual.

The concert became an emblem of the moment of irrationality and hysteria essential to the way in which the culture industries operated in the twentieth century. The entertainment industries sought moments where there was a massive effect; in popular music, this patterning came to be described as the hit, where something in the performance produced a huge outpouring of affective connection. The objective of cultural production, as it was organized through the interests of consumer capitalism, was to replicate those moments of massive and collective connection to a particular phenomenon.

Despite the fact that the Beatles were never to perform in concert after 1966, the constitution of their audiences as a cultural memory has remained consistent. While their music may have transformed and adopted aesthetic pretensions and/or emotional maturity, the concerts were the signs of what the Beatles represented in their first years. Predominantly young (pre-pubescent and post-pubescent) girls dominated the image of these concerts and their public appearances on US television, such as *The Ed Sullivan Show*, in 1964. The significance of this representation of fandom is twofold for the organization of popular music personalities.

First, the Beatles produced an audience that helped to define the division between pop and rock in the following 30 years. Pop music, which maintained a closer lineage with Tin Pan Alley and the traditions of the recording industry, was primarily aimed at creating affective sensations that were clearly identified with a female audience. In contrast, rock music grounded itself through an emotional connection to performance that was inherently narcissistic, in that its male performers appealed predominantly to young, male audiences.

Secondly, the Beatles articulated a presentation of personality that played with the construction of public sexuality. Popular music as a cultural discourse of personality became fundamentally a discourse about the construction of gender itself. The female fans' overt and apparently highly emotional connection to their idols underlines the group's play with sexual ambiguity: the Beatles' youthfulness, their girlish moptop haircuts and proper suits made them an amalgam of sexual identity. In some ways, their demeanour made them unthreatening as love interests for young girls and promoted the devotional bedroom shrine that became *de rigueur* for the post-1960s female teenager; but throughout their small efforts to bend the constituent categories of male and female appearance, they were sustained by the media as pleasant boys with a well-developed and well-mannered sense of humour.

What the Beatles produced in those early years through their construction of emotionally charged audiences was a template for an industry. Popular music idols certainly predated the Beatles' emergence; but the concerts and the circulation of images of fan solidarity with, and devotion to, the Beatles became models for the recording industry to replicate. Pop music became the site for producing the teen idol as a phenomenon in the way that movies might have operated more centrally in the 1930s and 1940s. The idols who postdated the Beatles continued the group's play with sexual identity that characterized its international emergence. The Monkees, David Cassidy, Leif Garrett, the Bay City Rollers, New Kids On The Block, Take That, the Backstreet Boys and many others point to the manner in which the affective, even hysterical, moment of the Beatles was routinized into an industrial strategy. (In many ways, this routinization of massive affective moments parallels Weber's [1968] discussion of the routinisation of charisma into political institutions.) The sexual identity of these popstars has been decidedly between boys and men, and in their play with active sexuality the pop stars who followed the Beatles have tried to repeat the close connection to the pre/post-pubescent girl.

Fabrication and authenticity

A central tendency that was further refined by the Beatles was the division between the obviously constructed nature of the celebrity of traditional popular music and some new sensibility of the music performer. The Beatles were instrumental in making the persona of popular music an issue. Unlike folk performers emerging from the USA at roughly the same time, the Beatles were not clearly a public sign of sincerity or authenticity – they operated as signs over the contestation of their own significance. Chambers has underlined the fact that their early music was much more closely aligned with traditional themes of pop tunesmiths (1985: 63). 'Love Me Do', for example, was not a creative advance over the songs produced for Hollywood musical stars of the 1930s and 1940s. But there were differences in the way the Beatles *presented themselves* that established markers for shifts in the meaning of popular music in contemporary culture.

Their media moniker – the Fab Four – provides a clear indication of how the Beatles trod the line between something authentically wonderful and significant (*fabulous*) and something manufactured and created by an industry (*fab*rication). Their effective blend of this binarism operated through a number of channels. The discourse of the artist as genius-creator was a prevalent definition of something culturally authentic both in contemporary art and, increasingly, in the folk-inflected music cultures of the 1950s and early 1960s. The Beatles were able to ride that form of authenticity predominantly through Lennon and McCartney's songwriting and, in so doing, connected the cultural connotations of the group to the singer-songwriter tradition. Having that control over the production of their music provided a route through which they received a certain credibility in the 1960s and which challenged the traditional Tin Pan Alley distinction between composer/writer and performer. They were also distant from those fabricated singing groups who depended on a manager to orchestrate their music, their venues, and their look; in this way, for example, the Beatles were in clear contrast to girl groups like the Supremes, constructed by Motown. Their ability to play their own instruments positioned them within subsequent definitions of rock performers as opposed to pop performers; their extensive prefame work in Hamburg nightclubs accentuated their independence and authenticity as they developed a style and a musicianship which gave them a degree of autonomy from the industry; the fact that they formed their group as schoolboys in Liverpool without the initial help of a manager emphasized that they had roots which predated any Svengali-like transformation.

Despite these impressive claims to the authentic, the Beatles did at the same time represent something contrived and manufactured by an industry that worked to accelerate the power of a new entertainment act. Although their hairstyles came from their Hamburg days and the influence of artist-friends, the suits of the early years (at the insistence of Epstein) were a sign of moulding their personalities into a successful industrial act. Their musical style may have relied on a 'leather and rockers' image; but they traded their leather jackets to present something less threatening. Where Elvis had constructed a more palatable white image for rock and roll, the Beatles moved that image still further, from its African-American creative-though-culturally-threatening source to the boys-next-door. The Beatles, in a very real sense, allowed themselves to be shaped into a product for the proliferation of their fame.

All of these conflicting discourses about the nature of their celebrity converged in their first moments of international fame and, in some ways, their presentations of self did influence definitions of the authentic in contemporary culture. Expansive patterns of fame which represented the antithesis of genuine achievement or real heroism have been presumed to be a source of inauthenticity since the nineteenth century. In the twentieth century, fame through film or popular music reflected a connection to the masses, and was even more clearly associated with something of fleeting importance or a form of commodity fabrication. Fame represented a double breakdown in culture: first, the forms of knowledge of the celebrated personality bore little connection to the deeper structural knowledge of the person associated with the traditional community; secondly, the former elites of state and church were no longer in complete control of those who might be celebrated or venerated. What the Beatles signified was a re-reading of the cultural value of fame and celebrity. Instead of possessing a negative connotation, the Beatles became a democratic celebration of the new power of fame. The commodity could no longer be seen as some form of corruption of artistic practice, but it was more *part* of the artistic process. Andy Warhol's blank parodies of fame in his Marilyn and Elvis series was an art-parallel to the Beatles' engagement with their public through the media.

The new authenticity that the Beatles expressed through their own commodification can best be seen in their interviews and in their two Richard Lester movies. The early interviews were an elaborate game with the various press scrums, in which each Beatle performed an evasive manoeuvre as he answered the questions put to him with his own questions or nonsensical answers which played with the rhythmic quality of the original questions. Lennon became infamous for his ability to make nonsense – but funny nonsense. It should be noted that the form of humour followed a long tradition in British comedy, from the music hall to BBC radio's *The Goon Show* in the 1950s. What was new was its deployment in the presentation of the self for media and public consumption. The evasive but funny interview marked by its sense of non-cooperation with media powers became one of the most dominant patterns in rock and popular music in television and film.

The Lester-directed movies *A Hard Day's Night* and *Help!* served a similar purpose. The basic premise of each film was that the Beatles were playing themselves. Their 'acting' was thus an elaborate variation on their public 'everyday' selves which had grown from these media interview personae. As a narrative, the films represented the capacity of the Beatles to maintain their humour, and thus their authentic selves, in a world which had tipped towards a hysterical relationship to their personalities.

The expression of individuality

These origins of a new authenticity that the Beatles express a mutated somewhat over the 1960s and affected their status as a group. Indeed, the central narrative of the Beatles as public personalities in that decade was to achieve a form of legitimacy that transcended their group definition and moved the reading of the Beatles into an interpretation of *individual* personality.

The Beatles' migration from a collective identity to a focus on the individual is nothing new. It expresses more than anything else the resurgence of modern conceptions of the individual and their articulation through public personalities. It also reiterates a form of search for authenticity through many of the classically modern motifs – such as scandal.

The development of scandals enveloped the Beatles at various moments of the group's life; there were hints of scandals concerning liaisons with women, and numerous reports of drug use. The greater scandal was the misinterpretation in 1966 of a John Lennon interview in which he offered the observation that the Beatles were more popular than Jesus Christ. I am less concerned here with the validity of the story, and more interested in the effects of the idea of scandal on the celebrity. Viewed in the usual way, scandal implies deleterious effects; but what has to be understood about the Beatles as celebrities is that scandal, within the discourse of popular music as rock, actually works towards a form of legitimation. This was an emerging part of the idea of rock music as oppositional. Generational divides can become more clearly demarcated through such emotionally charged incidents. The scandal itself can produce a form of publicity that makes the celebrity a richer and deeper text and may allow a form of politicization to emerge from the process. Lyrics may be listened to more closely for intentionality and for their potential political and cultural impact.

Scandal also worked to give the Beatles a sense of autonomy. Again, this conception of autonomy seems to operate counterintuitively to the meaning of scandal. However, in the case of the Beatles their construction as pleasant, fun-loving personae actually situated them within a clear 'entertainer'–orientated presentation of self – what I have earlier characterized as a clear lineage to the Tin Pan Alley tradition of popular music. In a very real way, the image of the Beatles provided a stereotype that was a form of public strait-jacket for the group. Although Paul McCartney seemed the most comfortable with the tunesmith role, their believed-to-be authentic personae restricted their connection to broader social and cultural movements. Large-scale media scandals actually allowed the group to exercise an independence from the industry it had spawned.

Apple is the most obvious example of this stretch to autonomy. Established in 1968 to foster innovative cultural productions and technological projects – as Paul McCartney labelled it, 'a kind of Western communism' (Burrows 1996: 154) – Apple was crafted to a new cultural politics emerging from the power of the Beatles' contemporary celebrity formation that had emerged from the culture industries themselves. Although generally deemed to be a failure, its status is an important marker of the Beatles' legacy to corporate/artistic autonomy in popular music, if not in other highly commodified cultural forms. Contemporary examples of this exercise of cultural individuality within the corporate structure abound, but probably the most successful in her articulation of a sense of autonomous artistry is Madonna. On more modest scales, the clearly clichéd setting up of the home recording studio is an example of the individual artist reprising some of the power of the corporate music industry world at the level of production.

The invocation of the artist in all its nineteenth-century vaingloriousness is deeply imbedded in the Beatles' celebrity legacy. The artist has served as modernity's and modernism's heightened expression of individuality. Creativity and innovation have been celebrated in the liberalist conception of the individual and the Beatles were driven to perpetuate the genius-creator myths within a new popular cultural form. In conjunction with their producer George Martin, the Beatles worked towards a differentiation of their text out of the patterned rhythms of popular music where repetition and appropriation of the popular and the non-commodified folk traditions were well established; collectively and individually, they worked to construct *difference* in their music. *Sgt Pepper's Lonely Hearts Club Band* must be seen as a milestone, not only in popular music production, but also in the shift in audience perceptions of the popular music celebrity. Complicit in this transformation of the meaning of popular music icons was the music press which began to investigate and invest in the inner lives of performers for the inspiration of their artistry in a way which echoed the achievements of their jazz precursors; the fundamental difference was that popular music performers were imbued with the new authenticity of democratic celebrity. Their inner lives became an expression of cultural anxiety, a journalistic shorthand for understanding generational change. Because of their overwhelming popularity, the Beatles were seen – and used – as beacons from which to understand the contemporary. Thus, their experimentation with Eastern mysticism in their Indian pilgrimage heralded a different period of intense scrutiny of the Beatles, when their work and their lives became a journey of self-discovery through which their dispersed and massive Western audience vicariously travelled towards some inner truth about the group and contemporary existence itself. It was a combination of pop psychology, Eastern religion, Freudian psychoanalysis and more traditional forms of celebrity gossip. The will to discover the true Beatles was jointly organized by the media, by their fans, and by the Beatles themselves.

The actual fragmentation of the Beatles was a further expression of the role of individuality in popular music celebrity identity. The idea of the pop group continues to be the starting point of the rock/pop music celebrity; but progression is often defined by the movement to solo careers. The Beatles became an unworkable group for all sorts of reasons and it is important to note how the breakup connected to their public roles as celebrities. The Beatles as a phenomenon became, like McLuhan (another 1960s icon), a victim of their own sign crime (Kroker 1984). Ironically, because of their huge success, the Beatles embodied a series of cultural memories that overwhelmed their own present as a group. In a very real sense, the Beatles had to reinvent themselves – as an experimental artist (Lennon), an Eastern-influenced guitarist (Harrison) or an actor (Starr). Re-invention has since become the routine form of renewal for the popular music celebrity. David Bowie's chameleon-like shifts in persona, Madonna's costume and attitude transformation, and U2's trawling of the popart tradition are all examples that have drawn on the transformations of character developed by the Beatles within the lifetime of the group and in the post-Beatle era.

Conclusion

The Beatles in their various presentations of self provide a road map for the organization of the contemporary popular music personality. They successfully integrated previous representations of the popular music performer into a transformed role in the middle of the twentieth century. The constitution of that celebrity form is very much linked to the rejuvenation of modernity in the context of the popular. Although it is difficult to unify the project of modernity, it does have some defining characteristics in terms of social improvement, progress, and positive change towards the future. The Beatles were instrumental in shifting the domain of the modern into the significance of popular culture for the politics of contemporary culture. I have described this shift, expressed through the discourses that developed around their personalities, as a new authenticity that could be best characterized as a democratic celebration of the celebrity. The Beatles demonstrated a new cultural power that was clearly connected to cultural transformations.

This new authenticity of the popular music celebrity has provided a legacy for the meaning and significance of popular music within a broader social context. Popular music has become a major site for debates about sexuality, youth, and the general theme of identity politics. Succeeding generations of popular music celebrity figures (in their invocation of a form of liberalist individualism as artists in conjunction with their popular connection to an audience) have continued to be intense sites or channels for working out contemporary political and cultural meaning. The artistic phenomenon of Beck in the late 1990s, the scandal of Public Enemy in the early 1990s, and the sexual politics of Madonna through the 1980s are all articulations of what the Beatles brought together in their personae. Popular music, through its celebrity icons, became simultaneously the location for the examination of the self, the continuing discourse of entertainment and pleasure, and the recognition of the cultural power of popularity.

Chapter 28

Richard Johnson

EXEMPLARY DIFFERENCES
Mourning (and not mourning) a princess

THIS CHAPTER LOOKS AT 'Mourning Diana', with the emphasis on the 'Mourning'. It addresses the puzzlement, expressed by many commentators, about the intensity of popular feelings around her death. My interest derives, in part, from personal experiences. The death of Jill, for thirty-three years my partner, lover and wife, in January 1992, thrust me into the turmoil and practices of grief, which became, in turn, objects of reflection. As often in cultural inquiry, personal experiences provide clues to wider investigations.[1]

In mourning Diana (and in not-mourning) many other issues were involved. The mythologies around her are hard to grasp without an awareness of the power of sudden death over those who live on; but the mourning patterns also depended on a life which was colossally, excessively, represented. This was a life in which sexual relations 'in private' were often public, in which death itself was in, or by, the camera's eye, and in which the scale and significance of happenings was grandiose – national at least, often international or global. I argue later that this episode – and the figure of Diana in general – was particularly rich in cultural themes and political issues.

How can we comprehend the peculiar intensity of this moment, organized through the dynamics of mourning? And how did mourning Diana, as a cultural and psychic process, interact with significant contemporary themes, especially the politics of the sexual and the dialectics of the national/international? In what follows I explore the mourning process first; then, working out from this centre, tease out the national–sexual themes.

Some emotional dynamics of mourning

When Jill died I was working with a group on the politics of sexuality. Grieving for Jill and thinking about the sexual went hand in hand, so that when the group published its book, *Border Patrols: Policing the Boundaries of Heterosexuality*, the poems I wrote to grieve for Jill were published in it, alongside an autobiographical commentary. In the commentary I wrote:

> it seems to me that death is another kind of 'border' and that grieving and its accompanying activities are another kind of 'patrol'. Like all 'border patrols' grieving rituals and practices are there to police the boundaries. At the same time, even the best defended frontier guards may tremble at the perils of dwelling in the borderlands. They are dangerous places where new identities − neither One nor the Other − may arise . . . [So] From one point of view, grieving is a work of reassurance and boundary-maintenance against the shock of death and loss. But the reassurance is necessary − even though it may not succeed − because the death of some-one close to us produces a 'madness': overwhelming emotions, that throw into giddy, vulnerable, high relief all our current identities.
>
> (Steinberg, Epstein and Johnson 1997: 234–5)

In my case, grieving destabilized my investments in heterosexuality and certain kinds of masculinity. We had struggled for a long time over gender power and domestic roles, over the greedy tyranny of my life over hers and of my professional occupation over our marriage, about monogamy and constancy, about intellectual equality and respect. When she died we had − in my opinion, I cannot speak for her − been taking on these issues with some success, made some crucial decisions anyway, including my early retirement. Her dying, and my sense that I was responsible for her death, brought out the old contradictions and put all the 'solutions' in doubt.

Grieving for Jill involved powerful feelings of love, sorrow, guilt and personal disorganization; it also involved attempts to control these feelings, and to recompose myself. I tried, in vain, to contain overwhelming feelings to the hours around 4.30 a.m. when I always awoke, in unconscious fear of my own death or, perhaps, in hope of saving Jill. I kept a diary which became the space for writing poems. I made a photographic record of Jill's life. I went to bed in or with her clothes. I haunted her spaces, searched out her things, her creations, and used them, assumed her roles, became more like her − tidier, more 'careful' about money, more practical, more domestic, more 'caring', you could say more 'feminine'. Much of this was done out of necessity and in desperation, but many activities were also intensely pleasurable. Doing what Jill did was getting, staying closer to her. I was also doing what I should have done before or should have done better. I was showing her I could. In a way, I was appropriating her things, her job, her roles − her very Self? Mourning activity was fiercely concentrated, wholly engrossing, 'obsessive'. In speaking and writing about Jill in public, I felt I was 'doing her justice' in ways I had failed to do in life.

Later I started to read about death, loving and mourning, especially psycho-analytic works. I found Melanie Klein's accounts moving and illuminating (especially Mitchell 1986). Her discussion of 'the depressive position' (a 'normal' psychic state, a key moment of infantile experience, but available to adults too) shows the closest of associations between feelings of loss and mourning on one side and love and reparation on the other. Klein sees 'inner chaos', intense activity and infantile feelings as key features of mourning (*ibid.*: 146–74). She understands this as a loss of identity − more precisely 'the loss of *internal* "good" objects'. 'Objects' here are the images or versions of 'real' others we have introjected. In this intensely relational version of psycho-analysis, developed further by the school called 'Object Relations', we internalize a version of significant others, and this becomes the site of the working out, the splitting off, and at best the reconciliation, of our emotional ambivalences, our loving and our hating. When a loved one dies, we try to recreate and re-embody the lost one, more or less consciously, as an object we can love (again) as a 'good' object. This repeats struggles in our earlier life, especially our struggle to save our internal good objects from our own destructive feelings towards carers in infancy. In my grief I too was 'setting up the lost loved object inside himself'. I was constructing and embodying, including 'becoming like', my 'best Jill', a perfected, idealized version. The emotional complexity of this process was the complexity of our turbulent relationship relived in the mo(u)rning. Ethically, politically, mourning was complicated too: it involved deepening attempts at reparation, and acts of appropriation, possession, even 'tri-umph'. My grief could also function as a more general catharsis – as a focus for other griefs. When I cried for Jill, part of the torrent came out of an eight-year-old who was sent away to boarding school and put up with abandonment in dutiful silence. The restoration of 'good objects' associated with loving Jill worked on the older damage too. Not surprisingly, I emerged from the most intense period of grieving without the undertow of constitutional melancholy that had been habitual. Mourning was a last inequality between us. Not only did she die and I live, I lived to benefit from her dying, or, to see it rather differently, she left me this as a possibility.

Talking to other mourners showed the importance of the precise circumstances of dying. Patterns of mourning follow from our lives together but also from the *how* of dying itself. Jill awoke early one morning with pains in her chest and died in an ambulance on her way to hospital. She had no chance to reflect upon her own death. The rest of us carried the burden of comprehending the impossible.

Clues to mourning Diana: emotional dynamics and critical differences

I was moved by Diana's death and by the actions of other mourners. I was caught by surprise by my own tears. Partly, I thought, this was because I had learned to cry, perhaps to cry too easily. I realized there were convergencies between the two situa-tions that might have aided a process of transference: Jill's second name was 'Diana', a name resonating with some of the same mythological references noted for her namesake; she was 'elegant', liked clothes and was full of energy and life; like Diana, she lived through a major crisis in her marriage (though not a divorce); our marriage was not aristocratic or royal, but it was (or had been?) patriarchal; Jill struggled for and achieved a large measure of independence and a 'project' of her own; they were both courageous, risk-taking, resourceful women. These parallels, and my 'feminism', put me in the pro-Diana camp, though I had some countervailing feelings: why should this woman receive so much attention when women like Jill or women much poorer and living more difficult lives, achieving so much, were forgotten?

None of these feelings was intense or lasting. And I was not unaware of the possible transferences – and their inappropriateness. Many people seemed more deeply moved than I was by events, though I noted a measuredness, a certain 'good sense', in their mourning too. We watched the funeral on television, but I never thought of joining the crowds in London or going to one of the local 'shrines' – Leicester Town Hall Square in our case. But in two clear ways the stories do converge: first, my own grief made me sympathetic to 'mourning Diana', especially to its 'madness' or excess, more sympathetic, perhaps, than many 'intellectual' contemporaries; second, reflection on my personal grieving does provide clues, I think, to the public occasion.

Of course, it will not do to neglect differences, including the massively mediated nature of the royal Diana figure. Yet I disagree with critics of the mourning who make an in-principle distinction between 'face-to-face' and more 'mediated' mourning, between for instance, 'the death of someone who was actually a friend and the more ethereal loss of someone known only as a media figure' (Wilson 1997: 136). It is not clear why mourning with a mediated aspect must be 'more ethereal', less real. For many Diana mourners, and not only for those who had met her face-to-face, mourning was 'real' enough to produce significant actions and discussions within everyday spaces. Similarly, Diana's celebrity, even her privilege, does not in itself inauthenticate the feelings woven around her. It is often argued that there was a surplus of 'fantasy' in people's relationships with her, fantasies heightened by media representation.[2] Yet fantasy accompanies all our relationships: we idealize, install as 'good objects', the living and the dead, our companions and our public hero/ines. We also seek to ground our imaginings, to test them against reality. This may be easier when we can meet face-to-face, but contemporary citizens are probing, sceptical readers of media representations and have ways of checking them out. Moreover death itself, as both Freud and Klein argued, is the decisive 'reality test' – mourning involves coming to terms with the real absence of the loved one (Mitchell 1986: 147).

Clues to the mourning process are needed because so much of the commentary has been incomprehending. Acute observers were surprised and shaken by the public response (e.g. Mckibbin in Merck 1998: 15). There was a widespread sense of a popular initiative which was out of everyone's control (e.g. *The Independent* in MacArthur 1997: 39). This is the best evidence against the argument that the grieving was merely a media event.

More sympathetic interpreters focus on the thematics of Diana's life, her struggle with royal and patriarchal institutions including an exploitative relationship with an unloving husband, and her search for a personal and royal role. (See many of the accounts in MacArthur 1997, especially Moore: 33–5; Burchill 1998; Campbell 1998.) Less sympathetic accounts show an angry impatience, even a disbelief, towards pro-Diana popular reactions and most media coverage. Elizabeth Wilson, for example, 'could neither understand nor share the apparent outpouring of grief'. She was 'baffled and deeply alienated by the public response' (Wilson 1997: 136). Several critics make a sharp distinction between Diana's strategies and public admiration for her on one side and a rational politics on the other. As Linda Holt put it, feminist columnists who praised Diana's emotional authenticity 'cleared a blank space where myriad fantasies could be projected and ring-fenced against reason'. It followed that 'Diana's death and suffering had no political consequences' (Holt in Merck 1998: 190 and 196). Similarly, John Pilger has published an angry denunciation of 'women's writing' and 'feminist journalism' for wasting time, opportunistically, in 'the Diana Supermarket' and ignoring more important issues (Pilger 1998: 19).

Neither side deals self-reflexively with the fact that the debate itself was part of a process of mourning (and not mourning) Diana's death. The strong and contradictory feelings — Elizabeth Wilson's or John Pilger's political passion as much as Julie Burchill's or Suzanne Moore's — were the feelings associated with mourning. 'Inner chaos' was painted large in collective public acts which I found strangely reminiscent. Many popular actions were dramatic, passionate, 'mad' or unusually expressive. There was lots of poetry again. The lost one's spaces were occupied — Kensington Palace, royal places, Spencer places, Al Fayed places. Most places had their shrines. Familiar boundaries were broken by gestures that seemed melodramatic, operatic — flower throwing, clapping a funeral procession, besieging royal buildings, criticizing com- memorative practices, or the lack of them, even watching television on a Saturday morning! There was emotional language and weeping in public. When people in London left their television sets to walk towards Westminster Abbey, it was to experience 'the atmosphere, the silence, the emptiness of the city, the strangeness of it all' (Silverstone in *Screen* 1998: 82). There was concentrated, 'obsessive' activity: queuing for condolence books, buying or picking flowers, writing cards and messages, choosing memorabilia, placing them. The crowd was possessive: they claimed 'owner- ship of an event' by performances 'for the self' and performances 'for the other' (*Screen* 1998: 84). Mourning was a collective social action fuelled by private but shared feelings and meanings: a particular alliance was activated. Nor is there a good enough reason to exclude the colossal media coverage, as much a social response, from all this: press, television, radio phone-ins, magazines, and, later, the commemorative objects from books to porcelain figures. Some of the most interesting material was 'local' or communal — the coverage in the gay monthly magazine *Gay Times* ('Diana: A Tribute', October 1997), or the depiction of Diana as an eight-armed Goddess by Asian artists (*Eastern Eye*, 25 September 1998), or the Special Debate in the academic film magazine *Screen*, part critical commentary, part 'an act of mourning in the classic sense' (1998: 67).

To argue that these forms broke from 'reality' — to dismiss them as 'manu- factured' and 'fantasy' — is to neglect the way they referenced the familiar, used existing codes and repertoires. There was little new about poems or flowers, espe- cially when we take into account the growing popular practice of creating little shrines at sites of fatal car accidents.[3] The sources of inspiration were sometimes surprising but none the less everyday — of course, because we live in an intricately inter-discursive and intertextual culture where media moments are mixed up with unmediated ones, where this distinction remains but shifts about. The connection between royal representation and soap opera narratives, familiar since Ros Coward's comments in *Female Desire*, is a case in point (Coward 1984: 164–71). As Christine Geraghty shows, soap opera was a main form of narrative by which the Diana story was written and understood, especially among women. But values drawn from soap opera, among other sources, also set the dominant terms of popular mourning:

> what is striking . . . is the dominance of soap opera values in the way that
> people spoke about Diana's death. Talk about private feelings — the staple

of soap opera – was valued as the best way of expressing grief, and indeed as a sign of grief itself.

(Screen 1998: 73)

'Soap' is not used dismissively here. It is understood that 'soap' forms arise from ordinary living, are appropriated and changed by media production and return to us as audience members. They influence our sensibilities, responses and outcomes – including our face-to-face encounters, without however, determining them. In this case, soap-opera-like sensitivities acquired a kind of dominance:

> In this discourse the refusal of the Queen and Charles to speak was taken to signify a lack of grief, and was harshly criticized . . . For those outside this 'feminine' discourse, there was very little space in which to speak.

(Screen 1998: 73)

Geraghty also suggests that mourners sought ways of checking out the reality of the meanings of Diana's death. Popular scepticism about the media image fed an appetite for direct witness from those who had met Diana, hence the movement from television set to street. Witnesses emphasized physical proximity and touch against 'the media's endless use of photographs'. Physical presence at sites of mourning seemed the fuller experience: 'television offered a better view, but not the smell of the flowers, the touch of the crowds'. Even then, mediated and unmediated truths chased each other in endless circles: 'the crowds at the palaces became a media event in which those present used the media to tell those who relied on the media what they were missing' (*Screen* 1998: 73). Yet as Jenny Kitzinger puts it in the same edition of *Screen*, 'public response, though choreographed by the media, sometimes exceeded its mediation' (78).

Both sides of mourning – chaos, policing – were there in August 1997. Diana's sudden, accidental, initially inexplicable death shook existing identities, erased borderlines. Royal power and conventions of grieving were thrown into crisis; media struggled to find appropriate rhetorics. Death's diminution of the human was unusually strong and pervasive. If someone so hugely present and protected could suddenly disappear – 'no more photographs' – what chance of survival for me? Is the death line so fine? From the beginning, however, there were also 'border patrols', regulating and containing panic. Denial was offered, or solace. How often it was said that she could 'live on through our memories', had 'gone to heaven' or was an 'angel' or 'saint'? More rationalistically, the cognitive challenge of a sudden 'accidental' death was taken up: why did Diana die? In hostile accounts, for example, much easier to articulate a year later, Diana's last month was presented as 'a hurtling towards chaos', as though the chaos had belonged to exclusively to her and not at all to us (Flett 1998).

As this example suggests, the more analytical, 'political' responses, feminist or left-wing for example, were not immune from instability. There was a marked splitting into 'good' and 'bad' Dianas. She was much idealized. In a beautifully designed book full of fascinating photos, she is Julie Burchill's 'sweet princess' – a 'spirited, compassionate and beautiful Englishwoman' (Burchill 1998: 9 and 236). For Andrew Morton, she was 'flag-bearer for a new generation, a new order and a new future' no less (Morton 1997: 9). For both these popular journalists, feelings about their exploitation of an icon may well accompany their unreserved praise. As Klein puts it: 'The ego feels impelled . . . (by its identification with the good object) to make restitution for all the sadistic attacks that it has launched on that object' (Mitchell 1986: 120). Idealization is expressed in a hyperbolic style which no one could mistake for measured judgement.

On first reading, the anti-Diana writing seems to invert all this. It presents a sternly super-egotistical damming up of emotions that threaten to spill out, drowning out a thoughtful politics. The Other here is the tyranny of 'feelings': emotional self-indulgence in Diana's own life but public mourning and pro-Diana writing is implicated too. Reviewing Beatrix Campbell and others, John Pilger spits out the familiar epithets with reiterative disgust: 'agony aunts', 'the therapist's couch', 'self-pitying' and 'emotional grandstanding'. Such indulgence contrasts with 'real feminism' that connects with the issues of a global class politics. Clearly the boundaries of 'real politics' are being patrolled here.

Yet the mounting of these patrols suggest another kind of madness going on. By expostulating about *not* mourning Diana, critics add to the attention they so much deplore. Reason sits oddly with heavy, angry satire or plain disgust. Pilger, for instance, reads Beatrix Campbell's committed but analytical and explanatory book on royal and aristocratic patriarchy as 'a rant against Charles the Wicked Prince' and constructs his own intra-feminist opposition between feminist writers tricked by 'celebrity consumerism' and his 'honourable exceptions' who are treated as heroines, who celebrate heroines (Pilger 1998). His own passion in and for a politics is unacknowledged: a passionate polemic in which good and bad are starkly defined, much too starkly in this case. What is problematic in the attack on mourning is the (impossible) splitting off of thought and feeling, all too familiar in 'science', 'intellectual seriousness' and in the political left.

The differences between pro- and anti-Diana camps illustrate variant psychic dynamics in mourning and refusing to mourn, different ways in which political identities are constructed. But they are also important 'in their own terms'. They are one of the ways in which the figure of Diana condensed an extraordinary clustering of cultural meanings and political issues: here, differences over reason and emotion in politics, over modern and postmodern political styles, between a puritan or purist choice of issues and a certain opportunism or 'strategy' about 'interventions'.

These differences run through both feminist and left-wing politics. They also divide cultural researchers. One strand has been preoccupied with uncovering Diana's 'popularity' by unwrapping the political and cultural contents of support for her, drawing on different frameworks, materialist, poststructuralist, psychoanalytic (e.g. *Screen* 1998; Campbell 1998 [. . .]). Another has been concerned to interpret events according to a theory about 'celebrity', 'sainthood', 'glamour', 'paranoia', 'the operatic', emotionality or soap opera – pushing these categories as far as they will go, and often applying them rather dismissively (e.g. many but not all contributions in Merck 1998). The debate about Diana is an example of the continued tension between a 'mass culture' perspective, ultimately contemptuous of popular forms and idols, and an identification with the popular, sometimes criticized as an unthinking 'cultural populism' (e.g. McGuigan 1992). Diana's privilege obscures her popularity or encourages critics to override it; but the debate shows how active the mass culture framework remains and how important it is to keep contradictory political spaces open by critiquing it.

Other issues that clustered around 'Diana' included the future and (un)popularity of the monarchy, the media's role in the lives of public persons, many questions of 'sexual politics' including patriarchy and class, marriage, sexual morality, monogamy, 'adultery', and what constitutes feminine 'independence', the politics of HIV, AIDS and homophobia, the production and use of landmines (and so the long-term consequences of warfare), the politics of royal representation in Britain and abroad, the political role of 'charities' and the differences between 'humanitarianism' and 'politics'. Within the last two issues nestle many of the concerns – about the global class system predominantly – that animate the politics of the sharpest materialist critics.

If mourning Diana was a hugely over-determined event, its ruptural character was secured by two main eventualities. The first – which we have discussed – was simply her dying – her dying as she did, when she did. The second, to which we now turn, was Diana's extraordinary availability as a figure or 'object' in the identity work of others.

Diana represents the nation: the emotional and the global

Diana was unusually 'available' in two main ways. Most obviously she was extensively represented in public media throughout the world; she was 'the most famous woman in the world'. But she was also available 'subjectively', in that so much of her personal story, sometimes in her own words, was reported and discussed. Areas usually regarded as private – family relations, sexual relationships, food problems and visits to the gym for instance – were in her case made conspicuously, selectively public. Her fame was matched by her evident vulnerability. She was vulnerable as an inexperienced young woman cheated and scorned by her husband, as a bulimic, as someone who damaged her own body and attempted to kill herself, as what she called 'a media toy', as a 'outsider' (of a kind) in the royal circles. Even her points of strength, her motherhood for example, were points of danger: would she be allowed to bring up William and Harry, to be gentle princes, as she wished? Popular availability was also part of a survival strategy. She appealed to her publics for love and for support in a difficult life, most evidently in the wounded, wooing looks and sensational personal disclosures of the interview she gave to the prestigious BBC current affairs programme *Panorama* in 1995 and in the tapes that informed Andrew Morton's biography (Morton 1997: 23–69).

So Diana, or the Diana figure, was available to a vast and differentiated public. This made her a rich resource for the cultural and psychic work of others. I want to draw attention, here, to four main forms of attachment. All four categories are relational or dialogic: they express relationships between Diana and her publics.

First, she related to others as a representative. She represented 'us' to others, especially people in Britain to others 'abroad'. This was inscribed in her official role as a royal, but also in her self-ascribed identities as 'a Queen of Hearts' and as 'an ambassador for this country' (*Panorama* interview, quoted Morton 1997: 257–8) and in her posthumous title as 'the People's Princess'. The *Panorama* interview typically combined vulnerability and strategy:

As I have all this media interest, let's not just sit in this country and be battered by it. Let's take them, these people, out to represent this country and the good qualities of it abroad.

(Morton 1997: 258)

How, then did Diana's strategy or being a new kind of national representative effect the work of identity of others around her, processes both global and national?

One important moment in national identity as a process is its production 'as against' others, especially as against other national identities. In the most literal versions of this argument, the relation with national others is seen as external: Englishness is defined against Frenchness, Irishness, Americanness, etc. Contemporary theories of cultural identity, especially when they extend to psychic dynamics, show how little 'external' these relations actually are.[4] Defining yourself against an other, itself only one of the psychic dynamics of identity, involves several different operations. The other must first occupy the same psychic or cultural space as the self. A version of the other is internalized or introjected; it becomes an image or 'object' – the Other.[5] But the image of the Other must also, in this paranoid pattern of self-production, be disavowed, expelled, projected 'outside'. Such processes are imaginary but have literal, spatial accompaniments and consequences: internal others are thrust 'beyond the pale', outside the bourgeois spaces, or the all-white spaces, or the men-only spaces. These spaces must in turn be policed. The tortured history of war, conquest, pogroms, genocide, lynchings, 'ethnic cleansing' and forced exclusion shows the consequences for groups who figure as Others in powerful collective imaginaries. Yet for the most powerful categories even physical expulsion is self-defeating or self-depleting. External boundaries are, as Slavoj Žižek argues, also internal limits (Žižek 1991). An identity that holds itself in place by expelling others is doomed to the constant repetition of similar processes. Its relation to Others remains peculiarly intimate or proximate; the struggle for purity is a struggle with itself. Given the porosity of boundaries – social, cultural and psychic – in the modern period, such paranoid externalization has to be repeated unendingly.

Paranoid patterns were certainly present in the representation of Diana's life and death. On the side of pro-Diana sentiment they flourish in the elaborate conspiracy theories around her death (e.g. Benton in Merck 1998). They are especially evident in anti-Diana representations. We have already noted the splitting and projection which accompanies the sometimes justifiable arguments about emotionality. In the weeks before they both died, the British press was also starting to issue public warnings around the relationship with Dodi Al Fayed. As the tabloid newspaper *The Sun* put it: 'Please tread carefully Di. A new love affair can be as dangerous as the Bosnian minefield' (quoted in Flett 1998). Had the couple lived and their relationship continued, the press's narrative might well have swung much further in an anti-Diana, anti-Muslim, nationalist direction. The possibilities of a racist–nationalist closure here were strong. It is important to remember too that another Diana had loomed large in the public myths of the early 1980s, the heyday of Thatcherite nationalism, the era of the heightened fantasies of Wars and Weddings, of the Falklands adventure and Charles-an'-Di.

The later Diana was not, however, a nationalist icon of this kind, opposed to foreign others. Her liberation from royal wifedom was accompanied by a redefinition of her national significance. 'Dianaized' versions of the nation were not typically nationalistic, militaristic or paranoid; if anything they were 'depressive' or introjective. They involved taking in, or 'taking on', versions of the other or versions of the self seen through the other's eyes. This shift can be elaborated both negatively and positively.

Attempts to produce the later Diana as exclusively British or English were often forced or confused. There was the obvious anomaly that the 'English Rose' of the Elton John song was also the Princess of Wales. This was confusing when, in the historical semiology of the nations, 'Englishness' works best in its domestic oppositions to Welshness, Scottishness and Irishness(es). Christine Gledhill has analysed a larger confusion or transition in the mourning speeches of Tony Blair. Sometimes he claimed Diana as British, implicitly underlining an opposition to others. Sometimes he included, in 'the People's Princess', the rest of the globe: 'the people everywhere, not just here in Britain but everywhere' (Gledhill in *Screen* 1998: 79).

Nor could the later Diana be recruited very effectively to serve Conservative political mythologies. This was mainly because of her ambiguous relation to monarchy, a central nationalist definer. She shifted from being a queen-in-waiting to being the ex-wife of a prince (whose own claim to succeed was not unquestioned). Despite attempts to disguise the fact, their divorce meant more than a change of titles. Diana's strongest claim to royalty was as mother of a future king. Even this claim was being attacked, morally, in her last months, when some journalists dubbed her 'a trash icon for our times', 'the Queen of England manqué' (Nigel Fountain quoted in Flett 1998) and, in classically sexualized language, a 'fast woman' (*Sunday Telegraph* quoted in Flett 1998). I agree that Diana was never a plausible republican heroine, but also with those that argue that her painful struggle for recognition and for a liveable place in a bizarre world highlighted many of contradictions of royal institutions, especially its particular and oppressive forms of aristocratic patriarchy (Campbell 1998). For one royalist section of pro-Diana opinion, she came to represent not what monarchy was but what it might be. She was a kind of royal promise. The promise was offered first through herself, by performance as much as vows; but a promise was also made through or on behalf of her children, in her own lived fantasy of William as a 'once and future king' of a new kind. To another kind of pro-Diana sentiment, her life and struggles showed up the oppressive roles of royalty, strengthening a preference for republican solutions.

It was hard, anyway, for such a figure to represent the 'historic' nation, replete with its residual themes. It was hard to use Diana for the anti-Europeanism of the popular Conservative press, for example. The figure of the Queen (or better still the Queen Mother?) can still be recruited to British Euro-phobia, as in panics over whether the royal portrait can appear on the new Euro currency, or rows about attempted reconciliation with Germany in the commemoration of the Second World War. As a fully postwar figure, Diana was more distant from British Germano phobia and the safe, un-self-critically affirmative version of 'the War We Won'. Moreover, as a divorced woman and a single mother and as the socially compassionate 'Queen of Hearts', she was in tension with key themes in Thatcherite nationalism, especially the reckless stress on 'enterprise' and the moral traditionalism of 'the family'. Even Douglas Hurd, a 'moderate' Conservative ex-foreign-secretary and a pro-European, had to work hard to 'nationalize' Diana through her royalty:

> Diana, Princess of Wales used to the full the traditional manners and
> methods of the Royal Family. She spoke and carried herself like an English
> girl from the background that was in fact hers, adding the particular
> personal flair that made her a star.
>
> (Hurd in MacArthur 1997: 98)

Hurd must expunge the massively publicized antagonisms between Diana and
Charles and the struggles with royal institutions. He must represent everything in her
life which is out of the (royal) ordinary as purely personal – including her 'bitterness'
for example. His national ascriptions ('an English girl') work best where they are
personal, implicit, feminine and bodily ('carried herself') not projected outwards into
the public or registered against an Other.

Positively, this meant that grieving for Diana was, for many liberal royalists, a
mourning, as Dorothy Thompson put it, 'for a better monarchy' (Merck 1998:
33–40). Grief accumulated around lost possibilities, or possibilities not recognized in
Diana's lifetime, or not properly credited to her as her contribution. The forms of
mourning brought this out. The ceremonial trappings of war (gun-carriage, soldiers,
pacing male mourners) seemed inappropriate contrasted with her own disassociation
from the royal culture of soldiering and of 'hunting, shooting and fishing', and the
implied pacifism of the mines campaign. Yet other Dianas were present too in the card
to 'Mummy', in the obviously civilian charity workers, the marked gay presence, the
multi-ethnic composition of crowds, the clapping and the flowers. It was as though
Diana was being recognized for what she had done, for what she was, in 'national'
terms – but, in that characteristic depressive regret of grief, too late. So there was
much in the official mourning not only to feel with (as the critics have it) but also to
think on. It was hard to articulate these weirdly coexisting elements at the time. Yet
the new, as carried by Diana, had died. What did it all mean?

Some concluded that a chance for reform was lost; others that Diana had shown
the limits of royal institutions, their historical redundancy. Most commonly, perhaps,
in the absence of an explicit answer, the meanings, were performed, acted out. A
large part of the popular emotional drive to mourn Diana was expressed in copying
her, not in an abject dependency but out of respect. Just as Diana had opposed
traditional royalty with her more democratic princely or knightly promise, so we,
the mourners, reproached Queen and Establishment for unjust neglect, and acted
out our different way of mourning. We represented the representative. We recognized
the recognizer.

But the central difficulty of a nationalist appropriation of Diana's symbolic value
lay in her standing as an international celebrity. Her celebrity has been discussed as
a limit to her political significance, involving those who loved her, apparently, in self-
defeating narcissism (e.g. Mark Cousins in Merck 1998: 77–86). Less often appreciated is the way celebrity blocked nationalism and fuelled an internationalism. She was
internationally famous, it is true, as a British royal, but she carried her royal ambiguities into this international domain. She was famous also as a media celebrity, a worker
for international charities, a campaigner on landmines, AIDS and other issues and,
latterly, as the lover of an international playboy from a wealthy (would-be) British-
Muslim dynasty. She was, according to her brother's tribute, 'a very British girl who
transcended nationality' (Earl Spencer in MacArthur 1997: 179). She also 'talked

endlessly of getting away from England mainly because of the treatment that she received at the hands of the newspapers'.

The discovery of Diana's fame abroad, sometimes by surprising routes, was a common theme in the aftermath of her death. On visits to Amsterdam, in 1998, for instance, a friend told me about a regular newspaper series called 'Dianarama' – a series that continues today. Later she sent me a Dianarama clipping, with a photograph taken in Aleppo, Syria, by a Dutch photographer, of an advertisement for Muslim women's headwear, featuring Diana's face (Dianarama 60, *de Volkskrant*, 16 June 1998).[6] Mary Dejevsky's round-up of US and French responses for *The Independent* showed the extent of the impact of her death on other close cultural neighbours. Reassuringly perhaps, similar patterns were observed as in Britain: the queues (!) to sign books of condolences at embassies, the high proportions of gay men and lesbians and 'people of colour' in the crowds, the sense that Diana was on the side of 'ordinary people'. Her conclusion was less reassuring:

> This creates for Britain abroad a problem similar to the one that now faces the Royal Family at home. The monarchy has lost at a tragic stroke all that was young, beautiful, sympathetic, accessible and even relevant about British Royalty.
>
> That is also what Britain has lost in the world. For millions of people who knew or cared little for international diplomacy, Diana was the lively, modern and humane face of Britain.
>
> She was a global Ambassador on a scale that is only now apparent.
>
> (Mary Dejevsky in MacArthur 1997: 43)

While 'Britain' is yet again produced as a unity in this account 'we' are also invited – through Diana's international celebrity – to adopt an unfamiliar gaze. We are not looking outward at the Other, or even boasting about our Queen of Hearts. Our subjective position is more 'depressive' than paranoid, self-doubting not self-aggrandizing. Diana's death invites us to look at ourselves through Other eyes, eyes rather like our own, that recognize our loss, but judge it according to our ability to be seen and heard. In this gaze the self is relativized, seen as changeful and historical. The conclusion is decidedly melancholy. Consider how our 'face' must now appear outside, now that our best self, according to outside observers, is eclipsed: as 'all that is' ugly, insensitive, inaccessible, dull, archaic, inhumane and irrelevant! Again, the loss of Diana bears on national identity but in a self-reflexive, thought-inducing way. Again the mourners' response is to remember, to hold on to this 'good-object-in-the-eyes-of-others', to make it part of our new self. The whole pattern suggests a very different relation to the other than in the usual nationalistic excess.

It is important too that Diana's representative function was not limited to the national frame, even when her royal repertoire was mobilized. Diana could also represent *sections* of 'the people' to the rest. Both 'the sections' (the represented subject) and 'the rest' (the addressee) could be transnational as well as national. Some of her most dramatic representational acts were performed in the United States, and later in the anti-mines campaigns in Angola and Bosnia. In her more sectional representational acts, there was a definite pattern. She typically represented groups that had been othered or marginalized in power relations and in representational processes.

When she concentrated her charitable activity after her divorce, she focused on The Leprosy Mission, Centrepoint (a London-based charity for the homeless), The National AIDS Trust, the Royal Marsden National Health Service Trust (a cancer hospital) and the Great Ormond Street Children's Hospital (Morton 1997: 252–3). Later she took a leading role in the Red Cross's campaign against landmines.

From a left political perspective, her 'charitable' relations were deeply problematic because of the inequalities between her and her 'subjects' and because of the proximity of the relationships to royal and aristocratic condescension. It was in this context, however, that she developed her personal styles of interaction – touching and, more important, being touched, concentrating hard on listening to others, approaching people through shared 'human' territory (through her fanship of soaps, for instance!), using humour and a general informality to break the royal distance – but still use it. Her own self-ascriptions – 'I am a humanitarian. I always have been and I always will be' (quoted Katharine Graham in MacArthur 1997: 95) – and her wishes for her royal boys – 'I want them to grow up knowing there are poor people as well as palaces' (quoted W. F. Deedes in MacArthur 1997: 69) – were hardly socialist or republican (palaces and poverty it seems will remain). But she was a representative who sought out the hidden and tragic sides of those she represented, authenticating them to her own publics. This, once more, made her available for other kinds of relationship, real and imaginary. Especially important were the intersections of her role as a representative with her role as a recognizer of the other.

Diana and the other: recognition

Our second relational category is recognition. It is one peculiarly appropriate to Diana. A main theme of sympathetic commentary – and of most of those who speak of actually meeting her – is her ability to recognize others, to say and do things related to their needs. Christopher Spence, founder of the AIDS charity The London Lighthouse, called her 'a natural counsellor':

> She knew how to pay attention, the most dignifying thing that one person can do for another. Time after time over a ten-year period I watched her intuitively knowing what to do and say in order to come close to another person – often people very near to death. She knew how to make a real connection, enabling people to talk to her from their hearts about what really mattered. She could sense what someone, or even a whole group of people, might need with unfailing accuracy.
>   She would usually ask a simple question: 'Hello, how are *you*?'
> (MacArthur 1997: 101)

Perhaps the source of this gift, or of the intensity and generosity of its employment, is that the woman who was often a 'good object' in the minds of others so badly needed to restore the 'good objects' inside herself. The urgency of this need was not directly articulated, often. It was expressed, practically, as risk, in the 'lengths she was prepared to go'. It is interesting how much of her charitable work explored the borderlands of dying: from AIDS and other dangerous diseases to the sudden immolation or death from explosive charges to the work in children's hospices. It is interesting too how often she dealt in 'social death' – in recognizing the unrecognized or unrecognizable, in touching the untouchable. It is quite wrong to imply that everything this celebrity did was self-seeking in a narcissistic way, not least because much of her charitable work was, when the media would allow, private and hidden. It was also often beyond the call of duty. In these dangerous places, she seems to have sought recognition too, not least for her 'professionalism'. Her own descriptions of such moments – when she connects with people and they cling to her and cry – stress her own comfort too, her unwillingness, even, to leave:

> He was crying his eyes out and clung on to my hand and I felt so comfortable in there. I just hated being taken away.
> ('In Her Own Words', published in Morton 1997: 65)

Even in more public encounters where she seems 'like a pop star', the word 'comfortable' returns, if discomfortingly:

> People thanking me for bringing happiness in their lives; little sentences that put together make a very wonderful, very special day. Thanking for coming; thank-you for making the effort; thank-you for being you and all those things, [I] never used to believe. Now I'm more comfortable receiving that sort of information whether or not it's true. I can now digest that sort of thing whereas I used to throw it back.
> (Morton 1997: 67)

That Diana was intensely needy, but expressed her need by recognizing the needs of others, was part of a popular common sense about her, especially among women familiar with this psychic economy. More technically, we could say that she projected her needs on to others and tried to meet her own needs by caring for them. Such a strategy, which is central to conventional gender relations in our culture, is posited in risk – the risk of one-sidedness for the carer, who is usually a woman. She risks exploitation of her emotional labour and a personal depletion. This unrequited pattern is also clear in Diana's own account:

> No-one has ever said to me 'Well done'. Because I had a smile on my face everyone thought I was having a wonderful time. That's what they chose to think – it made them happier thinking that.
> (Morton 1997: 67)

On the other hand, where recognition *is* returned by the object of caring it can create powerful bonds of love. Recognition, then, has some measure of mutuality in it. Diana's plentiful self-revelations were surely bids for mutual recognitions of this kind. Were they often responded to? Did she think they were? Does the deficit here explain something of why she was so loved and mourned, or loved-in-the-mourning? Did we try to make some reparation for her desperate giving, often one-sided, when she died? I believe that all these moments were active in the mourning process.

Identification, dis-identification and transference

Though representation and recognition have emotional and psychic dimensions, they also express social relations in quite a direct way. Our third and fourth relationships — identification and transference — often operate, by contrast, quite unconsciously. It was clear, however, that the figure of Diana was the object of a continuous play of *identification* and *dis-identification*. Many members of her public defined their own identities in relation to her, sometimes as very different, sometimes as like her in some way. Identification of this kind is never total, or fixed or without ambivalences. It can also cross social categories — including rich and poor, royal and not-royal — in surprising ways. We will return in a moment to the concrete pattern of these identifications or dis-identifications in considering the version of nation which mourning Diana produced.

Finally, in terms of forms of attachment, Diana was clearly the object of many *transferred feelings*, feelings that had little to do with her own life and death, and everything to do with the lives of members of her public. Many people told television interviewers or radio chat-show hosts how they had cried for Diana, but also at the same time for some other loss, unmourned at the time, rather as I cried for my own (parental) loss in mourning Jill.

Such transferences are aided by relations of representation, recognition and/or identification in very complex interactions. Diana's relationships with gay men and with gay community organization is a striking example here. According to Jonathan Grimshaw, founder of the Landmark Centre in London, Diana's HIV/AIDS interventions were crucial:

> When society rejects you, the symbolic importance of having a member of
> the Royal Family, a representative of the nation, talking to you and saying
> 'I want to hear what you have to say' is enormous.
>
> (quoted in *Gay Times* 1997: 51)

For Susie Parsons, current chief executive of the London Lighthouse, Diana was not only a representative but also a 'champion for people with HIV' and 'a friend' to them too (*Gay Times* 1997: 51). Her recognitions — listening, holding hands, hugging and joking — were crucial in breaking the massive non-recognitions, the active homophobia that was rampant in the mid-1980s. In a fascinated and fascinating essay, Richard Coles, formerly of the Communards and now a Radio 3 broadcaster, critiques and satirizes dependence on 'feelin's', but also does justice to her gay alliances. It was not just that she managed to be royal and not-royal at the same time, but that she keyed into, used and lived indeed, a gay style and repertoire. 'Diana', writes Coles, 'was a gay man,' (Coles in Merck 1998: 176). This element can be seen in Diana's 'coming out' on television, in her narration of her life as 'redemption' from oppression, and in her fascination with glamour and the 'fabulousness' of gay men in show business and the arts. Coles stresses how Diana identified with gay men, but it must also be the case that many gay men found in her life, too, grounds for identification and for a transference of feelings. Again this connection was particularly poignant in her dying, since gay culture was perforce so expert in the dying game. No wonder that Diana was mourned with a special intensity within the gay community and that there was so marked a gay presence and flavour in the rituals of mourning. As the playwright, actor and director Neil Bartlett put it, 'We were being included in Diana's funeral not as spokespersons for a cause, but as honoured guests' (quoted in *Gay Times* 1997: 52).

It is important to end the discussion of 'attachments' by stressing the political power of Diana's strategies. Her life and the mourning of her death do *not* collapse down into 'feelin's', important – in politics – though feelings are. By recognizing the unrecognizable, she extended the boundaries of effective citizenship. She could bring marginalized groups into a centre of concern and self-activity. In single acts – touching and being touched by men and children with AIDS for example – she could shift the relations of force in public representations, re-establish a sense of worth in those she recognized and challenge her publics, individually and collectively, to do likewise. Her strategies certainly stemmed from a particular psychic economy, but one within which a definite politics was embedded.

Diana's Britain: (not) one nation, (more) the differences among Us

I want to end this chapter by pulling together some themes around the 'Dianaized' nation.

Most accounts of national identity have stressed the production of the nation as a unity, emphasizing cultural homogeneity and cohesion. This goes for traditional Conservative cultural theory, of course, but for critical writing on national identity too. Homogeneity is constructed but it is still a distinctive feature of nations. It is produced by social networks or by 'complementarity of social communication' (Mackenzie 1978, Deutsch 1966) or by common symbolic imagining through modern media (Anderson 1983), or by nationalist movements, political intellectuals and educational institutions (Gellner 1983) or by the political working up of pre-existing cultural commonalties or 'ethnicities' (Smith 1979). In many accounts it is also a rather top-down construction. For Gellner, for example, national identity is produced through the diffusion and imposition of a universal 'high culture' – a 'school-mediated, academy-supervised idiom, codified for the requirements of reasonably precise bureaucratic and technological communication' (Gellner 1983: 57).

The language of national unity suffuses accounts of the Diana phenomenon and not only in tabloid newspapers: 'the emotions which overwhelmed the country' (Ignatieff in MacArthur 1997: 187); 'a nation in a state of shock' (Tony Blair in MacArthur 1997: 17); Diana as 'our common creation and national possession' (*Independent*, MacArthur 1997: 21). The forms of mourning – especially their expressivity – are seen as marking a shift in national character, dubbed 'American' or 'Neapolitan' or perhaps a pre-Victorian recovery. For John Gray, the mourning is 'a revelation of the country we have become . . . already more modern than its politicians have yet understood' (MacArthur 1997: 187). 'The British', with or without a hint of parody, conform to type, or break from stereotype, as a 'country' or a 'people' as a whole:

> Uncertain what to do next, the British followed their instincts and began
> to queue . . . By lunchtime the official waiting time was two hours . . . By

9pm the wait was seven hours, and many prepared to wait all night. Foreign tourists did not seem enthused by this prospect. The British, however, reacted differently.

(Matthew Engel, in MacArthur 1997: 26)

Most accounts of the mourning crowd stressed its inclusiveness. Engel again:

The waiting crowd seemed as near as it was possible to get to a cross-section of the country: young and old, men and women, rich and poor, black and white. Many of them were carrying flowers. Only the time-pressed and the hyper-sophisticated were missing.

Even those who recognized the specificity of the crowds – as *The Daily Mail* characteristically recognized its femininity for instance – felt the pressure to include everyone: 'Who were they? Anyone or everyone probably a better cross-section of the British people than you could find at any comparable event' (MacArthur 1997: 30). It was only really those commentators – on left and right – who felt excluded from the mourning process who doubted the 'unities' it was supposed to produce. As Elizabeth Wilson put it. 'I [did not] believe that the tragic event had in any real or permanent sense "united the nation" as we were being told' (Wilson 1997: 136).

It is doubtful if national identities are *ever* fully formed and entire in 'a real or permanent sense'. I agree with Beth Edginton who concludes that 'the nation really is an extremely delicate construct' (*Screen* 1998: 81). Even moments of national unity passed down as 'historic' – Britain in the Second World War for instance – reveal fractures when explored more closely. Given the actual diversity of ways of living within any space marked out as national, such descriptions are bound to be selective and partial. They ignore those who stay away. They flatten contradictions and coexisting differences. They may be insensitive to what is hidden but emergent or subversively 'supplementary' in national formations. Alternatively, as often the case in Diana representations, picking on one feature, they exaggerate the import of the 'new' by representing it as the whole future.

In this chapter I have pursued a different strategy and I have found it valuably explanatory. I have focused not on *unity as a product* but on the *processes of the production* of identity *in and through social difference*. This process involves psychic dimensions, particular forms of emotional investment that flow between persons and between persons and public representations. The construction of the nation on the basis of difference was not a unique feature of 'Dianaization'. In unequal societies all cultural renderings of nationality work in and through difference in this way. Some social categories are always rendered central or exemplary; others are pushed to the social margin; others still are treated as Other, different from Us. The citizens, in other words, are put in their places. In Thatcherite Britain the preferred sexual categories, for instance, were heterosexual, monogamous and married, the preferred gender and child–adult social ordering was a traditional (and strongly wishful) version of 'the family'. The splitting off and political exclusion of homosexualities, as viable alternative ways of living, were crucial to this formation. In a long historical perspective, this may represent the last phase of a particular modern articulation of the heterosexual procreative couple to the modern nation-state (Epstein and Johnson 1998).

What finally fascinates me about the story of mourning Diana is not that differences were made, but that the nation was composed in such a different pattern. This overall difference, a difference from a very oppressive 'norm', is everywhere in our analysis.

It can be seen first in the chagrin of marginalized intellectuals of the left, unable to identify with Diana and therefore unable to see the democratic underside of her politics beneath the privilege and the hype. Left-wing rationalism is often accompanied by a righteous anger on behalf of the unrepresented poor of the world, yet many critics could not see how poverty and oppression figured in the alliance that Diana had begun to make. They could not see the phenomenon as 'political' at all: as Linda Grant puts it, in a terrible simplification of issues of thought and emotion:

> The problem, as much for Diana and the 'ordinary people' who shed tears over her death as for the feminists cited above, is that feelings are not politics.
>
> (Grant in Merck 1998: 190)

Such a statement can make sense only if we cling possessively to our own (intellectual's) definitions of politics: politics as highly articulated, coherent, thought-throught, pure. The politics around Diana and much of her way of life was by contrast embedded, implicit and under-articulated, contradictory because engaging with a contradictory world.

The 'Dianaized' nation seems to have excluded much (but not all) critical intellectual opinion. I guess that this excluded group included large sections of the educated or college-going middle class, especially perhaps their men. There was little for them to identify with in Diana's life or death. There was plenty to despise in her very un-academic, un-high-cultural persona. The other identifiable source of opposition came from right-wing royalists and conservative liberal Charles-ites who saw Diana as a competitive spoiler of royal dignities and princely projects. From these sources the attempt to curtail mourning ('enough is enough' said on behalf of her boys) and really to bury the Princess and her promise continues.

Most strikingly, in Diana's Britain, previously central categories were thrust to the margins: especially the 'old' royals with their huge privileges and awkward condescensions. The fleeting hegemony of the Diana moment was popular or populist in two senses. It was 'anti-intellectual' in an important sense, but also as Beth Edginton argues, 'the anti-thesis of the Nation-as-Establishment' (*Screen* 1998: 79). The people made their demands as 'citizens' not 'subjects', with the Queen as subject to Her, and the whole royal crew awaiting the dead Princess at the Palace gates.

The dynamics of representation, recognition, identification and transference which focused on Diana shifted the pattern in other ways. It made marginalized categories integral to an exemplary relationship. In terms of sexual categories it was not the Thatcherite 'family' (or even its Blairite version) which was exemplary, but the independent woman seeking to represent herself and have her own project. This independent heterosexual woman made a close alliance with gay and lesbian styles and politics. Gay identities were not simply 'tolerated' but affirmed. Other social identities, usually more marginal still, like the ill and the dying, the mutilated and the disabled, the war victims, the anorexic and the bulimic, were included in Diana's world, and through her in the nation. Many commentators have noted the interracial multicultural composition of the mourning crowds, and in Birmingham and other cities Diana was commemorated in inter-faith religious services.[7] Her relationship with Dodi Al Fayed gave points of identification for Islamic communities within and beyond the British-based diasporas. Again, a category often treated as Other in contemporary nationalist and occidentalist polemics was brought within the nation and the wider 'Us' by Diana's politicization of intimacies.

All this is consistent with our analysis of psychic dynamics. Traditional nationalist paranoias are historically associated with racism and xenophobia. The view of the nation through other eyes is much closer to the positions adopted by those who have the experience of being members of an 'ethnic minority' and who may also be particularly conscious of the mirroring of their place of settlement by public media in other countries. Most important, perhaps, was Diana's style of relationship to the Other, and to the rest in relation to the Other. This was a way of relating that embodied and internalized the Other as a 'good object' and invited others to do the same. It is difficult to say how Diana's 'humanitarian' politics would have developed and how its limits would have been revealed in situations, especially, of marked social antagonism. Yet once the reality of the lives of oppressed groups are really listened to, once 'difference' is really grasped, it is hard for the dominant social categories to remain the same. Of some of this Diana seems to have been aware, within the limits of her politics of 'comfort': 'You can't comfort the afflicted without discomforting the comfortable' were words written on a piece of paper a friend found on her desk beside momentoes of her visits to the Pope and Mother Teresa (Rosa Monckton in MacArthur 1997: 62).

Diana was mourned so intensely because she was widely available – famous and vulnerable – for others to invest in as a source of pleasure, identity and recognition. She combined a powerful redefinition of a traditional (royal) representative function with the ability to acknowledge something of the reality of other people's lives, especially of those suffering from major oppressions and ill-fortune. This endeared her to large numbers of people, especially those who had endured formative experiences of grief and subordination in their own lives. The widespread identifications, face-to-face or through media which always sought to possess even her private selves, set the terms of a passionate, political mourning. Even in her death, Diana bequeathed to others the opportunity to grieve for ungrieved bereavements of their own. Misrecognized by critics as manufactured or sentimental, this mourning was a typical expression of public grief and personal loss, magnified as much by the intimacy and extent of Diana's social connections (face-to-face and mediated) as by modern global media themselves. Above all, perhaps, we grieved, for what we had lost so suddenly and recognized too late. We mourned her lost promises: for some a reformed and more democratic monarchy; for others the non-royal forms of an equalizing public recognition immanent in her 'testing' of monarchy; for all a social order based on care; and a relation to a wider world founded on the respect of ordinary citizens abroad, not on xenophobia, colonial attitudes and militarized missions. Whatever our subsequent histories, the extent and intensity of the mourning for Diana remains as a testimony to the appeal of this version of the future.

Notes

1   I am grateful, however, to many others with whom I have discussed *Mourning Diana*, especially to Mariette Clare, Ali Mohammadi, Barbara Henkes and members of my Research Practice Group and the MA in Heritage Studies at Nottingham Trent University. Special thanks to Deborah Steinberg, who, as a critical reader and editor of this volume, encouraged me to develop further several of the themes in this essay. I haven't always been able to do this within the limited time available.

2   This is a leading theme of several of the essays in Merck 1998, a collection the subtitle of which, *Irreverent Elegies*, signals a certain intention to debunk.

3   It is common in Britain today to see little piles of flowers and messages at the roadside where an accident happened. Commentators have suggested a connection with the major disaster at the Hillsborough football stadium in 1989 where many people were killed – and a major spontaneous commemoration was held (e.g. Matthew Engel in MacArthur 1997: 27).

4   The paragraph that follows is based on a reading of key texts in contemporary identity theory. Particularly formative for my own approach have been Said 1978, Stallybrass and White 1986, Žižek 1991, Benjamin 1990, Dollimore 1991, Bhabha 1994, Sedgwick 1994, Hall 1997.

5   Versions of this process differ according to the type of psychoanalytic theory underpinning the account. The contemporary revival of psychoanalytic thinking in cultural studies is a major presence in theories of Self and Other. In Kleinian theory, for example, introjection is based on an initial projection into the other – so-called 'projective introjection' (e.g. Mitchell 1986: 185). This is critical for processes of identification.

6   I am grateful to Barbara Henkes for drawing my attention to Dianarama, for discussions on Diana, and for sending me clippings.

7   I am grateful to Deborah Steinberg for discussions and information on these themes.

Chapter 29

Catharine Lumby

VANISHING POINT

Diana seemed to have reached a vanishing point where she was five parts iridescence to one part flesh – truly a heavenly ghost.[1]

LEANING INTO THE LENS, her torso bare bar a single strand of pearls, her naked arms braced across her legs, Princess Diana phosphoresces. Skin, teeth, eyes, hair – even her nails are charged with a luminous glow. It's one of those rare pictures which reminds us what it is to be photogenic, an image in which the subject herself actually appears to give off light. (The word 'photogenic' is derived from the Greek words *photo*, meaning light, and *genes*, meaning to beget or produce.)

The photograph, taken by Patrick Demarchelier, graced the cover of Australian magazine *Who Weekly* a fortnight after Diana's death. A black and white image unencumbered by text, it stood out from the bellowing mardi gras of glossy tributes and commemorative colour liftouts which festooned news stands. A deceptively simple picture, it's true subject is less Diana than the peculiar pull of her image itself.

It's now received wisdom that Princess Diana was literally driven to her death by the public's fascination with her image. As Martin Amis put it in *Time* magazine, she died on the 'pointed end' of her own celebrity pursued by 'the high-tech dogs of fame'.[2] In terms of public impact, perhaps the most damning criticism of the media came from Diana's brother, Charles Spencer, who said:

> I always believed that the press would kill her in the end. But not even I could imagine that they would take such a direct hand in her death, as seems to be the case. It would appear that every proprietor and editor of every publication that has paid for intrusive and exploitative photographs of her, encouraging greedy and ruthless individuals to risk everything in pursuit of Diana's image, has blood on their hands today.[3]

The intense media interest in Diana – perhaps unparalleled in its concentration – was a source of deep community concern in the days following her death. But it was also a source of great interest for many people and a focus for global grief.

In many respects, Princess Diana has become a symbol of our anxieties about the way the mass media has changed our lives and confused our sense of what information is private and what should properly be made public. A member of the British Royal Family, Diana was equally a celebrity in the mould of Hollywood stars. A public figure who often expressed personal pain, she both resented and courted the attention of the press and the television cameras. Even the circumstances of her death illustrated this paradox. In the days that followed the accident, the media was consumed by a debate about its own role in her demise. Yet it was an analysis of the global media's feeding frenzy over Diana which took place in the context of a global media feeding frenzy of its own. And many of the same people who attacked the media for hounding Diana watched and read, avid to consume her image over and over again.

Diana has often been dismissed as a superficial figure: as a narcissistic, excessively emotional, hyperfeminine, wealthy woman whose charitable gestures were a pointless diversion of media attention away from the real structural causes of inequality and poverty. Diana's fans, and those who participated in the global mourning after her death, have also been caricatured as a mob of sentimental, weepy idiots brainwashed by a load of pretty pictures of a princess.

The day Diana's death was announced I appeared on an ABC radio panel with *Foreign Correspondent* presenter George Negus. Negus declared himself 'astounded' at the global outpouring of emotion over her passing and said he was initially shocked to discover a close female relative in tears about the news. His response is both understandable and typical of someone who works in a profession which habitually divides the world into important public issues and trivial, soft, lifestyle matters.

But there is another way to understand the public's fascination with Diana and the overwhelming emotion displayed at her funeral. Diana was an enormously privileged charismatic public figure who nonetheless became best known for her struggles with private unhappiness. Her battles were ones many ordinary people could relate to: family breakdown, eating disorders, an unhappy marriage, the desire to break free of an oppressive working life. To dismiss the obsession a large section of the community had with Diana is to symbolically dismiss issues which dominate the lives of many people, particularly many women.

In a broader sense, Diana is also an important symbol of the way the media is changing public life. Her life and death offer a textbook case study of the way the media has put celebrities at the centre of public life, and of how and why they hold such fascination. Diana illustrates the way issues which were formerly considered purely private or personal are increasingly seen as political issues, and the belief that airing such issues has therapeutic value for the individual concerned and serves to raise public awareness of the problem. Diana's devastation over her parents' divorce, her battles with anorexia, her struggle to extricate herself from a failed marriage, and her attempts to remake an independent life for herself and her children were all chronicled in numerous magazine articles, television documentaries and a host of biographies. And while these stories often germinated as tabloid scandals, Diana herself eventually confirmed many of them publicly and wove the public's awareness of her various personal struggles into her public image.

Far from being an icon of the banality of contemporary culture, Diana is a complex symbol whose image embodies many of the contradictions of living in a global media age. I'm not concerned here with getting to the 'truth' about Diana, in either demonising or canonising her. My interest lies not in Diana the person, but in Diana the icon. Viewed metaphorically rather than literally, Diana emerges as a key figure in twentieth-century Western culture – as someone who symbolised the massive changes the globalisation of information flows has wrought in our social, political and cultural life.

Divinely popular

In his book *Celebrity and Power* Canadian media theorist David Marshall offers the most detailed analysis to date of the fascination celebrities hold for the public gaze. He examines various kinds of stars and asks what role they fulfil in our lives.

Celebrities, according to Marshall, were an invention that heralded a democratic era in the fame business. The contemporary understanding of the term 'celebrity' developed in the nineteenth century. Comparing prior usages of the term, Marshall discovers a transformation of meaning that parallels some important shifts in social and cultural structure. In the seventeenth and eighteenth centuries, the term 'celebrity' carried connotations of solemnity and religious significance, but by the mid-nineteenth century it had begun to carry a familiar double meaning – it suggested both fame and notoriety, was a word stained with the potential for vulgarity. Marshall notes that the roots of the word are contained in the Latin *celebrem*, which suggests two meanings: being well-known and being thronged by the public. Marshall writes:

> The celebrity, in this sense, is not distant but attainable – touchable by the multitude. The greatness of the celebrity is something that can be shared and, in essence, celebrated loudly and with a touch of vulgar pride. It is the ideal representation of the triumph of the masses.[4]

Celebrities, according to Marshall, have taken over the role once played by kings, war heroes and prophets – they're invested with an aura of public authority which was once reserved for people elevated by birth, the State or the Church. The important difference is that the celebrity is someone whose authority appears to emanate directly from the masses and whose power, as a result, is dependent on maintaining the illusion of contact with their public.

Queen Elizabeth is clearly not a celebrity in modern terms. She's widely known, loved by many, and often goes out and shakes hands with the public. But she is not, in any sense of the word, *available*. Her public authority is grounded in her ancestry and in the historically divine right of kings and queens to rule their subjects. The distinction between royalty and celebrity was amply illustrated when Paul Keating, then Prime Minister, inadvertently touched the Queen's lower back when she was visiting Australia and the British press expressed outrage.

In stark contrast to Queen Elizabeth, Princess Diana frequently hugged and kissed her public. In 1987, at a time when many people still erroneously believed that the HIV virus could be contracted from casual contact, Diana offered her ungloved hand to an AIDS patient in a London hospital. And in 1993 she made a point of touching people with leprosy while visiting Nepal. She also became known for making spontaneous personal gestures to people she met through charity work, sending them cards and photographs and comforting bereaved families. Unlike her husband Charles, she also made a point of showing physical affection to her own children in public.

This emphasis on touching the sick and underprivileged symbolically aligned Diana with religious figures like her friend Mother Teresa. But the perception that she had a gift for healing wasn't grounded in her supposed connection to royalty or God, but in the belief that Diana channelled humanity through her displays of love and empathy. In this sense, Diana might be seen as a humanist version of Mother Teresa – as someone who secularised religious touch and symbolised the way many of the rituals and functions once embodied by the Church have moved outside organised religion into public life. Diana's own funeral was a case in point. The media operated as a proxy global church, offering a place where millions could focus their grief and come to terms with their loss.

Diana's talent for bringing private emotions into the protocol-bound corner of the public sphere reserved for royalty cemented her status as 'the People's Princess' and 'the Princess of Hearts'. And the gulf between Diana's style and that of traditional royalty was brought sharply into focus by the Royal Family's response to her death. Two months before she died, Diana had sat at the funeral of designer Gianni Versace with her arm around performer Elton John. Her public gesture of comfort was in stark contrast to television images beamed around the world of Prince Charles accompanying his sons to church on the morning that he told them of their mother's death. Charles sat upright and looked straight ahead without touching either boy.

As British cultural studies theorist Mica Nava notes, Diana's style radiated not only a willingness to touch, but an *in-touchness*.[5] She functioned as a symbolic link between the monarchy and contemporary life. And, despite the fact that she lacked tertiary education, and had married extremely young by contemporary standards and promptly produced two children, Diana was still seen as a quintessentially modern woman.

To understand Diana as a purely conservative figure because she was white, privileged and embraced the traditional roles of wife and mother ignores a central element of her appeal. Diana might have begun her public life as a model of feminine acquiescence, but she became something else. Her claim to modernity – or, more accurately, to postmodernity – lay in her ability to reinvent herself. She might have entered the public imagination as an unreconstructed fairytale princess but she left it as a far more contemporary symbol: a woman who rewrote the fairytale and, with it, the future of the British monarchy.

Mica Nava notes that images of Diana's mourners included a large number of non-Anglo faces, that almost all British newspapers at the time commented on the 'multi-ethnic' character of crowds lining the streets, and the way that different groups set up their own shrines. She writes that:

> Buckingham Palace was for middle-Englanders and the tourists; Kensington Palace, the most densely packed with flowers and other offerings, provided, as Diana's home, the pull for her supporters and the critics of the Royal Family; and the department store Harrods was for those who

celebrated the coupledom of Diana and Dodi and wanted to commiserate with the Al-Fayed family.[6]

As Nava points out, the affection didn't just flow one way. In both her professional and personal life Diana established a series of relationships with foreigners and non-Anglo British people. When she gave her infamous BBC *Panorama* interview in which she talked about her eating disorders and the breakdown of her marriage, she chose a low-profile journalist of Indian Muslim origin, Martin Bashir. Prior to beginning her affair with Dodi Al-Fayed, she had retained a friendship with his father following her own father's death. She also visited Pakistan frequently and spent time with her friends Jemima and Imran Khan, and it was during one of her visits there that she became romantically linked with Hasnat Khan, a Pakistani heart surgeon. Her final relationship, with Dodi Al-Fayed, was in flagrant breach of British establishment protocol.

Despite owning Harrods, Dodi's father, an Egyptian Muslim, was never fully accepted into British society and found himself unable to obtain citizenship, regardless of the large tax bill he paid in the UK. By linking herself with the Al-Fayed family, Diana was linking herself with one of the most distrusted and misunderstood religions in Britain and flouting social convention. It was a relationship which her public nonetheless warmed to because of the perception that Diana, a deposed Royal Family member, was aligning herself with people outside the British establishment. Many of her highest profile humanitarian campaigns concerned controversial and global issues – AIDS, landmines, poverty in the Third World. In the wake of the crash which killed her, black British television executive Trevor Phillips described Diana as a 'heroine' who 'embraced the modern, multicultural, multiethnic Britain without reservation'.[7]

Writing in *Newsweek* in November 1997 Michael Elliott argues that Diana symbolised a shift in the self-perception of many Britons. When she married Prince Charles, Elliott writes, 'The country was in crisis. Race riots flared in the cities. Whole areas of the industrial Midlands and North had been reduced to rusty wastelands', but during her reign as Princess of Wales 'Britain itself got progressively richer and more self-confident' and it 'grew and changed with her'.[8] Elliott's statement about the way England has changed is highly reductive, and it glosses over the very real social and economic divisions which continue to mark the country, but his general point about the reconfiguring of British identity in a symbolic sense makes sense. Diana's willingness to embrace a global and multicultural vision of the world, if only in her personal dealings with individuals, was in tune with progressive elements in British culture. England may still be ruled by the Queen, but it's equally a nation where almost as many people attend mosques as the Church of England.

For all of these reasons, Diana fulfilled an essential criteria of modern celebrity in its fullest sense: she acted as a kind of screen onto which a wide variety of individuals could project their own changing sense of self and community. Her transformation from awkward and insular Sloane Ranger, notable only for her traditional British complexion, fussy wardrobe and plummy accent, to a confident and cosmopolitan ambassador mirrored a slow shift in the perceptions of many Britons about what it means to be British in a post-colonial world.

Her trembling lower lip

If Prince Charles' stoicism and devotion to royal duty exemplifies the British stiff upper lip, Diana offered the public a glimpse of the trembling lower lip hidden beneath it. A modern princess who frequently gave speeches about the emotional needs of others, she was equally admired for revealing the ordinary problems which lay behind the extraordinary life led by the Windsor family.

After years of press speculation about her marriage and her eating disorders, Diana took the unprecedented step of secretly telling 'her story' to biographer Andrew Morton in a series of taped responses to his written questions. Morton's biography begins with an anecdote which epitomises the symbolic bridge Diana built between public status and private pain. The six-year old Diana Spencer sits quietly at the bottom of the cold stone stairs of her home and listens to her mother leave her father. It's a vivid picture of a young girl listening to simple sounds which herald a cataclysmic event in her life. Morton writes:

> She could hear her father loading suitcases into the boot of a car, then Frances, her mother, crunching across the gravel forecourt, the clunk of the car door being shut and the sound of a car engine revving and then slowly fading as her mother drove through the gates of Park House and out of her life.[9]

The fact that Diana's home was a ten-bedroomed residence with attached staff cottages, a swimming pool, tennis court and cricket pitch which was granted to her grandfather by King George V only adds to the poignancy of her story, at least as Morton tells it. A wealthy child who longed for 'cuddles and kisses', she was given 'a catalogue from Hamleys toyshop'.[10] A woman whose wedding day was watched by millions around the world, she endured a tortured marriage and cold in-laws. A princess with servants, numerous homes and a large wardrobe, she was denied the things she claimed she craved most: to mix freely with her friends and to walk down the street without a bodyguard or the press following her.

But given the advantages she already had, why did so many people care about her private life? Why, as Rosanne Kennedy asks, did so many 'mourn the death of a young, rich, white woman, when they weren't mourning the civilians who had just been killed in a market bombing in Israel or the men, women and children who had been massacred in Algeria?' One of the answers lies in the fact that Diana not only impressed her personal pain on the world – she came to symbolise the 'victim-turned-survivor' narrative.[11]

Diana was at the centre of hundreds of media scandals and speculations during her lifetime, but she also greatly contributed to public interest in her private life by making a series of public confessions, firstly to biographer Andrew Morton and then in the *Panorama* interview, after which she continued to pepper her public speeches with references to her private experiences.

Confession was once a preserve of the Christian Church or the therapist's couch, but over the past two decades it has increasingly moved into the public domain. From the most literary of memoirs to the trashiest of talk shows, telling all in public has developed a quasi-spiritual significance. In popular therapeutic terms, confession has become an important part of self-recognition and definition. You discuss your old life and the lessons you've learned in order to make a new one. In religious terms, confession can also have a redemptive function – when Diana confessed to having an affair she was, in effect, directly asking her public for absolution.

Diana was also an aficionado of astrology, herbal medicine, aromatherapy and clairvoyance, and there's an important link between the popularity of public confession and the growth of alternative therapies and philosophies. Public confession of private pain or misbehaviour has come to symbolise a willingness to change. Likewise, alternative therapies, mysticism and self-help theories claim to offer new ways of living and understanding the self. At the heart of many New Age philosophies and therapies is the belief that individuals, given the right tools, can identify and alter their destiny. 'Self-help' is a term which encapsulates this claim – it suggests that, while the self may be preordained, it can be altered.

Diana's involvement in self-help theories, alternative therapies and New Age philosophies put her interests perfectly in synch with much of her core public. From Australia's *Woman's Day* to the US *National Enquirer*, many popular women's magazines now focus heavily on these subjects – a focus which suggests their readers are hungry for alternatives to Western expert discourse in the area of relationships, health and finance. It's easy to dismiss columns on numerology or articles on the healing power of crystals as superstitious nonsense, but to do so evades the question of why these philosophies and therapies have become so vastly popular with readers of magazines which once filled their pages with the advice of Western doctors, psychologists, and 'home scientists'. One answer, perhaps, is that many women have become increasingly disillusioned with the paternalistic advice of predominantly male experts and are looking for alternative ways to assert control over their lives.

As a relatively uneducated person who was thrown into the rigours of marriage and child-bearing before she had a clear sense of her own goals in life, Diana had something in common with many ordinary women. In feminist terms, her life reads like a consciousness-raising narrative. Unhappy in her marriage, feeling perpetually inadequate and self-destructive, she gradually recognised that many of her personal problems were rooted in a system which required her to conform to other people's expectations without acknowledging her own needs. But unlike women schooled in feminist politics, Diana relied on quasi-spiritual theories and therapies to help her escape from a suffocating life and reinvent herself.

There are correlations between many of the self-help theories and New Age practices and the consciousness-raising technique used by feminists in the '70s. At its most basic, consciousness-raising offered women an alternative story about their lives, a story which gave radically different explanations for their personal unhappiness than those they were being offered by their husbands, mothers, psychiatrists and family doctors. The agenda of the feminist consciousness-raising groups which proliferated in suburbia during the '70s obviously differed sharply from New Age philosophies in that they regarded women's personal unhappiness as a symptom of the deep-rooted systemic inequality of the sexes. To invoke a famous feminist slogan, they were grounded in the belief that 'the personal is political'. Self-help and New Age theories and therapies, in contrast, are marked by a highly individualistic account of personal experience. Nonetheless, both movements have borrowed rituals traditionally associated with organised religion, including the power of confession, group witnessing and talismans.

It would be simplistic to equate Diana's conversion to self-help/New Age therapies with a straightforward narrative of feminist consciousness-raising, but it's important to acknowledge that both movements have appealed to many women for common reasons. Both rely on self-discovery and an awareness of alternative lifestyles as the basis for change – and it was Diana's capacity to reinvent herself in the face of systemic opposition which so many women admire.

British novelist Martin Amis voiced an opinion common to many educated people when he wrote of Diana: 'Her enthusiasms were crankish, hypochondriac, self-obsessive: aromatherapy, colonic irrigation, the fool's gold of astrology.'[12] What his analysis avoids examining, however, is why so many people have turned away from both Western expert knowledge and traditional religions in the first place. Because, while alternative therapies and philosophies are easy to deride, their popularity in the late-twentieth century, particularly among women, suggests that many people think conventional Western disciplines are not addressing their needs.

While Diana's image as a victim-turned-survivor humanised her, it also invested her with an other-worldly aura. In an essay examining the saintly qualities often attributed to Diana, cultural studies writer Kath McPhillips argues that saints are traditionally people who are perceived to have challenged institutional structures, and that it was Diana's willingness to challenge the monarchy which invested her with this religious aura.[13]

If Diana was sometimes characterised in quasi-religious terms during her lifetime, it was in death that the spiritual metaphors really began to multiply. A much-quoted card left at Kensington Palace read: 'Born a lady, became a princess, died a saint.'[14] Mourners queuing up to sign the condolence book at Buckingham Palace reported seeing her image shimmering on the glass of an old painting.[15] It's surely not the last we'll hear of strange Diana sightings. If celebrities are ordinary people rendered extraordinary through media coverage, in death they can become positively supernatural.

The other side of the screen

Diana's willingness to reveal her private emotions and fears rendered her human in life and saintly in death, but the unbidden instrusions on her privacy saw the media demonised. Diana's death was particularly significant as a media event because it was one which required everyone who participated in it, whether as a producer or a consumer, to reflect on the role media events play in real life – to consider their reality effect. It was a meditation which undoubtedly intensified the sense of anger and disbelief immediately following the accident. The grieving masses outside Buckingham Palace were also an indignant mob baying for media blood, and, to many who breathed the frequently smug and relentlessly cynical atmosphere of daily journalism, it must have looked as if the unwashed masses had got a glimpse inside the media palace and weren't impressed with the calibre of their masters.

More important was the persistent and unwitting challenge that the media coverage of Diana's death offered to many of the assumptions that ground much media commentary on the media itself. Chief amongst these was the notion that good media is media which stands apart from reality, faithfully reflecting and analysing it; media, in other words, that puts everything carefully back in its place in the social order. Yet the enormous attention that Diana's death focused on the media itself made it extraordinarily difficult to maintain this outsider fiction.

Moments of transparent hypocrisy kept bubbling to the surface of media coverage, drawing attention away from the event and back towards the media. On the morning following Diana's death, for instance, a BBC commentator interrupted a friend of hers midway through his answer to a question about whether photographers had hounded her to her death, to cut away to live images of the press photographing grieving people outside Buckingham Palace. Even a discussion about media intrusiveness, in other words, was illustrated by media intrusiveness.[16]

One response to this is to argue that the media ought to simply stop intruding. Unfortunately, drawing the line between justified and prurient coverage isn't always so simple, as the BBC cut-away to Buckingham Palace illustrated. At what point, for instance, do images of a grieving crowd shift from being legitimate news coverage of the reaction to Diana's death and become intrusions into personal grief? And what incentive is there for the news media to make these decisions when it's competing for ratings in the midst of one of the biggest stories of the century? (In the final chapter, I'll take a much more detailed look at this issue and offer some practical suggestions.)

The problem of covering a story in the midst of the widespread hostility to the media which flowed from the circumstances of Diana's death fuelled a rush to find some high, dry moral ground. Media commentators began justifying their own coverage by separating the bad media from the good media. In a segment following the incident mentioned above, BBC's media analyst Nick Hyam was quick to note: 'You have to distinguish between, on the one hand, the activities of the photographers on the ground who are, for the most part, freelancers, and, on the other, the newspapers and their staff reporters and photographers.'[17]

Hyam's desire to separate the media into a hierarchy of responsibility gestures to a far more deep-rooted problem: how do you attack the media without attacking its consumers? Where, in other words, does the circle of production and consumption end?

Sydney Morning Herald columnist Mike Carlton attempted to break the Gordian knot by singling out a particularly culpable group of producers and consumers. He blamed 'the editors and media barons who funded their intrusions and the millions of readers who bought the stuff, avid for ever more salacious scandal'. The Australian women's magazines who habitually published photographs and stories about Diana's private life, according to Carlton, were 'wet Kleenexes of junk journalism – which have fallen over themselves in panicky retreat from their customary soft-porn voyeurism'.[18]

Carlton's choice of words is revealing. Soggy tissues make us think of the irrational weepy women who supposedly buy magazines like *Woman's Day*, but they're also associated with the masturbatory habits of sexually frustrated teenage boys. Both are familiar figures in attacks on the base appetites which supposedly drive consumers of popular culture. On one hand, these media consumers are supposedly passive, lonely, irrational and easily manipulated, but they're just as easily portrayed as a voracious, amoral, devious and compulsive swarm.

The qualities Carlton identifies in the public who avidly consumed Diana's private life – excessive emotion, voyeurism, a taste for the banal, and herdlike behaviour – are qualities which have been cited in attacks on the public taste for popular culture throughout the twentieth century. Female consumers have been particularly vulnerable to such attacks – indeed it's women who are most often pictured as consumers, while men are routinely portrayed as producers. This gendering of consumption is typified by annual stories on post-Christmas sale 'hysteria', when women supposedly give in to their basest natures. As Elizabeth Wilson has argued, female consumerism is often portrayed as:

> . . . a compulsive form of behaviour, over which we have little conscious control. According to this puritanical view, we are squeezed between the imperatives of the market and the urges of an unconscious whose desires are warped and invalidated by the culture in which we live.[19]

According to this scenario, women's symbolic proximity to nature and their lack of rationality makes them ideal targets for manipulation by advertisers and retailers, but it also renders them an unpredictable and potentially voracious force whose desires are capable of threatening the social order. Being weak-minded, the story goes, women consumers don't really know what they want – they need to be seduced, to be sold stuff by savvy advertisers, retailers and editors. Once they get a taste for something, however, whether it's a new perfume or a new celebrity, then everybody better watch out. Women's lack of intellectual or moral substance makes them potential addicts, and they'll go to any lengths to possess the objects of their desire.

In the weeks following Diana's death, both representations of Diana's female public were in evidence. William Shawcross, for instance, wrote about the 'Cult of Diana', a term which suggests that zombielike masses were being brainwashed by the tabloids into devouring her image.[20] Writing in the *Australian*, Tom Gilling ridiculed the women's magazines for their 'solemn vows of self-censorship and photographic chastity' and predicted that personal reminiscences of Diana would soon be 'hustled into print' with 'brassy' headlines.[21]

All these attempts to pass the blame to women's magazines and their consumers were, however, already doomed by the way Diana's image had already cut across the grain of the traditional quality–tabloid split. In the days immediately following her death, almost all media sources were careful to emphasise images of Diana in official, public roles: marrying the Prince of Wales, accompanying her children to school functions, comforting the sick and dying, and assessing the landmine problem with Red Cross officials. These images provided a crucial justification for the intense media focus which followed the accident, given the simultaneous debate about precisely this kind of intense media focus.

This attempt to split sanctioned public images of Diana from illicit private images ignores the fact that the two have always been inextricably linked. As a former royal, the mother of the heir to the British throne, and an ambassador for Britain, Diana was always a legitimate object of traditional news interest. But her immense appeal, and the grief which followed her death, wasn't grounded in her official status, it was attached to her unexpected *departure* from it. In a sense, all media outlets who devoted intense coverage to Diana's death – whether they were broadsheet newspapers or weekly celebrity magazines – were feeding the same public appetite for information about the dead princess. The whole point about Diana's appeal is that it was, and remains, grounded in the way her image transgressed the split between the public and the private, the highbrow and the lowbrow, the quality press and the tabloid weeklies.

The eloquence of crowds

Eloquence is not a quality we readily associate with crowds. In conventional terms, crowds don't speak – they cheer or boo. They express themselves in a blunt, almost animalistic fashion. They're supposedly illogical, easily swayed and given to panic. Indeed, a great deal of twentieth-century sociological literature has been devoted to the subject of controlling crowds and preventing riots.

Elegant, persuasive speech is supposedly the domain of politicians, opinion makers and writers seeking to reassure or persuade the masses. Yet in her introduction to a collection of essays on Princess Diana, Helen Grace notes a curious reversal of this hierarchy in the weeks following Diana's death. The massive outpouring of public emotion, she says, precipitated an 'anxiety of speech' among academics and public commentators who were asked to speak about it. She concludes that 'spontaneous popular response was far more eloquent in this context than expertise could ever hope to be'.[22]

Writing in the same collection, Ruth Barcan argues that the crowd response to Diana's death was a sudden eruption of 'the popular feminine' into a masculinised rational public sphere. Barcan's alignment of the emotional masses with an emotional feminine world, and the public sphere with a masculine rational world isn't an endorsement of this division. Rather, Barcan is referencing a large body of feminist work which has explored the way the public and private spheres have been split along gendered lines. In conventional terms, the domestic sphere is the domain of women and children: it's symbolically aligned with the body, intimate relationships and emotions. The public sphere, on the other hand, has conventionally been identified with men: it's symbolically aligned with the mind, contractual and commercial relationships, and reasoned debate.

In Barcan's terms, the mass outpouring of grief over Diana's death suspended this split and saw personal emotion spill over into the public arena. It made it clear that 'grief can be rational, that emotion can be political, that governing systems might have to configure human feelings as central to politics and not as an excessive outside to their "real" concerns'.[23] It was an event, in other words, which demonstrated that the conventional division of the world into reason versus emotion, public versus private, or male versus female, is a construct.

Barcan's analysis of the symbolic weight of the enormous reaction to Diana's death raises an important question: to what extent does it make sense anymore to talk about the public and the private as separate realms in the first place? Because if, as I argue in this book, they've already thoroughly contaminated each other, then the personal character of the public's response wasn't a revolutionary moment but an illustration of how far the public sphere has strayed from the model many academics and opinion makers still use to understand it.

What if the public has already escaped the terms conventionally used to define and govern it? What if opinion makers, cultural commentators and politicians are operating in a vacuum of their own design? One look at the Queen's faltering composure when she finally addressed the world, under obvious duress, to express her sadness at Diana's death suggests she was shaken by something more fundamental than the loss of a former daughter-in-law. She looked more like a monarch in the throes of coming to terms with her subjects' wrath.

'Global mourning' is a term which already suggests that it's no longer possible to separate the worlds of emotion and rationality, the individual and the collective, the public and the private. Mourning, at least in recent Anglo-Saxon history, is an emotion which has been traditionally defined by the closeness a mourner has to the deceased. It's regarded as one of the most private emotions. A graphic illustration of this is the advice the father of a friend of Prince William gave his son when he returned to school with the prince. The son protested that all the photographs of Diana which adorned local shop windows would upset William. His father reportedly replied, 'Well then, it will be your duty never to mention her. You must pretend that nothing has happened and just carry on'.[24]

If mourning is meant to be intensely personal, at least in Western culture, globalism signifies everything conventionally opposed to the personal, including locality, individuality, nationality and culture. It's a zone of protocol, legality, diplomacy and political bargaining. What Diana's funeral brought home was how profoundly these two terrains, the local (or personal) and the global (or public), are implicated in each other. It reminds us that communication, on any scale, always has an affective as well as an effective dimension, and that the global nature of the media has already traversed boundaries which diplomats and trade officials are still labouring over.

Rather than seeing the massive response to Diana's death as an extension of 'real life' or local emotions to a figure known only via the global media, we can also see it as a sign of a subtle but important reversal of the relationship between these two zones. In a world where our sense of reality is constantly filtered and informed by the media, media celebrities come to seem literally larger than life. As one man said in a radio talkback session, 'I didn't cry this much when my wife died'.[25] His remark illustrates a strange possibility: that the vast media coverage of Diana rendered her more real to many people than real life itself.

It's a scenario which might better explain why so many cultural commentators were at a loss to understand the response to Diana's death, because the terms of their analyses rely on a separation between reality and its representation, and on the belief that they themselves occupy a critical space outside the media and its relentless circulation of images.

At the heart of the global fascination with Diana is the fact that she herself symbolised the difficulty of living in a world increasingly made up of appearances. As an individual whose body, emotions and intimate relationships were under continual scrutiny, she literally lived on a fault line between the public and the private.

The desire to get to the truth behind Diana's marriage, her divorce, her eating disorders, her relationship with the Royal Family, her love affairs, and now, in predictable perpetuity, her death, is all part of a social hunger to uncover the real person behind the image. As Richard Dyer observed in *Heavenly Bodies: Film Stars and Society*, the whole media construction of stars encourages us to ask what they are 'really' like.[26] The irony, of course, is that whenever a fragment of the celebrity's private life is reported, it becomes part of their public persona. Separating the public from the private in this context is ultimately futile. Diana's popularity rested on the public's knowledge of her personal life and their resulting sympathy for her. And it's precisely the undecidability of where the public stops and the private begins which defines the fascination of contemporary celebrity.

The circumstances of Diana's death suddenly brought into focus the nature of this fascination and the anxieties that accompany it. In a broader sense, it is only in this context that the enormous worldwide outpouring of grief and disbelief following the accident begins to make sense. For the vast majority of her fans, Diana only ever existed as an image – and little has changed. In the year following her death, Diana's face has continued to appear weekly on the covers of magazines around the world. In death, she quite literally lives on.

Life after death

On August 31, 1998, exactly a year after Diana's death, a musical titled *Queen of Hearts* opened off-Broadway in New York. Billed as a tribute to Diana, the production featured a cast of characters which included Prince Charles, Princes William and Harry, and Charles' mistress Camilla Parker-Bowles. At the conclusion of the first act, Diana, Charles and Camilla get together for a joint singalong. And in a final bizarre twist, the late Princess Grace of Monaco (who also died in a car crash) turns up as Diana's guardian angel.[27]

The Diana industry didn't end with her death – if anything it escalated. Her image has continued to grace magazine covers, books and documentaries, and sell a slew of posters, souvenirs, compact discs and items at auction. The anniversary of the car crash spawned a whole new rash of Diana tributes, tours and memorabilia.

In July 1998 Diana's brother opened the grounds to the family estate of Althorp and a brand new, three-million-pound Diana museum. For just under ten pounds visitors can take a tour of the museum, which documents various stages of Diana's life. Exhibits include her school uniform, family home-movie footage, her wedding dress, and (somewhat ironically) the original draft of the speech her brother gave at her funeral attacking the media for invading her privacy. Visitors get to take home souvenirs in a purple carry bag bearing the legend 'Althorp' in gold. The museum was launched with a concert tribute to Diana attended by 15 000 people at which David Hasselhoff, the star of *Baywatch*, asked Diana to stop the rain.[28]

The Althorp museum is only one cog in the massive engine which drives the Diana industry. From the most humble plastic souvenir Diana thimble, to the million-dollar Christies auction of Diana's gowns, the princess's name, face and signature have become a blue-chip commodity.

Criticism of this cashing-in on Diana's death has been widespread, with British Prime Minister Tony Blair leading a campaign against what he called tacky and inappropriate souvenirs, and calls by other MPs for legislation to prevent the sale of such items. Writing in the *Sydney Morning Herald* in 1998 Christopher Henning typified the response of many media commentators when he condemned 'the tone of treacly kitsch which, since her death, seems to flow over everything to do with Diana'.[29]

The criticisms of the Diana memorabilia and tribute industry precisely echo criticisms of media coverage of Diana when she was alive. The official, unemotional and authorised use of Diana's image and name by the Diana Memorial Fund on a coin and to fund a scheme for community nurses is generally seen as acceptable. What arouses the ire and scorn of many critics is any open sign that individuals and organisations are milking Diana's legend for personal gain, cheapening her image by associating her with kitsch or downmarket products or sentimental tributes. It's a division which mirrors the division of Diana stories and images into those which legitimately show her performing her public duties (and are therefore in the public interest) and those which inappropriately delve into her private life (and therefore sully both the princess and the people who consume them).

While it's true that the official Diana Memorial Fund can claim to be redistributing monies received to charities the princess supported during her life, there are other issues at stake in the condemnation of the non-authorised arms of the Diana industry. To begin with, Diana's persona hasn't been turned into a commodity by the vendors of cheap souvenirs, it was already a well-established commodity during her lifetime. Certainly, the directors of the Memorial Fund were under no illusions about the value of her image when they applied to the British Patent Office to register twenty-six well-known photographs of Diana as their intellectual property. What's more, much of the criticism of unofficial Diana souvenirs is rooted in class-ridden notions of what constitutes good taste. A souvenir which may seem ludicrously kitsch to an educated, middle-class media commentator – a porcelain doll made in Diana's image, say, or a book of sentimental Diana tribute poems – may be genuinely precious to Diana fans from other backgrounds. It's somewhat ironic, to say the least, that the commentators who attacked the kitsch memorabilia industry made no comment on plans to place Diana's head on a five-pound coin – an act which quite literally gives the image a monetary value.

In reality, the preciousness, aesthetic quality, or authorised nature of a given piece of Diana memorabilia is no indication of the value it has for its owner. The rich buyers at the official Christies gown auction are no less consumers of Diana's memory than working-class people swapping 'Queen of Hearts' playing cards in a magazine. The desire to divide the Diana industry into an authorised, appropriate camp and an inappropriate, cashing-in camp is ultimately a desire to evade an obvious truth: Diana's memory in death, just like her image was in life, is a commodity, regardless of how that memory is marketed.

The same kinds of criticisms that have been levelled at the unofficial Diana memorabilia industry have been levelled at the purveyors of the inevitable conspiracy theories which have circulated in the wake of Diana's death. Within hours of the car accident, rumours had begun to circulate that the princess had been assassinated by British secret service agents acting on behalf of the Royal Family. Six months after her death came the book *Death of a Princess: An Investigation*, which renewed speculation that Diana was pregnant at the time of the accident and that her life could have been saved were it not for the outmoded medical techniques of attending doctors. The father of Dodi Al-Fayed, Mohamed Al-Fayed, also made public claims that his son and the princess were victims of a conspiracy by the British establishment to prevent them marrying.[30]

The circulation of wild conspiracy theories and unofficial memorabilia may seem unrelated, yet both perform the same function: that of preserving and mythologising

Diana's image. It's extraordinarily fitting that Elton John chose to rewrite 'Candle In The Wind', originally a tribute to actress Marilyn Monroe who died at the age of thirty-six, for Diana, who also died suddenly at the same age. Monroe invites a number of unexpected comparisons with Diana. A celebrity who was often dismissed as a dumb, sexy blonde actress in her lifetime, Monroe acquired a far more complex status in death. It was only in the years after her death that her image evolved into a fully fledged legend, as a result of endless biographies, documentaries, photo collections, conspiracy theories, plays, films, novels and academic essays celebrating, analysing and attempting to reclaim Monroe for a thousand different causes. What so many of these archaeological expeditions into Marilyn's life and work share is a belief that, given sufficient elbow grease, they can exhume the truth about Monroe. Gloria Steinem sums up this approach when she dedicates an essay on the actress: 'To the real Marilyn and to the reality in us all.'[31]

The irony is that, far from stripping back the veil, every fresh foray into the Monroe myth merely adds to the legend. There's no definitive Monroe, in other words, just an ever-accumulating pile of perspectives. Conspiracy theories are the most obvious illustration of how this process works. They do anything but reveal the real story behind the alleged cover-up; they muddy the waters further, blurring the boundary between fact and fiction, and engender a whole new set of conspiracy theories.

The sudden death of a celebrity offers particularly fertile soil for the conspiracy theorist. The dead are always ideal candidates for wild speculation, since they don't talk back, correct factual errors or sue for defamation. And speculation on the truth behind the death of a celebrity is, in many ways, simply an extension of the obsession with finding out who a star really is when they're alive.

We can be sure that the facts of Diana's life and the circumstances of her death will be endlessly sifted and resifted in the decades to come. Long after the French police have bagged the last flake of paint from the crash scene and closed the file, fresh 'evidence' will be adduced to support claims that Diana was assassinated by a myriad malevolent forces.

Conspiracy theories are routinely attacked as a superstitious, paranoid and politically regressive phenomenon.[32] While it's certainly true that conspiracy theories can ignite and fuel reactionary politics (the pro-gun lobby in both the US and Australia are enthusiastic marketers of conspiracy theories), there's another way of thinking about their broader cultural appeal. The idea that we're not being told the whole truth about a particular celebrity offers a covert justification for our continuing fascination with their image. Conspiracy theories, then, are a populist version of the highbrow investigative news. Both base their right to investigate and circulate stories on the claim that the information is in the public interest. Indeed, the lines between investigative journalism and conspiracy-mongering are not always so clear. Both forms rely on anonymous sources and whistleblowers, and stories which are originally dismissed as paranoid fantasies are sometimes revealed by trained reporters to have substance.

The belief that the truth is being systematically hidden from us and that we need to know more appears, on the face of it, to contradict the equally pervasive belief that we live in a prurient media culture which tells us far too much. In fact, these two beliefs are two sides of the same coin. Both are responses to living in a mass-mediated age – an age in which so much of our daily reality is penetrated by stories about people and events we have no direct experience of. Trying to separate what we know from what we're told – getting to the truth behind media images – is a Sisyphean task. On the one hand we're saturated with information, and on the other we're so rarely in a position to directly evaluate its truth value. Celebrities arguably function as a kind of screen for the anxiety generated by this scenario. At once real people and media-generated images, celebrities embody this paradox. The desire to get to the real person behind the image is a direct echo of the desire to get behind the media screen which increasingly swaddles our globe. A woman who lived and died amid a frenzy of flash-bulbs, Diana is a peerless icon for our times.

Notes

1   Allison Pearson, London *Daily Telegraph*.

2   M. Amis, 'The mirror of ourselves', *Time*, 15 September, 1997, p. 57.

3   W. Shawcross, 'Patron saint of the global village', *Sydney Morning Herald*, 6 September, 1997, p. 32.

4   D. Marshall, *Celebrity and Power: Fame in Contemporary Culture*, University of Minnesota Press, Minneapolis and London, 1997, p. 6.

5   M. Nava, 'Diana: Princess of Others', *Planet Diana: Cultural Studies and Global Mourning*, ed. Re:Public, Research Centre in Intercommunal Studies, Sydney, 1997, p 21.

6   *ibid*. p. 20.

7   M. Elliott, 'Heroine of a new Britain', *Diana: a Celebration of Her Life*, Newsweek, Sydney, 1997, p. 107.

8   *ibid*. p. 106.

9   A. Morton, *Diana: Her True Story – In Her Own Words*, Michael O'Mara Books Limited, London, 1997, p. 70.

10   *ibid*.

11   R. Kennedy, 'Global mourning, local politics', *Planet Diana: Cultural Studies and Global Mourning*, ed. Re:Public, Research Centre in Intercommuinal Studies, Sydney, 1997, p. 50.

12   Amis, 'The mirror of ourselves', p. 57.

13   K. McPhillips, 'Postmodern canonisation', *Planet Diana: Cultural Studies and Global Mourning*, ed. Re:Public, Research Centre in Intercommunal Studies, Sydney, 1997, p. 89.

14   L. Deegan, 'Born a lady, died a saint', *The Daily Telegraph*, 2 September, 1997, p. 4.

15   D. Burchell, 'Ensigns taken for wonders', *Planet Diana: Cultural Studies And Global Mourning*, ed. Re:Public, Research Centre In Intercommunal Studies, Sydney, 1997, p. 28.

16   *BBC News*, BBC, London, 31 August, 1997.

17   *ibid*.

18   M. Carlton, 'Diana: media's sickening u-turn', *Sydney Morning Herald*, 6 September, 1997, p. 34.

19   E. Wilson, *Adorned in Dreams: Fashion and Modernity*, University of California Press, Berkeley, 1987, p. 245.

20   W. Shawcross, 'Patron saint of the global village', p. 32.

21 T. Gilling, 'How to knit yourself a brand new Diana', *The Australian*, 1 October, 1997, p. 13.

22 H. Grace, 'Introduction: the lamenting crowd', *Planet Diana: Cultural Studies and Global Mourning*, ed. Re:Public, Research Centre in Intercommunal Studies, Sydney, 1997, p. 3.

23 R. Barcan, 'Space for the feminine', *Planet Diana: Cultural Studies and Global Mourning*, ed. Re:public, Research Centre in Intercommunal Studies, Sydney, 1997, p. 40.

24 J. Adler, and D. Foote, 'The young princes' ordeal', *Diana: A Celebration of her Life*, Newsweek, Sydney, 1997, p. 104.

25 D. Burchell, 'Ensigns taken for wonders', p. 28.

26 R. Dyer, *Heavenly Bodies: Film Stars and Society*, British Film Institute, London, 1986, p. 18.

27 M. Riley, 'Anniversary madness – global village', *Sydney Morning Herald*, 15 August, 1998, p. 31.

28 C. Henning, 'The Diana business', *Sydney Morning Herald*, 2 July, 1998, p. 13.

29 *ibid.*

30 A.F.P., 'Cyber Di car crash top of tack parade', *The Australian*, 17 February, p. 11.

31 G. Steinem, *Marilyn*, Henry Holt, New York, 1986.

32 E. S. Bird, 'What a story', *Media Scandals*, ed. J. Lull & S. Hinerman, Polity Press, Cambridge, 1997, p. 117.

Narcissism, fandom and the will to celebrity

Introduction to part five

■ P. David Marshall

THE CAMERA AND THE eye are always trained on the famous. Their movements are mapped. Paparazzi will stalk celebrities with telephoto zoom lenses to capture their private moments and with flashes to memorialize their public displays and promotions. Perhaps celebrities represent the vanguard of the surveillance society, where one's anonymity is surrendered to the benefits of the cybernetic consumer culture: Our desires are mapped, recorded and thereby become the material for more precise and directed appeals than the blunt instrument of mass advertising could ever achieve.

Despite their regular protests about the invasion of privacy, celebrities are complicit in being surveilled and monitored: It is part of their job. The camera thus becomes their mirror and the celebrity's cultural reflection via the camera is internalized into celebrity culture itself. It is a form of narcissism, an obsession with image and the body, and concern over presentation and representation that pervades a city such as Los Angeles. The ripples of this reflecting pool widen outwards to the audiences themselves into a much more expansive internalization of the look and the desire to be looked at. In the era of new media where blogs and webcams spar for our affections with film and television, the reflections of the private self sometimes become the material for the individual's desire to be recognized in the public world – to be famous.

Returning and acknowledging the internalized look of the famous are the audiences. Fans invest in the relationship and work – sometimes desperately – to correct the imbalances in reciprocation through an abundance of attempts at connection with celebrities. In their hyper-activity, fans embody the active audience and transform the narcissism in celebrity culture into an exchange, a form of communication and an expression of love within the boundaries and confines produced by celebrity's highly mediated reality intertwining with a fan's often everyday expressions of affection and devotion.

Chapter 30

Elizabeth Arveda Kissling

I DON'T HAVE A GREAT BODY,
BUT I PLAY ONE ON TV
The celebrity guide to fitness and weight loss in the United States

IN LIGHT OF CURRENT interests in dieting and physical fitness among North American women, and the phenomenal success of Jane Fonda's exercise records, videos, and books, it is neither surprising nor coincidental that many women celebrities have begun to produce their own related consumer products. Although many now star in their own fitness and exercise videos, self-help books remain a popular and accessible forum through which celebrities dispense weight loss and fitness advice. Jane Fonda, for example, has written three books, Victoria Principal has written two, and Raquel Welch, Linda Evans, Elizabeth Taylor, Stephanie Powers, Angela Lansbury, Brooke Shields, and Cher one each.

My interest in this particular genre of self-help books grows out of my personal and professional interests in women and body-consciousness and the ways in which the mind-body relationship is mediated through language. This analysis focuses on the rhetorical construction of these issues in celebrity diet and fitness books, and how such advice literature addresses and positions women. Humans understand the world through communication. Leslie Miller and Otto Penz (1991) identify the special irony of this insight with respect to the human body: "despite its apparent immediacy, [the body] is never knowable in direct, unmediated ways" (p. 148). The use of a particular vocabulary of bodies suggests particular ways of believing about, acting toward, and knowing bodies. A feminist critical perspective asserts that these communication patterns are not neutral but reflective of male biases encoded in language and social practices (Penelope, 1990; Spender, 1985). A feminist critical perspective also asserts that critical analysis of language and the social practices in which it is embedded is a vital component of social change (Penelope, 1990). It is from this perspective that I approach the language of dieting and embodiment.

The language of dieting and embodiment contained in these celebrity self-help books promotes anti-feminist views. The following analysis identifies three recurrent themes that work against women's interests: celebrity fitness books present contradictory advice about the mind/body relationship, associate self-esteem with beauty, and conflate the relationships among health, fitness, and beauty.

Themes of celebrity advice

Aside from superficial differences, celebrity self-help books are similar in substance, format, and advice; most feature authors who all are white, Euro-American heterosexuals. Their writing addresses readers with the presumption that they are also white and heterosexual. Each author typically begins with a "how-I-came-to-write-this-book" introduction that outlines her experience with weight gain and low self-esteem, followed by how she developed an exercise-diet regimen in response to her frustration. The middle section, usually the longest, provides detailed instructions for following her program. The book ends with a restatement of the importance of physical and mental health and an affirmation of the joy of slimness. These books also share three recurrent themes that present disturbing messages to their targeted audience of women.

Mind/body relationships

Like other diet books, these celebrity texts promote contradictory images of the relationship between mind and body. Carole Spitzack (1987) observes that to lose weight, or to desire weight loss, women must first distance themselves from their bodies to recognize their bodies as deviant. Then, one must keep her body under constant surveillance – displaying mind over matter – in order to lose weight. Hence, diet books portray the body as an object that must be controlled, or even as an enemy that must be avoided.

Celebrity diet books in the United States conform to this pattern. But while many of these famous authors articulate views of the mind and body as unified and inseparable, their own texts undermine these stated claims. For example, Raquel Welch (1984) writes that "the mind and body are interrelated – they never stop interacting. Everything we think and feel is related to our physical form; . . . the physical and mental aspects of each of us are inseparable" (p. 2). A few pages later, however, she advises readers to separate mind from body: "[T]ell yourself this is the last time you're going to look this way. Those bumps and bulges aren't *you*, anyway – they're just excess baggage that you're about to unload" (p. 22). Similarly, in *The Body Principal* (1983), Victoria Principal claims that "mental peace" can be obtained only with "physical peace," which requires exercise (p. 185). Yet in her discussion of choosing appropriate food, her body is unmistakably an object: "I consider my body my most valuable possession – a machine, if you will – and thus the food I put into it has to be the best of all possible fuels and nutrients" (p. 168). Cher (1991) uses the same analogy, claiming that

> [o]ur bodies are like engines. What happens if you pour cheap gasoline into your car engine? Doesn't your car just fall apart? We can't keep dumping poison into our bodies from every angle . . . (p. 8).

This simile comes just a few pages after *her* discussion of the inseparable connection between mind and body.

Linda Evans (1983) claims to be so convinced of mind/body interdependence that she was unwilling to write a beauty book unless it incorporated what she calls inner beauty: "I believe outer beauty is a direct result of how we feel inside" (p. 11). Yet, apparently, inner beauty and outer beauty are distinct enough to require a division of the book into two parts. The body is implicitly and explicitly objectified in *Linda Evans' Beauty and Exercise Book*:

> Looking the very best that I can helps me to feel positive about myself, while staying in shape and keeping healthy gives me the freedom to take my mind off myself, and enables me to concentrate on the important things in life.
>
> There are certainly enough trying experiences to go through, to absorb and comprehend, without having our bodies as an obstacle (p. 53).

In less than one page, the body moves from inclusion in "myself" to an objectified self, then to an unimportant object, finally to be dismissed as an obstacle. Raquel Welch (1984) takes this progression even further, noting that once she has "taken care" of her body (through diet and exercise), then she can forget about it to be "free to escape the physical and let my mind settle on other, more engaging things" (pp. 2–3).

Arguments for a unified, inseparable mind/body are continually subverted by the discourse of *control* in these celebrity diet and fitness books. Bodies must be controlled through diet and exercise, in order to be pretty, to be thin, to maintain a positive self-image, to win others' praise, and even, ironically, "to overcome the alienation from our bodies that many of us feel" (Fonda, 1986, p. 11). Jane Fonda encourages us to work out so that "you can have a little control over your physical self in a positive way" (1986, p. 11). Elizabeth Taylor (1987) finds such self-discipline empowering: "There is no greater boost to the self-esteem than to have others acknowledge that you are in control" (p. 247).

Indeed, the restoration of control over the self is the motivating force behind these self-help books. For example, Elizabeth Taylor's stated goal in writing *Elizabeth Takes Off* (1987) is to "give others the impetus to regain control of their lives and their looks" (p. 21). Loss of control, of course, *is* why Liz became fat in the first place: "I may be a 'movie star,' but my reasons for reaching this sorry state were the same as any woman who has, literally, let herself go" (p. 25). Likewise, Victoria Principal's second book, *The Diet Principal* (1987), details her own weight gain after "just plain letting [myself] go" (p. 12), and her strategy for regaining control.

The emphasis on the power of the mind over the body creates a division in which the body becomes an object for the mind to control. This is made explicit, for example, in Cher's (1991) view of exercise as a winning battle strategy in the war between mind and body. "People I know who have had a war going on with their bodies begin to work out, and suddenly they start to love the new power they have over their bodies" (p. 2). The mind/body dualism in these books parallels other dualisms pervasive in Western thought: reason/emotion, culture/nature, objective/subjective, male/female. In these cases, the first item of the pair is seen as both more valuable than and dominating of the second item. Such dualisms are artifacts of a binary world view; they promote division and deny interdependence (Ursula LeGuin, cited in Kramarae & Treichler, 1985). By encouraging women to objectify and separate their selves from their bodies, these self-help books perpetuate dualistic, anti-feminist ways of thinking.

Self esteem and beauty

These texts are also anti-feminist in their passive acceptance of sexist standards for appearance. Most, for example, urge women to trade on their looks. Brooke Shields (1985) straightforwardly proclaims that what is inside is important *"but looks do count. Why else is there so much emphasis placed on fitness, health, and beauty?"* (p. 57, emphasis original). Cher defensively adds: "Look, we're a visual society. I didn't make this society. I just live here. I adapted to it" (1991, p. 161). Elizabeth Taylor (1987) concurs, saying "It always matters how you look" (p. 122) and encouraging women to attend to their appearance continually, regardless of their weight. The authors' advice stems directly from their conformity to, not their challenge of, prevailing attitudes about the importance of looks in defining women's value.

As many feminists contend, in a patriarchal society where women are judged and valued first for their appearance, women often feel they have little choice but to be concerned with and continually working on their looks (Wolf, 1991). In the current climate of backlash against feminism, oppressive and unachievable standards of slenderness and beauty serve to keep women political prisoners, captive to diets and beauty regiments that drain their energies from social, political, and economic work to work on appearance (Faludi, 1991; Wolf, 1991). In an intriguing correlation, as women become more powerful politically and socially, the idealized female body size in America grows ever slimmer (Kissling, 1991; Orbach, 1986; Seid, 1989; Wolf, 1991).

However, attractiveness is not only the criterion by which men evaluate women, but is a defining criterion of self-worth for women themselves (Finkelstein, 1991; Wolf, 1991). Collectively, these celebrity books advance the position that women not only do but should derive their self-esteem from their looks. Exercising and working out, then, are motivated primarily by vanity. Victoria Principal's axiom is telling: "I look better, I *am* better" (1983, p. 18, emphasis original). For Cher, looking good means being happy (1991, p. 2), while, for Linda Evans, an attractive appearance is associated with "feeling positive" about herself (1983, p. 53). Elizabeth Taylor also recognizes the "inextricable" link between self-image and self-esteem, a relationship that all women will admit as long as they are "honest enough" with themselves (1987, p. 14). Such views go against the grain of much feminist thought. As Kissling (1991) notes, writers like Kim Chernin and Laura Brown argue that the relationship between self-esteem and looks – especially slenderness – induces self-hatred in women because they cannot live up to the unrealistic ideals of beauty admired in North American culture. Celebrity authors try to minimize their role in contributing to this problem with weak caveats: Jane Fonda (1986), for example, states that one's "goal is not to get pencil-thin or to look like someone else" (p. 86) while Victoria Principal (1983) wants to discourage women from "looking like me" (p. 18). At best, these are mixed messages, at worst misleading, given each author's detailed instructions for following her personalized exercise and diet regimens exactly and each book's abundance of photographs of the author looking her Hollywood best.

Health, fitness, and beauty

The relationship between looks and self-esteem is further complicated by the conflation of beauty, health, and fitness in these texts. Beauty is achieved through health and physical fitness; mental and physical health come from beauty. Raquel Welch (1984) proclaims that "glowing health is the best beauty treatment" (p. 259). Victoria Principal (1983) contends that mental peace requires physical peace which can be achieved only through exercise. Linda Evans (1983) states that women who are not thin possess neither health nor self-esteem. These texts consistently promote exercise and diet as the true paths to beauty and health. Thin equals health; health equals beauty. The reverse is clearly implied but not stated: fat equals unattractive, unattractive equals pathological.

Fat is not merely pathological in celebrity fitness books but immoral. Following a healthy diet, then, is also a path to moral superiority. Many North American women are already familiar with the rhetoric of sin that describes their eating habits (Bringle, 1989). Led into temptation, women consume bad foods, then feel guilty and confess, assigning themselves caloric or physical penance and promising to be good in the future. Celebrities also embrace this metaphor and its implications. Elizabeth Taylor (1987), for example, warns that "lapses can begin insidiously, so a dieter must be on National Guard duty twenty-four hours a day" (p. 140). Brooke Shields (1985) admits her obsession with weight, and confesses her dieting sins:

> I'll start mentally punishing myself for what I've eaten during the week; how I had three helpings of salad at one meal, with all the salad trimmings, or maybe too much granola, which is one of my favorite foods and is extremely high in calories. And, even though I haven't binged on junk food, overeating any one type of food is just indulgent (p. 101).

Brooke Shields is not alone in attributing inherent goodness or badness to particular foods. Jane Fonda (1986) emphasizes the importance of eating the "right stuff"; Victoria Principal (1983) labels the eating of unhealthy foods as *abuse*, and in her diet book (1987) divides food into categories of perfect, maybe/sometimes, and forbidden. Cher (1991) sees all food as "just another substance that people can abuse during weak, stressful, or self-destructive phases" (p. 13), and discusses at great length her efforts to resist such "bad" foods as Haagen-Dazs ice cream and M&Ms candy. If certain foods are bad, the logic goes, then people who eat them or want to eat them also are bad. In this rhetoric of evil eating, a sweet tooth becomes a deadly sin. The path to righteousness and redemption is denial of hunger and discipline of the body through exercise.

When women are encouraged to see fat as both pathological and immoral, it is no surprise that women who are not thin often have low self-esteem. As Victoria Principal (1987) states, "[a]nyone can gain weight. . . . But it had never happened to me, and I was scared. I was also heartbroken. And, frankly, ashamed" (p. 12). Elizabeth Taylor (1987) concurs:

> [M]ost women know their appearance affects their self-image, and in our society looking good means looking slim. Weight gain affects our feelings about ourselves as much as it affects our looks. Weight loss can provide an immediate boost to our self-esteem (p. 14).

These themes are familiar to many North American women. Self-help books purportedly assist women readers in their quests for physical fitness, beauty, and self-esteem. By equating the three, these celebrity writers have made them even less attainable. Presented as a tool for women's liberation and independence, the equation of fitness, beauty, and self-esteem instead contributes to a climate of oppression by encouraging women to participate in the objectification of their own and other bodies. Focusing on diet and fitness increases the chasm between mind and body. When the body image they recommend for women is difficult to achieve and unattainable for most, and then presented as essential to self-esteem, these texts shame women for failure to meet these ideals.

Conclusion

Like other self-help texts, celebrity diet books locate women's unhappiness within themselves. The presentation of slenderness as a choice, achievable through mind over matter, makes troubles with body image an individual problem. The systemic problems created by a society that values female appearance more than female accomplishment are not held accountable. In spite of their stated intentions, celebrity authors perpetuate sexist standards of beauty and a destructive symbiotic relationship between self-esteem and appearance. Although some may argue that these women earned their celebrity status because of their idealized appearance, their success in film and television clearly requires much more: the discipline to pursue their dreams, the intellect to manage their careers and business ventures, and at least a modicum of talent. One might hope that such successful, well known women would be in a position to challenge the idea that a woman's most important source of self-esteem in her looks rather than her talent and achievements. But their own words confirm their vulnerability to the self-esteem=beauty=slenderness=health equation that victimizes many other woman in the United States. Cher, an accomplished, award-winning performer, makes this painfully clear: "I never liked the way I looked much, but it's okay. I've done the best I can do with it. If I had been given a choice, I don't think I'd have picked this look. I might have gone more with Michelle Pfeiffer's look" (1991, p. 162).

Chapter 31

Kathy Davis

BEAUTY AND THE FEMALE BODY

BEAUTY AND THE FEMALE body go hand in hand. In Western culture, beauty was treated as a virtue which was associated with the female sex (Lakoff and Scherr 1984; Suleiman 1985). Since Plato, feminine beauty has been idealized as representing moral or spiritual qualities. The medieval cult of chivalry extolled the fair damsel as a symbol worth fighting and even dying for. During the Renaissance, the female sex was linked to the divine. The female nude represented beauty in its purest form. Throughout the nineteenth century, Romantic poets, novelists and philosophers sought their inspiration in beauty, adopting a beautiful woman as their muse.

The alteration of the physical body in the name of beauty also has a long tradition – a tradition which has fluctuated in accordance with changing configurations of power. Although beauty practices are at present primarily the domain of women, this has not always been the case. Historically, both sexes went to great lengths to beautify and decorate their bodies. The French historian Perrot (1984) provides an arresting account of shifting practices in the alteration of the body in Western Europe. For example, in the eighteenth century the cultivation of appearance was limited to the aristocracy. There was little difference between the wealthy Parisian lady and her male counterpart. Both sported heavily powdered faces, brightly painted lips, false hair and enormous whigs, and high heels. The French revolution abolished this accentuation of class difference through appearance. In the late eighteenth century, sexual difference became the central organizer of social asymmetries of power (Laqueur 1990). This was reflected in changes in appearance. Men began to dress soberly, paying little attention to their physical appearance, while women were increasingly concerned with altering and beautifying their bodies. The corset became the symbol of the nineteenth century – literally imprisoning women in their bodies (Kunzle 1982). Assembly line production of clothing and the department store made fashion available to the masses, the beauty salon was born, and the invention of the camera made it possible for images of beauty to proliferate on a mass scale — from women's magazines to the movie industry (Lakoff and Scherr 1984; Wilson 1985; Bowlby 1987).

By the twentieth century, the cultivation of appearance had become a central concern for women of different classes, regions, and ethnic groups, simultaneously uniting them in the desire for beautification, and setting up standards to differentiate them according to class and race (Banner 1983). For example, Peiss (1990) shows how the burgeoning cosmetic industry used a combination of a universal standard of feminine beauty ("beauty through the ages") and cultural constructions of gender, class, and race to sell beauty products. The exotic vamp with the Cleopatra look became a cult figure emulated by thousands of American women, while the association of light skin and straight hair to social success, refinement, and superiority held women of color in its sway. By exploiting the tension between the appearance of Anglo-Saxon gentility and foreign exoticism, advertisers could appeal to women of different class and ethnic backgrounds, while, at the same time, creating a conception of beauty which drove a wedge between them.

As the twentieth century progressed, the standards for feminine beauty shifted in rapid succession. In the U.S., for example, the stately Gibson girl with her hourglass shape made way for the perky, flat-chested flapper of the twenties. The businesslike, assertive beauties of the forties as represented by Hollywood stars such as Joan Crawford, Katherine Hepburn, and Bette Davis were replaced by the sex symbols and Playboy bunnies of the fifties. Thin was in with Twiggy in the sixties and muscles and the healthy look were added in the late seventies as the fitness craze emerged and Jane Fonda became the symbol of feminine beauty (Banner 1983; Lakoff and Scherr 1984; Marwick 1988).

Despite the changes in cultural beauty ideals, one feature remained constant; namely, that beauty was worth spending time, money, pain, and perhaps life itself. Beauty hurts, and it appeared that modern women were willing to go to extreme lengths to improve and transform their bodies to meet the cultural requirements of femininity. Comparing contemporary Western beauty practices to the ostensibly more painful practices of other cultures (like binding feet, stretching lips, elongating necks, or filing the teeth to sharp points), Lakoff and Scherr (1984) note that:

> the pain tends to be of a long, even lifelong duration: rather than the quick prick of the needle, we have the squeezing of the tight-laced corset, the stab of the pointy toe, the asphyxiation of the collar and tie, or the scrape of the razor blade, day in and day out. The pain is perhaps less agonizing at any one moment in our beauty rituals than in theirs, but over time it evens out (p. 60).

Whether a practice is labeled mutilation or decoration, bizarre or normal depends more upon the discourses of beauty in a particular culture than any innate quality of the practice itself. Moreover, the amount of damage inflicted in the course of beautifying the body tends to be directly related to the development of technology. As Perrot (1984) has noted, the nineteenth century corset may have been unhealthy, causing breathlessness, fainting spells, and shifting organs, but the twentieth century has produced an even more constraining corset – the woman's own skin. Cosmetic surgery has become, if not routine, at least acceptable as a method of body improvement for contemporary Western women.

This chapter deals with women's willingness to suffer for the sake of beauty. First, I take a brief look at explanations put forth in the social sciences for this phenomenon, showing how these accounts are inadequate primarily due to their neglect of issues concerning gender and power. I then turn to several feminist theories which place the relationship between beauty and the female body in the context of the social reproduction of femininity and power relations. Drawing upon a critical appraisal of these theories – as well as a dash of feminist fiction – I assemble a theoretical perspective which can help me tackle women's involvement in the most drastic beauty practice of all – cosmetic surgery.

Social psychology and beauty

In social psychology, appearance has been a standard topic. Empirical studies abound which show that beauty is linked to a host of positive social and cognitive characteristics (Berscheid et al., 1971; Berscheid and Walster 1974; Hatfield and Sprecher 1986). The attractive person is happier, more successful, more well-adjusted, and generally better liked. In a society where first impressions are increasingly important, attractive people get preferential treatment in everything from getting jobs to finding a residence. Good looks are important throughout the lifespan for shaping self-esteem, ensuring happiness, and determining how a person will be treated by others.

Although social psychologists portray attractiveness as advantageous for everyone, they are quick to note that there are sex differences. Studies show that men seem to profit more from being attractive and care less, while women, regardless of how they look, have difficulties reaping the benefits of physical attractiveness (Hatfield and Sprecher 1986). Men have consistently better body images than women. Even at an early age, girls admit to feeling less attractive than their sex peers and this sense of physical inferiority increases with every passing year (Freedman 1986). Women consistently perceive their bodies inaccurately or experience them as having an abnormal shape, size, or appearance (Miller et al., 1980). This faulty body image is related to a host of typical female body disorders like anorexia nervosa, obesity, agoraphobia, frigidity, and depression. It contributes to psychosomatic symptoms, stress, and feelings of shame and guilt (Freedman 1986).

Many researchers cite women's lack of self-esteem as the reason they do not profit from the advantages of physical attractiveness. Social norms of female inferiority have been internalized to the extent that even physical beauty does not bolster a women's pride (Sanford and Donovan 1984). The beautiful woman is never really free of the fear that she will lose her looks or that she is only valued for her body. Marilyn Monroe is the paradigm example of the difficulties which can befall the beautiful woman (Lakoff and Scherr 1984). The general female propensity toward feelings of self-worthlessness make the plight of both beautiful and plain women remarkably similar. Whereas attractive men can enjoy their appearance, attractiveness is not a source of well-being for the female sex.

This is particularly disturbing in the light of findings that both sexes value physical attractiveness more highly in women than in men (Freedman 1986). Women believe that beauty is important in their everyday social interaction as well as their relationships, while men are more likely to find their attractiveness of importance in intimate relationships alone. Men especially value beauty in their relationships, while men are more likely like kindness, empathy, or having the same interests on the top of their lists (Lakoff and Scherr 1984). It is assumed that women are aware of this discrepancy and in the interest of finding a male partner will be prepared to invest time and energy in maintaining their appearance.

Social psychology tends to explain such sex differences in terms of role socialization. If society – for whatever reason – requires physical attractiveness in women, girls will be socialized to comply with the norms of beauty. Sex-specific expectations concerning appropriate behavior or feelings will be internalized by the individual woman who will find beauty essential for her well-being. In a context where female inferiority is the norm, women will suffer from a low self-esteem, making them vulnerable to what others think about them.

Social psychological explanations treat women's preoccupation with their appearance as an individual, psychological problem. They do not explore the social pressures on women to be beautiful; nor are they concerned with why the social sanctions on women to comply with the norms of beauty have emerged at this particular moment in time. It therefore remains unclear why women are willing to go to such lengths to improve their appearance. By the same token, it is difficult to explain why women who have managed to defy social conventions in other areas of their lives are unable to resist the norms of beauty. In short, social psychology tends to minimize the problematic dimensions of beauty for women, while blaming the individuals who become overly concerned with their appearance.

Psychoanalysis and beauty

In psychoanalytic thought, the cultivation of appearance is associated with narcissism. Freud (1957) referred to narcissism as the "original disposition of the libido" (ibid., 81) whereby the individual achieves gratification through looking at or touching her or his own body – literally, treating it as though it were a sexual object. Children of both sexes start out with a capacity to take pleasure in their own bodies and a certain degree of narcissism is considered necessary for both sexes as a defense against feelings of worthlessness or shame. Narcissism, however, can take on a pathological hue when the individual has to shore up his or her psychic boundaries through an omnipotent sense of self-worth or an insatiable need for admiration from others (Kohut 1977). Grandiosity becomes a neurotic cover-up for a fragile identity which is too easily overwhelmed by feelings of shame or despair.

Although narcissim has its origins in the Greek myth about a young man who fell madly in love with his own reflection while bending down to drink from a pond, the narcissistic cultivation of appearance is most often associated with women, conjuring up the image of "a woman primping in front of a mirror imagining her sexual desirability to real or fantasized men" (Garry 1982: 148). Indeed, psychoanalytic thought regards narcissism as essential to women's sense of self – along with masochism and passivity, the sine qua non of femininity (Freud 1933; Deutsch 1930). Narcissism begins with the girl's fatal discovery that she lacks a penis. She is castrated; her body is deficient. This crushing blow to her pride in her body and, more generally, her self-esteem initiates a lifelong cycle of excessive vanity, alternating with bouts of shame and self-hate.

As one psychoanalyst succinctly puts it:

> I assume that the little girl who compares her genitals to those of the little boy finds her own ugly. Not only the greater modesty of women but their never ceasing striving toward beautifying and adorning their bodies is to be understood as displacement and extension of their effort to overcompensate for the original impression that their genitals are ugly.
>
> (Reik, quoted in Firestone 1970: 66)

In psychoanalysis, feminine narcissism is treated as a necessary defense and even a partial corrective to the problems of femininity. By taking an excessive pride in her appearance and enjoying her own image as seen through the eyes of another, a woman can defend against the feelings of shame and inferiority which are her anatomical lot in life. Female beauty becomes a consolation prize for phallic loss.

The line between narcissism as a normal feature of femininity and narcissism as a character disorder is a thin one, however. The pride a woman takes in how she looks is, after all, little more than a thin veneer, covering a deep-seated sense of unworthiness. The cultivation of bodily appearance is a form of adaptation to the difficulties central to womanhood – a way to keep depression at bay, at least for the moment. It does nothing, of course, to eliminate the wound which women receive to their core feeling about their bodies and sexual identities. Femininity, by definition, creates a precarious balance between narcissistic gratification and an ever-present dissatisfaction, fuelled by a deep-seated self-hate.

Unlike social psychological explanations for women's concern with their appearance, psychoanalysis asserts that women have little choice but to pursue beauty. Their very identity, not to mention their happiness and well-being, depend upon how they look. However, by treating narcissism as an essential feature of femininity, it gives it an ahistorical, universal quality, independent of specific constellations of power or cultural contexts.[1] And, finally, psychoanalytic approaches to feminine narcissism construct and reproduce a double standard of mental health: to be normal, a woman must be feminine. However, being feminine, she automatically becomes maladjusted and disturbed (Broverman et al., 1970; Smith and David 1975). A woman who cultivates her appearance is damned-if-she-does and damned-if-she-doesn't.

Sociology and beauty

Although women's relationship to their bodies and their problems with beauty were on the agenda of feminist sociologists for nearly two decades (Henley 1977; Millman 1980; Chernin 1981; Brownmiller 1985; Collins 1990; Smith 1990b), the body seems only very recently to have become a topic for the sociological mainstream (Turner

1984; O'Neill 1985; Featherstone 1991; 1992; Finkelstein 1991; Giddens 1991; 1992; Scott and Morgan 1993; Shilling 1993). Sociology is primarily concerned with institutions, social structure, the constitution of society, and social change – subjects which were apparently far removed from the individual's relations to his or her body. As Turner (1984) explains:

> The human body as a limiting point of human experience and consciousness seemed less important than the collective reality of the social world within which the self was located. The legitimate rejection of biological determinism in favor of sociological determinism entailed, however, the exclusion of the body from the sociological imagination (p. 31).

Bodies, however, are back. Frank (1991) traces this sudden return of the body as a respectable topic for sociological inquiry to the contradictory impulses of modernity as carried forward in postmodern theory. This is the backdrop for considerable research on the importance of beauty in consumer society as well as on women's particular involvement with the cultivation of appearance.[2]

Interest in the body is the product of a typically modernist conflict. On the one hand, modernity spawned positivism which treats the empirical world as an objective mirror of reality. On the other hand, it launched the Enlightenment quest for a transcendental reason which would provide the stable foundations for knowledge and politics. At the same time, however, the actual (post) modern world is characterized by impermanence, fragmentation, and constant flux.[3] There are many versions of reality in it and the tendency toward political relativism and even nihilism lurks just around the corner. The contradiction between modernist certainty and (post) modernist uncertainty is played out in sociological perspectives on the body. On the one hand, the body is treated as the biological bedrock of theories on self and society. It is the "only constant in a rapidly changing world, the source of fundamental truths about who we are and how society is organized, the final arbiter of what is just and unjust, human and inhumane, progressive and retrogressive" (Frank 1990: 133). On the other hand, the body itself seems to provide the most convincing proof for radical constructionism. It has become increasingly untenable to speak of a natural body. The work of social scientists like Douglas (1966; 1973) and Goffman (1959; 1963; 1967; 1976) demonstrate that the body's surface and comportment as well as the cultural beliefs and technologies concerning its maintenance, alternation, or improvement vary radically, both within and between cultures. The body as social construct appears to be suited for use as a ground for launching criticisms against claims of universality, objectivity, or political correctness.

The contradiction between the body as bedrock and the body as construct can also be found in postmodern theory. For example, in the "high theory" of Barthes (1985), Lacan (1977; 1982), Deleuze and Guattari (1983), and Baudrillard (1988), the material body makes room for the body as metaphor, but the tension remains.[4] The body is treated as the ideal location from which to criticize Enlightenment philosophy and its tendency to privilege the experience of a Western masculine elite which had devalued the body. By "embody-ing" knowledge, these critics deconstruct the faulty universalist pretensions of such narratives as merely one version among many.

In the work of Foucault (1978; 1979; 1980; 1985; 1986; 1988), which has made an even greater impact on recent sociological theory, the body is treated as a primary site for investigating how power works. Modern power is no longer deployed from above, but works at the micro-level of the body, through discipline rather than oppression. The body is a good place to explore how different subjectivities are constructed and authorized as the truth through the disciplinary discourses of power. Thus, the body in postmodern theory is both reference point in a world of flux and the epitome of that flux (Frank 1991: 40).

The revival of interest in the body has formed the backdrop for recent studies on the importance of appearance in Western consumer culture (Turner 1984; Featherstone 1983; 1991). Postwar improvements in organization of production, a general increase in wages, the improved distribution of commodities through department stores and buying on credit, and the rise of advertising all contribute to the creation of a mass consumer market for personal goods and services. The Protestant ethic of the nineteenth century, with its emphasis on hard work, thrift, and sobriety, makes way for an ethic of leisure, consumption, and "calculating hedonism" (Jacoby 1980).

> The imagery of consumer culture presents a world of ease and comfort, once the privilege of an elite, now apparently within the reach of all. An ideology of personal consumption presents individuals as free to do their own thing, to construct their own little world in the private sphere.
>
> (Featherstone 1983: 21)

The locus of control has shifted from society to the individual (Crawford 1984). An emphasis on life style change holds individuals responsible for their own fate. They expect to be happy, to achieve a glamorous life style, and to cultivate an attractive body through discipline and denial. Controlling appearance through the daily regime of body maintenance (jogging, diets, keeping fit) is a primary means for the individual to eke out his or her identity under the conditions of modernity (Giddens 1991). Through the cultivation of the body, individuals enact and display their desire for control.

> We cut out the fat, tighten our belts, build resistance, and extend our endurance. Subject to forces that lie beyond individuals control, we attempt to control what is within our grasp.
>
> (Crawford 1984: 80)

Although these social scientists frame their analysis of body maintenance and improvement as a general phenomenon in Western consumer culture, something affecting the modern self, they willingly concede that women are the primary targets and "most clearly trapped in the narcissistic, self-surveillance world of images" (Featherstone 1991: 179).

The explanation for the feminine susceptibility to the promises of happiness through body improvement is sought in the sexualization of the female body by the media in order to sell products. Bombarded with images of themselves on billboards, in magazines, and on the screen, women are easy prey for the lures and false promises of consumer culture. However, lest we become too alarmed, we are assured that cosmetic and fashion industries are currently directing their efforts at a male market. It is presumably only a matter of time before men and women enjoy "dubious equality" in the area of body cultivation (Featherstone 1991: 179).

Taking this argument a step further, some have suggested that women are not merely the primary objects of consumer culture but that culture itself is in the throes of "feminization" (Huyssen 1986; Featherstone 1992). The masculine or "heroic" values of action have been replaced by the "idols of consumption." The world of Hollywood celebrities, soap opera stars, and royalty – the cultural favorites of the female consumer – are the new cultural symbols – admirable for who they are rather than what they can do. They are ideally suited to promoting the glamorous life, replete with fancy hair styles and makeup, electrolysis, teeth capping and cosmetic surgery. In the feminization of culture, women are the victims and the perpetrators, all in one.

Other sociologists place women's concern with appearance in the context of their emancipation (Turner 1984; Giddens 1991; 1992). Having broken free of the constraints of domesticity and entered the public sphere of waged labor, women have for the first time the material means to enjoy themselves. The sexual revolution and feminism provide the finishing touches, encouraging them to make the most of themselves and take their own needs seriously. Women continue to be excluded from full participation in the public realm, however, and the cultivation of the body becomes one of the only ways they can achieve the exciting life which they had come to expect was within their reach. As the contemporary epidemic of anorexia nervosa attests, controlling the body can become a dangerous and destructive way to master an insecure environment. In a world of many promises and few real options, freedom under conditions of modernity is, at best, a "risky business" (Giddens 1991: 107–108)[5] and, at worse, only a "pseudoliberation," with the old chains of patriarchal authority replaced by the new ones of consumer culture and neuroticism (Turner 1984: 203).

Unlike social psychological or psychoanalytic approaches, sociological perspectives on beauty do not individualize women's concern with appearance as a personal lack of self-esteem or as a woman's psychosexual predisposition toward narcissism. The cultivation of appearance is treated as an artefact of consumer capitalism which, in principle, affects us all. The specific relationship of women to their bodies, however, tends to be ignored or overemphasized as the feminization of culture in general. Women are treated as the brain-washed victims of media hype or of their own deluded search for emancipation. Sociologists, like psychologists, tend to blame the victim rather than explore how women actually experience and negotiate their bodies in a context of many promises and few options. Beauty is linked to women's illusory quest for happiness rather than the more mundane reality of discomfort and suffering which most actual beauty practices entail. Power relations between the sexes tend to be glossed over or dispatched conveniently to some shadowy and distant patriarchal past. Although some concession may be given to the "greater premium" placed on physical attractiveness for women as opposed to men (Giddens 1991: 106), the significance of gender for these different beauty norms (or the norms for sexual difference) is left unexplored. Thus, while sociological approaches provide insights into the social and cultural context in which body improvement is situated, its explanations fail to account for women's specific relationship to their bodies and for their involvement with the practices of body improvement. To do so would require a perspective which links a sociological analysis of the contradictions of modernity and consumerism to an analysis of the social construction of femininity, the control of women through their bodies, and the politics of beauty.

Femininity and the politics of beauty

Within feminist scholarship, women's preoccupation with their appearance is invariably explained as an artefact of femininity in a context of power hierarchies between the sexes and among women of different social and cultural backgrounds. Feminists have tended to cast a critical eye on women's quest for beauty, which is described in terms of suffering and oppression. Women are presented as the victims both of beauty and of the ideologies of feminine inferiority which produce and maintain practices of body maintenance and improvement. Originally, the culprit was sought in what was described as a system of cultural beauty norms. These norms demanded eternal youth and impossible beauty from women: slender but voluptuous shapes, faces unmarked by the passage of time, and, most of all, an appearance in keeping with the conventions of upper-class, Western femininity (Perutz 1970; Henley 1977; Millman 1980; Baker 1984; Brownmiller 1985; Chapkis 1986; Wolf 1991).[6] By linking the beauty practices of individual women to the structural constraints of the beauty system, a convincing case was made for treating beauty as an essential ingredient of the social subordination of women. Beauty was seen as an ideal way to keep women in line by lulling them into believing that they could gain control over their lives through continued vigilance over their bodies.

In recent years, feminist scholarship on beauty as oppression has begun to make way for a more postmodern approach which deals with beauty in terms of cultural discourses (Suleiman 1985; Probyn 1987; Haug et al., 1987; Diamond and Quinby 1988; Jaggar and Bordo 1989; Jacobus et al., 1990; Spitzak 1991; Bordo 1993). In this framework, routine beauty practices belong to the disciplinary and normalizing regime of body improvement and transformation, part and parcel of the production of "docile bodies" (Foucault 1980). The focus is on the multiplicity of meanings attributed to the female body as well as the insidious workings of power in and through cultural discourses on beauty and femininity. The body remains a central concern, this time, however, as a text upon which culture writes its meanings. Following Foucault, the female body is portrayed as an imaginary site, always available to be inscribed. It is here that femininity in all her diversity can be constructed – through scientific discourses, medical technologies, the popular media, and everyday common sense.

Although the theoretical perspectives for understanding women's beauty practices differ in their emphasis on beauty as oppression or as cultural discourse, the focus remains on how these practices work to control or discipline women.[7] In the first perspective, femininity is defined in terms of women's shared experiences of which the most central is oppression. Power is primarily a matter of male domination and female subordination. In the second perspective, the unified category "woman" is abandoned in favor of a diversity of femininities. Femininity is regarded as a (discursive) construction with power implicated in its construction. Power is no longer a matter of top-down repression or coercion, but the vehicle through which femininity is constituted at all levels of social life. In both perspectives, women's

preoccupation with their appearance is viewed as part of a complex system of structured social practices, variously referred to as the politics of appearance (Chapkis
1986), the technologies of body management (Bordo 1989), the beauty system
(MacCannell and MacCannell 1987), the aesthetic scaling of bodies (Young 1990a),
the fashion-beauty complex (Bartky 1990), or the beauty backlash (Wolf 1991). This
system includes the myriad procedures, technologies, and rituals drawn upon by
individual women in their everyday lives, the cosmetic industry, the advertising business, and the cultural discourses on femininity and beauty. Beauty is central to femininity, whereby Woman as sex is idealized as the incarnation of physical beauty, while
most ordinary women are rendered "drab, ugly, loathsome or fearful bodies" (Young
1990a: 123). This ambivalence concerning the female body is implicated in the reproduction of unequal power relations between the sexes. It aids the channeling of
women's energies in the hopeless race for a perfect body. As Bartky has noted, the
"fashion-beauty complex," like the military-industrial complex, is a "major articulation of capitalist patriarchy" (Bartky 1990: 39–40).

The beauty system also articulates social hierarchies based on class, race, and
ethnicity (Lakoff & Scherr 1984; Chapkis 1986; Collins 1990; Peiss 1990; Young
1990a; Bordo 1993). In Western culture, dominant discourses of the body enable
privileged groups – notably, white, bourgeois, professional men – to transcend their
own material bodies and take on a god's eye view as disembodied subjects. They
become the ones who set the standards and judge, rather than the ones who are judged
against standards they can never hope to meet. Subordinate groups are defined by their
bodies and are defined according to norms which diminish or degrade them. Those
designated by the dominant culture as Other (old, homosexual, disabled, fat, and/or
female) become imprisoned in their bodies.

Beauty standards set up dichotomies of Otherness and power hierarchies between
women.

> Blue-eyed, blonde, thin white women could not be considered beautiful
> without the Other – Black women with classical African features of dark
> skin, broad noses, full lips, and kinky hair.
>
> (Collins 1990: 79)

White, Western women are trapped by the promise that they are special, which
gives them a vested interest in maintaining the beauty system. The norms which
equate the light-skinned, Western look with beauty permeate relations between white
women and women of color, as well as between women and men of color. Women of
color are bombarded with cultural messages which not only link whiteness to feminine beauty, but, more importantly, to "gentility, female domesticity, protection from
labor, the exacting standards of the elite, and Anglo-Saxon superiority" (Peiss 1990:
164) – in short, to power.

In conclusion, feminist approaches place the social production of femininity and
power processes of domination and subordination at the heart of their analysis of
beauty. I shall now take a closer look at how women's involvement in the norms
and practices of the beauty system has been analyzed in the two main perspectives
within feminist scholarship on beauty: beauty-as-oppression and beauty-as-cultural-
discourse. Feminist scholarship from these two perspectives is predictably diverse and

rarely fits neatly into one perspective. I have chosen to focus on two specific examples which are particularly good representatives of each perspective. In addition to showing how beauty can be analyzed in terms of gender and power, they enable me to explore the strengths of each framework for understanding women's specific participation in the beauty system.

Beauty as oppression

In *Beauty Secrets* (1986), Wendy Chapkis tackles beauty as a central feature of women's oppression. Her primary aim is to analyze beauty as a political phenomenon – a "politics of appearance" – and to this end, she employs two strategies. First, she takes women's concern with appearance out of the realm of individual psychology. She shows how advertising, the communications media, and the cosmetic industry have joined forces to become a "global culture machine," which makes a Western model of beauty and the Good Life mandatory for women all over the world (Chapkis 1986: 37).

Second, she explores the beauty secrets of women of various ages, ethnic backgrounds, and social classes. Adopting a "personal is political" stance, she uses their everyday battles with hated bodily features (facial hair, blemishes, bulges) as a starting point for a powerful commentary on the suffering which women experience when their bodies do not meet the standards of conventional femininity. She uncovers the diversity of expensive and painful rituals which women routinely undertake in the name of beauty.

According to Chapkis, the cultivation of appearance is one of the primary ways that gender difference is created and maintained. Beauty belongs to the sex/gender system (Rubin 1975), whereby both sexes negotiate conflicts between gender identity and anatomical reality through the alteration of appearance.[8] For example, the mustached woman contemplates depilatories or electrolysis to avoid being addressed as "sir." The small-chested woman receives a breast augmentation in the hopes that she will feel more "womanly." The professional woman dresses for power, while looking for ways to maintain a "feminine look." Men, too, must toe the line, however. The short man wears elevator shoes or takes up body building; the balding man buys a toupee or has a hair transplant. In short, gender and appearance are mutually sustaining.

Like other proponents of the oppression model, Chapkis employs a top-down model of power. She treats the beauty system as a repressive collection of structures and practices which work through the mechanism of internalized oppression. Women are lulled into believing that by controlling their bodies they can control their lives. They are compelled to conform with standards of feminine beauty which are not only impossible to meet, but have to be met, paradoxically, "naturally" – that is, without effort or artifice. Herein lies the most pernicious feature of most beauty rituals: they are performed in secrecy. For the feminist, of course, such rituals are especially shameful. Knowing that the beauty norms are oppressive and yet hopelessly caught up in them herself, she is in for double trouble. As Chapkis notes, describing her own experiences with electrolysis:

> I am a feminist. How humiliated I then feel. I am a woman. How ugly I
> have been made to feel. I have failed on both counts.
>
> (Chapkis 1986: 2)

Despite women's entrapment in the beauty system, Chapkis is convinced that
there are possibilities for change. She illustrates this optimism with instances of
women who manage to find ways to beat the system – for example, by dressing to
please themselves or celebrating their wrinkles, flat chests, or stretch marks. The key
to liberation lies in women casting aside the oppressive yoke of femininity – and along
with it their own self-defeating obsession with beauty – and accepting themselves and
their bodies as they really are. This means breaking the silence and subjecting our
beauty secrets to a clear-headed feminist analysis.

The major strength of Chapkis's analysis and, more generally, the oppression
model from which she draws, resides in placing a hitherto privatized phenomenon like
beauty on the political agenda. She shows why beauty is relevant for all women –
including feminists. Appearance is one of the central ways that gender difference is
constituted in a sexually, racially, and economically divided society. By drawing upon
women's personal experiences, Chapkis makes a convincing case for the importance
of linking the structural and cultural constraints of the beauty system to women's
lived experiences with their bodies. She situates resistance to the beauty system in
refusal and provides examples of individual women who, indeed, manage to free
themselves from the dominant norms of feminine beauty. Although her solution to
women's beauty problems is utopian – a feminist aesthetic of appearance – her
portrayal of their everyday struggles indicates that even in a context of oppression
there are always some possibilities for action.

Beauty as cultural discourse

Like Chapkis, Susan Bordo assumes that beauty cannot be understood without taking
gender and power into account. She does not immediately link the feminine quest for
beauty to oppression, however. Instead she focusses on images of the female body as a
site for exploring how gender/power relations are constituted in Western culture
(Bordo 1993). Drawing upon Foucauldian notions on power, Bordo treats the female
body as a kind of text which can be "read as a cultural statement, a statement about
gender" (Bordo 1989: 16). In order to understand why women are preoccupied with
their appearance, she describes several intersecting cultural discourses, showing
how they converge in contemporary bodily phenomena associated with femininity –
hysteria, eating disorders, agoraphobia, and the more routine beauty practices like
dieting and body building (Bordo 1988; 1989; 1990b; 1990c).[9]

The first discourse centres around the mind–body dualism which permeates
Western thought, dividing human experience into a bodily and a spiritual realm. The
female body becomes a metaphor for the corporeal pole of this dualism. Images of the
dangerous, appetitive female body, ruled precariously by its emotions, stands in
contrast to the masterful, masculine will, the locus of social power, rationality, and
self-control. The female body is always the "other": mysterious, inferior, threatening
to erupt at any moment and challenge the patriarchal order (Bordo 1990a: 103).

The second discourse focusses on the preoccupation with control and mastery in highly industralized Western societies. Like the sociologists mentioned earlier, Bordo situates the explosion of techniques for body maintenance or improvement in the "collective cultural fantasy" that death and decay can be defeated and an increasingly unmanageable culture brought under control (Bordo 1988: 100). The notion that the body can be controlled through a little will power ("mind over matter") sustains power relations between the sexes. Women believe that by controlling or containing their bodies and their appetites, they can escape the pernicious cycle of insufficiency, of never being good enough. Moreover, by controlling their bodies they can take on "male" power – power-as-self-mastery (Bordo 1990a). Thus, women paradoxically feel empowered or liberated by the very beauty norms and practices which constrain and enslave them.

The third discourse focusses on femininity. The female body is a medium through which different cultural discourses of femininity are expressed. Whereas the norms for femininity, and by implication, beauty and how women should adorn or alter their bodies, have varied immensely, the discourse of feminine beauty works to erase differences between women under the homogenizing banner that any body will do (as long as it is different than the one you have.) For example, corn-rows on the unimpeachably white Bo Derek lend an "exotic touch of Otherness" while a black woman is magnanimously offered the "choice" of having her hair straightened. This ostensible sameness in opportunity ignores a history of racist body discriminations and acerbates inequalities based on ethnicity, class, or sexuality (Bordo 1990b: 659). The erasure of specific cultural meanings robs beauty practices of their political significance and makes them ideally suited to the normalization of femininity in all its forms.

Bordo is more pessimistic than Chapkis about women being able to beat the system. Their preoccupation with beauty is not something to be shed with a little feminist rhetoric along the lines of accepting the "real me," that autonomous feminist subject lurking underneath or outside the constraints of culture. Women are embedded in and, indeed, cannot help but collude in the beauty system which oppresses them. Gender power is oblivious to the goals and motivations of individual women. As feminist strategy, Bordo advocates analyzing the "collusions, subversions, and enticements through which culture enjoins the aid of our bodies in the reproduction of gender" and recovering the body as a "political battleground for feminist practice" (Bordo 1989: 28). It is not at all clear, however, how any practices, feminist or otherwise, might escape the hegemony of cultural discourses in which the female body is enmeshed. While Bordo distances herself from an exclusive focus on cultural representations of the body to the detriment of women's practical relationship to their bodies, she remains oriented to how women collude or comply with the norms and practices of feminine beauty.[10] It is easy to lose sight of how women manage, individually or collectively, to resist or even subvert the beauty system.

The major strength of Bordo's analysis resides in her sophisticated framework for linking individual beauty practices to a broader context of power and gender hierarchies. By analyzing the complex and contradictory workings of cultural discourses around the body, control, and femininity, Bordo shows why women are especially susceptible to the lures of the beauty system. Since women do not stand outside culture, Bordo makes a convincing case for why feminists have to be suspicious of the possibility of discovering an authentic feminine self who is able to free herself from the constraints of the beauty system. She alerts us to how women's attempts to liberate themselves are continually in danger of being reabsorbed into repressive discourses of femininity.

In conclusion, feminist perspectives take social scientific explanations for women's concern with their appearance a step further. The feminine predilection for body improvement is not reduced to undesirable role behavior, to be shed with a little more willpower. Nor is women's concern with their appearance relegated to an immutable and pathological feature of femininity itself. The feminine beauty system is not simply a gender-neutral artefact of consumer capitalism, the feminization of culture, or of the contradictions of modernity; it is central to the production of relations of domination and subordination as well. By adding gender and power to their theoretical frameworks, feminist approaches can uncover why women engage in the beauty system and how their participation perpetuates the constraints and disciplinary effects of femininity without blaming them for their collusion. Both the oppression and the cultural discourse perspectives on beauty provide valuable insights into why women persist in improving or altering their bodies despite the dangers and drawbacks of most beauty practices. For this reason, they are foundational for analyzing women's involvement in cosmetic surgery. At the same time, however, they leave several questions unanswered. It is to these questions that I now turn.

The problem of the cultural dope

I began this book with a story about my own discomfort and puzzlement when a feminist friend informed me that she wanted to have cosmetic surgery. Confronted with the contradiction between my critical stance toward cosmetic surgery as dangerous and demeaning for women and my desire to take my friend at her word that it was, nevertheless, the best course of action for her under the circumstances, I looked to feminist theory for help. I wanted to take my friend's reasons for having cosmetic surgery seriously without condoning cosmetic surgery as a practice. While contemporary feminist scholarship on beauty enables me to be critical of cosmetic surgery and the beauty system it sustains, it falls short when it comes to making sense of my friend's experience. For example, how can I reconcile her determination and even exhilaration at having decided to have cosmetic surgery with her knowledge of its risks and dangers? How can I explain that she avidly subscribes to the feminist case against the beauty system and yet defends cosmetic surgery as the only solution to her own problems with her appearance? How can I take her suffering seriously, without undermining as mistaken or misguided her decision to alleviate this suffering?

The feminist approaches described above do not do justice to these kinds of questions – questions which concern women's active and knowledgeable involvement in practices which are also detrimental and/or degrading to them. Despite their differences, both oppression and cultural discourse models of beauty account for such ambivalencies by assuming that women who choose to have cosmetic surgery do so because they have had the ideological wool pulled over their eyes. They are cultural dopes.[11]

It is my contention that there are (at least) three reasons why a cultural-dope approach to beauty obstructs an understanding of women's involvement with cosmetic surgery.

First, it reinforces dualistic conceptions of feminine embodiment. Contemporary feminist theory has paid considerable critical attention to the masculinist under-pinnings of epistemologies which split mind from body (Jaggar and Bordo 1989). Ironically, however, women's active and lived relationship to their bodies seems to disappear in feminist accounts. Cosmetic surgery becomes a strangely disembodied phenomenon, devoid of women's experiences, feelings, and practical activities with regard to their bodies. Without embodied subjects, there is no space for experiences of excitement or triumph which might be part of the act of altering one's body surgically. Cosmetic surgery can only be a transformation of the body as object, never as self.

Second, it rests on a faulty conception of agency. Whether women are viewed as oppressed victims of patriarchal capitalism or as embedded in the cultural discourses of feminine inferiority, cosmetic surgery cannot be explored as something which can, at least in part, be actively and knowledgeably chosen. Women's actions can only be construed as compliance, serving to reproduce the conditions of their subservience. It is impossible to even entertain the possibility that cosmetic surgery might be a solution for a particular woman under the circumstances.

Third, it ignores the moral contradictions in women's justificatory practices. Given the totalizing and pernicious character of the feminine beauty system, women's reasons tend to be heard as ideologically contaminated, having nothing of relevance to offer for a feminist response to cosmetic surgery. By ignoring how women defend, legitimate, but also criticize their decision to have cosmetic surgery, those feminist approaches make it difficult to imagine not only what tips the scales in favor of cosmetic surgery, but also what makes the surgery problematic for the recipients themselves. Feminist intervention in cosmetic surgery becomes restricted, on the one hand, to the moralistic strategy of propagating self-acceptance in the hope that women will see the error of their ways or, on the other, to waiting until some miraculous shifting in the discursive constellations enables this particularly nasty cultural phe-nomenon to make way for other – less oppressive, it is hoped – cultural practices.

In conclusion, while contemporary feminist scholarship has made a strong case for linking beauty to an analysis of femininity and power, it has been less successful in finding ways to understand women's lived experience with their bodies, how they actually decide to have cosmetic surgery, and how they access their actions after the fact. Thus, my brief foray into feminist scholarship on beauty leaves me with a problem. While I am now armed with a critical perspective on cosmetic surgery, I am left empty-handed in terms of how to take women who have cosmetic surgery ser-iously. In order to avoid relegating women who have cosmetic surgery to the position of cultural dopes, I would need to be able to explore their lived relationship to their bodies, to recast them as agents, and to analyze the contradictions in how they justify their decision to have cosmetic surgery.

I found the theoretical antidote I was looking for in the work of Iris Young, Dorothy Smith, and Sandra Bartky. Each has dealt with the practices and discourses of the feminine beauty system. Although they also draw – albeit somewhat eclectically – from the oppression and cultural discourse perspectives described above, they avoid the pitfalls of a cultural-dope approach to beauty. Although they do not explicitly deal with cosmetic surgery – and, indeed, stop short in applying their theoretical insights to that particular phenomenon – they provide the theoretical building blocks for a critical analysis of women's involvement with cosmetic surgery without undermining the women who decide to have it.

Embodied subjects

The political theorist Iris Marion Young (1990a; 1990b) provides a theoretical framework for understanding how women negotiate a sense of self in relation to their bodies. Drawing upon phenomenological theories of embodiment (Merleau-Ponty, Sartre, de Beauvoir), she explores the typical tensions of feminine embodiment as women attempt to become embodied subjects rather than "mere bodies."[12] On the one hand, women participate in a gendered social order where they are continually defined through their bodies. The female body is the perennial object of the intentions and manipulations of others. Women often adopt this attitude themselves, viewing their own bodies at a distance through the critical eyes of others.[13] It is easy for women to feel "mired in materiality," to experience their own body as a thing or as an encumbrance to their projects (Young 1990b: 155). On the other hand, women, like men, experience their bodies as vehicles for enacting their desires or reaching out in the world. Whereas they do not transcend their bodies as men presumably can, as subjects women can never be entirely satisfied with a rendition of themselves as nothing but a body.[14] This tension accounts for the unease many women experience with their bodies and, through their bodies, with themselves.

> [B]ecause she is a human existence, the female person necessarily is a subjectivity and transcendence, and she knows herself to be. The female person who enacts the existence of women in patriarchal society must therefore live a contradiction: as human she is a free subject who participates in transcendence, but her situation as a woman denies her that subjectivity and transcendence.
>
> (Young 1990b: 144)

Young takes the tension between the female body as object and the embodied feminine subject as a theoretical starting point for understanding women's everyday struggles with their bodies and imagining how this tension might provide possibilities for subverting or disrupting the objectification of women's bodies. Her analysis of the feminine experience of "being breasted" is a case in point, particularly in view of the rising incidence of cosmetic breast surgery (Young 1990b: 189–209). In Western culture, breasts are probably the most visible symbol of femininity and, therefore, central to women's identity and bodily self. More than any other body part, breasts are "up for judgement," problematic, and subject to various forms of correction, ranging from the padded bra to the surgical lift or augmentation (Young 1990b: 190). Breasts are also a source of pleasure for women, a part of their body which distances them – at least in part – from the cultural norms of beauty. "However much the patriarchy may wish us to, we do not live our breasts only as the objects of male desire, but as our own, the sproutings of a specifically female desire" (Young 1990b: 192). Women's breasted experience can disrupt the patriocentric dichotomization of mothering and female sexuality, for example, in the experience of nursing where the image of the nurturant, giving mother is united with the image of the sexual, desirous woman who takes her pleasures without a man. Thus, Young's analysis shows that breasts do not have to be viewed as symbols of women's objectification, but can be seen as a source of empowerment and subversion as well.

Young's notion of feminine embodiment enables me to situate women's experience of their bodies as potential objects for surgical manipulation in a broader context of the tensions of feminine embodiment in Western culture. I can explore cosmetic surgery as symptomatic of a culture where it is possible to view one's body as separate from who one is or would like to become and as site, particularly for women, to negotiate their identities in a context of structured hierarchies of power. Cosmetic surgery becomes both an expression of the objectification of the female body and of women's struggles to become embodied subjects rather than mere bodies.

Secret agents

The sociologist Dorothy Smith (1990b) is concerned with femininity as an active and knowledgeable accomplishment of the female agent. Like Chapkis, Smith situates women's dissatisfaction with their appearance as well as their involvement in the beauty system in the context of patriarchal and capitalist relations of ruling. Women's energies and activities are channeled into the all-consuming business of creating an acceptable feminine appearance, while, at the same time, waiting passively and with apprehension for the male stamp of approval. Smith rejects the notion, however, that women blindly internalize the dictates of femininity. On the contrary, women are always agents – agents who, as she puts it, "give power to the relations that 'overpower' them" (Smith 1990b: 161). Like Bordo, Smith treats femininity as a discourse. However, she is not primarily concerned with cultural discourses per se, but rather with the ways that femininity is discursively mediated through women's practical activities.[15] While femininity is textually mediated, women are not simply entangled in its discourses; they have to actively "do femininity."

Smith shows how even the most mundane texts – for example, an advertisement, a fashion photo, or instructions for cosmetics – require complex and skilled interpretative activities on the part of the female agent. For example, in order to create an acceptable appearance according to the current norms of femininity, a woman must possess specialized knowledge about makeup and fashion. She must be able to indexically imagine how her present body looks as well as how it would look following the application of a particular product or procedure. She has to plan a course of action, making a series of on-the-spot calculations about whether the rigorous discipline required by the techniques of body improvement will actually improve her appearance given the specifics of her particular body. In short, she has to know what she is doing for the text to have any impact at all (Smith 1990b: 201).

Smith does not limit agency to women's ability to process texts on feminine beauty, however. She shows how the texts themselves are organized around the notion of a female agent. By projecting an ideal image of the female body (perfect skin, slender figure, expensive clothing), a woman is confronted with the imperfections of her own body. Dissatisfaction breeds the desire for transformation, for a different body than the one she has. At the same time, the text instructs her in how her body can be improved upon. The body is remediable, once the female agent has discovered how to go about it.

> Discontent with the body is not just a happening of culture, it arises in the relation between text and she who finds in texts images reflecting upon the imperfections of her body. The interpenetration of text as discourse and the organization of desire is reflexive. The text instructs her that her breasts are too small/too big; she reads of a remedy; her too small breasts become remediable. She enters the discursive organization of desire; now she has an objective where before she had only a defect.
>
> (Smith 1990b: 185–186)

The female agent is the sine qua non of the feminine beauty system. Without agency, texts would fail to motivate women to participate in activities of body improvement. By creating a gap between a woman's perceived bodily deficiency and an objective which promises to overcome it, her dissatisfaction becomes an active process. Rather than immobilizing women, bodily imperfections provide the opportunity for action. Women relate to their bodies as objects – not as sex objects for others – but rather as objects of work, as something to be improved, fixed, or transformed. While women cultivate the appearance of beauty without effort and adopt a passive attitude of waiting until the masculine subject finds them attractive, such appearances are deceiving. In reality, women are agents, albeit secret ones.

> There is a secret agent behind the subject in the gendered discourse of femininity; she has been at work to produce the feminine subject-in-discourse whose appearance when read by the doctrines of femininity transfers agency to the man.
>
> (Smith 1990b: 202)

Smith's notion of agency allows me to tackle several issues concerning women's involvement in cosmetic surgery which are obscured by a cultural-dope approach to beauty. I can explore women's decisions to alter their bodies surgically in the context of their having to "do femininity." I can begin to look at how they actively and knowledgeably transform the texts of femininity into a desire for cosmetic surgery. Cosmetic surgery becomes viewable as a possible remedy – a way for women to do something about their dissatisfaction. And, finally, I can explore the decision to have cosmetic surgery as a way for women to take action – paradoxically, perhaps, to become female agents.

Ontological shocks

The feminist philosopher Sandra Bartky (1990) has offered a penetrating analysis of how women actually grapple with femininity as moral actors rather than the victims of false consciousness. Like Smith, she regards agency and the sense of mastery which accompany women's involvement in the beauty system as essential to femininity. And, like Young, she draws upon phenomenological frameworks to explore how women's struggles with femininity might actually feel. Unlike Smith and Young, however, Bartky is particularly concerned with how women become embroiled in the moral contradictions posed by practices which are both desirable and denigrating, seductive and disempowering (Bartky 1990: 2). Taking the prototypical experiences of masochism, narcissism, and shame as objects for her analysis, she shows how women's everyday struggles to make sense of needs which are in conflict with their (feminist) principles can be a resource for a critical intervention in the oppressive practices of femininity.

Her analysis of shame is a case in point. Shame is one of the most profoundly disempowering features of feminine experience. It is the gut-level sense of being flawed or at fault which structures a woman's image of her body, her perception of who she is, her interactions with others, and her capacity to move about freely in the world. It can be read in women's bodily demeanor: their hunched shoulders, bowed heads, hollowed chests, or flushed faces. Without being linked to a specific act or a negative reaction, it evokes silence, hiding, evasion, and the "confused and divided consciousness" which sabotages women's intentions and politics (Bartky 1990: 93–94). In short, shame is the feminine emotion par excellence.

In view of this pervasive sense of bodily deficiency, it is not surprising that women become committed to the rituals and practices of body improvement: the "sacraments" which provide "the closest thing to a state of grace" (Bartky 1990: 41). Femininity is a need which is no less real for being repressive. Despite the "repressive satisfactions" of femininity and the "fashion-beauty complex," women would feel lost and abandoned without them.

The experience of having to make sense of needs which are both heartfelt and harmful is morally unsettling, however. The contradictory lures and oppressions of femininity can be experienced as "ontological shocks" – that is, disjunctures between a woman's values and beliefs and her practical or lived consciousness of being-in-the-world, between how she thinks she *should* feel and how she, in fact, *does* feel.[16]

Bartky is critical of attempts to resolve these troublesome ontological contradictions discursively – for example, by propagating the freedom of the individual to "do her own thing" without concern for the structural constraints of femininity or by providing a radical code of ethics for feminist behavior "which divides women within the movement and alienates those outside of it" (Bartky 1990: 61). Both solutions are inadequate for coming to terms with women's struggles as moral actors to make sense of the troubling or painful dimensions of their experiences. She proposes instead an approach which takes women's "ambiguous ethical situation" (Bartky 1990: 20) as an opportunity for reflection and, ultimately, for "exorcising one's own demons."[17] Although Bartky's approach might be seen as pessimistic and non-utopian, it offers a program for feminist analysis which is grounded in women's everyday moral experience in a gendered social order.[18]

In conclusion, Bartky's work is useful for uncovering women's ambivalence concerning cosmetic surgery. It can help me pinpoint the ways that a woman's gut-level sense of bodily deficiency might sabotage her reservations about cosmetic surgery as well as her critical stance toward the feminine beauty system in general, enabling me to understand what makes cosmetic surgery both desirable and morally problematic for the recipients themselves. I can treat women's ongoing struggles to justify a contradictory practice like cosmetic surgery as a resource for developing a feminist response which speaks to women's experiences rather than simply reiterating the correct line on women's involvement in the beauty system.

Taken together, the work of Young, Smith, and Bartky provide the theoretical tools necessary for a feminist analysis of cosmetic surgery which avoids viewing recipients as the duped and passive victims of the feminine beauty system. They show that embodiment, agency, and moral contradictions are central to understanding women's problems with their appearance as well as their decisions to have their bodies altered surgically. Interestingly, none of these authors extend their theoretical insights to women's involvement in cosmetic surgery. While their reluctance to explore this particular phenomenon is somewhat puzzling [. . .] I see no reason why their theoretical insights concerning embodiment, agency, and women's struggles with morally problematic practices might not be applied to understanding cosmetic surgery. Drawing upon feminist perspectives on femininity, power, and the cultural norms and practices of the beauty system, I attempt an analysis of cosmetic surgery which is critical without undermining the women who have it. Before getting started on this endeavor, however, let me leave feminist theory for the moment and take a brief look at some feminist fiction as – paradoxically – a way to get closer to the facts of women's involvement in cosmetic surgery.

The demise of the cultural dope

Fay Weldon's *The Life & Loves of a She-Devil* is a feminist satire about cosmetic surgery. The heroine of the story, Ruth, is a fat, ugly, middle-aged housewife, mother, and drudge, whose husband Bobo leaves her for Mary Fisher – rich, beautiful, successful, and, of course, thin. Initially devastated, Ruth gathers together her courage and decides to get even. Her revenge involves, among other things, a series of cosmetic surgery operations. Over a period of several years, she has her entire body remade surgically, transforming her into a beautiful woman and enabling her to vanquish her rival. She exacts her revenge, winning her husband back. This time, however, he is a broken man who is firmly and irrevocably under her thumb.

Weldon's novel leaves the reader with several puzzles. It is a feminist novel about sexual politics, replete with shocking examples of female oppression and male treachery. However, it a tale with a surprising twist – a female protagonist who wins; that is, who comes out on top in the battle of the sexes. It is the story of a woman who suffers to such an extent under cultural norms of feminine beauty that she is willing to undergo the pain and expense of cosmetic surgery to alter every part of her body. However, the heroine also uses cosmetic surgery as a source of empowerment, a way to regain control over her life. Ruth is both a victim of the feminine beauty system and one of its most devastating critics. Her decision to undergo cosmetic surgery supports the status quo of feminine inferiority, while, at the same time, it shifts the power balance – temporarily, at least – in her own relationships.

Ruth could, of course, be discarded as merely a fictional character, hardly representative of women who really undergo cosmetic surgery. Her quest for power and beauty then would become just another instance of feminist (science) fiction, to be enjoyed but otherwise ignored. However, before relegating Weldon's heroine to the world of make-believe, I propose taking the imaginary more seriously. It is my contention that her book contains some important lessons about why women might insist upon altering their bodies surgically, even at great cost to themselves – lessons that could profitably be incorporated in feminist accounts of femininity and beauty.

To begin with, Weldon's tale is a bitter commentary on the constraints of normal femininity as well as the institution of heterosexual love. Discussing her plans to have cosmetic surgery, Ruth compares herself to Hans Christian Andersen's little mermaid:

> I am paying with physical pain. Hans Andersen's little mermaid wanted legs instead of a tail, so that she could be properly loved by her Prince. She was given legs, and by inference the gap where they join at the top, and after that, every step she took was like stepping on knives.
>
> (Weldon 1983: 148)

This is a fairy tale which links, as no other, women's subordination in heterosexual relationships with beauty. It is about women's compliance with the beauty system and their willingness to undergo terrible suffering for the love of a man. The tale has a subtext, however. It is also a story about feminine wiles and subterfuge – the woman who applies deceit knowledgeably and with forethought in order to get her way. The little mermaid knows the rules of the game and plays by them. So, too, does Ruth.

> "Of course it hurts," she said. "It's meant to hurt. Anything that's worth achieving has its price. And, by corollary, if you are prepared to pay that price you can achieve almost anything".
>
> (Weldon 1983: 148)

This is no cultural dope, blinded by social forces beyond her control or comprehension. She does not see cosmetic surgery as the perfect solution and she is well aware of the enormous price for women who undertake it. Under the circumstances, however, it is the best she can do. For she knows only too well that the context of structured gender inequality makes this solution – as perhaps any solution – at best, a temporary one. In other words, she plays the game, assessing the situation with its structural constraints and making her choices, knowledgeably, within the context in which she lives. She knows what she wants, but, at the same time, she knows how limited her choices are. Within the context in which she lives, Ruth makes her choices – perhaps not freely, but at least knowledgeably.

Cosmetic surgery thus becomes a resource of sorts in the power struggle between the sexes. Whereas no one (including Ruth herself) particularly likes the means to the end, it cannot be denied that, by the time the book comes to a close, Ruth has a better bargaining position than she had earlier. She not only has more control over her immediate circumstances, but she has gained a different perspective on her future. As she notes at the end of the book, it was, after all, just a matter of power: "I have all, and he has none. As I was, so he is now." (Weldon 1983: 240). In this way, Weldon's novel offers a scathing portrayal of the feminine beauty norms without reducing women to the position of deluded victim. Her protagonist is a "she-devil" and, if we might wish her a better life, the matter of her agency cannot be ignored.

Weldon's portrayal of cosmetic surgery provides a view of the subject which does not fit into feminist perspectives on beauty. Ruth is neither as embedded as Bordo would have us believe, nor has she liberated herself along the lines that Chapkis would suggest. Caught off guard by a literary ploy – "a comic turn, turned serious" (Weldon 1983: 240) – the reader must begin, perhaps in spite of herself, to entertain issues that tend to be skipped over in the more straightforward rhetoric of academic feminism. Previously held notions of the docile female, trapped by the constraints of beauty, are forgotten – at least for the moment – in favor of a vision where women as knowledgeable agents and cosmetic surgery can go together. By combining the contradictory and disturbing dimensions of cosmetic surgery with a feminist critique of the power relations between the sexes, Weldon shows how ambivalencies can be embraced rather than dismissed or avoided. It is precisely at this point of discomfort – our own and other women's – that a feminist analysis of cosmetic surgery needs to begin. We need to find ways to explore cosmetic surgery as a complex and dilemmatic situation for women: problem and solution, oppression and liberation, all in one.

Notes

1   This critique does not apply to feminist approaches to narcissism which place it in the context of the social constraints of femininity and power relations between the sexes. See, for example, Bartky (1982); Garry (1982); and La Belle (1988). Lasch (1979) also situates narcissism in a broader context by linking it to modernity and the problems of the the promiscuous and bored individual in search of intimacy and eternal life. See also Giddens (1991; 1993).

2   Frank also gives feminism some credit for bringing bodies back in. Feminist scholarship on the body has also struggled with the legacy of modernity in the face of the postmodern turn. Moreover, feminist perspectives on beauty generally situate beauty practices in Western consumer culture. Both sociological and feminist perspectives share a concern for how the social order is reproduced in the individual's embodied social experience. I will be considering feminist scholarship, including the split between modernist and postmodernist traditions, in the next section.

3   This point is made by sociologists who proclaim that we have entered the age of the postmodern as well as those who claim we are still hovering in the final stages of modernity. See Giddens (1990).

4   The point has been made – and it is an apt one – that, despite the centrality of the body in postmodern theory, material bodies seem to have disappeared altogether. The body is used to stand in for something else – the opposite of reason, the

incarnate Feminine, or whatever. This same critique applies to much feminist postmodern theory of the body. See, for example, a recent issue of *Hypatia* on feminist theory and the body as case in point. See also note ten in this chapter.

5   Like Featherstone, Giddens is more likely to emphasize that this imbalance is changing (1991: 105–106) or even that women have already succeeded in transforming themselves (Giddens, 1992).

6   Naomi Wolf (1991) does not belong to the group of second-wave feminists who were originally concerned with beauty. However, she does make similar arguments in her critique and, indeed, calls for a "feminist third wave" and some "generational mending" if we are to overcome the damage inflicted upon women by the beauty myth.

7   I have borrowed the terms "oppression model" and "discourse model" from Komter (1991) who has analyzed them in the context of recent developments in feminist theory in general. See also Davis (1991b).

8   Chapkis is one of the only theorists on beauty who link women's preoccupation with appearance to the struggles of transsexuals with their bodies. The theme of the ordinary body in a gendered social order links the experiences of women who have cosmetic surgery with those of transsexuals who have sex change operations.

9   I have translated Bordo's (1988: 90) term "axis" as "discourse." She uses axes to refer to "cultural streams or currents" which converge in a particular phenomenon. By exploring their interconnections we can understand why contemporary feminine disorders of the body emerge at this particular point in time, as well as make historical connections.

10 Bordo (1990b) is somewhat ambivalent about theorizing resistance. She is critical of postmodern cultural critiques which treat the body as a playground for experimenting with different subjectivities, while losing sight of the political valence of the options open to different groups. Moreover, she rejects the tendency within contemporary feminist theory to explore cultural representations of the female body without their relation to women's lived bodies. While she sees possibilities for resistance, she does not explore them herself.

11 This term was coined by Harold Garfinkel (1967) in criticism of functionalist or Parsonian conceptions of agency where the human actor has so completely internalized the norms and values of society that his or her activities become limited to acting out a predetermined script.

12 It is the contribution of the existential phenomenology of Merleau-Ponty and Sartre to discard the notion that the human mind is the locus of consciousness and the body the locus of experience. Instead, the subject is situated in the world and it is through this physical being-in-the-world, the "lived body," that we can act upon and give shape to our situations. According to existential phenomenology, it is the international or active capacity of reaching out into the world which enables us to transcend the body and to structure our situations, thereby becoming subjects. It is de Beauvoir's notable contribution to existential phenomenology to point out that subjectivities are structured by the situations in which we live. For women, the historical context of our subordination makes it difficult for us to transcend our bodies, to reach out, and, ultimately therefore, to become subjects. In addition to Young (1990b), see Allen and Young (1989), and Butler (1987) for a further discussion of feminist appropriations of phenomenology.

13   Young could be criticized for speaking of "typical" experiences of feminine embodiment – hers include throwing balls, pregnancy, or being breasted – given the enormous variability of bodily experience. She herself provides the necessary disclaimers, explaining that the tension between body as object and the subject acting on the world is a product of a specifically Western world view with its Platonic-Aristotelian doctrines of reason and substance and modernist conceptualization of a Cartesian egology (Young 1990b: 191). Nevertheless, her emphasis remains on the commonalities of embodied identities and on a politics of identity which focuses on collective difference rather than the particularities of individual body experience. See Young (1990a).

14   Obviously, men never fully transcend their bodies. The notion of the disembodied masculine subject – the mind without a body – is, like that of the objectified female body – the body without a mind – a fiction and has been amply criticized in feminist theory. See for example, Bordo 1987; Code 1991.

15   Although Smith claims a certain affinity with Foucauldian notions of discourse, she employs an ethnomethodological perspective which takes specific texts as a starting point for analyzing how people actually interpret texts and how these texts organize their interpretative practices.

16   In her discussion of racism, Young (1990a) makes a similar distinction between discursive consciousness and practical consciousness, whereby the former refers to aspects of experience which can be explicitly or easily verbalized and the latter to aspects of experience which are located at the fringe of a person's awareness. She uses this distinction to account for the involuntary aversion which members of dominant groups can experience toward other groups, even when this contradicts their conscious commitment to egalitarianism.

17   Bartky (1990: 10) uses this expression to refer to her own task as philosopher as well as to ordinary women's struggles with the contradictions of femininity. In her framework, any woman confronted with her demons and willing to reflect upon them should be able to engage in some feminist exorcism.

18   See, for example, a recent forum devoted to Bartky's work in *Hypatia*, (8 [1], 1993) where responses were mixed concerning her pessimistic approach toward transformation, ranging from regret that Bartky had neglected to provide "constructive suggestions of ways out from under" (Mickett 1993: 173) to praise that her analysis places estrangement and self-reflection at its center rather than a naive call for change based on a feminist identity politics (Bar On 1993a: 161).

Chapter 32

Lawrence Grossberg

IS THERE A FAN IN THE HOUSE?
The affective sensibility of fandom

THERE IS SOMETHING ODD about 'fans.' I remember when I began teaching university classes on rock-and-roll, a number of colleagues tried to sabotage them, by arguing that such forms of culture did not belong in the university curriculum. When this argument was defeated, they took a different strategy: they argued that, as a fan of rock, I was not the appropriate person to teach the class. While I disagreed with their implicit assumption that fans could not have any critical distance, I was fascinated by their insight that, somehow, being a fan entails a very different relationship to culture, a relationship which seems only to exist in the realm of popular culture. For example, while we can consume or appreciate various forms of 'high culture' or art, it makes little sense to describe someone as a fan of art. How, then, do we understand what it means to be a fan? The easiest answer, one that I reject, is that it is all a matter of what forms of and relationships to culture are legitimated within the existing relations of power. This assumes that it is all a matter of status and that there are no real distinctions that mark the 'fan.'

How then do we look for those distinctions? One way would be to consider what differences if any define the sorts of texts that fans are fans of. Or in other words, we can try to understand what makes popular culture popular? The question seems innocent enough but, as soon as we begin to look for an answer, we are confronted only by ambiguity and uncertainty. What is it, after all, that we are attempting to explain? Is it a matter of aesthetic or moral criteria which define the differences between popular texts and other forms of cultural texts (for example, high culture, mass culture, folk culture)? But history has shown us that texts move in and out of these categories (for example, what was popular can become high art), and that a text can exist, simultaneously, in different categories. There are no necessary correspondences between the formal characteristics of any text and its popularity, and the standards for aesthetic legitimacy are constantly changing. Is it then a matter of where the text comes from, of how and by whom it is produced? But again, there are too many exceptions to this assumed correlation. The mode by which a text is produced, or the motivations behind it, do not guarantee how it is placed into the larger cultural context nor how it is received by different audiences. So perhaps the answer to our question is the most obvious one: what makes something popular is its popularity; it is, in other words, a matter of taste. This formulation begins to point us away from the texts, and toward the audiences of popular cultures. But, in the end, it does not help us very much, for the same questions remain, albeit in different forms: how much popularity? whose tastes? and what do different tastes signify?

A second approach attempts to begin by characterizing the particular sorts of people who become fans, and the basis on which their relationship to popular culture is constructed. In this model, it is often assumed that popular culture appeals to the lowest and least critical segments of the population. These audiences are thought to be easily manipulated and distracted (not only from 'serious' culture but also from real social concerns), mobilized solely to make a profit. The various forms of popular culture appeal to the audience's most debased needs and desires, making them even more passive, more ignorant and noncritical than they apparently already are. Fans are simply incapable of recognizing that the culture they enjoy is actually being used to dupe and exploit them. A second, related view of fans assumes that they are always juveniles, waiting to grow up, and still enjoying the irresponsibility of their fandom.

For many years, the only alternative to this image of fans as cultural dopes came from various arguments that divided the audience for popular culture into two groups: the larger segment is still assumed to be cultural dopes who passively consume the texts of popular culture. But there is another segment, much smaller and more dispersed, who actively appropriate the texts of specific popular cultures, and give them new and original significance. For example, one small part of the audience for comic books or popular music might approach such forms as art; or another group might take them to be the expression of their own lived experience. And still others may use them to resist the pressures of their social position and to construct new identities for themselves. According to this 'subcultural' model, any of these groups would be considered fans; fans constitute an elite fraction of the larger audience of passive consumers. Within this model, the fan is able to discriminate between those forms of popular culture which are 'authentic' (that is, which really are art, which really do represent their experience, etc.) and those which are the result of the efforts of the commercial mainstream to appropriate these forms and produce tainted versions for the larger audience. Thus, the fan is always in constant conflict, not only with the various structures of power, but also with the vast audience of media consumers. But such an elitist view of fandom does little to illuminate the complex relations that exist between forms of popular culture and their audiences. While we may all agree that there is a difference between the fan and the consumer, we are unlikely to understand the difference if we simply celebrate the former category and dismiss the latter one.

We have to acknowledge that, for the most part, the relationship between the audience and popular texts is an active and productive one. The meaning of a text is not given in some independently available set of codes which we can consult at our own convenience. A text does not carry its own meaning or politics already inside of itself; no text is able to guarantee what its effects will be. People are constantly struggling, not merely to figure out what a text means, but to make it mean something that connects to their own lives, experiences, needs and desires. The same text will mean different things to different people, depending on how it is interpreted. And different people have different interpretive resources, just as they have different needs. A text can only mean something in the context of the experience and situation of its particular audience. Equally important, texts do not define ahead of time how they are to be used or what functions they can serve. They can have different uses for different people in different contexts. The same text can be a source of narrative romance, sexual fantasy, aesthetic pleasure, language acquisition, identity or familial rebellion. Given contemporary recording technology (whether audio or video), a text can be remade and even remixed to conform to the audience's expectations and desires. How a specific text is used, how it is interpreted, how it functions for its audience – all of these are inseparably connected through the audience's constant struggle to make sense of itself and its world, even more, to make a slightly better place for itself in the world.

Audiences are constantly making their own cultural environment from the cultural resources that are available to them. Thus, audiences are not made up of cultural dopes; people are often quite aware of their own implication in structures of power and domination, and of the ways in which cultural messages (can) manipulate them. Furthermore, the audience of popular culture cannot be conceived of as a singular homogeneous entity; we have to take seriously the differences within and between the different fractions of the popular audience.

This view of an active audience only makes it more difficult for us to understand the nature of fandom, for if all consumers are active, then there is nothing against which to measure the fan. Such views cannot explain the significance of the fact that some people pay attention to particular texts, in ways that demand particular sorts of interpretations, or that some texts are granted an importance and perhaps even a power denied to others. We need a different approach, then, to the question of fandom and popular culture. If we cannot locate a viable response in either the nature of the cultural forms or the audience, then perhaps it is necessary to look at the relations that exist between them. But we have to consider the relationship without falling back into theories which privilege either the text or the audience by giving one the power to determine the relationship. For even if it is true that audiences are always active, it does not follow that they are ever in control.

The relations between culture and audiences cannot be understood simply as the process by which people appropriate already existing texts into the already constituted context of their social position, their experience or their needs. Nor can it be described in terms which suggest that the audience is simply passively acceding to the predetermined nature of the text. In fact, both audiences and texts are continuously remade – their identity and effectiveness reconstructed – by relocating their place within different contexts. The audience is always caught up in the continuous reconstruction of cultural contexts which enable them to consume, interpret and use texts in specific ways. It is these 'specific ways' that concern us here.

Audiences never deal with single cultural texts, or even with single genres or media. Culture 'communicates' only in particular contexts in which a range of texts, practices and languages are brought together. The same text can and often will be located in a number of different contexts; in each, it will function as a different text and it will likely have different relations to and effects on its audience. For example, a typical context of rock-and-roll – and there are many of them at a single moment – brings together musical texts and practices, economic and race relations, images of performers and fans, social relations (for instance, of gender, of friendship), aesthetic conventions, styles of language, movement, appearance and dance, media practices, ideological commitments and, sometimes, media representations of rock-and-roll itself. It is within such contexts that the relations between audience members and cultural forms are defined.

We can call the particular relationship that holds any context together, that binds cultural forms and audiences, a 'sensibility.' A sensibility is a particular form of engagement or mode of operation. It identifies the specific sorts of effects that the elements within a context can produce; it defines the possible relationships between texts and audiences located within its spaces. The sensibility of a particular cultural context (an 'apparatus') defines how specific texts and practices can be taken up and experienced, how they are able to effect the audience's place in the world, and what sort of texts can be incorporated into the apparatus. Different apparatuses produce and foreground different sensibilities. This assumes that human life is multi-dimensional, and texts may, in various contexts, connect into certain dimensions more powerfully than others. There is, in fact, more to the organization of people's lives than just the distribution or structure of meaning, money and power.

I want now to describe the dominant sensibilities of contemporary popular culture in order to identify the sensibility within which fandom is located. Just as the same text can exist in different contexts and thus, different sensibilities, so too can different audience members. The different sensibilities are not mutually exclusive; people always exist in different sensibilities, and their relations to a particular set of cultural practices (for instance, rock-and-roll) may be defined by an overlapping set of sensibilities. Nevertheless, it may be useful to make some basic distinctions here.

The sensibility of the consumer operates by producing structures of pleasure. Of course, pleasure is itself a complex phenomenon, and there are many different relations operating in this notion of consumption: there is the satisfaction of doing what others would have you do, the enjoyment of doing what you want, the fun of breaking the rules, the fulfillment – however temporary and artificial – of desires, the release of catharsis, the comfort of escaping from negative situations, the reinforcement of identifying with a character, and the thrill of sharing another's emotional life, and so on. All of these are involved in the 'normal' and common relationship to popular culture and the mass media. We are engaged with forms of popular culture because, in some way and form, they are entertaining; they provide us with a certain measure of enjoyment and pleasure.

I am suggesting that our most common relationship to popular culture is determined by the cultural production of pleasures. But again, this consumerist sensibility rarely operates in total isolation. It is quite usual, for example, to find that such pleasures depend upon the production of other sorts of effects. The culture of the mass media often depends upon the production of meanings and, more specifically, of ideological representations. Ideology refers to the structures of meaning within which we locate ourselves. That is, ideologies are the maps of meaning which we take for granted as the obviously true pictures of the way the world is. By defining what is natural and commonsensical, ideologies construct the ways we experience the world. A consumerist sensibility might, in specific instances, be connected to ideological sensibilities, either by making certain experiences pleasurable, or through the pleasures of ideological reinforcement. Nevertheless, I still believe that the real source of the popularity of the culture of the mass media lies, not in its ideological effects, but in its location within a consumerist sensibility emphasizing the production of pleasure. We can find some evidence for this claim in the existence of a variant of the consumer relation, one that we might call the 'hyperconsumerist' sensibility. This describes the seemingly compulsive consumption of mass media, regardless of whether any actual single text provides pleasure. That is, hyperconsumerism describes the situation in which the very activity of consuming becomes more important, more pleasurable, more active as the site of the cultural relationship, than the object of consumption itself (for instance, 'couch potatoes,' collectors, and so on).

The category of the fan, however, can only be understood in relation to a different sensibility. The fan's relation to cultural texts operates in the domain of affect or mood. Affect is perhaps the most difficult plane of our lives to define, not merely because it is even less necessarily tied to meaning than pleasure, but also because it is, in some sense, the most mundane aspect of everyday life. Affect is not the same as either emotions or desires. Affect is closely tied to what we often describe as the feeling of life. You can understand another person's life: you can share the same meanings and pleasures, but you cannot know how it feels. But feeling, as it functions here, is not a subjective experience. It is a socially constructed domain of cultural effects. Some things feel different from others, some matter more, or in different ways, than others. The same experience will change drastically as our mood or feeling changes. The same object, with the same meaning, giving the same pleasure, is very different as our affective relationship to it changes. Or perhaps it is more accurate to say that different affective relations inflect meanings and pleasures in very different ways. Affect is what gives 'color,' 'tone' or 'texture' to our experiences.

Perhaps this can be made clearer if we distinguish two aspects of affect: quantity and quality. Affect always defines the quantitatively variable level of energy (activation, enervation) or volition (will); it determines how invigorated we feel in particular moments of our lives. It defines the strength of our investment in particular experiences, practices, identities, meanings, and pleasures. In other words, affect privileges volition over meaning. For example, as one ad campaign continuously declares, 'Where there's a will there's an "A".' But affect is also defined qualitatively, by the inflection of the particular investment, by the nature of the concern (caring, passion) in the investment, by the way in which the specific event is made to matter to us.

Within an affective sensibility, texts serve as 'billboards' of an investment, but we cannot know what the investment is apart from the context in which it is made (that is the apparatus). While critics generally recognize that meanings, and even desires, are organized into particular structures or maps, they tend to think of mood as formless and disorganized. But affect is also organized; it operates within and, at the same time, produces maps which direct our investments in and into the world; these maps tell us where and how we can become absorbed – not into the self but into the world – as potential locations for our self-identifications, and with what intensities. This 'absorption' or investment constructs the places and events which are, or can become, significant to us. They are the places at which we can construct our own identity as something to be invested in, as something that matters.

These mattering maps are like investment portfolios: there are not only different and changing investments, but different forms, as well as different intensities or degrees of investment. There are not only different places marked out (practices, pleasures, meanings, fantasies, desires, relations, and so on) but different purposes which these investments can play, and different moods in which they can operate. Mattering maps define different forms, quantities and places of energy. They tell us how to use and how to generate energy, how to navigate our way into and through various moods, and how to live within emotional and ideological histories. This is not to claim that all affective investments are equal or even equivalent; there are, at the very least, qualitative and quantitative differences among them.

The importance of affect derives, not from its content, but from its power over difference, its power to invest difference. Affect plays a crucial role in organizing social life because affect is constantly constructing, not only the possibility of difference, but the ways specific differences come to matter. Both ideology and pleasure depend on defining and privileging particular terms within various relations of difference. But it is affect which enables some differences (for instance, race, and gender) to matter as markers of identity rather than others (foot length, angle of ears, eye color) in certain contexts and power relations. While we might notice these latter sorts of things on certain occasions, we would think it ridiculous to imagine a world in which they mattered. Those differences which do matter can become the site of ideological struggle, and to the extent that they become common-sense social investments, they are landmarks in the political history of our mattering maps.

Through such investments in specific differences, fans divide the cultural world into Us and Them, but the investment in – and authority of – any identity may vary within and across apparatuses. In fact, as individuals and as members of various social groups, there are many axes along which we register our difference from others – some are physical categories, some are sociological, some are ideological and some are affective. We are women, black, short, middle-class, educated, and so on. Any particular difference, including that marked out by being a rock fan, is always augmented and reshaped by other differences. At different points and places in our lives, we reorder the hierarchical relations among these differences. We redefine our own identity out of the relations among our differences; we reorder their importance, we invest ourselves more in some than in others. For some, being a particular sort of rock fan can take on an enormous importance and thus come to constitute a dominant part of the fan's identity (this is how we often think of subcultures). For others, it remains a powerful but submerged difference that colors, but does not define, their dominant social identities.

The most obvious and frightening thing about contemporary popular culture is that it matters so much to its fans. The source of its power, whatever it may seem to say, or whatever pleasures one may derive from it, seems to be its place on people's mattering maps, and its ability to place other practices on those maps. For the fan, certain forms of popular culture become taken for granted, even necessary investments. The result is that, for the fan, specific cultural contexts become saturated with affect. The relations within the context are all defined affectively, producing a structure of 'affective alliances.' And the apparatus, as an affective alliance, itself, functions as a mattering map within which all sorts of activities, practices and identities can be located. It is in their affective lives that fans constantly struggle to care about something, and to find the energy to survive, to find the passion necessary to imagine and enact their own projects and possibilities. Particular apparatuses may also provide the space within which dominant relations of power can be challenged, resisted, evaded or ignored.

Consequently, for the fan, popular culture becomes a crucial ground on which he or she can construct mattering maps. Within these mattering maps, investments are enabled which empower individuals in a variety of ways. They may construct relatively stable moments of identity, or they may identify places which, because they matter, take on an authority of their own. Fans actively constitute places and forms of authority (both for themselves and for others) through the mobilization and organization of affective investments. By making certain things or practices matter, the fan 'authorizes' them to speak for him or her, not only as a spokesperson but also as surrogate voices (as when we sing along to popular songs). The fan gives authority to that which he or she invests in, letting the object of such investments speak for and as him or her self. Fans let them organize their emotional and narrative lives and identities. In this way, they use the sites of their investments as so many languages which construct their identities. In so far as a fan's investments are dispersed, his or her identity is similarly dispersed. But in so far as fandom organizes these investments – both structurally (as a mattering) and intensively (as different quantities) – so it establishes different moments of relative authority, moments which are connected affectively to each other (for example, the investment in rock may make an investment in certain ideological positions more likely although it can never guarantee them). The fan need not – and usually does not – have blind faith in any specific investment site, but he or she cannot give up the possibility of investment as that which makes possible a map of his or her own everyday life and self.

The image of mattering maps points to the constant attempt, whether or not it is ever successful, to organize moments of stable identity, sites at which we can, at least temporarily, find ourselves 'at home' with what we care about. The very notion of a fan assumes the close relationship between identity and caring; it assumes that identity matters and that what matters – what has authority – is the appropriate ground of stable identity. But mattering maps also involve the lines that connect the different sites of investment; they define the possibilities for moving from one investment to another, of linking the various fragments of our identity together. They define not only what sites (practices, pleasures, and so on) matter, but how they matter. And they construct a lived coherence for the fan.

Moreover, the affective investment in certain places (texts, identities, pleasures) and differences demands a very specific ideological response, for affect can never define, by itself, why things should matter. That is, unlike ideology and pleasure, it can never provide its own justification, however illusory such justifications may in fact be. The result is that affect always demands that ideology legitimate the fact that these differences and not others matter, and that within any difference, one term matters more than the other. This is accomplished by linking specific mattering maps to an ideological principle of excessiveness. Because something matters, it must have an excess which explains the investment in it, an excess which ex post facto not only legitimates but demands the investment. Whatever we invest ourselves into must be given an excess which outweighs any other consideration. The more powerful the affective investment in difference is, the more powerfully must that difference be ideologically and experientially legitimated, and the greater the excess which differentiates it. This excess, while ideologically constructed, is always beyond ideological challenge, because it is called into existence affectively. The investment guarantees the excess.

For example, what defines rock's difference — what makes it an acceptable and, for its fans, absolutely necessary investment — is simply the fact that it matters. It offers a kind of salvation which depends only on our obsession with it. It constructs a circular relation between the music and the fan: the fact that it matters makes it different; it gives rock an excess which can never be experienced or understood by those outside of the rock culture. And this excess in turn justifies the fan's investment in it. Rock refers, in this sense, to the excess which is granted the music by virtue of our investment in it. By virtue of the fact that rock matters, rock is granted the excess which justifies its place on our mattering maps, and its power to restructure those maps. Thus it is not so much that rock has a 'real' difference but, rather, the fact that it matters calls its difference into existence. Consequently, the ideology and even the pleasure of rock are always secondary to, or at least dependent upon, the fan's assumption of rock's excess, an excess produced by the ways rock is placed in the fan's everyday life. The place of rock defines possible mattering maps, maps which specify the different forms, sites and intensities of what can matter, maps which chart out affective alliances. Rock positions not only the elements of rock culture, but other aspects of everyday life. It can determine how other things matter. Thus, for example, within rock's mattering maps, entertainment matters but in a very different way from rock, as something to be consumed and to produce pleasure. Rock works by offering the fan places where he or she can locate some sense of his or her own identity and power, where he or she can invest his or her self in specific ways.

But how are we to understand rock's excess? Rock, like any other culture of fandom, is organized around a particular ideology of excess, an ideology which distinguishes certain kinds of musical — cultural practices and certain kinds of 'fans' (although the two dimensions do not always correspond). This ideology not only draws an absolute distinction between rock and 'mere' entertainment, it says that it is the excess of the difference — its authenticity — that enables rock to matter. Every fan — of whatever forms of popular culture — exists within a comparable ideology of authenticity, although the difference need not operate in just the same way, and the ideological grounds of authenticity may vary considerably. This ideological difference has taken many forms, which are not necessarily the same: the center vs the margin, rock vs pop, the mainstream vs the periphery, commercial vs independent, coopted vs resistant. Moreover, the same distinction can be applied in very different ways to describe the same musics. In different rock apparatuses, the difference can be explained in different ways; for example, the line can be justified aesthetically or ideologically, or in terms of the social position of the audiences, or by the economics of its production, or through the measure of its popularity, or the statement of its politics. In all of these cases, the line serves, for the fan, 'properly' to distribute rock cultures. On the one side, entertainment, on the other, something more — an excess by virtue of which even mere fun can become a significant social statement. The excess links the social position and experience of musicians and fans with rock's ability to redefine the lines of social identity and difference. That is, the excess marks the rock fan's difference. Rock fans have always constructed a difference between authentic and coopted rock. And it is this which is often interpreted as rock's inextricable tie to resistance, refusal, alienation, marginality, and so on.

However, we must be careful, for sometimes 'authenticity' is used to refer to a single definition of authenticity. But there are many forms of authenticity, even within rock culture. One need only compare the various contemporary performers who might qualify as authentic rockers: Springsteen, U2, REM, Tracy Chapman, Sting, Prince, Public Enemy, Talking Heads and even the Pet Shop Boys. In general, it is possible to isolate three versions of this ideological distinction. The first, and most common, is usually linked to hard rock and folk rock. It assumes that authentic rock depends on its ability to articulate private but common desires, feelings and experiences into a shared public language. The consumption of rock constructs or expresses a 'community.' This romantic ideology displaces sexuality and makes desire matter by fantasizing a community predicated on images of urban mobility, delinquency, bohemianism and artistry. The second, often linked with dance and black music, locates authenticity in the construction of a rhythmic and sexual body. Often identifying sexual mobility and romance, it constructs a fantasy of the tortured individual struggling to transcend the conditions of their inadequacy. The third, often linked with the self-consciousness of pop and art rock, is built on the explicit recognition of and acknowledgment that the difference that rock constructs (and which in turn is assigned back to rock) is always artificially constructed. That is, the difference does not exist outside of the consumption of rock itself. Such music, which is increasingly seen as 'avant garde' or 'postmodern,' celebrates style over music, or at least it equates the two. But despite its self-conscious negation of both romantic transcendence and transcendental sexuality, it still produces real and significant differences for its fans.

I do not mean to suggest that the category of the 'fan' exists in the same way in every historical situation. The fan can only be understood historically, as located in a set of different possible relations to culture. In fact, everyone is constantly a fan of various sorts of things, for one cannot exist in a world where nothing matters (including the fact that nothing matters). In fact, I think that what we today describe as a 'fan' is the contemporary articulation of a necessary relationship which has historically constituted the popular, involving relationships to such diverse things as labor, religion, morality and politics. Thus, there is no necessary reason why the fan relationship is located primarily on the terrain of commercial popular culture. But it is certainly the case that for the vast majority of people in advanced capitalist societies, this is increasingly the only space where the fan relationship can take shape. It is in consumer culture that the transition from consumer to fan is accomplished. It is here, increasingly, that we seek actively to construct our own identities, partly because there seems to be no other space available, no other terrain on which we can construct and anchor our mattering maps. The consumer industries increasingly appeal to the possibilities of investing in popular images, pleasures, fantasies and desires. The fact that we relate to these appeals, as either consumers or fans, does not guarantee our subjugation to the interests or practices of the commercial sector. One can struggle to rearticulate effective popular appeals but I think it is also true that the consumer, however active, cannot remake the conditions of their subordination through their act of consumption.

The fan, however, is a different matter altogether. For the fan speaks from an actively constructed and changing place within popular culture. Moreover, because the fan speaks for and to the question of authority, and from within an ideology of excess (which constructs a certain critical distance), the politics of the fan never entails merely the celebration of every investment or every mattering map. The fan's relation to culture in fact opens up a range of political possibilities and it is often on the field of affective relations that political struggles intersect with popular concerns. In fact, the affective is a crucial dimension of the organization of political struggle. No democratic political struggle can be effectively organized without the power of the popular. It is in this sense that I want to say that the relationship of fandom is a potentially enabling or empowering one, for it makes it possible to move both within and beyond one's mattering maps.

Empowerment is an abstract possibility; it refers to a range of effects operating at the affective level. It is not synonymous with pleasure (for pleasure can be dis-empowering and displeasure can be empowering); nor does it guarantee any form of resistance to or evasion of existing structures of power, although it is a condition of the possibility of resistance. Empowerment refers to the reciprocal nature of affective investment: that is, because something matters (as it does when one invests energy in it), other investments are made possible. Empowerment refers to the generation of energy and passion, to the construction of possibility. Unlike the consumer, the fan's investment of energy into certain practices always returns some interest on the investment through a variety of empowering relations: in the form of the further production of energy (for example, rock dancing, while exhausting, continuously generates its own energy, if only to continue dancing); by placing the fan in a position from which he or she feels a certain control over his or her life (as a recent ad proclaimed, 'shopping puts me on top of the world'); or by making fans feel that they are still alive (as Tracy Chapman sings, 'I had a feeling I could be someone').

In all of these cases, fans are empowered in the sense that they are now capable of going on, of continuing to struggle to make a difference. Fans' investment in certain practices and texts provides them with strategies which enable them to gain a certain amount of control over their affective life, which further enables them to invest in new forms of meaning, pleasure and identity in order to cope with new forms of pain, pessimism, frustration, alienation, terror and boredom. Such empowerment is increasingly important in a world in which pessimism has become common sense, in which people increasingly feel incapable of making a difference, and in which differ-ences increasingly seem not to matter, not to make any difference themselves. Fandom is, at least potentially, the site of the optimism, invigoration and passion which are necessary conditions for any struggle to change the conditions of one's life. At this level, culture offers the resources which may or may not be mobilized into forms of popular struggle, resistance and opposition. The organization of struggles around particular popular languages depends upon their articulation within different affective economies, that is, upon the different investments by which they are empowered and within which they empower their fans. While there is no guarantee that even the most highly charged moments will become either passive sites of evasion or active sites of resistance, without the affective investments of popular culture the very possibility of such struggles is likely to be drowned in the sea of historical pessimism.

Chapter 33

Stephen Hinerman

'I'LL BE HERE WITH YOU'
Fans, fantasy and the figure of Elvis

We have lost the relative strength and security that the old moral codes guaranteed our loves either by forbidding them or determining their limits. Under the crossfire of gynecological surgery rooms and television screens, we have buried love within shame for the benefit of pleasure, desire, if not revolution, evolution, planning, management – hence for the benefit of Politics. Until we discover under the rubble of those ideological structures – which are nevertheless ambitious, often exorbitant, some-times altruistic – that they were extravagant or shy attempts intended to quench a thirst for love. To recognize this does not amount to a modest withdrawal, it is perhaps to confess to a grandiose pretension. Love is the time and space in which 'I' assumes the right to be extraordinary. Sovereign yet not individual. Divisible, lost, annihilated; but also, and through imaginary fusion with the loved one, equal to the infinite space of superhuman psychism. Paranoid? I am, in love, at the zenith of subjectivity.

Julia Kristeva (1987, 5)

Although Elvis Presley has been dead for more than 10 years, fans who believe that he is alive send him an average of a letter a day.

Newspaper report (*San Francisco Chronicle 1987*, p. A10)

Introduction

PERHAPS NO MODERN FIGURE has held our attention like Elvis Presley. In life, he was held responsible for: building the populist base of rock 'n' roll by mixing black and white musics; articulating the sound of a youth rebellion; taking rock into the world of traditional entertainment; showing that a rock career could sustain longevity with a consistent fan base; practically inventing the idea of rock music 'selling out'; and finally showing how it was possible to be relevant, then irrelevant, then finally relevant again before becoming a caricature of his early image-making and dying a spectacularly inflated death. With Elvis Presley alive, it always depended on 'who you asked' as to what any of this meant; and when you did, the response always showed that whoever and whatever Elvis was said to be, he always appeared to matter. But the significance of Elvis Presley did not end when his life did, for in death he remains: an icon for fan worship; a textual mine for artists of various media; a subject of in-jokes; a signifier of both hipness and the retrograde; and a viable commercial marketplace. And now, Elvis (all one ever needed, *especially now*, is the first name) has become a country unto himself; he has shown that in matters of commodity capital, death is of no importance whatsoever.

One is tempted, in this atmosphere where the difference between cliche and subversion is barely visible, to stay away from the Elvis phenomenon altogether. How can one say anything new about Elvis or his fans? Is there anything worth saying that can escape tedium, self-parody, the mundane or pretension? Haven't we, to put it another way, had enough of this Elvis-thing?

The answer appears to be 'no.' The writing goes on, the tabloid articles continue, the books are still published, new combinations of previously released material appear on CDs, and Graceland continues to play host to apparently unending battalions of the curious and the ceaselessly devoted. There is a continuing appetite for what-has-become-Elvis and it shows no sign of abating.

How could anyone, then, who seeks to understand what it might mean to be a 'fan' today pass over the site of Elvis? Not only does the Country of Presley contain virtually every type of media relationship between a star and his consumers, it also contains some of the most pronounced structures of feeling in all of popular culture. Every fan may be like Elvis fans; but there are no fans like Elvis fans.

My own interest here is to explore a certain type of fan encounter: the particularly active fantasies of fans whose interactions with a star are generated with either memory or secondary material. In this light, I am interested in what lies behind or within a few of the encounters that fans have had with Elvis since his death. The accounts I have chosen are often extreme, exhibiting just how far some fans *can* go with fantasy material. Some of these are paranormal; some are simply daydreams. While not all Elvis fans have such encounters, I would maintain these represent a generalized set of responses that fans can have to media figures today when they engage in what we commonly refer to as a full-fledged fantasy narrative. With Elvis, the juice often gets turned up and the stakes are raised; and because of that, the results become particularly enlightening in trying to understand both the nature of 'fandom' and that of the 'fan-star fantasy.'

First, in order to provide a theoretical framework with which to approach these after-death fantasies of Elvis and his fans, I will elaborate a psychoanalytic perspective of fantasy out of Freud and Lacan. Then, I will attempt to use this perspective to 'read' some Elvis fantasies, making the argument that fantasies centered around Elvis (or any other media figure) are not delusional or maladjusted scenes, but are instead statements that serve at least two functions. First, they 'suture' a potentially traumatic threat to a person's psychological identity, reassuring the fantasizer that full presence, satisfaction and sense might one day be obtained. Second, fantasies engage the world ideologically from a specific political place, speaking a language of individuals and classes who are denied more 'direct' and confrontive solutions to crisis. Some implications for the study of fans and fantasy arising out of these tendencies are then offered.

The nature and function of fantasy

Laplanche and Pontalis (1973) offer the following definition of fantasy (or, as they call it, 'phantasy'):

> Imaginary scene in which the subject is a protagonist, representing the fulfillment of a wish (in the last analysis, an unconscious wish) in a manner that is distorted to a greater or lesser extent by defensive processes.
>
> Phantasy has a number of different modes: conscious phantasies or daydreams, unconscious phantasies like those uncovered by analysis as the structures underlying manifest content, and primal phantasies. (p. 31)

I would argue that many of the scenes in which fans confront the images of a star today are well within the parameters of this definition and conform to the description of fantasy. From daydreaming about a particular figure to experiencing extra-sensory encounters (both of which fill the literature of Elvis fans), part of what it means to be a fan for some people in some places clearly involves fantasy-work. We may be able to gain valuable insight into the process of what it means to be a fan by exploring the psychoanalytic roots of fantasy.

Fantasy occupies a central place in the project of analysis undertaken by Freud.[1] From his early studies of women's hysteria, the questions of fantasy as illusory episodes were of paramount importance. Daydreams, scenes, romances and fictions which were recounted by the hysteric while awake were raw material for his analysis. While this work has its share of problems, we can sketch a useful foundational explanation of how fantasy begins and what paths it takes as psychosexual development occurs, building upon the work undertaken by others following in Freud's path.

Mitchell (1984) offers the following scenario as a prime instance where Freudian psychoanalysis seeks to explain the origins of fantasy using the 'oral stage' as an idealized example of the pre-Oedipal. She argues that in the oral stage, when a child first experiences the sucking of the Mother's breast, a certain undifferentiated satisfaction is produced. The child feels at one with the breast. The child *is* what it experiences; it is its own universe.

However, when the biological need is fulfilled and the breast is removed, the child experiences a lack. Because the child not only enjoyed the nourishment of the breast but the act of sucking itself, the child misses the sucking and the pleasure it granted. This longing for pleasure-for-pleasure's-sake (or sucking for the sake of sucking) is posited by psychoanalytic theory as the beginning of the erotic. The wish for pleasure is now present where before there was once only the need for nourishment. From this moment on, the child begins to learn to tend toward those acts which reduce tension and maximize the seeking of pleasure, a tendency Freud called the 'pleasure principle' (Freud 1928).

The child, now missing the satisfaction of the breast and longing for its return, is left with a 'memory-trace' of the pleasure object and a sense of loss that 'something which was here is no longer here.' The child therefore begins to experience absence; a sense which is, at this point, internalized in a feeling that 'I am not whole or complete.' A lack is felt, and it is in the 'space' of this lack (for Lacan and others following Freud) that there comes the beginning of a gap, a growing sense that the 'world is not simply my pleasure experience' but, in fact, is made up of both the presence and absence of pleasure. If we explain this in linguistic terms, the child begins to see the difference between 'I' (my pleasure experience) and 'not/I' (the absence of my pleasure). The young child, both pre-Oedipal and pre-language, cannot formulate or express this feeling of lack or difference, but in the movement toward the Oedipal stage, this condition will be elaborated until at the Oedipal moment it is expressed and felt with the development of the unconscious.

Before the Oedipal moment, however, the child is motivated by 'drives' which are simply 'movements' toward full satisfaction. The child tends toward the reenactment of the moment of undifferentiated pleasure; she is *driven* in that direction. The pre-Oedipal child is, therefore, marked by the drive toward pleasure.

Such a simple formulation of drives and unity cannot last. The child must 'take its place' in a world where undifferentiated pleasure is not possible, where there are not only 'I's' but 'Others,' where one must experience limits upon subjective satisfaction. In order to elaborate this development and its role in the formation of fantasy, we turn to the work of Jacques Lacan and his discussion of psychosexual development.

For Lacan, following Freud, the gap or lack we have been discussing becomes the foundation for the child's entrance into the social.[2] The child, in the Lacanian world-view, begins in the realm of the Imaginary, which is his term for the undifferentiated experience of pleasure when the child and Mother were one. However, this experience is quickly changed in child development. For Lacan, the child moves from the Imaginary into a world of differences (or presence/absence) which he terms the Symbolic.

Instead of the story of the breast, Lacan makes use of the example of a child who looks in a mirror (Lacan 1977, 1–7). When a child first looks into the mirror, he or she thinks that the image reflected back is the self. Yet, this is clearly not the case; the image is of the child yet not the child itself (it is, if you will, a re-presentation of the child). But the child at first mistakes (misrecognizes) the image as if it were simply an extension of the child. The child continues this basic process and begins to interact with the whole of the outside as if it were simply an extension of its own 'I' (which implies, for Lacan, that identity is always somehow grounded in narcissism and misapprehension). As in the story of the breast, the child begins in full presence, without a sense of subjectivity. But, for Lacan, such an understanding is a misreading, a missed-take on the image.

This perception of the outside as narcissistic is the way, Lacan argues, that the ego is built, beginning with childhood but carrying throughout adulthood. We build what Eagleton (1983, 165) calls a 'fictive sense of unitary selfhood' by identifying with objects in the world, apprehending them as extensions of self and therefore stable in their identity. Yet, as we have seen, this is hardly the 'reality' of the world. The stability of the outside world is only a fiction, a fiction organized around our sense that the Other (the external) is a reflection of our own unitary identity and therefore as apparently stable as the 'I' we experience.

As the child enters the world of the parents, the split in identity between I/Not I (the I/Other) will become more pronounced and the early unity of self/other will be finally shattered. When the child moves from the duality of Breast-Absent/I (or Mirror/I) into the triangular relationship of the Oedipal situation, the separation of the child from the Mother is moved toward completion. Now, the child must recognize that, in order to 'fit' and attain full identity in the social world, represented in the first instance by the family, she must respect the family order and the world of language already in place. She must recognize in a fuller sense than ever before that her drives will not always be granted priority; that she must face a world with full prohibitions on continuing a certain kind of relationship with Mother; and one with certain 'laws' against the total expression of drives. In a larger sense, she must realize that the world is no longer fully 'I' but is made up of 'I' and 'Other.' Drives, which are not going to be automatically satisfied and will even be prohibited, must be submerged.

Lacan calls this mechanism of prohibition which enforces the split the 'Law of the Father'. It causes the child fully to repress its drives to recreate the undifferentiated pleasure of the breast (creating unconscious desire) and accept the system of differences which first appeared in the mirror-stage (or the absent breast). The child emerges from the Oedipal situation understanding that the world is made up of less-than-total satisfaction and an always present feeling of absence.

As I have mentioned, for Lacan, this developmental process is intimately bound up with the idea of language. Language, from his perspective, makes use of a system of differences (much like the 'I/Not I') in order to create meaning. Eagleton (1983) explains the process in the following:

> We can think of the small child contemplating itself before the mirror as a kind of 'signifier' – something capable of bestowing meaning – and of the image it sees in the mirror as a kind of 'signified.' The image the child sees is somehow the 'meaning' of itself. Here, signifier and signified are as harmoniously united as they are in Saussure's sign. . . . It is a world of *plenitude*, with no lacks or exclusions of any kind: standing before the mirror, the 'signifier' (the child) finds a 'fullness,' a whole and unblemished identity, in the signified of its reflection. No gap has opened up between signifier and signified, subject and world. . . .
>
> With the entry of the father, the child is plunged into post-structuralist anxiety. It now has to grasp Saussure's point that identities come about only as a result of difference – that one term or subject is what it is only by excluding another. Significantly, the child's first discovery of sexual differ- ence occurs at about the same time that it is discovering language itself. . . . In gaining access to language, the small child unconsciously learns that a sign has meaning only by dint of its difference from other signs, and learns also that a sign presupposes the absence of the object it signifies. (p. 166)

Such a realization, as we have seen, is implied from the first moment of the child realization of absence with the breast. But it reaches a full flowering in the world of the social (the world of language, the world of the Oedipal). In this world, language awaits the child, ready as a pre-existent system to assign a 'place' to the child. Parents await, in much the same way, with a pre-existent system of rules and roles ready to have the child 'fit' its drives in certain socially acceptable ways. All of this pushes the child's drive for unity and pure pleasure into the framework of desire, repressed and formed in the unconscious.

Therefore, we can see that in the moment of the Oedipal (which is simultaneously a moment of language), a child is formed as a social creature. Drives are displaced by desire; the ego is formed which allows the child to 'fit' into the world of language and family while the unconscious is formed to house repressed desire.

Yet, repressed desire, a longing for full satisfaction, for merging, for plenitude, for oneness, for full identity of self, remains. And it must, on occasion, to a greater or lesser degree in each person, reemerge. We call this reemergence fantasy. Fantasy expresses the desire for fullness and the hope for the eradication of the troubling Absence. Fantasies promise a full satisfaction and total meaning in a world marked by separation, absence, and traumatic disruption.

This implies, among other things, that fantasy, in so far as it is the seeking of pleasure of the absent Other which promises full satisfaction, marks us as social creatures, as meaning producers. Just as being able to repress drives is necessary to life, so too is the functioning of desire and the want to increase pleasure towards satisfaction. Fantasy, then, may well be a foundational mark of human existence. The absence of fantasy in a life would be the mark of full repression and a sign of the 'non-human.' It would be as impossible to imagine as a person who never dreams.

Other aspects of fantasy also must be commented on. First, since the desired object is absent and the beginning of desire is in the Oedipal situation, the site of desire is also a site of prohibition. Something (more properly, the feeling of full satisfaction, total subjectivity and complete presence) has been taken away and is denied a return. Drives are repressed in order to fit into the social structure. Because repression is so linked with the Law of the Father, the child quickly learns that punishment is a possibility for feeling desire and certain desires are prohibited. Fantasy will, therefore, always gather around what is outlawed. This means that the site of fantasy will also be the site where defense mechanisms develop. These aid the child (and later the adult) in coping with absence and the possibility of prohibition and punishment.

But since desire never completely goes away, one finds that there are ways to 'disguise' the feeling of desire in various forms of fantasy. In other words, fantasies allow one to 'get around' the outlawing and prohibition. This 'disguising' of desire in fantasy form will inevitably distort and 'hide' the desiring wish, but that wish always remains present for us to access in the fantasy narrative.

Fantasies are, then, one way humans have to negotiate a troubling situation. They bridge the gap that is created when desire is prohibited but the longing for full satis-faction is still there. Fantasies allow us to 'close the distance' between what we need or want and what we can have. When the unconscious desires and the ego prohibits, throwing open questions of identity and the self, fantasies step into the breach.

In this sense, fantasies work much like a 'suture' that a doctor uses to close a 'gap' in a wound. The use of the term 'suture' has been explored in Lacanian theory by Miller (1977/8) and in film theory by Oudart (1977/8) and Heath (1977/8) but

I would argue that it also has a place in fantasy theory. It stands to reason that if fantasy is a way of negotiating a space that grows up between the unconscious and symbolic worlds, it would be particularly present when desire is blocked by prohibition. Fantasy can act as a way the individual sutures his or her own identity back together (bonding the ego to the unconscious) when it is most vulnerable.

For instance, when an event happens where I 'feel' dissatisfied or threatened (where desire is prohibited), my whole sense of self can be disrupted. If this disruption is prohibited direct expression, then the fantasy can be a way to 'travel' the disruptive area, allowing me to 'stitch' my identity back together without being banished from the culture in which I live and regain my sense of self. When in doubt, in other words, I can always dream.

This suggests that we should find fantasies around particularly traumatic situations which involve real threats to identity, where the sense of a stable 'I' is facing the Absence which stands ready to destroy it. Situations (following Freud) around the issues of death or sex, which can raise traumas around the crisis of identity, would cry out for fantasy as a way of suturing the self 'back together.' Because both situations are often culturally prohibitive (people are not necessarily, in certain cultural formations, allowed to speak freely on either subject), fantasy becomes even more important as a 'safe' way of giving the self the 'answers' required to go on believing in the stability of the 'I' who believes.

One can immediately see, however, how much of the above is reliant upon various cultural forms of life. In the first place, sites of prohibition might change depending upon the culture and the place of the individual within it. What is seen as a 'prohibitive expression of desire' in one place may not be in another. The options open for an individual to suture around trauma may vary within cultural formations. In some cultural 'places' one may be allowed a visit to an analyst; in another, Elvis might have to arrive from outer space. In both cases, albeit through different techniques, an ongoing, provisional sense of identity is restored.

Finally, the narratives themselves which make up dreams and daydreams are linguistically-bound scenarios, and as such, I would argue that both the form and content would vary from culture to culture. So, while the latent desire of fantasy may be a fundamental mark of the human, the manifest form and content will often be highly cultural.

This is what allows us to move from a theoretical discussion of fantasy to specific fantasies concerning, in this case, Elvis Presley. It is no secret that since the rise of mass media in Western-style commodity capitalism, one way fantasies get 'cast' are with star figures. These star images often become wrapped up with the life of the individual who fantasizes and become crucial signs of repressed desire seeking fullness. So, in America, it causes few eyebrows to be raised if one 'dreams' of a sexual encounter with Paul Newman or daydreams about fighting in the streets alongside Sylvester Stallone. Star fantasies are now a matter of cultural course, from childhood on.

Yet, just because they are so common, we should not be blind to the cultural forces at work in these fantasies. Dyer (1986) observes that:

> We're fascinated by stars because they enact ways of making sense of the experience of being a person in a particular kind of social production (capitalism), with its particular organization of life into public and private

spheres. We love them because they represent how that experience is or how it would be lovely to feel that it is. Stars represent typical ways of behaving, feeling and thinking in contemporary society, ways that have been socially, culturally, historically constructed. Much of the ideological investment of the star phenomenon is in the stars seen as individuals. . . . [What] makes them interesting is the way in which they articulate the business of being an individual. . . . Stars are also embodiments of the social categories in which people are placed and through which we make our lives – categories of class, gender, ethnicity, religion, sexual orientation, and so on. (pp. 16–17)

This is particularly true of the presence of stars within fantasy. Why do we pick one figure over another to fantasize about? What do they 'do' in the fantasy, and what do those behaviors reveal about the prohibitions being invoked, the traumas involved or the desire and longing being fulfilled?

These questions only begin to raise others, which move us further in the cultural forces at work in the star fantasy. If American culture tends to 'traumatize' adolescent sexuality, for instance, would it not also be a site where we find many fantasies and fantasizers? Are other stages of life particularly ripe for fantasy? If our culture is heavily patriarchal, then do biological males and females have different forms of fantasy, which raise different questions around desire? Does the patriarchy make it more inviting for women to articulate their fantasies publicly, and does that artic-ulation also invoke sanctioning from the rational (often privileged) side of cultural discourse?

The discussion that follows can only hint at some of the answers to these ques-tions. Still, it is my belief that viewing specific fantasies concerning Elvis can give us a start toward finding those answers.

The Elvis fantasies

Images of Elvis live on to one degree or another in the fantasy life of almost all who live in the Western world. Since his death, that image has been displayed by some as a way of playing any number of social roles, from 'true fan,' to 'rebel,' to 'hip,' to 'hipper-than-you.' It has been used to sell products both related and unrelated to his music. It has even become a text which weaves its way through any number of films and any number of comedy routines. It is no wonder that so many access the man in their waking and sleeping moments.

In the midst of this, many accounts have appeared which place Elvis as either a paranormal figure, a guide to the world beyond, and/or an image of salvation. All are, in essence, fantasy accounts. (It is important to stress once again that this is not a judgement as to their 'truth' value; all fantasies are outside of the categories of truth.) I will discuss five such accounts here, citing other fantasy accounts when relevant. In doing so, I am not arguing that they represent the totality of Elvis fantasies; simply that they begin to illuminate the nature of stars and fantasies in our own cultural formation. In recounting the fantasies, I will show how they serve as sutures which, gathering around trauma and prohibition, attempt to resolve a crisis of identity and desire.

Before beginning, however, I want to refer back to the preceding discussion of the impact of patriarchal structures on fantasy. Out of the five fantasies discussed below, women predominate. This is also true of the literature which is extant. The phenomenon is not due to the fact that men have no Elvis fantasies; after all, there are, at last count, some 3,000 Elvis impersonators in America, all of whom must be said to be living out some kind of fantasy relationship to Presley. Yet, when one surveys the Elvis literature, women not only speak their fantasies more freely and in more detail, they speak them more often.

Perhaps this is the impact of culture which we mentioned earlier. Perhaps in a patriarchal society, with many men raised to cling to the 'rational/concrete' side of discourse, women are simply more comfortable speaking about fantasies. Perhaps women, being denied in certain social classes certain forms of emotional support, are forced to turn to the fantasy with idealized male figures more often. The subject of Elvis himself, as suggested below by Jimmy Reed, may be more easily accessed by women in our culture. Perhaps, finally, given the demands of the marketplace and the wrongheaded tendency to link fantasy with 'emotional instability,' the preponderance of women's fantasies in the public domain is just one more example of the power of patriarchal culture to 'display' women as 'emotional subjects.' Whatever the reason, the fact that women speak more of Elvis here is only a sign of the available data and should not be linked to arguments which tie fantasy to positive or negative social judgements about the individual who 'tells' of Elvis.

One other caveat is necessary. By necessity, the fantasies below work with material that is highly personal and emotionally charged. It is also material that is incomplete. A full psychoanalytic reading would involve a level of disclosure that is virtually impossible without extensive therapeutic work, which may not even be desired by those who fantasize. Consequently, my 'reading' of the fantasies below involves certain leaps and presumptions that I hope the data justifies. The 'point' of these readings is not to pass judgement or articulate a 'truth' about the meaning of the fantasy; it is simply to illustrate how such readings might be accomplished and to theorize larger structures of the possible relationship forms between fans and stars.

The first fantasy I will consider is one recounted by Moody (1987) involving Vanessa and Harry Grant. The Grants' fantasy is one which takes a very traditional form, that of the 'daydreaming fan.'

It seems that Vanessa Grant began a fantasy life around the figure of Elvis when she was in high school in the 1960s. At that time, she would daydream that Elvis 'and I were friends and he would invite me to come to Graceland and we would ride horses together' (p. 108). This fantasy relationship was so important that when she met her husband-to-be during this time, she made sure that he understood her 'love' for Elvis and that marrying her involved, to some extent, 'sharing' her with Elvis.

The Elvis fantasies increased for Vanessa. After marriage, she says that she would fantasize about Harry, Elvis and herself 'being friends.' 'In the daydream,' she states, 'Harry got a job with Elvis on the soundcrew, because Harry has always been good with electronics, and we would travel around with Elvis as he gave concerts' (p. 108).

Three traumas then came into Vanessa and Harry's life. First, Vanessa found that she was unable to bear children. This saddened both, and as a response to the situation, they decided to travel more and more to see Elvis perform in person. Then, Elvis died, followed six weeks later by a painful death of Vanessa's step-sister. Vanessa remembers 'Nobody knows what a hard year that was for me, the year that Elvis died. . . . (My) step-sister died six weeks later. She had been one of my best friends since I was seven years old. After she died I could hardly get out of bed for a month. I would stay in bed and try to sleep and forget it all' (p. 107).

Within the next year, fantasies increased. Vanessa recalls: 'I would have these little imagined conversations in my head with Elvis. I would ask him what he was doing, and where he was, and things about his life, personal things mostly, and then I would imagine him giving his answers back to me. I would try to imagine what his voice would sound like as he gave his answers back to me' (pp. 107–8). She reports that these fantasies began to help her recovery, while at the same time placing some strain on the marriage as she withdrew into her inner conversations.

In an effort to help his wife, Harry invented a computer program which allowed Vanessa to communicate with an Elvis-like program, asking it/him questions while he/it 'answered' from a programmed set of responses. With the fantasy moved from individual daydream to the social setting of their basement, Vanessa began to brighten. Her solitude lessened and she finally recovered from the various traumas. Vanessa and Harry now spend hours communicating with their version of Elvis Presley, which makes Vanessa, 'actually feel that he really does talk to me . . . through the computer' (p. 113).

Vanessa has recounted a daydream, a fantasy which is much like the fantasies many fans recount in Fred and Judy Vermorel's collection, *Starlust* (1985). Elvis becomes a conversational partner, taking an active role in the life of the fan while the fan generates responses based upon his or her memory and his or her knowledge of the star's tendencies, history and images. Yet, it is clear that for Vanessa Grant, particularly, the Elvis-relationship is a response to a set of traumatic events in her life. Fantasies clearly accelerate around her experience of high school and the death of Elvis and her step-sister.

Both events are potential sites for prohibitions. In American middle-class culture (to which the Grants belong), high school represents a place and time when adolescent sexuality is worked through. Vanessa clearly sees Elvis in such a light; not only does she fantasize being 'singled out' by the romantic male figure of Elvis, she sees him in competition with her husband-to-be, a competition resolved only when Harry agrees to 'share' her with Elvis. While the data is less than complete, it is not unreasonable to think that this is the way many young girls in the 1950s and early 1960s employed the image of Elvis. He became an 'idealized male hero,' a pin-up, a male who offered to resolve the confusions of adolescent sexuality, allowing it full (imaginary) expression while keeping the fantasizer from having to enact the fantasy with nearby (and often unpredictable) boys.[3] I will return to this point in detail later.

The real acceleration in fantasy material, however, comes with the depression Vanessa experiences around the real deaths of her fantasy hero and her step-sister. The fact of death, the way in which death (particularly the death of a sibling who is still young) often seems to call into question the very structures by which we make sense of things, only highlights the prohibitive place of death in our culture. Death tends to be 'talked around,' and the grieving spend tremendous resources trying to 'make sense' of the death. In a very real way, death is the 'Not I' made nervously present, and carries with it the real anxiety that full presence may never be fully obtained again, that desire will one day extinguish without reaching its *telos*.

Obviously unable to communicate with the world in a way that provided satisfaction, Vanessa begins to conduct fantasy conversations with the figure who once had resolved an equally troubling moment. The deaths (and whatever else may have led to this moment) have left her in need of the fullness of the 'I' one experiences early in life, the moments when one feels full connection, identity and sense. Denied other ways to articulate her need (and the reasons why are not clear), she turns back to Elvis, who provides her with a sense of identity, of self. Elvis becomes the way to deal with the prohibitive site of death while restoring the hope for life. Through her conversations with Elvis, she begins to feel identity regained and a 'sense' of life restored.

Harry's creative technological solution to the fantasy work allows Vanessa to be social in her expression of longing, thereby brightening her mood. But whether she does it alone or with Harry at the computer, the fantasy work she undertakes is clearly a longing for security and stability in the face of changes that cannot be spoken in her cultural milieu. Around the prohibition of death (and earlier, sexuality), Elvis provides a way for desire to find some satisfaction and still allow her to function in the non-fantasy world.

Sherry and Jimmy Reed offer a more elaborate version of Elvis-as-the-resolver-of-trauma. As recounted by Moody (1987), both Sherry and Jimmy are fans of Elvis from their adolescence. Sherry's account sounds a familiar note to readers of the Elvis fan literature.

> I remember it like it was yesterday. I was in the sixth grade, and my friend Susan Logan was having me and several other girls over to her house for a spend-the-night party. Susan was playing some records on her record player, some Perry Como ones and some Tennessee Ernie Ford, I believe, that belonged to her parents, and then she got one out of her drawer and she said, 'Have you heard Elvis Presley yet?' None of us had and she played 'Blue Suede Shoes.' It was just terrific, of course, and we must have played it ten or fifteen times that night until Susan's mother and father came in and told us we had to be quiet and go to bed. For the rest of my life, since that night, I have liked Elvis Presley. (pp. 49–50)

Sherry's account is mirrored over and over again by women growing up in America of the 1950s. Witness the following, from a woman who became a friend of Elvis later in life:

> When Elvis made it big I was in elementary school. I lived in Corinth, Mississippi, right on the Tennessee line, and we didn't have any theatres, except the one with rats that nibbled our toes, but we did have the Skyline Drive In. When I couldn't get Mama to take me to see Elvis movies (which she didn't like because he 'made that motion' with his hips), I'd go over to Patti's and we'd sit out in her back yard where we could see the screen for free. We'd call over the fence for someone to turn up the speaker for free. On the back row, no one watched the movie. Some didn't even get the speaker off the pole. Anyway, when Elvis sang, Patti would moan and groan and I'd do the twist.
>
> (Deen 1979, 169)

The literature of Elvis is full of similar accounts. Elvis records are hidden away in bedroom drawers until the crucial moment when they emerge among girls who dance in secret from their parents' gaze (Hecht 1978, 60). Girls sneak out of church to view clandestinely Elvis's first TV appearance (Lasker 1979, 205). These accounts make clearer what Vanessa Grant hinted at, that Elvis is linked for many females of the 1950s and 1960s to adolescent sexuality (as a promise that desire will indeed find total fulfillment and as a seductive presence) and to sites of prohibition (much of his appeal is that such sexuality/resolution is displayed *away from* the adults, in the presence of other girls but outside of the possible punishments of the Law of the Father). Elvis is, to these women, the promise of full sexuality and passion, the desire-that-must-be-hidden made manifest, who promises a solution to the trauma of adolescent sexuality. As such, he can then be accessed in narratives later in life to suggest the solution to other problems which grow around later traumatic prohibitions.

Jimmy Reed, Sherry's husband, was also an Elvis fan. But as a man of the South during the 1950s, his fantasies were not given as free a rein. He remembers that during a party in the sixth grade, Elvis records were played and he was 'impressed.' But, Jimmy continues, 'several of the boys said they didn't like it and so I went along with the guys because I didn't want to seem different. . . . (In) secret, of course, yes, I did like Elvis from the very beginning. . . . Later on, in my twenties, well, then I got over that envy and could enjoy Elvis in public, just like anyone else' (pp. 50–1).

Jimmy and Sherry Reed illustrate the way cultural pressures can shape fantasy and its expression. Sherry and her girl friends 'hid' away together, but in doing so were communally building elaborate fantasy interests in the figure of Elvis. Jimmy simply hid his enthusiasm, channeling, no doubt, his fantasies into more culturally sanctioned models (say, wearing his hair like Elvis, dancing like Elvis, and so on) when he finally displayed such interests.

Jimmy and Sherry later married, both now 'out' Elvis fans. Then, a tragedy struck. Their daughter was born with Down's syndrome. A week later, they find the baby was born with a defective heart. In the midst of this trauma, the Reeds adjusted as best they could. But one thing they claim they did that had a real impact on their daughter was the way they immersed her in the images of Elvis which they had carried forward from their own youth.

> Naturally, Jennifer (the daughter) loved Elvis. We played Elvis records all the time for her and sang his songs for her. The first time she saw him perform, I think, was on his TV special from Hawaii, and she smiled and laughed and danced the whole way through. She would watch Elvis movies on TV and I would show her pictures of Elvis from magazines. (p. 53)

When she was ten, Jennifer was rushed to the hospital near death. Right before her death, her parents recall that she looked upward, stretched out her hands, and said, 'Here comes Elvis.' Then she died.

For the Reeds, the signs are clear. Sherry says, 'Elvis came to meet her and help her as she died' (p. 55). For Jimmy, 'God came through and he sent Elvis' (p. 56). Both parents now feel their minds clear on the death of their daughter, and they feel as if her death is not a thing to fear, but an event ensuring her eternal life. Both are sure that Elvis appeared to their daughter in the operating room and escorted her to Heaven.

Again, an absence has been felt around a prohibitive site. Death has taken a child and rational explanations fail. Jimmy, Sherry and (before) Jennifer Reed all return to a figure who stands for identity (the identity of Jennifer's growing up against the odds, the presence of the pre-Oedipal, the miracle of survival and growth). The image of Elvis has allowed the couple to 'suture' the narrative of Jennifer, disrupted so violently by disease. By recreating a narrative where Elvis becomes a central 'sense-making' image, the desire for fullness, sense and identity is (temporarily) satisfied. Life can go on for the Reeds with the knowledge that Elvis's role in their daughter's death 'makes sense' as an ongoing event which stamps 'meaning' upon tragedy.

Dorothy Sherry's fantasy is even more elaborate. She began as an Elvis fan around the age of ten or eleven. While she was a real fan at that age, as she became older, the passion for Elvis subsided. She was married and had children. Then, when she was 32, Elvis came to visit.

According to Dorothy (Holzer, 1978), Elvis appeared to her in a vision and told her that they had once been married. He tells her he is at the end of a long search for her and explains to her that their marriage has been going on throughout 'many, many lives' (p. 86). Somehow in this life, however, things have gone wrong and they have become separated. In order to be with her and re-establish their rightful connection, Elvis takes her on a series of journeys to the Other Side, showing her the world of the souls.

Dorothy's fantasies with Elvis occur with more and more frequency as Elvis takes Dorothy on many trips throughout the psychic realm. These place a strain on the Sherry marriage. Dorothy's mother has her get in touch with psychic Hans Holzer, who interviews her, while at the same time exploring with her the ramifications of the encounters, which take Dorothy from automatic writing to seances with Elvis's relatives financed by the *National Enquirer*.

The main narrative features of Dorothy's highly detailed fantasies are simple. Elvis, as stated earlier, claims that he and Dorothy have been married. (This is only 'the second time' they have been apart in Time.) With the onset of the fantasies, Elvis has arrived, according to Dorothy, to 'take care of me, now' (p. 93). She meets Elvis's caregiving reasoning with some protest, arguing with Elvis that she is a 'nobody': 'I said, do you realize who you are and I'm a nobody. I'm a housewife from New Jersey, I said, which is no big thing. You are a popular man. I said, how come you're coming to me. He said, I explained this to you over and over, up there I'm like everybody! I'm no star or shining light' (p. 48).

But Elvis clearly disagrees with her assessment of herself as a 'nobody,' and does several things to show her her own 'special' place in the universe. Elvis tells Dorothy that he has 'special permission' to visit her (p. 52). He speaks to Holzer through the medium of Dorothy and tells him: 'At times there are mistakes. But I will wait for her. The bond between us is very strong' (p. 33). And he tells Dorothy that even if she doubts now, she will get 'stronger' in the days ahead (p. 85) and more convinced of her special place in Time.

A bond grows between Elvis and Dorothy. She now wants the relationship to 'go on' (p. 55) and wonders what to do. (Should she divorce? Leave town?) Elvis finally gives her a message to stay in her current situation for now 'because I have to raise those children,' but after they are grown, he assures her that 'we will be together' (pp. 47–8).

If fantasy is a suturing event, then it should be a response to some kind of trauma surrounding identity for Dorothy Sherry. While she voices none (claiming that the marriage problem came after the fantasies started, not before), the message Elvis delivers certainly indicates something more. The structure of the fantasy narrative is one where the individual is 'found.' She at first feels a 'nobody' in the face of her fantasy, but the figure of Elvis manages to give her a sense of mission, granting her a purpose and even an agenda for the future. In other words, a new, stronger sense of identity is granted through the Elvis fantasy.

The fantasy seems to function like many media fantasies, in that it appears to resolve a crisis of meaning of the self. In this sense, it functions as an empowerment, suturing a place where absence has become so powerful a threat that the ego appears in danger of dissolution. Was Dorothy Sherry feeling an increasing sense of crisis? Was her life lacking direction, focus? Was she losing any idea of who 'she' might 'be'? Was her very ego falling apart?

The best way to answer is simply to look at how the fantasy functions and what its results are; and in Dorothy Sherry's case the fantasy clearly leads to increased ego-maintenance and a renewed sense of presence (exhibited in her newfound beliefs in the ideology of Romance and the conviction that she now must carry Elvis's message of peace, love and happiness to the world). The fantasy obviously changed Dorothy Sherry and gave her a new sense of identity over what certainly must have been prohibited before in her life: the idea that both Romance and Mission were impossible for someone who was a 'nobody.'

Another Elvis fantasy involving the paranormal is related by Bess Carpenter (in Moody 1987). According to Carpenter, Elvis had always been special to her. As she says, 'I have a thing about Elvis. He was the man of my dreams from the time I was fourteen. At my fifteenth birthday party, my girlfriends gave me a cake that had "ELVIS and BESS" written in pink icing on the top of it. Our names were enclosed in a heart. I love Elvis' (p. 44). Again, Elvis has functioned as a fantasy figure around the issue of adolescent sexuality and the ideology of romance which attempts to resolve the struggle.

So, when Ms. Carpenter found herself, in 1979, pregnant, unmarried and deserted by the child's father, it is not surprising given our other examples that Elvis returns to function in another prohibitive site of trauma. While Ms. Carpenter has had two children previously and wished to give birth to this one, when she told her parents of her condition, they 'freaked out.'

This 'disowning,' coupled with the father's desertion, leads to a traumatic condition. The culture has left Carpenter isolated. She enters into a self-described 'depression,' which is broken only on the day of the birth and Elvis's appearance. This is her account of her Elvis fantasy:

> When they wheeled me into the delivery room, they put this mask on me and I breathed the anesthetic. I was conscious the whole time, but I had a weird experience. The doctors and nurses were all around me in these white gowns, looking at me. Right there among them, Elvis Presley

appeared. He smiled and winked at me. He said, 'Relax, Bess, it's O.K. I'll be here with you.' It looked just like him. I stared into his face, then I would blink and look away, but when I looked back he was still there. The others had on surgical masks but Elvis didn't. It was his voice, too. I'm certain of it. When you hear Elvis Presley's voice speaking to you, there can't be any doubt whose voice it is.

I stared into his face the whole time. He was so sweet. He stood there the whole time. Then, when the baby came, it was he who said, 'It's a boy!' For an Elvis Presley fan, there can't be a bigger thrill than hearing Elvis himself telling you you have a new baby.

All the commotion started then. Doctors and nurses were running here and there, checking the baby and sewing me up and I sort of lost Elvis in the crowd. I didn't see him anymore after that . . . I feel like he came through for me when I was feeling low. (p. 6)

The Elvis fantasy has sutured another prohibitive site. He has granted a sense of presence to the crisis of the ego encountered by desertion and anxieties around childbirth (which invoke both questions of sex and death). Through Elvis, Bess Carpenter's sense of ego is restored. By his role in her fantasy, he has sutured the battering crisis around the ego caused by the desertion of all outside support systems from Bess Carpenter's life.

Of course, there are patriarchal issues abounding in this account as well as running through previous ones. Is is necessary for these women that a male *always* act as a 'suturing/fantasy agent'? Hopefully not. Isn't such a use a comment on how deep male authority both causes and permeates the prohibitive sites of fantasy? Certainly. Yet, if these women live in cultural situations where more 'liberating' practices are not available, does the difficulty lie in the figure of Elvis, or in a culture that proscribes the set of available fantasy practices and images?

The image of Elvis obviously functions for many fans as an initial figure around the question of what it means to be 'female' or 'male' in our culture. Women have a series of options by which they may respond to him; men another series. Some overlap, some appear widely apart. One Elvis may be used by gay men, another by heterosexual men; one Elvis may be used by lower-class Southern women, another by bohemian New York artists. But the use of the Elvis image as a fantasy figure brings with it a whole range of commentary on the culture, on prohibition and the sites of trauma over identity in our everyday lives.

To illustrate this point further, one final fantasy must be considered. Since its publication, Lucy De Barbin and Dary Matera's (1987) account of a 'secret life' between Lucy and Elvis (and a resulting child) has been controversial. Many in the Elvis 'camp' deny the book's claim; even Geraldo Rivera spent air-time on 'Entertainment Tonight' investigating the claims only finally to doubt their truth.

Such arguments over truth and fiction do not concern us here.[4] De Barbin's account *is* a narrative, and we can assume it has traces of desire throughout. The question we will ask is simply: if we treat the account as fantasy, will it further illuminate the problem this paper addresses?

De Barbin's story certainly has all the marks of a fantasy. Her narrative of Elvis begins with a trauma around a site of prohibition (that of sexual seduction) and ends with the figure of Elvis offering to suture a return to pre-Oedipal plenitude and identity.

The initial trauma of De Barbin's life is a forced seduction. At the age of twelve, she is sold to an older man to be his wife. He repeatedly rapes her and denies her any sense of her own pleasure. That this has occurred after her own father (whom she idolizes in pre-Oedipal memories) dies while she is very young only serves to make the account more 'tragic.' De Barbin's life is, in many ways, a classic one: a lower-class girl, who early in life loses her loving Father, finds herself tyrannized by a male dominator.

In one way, De Barbin's account differs from the others we have considered, in that she has no knowledge of Elvis as a singer/star when she first meets him. But in every other way, particularly the role Elvis will play in her own sexual/romantic reawakening, her fantasy is similar.

Elvis, as in other fantasy narratives, is always met in secret. In fact, De Barbin claims that only the two of them knew of the affair until Elvis's death. But in this secret place, Elvis becomes the 'gentle' lover that De Barbin has been denied by the conditions of her existence. When she meets him, early in the relationship, her account illustrates Elvis's 'difference' from other men she has met. (It also reverberates with many other fantasies in the Elvis literature.)

> Elvis came into the room fifteen seconds later, hardly discreet. His presence changed the entire room. It was as if a warm light flashed on, softening all the hard edges. He held me, and I inhaled his nice clean smell. I didn't know if it was his soap or the hair tonic he carried in a tall, skinny bottle with a shiny silver top, but it was enough to drown out the rug (which was musty).
>
> I fought to keep my emotions in check. (p. 50)

For some time, De Barbin continues to have an affair with Elvis while living with her husband, who she refers to as The Man. Elvis offers her sexual awakening, compassion, sensitivity. The Man beats her. As she states it, 'Elvis was Heaven. Home was Hell' (p. 7).

Things obviously change as Elvis is said to change. He comes under more 'pressure' to be all things to all people and keep up a public image, while De Barbin resists the temptation to become more attached publicly to Elvis, fearing a scandal. Still, throughout the fantasy, Elvis embodies characteristics which allow De Barbin to suture the trauma that abuse causes her ego: 'He was a man beyond the image everyone saw. The only man I could love without being afraid. Before him, I was so afraid. He came and took the pain away. He was strong, indomitable, and sure of himself and his beliefs. He was tender, kind, gentle, and loving. He was my lover, my inspiration, my deliverer' (pp. xix–xx). Elvis saves De Barbin from the world of forced seduction, from male violence and power, and allows sexuality to flourish in a context of romance and passion. Through Elvis, Lucy De Barbin grows in ego strength that allows more commonly accepted practices for the display of desire.

In this sense (and this holds true for all the fantasies), Elvis is truly a 'deliverer.' If the fantasy is the wish for plenitude, Elvis seems to deliver such plenitude to the fantasizers, standing as a site of completion, an alternative to the world which prohibits or circumscribes full expression of desire. In this sense, Elvis Presley is a continuing figure bringing the salvation which desire always asks for in any situation of trauma.

Conclusion

This paper is an attempt to rehabilitate the fantasies of fans in light of media studies. For too long, we have dismissed many of the practices of both sexes in relation to star commodities. We have failed to treat them as serious attempts to address life-situations, choosing instead to characterize them as sometimes laughable, sometimes delusional products of 'weaker' minds.

Instead, I have argued that fantasy is a necessary component of the fundamental tension between the Imaginary and Symbolic in life, between the unconscious and ego formations. Every individual will be driven by desire toward presence just as the social formation of the ego seeks to repress and redirect that desire. At sites of trauma, marked by social prohibition, the gap between desire and ego will be marked, calling Identity and Self into question. At this point, fantasy can be a way in which Identity is sutured together, a way in which desire and ego are stitched and which allows healing.

The use of media figures in fantasy does bring with it a host of questions, some of them as troubling as the culture which both prohibits and provides images. Some of these questions are political, and spin from those asked in another context, that of fantasy-romance novels, by Modleski (1982, 113). She observes, for instance, that, 'while popular feminine texts provide outlets for women's dissatisfaction with male–female relationships, they never question the primacy of these relationships. . . . Indeed, patriarchal myths and institutions are, on the manifest level, whole-heartedly embraced, although the anxiety and tensions they give rise to may be said to provoke the need for the texts in the first place.'

To say this another way, the female fantasies around Elvis discussed here, while often constituting a critique of male inadequacy and female sexual repression, never raise the question that the conditions *creating* the need for such fantasies are engendered by institutional and social systems of power and control. This will immediately make the texts somewhat 'suspect' for many feminists, who believe that the critique of patriarchy must take place at an institutional level as well as a personal one.

Yet, perhaps these women (and some men, no doubt) who fantasize about Elvis are of a class and social formation that experience the domination of men firsthand, in such a way that the idea of an 'institutional critique' seems impractical. Certainly, it is hard to believe that someone like De Barbin could have faith in institutional critiques of patriarchal power when she is being beaten regularly by a powerful male in her household. It may be that her only option was the promise offered by the figure of Elvis. And while that promise may not change the system which created The Man and his violence, it does, in some sense, help her redeem her life.

For whatever else you can say, fantasies of Elvis fans are important to many of them as signs of *personal* liberation. We may quarrel with the form, but we cannot deny their power as testified to by thousands of fans who speak of being transformed by Elvis's voice, his visage, his magnetism. For these women and men, he is, in certain ways, the light of the world and the glory of glories. And still, they line up, row upon row, at his altar locations, dreaming their dreams, making their wishes. For them, there is absolutely no doubt. Elvis will always be alive.

Notes

1 Much of the following review of fantasy and Freud is indebted to Laplanche and Pontalis (1973).

2 A full explanation of post-structural linguistics would take us even further afield, but for a more complete explanation of this initial formation stage, see Lacan (1977, 1–7).

3 There is a substantial body of literature on this particular facet of fantasy. I refer the reader, in particular, to Radway (1984) and Modleski (1982). Connell *et al.* (1981) offer a more 'personal' reading of the issue, while Kaplan (1986) makes important qualifications on the tendency to make such analyses too general and outside of social formations of class. Finally, Coward (1985) offers a specific reading of 'male crooners' that could certainly be applied in this situation to Elvis as a 'male idealized' figure who promises certain women fulfillment.

4 Laplanche and Pontalis (1964/87) argue that such judgements are, in fact, definitionally impossible.

Chapter 34

Chris Rojek

THE PSYCHOLOGY OF ACHIEVED CELEBRITY

SINATRA WAS AN ACHIEVED celebrity, arguably one of the most resplendent in
the field of American popular entertainment in the twentieth century. This popularity derived in part from his relatively humble beginnings. Yet he was both insuffer-
ably proud of and tormented by his parvenu status. This left an indelible mark on his
psychology as an achieved celebrity. Until the end of his days he made no bones
about emerging from the ranks of the people. Yet at the same time he was fully aware
that the scale of his success estranged him from them. This sense of the loss of his roots
was not replaced by corresponding feelings of belonging to the higher echelons of the
wealthy of which his material success now made him a part. As a member of the
Hollywood celebritariat he was regarded as a rough diamond by old money. This
reinforced his desire for legitimacy and this was expressed in his obsession with power.

Sinatra learned that financial achievement and celebrity status are not sufficient to
open all doors in American life. His relations with the establishment bear the water-
mark of not being acknowledged as "one of us," a lack of acceptance that was a
continuous thorn in Sinatra's side. Arguably, it is the American dilemma, especially of
first born citizens, who more than the native born suffer from a sense of displacement
and estrangement: achievement without acceptance. After all, why had Sinatra's
parents left Italy? To find a new life or to escape the shame of being rejected by the
homeland? The sense of what might be called, perhaps portentously, *primordial* rejection never left Sinatra. However good he was as an entertainer, businessman or
political fixer, however rich he became, he could never overcome the sense of belonging to cast-off stock. The anxiety of being profoundly, unutterably *dispossessed* arguably
haunts the psyche of migrants into the American melting pot. If so, Sinatra dealt with
it by developing a relationship to politics and public respectability that was at once
passionate and lethally tenuous.

Notoriously, in his middle and later years he switched from youthful evangelical-
ism for the Democrats to dyed-in-the-wool support for the Republicans. In truth his

attitude to power was promiscuous and ultimately self-serving. He was attracted to power as an end in itself, for the bearing it gave the holder in public. Leaving aside the desire to perfect his vocal art, one of the few consistencies in Sinatra's career was the determination to be recognized as a person of cultural and physical substance, a man able to fix problems swiftly and decisively, a man indeed who craved acceptance. To some degree this reflects the Sicilian male ideal, which fulfills its most extreme expression in the figure of the mafioso. But it also reveals the flexibility of an achieved celebrity of Sinatra's stature, who is positioned to move relatively freely between the interlocking circles of economic, political and military influence, and whose fame yields a measure of immunity from prosecution.

Achieved celebrities frequently complain that their psychology is uncomfortably displaced. They are not at home in themselves, and they feel themselves to be expatriates from their home background. While they often make extravagant public displays about the decency of ordinary folk and family values, most of them would no more dream of returning to live in their home neighborhoods than abandoning their celebrity status. Achieved celebrity is a different world. While sentimental expressions of the old days come easily to many achieved celebrities, they maintain great care to protect their wealth, lifestyle, and celebrity status. It is given to relatively few people to walk into a room and be immediately recognized as the unequivocal centre of attention. Still fewer receive the economic riches that are the due of the highest echelon of achieved celebrity. The honor and wealth distributed to achieved celebrities are intoxicating. They literally give the recipient a drunken sense of his or her self-importance.

Conversely, they also involve excessive intrusion, leaving the celebrity with a sense of being harassed by the public or dogged by counterfeit relations with others. Achieved celebrities frequently testify to the emptiness of the honorific rituals of celebrity status and materialism. They compare achieved success to a no man's land in which they are neither fish nor fowl. Chris Evans, the British disc jockey, show business tycoon and game show host, is reported to have said that when you get to the top you find there is nothing there (Gray 2002: 7). This point of view abounds in the literature of celebrity with such profusion that it has become a cliché. Even so, it remains an indispensable insight into the psychology of achieved celebrity.

Sociologists use the term *anomie* to describe a condition in which there is a lack of certainty about values and goals, and an absence of a binding moral, normative framework to guide choice and action. Achieved celebrity is inherently *anomic* since it plucks the individual from the ground rules of domestic life and elevates him or her into a world in which the boundaries of conduct are infinitely more elastic. One coping strategy is to offer exaggerated panegyrics to one's roots from the dizzy heights of one's achievement. The abandoned home becomes the imaginary moral anchor for relations in the new and uncertain world of glamour, power, prestige, and wealth. Celebrities often invoke the moral certainties of home against the glittering, meretricious world of fame, conveniently forgetting the determination that they generally harnessed to escape the trappings of their family and neighborhood of origin, and overlooking the tenacity with which they strive to hold on to their achieved status.

In Sinatra's case, he offered countless tributes to the values of his family and the Italian-American community of his youth. He credited them with instilling in him beliefs in fair play, racial tolerance, and giving a break to the little man. He was less supportive of Hoboken, a town that he rarely visited after achieving his success and which he regarded as having held him in insufficient esteem. In public declarations he offered the traditional gospel of self-help as his philosophy of making good. For example, in the 1970s he went on record with a German interviewer as maintaining: "You've got to put the most into everything that you do. You must try to do the best, with a decency and a dignity and compassion for your fellow man. I think that if you do the best you can in your life, you get your just reward" (quoted in Zehme 1997: 246).

Sinatra believed in concepts of "dignity" and "compassion," but he did so on his own terms. His moral code was paleolithic. In his business and personal relationships he punished infraction and transgression with violence, occasionally with physical attacks and usually with implacable social and psychological rejection. He held a black-and-white view of friendship and love, demanding total loyalty but keeping his corresponding options open.

For example, onstage in 1966, during a performance at the Sands Hotel, he said of his third wife, Mia Farrow, 30 years younger than he was: "Maybe you wondered why I finally married her. Well, I finally found a broad I can cheat on" (cited in Freedland 1997: 233–4). This is a callous and mean-spirited remark which caused Farrow considerable public embarrassment. It is not only sexist, it relishes the age difference between the couple in a boorish, self-regarding way, relegating Farrow to a mere *naïf* and casting himself in the role of a world-weary, gin-marinated *savant*. He acts as if his glamour and fame insulate him from the ordinary duties of respectable marital behavior.

The achieved celebrity indeed passes from the ordinary world of habitual mutuality, reciprocity and respect into an altogether more imprecise world of inexhaustible possibility, global intrigue and fabulous wealth. Accountability to fans persists, but this is generally an abstract relationship managed by cultural intermediaries such as publicists, stylists and managers and punctuated by public performances designed to *elevate* the celebrity above the public rather than to engage in genuine mutuality and reciprocity. Achieved celebrities live on a different plane to the rest of us. Their sense of psychological integrity is undermined by public representations of their fame. For the public face is always an assisted, artificial construction, a design intended to have a cultural effect in stimulating desire and worship in the audience.

In presenting a public face, achieved celebrities often complain of symptoms of psychological disassociation. The public responds to a carefully constructed external face, but the real self is elsewhere and suffers from annihilating feelings of nonrecognition and, in some cases, invalidation. In the private life of celebrities accountability and loyalty are frangible and strategic. This is why so many of them experience divorce, addictions to drugs and alcohol, and difficulties with siblings.

Sinatra himself divorced three times and had a somewhat thwarted relationship with his son, Frankie Junior. Junior was a more introspective, thoughtful character than his father. In choosing to be "his father *manqué*" by following a performing and recording career with the Tommy Dorsey Band, he opened himself up to the full range of Sinatra's invective, spite, and fatherly praise. Two weeks after the assassination of John F. Kennedy, Frankie Junior was the subject of a bizarre kidnap. He was held for some days and a ransom of $240,000 was paid. The kidnappers were eventually captured and most of the money was recovered.

In the final five years of his performing career Sinatra appointed Frankie Junior as his music conductor. But the public always regarded the relationship as uncomfortable. Sinatra seemed not so much to be assisting his son as adding a new layer in his overbearing attitude toward him. Perhaps his son made him competitive and over-conscious of his own mortality. For an achieved celebrity of Sinatra's stature, physical disappearance – death – after having struggled so hard and with such accomplishment to attain achievement is an appalling prospect. This is why the charities and founda-tions they create cannot be read as simple acts of generosity. They are also investments in their enduring fame and cultural presence. This was certainly the case with Sinatra who feared death greatly and engaged liberally in charitable works in the last 25 years of his life.

Contra his troubled relationship with Frankie Junior, Sinatra was notably more affectionate and indulgent with his daughters, Nancy and Tina. Kitty Kelley (1986: 285) makes much of his favoritism to the girls, noting that they always received presents galore at Christmas, whereas Frankie Junior received scarcely $500 worth of gifts. Sinatra aided Nancy's singing career, duetting with her on the number one single *Somethin' Stupid*, a somewhat incestuous, ill-judged love song for a father and daughter to sing.

Sinatra's narcissism

Sinatra demonstrated the classic hallmarks of the narcissistic personality. It should be no surprise that achieved celebrity and narcissism are closely related. The achieved celebrity wins fame by reason of his or her accomplishments on earth. But these accomplishments also detach the individual from the earth. Society does not exert a sufficient hold upon the celebrity to guarantee the regulation of desire and emotions. In successfully going beyond general mores and reciprocities and achieving intense acclaim and tributes from fans, the celebrity develops an idealized public face which is projected over all aspects of his or her private and public life. The sense of standing above the world as a role model or figure of popular desire and fantasy, and simul-taneously rejecting worldly values since they belong to a less exalted realm, can be psychologically difficult to reconcile. The narcissist may sublimate frustration at being forced back into himself by having providential dreams of social improvement for mankind, or turn to religion as a means of personal salvation. While Sinatra remained a lifelong Catholic, he was not a devoutly religious person. The closest he came to delivering a religious testament to the future is the third disc on *Trilogy* (1980). Part space odyssey, part muddled, vapid, embarrassing, woolly-headed aspiration, the disc is justly described by Sinatra's best music critic, Will Friedwald, as "the most spec-tacular disaster of his career . . . [Sinatra] blew it by addressing ideas that were at once too grandiloquent and too stupid" (1996: 356). The vision of the future that it presents is, indeed, piffle, with seemingly universal amity and the end of ignorance and want gracefully descending upon humanity by an act of divine consent.

Meliorist fantasies of general improvement, in fact, often amount to a disguised yearning for immortality, since they presuppose that the defects of this world will be replaced by the bountiful world to come, in which the narcissist can expect, at last, to gain the recognition he or she deserves. But Sinatra's wayward politics suggests that he was unable to adhere to any durable ideal of the good society. To be sure, as he grew older, he became notably more skeptical about schemes of social improvement. Arguably, his respect for the aggression and guile he learnt on the streets of Hoboken expanded. Inversely, his fugitive pleasures delivered diminishing returns. In the final decade of his life, the drinking sessions were often maudlin, lachrymose affairs, as he morosely toasted absent friends. Sinatra remained the center of ceremonies, if no longer, for reasons of apparent dementia, the master. He was still the object of success by which his drinking buddies were urged to measure their own worth. His story was still, in the final analysis, the only relevant *his-story*.

Inasmuch as this is so, it is appropriate to see Sinatra as an orthodox narcissist. The narcissist has problematic relationships with the external world because he places himself at the unequivocal center of it. This is actually a state of withdrawal because it does not engage with the real external world but replaces real relationships with fantasy substitutes. After achieving celebrity, Sinatra's relationships with women, peers, the Mafia, and presidents possessed a high level of fantasy content. He imagined himself to be irresistible and omnipotent. He saw himself as beyond the rule of law and dealt with any friction of conscience by identifying the common good with the fulfillment of his self-interest.

This is a point of view that requires considerable displays of sociability. Although the narcissist feels fundamentally cut off from worldly life since it fails to measure up to his perceived superior status, he needs company because it provides a forum for the giving of tributes and honors.

Sinatra's appetite for partying and clubbing was legendary. He lived for the nightlife and performing. Habitually, he made it a point of honor to stay up until dawn. His dress sense was generally fastidious and arguably obsessive, which is why I earlier described the mid-1960s episode involving the love beads and Nehru jacket as excruciating. His suit maker was Carroll & Co. of London and Beverly Hills. When he wore a tuxedo he insisted that the shirt cuffs extended no more than half an inch from the jacket sleeve. His trousers were not permitted to extend further than the top of his shoe. He tried to avoid sitting down because this wrinkled the cloth. His custom-made shirts were buttoned beneath the crotch. His trouser pockets were carefully arranged: an inside pocket held a white linen handkerchief and little mints, and he carried individually folded tissues in the outer left and a single key on a fob. His paper cash was held in a money clip. He never carried credit cards. He usually wore a pocket handkerchief, generally orange, because it was his favourite colour. Cufflinks were *de rigueur*. His favored supplier was one Swifty Morgan based in Florida. Although he was oddly averse to some perfumes on women, he usually smelled of *Yardley's English Lavender* or the Spanish cologne *Agua Lavanda Puig*. His closets were meticulously arranged. The state of dishabille was anathema to him, provoking complaints of toxic manners and a lack of self-respect when he encountered it in others. As Tina Sinatra recollects:

> I would marvel at the way things were hung together in categories. Sweaters were folded on shelves; the hats were perched in rows up on the highest shelf; shoes with shoe trees lined the floors. Everything smelled like him. He had a scent and a style and an order to his life always.
> (Quoted in Zehme 1997: 128)

The process of tipping was likewise primed and orderly. He referred to his tipping as "duking." The term derives from Tin Pan Alley where skimming cash was known colloquially as "dipping his duke in the tambourine." Typically, Sinatra's tips were $100 bills, which is why his behavior on the 1974 tour to Australia when he dispensed $200 bills to all hotel and valet staff was out of character. Perhaps this was his way of diffusing the intense hostility directed at him by the Australian media at this time. According to Tina Sinatra (2000: 228), in his usual social life he gave $100 for a round of drinks and $200 for valet parking. The bills were folded three times into small squares to make it easy to pass them unobtrusively in a handshake. Among Sinatra's tribe, Jimmy Van Heusen, Jilly Rizzo and Hank Cattaeno were delegated the task of carrying and dispensing the money. His generosity was kingly, showering not merely money but also his blessing upon the recipient. Even in old age, Sinatra was concerned with making his mark, with leaving an impression on everyone he encountered.

The tensions between the public and the private face

George Herbert Mead (1934) held that it is useful to divide the individual between the "I" (the veridical self, or I as I am) and the "Me" (myself as seen by others). The "Me" is assembled from the attitudes and values of the social group and, as such, amounts to the internalization of the generalized other. The healthy individual maintains equilibrium between the "I" and the "Me," so that neither side is permitted to overshadow the other. For the narcissist this equilibrium can often be very precarious indeed. Public acclaim inflates the "Me" so that the "I" feels engulfed and under threat of annihilation. This is especially acute in the case of achieved celebrity. In normal circumstances the I/Me confronts the frailty and vulnerability that is part of the human lot as a mutual partnership. Conversely, for achieved celebrities, the "I" remains locked in the condition of frailty and vulnerability because its true worth is scarcely recognized by the public, while the "Me" is pumped up to appear seductive, radiant, and serenely untouchable.

Moreover, the multiple and conflicting claims of the public introduce schism in the construction of the "Me," so that stable internalization of the generalized other is obstructed. Achieved celebrities are often prey to deeply distressing anxieties and fears about their status with the public. They are more likely to have cosmetic surgery to defend the public's image of the "Me" and to falsify frailty and vulnerability. Statistically, they are also more likely to develop dependence on drugs and alcohol, and resort to psychoanalysis to maintain a public face of equilibrium. The consequence of this is to further undermine the sense of "I as I am." The "I" responds to the public inflation of the "Me" by heightening anxieties concerning annihilation and disappearance. In some cases achieved celebrities resort to regarding the public as a monster that inexorably threatens to devour them. One coping strategy is to withdraw inwardly so as to restore the resources of the "I." Arguably, the classic example of this is Greta Garbo, who withdrew from the limelight at the height of her career for reasons of self-preservation.

Even in the "Dark Ages," when Sinatra's relationship with the public was the most perplexed, his narcissism prevented him from following the Garbo route into voluntary obscurity. Despite declining record sales, film roles and nightclub bookings he continued to court public attention and present himself as the center of the world. He dealt with the disequilibrium between the "I" and the "Me" by two strategies. First, he subjected himself to fulsome self-exculpation. For example, in 1955, during an interview with the writer A. E. Hotchner which touched on the causes behind his career collapse between 1947 and 1953, he observed:

> I did it. I'm my own worst enemy. My singing went downhill and I went downhill with it, or vice versa – but nobody hit me in the throat or choked me with my necktie. It happened because I paid no attention to how I was singing. Instead, I wanted to sit back and enjoy my success and sign autographs and bank the heavy cash. Well, let me tell you, nobody who's successful sits back and enjoys it. I found that out the hard way. You work at it all the time, even harder than when you were a nobody. Enjoyment is just a by-product of success – you get a kick out of it, fine, but the only real fun in being successful is working hard at the thing that brings you success . . . You hear all the time about guys who showed big promise or who even made it to the top and then suddenly they flub out. Everybody says they must have developed a block or lost their touch or one of the guys at the office was out to get them or whatever: Well, maybe that's just a fancy way of saying the thing I found out: The only guy can hurt you is yourself. (Quoted in Zehme 1997: 218)

In this passage Sinatra denigrates himself only as a pretext to holding that an enlarged, richer personality was given to the world through his suffering, a typical strategy of the narcissistic personality.

Sinatra's second strategy was to construct an inner circle, an allotment of confidantes, to act as a buffer between his exalted state and the fleshy world of the unexalted. As a narcissist, he kept most people at arm's length. When he allowed you into his inner circle and private life he required absolute obedience with his code of honor. Since this code was articulated through example rather than instruction, it was notoriously difficult for others to fathom and apply. Sammy Davis Jr first broke the code in 1959 when, in the course of Jack Eigen's radio show in Chicago, he ventured:

> I love Frank and he was the kindest man in the world to me when I lost my eye in an auto accident and wanted to kill myself. But there are many things he does that there are no excuses for. Talent is not an excuse for bad manners . . . it does not give you the right to step on people and treat them rotten. This is what he does occasionally. (Quoted in Quirk and Schoell 1998: 170)

Sinatra punished Sammy for this soliloquy in his customary fashion. He ceased to speak to him, banned him from attending any of his public performances, and arranged for MGM to replace Sammy with Steve McQueen in the film *Never So Few* (1959). Sammy was forced to make a humiliating public apology during a TV interview. Only then was Sinatra prepared to relent.

Later in the 1960s and early 1970s, Sinatra broke with Sammy again. This time the cause was Davis Jr's addiction to cocaine, which Sinatra abhorred as unmanly. After a long period of rejection, Sinatra instructed Davis Jr to quit the drug if he wanted to regain the friendship. Sammy complied and in the last few years of his life good relations with Sinatra prevailed.

Sinatra's cruelty had a casual, desultory aspect. It could be articulated thoughtlessly and without apparent premeditation. It was as if he relished pushing relationships to breaking point by using abuse and invective to precipitate a crisis in which loyalty to him would be tested. Sinatra seemed unable to draw the line between what would pass for ribald banter within his circle and wounding abuse in public. He was so used to being king-of-the-castle among his intimate associates that his judgment about the face he showed to these confidantes and the face he showed to the public was often faulty. The inner cabinet of Sinatra's tribe was the Rat Pack. With Dean Martin, Sammy Davis Jr, Peter Lawford and Joey Bishop, between the mid-1950s and mid-1960s, Sinatra achieved a legend of ensemble performance that defined male values in consumer culture. In the words of Quirk and Schoell:

> In 1960, Frank and the Rat Pack were the epitome of cool. Men wanted to be like them, live like them, make love like them: they wanted to stay out all night like they did, bed a different broad whenever they felt like it, and never fear any consequences. They wanted to smoke and drink until it made them sick, throw money around like it was meaningless and feel like irresponsible, irrepressible college boys again. (1998: 184)

The Rat Pack appeared to work for fun, and they earned vast sums of money in so doing. They hinted at limitless sexual licence. They placed themselves on the wheel of conspicuous consumption and unapologetic hedonism. They ridiculed pomposity and formality. Their unvarying attire of evening dress was presented as a mark of respect for the audience. The sentiments of the stage act were generally self-mocking, licentious and occasionally bawdy. Yet there was a code of honor behind Rat Pack repartee. It was based on the male clannish recognition that all five performers had been bruised by faulty relationships with women, drink, bad business deals, and entertainment business double-think. Dean Martin described the Rat Pack as "like the PTA – a Perfect Togetherness Association" (Levy 1998: 186).

Perhaps the best way to think about it is as the public variant of Humphrey Bogart's famous "Fuck You Fund." Throughout his career Bogart was careful with money, always saving a large proportion of his film fees. When a reporter asked him why he was building up large reserves of money instead of enjoying spending it, Bogart replied that the money was going into his "Fuck You Fund." Whenever, a movie mogul tried to inveigle him to play a role he was not interested in, or a director became insolent or boorish, the fund gave Bogart leave to say "Fuck You." It gave him the luxury of walking away from the venture, without needing to worry how he could continue to pay the bills. It was the achieved celebrity's charter for doing as he pleased.

Similarly, the Rat Pack "Perfect Togetherness Association" was akin to a performers' combination against the cutthroat entertainment industry. They aimed to maximize control over the stage act, recordings and films, and their earnings from them. The Rat Pack was therefore a form of both financial and emotional protectionism. Its style was to emphasize minimal constraint from the financial and managerial fetters that bound other performers. As such, it was an important precursor to the more informal and personally advantageous financial and artistic deals sought by independent film stars, directors and musicians in the 1960s.

Chapter 35

Alison Hearn

"JOHN, A 20-YEAR-OLD BOSTON NATIVE WITH A GREAT SENSE OF HUMOR"

On the spectacularization of the "self" and the incorporation of identity in the age of reality television

Introduction

IN THE FALL OF 1996, Steelcase, a manufacturer of office furniture, installed an unusual piece of "art" in the lobby of its headquarters: a giant colony of 1,500 harvester ants encased in a large beveled steel and glass structure. According to company spokesman, Dave Lathrop, the colony was intended to function as a metaphor to describe how people work and live: "Work is dramatically different than it used to be. For more people, work and non-work are blending. Ants live to work, and work to live. We enjoy the ability of the ants to silently represent that, simply by doing what they do" (Petersen 1996: B1).

Multi-level marketing companies, such as Amway and Mary Kay, would certainly appreciate such a potent metaphor. After all, these organizations are notorious for encouraging their participants to integrate work into every aspect of their lives and to develop deep affective bonds to the company. They employ very specific management strategies in order to "transform work–family conflict and general ambivalence about work into commitment" (Pratt and Rosa 2003: 395). Like the colony of ants, these organizations "harvest" ambivalence and conflict, recognizing that, once converted, conflicted participants adhere to their "new faith more strongly than born members" (Pratt and Rosa 2003: 414). These harvesting strategies are intended to bind workers tightly, body and soul, to the company. As one enthusiastic Amway worker has said: "People say we brainwash people. That's true! We are talking about brainwashing to make you all more positive people!" (Pratt 2000: 456).

In effect, and unbeknownst to them, the ants at Steelcase and multi-level marketing companies like Amway work to signify the conditions of what Antonio Negri and other autonomist Marxists have famously called "the social factory" (Negri 1989, Hardt and Negri 2000). Here work is dispersed into all areas of life and the social becomes the site for the creation of new forms of productive activity and their transformation into commodities. These new forms of productive activity involve immaterial labor, defined as the expression and development of human communicative capacity: "the kinds of activities involved in defining and fixing cultural and artistic standards, fashions, tastes, consumer norms, and . . . public opinion" (Lazzarato 2005). Immaterial labor is based on what Paolo Virno has termed "virtuosity" – "an activity which finds its own fulfillment (that is, its own purpose) within itself" (Virno 2004: 52) which, under post-Fordist capitalism, has become waged activity. Immaterial labor, while often invisible, works "to promote continual innovation in the forms and conditions of communication. It gives form to and materializes needs, the imaginary, consumer tastes" (Virno 2004: 52). It generates not only concrete products but new relations and conditions of production as well. According to autonomist Marxist critics, the conditions of the social factory, marked as they are by ever-developing forms of immaterial labor, constitute "the real sub-sumption" of all social existence by capital.[1] Just as in the colony of harvester ants, or in an Amway marketing scheme, life in the social factory is, quite simply, all labor all the time.

What distinguishes the worst multi-level marketer from the best harvester ant, however, is that his work is formed, not only within his singular imagination, but also within the abstract, imaginative ethos of "work" under capital: the *story* of the social factory, which depicts life as a non-stop entrepreneurial venture, predicated on virtuosic communicative capacity, inevitably leading to self-fulfillment and auton-omy. While the harvester ant serves as a metaphor for work, the Amway partici-pant embodies this new form of labor every day within an abstract imaginative ethos both modeled and produced by the paradigmatic industry of the post-Fordist era – "the quintessence of the mode of production in its entirety" (Virno 2004: 60) – the culture industry.

In what follows I will explore the ways in which "reality" television programming, which has initiated a new business model for, and a new genre within, the culture industry, works to harvest the conditions of the social factory by simultaneously narrating these conditions and producing new forms of immaterial labor in and through them. I will argue that the form of work performed by the shows' partici-pants involves the self-conscious development and management of a public persona based on templates of the "self" supplied by corporate media culture. I will trace some of the ways in which this work of self-presentation is understood to be the work of self-commodification: a process that operates simultaneously as labor for the television industry and as a form of image-entrepreneurship for the individual participants. I will also argue that this form of work, insofar as it involves the alienation of embodied subjectivity into image commodities with recognizable market value, constitutes a form of self-spectacularization.

Reality television programming provides the templates for these forms of token-ized persona within a distinct corporate culture, which aims to contain and control individuals' virtuosity. In light of this, I will explore some resonant connections between the content and labor practices of reality television and established corporate management strategies for successful employee socialization and commitment. *The Apprentice* and *Joe Schmo* are offered as examples of "reality" shows that dramatize and embody the collapse of any meaningful distinction between notions of the self and capitalist processes of production. As narratives that both tell the story of the social factory and produce its social relations and conditions through immaterial labor, reality television programs involve what we might call the "incorporation of identity." Finally I will briefly speculate about the ways we might understand this process of both narrating and producing a branded "self" as part of a broader multi-level marketing campaign we could call "the corporate colonization of the 'real' ".

The spectacularization of the self

1

I'm in Boston at a popular bar called "The Rack". The bar is full of young adults, all sitting at tables writing intently. These 18- to 24-year-olds are not studying for exams in this famous college town; they are filling out applications to audition for an MTV "real movie" called *The Real Cancun*.

I slide in next to some kids at a booth and introduce myself. I have a tape-recorder with me, am middle-aged and, I assume, reasonably legitimate-looking. Before I get a chance to explain my project and directly ask for their consent, one of them says, "YES! I'd love to be interviewed, what do you want to know?" The others perk up and pay attention. I sense they think this is part of the audition. I turn on the tape recorder and ask for their names. They all reply eagerly, sitting up straight, flipping their hair, and, with cadences down pat, like car salesmen trying to close a deal, they offer me their best pitch:

> "My name's John and I'm a 20-year-old Boston native with a great sense of humor and an adventuresome spirit."

> "I'm Jenny. I'm planning to be a nurse, but being in this movie is my destiny! It would be a dream come true . . ."

> "Hi, I'm Matt. I'm 19 years old and I really feel I have something special to share with the world . . ."

I recall Jean Baudrillard's "Disneyworld Company", in which he writes: "We are no longer alienated and passive spectators, but interactive extras (*figurants interactifs*); we are the meek, lyophilized members of this huge 'reality show' "(Baudrillard 1996). Lyophilized, meaning "freeze-dried", seems an apt description of the responses I receive that day in Boston; they are pre-set, freeze-dried presentations of self, molded by prior knowledge of the dictates of the reality television genre and deployed strategically to garner attention and, potentially, profit.

2

One way to understand the work of reality television is as a narrative legitimating the cultural transition into the post-real visual world of new media technology and the new surveillance economy.[2] The rhetorical deployment of the term "reality" as a name-brand for a genre of television shows, as signifying just another realm of image-making, might be read as ideological assurance that we are, indeed, beyond the "real" in and of itself. This colonization of the word "reality" by corporate media and its application to the processes of televisual image-making tacitly affirms the ascendance of the virtual-life, the priorities and values of techno-capital, and, more importantly, legitimates all forms of economic and political maneuvering being done in their name.

Part of the cultural work of reality television, then, is to tell us stories about the new immersive experiences of on-line culture and virtual worlds. Reality television does this by self-consciously revealing the internal workings of its production practices, incorporating "regular people" into the shows, and offering us facsimiles of technologies-to-come through voting rituals and interactive appeals. Insofar as these shows are crude imitations of immersive post-real environments, we might argue that participating in them is more akin to going to a theme park, such as Disneyworld, than anything else; participants on reality television are simply taking a trip to TVLand.

Exposing the inner workings of the television industry is not new. In his 1961 book *The Image*, Daniel Boorstin claims that "some of the most effective advertising nowadays consists of circumstantial descriptions of how the advertising images were contrived . . . the stage machinery, the process of fabricating and projecting the image fascinate us" (Boorstin 1961: 194). He goes on to argue that "paradoxically . . . the more we know about the tricks of image building, about the calculation, ingenuity, and effort that have gone into a particular image, the more satisfaction we have from the image itself" (Boorstin 1961: 195).

What is new about reality television production is the way in which viewers themselves are summoned to get inside the mechanics of the industry and offer their bodies and labor up to the image making machinery for free.[3] Much like donning Mickey Mouse ears at Disneyland, becoming a part of the immersive television experience involves adopting a "persona" consonant with its dictates: the jock, the vixen, the asshole, the gay guy, the rich bitch, the grizzled vet, the buddy. Reality television entices viewers to go on its various "rides" and calls this "real". As Baudrillard writes: "It is no longer the contagion of spectacle that alters reality, but rather the contagion of virtuality that erases the spectacle" (Baudrillard 1996).

3

While reality television programming works ideologically to legitimate the new surveillance economy and the ascendance of techno-capital, it also functions more concretely to produce new forms of labor. What is the nature of this labor and what kind of value are laborers hoping to produce?

In his essay "Phantasmagoric Capital," Ernest Sternberg maps three distinct discourses of labor since the dawn of the industrial age. The discourse of romantic labor is based on the exhibition of "character": depth, fortitude, moral upbringing, perseverance, obedience, and humility. All classes of workers labor to express these values. Modernist labor is embodied in the ideals of Taylorism. Here labor is atomized, individualistic and valued only in terms of quantitative outputs. Workers obey management not out of "inner-developed" notions of loyalty and morality, but because it is patently in their self-interest to do so; submission to standardized systems increases output and benefits everyone eventually (Sternberg 1998:3–21).

In the new phantasmagoric workplace, as Sternberg calls it, workers labor to produce persona consonant with the dictates of their particular jobs. Just as we accept the loading up of goods with evocative emotions and meanings by advertisers, we understand that we, ourselves, must also consciously self-present. We load ourselves up with meaningfulness; we work hard at issues of self-image in an effort to constitute ourselves as "significant" iconic-workers. It is just as important to be seen as a good nurse, executive, flight attendant, as it is to actually do the tasks that make up the job; the "capacity for calculated posing" has become a routine job requirement. Sternberg writes: "The new firm must reward the iconographic capabilities in the workforce. Whether the firm sells services, or packaged vegetables, or residences, workers must have the iconographic capability to heighten product value. Workers must act out their persona on the job" (Sternberg 1998: 11).

Under phantasmagoric capitalism, notoriety and recognition serve as "proxy indicators" of personal ability. If a person is well known, then their persona-producing capacity must be good; therefore they must be a good bet, a good worker and a good hire. In this new economy of the image, we are always already engaged in "face-work" (Goffman 1967).

Paul du Gay and Colin Gordon have mapped the ways in which the workplace has become "customer-saturated," arguing that the discourses of consumer society have infiltrated our approach to work. This results in a workplace where "work becomes an arena in which people exhibit an 'enterprising' and 'consuming' relationship to self, where they 'make a project of themselves' " (du Gay 2000: 70). Dominant forms of social control and governance express the logic of the market system and operate through the soul of the worker, thus promoting a view of the individual as an "entrepreneur of the self," engaged in the "continuous business of living to make adequate provision for the preservation, reproduction, and reconstruction of (their) own human capital" (Gordon 1991: 44).

Sternberg's characterization of the phantasmagoric workplace as dependent on the persuasive performance of the self, and du Gay's and Gordon's description of the entrepreneurial self, resonate with Paolo Virno's claim that the post-Fordist workplace is marked by virtuosity put to work for capital.[4] For Virno, individual virtuosity involves a capacity for improvised performance, linguistic and communicative innovation, and inevitably requires the presence of others. Virno argues that, under post-Fordist capitalism, "productive labor, in its totality, appropriates the special characteristics of the performing artist" (Virno 2004: 54–55). Here Virno makes a link between the entrepreneurial self and the culture industry. He argues that it is the culture industry, in particular, where "the virtuoso begins to punch a time card" (Virno 2004: 56). The practices of the cultural industry have become "generalized and elevated to the rank of *canon*" (Virno 2004: 58). The culture industry, then, is the exemplary mode of production, as it provides templates for effective performance, communicative, and image skills, all requisite for the production of the entrepreneurial self.

At the level of narrative, reality television shows offer instruction about how to become a media celebrity. Many of these shows, such as *American Idol* (Frot-Coutaz et al. 2002–), *Making the Band* (Singer and Mok 2000) *America's Next Top Model* (Mok and Banks 2003), and *Tough Enough* (Mok 2001) have the story of celebrity shaping as their central theme. The body makeover shows, of course, are the literal enactment of face work, involving the material construction of the body according to the dictates of celebrity culture, illustrated in shows like *I Want a Famous Face* (Sirulnick and Lazin 2004), or the beauty pageant standard, as in *The Swan*. (Weed *et al.* 2004–). The endless list of transformation shows, such as *Extreme Makeover Home Edition* (Armstrong *et al.* 2004–), *Trading Spaces* (Cohen-Dickler *et al.* 2000–), or *What Not to Wear* (Harvey 2003–), to name only a few, offer instruction on how to achieve the appropriate body, home, and personality for success on the more general market in social status.

At the level of production, however, it is possible to argue that when viewers become participants they are not only laborers for the television industry, but have also become image-entrepreneurs, representing the ultimate socialization of labor, in which "the activities of people not just as workers, but as students, consumers, shoppers, and, most notably, viewers are directly integrated into the production process" (Dyer-Witheford 1999: 158). Reality television programs provide the mechanism whereby participants can effectively construct personae and put them to commercial use. Participants are laboring to create a product they know has market value – fame.

4

American courts have recognized fame as a commodity since 1953. At this time the courts established that the commercial use of an individual's persona without their consent did not constitute an invasion of their privacy, but, rather, an appropriation of a valuable asset: "the ability to profit from the commercialization of one's persona is less a privacy interest and more a kind of property interest, fully alienable, and, in many jurisdictions, descendible, as well" (Jacoby and Zimmerman 2002: 1229–1330). The courts have called these "publicity rights." When a celebrity grants exclusive rights in his persona to someone else, "what has occurred is the transfer of his property" (Jacoby and Zimmerman 2002: 1330).

Recent court cases have underscored the notion of fame as commodity. Joe Piscopo's wife was able to sue for half his publicity rights in their divorce. Every time he trades on his name, his ex-wife gets half the profit (Jacoby and Zimmerman 2002: 1339). Other examples of the market in fame include David Bowie's 1997 offer of Bowie Bonds, where his fame and iconic status were offered as bond security on the open market.[5] Product endorsement deals often constitute more income for sports and entertainment celebrities than the work that made them famous in the first place. Tiger Woods made 63 million dollars in 2001 trading on his fame alone (Craig 2002).

Fame is a saleable commodity in its own right. It can be reasonably argued that reality television provides a quick and easy way for individuals to self-commodify: to generate and brand their own personae and "get" fame, which can be exchanged for cash down the line. Participants on reality television function both as image-entrepreneurs, as they work to produce branded versions of themselves, and as unpaid laborers for the networks who reap huge financial rewards as a result of lowered production costs. The immaterial labor of the construction of persona is simultaneously enacted in reality television's narratives and on their shop floors.

5

The notable thing about the kinds of personae generated on reality television is that they are not tied to any particular kind of work or specific skill set we might recognize. Instead they are lyophilized images of various types of "modern individuals", versions of the everyday self, generated inside the structural limits set by reality television show producers and editors. Mark Burnett reveals his repertoire of 16 character types in *Survivor 2: The Field Guide*: "the entertainer, the leader, the flirt, the underdog, the professor, the zealot, the mom, the athlete, the wild and crazy guy/girl, the quiet one, everybody's friend, the feral child, the introvert, the redneck, the slacker and the snake" (Burnett 2001: 69). As Burnett describes them, these character types are strategic choices made by the contestants, generated out of their own unique personalities (Burnett 2001: 89). We might also see these character types as rendered from individuals' virtuosity; they are the result of creative and communicative improvisation, which takes place inside a tightly controlled corporate context.

The freeze-dried versions of the self that emerge in the finished product, however, are not freely chosen but are determined by agents of the industry during editing and eventually become fully alienable – legally subject to all kinds of ownership issues. Participants sign away control of their voices, images and likenesses, often in perpetuity. A section of an *American Idol* contract reads: "other parties . . . may reveal and/or relate information about me of a personal, private, intimate, surprising, defamatory, disparaging, embarrassing or unfavorable nature, that may be *factual and/or fictional*."[6] As Jacoby and Zimmerman warn, "the choice to convert the human persona into an asset subject to market exchange not only provides a vehicle for channeling extra benefits to the famous and to their voluntary transferees but also opens the door for others – whether spouses, the IRS, or unsatisfied creditors – to assert actual claims to the value of that fame" (Jacoby and Zimmerman 2002: 1445).

Here we see persona tokenized. It is now a product with market value, forged in the machinery of the commercial television industry. The image tokens produced are resonant with the image-thinking characteristic of phantasmagoric capital and its interests. Following Daniel Boorstin, these image tokens are "synthetic, believable, passive, vivid, simplified, and ambiguous" (Boorstin 1961: 185), and they are thoroughly detachable, "alienable," from the bodies that may have initially generated them. The successful work of persona is conflated with the production and circulation of the image in capitalist exchange.

If, with Virno, we allow that the spectacle involves "human communication which has become a commodity" (Virno 2004: 60), and we maintain Debord's insistence that the spectacle describes both a process whereby "images detached from every aspect of life merge into a common stream," and "a social relationship between people that is mediated by images" (Debord 1994: 12), we might understand the creation of a tokenized persona as constituting a practice we could call the "spectacularization" of the self.

The incorporation of identity

1

In the past few decades we have seen the restructuring of capital to contain the insubordination of labor from below. New communication technologies produce increasing knowledge bases and the need for collective and cooperative innovation, but capital cannot allow their growth and development to go unchecked. Although human innovation and unruly virtuosity will always and inevitably exceed the reach of capital, capital continues to do its best to tame this growth of the general intellect and put it to profitable work.[7] Innovative knowledge, communication skills, and affective skills are contained and conditioned within traditional corporate work sites by participative management programs such as quality circles, team concepts, and total quality management initiatives. Management works hard to incorporate workers through strategies of "organizational seduction" (Lewicki 1981: 5–21).

These management programs address the individual subjectivity and will of the worker. A worker's commitment to the organization is generated by involving them in small-scale decision-making, asking them to take more responsibility for quality control and to get involved in the various relationships and hierarchies within the company. As Maurizio Lazzarato writes, "the worker's personality and subjectivity have to be made susceptible to organization and command . . . today it is the soul of the worker which must come down into the factory" (Lazzarato 2005). In this way, while workers become master communicators and may feel as though they have become entrepreneurs of the self, they only do so according to the dictates of capitalist management structures. Charles Sabel argues that, while "employees . . . are encouraged to think of themselves as entrepreneurs," their "enhanced autonomy is simultaneously qualified by the same situation that produced it" (Sabel quoted in du Gay 2000: 71). Participative management programs remain authoritarian: "one *has* to express oneself, one *has* to speak, communicate, cooperate, and so forth. The 'tone' is that of the people who are in executive command" (Lazzarato 2005).

Studies of multi-level marketing companies, in particular, note the development of organizational socialization strategies intended to strengthen the affective bonds between workers and their organizations. Companies like Amway construct narratives that emphasize the importance of the link between familial bonds, self-expression, entrepreneurship, and capital. Amway participants are encouraged to get involved in an on-going process of "dream-building," which helps recruits set personal and sales goals, and "positive programming," which involves surrounding recruits with uplifting messages and supportive people. Through "dream-building" rituals these companies encourage "seekership" in their members. "Seekership" involves acknowledging the shortcomings of one's life situation, and searching for "more meaningful meanings" through work for the company. "Sense breaking" of previously held meanings is encouraged in recruits as they embrace their "seekership." Within the dream-building paradigm, a recruit is always running an "identity deficit," striving to attain ideals that remain just out of reach. All dreams at Amway, however, are not created equal. Amway dreams must involve attaining financial security and personal autonomy through entrepreneurial rigor (Pratt 2000: 456–470).

In a foundational article of management literature entitled "People Processing," John Van Maanen identifies several standard strategies of organizational socialization. These include "collective" socialization techniques, whereby individuals are trained and socialized in groups. "Tournament" socialization techniques involve tracking employees according to differences in skills, ambition and background, pitting them against each other, and offering no recourse should they lose: "when you win, you win only the right to go on to the next round; when you lose, you lose forever" (Van Maanen 1978: 30). Van Maanen argues that this form of socialization "can shape and guide ambition in powerful ways" (Van Maanen 1978: 30). Another well-known socialization technique involves the process of "divestiture" where personality characteristics of the entering recruit are systematically dismantled. Recruits "must often suffer considerable mortification and humiliation, to pay the dues necessary before they are considered equal and respected participants in their particular professions" (Van Maanen 1978: 33). In extreme cases, recruits are isolated from established friendships, put through initiation rituals, and forced to abstain from certain types of behaviour. They "must publicly degrade themselves and others through various kinds of mutual criticism, and must follow a rigid set of . . . rules and regulations" (Van Maanen 1978: 34). The ordeal aspects of divestiture are identity building as well as identity destroying. According to Van Maanen, collective, tournament, and divestiture strategies, taken together, will deliver a "passive group of hard-working but undifferentiated recruits" (Van Maanen 1978: 35). As Roy Lewicki notes in his article "Organizational Seduction," if the socialization program has worked, the organization "does not have to kick you, you kick yourself" (Herzberg quoted in Lewicki 1981: 14).

2

These socialization strategies resonate strongly with the narrative themes and labor practices of reality television shows such as *The Apprentice* (Burman *et al.* 2004–) and *Joe Schmo* (Ross *et al.* 2003). Originally aired in North America during the 2003–2004 season, both of these "reality" shows tell stories about work. Both shows employ many of the management strategies described above, including collective training, tournament play, and identity breaking and building practices.

These strategies are most obvious with *The Apprentice*, a reality show about corporate training, in which contestants compete to win a job from uber-corporate persona Donald Trump. The show demands that contestants work together, competing in teams on a series of "business" tasks. The losing team must meet with Trump, where they are asked to evaluate and betray each other. Finally one member of the losing team must submit to the ultimate degradation of being fired by Trump. The aspirational discourse of *The Apprentice* reflects the strategies of dream building and seekership. As winners of challenges are treated to the high life aboard helicopters, in country clubs and lavish restaurants, participants are constantly exhorted to "get into the mindset" of being rich.

While *The Apprentice* requires the same gaming skills as shows like *Survivor* (Burnett 2000), it abandons their highly fictionalized conceits by situating the game inside its presumed natural habitat – the cut-throat world of corporate capitalism.

With the tagline "It's nothing personal, it's just business," *The Apprentice* markets itself as the real face of contemporary competition, eschewing all other reality television diversions, such as interpersonal melodrama or physical stunts. *The Apprentice* appears to transcend its role as entertainment and move into the realm of public pedagogy, as business schools across the US have used it as a teaching tool in the classroom (Associated Press 2004).

Pedagogical merit aside, the fact remains that the show itself is an exemplary business venture, offering a distinctive line of products. First, *The Apprentice* functions as an extended advertisement for Donald Trump's own various business interests: golf courses, casinos, hotels, bottled water, as well as for his own branded persona. Through the use of strategic product placement and narrative design, the show produces an elaborate marketing campaign for Trump.[8] *The Apprentice* also self-consciously produces itself as a branded form of entertainment or "advertainment" by integrating other corporate brand names and their products into the narrative of the shows. Contestants must develop an advertising campaign for Crest toothpaste, or a new toy for Mattel as a part of the job competition. As a form of branded entertainment, *The Apprentice* serves as a commodity in itself; it now exists simply as branded format, available for sale in media markets across the globe.[9] The sale of cultural content to corporate sponsors functions in tandem with the show's more traditional work of carefully targeting and capturing audiences and selling them to advertisers. The audience commodity is created by producing a distinct cultural text that, on the surface, tells a story about how to succeed in the corporate world as a hard worker. As a constructed narrative, however, the show still functions metaphorically, no matter how appropriate its setting might seem. So, behind the story of work, lies another story for the viewers: a story about who can most successfully construct a notable image persona, which will, by extension, produce profit. Most of the cast members from the first season have gone on to lucrative jobs and endorsement deals based on their "realistic" portrayals of high-flying corporate wannabes on TV. As Omarosa, the "bad girl" of the first season of *The Apprentice* has publicly stated:

> The best thing about the experience was my great sense of accomplishment after (1) being selected out of 250,000 applicants (2) participating in such an awesome game show and (3) truly turning a bad situation into a very lucrative one!! Who knew that being soo bad could be soo good$$!!
>
> (In Anon. 2005)

Here we can see corporate socialization practices hard at work. Omarosa has been flattered by her selection to be on the show. As a result, she expresses her allegiance to the "awesome game show" and its corporate bosses, while simultaneously recognizing that her labor is actually immaterial at its core. Omarosa's performance of herself as "bad" proved to be a "good" (read profit-producing) decision. Herein lies another product of the show; while laboring at performing themselves as corporate moguls-in-training, contestants produce their own branded image tokens.

Joe Schmo tells a story of a "real" person, Matt Kennedy Gould, who believes he is a participant on a reality show entitled *The Lap of Luxury*. The show, however, is an elaborate ruse designed to trick Gould. All the other participants on the show are paid actors. The premise of the "faux-show", *The Lap of Luxury*, is that contestants are locked into an extravagant mansion and must endure grueling competitions and intense psychodrama in order to "outdo, outshine and outperform" their opponents. *Joe Schmo* narrates Gould's experience as he participates in what he believes to be a "real" reality show, as well as the trials and tribulations of the actors, producers and writers as they continually try to keep Gould from catching on. In this way *Joe Schmo* also tells a story about working. The site of this work, however, takes place not in the corporate boardroom, but on the set of a television show.

While it can be argued that *Joe Schmo* is of a different order than *The Apprentice* because its appeal is not competition-based and it overtly recognizes its strategic and satirical deployment of the "reality show" motif, its aesthetic markers – music, editing, use of the confessional camera – are all standard reality show style. The confessional camera captures the actors talking about their acting troubles and their concerns about deceiving Gould. Split screen shots regularly depict the producers and director in the control room, nervously conducting what they have called their "elaborate social experiment." The opening credits display the actors as their clichéd characters – the bitch, the vet, the buddy, the gay guy, etc. – and a voice-over describes the complicated deception being undertaken by the producers of the show.

The dramatic content of *Joe Schmo* does not come from games or competition, or even from social conflict, but from watching Gould participate in what everyone else knows is an illusion, from witnessing his attenuated duping, and from the struggle by the actors and producers to make sure that the deception is not revealed. The central theme of the show, then, becomes the challenge of its own construction. This is most pointedly illustrated at the climax of the show, when the "truth" is revealed to Gould. Here the host states over and over again that the whole ruse has been for Gould's *good*. They have done it all *for* him. The cast and crew, the producers and the network have selflessly constructed this elaborate ruse in order to turn "the nice guy next door, into television's hottest new star" (Ross et al. October 9 2003, Episode 9).

Joe Schmo is not a satire of reality television, but a story about the challenges of reality television production. It asks for viewers' emotional investment in a story about how to succeed on that terrain, and focuses on narrativizing the difficult kinds of face work and persona construction required by TVLand. It employs methods of tournament socialization, and, most notably, of divestiture to bring Gould into the fold of the television industry. And, in the end, after destroying his identity, it dream-builds with him, hoping to encourage his seekership in the world of the image industry. In many senses, *Joe Schmo* is a more honest representation of the contemporary working world, as it fixes our gaze and interest away from the boardroom and onto the television studio as the real site of cultural competence and success.

3

Given these descriptions of the labor and narrative practices of reality television programming and their resonance with corporate socialization strategies, it makes sense to consider the ways in which we might see reality television itself as part of a multi-level marketing campaign for the corporate "real." Multi-level marketing depends upon the recruitment of participants to initially buy a product, and then to become distributors themselves. It has been defined as "a way of distributing products or services in which the distributors earn income from their own retail sales and from retail sales made by their direct and indirect recruits" (Vander Nat and Keep 2002: 41). "The party who recruits another participant is the 'upline' of the recruit. The recruited party is the 'downline' of the recruiter" (Koehn 2001: 153). Each person down the chain receives a percentage of the sales of all those they have successfully recruited, while those at the top of the chain of distribution reap the majority of the profit.

With the growing recognition that television content can no longer simply function as a "free lunch inducement"[10] for viewers to watch advertisements, television producers increasingly see programming as a clearing house for products and services and as a source of diverse revenue streams beyond the shows themselves. For example, the profit-making opportunities attached to Mark Burnett's latest reality series *The Contender* (Burnett *et al.* 2005) include: "the sale of ads, an equity stake in boxing brand Everlast as well as more traditional product integration fees, ticket sales from the Contender boxing finale at Caesar's Palace in Las Vegas and future rights to the fighters who star on the show" (Schiller, February 10 2005).

The most lucrative and long lasting of these revenue streams involves securing "rights" to the people laboring on the programs, their production as minor celebrities, as well as the dissemination of a more general set of guidelines about how to become an image-entrepreneur. Similar to the singing contestants on *American Idol*, struggling boxers on *The Contender* not only participate in the reality game show, but also allow producers Burnett and Jeffrey Katzenberg to control their future careers. Burnett and Katzenberg have become registered boxing promoters in the State of California in order to create live boxing events featuring contestants from the series; these live events will have network specials and pay-per-view deals attached to them (Carter 2005). In their attempt to "resurrect boxing as a sport" (Carter 2005), Burnett and Katzenberg effectively colonize it by producing and shaping potential boxers within their strict commercial controls and spectacular logic.

In a recent *New York Times* article Burnett laments the fact that he has been unable to control the future earnings of the non-actors on his other reality shows who have since become famous. About Omarosa, the celebrity villain from the first season of *The Apprentice*, he muses wistfully, "She's not an actress. I don't have access to her future value" (Carter 2005). Burnett recognizes that the profit-making potential from participants on shows like *The Apprentice* extends only as far as the specific "reality" they have been recruited to enact.

What Burnett does not recognize, however, is that the logic of the branded or promotional self is being extended further and further into the population at large through the production and distribution of his shows and their colonization of generalized character types. As previously mentioned, participants on reality shows frequently go on to "represent themselves" in the industry as image entrepreneurs via speaking tours, corporate engagements, and diverse business ventures.[11] As they do so, they indirectly produce profit for those in the industry who are "upline" of them by summoning others to join them "downline." They do this by recounting their experiences and offering instructions on how to engage in the practice of self-branding via the opportunities on offer through "reality" television.

As the practice and promotion of self-branding works its way down the chain of distribution, it eventually ends up in the minds and bodies of non-spectacularized individuals, like John, Jenny, and Matt, the young people I met in Boston. While they have not yet been "chosen" to "seek" and "dream-build" with the corporate culture industry, it is clear that they have already learned to emulate its discourses and values. In mimicking the cadences and platitudes characteristic of the lyophil-ized character types produced by reality television conventions, they clearly recog-nize that these corporatized, promotional versions of the self constitute a distinct form of labour, have market value, and, as such, constitute the only "reality" that matters.

Conclusion

While not all participants on reality television happily accept their constructed image-persona or go on to claim their fame, and viewer response is, inevitably, diverse and uneven, this form of programming continues to successfully recruit "image entrepreneurs" into its service.[12] Both the labor practices and narratives of reality television are a part of the broader aesthetic, institutional, and structural "make-over" of the television industry in recent years. As a medium-in-eclipse, threat-ened by legislative deregulation, global competition, neglect of public broadcast-ing, new media technologies and on-line grass-roots forms of entertainment, main-stream network television in the United States, especially, has focused on developing its role as a promotional and commercial vehicle par excellence. We have seen how reality television programming, specifically, expresses the logic of commodifica-tion and promotion in all of its facets: its institutional origins and processes of produc-tion, its narratives and aesthetics, its strategic management of audience attention and savvy and, most notably, its production of new forms of virtuosic labor. Indeed, the growing trend in branded entertainment marks the overt mythologizing of promo-tional culture itself, whereby the values and logic of promotional activity within the social factory become the content and message of the stories being told, as well as their end product.

Paolo Virno contends that communicative ability is the primary skill required under the post-Fordist mode of production. The "mode and action of the culture industry" then becomes "exemplary and persuasive" (Virno 2004: 58). The spectacle, as expressive of the logic of the post-Fordist system, "portrays labor in itself, the present tense of labor" (Virno 2004: 61). "Reality" television programming both generates and portrays new forms of immaterial labor. In this way, it plays a central role in containing and controlling individual innovation and virtuosity in the post-Fordist era, subjecting them to incorporation inside the logic of capitalist manage-ment conventions and generating narratives and guidelines for a more generalized form of self-branding.

We have seen how the internal needs and logic of reality television summon a notion of the self as a strategic image-invention devised for future profit. As the work of persona becomes both a form of spectacle and an overtly recognized form of labor, we might say, in true post-modern fashion, and not very interestingly, that subjectivity ceases to be a concept located in the body, warranted to an individual, but is displaced, indeterminate, multiple. Certainly subjectivity is an ideal, a "truth" about the self that has been displaced and fractured, but it is also a "truth" that has been overtaken by the logic of the image and put to work for capital. The constitution of the self is now an outer-directed process, which involves our skill at self-production as saleable image tokens. The "self" has become yet another commodity-sign, generated and deployed in a manner akin to other multi-level marketing campaigns.

Unlike the silent demonstration of the harvester ants, the people we see on reality television are involved in a kind of labor that is simultaneously defined by and defining of the imaginative ethos of capital as it takes place within a corporate colony called "reality." As these workers craft their individual persona with an overt understanding of the power and profit associated with notoriety and branded subjectivity, they must also recognize that their labor does not produce commodities per se, but "first and foremost, produces the capital relation" (Lazzarato 2005), furthering the corporate colonization of the "real," the elision of person and thing, the reach of reification, and the real subsumption of social existence by capital.

Notes

1   Nick Dyer-Witheford in *Cyber Marx: Cycles and Circuits of Struggle in High-Technology Capitalism* (Urbana and Chicago: University of Illinois Press, 1999) describes the process of subsumption as "the degree to which labor is absorbed into capital's process of value extraction" (57). "Real" subsumption marks the phase of capital in which all human activity is subject to the extraction of value, and the individual laborer becomes a part of a collective worker "made up of labor power, socially combined."(57). All forms of labor are aggregated to generate the ever-expanding productive "machine" of capital.

2   Mark Andrejevic in his excellent book *Reality TV: The Work of Being Watched* (New York: Rowman and Littlefield, 2004) makes a similar argument when he states that reality television "serves . . . as a form of acclimatization to an emerging economic regime predicated on increasingly unequal access to and control over information" (111). Andrejevic emphasizes the way in which reality television is embedded within a surveillance society based on "mass customization" and "hyper individuation." While entirely sympathetic with Andrejevic's reading, the approach taken here focuses on the way in which reality television, a meta-genre that refers primarily to new types of production practices in the television industry, works to narrativize and enact the productive conditions of the social factory.

3   At the time of writing, there have been over 200 reality television shows produced and aired, and many of these have seen multiple seasons. For a reasonably complete list of these shows see <http://www.realitytvworld.com/realitytvworld/allshows.shtml> (accessed April 23, 2005).

4   It goes without saying that debates about the nature and/or construction of the "self" have preoccupied theorists for centuries. John Locke explicitly recognized the self as a form of property that can be put to work for capital in *The Second Treatise of Civil Government* (Indianapolis: Hackett Publishing, 1980, chapter 5, section 25). Recent and influential theorists such as Michel Foucault in *History of Sexuality Volume One: An Introduction* (New York: Random House, 1978) and *History of Sexuality Volume Two: The Care of the Self* (New York: Random House, 1986) and

Judith Butler, *Gender Trouble* (New York and London: Routledge, 1990) have contributed significantly to debates about the non-essential self: its social construction or performative nature. These debates are not my focus here, however. I wish to describe a more conscious and instrumental human activity, which may or may not have anything to do with a "deeply felt" self or even with some generic and deeply entrenched performative identity such as "man" or "woman." This activity is an outer-directed process of highly stylized self-construction, a cynical kind of labor of the self directly tied to the promotional mechanisms of the post-Fordist market. We might understand this process as involving the addition of a "promotional supplement" to Locke's commodity-self, thereby extending and transforming its "original" commodity form. This "persona produced for public consumption" reflects a "self which continually produces itself for competitive circulation" (Andrew Wernick, *Promotional Culture*, London: Sage, 1991: 193).

5   The trend in bonds secured by the work of artists, musicians and writers is catching on. David Pullman, the Wall Street maven who developed the Bowie Bond, has since done the same for James Brown, Marvin Gay and Motown songwriters Holland and Dozier. See Daniel Kadlec, "Banking on the Stars", *Time.Com*, <http://www.time.com/time/innovators/business/profile_pullman.html> (accessed April 23, 2005).

6   Quoted in Eric Olsen, "Slaves of Celebrity," *Salon* (September 18, 2002), <http://salon.com/ent/feature/2002/09/18/idol_contract/index.html> (accessed April 23, 2005).

7   For a full description of this process of resistance and containment see Lazzarato (2005) and Dyer-Witherford (1999).

8   For an extended discussion of the history of financing practices of reality television, including innovative direct deals between producers and sponsors and the full integration of product placement strategies, see Ted Magder, "The End of TV 101," *Reality TV: Remaking Television Culture*, Susan Murray and Laurie Ouelette (eds) (New York: New York University Press, 2004).

9   For more on the trend to branded entertainment, or "advertainment," which essentially names the flurry of cross-promotions, synergies, and sponsorships now marking the work of the culture industry, see June Deery (2004) "Reality TV as Advertainment," *Popular Communication*, 2 (1): 1–20, Joe Mandese, "NATPE: Branded Entertainment is Topic A", *Broadcasting and Cable*, (January 17, 2005), <http://www.broadcastingcable.com/article/CA496808.html> (accessed April 23, 2005), Gail Schiller, "Product Placement in TV, Films, Soar, Study Finds," *Reuters.com* (March 30, 2005), <http://www.reuters.com/newsArticle.jhtml?type=industryNews&storyID=8031889> (accessed April 23, 2005), or Mark Lasswell, "Brand Me Baby!", *Broadcasting and Cable* (August 23, 2004), <http://www.broadcastingcable.com/article/CA446675.html> (accessed April 23, 2004).

10   This phrase is drawn from Dallas Smythe's famous essay on the audience commodity "Communications: Blindspot of Western Marxism," *Canadian Journal of Political and Social Theory*, 1 (3), Fall (1977): 1–27.

11   Booking agents such as Nykole Lynne (http://www.nykolelynn.com/tvstars4.html), All-American Speakers (http://www.allamericanspeakers.com/celebrity_booking_agency/Reality_TV_ Stars.php) or Reel Management (http://www.reelmanagement.net) promote reality TV stars for all kinds of speaking engagements, campus visits and corporate events.

12   It is beyond the scope of this essay to tackle the sociological effects of this form of programming. Certainly more work is to be done to determine the degree to which this "multi-level marketing campaign," as I have chosen to call it, is catching on. The goal here is simply to draw attention to the ways in which reality television programming is putting virtuosic communicative capacity to work for capital at the same time as it is "mythologizing" these same processes.

Chapter 36

P. David Marshall

NEW MEDIA – NEW SELF
The changing power of celebrity

CELEBRITY, IN ITS ELEVATION of particular personalities to public acclaim and recognition, has relied on a relatively stable media system to circulate its images and stories. Thus, even a decade ago one could confidently write about how industries such as film, television and popular music patterned the production of celebrities. To be sure, celebrity, in its focus on the extra-textual dimensions of the public persona, has always had elements that were out of control of an industry, an apparatus or a system of production. Scandals and gossip were part of the highly structured world of Hollywood studio-era celebrities that sometimes were with the consent of the industry, but also were moments where different configurations of power and influence were revealed. Nonetheless, there had developed by the 1980s a maturity in the structure of a celebrity system of promotion: what could described as a "modern" celebrity in the context of television, film and popular music had emerged: a coherent system of promotion of celebrities was in place that was supported by the industries of print and entertainment television. Audiences were organized carefully and discretely around an array of celebrities and closely connected to cultural commodities. Celebrities themselves were also highly organized as commodities even when they exited the world of cultural commodities and only existed in the tabloid press.

The symbiotic relationship between media and celebrity has been ruptured somewhat in the last decade through the development of new media. The discrete and carefully controlled and distributed structure of the culture industries, where cultural commodities and their promotional extensions are a tightly interwoven tapestry, have been elasticized by the different flows of information that have developed via the Internet and the Web as well as new media forms such as mobile phones, iPods, MP3 players, PDAs, and video and computer games. What follows is an exploration of the intersections between new media and celebrity in an era where media is produced increasingly by the user and the audience. The changing structure of fame has had repercussions that are evident in the proliferations of blogs and webcams as well as fan web sites, and official celebrity sites that are changing the relationships and mediations between user and public personality.

To identify this change, it is worthwhile backing up and identifying how the celebrity has operated in contemporary culture. First of all, we need to understand how celebrity is a "source of the self" (Taylor, 1991). Individuality is one of the ideological mainstays of consumer capitalism where, through consumption, we as individuals can have the serial frisson of transformation and change *and* the sensation of choice and possibility even when we do not act on that possibility. Individuality is equally one of the ideological mainstays of how democracy is conceived through the plaint and appeal to the individual voter/citizen. To maintain this ideology of individuality, there are powerful support structures, institutions, and discourses that work to make the cultural centrality of individuality concretely real. Celebrity and the celebrity culture it spawns can be thought of as one of these discourses of the self that makes individuality concrete and real. It moves the representation of individuality outside of the film, television, sport, politics, or popular music text into what I would call the *extraordinary everyday* as it maps and explains celebrated individuals' activities.

Although I am condensing a great deal here, I want to highlight a couple of key concerns. First, celebrity culture as a discourse is a focus on individualism and identity. Second, it is also a discourse of identification or implied identification by an audience. As I have developed elsewhere, the celebrity's power is its capacity to embody an audience and more specifically the "affective investment" of an audience (Marshall, 1997: 73–75). And third, celebrity is a discourse of becoming and transformation: celebrities' origins are from the populace, their fame is not necessarily derived from prior social status, and their current status is achieved in a lifetime.

These elements of individuality, identification and transformation have been the cornerstones of the celebrity system that have been developed and really institutionalized in our culture industries for most of the twentieth century. The myriad stories about celebrities have become recognized components of our press and our news as entertainment. Supporting the production of celebrities, where the texts of stars are deepened and made more significant than their film, television, music or sporting roles for example have been the background features in newspapers, the gossip magazines, the celebrity profiles and biographies in book publishing, the television talk shows, the celebrity interview which has populated television production, magazine cover stories and newspaper sections. Each of these forms of the extratextual dimensions of stars that work to transform them into celebrities have developed subgenres and categories as well as extensions of a celebrity system further into the arts, politics, sciences, medicine, business, and the academy. The celebrity system is in some sense ubiquitous.

This elaborate system has always generated remarkable connections to its audiences. Fan mail and fan clubs emerged with and alongside Hollywood, and in a similar way, alongside the development of professional sports. This connection underlined the investment — affective investment — that helped the celebrity system establish its economic power in the production of cultural forms. And in many ways, the celebrity system was part of the feedback system for industries such as the film industry to gauge value, impact, and investment in their films. This idea of investment by an audience takes on a more critical dimension in the era of new media precisely because investment and engagement in cultural forms is what new media is altering through an intensification of the cultural experience.

So, the question that I want to answer, but recognize that I can only answer it partially, is whether the elaborate discourse of celebrity – this system as I call it – is challenged by the shifts in the way that we use media in this era of new media cultures? If there are shifts in the sources of the self that new media alter or intensify through experience and use, does this also shift the structure of a celebrity system built on what we would now call traditional media, or is the celebrity discourse impermeable or malleable in its connection to audiences and its expressions of identification?

Differences in subjectivity: audience subject and celebrity power

Traditional media forms such as film, television, and popular music in particular have produced interesting relations between celebrities and their audiences. From film analysis perspectives in the tradition of Christian Metz, the entire cinematic apparatus of film produced larger than life forms of identification for the audience that allowed a kind of projection of the self from the screen icons back into a parallel dream-state for the individual. Film "sutured" a relation between the stars presented and the audience in a powerful form of identification where the audience pleasure is imagining him or herself as the active agent/character on screen.

Television's form of identification has rarely been analyzed as having the same capacity to transform the viewer into a dream-state and substitute ego-ideals in that condition of watching. Television's usual point of consumption has meant that its images have been integrated somewhat into the everyday and the domestic flow of life. Even the interruptions of television, whether in the form of commercials or promotions for other programs, frustrate the coherence of identification of the viewer with the characters and personalities presented. I have described this kind of identification as a form of familiar connection with the audience (Marshall, 1997: 131–132, 190–193) in contrast to the aura of identification that film is often able to produce as an apparatus (Marshall, 1997: 187–190).

Popular music has generally relied on a form of identification that makes the star one of the audience. The age of the performer, their sensibility and attitude are often closely aligned with the audience's and produce a resounding discourse of authenticity. The experience of popular music is one of close relationship to the artist via the concert as the ultimate moment of authentic connection (Marshall, 1997: 193–197).

Collectively, traditional media have produced "audience-subjectivities" that imply the engagement of the audience with particular celebrated personas. The key collective subjectivity developed here is through the category of the audience. Via that category of the audience, the production of our celebrity culture can be characterized as one modalized through an elaborate system of representation. Celebrities in a sense "represent" audiences in various public worlds. In terms of the industry itself, celebrities embody the power of the audience members: the audience's power – their economic clout – is represented by the celebrity and their capacity to deliver that audience for the industry. Often in the political world, celebrities are agents and proxies around particular issues: for instance, Bono of U2 fame represents a large audience's emotional connection and translates that emotional investment into focusing attention on world poverty. Indeed, politicians attempt to produce that same emotional connection to particular issues in order to represent the populace.

Representation, through an elaborate network of public figures, describes the operation and the continued presence and power of our celebrity system and possibly how it has migrated so easily into other realms beyond entertainment. Supporting this organization of representation have been media systems, whether television, radio, print, or film which in their technology are designed to "broadcast" from one to many. In this way, the systemic qualities of the media industry help reinforce the capacity for representation to operate efficiently. The media help focus audiences on particular personae that represent them culturally, politically, and socially.

New media subjectivities: the rise of presentation

In contrast to the traditional media promotion of representational regimes that have supported the organization of a celebrity culture, new media forms help produce a very different subjectivity that advances a *presentational regime*. To understand this difference and its effect on what I would call the very modern and relatively organized world of celebrity culture, it is best to analyze the various new media forms that highlight the presentational over the representational.

The Internet would be difficult to define as a single media form, but it perhaps best embodies the way that a new media subjectivity has emerged. Definitionally, it is simply a network of networks that connect personal and mainframe computers throughout the world for the exchange of information. Nonetheless, this simple description uncovers one of the fundamental changes in which this extensive media form is distinctive from its predecessors, such as television or film. Through sending packets of information in both directions – that is, uploading and downloading from any individual computer – the Internet does not resemble the broadcast model of communication. It permits movement of information in both directions and in many of its forms can be defined as a many-to-many form of communication, in contrast to broadcast technologies' structure of one-to-many. This difference in the capacity to both receive and send information is the first challenge to the representational regime that has become so familiar to us through celebrities.

Equally significant in defining the different relationship people have to technologies such as the Internet is that the information has been digitalized for its exchange among users. The digitalization process has allowed the conversion and manipulation of that information by the myriad users of the Internet. Thus the digital media form is unstable or what I would describe as indiscrete as opposed to the more discrete and defined forms and commodities – films, television programs, albums – that the media industry has produced in the past. In other words, digital media in combination with the many-to-many distribution of the Internet allows for the dispersion of any unitary message as users manipulate the codes for slightly different objectives and ends.

What is emerging from the many practices of the Internet is a changed subjectivity: the technology and its various practices or forms of interaction interpellates or hails us quite differently than a television program or film. The social category of the audience is challenged in the uses made of the Internet. Several writers have tried to define this subjectivity with neologisms such as the pro-sumer (Toffler, 1980), where the idea of the producer and the consumer are wedded together, or the prod-user, where the user and producer are merged (Bruns, 2005: 23, 315–316). In all these efforts to understand the experience and engagement of new media what is underlined is that the "audience" member has become a producer of their content. In some instances, that action of producing is quite limited to just moving from website to website in a particularly individual and idiosyncratic way; in other cases, the user is actively transforming content for redistribution. New media culture thus is generative of a new type of individualism: a will to produce that formulates a shifted constitution of desire and a different connection to the contemporary moment.

Cultural production in this broad characterization is democratized under new media. In that dispersion of sources of cultural production across the users of the Internet, there is an increasing desire to personalize media. This personalization is enacted further through the use of iPods and MP3 players that allow individuals to download and then program their playlists and thereby eliminate the mediating world of broadcast radio. The rapid expansion of mobile phones, PDAs and Blackberries, with a variety of features including cameras, downloadable ringtones, different skins to accessorize their look, email, note-taking, and Internet capacity further underlines how new media personalizes one's media use and environment. Text messaging, email, and chat programs also express the personalization of media use.

New media's democratization of cultural production has also opened the door to not only personal use but also personal expression. Beyond email and other semi-private forms of communication, there has been an explosion in practices of presenting one's self online in the most public way. For well over 10 years, personal websites have been forms of personal if not intimate expression. One's interests, photos of home and family members, along with a commentary on what it all means, have become emblematic of the personal web page. For some, the website actually reconstructs "home" into a virtual space that is both public and private, where the web is a place of performance and staging of the self (Zalis, 2003). These website missives via the Internet's capacity for distribution imply in their own production equivalent status to other media forms.

Andreas Kitzmann has explored these efforts of publicizing the self and has identified these kinds of web sites as a new dimension of what he labels "public privacy" (Kitzmann, 2004: 80–87). For Kitzmann, public privacy developed with the use of the camera and its blending of recording private moments but through the technology allowing for the possibility of these images to be used in the public world. Lalavani explains Kitzmann's position that "what needs to be understood is that portraiture is always about public display, even if the photography is limited to private consumption" (Lalavani in Kitzmann 2004: 83). Similarly, according to Kitzmann home movies (through the instructions of the Kodak guides) encouraged people to maintain the "entertainment value" (84) of their productions and thereby advance the notion of the public privacy of personal productions where "a version of the private [is made] suitable for public consumption" (85–86).

In the era of webcams, the notion of public display of the private is accentuated and presented. Web log or blogs also present the self in a manner that goes beyond the former diary – even though the diary from previous centuries was similarly designed for public consumption. Not only are individuals revealing a great deal about their innermost thoughts and feelings via their blogs, they are designing those renditions for others to read *and* respond to. Jennicam, one of the ur-texts of webcams, documented Jennifer Ringley's life, with cameras positioned throughout her apartment. Her webcam site became celebrated and Jenni became a new media form of celebrity (Marshall, 2004: 54–55). There was nothing particularly special about Jenni other than she was willing to display her home life on camera which allowed the possibility of nude or semi-nude depictions of Jenni and partners on occasion. Kitzmann identifies the elaboration of the mediatization of the self through the example of Amandacam, where Amanda, through a web log and camera, presents herself each month in different cover-girl poses "for the home page, which are modeled after fashion magazines" (Kitzmann 2004: 87). Kitzmann concludes his study of public privacy with the following:

> Whatever the mechanism, its basic function appears to be the creation of a kind of economy of recognition, which often borrows from the tropes of mainstream media and the embedded discourses of control, categorization, and rationalized order. Private space thus undergoes an important mutation by virtue of being coupled with the very public spaces of performance, celebrity, and commercial media
>
> (Kitzmann, 2004: 87)

The mediatizing of the self through new media forms has a couple of dimensions that begin to challenge the relatively structured and controlled world of celebrity culture. First, when developed from more traditional media sources, celebrity produces an eerily similar discourse to blogs and webcams that can also be labeled "public privacy". Celebrity, as we have explained, is often specifically about the extra-textual dimensions of the public persona. Those extra-textual dimensions are discourses of revelation of the private self and we read these to uncover the "real" and authentic person behind the public display. In magazines, entertainment programs and tabloid journals we are led into a world of gossip and background information on the private trials and tribulations of celebrities. As an audience, we use celebrities to talk about sometimes very intimate and private issues but in a very public way. Blogs and webcams break down this representational layer of dealing with the private self in public via celebrity discourses through the display of many selves who present their private worlds for public consumption and talk. Moreover, through web rings and other means of associating different web logs and web sites, the Internet produces communities where different expressions of the self are discussed by others. In pure media economy terms, the presentation of the self via blogs and webcams has produce an incredible surplus of sources of the self that in effect discounts the value of the many celebrity discourses that now circulate.

It is important to realize that not everyone that uses new media forms produces or even peruses blogs and webcam sites; but it is equally important to realize that there is a general expansion in placing one's personal self for public display on the Web. For instance, among American university students the pervasive use of Facebook.com and Myspace.com is remarkable. These sites are organized to connect friends, but also provide techniques for checking out others. In a vague sense, it may be used for Internet dating, but it is also a quasi-public site. These kinds of sites describe the wider proliferation of the presentation of the self. With photos and other personal details, Facebook and Myspace generate public privacy into a new form of narcissism. This narcissism is actualized through new media and it is specifically modalized around a mediatized version of the self: the representations of celebrity have now been liberated to become the basis for the potential public presentation of the self.

Added on to these shifts in identity that have been produced through the practices of the Internet are the identities and relationships to representation produced by video and computer games. Electronic game playing should be understood as a subjectivity that depends on two interrelated components: the structure of inter-activity and the capacity to become the protagonist. The electronic game has grown in sophistication in its true-to-life depiction of game characters. Players are involved in choosing their player and customizing their look as they conjoin the game identity with their own. The play of representation is articulated through the actions of the individual, elevating the individual into a kind of DIY subjectivity (McKay, 1998). In electronic games, the shift is that the individual is the agent, the actor, the avatar. His skin may be different and may be the hyperversion of self in its capacity to super-herodom or in its ability to have many lives. Nonetheless, the becoming quality of the player where the player and its image are unified through action and choice is enacted through play and not the representational field. A 2005 *New York Times* article indicated that while there has been a decline in youth watching professional basketball on television, there has been a notable increase among the same demographic of playing of Playstation versions of professional basketball (*New York Times*, 2005: A1). Both are mediated representations of the game, but in Playstation games one becomes the player and/or the team and is involved in the outcome of the game itself. What makes this practice of even greater significance is that this decline in watching basketball was occurring during the televised championship series.

New media forms have also allowed the meaning of celebrities produced by traditional media to be altered and engaged with differently: in other words, the representational gap is narrowing. On one level, the many fan websites for particular stars indicate a continuity to the past fan–celebrity relationship that developed around film and television stars. On another level, there is clear evidence that the gap between fan and celebrity is narrowing quite dramatically. For instance, particular celebrities have their own websites where they post information and occasionally more personal details and responses to fans. There have also been countless instances where the actual celebrity responded to comments on a fan's blog. Although this is not a per-vasive phenomenon, there are enough examples to indicate that a changed relation-ship between celebrity and fan is developing and, in some popular music and sport circles, is an expected component of the fan–celebrity relationship. For instance, the Association of Tennis Professionals website has a blog posted by a different popular player for each tournament: the technique draws the fan closer on a more regular and everyday fashion to the tennis celebrity.

The closeness to celebrities is further manifested by the manipulation of celebrity images throughout the web. Countless images of major celebrities are transformed using basic photoshop alterations and video cut and paste. For instance, a Liza Minelli television interview was reconstructed into a series of bizarre outbursts that in the editing transformed the original interview into something designed to question the sanity of Ms Minelli (Ifilm.com 2006). The famous 2005 interview of Tom Cruise with Oprah Winfrey was transformed into the vignette entitled by its maker "Tom Cruise kills Oprah" and made to appear that when Tom grabbed Oprah he actually electrocuted her with massive arcs of lightning (Ifilm.com, 2005). In another video, an animated parody of Tom Cruise's and Katie Holmes' romance is presented with the two actors singing to 50 Cent's *Candyshop* with transformed lyrics that openly suggest that their declarations of love may have been designed for publicity reasons (Liquidgeneration 2005). A more common and mundane reconstruction of celebrities is the fabricated "nude" photos of particular personalities designed to draw the web surfer into particular mildly pornographic sites. Political personalities such as Arnold Schwarzenegger have been reconstructed as dance club stars raving on the beach with fluorescent namchucks (Ifilm, 2003). Moveon.org sponsored a campaign for political advertisements called "Bush in 30 seconds" that generated thousands of entries that reconstructed, edited, dubbed and sometimes animated George Bush for their own often humorous and parodic ends. One video produced by Johan Soderberg for Swedish television in 2003 has circulated widely on the Web: to the Diana Ross and Lionel Ritchie ballad "Endless Love", Tony Blair and George Bush declare their clear devotion to each other (Soderberg 2003). Much of this content has been labeled by the industry as consumer generated media when it is relatively innocuous, and viral video when it is seen as something subcultural. With the success of these various videos migrating from personal computer to computer for viewing, there have been many efforts to reinscribe the creativity and production desires of these internet users back into the consumer culture. Indeed, fame and celebrity sometimes emerge from video on websites and blogs that, because of the idiosyncrasy of a particular individual's performance on a web cam or fabricated video, become downloaded and passed on via email throughout cyberculture. User generated media is a further example of the breakdown in control of mediated culture by the major players in the entertainment industry. The implications for the meaning of celebrity in contemporary culture who represent and embody the entertainment industry are equally far-reaching.

Reactions and repercussions in celebrity culture

The shift to a more presentational and personal mediation of culture from its more representational structure reverberates throughout celebrity culture. The media entertainment industries are now reacting to this less discretely controlled cultural world. In contrast to traditional media, it is less clear where a product begins and where it ends as this new system of production implies multiple forms produced by users. Songs are transformed and mutated ad infinitum. For instance, Bananarama's 1980s kitsch pop hit *Venus* has multiple mixes and add-on versions that rely on the core of the song's beat and singing but alter its flow in countless ways. This is in obvious contrast to the generally discrete and structured quality of past film, television, and popular music. Perhaps what is even more interesting is that these indiscretions of reproduction and remaking have legal implications related to when a user actually possesses and makes a cultural form his/her own. This challenge to ownership and the commodity status of cultural forms is in contrast to the discrete quality of past film, television, and popular music. The digitalization and the reduction of cultural forms to code produces an open source environment. The traditional media industries are now circling and recircling to stop the bleeding of their formerly discrete commodities.

Celebrity as a discourse in some ways dovetails into this indiscrete new media culture. Where the discrete product and narrative of, say, a film or popular song ends is exactly where celebrity culture begins and proliferates. Its presence in the public world or its presentation of the private world of celebrities for public consumption parallels the breakdown of the discrete cultural commodity of new media. However, the originary texts and industries – the commercial products that are the source of celebrity status and that at least begin the play of representation in an audience – have been shaken and their economic models have been challenged.

The audience-subject, what I have indicated is produced by the celebrity system and services the various cultural industries by demonstrating the economic value of a personality in a cultural production, no longer works as smoothly. Celebrities are a kind of guarantee of economic value as audiences are bought and sold throughout the entertainment industry. The advertising industry is at the center of this exchange process and it is here that one can see the greatest upheaval. For instance, advertisers now have a "crisis of confidence" in the spot advertisement which has been the cornerstone of commercial radio and television (Klaassen, 2006). Agencies are now emerging to serve advertisers in new ways. Product placement, whether in electronic games, films, popular music, or television is expanding rapidly. Word-of-mouth marketing and communication both via the Internet and direct face-to-face efforts is also growing as advertisers begin to disconnect the relationship of entertainment forms to the selling of their products. Complete branding of television programs, where the producers are the advertisers in the tradition of 1930s and 1940s American soap operas, are on the rise.

Although the fluctuations in the economic models of the various culture industries are now easy to discern, it is harder to identify the effects these changes have had on celebrity culture. The recording industry, which had depended on products such as CDs, is now fundamentally organized around downloads and the uses made of music through a variety of venues and formats, such as the personal computer, MP3 players and iPods. The former powerhouses of the music industry are not as well positioned to produce the musical stars that feed into the celebrity system and structure the range of performers who are promoted heavily. There is a dispersion of cultural power into the new technologies of distribution that break down the capacity of the industry to produce the iconic and celebrated representations of contemporary music. There is simply less coherence in popular music generally as their music stars tend to embody smaller audiences that can be geographically dispersed.

In a similar vein, the film industry is transforming. Film is losing its centrality and its cultural cachet as the first window of the cultural commodities' series of exhibitions. Over successive years there has been a decline in the theatrical box office as audiences disperse (Jaworoski, 2006: C3). The gap between the theatrical release of a film and the release of its DVD version has consistently narrowed. The film industry continues to try and produce event films to attract massive audiences, organized around simple films and a cluster of A-list stars. In order to maximize and concentrate the expenditure on advertising and promotion and its effect as well as circumvent the possibility of piracy and Internet distribution, event films' theatrical releases are now much shorter.

In this transformed industry, there is a correlated downgrade in the significance in the film celebrities produced. The immediate repercussion of this change has been an intensification of film celebrity stories and publicity. In the summer of 2005, we witnessed a publicity fight-back more or less articulated, not through the rather discrete promotions of the films but through the bizarre publicity-hungry behaviour of Tom Cruise and Katie Holmes (which obliquely connected to the release of *War of the Worlds* (2005) in which Cruise starred and *Batman Begins* (2005) where Holmes headlined) (Waxman, 2005: B1) and the equally operatic love triangle of Angelina Jolie, Brad Pitt, and Jennifer Aniston (which related in a major way to the action-comedy *Mr. and Mrs. Smith*). Cruise's tour was populated regularly with stunts that produced extensive news coverage. From his couch-jumping on Oprah's talk show and his attacks on Brooke Shields to his Eiffel Tower marriage declaration, Cruise ensured that cameras, commentators, and bloggers were regularly talking about his brazen public actions. We are seeing an acceleration of scandal not between acting assignments for major stars but during the release of films to generate parallel publicity. The film star's aura of distance and distinction is breaking down as the film commodity's capacity to generate unique cultural capital dissolves. For actors, this is a new level of publicizing to strengthen their own presence and capital – but it betrays a decline in overall significance of the industry and their stars. It also underlines the dispersal of information about celebrities as it proliferates via the Web and its blogs, via fan websites and through the new mediascape more rapidly and with less possibility for industry control.

Television's reaction to the new subjectivity of the user and its play with its own construction of personalities and celebrities is perhaps even more complex and interesting. Television, via the proliferation of cable channels, had already gone through a dispersion of its audience and partial breakdown of its coherent production of celebrity. But more recently, there has been a massive move to reality television. Reality television represents commercial television's efforts to react to new media. Like the game show and the talk show that predate it, reality television makes the audience the show itself. Although it is through the elaborate construction of television production, reality television is television's effort to make the user more central and more engaged with the experience. Despite the many incarnations, a dominant trope of reality programs is that the "cast" is derived from supposed everyday people. The show's content – whether *Big Brother, Survivor*, or the various versions of *Pop Idol* shows around the world, provide techniques for engagement by the audience beyond the usual fan sites (Marshall, 2004: 96–100). These programs themselves are very controlled and contrived constructions of celebrity discourse in and of themselves. Television, through these programs, has dispensed with the originary text that defines and makes the star and has begun constructing "celebrities" through its narratives of the intimate via a plethora of strategically placed cameras and microphones. It should also be noted here that this construction of celebrities of the moment by television has demanded the development of contracts that resemble the old film studio era in their control of their talent (Mole, 2004).

Conclusion

What we are witnessing is a frenzy of celebrity stories and an incredible discourse that proliferates in a variety of venues. What we are missing is why this is occurring now. Celebrity has defined in many senses our profound interest to reveal the self, sometimes the intimate self, in the most public of ways. Its 100-year past has been very much tied and wedded to identification and representation where audiences use celebrities to be their conduit between themselves and contemporary culture. Something has shifted and is continuing to shift, and I have called it a user-subjectivity that now informs the production of the self that doesn't necessarily replace the way that celebrities operate, are deployed and engaged with by people, but has begun to modify the sources of our celebrity. We are in an era of a new narcissism with the production of the self at its centre that allows for the migration via new media forms of presentation over representation. We are also at the zenith of older media industries attempting to hold on to their forms of cultural power and influence in conveying the enduring ideology of individualism. The outcome of this attempt to attach is in fact an expansion of celebrity discourse as new constitutions of cultural value and cultural capital are developed. What I have argued here is that we are seeing reactions by older media such as television (the development of a celebrity system organized through reality television where the audience is made "famous"), film (where increasingly established stars are clamouring for attention), and popular music (where distribution of the form and the background information on stars is paralleling the music's own movement through downloading, podcasting, and websites).

We are in the era of the new indiscretions of public personalities where the hold on public identity as a property right of the entertainment industry is under threat and there are intense reactions to maintain the brand identities system of celebrity – what I have called the "modern" celebrity – by that same industry. New media has modified the sources of the self as we move from a representational culture epitomized by celebrity to a presentational culture where celebrities are being reworked and reformed in terms of their value and utility by audiences and users.

PART SIX

The celebrity industry
The management of fame

Introduction to part six

■ P. David Marshall

IT TAKES EFFORT TO be famous.

The celebrity industry has two interlocking components. First, there is the production of the public individual. For an individual with international celebrity stature, a veritable team of managers, agents, and publicists are part of the production and positioning process. Whether it is the managing of an international tennis star and organizing their appearances, endorsements, and tournament schedules or the selective shielding of a film star, there is a manufacturing element to the contemporary celebrity.

The second component is the media industry that disseminates the texts, images, and scenarios for the public presentation of the individual. Historically, there have been particular individuals (such as Walter Winchell) and media outlets (such as *People* magazine and the *National Enquirer*) that have operated as the source for celebrity gossip. There are the paparazzi, who freelance for an opportunity of catching a celebrity in a compromising position, and there are the official images and stories that are provided by the managers/publicists of the famous. The celebrity press, then, is sandwiched between the exclusive that is structured and provided by the celebrity entourage and the effort to capture the uncontrolled moments which become more clearly demarcated as news.

Somewhere between these interlocking components is the celebrity, who may or may not be comfortable with the yokes that are placed around them in order for them to be the engines of an even more elaborate entertainment industry. Celebrity stories are deployed for very direct publicity purposes, sometimes driven by the economic exigencies of the news media and sometimes by the needs of the entertainment industry. And many times, these two purposes coincide whether the story is planned or unplanned.

Celebrities are magnets for the collection of affect that are exchanged by these interlocking industry components in a bizarre economy that is very often close to the profit core of these industries. It is as irrational and rational an organization of an economy as world stock exchanges.

Chapter 37

Kembrew McLeod

THE PRIVATE OWNERSHIP OF PEOPLE

The private ownership of the celebrity's image

ALONG WITH NUMEROUS OTHER changes in the nature of fame in the twentieth century, a pivotal transformation in the way the celebrity is constructed was enabled by a new type of property law. The "right of publicity," essentially, has enabled celebrities to privately own and control the use of their image within the marketplace. I do not argue that the celebrity's image was never commodified in previous centuries – it certainly was. But commodification coupled with legal protection has altered fame in ways that have changed the nature of fame dramatically. Today, a celebrity's image generates economic value for industries that produce news, gossip, biographies and interviews that are highly sought after by the media and the public. There is a huge market for the merchandising of celebrity images, and celebrity appearances in advertisements enhance the marketability of the products with which they are associated.[1]

An entertainer makes a significant amount of income from appearing in advertisements and from licensing his or her image for T-shirts, posters, etc.[2] Obviously, this was not always so, something I will illustrate with an example. The Berkeley Pop Culture Project documents that "Mickey [Mouse]'s image is the number one most-reproduced in the world, with over 7,500 items bearing his cheerful little image. Jesus is number two, and Elvis is number three."[3] Disney aggressively guards against the appropriation of Mickey Mouse's image and protects its trademarks in court, as does the Presley estate on behalf of Elvis's image.[4] But no single corporate entity collects royalties from the reproduction of Jesus' image in the same manner Disney and the Presley estate do, even though Jesus' image, like Elvis's, has been commodified in many ways, such as in those mass-produced black velvet paintings.

As much as some televangelists may have desired it, Jesus Christ cannot be trademarked. Without any intellectual property protection for Jesus' image, churches cannot prevent the presentation of artist Andres Serrano's *Piss Christ* – the controversial photograph of a crucifix submerged in a glass of urine – in the same way that Disney can legally enjoin an offensive work of art that appropriates its trademarked characters. Just as it is impossible for churches to trademark the image of Jesus Christ, it is unthinkable that the Bible could be copyrighted. The Church of Scientology – a religion that emerged in the age of intellectual property law – copyrighted its religious writings, and it has filed numerous copyright infringement lawsuits throughout the past few decades to maintain control over the context in which those writings are presented.[5]

In recent years, the Internet has been a place where Scientology dissidents have organized and traded information, and many of the online critiques that have used Scientology's copyrighted and trademarked images have prompted intellectual property lawsuits.[6] For instance, in 1996 a judge ruled in favor of the Church of Scientology when a critic of the church published copyrighted Scientology writings on the Internet as part of an ongoing discussion among church dissidents. Citing the example of a person who wants to engage in a critique of Christian religious beliefs needing Bible text to work from, one defendant's lawyer unsuccessfully argued that the use of the copyrighted documents were necessary to engage with the Church of Scientology's ideas.[7]

The Church of Scientology has won numerous copyright cases against those who critique the church, and its court battles pertaining to the Internet helped set the first precedents concerning copyright and cyberspace.[8] The Internet is an increasingly significant venue for individuals to use celebrity images to help make meanings and build communities among people with common interests. It is also a site where celebrities have intervened to shut down uses of their image of which they do not approve. I will return to the way intellectual property law is used ideologically to manage celebrity images, but first I will give a brief history of the reproduction of celebrity images.

Early stages of the commodified celebrity image

The mass dissemination and sale of famous people's images are commonplace in capitalist societies, but before the twentieth century there was little to no litigation surrounding what is now considered unauthorized appropriation. Perhaps the earliest examples of the mass production of famous people's likenesses are coins. The likenesses of Roman emperors were common on coins and in sculptures throughout the empire – Caesar, Alexander, Augustus and others took advantage of the publicity value this gave them. For instance, Alexander the Great's image was featured in numerous public objects during his lifetime (sculptures and coins included) and after his death Alexander's image was appropriated by his successors in an attempt to suggest the late emperor's sanction of the current ruler's regime. Augustus took note of Caesar's program of publicity and made his likeness virtually omnipresent throughout the empire, something that later political rulers did as well, especially on coins.[9]

Images of famous people that appeared on various consumer-related items were common in centuries previous to the twentieth, especially in the years following the invention and proliferation of the printing press in the late fifteenth century. Elizabeth

Eisenstein documents that sixteenth-century mass-produced portraits of Erasmus and Martin Luther were duplicated frequently. At the same time, she noted, "the drive for fame moved into high gear; the self-portrait acquired a new permanence, a heightened appreciation of individuality accompanied increased standardization, and there was a new deliberate promotion by publishers and print dealers of those authors and artists whose works they hoped to sell."[10]

During this period, the economic status of the artist and engraver was in the process of shifting from control by the patronage system funded by members of the aristocracy to the need for an audience of individual buyers in a marketplace system. Out of economic necessity, the printer now sought to please mass audiences, helping to develop new tastes in hero-worship that no longer solely belonged to people in traditional positions of power.[11]

The sale and distribution of the likenesses of celebrities had become big business by the second half of the eighteenth century in America – especially during and after the American Revolution.[12] For instance, in 1774 businessman Josiah Wedgwood began a line of portrait-medallions called "illustrious moderns" aimed at a more popular, less affluent audience, and by 1779 the medallions outsold the tea services that had been Wedgwood's primary business. His 1779 catalogue included numerous different heads for sale, including classical music composers, popes, monarchs, poets and artists, as well as Ben Franklin and George Washington.[13] In the nineteenth century, Madow writes:

> We can again find manufacturers making widespread use of the names and faces of famous and prominent persons. For example, after John Brown was hanged by the State of Virginia for his role in the raid on Harper's Ferry, entrepreneurs marketed lithographs, prints, busts, and photographs of him. During Sarah Bernhardt's 1880 American tour, manufacturers and merchants "cashed in with Sarah Bernhardt perfume, candy, cigars, and eyeglasses." Two years later, when Oscar Wilde visited the United States on a much-publicized and controversial lecture tour, advertisers put his image on trade cards for such products as Marie Fontaine's Moth and Freckle Cure.[14]

To use another comparative example, it would have been inconceivable for Martin Luther (the religious zealot who nailed his "Theses" to Wittenberg's church door back in 1517) to regulate the reproduction of his image in the same way that the estate of black leader Martin Luther *King Jr.* regulates his. Phillip Jones, president of the firm that manages the King estate and searches for possible infringements, stated: "King may belong to the public spiritually, but King's family is entitled to control the use of his image and words."[15]

The image of Ben Franklin, who promoted himself throughout Europe after the American Revolution, quickly appeared on fans, perfume bottles, and over a hundred other items of fashion. By the time Franklin was an old man, "his own face was displayed all over Europe in the shape of engravings, busts, statues, paintings, and even little statuettes and painted fans that looked like souvenir keepsakes."[16] Although Franklin could capitalize on his high visibility, he could not directly profit from the sale of his image on a perfume bottle in the same way that Elizabeth Taylor (who flatly acknowledged "I am my own commodity") does today with her line of perfumes.[17]

Nevertheless, Franklin's face *certainly was* a commodity that was exchanged in the marketplace, but without the extensive juridification of this sphere of cultural production it could not be privately owned and controlled by a single entity. It was perceived, instead, as being in the public domain. At this time, and even up until the early twentieth century, there was no conceptual framework to even conceive of one's own image as private property. The merchandising and commodification of the celebrity image continued through the twentieth century with little public outcry and virtually no litigation.[18] Harris writes:

> During previous centuries fads and manias had often swept large masses of people, caught up in enthusiasm for a cause, a hero, or a work of art. Actors, generals, opera singers, politicians, artists, ballerinas, novels, all had demonstrated a capacity to influence daily fashions, social customs, or habits of consumption. From Jenny Lind to Georges du Maurier's Trilbymania, from Louis Kossuth to Lillian Russell, celebrities stood at the center of temporary epidemics. Hats, dolls, canes, bicycles, theaters, toys, dinnerware, furniture, cigars, liquors bore the likenesses, names, or special symbols of various personalities. . . . Yet all this stimulated little litigation. Some unspoken assumption made famous people and literary characters a species of common property whose commodity exploitation required little control.[19]

It was during the last 2 decades of the nineteenth century that the assumption that the celebrity's image is common property was challenged in the courts and criticized in legal journal editorials. Around this time were the first reported lawsuits initiated by well-known people who were disturbed by the fact that their likenesses had been used in commercial products without their approval. Although it was increasingly considered wrong to appropriate these images, the courts were undecided and confused as to what legal right, if any, could protect a celebrity's image. Some courts believed that the use of a celebrity's likeness constituted an invasion of privacy, and some rejected that argument, while other courts couched these ideas in different legal concepts.[20]

A 1907 ruling on the unauthorized use of Thomas Edison's image on a medicine label framed the issue in terms of "property," and it represents what is likely the first such judicial recognition of a person's image. The court stated, "If a man's name be his own property, as no less an authority than the United States Supreme Court says it is, it is difficult to understand why the peculiar cast of one's features is not also one's property, and why its pecuniary value, if it has one, does not belong to its owner, rather than to the person seeking to make an unauthorized use of it."[21]

The emergence of celebrity image ownership

In the early twentieth century, protection from the commercial appropriation of one's image was far from a universally protected right, but contracts began to emerge that attempted to exclude others from freely appropriating a celebrity's likeness. Perhaps because the movie star emerged from a highly visual medium, it is logical that this was one of the first realms of fame that recognized the commercial value of the image. Contracts enabled movie studios to use a star's name, voice and likeness to promote the film, and more underhandedly, it allowed for the use of a star's image to be licensed for product endorsements, even in the most questionable and tangential circumstances.

Movie studios could use a star's image as it related to a particular film, and could license that image to businesses that produced greeting cards, toys and a myriad of other kinds of products in exchange for a royalty payment to the star image's owner, the studio. In fact, studios vehemently policed the unauthorized use of their property by outside businesses. By the 1940s a few stars who had the power to negotiate with the studios succeeded in contractually limiting the use of their image only to areas directly related to the promotion of a film, but these cases were extremely rare. Even Betty Davis's contract enabled a producer to use her image without any connection to the movies in which she appeared.[22]

At the height of her fame in the 1930s, Shirley Temple was able to secure merchandising arrangements that were disconnected from the studio she worked for in order to personally profit from the sale and distribution of her image.[23] Another exceptional early case was Roy Rogers – a pioneer in the licensing and merchandising of one's own image. His 1940 contract allowed him to create his own separate business completely independent of the production house that employed him. This laid the foundation for a merchandising empire in which Rogers appeared in advertisements endorsing Wheaties cereal and began promoting such items as electric ranges and dog food. Rogers licensed thousands of products – from records and comics to cowboy hats and harmonicas – that reaped millions of dollars in revenues during, and after, his lifetime.[24]

In 1953, the U.S. Court of Appeals for the Second Circuit handed down an opinion that defined a type of legal protection – the "right of publicity" – that celebrities could invoke in the face of unauthorized commercial appropriation. This court ruled on *Haelan Laboratories, Inc. v. Topps Chewing Gum, Inc.*, a breach-of-contract case involving two competing baseball card manufacturers that both printed a card with the same player's photograph. Haelan Laboratories argued that the right to privacy did not prevent their company from using that baseball player's image, regardless of any exclusive contract the player signed with another company.

The court's opinion stated that "a man has a right in the publicity value of his photograph, i.e., the right to grant the exclusive privilege of publishing his picture, and that such a grant may validly be made 'in gross,' i.e., without an accompanying transfer of a business or of anything else."[25] The court suggested "right of publicity," which grants "a person the exclusive right to control the commercial value and exploitation of his name, picture, likeness, or personality, and to prevent others from exploiting that value without permission, or from unfairly appropriating that value for their commercial benefit."[26]

The "right of publicity" has been enthusiastically embraced by the legal community; over half the U.S. states recognize the right of publicity, and that recognition has expanded to foreign jurisdictions as well.[27] Numerous court cases since the 1953 *Haelan Laboratories, Inc. v. Topps Chewing Gum, Inc.* decision have expanded what is considered to be legally protected – far beyond one's likeness. For instance, in the 1950s a U.S. appeals court ruled in a suit brought by Ed Sullivan that the name "Ed" could not be adjoined to "Sullivan" when the likelihood of confusion might occur.[28] The "right of publicity" case law has developed to include not just one's name but other characteristics unique to a particular person such as certain traits, characteristics, mannerisms or paraphernalia.[29] For instance, in 1996, basketball star Dennis Rodman sued the manufacturer of a long-sleeved T-shirt that bore replicas of his tattoos as they appear on his own body.[30]

There are many areas that fall under the domain of "right of publicity." Coombe writes, "It is no longer limited to the name or likeness of the individual, but now extends to a person's nickname, signature, physical pose, characterizations, singing style, vocal characteristics, body parts, frequently used phrases, car, performance style, and mannerisms and gestures, provided that these are distinctive and publicly identified with the person claiming the right."[31] For instance, Johnny Carson successfully sued a company that appropriated the famous opening phrase used to introduce Carson – "Here's Johnny" – in conjunction with the promotion of its portable toilets. In this case the court held that "Carson's identity may be exploited even if his name or his picture is not used."[32]

As far back as 1974, the U.S. Court of Appeals for the Ninth Circuit deemed actionable the use of a well-known race car driver's car in a cigarette advertisement. It was successfully argued that the use of the car was intended to associate that driver with the product – even though the driver was unseen.[33] More recently, in the *Vanna White v. Samsung Electronics America, Inc.* case, the U.S. Court of Appeals for the Ninth Circuit expanded publicity protection even further to include any commercial appropriation of the distinctive features of a celebrity. In that case, a Samsung commercial featured a robot wearing a blonde wig, jewelry, and an evening gown that stood in front of a display board that resembled the set of the game show – *Wheel of Fortune* – that featured Ms. White. The court decided that the commercial infringed on White's right of publicity, even though the commercial clearly employed parody.[34]

"Right of publicity" has expanded to protect a singer's voice from *imitation*. Previous to 1988, courts had rejected the notion that vocal style could be protected under a right of publicity theory, but today there are two significant precedents that have expanded that right.[35] In 1988, pop star Bette Midler brought suit against Ford Motor company and its advertising agency for the deliberate imitation of a Midler song by another singer for a television commercial. In *Midler v. Ford Motor Co.*, the California court held that "Midler had a legitimate claim under the common law right of publicity."[36]

This is quite different from the outcome of an earlier, similar case in which Nancy Sinatra's biggest hit, "These Boots Are Made for Walkin'," was performed by a female vocalist who was directed to imitate Sinatra in a Goodyear Tire commercial that also featured four women dressed in 1960s "mod" fashions (i.e., short skirts and high boots). In *Sinatra v. Goodyear Tire & Rubber Co.*, the U.S. Court of Appeals for the Ninth Circuit decided that "imitation alone does not give rise to a cause of action."[37] But when Midler's lawyers couched their arguments in terms of "property," she won.

After the Midler decision, Tom Waits successfully sued Frito-Lay for using a singer who imitated his raspy style for a radio commercial. The Ninth Circuit reaffirmed the Midler decision and awarded $2 million in punitive damages to the plaintiff. Stamets points out that this decision "represents a dramatic expansion of the publicity right defined in Midler. In the Midler case, Ford's advertising agency admitted trying to imitate Midler in a version of a song she made a hit. . . . Unlike Ford, however, Frito-Lay's sound-alike was given an original tune to sing, a tune never associated with the plaintiff."[38]

The right of publicity and celebrity image management

Elvis Presley is a quintessential American celebrity who means many things to many people, and the history of the struggles over the use of his image is representative of the way a celebrity's image is managed today. Even though Elvis is no longer alive, his image remains tightly controlled by his estate, which went so far as trademarking "Elvis," "Elvis Presley," "Elvis in Concert" and "Graceland," among other things. Not only has the King's epitaph been copyrighted, but so has the inscription on Grandma Minnie Mae Presley's tombstone.[39] Since it was founded in 1979, Elvis Presley Enterprises (EPE) has filed hundreds of lawsuits pertaining to the unauthorized use of Elvis's image in a variety of contexts.

Recently, in 1998, a U.S. Circuit Court of Appeals barred a tavern from using the name "The Velvet Elvis." The establishment's owner argued that it parodied 1960s kitch, more generally, but the court rejected the argument, stating: "Without the necessity to use Elvis's name [to target the 1960s], parody does not weigh against a likelihood of confusion in relating to EPE's marks. It is simply irrelevant."[40] Despite this and many other successes, EPE has not been universally successful in court (it hasn't been able to stop Elvis impersonators). Nevertheless, it has won numerous court battles – enough to create the perception that, for Elvis's image to be used in any sort of commercially oriented artistic product, permission must be granted by EPE and the image must be licensed.[41]

To give a few examples, the 1980s television sitcom *Cheers* sought the permission of EPE for a planned episode in which a character had a dream about Elvis, and EPE made sure both the actor who portrayed Elvis and the script met with its approval. Similarly, before the ghost of Elvis was used in the movie *True Romance*, producers sought the permission of EPE. Elvis Presley Enterprises so emphatically protects the use of the King's image that it seriously considered suing the company that distributed the book *Elvis Alive?*, which came with an audiocassette that supposedly contained a conversation with the deceased Elvis Presley. As ludicrous as this sounds, because EPE owns Elvis's "performance rights," EPE lawyers felt justified in claiming that if this truly was a recording from *beyond the grave*, its reproduction infringed on the estate's proprietary rights. The idea was dropped after the book sold poorly.[42]

In addition, the threats contained in EPE's intimidating letters, combined with EPE's financial muscle, convinced the producers of a play, *Miracle at Graceland*, which was being staged at a small community arts center, to drop the word "Graceland" from the title and remove all images of Elvis from the set. While EPE's charges might not have held up in court, as is the case with many intellectual property lawsuits (or threats of suits), the producers complied because they lacked the resources to sustain a court battle.[43] As "right of publicity" has expanded to allow celebrities (and their families) more power to control the use of their images, it has at the same time affected the way everyday people appropriate celebrity images to generate meanings within their own lives and communities.

Celebrities and audiences

Madow argues that, in their everyday lives, people "make active and creative use of celebrity images to construct themselves and their social relations, to identify themselves as individuals and as members of subcultural groups, and to express and communicate their sense of themselves and their particular experience of the world."[44] One of many examples of this use of celebrity images is Dyer's analysis of how 1950s urban gay culture reinterpreted the image of Judy Garland as a symbolic icon whose ambiguous masculine/feminine coding provided a way for gay men to engage in a dialogue about themselves and others.[45]

Because mass-media audiences are not lifeless sponges, it is no surprise that people draw on these images and texts to actively make sense of their own lives and the world that surrounds them. But "right of publicity" law centralizes the celebrity's decision-making power in determining what he or she "means" to an audience by allowing that celebrity the ability to decide what parts of his or her image to magnify, what parts to distort, and what parts to delete. This contemporary legal climate makes it more difficult for an audience to actively engage with star texts, let alone to produce and distribute alternative readings that generate effective, resistive cultural practices.

Before I examine the way the management of celebrity images affects the celebrity-fan relationship, I want to discuss the line of thinking that asserts audiences are not passive consumers who soak in media images without thinking. De Certeau,[46] Silverstone,[47] Jenkins,[48] and Fiske[49] argue that people actively "read" media texts using celebrity images, among other things, to actively create shared meanings within communities of fans.

De Certeau, who focuses on book-reading rather than other media, reminds us that we must not take people for fools. He attacks the perception that book-reading audiences are passive "sheep" who are content to graze in the pastures of a field they did not participate in creating. He finds this notion unacceptable, taking the stance that, far from being passive, reading is a productive act that is as creative as that of the novelist. De Certeau positions the reader as a nomad who occupies and wanders into different territories, "poaching" meanings that are perhaps unintended by the author and the elite class who "police" preferred meanings through a variety of social mechanisms.[50]

Silverstone, in his fondness for militaristic metaphors, takes de Certeau's arguments as a call to arms. He claims that what is considered mundane, daily life is a kind of guerrilla war that is waged by the subjugated against oppressors in the field of everyday life, and he sees a revolutionary potential in the seemingly trivial practices of watching television. Rather than being a passive activity, television viewing, according to Silverstone, is the site of an enormous amount of cultural work on the part of both the producers and the receivers. He notes studies that demonstrate how television watchers integrate its texts within their own lives in a variety of ways, and he argues that even though the cultural power of institutions is deeply imbedded in the texts and the writer-reader relationship is unequal, there is still room for move-ment and some freedom.[51]

Similarly, Fiske argues that fans are extremely creative and active. He points out that the notion of a productive audience does not necessarily provide the basis for a movement that can change society; he conceptualizes resistance, instead, as producing a form of consciousness. Fiske argues that just in the act of listening to or watching a mass-media venue, fans are engaged in constant symbolic meaning formation. Audiences also talk about music or television shows with others, creating shared and constantly metamorphosizing communal meanings. Finally, fans engage in productive behavior when they create fanzines, videos, songs and other cultural products that are shared within their community.[52]

In one case, a fan video incorporated Jimmy Buffet's song "Leaving the Straight Life Behind" as the narrative that held together carefully selected clips of television cops Starsky and Hutch, edited to portray them humorously in a homoerotic relation-ship. The clips include images of the officers playing chess in their bathrobes, disco dancing together, embracing each other and jumping into bed together. Jenkins sug-gests that the activities of fans should be viewed as "poaching" rather than mindless consumption, and maintains that fandom is "a vehicle for marginalized subcultural groups (women, the young, gays, etc.) to pry open space for their cultural concerns within dominant representations."[53]

By generating alternate readings of mass-culture materials, Jenkins claims, these groups can transform the products of the media to serve their interests. His empirical study focuses on the participatory fan (re)writings of *Star Trek* storylines by largely female fans, which were written in a way that recognized and validated the authors' (and their audience's) experiences. He argues that resistance comes not from the original media texts themselves, but from the *practice* of writing new texts, distributing the fanzines and community building. Jenkins concludes:

> Nobody regards these fan activities as a magical cure for the social ills of postindustrial capitalism. They are no substitution for meaningful change, but they can be used effectively to build popular support for such changes, to challenge the power of the culture industry to construct the common sense of a mass society, and to restore a much-needed excitement to the struggle against subordination.[54]

The positions of de Certeau, Silverstone, Fiske and Jenkins are, to a certain extent, polemical – a reaction against Frankfurt School theorists such as Adorno who saw the products of mass culture as nothing but oppressive. Even if their arguments may be exaggerated, they were a necessary tactical move away from the deeply ingrained notion that everything is determined, that there is no opening that allows for social transformation. The above-mentioned authors were attempting to give agency back to social actors who had been stripped of it by critics of mass culture. But, as is often the case, polemics do not translate well into empirical research, and some of the more extreme claims made by the authors do not hold water.

I believe that in choosing to study the specific practice of *Star Trek* fanzine writing, Jenkins paints a much more optimistic picture of this type of cultural activity than actually exists because, as he acknowledges, Paramount (*Star Trek*'s copyright owner) tended to treat these unauthorized materials with "benign neglect" if they were non-profit and relatively low profile. Most corporate owners of mass-distributed and highly profitable cultural texts *do not* react with "benign neglect" over the distribution of materials that use their privately owned property without permission.

There are many areas of mass culture (Disney and Lucasfilm are only the tip of the iceberg) in which this kind of fan activity is made very difficult and financially hazardous for the producers of texts who incorporate copyrighted and trademarked images. Because a large portion of the same type of cultural activity that fans engage in has moved from the medium of reproduced photocopies quietly mailed through the U.S. Postal Service (in the form of zines) to the very public forum of the Internet, this difficulty has intensified. The products of the fanzine-trading community were more difficult to detect by intellectual property-holding companies when they were distributed through the mail, simply because this community was more underground and difficult to keep track of.

While photocopied, hand-stapled fanzines certainly still exist, now much of the same kind of fan production has shifted to the Internet in the form of web sites, something that is easy to monitor with a simple keyword query on an Internet search engine [. . .]. Again, I agree with the above-mentioned authors that receivers of media texts are productive and that people use these texts in meaningful ways. But it is difficult to use these texts to build support for social change and, in Jenkins' words, to "challenge the power of the culture industry" when owners religiously use intellectual property law to suppress the uses of texts that challenge dominant ideologies.[55]

The ideological management of celebrity images

When a T-shirt manufacturer began selling shirts that appropriated images of Mr. Rogers juxtaposed with the captions "Pervert" and "Serial Killer," Rogers sued the company, invoking "right of publicity" and trademark infringement. In addition, Rogers sued another company that allegedly sold a T-shirt of Rogers holding a gun. His lawyers stated, "It is antithetical to Rogers' and FCI's philosophy, image and business practice to be associated with the corrupted depiction of Rogers shown in defendant's shirt."[56] Similarly, Muhammad Ali successfully sued under "right of publicity" when *Playgirl* magazine published a drawing, subtitled "the greatest," of a nude black man seated in the corner of a boxing ring.[57]

Yet another case that highlights the way "right of publicity" is invoked in an ideological manner is the following. When the New York state legislature held hearings on a bill that would make the right of publicity something that can be passed on to one's descendents, John Wayne's children cited a greeting card sold primarily in gay bookstores that featured a picture of the late actor with the caption, "It's such a bitch being butch." While they objected to the card on the grounds that it siphoned off money that should go to the estate, more importantly, they saw the card as "tasteless" and believed it worked against their father's conservative image.[58]

John Wayne carries a lot of semiotic baggage; he is for many people the archetype of the ultimate American tough guy, representing a certain ideal of masculinity. But against this "preferred reading" can exist a resistive reading, such as what is embodied in the greeting card (which was considered so subversive by his family that they took their exception to it to the halls of New York state legislature). This resistive reading recodes popular conceptions of masculinity and heterosexuality in a way that many might find offensive, and is obviously something that Wayne Enterprises wanted to silence.[59]

The success of celebrity icons depends, in part, on their reworking of previous celebrity images and other resonating signifiers. For instance, Coombe rhetorically asks how much Elvis Costello owes to Buddy Holly, or Prince to Jimi Hendrix. Madonna reconfigured many twentieth-century sex goddesses and ice queens, including (but not limited to) Marilyn Monroe, Jean Harlow, Greta Garbo and Marlene Dietrich.[60] But, Coombe argues:

> If the Madonna image appropriates the likenesses of earlier screen goddesses, religious symbolism, feminist rhetoric, and sadomasochistic fantasy to speak to sexual aspirations and anxieties in the 1980s and 1990s, then the value of her image derives as much, perhaps, from the collective cultural heritage on which she draws as from her individual efforts. But if we grant Madonna exclusive property rights in her image, we simultaneously make it difficult for others to appropriate those same resources for new ends, and we freeze the Madonna constellation itself. Future artists, writers and performers will be unable to creatively draw upon the cultural and historical significance of the Madonna montage without seeking the consent of the celebrity, her estate, her descendants or her assignees, who may well deny such consent or demand exorbitant royalties.[61]

"Right of publicity" law has opened up another area of culture to privatization, allowing for celebrities and their lawyers to police representations they do not approve. As cultural production and creative activity takes place more and more in the sphere of the marketplace, it becomes increasingly difficult to argue that the appropriation of celebrity images falls under "fair use," particularly because, like trademark law, it contains no developed "fair use" statute or exception. Moreover, "right of publicity" law is more ambiguous and inconsistent than trademark law, and it has even more potential to silence a number of different expressions having to do with celebrity images. When certain types of cultural production are engaged within the marketplace, the owners of privatized cultural texts – in this case, celebrities – have greater power to (if not win court cases) exert enough financial muscle to wipe out appropriations that are not to their liking.

Conclusion

The three primary examples of the private ownership of people in this chapter – via gene patenting, proprietary consumer databases, and "right of publicity law" – are extremely different. In each case, there are varied articulations of labor relations, battles between large corporations, notions of authorship, and government policy, among other things. As we have seen, the consequences of privatization vary quite a bit throughout the above-mentioned contexts, and this illustrates that the privatization of culture is not a highly determined, ahistorical process that generates uniform actions.

One advantage of using articulation theory is that it allows us to make connections across disparate areas of cultural production [. . .]. Perhaps most importantly, these connections all are articulated differently with intellectual property law because there are conflicting operating notions of *what* is being authored, *how* it is authored and *who* is doing the authoring. These distinct concepts, which have arisen out of situated historical circumstances, have helped construct who has control of the means of production, and control of the means of production has worked to enforce a definition of authorship in each particular area. Database owners most certainly define themselves as authors because they own the software and hardware that can organize information relating to consumer behavior. To many, this fact makes ascribing authorship and ownership of these data images to a corporation that has invested lots of money an obvious choice.

But, from another perspective, it was the labor of the consumers (i.e., in their trips to the shopping mall) that enabled the information to exist in the first place. When individuals work 40 or more hours a week to be able to consume the things they want or need, they also work as laborers for the corporations that collect data on their purchasing behavior, data that is in turn used to try to persuade them as consumers to buy more. The companies merely trace and map the data trails that consumers leave, organizing that information in particular ways that allow for the useful and profitable manipulation of that data.

Consumers *don't* control the means of production of their data image, nor are they considered the authors of their data image. Moreover, very little legislation has been passed to empower American consumers in any way, and for them certainly nothing like "right of publicity" law exists that would allow consumers the right to similarly control their own electronically stored consumer profiles within the marketplace. The privacy laws that do exist protect individuals from a variety of invasions of privacy, but they do little to prohibit the collection of personal information – nor are they intended to. Large corporations not only recognize the economic power that access to consumer data images gives; they have successfully secured their control of the means of production over the construction of consumer data images, though they have yet to secure a type of intellectual property protection.

Because the methods of organization used by consumer database companies are not considered to be very inventive, database owners have not won full copyright protection for their property in recent court battles. In the 1991 *Feist Publications, Inc. v. Rural Telephone Service* U.S. Supreme Court decision, the court ruled: "There is nothing original in Rural's white pages. The raw data are uncopyrightable facts, and the way in which Rural selected, coordinated, and arranged these facts is not original in any way."[62] Because they lack originality, according to the court, the companies that own these databases do not qualify for authorship status and, therefore, the materials are not copyrightable. Another important reason for this lack of protection was the lobbying efforts of very powerful companies that would be negatively impacted by tighter database protection.

Just as noncelebrity individuals, as they exist as consumers, are alienated from the data image that they labored to produce, individuals are also deprived of the control of their own flesh as it is used by medical and scientific researchers. The case of John Moore – the man whose spleen provided the basis for a medicine that has generated over $3 billion in revenues – is instructive. As was discussed earlier, the California Supreme Court decided that John Moore had no right to claim any proprietary rights over his own body. Other exploited non-Western, noncelebrity people enjoy even fewer rights than a U.S. citizen like Moore because of Eurocentric intellectual property laws that perpetuate colonialist relations between the First and Third Worlds.

The precedent established by the successful patenting of plant and human genes has ensured that biological material is considered a legally protectable form of intellectual property. Because the notion of private property is hegemonic, groups who hold economic power have more control in defining *who* is considered an author, and, therefore, an owner. This particular definition of authorship and ownership has been employed by the U.S. court system and the Patent and Trademark Office, and that definition has increasingly shaped the content of the international trade treaties forced on foreign countries. Owning the means of production of scientific knowledge establishes author rights for companies that can afford the technology that isolates and analyzes genes. This provides a rather clear-cut example of how the balance of power is further shifted in favor of wealthy individuals, rich companies and the more powerful Western economies, all at the expense of powerless individuals and countries with few economic resources.

The battle between studios and film stars was first and foremost a labor struggle, one that actors won, in part, because of the leverage their relative economic privilege gave them. After movie stars and other celebrities successfully altered the contracts between themselves and their employers, they lobbied to expand the legal protection of their images from commercial appropriation. "Right of publicity" developed to meet the celebrities' desire to control their own images within the marketplace in order to profit from it, and this law recognizes that celebrities own the means of production of their own image. Elizabeth Taylor acknowledged this to a certain extent when, in discussing the marketing of her own line of "Liz Taylor" perfume, she asserted, "I am my own commodity."[63]

The celebrity can be seen as the singular author of his or her image, but, as Dyer argues, the celebrity image is constructed from multiple discourses originating from a variety of sources.[64] In *Heavenly Bodies*, Dyer traces the intersections of ways of talking about a celebrity persona, and he reminds us that film stars' images are not simply created directly by them or by the films in which they appear. The star's image is also created from texts relating to the promotion of the films (press photos, pin-ups, public appearances), as well as interviews, biographies, and the press coverage of a star's "private" life. The star's image is also comprised of what critics and commentators write or say about him or her in the media, as well as the way a star's image is used in "advertisements, novels, pop songs, and finally the way the star can become part of the coinage of everyday speech."[65]

In other words, in a critical sense the celebrity is no more the author of his or her image as it is reconstructed within popular culture than is the fan, whose intertextual associations work to construct meaning for an individual and a community. But through the labor battles between actors and studios that occurred in the first half of the twentieth century, and then through numerous lawsuits that created a strong body of case law, celebrities were able to gain control of the means of production of their own image. This form of ownership legitimizes the argument that the celebrity is the sole author of his or her image and, in turn, the establishment of the celebrity's authorship justifies his or her complete control over the valuable cultural product that is his or her image. Personal economic power allowed celebrities to gain control, through a long series of court battles, of the means of production. The same is true of the fields of genetics and consumer data collection.

The economic power of large corporations gave them the power to influence the way TRIPS was written, therefore helping to define authorship in ways that privilege corporate owners. But given the hegemony of the idea of private property in our culture, it is hard to argue against the logic that underpins the notion that database owners, scientists and celebrities should enjoy the fruits of their labor. As the president of the Sequana stated: "Gene discovery is just the first step in a 1,000-mile journey to find a therapy. It's a process that costs us millions and takes years of work. So how much does somebody who gets his arm pricked deserve?"[66] My intention here, more generally, is to complicate this common sense, ideologically charged notion of authorship and ownership by showing how power and access to capital have been key factors in the way various spheres of cultural production have become differently (and similarly) articulated with intellectual property law.

Celebrities, consumers and individuals whose genetic materials have been appropriated are all differently articulated with intellectual property law in a fundamental way. As I have argued in regard to the copyrighting of world music, and with plant and human genetic patenting, intellectual property law only recognizes certain types of authorship. So, for instance, under Western intellectual property laws, indigenous peoples who have their music or their blood "sampled" do not have the right to claim ownership over what they produce (be it their songs or their own genetic material). But those who have the capital to purchase a recording device or piece of scientific equipment – but who merely press the record button or run genetic data analysis programs – are recognized as authors and therefore as owners of these cultural products. Intellectual property law, like any property law, handicaps those who have few material resources and no access to the means of production, and it works to maintain unequal power relations.

Notes

1   Madow, M. (1993). Private ownership of public image: Popular culture and publicity rights. *California Law Review, 81*, 125–; Fowles, J. (1992). *Starstruck: Celebrity performers and the American public*. Washington: Smithsonian Institution Press.

2   Madow, M. (1993). Private ownership of public image: Popular culture and publicity rights. *California Law Review, 81*, 125–.

3   Ibid., p. 208.

4   Stern, J. & Stern, M. (1992). *The encyclopedia of pop culture*. New York: HarperPerennial.

5   Mallia, J. (1998, March 4). Inside the Church of Scientology. *Boston Herald*, p. 25.

6   Global struggle over truth and eternal life. (1995, August 20). *South China Morning Post*, p. 4.

7   Copyright law applies to internet; Judge rules Scientologists win U. S. lawsuit. (1996, January 21). *Toronto Star*, p. A13.

8   Church satisfied with copyright judgement. (1996, October 16). *Phoenix Gazette*, p. A5.

9   Braudy, L. (1986). *The frenzy of renown: Fame and its history*. New York: Oxford University Press.

10 Eisenstein, E. L. (1983). *The printing revolution in early modern Europe*. Cambridge: Cambridge University Press, p. 131.

11 Braudy, L. (1986). *The frenzy of renown: Fame and its history*. New York: Oxford University Press.

12 Madow, M. (1993). Private ownership of public image: Popular culture and publicity rights. *California Law Review, 81*, 125–.

13 Braudy, L. (1986). *The frenzy of renown: Fame and its history*. New York: Oxford University Press.

14 Madow, M. (1993). Private ownership of public image: Popular culture and publicity rights. *California Law Review, 81*, 125–, 151–152.

15 Ibid.

16 Braudy, L. (1986). *The frenzy of renown: Fame and its history*. New York: Oxford University Press, p. 377.

17 Wolmuth, R. (1987). Liz Taylor leaps into a vial business with passion. *People Weekly, 28, 14*, 38.

18 Madow, M. (1993). Private ownership of public image: Popular culture and publicity rights. *California Law Review, 81* 125–.

19 Harris, N. (1985, Summer). Who owns our myths? Heroism and copyright in an age of mass culture. *Social Research*, 241–267, 251.

20 Gaines, J. (1991). *Contested culture: The image, the voice, and the law*. Chapel Hill: University of North Carolina Press; Madow, M. (1993). Private ownership of public image: Popular culture and publicity rights. *California Law Review, 81*, 125–.

21 Madow, M. (1993). Private ownership of public image: Popular culture and publicity rights. *California Law Review, 81*, 125–, 153.

22 Gaines, J. (1991). *Contested culture: The image, the voice, and the law*. Chapel Hill: University of North Carolina Press.

23 Ibid.

24 Phillips, R. W. (1995). *Roy Rogers: A biography, radio history, television career chronicle, discography, filmography, comicography, merchandising and advertising history, collectibles description, bibliography and index*. Jefferson: McFarland & Company, Inc.

25 Hetherington, L. H. (1993). Direct commercial exploitation of identity: A new age for the right of publicity. *Columbia-VLA Journal of Law and the Arts, 17*, 1–49.

26 Right to privacy and publicity. (1996). In *Corpus Juris Secundum (Vol. 77)* (pp. 481–544). St. Paul: West Publishing, pp. 539–540.

27 Ferri, L. M. & Gibbons, R. G. (1999, April). The growing right of publicity. *The Intellectual Property Strategist, 5, 7*, 7.

28 Schwartz, H. (1996). *The culture of the copy: Striking likenesses, unreasonable facsimiles*. New York: Zone Books.

29 Halpern, S. W. (1996). The right to publicity: Maturation of an independent right protecting the associative value of personality. *Hastings Law Journal, 46*, 853–873.

30 Rodman sues manufacturer, distributors over shirts depicting his tattoos. (1996, July 31). *Entertainment Litigation Reporter* [Online]. Available: Lexis-Nexus.

31   Coombe, R. J. (1998). *The cultural life of intellectual properties: Authorship, appropriation, and the law*. Durham, NC: Duke University Press, p. 90.

32   Rahimi, T. J. (1995). The power to control identity: Limiting a celebrity's right to publicity. *Santa Clara Law Review, 35*, 725–753.

33   Halpern, S. W. (1996). The right to publicity: Maturation of an independent right protecting the associative value of personality. *Hastings Law Journal, 46*, 853–873.

34   Giftos, A. C. (1994). The common law right of publicity and commercial appropriation of celebrity identity: A whole new wardrobe for Vanna. *Saint Louis University Law Review, 38*, 983–1008.

35   Stamets, R. A. (1994). Ain't nothin' like the real thing, baby: The right of publicity and the singing voice. *Federal Communications Law Journal, 14*, 347–373.

36   Giftos, A. C. (1994). The common law right of publicity and commercial appropriation of celebrity identity: A whole new wardrobe for Vanna. *Saint Louis University Law Review, 38*, 997.

37   Gaines, J. (1991). *Contested culture: The image, the voice, and the law*. Chapel Hill: University of North Carolina Press, pp. 108–109.

38   Stamets, R. A. (1994). Ain't nothin' like the real thing, baby: The right of publicity and the singing voice. *Federal Communications Law Journal, 14*, 347–373, 349–350.

39   O'Neal, S. (1996). *Elvis Inc.: The fall and rise of the Presley empire*. Rocklin, CA: Prima Publications.

40   Soocher, S. (1998, May). Blue Velvet. *Entertainment Law & Finance, 14, 2*, p. 5.

41   O'Neal, S. (1996). *Elvis Inc.: The fall and rise of the Presley empire*. Rocklin, CA: Prima Publications.

42   Ibid.

43   Ibid.

44   Madow, M. (1993). Private ownership of public image: Popular culture and publicity rights. *California Law Review, 81*, pp. 125–, 143.

45   Dyer, R. (1986). *Heavenly bodies: Film stars and society*. New York: St. Martin's Press.

46   de Certeau, M. (1986). *Heterologies* (B. Massumi, Trans.). Minneapolis: University of Minnesota Press.

47   Silverstone, R. (1989). Let us then return to the murmuring of everyday practices: A note on Michel de Certeau, television and everyday life. *Theory, Culture and Society, 6, 1*, 77–94.

48   Jenkins, H. (1988). Star Trek rerun, reread, rewritten: Fan writing as textual poaching. *Critical Studies in Mass Communication, 5*, 85–107; Jenkins, H. (1992). *Textual poachers: Television fans and participatory culture*. London: Routledge.

49   Fiske, J. (1987). *Television culture*. New York: Routledge; Fiske, J. (1992). The cultural economy of fandom. In L. Lewis (Ed.), *The adoring audience: Fan culture and the popular media* (pp. 30–49). London: Constable.

50   de Certeau, M. (1984). *The Practice of Everyday Life*. (S. Rendall, Trans.). Berkeley: University of California Press.

51   Silverstone, R. (1989). Let us then return to the murmuring of everyday practices: A note on Michel de Certeau, television and everyday life. *Theory, Culture and Society, 6, 1*, 77–94.

52   Fiske, J. (1987). *Television culture*. New York: Routledge; Fiske, J. (1992). The cultural economy of fandom. In L. Lewis (Ed.), *The adoring audience: Fan culture and the popular media* (pp. 30–49). London: Constable.

53   Jenkins, H. (1988). Star Trek rerun, reread, rewritten: Fan writing as textual poaching. *Critical Studies in Mass Communication, 5*, 85–107, 87.

54   Ibid., p. 104.

55   Ibid.

56   Mr. Rogers seeks beautiful day in court in trademark suits. (1999, February). *Sports & Entertainment Litigation Reporter*, 10, 10, 6.

57   Grossman, M. (1998, April 17). Right of publicity tested on the net. *Broward Daily Business Review*, p. B1.

58   Madow, M. (1993). Private ownership of public image: Popular culture and publicity rights. *California Law Review, 81*, 125–.

59   Ibid.

60   Coombe, R. J. (1998). *The cultural life of intellectual properties: Authorship, appropriation, and the law*. Durham, NC: Duke University Press.

61   Ibid., p. 98.

62   Branscomb, A. W. (1994). *Who owns information?: From privacy to public access*. New York: Basic Books, pp. 38–39.

63   Wolmuth, R. (1987). Liz Taylor leaps into a vital business with passion. *People Weekly, 28, 14*, 38.

64   Dyer, R. (1986). *Heavenly bodies: Film stars and society*. New York: St. Martin's Press.

65   Ibid, p. 3.

66   Salopek, P. (1997, June 22). Gene hunters taking hits the global scramble for genetic cures in the DNA of small ethnic groups has provoked cries of protest – and they are getting louder. *Toronto Star*, p. F8.

Chapter 38

Neal Gabler

WALTER WINCHELL
Stardom

I

WALTER WINCHELL HAD CHANGED remarkably in the fifteen years since he arrived back in New York late in 1920 as a naive but aggressive young vaudevillian trying to make his name in the world. He was still handsome, still with fine features and penetrating blue eyes that locked so intently on a listener that they often unnerved those who met him. He still talked like a "magpie," in Ben Grauer's words, and he still sent off waves of electricity that could set a whole room buzzing. He was still fearful and insecure, still always worrying about money. He was still much more outwardly than inwardly directed, still campaigning for himself every chance he got, still at turns sycophantic and resentful.

But he had changed. Physically he was trim, but his five-foot-seven-inch body was no longer lithe. His hair was rapidly turning gray, his hairline receding. He looked older than his thirty-nine years, even if his aging had imparted a certain distinction — something no one could have imagined thinking back on the ambitious, glad-handing young Winchell. The larger change one detected, however, was in his temperament. Though quick-witted and often funny, he had become much more self-conscious about his growing status as a political commentator and much more concerned about preserving his image as an American institution. There was a sobriety one seldom found in the younger Winchell, a sense that he could no longer stand on the sidelines heckling, that to be taken seriously he had to grapple with weightier issues.

Yet at the same time that he was completing his transformation from imp to institution, he realized that he still couldn't rest. He had to move or someone would catch up to him, even surpass him. That, he knew as well as anyone, was how celebrity worked; there was always something new coming along, something hot. So one always had to reinvent oneself. It was out of this impulse that he had first ventured into radio when he felt he had reached a ceiling with the column. Now that he was preeminent in both radio and print, he needed to master another medium to stay ahead of the pack. And this time he looked to Hollywood. This time he was going to become a movie star.

As preposterous as this might have sounded for any other journalist, it was far more than a pipe dream for Winchell. His film shorts aside, he had been courted by Hollywood for starring roles since his first trip there, but he had always rebuffed the studios by asking for a prohibitively high salary. By 1935 Walter was listening more attentively, not only because he wanted something to rejuvenate him but because he thought he had found a way to reduce the risk of failing while he tried: Ben Bernie.

Over the years Walter and Bernie had had their real-life disputes – when Bernie wrote for permission to mention Walter's name in a trailer for a film he was doing at Paramount, Walter refused and warned, "[I]f you persist then I'm washed up with you forever"[1] – but their radio feud had continued unabated since those few weeks back in 1933 when the sponsors temporarily ordered them to desist, and Bernie spent part of 1935 in Hollywood prospecting for movie projects for the two of them. By the fall Walter, obviously over his anger about *Broadway Through a Keyhole*, was also pressing Darryl Zanuck at Twentieth Century-Fox to come up with a vehicle for Bernie and Winchell. "Reliance films have been writing me for weeks for an interview, claiming they have three scripts for me," Walter said. "Thalberg [of MGM] and Harry Cohn of Columbia are also interested but I think you are top man and our alleged prestige would be safer with you."[2]

Zanuck had promised Walter that he would find the "proper and correct vehicle for you and Bernie,"[3] but it wasn't until September 1936 that he found it. Zanuck was clearly excited. He dispatched Fox Vice-President Joe Moskowitz to New York with a temporary story treatment and instructions to contact Walter the minute Moskowitz arrived. Less than three weeks later, with Moskowitz trailing Walter on his rounds and by one account pleading with him to agree so that Moskowitz could return to California,[4] Walter signed for his first starring film role. The salary was to be $75,000. "I hope I haven't been swindled!"[5] Walter wrote Zanuck three days later. Walter also asked that he not be forced to come to Hollywood much before actual production began, since his syndicate had complained of too much Hollywood gossip and not enough New York. Zanuck cheerfully agreed. "I will not send for you until I actually need you and you will receive script far in advance so you will have plenty of time to build up your own dialogue and cut down Bernie's," Zanuck joked.[6] To Fox publicist Harry Brand, Walter made one more request: that he be given a bungalow on the lot to race to between takes so he could "get another couple of paragraphs done."[7]

Walter departed New York on December 14, 1936, from Penn Station and arrived in Los Angeles three days later.[8] Though Eddie Cantor, who was to costar, had begged off the picture – Walter later said because Cantor thought it would fail[9] – Walter arrived in high spirits. The story, adapted by Curtis Kenyon from Dorothea Brande's novel *Wake Up and Live*, was a farce about a timid page at a radio station who has a lovely singing voice but gets "mike fright." The beautiful hostess of an inspirational radio program (Alice Faye) encourages him to conquer his fear by practicing in front of the microphone. One day while he is singing to himself, his voice is accidentally broadcast on Ben Bernie's program. The public response is overwhelming, but the page is unaware that he is the object of its affection, and so is Bernie. Inundated by calls and telegrams demanding the singer's name, Bernie decides to call him "The Phantom Troubadour." Suspicious, Winchell demands that Bernie produce the troubadour. When Bernie tries, hiring a stand-in, Winchell reveals the hoax and humiliates his rival. Meanwhile, an unscrupulous agent, who has discovered the truth, kidnaps the page. By the end the page has been freed and, with the help of the hostess, sings publicly at a nightclub while Bernie and Winchell declare a truce. All this was to be punctuated with songs by Mack Gordon and Harry Revel. But as Zanuck had told Walter, "The beautiful part about this story is that neither you nor Bernie have to carry the plot, the plot is carried for you and yet you are an integral part of it without being dragged in. . . ."[10]

"I have just seen the final script on 'Wake Up and Live,' " Walter wrote *Variety* editor Abel Green enthusiastically the first week of 1937, "and really think it is one of the swiftest paced I have ever read or seen . . . I am playing a semi-menace with the usual windup. 'Why Walter we didn't know you were using it for That reason!' "[11] Walter's confidence, however, rapidly ebbed the closer he got to production, and his mood was souring. "From the office-dressing room windows," he wrote, "it [Hollywood] looks like the front of the Palace used to look . . . The same agents, actors, hangers-on, lobbygows, phonies, front-putter-uppers . . . Strange, too, seeing so many falsefaces . . ."[12] He admitted he was overtaken by nerves and began suffering a severe case of lumbago. The night before his screen test he had slept only three and a half hours, which "certainly isn't enough to make a guy feel like doing anything but committing a murder."[13]

Zanuck tried to bolster his spirits. After seeing Walter's test, the studio head declared himself "very happy."[14] "Your personality is swell on screen and you have the best pair of eyes I've seen on an actor in a long while," he gushed to Walter. "This is no bull, I mean it. The way they have darkened down your hair looks good. If you know your dialogue and do not let Bernie step back on you, I'm afraid you are going to be a bit of all right." Walter had also objected to several of his lines, and Zanuck readily agreed to change all but one. He had even given Walter the star dressing room.

But for all Zanuck's attempts at accommodating him, Walter was not reassured. One rumor had him fainting on the set his first day.[15] Walter vehemently denied it, saying that he had been on the set for only two minutes that day – just long enough for Patsy Kelly, who was playing his secretary, to nudge him after a crack by Bernie, run a finger across her throat and say, "Hmmm, your pal!" Nevertheless, the film's director, Sidney Lanfield, who had known Walter from the NVA days, said he was always having to shoot around his star in the morning because Walter was too jittery to sleep and usually arrived late. And when he did arrive on the set, he was still so nervous and uncertain that Lanfield usually had him perform the first take to an empty camera until the actor calmed down.[16] Bernie told an interviewer that the technicians on the picture had been bothered for ten days by a strange noise that kept drowning out the dialogue. "We found out it was Winchell's knees rattling madly against each other!"[17]

He finished shooting in late February with high praise in the column for Lanfield, who "finally got what the authors intended, we think, after perspiring blood and dying a little every day . . . It seemed a dirty trick to play on a man – handing him two 'actors' such as Bernie and us."[18] Lanfield was so moved by this little tribute that he wired Walter his thanks rather than phone him, for fear he would lose his composure: TO THINK THAT IT TOOK THE TOUGHEST GUY FROM THE TOUGHEST CITY TO COME OUT

HERE AND SOFTEN UP A LOT OF CALLOUSED FARMERS STOP WE ALL LOVE YOU AND WE'LL MISS YOU LIKE HOLY HELL YOU LOUSE.[19]

Walter lingered for several weeks, adjusting his sleep schedule and hitting the clubs again. By the time he returned to Broadway, Zanuck's publicity machine was already cranking up for *Wake Up and Live*. "Prepare yourself for the kick of your life," Zanuck told a journalist even before the picture was cut.[20] "When you see 'Wake Up and Live' you are going to see a new screen actor the like of whom has never been on the screen. Forget that he is Winchell, look at him under the name of Joe Doakes, if you wish, but look at him and you will agree with me he is one of the greatest picture possibilities that has come to the screen in many a day."

At Grauman's Chinese Theater in Hollywood on April 4, two weeks after Walter's return to New York, *Wake Up and Live* received its first press screening. "It is sheer entertainment, fast stepping, sparkling, without a foot of waste material or a dull moment," rhapsodized *Daily Variety*.[21] "Dust off all your SRO signs," joined the Hollywood *Reporter*. " 'Wake Up and Live' will make the box offices of the nation do exactly that. It is headed for record-breaking business." I HAVE TO ADMIT PREVIEW GREAT, Lanfield wired Walter that night. ALL NOTICES RAVES[.] DOUGLAS FAIRBANKS[,] ZANUCK [,] [ADOLPHE] MENJOU AND HUNDREDS OF OTHERS SAY BEST MUSICAL THEY HAVE EVER SEEN.[22]

Walter seemed to have won his gamble and should have been ecstatic. But the day after the preview he was rushing back to Hollywood to confront a new crisis. While he had been in New York, his family had fallen ill. To those to whom he mentioned the crisis, he didn't specify what was wrong, but by way of explaining his sudden trip west, he wrote Hearst, "My wife is pretty sick,"[23] and he informed columnist Leonard Lyons that June was going to be operated on the following Monday. "She's a pretty sick girl and so I belong here with them," Walter said, adding that he had already told his radio bosses that his family must come first and that they had graciously agreed.[24]

The nature of the operation or the degree of its seriousness Walter again did not divulge in his letters, but whatever June was undergoing was complicated by another development. The very day that she went into the hospital, Walter tersely ended his column: "The W.W.s anticipate a blessed event in the Winter."[25] June had now lost the baby and possibly the ability to have any others. "The Walter Winchells aren't that happy," he wrote in the column a week after the operation.[26] "Mrs. Winchell was suddenly rushed to a surgeon's stiletto but is on the mend." Privately, he wired his secretary: WE WOULD RATHER HAVE BABIES THAN MONEY.[27]

As June convalesced, Walter remained in California, missing, as it turned out, the New York premiere of *Wake Up and Live* at the Roxy later that month. The critics there had been as enthusiastic as the ones in Hollywood, but they reserved their loftiest encomiums for Walter. Regina Crewe in the New York *American* said that "the Winchellian personality dominates the screen when Walter is in camera range. The qualities that have won him fame in two media are apparent in the third. His acting has the fine virtue of appearing natural."[28] (She added that he was turning down offers of $15,000 now for personal appearances and that his fan mail equaled that of Fox's biggest star, Shirley Temple.) Frank Nugent in *The New York Times* called *Wake Up* a "blessed event at the Roxy."[29] "He runs through 'Wake Up and Live' with the assurance of an ex-vaudeville hoofer and the high tension we always have associated with Broadway's Pepys," Nugent wrote. Producer Billy Rose, then in Fort Worth, Texas, for the state centennial fair, saw the picture the same night as its New York opening and sent Walter a glowing telegram offering to back a revival of *The Front Page* starring Walter. He even promised to donate the profits to any charity Walter designated.[30]

Louella Parsons, Hearst's Hollywood gossip, was so impressed that she devoted an entire column to an interview with Walter – a rare beneficence. No longer hedging about his future in pictures – after returning from California he had said that "wild horses couldn't drag another picture out of him"[31] – he openly discussed with her his jitters while the film was being made and said he thought his second movie would be less nerve-racking.[32]

Audiences swarmed to the picture. On opening day more than 6,000 patrons attended a midnight screening at the Roxy,[33] helping set a one-day attendance record of 38,825.[34] More than 1,500 people were in line at ten o'clock the next morning. It broke house records at the theater on Saturday and Sunday by more than $2,000 each day and broke another the following Tuesday despite a continuous rain.[35]

As years passed, however, the luster of *Wake Up and Live* would diminish until the film virtually vanished, as most of Walter's work would. Certainly no one any longer would be calling it one of Hollywood's greatest musicals. Once past the flush of initial excitement and Winchell's power of intimidation, the picture receded as forgettable froth with some tuneful songs, none of which became a standard, and some winning performances by veteran character actors Patsy Kelly, Ned Sparks, Walter Catlett and Jack Haley as the Phantom Troubadour – the same Haley of Haley & Craft who had provided Walter jokes back in vaudeville.

Despite its impermanence, *Wake Up and Live* may have had one effect: Some observers thought that Walter's performance had a lasting influence on screen acting. "Walter Winchell is so positive an acting personality that professional actors imitate him," drama critic George Jean Nathan wrote after seeing the film, citing twenty-seven plays and forty-three movies over the last few years in which actors patterned themselves after Winchell.[36] To the extent that he symbolized the city in the thirties, Walter did seem to define an urban style for actors. Something in his clipped, nasal voice, something in the fast, kinetic, herky-jerky way he moved, something in his snap-brim fedora and the double-breasted blue suits he wore, something in his wise-cracking and his slang, something in his bantam size and sharp features, provided a model of tough-guy urban America, and there would be a little of Walter Winchell in James Cagney, George Raft, John Garfield, Edward G. Robinson, even Humphrey Bogart, all of whom rose to prominence after he had become a national figure.

Whether he could actually have become a successful movie star is a moot point. Though he waffled, he really seemed to have no desire to do any more pictures. In any case a friend had warned him to take his time before making another film. "I think you're a chump to hurry back before the cameras," the friend wrote. "You're in a spot where audiences want more of you, but if you oblige too fast, I'm afraid you might weaken the grand value you have won. You're not a hungry actor who must work to be remembered."[37] "This is very difficult for me to tell you," Walter wrote Zanuck, taking the friend's advice to heart, "but I would be happier if you wouldn't take up my option."

"Whoever wrote you that letter that you quoted in your letter to me should have his head examined," Zanuck indignantly wrote back the same day.[38] "I think your attitude, as expressed in the letter – if you are sincere about it – is certainly a slap in the face at me and ungrateful to say the least." Zanuck promised not to "mince words" with Walter. "In the first place, you asked me to find a picture for you when you were out here last year. I did not ask you. I found a picture and paid the price that you wanted without quibbling. I designed the picture and spent over $850,000 to find out whether I was right or wrong. No one took a gamble except Twentieth Century-Fox and Darryl Zanuck." He said that the studio had extended Walter every consideration, and he ended, "I am surprised at you, Walter." Two months later Joe Moskowitz sent Walter an agreement, exercising the option and ordering Walter to California on September 23 to begin a movie to be called *Love and Hisses*, once again costarring Ben Bernie.[39] Now he was enslaved not only to the column but to Hollywood as well.

Actually he had been in New York only once – a week in mid-July – since June's surgery, and in all likelihood it was only the operation and her convalescence that saved him from the *Mirror*'s usual dunning that he return to New York and write a Broadway, not a Hollywood, column. In late June, he made an appearance on Cecil B. De Mille's "Lux Theater" playing reporter Hildy Johnson to James Gleason's editor Walter Burns in a radio adaptation of *The Front Page*.[40] As Johnson, a reporter whose soul belongs to journalism but who struggles futilely to extricate himself from it and live normally, Walter was clearly playing a role wrenched from his own life, and he was brilliant at it. When Hildy's fiancée scolds him for being on the job every time she calls for his presence, it could have been June talking to Walter, and when Burns, after being excoriated by the fiancée, admits, "I'm a bum," Hildy chimes in, "I'm a newspaperman!," again sounding one of Walter's own defenses. There are not many Hildy Johnsons left, not many journalistic "swashbucklers," Walter told De Mille in an on-air interview after the play, but Walter left little doubt that he considered himself one of that dying breed whose chief dedication was to the paper, and he promised that he would be back on Broadway as soon as he finished his film obligation, probably in October.

But as the starting date for *Love and Hisses* approached, Walter was clearly growing apprehensive again – this time less over his acting than over his workload. He couldn't help remembering how difficult it had been to balance the film, the broadcast and the column during *Wake Up and Live*, and in mid-September Walter advised Jergens that his health would prevent him from doing the broadcast for the next eight weeks. Always protecting himself, however, he asked Jergens not to replace him with another commentator but to do another kind of program entirely. Jergens granted the leave but not the request for a different program. OUR INTEREST REQUIRES US TO PROTECT THE GREAT INVESTMENT MADE IN DEVELOPING THIS PERIOD AS A NEWS SPOT, Robert V. Beucus of Jergens wired him.[41] He got the same consideration from the *Mirror*, with Louis Sobol taking over the column for syndication in his absence.[42]

Now Walter was forced to deny rumors that he was going to let his contract lapse and finally scale back, as he had been promising June for years. He insisted that he was simply going to recharge. "The odds are a good ten to one that if I had not received this leave I would have been a very sick fellow," he wrote a friend.[43] A press release from Fox reported that Walter was suffering from "nervous exhaustion" and that aside from the suspension of his broadcast and column, precautions were being taken on the set to ensure his well-being.[44] A physician was to be present at all times, and the start of shooting had been pushed back from 9:00 a.m. to 11:00 a.m. to accommodate Walter's sleep. But none of these things seemed much to appease him. If he had been nervous and sick with anticipation during his first film, he was ill-tempered and bored during the second, knowing he had already proved himself, and tired of the whole thing. "All I know is that I sit around fifty minutes out of every hour waiting to do a scene that is seldom over four or five lines," he wrote Abel Green. "My God, how they waste time out here! . . . I need more action than that, Abel, or I fall asleep."[45]

THE DAY after he wrote Green, Walter received a letter from a ghost of his youth. It had been years since he had had any contact with Rita Greene. He had expunged her like so much of his past, readily agreeing to an increase in her stipend fourteen months after their divorce and then, less readily, to another in 1931, but neither seeing her nor writing her in the six years since. (Evidently Walter had been so angry over her second request that he instructed his secretary not to put her calls through.)[46] Those years had not been kind to Rita. After the divorce she had continued in vaudeville, but she was exhausted and frequently ill with a thyroid condition, and she finally quit on her doctor's advice. Eventually she enrolled in business school, and on August 11, 1930, her eleventh wedding anniversary, she set out for an employment office and wound up landing a job in the New York branch of Pathé Pictures where, out of consideration for Walter, she dropped the name Winchell.[47]

It was never easy. With one sister married and gone and another unmarried and working only fitfully, Rita became the main provider for her family, living in an airy house on Staten Island. Her life revolved around her job, first at Pathé and later as a legal secretary, around her obligations to her family and around the local church. She and her family huddled in front of the radio each week to listen to Walter's broadcast, but he was never mentioned in the household in any context other than as a reporter and gossip.[48]

Then she got the news, the news of which she wrote Walter that October while he was filming *Love and Hisses*. "Sometime back I found out I had a tumor in my breast," went the letter. "I have been taking treatments for this tumor in the hope that it would dissolve, but I am now of the belief that it must come out." The operation, which doctors advised she have immediately, would cost roughly $500, and she was now asking Walter if he might see his way to giving her $300 toward it. The response, whether Walter authorized it or not, was unspeakably cold. His secretary in California wrote: "[W]e are doing our best to simplify his routine as much as possible for him. . . . I have been given strict orders not to bother him with any mail at the present time. . . . I'm sure you understand."[49]

Of course, all Rita understood was that she had cancer, that Walter had promised years ago he would help her if she needed it and that now she needed what amounted to a pittance, though Walter, always suspicious, probably believed the tumor was a ruse to pry more money from him. Rita angrily wired back that if Walter was too busy to answer his mail, could his secretary please see to it that his *wife* got the request? Within a few days Rita got her money and soon after had a radical mastectomy that saved her life.[50] But she could never forgive Walter his insensitivity, and she bridled at the injustice of her supporting a family on her wage of less than $20 a week and Walter's stipend of $75 while he boasted of making thousands of dollars a week. At any rate, she believed that by getting her to agree to forgo alimony, Walter had conned her into accepting less than what she was entitled to.

After the operation Rita attempted to contact Walter for redress. Again and again she found he was "too busy, or in other words can't be bothered."[51] "My hours are never regular," he wrote her after a year of her trying to arrange a meeting. "I sleep when I can and get up when I can. . . . I just can't make dates."[52] It was, Rita said, after another year of these rebuffs that she devised a new plan. She would write a book about her life with him. She would reveal the secrets he had worked so desperately to conceal. "I am not getting any younger," Rita wrote in her manuscript by way of explanation. "I am getting older, my health is nothing to write about, and I have come to the time when I must have some security. . . . [A]s everyone has written about Winchell, and it appears that he is such good copy, I have tried my hand at it, and perhaps it will give a few people a laugh when they read why Winchell's life is more interesting than the others."[53]

Rita wrote her manuscript, leaving little doubt that she intended it less as a literary effort than as a means to coerce Walter into increasing her stipend. But then she locked it away in a trunk with an old photo album, clippings, letters and other mementos of her life with Walter. For in the end, no matter how desperate her plight and no matter how cold-hearted Walter's treatment of her, she loved him. Rita Greene never stopped loving Walter Winchell.

WITH *Love and Hisses* completed, Walter returned to New York in November and resumed the broadcast on November 14, after his eight-week hiatus, vowing yet again that his days as a movie star were through.[54] In all, he had spent eight and a half months in Hollywood that year, the longest stretch of time he had been away from New York since his last vaudeville tour in 1920, and he had become increasingly disenchanted with it, increasingly restless over its pace and its social life. "There's nothing for me to do in California," he told *Time* magazine. "I can't go to people's homes and then write about them."[55] He was especially struck by Walda's reluctance to tell him anything about her friend Shirley Temple. "You would just put something in the paper about her," she said.

In California, *Love and Hisses* was being previewed. Based on an original story by Walter's friend Art Arthur, who had been the Broadway columnist for the Brooklyn *Eagle* before heading to Hollywood to write pictures, *Love and Hisses* was in the vein of *Wake Up and Live* but even slighter. The plot is triggered when Bernie asks Walter if he will promote a new find of Bernie's, a pretty French singer who, Bernie claims, has entertained the crowned heads of Europe. Discovering otherwise, Walter blasts her on the air instead. The next day a worried French aristocrat arrives at Walter's office, asking the columnist's assistance in finding his daughter, who has run away to Broadway. Walter promptly finds her at a casting call at Bernie's club and is wowed by her voice. What Walter doesn't know is that this has all been part of an elaborate deception by Bernie to make Walter eat crow, since the girl (Simone Simon), whom Walter now promises to publicize, is the same one he has criticized. But before Bernie can make a fool of him, Walter discovers the plot and springs a practical joke of his own on Bernie. He has some gangsters kidnap Bernie and threaten to kill him unless Walter hands over $50,000 in ransom money. At film's end, Bernie, blindfolded, is pleading for his life, not realizing he is onstage at his club before a full house. With Walter now having regained the upper hand, the French girl sings to an appreciative audience. "I'm the guy who brought her over," says Bernie. "But I'm the guy who *put* her over," replies Winchell.

Sidney Lanfield, who directed *Love and Hisses*, wrote Walter that "the consensus out here is that it is much better than 'Wake Up and Live,' " and he added that he had received "fifty rave wires from people who said the audience screamed from beginning to end." When the picture opened early in January, however, the consensus was anything but the one Lanfield had described.[56] Frank Nugent in *The New York Times* was kindest, saying, "As sham battles go, this one is not quite up to the standard of their [Winchell and Bernie's] previous engagement, but it still must be reckoned a lively, well-scored, amusing show. . . ."[57] More typically, *Newsweek* called it "uninspired entertainment," which "misses by a considerable margin" the success of *Wake Up and Live*, but the magazine spared Winchell and Bernie responsibility.[58] Howard Barnes in the New York *Herald Tribune* found a cruelty in the banter between Walter and Bernie that the critics had surprisingly overlooked in the first picture. "Their continual heckling of each other has already lost its freshness."[59]

Lest the film be perceived a failure and a blow to Walter's seeming indestructibility, he was at some pains in the following weeks to tell listeners that *Love and Hisses* was actually outperforming *Wake Up and Live* at the box office.[60] At the same time he was now insisting that he would have continued making movies if the tax bite hadn't been so deep and left him so little return.[61] Yet whatever gloss he put on it, *Love and Hisses* had been a disappointment after *Wake Up and Live*, and the willingness of critics to say so could be laid partly to Walter's long sabbatical without his column and broadcast. Defenseless, he was fair game.

II

"The Column." It was always "The Column," as if it were something holy and inviolable, as if the others were pretenders, which, in a sense, they were. Everyone read "The Column." "I have never been able to get far enough into the North woods not to find some trapper there who would quote Winchell's latest observation," Alexander Woollcott wrote as early as 1933, and he recalled a "painful" scene in Hatchard's bookshop in Piccadilly where a lord was in a dither because his orders to have Winchell's Monday column rushed to him as soon as it arrived had been disobeyed.[62]

But however popular it was elsewhere and however much civilians enjoyed it, it was in New York and especially among show people and café socialites that "The Column" was devoured with the avidity of a child racing to the tree on Christmas morning to see what gifts had been left. By eight o'clock each evening, press agents and other show business personalities were queuing up at the newsstand, waiting for the early or "green" edition of the *Mirror*. "Before anything you turned to page ten," a press agent recalled, referring to the page on which "The Column" was found. "A press agent would grab the *Mirror*, run through it like a dose of salts and run to the telephone and say, 'Pete, you're in Winchell today!' "[63]

And the interest went beyond ego gratification or professional advancement. "The Column" was so sacrosanct and café society's faith in publicity so devout that Winchell's items had an oracular authority. "If Winchell says so, it's gotta be true," Lucille Ball said about a report of Walter's that she was expecting a child.[64] (She was.)

Others learned of unhappy spouses and impending divorces or soured romances. David Brown was shocked to read in Winchell that his wife was divorcing him, then heard from her lawyer the next morning.[65]

Walter himself seemed to regard "The Column" with a kind of reverence, too, as if he were merely its custodian and not its creator. "Other columnists have jocular moments when they suggest to a very limited group of intimate friends, that perhaps there are more important matters on earth than their daily essay," wrote one press analyst. "When Winchell says something about 'The Column' it is as if he were discussing an immutable force which he had miraculously unleashed but scarcely understood."[66]

For Walter, everything had to be seen through the scrim of "The Column"; life was reduced to column fodder. As Emile Gauvreau put it in one of his novels, "The interests of others concerned him only in so far as he could make capital out of them."[67] Once Walter was strolling down the beach in Miami while composer Richard Rodgers was discoursing to some friends on an investment he had made. Seeing Walter, Rodgers offered a brief summary, but Walter stopped him after a moment. "Never mind, never mind," he said, holding up his palm. "It's no good for the column."[68]

In one sense his reverence for "The Column" enslaved him to it; in another sense it liberated him from responsibility for it. Walter's "wrongoes" on both the broadcast and in "The Column" were numerous, as might be expected from a column that could contain well over fifty items each day. He repeatedly reported that Judge Joseph Force Crater, a New York jurist who had suddenly disappeared, was still alive.[69] A week after reporting that Douglas Fairbanks, Jr., had given an engagement ring to Vera Zorina, he announced that Zorina had married George Balanchine two weeks earlier, without ever referring to his own blooper.[70] He spent months and even years tracking the romances of Katharine Hepburn, once publishing an "unconfirmed report" that she had married agent Leland Hayward after both had obtained Mexican divorces.[71] Boarding a train in Newark for New York upon her return from the Yucatán, Hepburn instructed her traveling companion to hand a reporter a Mexican peso. "You give that to Mr. Winchell," snapped Hepburn. "It's worth 30 cents. That's what I think of Mr. Winchell."[72]

Walter conveniently managed to ignore most of his mistakes or attributed them to erroneous "reports," as if he hadn't been the one circulating them; when he did correct errors, he did so circuitously by assailing sources. *He* never made errors, never retracted, not necessarily because he was infallible but because "The Column" had to be infallible. That might not have pacified anyone stung by Walter's "wrongoes," but readers and listeners never remembered the mistakes anyway, and his credibility never suffered. They seemed to realize that accuracy was beside the point. The point was creating a sense of omniscience. And for this, Winchell understood, seeming to predict events was just as good as actually predicting them.

WITH "THE Column," the broadcast, the personal appearances and movies, Winchell in the mid-thirties had become his own cottage industry, and though he liked to give the impression that he managed all these activities with a minimum of help – as was somewhat true – he still, of necessity, had gathered around him a small coterie to feed the maws. Ruth Cambridge continued to run the office in her relaxed fashion.

Vivacious and carefree, Ruth had met dancer Buddy Ebsen the summer Walter was away in California with June after Gloria's death. Three weeks later they eloped. "Now I know why you've been sending my mail to Chicago (where Buddy was) instead of to California where I am!" Walter quipped in the column.[73]

Ruth enjoyed the tumult at the Winchell vortex. Even after she married, she stayed with Walter, running the office single-handedly except for an occasional temp, until May 1935, when she left for Hollywood, where her husband had landed a film contract. Her replacement couldn't have been more different from Ruth. She was a petite, dark, chain-smoking young woman, nervous and birdlike, named Rose Bigman, who was conscientious where Ruth was convivial and who had a manner and voice almost as sharp as her boss's.[74]

Rose's father had died when she was two, her mother when she was seven. She and her older sister spent their childhood unhappily bouncing from one aunt to another until the girls were old enough to work. Rose had worked as a secretary at a real estate firm for several years until "economic conditions made it necessary to dispense with my services," as she wrote in her letter of introduction, then as the secretary to the man in charge of the New York office of Westinghouse radio stations until these were sold to NBC, and then as secretary to an executive at the Columbia Phonograph Company until her division was closed down. A son of one of her bosses was dating Ruth Cambridge at the time and recommended Rose for a temporary position to help with an overflow of mail. She pounced on the opportunity – for years she had carried a clipping of a lovelorn poem from Winchell's column – and arrived for her interview in a large borrowed coat so she would look older than her years. Ruth hired her at $5 a week, and she began work on December 4, 1932, the day Walter debuted his Jergens program.[75]

Though the job was supposed to last only a few weeks, Rose wound up staying nearly a year before Walter decided that the office work no longer warranted two secretaries. Fortunately Bernard Sobel, the *Mirror*'s drama critic now that Walter had surrendered the job, decided to hire her. But Rose never lost her bond to Winchell – even though she hadn't seen him during her first six months on the job – and Sobel was careful not to disparage him in front of her.[76] When Ruth left for Hollywood, as Rose later told it, "Winchell yelled up to Bernie, 'Send Rose down to me!' " From that day, for the next thirty-five years, Rose Bigman was Winchell's gatekeeper, carving out her own small legend among the Broadway cognoscenti.[77]

By his own admission, he was a tyrannical boss. "Nobody's Girl Friday, I am sure[,] has taken so much from a boss who can blow his top faster than I – before orange juice," he wrote in his autobiography, describing a typical phone call. " 'Fercrisssakes! You let me run the leading item when two of the opposition rags had it the day before! I thawt you read all of them. I can't read every paper every day. I don't mind getting it second. I just don't like getting it third!' (Bang! Hanging up.)"[78] Rose called him the "bantam rooster" when he flared up this way.[79] "We'd have these big fights," she recalled. "But when he'd call again, we never mentioned it. Everything was like a new day."

Even so, she was terrified of leaving the office for fear he would phone. "I never went out to lunch. I would practically die before I would have to go to the ladies' room or anything . . . because I never knew from one day to the next what time he would call. It could be ten o'clock in the morning or six o'clock at night. But I'd have to sit there all day to wait for him, you see."[80] If she did happen to miss his call, he would bark, "Where the hell were you?" She worked seven days a week, including holidays, recovering only when he took his four-week summer vacation.

"Don't let the Boss frighten you – talk back to him when he starts shouting," Ruth counseled from California.[81] But Rose was nowhere near as assertive as Ruth, and she fretted over every little mishap. "You have found out what a worrier I am," she wrote Walter shortly after assuming her duties. "I worry about the column every minute of the day and when I get up in the morning my first thought is 'Did WW leave me any notes? Did I do all right yesterday and other silly things like that?'

"What I'm trying to say is please have a little patience with me. . . ."[82]

At the bottom of the note, Walter typed: "Stop worrying. You're doing bigtime work and I appreciate it. I'm just a nervous guy, get used to me. Love and kisses, Walter." And he gave her a $50 raise.

The routine was killing. Rose arrived at the office at 10:30 each morning and seldom left before 7:30 or 8 o'clock. Each day brought hundreds of packets from press agents. Rose read them and began sorting them by column heading: "Man About Town," "Things I Never Knew till Now," "New York Heartbeat," "Notes from a Girl Friday." The best material she sent to Walter's apartment in what she called the "nightly envelope." Then he composed the column, either at home or in the office late at night after Rose had left, and sent back the rejected items circled in red with comments scrawled in the margins. He also enclosed drafts of letters he wanted typed.

A messenger brought the finished column down from Walter's apartment to the *Mirror* offices on 45th Street. "He'd make so many changes," Rose said. "He crossed out things. He x'd them out. Nobody could read it but me."[83] Frequently he phoned with last-minute emendations. So Rose would retype the column and send a copy to the composing room and another to the Hearst lawyer, who vetted it for libel and sent it on to the editor for another review. It was Walter's expectation that Rose would protect the column from these censors. At first it was "awful," in Rose's word. "I'd be so scared and I'd sit and wait for him [the editor] to call and I'd say, 'What am I going to take out? What am I going to take out?' " But after a while she learned to "fight like mad."[84]

Her most important assignment, however, was not shepherding the column to print or even protecting it against Hearst. Her most important assignment was controlling access to Walter. She learned early that he was never to be disturbed. Ruth was on one of her long lunch breaks one day as a meeting between Walter and some Paramount Picture executives was rapidly approaching. Rose felt a wave of panic. Should she disturb Walter at home to remind him of his appointment or should she let him miss it? She decided she really had no choice but to phone him. Walter was furious at being awakened. He gave her such a dressing-down that she decided thenceforth she "wouldn't call him even if the building was burning."[85] Not even Hearst himself got through. "I'm sorry. Mr. Winchell is sleeping," she told Hearst when he phoned once and demanded that Walter be alerted immediately. "This is William Randolph Hearst," he insisted. Still, Rose refused. Later Walter sent Hearst a note saying that he had been unavailable because he had fallen out of the window.[86]

"Everyone thought I was a battleax until they met me," Rose admitted.[87] When they did meet her, they discovered an unprepossessing young woman – everyone assumed from her phone manner that she was much older – who fully realized that while she was to run interference for Walter, she had also to mediate between Walter and the press agents who serviced the column. When Walter was about to blacklist a press agent from the column for some offense, real or imagined, it was Rose who said, "C'mon, Boss. Wait a minute. Don't put him on the list. He really didn't mean it."[88] In this way, onetime press agent Ernest Lehman believed, she "kept Walter from going to extremes." On the other hand, it was also Rose who, after Walter had erroneously printed that the Lehmans were "writing their own unhappy ending" – he had confused Ernest with another Lehman – begged Lehman not to demand a retraction. "Please don't ask him to retract," she importuned. "Just forget it."[89]

Rose answered the phones, opened the mail, wrote the letters, retyped the column and broadcast, even changed the ribbon on Walter's typewriter. Yet there was still the enormous job of feeding the maws, and these duties fell to hundreds, if not thousands, of contributors, none of whom expected or received monetary compensation; the mention was compensation enough.

One of the most faithful of these contributors, a thin, painfully shy clerk for the Brooklyn Edison electric company named Philip Stack, began mailing poems to the column under the pseudonym "Don Wahn" in 1929. His verses were both melancholy and cynical, about lost romance and jaded lives, but Walter loved them – they may have reminded him of his own *Vaudeville News* doggerel – and they became a regular feature, running just under Walter's by-line and making "Don Wahn" possibly the best-known poet in New York. Still, Stack was never paid. "I think that contributors to columns like you ought to be paid for their work – by book publishers, I mean," Walter wrote in the introduction to a collection of Stack's poems.[90] "For you never heard of a columnist paying for his contribs – and you never will. Never give a sucker an even break, Barnum is supposed to have said.

"But as that Guinan Gal taught me: 'Never even give a sucker (a contributor) ANYTHING!' "

For Walter it had always been part of the Winchell myth as well as a point of honor that he composed the column virtually by himself and that he never paid for items. But both claims were fallacies. In the early thirties he asked his old roommate Curley Harris to collect items for him at $50 a week. Harris agreed. "Sometimes I'd pick up the column, a third of it would be mine. Sometimes more," Harris recalled.[91] So he asked Walter to revise the arrangement up to $100 a week. Money-conscious as he was, Walter acquiesced. But Harris was soon dissatisfied again. "Eventually I thought the hundred wasn't enough," Harris remembered. "He was making a lot of money. He went up pretty fast, you know. . . . So we finally made an arrangement that he would pay me I think it was $10 or $20 for things on the radio and $10 or something for things in the column. Five items would be $50. So we worked that way for a long time." Others worked on the same basis – author Jim Bishop, then a copyboy, made $5 for each "Oddity in the News" Walter used – but always secretly, lest anyone discover that Walter was not the one-man band he made himself out to be.[92]

Regardless of the number of contributors, it fell to Walter to distill and shape the contributions into columns, and no one ever denied that his sensibility governed. One friend recalled watching Walter intently sitting on the bed in his apartment, brandishing scissors, clipping away at press agents' sheets and then connecting strips with Scotch tape, papers strewn everywhere. "It looked like a kindergarten class," observed the friend. "But he knew what was important. *He knew* that."[93] "He could take any guy's twelve lines and reduce it to six lines and make it far more readable, far more pointed, and it hadn't lost a thing that the original writer put in it," remembered Arnold Forster, the Anti-Defamation League attorney who often contributed political material to the column.[94] Just how good an editor he was may have been most apparent when he was on vacation. "The press agents would send the same material that they sent to Winchell when Winchell was around," remembered one associate, "but none of the other columns ever improved. . . . None of them ever had his style. . . . When he came back, it became Winchell again."[95]

Early in 1937, when he was in Hollywood making *Wake Up and Live* and unable to devote as much time as usual to his column, Walter realized that his ad hoc system would no longer be sufficient. He needed someone who could compose portions of the column and the broadcast for him, someone who was young and hungry and discreet, someone who could be trusted. And he already had a candidate in mind: a tousle-haired, bespectacled twenty-year-old gag writer named Herman Klurfeld.[96]

Like Walter, the Bronx-born Klurfeld was the elder son of Russian Jewish immigrants – his father a house painter, his mother a housewife. He spent his youth in Jewish enclaves around the Bronx, speaking Yiddish until he was taught English in the first grade. During his senior year of high school, he was stricken by a lung abscess and was bedridden for two months, passing the time listening to radio comedians and then penning his own gags, which he never mailed. When he graduated, he planned to become an accountant, but with his father frequently out of work and the family in desperate need of money, he took a job pushing handcarts in the garment district. At night he still wrote gags, scribbling them on index cards. Finally a friend convinced him to send a few of his choicest jokes to Leonard Lyons, the new Broadway columnist at the New York *Post*. Klurfeld sent six. Lyons published one: "Girls used to dress like Mother Hubbard. Now they dress like a cupboard." Klurfeld was ecstatic. "To see my name in a Broadway column in the New York *Post* for a kid who lived in the Bronx tenement area – this was startling for me and all of my friends," he remembered.

He kept submitting, and Lyons kept publishing. "Herman Klurfeld at the Stork says . . ." Finally, after six months, Lyons wrote him asking if he would like to become a PR man. Klurfeld hadn't the slightest idea what a PR man was, but he went to Lyons's office, dressed in the same tattered sweater he wore to his job in the garment district. Lyons explained that a press agent named Dave Green had noticed Klurfeld's contributions and wanted to see him. Klurfeld was so dumbstruck by Green's sumptuous office in the RKO Building and by the celebrity photos decorating the walls that he immediately accepted an offer of $10 per week, even though it was $2 less than he was earning in the garment district. When he raced home and told his parents that he was going to work as a gag writer, they were stunned. "But I loved it. I couldn't wait."[97]

Klurfeld was raw and untutored – Green had to buy him a suit so he wouldn't embarrass the office – and he landed so few gags in the columns in those first months that Green kept cutting back his salary. But when Walter returned from his annual vacation at summer's end and received several months' worth of gags that Green's office had stockpiled for him, he made a point of phoning Green to tell him how much he liked the young man's work and told Green to send him over to the office. When he arrived, as Klurfeld remembered it, Walter was in his fedora pecking away, two-fingered, at the typewriter.[98] The office "didn't look at all the way I had imagined. Dingy, narrow, cluttered, it was sparsely furnished with several hard chairs, a row of files, a long table and two desks."[99] He was struck immediately by Walter's handsomeness, especially his mesmerizing blue eyes. On either side of the columnist sat two burly men, who Klurfeld later learned were bodyguards: one from the FBI, the other from the mob. Glancing up, Walter pushed himself away from the typewriter. "You have a way with words, kid," he told Klurfeld. And Klurfeld "glowed, simply awed to be in his presence."[100]

For the next hour Walter expatiated about everything from the Stork Club to "The Column" to the movies Zanuck wanted him to make. But he also questioned Klurfeld about his family, his background, and his aspirations, and he seemed especially to approve that Klurfeld's family was so much like his own. Afterward, ducking into a cab, Walter promised they would be seeing more of each other. Two weeks later Walter asked Green to send Klurfeld to the Stork Club. They ate in a private room, only three or four tables, where Walter introduced him to Tallulah Bankhead ("Go fuck yourself" were her first words) and gangster Bugsy Siegel. Again, Klurfeld was dazzled. When, on another occasion, Klurfeld expressed his admiration for the playwright Clifford Odets and cited him as an inspiration, Walter arranged for Odets to join them at Lindy's for breakfast.[101]

If Walter was trying to seduce the young man into the orbit of W.W., he succeeded masterfully. After the Stork, Klurfeld started dropping by the office several times a week in the early evening, before heading off to night school, where he had enrolled in accounting courses. ("Accountant?" Walter had asked him incredulously when he heard. "Accountants don't have fun."[102]) A short time later Walter left for Hollywood. Shortly after that Klurfeld submitted to the column a paragraph he called "The Headliners," which was a series of quotes from famous individuals, followed by a wisecrack. Walter phoned him, which wasn't unusual by now, but this time "he seemed to be very excited," as Klurfeld remembered it. "He said, 'Kid, I loved those "Headliner" things. From now on I don't want you to contribute to any other columnists. I want you to go to work for me. How much are you making?' " $25 a week, Klurfeld told him. "I'll double it," said Walter. It was understood that no one but Dave Green and Rose were to know about the arrangement. Klurfeld was to work at home. Rose even cashed his checks lest anyone wonder why Winchell would be giving a weekly stipend to Herman Klurfeld.

As Herman quickly discovered, working for Walter Winchell was never merely a job; it was a way of life. "I would write the Sunday column, which we started calling 'The New York Scene' and then 'Notes from an Innocent Bystander,' " he recalled. "I would write ninety-nine percent of that column, which was what the critics said about the [Broadway] shows. We boiled it down, you know . . . I did very little [on Monday] except punch up the Monday 'Man About Town' column – the gossip stuff. I would just punch it up with little phrases to make it more readable. The Wednesday column – the 'New York Heartbeart' – that was for press agents. That was a payoff for press agents. That he mostly did on his own."[103] Of the seven columns that Walter submitted each week, then, Klurfeld said he wrote the better part of three, though Walter edited them all. "Some weeks I did four. Some weeks I did two."

On Thursdays, while he was drafting the Sunday column, Klurfeld also began wrestling with his main contribution to the broadcast in those early days – the lasty.[104]

Because of Walter's adamance that listeners remembered most what they heard last, his sign-off – "With lotions of love, this is your correspondent Walter Winchell who . . ." – was given assiduous attention. "How about a hundred [submissions]?" Klurfeld said of the number of lasties he wrote each week before Walter was satisfied. "And sometimes he didn't like anything I gave him of the hundred. And very often I'd give him one and he said, 'That's it.' " But even then Klurfeld couldn't trust that his mission was complete; he was on twenty-four-hour retainer. "I'd say, 'I'm going to have a Sunday off. Terrific!' Well, Sunday morning I get a call from Rose: He changed his mind. He needs a new lasty . . . And there went my whole Sunday. I sat at that goddamned typewriter and turned them out until he got one he liked. Some days he didn't like it and used the one he had on Friday anyhow. . . . I worked harder on that goddamned one line than I did in writing four columns."

For both Klurfeld and Rose, the demands were ceaseless, the work was grueling and slavish, the pay good but not great, and Walter seemingly ungrateful. So why did they subject themselves to it for as long as they did? They often asked themselves this question as the years passed. One answer was action. Working for Winchell, even surreptitiously as Klurfeld did, put one at the center of action and connected one, if only vicariously, to power. "Psychologically I got the joy of working for a man who was to me almost godlike, who could change the world, change people's lives," Klurfeld reflected years later. "He was the king of the world and I was one of the assistant kings."[105]

Rose too enjoyed being at the eye of the storm, swept up in the turbulence. It gave her life momentum and meaning. It also gave her deference and perks, like show tickets and free meals at fine restaurants. And when Walter was inundated with Christmas presents, all of which he felt ethically obliged to return, Rose convinced him to let *her* keep them.[106]

But there was another force that bound both Herman Klurfeld and Rose Bigman to Winchell: the force of family. Like Nellie Cliff, Rita Greene, June Magee and Ruth Cambridge before them – like Broadway in the twenties and America in the thirties – Klurfeld and Bigman were young and adrift and looking for a community that would have them. Walter provided it. "He was sort of a father image to me," Rose said. "I think that's why I took the yelling and everything. I didn't have a father, so I took it from him."[107]

Klurfeld also described his relationship to Walter as one of a father to a son.[108] Walter was the one he wanted to please. "If I've made any kind of headway, I'm grateful to you," Klurfeld wrote Winchell shortly after going to work for him.[109] "You've been a sort of guide and teacher for me. You made me do a lot of things I never dreamed I was capable of performing." A year later he wrote again: "I want to thank you for being so nice to me. I hope that someday I'll be able to afford to contribute material without getting anything for it, simply because I don't consider that work. And the pleasure I get[,] the things I learn from you are worth more to me than anything else. That may sound Pollyannish, but it's the way I really feel."[110]

Sometimes Herman even allowed himself to imagine that he was being groomed for the day when Walter would fulfill his longtime promise to June and retire.[111] To Rose, Walter was less paternal and more abusive, and she thought he regarded her only as a "necessity," but he also referred to her only half-jokingly as his "other wife," and in any case, what she mistook for lack of intimacy was simply the way

Walter dealt with people, warily, never letting down his guard. He trusted Herman and Rose about as much as he would ever trust anyone besides June. Everyone else wanted something. Herman and Rose wanted only to bask in the reflected glory of Walter Winchell.

III

It wasn't only Winchell, Bigman and Klurfeld who were indentured to "The Column." So were the press agents. "We regarded that column as number one, and we broke our backs to get in there," remembered one.[112] At one agency the going rate for landing a joke in Winchell's column was $75; for landing an "orchid," Walter's method of bestowing praise, $150;[113] and a single mention would hold a client for weeks.[114] That was why the press agents got what they called "seven o'clock stomach" waiting for the first edition of the *Mirror* to hit the newsstands. One press agent recalled rushing his pregnant wife to the hospital to have their baby, then picking up the *Mirror* while he waited for the delivery. When his wife emerged, she beamed and said, "It's a little girl!" and asked if he was happy. The press agent said, "Happy? I got five items in Winchell."[115]

There were, in the late thirties, hundreds of these press agents – some of them joke and pun writers, others news gatherers, still others outright promoters and ballyhoo artists. "In those days being a press agent was like a girl being a model," said one veteran publicist. "When a guy was arrested and they asked him what he did, he'd say 'publicity.' Everybody was in publicity."[116] Press agents had first materialized around the turn of the century to exploit free publicity in the expanding press.[117] Though a bill was introduced in Congress in 1913 seeking to outlaw press agentry and though the New York legislature passed a law in 1920 restricting publicists' activities after one of them had faked the suicide of an actress to promote her new film, press agentry remained a growth industry not only among the august public relations counselors who ministered to corporate clients but among the low-rent hustlers who promoted bandleaders, stripteasers, banjo players and restaurants.[118] It was the rise of the mass media and the concurrent rise of the idea of celebrity that did it. Even the most minor performer realized that publicity, not necessarily talent, was the way to fame, fame the way to success, and a press agent was the first step along the way.

Virtually all these press agents sent material to Winchell – scores of items, pages of items, thick packets of items – every day. Rose Bigman said admiringly that she didn't know how they did it.[119] But the fact was that they had little choice. "You *had* to service Winchell every single day – 'Sounds of the Night,' or funny stories or observations," said Coleman Jacoby, later a comedy writer.[120] Jacoby submitted five pages of jokes to Winchell each day. Press agent Eddie Jaffe submitted as many as ten pages, others even more. "I realized that competing to get into Winchell's column was like a third university for me because you were competing against four hundred other minds every day," said press agent Gary Stevens.[121] Searching for an advantage, Jaffe printed up stationery: "Exclusive to Walter Winchell." Emmett Davis sent his items on pumpkin-colored paper until Winchell scribbled back, "I've had enough of yellow journalism. USE WHITE PAPER!"[122]

Even greater ingenuity was applied to the items themselves. A press agent named Milton Berger once financed a divorce so that the aggrieved husband could sue Berger's client, muscleman Charles Atlas, for alienation of affections.[123] Another time, representing a toupee firm, he planted the story of a man who fell asleep in his barber's chair during a shave and wound up getting his toupee cut. When Marlene Dietrich's press agent was having difficulty keeping her name in the papers, he called on Eddie Jaffe for help. Jaffe, who knew you could always get clippings in the sports department, concocted the "Marlene Dietrich Award" for the race-horse with the best legs, then found a racetrack willing to present it.[124] Another legendary press agent, Jack Tirman, was representing the Kit Kat Club, where "if you didn't get in the papers," the owner "beat you up. He didn't fire you."[125] To keep the Kit Kat in the columns, Tirman began inventing nonexistent acts. One of these, a dance team, wound up getting orchids in Winchell's column as well as a review in the *Post*. When Walter discovered the ruse, he was furious, but Tirman deflected the anger by telling Walter that *if* the dance team had actually existed, Tirman *would* have come to Walter first.

"We and the other press agents fought with each other to see who was in Winchell's favor," remembered Ernest Lehman.[126] Those who weren't in favor had to devise methods to land their client's plugs anyway. This often resulted in elaborate deceptions by which the outcasts routed items through the favored press agents.[127] This way the out-of-favor press agents got the mentions they wanted, and the favored ones were rewarded with mentions for *their* clients because Walter believed they had given him "free" items – that is, items about people and places they didn't represent. The rule of thumb was that Walter would give a press agent one plug for every five "free" items the agent delivered.

There was always more anxiety than honor, more pressure than respite, for the press agents. "We lived in a dangerous world," Lehman said.[128] Clients were seldom satisfied; they always wanted more. Press agents loved to tell the story about dance king Arthur Murray, a dour, laconic man whose press agents got him in the columns by making him the vehicle for their snappy one-liners. Then came a fallow period when Murray wasn't in the papers. So he called his press agent, Art Franklin, and complained, "What happened, Art? Did I lose my sense of humor?"[129]

Even when clients were reasonably satisfied – and the turnover was great in the best of times – press agents found themselves in a daily pincers between competing columnists. That was because columnists seldom returned items, and press agents were forced to guess how much time to let pass before submitting the same items to another columnist, the damage of having the same item run in two columns being incalculable. Of course, Walter received all material first, and press agents appreciated that he alone among columnists always returned unused items promptly, usually no later than a week after submission, frequently with the reason for rejection. Press agents in good standing also appreciated that Walter occasionally sent along a scurrilous item he had received about one of their clients, placing a question mark beside it to show that he wasn't using it.[130]

Still, he inspired terror. Once, at a time when Walter was especially enamored of the rhumba, he was watching a couple on the dance floor and remarked how much he was enjoying them to press agent Sid Garfield, who quickly chimed in, "Look, Walter, I'm enjoying them too."[131] Another time, when a few disgruntled press agents began griping about Winchell, Jack Tirman looked skyward and blurted, "I'm not listening, Walter."[132] Another press agent remembered instinctively checking his car's rearview mirror when a passenger criticized Winchell, fully expecting to find Walter tailing him.[133]

The greatest fear was of winding up on what Walter called the "Drop Dead List." Any one of a number of petty offenses could land a contributor on the DDL, a Coventry that could last months or even years and that would undoubtedly cost the transgressor clients and money and possibly his job. One common offense was giving Walter an item that had run in another column, something that happened occasionally when a press agent or contributor mistakenly thought he had already rejected an item. Another was giving him an erroneous item — a "wrongo." "Sometimes people give you a wrong steer," Walter frankly told an interviewer in 1937. "When I find that a contributor has done that, I never use his stuff again. I don't know why. It's like finding that a girl has been unfaithful."[134] (This was also the main reason why he seldom confirmed items with the subjects, despite claims that he did; contributors knew they gave him false information at peril of being put on the Drop Dead List.)

Like veterans telling war yarns, every press agent had his favorite story about landing on the DDL or narrowing escaping it. Marty Ragaway earned a place on the DDL when, on meeting Walter, he casually mentioned that he had been sending gags to the column since he was in high school. "Well, how dare you do that to me?" Walter fumed. "How dare you send me copy and let me use a kid in high school's material?"[135] Ben Cohn, under pressure from Walter to supply "novelettes," invented one about a showgirl who was about to jump from her hotel room window because she could not pay the bill. Then she got a call to report to rehearsal, but as she walked through the lobby, the house detective stopped her and told her to forget the rehearsal. He had called the producer and said she couldn't do it.[136]

The story had immediate impact. Producer Billy Rose offered her a job. Radio columnist Nick Kenny wrote a poem to her. The Chez Paree took up a collection. Now Walter wanted to meet her. "My world shattered," Cohn said. So Cohn typed a letter, had the receptionist rewrite it in her hand, put it in an envelope, pricked the envelope with two pins and brought it to Walter. When Walter demanded to see the girl, Cohn said he had let her have his room, then returned to find his money gone, his bridgework missing and the note pinned to his pillow, saying that she had been through so much and was now taking a few things of his. "And so you were only stuck for a story," Girl Friday wrote in the column. "Ben Cohn was stuck for $32 and his bridgework." But he escaped the DDL.

Cohn was among the lucky ones. Gary Stevens was representing a singer named Patricia Gilmore, who was conducting a discreet romance with bandleader Enric Madriguera. The Associated Press had reported that the two had wed, but Gilmore, whose Irish Catholic parents disapproved of the relationship, phoned Stevens to dispute it, and Stevens in turn sent on a denial to Walter, who published it along with a dig at the AP. The AP retaliated by publishing a photostat of the marriage certificate. When Stevens confronted Gilmore, she confessed that they had gotten married but wanted to keep it secret.

Now came the storm. Rose phoned Stevens immediately to ask how he could have made such an error. The next day Walter himself phoned, spewing expletives and demanding that Stevens meet him at the Stork Club that afternoon. When Stevens arrived at the club, it was empty except for the waiters and Walter, who was eating. Walter ordered him to sit and began lecturing him, almost paternally at first as Stevens remembered it, about the responsibility to check facts. Then he turned angry. "You're on my shit list for one year," Walter said, and quickly dismissed him.

Every day Stevens sent contributions to Winchell, and three days later they would come back, untouched and unclipped and always with the same note: "Don't send these to anyone else." (Stevens circumvented the ban by rewriting items and submitting them to Dorothy Kilgallen at the *Journal* and to Sullivan and then trading items with other press agents.) Months after the imposition of the ban, Walter was dancing at the Stork with a girl whom Stevens was dating at the time. "Tell your friend to call me," Walter said to the girl. Stevens did, and Walter, as if compensating, published seven or eight of Stevens's items in the first few weeks. Bringing up the incident years later, Walter laughed, punched Stevens playfully on the shoulder and said, "I was wrong and you were wrong."[137]

Usually contributors pleaded with Walter to reinstate them. "I am sorry that you think I deliberately tried to palm off someone else's gag on you as my own, and that as a result you feel toward me as you do," comedian Henny Youngman once wrote him abjectly. "Certainly I respect you too much to try to pull anything as raw as slipping you a gag from another column," and he promised that he would hence-forth be "doubly careful in checking on any material submitted to me. . . . I cannot risk incurring your displeasure for a mere line."[138] Eventually all but a few were reinstated. The only capital crime for which there was no reprieve was boasting that one could get an item into the column.[139] Walter made it clear that no one had that ability; anyone who believed he did would be making Walter out to be a dupe.

He was most lenient with young press agents. A new publicist at Warner Bros. named Robert William was assigned to provide Winchell with material, and William's boss invited him to dine with Walter at the Stork. Beforehand, however, the two stopped at the Astor Hotel for drinks. William, a novice drinker, downed a scotch and soda "like a malted" and within five minutes was in "the most advanced state of euphoria you could imagine." By the time he arrived at the Stork, he was goggle-eyed, and while he managed to keep himself composed during dinner, after dinner he was "stricken with the greatest case of narcolepsy." William's boss was irritated, but Walter was understanding. "When I was your age I went to sleep right under the table," he said. William believed "he saved my job."[140]

Otherwise Walter was largely contemptuous of press agents. He hated their sycophancy, their mewling, their obvious insincerity, their desperation, which may have reminded him of his own. "The press agents were all over him," recalled David Brown.[141] He walked around "like a shark with little fish around him" was press agent Maurice Zolotow's description.[142] Above all, he hated his dependence upon them.

For the press agents the feeling was mutual. Most of them deeply resented the power Walter held over them, the peremptory banishments, the constant demands, the need to today and bootlick. Their resentment toward Winchell may have been exceeded only by one other hatred: their own profound self-loathing. On the face of it, press agents were a strange, colorful breed who prided themselves on being characters in the Damon Runyon mold. But just beneath the surface of the image, one found an unsavory and largely forlorn group of men. Some were lapsed journalists in mid-career who were frantically searching for a way to make money. Some were fresh high school kids who liked to wisecrack and hoped they might become humorists or even columnists. Others were orphans and vagabonds who had drifted into publicity because they didn't know how to do anything else. "A lot of these guys couldn't write their own names," Ernest Lehman said.[143]

They spent their evenings, as Walter did, hanging out at clubs and restaurants, hunting for clients, picking up gossip, trading stories, cadging drinks, pressing items on columnists. They lived with a sense of their own corruptibility, often having to bribe their way into columns. At Walter's own *Mirror*, for example, $25 could buy a picture on the center "split page." For $2, radio columnist Nick Kenny would mention a birthday. Kenny's secretary, who happened to be his niece, would demand tickets to radio programs. His brother, who was married to a radio actress, would demand that press agents help her get jobs. A cartoonist for the column named Bill Steinke ("Jolly Bill" he was called) demanded $10, he said, to make a plate. And Kenny himself was a songwriter who plugged those clients who helped get his songs on the radio.[144]

The whole process was grubby and humiliating, and it was no different at many of the other papers. The submissiveness hurt, and the agony of knowing that you were chasing trivia, leaving nothing. Stanley Walker in a scathing dissection of the press agents in *Harper's* magazine wrote of hearing them "cry softly into the beer, ale, Scotch, and rye along Broadway for years and curse their own strange calling. . . . They do become ashamed of themselves at times, though the majority, if they keep at it long enough, manage to smother their consciences."[145]

They tried, some of them, to boost their status by calling themselves "public relations men" or "press representatives," but the terminology of their trade betrayed them. Press agents talked of "servicing" a column and of "scoring" when one had a successful plant in a column. The metaphors were sexual because the press agents saw themselves as procurers with a stable of clients they had to sell and columnists they had to sell them to. And what added insult to the insult was that clients frequently failed to pay; by Eddie Jaffe's estimate, 50 percent of his clients welched.[146]

Yet however shabby the system, however meager the influence of any one individual, save Winchell, they were all locked in an immense cycle of promotion and dissemination and creation which for better or worse helped define the country. "Publicity is the nervous system of the world," wrote Harry Reichenbach, who was one of its earliest and best practitioners.[147] "Through the network of press, radio, film and lights, a thought can be flashed around the world the instant it is conceived. And through this same highly sensitive, swift and efficient mechanism it is possible for fifty people in a metropolis like New York to dictate the customs, trends, thoughts, fads and opinions of an entire nation of a hundred and twenty million people."

Most of the press agents themselves were so absorbed in the details they were myopic to the rest; they never saw the system whole this way or gave a moment's thought to its effect. But a few did. A few knew. "I always believed that a great deal of our news was shaped by a rather small group of press agents," observed Ernest Lehman. "If I ever saw a feature story in a New York newspaper I knew that that was not the result of some editorial board saying, 'Let's do a feature on so-and-so,' or that the feature writer said, 'I've got a great idea. I'd like to do a feature on so-and-so.' I felt it always started with a press agent calling someone and saying, 'Look, I've got a story for you. Here it is.' "[148]

That is the way the system operated. That is the way the world worked in an age of gossip and celebrity. And the press agents, for all their abasement, were the ants that moved the mountain. For without them, there was no celebrity, no gossip, no mass culture really. And, as he knew only too well, no Walter Winchell either.

IV

He never called them rivals. To Winchell his fellow columnists were always "imitators," riding on the coattails of his popularity. He loved to read their columns aloud in front of an appreciative audience and provide a running commentary.[149] When he saw items and jokes he had rejected appearing in other columns, he would crack, "I see my rejects are ending up in the garbage pails."[150] But this was more than public entertainment. David Brown, then an obscure young journalist writing a column for *Pic* magazine, was shocked to receive tear sheets of his pieces with comments and criticisms from Walter even though Brown had never met him.[151]

"[M]y impression of the Broadway columnists[,] judging from their output, was that they were, by and large, a rather venomous lot, forever clawing at each other," wrote one, recalling his feeling as he was about to join their ranks.[152] By the late thirties there were many more of them clawing, nearly all of them marginalized Americans – Jews, Catholics, women, homosexuals – venting national frustrations through their own. The *Daily News* had both Ed Sullivan and Sidney Skolsky. When Skolsky was fired for insubordination, he was replaced by a aristocratic-looking Georgian named Danton Walker, who had once served as assistant to Alexander Woollcott and then to Harold Ross of *The New Yorker* before joining the *News* as an assistant to the financial editor.[153] Genial Louis Sobol still covered Broadway for the *Journal*, but when O. O. McIntyre died suddenly, early in 1938, Sobol, who had never really had the stomach for the sort of bare-knuckles journalism that Walter loved, took over as the *Journal*'s resident nostalgist. He, in turn, was replaced on the Broadway beat by Dorothy Kilgallen, the twenty-five-year-old daughter of veteran Hearst reporter Jimmy Kilgallen, and a valued reporter in her own right. Lee Mortimer, who had once written the Sunday column in the *Mirror* while Walter sulked, now had his own column. Hal Conrad wrote Broadway gossip for the Brooklyn *Eagle*, and within a few years producer Billy Rose was to launch a syndicated Broadway column.

"Did you know L. Lyons is now a columnist?" Girl Friday asked in May 1934.[154] Leonard Lyons, who had landed on the *Post* that month, was one of the few with whom Walter didn't quarrel.[155] He had been born in 1906 Leonard Sucher, youngest of seven children of an impoverished garment worker from Romania who died in a sweatshop when Leonard was eight years old. To support the family, his mother set up a candy stand at Ridge and Rivington streets on New York's Lower East Side while Leonard, a bright student, sailed through P.S. 160, skipping four grades. He worked his way through high school, making keys at the Segal Lock Company and during summers running errands at the Palisades Park Commission, where one of his brothers was head bookkeeper. After high school he took accounting courses at City College, then went to St. John's Law School, where he graduated second in his class. He joined a law firm and left two years later to start his own practice.

Soon, however, he realized that the law exerted a weaker claim on him than journalism. One reason why, evidently, was his fiancée, Sylvia Schonberger, whom he had met at a party during his senior year of law school and whom he had instantly resolved to marry.[156] Sylvia, moved by the beautiful letters he had written her, was convinced Leonard could be a writer. In June 1930 he landed a column in an English-language insert in the Yiddish *Jewish Daily Forward* at $15 per week. It was the editor there who renamed him Leonard Lyons.[157]

Six months later the section folded. Lyons was now contributing items to the Broadway columns, including Walter's, but he hadn't lost hope of getting another column of his own. "It was the mad dream – the terrific longshot," he later said.[158] Early in 1934 New York *Post* publisher David Stern put out a call for a Broadway columnist. Lyons submitted his clippings and won the job from among five hundred applicants. (Walter claimed to have recommended him.[159]) He was sitting at a night-club one night that May batting around possible names for the columm when Walter said, "Here's a natural for you. The Lyons' Den."[160] Lyons liked it and joked that Walter had won the name-the-column contest, the prize being a night on Broadway.

"Why would a lawyer become a columnist?" his son Warren reflected many years later of his seemingly modest and unambitious father.[161] "I asked him this many times. His answer was, 'I don't know.' That's what he said to me. 'I don't know.' " There was always a lingering suspicion both within the Lyons family and without that Lyons hadn't really wanted to be a columnist, that his wife, Sylvia, was the driving force behind his career and the one who stoked his ambition. Lyons would admit only that he liked the excitement of being a columnist, and there certainly were perks.[162] But he may have been unwilling or even unable to admit the deeper attraction that a Broadway column held for a poor boy from the Lower East Side who devoutly wanted to be accepted, and for his wife as well: a Broadway column allowed them to circulate among the famous.

Walter hated having to mix with celebrities; he thought of them as unavoidable nuisances. "I just don't like celebrities," he told an interviewer.[163] "I'm like the violin-ist in the story who played with the orchestra for forty years, and when the conduc-tor asked him why he made such faces he replied, 'Because I hate music.' " Lyons, on the other hand, loved to mingle with them, and in his column he told tales *about* the famous rather than *on* them, lest he offend. "My father never printed gossip," said Warren Lyons.[164] "If you look through his columns, you'll never find a blind item. . . . You'll never find anything 'who was going out with whom.' . . . He prided himself on not printing gossip." Lyons printed anecdotes instead, which is the main reason Walter was so magnanimous toward him. "You are the first column to come along who [*sic*] doesn't copy me," Walter wrote Lyons his first week on the job.[165]

Lyons cultivated a different image, too, from the pugnacious one that Walter had perfected and that the others copied. He avoided the crossfire that was a staple of the columns, and one of the few times he did attack was to scold Louis Sobol for hosting vaudeville shows because he thought that using celebrities and then writing about them was unethical.[166] Lyons was "a real gentleman," said press agent Robert William.[167] "Pleasant," Eddie Jaffe called him.[168] "Made a real *effort* to be pleasant." *The New Yorker* closed its profile of him by saying, "Everyone is Lyons' friend."[169] And one of those friends, the playwright William Saroyan, observed, "There is not a great deal of desperation in him – if there is any at all."[170]

But anyone watching the tiny man with the prominent nose flitting restlessly from nightclub to nightclub and from table to table, scribbling notes – he was famous for mangling stories to the point of nonsense – knew there was quite a bit of desperation in him, whether his own or Sylvia's. "Driven, dedicated," were words used to describe him.[171] "The hardest-working newspaperman I ever met," said one Broadwayite.[172] "Lyons never drinks, not even coffee," wrote Westbrook Pegler admiringly, "and he tells how when he gets home at 6 A.M. and says 'Good night' the elevator man thinks he is drunk and how his baby is just waking up when he gets in and just being put down when he starts back to work at four in the afternoon – the gay life of a Broadway bon vivant."[173]

Of course, it wasn't gay. It was long and arduous, and by the late thirties even members of the fraternity were questioning whether a Broadway column was worth the effort. In the twenties and early thirties Broadway, pulsating with uninhibited energy, was undeniably the center of the celebrity universe, and the Broadway columnist at the center of the center. But the evolution of café society couldn't conceal that the center was gradually shifting westward to Hollywood, where the movie stars dwelt. More and more, that seemed to be the place for a gossipmonger.

Partly in recognition of the changing order, the *Daily News* had dispatched one of its Broadway columnists, Sidney Skolsky, to California for what was supposed to be a year's tour of duty. Four years later, Skolsky was still in Hollywood. But then Ed Sullivan, jealous of what Walter had accomplished in the movies, convinced *News* editor Frank Hause to recall Skolsky at long last and send Sullivan instead. "I pleaded with him by wire and phone to return," Hause later wrote Walter of the efforts to bring Skolsky back, "but no dice. I guess the competition on the Broadway beat was too much for the Little Mouse, and he liked the easier tempo and climate of Hollywood."[174] Skolsky saw it differently. He fired back a letter of resignation, saying that "Broadway columns are as passé as Broadway"[175] and closing with a slight variation on the tag line of his column: "They got me wrong. I love Hollywood." Skolsky then switched to the *Mirror*, Sullivan left for California and Danton Walker took Sullivan's place on Broadway.

Wisely Walker began by soliciting advice from Walter on how to conduct his column. "Well, how shall I start?" Walter wrote back.

> I think it's important for anyone on a newspaper, particularly one who is doing a column, to "build his fences." The politicians do this a great deal, and it is a wise thing. Of course I mean make as many friends as you can. You never know from where the next line or paragraph is coming. One of your best stories may come from a fellow whose face you never liked, but whom you were nice to – and he appreciated your being civil to him, which is why he gave you the break.[176]

And he issued a warning about press agents: "Try your best to avoid the shyster press agent. There are many of them on our beat, and they think nothing of using one's column to spoil it if it will help them gain something." As for finding the right voice, "Try to be yourself as often as you can. I mean in style." He closed with an ethical consideration: "Never permit anyone to give you a gratuity because if you do, Danton, you will be putting yourself where they want you – in a spot."

Meanwhile, out in Hollywood, Sullivan was exploiting the film industry even more aggressively than Walter had. In short order, he sold three story ideas and appeared in the film of one of them, *Big Town Czar*. (*The New York Times'* Frank Nugent wrote, "[T]he only word for Ed Sullivan's portrayal of Ed Sullivan is 'unconvincing.' "[177]) But as with Skolsky, Sullivan was eventually recalled to New York, and as Skolsky had, Sullivan refused the order. Frank Hause was visiting Sullivan at the time the wire arrived from *News* publisher Joseph Medill Patterson. "I pointed out to the great Port Chester athlete the advantages of the Broadway beat and the *News* growth and prestige," Hause remembered, "and then dictated a wire to JMP, in which Sullivan stated, 'I acted hastily [*sic*]. Please ignore earlier telegram. Am returning New York.' He did return, and Patterson, flattered, made Sullivan the fair-haired boy."[178]

Skolsky, in the meantime, was finding Hollywood less hospitable than he had at first thought. Working on the *Mirror* had brought him into direct competition with Hearst's veteran Hollywood columnist, Louella Parsons. Skolsky had been on the paper only a short time when Parsons published a front-page story announcing that Greta Garbo and conductor Leopold Stokowski were to be married. In the very same paper, Skolsky's column reported that the rumours were false. Infuriated, Parsons labeled Skolsky a Communist, and Hearst refused to hear his defense: He would be fired as soon as his contract expired. Three months later he spotted Parsons at Chasen's restaurant with her niece – a movie publicist named Margaret Ettinger – and the journalist Alva Johnston. Johnston and Fttinger waved him over. As Skolsky told it, he spent the next fifteen minutes pleasantly conversing, never addressing a word to Parsons, until she finally chirped, "If I'd known you were so nice, I wouldn't have told Mr. Hearst you were a Communist." Skolsky was so angry he bit her. All told, he was out of work for eight months.[179]

Skolsky should have known better than to take on Louella Parsons. There were others purveying gossip in Hollywood in the mid-thirties, notably a onetime actor and movie publicist named Jimmy Fidler who had a fifteen-minute radio show, but Parsons was the undisputed queen, the Walter Winchell of the West. "I've always claimed a story wasn't a story unless I got it first," she wrote.[180] She had set her sights on being a reporter from the time she was a young girl in Dixon, Illinois. In 1896, at fifteen, she got a job moonlighting as church, social and sewing circle reporter for the Dixon *Star* while she taught school. At twenty-four she married John Parsons, a wealthy real estate agent eight years her senior, who moved her to Iowa, installed her in a boarding house, gave her a daughter and then abandoned her. At twenty-nine, she moved to Chicago, where she wrote articles for the Chicago *Tribune* by day and dreamed up screenplays at night. In the meantime, she married again, this time to an impoverished but attractive sea captain. Eventually she was hired by the Chicago *Record-Herald* to write film reviews and features, but when the *Herald* was folded into Hearst's *American*, Parsons left for New York and landed the job as motion-picture editor on the *Morning Telegraph*, whose current editor had left for the war. Five years later she assumed the same duties on Hearst's New York *American*.[181]

The dominatrix of the relatively small but rapidly growing field of movie news, Parsons worked tirelessly not only building her column but cultivating contacts. Chief among them was William Randolph Hearst's paramour, the actress Marion Davies. It was Davies who invited Parsons to join her on an excursion to Hollywood in May

1925. Parsons was captivated. Feted by the Hollywood community, which respected both the power of her column and her relationship to Davies, the plain, plump, unsophisticated woman from rural Illinois had found her spiritual home. She returned to New York at summer's end, but a bout of tuberculosis sent her back to California for convalescence that fall. When she recovered, Hearst insisted she remain in Hollywood as motion-picture editor of his Universal News Service. It was the syndication of her column in the Hearst papers that cemented her status as the most important of the Hollywood journalists.

In New York the premier gossips were the ones, like Walter, whose tongues were the sharpest and whose scruples the lowest. Power there was a function of one's insolence. In Hollywood, a one-industry town as far as gossip was concerned, things were entirely different.[182] Parsons was part of Hollywood's social order, not antagonistic to it. Her power derived from her relationship with the studio establishment, and her column was largely a compendium of trade news, interviews and other information which the studios wanted to have disseminated. As a result, stars and other employees feared her not because her column could harm them with the public (though it could) but because her coziness with the men who ran the studios could destroy them with their employers. Even so, she was ordinarily quite benign, despite her despotic reputation. "The only time she would get burned up with a star was if they [sic] had a big scoop and didn't give it to her," recalled her longtime assistant Dorothy Manners. "She'd ask if they'd lost their minds."[183]

"She was always in the swim," said Manners.[184] She began working the phones at nine each morning, tramping to her desk in her office, which adjoined her bedroom, sometimes still in her robe. The phones rang constantly, and each of her two secretaries had two. As the secretaries fed her information from the studios and from her legman, Neil Rau, Parsons composed the column, then read it to her staff for suggestions. (When a messenger glanced at the column one day and said he didn't understand something, Parsons began reading the column to him too.) By one o'clock in the afternoon the column was filed, and Parsons began her rounds of the studios. By late afternoon she had returned to the office for her hairdresser, and then it was off to Romanoff's or Chasen's or a party.

Once a month she hosted a large gathering of her own, putting up a tent in the yard of her Beverly Hills mansion and inviting as many as two hundred guests. (Later she bought a farm outside Los Angeles, built an oversized porch, outfitted it with bunk beds and entertained on weekends there.) She lived regally with a maid, a cook and a chauffeur, and she expected from the community the deference due a sovereign. Unsurprisingly, everyone paid tribute. Warner Bros. publicist Robert William remembered Parsons's coming to the studio lot at Christmastime to collect her bounty. He filled her station wagon with presents. "And she took it as a kind of princess [from her] devoted crowd," he said.[185]

The princess treated Walter like visiting royalty – at first, no doubt, because they were both members of the Hearst family and thus technically noncompetitive, and later because she had a fifteen-minute radio program that followed Walter's and she realized she inherited part of his massive audience.[186] If she ever said an ill word of Walter, no one could recall it, and she even offered to send him hot stories. "Sometimes things break out here that you could have on the air before they are printed in New York," she told him.[187]

Her spite, all of it, was reserved for Hedda Hopper, a former actress who, in 1937, had the temerity to begin a Hollywood gossip column of her own. Parsons "hated her guts," said Dorothy Manners.[188] Hopper, born Elda Furry, was one of nine children of a butcher in Hollidaysburg, Pennsylvania, in Quaker country just outside Altoona. Her childhood dripped with bitterness and resentment; her seminal experience was nursing her wealthy grandfather back to health after his eyesight had failed and being rewarded for her months of effort with a silver dollar. Bored with school and angry at the favoritism shown her brothers, she ran off to New York to become an actress and met De Wolf Hopper, an aging, physically imposing thespian with the voice of a church organ.

De Wolf Hopper, already four times married, doted on pretty Elda. "To him I was a new audience. I was as fresh as an unhatched egg. He enjoyed the attention he got from his raw recruit, went all out to give a continuous performance."[189] When she landed roles in two shows and toured the country, he wrote her ardently at every stop, and when she returned to New York, he met her at the station and immediately drove her to New Jersey to marry him. De Wolf was so much older than Elda's own father and such a notorious philanderer to boot that a friend of hers wept uncontrollably at news of the marriage. Meanwhile, he had such a difficult time distinguishing his new wife's name from those of his previous wives that Elda consulted a numerologist who, after much deliberation, dubbed her Hedda. Hedda said she hated it, but "I never heard him call me Ella, Ida, Edna, or Nellie again."[190]

Thin and delicate where Parsons was round and thick, pretty where Parsons was snaggle-toothed and jowly, Hedda found work in movies and on the stage through the twenties and early thirties, but by the time she turned fifty in 1935, she was divorced and jobless with a child to support. Eleanor "Cissy" Patterson, an old friend and the publisher of the Washington *Herald*, suggested she write a weekly "letter from Hollywood," and Hedda eagerly seized the chance. She lost the column in an economy move, but in 1937, on the recommendation of a publicist at MGM who claimed that Hopper seemed to have the best intelligence network in the film community, the Esquire Feature Syndicate signed her for a new Hollywood column. When the Los Angeles *Times* picked it up early in 1938, Parsons for the first time had real competition.

There were those who believed that Hedda Hopper had been energetically, if secretly, promoted by the studios as a way of balancing Parsons's power and keeping her in check. If so, Hopper eventually proved less compliant than Parsons and drove her into being less manageable too. Together the two guarded their domains, terrorizing stars, demanding scoops, punishing those who wouldn't provide them and creating a terrible dilemma for the unfortunates who wanted to stay in the good graces of both. "[H]alf the movie colony has gone schizophrenic handling those two old bags," Errol Flynn allegedly complained once. "You've got to please one without alienating the other!"[191]

But however much they loathed each other, Louella Parsons and Hedda Hopper were really very much alike. They were both conservative, prudish, narrow-minded small-town women in an essentially conservative and prudish community, and they used their gossip as a club to keep celebrities in line rather than as a needle to make celebrities scream. This was also one reason why Parsons and Hopper never had anywhere near the impact that Winchell had, even though their names became almost as well known as his. Winchell took on the world. As members of the establishment, Parsons and Hopper, like two biddy schoolmistresses, always fought to conserve the old order until the world passed them by.

Notes

1   Note on telegram Bernie to W, Dec. 22, 1934; W to Bernie, n.d., Bernie file, Winchell papers.
2   W to Zanuck, Oct. 15, 1935, Twentieth Century-Fox file, Winchell papers.
3   Telegram Zanuck to W, Sept. 19, 1936, Zanuck file, Winchell papers.
4   NY *American*, Sept. 30, 1936.
5   W to Zanuck, Oct. 3, 1936, Zanuck file, Winchell papers.
6   Telegram Zanuck to W, Oct. 5, 1936, Zanuck file, Winchell papers.
7   W to Brand, Oct. 14, 1936, Zanuck file, Winchell papers.
8   Leonard Gaynor, Twentieth, to Richard Hyman, King Features, Dec. 11, 1936, Zanuck file, Winchell papers.
9   "Jergens Journal," Sept. 11, 1938, NBC Blue, roll 712, NBC records.
10   Zanuck to W, Sept. 19, 1936, Zanuck file, Winchell papers.
11   W to Abel Green, Jan. 4, *Variety* file, Winchell papers.
12   NY *Mirror*, Jan. 8, 1937.
13   Ibid.
14   Zanuck to W, Jan. 8, 1937, Zanuck file, Winchell papers.
15   NY *Mirror*, Jan. 19, 1937.
16   *NY Times*, Feb. 7, 1937.
17   Clipping, n.d., MWEZ + n.c. 11, 680, NYPL at Lincoln Ctr.
18   NY *Mirror*, Feb. 26, 1937.
19   Telegram, Lanfield to W, Feb. 26, 1937, L file, Winchell papers.
20   Whitney Bolton, "The Stage Today," NY *Morning Telegraph*, Jan. 27, 1937.
21   Clipping, n.d., Scrapbook 1936–37, NYPL at Lincoln Ctr.
22   Telegram Lanfield to W, April 7, 1937, L file, Winchell papers.
23   W to Hearst, April 9, 1937, Hearst file, Winchell papers.
24   W to Lyons April 8, 1937, Lyons file, Winchell papers.
25   NY *Mirror*, April 12, 1937.
26   Ibid., April 19, 1937.
27   Telegram W to Rose Bigman, April 18, 1937, Bigman coll.
28   NY *American*, April 24, 1937; April 25, 1937.
29   *NY Times*, April 24, 1937.
30   Telegram Billy Rose to W, April 25, 1937, NYPL at Lincoln Ctr.
31   *NY Times*, March 28, 1937.
32   NY *American*, April 26, 1937.
33   Press release, Twentieth Century-Fox, Scrapbook 1936–37, NYPL at Lincoln Ctr.
34   *Motion Picture Daily*, April 27, 1937.
35   Harry Brand to W, April 26, 1937; Brand to W, April 28, 1937, Zanuck file, Winchell papers.
36   Quoted in Irving Hoffman, clipping, MWEZ + n.c. 11, 680 in NYPL at Lincoln Ctr.
37   Quoted in W to Zanuck, May 5, 1937, Twentieth Century-Fox file, Winchell papers.

38 Zanuck to W, May 5, 1937, Twentieth Century-Fox file, Winchell papers.

39 Moskowitz to W, July 19, 1937, Twentieth Century-Fox file, Winchell papers.

40 *The Front Page*, "Lux Radio Theater," June 28, 1937, Cassette 13646, Sound Div., Library of Congress.

41 Beucus to W, Sept. 16, 1937, Layer coll.

42 *Editor & Publisher* (Sept. 18, 1937), 20.

43 W to Abel Green, Sept. 24, 1937, *Variety* file, Winchell papers.

44 Press release, "Love and Hisses," Sept. 22, 1937, Winchell file, Margaret Herrick Lib., AMPAS.

45 W to Green, Oct. 1, 1937, *Variety* file, Winchell papers.

46 Rita Greene, unpub. ms., 46A–47A, Pat Rose coll.

47 Ibid., 72–73. Pat Rose, niece of Rita, int. by author.

48 Rita Greene to W, Oct. 2, 1937, Pat Rose coll.

49 Margarie Hockley to Rita Greene, Oct. 4, 1937, Pat Rose coll.

50 Ibid., 52; PR.

51 Ibid., 52.

52 W to Rita Greene, Sept. 29, 1938, Pat Rose coll.

53 Greene, 52A.

54 "Jergens Journal," Nov. 14, 1937, NBC Blue, roll 694, NBC records.

55 *Time*, July 11, 1938, 36.

56 Lanfield to W, Dec. 21, 1937, L file, Winchell papers.

57 *NY Times*, Jan. 3, 1938.

58 *Newsweek*, Jan. 3, 1938, 34.

59 NY *Herald Tribune*, Jan. 3, 1938.

60 "Jergens Journal," March 20, 1938, NBC Blue, roll 701, NBC records.

61 *he would have continued making movies* . . . Ibid., March 6, 1938, roll 701

62 Alexander Woollcott, "The Little Man with the Big Voice," *Hearst's International Cosmopolitan*, May 1933, 143.

63 Al Rylander, int. by author.

64 Lucille Ball int., Apr. 22, 1970, Thomas coll.

65 DB.

66 Charles Fisher, *The Columnists* (NY: Howell, Soskin, 1944), 103.

67 Emile Gauvreau, *The Scandal Monger* (NY: Macaulay, 1932), 187.

68 St. Clair McKelway, *Gossip: The Life and Times of Walter Winchell* (NY: Viking, 1940), 28–29.

69 "Jergens Journal," Nov. 17, 1935, roll 650; Sept. 6, 1936, roll 667, NBC records.

70 Ibid., Jan. 15, 1939, NBC Blue, roll 720, NBC records.

71 NY *Mirror*, Dec. 3, 1934.

72 Clipping, "Hepburn Home and Happy with Boo for Walter Winchell," n.d., Scrapbook 1933–34, NYPL at Lincoln Ctr.

73 NY *Mirror*, July 7, 1933, 19.

74 Rose Bigman to Gordon Van Ark, Nov. 28, 1933, Bigman coll.

75 Rose Bigman int. by author.

76 Bernard Sobel, *Broadway Heartbeat: Memoirs of a Press Agent* (NY: Hermitage House, 1953), 303.

77 RB.

78 Walter Winchell, *Winchell Exclusive: "Things That Happened to Me—And Me to Them"* (Englewood Cliffs, N.J.: Prentice-Hall, 1975), 92.

79 RB.

80   Ibid.
81   Cambridge to Bigman, n.d., Bigman coll.
82   Rose Bigman to W, n.d. [1935], Bigman coll.
83   RB; McKelway, 35.
84   RB.
85   Ibid.
86   Ibid.
87   Ibid.
88   Ernest Lehman int. by author.
89   Ibid.
90   Winchell in intro., Philip Stack, *Love in Manhattan* (NY: Liveright, 1932), v.
91   Curley Harris int. by author.
92   Jim Bishop, Miami *Herald*, Feb. 21, 1972, 14–C.
93   Joel Landau int. by author.
94   AF.
95   Herman Klurfeld int. by author.
96   Ibid.
97   Ibid.
98   Ibid.
99   Herman Klurfeld, *Winchell: His Life and Times* (NY: Praeger, 1976), 72–73.
100 HK.
101 Klurfeld to author, Dec. 5, 1992.
102 Klurfeld, 73.
103 HK.
104 Ibid.
105 Ibid.
106 RB.
107 Ibid.
108 HK.
109 Klurfeld to W, Feb. 14, 1937, Klurfeld file, Winchell papers.
110 Klurfeld to W, Nov. 29, 1938, Klurfeld file, Winchell papers.
111 HK.
112 Sid White int. by author.
113 Maurice Zolotow int., Apr. 18, 1970, Thomas coll.
114 Leo Guild int., Apr. 13, 1970, Thomas coll.
115 Sam Wall int., Apr. 7, 1970, Thomas coll.
116 Lee Meyers int. by author.
117 Eric F. Goldman, *Two-Way Street: The Emergence of the Public Relations Counsel* (Boston: Bellman Publishing Co., 1948).
118 Candice Jacobson Fuhrman, *Publicity Stunt: Great Staged Events That Made the News* (San Francisco: Chronicle Books, 1989), 24–26.
119 RB.
120 Coleman Jacoby int. by author.
121 GS.
122 Lee Israel, *Kilgallen* (NY: Delacorte, 1979; rep. Dell, 1980), 209.
123 CJ.
124 Eddie Jaffe int. by author.
125 Jack Tirman int. by author.
126 EL.

127 Bill Doll int., May 29, 1970, Thomas coll.
128 EL.
129 CJ.
130 Al Rylander int. by author.
131 Ibid.
132 JT.
133 CJ.
134 Henry F. Pringle, "Portrait of Walter Winchell," *American Mercury*, Feb. 1937, 143.
135 EJ.
136 Ben Cohn int., March 25, 1970, Thomas coll.
137 GS.
138 Henny Youngman to W, May 5, 1938, comedian file, Winchell papers.
139 Milt Josefsberg int., April 16, 1970, Thomas coll.
140 Robert William int. by author.
141 DB.
142 Maurice Zolotow int., April 8, 1970, Thomas coll.
143 EL.
144 *Bribes*. Hal Conrad, Gary Stevens, Lee Meyers int. by author.
145 Stanley Walker, "Playing the Deep Bassoons," *Harper's Monthly Magazine*, vol. 164 (Feb. 1932), 373.
146 EJ.
147 Harry Reichenbach, as told to David Freedman, *Phantom Fame: The Anatomy of Ballyhoo* (NY: Simon & Schuster, 1931), 165.
148 EL.
149 Ed Weiner, *Let's Go to Press: A Biography of Walter Winchell* (NY: Putnam, 1955), 16.
150 Jack Ellinson int., April 10, 1970, Thomas coll.
151 DB.
152 Danton Walker, *Danton's Inferno: The Story of a Columnist and How He Grew* (NY: Hastings House, 1955), 13.
153 Ibid., 48 passim.
154 NY *Mirror*, May 11, 1934.
155 Russell Maloney, "Profile," *New Yorker* (April 7, 1945), 30; Mary Braggiotti, "Keeper of the Lyons Den," NY *Post*, Nov. 4, 1947; Warren Lyons int. by author.
156 Braggiotti.
157 Nathan Zalowitz to Lyons, June 19, 1930, quoted in Maloney, 30.
158 Braggiotti.
159 Sid White int. by author.
160 Lyons to W, June 13, 1934, Lyons file, Winchell papers.
161 WL.
162 Braggiotti.
163 J. P. McEvoy, "He Snoops to Conquer," *Saturday Evening Post*, Aug. 13, 1938, 10.
164 WL.
165 NY *Post*, Oct. 8, 1976.
166 Louis Sobol, *The Longest Street: A Memoir* (NY: Crown, 1968), 367.
167 RW.
168 EJ.
169 Maloney.
170 Ibid.
171 EJ.

172   AR.

173   Westbrook Pegler, *Dissenting Opinions* (NY: Scribner's, 1938), 245.

174   Hause to W, May 5, 1953, Bigman coll.

175   *Variety*, Sept. 15, 1937; Jerry G. Bowles, *A Thousand Sundays: The Story of the Ed Sullivan Show* (NY: Putnam, 1980), 98.

176   W to Danton Walker, Sept. 4, 1937, Walker file, Winchell papers.

177   Bowles, 99–100.

178   Hause to W, May 5, 1953, Bigman coll.

179   Sidney Skolsky, *Don't Get Me Wrong – I Love Hollywood* (NY: Putnam, 1975), 42–45.

180   Louella O. Parsons, *Tell It to Louella* (NY: Putnam, 1961), 13.

181   Parsons, 121; George Eells, *Hedda and Louella: A Dual Biography of Hedda Hopper and Louella Parsons* (NY: Putnam, 1972), 35 passim.

182   Always toothless, Hollywood gossip became even more so in the mid-thirties, when the studio chiefs issued an informal edict compelling writers to submit stories to the studios for approval. Newspapers and magazines complied on threat of losing movie advertising.

183   Dorothy Manners int. by author.

184   Ibid.

185   RW.

186   Parsons, 126–27.

187   Parsons to W, Aug. 30, 1943, Parsons file, Winchell papers.

188   DM.

189   Hedda Hopper, *From Under My Hat* (Garden City, NY: Doubleday, 1952), 10.

190   Ibid., 13, 20.

191   Quoted in Marlo Lewis and Mina Bess Lewis, *Prime Time* (Los Angeles: J. P. Tarcher, Inc., 1976), 22.

Chapter 39

Joshua Gamson

THE NEGOTIATED CELEBRATION

With Isabel Adjani, I was having the worst time. All of a sudden we're seeing in the gossip columns that Warren Beatty was at the hotel at two in the afternoon, and so and so had come by at three o'clock, and Daniel Day-Lewis was around. It was like, who the hell got paid in that hotel? Someone was getting paid under the table to find out just what was going on. Yes, Beatty was showing up. They're friends. Yes, Daniel Day was there, too, and God knows who else. There's nothing you can do. But you just sit there going crazy trying to stop this from happening, and sometimes you have no control over it. Isabel Adjani is supposed to be a class act, so why would we want to see the *National Enquirer* saying all these guys are trudging along in the hotel? We're protecting the image of her as a class act, and that's what she wanted. Then on the night of the big premiere I took her and Warren through a back route just to make it safer, since it was paparazzi out of control. So the car takes off without me, and the next thing I know around the corner come all the paparazzi, screaming at me. I am chased to my car, and stones are being thrown. They were throwing stones because I wouldn't let them have her. To get a Warren Beatty photo with Isabel Adjani, maybe embracing, that's worth some good buckeroonies. And I took away whatever chance they had. Not one photo came out. I was always in the way.

Janine Rosenblat, independent film publicist

In real-life journalism you call up the source and you say, "Can you talk?" In celebrity journalism you call up the publicist, you negotiate, you negotiate, set ground rules, negotiate.

Miriam Ross, entertainment magazine editor

Adjust the picture. Looking closely at the celebrity industry, one sees not the smooth assembly-line manufacture of commodified human sales pieces but intense back-stabbing and back-scratching, negotiations and skirmishes. The language is often not only of sales and industry but also of combat and arbitration. Entertainment journalists — writers, editors, television producers, and bookers — most commonly describe their relationship with publicists in terms such as "battles" and "bargaining." In these relationships, intense mutual hostility coexists with intense mutual buttering-up. Powerful female publicists are on the one hand referred to by respected journalists as "dragon ladies." Stone throwing is an exaggerated image to summarize the publicist-media worker relationship, but it works metaphorically. On the other hand, an editor at *Forbes* points out, it is very difficult to think of another "beat where your sources air-kiss you."[1] Although the workers in the various celebrity-producing industries are in many ways tightly allied, the relationships among those actively producing celebrity representations also pull in a variety of directions. Understanding these relationships, their tensions, and their resolutions is critical for understanding precisely what sort of representations they produce.

Sponsors and teams: celebrity versus spokesperson

In order to most effectively manage the manufacture of celebrity, like the manufacture of any product, the production process has to have, first of all, a unified goal. Either through an identity of interests or through centralized, hierarchical control, those in the production process need to set out to produce the same product. This was generally the case during the days of tight studio control, but there is no longer a single organization in control of the celebrity and the celebrity image. Even if the interests of all parties were completely aligned (and at times they come close), coordinating the production process is cumbersome because it is decentralized and nonmonopolistic. In fact, despite a general correspondence of interests in the production of celebrities, the various parties (the celebrity and her team, the sponsoring entertainment organizations) do not all have the same particular type of product, and the same particular types of uses, in mind.

A certain nostalgia for the studio system, along with behaviors that try to reinstate some of its elements, is heard in discussions with studio and network publicists. Diana Widdom is senior vice-president for worldwide special publicity planning at Paramount Studios. "In many respects," she says, "I wish those days would come back again."

> In the good old days, it was, "You report to Stage B and you have your photograph taken at 2:30." And they did. That's the way to get the most out of your talent and make sure they'll do what you want them and need them to do to publicize a film. There is no substitute for a star really working for a film. It is terribly, terribly important. And studios now know that going in, and they're sort of backing away from making films with actors who won't do publicity. They're not under any legal obligation, which is a sore point. The Paramount legal department very much wants to introduce back into contracts that the star will have an obligation

to promote their film. We have no *real* way of getting an actor to do anything he doesn't want to do.

This last sentence sums up the tensions in the celebrity-production scene: struggles between a variety of parties over what a celebrity should do and be and over the capacity to make him or her do and be.

The question of what a celebrity should be involves more than the constant daily disagreements over what will work (that hairstyle is too young, this role is too much against type); more fundamental disagreements are rooted in different interests. Key players with short-term interests tend to emphasize a performer's vehicles over her career, while players with long-term interests will emphasize career over vehicle. The result is a push in different directions: both toward and away from a celebrity divorced from her particular vehicles and roles, known for her self alone; and both toward and away from interchangeability.

As long as performers are hired on a project-by-project basis, studios, networks, and production companies will want the celebrity to be tightly linked in the short term to a particular project. For one thing, the publicity they sponsor is always geared toward selling the vehicle. "If you went on a talk show and talked mostly about your life and not the film," says Widdom, "that would not be our best case at all. There's a certain way the marketing department is going to sell the film, and we want the talent also to sell the film in that same way." As Bob Merlis of Warner Brothers points out, while the company benefits from a celebrity's notoriety ("the fact that Madonna is written about in a given magazine is good because it raises the consciousness of her as an entity"), fame itself is not enough. "The fact that you're famous is thrilling," he says, "but could we sell something please?" Moreover, to the degree that they do make use of a "personality sell," sponsoring organizations tend to want to use personality to link celebrities to their vehicles (again, as earlier studios did in the blurring of "reel" and "real" lives). Nia Peeples is a recording artist, dancer, actress, and hostess (until its cancellation) of a late-night, youth-oriented, television dance-party program called "The Party Machine with Nia Peeples." Paramount, the studio that produced the show, pushed her to make public appearances and conduct interviews that painted her as a party girl. "Paramount doesn't care about the rest of my career," Peeples said in an interview before the show's cancellation. "They care about 'The Party Machine,' and that's it. So to have me be a hostess out there partying all the time and giving that image is what they would love. But I won't. It's not me. It's just their vision of the ultimate party host." In large part, sponsoring organizations try not only to consistently establish a link between the celebrity and the vehicle but also to line up their celebrity's public personality with the celebrity's character and tone in that vehicle.

Such a strategy can be hazardous for performers and their managing teams. First of all, they may be asked to associate themselves enthusiastically with what turns out to be an ill-received project; the closer the association, the lower drops their market value. Second, being too closely associated with a project may cut off future options. For the celebrity emphasizing "performer" over "star," a commonly cited danger is that of being "typed." As a manager, David Spiro has his eye on what's "good for you long term." For him, this means the ability to diversify.

> In the industry they're very short-sighted, and they pigeonhole. It's the only way they can work with you. People have in their head what Eartha Kitt is going to do. It's "Batman" or it's camp. If you're young and put yourself in a position where you're doing lots of slasher movies, it's hard to break out of that. When the industry looks at Joan Collins, they're going to see someone who's beautiful, glamorous, bitchy. Therefore you're not going to see Joan Collins doing *Driving Miss Daisy*, because no one's going to want to invest ten million dollars in a film where Joan Collins is going to play a kindly old woman dressing in rags. They don't think the American public is going to believe it.

Nia Peeples's concerns are both personal ("it's not me") and professional ("the rest of my career"). Paramount's desires, in addition to conflicting with her self-image, may be damaging to her credibility as a more serious and versatile performer and thus harmful to her future value. She runs the risk of giving people in the industry "just that image in their minds of a sexy, energetic, party-going person, that Nia Peeples is a party animal." Not only is that not accurate, she says, but "my goal in life is not to become Downtown Julie Brown or Martha Quinn" – that is, to become locked into the role of "television personality."

For those pursuing bankability based primarily on personality rather than ability, being linked to specific projects and roles carries an even more fundamental risk. The most valuable type of celebrity – commonly referred to as the "real star" – is the one liberated from particular projects and abilities who can gain attention and loyalty for his self, for being "unique" and unprecedented. "It's kind of degrading to think that you're just famous for singing, or just famous for acting, or just famous for dancing, or just famous for being funny," says Los Angeles's Angelyne. "I want to be famous for the magic I possess. I've never happened before." Her assistant, Scott Hennig, even more clearly articulates this notion.

> Stars are people whose own personality is so strong, and their own visual image is so strong, that they come across as themselves no matter what they're doing. The people who have been consistent stars throughout time, even after they died, are people who established a certain persona. John Wayne was John Wayne in every movie, no matter what. No matter what Marilyn was in, she was Marilyn.

Angelyne's approach is to "only take projects that allow her to be strictly Angelyne." This strategy severely limits job options, of course, something the vast majority of aspirants aren't willing to do. But to the degree that they and their strategists take this route of developing a transcendent "persona," the constant need to be associated with their particular vehicles gets in the way.

A second set of conflicting interests runs parallel to the conflict between personal promotion and vehicle promotion. Although they clearly want a celebrity with demonstrated attention-getting capacity, entertainment-industry buyers do not necessarily need one with the demonstrated capacity of audience *loyalty*. The ubiquitous term "hot," evoking a temporary, passing condition, captures this short-term interest well. A flash in the pan, as long as it is made use of in its hot period, does no damage to an organization whose use of the performer is temporary. Indeed, a celebrity who is hot and recognizable but not established is easier to come by and less expensive to employ than a major star; the latter, of course, with an established audience, is still a safer form of insurance and can draw a much higher price. A celebrity and his team are obviously damaged by interchangeability; being replaceable is not only a tremendously unstable position but also one that vastly decreases one's value. Relinquishing control of the production process to someone with a short-term interest can damage future prospects in this way as well: those driving toward the safe bet of the formulaic tend to produce imitative celebrities, with a short shelf life. "Your individuality is what sends you to the top and makes you stay there," says Peeples. "Being the most of what I am. Nobody does Tina Turner better than Tina Turner. Nobody is what I am better than I am." Those who would use her, however, "can only hear the hit that's happening right now."

> It would be very simple for me to do that. When I was shopping for a record deal, I had a lot of record companies say, "This is great. You dance. You have a great look. Paula [Abdul] and Janet [Jackson] are happening right now, that's the biggest thing. We could put you in this machine, this formula that already works, and spit you out to the public, and we know that you can perform in front of it."

Peeples fought against this, first of all, because as a born-again Christian she cares about the content of what she's putting out; more revealing, she resisted it because it goes against the individuality she believes is necessary for success. Robbed of the ability to be "wholly Nia" (like many celebrities, she refers to herself periodically in the third person), she believes she is robbed of the chance to become a performer with longevity. The choice to be sponsored, or to appeal to sponsors, often involves a greater risk – being a "one-hit wonder."

We are beginning to see an odd mix of conflicting interests: sponsors are interested in making use of performers as celebrities but want to see them consistently linked to work; the performer who wants to increase his performance marketability often is interested in deemphasizing the particular performance vehicle; the performer who wants to increase her marketability as a celebrity persona is also resistant to the link to work, preferring personality alone; the short-term entertainment-industry interests push toward formulaic, interchangeable performers, while those celebrities and celebrity teams with an eye on the long haul have an interest in resisting that. The relationships pursued between celebrities and their performances and roles (are performances and roles an important part of their public images or not? are roles and lives conflated?), and between celebrities and distinction (are celebrities produced as genres or as individuals?), are not nearly as simple and clean as they first appeared. Indeed, they are disputes built into the celebrity production process.

Publicists, celebrities, and outlets: who keeps the gates?

> A couple of weeks ago we were going after a big star in a big movie. I thought automatically he would do an interview. I was told, "Well, he's

going through a different publicity phase on this." Between the lines, it was, "He's going to try to take the high road on this," go for the cover of *Vanity Fair* or *Rolling Stone* rather than "Entertainment Tonight." I was told he wasn't going to do a lot of other things. In the meantime, we were offered three other costars from that film, and we did them, and arranged to do the premiere and all that stuff. Then when it came time to start running them, this actor suddenly started showing up on our competition, on Oprah, Donahue, the morning shows. So I was told by my producers, "Tell them we're not running any of the stuff we've done unless he agrees to an interview." I told the studio and the personal publicist. I was accused of blackmail. It wasn't blackmail, because it was one thing when it started and then all of a sudden the rules changed. So the publicist went to the star, and the star said, "No way," got really mad. So we pulled out of covering the premiere that night. It was a big deal. A day and a half later he agreed to do an interview, and he couldn't have been nicer during the interview. So we aired two pieces, and we reinstated our other ones.

Pete Hammond, segment producer, "Entertainment Tonight"

It's a very fine line we have to tread between doing journalism and just being an outlet for whatever a celebrity wants to say. It's very hard to have any integrity and cover Hollywood, because so many people are trying to manipulate image.

Michael Alexander, staff writer, *People* magazine

I am my own industry. I am my own commodity.

Elizabeth Taylor

The celebrity industry is the scene of constant battles for control. The most central ones, guided by the variety of interests already described, are struggles for control of the commodification process, the direction and content of the attended-to: Who gets to decide what the celebrity will look like, what she will talk about and with whom? Who, finally, gets to produce the commodity for profit? Because the celebrity has so many producers, the industry so many subindustries, the answer is ambiguous and contested. Parties persuade, cajole, and flatter each other; they barter and trade; when all else fails, they battle. This is the environment in which the celebrity text is created – particularly as it takes form in celebrity-based television "reality" programming and newspaper and magazine reporting. It is, first of all, not a smooth production system. More important, the relationships within it push both toward and away from a pursuit of the "true" celebrity personality. The result, we will see, is most commonly a compromise on the part of entertainment-reporting organizations, and the compromise dovetails with the dominant strategies of celebrity teams: celebrities are reported as semifictional texts.

Journalists in celebrity-based media institutions experience a dilemma in their work lives. Los Angeles bureau chief Stan Meyer hears again and again from members of the entertainment industry that his magazine, a weekly personality-based publication, is "fair with people." For him, the compliment carries an insult. "As a journalist you think, 'Gee, did I not dig deep enough?'" Journalism and public relations, he believes, "should be at odds with each other, not walking hand in hand down the aisle." It is a source of discomfort, therefore, for him to be told by his adversaries that they are happy with his work. If he were doing the job of a "real" journalist, if his work were going "deep enough," his subjects would not be forever thanking him. Like Michael Alexander, quoted above, he's never quite sure if he's "doing journalism" or "being an outlet."

Both the discomfort and the blurry line between serving and reporting on the industry stem from the fact that Meyer's work *does* depend heavily on public relations; if the two are not married, they at least enjoy an unhappy, rocky, but deeply committed and long-standing relationship. As we have seen, they share fundamental commercial interests and are linked institutionally and through day-to-day routines. Publicity professionals, whose careers are plainly dependent on mass-media coverage, also provide services of value to those reporting on the entertainment industry. They suggest angles and stories, provide quotes and art work, offer written and video press releases, arrange and sit in on interviews and photo sessions, train and coach clients to give better interviews. They supply an "information subsidy," usable written and visual information that the reporter would otherwise have to spend valuable time locating and writing up and that the organization would otherwise have to spend money acquiring.[2] They find, mold, and provide precisely what the media covering them need. Television bookers and magazine editors, for example, constantly emphasize their need for celebrities with "name recognition" or "identifiability." Publicists do what they can to provide this. "When I dress a party for video consumption," says Bob Merlis, vice-president of publicity for Warner Brothers Records, "I want to have people who look like who they're supposed to be. You want instantly recognizable people." As Pete Hammond of "Entertainment Tonight" says, "Couldn't do it without them."

At the root of these behaviors is the fundamentally uncertain business environment in which celebrity is developed. Paul Hirsch, providing an organizational model for the analysis of cultural industries, argues that industry workers face first the difficulty of knowing what will succeed in the marketplace; the activities described in the previous chapter are attempts to cope with this difficulty. Here I focus on the second central uncertainty to which Hirsch points: the control of decisions by organizations (primarily mass-media "gatekeepers") "whose actions can block or facilitate communication" and therefore "wield great influence over the access of artist and audience to one another."[3] To ensure that designated persons get a certain amount of attention, that the story lines and images designated as those that will attract and retain consumers get disseminated, and that a consistent and appealing celebrity is produced, decisions regarding coverage must be controlled. As Hirsch argues, legally and normatively these gatekeeping organizations are autonomous, and therefore the vertical integration of a product's manufacture and exposure to consumers is blocked. Producers develop strategies to control this "checkpoint" within these limits, most notably by "co-optation" of mass-media functions.

Although they speak generally of "creating an awareness" and euphemistically of "appropriate exposure," publicists' activities are plainly geared toward control of the gatekeeper role. By preparing their products according to the perceived specifications of the mass media, the publicity industry attempts to increase the likelihood of coverage. "I know how editors think and I come at them from their own angle," says personal publicist Amanda Weber. "I'm talking to them like I'm a writer pitching them a story. I know what they need and we provide it for them before they need to ask for it." By practicing many journalistic tasks (writing press releases, producing electronic press releases into which reporters can insert their own scripted voice, suggesting angles, attending interviews), publicists decrease the uncertainty of coverage content. As Jerome North, a publicist at a large PR firm, says matter-of-factly:

> There are certain writers who have reputations for being a hardass or for really getting into areas they shouldn't, or who have a history of writing unflattering portraits. If we get an assignment and it's one of those people, we may go back to the editor and ask for another writer. We want somebody the client's going to be comfortable talking to, to try and get the best piece.

A *Rolling Stone* editor complains that more than twenty writers were approached for a cover story on Tom Cruise and were either vetoed by Cruise's publicist or opted out rather than work under the publicist's restrictions. "Publicists think of themselves as the editors," complains another magazine editor. "They want to make all the editorial decisions."

In fact, the oft-repeated cliché that "Hollywood is all relationships" contains the reality of informal co-optation. "It's all relationships," says Sarah Tamikian, a cable network publicist, describing a "publicist's nightmare," an interview in which a celebrity bad-mouthed her vehicle to "Entertainment Tonight." Tamikian's response was to call the producer and ask her to remove the quote. "I have a relationship with her," Tamikian says, "and I knew that she would do what she could to make the piece better for me." Jordan Kamisky tells of a client who was asked by a syndicated columnist why he went into acting:

> He said, "Because there were a lot of pretty girls I wanted to fuck." My mouth fell open and I kicked him under the table. I thought, what a fucking idiot. It made him seem like an idiot, like he wasn't serious about acting. What he should have said, whether it was true or not, was "I watched Marlon Brando when I was a child and he was so amazing in *On the Waterfront*." He needed an answer like that. Luckily, I had a relationship with this journalist. I said, "Do me a favor, either don't use it or at least tone it down," which he did.

The relationship is used for damage control. Formal co-optation of media decision making is ethically and legally constrained, so informal co-optation via relationships takes on a central and daily importance.

Mutual co-optation and the drive toward "fluff"

Co-optation is neither easy nor complete, and much of the activity involves simple persuasion. Often, when interests overlap, co-optation is unnecessary. In Tamikian's story, for example, the producer who excised the negative quote responded, "it doesn't do us any good as 'Entertainment Tonight' to have an artist who's not really convinced with what she's saying." Both the media and the publicist want the same outcome.

More significantly, co-optation is mutual and two-directional. Celebrity-based media are not simply "bought" through time- and money-saving devices and camera-ready celebrities. Most entertainment media are not in fact "autonomous" gate-keepers. Although they are formally autonomous from commercial culture producers, they are institutionally dependent on them. "We use them, they use us," says a newspaper reporter who covers television. "It's a symbiotic relationship." Whereas the media guard the gates of exposure, the publicists guard the gates of access.

Indeed, since celebrity providers control access to a large degree, it is a professional and institutional necessity for entertainment media to build and maintain successful working relationships with them.[4] "People basically deliver for you," says Ann Sandberg, who books entertainment guests for a national morning show. "I might be close to the head of publicity at a movie studio, and they commit a star to me because they like me and they like the show, and even if we were number two I'd still get it. Those are the things that can really make or break you, your relationships." Here, relationships are used not by the publicist to control media exposure but by the media to control publicist delivery.

The more dependent a magazine or program is on celebrity images for sales, of course, the more powerless they are to make editorial evaluations and control content. "Just to get the face on the cover," complains an *Us* magazine editor, "a lot of times it becomes really secondary what the piece says."

> The issues that have the ten hottest men, the ten most beautiful women, the ten most this or that, those are the ones that sell off the stands. Go figure. To me they're insubstantial fluff, these beefcake or cheesecake pieces with big, glamorous photographs and some text about what nice guys they are and what their marital status is. It's nobody's ambition to be generating these kinds of things, but we can't get away from it. They sell.

He pushes for "people who are worth taking a look at," but the answer is usually, "Yes, but they don't sell magazines." *Rolling Stone* senior writer Bill Zehme tells of profiling Albert Brooks, who will never be on *Rolling Stone*'s cover but who, "if you put people on the cover because of merit instead of what will sell, should be on everybody's cover." Instead of subjects such as Brooks, in Zehme's eyes a "comic genius," many of his subjects are like actor Johnny Depp: nice, talented, but attended-to because he is "an image that sells" when "his body of work is almost nonexistent." Editorial control (in this case, the power to cover people who in the opinions of editors "merit" interest, to write stories where content is not "secondary") is trumped by salability and marketing department control.

Fluff writing, these "beefcake or cheesecake pieces," is not so much a result of perceived reader preferences for contentless profiles; the lack of substance comes more from the dependence on celebrity images and the subsequent weak bargaining position against those who regulate access to them. The dependence is clearest and most developed in the relationships between mass-media workers and personal publicists, hired either to facilitate or retain control of coverage. In recent years, both publicists and journalists commonly note, the balance of power has tipped toward the publicists. "As much as we fight it, and we fight it, publicists know that we need the people to sell the magazine," says Zehme. "So they play games with us, they extract things."

Negotiating fills in where relationships are insufficient. One editor demonstrates both the types of demands and the power of publicists to extract them:

> When we assigned a staff writer to do a profile of Candice Bergen, PMK [Bergen's publicity firm] said, "While we respect this writer we don't think that she would appreciate Candice Bergen's sense of humor." The image they were trying to create for Candice Bergen was that she was funny, and they didn't think this particular writer would do their bidding on that. The editors basically said, "Screw you. If you want to pick your writers, why don't you start your own magazine?" The epilogue is that shortly after this [a new owner] took over, the editor who said fuck you to PMK was fired, and the new people said, "Okay, who do you want for the piece?"

The answer, presumably, was a writer who would "do their bidding." Even if the media workers *want* to cut themselves off from publicity operatives, it is simply not practical for their professional well-being. Cutting oneself off from publicists means cutting oneself off from the main pipeline to celebrity interviews and information. Perhaps more critical, one risks being blocked from getting the article or segment in process completed as one would like, when one would like. "It's very present-oriented," says entertainment-magazine writer John Rider. "Their power is what they can do or not do then and there." The stronger the journalist's and organization's relationship with publicists, the less can be extracted in these negotiations.

We arrive at one compelling set of celebrity-industry dynamics: the drive against pursuing "truths" and toward celebrity- and entertainment-product promotion. In many cases, developing successful and useful relationships with publicists means developing a reputation for presenting their clients in the desired light. It means avoiding the "hardass" reputation, editing out the complaint about a bad script, replacing "I wanted to fuck pretty girls" with "I wanted to be just like Marlon Brando," granting photo approval, promising a cover. Several large publicity firms handle, in fact, the bulk of the most salable subjects. Therefore if you do "some scathing thing" on a star, says Stan Meyer, "you're not only pissing off an individual, you're pissing off a publicist who has a stable of people that [he] may withhold from you." A publicist who is confident, either because of bargaining or prior relationships, that the outcome will be favorable (the photos will be right, the cover will be theirs, the appropriate areas will be covered, the writer will not write an "unflattering" portrait), is the publicist who will "deliver." This, finally, is the practical, institutional push toward producing promotional fluff, or, in the terms of Stan Meyer's would-be enemies, "fair" reporting.

The drive toward the "inside" and the economy of the tidbit

The struggles, however, are bitter and the animosity strong. Why isn't the marriage happy? Given all of the overlap in commercial interest, the closeness in informal networks, the interdependent institutional networks, why not simply become a promotional outlet, a fluff factory? Why fight it?

To begin with, there is clearly a genuine sense of threat to many journalists' sense of integrity and professional identity, a resentment of publicists' attempts to do their jobs for them. One overview of studies of journalism distinguishes two types of reporters: "straight reporters," who are "content to collect the facts through recognized channels and to leave to the reader the task of interpreting or evaluating them," and "committed journalists," who "believe more attention should be paid to news-gathering, investigation, to providing background and analysis, even to making judgments on behalf of the reader about the relative worth of different accounts or the implications of particular statements and events."[5] To these a third might be added, the "artistic" journalist, whose professional identity is linked to creative criteria. The identities of the last two are particularly threatened by an alliance with publicity managers.[6] Bill Bruns of *TV Guide*, fighting with a publicist over the assignment of a writer, tells her, "Forget it. You guys are trying to dictate. This is First Amendment kind of stuff." Writer Patrick Goldstein points out the limits set on investigation and depth, both of which he takes to be his job:

> Whoever controls the information has a lot of power, and the publicists do control a lot of information. They control your access to it, the way it's disseminated, the timing, the amount. They try to control the image in the sense that they don't want me to get too much of a glimpse of the celebrities' private lives. Then it's just kind of a battle between me and the publicist over how much access I have. The more access you have, the more in-depth, the more texture it's going to have. If you only give somebody an hour to talk, in an office somewhere, you control the environment completely.

Similarly, Stan Meyer's description of a photo shoot with Michael J. Fox points out the limits set on creativity:

> The photographer, always wanting to try something different, brought along a very high-powered magnifying glass and for one shot wanted him to just hold it up to his face. I guess the image would be of this really big head and this little body. I don't know what he was after exactly, but he was just messing around. Of course, the publicists were there for this whole thing, and they plotzed when they saw what he was trying to do. They said, "No, no, we're not doing anything like that. Just a regular old shot, the old Michael Fox head shot." And I was trying to help the photographer out so I said, "Michael's trying to stretch in his roles, and we're just trying to get something that will make people stop when they see his picture in the magazine." The publicist looks at me with daggers saying, "People *always* stop when they see his picture."

Giving in to publicists' power undermines the bases of many journalists' professional identities: access to investigation is largely blocked, the possibilities of writing a textured or nuanced story impeded, interpretation and analysis discouraged, the integrity of free and creative expression compromised. These are matters not only of identity, of course, but of interest. Control of defined professional activities as a means of building and protecting status and money is an important force in all lines of work, and here it is clearly threatened.[7]

The push away from allying with publicists goes beyond professional identities and professional control, however, to institutional and commercial requirements. The problem is not only that publicists want to "write the story themselves" but that the story they would like to write is not distinctive enough or "inside" enough to meet the media organization's commercial needs. To be competitive in the marketplace, many programs and publications promise audiences something they cannot get else-where: the exclusive, inside story, a look at the "reality" behind the image. "If you are giving your readers a cover story," says Miriam Ross, "you have to deliver. There's an unwritten agreement. If you cheat them, they know, and they're going to remember next time. I think readers know when it's not a real story." When they cannot fulfill that promise, they must at least provide a story that is distinguishable from all the others. The question, says Pete Hammond of "Entertainment Tonight," is always "how can we make this different from ten other interviews he's going to do sitting next to a plant in a hotel room talking about his latest movie? We're going for ratings, and we don't want to put on stories that are unappealing to viewers who've seen them on twelve other shows. We want an audience grabber." When Bill Bruns describes his fight to assign a writer the publicist thought would "ask uncomfortable questions," his description slides immediately from the First Amendment to the practical require-ments of the magazine. "The writer is supposed to ask those questions," he says. "We don't want to have someone just talk about being an actress and how she does her role. That's boring." Maintaining control of the story is often demanded not only by professional identity but by competitive viability.

The danger of producing promotional fluff is that it will be seen by audiences as such, dismissed as the same old same old, akin to the ubiquitous and free-of-charge advertisements. Publicist control can get in the way of delivering competitively to the consumer. Publicity workers get in the way of this promise quite literally, first of all, by sitting in on interviews, blocking photos at opportune moments, asking for questions in advance, acting as spokespeople, trying to veto writers and photographers.

Second, with their interests primarily pushing toward safe promotion ("appropri-ate exposure"), what publicists offer most generally is the celebrity in a standardized, controlled, packaged form. (As we saw earlier, this overriding tendency is supported by the short-term uses of entertainment-industry buyers.) The coached and trained and much-used celebrity works against the promised delivery of "real goods." "Some of these publicists coddle so badly and try to protect their clients," says *TV Guide*'s Bruns, "that they've created a lot of really bland personalities." What to a publicist and celebrity is careful and safe is bland to him; bland does not serve his purposes. What he needs is people who will "open up a little bit with the press" – that is, provide distinctive pieces of personal information. "It's appalling to me," says Stan Meyer, "that as I'm interviewing them I start hearing the quotes I've read a thousand times. The challenge is to get them to get away from their habit of bullshit." *People* writer Michael Alexander underlines the same experience:

> For a lot of these celebrities, it's just part of the shtick. You know, "How did it feel doing that scene wrapped in plastic?" "Blah blah blah blah. It was very cold. I had to drink hot tea. Blah blah blah." They start regurgitating the same answers and they give everybody a very limited idea as to who they are. It's this tug-of-war. You try to get as much stuff out of them as you can, and they try to give you as little as they can.

What the media organization needs is a convincing presentation of "who they are." Alexander tells a story of a *People* reporter's interview with television's Paula Zahn where "the whole thing was, 'Life is just great, life is fabulous.' " For ten minutes the reporter dug, worried that "this story's going to get killed because there's nothing to differentiate this woman from lots of other people." Then, finally, Zahn "started babbling about how her father died of cancer and now her mom has cancer, and the reporter was like, 'Okay, a cancer story.' " The reporter had won the tug-of-war, found the piece of personal information that could distinguish the story and offer more than the publicist-controlled idea of the subject. Competing with the push to present publicist-friendly material that keeps access open, then, there is a strong commercial and organizational push to dig beyond the fluff, to pull the cancer story from the fabulous life. To be competitive, media organizations need access not only to the celebrity image but to unmined pieces of the celebrity personality. For this, they must on some level fight the publicist and the celebrity. They face the dilemma, then, of fighting those on whom their work activities and livelihoods depend.

These battles between publicists and journalists are part of a war in an economy of information – specifically, an economy of tidbits. Bits of personality information, either written, spoken, or photographed, are the primary currency circulating and fought over between those seeking exposure and those providing it. The celebrity is divided up into pieces, and those pieces move between parties, are exchanged, invested, cashed in. Each party wants in some sense to establish usage and ownership rights over the celebrities and their images and information.[8] The celebrity and publicist know the value of the information commodity, and they control its scarcity to maintain its value in extracting exposure. The journalist and media organization try to attain it in order to attract audiences. Significantly, media organizations are motivated to win only the individual battles. If the war were won, it might therefore be lost: the information's value as an audience-attractor, and therefore as a money-maker, depends on its scarcity.

Resistance, selling out, and the pursuit of the semitrue

> "Dirt" is a term that means all information that stars might not want me to write, which could be just revealing that they're pregnant before they tell anyone, or their secret engagement, or who they're dating, or maybe just an inside, personal story of someone having a tantrum backstage or something. Dirt is not necessarily a negative thing, it's just stuff that for whatever reason they don't want you to know, or don't want to have in print yet. It's my job to get it. I'll pay money to try to get the story before anyone else has it.
>
> Mary Morgan, tabloid gossip columnist

If we asked embarrassing questions, we'd be out of business tomorrow.
Lee Masters, president, E! Entertainment Television

My theory is that once you sit down with them, everyone is interesting.
Sometimes it takes longer than others, but I really do believe that if you sit
down with anyone you can get a pretty good story.
Michael Alexander, staff writer, *People* magazine

Not all entertainment-media institutions are positioned alike in this economy of
information. Some choose sides, either resisting or giving in to the bids by others to
control coverage. Those that resist can do so largely because their commercial interests do not coincide with those of the publicity operations; they are genuinely
autonomous. Conventional news operations resist where they can; for them, maintaining a reputation as independent pursuers of facts remains more critical for sales than
celebrity information and images. Like several other publications, the *Los Angeles Times*
is perceived as especially important and thus retains an upper hand facing publicists'
demands. Moreover, the *Times* can set terms because "we're not selling newspapers
with celebrities, we're not using celebrities to try to build our circulation." The
position is thus simple. "If you're going to do these interviews," a *Times* editor says,
"you're going to do them on our terms." Speaking to a meeting of the Publicists'
Guild, he told them "in as professional and nice a way as I could" not only that they're
unwanted but that they're unnecessary:

> I said, "If I had my way, receiving your pitches would be zero percent of
> my job. If you guys never sent me another pitch I'd be happy." And they
> were shocked to hear that. They think I need it. They're sure that what
> they do is a service. I had breakfast with a publicist the other day who
> basically wanted to know how to pitch me. Finally I said, "I know that
> every time you're given an assignment you've got to get as much as you
> can, and you have to file a report to someone that says you called the *Los
> Angeles Times*. Just cut me out of the process. I'll give you a carte blanche
> rejection. You can say I said no to everything you've got."

The *Los Angeles Times* and publications like it can for the most part dig or skip the story,
using some but ignoring much of PR. They can and do, in fact, even investigate and
expose those attempts by the publicity industry to control stories.[9]

Ironically, tabloids are also in an autonomous position. "I get my stories *in spite* of
publicists, not because of publicists," says gossip columnist Mary Morgan. "I try to
avoid them, frankly, because I find when I call them up with a great story to validate it,
they'll steal it and turn it over to a daily paper and scoop me. They have no ethics."
Morgan's paper is built on "dirt." Inside information – for which the paper pays from
$100 to $1000 – is the source of its profits.

The activity of "digging" is alive and well, as it is in conventional newspaper
reporting, though in a different form. Morgan's column, for example, is made up
mostly of information bought from sources. She supplements it by going to events
where there may be gossip and gossips to be found.

You'll find some crew member, someone who works in public relations, someone who works as a makeup artist, a hairdresser. I head for those people, and I start talking to them. And if I find out they're gossipy-talkative, I get a feeling for their observational powers, and how open they are about talking. I give them my card. If someone's an extra on the set the day Kirstie Alley walks in and says, 'Well, I'm pregnant," that could be a big front page story, it's harmless, and a lot of money. People beat each other up to get to the phones first to call me and get the money. And sometimes I just feel like putting on a wig and I go out and chitchat with people. People will tell you the most amazingly intimate things if you're just a talkative person at a party.

Since it is precisely these intimate tidbits that celebrities and publicists use in the exchange for exposure control, tabloids are their ultimate enemy in the economy of information. "I keep my clients out of the *Globe* and the *Enquirer*," says personal manager Arlene Dayton.

There's outlets and there's outlets. Once they start with you, you become fair game. I tried to explain this to a publicist who does work with them, and he said, "Wouldn't you rather control?" I said, "What control? There's no control. It's like controlling mad dogs." They don't care about you, they only care about exposing whatever there is about you to expose.

Morgan, however, counters that tabloid coverage can be extremely valuable to celebrities. "I think I'm doing them all a favor," says Morgan, "because I know for a fact that their prices go up. The better their name is known by the public, the more money they get paid." Publicist Kathie Berlin agrees they can be useful: "If I had a movie with a female audience, the best thing I could get would be a color layout in *The Star*."[10] Yet while this mutual *commercial service* still exists, tabloids are structured on an *institutional divorce* from those in the entertainment industry trying to control publicity.

On the other side are those businesses structured from the outset on serving and being served by publicists. *USA Today*, for example, says an entertainment editor who was there at its inception, was "almost designed as an outlet," and publicists love it. "Entertainment Tonight," says a television critic, is "a publicist's dream." At the furthest extreme is "celebrity-friendly" E! Entertainment Television, a twenty-four-hour network devoted to celebrities, with a format described by a *Newsweek* writer as "endlessly rotating plugs, previews, and puff pieces," like "a science-fiction movie in which a Hollywood publicist takes over your brain."[11] Resembling teen-idol magazines, E! profits by providing an outlet for celebrities, gaining easy access to them by relinquishing control of coverage content almost entirely to the industry it covers.

Where E! and businesses like it thrive by providing an ideal venue for the celebrity as a product promoter, glamour-oriented programming such as "Lifestyles of the Rich and Famous" is built on providing an outlet for the celebrity as self-promoter. Designed for viewers who "want glamour, who want a star to be a star and live in an incredible house and have fancy jewelry and drive a Rolls Royce," "Lifestyles" is a safe environment for celebrities, says Robin Smalley, a director for the show. No probing questions are asked, no negatives are allowed. "You don't do anything that's reality-based," says Smalley. " 'Lifestyles' is deliberately 'nice' television. We use every kind of enhancement we can. We use wide-angle lenses to make the rooms look bigger, star filters to make everything look glitzier, fog filters to make people look better and rooms look softer. It's all there to make everyone look wonderful and glamorous and happy and carefree." Thus, although plugging a project is excluded, "it's a good show for somebody who wants to project or foster a certain image."

Although some institutions choose sides, what one analyst has noted of the art/ commerce dilemma in cultural production is true in the parallel fluff/dirt conflict as well: "There are more complex adaptations to it than the polar opposites of alienation or acceptance."[12] The bulk of entertainment-media organizations are semiautonomous, and the most common resolution to conflicting pulls is a compromise. Entertainment journalism tends to shy away from criteria of truth and worth. Though not dismissed, they are limited to the pursuit of technical accuracy: facts are tirelessly checked, questions of legality carefully considered. But, faced with a need to deliver inside information where digging for it can threaten essential industry relationships, celebrity-based media work with entertainment criteria that bridge these interests.

Traditional journalistic criteria are here reversed.[13] In coverage decisions, the primary question is not which people are most deserving of examination but which will be most appealing, which are "hottest" and fit current production needs best. Entertainment-media workers, like their counterparts in the entertainment-production fields, categorize celebrities into levels of popularity. "It's a pyramid," says Don Roca, who books guests on a local morning show.

> It's like a cumulative knowledge or awareness. We talk with "A-list" and "B-list," "A-minus celebrities," "B-plus celebrities." We have no shame. Everybody's always arguing it out. "Oh, he's hot." "Oh, who gives a shit," Talent as an issue comes into play, but not very much unless it adds to someone's level of hotness. If you're hot *and* talented, then great.

Similarly, in approaching a subject, the primary question is not what is most important to know about them or what will reveal them most truthfully but what about them will be most interesting. The interview is primarily used neither to make a coverage decision (is this person a worthy subject?) nor to search out the depth of a subject (what makes this person worth lavishing attention on?). "It's just any quirk," says Michael Alexander. "It's like, oh, came from a family of twelve kids, started working when you were three." His description of "a great story," on Miguel Ferrer from television's "Twin Peaks," is a revealing summary of typical criteria:

> He has famous parents plus he had a lot of family problems. His mom, Rosemary Clooney, was married to Jose Ferrer, they had five kids in a row, split up, then got remarried, then she had a big breakdown, and Miguel was the oldest and was sort of the man of the house at age twelve. These were fabulous details. Now everybody's hunky-dory and he's very successful and so forth. We love people overcoming something. It was the perfect situation. Here was a guy with a high visibility role on at that point a very hot show, and he had a great story to tell.

Once you've selected whom to cover according to the product categories called for by the magazine's format ("big male star, blonde bimbo, rising young ingenue, they fit a niche"), another *People* worker says, "you try and get them to say something real." Investigation provides amusing, distinctive details about a subject dictated by commercial appeal.

The "good story" is thus a narrative resolution somewhere between promotional "puffery" and "serious" investigation, a resolution that balances opposing organizational pulls. Important is the fact that this resolution keeps the economy of information flowing. First, by largely sidestepping criteria of worth for coverage decisions, it allows journalists to pursue commercial appeal and minimize the threat to publicity seekers posed by evaluation. Under entertainment criteria, a critical stance – the evaluation of a celebrity's claim to attention, for example – is bypassed, opening up a nearly endless field of "interesting" candidates. Nearly anyone is an eligible candidate since almost anyone has a good story in them *somewhere*. This is in the interest both of cultural producers, for whom the likelihood of "hitting" is increased as the number of shots increases, and those reporting on the industry, who reduce the risk posed by relying on a small set of subjects.

Second, the good story's deemphasis of authenticity in favor of an engaging narrative relieves the tension brought by zero-sum-game fights accompanying pursuits of "the real goods." "Interesting" is a different informational realm. In daily journalistic practice, investigating-for-interest behaviors are directed toward the "fabulous details" and the "great story," toward narrative elements rather than truth content. As long as the story is deemed sufficiently interesting or amusing – and technically accurate – and enough personal-information "goods" are relinquished to establish an "inside" stance, the purposes of the journalist are served. There are plenty of good stories and interesting tidbits to go around. More fundamentally, investigation, which for institutional reasons must not dig too far, does not need to dig too far to be practically useful. "You as a reporter have some goods, but you don't have the real goods," says personality magazine writer and editor Miriam Ross. "There's a limit to how inside you're going to get. That's the bargain you make." The bargain is a comfortable one: "some goods" are enough. And what is important is that these goods can be easily acquired *within* the bartering network between the media and the entertainment industry without threatening that relationship.

We saw earlier how celebrity producers often use the strategy of Dramatic Reality to increase the chances of selling their celebrity. Outlets that see themselves as amusement are driven toward the same strategy. Clues can be taken from the arena of photographic images, in which the industry–news media alliance works almost without tension. Since the products celebrities appear in and are used to sell are in the visual media of film and television, most in the entertainment industry agree that pictures are the most important component of image making. Publications and programs also depend on an appealing visual image. Questions of "truth" and "integrity" hardly arise in this arena, possibly the most important one, because suppliers and buyers of celebrities are joined here without tension. "When I wrote about Julia Roberts," says Patrick Goldstein, "I said she looked like a librarian. But the picture we ran of her, she had her makeup on, our photographer put up the right lights. His job is to get a nice picture." Because photographic images are widely assumed to "tell the truth," the camera widely assumed to "never lie," there is little need or incentive for the entertainment-news industry to fight the manipulation of visual images. In fact, the industry and journalism together build salable visual images, through both simple techniques such as makeup and touch-ups and more dramatic techniques; *TV Guide*, for example, was caught melding Oprah Winfrey's head with Ann-Margret's body. The obligation to "dig" is erased, questions of what this person looks like in day-to-day life are bypassed. His magazine, Stan Meyer says, is "very photo-oriented" and uses "the cream of the crop of portrait photographers." Thus celebrities and their handlers tend to be attracted to the magazine "because they know they're going to end up looking good." (Compare this to those whose livelihood depends on revealing celebrities as they do *not* like to be seen, the tabloids who are as happy to put a fat Oprah Winfrey on the cover as a svelte one, a strung-out-looking star as a glamorous one. They do not work with celebrities and their handlers to create these photographic images but instead depend on paparazzi to catch them unawares.)

Good-story pursuits effect a similar working alliance. Semifiction becomes a meeting ground for groups with a variety of interests. Focusing on narrative rather than on truth elements also allows *both* parties greater control over the journalistic output. Both sets of commercial enterprises seek to exploit audiences' involvement with celebrities; they do so through a search for a realm between fact and fiction, a realm that, with its dependence on discernible narrative elements and semi-independence from truth, is much more easily controlled than "real life" but looks much like it. The news and entertainment industries often work together day to day to develop and represent a version of celebrity selves that is more explicitly staged than behaved: the actor playing himself for the cameras, writing his life along with the reporter such that both will benefit. It is important to notice that this is rarely a conscious conspiracy to deceive but instead a set of compromises between conflicting but interdependent parties. Staged events, for example, are effective exactly because they are still events: "If Tom Cruise is getting a star on the Walk of Fame," says "Entertainment Tonight" producer Pete Hammond, explaining the program's coverage of events they know are promotional, "Tom Cruise is getting a star on the Walk of Fame." It's a good story. The alliance is not so much around developing lies as developing performances of celebrity selves.

The talk show and predictable spontaneity

> With television the viewer gets the impression that it's the real person, but it's not. It's acting. Anyone who's done a talk show can tell you that. It's performing. Once a week I'm on a television program, and 80 percent of the time when I finish I feel this sense of incompletion. It's kind of like sex without the orgasm. I wind up automatically saying what they want me to say, not necessarily what I mean to say or what I want to say. It's an unconscious thing. I just do it. I know the medium, I know how it works, so I wind up cute and catchy, the way they want it.
>
> Stuart Stein, newspaper television critic

Nowhere is the outlets' drive toward semifiction clearer than in the celebrity-based talk show. Talk-show producers perceive their projects as entirely entertainment and thus as exempt from criteria of evaluation other than popularity and amusement. They are not bound by journalistic criteria, only by the need to present amusing people out of their usual fictional roles. Don Roca, a producer and booker for a local celebrity talk show, sums up what he is looking for.

> It's my job to bring on the most provocative, intriguing, fascinating, interesting people that the viewership is actually going to want to watch. You want celebrities that have some kind of name recognition, or a celebrity that happens to be so hot at the moment that people are talking about them. If you have to say "Who?" they're almost dead in the water. And you always want a guest who's energetic, vibrant, and is willing to speak freely and openly. That's a great guest, because you're going to watch that person and you're going to see engaging conversation, regardless of what they're talking about. Ultimately, who's really going to care about what celebrities have to say anyways? At least that person, whatever they're talking about, they're doing it in an interesting way. You'll stay tuned, you'll stay with the show. The consideration is how best to entertain the audience and how to have the audience like you and stay with you.

Bob Dolce, who books guests for "The Tonight Show," tells a similar story.

> Before we have somebody come in we've done a little bit of research on them to see if we think the potential is there, no matter how much we respect the work, to be an entertaining talk-show guest. And I'm underlining the word "entertaining." That's the primary thing. There are a lot of people whose work we really, really respect who aren't particularly entertaining when it comes to talking. Our primary interest is in people who talk. The primary objective is to get talk time that is light. We're surfacey.

Celebrities on these programs are selected on the basis of their entertainment value, either because they are established figures ("You always want the Pope, the Queen, and the President," says Dolce) or because they can "talk." The quality of a guest's work is irrelevant; under entertainment criteria there is no necessary connection between achievement and exposure.

The guest needs less to have *done* something than to be able to *be* something in the moment. His job is to perform. "This is sort of heightened life," says Dolce. "It all happens in between six and eight minutes. It's forced casual conversation, really more like a performance than a visit, like talking in headlines. It can only look like a conversation. We need someone who can do that, who understands what this is about and is comfortable doing that." Don Roca echoes, "[I'm] almost like a movie director," making sure that the guests each "deliver" in their five-minute performances. The task is not too difficult. "Celebrities are performers, and performers can deliver, if not shtick at least likability. If you're telling them, 'You're really going to have to bring your energy up and have a lot of fun out there,' they'll understand that. It's like a performance. It's a business." Indeed, Roca's program for some time used actual chefs for its cooking segment. Some of them, however, were "real drips on the air," so a change was made to ensure that the segments would be conducted by celebrities who could be "very upbeat, engaging, funny. The recipe is secondary, what they cook is secondary, whether they even know how to cook is secondary. As long as they can fake their way through a recipe in a fun way, we'll have them on." Celebrities are chosen for their ability to perform themselves amusingly.

A performance is clearly more manageable than a spontaneous appearance. To help ensure a predictable performance, talk-show producers conduct a preinterview with the guests and provide the hosts with an interview structure. In the preinterview the booker first pokes around for fresh tidbits or stories that make the guest distinctive. "I look for what I call fingerprints," says Dolce. "Something that applies only to that person, something you haven't heard before or couldn't hear from five other people." The challenge of established icons – worn-out, over-used commodities, in a sense – is that "although you may have a guaranteed audience, you don't have a guaranteed conversation." To find something Jimmy Stewart or George Burns have not "shared before" is "a great accomplishment."

The talent coordinators then try to shape the conversational content into a "successful appearance" by going over "some possible lines of conversation" and making suggestions ("That line, or that thought, might be sort of fun"). Producers also present the host with a "structure." As Dolce describes it, the structure involves

> five to eight areas, guidelines, in which you have weeded out anything that
> is going to be unproductive and removed any area that the guest might
> consider to be sensitive. [The structure] has questions and a general area of
> response. I don't punch lines in. I won't reveal where it's going. And the
> guest basically has also been briefed about what the host might be looking for.

Although the hosts and guests are briefed, spontaneity is part of the show. "Often the hosts will take a completely different tack," says Roca. In looking for conversational skills, a preinterviewer will check for a guest's ability to handle unpredictable moments. The challenge here, says Dolce, is new people. "You don't know what's going to happen, you don't know what their on-air judgment is like. So I have to see how this person handles obstacles, a different direction. What happens if a curve comes in, how fast do they respond, how playful are they, how programmed are they?"

Why *not* script and perform the entire show? If controlling the outcome is desirable, why leave it partially uncontrolled? Why allow curves? The answers are again found in the commercial drive toward pursuing "real" or "honest" moments. Spontaneity is necessary because it provides distinctiveness. A predictable perform-ance can be a dull one. Dolce complains about the new crop of "generic" talent who come into his office "totally prepared."

> They're like automatons. I want their real selves. The kids who come in
> are bright, articulate, attractive, likable – and interchangeable. And that is
> a problem for me. They don't say anything. They just do everything right.
> You can't remember whether it was this blonde or that blonde. Was that
> the redhead? Was this him, or was it that other guy?

Moreover, a performance that is too performed can appear unreal on a program that claims to provide reality. With "civilians," Dolce says, "you get something much more honest. They're unpredictable. They're excited about being here and they're not promoting anything. They're not selling an image, and they're not selling a movie or a record. They're just here. So you get something much more honest, and you don't know what's going to happen." The spontaneity, though, is "terrifying," high-risk. Dolce prefers working with celebrities because, despite the risk that they will appear more canned, "they're going to be anxious to please, anxious to do it right."

The dilemma for talk-show coordinators, then, is that spontaneity and performance are both necessary and risky. The result is practical behaviors aimed at managed spontaneity, a sort of live performance of the semifictional. On one level, like the good story, this set of criteria and behaviours allows the symbiotic supplier-outlet relations to flow relatively smoothly. Besides trading access for promotion, suppliers and outlets reach a compromise on how far into the "real" person the exposure will extend. Taboo subjects, areas the guest and his team feel are "sensitive," are discovered and sidestepped in exchange for a performance that suits the program's needs. As long as "some goods" are offered, image control is left in the hands of the team. On another level, independent of the relationships with publicists, talk shows pursue the middle realm of simulated selves based on their *own* production requirements, the need for safe, structured spontaneity and predictable performances.

The adjusted picture

Celebrity is an industry like many others. Celebrities are manufactured as attention-getting bodies, a process complicated but not negated by the fact that celebrities are human beings. Knownness itself is commodified within them. To be more certain of their successful marketability, those producing and profiting from them – they and their team, one set of "authors" – adopt strategies of image management that blur fiction and nonfiction. Celebrity building is a complex task riddled with conflict, and the messiness is telling. In the absence of a single organizational monopoly on the production and distribution networks, various competing interests vie for control. These interests and the relationships that develop from them, when examined, reveal tensions in the process through which celebrities are given meaning. Abstract familiarity, knownness for the self rather than for works or roles, is not something all celebrity-producing parties desire. Celebrities are simultaneously linked to and divorced from the activities for which they are ostensibly famous.

With the introduction of the second set of "authors," mass-media institutions that publicly represent celebrities, an even more developed set of conflicts over control of representation can be seen. Business uncertainties lead both those pitching celebrities and those covering them toward mutual dependence, mutual co-optation, battles, and negotiation. Celebrity-based media organizations, locked to varying degrees into the economy of tidbits, are pulled both toward and away from activities that pursue "truth" or "reality." Although the legal system sets a bottom-line constraint on out-and-out lying and outlets seek accuracy if only for that reason, those whose profits explicitly depend on pleasing celebrities' gatekeepers are not fundamentally pursuing truth, and they make no bones about it. These organizations are concerned with gaining readers and viewers through the exposure of celebrities in nearly *any* form. They serve as promotional outlets for carefully managed and produced publicity;

indeed, this is the only institutional arrangement that will allow them such constant access to celebrities. They do not investigate, they publicize. On the other hand, those organizations that do not require celebrity images for sales, and who are thus not highly dependent on cultural producers for subjects, are clearly in a position to investigate. Having less stake in the promotional, they tend to chase what they see as "the facts" or take an evaluative, critical position. These are journalists as investigators in the more traditional sense. Their business depends on a reputation for "seriousness": reporting that seems to be presenting facts rather than advocating, criticism and revelation of their subjects, and a demonstration that their subjects are worthy of attention. There is little in their organizational arrangement to inhibit these activities.

Finally, the most common arrangement – the semiautonomous journalistic organizations caught on the horns of the puff/dirt dilemma – pushes toward a middle ground between artificial image and authentic reality in which the two are difficult to distinguish. The construction of the good story, guided by criteria of amusement, interest, and restricted revelation, characterized by choreographed performances and restricted investigation, largely displaces the pursuit of truth in celebrity writing and programming. It is not so much that pursuing truth is avoided or impossible here but that it becomes largely unnecessary. This, I have argued, has happened because such a displacement is *necessary* for institutional survival.

Perhaps the most revealing arrangement is the tabloid. Institutionally independent in large part, commercially driven to reveal, the *National Enquirer* would seem to be organizationally better equipped for pursuing truth than its counterparts, such as *People*, which are perceived as more legitimate and truth telling. The tabloids are virulently attacked by both those counterparts and entertainment-industry workers not because they *lie* but because they *break the rules* of the information economy, grabbing valued pieces of information without offering the payment of controlled publicity. Why, then, the reputation as the nation's biggest liars? Joined with the organizational freedom to pursue truth is the commercial requirement to provide celebrity "dish." While they are not institutionally bound to serve as promotional outlets, they are commercially bound to amuse through inside information rather than to reveal through it. Rather than "truth," they pursue the "inside scoop" in good-story form – usually the free-wheeling form of rumor and gossip – within the legal limits. "What could be better than that Danny Bonaduce story about picking up a transvestite prostitute and robbing him? I get enough stories that are true," says Mary Morgan. "So I don't have to make up stories." The implication, of course, is that a made-up story does the trick on a bad day – true ones are just less work. Tabloids are, in a sense, commercial-entertainment journalism at its most pure and free: acting in opposition to publicists by pursuing "dirt," they are also liberated from reality by the pursuit of amusement.

What the adjusted picture reveals is a cultural industry in which the creators, the authors of the celebrity text, are far from constituting a monolithic elite manufacturing standard celebrity products. Interests diverge, and the workers actively battle each other throughout the production process; the texts created are filled with the conflicts from which they are born. Yet again and again interests are realigned and conflicts resolved through a central compromise. Either because it is more controllable or because it solves an institutional dilemma, the realm of the semifictional is one in which nearly everyone has a stake. Most roads, however roundabout and bumpy, lead there.

Notes

1   Lisa Gubernick, quoted in Neal Koch, "The Hollywood Treatment," *Columbia Journalism Review* (January/February 1991): p. 31.
2   Oscar Gandy, *Beyond Agenda Setting* (Norwood, N.J.: Ablex Publishing, 1982).
3   Paul Hirsch, "Processing Fads and Fashions: An Organization-Set Analysis of Cultural Industry Systems," *American Journal of Sociology* 77 (1972): 640.
4   Moreover, says David Israel, a newspaper columnist turned television producer, the push to maintain good relationships is underlined by the lure of eventually becoming what you're reporting on: "Covering Hollywood is the only job where reporters aren't sure whether to pitch or catch. All those people who, while they're doing journalism, would like to think that they're being objective, many, in the back of their minds think, 'These guys buy screenplays; maybe I have a shot' " (quoted in Koch, "The Hollywood Treatment," p. 31).
5   Philip Elliott, "Media Organizations and Occupations: An Overview," in James Curran, Michael Gurevitch, and Janet Woolacott, eds., *Mass Communication and Society* (Beverly Hills: Sage Publications, 1977), p. 149.
6   This is often expressed through a cynical sense of humor. Patrick Goldstein will call his friend at Associated Press and pose as the publicist who can always be counted on to call with a quote from a celebrity client. "Mickey Rooney is deeply saddened," Goldstein will tell the other writer in his mock-sincere publicist's voice, "by the death of his very good friend." Their discomfort with their dependence on publicists comes through in ridicule.
7   See Eliot Freidson, "The Changing Nature of Professional Control," *Annual Review of Sociology* (1984).
8   This is not simply an implicit interest. In numerous cases, in fact, image-ownership and celebrity-as-commodity battles have found their way into the court system. Questions of individual versus corporate ownership of an image, and celebrity as financially valuable property to be divided upon divorce, for example, have been legally disputed. For an interesting treatment of these sorts of contests, see Jane Gaines, *Contested Culture: The Image, the Voice, and the Law* (Chapel Hill: University of North Carolina Press, 1991).
9   See Michael Cieply, "Hollywood's High-Powered Image Machine," *Los Angeles Times Magazine*, July 10, 1988; Jonathan Alter, "The Art of the Deals," *Newsweek*, January 9, 1989.
10 Kathie Berlin, quoted in Aimee Lee Ball, "The Starmakers," *New Woman*, November 1988, p. 123.
11 Yoffe, "E! Is for Entertainment," *Newsweek*, August 12, 1991, p. 58.
12 Elliott, "Media Organizations and Occupations," p. 148.
13 To think that commercial news organizations operate according to such traditional criteria is naive; what I am describing here is not exclusive to entertainment news. The point is the distinctive degree to which criteria of "newsworthiness" and the pursuit and provision of "truth" simply do not circulate in these environments.

Chapter 40

Rosemary Coombe

AUTHOR(IZ)ING THE CELEBRITY
Engendering alternative identities

The white kids had the counter-culture, rock stars and mysticism. The blacks had a slogan which said they were beautiful, and a party demanding power. Middle America had what it always had: Middle America. The hawks had Vietnam, and the doves the Peace Movement. The students had campus politics, and the New Left had Cuba and the Third World. And women had a voice. I had rejection from each of them. I also had Judy Garland. – Drag Queen, a character in *As Time Goes By*, by Noel Grieg and Drew Griffiths[1]

Sex imposes a uniformity upon bodies for the purposes of reproductive sexuality. This is also an act of violence. – Angela McRobbie on Judith Butler, in *Postmodernism and Popular Culture*[2]

. . . new queer spaces open up (or are revealed) whenever someone moves away from using only one specific sexual identity category – gay, lesbian, bisexual or straight – to understand and to describe mass culture, and recognizes that texts and people's responses to them are more sexually transmutable than any one category could signify – excepting perhaps, that of queer. – Alexander Doty, *Making Things Perfectly Queer*[3]

Having categorized the right as property, some courts seem to think that they have little or no choice but to recognize its survivability. After all, an assignable interest that dies with its assignor is a very queer sort of property. – Michael Madow, "Private Ownership of Public Image: Popular Culture and Publicity Rights"[4]

WHO AUTHORS THE CELEBRITY? Where does identity receive its authorization? I shall argue that the law constructs and maintains fixed, stable identities authorized by the celebrity subject but that the celebrity is authored in a multiplicity of sites of interpretive practice. The celebrity image is a cultural lode of multiple meanings, mined for its symbolic resonances. Focusing on cultural practices that appropriate celebrity images in the service of unanticipated agendas, I suggest that in such processes, unauthorized identities are produced, both for the celebrity and for her diverse authors.

In societies characterized by mass production, consumer capitalism, and mass-media communications, the celebrity image[5] holds both seductive power and significant economic and cultural value. Legal regimes simultaneously create, legitimize, and enable the realization of this value through doctrines of personality or publicity rights (and, less directly, through trademark and copyright laws). Celebrity names and images, however, are not simply marks of identity or simple commodities; they are also cultural texts – floating signifiers that are continually invested with libidinal energies, social longings, and, I will argue, political aspirations. The names and likenesses of the famous are constitutive of our cultural heritage and resonate with meanings that exceed the intentions or the interests of those they identify or resemble. I will very briefly summarize the legal doctrine of publicity rights[6] as it has developed in North America and the trend toward increasing the scope and duration of these rights. The social and cultural value of the celebrity image will be situated in the larger historical, political, and economic context of postmodernity and cultural practices characteristic of postmodernism.

In the cultural conditions of postmodernism, the commodification of cultural forms creates both generative conditions and prohibitive obstacles for the formation of alternative subjectivities. Celebrity images provide meaningful resources for the construction of identity and community. The law commodifies the celebrity subject and provides the means through which the celebrity may attempt to fix the identity and meaning of her persona. But in so doing, the law produces the possibility of the celebrity's polysemy. Focusing on a number of cultural practices that engage, reproduce, ironize, and sometimes transform the meaning of celebrity personas in order to produce and assert alternative gender identities for those who are socially marginalized, I argue that through its prohibitions, the law provides the means by which unauthorized identities are both engendered and endangered.

Popular cultural practices that engage celebrity images in innovative fashions illustrate the vibrant role played by these cultural icons in the self-authorings of minority, subaltern, or alter/native social groups. Gay male appropriations of female stars in camp subculture, lesbian refashionings of James Dean, and middle-class women's use of the *Star Trek* characters in the creation of fanzines are practices that recode pervasive images in a subversive but politically expressive manner. Investing celebrity personas with new and often oppositional meanings, subordinate groups assert unauthorized gender identities. They thereby affirm both community solidarity and the legitimacy of social difference by empowering themselves with resources afforded by mass media, which are nearly always the authorial properties of others.

The value of the celebrity persona

> What's the difference between Vanna White and a robot? Not much
> according to White, that woman of letters. The longtime gameshow cubist
> is suing Samsung Electronics America and its ad agency because of a
> humorous print advertisement that she claims pirated her celebrity.
> Several years ago the company ran a VCR ad that depicted a robot with a
> blonde wig, jewelry and alluring evening gown, turning giant letters on a
> video board . . . White was not amused . . . she [successfully] argued they
> had misappropriated her "identity." – *Newsweek*, April 5, 1993

Anglo-American legal jurisdictions recognize the right of individuals to protect publicly identifiable attributes from unauthorized and unremunerated appropriation by
others for commercial purposes or economic benefit. In Canada and Britain, this right
developed at common law into a distinct cause of action known as the tort of
appropriation of personality. Some Canadian provinces also recognize the right in
privacy statutes.[7] In the United States, the right of publicity arose as a category of
the right of privacy that protects the individual against misappropriations of her
name or likeness.[8] Various states have also incorporated these rights in privacy
statutes and state constitutional provisions.[9] In both Canada and the United
States, federal trademark legislation provides additional protections.[10] The literature detailing the origins and developing scope of these rights is so voluminous
that a 256-page *bibliography* of relevant American literature was published in 1987.[11]
Today the literature is even more extensive, and I make no effort to summarize the
entire field.

Originally developed primarily to deal with an unauthorized use of a person's
name or picture in advertising that suggested the individual's endorsement of a product, the right of publicity has been greatly expanded in the twentieth century. It is no
longer limited to the name or likeness of an individual, but now extends to a person's
nickname,[12] signature,[13] physical pose,[14] characterizations,[15] singing style,[16] vocal
characteristics,[17] body parts,[18] frequently used phrases,[19] car,[20] performance style,[21]
and mannerisms and gestures,[22] provided that these are distinctive and publicly identified with the person claiming the right. Although most cases still involve the unauthorized advertising of commodities, rights of publicity have been evoked to prohibit the
distribution of memorial posters, novelty souvenirs, magazine parodies, and the presentation of nostalgic musical reviews, television docudramas, and satirical theatrical
performances.

Increasingly, it seems that *any* publicly recognizable characteristic will be legally
legitimated as having a commercial value likely to be diminished by its unauthorized
appropriation by others. As we saw in the case of trademarks, recognition by the
public is appropriated by the celebrity as intrinsic parts of a personality over which
proprietary claims are made; again, *social* knowledge and *social* significance are
expropriated as private properties. Some have even recommended that "any distinctive aspect of personality that sets that individual apart in the marketplace and imbues
that unique human identity with commercial value" should be protected, such that if
tomorrow's rage is "t-shirts sporting a shorthand reference to the DNA makeup of
movie box-office idols," a celebrity would be protected against such (ab)use.[23] As

other scholars assert, the right of publicity has grown massively in scope in the late twentieth century without clearly articulated grounds that would provide reasonable limitations for its scope and duration.[24] The rationales traditionally offered for recognizing and protecting rights to the celebrity persona cannot be empirically supported and certainly don't justify the extent of the protections legally afforded celebrities, their estates, or their assignees.

The right has been recognized as proprietary in nature[25] and may therefore be assigned and the various components of an individual's persona may be independently licensed. A celebrity could, theoretically at least, license her signature for use on fashion scarves, grant exclusive rights to reproduce her face to a perfume manufacturer, voice to a charitable organization, legs to a pantyhose company, particular publicity stills for distribution as posters or postcards, and continue to market her services as a singer, actor, and composer. The human persona is capable of almost infinite commodification, because exclusive, nonexclusive, and temporally, spatially, and functionally limited licenses may be granted for use of any valuable aspect of the celebrity's public presence. Furthermore, the right of publicity has been extended beyond the celebrity and his or her licensees and assignees to protect the celebrity's descendants or heirs.[26]

Although constitutional protections under the First Amendment privilege certain uses of celebrity names and likenesses, the definition of free speech that has developed in right of publicity cases is both narrow and inconsistently applied.[27] Focusing almost exclusively on the newsworthiness of the alleged appropriation and its ability to disseminate truthful information, courts have failed to consider other values that underlie our commitments to freedom of speech [. . .]. Freedom of expression is generally understood as essential to democratic self-government and as integral to the self-realization and self-expression constitutive of freedom in liberal societies. The recognition of exclusive proprietary interests in celebrity personas may impose real limits to the self-realization of those with alter/native agendas.

Celebrity authorship

> Cliff and Norm, the buffoon barflies on "Cheers," may have a sense of humor, but apparently the actors playing them don't. John Ratzenberger and George Wendt are suing Host International, which operates a chain of "Cheers" airport bars . . . Each has dark wood panelling, the wood-carving of a Native American near the door – and replicas of Cliff and Norm. While the talking robots are named Bob and Hank, they have physical similarities to the television characters and their conversation is equally insipid. So Ratzenberger and Wendt say they're being ripped off. – *Newsweek*, April 5, 1993

It is impossible to deny the potential value of the celebrity persona. The aura of the celebrity is a potent force in an era in which standardization, rationalization, and the controlled programming of production characterize the creation and distribution of goods. Mass-media communications convey imagery and information across vast distances to produce consumer demand. As mass-market products become functionally indistinguishable, manufacturers increasingly promote them by symbolically associating them with the aura of the celebrity – which may be the quickest way to establish a share of the market.[28] It takes years to establish a brand name but only months to capitalize on celebrity. It is suggested that fame has become the most valuable (and also the most perishable) of commodities[29] and that celebrity will have been the greatest growth industry in the nineties.[30] With its "alchemical power to turn the least promising of raw materials into alluring and desirable artifacts" (designer jeans, sunglasses, deodorants, architects' teakettles and coffee mugs), "fame's economic applications are limitless."[31] Originally a by-product of a successful film or athletic career, we now have celebrities famous simply for being famous (Gloria Vanderbilt, Paloma Picasso, and Vanna White come to mind). The value that a famous name adds to a product may be astronomical; London outworkers knit pullovers for £6 – with a Ralph Lauren tag they sold for $245 in New York – but Lauren had a $17 million annual advertising budget to cover.[32]

Celebrities, then, have an interest in policing the use of their personas to ensure that they don't become tainted with associations that would prematurely tarnish the patina they might license to diverse enterprises. Indeed, a new breed of lawyer has emerged, one who scouts remote corners of metropolitan areas for unauthorized commercial uses of celebrity images. This postmodern ambulance chaser advises the estates of the famous of potential avenues for successful lawsuits, demanding only a portion of eventual damages for a fee. Scouring the urban landscape for signs of renegade Elvis restaurants, unlicensed Marilyn likenesses, and other profitable piracies has become a lucrative occupation made possible by the legal recognition of publicity's value.

This potential commercial value is generally offered as reason in itself to protect the star's control over his or her identity through the allocation of exclusive property rights. Most commentators have defended the recognition and enforceability of exclusive property rights on the grounds of exigent economic necessity: because such interests have market value, they deserve protection.[33] Indeed, until the 1990s it was virtually impossible to find any alternative perspective on the right of publicity. Others, like myself, see this as "a massive exercise in question begging."[34] As Wendy Gordon notes, to propose that a right follows from the existence of potential value is to propound a principle with no coherent parameters.[35]

Market values arise only after property rights are established and enforced; the decision to allocate particular property rights is a prior question of social policy that requires philosophical and moral deliberations[36] and a consideration of social costs and benefits:

> It is sometimes said that the right of publicity rests on the commercial value of the interest itself, but that explanation is nonsense without something more. A claim of this sort will have commercial value only if it also has the protection of the law. In a sense, the value of this property stems from the fact that the law recognizes and protects it. Perhaps the question to be considered, then, is really two questions: first, whether there is a sensible basis upon which a claim can be made to rest beyond the value which protection undoubtedly will confer, and second, whether there is any offsetting consideration which might lead one to conclude that

protection ought not be granted even though there is some legitimacy in the claim.[37]

In determining whether there is a sensible basis for granting a property right in a celebrity's persona, we might consider traditional liberal justifications in support of private property. The idea that people are entitled to the fruits of their own labor and that property rights in one's body and its labor entail property rights in the products of that labor derives from John Locke[38] and is persuasive as a point of departure. It does not, however, very far advance the argument in favor of exclusive property rights. As Edwin Hettinger remarks, "assuming that labor's fruits are valuable, and that laboring gives the laborer a property right in this value, this would entitle the laborer only to the value she added, and not to the *total* value of the resulting product."[39]

Publicity rights are often justified on the basis of the celebrity's authorship: his or her investment of time, effort, skill, and money in the development of a persona.[40] Such claims, however rhetorically persuasive, are rarely supported by any empirical data. How much of a star's celebrity and its value is due to the individual's own efforts and investments? Clearly, individual labor is necessary if the persona is to have value, and we could not appreciate celebrities without their expenditure of effort – but it is not usually sufficient for the creation of publicity value. But, as Hettinger argues with regard to intellectual properties more generally, "it does not follow from this that all of their value is attributable to that labor."[41]

Celebrity images must be made, and, like other cultural products, their creation occurs in social contexts and draws upon other resources, institutions, and technologies. Star images are authored by studios, the mass media, public relations agencies, fan clubs, gossip columnists, photographers, hairdressers, body-building coaches, athletic trainers, teachers, screenwriters, ghostwriters, directors, lawyers, and doctors. Even if we only look at the production and dissemination of the celebrity image and see its value as solely the result of human labor, this value cannot be entirely attributed to the efforts of a single person.

Moreover, as Richard Dyer illustrates, the star image is given value by its consumers as well as its producers; the audience makes the celebrity image the unique phenomenon that it is.[42] Selecting from the complexities of the images and texts they encounter, they produce new meanings for the celebrity and find in stars significative values that speak to their own experiences. These new meanings and significations are freely mined by the media producers of the star's image to further enhance its market value. As Marilyn Monroe said, in what are alleged to be her last recorded words in public, "I want to say that the people – if I am a star – the people made me a star, no studio, no person, but the people did."[43]

As Hettinger remarks, "simply identifying the value a laborer's labor adds to the world with the market value of the resulting product ignores the vast contributions of others."[44] The star image is authored by multitudes of persons engaged in diverse activities. Moreover, the star and her fame are never manufactured from whole cloth; the successful image is frequently a form of cultural bricolage that draws upon a social history of symbolic forms. Consider the Marx Brothers. Clearly, the construction of their characters involved creative activity and their characters were successful in the market:

But what we cannot know in fact, and what I suspect strongly could not be proven now if one set out to do so with the best will in the world, is how much the characters created by the Marx Brothers owe to the work of tens, scores, perhaps hundreds of other vaudeville and burlesque performers with whom they came into contact during their early years in the business. What we do not know, in short, is how much of these characters the Marx Brothers themselves appropriated from others. All that is certain is that they created themselves, individually and collectively, as a kind of living derivative work. That much Groucho himself has told us, but even without his candid admissions, it would be foolish and indeed ignorant of the history of burlesque and vaudeville to doubt that they took what they wanted from what they observed among the performers they grew up with, perhaps adding, in the process, important new material of their own. To be sure, the Marx Brothers became celebrities as most vaudevillians did not. But surely we are not rewarding them on that ground alone. Even in an age as celebrity-haunted as this, we cannot mean to establish dynasties on the memory of fame.[45]

The "authorship rationale" for publicity rights goes beyond the contribution of labor, however, to stress the unique singularity of the individual's efforts in creating a persona. In a recent defense of the right, Roberta Rosenthal Kwall suggests that "fostering creativity" is one of the reasons for extending publicity rights, and asserts that, "whatever the means through which an individual's persona comes to have value, that value should be attributable to the persona of the publicity plaintiff . . . Thus even if others help mold a celebrity's image, the celebrity herself is still responsible for the vast majority of the profit potential of her persona. Those who assist the plaintiff in creating a marketable persona typically are paid for their efforts. Further, when a celebrity borrows from the cultural fabric in creating her persona, it is still the unique combination of the past and the persona's original contributions that give the persona its present appeal."[46]

The attributes that are legally protected as an individual's "persona," however, are those that are *publicly identified* with him or her; it is the degree to which the particular attribute is socially distinctive or publicly recognizable that determines its protection against unauthorized use. It does not follow that that which is most appreciated or distinctive in the public sphere is the attribute in which the celebrity has invested his or her labors, or that the celebrity himself or herself was not paid for efforts in the activities that made him or her famous. There is no guarantee that it is the celebrity's "original" contributions that give his or her image its "appeal" or even its profit potential. It might be an image's conformity to a conventional stereotype and a particular social attachment to that stereotype that give the persona its social meaning and value. Certainly any number of individuals have attempted to achieve celebrity with diligent effort, great investment, and the utmost originality and still failed to achieve any public recognition or social distinction. The social production of meaning and the totally unpredictable generation of public distinction are here neatly attributed to the unique and singular efforts of an author who, in addition to salary and fees, is also ascribed with a new form of cultural authority in the public sphere.

Dynasties established on the memory of fame have also provided sinecures for many who have merely inherited this authority. In Groucho Marx Productions, Inc. v. Day and Night Co., Inc., the successors to rights in the names and likenesses of the Marx Brothers made a successful publicity rights claim against the production company, producers, and authors of the Broadway play *A Day in Hollywood, a Night in the Ukraine*.[47] The authors of that play intended to satirize the excesses of Hollywood in the thirties and evoked the Marx Brothers as characters playfully imagined as interpreting a Chekhov play. The defendants were found liable for appropriating the Marx Brothers' personalities or violating their publicity rights, and their First Amendment privilege was dismissed on the ground that the play was an imitative work.[48]

The Marx Brothers *themselves* might be seen as imitative or derivative works, whose creation and success as popular cultural icons derives from their own creative reworkings of the signifying repertoire of the vaudeville community. Contemporary stars are authored in a similar fashion. How much does Elvis Costello owe to Buddy Holly, Prince to Jimi Hendrix, or Michael Jackson to Diana Ross? Take the image of Madonna, an icon whose meaning and value lie partially in her evocation and ironic reconfiguration of several twentieth-century sex goddesses and ice queens (Marilyn Monroe, obviously, but also Jean Harlow, Greta Garbo, Marlene Dietrich, Gina Lollobrigida, and perhaps a touch of Grace Kelly) that speaks with multiple tongues to diverse audiences. Academic descriptions of Madonna as semiotic montage abound,[49] but the following somewhat hyperbolic extract from a *Village Voice* article appeals to me: "What Madonna served up in the name of sexuality was not liberation as I'd known it, but a strange brew of fetishism and femininity. Only later would I understand that the source of her power is precisely this ambiguity. It's a mistake to think of any pop icon as an individual . . . Madonna is a cluster of signs, and what they add up to is precisely the state of sex in the culture now: torn between need and rage and unable to express one without the other . . . Madonna raids the image bank of American femininity, melding every fantasy ever thrown onto the silver screen and implanting them in the body and voice of every-babe."[50]

In an era characterized by nostalgia for the golden age of the silver screen and an aging baby boom generation's fascination with the television culture of its youth, successful texts and images are often those that mine media history for evocative signifiers from our past. This is not to deny that such appropriations and reconstructions are creative productions; it is to stress emphatically that they *are* and to assert that such creative processes ought not to be frozen, limited, or circumscribed by the whims of celebrities or the commercial caprice of their estates or assignees.

The Marx Brothers scenario illustrates the danger well. The producers of *A Day in Hollywood* used the Marx Brothers characters to speak to our relation to Hollywood in its heyday, much as the Marx Brothers brought the spirit and forms of vaudeville to speak to Depression America. As Lange sees it:

> What they sought to do, by their own account, "was to work a satiric comment on Hollywood movies using a parody of the Marx Brothers movies as one of the literary devices." The work they produced earned substantial public acceptance, and despite the court's opinion, has at least some claim to acceptance as a creative success as well. Yet the result of this litigation is that the work no longer can be performed as written without

accommodating the plaintiffs in some fashion. In a case like this, then, what society loses is a right of access amounting to an easement. In at least a preliminary sense, this is always the result of upholding a claim to a right of publicity.[51]

Lange argues forcefully that the proliferation of successful publicity rights claims has occurred at the expense of individual rights in the public domain. The public domain is inadequately considered and rarely conceptually developed in juridical contexts; no one represents the public domain in intellectual property litigation or acts as its guardian, and rules of civil procedure currently prohibit the participation of third parties who will ultimately be affected (other artists, writers, and performers of current and future generations). As a consequence, access to the public domain is choked or closed off, and the public "loses the rich heritage of its culture, the rich presence of new works derived from that culture, and the rich promise of works to come."[52]

If the Madonna image appropriates the likenesses of earlier screen goddesses, religious symbolism, feminist rhetoric, and sadomasochistic fantasy to speak to sexual aspirations and anxieties in the 1980s and 1990s, then the value of her image derives as much, perhaps, from the collective cultural heritage on which she draws as from her individual efforts. But if we grant Madonna exclusive property rights in her image, we simultaneously make it difficult for others to appropriate those same resources for new ends, and we freeze the Madonna constellation itself. Future artists, writers, and performers will be unable to creatively draw upon the cultural and historical significance of the Madonna montage without seeking the consent of the celebrity, her estate, her descendants or their assignees, who may well deny such consent or demand exorbitant royalties.

We might consider whether certain celebrity images are so deeply embedded in the North American psyche and cultural subconscious that they constitute parts of a collective cultural heritage that should not be subject to control by the parochial interests of the celebrity's estate and assigns. Elvis Presley provides an apt example. In the film *Mystery Train*, Jim Jarmusch explored the cultural and psychological significance of Presley in the depressed economy of Memphis, Tennessee, and in the consciousness of those who live on its social margins. The film also addresses his charisma for those in other countries whose fascination with American media images manifests itself in pilgrimages that have turned Memphis into a late-twentieth-century mecca. Even the possibility that Elvis Presley's estate *might* seek to prohibit the production and/or distribution of a film such as this[53] while simultaneously arranging to market cologne designed "for all the King's men"[54] alludes to the parameters of the problem. The opportunity for the celebrity's heirs or assignees to behave in such a manner has, in fact, been seized in similar circumstances. When the city of Memphis decided to erect a bronze statue to memorialize Elvis as part of a city redevelopment scheme, and a nonprofit city corporation offered pewter replicas of the King in return for donations to finance the monument, owners of rights to commercially exploit the Presley likeness were quick to seek and obtain an injunction.[55] Neither Elvis Presley's manager's corporation, Factors, Inc., nor his family can completely control the uses to which his image is put, however. Elvis impersonators and fans create an ever-evolving Elvis folklore and collectively sustain a deep distrust for those mass-media versions of

Elvis from which his estate and their official licensees continue to profit. Others author Elvis and forge their own norms of propriety about the use of his image.

A Lockean labor theory justifying property rights in the celebrity image is inadequate to establish a right to receive the full market value of the star persona or to establish exclusive rights to control its circulation and reproduction in society. Although a moral right to the fruits of one's labor must encompass a right to possess and personally use what one develops for one's own benefit and, perhaps, to exchange it on the market, this right need not necessarily be exclusive nor yield the full market value of such exclusivity.[56] Liberal values protecting individual freedom guarantee the possession and personal use of the product of one's labors only insofar as the exercise of this right does not harm the rights of others. As Wendy Gordon argues, deprivation of public domain and loss of access to cultural heritage are forms of harm that might be contemplated.[57] Moreover, rights to possess and personally use the fruits of one's labor do not necessarily entail the imposition of full property rights or rights to perpetually garner the full profits that such a product would yield in the market: "This liberty is a socially created phenomenon; the 'right' to receive what the market will bear is a socially created privilege, and not a natural right at all."[58]

If traditional liberal philosophy appears inadequate to encompass the range of social and cultural considerations that need to be addressed when defining the scope of publicity rights, other fields of intellectual property protection might seem to afford more guidance. However, if we examine traditional rationales for extending property rights to other forms of intellectual property, it becomes clear that the extension of property rights in cultural works is recognized as a socially bestowed privilege granted in exchange for social contributions and the bestowal of public benefits. (To spare the nonlegal reader, I have confined my comparison of the scope of publicity rights with other forms of intellectual property to an extended footnote.)[59] Publicity rights may be loosely analogized to rights granted by copyright, patent, and trademark laws, but none of these doctrines provides a degree of protection against unauthorized appropriation equal to that afforded celebrities. Moreover, all of these other areas of law contain limitations, exemptions, and defenses that recognize competing social and cultural interests.[60] Intellectual property protections were designed to provide limited rights in order to serve community goals and purposes; they make the exercise of individual property rights contingent upon the fulfillment of social responsibilities. Neither traditional liberal theory nor our rationales for recognizing limited property rights in artistic, literary, commercial, and scientific expressions justify the extent of contemporary publicity rights. Moreover, enabling celebrities, their estates, and their assigns to exercise absolute rights to control the celebrity image may have adverse consequences, both for the preservation of our collective cultural heritage and for our future cultural development. Judicial authority (albeit in dissent) is now available to support this claim: "Millions of people toil in the shadow of the law we make, and much of their livelihood is made possible by the existence of intellectual property rights. But much of their livelihood – and much of the vibrancy of our culture – also depends upon the existence of other intangible rights: The right to draw ideas from a rich and varied public domain, and the right to mock, for profit as well as fun, the cultural icons of our time."[61]

The celebrity form and the politics of postmodernism

> The fact that celebrities haul so much semiotic freight in our culture
> has a number of important consequences. – Michael Madow, "Private
> Ownership of Public Image"[62]

Systems of mass production and mass-media communications have afforded opportunities for talented, beautiful, and/or charismatic individuals to achieve reknown across
unprecedented distances and to have their fame survive for generations. These
opportunities have been seized by individuals who seek to maximize their economic
return. By recognizing the ability to exploit one's persona as an exclusive property
right, the law has created a significant new source of economic value. In the process of
developing individual economic rights, the law deprives us of collective cultural
resources. The social value and cultural meaning of the celebrity image have their
genesis in the same historical conditions that created the possibility of its economic
value. In this section, I address the cultural significance of the celebrity image generally, and then explore the specific significance that particular celebrities have to select
social groups. As it proceeds, this section becomes more ethnographic as I submerge
the reader in unfamiliar realms of "subculture" (although I might prefer to simply call
them queer spaces)[63] before returning to the legal dilemma.

In his illuminating essay "The Work of Art in the Age of Mechanical Reproduction,"[64] Walter Benjamin suggested that technologies of mechanical reproduction and
systems of mass production changed modes of human perception and evaluation, fundamentally altering our aesthetic responses. These changes, I would suggest, are integrally related to the cultural value of the celebrity image in contemporary social life.
Benjamin argued that our experience of cultural imagery changed dramatically with
lithography and photography. The work of art traditionally had a tangible individuated
presence in time and space, a singular history, and a situation in a cultural tradition. This
notion of the original, necessary to the idea of authenticity and to the work's authority,
was maintained during the era of manual reproduction, but increasingly became irrelevant in an age of technical reproduction. Mass reproduction creates copies that possess
an independence from the original; they can transcend the spatial and visual limitations
of the original's physical tangibility and susceptibility to temporal and material processes of age and deterioration. As the artwork's substantive duration ceased to matter,
the art object lost its authority or its *aura* – "the unique phenomenon of distance
however close it may be."[65] The aura embodied the work's value by engaging the
beholder's affective, reflexive relationship to the cultural tradition in which the work
was situated. The artwork was unapproachable; both in its physically unique embodiment and in its tangible history in a cultural tradition, it resisted too intimate an
appropriation by the beholder into his or her own physical and cultural lifeworlds.

The work of art's aura was lost in the age of mechanical reproduction because
"the technique of reproduction detaches the reproduced object from the domain of
tradition."[66] By substituting a plurality of copies for a unique existence it enabled the
consumer to position the reproduction in his or her own domestic, social, and historical milieus without any necessary cognizance of an original or its historical situation.
The photograph and the film, for Benjamin, represent the culmination of the destruction of the aura because they are designed for reproducibility: "From a photographic

negative, for example, one can make any number of prints; to ask for the 'authentic' print makes no sense."[67] The criterion of authenticity ceased to be applicable to artistic reproduction. The uniqueness of a work of art was due to the work's situation in a traditional ritual context, whether that context was magical, religious, or secular. The "contextual integration of art in tradition found its expression in the cult"[68] that defined its use value. Technologies of mass reproduction enabled copies to transcend the work's historical use value in social cults of ritual and to become pure objects of exchange value or commodities.

Benjamin's reflections on the historical development of the work of art and the decline of its aura may help us to understand the cultural significance and seductive powers of the celebrity image. Here I want to go beyond Benjamin's own disjointed observations on the topic. He saw the screen actor as one whose performance was fragmented by the camera, alienated from the audience, deprived of his corporeality, and dissolved into flickering images and disembodied sounds.[69] The effect of film was to engage the whole living person but to replace the actor's aura with an artificially produced "personality" that was only the "phony spell of the commodity."[70] Benjamin alludes to the possibility of another, alternative understanding of the celebrity when he refers to "the cult of the movie star,"[71] however, an allusion that provokes one to ask whether celebrities might represent residual vestiges of the "auratic" in contemporary mass culture.

If the work of art's aura derives from its unique, embodied, or tangible presence in time and space, an individual history, and a situation in a cultural tradition, then it is difficult to deny the aura of the celebrity. However often a celebrity's likeness is reproduced, there remains a social knowledge of the celebrity as an individual human being with an unapproachable or distant existence elsewhere, a life history, and a mortal susceptibility to the processes of heartache, injury, illness, aging, and, ultimately, death. For example, it is difficult to envisage Elvis Presley without conjuring up images of health, vibrancy, and sexual energy followed by self-inflicted injury, gluttony, corpulence, and decay. Arguably, celebrities evoke the fascination they do because however endlessly their images are reproduced, their substantive duration – that is, their life – never becomes wholly irrelevant. They never lose their autonomy from the objects that circulate in their likeness.

Moreover, the star is historically situated and lives his or her life in social conditions that give his or her image meaning, resonance, and authority. Part of the celebrity image's value might reside in its exemplifying a particular human embodiment of a connection to a social history that provokes its beholder to reflect upon his or her own relationship to the cultural tradition in which the star's popularity is embedded. We all consider celebrities from different social positions; as a feminist and social democrat, for example, I cannot perceive Marilyn Monroe without reflecting upon my own troubled relationship to male definitions of female sexuality, the femininity of sexual innocence, the Playboy tradition, the cold war, and Monroe's own left populist politics.[72] Celebrity images, I would contend, always maintain their aura because they bind subjects in affective and historically mediated relationships that preclude their appropriation as pure objects.

Stewart Ewen sees the power of the celebrity image as rooted in photography's simultaneous affinity to reality and fantasy: "As Oliver Wendell Holmes had observed, the power of the disembodied image is that it can free itself from encumbrances posed by material reality and still lay claim to that reality. At the same time that the image appeals to transcendent desires, it locates those desires within a visual grammar which is palpable, which *looks real*, which invites identification by the spectator, and which people tend to trust. According to John Everard, one of the pioneers of commercial photography, it is this trust that makes photography so forceful as an advertising medium."[73]

The personal lives of celebrities, closely monitored and continually represented in the mass media, perform a function similar to that of commercial photography and similarly emerged with the image-making machinery stoked to maintain the perpetuation of contemporary consumer culture.[74] Ewen also sees the celebrity as a cultural response to modern social experiences of alienation and anomie – an icon of the significance of the personal and the individual in a world of standardization and conformity and the embodiment of the possibility of upward mobility from the mass: "Celebrity forms a symbolic pathway, connecting each aspiring individual to a universal image of fulfillment: to be someone, when 'being no one' is the norm."[75] The social potency of celebrity auras and the ubiquity of their presence in contemporary North American society make the celebrity persona a compelling and powerful set of signifiers in our cultural fields of representation. Simultaneously embodying the fantastic and the real, utopian ideals and quotidian practices, and the realization of popular aspirations for recognition and legitimacy, the celebrity form attracts the authorial energies of those for whom identity is a salient issue and community an ongoing dilemma.

But what meaning do particular celebrities have in the cultural lives of specific social groups in North American society? Focusing on a range of practices, engaged in by marginal social groups in nascent constructions of alternative identities, I attempt to make socially concrete the philosophical arguments I asserted earlier about the cultural losses contingent upon the commodification of the celebrity image. Moreover, I shall suggest that this foreclosure on the use of cultural resources has political dimensions. The practices I examine are those of gay male camp subculture in the preliberation era, lesbian refashionings of pop icons, and finally, middle-class women's engagement in the reading, writing, and circulation of *Star Trek* fan magazines ("fanzines"). These practices involve the redeployment of celebrity images, an aspect of that rearticulation of commodified media texts that has been defined as the essence of popular culture. Many of the people I'll describe here are "fans," and fandom is often "a vehicle for marginalized subcultural groups to pry open space for their own cultural concerns within dominant representations . . . a way of appropriating media texts and rereading them in a fashion that serves different interests":[76]

> fans enthusiastically embrace favored texts and attempt to integrate media representations into their own social experience. Unimpressed by institutional authority and expertise, the fans assert their own right to form interpretations, to offer evaluations, and to construct cultural canons. Undaunted by traditional conceptions of literary and intellectual property, fans raid mass culture, claiming its materials for their own use, reworking them as the basis for their own cultural creations and social interactions. Fans seemingly blur the boundaries between fact and fiction,

speaking of characters as if they had an existence apart from their textual manifestations, entering into the realm of fiction as if it were a tangible place they can inhabit and explore. Fan culture stands as an open challenge to the "naturalness" and desireability of dominant cultural hierarchies, a refusal of authorial authority and a violation of intellectual property.[77]

In conditions of postmodernity, cultural consumption is increasingly understood as an active use rather than a passive dependence upon dominant forms of signification. As Michel de Certeau[78] and Paul Willis[79] argue, consumption is always a form of production and people continually engage in cultural practices of bricolage – resignifying media meanings, consumer objects, urban spaces, and cultural texts in order to adapt them to their own interests and make them fulfill their own purposes. The consumer is seen as actively reworking everything from the design of the shopping mall[80] and the rhetoric of the romance[81] to mass-marketed toy culture[82] in the articulation of alternative meanings and identities. Commodified signs become cultural resources with which new social and political realities are forged.

Hal Foster,[83] for example, views these practices of appropriating or "recording" contemporary cultural forms as the essence of popular culture, central to the political practices of those in marginal or subordinated social groups, who construct subcultures with resources foraged from the mediascape.[84] Steven Connor sees postmodernism as (among other things) manifestations of "the central paradox of contemporary mass culture."[85] On the one hand, mass culture has enormous influence due to its global reach and penetration into the daily lives of millions of people, thus posing the possibility (or specter) of cultural unification and homogeneity. On the other hand, it provides resources for and contains the "capacity to tolerate, encourage, and engender a plurality of styles and identities."[86]

Cultural studies theorists defined subcultural practices to involve practices of appropriation and innovation of existing cultural forms in improvisations that provide opportunities for the affirmation of emergent cultural identities.[87] Dick Hebdige, for example, described the manner in which music styles like rap and hip hop deployed available symbolic and material forms using principles of parody, pastiche, and irony to articulate mixed, plural, or transitional identities for social groups at the margins of national or dominant cultures.[88] Angela McRobbie makes a similar case for optimism about the penetration of media imagery and communications into our psychic and social lives, arguing that the frenzied expansion of mass media enables new alliances and solidarities across traditional spatial, racial, and cultural boundaries as well as resources for producing new meanings and new identities.[89]

The constitution of provisional identities through the invocation of mass-media images, texts, and symbols is made possible when an audience is simultaneously absorbed and capable of ironic detachment. Lynda Hutcheon feels that this attitude defines postmodernism, "the name given to cultural practices which acknowledge their inevitable implication in capitalism without relinquishing the power or will to intervene critically in it."[90] This was an attitude Susan Sontag earlier described as the essence of camp, but one that McRobbie sees as shared by many consumers of mass culture in the condition of postmodernity:

Sontag's linking pastiche with its favoured audience, gay men, is instructive because she shows how a relationship evolved around a social minority
making a bid for a cultural form in which they felt they could stake some
of their fragmented and sexually deviant identity. The insistence, on the
way, on both style and pleasure made the product attractive to those
outside as well as inside . . . Sontag's approach is useful because she is
talking not so much about pure or original "artistic" invention. Rather she
is describing how forms can be taken over, and re-assembled so as to suit
the requirements of the group in question. This often means outstripping
their ostensible meaning and ostensible function . . . And if media forms
are so inescapable . . . then there is no reason to assume that consumption
of pastiche, parody or high camp is, by definition, without subversive
or critical potential. Glamour, glitter, and gloss should not so easily be
relegated to the sphere of the insistently apolitical.[91]

Ours is a world in which spatial and temporary distances can be quickly bridged
through instantaneous communications. Ethnic, racial, class, and cultural boundaries
are becoming less easily defined as a consequence of mass migration, immigration,
transnational flows of labor and capital, and the expansion of mass markets. In this
context, allegiances and identities are reconstructed. The breakdown of traditional
communities has not resulted in social homogenization, however, but in a proliferation
of differences organized along nontraditional lines. As Willis suggests, organic communities and organic communications are breaking down in the late twentieth century, and "proto-communities" are emergent.[92] Proto-communities "start and form
not from intentioned purposes, political or other, but from contingency, from fun,
from shared desires . . . they form from and out of the unplanned and unorganized
precipitations and spontaneous patterns of shared symbolic work and creativity."[93]
Such communities may evolve around a "consuming interest" in cultural commodities
such as products of the communications media, with which new meanings are
minted: "All popular audiences engage in varying degrees of semiotic productivity,
producing meanings and pleasures that pertain to their social situation out of the
products of the culture industries. But fans often turn this semiotic productivity into
some form of textual production that can circulate among – and thus help to define –
the fan community."[94]

   Mass-media imagery allows people who share similar social experiences to simultaneously express their similarity by emotionally investing in a range of cultural
referents to which media communications have afforded them shared access. It also
enables them to author(iz)e their difference by appropriating and improvising with
these images to make them relevant to their social experiences and aspirations. These
images may serve to present these emergent identities in the public sphere in a
manner that may be both aesthetically appealing and politically charged; we are culturally drawn to the image because of its presence in our own lifeworlds and, arguably,
are therefore more likely to be sympathetic to the legitimacy of the forms of
difference and aspirations expressed in its renarrativization by subaltern groups.

Doing gender

> I want to recall Benjamin's critique of the state's techno-fetishization of
> technologies of reproduction in the context of contemporary lesbian
> bodies – bodies working under a signifying regime of simulation and
> within an economy of repetition. Jean Baudrillard has defined post-
> mechanical reproduction as the precession of simulacra, the accession of
> post World War. II, postindustrial culture to a state of hyper-reality . . .
> The cultural reproduction of lesbian bodies in the age of (post)mechanical
> reproduction, that is, in an economy of simulacral repetition, has more
> than ever destroyed any aura of an "original" lesbian identity, while expos-
> ing the cultural sites through which lesbianism is appropriated by the
> political economy of postmodernity. – Cathy Griggers, "Lesbian Bodies in
> the Age of (Post) Mechanical Reproduction"[95]

Let us turn to specific examples of the cultural politics of authoring social identities
through the improvisational use of celebrity images. The phenomenon of projecting
new meanings upon celebrity images is no doubt widespread, because, as I suggested
earlier, the celebrity is an image that is both fantastic and real and embodies the
realization of popular aspirations for recognition and legitimacy. The star persona is
especially likely to attract the energies of those in subordinate or marginal groups for
whom social recognition and a positively evaluated identity are pressing concerns.
Although the recoding of celebrity images is in no way limited to a concern with
gender identity, I will focus on practices that question traditional formulations of
gender and express desires to construct alternatives.

The social construction of gendered subjectivity is the central premise of an anti-
essentialist feminism that understands sexual difference to be "a complex, ever-shifting
social practice."[96] If sexual identities are culturally, constructed, then we need to
explore how specific gendered subjectivities are produced. Feminist poststructuralism
has been characterized by a concern with the formation and reformation of gendered
social subjectivities in fields of power and knowledge. Earlier I suggested that legal
scholars needed to reconceptualize subjectivity in a manner that avoided both liberalism and essentialism and recognized the discursive constitution of subjectivity. I think
this is particularly important for feminist legal scholars, for "one of the initial insights
of the women's movement and one of the tenets of feminist discourse – that the
personal is political – involves a recognition that there is a direct, albeit complex,
relation between social life and subjectivity and between language and consciousness.
The relation of experience to discourse is central to the very definition of feminism.
The parameters of feminism correspond to certain subjective limits, limitations on
possible subjectivities imposed by the constraints of language and sociohistorical structures of meaning. Within this range of constraints, however, women find possibilities
for new configurations of subjectivity . . ."[97] Feminist historian Joan Scott suggests
that we ask *how* categories of gender identity are constructed.[98] I take this question to
contemporary domains of popular culture to consider the possibilities for new configurations of gendered subjectivity emergent there.[99] The celebrity icon figures centrally in many constructions of alternative gender identities; the law simultaneously
enables and constrains these popular cultural practices. The law both engenders and

endangers the production of alternatively gendered subjectivities; fortunately, it can never fully contain or control the direction of this cultural energy.

The concept of alternative gender identities is borrowed from Judith Butler's pathbreaking work *Gender Trouble*,[100] in which she suggested that a feminist politics required an inquiry into the political construction and regulation of gendered identities, a radical critique of the limitations of existing categories of identity, and an exploration of practices in which alternatively gendered worlds are imagined. The practices I explore here are active gender performatives "that disrupt the categories of the body, sex, gender, and sexuality and occasion their subversive resignification and proliferation beyond the binary frame."[101] Before we delve into these, we might ask why Butler believed such practices to be politically significant. One problem that has plagued feminist theory has been the effort to locate a common identity for a feminist politics. Traditionally presupposing "some existing identity, understood through the category of women, who not only initiates feminist interests and goals within discourse, but constitutes the subject for whom political representation is pursued,"[102] feminist theory has been challenged by poststructuralist theorists suspicious of the category of the subject, and by those (women) who refuse the category (woman) as insufficient to represent the complexity of their political identities.

Theoretically, Butler accepted the Foucauldian claim[103] that systems of power *produce* the subjects they supposedly served to represent, and they did so through political practices of domination and exclusion.[104] The feminist subject may "be discursively constituted by the very political system that is supposed to facilitate its emancipation"[105] and may, then, be defined, limited, and restrained by the requirements of these structures of power. Empirically, the insistence on a stable subject of feminism "generates multiple refusals to accept the category"[106] and "feminism thus opens itself to charges of gross misrepresentation."[107] Butler engaged in a genealogical critique to expose the foundational categories of sex, gender, and desire as the artifacts of a patriarchal, heterosexist system of power, invested in the maintenance of an exclusively or primarily reproductive sexuality.

Feminist theory long recognized a distinction between sex and gender, asserting "that whatever biological intractibility sex appears to have, gender is culturally constructed."[108] Even if we assume the stability of binary sex, it does not follow that genders will accrue to sexed bodies in a one-to-one mimetic relationship (i.e., that "women" will interpret only "female" bodies). The recognition of gender as cultural construct enables the possibility of a multiplicity of genders, and also raises the question of whether sex itself may not be produced through the limitations that restrict the performance of gender to a binary economy. In other words, if gender is a cultural or discursive construction, it is perhaps this very act of production that establishes sex as a "natural" fact, and provides the means by which it could be established differently. For Butler, identity is *articulated* from within existing cultural forms; regimes of power institute, maintain, and stabilize naturalistic and causal relations of coherence among and between sex, gender, sexual desire, and sexual practice, but such correspondences are neither "natural" nor inevitable.[109] Other identities that express discontinuous relations between biological sex, cultural gender, and the "expression" or "effect" of these in sexual desire and practice are persistent; their proliferation may provide critical opportunities for subverting and denaturalizing the cultural matrix that supports heterosexual and medicojuridical hegemonies.[110]

Gender, then, is *performative* (but not a performance), a doing and constituting of the identity it is purported to be: "there is no gender identity beyond the expressions of gender; that identity is performatively constituted by the very 'expressions' that are said to be its results."[111] Such enactments must of necessity draw upon existing cultural forms; sexuality and gender are always constructed within the terms of discourse and power, and thus must engage heterosexual cultural conventions:[112] "If sexuality is culturally constructed within existing power relations, then the postulation of a normative sexuality that is 'before,' 'outside,' or 'beyond' power is a cultural impossibility and a politically impracticable dream, one that postpones the concrete and contemporary task of rethinking subversive possibilities for sexuality and identity within the terms of power itself."[113]

Butler is interested in modes of "doing" gender that evoke but do not constitute simple imitations, reproductions, and consolidations of the terms of power but displace, subvert, and confuse the very constructs they mobilize, "displacing those naturalized and reified notions of gender that support masculine hegemony and heterosexist power."[114] The constructed character of sex and gender provides conditions of possibility for their deconstruction; as ongoing discursive practices, they are open to intervention and resignification. For example, "numerous lesbian and gay discourses understand lesbian and gay culture as embedded in the larger structures of heterosexuality even as they are positioned in subversive or resignificatory relationships to heterosexual cultural configurations."[115] The repetition of heterosexual cultural forms *may* also be the site of their denaturalization, bringing "into relief the utterly constructed status of the so-called heterosexual original."[116] As we shall see, celebrity images provide important cultural resources for practices of "doing" gender that subvert and reconstruct dominant forms of gender identity. Such practices, which do not choose, in any voluntarist or intentional way, to resist the normalization of sex/gender,[117] nonetheless pose the promise of an alternatively gendered world that displaces heterosexist cultural conventions even as it ironically evokes their forms.

Respecting Judy

The denaturalization of heterosexual cultural forms is readily apparent in gay camp subculture, a phenomenon I have already alluded to as involving an engagement with media-disseminated celebrity images. Andrew Ross argued that gay camp had a significant influence on changing social definitions of masculinity and femininity from the late 1950s, working "to destabilize, reshape and transform the existing balance of accepted sexual roles and sexual identities."[118] Whatever its ultimate cultural effects, its origins must be understood in the context of gay urban life in the preliberation period. In the 1950s and '60s, a sophisticated gay male subculture evolved around a fascination with classical Hollywood film stars such as Judy Garland, Bette Davis, Mae West, Greta Garbo, and Marlene Dietrich. As Richard Jackson put it, "in an age when their ability to be open about the fact that they were gay was circumscribed, gay men's 'use' of certain star images constituted a kind of 'going public' or 'coming out.' "[119] Camp contained a kind of commentary on the ongoing feat "of survival in a world dominated by the tastes, interests, and definitions of others":[120] "In its pre-Stonewall heyday (before 'gay' was self-affirming) [camp] was part of a survivalist culture which found in certain fantasmatic elements of film culture a way of imaginatively communicating its common conquest of everyday oppression. In the gay camp subculture, glamorous images culled straight from Hollywoodiana were appropriated and used to express a different relation to the experience of alienation and exclusion in a world socially polarized by fixed sexual labels. Here, a tailored fantasy, which never 'fits' the real, is worn in order to suggest an imaginary control over circumstances."[121]

This is explicated by Esther Newton, whose ethnographic study of drag queens and urban camp subculture in the late 1960s indicates that camp humor grew out of the incongruities of living gay and male in a patriarchal and heterosexist society during a period when the stigma of being gay was largely accepted and internalized rather than rejected as illegitimate. Drag queens were homosexual men performing the social character of "women" (that is, the signs and symbols of a socially defined American category) by artifically creating the image of glamorous women (often celebrities publicly affirmed as glamorous). Drag queens were often preeminent "camps," engaging the opposition between inner (subjective) self and outer (social) self in an assertive, theatrical, humorous, and stylized manner that defined a creative strategy for dealing with the homosexual situation.[122] As a practice, drag may perform a subtle social critique:

> the effect of the drag system is to wrench the sex roles loose from that which supposedly determines them, that is, genital sex. Gay people know that sex-typed behavior can be achieved, contrary to what is popularly believed. They know that the possession of one type of genital equipment by no means guarantees the "naturally" appropriate behavior . . . one of the symbolic statements of drag is to question the "naturalness" of the sex role system in *toto*; if sex role behavior can be achieved by the "wrong" sex, it logically follows that it is in reality also achieved, not inherited, by the "right" sex . . . [it] says that sex-role behavior is an appearance [or performance].[123]

Stars who were most popular in the camp pantheon, and the subject of most frequent impersonation, were "glamorous" in highly mannered ways that indicated an awareness of the artifice in which they were engaged: Bette Davis, Mae West, Greta Garbo, Marlene Dietrich, and, to a lesser extent, Marilyn Monroe. The most popular stars were those who acted in subtle ways "against the grain of the sexually circumscribed stereotypes they were contracted to dramatize."[124] This celebration of the personas of those "whose screen identities could not be fixed by the studio machine,"[125] who often fought for their own roles[126] and subtly mocked the "corny flamboyance of femaleness . . . defetishized the erotic scenario of woman as spectacle."[127] Thus, they explored the relation between artifice and nature in the construction of sexuality and gender long before these issues were recognized as part of the political agenda: "To nonessentialist feminism and the gay camp tradition alike, the significance of particular film stars lies in their challenges to the assumed naturalness of gender roles . . . Each demonstrates how to *perform* a particular representation of womanliness, and the effect of these performances is to demonstrate, in turn, why there is no 'authentic' femininity, why there are only representations of femininity, socially redefined from moment to moment."[128]

Greta Garbo, for example, was (and perhaps still is) regarded in the gay community as "high camp," according to Newton; as Parker Tyler put it, "Garbo 'got in drag' whenever she took some heavy glamour part, whenever she melted in or out of a man's arms, whenever she simply let that heavenly flexed neck . . . bear the weight of her thrown-back head . . . it is all impersonation whether the sex underneath is true or not."[129] Just as the covert homosexual must impersonate a "man" (or that social role as defined by the straight world), Garbo playing a "woman" was in drag, and life was theater. (As a performance, rather than a performative, such activities might simply reinforce and reidealize normative sex/gender systems, however.)

Judy Garland had a special place in gay culture as the symbol gay men used in the pre-Stonewall period to speak to each other about themselves.[130] She also symbolizes an important historical era. The period of camp's heyday is punctuated by Garland's repeated suicide attempts (1950–1969), and the Stonewall riots (which inaugurated a new gay political praxis and a rejection of camp) took place on the evening of Garland's funeral. Moreover, Garland occupies a unique role "expressing camp attitudes" because of her repeated shows of resilience in the face of oppression, her strength in the face of suffering, her determination to carry on with the performance no matter how exhausting and debilitating, and the disparity between her ordinariness in film roles and her extraordinary private life.[131] All of this resonated with gay men living on the edge between a stigmatized gay identity and the daily fragile performance of passing for straight.[132] Her failure at femininity and the hints of gender androgyny in her film performances also served to make the Garland image a compelling vehicle for gay men to use as a means of going public or coming out before less heavily coded assertions of identity became possible.[133]

Camp lost its appeal with the arrival of a militant gay politics that asserted the "natural" quality of homosexuality, revived "masculine" styles, and sought to undermine the "effeminacy" of the stereotypical gay image. As Al La Valley noted in 1985, the movement from negotiating gay sexual desire through strong women stars to a more direct appreciation of male celebrities was coincident with Stonewall: "the natural-man discourse with its strong political and social vision and its sense of a fulfilled and open self, has supplanted both the aesthetic and campy discourses."[134] The finale of Michel Tremblay's acclaimed play *Hosanna*[135] well illustrates the new attitude toward camp. Hosanna, an aging drag queen who identifies with and projects her identity upon Elizabeth Taylor, is humiliated and forced to renounce her attachment to the star and disarm herself of her Taylor impersonation. Stripped naked, he declares "I'm a man," and, at long last, it is implied, allows his lover to embrace his "true" "masculine" self. Camp has, however, enjoyed something of a resurgence in the 1980s, confluent, perhaps, with the influence of Foucault, poststructuralism, and a revival of the credibility of the notion of the socially constructed subject and the historical contingency of sexual identities. Judy Garland has survived the vicissitudes of gay politics, continuing as an icon of struggle into the 1990s. As Douglas Crimp writes of his longtime friend, "quintessential gay activist turned AIDS activist"[136] Vito Russo, "a very funny queer": "Reminiscing about Vito's pleasure in showing movies at home to his friends and about his unashamed worship of Judy Garland, Arnie summed up Vito's brand of gay militancy (or perhaps I should say, his gay brand of militancy): 'In Vito's house,' Arnie quipped, 'either you respected Judy . . . or you left.'[137]

Lesbian engagement with celebrity images is a less documented and more recent phenomenon (although, as well shall see, "Judy" also has a certain significance here). Just as gays dignified and reclaimed Garland from the clutches of the star-making machinery that victimized her, there is some indication of lesbian identification with and resurrection of sixties female pop stars and "girl groups." In Toronto a band called the Nancy Sinatras reworks her songs and in a Queer Culture skit give Sinatra a lesbian identity and the opportunity to strike back at the patriarchal figures who controlled, contained, and ultimately, they suggest, crushed her in the sixties.[138]

> nine women, speaking singly or in groups, tell the story of an evening at the Lower East Side performance space P.S.122 when lesbian comedian Reno was performing. What made the occasion worth talking about was that someone special was in the audience . . . Nancy leaned over to say, "Fran Liebowitz is over there . . ." "We're both, you know, we both kinda have a thing for Fran . . . there was a commotion on the stairway as the audience was leaving . . . and all I see is this giant hair. It's almost like it could have been hair on a stick passing by, this platinum huge thing on this little black spandex." In case we haven't yet figured out what the commotion is about, Zoe adds another little clue: "I turned around, and I saw her breasts, I saw this cleavage, I saw this endowment, and, oh my God, I saw the hair, and it was . . . Dolly Parton."[139]

Crimp proposes that the discussion in the video isn't really about Dolly Parton but about gossip and its significance in the construction of lesbian subjectivity and visibility; "Dolly is the absence around which a representation of lesbianism is constituted."[140] Communities are always constructed around identifications of particular kinds. Although Dolly Parton's rumored lesbianism makes her a more likely choice of object,

> the emphasis on signifiers of Dolly's feminine masquerade – huge hair, huge cleavage, tiny spandex miniskirt – by a group of women whose masquerade differs so significantly from hers implicates their identifications and their desire in difference. None of the lesbians visable . . . looks femme like Dolly; compared with her absent image, they are in fact a pretty butch bunch. Identification, is, of course, identification with an other, which means that identity is never identical with itself. This alienation of identity from the self it constructs, which is a constant replay of a primary psychic self-alienation, does not mean simply that any proclamation will be only partial, that it will be exceeded by other *aspects* of identity, but rather that identity is always a relation, never simply a positivity . . . perhaps we can begin to rethink identity politics as a politics of relational identities formed through political identifications that constantly remake those identities.[141]

Gossip, he suggests, serves important functions in the construction and reconstruction of queer identities. The experience of recognizing oneself when someone else is gossiped about as a fag or a dyke ("So that's what I am") enables identifications to emerge from derogations, confirmed as self-derogations that are then positively nuanced in queer communities through new identifications forged in gossip.[142] Such gossip often involves celebrities; their circulation makes them shared cultural knowledge, and the esteem in which they are generally held, as well as the iconic and semiotic dimensions of their personas, invite such identifications.

Fictionalized sexualities

> There is nothing much deader than a dead motion picture actor, and yet
> . . . – John Dos Passos, *Midcentury*[143]

> . . . more than any time since the fifties, James Dean now represents *the* coherent icon of our time. He is an American object whose nature is condensed energy, an objectification of attitudes simple and immediate enough to become a brand whose implicit value, like the Coke bottle, is reinforced through repetition . . . In the eighties, Levi Strauss made a series of commercials using James Dean look-alikes . . . one of the commercials features an actress wearing a cowboy hat and Levi jeans, with her boots up in an antique Rolls Royce convertible – imitating the classic James Dean pose in *Giant*. – David Dalton, *James Dean: The Mutant King*[144]

One lesbian challenge to the "truth" of sex, gender, and desire and the restrictions of a binary sexual economy is given voice and celebrated by Sue Golding in her discussion of a performative gender identity she calls lesbian hermaphrodism.[145] This "erotic sensibility," worn, felt, and enacted by a number of lesbians, is a "fictionalized sexuality" that finds its performative significations in mass-media icons that it replicates in ironic, playful, and assertive reconfigurations:[146]

> no tits, no cock, oozing with a kind of vulnerable "masculinity," sheathed in a 50's style black-leather motorcycle jacket. Or to put it slightly differently, it's James Dean, with a clit . . . What emerges is the "virile girl," the butch baby, full of attitude but not of scorn, lots of street smarts and a bit of muscle. This new hermaphrodite embodies forever the image of the destructive adolescent dramatically and in one being, teeming with a creative, raw-energy, and beckoning with the possibility of a new era. She's the Peter Pan who reaches puberty and survives – her boyhood and her cunt intact, and ready. Most of all, she's public. But she's public in quite a different sense than meaning simply "out of the closet." For she is the orphan of a people's imaginary; a peculiar offspring of the avant-garde art world, the butch 50's "diesel dyke," and that kind of feminism which knew above all that sexual difference was ever only a *political* and not biological category. She is public in the most profound sense of the term: a composite copy of a mass invention, a replica of our own societal icons, which are themselves never anything other than a public fiction. She is James Dean over and over again: James Dean with his arrogant hair, James Dean with his tight black denims, James Dean with the bitter brat look,

James Dean with the morbid leather boots, James Dean against the whole boring suburban middle class . . .[147]

As Golding makes clear, this is an erotic sensibility or sexual identity that rejects the truth of anatomical sex and goes well beyond the idea of gender as a cultural construction built upon a naturally sexed body that provides a politically neutral surface for multiple significations. Or, as Butler poses it:

> The cultural matrix through which gender identification has become intelligible requires that certain kinds of "identities" cannot "exist" – that is, those in which gender does not follow from sex, and those in which the practices of desire do not "follow" from either sex or gender . . . Indeed, precisely because certain kinds of "gender identities" fail to conform to those norms of cultural intelligibility, they appear only as developmental failures or logical impossibilities from within that domain. Their persistence and proliferation, however, provide critical opportunities to expose the limits and regulatory aims of that domain of intelligibility, and, hence, to open up within the very terms of that matrix of intelligibility rival and subversive matrices of gender disorder.[148]

Demonstrating that gender identity (construed as a causal or natural relationship among sex, gender, sexual practice, and desire) is the effect of a regulatory practice that reproduces medical and juridical hegemonies, this gender rebel without a cause also rejects prior forms of "gender trouble" that accepted and worked within the terms of the natural sex/cultural gender dichotomy. This hermaphrodism bears no relation to a biological hermaphrodism "connected to some formulaic equation of the x and y chromosome, scientifically tested in relation to the size and shape of the breast and clitoris"[149] (except insofar as nineteenth-century science labeled *all* women hermaphroditic whose sexual orientation was nonheterosexual, insufficiently submissive, or masturbatory). Neither, Golding makes it clear, is this a '60s androgny that built around an absence or sameness of the sexual organs, nor a '70s sexual aesthetic "born out of an acknowledged irony of the ways in which society enforces gender specific clothing."[150] Rather, this gender rebel performs with her body an erotic identity that is an embodied performative: " 'a fiction as "real" as the specific body parts of her hermaphroditic predecessor. Only this time, her "truth," the clues to her sexual transgression will never be found in the physical attributes of her body *per se*, but only in their "look," only in the defiant aesthetic of the erotic masculine shot through with the voluptuousness of the female sexual organs' [and] 'the celebration of female genitalia' that refuses definition as 'a bleeding wound of castrated cock.' "[151] An "erotic mutant," "a fractured playfulness of social icons [like the Dean image, although Elvis Presley offers other possibilities, as k. d. lang might suggest] copied over and over again,"[152] the lesbian hermaphrodite enacts a performative signification that parodies, proliferates, and subverts gendered meanings. To what extent this particular performative engenders communities as well as identifications, however, is never made clear.

"Doing gender" is not the exclusive preserve of gays and lesbians, however more likely the social conditions of their existence are to incline them to contest hegemonic norms of gender identity. This will be clarified by an examination of the activities of certain groups of North American science fiction fans who articulate new gender identities and construct communities by literally rewriting their favorite television series characters into narratives that express their fears and aspirations.

Enterprising women

The science fiction fan world structures itself around a series of conventions; media fans constitute a distinct fan world and *Star Trek* is one of a number of television and movie series around which a fan community has emerged. *Star Trek* fans constitute a social and cultural network that is international in scope. Within this community itself, there are distinct groups of fans that organize around the production, circulation, and consumption of fan magazines.[153] The fanzine community is almost exclusively female and predominantly heterosexual. It involves middleclass women who work as housewives and in nursing, teaching, and clerical and service occupations.[154] Fans exchange letters, distribute newsletters, create artworks, make videotapes, and produce and circulate fanzines that contain original fiction, poetry, and illustrations by women across North America, Britain, and Australia. I will focus here on the *Star Trek* fanzine community, a subculture explored with great sensitivity by Camille Bacon-Smith in her sparkling ethnography *Enterprising Women*.[155] As well as attending conventions, fanzine community members may belong to clubs that distribute newsletters, and see themselves as members of a larger fan community or interest group (250 to 500 participants) and its constituent parts — local circles (of ten to thirty women) who gather at weekend house parties where they talk, watch videos, read fanzines, work out stories, and establish interpretive norms for their reading and writing activities.[156]

Usually produced out of women's homes, fanzines are generally mimeographed or photocopied productions, but some have become more sophisticated with the introduction of computerized desktop publication technology; most issues are more than a hundred pages long.[157] In 1988, it was estimated that there were 300 publications that enabled fans to explore aspects of television series, 120 of them centered on *Star Trek*,[158] a number that no doubt *underestimates* the production of fan literature because it doesn't include literature circulated only in photocopy circuits or the more covertly circulated publications.[159] These publications are sold at cost, relying on subscriptions and often prepayment to finance production and distribution costs; producers are motivated more by the desire to express identity and establish community than any monetary interest and often operate at a loss.[160] Fans are aware of the copyright status of the source products on which they draw and know that neither writers nor publishers may legally profit from their work.

In their writings and drawings, contributors to the fanzine employ images, themes, and characters from a canonized set of mass-culture texts (the *Star Trek* television series episodes, films, and commercially produced novels) to explore their own subordinate status, voice frustration and anger with existing social conditions, envision and construct alternatives, share new understandings, and express utopian aspirations.[161] In so doing, they force media texts to accommodate their interests, to become relevant to their needs, and thereby empower themselves with mass-culture images. In their creative reworking of *Star Trek* imagery, fanzines create new female communities, new personal identities, and, I will argue, alternative gender identities. These activities create new relationships between those who contribute to fanzines and the larger world, forge a sense of community and extensive social networks, and provide new possibilities for individual expression.[162] Above all, these are shared *social* activities:

> Elaine Showalter picks up the metaphor of quilt-making when she des-
> cribes women writing commercially and her analysis applies equally to fan
> writers. Using well known communal patterns, the craftsperson creates a
> work like a quilt top, unique in the way it combines the familiar elements
> with the distinctly personal statement she makes through her selection of
> elements . . . Women fan-writers, like the women who wrote gothic
> romances in the 1850's, value their workmanship in the community, but
> place little or no emphasis on the concept of "auteur" as solitary creator of
> an aesthetically unique piece of art. In the fan community, fiction creates
> the community. Many writers contribute their work out of social obliga-
> tion, to add to the discourse, to communicate with others. Creativity lies
> not in how a writer breaks with the tradition of the community's work,
> but in how she uses the language of the group to shed a brighter light on
> the truth they work to communicate. Commercial television fits uniquely
> into this scheme of women's culture . . . television is a readily available
> source of infinitely combinable but specifically not unique elements. They
> borrow wholesale from the television sources [to construct fictional "uni-
> verses" with which they organize their own social worlds].[163]

Star Trek fans characterize their entry into fandom as a movement from the social and cultural isolation imposed on them (both as women in patriarchal society occupy-ing low-paid jobs and as seekers of pleasure within media representations) toward more active participation in a community where cultural creativity is encouraged and appreciated.[164] *Star Trek* episodes and characters are revised and reworked and new texts are authored to reclaim female interests, experiences, and feelings from a set of common references that women separated by great distances can share. Issues of gender roles, sexuality, and the tension between family obligations and professional ambition are explored. The *Star Trek* future world holds out the promise of opportun-ities for nontraditional female pleasures, active involvement in decision making, and a state of sexual equality in which emotional needs and professional responsibilities are taken seriously by men and women alike.[165]

Many early stories featured a young, well-educated woman who was desirable, competent, and moral, simultaneously winning the love and respect of the *Enterprise* crew and ultimately the romantic interest of one of the major male characters. These "Mary Sue" stories, however, produced great discomfort and ambivalence in the community, although most fan writers have written at least one, usually early in their careers.[166] Contemporary fanzine editors now refuse to publish them. Bacon-Smith suggests that in this writing, women are engaged in re-creating adolescent selves that they may now feel shame or pain in recalling:

> Fans often recount the scorn they experience for their "masculine" interest
> in science fiction and action adventure. These readers grew up in a period

during which active, even aggressive behavior was acceptable for prepubescent girls who were expected to put away their grubby corduroys and baseballs, their books that chronicled the male fantasies of exploration and adventure, when they entered adolescence. With the teen years girls were expected to turn to make up, curlers, and high heel shoes to attract the attention of boys . . . The teenaged girl had to be not just seductive, but non-threatening; she could not challenge the supremacy of the male or in the classroom.[167]

Many women in fandom couldn't successfully make this transition – they were too tall, too "serious," wore glasses, were unable or unwilling to mask their intelligence – and "Mary Sue" reconciles the felt anomalies of their identity. Combining the characteristics of active agent with culturally approved traits of beauty, sacrifice, and self-effacement, she wins the love of the hero: "We can easily see that Mary Sue is a fantasy of the perfect woman created within the masculine American culture. Men are served by Mary Sue, who ideally minimizes her own value while applying her skills, and even offering her life, for the continued safety and ease of men. Even in her superiority Mary Sue must efface her talents with giggles and sophomoric humor. She must deny that her solutions to problems are the result of a valid way of thinking, modestly chalking up successes to intuition."[168] "The writer, become reader, recognizes Mary Sue's childish behavior as a coping mechanism she has used herself or observed in her friends to mask the threat their own intelligence and competence poses to men."[169] But once in fandom, women encourage each other to leave such camouflage behind and construct alternative roles: "Women in the fan community have rejected Mary Sue and the cultural role of precocious child, and in many cases have replaced her with the Matriarch in the genre referred to as "Lay" stories, so named because the alter-ego heroine develops a sexual relationship with the hero. Her adventures are an adjunct to his world and her demeanor is one of matriarchal dignity outside of the bedroom and politically correct sensuality within it."[170]

In "Lay" stories, however, women appear to be more engaged in rewriting the masculine gender than in imagining alternative feminine ones. In particular, the stories teach women how to deal with male sexuality – an uncontrolled or unpredictable internal physical urge coupled with a controlled, emotionless exterior. The female heroine is an intelligent, supportive woman who (often after a period of subjugation and oppression) helps her partner to accept his emotions and recognize that true love and sexual satisfaction grow out of mutual respect and trust. Even these women, however, are being increasingly dismissed as falling into the contemptuous category of Mary Sue, and the lack of strong female characters in most fanzines "signals a continuing dissatisfaction with the options available to women characters and to women in society."[171]

Stories focusing on women represent very few of the stories fanziners read and many more stories involve male friendships. Two significant genres of fanzine fiction are "Slash" (or homoerotic) and "Hurt/Comfort" stories, both of which center on relationships between the male characters in the series. In all of these stories, the links among anatomy, gender, desire, and sexual practice are sundered. In the male friendship stories, the male characters are alternatively engendered; stripping them of a rationalist, ego-centered individualism, the fans imbue them with emotionality and empathy, knitting them into close family and community relationships as well as intimate caring friendships that nurture and support them in their adventures.[172]

In "Slash" fiction, women write erotic stories and draw illustrations depicting a love relationship between Kirk and Spock (erotic fiction is also written about the *Starsky and Hutch*, *Blake's 7*, *The Man From U.N.C.L.E*, *Miami Vice*, and *The Professionals* characters). Fearing social ridicule, loss of employment, and potential legal repercussions, fanzine writers often write such stories under pseudonyms, although within the community most of the authors' identities are known. Some of this literature circulates only through complex subterranean photocopying networks in order to evade exposure outside of the group.[173] So well-hidden is the circuit that only the most experienced readers and writers have access to it. Within this realm of secrecy and risk women explore and express personally painful and significant themes: "Homoerotic fiction addresses some of the most risk-laden questions in the community. It protects the questioner from direct exposure of some of her deeper anxieties, but conserves the risk with a level of metaphor that offers the greatest distance but which itself poses the greatest danger from within and without the community."[174] Some fans oppose these stories on religious or moral grounds, others find them "untrue" to the source or canon, some find them too explicit, and others worry about exposing the original actors to ridicule. Both outside and within the community, writing "Slash" fiction is risky business. Similarly, in the relationships depicted, "romantic love is fraught with risk – of trust broken, of exposure or even loss of the self, of society's disapproval, or of misinterpretation of the intent of the partner – and the prize for risking all is perfect physical and psychic fulfillment,"[175] represented by the mind meld or telepathic union.

Bacon-Smith describes a number of tasks performed by the homoerotic romance in the communication of personal needs and experiences and rejects the idea that the male characters are surrogate women, an idea popularized by Joanna Russ when she argued that because of the overriding importance of touch, to the slow thoroughness and sensitization of the whole body, the sexuality expressed is female.[176] For Russ, "the penis is a sign, literally, behind which the woman can express femaleness free of male domination."[177] Bacon-Smith, however, asserts that these women are writing consciously and deliberately about men,[178] exploring who men are and reconstructing them into people with whom it might be more comfortable to share life, love, and sexual relationships.[179] Certainly, "sexual experiences with men, as they are presently enculturated, can seem intimidating to heterosexual women," and a number of fans "openly express a need for more satisfying sexual relationships."[180] These women also want to explore relationships between powerful equals while tearing "down the very institution of hierarchical power that constructs men as individuals" – reconstructing power itself as an integrated union of mutuality with full and open communication.[181]

In both "Slash" fiction and "Hurt/Comfort" stories,[182] as well as the friendship stories described earlier, the "male" characters are given a combination of gender traits: Kirk's "feminine" traits are matched to Spock's "masculine" ones and vice versa. Each shares aspects of traditional gender roles. In this way, new genders are inscribed on "male" bodies, and new desires, experiences, feelings, and practices may therefore proliferate.[183] Men's suffering, rage, and need for comfort can thus be acknowledged as well as male violence and the need that women feel to be the recipients as well as the bestowers of comfort.[184]

As well as being alternatively engendered, the male characters are freshly embodied; their bodies are inscribed with ranges of sensitivity, zones of erogeneity, and a heightened receptivity to tactile pleasures and physical comfort: "women in the fan community prefer images that reclaim the sensuality of the whole body . . . hands are perceived as sensual, and faces as vulnerable, hands touching a face in an environment of trust symbolize sensuality as protective . . . kisses to the neck, the wrists, the inner arm elicit as strong a reaction as mouth to mouth osculation; women viewers seem to value the rediscovery of some of these more neglected erogenous zones."[185] Their heroes' pain, decontextualized in the mass media, is reunited by fanzine writers with both physical and psychological suffering. The male characters, then, are reconstructed as fully emotional and sentient beings. Perhaps the fanzine writers perform the most thorough practices of "doing gender" that we have examined. Constructing new connections among novel (male?) bodies, new masculinities, erotic desires, and sexual practices, they simultaneously situate these newly engendered creatures in personal and social relationships, empowering themselves and their communities as they do so.

In writing about gender and fanzines as an academic engaged in the production of an authorial work, however, one's authority and one's work are themselves open to the subversion of other authorial energies. Postmodernism is a condition in which genres blur, popular culture and high culture dance seductively, academic commentators can become celebrities, and academic critique can itself become the stuff of parody and fanzine fantasy. One fanzine has turned Judith Butler's own persona into a celebrity image available for the fantastic fabulations of its apparently lesbian graduate student readership. Simply titled *Judy*, the first issue proudly proclaims that all of its texts are anticopyright: "Copy this whole thing if you want; send it to your friends, that's cool – saves me money. Isn't this whole copyright thing out of hand? Go ahead, copy it at Kinko's."[186]

The fanzine features two pictures of Judy Garland with the apology that "it's really hard to find pictures of Judith Butler so here is another Judy."[187] It also features ironic and lusty commentary on several other theorists of gender and sexuality. Declaring itself "a non-academic, sex-oriented, wish-fulfillment magazine,"[188] it includes, in true *Cosmopolitan*® fashion, a special quiz to determine whether you're "a theory-fetishizing biscuithead" or "an illiterate pre-theory peon." This author finds herself guilty, as charged.

Engendering and endangering alternative identities

> . . . the very conceptualization of "sex" and "gender" underlying legal categorization creates difficulties that cannot be resolved through resort to static, binary, essentialized approaches. Instead . . . it will be necessary to challenge the system of classification itself in fundamental ways to take account of the ambiguities of homosexual and transsexual identity . . . these identities [are] themselves a challenge to the stable system of identity formulation that lies at the heart of U.S. legal discourse – a challenge that could be destablizing if not contained – Elizabeth Mertz on Lisa Bower, in "A New Social Constructionism for Socio-legal Studies"[189]

These subcultural or alter/native practices at first seem distant, if not divorced, from the legal regime of publicity rights, but they do occupy cultural spaces in the social fabric intersected and influenced by relations of law, commodification, and cultural form. We need to think about law not simply as a set of prohibitions, but as an authoritative and pervasive discourse that defines, shapes, and is imbricated within the everyday life of cultural practice. The risks these people run under legal regimes of prohibition *are* certainly significant ones. So are the ethical risks of writing about their practices. Bacon-Smith, Jenkins, and Penley have been very careful not to reveal details about or examples of particular fanzine writing, filming, and drawing practices or the identities of practitioners. I respect their circumspection and similarly will not, as a matter of ethical principle, delineate the precise ways in which fanzine writers or those in gay and lesbian subcultures could be held to violate either publicity rights or the copyright and trademark rights held by the commercial producers of the media products on which they draw. To do so would be to provide the legal resources with which to prosecute them, or with which they might once again be threatened with the prospect of legal action.[190]

It is important, however, to recognize that juridical power is productive as well as prohibitive; the law, as discursive cultural practice, is generative of categories, distinctions, and valuations – of knowledges, spaces, identities, and subjectivities.[191] As Lisa Bower suggests, law simultaneously limits the aspirations and claims of individuals and groups and provides resources for the marginalized to refigure identities; people recreate law in their everyday lives as they draw upon its norms and forms in both conventional and transformative practices.[192] Bower goes beyond such claims, however, to add that law also plays a constitutive role in creating cultural spaces for politicization and community formation.

The law of publicity rights functions in just such a fashion – or at least these are some of its unanticipated consequences. By prohibiting public reproductions of the celebrity image for another's advantage, it promotes the mass circulation of celebrity signifiers by ensuring that they will have a market value; if the image were freely available for mass reproduction, there would, presumably, be less of an incentive to engage in the investments necessary to disseminate it through media channels (the same argument might be made for copyright and trademark). Ironically, then, the law creates the cultural spaces of postmodernism in which mass-media images are authorized and become available for the authorial practices of others. It produces fixed, stable identities authored by the celebrity subject, but simultaneously creates the possibility of places of transgression in which the signifier's fixity and the celebrity's authority may be contested and resisted. Authorized and unauthorized identities are both, therefore, engendered in relation to this juridical regime. The law, however, lends its authority only to those meanings that the celebrity wishes to appropriate, attributing these to his or her own efforts, and denies that legitimate cultural value may be produced elsewhere.

Power may be in a productive relation with forms of resistance, but it does not determine the content of the practices that transgress its strictures. Through its prohibitions, the law may produce the means by which unauthorized identities are both engendered and endangered, but these practices are not simply effects or consequences of juridical regimes. People's interests and inclinations to engage in the construction of alternative gender identities are shaped by multiple hegemonies.

Performative enactments of erotic identity are unlikely to be direct or univocal statements of opposition to any singular structure of power; more often they effect diverse forms of cultural "resistance" to multiple sites and forms of power. Through irony, mockery, parody, pastiche, and even alternative modes of appreciation, activities of creative appropriation enable fans to comment indirectly not only on gender ideology, but on law, culture, authorship, authority, and the commodity form.

Such commentary is especially cogent in the fanzine context. Fans don't see *Star Trek* as something that can be reread but as something that must be rewritten in order to make it more responsive to female needs and a better producer of personal meanings and pleasures.[193] According to Henry Jenkins, fans expressly reject the idea that the *Star Trek* texts or the Kirk/Spock characters are a privileged form of exclusive property, but at the same time they have developed a complex moral economy[194] in which they legitimize their unorthodox appropriation of the texts, characters, and personas drawn from the television series. Despite the potential for legal prosecution, they see themselves as loyalists, fulfilling the inherent promise and potential of the series – a potential unrealized or betrayed by those who "own" the intellectual property rights in it. Fans respect the original texts, and regularly police each other for abuses of interpretive license, but they also see themselves as the legitimate guardians of these materials, which have too often been manhandled by the producers and their licensees for easy profits.[195] As one fan writes: "I think we have made Star Trek uniquely our own, so we have all the right in the world . . . to try to change it for the better when the gang at Paramount starts worshipping the almighty dollar as they are wont to do."[196] Fan writers exercise an ethic of care with regard to the characters – a care they fear that more commercially motivated parties frequently do not share.

In *Enterprising Women*, Bacon-Smith also illuminates the complexities of the attitudes fanziners hold with regard to the legal status of the source product. On the one hand, they are aware that the characters, plots, films, television episodes, videos, logos, and dialogues with which they work are the properties of others. On the other hand, they take quite seriously the philosophy of IDIC (Infinite Diversity in Infinite Combination), propagated by Gene Roddenberry, the originator of *Star Trek*. They respect the legal prohibition against selling their writings, videotapes, and artworks for profit, but the possibility that many of their activities might still be enjoined on copyright, trademark, or publicity rights grounds does not appear to operate as a serious deterrent. These women know they assume risks of legal prosecution, but legal risks are only a very few and possibly the most distant of the risks they face; indeed, Bacon-Smith implies that the assumption, management, and shared exploration of risk is the central ethos of the community and constitutive of the construction and reconstruction of culture in which they engage.

Bacon-Smith also discusses the moral economy in which fans operate (although she does not expressly employ the term). She suggests that fans have a respect for the characters and relationships as they are presented in the source product devised by the commercial producers, which serves as "the source of infinitely combineable but specifically not unique elements. A fan does not change the status of the characters by adding permanent wives or children, or killing or maiming one of the main characters. The writer works hard to create in her stories characters that speak like the ones on television, and whose personalities match the screen product.

Consonant with the science fiction assumption that any change from the known history splits off a timeline, or universe ongoing simultaneous to all others, writers who do permanently change the status of a character or characters are said to create a new universe . . . [creating] their own universes, with characters and relationships that exist only in the stories their creators write."[197]

There *are* aspects of the original story and episodes that fans reject, however. For example, fans insist upon seeing characters grow and evolve and engage in relationships that change them as people. They reject linear narratives, aperspectivity, and closure. They don't see either the original episodes or their own stories as a self-sufficient work but as an expression of a continuing experience. At the end of the story characters go on living and changing; later in their lives they may recall the events of the original story differently, or perhaps the events, told from the perspective of another character, tell a different story. There is, then, no final or authoritative account of an event or experience; stories can and must be rewritten according to new perspectives: "The linear story with a single narrative perspective per scene is so alien to this group that they use their fiction to 'correct' the error of linearity in the source products. The fan writers see life as a sea of potentialities, many of which can be realized simultaneously, many of which spread out like ripples across the lives of others, and all of which must somehow be encompassed in the literature if it is to express any kind of truth . . . a worldview that sees every interaction as a multi-layered experience out of which reality is negotiated."[198]

Fans clearly engage in moral deliberation and dialogue when considering the legitimacy of particular activities. These amateur writers and the professional science fiction writers on whose works they have drawn have had to consider the vexed question of what distinguishes the activities of "a community in dialogue" from simple copyright infringement: "Many writers who express concern about the loss of autonomous control of their creation actually embrace the idea of sharing their worlds with their friends — we are not speaking of two groups of professional writers at odds, but of battles being waged within the heart and mind of each individual."[199]

Moreover, the fan community has a relationship with the stars of the various series from which they borrow. Although I know of no publicity rights suits, it is clear that celebrities regard these fan activities with some ambivalence. Stars are often asked to appear at conventions and many of them feel a sense of obligation to the fans for their support. Often they become aware of the fanzines and feel flattered by the attention. Robin Curtis (Saavik in the two *Star Trek* movies) said: "I really had no idea that this all existed . . . I don't know that I'll ever stop being amazed . . . really, the care and the time which people devote to something . . . It is really quite an honor to be the receiver of that kind of appreciation . . . [but] I haven't read it, to be honest with you."[200]

Other celebrities *have* read the literature and responses seem mixed. Constance Penley notes that Shatner and Nimoy have commented appreciatively on fanzines generally and found the homoerotic texts surprising but not inconceivable given what they now see as the "campiness" of some of the old episodes.[201] Other stars have viewed these texts less benignly. One actor in *Blake's* 7 encouraged fanzine writing, but upon discovering his fictive presence in homoerotic fiction, withdrew his support and attempted to blackball the writers within the fan community itself.[202] *Starsky and Hutch* fans worried that public exposure of "Slash" literature would hurt the reputations of stars they regarded with respect and affection; they insisted upon keeping the product underground to protect their heroes.[203]

Relations with the corporate producers of their source texts are more complex. Although some program producers and network executives celebrate the ongoing involvement of fans in the production of derivative texts, others see such activities as competitive and as threatening to their goodwill. In extreme cases, producers may try to bring fan activities under control:

> Lucasfilm initially sought to control *Star Wars* fan publications, seeing them as rivals to their officially sponsored and corporately run fan organization. Lucas later threatened to prosecute editors who published works that violated the "family values" associated with the original films. A letter circulated by Maureen Garrett (1981), director of the official *Star Wars* fan club, summarized the corporation's position: "Lucusfilm Ltd. does own all rights to the Star Wars characters and we are going to insist upon no pornography. This may mean no fanzines if that measure is necessary to stop the few from darkening the reputation our company is so proud of . . . You don't own these characters and can't *publish* anything about them without permission."[204]

Jenkins explores the ways in which the fan writing community responded to this threat, regarding it as "unwarranted interference in their own creative activity"[205] that attempted to impose male definitions of correct sexuality and prohibit works that explicitly challenged patriarchal assumptions. "Several fanzine editors continued to distribute adult-oriented *Star Wars* stories through an underground network of 'special friends,' even though such works were no longer publicly advertised or sold."[206]

Although fanziners, gay camps, and lesbian hermaphrodites are not necessarily engaged in practices directly opposing the law (however often they may unintentionally violate it), the law of publicity rights informs their performative activities. The knowledge that the cultural icons with which they express themselves do not belong to them, however affectionately they are adopted, is constitutive of these practices. The relationship of fans to the commodification of the texts and images whose meanings they simultaneously interpret and create may be one of admiration or antagonism, irony or parody, fear or nurturing, or even complicitous critique.[207] In any case, the law generates spaces for a proliferation of politics as well as identities, ethics as well as expressions, as people forge their own ethical distinctions between expression and theft, collectively negotiating community norms.

Legal forms and norms are socially engaged – embraced and rejected – in practices that do not seek legal recognition but do use legal narratives and forms in counterhegemonic activity. Such practices may coalesce, forging historically contingent (and continually emergent) identities and communities. It is in such activities that "culture" is made and "politics" practiced. Here, I am drawing upon an emergent conceptualization of politics that rejects the state as the singular site for identity claims and community coalition and transformation, and incorporates "the everyday enactment of social practices and the routine reiteration of cultural representations"[208] within its purview.

If we recognize the essence of democratic politics to be a dialogic process whereby social identities are actively articulated from contingent cultural or discursive resources, we must be sensitive to the critical role that commodified media texts – mass culture – play in shaping politically salient forms of difference. The subjects produced in popular cultural practice populate the social world with utopian and aspirational articulations. They pose the promise of an "alternatively gendered world" that displaces heterosexist cultural conventions even as it ironically evokes their forms. Those who control intellectual properties must always cope with the presence of others in the cultural spaces they attempt to colonize.

Notes

1   A character in N. Grieg and D. Griffiths, *As Time Goes By* (1981), cited in R. Dyer, *Heavenly Bodies: Film Stars and Society* 141 (1986).

2   A. McRobbie, *Postmodernism and Popular Culture* 70 (1994).

3   A. Doty, *Making Things Perfectly Queer: Interpreting Mass Culture* xviii–xix (1993).

4   M. Madow, "Private Ownership of Public Image: Popular Culture and Publicity Rights," 81 *California Law Review* 127, 173, n.229 (1993).

5   Throughout this chapter, I will use the term *celebrity image* to designate not only or exclusively a celebrity's visual likeness but rather all elements of the complex constellation of visual, verbal, and aural signs that circulate in society and constitute the celebrity's recognition value. The term *persona* will also refer to this configuration of significations.

6   I use the umbrella term *publicity rights* to encompass the tort of appropriation of personality as it has developed at common law, the proprietary right of publicity that has developed in U.S. law, and rights to prevent the appropriation of (*inter alia*) names and likenesses that have been enacted in provincial and state statutes as well as federal trademark legislation.

7   D. Vaver, "What's Mine Is Not Yours: Commercial Appropriation of Personality under the Privacy Acts of B.C., Manitoba and Saskatchewan," 15 *University of British Columbia Law Review* 241 (1981).

8   See American Law Institute, *Restatement (Second) of Torts* § 652A–652I (1977). Also, American Law Institute, *Restatement of the Law (Third) Unfair Competition* (1995) S. 46–49. As Christopher Pesce points out, the right of publicity is "a hybrid of privacy's tort of appropriation, the law of unfair competition, and the law of property" (C. Pesce, "The Likeness Monster: Should the Right of Publicity Protect Against Imitation?," 65 *New York University Law Review* 782, 792 [1990]).

9   See F.M. Weiler, "The Right of Publicity Gone Wrong: A Case for Privileged Appropriation of Identity," 13 *Cardozo Arts & Entertainment Law Journal* 223, 224–225, n. 14–17 (1994), for a list of state name-and-likeness statutes, a list of those states that have codified the right of publicity and recognize an independent common law right of publicity, a list of states that recognize the right only at common law, and the varying periods of protection afforded to the right in different American jurisdictions.

10   Trade Marks Act, R.S.C. 1985, c.T-13; Lanham Act, 15 U.S.C.A. § 1052.

11   L. Lawrence, "The Right of Publicity: A Research Guide," 10 *Hastings*

Communications and Entertainment Law Journal 143 (1987). See also F. Houdek, "The Right of Publicity: A Comprehensive Bibliography of Law-Related Material," 7 *Hastings Communications and Entertainment Law Journal* 505 (1985), and F. Houdek, "Researching the Right of Publicity: A Revised and Comprehensive Bibliography of Law Related Materials,"16 *Hastings Communications and Entertainment Law Journal* 385 (1994). Unfortunately, the latter author's summaries of the materials he includes are both inadequate and misleading.

12   Hirsch v. S. C. Johnson & Son, 90 Wis.2d 379, 280 N.W.2d 129 (1979) (athlete has right of publicity in his nickname "Crazylegs" and could sustain action against shaving gel manufacturer).

13   Cepeda v. Swift & Co., 291 F.Supp. 242 (E.D. Mo. 1968), aff'd, 415 F.2d 1205 (8th Cir. 1969); U.S. Life Insurance Co. v. Hamilton, 238 S.W.2d 289 (Tex. Civ. App.1951).

14   Athans v. Canadian Adventure Camps Ltd., 34 C.P.R.(2d) 126 (Ontario High Court 1977).

15   (1979) Lugosi v. Universal Pictures, 160 Cal. Rptr. 323.; Price v. Worldvision Enters., Inc., 455 F.Supp. 252 (S.D.N.Y. 1978) aff'd, 603 F.2d 214 (2d Cir. 1979); Price v. Hal Roach Studios, Inc., 400 F.Supp. 836 (S.D.N.Y. 1975).

16   Midler v. Ford Motor Co., 849 F.2d 460 (9th Cir. 1988) (singer awarded damages for television commercial's use of a "sound-alike" to imitate her voice and singing style).

17   In Lahr v. Adell Chemical Co., the court noted that Lahr had achieved stardom due to his "style of vocal delivery which, by reason of its distinctive and original combination of pitch, inflection, and comic sounds has caused him to become widely known and readily recognized." A television commercial using a similar voice was "stealing the thunder" of the performer (300 F.2d 256 (1st Cir. 1962) at 257).

18   Joseph v. Daniels, 11 C.P.R.(3d) 544 (B.C.S.C. 1986).

19   Carson v. Here's Johnny Portable Toilets, Inc., 698 F.2d 831 (6th Cir. 1983) (portable toilet manufacturer violated Johnny Carson's right of publicity by using phrase "Here's Johnny" with the slogan "The World's Foremost Comodian"); Ali v. Playgirl, 447 F.Supp. 723,3 *Media Law Reporter* (BNA) 2540, 206 U.S.P.Q. (BNA) 1021 (S.D.N.Y. 1978) (illustration depicting nude black male with caption "The Greatest" violated plaintiff's right of publicity because the phrase was known to be a common reference to the plaintiff).

20   Motschenbacher v. R. J. Reynolds Tobacco Co., 498 F.2d 821 (9th Cir. 1974) (plaintiff racing car driver had identifiable attributes appropriated because unique and distinctive decorations on his car were recognizable in cigarette commercial).

21   Lahr v. Adell Chemical Co., 300 F.2d 256 (1st Cir. 1962) (comic delivery style); Booth v. Colgate Palmolive Co., 362 F.Supp. 343 (S.D.N.Y. 1975) (imitation of Shirley Booth's voice and style of portraying television character Hazel).

22   Lombardo v. Doyle, Dane & Bernbach, Inc., 58 A.D. 2d 620, 396 N.Y.S. 2d 661 (N.Y. App. Div. 1977).

23   H. L. Hetherington, "Direct Commercial Exploitation of Identity: A New Age for the Right of Publicity," 17 *Columbia-VLA Journal of Law & the Arts* 1, 43 (1992).

24   See, e.g., J. R. Braatz, "White v. Samsung Electronics America: The Ninth Circuit Turns a New Letter in California Right of Publicity Law," 15 *Pace Law Review* 161 (1994); S. C. Clay, Note: "Starstruck: The Overextension of Celebrity Publicity

Rights in State and Federal Courts," 79 *Minnesota Law Review* 485 (1994); R. C. Dreyfuss, "We are Symbols and Inhabit Symbols, So Why Should We Be Paying Rent? Deconstructing the Lanham Act and Rights of Publicity," 20 *Columbia-VLA Journal of Law and the Arts* 123 (1996); P. B. Frank, Note: "White v. Samsung Electronics America Inc.: The Right of Publicity Spins Its Wheels," 55 *Ohio State Law Journal* 1115 (1994); W.M. Heberer, Comment: "The Overprotection of Celebrity: A Comment on White v. Samsung Electronics America, Inc." 22 *Hofstra Law Review* 279 (1994); Hetherington, *supra* note 23; J. F. Hyland and T. C. Lindquist III, "White v. Samsung Electronics America, Inc.: The Wheels of Justice Take an Unfortunate Turn," 23 *Golden Gate University Law Review* 299 (1993); D. R. Kelly and M. E. Hartmann, "Parody (of Celebrities, in Advertising), Parity (between Advertising and Other Types of Commercial Speech), and (the Property Right of) Publicity," 17 *Hastings Communications and Entertainment Law Journal* 633 (1995); Madow, *supra* note 4; G. A. Pemberton, "The Parodist's Claim to Fame: A Parody Exception to the Right of Publicity," 27 *University of California-Davis Law Review* 97 (1993); S. M. Perez, "Confronting Biased Treatment of Trademark Parody under the Lanham Act," 44 *Emory Law Journal* 1451 (1995); T. F. Simon, "Right of Publicity Reified: Fame as Business Asset," 30 *New York Law School Law Review* 699 (1985); L. J. Stack, "White v. Samsung Electronics America, Inc.'s Expansion of the Right of Publicity: Enriching Celebrities at the Expense of Free Speech," 89 *Northwestern University Law Review* 1189 (1995); Weiler, *supra* note 9. Most of these articles review the history of the doctrine and make suggestions for limiting the right of publicity and recognizing First Amendment concerns; I find many of the recommendations plausible and potentially effective, but my interest here does not center on law reform, but on the celebrity as a medium for the creation of alter/native identities. The slash here is meant to indicate that in the creation of such new identities, that which is "native" is altered. I prefer this to the term *subaltern*, for it suggests the potentially transformative effects that the margins may have upon the center and dominant understandings of what is natural or native to human being.

25   Canadian and British courts have not gone so far as to recognize the right as proprietary and continue to deal with it as a tort. This has not prevented celebrities from entering into licensing contracts and conveying merchandising rights, however.

26   American courts are divided on the issue of whether a right of publicity survives the individual's death and in what circumstances. Some courts have refused recovery for the relatives or assignees of a decedent where the name or likeness has been appropriated for commercial purposes on the grounds that an individual's personal right of privacy does not survive his or her death. Others have allowed recovery for invasion of privacy in similar circumstances. Decisions predicated upon rights of publicity range from those that hold that the right survives death in all circumstances, those that require the celebrity to have engaged in some form of commercial exploitation during his or her life before the right will be descendible, and those that unconditionally oppose descendibility in any circumstances. The tendency, however, has been toward greater recognition of the descendibility of publicity rights, and state legislatures have also inclined toward statutory recognition of the descendibility of such rights. The issue has yet to be determined or even seriously addressed in Canadian or British courts.

27   See discussion and cases cited in J. Gross, "The Right of Publicity Revisited: Reconciling Fame, Fortune, and Constitutional Rights," 62 *Boston University Law Review* 965 (1982), and R. T .E. Coyne, "Toward a Modified Fair Use Defense in Right of Publicity Cases," 29 *William & Mary Law Review* 781 (1988). In the case of celebrity images employed in commercial advertising, there are conflicting lines of authority. Historically, U.S. law accorded commercial advertising little or no value when it conflicted with an individual's privacy or publicity rights. Before 1976, this was consistent with the low constitutional value placed on commercial speech. As T. F. Haas, "Storehouse of Starlight: The First Amendment Privilege to Use Names and Likenesses in Commercial Advertising," 19 *University of California Law Review* 539 (1986) argues, however, the extension of limited First Amendment protection to commercial speech suggests that many of the cases involving appropriations of name and likeness in commercial advertising would now have to be decided differently.

28   D. Sudjic, *Cult Heroes: How to Be Famous for More than Fifteen Minutes* (1989). See also R. Schickel, *Intimate Strangers: The Culture of Celebrity, Where We Came In* (1985).

29   Sudjic, *supra* note 28, at 10.

30   *Ibid.*, at 15.

31   *Ibid.*, at 19.

32   *Ibid.*, at 83.

33   H. Gordon, "Right of Property in Name, Likeness, Personality and History," 55 *Northwestern University Law Review* 553, 555–557 (1960); Comment, "The Right of Publicity: Premature Burial for California Property Rights in the Wake of Lugosi," 12 *Pacific Law Journal* 987, 995–997 (1981).

34   D. Lange, "Recognizing the Public Domain," 44(4) *Law and Contemporary Problems* 147 (1981).

35   W. Gordon, "On Owning Information: Intellectual Property and the Restitutionary Impulse," 78 *Virginia Law Review* 149 (1992).

36   See M. Radin, "Market Inalienability," 100 *Harvard Law Review* 1859 (1987); M. Radin, *Contested Commodities* (1996); and E. Anderson, "Is Women's Labor a Commodity?," 19 *Philosophy and Public Affairs* 71 (1990), for philosophical discussions of the factors we need to weigh in determining if commodification is an appropriate mode of valuation.

37   Lange, *supra* note 34, cites S. J. Hoffman, "Limitations on the Right of Publicity," 28 *Bulletin of the Copyright Society* 111, 116–133 (1980), as asking a similar question. See also A. M. Weisman, "Publicity as an Aspect of Privacy and Personal Autonomy," 55 *Southern California Law Review* 727, 729–751 (1982).

38   J. Locke, *Second Treatise of Government*, ch. 5 (1978), [1690].

39   E. C. Hettinger, "Justifying Intellectual Property," 18 *Philosophy and Public Affairs* 31, 37 (1989).

40   For example, "the celebrity has invested time, money, and effort to develop a high level of public recognition. Therefore, the unauthorized use of the celebrity's persona . . . deprives the celebrity of the economic gain he or she deserves, unjustly enriches the user and reduces the celebrity's ability to control his or her public image" (A. Cifelli and W. McMurray, "The Right of Publicity – A Trademark Model for Its Temporal Scope," 66 *Journal of the Patent Office Society* 455, 462 [1984]).

41   Hettinger, *supra* note 39.

42   Dyer, *supra* note 1; and R. Dyer, *Stars* (1979).

43   D. MacCannell, "Marilyn Monroe Was Not a Man," 17 *Diacritics* 114, 115 (1987).

44   Hettinger, *supra* note 39, at 38.

45   Lange, *supra* note 34, at 162.

46   R. R. Kwall, "The Right of Publicity vs. the First Amendment: A Property and Liability Rule Analysis," 70 *Indiana Law Journal* 47 (1994). Professor Kwall's support of an "authorship rationale" for publicity rights is also shown in her belief that American copyright law in practice is inordinately concerned with pecuniary as opposed to personal interests and is to that extent incompatible with publicity rights protection. She suggests that *copyright theory*, to the extent that it acknowledges and protects an individual's authorial presence in his or her work and recognizes the personal interests of creators in their works, is compatible with publicity rights: "If copyrighted property can be said to represent the embodiment of a creator's heart, mind, and soul, this is even more true for attributes such as an individual's name and likeness that are protected by the right of publicity" (*ibid.*, at 59–60). The extent to which one's labor is embedded in one's name or likeness is questionable (except for some obvious examples), and a right to privacy, protection against defamation, and consumer protection laws would cover most objectionable usages of these attributes. Unfortunately, other attributes protected by rights of publicity go well beyond those that are most "personal" to include all attributes that are *publicly* recognized and hence, by virtue of mass exposure, the *least* intimate aspects of one's persona. The right, after all, does not protect one from alienation inasmuch as it fosters one's ability to engage in self-commodification.

47   523 F.Supp. 485 (S.D.N.Y. 1981), 689 F.2d 317 (2d Cir. 1982).

48   *Ibid.*, 523 F.Supp. 485, 492–494.

49   See T. Podlesney, "Blondes," in *The Hysterical Male: New Feminist Theory* 82 (A. Kroker and M. Kroker, eds., 1991), who argues that "the blonde" is the perfect post-WWII product and the ultimate sign of U.S. global supremacy, white patriarchy, and the triumph of American mass media and mass production. Madonna, she suggests, is the blondest blonde ever, "with forty years of the blonde phenomenon informing her every move." As Podlesney notes, Madonna has frequently been "heralded for mis(re)appropriating the iconography of the blonde bombshell in a cynical defiance of the rules of sexuality codified by patriarchy" (*ibid.*, at 84). On January 16, 1991, the *Washington Post* reported that Florida State University professor Chip Wells was writing a doctoral dissertation on Madonna as a "postmodern social construct." For a recent academic study, see S. P. Baty, *American Monroe: The Making of a Body Politic* (1995).

50   R. Goldstein, "We So Horny: Sado Studs and Super Sluts: America's New Sex 'Tude," *Village Voice* 16 October 1990, at 35, 36.

51   Lange, *supra* note 34, at 163.

52   *Ibid.*, at 165.

53   I have no idea whether Jarmusch sought the consent of the Presley estate or the corporate owners of his publicity rights and, if so, what royalties he agreed to pay. Nor do I know whether the Presley estate ever sought to enjoin the film's production or to demand royalties. The very possibility of such an injunction and its desirability is what is at issue here. Celebrities or their estates are not obliged to grant licenses for the use of their image regardless of the artistic or social merit of

the works in which these are deployed, and may withhold consent on any pretext. In this hypothetical scenario, *Mystery Train might* be privileged under the First Amendment, but then again, it might not, given the difficulties contemporary courts face in distinguishing between fact and fiction in consumer markets.

54   A party launching "Elvis Presley" cologne was held at the New York club Hot Rod in early October of 1990 (reported by M. Musto, "La Dolce Musto," *Village Voice* 26 October 1990, at 44). Wine is now marketed as "Marilyn Merlot," with the actress's likeness on the label (her image also adorns lingerie), and "Rebel" cologne is marketed with an image of James Dean's face, which, in Canada at least, is registered as a trademark. I am grateful to lawyers at Gowling & Henderson in Toronto for bringing this to my attention.

55   Memphis Development Foundation v. Factors Etc., Inc., 441 F.Supp. 1323 (W.D. Tenn. 1977). On appeal, the Sixth Circuit reversed and remanded, holding that the right of publicity was not descendible under Tennessee law 616 F.2d 956 (6th Cir. 1980). The Tennessee legislature responded by statutorily recognizing a descendible exclusive property right in an individual's name or likeness, terminable only upon two years of commercial nonuse (Tennessee Code Annotated [1988] § 47–25–1101–1108). The Tennessee Court of Appeals has since determined that Presley's right of publicity survived his death in 1977 and expressly rejected the Sixth Circuit's opinion on Tennessee law (Elvis Presley International Memorial Foundation v. Crowell 733 S.W.2d 89 [Tenn. Ct. App. 1987]). The Sixth Circuit then declared itself bound by the Court of Appeal's ruling in Elvis Presley Enterprises v. Elvisly Yours 817 F.2d 104 (6th Cir. 1987). For a discussion of some of the alternative moral economies in which Elvis figures in the American Midwest, see L. Spigel, "Communicating with the Dead: Elvis as Medium," 23 *Camera Obscura* 177 (1990).

56   Hettinger, *supra* note 39, at 39–40.

57   W. Gordon, "A Property Right in Self-Expression: Equality and Individualism in the Law of Intellectual Property," 102 *Yale Law Journal* 1533 (1993).

58   Hettinger, *supra* note 39, at 40.

59   Commentators seem eager to extend publicity rights using analogies to copyright, patent, and trademark, but they rarely carry such analogies through to the point of imposing either temporal limits on the right or permitting a range of defenses, exemptions, and opportunities for cancellation equal to those afforded the public in these other areas of law. In both copyright law and patent law, the grant of a property right is part of a socially beneficial bargain between the creator of the work and the public. Because we deem progress in the arts and sciences socially beneficial, we wish to encourage creative efforts and innovations. To induce individuals to invest their efforts in these areas, we grant such individuals exclusive property rights in their works and inventions for a limited period of time in order to recoup their investment costs. In exchange, the creator is obliged to disseminate these works and make them available to the public (sometimes by way of compulsory license) while the patent or copyright is in force, and bequeath the work to the public domain after the monopoly expires.

         The reasons we bestow property rights in literary, artistic, and scientific works, and the reasons we put limitations upon those rights, emerge from a history of social deliberation that is manifestly absent in our creation of publicity and personality rights. For example, if we extend property rights in the products of intellectual labor as an incentive to encourage socially desirable activities, then we need to address three questions: Is fame or celebrity a socially desirable product whose cultivation we wish to encourage? Are incentives necessary to encourage this activity? Does the necessity for incentives require the granting of exclusive property rights? The first question is the most difficult to answer; the celebrity phenomenon does appear to serve certain social needs and desires. However, to the extent that the celebrity aura is harnessed to develop wholly symbolic market distinctions among functionally indistinguishable goods (and may, therefore, concomitantly decrease incentives to improve product quality or encourage innovative product research and design), its social utility may be doubted. Such a qualification, however, already presupposes the answers to the second and third questions; only when exclusive rights to the image are granted will licenses of such rights have value in the market.

If we decide that the development of celebrity is socially desirable, then we need to determine if incentives are necessary to encourage these creative endeavors. Clearly the potential for financial reward afforded by the commercial exploitation of one's persona must glimmer on the horizon as a tantalizing possibility for some celebrities, especially those, like sports stars, whose professional lives are temporally limited. But again, this possibility begs the question. Those stars most likely and able to exploit their personas are those with successful careers in acting, singing, athletics, or politics who receive media recognition for their achievements. In the course of their careers they have been compensated with large salaries, lucrative bonuses, valuable perks, fees for public appearances, and fame itself. Arguably, they are already so well compensated (some would say overcompensated) for their activities that no additional incentives are necessary. Legal recognition of an exclusive right of publicity does not serve to induce, protect, or compensate the celebrity's achievements, but serves instead to give an additional and collateral economic value to the benefit of fame itself.

It seems doubtful that any further economic incentive is required to encourage the achievements of media and sport stars, and even more dubitable that such incentives should take the form of exclusive property rights. If required, such incentives might just as well take the form of higher salaries, public subsidies, reduced taxes, or free housing. But even if we *had* determined that an exclusive property right was a necessary incentive to have a celebrity bestow his or her fame upon us, the logic of intellectual property rationales would demand that the celebrity give us something in return. Copyright and patent laws insist that the work be made publicly available, whereas celebrities may insist upon seclusion and refuse to let their image circulate or price its use on the market so high that no one else can possibly have access to it.

Moreover, copyright laws enable fair uses to be made of a work, whereas we have no criteria or legislation enabling appropriators of a celebrity's image to claim that their use was a fair one. See K. E. Kulzick and A. D. Hogue, "Chilled Bird: Freedom of Expression in the Eighties," 14 *Loyola of Los Angeles Law Review* 57 (1980); K. S. Marks, "An Assessment of the Copyright Model in Right of Publicity Cases," 70 *California Law Review* 786 (1982); R. Kwall, "Is Independence Day Dawning for the Right of Publicity?," 17 *University of California-Davis Law Review* 191 (1984); Hoffman, *supra* note 37; Simon, *supra* note 24, and Coyne, *supra* note 27, for arguments in favor of a fair use defense in publicity cases. See Pemberton, *supra* note 24, and Weiler, *supra* note 9, for other potential copyright-based exemptions.

Copyright, furthermore, is limited to works of authorship fixed in a tangible medium of expression on the policy grounds that although expressions can be owned, ideas should be freely accessible to promote further creative endeavor. Many of the attributes protected by the right of publicity are intangible attributes of an individual that have become associated with that individual in the public mind. These associations are ideas in the public realm. By designating these public ideational associations the private property of individuals, we create individual monopolies in ever more ephemeral attributes and preclude these ideas from contributing to new creative works and the social goal of progress in the arts. Some commentators suggest that the copyright model is inadequate precisely *because* it cannot fully protect all aspects of the celebrity image, given that "the myriad of quirks and nuances that comprise the persona are not capable of being fixed in a tangible medium of expression" (B. Singer, "The Right of Publicity: Star Vehicle or Shooting Star?," 10 *Cardozo Arts & Entertainment Law Journal* 1 [1992]).

Moreover, not all of the elements that make up a copyrightable work are protected by copyright. Many components of the work are deemed to be in the public domain. See J. Litman, "The Public Domain," 39 *Emory Law Review* 965 (1990). Use of standard plot lines and stock characters, for example, are not considered copyright infringement because such devices are considered part of the public domain that must be available to future creators. We have more conceptual difficulty recognizing any recognized attribute of a persona to be in the public domain because these are understood to be bound up in the person, but if we think of celebrities as works we wish to promote, then some famous attributes will have to enter the public domain to provide resources for others. Otherwise, models such as Claudia Schiffer would have to receive licenses and pay royalties to ancestresses like Bridget Bardot and their estates and assigns.

Copyright and patent laws grant a limited term of exclusive rights on the basis that a temporarily limited monopoly satisfies the need for economic incentive and that the fruits of humanity's intellectual labors thereafter fall into the public domain and become the collective resources of humankind. The descendibility of publicity rights, however, raises the specter of human creative works owned and controlled in perpetuity by avaricious assignees ever more distant from the original creator, concerned only with a continuing stream of royalties and license fees. (For a longer discussion of the inaccuracies and inadequacies of comparing publicity rights to copy-right, see Simon, *supra* note 24.)

Some have argued that a right of publicity is more akin to a trademark than to copyright and patent, and, to a limited degree, the analogy holds. Few, however, have pushed the analogy to its logical conclusions. For trademark law, too, has social purposes, grants limited rights, and affords reasonable defenses, all of which serve to contain the property right in a manner that contrasts with the absolute nature of proprietary publicity rights. Trademark law is concerned with the protection of words and symbols as indicators of the source or sponsorship of commercial goods and services. Trademark rights arise through the extensive and continuous use of a brand name, image, or symbol in marketing particular goods or services. Once the trademark serves to distinguish a group of goods or services from other goods or services, the holder of the mark is given exclusive rights to use that mark in conjunction with that particular class of wares. He or she can then prevent others from using the mark on the same or similar goods on the basis that potential customers are likely to be confused as to the source of those goods and that the reputation of the trademark owner may be diminished by the use of the mark on inferior goods.

The value of a trademark is integrally related to the goods and services it represents. Rights to trademarks are never absolute property rights but exclusive rights to use the sign or symbol in conjunction with a particular class of goods or services. Thus, it is not a violation to use a mark in association with unrelated goods or services where there is no competition between the parties, no likelihood of customer confusion, and no suggestion in the public mind that the original trademark owner endorses the second group of goods. Trademark rights are linked to a certain line of goods and services; they cannot, for example, be assigned except in conjunction with the goodwill of the goods or services to which they pertain. Hence the rule that it is the trade and not the mark that trademark law serves to protect. Neither the common law nor trademark legislation recognizes a property right "in gross" (although [. . .] this may well be the *effect* of enforcing antidilution provisions and stretching the doctrine of confusion). To maintain a dilution claim, however, the symbol must at least serve as a trademark or trade name, whereas celebrities are enabled to enforce rights to icons even where these icons do not serve distinguishing roles in commodity markets. Even when trademarks are licensed, licensors were traditionally obliged to maintain control over the quality of the goods and services being rendered under the mark, because trademarks were intended to prevent the deceit of the public as to the source and quality of goods. Where there is no likelihood of confusion of sponsorship, and hence no possibility of public deception, the use of a mark would not be enjoined. Although consumer confusion is increasingly found by judges with alarming alacrity, these principles at least provide some guidance and limitations. Trademarks, moreover, must be monitored; they may be deemed abandoned, and they may be challenged for lack of use and loss of distinction.

Trademark rights, then, are limited rights, designed to serve social purposes – not absolute or exclusive property rights in a sign or symbol that can be evoked by a trademark "owner" in any context. Some aspects of publicity rights might be justified by analogy to trademark law. A celebrity might well use his or her name or likeness to market a particular class of goods or services. If the name or likeness came to identify and distinguish particular wares to consumers, a trademark right would be justified. However, the doctrine of publicity rights extends to celebrities a property right to their name and likeness before any marketing use of the celebrity image has been made and whether or not the public has come to recognize the image as distinguishing a group of goods or services. Moreover, a celebrity may attempt to prevent the use of his or her image even where there is no competition between the parties, no evidence that the defendant intended to pass off goods as those endorsed by the celebrity, and no evidence that the public was in any way confused by the use of the persona.

Indeed, whereas trademark laws (theoretically) attempted to prevent deceit in the marketplace, publicity rights may be exercised in a manner that contributes to consumer confusion. A celebrity can assign and license the attributes of his or her persona without having any relationship to the manufacture, production, and distribution of the merchandise to which he or she has linked his or her image, and he or she assumes no responsibility to the public for the quality of those goods. A well-known architect can license his name for use in the marketing of tea kettles, and the estate of an artist may collect royalties for the use of his name on perfume. If the public comes to associate certain attributes of quality with goods bearing these names, they may well be confused and disappointed when the architect's or the artist's estate later licenses these names to totally unrelated manufacturers who use them to market shoddy merchandise of inferior quality.

Celebrities may do nothing more than make a few carefully orchestrated public appearances every year to command a steady return of royalties from the licensing of their merchandising rights. They need invest no money of their own or have any involvement in the design, production, or dissemination of the products that bear their names. Once a famous designer, Pierre Cardin now earns a small fortune merely by capitalizing on his name. In 1987 he made $125 million from licenses to eight hundred licensees in ninety-three countries who sell merchandise worth more than $1 billion a year, from which he earns royalties of about $75 million. The Cardin name adorns products as diverse as cigarettes, clocks, and deodorants, but neither Cardin nor his company maintains much involvement in their design or production; Cardin's director of licensing admitted that "even we don't know all the products we license." (See discussion of Cardin in Sudjic, *supra* note 28, at 61.) Consumers were given no guarantee of source or quality; the goods bearing the Cardin name might have come from a Filipino factory or the former Soviet Union's Ministry of Light Industry (one of the hundreds of Cardin licensees), but still legitimately carried the celebrity's name. The recent controversy over celebrities' licensing their names to goods produced in sweatshop conditions makes it clear that such activities are only illegitimate in the court of public opinion and that publicity provides the only form of censure. For a longer discussion, see R. J. Coombe, "Sports Trademarks and Somatic Politics: Locating the Law in a Critical Cultural Studies," in *Competing Allegories: Global and Local Cultures of Sport* (R. Martin and T. Miller, eds., 1998).

Trademark law also incorporates a recognition that no sign or symbol can be taken out of public discourse except insofar as it actually continues to distinguish a particular range of goods. [. . . I]f a mark ceases to distinguish particular goods, a trademark holder may lose his or her exclusive rights to the mark unless he or she can show evidence of behavior indicating an intent not to abandon it. If the mark ceases to be used in connection with those goods with which it was acquired, or ceases to be distinctive in that it becomes a name in common parlance used to designate all goods of a particular class, then the mark holder will no longer have exclusive rights to it and the mark will be consigned to the public domain. A trademark owner is therefore obliged to police his or her mark in order to retain the rights to it. A celebrity or his or her estate is under no such obligation. A deceased star's estate or assignees, for example, might decide to use the star's likeness to market shoes years after his or her death, even though the likeness doesn't distinguish the shoes from others in the public mind, the celebrity's image has never been used to distinguish goods before, and the celebrity's image has become part of the popular culture used for a variety of entertainment and/or commercial purposes. Assignees may have done nothing to police the use of the likeness in the past yet suddenly claim exclusive rights to an image commonly understood to be part of a cultural heritage available to us all.

60   As Judge Kozinski put it in his acute dissent in White v. Samsung Electronics, 971 F.2d 1395 (9th Cir. 1992) at 1516:

> Intellectual property rights aren't free: They're imposed at the expense of future creators and of the public at large . . . This is why intellectual property law is full of careful balances between what's set aside for the owner and what's left in the public domain for the rest of us: The relatively short life of patents; the longer, but finite life of copyrights; copyright's idea-expression dichotomy; the fair use doctrine; the prohibition on copyrighting facts; the compulsory license of television broadcasts and musical compositions; federal preemption of overbroad state intellectual property laws; the nominative use doctrine in trademark law; the right to make soundalike recordings. All of these diminish an intellectual property holder's rights. All let the public use something created by someone else. But all are necessary to maintain a free environment in which creative genius can flourish.

The evocation of the Romantic "creative genius" aside, Kozinski's outrage with the unprecedented expansion of publicity rights effected by the decision (that a celebrity could claim damages and demand royalties from anyone who in any way *reminded* the public of his or her celebrity or evoked the celebrity's image in the public mind) was a welcome departure from judicial proclivities.

61   *Ibid.*, at 1521.

62   Madow, *supra* note 4, at 128.

63   Doty suggests that the term *subculture* reinforces marginality:

> we queers have become locked into ways of seeing ourselves in relation to mass culture that perpetuate our status as *sub*cultural . . . By publicly articulating our queer positions in and about mass culture, we reveal that capitalist cultural production need not exclusively and inevitably express straightness. If mass culture remains by, for, or about, straight culture, it will be so through our silences, or by our continued acquiescence to such cultural paradigms such as connotation, *sub*cultures, *sub*cultural studies, *sub*texting, the closet, and other heterocentrist ploys positioning straightness as the norm. Indeed, the more the queerness in and of mass culture is explored, the more the notion that what is "mass" or "popular" is therefore "straight" will become a highly questionable given . . . (*supra* note 3, at 104).

64   W. Benjamin, "The Work of Art in the Age of Mechanical Reproduction," in *Illuminations* (H. Arendt, ed., 1969).

65   *Ibid.*, at 221.

66   *Ibid.*, at 221.

67   *Ibid.*, at 224.

68   *Ibid.*, at 223.

69   *Ibid.*, at 228–229.

70   *Ibid.*, at 231.

71   *Ibid.*

72   See G. McCann, *Marilyn Monroe* (1988), for an extended elaboration of a male feminist's reflections on his relationship to her image, and Dyer, *Heavenly Bodies, supra* note 1, for an insightful discussion of her position in newly emergent discourses of sexuality in the 1950s. Monroe's ongoing dynamic presence in contemporary sexual politics is addressed by MacCannell, "Marilyn Monroe Was Not a Man," *supra* note 43, in a perceptive and scathing review of biographies written by Norman Mailer, Gloria Steinhem, Anthony Summers, and Roger G. Taylor. See also Baty, *American Monroe, supra* note 49.

73   S. Ewen, *All-Consuming Images: The Politics of Style in Contemporary Culture* 90 (1988).

74   *Ibid.*, at 91.

75   *Ibid.*, at 95–96.

76   H. Jenkins III, "Star Trek Rerun, Reread, Rewritten: Fan Writing as Textual Poaching," 5 *Critical Studies in Mass Communication* 85, 87 (1988).

77   H. Jenkins III, *Textual Poachers: Television Fans and Participatory Culture* 18 (1992).

78   M. de Certeau, *The Practice of Everyday Life* (1984).

79   P. Willis, *Common Culture* (1990).

80   See especially the studies in J. Fiske, *Reading the Popular* (1989), and J. Fiske, *Understanding Popular Culture* (1989).

81   *Loving with a Vengeance* (T. Modleski, ed., 1983); *Studies in Entertainment* (T. Modleski, ed., 1986); J. Radway, *Reading the Romance* (1984).

82   Conversations with Brett Williams. See also *The Politics of Culture* (B. Williams, ed., 1991).

83   H. Foster, *Recodings: Art, Spectacle, Cultural Politics* (1985).

84   The concept of the mediascape is borrowed from A. Appadurai, "Disjuncture and Difference in the Global Cultural Economy," 2 *Public Culture* 1 (1990), who asserts that we need to consider the complexity of the global flow of cultural imagery as producing new fields he defines as ethnoscapes, technoscapes, finanscapes, mediascapes, and ideascapes. For an overview of postmodernism and popular culture, see J. Docker, *Postmodernist and Popular Culture: A Cultural History* (1994).

85   S. Connor, *Postmodernist Culture: An Introduction to Theories of the Contemporary* (1989).

86   *Ibid.*, at 186.

87   *Ibid.*

88   D. Hebridge, *Cut 'n' Mix: Culture, Identity and Caribbean Music* (1987).

89   McRobbie, *supra* note 2.

90   L. Hutcheon, *The Politics of Postmodernism* (1989).

91   McRobbie, *supra* note 2, at 174–175.

92   Willis, *supra* note 79.

93   *Ibid.*, at 141–142.

94   J. Fiske, "The Cultural Economy of Fandom," in *The Adoring Audience: Fan Culture and Popular Media* 30 (L. Lewis, ed., 1992). See also H. Jenkins, "Strangers No More, We Sing: Filking and the Social Construction of the Science Fiction Fan Community," in *The Adoring Audience: Fan Culture and Popular Media* 208 (L. Lewis, ed., 1992).

95   C. Griggers, "Lesbian Bodies in the Age of (Post) Mechanical Reproduction," in *Fear of a Queer Planet* 178 (M. Warner, ed., 1993) at 180.

96   M. J. Frug, *Sexual Equality and Sexual Difference in American Law*, talk presented at
     the Symposium on Sexual Equality, Sexual Difference and Law at West Virginia
     University College of Law, Morgantown, West Virginia, 8 April 1988. See
     generally M. J. Frug, *Postmodern Legal Feminism* (1992).

97   T. de Lauretis, "Feminist Studies/Critical Studies: Issues, Terms, and Contexts,"
     in *Feminist Studies/Critical Studies* 1 (T. de Lauretis, ed., 1986).

98   J. W. Scott, *Gender and the Politics of History* (1988).

99   An alternatively gendered world was one that I imaginatively shared with the late
     Mary Joe Frug, a legal scholar and feminist who was shaping a postmodern
     feminist legal theory that recognized the iterative quality of gender identity and
     the significant role played by law in constructing a variety of gendered subject-
     ivities. We shared a belief that legal scholarship and legal thought should be
     characterized by a far greater variety of voice and a surfeit of style(s) that could
     evoke the irony, humor, rage, and sensuality that characterize everyday life and
     everyday struggle. We both regretted that commercial culture was so quickly
     dismissed and denigrated in academic circles. Mary Joe hoped that the voices of
     lesbian hermaphrodites and *Star Trek* fanziners might be heard, and that the cul-
     tural energy of the streets might one day invigorate legal debate. May her
     memory, her work, and her spirit continue to engender such utopian possibilities
     in the law.

100 J. Butler, *Gender Trouble: Feminism and the Subversion of Identity* (1990) (*hereinafter*
     Butler, *Gender Trouble*).

101 *Ibid.*, at *xii*.

102 *Ibid.*, at 1.

103 This argument is elaborated in M. Foucault, *History of Sexuality, Vol. 1: An Introduc-
     tion* (R. Hurley, trans., 1980).

104 In earlier work, I attempted to demonstrate how juridical systems of power
     produce the subjects they claimed only to represent. For a historical discussion
     and elaboration of the juridical production of gender and class subjectivities
     through representational practices in the adjudication of defamation claims, see
     R. J. Coombe, "Contesting the Self: Negotiating Subjectivities in Nineteenth-
     Century Ontario Defamation Trials," 11 *Studies in Law, Politics, and Society* 3 (1991)
     (*hereinafter* Coombe, "Contesting the Self").

105 Butler, *Gender Trouble, supra* note 100, at 2.

106 *Ibid.*, at 4.

107 *Ibid.*, at 5.

108 *Ibid.*, at 6.

109 *Ibid.*, at 17.

110 *Ibid.*, at 17–23.

111 *Ibid.*, at 25. For an elaboration of the meaning of performativity as used here,
     see J. Butler, "For a Careful Reading," in *Feminist Contentions: A Philosophical
     Exchange* 127 (S. Benhabib et al., eds., 1995), and J. Butler, "Critically Queer,"
     1 *Gay and Lesbian Quarterly: A Journal of Lesbian and Gay Studies* 17, 21–24
     (1993).

112 Butler, *Gender Trouble, supra* note 100, at 25–30. Butler's position here is
     congruent with my stance in "Room for Manoeuver," 14 *Law and Social Inquiry*
     69 (1989), where I argue that subjectivity is always constructed within the dis-
     cursive forms of prevailing structures of power, through the creative process of

bricolage – cultural practices that deploy existing cultural forms in ever-emergent new fashions that may transform structures of power even as they evoke its significations.

113   Butler, *Gender Trouble, supra* note 100, at 30.

114   *Ibid.,* at 33.

115   *Ibid.,* at 121.

116   *Ibid.,* at 31.

117   Butler clarifies the nonliberal character of the subject and the reiterative and rearticulatory (rather than original or intentional in any Romantic or modern sense) nature of the agency involved in *Bodies That Matter* (1993) at 15.

118   A. Ross, *No Respect: Intellectuals and Popular Culture* 159 (1989).

119   R. Jackson, *Modernist and Postmodernist Inscriptions of Camp*, paper presented at the Popular Culture Association meetings (7–10 March 1990).

120   Ross, *supra* note 118, at 157–158.

121   E. Newton, *Mother Camp: Female Impersonators in America* 3 (1979).

122   *Ibid.,* at 103.

123   *Ibid.*

124   Ross, *supra* note 118, at 159.

125   *Ibid.,* at 160.

126   *Ibid.*

127   *Ibid.,* at 159.

128   *Ibid.,* at 161.

129   P. Tyler, "The Garbo Image," in *The Films of Greta Garbo* 28 (M. Conway et al., eds., 1968); cited in Newton, *supra* note 121, at 108.

130   Dyer, *Heavenly Bodies, supra* note 1, at x.

131   *Ibid.,* at 148–154.

132   *Ibid.,* at 154, 160.

133   See Jackson, *supra* note 119.

134   A. La Valley, "The Great Escape," 10(6) *American Film* 71 (1985).

135   M. Tremblay, *Hosanna* (J. Van Burek and B. Glassco, trans., 1974).

136   D. Crimp, "Right On, Girlfriend!," 33 *Social Text* 2, 4 (1993).

137   *Ibid.,* at 3.

138   Lesbian identification with Sinatra does not appear to be limited to Toronto, judging from the New York "Lookout" Downtown Community Television's second annual Gay and Lesbian Video Festival. There, a video titled *Cruisin' the Rubyfruit Jungle* contained "a tribute to Nancy Sinatra that would make Irving Klaw blush" according to M. Dargis, "Being on the Lookout," *Village Voice*, 16 October 1990, at 51.

139   Crimp, *supra* note 136, at 12.

140   *Ibid.*

141   *Ibid.*

142   *Ibid.,* at 13.

143   J. Dos Passos, *Midcentury* (1960).

144   D. Dalton, *James Dean: The Mutant King* (1983).

145   S. Golding, "James Dean: The Almost-Perfect Lesbian Hermaphrodite," in *Sight Specific: Lesbians and Representation* 49 (D. Brand, ed., 1988).

146   *Ibid.,* at 50.

147   *Ibid.,* at 52.

148 Butler, *Gender Trouble, supra* note 100, at 17.

149 Golding, *supra* note 145, at 50.

150 *Ibid.*

151 *Ibid.*, at 52.

152 *Ibid.*

153 For a discussion of the social and institutional structures of particular fan communities, see C. Bacon-Smith, *Enterprising Women: Television Fandom and the Creation
of Popular Myth* (1992) at ch. 2. See also C. Penley, "Brownian Motion: Women,
Tactics, and Technology," in *Technoculture* 135 (C. Penley and A. Ross, eds., 1991).

154 Bacon-Smith, *supra* note 153, at 322; Jenkins, "Star Trek Rerun, Reread, Rewrit-
ten," *supra* note 76; C. Penley, *To Boldly Go Where No Woman Has Gone Before:
Feminism, Psychoanalysis, and Popular Culture*, lecture delivered at the Public Access
Series CAPITAL/CULTURE, Toronto, 24 April 1990.

155 Bacon-Smith, *supra* note 153, at 26–28.

156 *Ibid.*, at 16–31.

157 *Ibid.*, at 45.

158 Jenkins, "Star Trek Rerun, Reread, Rewritten," *supra* note 76, at 89.

159 In 1991, Constance Penley, *supra* note 154, estimated that there are 300 to 500
publishers of homoerotic fanzines alone. This number has no doubt increased with
the ease of electronic communications.

160 Bacon-Smith, *supra* note 153, at 45.

161 Jenkins, "Star Trek Rerun, Reread, Rewritten," *supra* note 76, at 104.

162 Fanzine writers face ridicule and hostility both in "mainstream" society and among
other (predominantly male) science fiction fans who see them as less than intelligent and as an embarrassment to fandom (Bacon-Smith, *supra* note 153, at 7–43,
77). For a more extensive discussion of their vilification in academia, the mainstream press, and the larger science fiction community, see Jenkins, *Textual
Poachers, supra* note 77, at 1–24.

163 Bacon-Smith, *supra* note 153, at 56–57.

164 Jenkins, "Star Trek Rerun, Reread, Rewritten," *supra* note 76, at 88.

165 *Ibid.*, at 93–97.

166 Bacon-Smith, *supra* note 153, at 94–98.

167 *Ibid.*, at 100.

168 *Ibid.*, at 101–102.

169 *Ibid.*, at 102.

170 *Ibid.*, at 102–103.

171 *Ibid.*, at 141–143.

172 *Ibid.*, at 145–147.

173 *Ibid.*, at 209–216.

174 *Ibid.*, at 334.

175 *Ibid.*, at 230.

176 J. Russ, "Another Addict Raves about K/S," 8 *Nome* 28 (1985), cited in Bacon-
Smith, *supra* note 153, at 371.

177 Bacon-Smith, *supra* note 153, at 245.

178 *Ibid.*, at 247.

179 *Ibid.*, at 246–249.

180 *Ibid.*, at 246.

181 *Ibid.*, at 249–250.

182   Hurt/Comfort stories are those in which one male character is hurt and suffers and the other comforts and nurses him (see discussion in *ibid.*, ch 10, at 255–281).

183   This would help to explain why fans don't necessarily see the sexual relationship between Kirk and Spock as a homosexual one (Penley, *supra* note 154). As some fans see it, there are forms of love that defy description; the sexual orientation of Kirk and Spock is irrelevant because their love is a matter of cosmic destiny (*ibid.*). For similar reasons, fans don't see even the most sexually graphic material as pornographic (Bacon-Smith, *supra* note 153, at 243). Such categories are simply inappropriate in these alternative universes.

184   Bacon-Smith, *supra* note 153, at 270–277.

185   *Ibid.*, at 195–196.

186   1(1) *Judy!* 1 (spring fever 1993) (unpaginated fanzine, P.O. Box 121, Iowa City, IA 52245–0121).

187   *Ibid.*

188   *Ibid.*

189   E. Mertz, "A New Social Constructionism for Sociolegal Studies," 28 *Law & Society Review* 1243, 1257 (1994).

190   It will undoubtedly be argued that if the individuals engaged in these subcultural practices were to be threatened with legal action, they could claim a defense under the First Amendment. Such responses evince an incredible naïveté about the obstacles that confront most people in even reaching a legal forum in which a constitutional challenge could be made. Moreover, First Amendment defenses in this area are rarely upheld and often dismissed out of hand. The case law in this area, moreover, is extremely confusing and often contradictory, as I will discuss in my concluding essay.

191   This insight finds its clearest articulation in the work of Michel Foucault. Although he dealt with the law as primarily repressive in his early work, he also argued that regimes of power were productive rather than merely prohibitive: they produce what they purport merely to represent. Others have extended this insight into the juridical domain. Clifford Geertz makes similar observations in *Local Knowledge: Further Essays in Interpretive Anthropology* (1983). These ideas are developed in G. Peller, "The Metaphysics of American Law," 73 *California Law Review* 1151 (1985), and elaborated in C. Harrington and B. Yngvesson, "Interpretive Social Research," 15 *Law & Social Inquiry* 135 (1990). For a discussion of the juridical production of class and gender subjectivities in the transition to industrial capitalism, see Coombe, "Contesting the Self," *supra* note 104.

192   L. Bower, "Queer Acts and the Politics of Direct Address," 28 *Law & Society Review* 1009 (1994).

193   Jenkins, "Star Trek Rerun, Reread, Rewritten," *supra* note 76, at 100.

194   This concept is developed in E. P. Thompson, "The Moral Economy of the English Crowd in the 18th Century," 50 *Past and Present* 76 (1971). The development of moral economies with respect to celebrity images – informal modes of regulation and sanction that grow up in the shadow of the law and with knowledge of the policing activities of those with legally recognized rights in the text – is not limited to the fanzine context. For example, it would appear that Elvis impersonators and fans are not deterred by the Presley estate's policing efforts (which have attempted to control and/or prohibit activities as diverse as black velvet art

featuring "the King," computer games featuring Elvis as street fighter, and at least one lesbian Elvis impersonator). However, some impersonators feel that they themselves have acquired rights by virtue of their transformative appropriations and, in at least one case, the law has supported the claim. In Flying Elvi v. Flying Elvises (unreported), one team of skydiving Elvis impersonators successfully sued another on grounds of potential consumer confusion. The defendants attempted to counterclaim "on behalf of anyone who wants to hit the silk in the name of the King" but lost. See M. Neill and A. M. Otey, "All Shook Up: Two Skydiving Groups Try To Chute Each Other Down," *People* (27 February 1995) at 50; "Look Up in the Sky. It's the Flying Elvises, er, Elvi," *The National Law Journal* (17 April 1995) at A27. For a discussion of the maintenance and social transformations of the Elvis image, see D. S. Wall, "Reconstructing the Soul of Elvis: The Social Development and Legal Maintenance of Elvis Presley as Intellectual Property," 24 *International Journal of the Sociology of Law* 117 (1996).

195 Jenkins, "Star Trek Rerun, Reread, Rewritten," *supra* note 76, at 100.

196 *Ibid.*, citing Schnvelle, 4 *Sociotrek* 8–9.

197 Bacon-Smith, *supra* note 153, at 58.

198 *Ibid.*, at 66.

199 *Ibid.*, at 40.

200 *Ibid.*, at 33.

201 Penley, *supra* note 154.

202 Bacon-Smith, *supra* note 153, at 35.

203 *Ibid.*, at 223.

204 Jenkins, *Textual Poachers, supra* note 77, at 30–31. Constance Penley told me in conversation that Lucasfilm threatened legal action on copyright grounds when they discovered that fanzine writers had depicted Luke Skywalker and Han Solo in an erotic relationship. Bacon-Smith, *supra* note 153, at 251, n.6, also notes that fandom has had an uneasy relationship with Lucasfilm but does not elaborate. A copyright claim would not require that the use be commercial to succeed and is thus a more flexible instrument for producers to use than trademark and more economically feasible than backing publicity rights claims by all of the individual actors to achieve the same ends.

205 Jenkins, *Textual Poachers, supra* note 77, at 31.

206 *Ibid.*

207 For a discussion of complicitous critique as an attitude symptomatic of post-modernism, see Hutcheon, *supra* note 90.

208 K. McClure, "On the Subject of Rights: Pluralism, Plurality and Political Identity," in *Dimensions of Radical Democracy: Pluralism, Citizenship, Community* 123 (C. Mouffe, ed., 1992).

Chapter 41

Graeme Turner, Frances Bonner and P. David Marshall

PRODUCING CELEBRITY

THIS CHAPTER HAS A classificatory objective: to sort out the various activities performed by publicists, agents, managers, and others. Importantly, it hopes to make these activities more visible. Unlike the celebrities they help to produce, those who work in publicity, promotion or management remain relatively private figures. They calculate their professional achievements through the exposure of their clients. How many column inches received in newspaper coverage, which television program appeared in, which magazine did a cover story, or what kind of contract negotiated – these are among the registers of success. Included within this calculation of success, however, is the invisibility of the work required to achieve it. People in this industry work long and hard, but a great deal of effort goes into masking that fact: into blurring the divisions between work and leisure while generating publicity, and between the constructed and the spontaneous in the outcomes. As a result, finding out what work is actually done constitutes an important part of the project of this book.

In a mature manufacturing industry, the delineation of jobs is relatively clear. Even in film production, through a combination of necessary skill development and union regulations, the categories of gaffers and script supervisors, best boys and editors are all well defined in larger productions. However, in the industry that produces Australian celebrities, job categories are in much greater flux. There are distinct names for some categories – agents, managers, publicists – but, on the ground, there is often considerable hybridity and no unequivocally clear system of nomenclature for describing what people actually do.

Unlike Hollywood, where the scale of the industry has necessitated the prolifera-tion of the categories of support required to manage the professional and public careers of the major stars, the Australian industry simply cannot support a great deal of differentiation. Jobs merge into each other and career trajectories take individuals from one sector of the promotions industry to another: Suzie MacLeod of Village Roadshow was in promotions before she moved into publicity; Tracey Mair, who now works mainly as a unit publicist, originally worked for women's magazines as a writer/editor; Georgie Brown has migrated from publicity at television networks to freelance publicity, management and public relations. Several, like Southern Star's Lesna Thomas, have moved from journalism into public (in this case, 'corporate') relations.

What follows has been drawn from our interviews with practitioners, most of whom learnt their craft through on-the-job training. They have been grouped into the categories they use to describe their principal activities. Our objective is not to nail down the categories or to prescribe a more consistent system of nomenclature. Rather, and at the most basic level, we are simply interested in using what our interviewees have told us as a means of describing in some detail the kind of work which goes on endlessly, frenetically, within an industry which depends on masking its processes in order to enhance the magical plausibility of its results.

The agent

It's very full on and it's very exciting; and some days it can be very frustrating and other days it can be exhilarating. Most days are fantastic.

Viccy Harper

Making connections

The oldest and most traditional job in this industry is the agent. There can be any number of adjectives qualifying specific areas of interest – one can be a talent agent, a sports agent, a theatrical agent – but the key task of the agent is to book talent. For this service, the agent receives what has become an international standard: 10% of the talent's fee. The role of Australian agents resembles that of their British and American counterparts and some of the agencies are global in their reach, although the vast majority are very small operations with limited international connections. The William Morris Agency, which began in the early twentieth century in New York and became a major Hollywood entertainment agency, has a small office in Sydney run by Anthony Williams. Trained in the William Morris style, Williams probably typifies the most 'classical' version of an agent in Australia. The traditional name for the craft comes from the pre-film era – Williams is a theatrical agent. In that tradition, the agent, in an unobtrusive dark-suited, white shirt and tie uniform, is an unseen figure who performs the task of getting employer and employee together:

ANTHONY WILLIAMS: [Theatrical] agent is a slight misnomer – it's what it is known as generally; but we represent actors, writers, directors in film, television, radio and we also represent book writers – fiction, biography, autobiography. And we're basically an employment agency. We find people whom we think that we can represent and sell. And we charge a commission on what we get for them.

Barbara Leane, who has run her own agency in Sydney for twenty years, is a slightly more visible figure in the entertainment scene than the traditional agent. She explains that a new wave of agents arrived in the late 1970s who did much more for their clients than book and pocket their 10% commission. In the pre-1970s era, a few agents such as Gloria Peyton had the market 'sewn up; they didn't have to go out and actively seek work. They could just sit there, the phone would ring . . .' The producer and the single agent would simply decide who would be in the production. This relatively cosy arrangement was transformed by the growth in the number of agencies throughout the 1980s and 1990s. Kristin Dale from Faith Martin, a major casting agency, estimates that there are now in excess of 150 agencies in Sydney and Melbourne. The agents who were the product of this highly competitive environment have therefore had to engage in a great deal more promotion of their clients to get them work.

As a result, professional connections to the casting agencies have become a crucial factor both for the aspiring actors and for their agents. Casting consultancies/agencies are on the other side – they work for the producers and the television networks, not the actor. The actor pays the agent to help them cross that divide. Since there may be a glut of agencies, professional reputations are crucial, as they determine which agency an actor will most prefer to represent their interests. For them, a successful agent is the first step to a successful career. The stories of how agents become successful at managing their network of connections are quite varied but often involve the agent having worked previously in some other part of the industry.

Gary Stewart of Melbourne Artists Management (whose clients include *Blue Heelers'* John Wood, and Rachel Griffiths) spent years working in live television productions such as *In Melbourne Tonight*. Sydney-based Kevin Palmer moved from acting to directing live theatre in England and Australia, before managing and then buying an agency:

KEVIN PALMER: To be quite honest I was an alright director, I wasn't a brilliant director – but I mean being a director sometimes is not being brilliant. Being a director is learning how to drive traffic on the stage and be able to talk to actors and communicate with actors. I was at an age where you thought, well, what else do you do. I wanted to stay in the industry so the best thing was to look for another sort of niche.

Palmer's ability to communicate with actors as a director as well as his wealth of production experience has helped to make him a successful agent, with a client list which includes Penny Cooke and Eden Gaha. Williams relied on his legal training in his move into the world of entertainment and agents. Leane began with an advertising agency and then occasional work with one of the key casting agents in the early 1970s to get a firm grasp of what being an agent entailed. She made contacts and developed what she now describes as her key asset: 'people skills'. Viccy Harper, of Hilary Linstead and Associates, worked her way into her position as director from being a receptionist when much of the firm's work was that of a casting agency. June Cann, the *grande dame* of Australian theatrical agents, was the script girl on the film *Eureka Stockade* and then did extensive voice-over work for the ABC before establishing her agency. Rebecca Williamson, who works with Cann, with her economics degree and her extensive family background in the arts (her father is the playwright David Williamson, and her brother is the actor Felix Williamson) had roots in the industry prior to becoming an agent.

As these examples indicate, broad backgrounds in the industry are undoubtedly helpful. The demands of making an agency a viable operation force the most traditional theatrical agency to recognise that they must understand the full range of possible forms of employment for their clients:

GARY STEWART: We cover all drama. We cover radio, film, television, theatre, commercials – we have to do the lot to survive really . . . I think most actors need to be able to do just about anything to make a reasonable living out of it. They must be able to voice-over commercials, if they sing and dance it helps. They've got to be good actors and we just kind of feed them into all those areas.

For the writer or the performer who loves the theatre, there is still the monetary pressure to do film or television. Palmer commented wryly that '10% [commission] of nothing is nothing', and indicated that 70% of an actor's 'income is in front of a camera one way or another'. Musical theatre, although infrequent and limited to large-scale productions, pays reasonably well; Harper explained that, in the post-10BA subsidisation of the film industry,[1] her firm became more focused on cabaret and musical theatre performance and they now represent a large part of the talent that performs, writes and directs for that market (they handled Tap Dogs, for instance).

The day-to-day running of an agency demonstrates the high level of involvement required to stay in touch with the industry. All the agents interviewed considered phones and faxes as virtual extensions of their bodies. Much like the talent scout for professional sports, the agent is always looking for new talent and therefore must attend a great number of plays, receptions and launches to keep connected to the industry and to read what it needs. Stewart went through his daybook for us to outline a typical 'day-in-the-life'. On the day we spoke to him, he was trying to circulate some photographs and biographies of Cerrian Clements, who was in the cast of Les Miserables in Melbourne for six months but wanted it to be known that she was available during that time for casual television work. He had to ring a contact for tickets to Chicago; he indicated that he had no clients in the musical but it was obvious that it was a scouting exercise. There were continuing discussions over a new contract with an actor (Jane Menelaus) who was in a play with the Melbourne Theatre Company. And he was preparing videotapes for four of his clients to send to the producers of a television lifestyle program who were seeking a new presenter. Stewart revealed that he has a backroom of videotapes of his actors; many of them he prepared himself from hours of television tape and dubbed on to individual show reels. He remarked that glossy photographs and a bio will get you in the door, but in the current state of play you need the videotape ready to send to secure a screen test.

This level of involvement is typical of what Barbara Leane calls the 'new-wave' agent. [. . .] The new-wave agent (or agent-manager) can be involved at a very personal level: Williamson acknowledged that she may be called upon for mundane support services, such as picking up her clients at the airport, and Harper admitted that she has had to make chicken soup for a client. As she recognises, this suggests that she has crossed a line into career or personal management: 'As an agent, you're a surrogate mother. We have to deal with mid-life crises sometimes. You have to deal with so much stuff because it all affects the bottom line — which is their careers.'

The new-wave agent — a response to the expansion in the size of the celebrity industry in Australia — provides probably the key example of job hybridisation. Their activities have expanded so that they now perform an analogous role to that of personal managers in the American entertainment industry.

Agents as scouts

One of the realities of the entertainment industry in Australia and elsewhere is that it operates on a massive surplus of labour. Unemployment for actors in Australia is a fact of life. Palmer admits that 'if you want to live comfortably you don't become an actor', and yet there is a swelling potential pool of actors to draw upon. He identified a real compulsion beyond the necessary ego ('that you are the most important person in the world at any moment') that operates 'like a drug that [the actor] cannot live without once they decide that's what they are'. The cultural value assigned to public performance of one kind or another is implicated in the constancy of this desire (but that may be another story).

Agents are part of a massive filtration system for the entertainment industry. According to Williams, many publishers also now prefer to handle only authors who have an agent. Stewart described dealing personally with at least half-a-dozen tapes a week from potential new clients — and these were the ones which were not screened out before they reached him. Similarly, Palmer received twenty to thirty letters each week requesting representation. The reality of this surplus of aspiring actors was reinforced by the number of times our interviews were interrupted by a cold call from an unknown, unrepresented talent.

The tertiary education system has built on these expanding aspirations. Initially, there was only the National Institute of Dramatic Art (NIDA), which accepted twenty-five students a year. After the Western Australia Academy of Performing Arts and the Victorian College of the Arts established-competing programs in the 1980s, virtually every university and many TAFEs have developed drama studies courses and programs which service and reinforce the desire for an acting career. While this might seem out of all proportion to the opportunities available, these programs have been surprisingly comprehensively integrated into the industry system. Most agents we talked to considered it a sign of commitment if a new client has trained for three years at a given institute. In the filtering game, most of the agents follow the graduating class from NIDA very closely to see whether they want to represent any of them. Like a debutantes' ball, their final showcase performances are attended by agents looking for future stars. Because many agents come from a theatrical tradition, they expect that training for the stage will provide the necessary range of skills that a future client needs for television or film. An odd anomaly in the training system is that there are few courses on film and television acting, even though this is likely to provide around 70% of their students' future income. Most agents we spoke with were drawn to performers who could act, sing and, preferably, dance as well. This implied what could be regarded as a slightly anachronistically vaudevillian model of the entertainment industry, where versatility was central and the capacity to perform credibly on stage was the issue rather than a specific set of skills.

Even with the best eye and the best contacts, however, it is a high-risk business. Agents deal with this by serving a surplus of clients:

BARBARA LEANE: Well, I had this dream . . . Wouldn't it be wonderful just to look after 50 people. That was the dream, totally impractical dream – totally, totally impractical dream. You can only charge, well, 10%. You're never going to get rich on 10%. The only way you're going to make any money on 10% is if you're fortunate enough to get someone in a big American movie with a lot of money, or a good ongoing American series.

At the time of our interview, Marcus Graham, the star of *Good Guys/Bad Guys*, was Leane's international hope as he had just completed a US television series, *City to City*, in Miami.

Other agencies are forced to play the same numbers game. Palmer's two-person agency was lined with photographs of his clients – hundreds of images – and yet he will only take on those who have theatrical training and who pass the test of his 'gut feeling'. Not all agents are looking for raw talent. Stewart might consider a potential client if they are good-looking; they can be employed in television commercials regularly because, often, this is all that is needed in a typical soap-advertisement shower scene.

As Stewart suggests, the choice of who gets the roles is at least partially determined by looks. This influence on casting is reinforced through *Showcast* (a massive casting book composed of glossy industry photographs of actors and performers, and their credits). As scripts and casting calls go out, the agent is part of the first screening process, determining who should be sent to the audition. Depending on the strength of their links with casting services and directors, a specific agent will begin to have a certain amount of influence in a certain sphere of production. So, agents themselves are also filtered. Leane felt that she had 'made it' (that she had the confidence of casting consultants, producers and directors) when she started receiving scripts to read. This exposure to the script gives her and therefore her clients an inside track, enhancing their chance of being employed on projects. Other, less well-connected, agents will be responding to general audition calls, where knowledge of the characters required will be much more restricted. As a result of this process, a level of specialisation can develop. Consequently, Stewart was more comfortable with musical performers, while Leane tended to represent actors. Other agents, not interviewed, specialised in getting extras and, presumably, one of their key skills was getting the right look for that shampoo commercial.

Considering that the agents interviewed readily agreed that the number of agencies had grown exponentially in the last twenty years, competition for talent must constitute a major part of their daily work. They generally denied the practice of poaching – after all, the Drama Agents Association forbids the practice. However, there was some finessing about whether someone had been poached (the jilted agent's position) or had looked for a new agent (the lucky agent). Leane, while protesting her innocence of poaching, indicated that Marcus Graham is a new client who has proven to be very lucrative for her. Williams suggested that the practice was common, if not routine: 'There are one or two agents who are enthusiastically poaching, particularly amongst . . . the glamorous sort of playwrights or writers'.

The contracts

Although most agents do not have any legal training, at the heart of their responsibilities to a client is the contract. Leane acknowledges that much of her job consists of working out contracts and determining whether they are in the best interest of her client; but she laments her lack of legal qualifications and envies Williams his training as a lawyer. Hilary Linstead and Associates finally hired an entertainment lawyer because of the proportion of their business that is fundamentally concerned with their clients' contractual obligations. Most learn on the job, and much of what they learn is about the requirements of different kinds of performances. Television contracts, for instance, may not pay much up front, but, as Stewart explained, the key factor is 'residuals': the income earned from repeated screenings and sales of the vehicle for that performance. This complicates matters for the agent attempting to set a price for an actor in a television commercial, for instance; it is hard to determine the long-term value of each performance. The requirements of a particular career, too, may influence the agent's judgement about which or how many contracts to pursue. Stewart points out that he has to be selective about which endorsement or merchandising contract he advises *Blue Heelers* star John Wood to accept. Not only is overexposure an issue for this actor, but he has also to be aware that any contract he signs now must help him deal with a period of virtual unemployability when he leaves the television series.

The level of involvement implied by the orchestration of Wood's public profile marks Stewart as occupying a transition point between the traditional and the new-wave agent. Like a manager, the new-wave agent may be involved in career building as opposed to just taking whatever money or deal is on offer. Rebecca Williamson explained the process that the actor/presenter Kimberley Joseph went through in working out her *Gladiators* television deal with Channel 7. Joseph had begun appearing irregularly on *Hey Hey It's Saturday* after the retirement of Ozzie Ostrich (Ernie Carroll). Her previous work had been as an actor on the soap opera *Paradise Beach*, but as a friend of Daryl Somers she had taken this casual, uncontracted work with his program. Although there were intimations that it might become regular, there had been no contract signed with Channel 9. In the intervening time, Channel 7 – possibly in a move to embarrass Channel 9 – had drawn up a contract for Joseph to appear in the first series of *Gladiators*. Williamson, acting as her agent, encouraged Joseph to sign the *Gladiators* contract.

The repercussions of that signing meant that the Nine Network had lost her services, just as they were using her to advertise *Hey Hey* (and promoting her in a story in *TV Week*). Williamson attempted to shield Joseph from the small-scale publicity scandal that the defection produced, as well as from Somers' wrath. Joseph did well financially through *Gladiators*, but it became clear to her agent that she wanted to return to acting, not presenting; she also did not want to become what Williamson described as 'a Seven girl', where she was contracted to perform or present whatever they were developing. Even though Channel 7 offered a longer development contract, Joseph turned it down in favour of greater autonomy and career independence. And she made a relatively successful transition back to acting through appearing as a regular character in a Village Roadshow production, *Tales of the South Seas*, which is destined for international release, and has now an American feature film behind her.

Handling and controlling publicity often falls into an agent's hands because of their contractual relation with a performer, although it is strictly speaking not part of their job. During our interview, Kevin Palmer was regularly distracted by having to screen press demands from women's magazines and daily newspapers for more information on the breaking story of former *A Country Practice* star Penny Cooke's pregnancy. Cooke did not in fact want her pregnancy to be widely known, so that requests for work would still come in, but Palmer acknowledged that the publicity at this stage (the last trimester of the pregnancy) was indirectly beneficial to her career. In general, and like most agents, Palmer felt that publicity itself was out of his jurisdiction, however much it affected a career. As we saw, though, the agent is often the first line of defence of an actor's privacy because the agent usually clears most press inquiries. They can also be placed in the position of protecting their clients from the consequences of some of their own choices and contractual obligations. When Noah Taylor, after having completed a small independent film, was being pressured by the distributors to engage in a major publicity drive, the June Cann agency tried to shield him from their demands. Eventually, this can stretch the role of the agent, even the new-wave agent, to breaking point. When a star reaches a certain level of prominence – particularly the kind of overseas interest that would surround, say, Rachel Griffiths – the agent will generally recommend the hiring of a manager.

While the overseas success of a client brings credit to an agent, it does have its downside. As a star moves internationally, contractual negotiations become more complex. According to most agents, it is the usual practice that, when an actor gets work in the United States or England, a local agent is involved. Instead of the entire 10% commission going to the Australian agent, there is a shared distribution. Occasionally, if the negotiations are done directly, the Australian agent picks up the full 10% from the international contract. Marcus Graham's recent success in *City to City* was all arranged between the casting director and Barbara Leane, who knew the casting director personally. The negotiations went on over a long period of time but, ultimately, Leane was able to claim the entire commission for the role. The usual case, however, is different; it is referred to as the 'Shanahan split' after the famous agent Bill Shanahan. If they successfully place one of their clients on an American film or television program, the local agent's share is 'two-and-a-half per cent of their [the American agent's] 10%; they hate to give it to you and you've gotta fight to get it – I always get it. If they want my actors, you've gotta do it – otherwise [they're] not coming.' Nevertheless, it has to be said that, if their actors land these large roles, even the regular 2.5% can keep an agency solvent. In the long term, though, such achievements are tempered by the reality that international stardom will move their clients out of their Australian orbit into the more elaborate agent-manager-publicist network of Hollywood.

The manager

> Management is a risk, clearly when you start the process, when you agree
> to manage, the best relationships between managers and artists occur
> when those artists have had nothing and so the growth has been together.
> Therefore the bad times have been shared by both, there's therefore no
> money for the manager let alone the artist for those years that it takes to
> get the income to that level.
>
> Peter Rix

Managers are much fewer in number in Australia than agents, and their clients are an
equally select group. The activities of managers vary significantly in the Australian
context. From our interviews and analysis of the way the industry operates, there
seem to be three general types:

- the classic manager of a star's complex engagements, with both financial and
  personal responsibilities;
- the role-specific manager, who might be engaged to line up speaking engagements; and
- the impresario manager, who plays an often public role while orchestrating or
  controlling the media presence of their clients.

The classic manager

Managing entertainment figures involves an intense and ongoing relationship. Consequently, the number of clients that any manager takes on is constrained by the
earning power of the client and the scale of the personal attention they will require.
Customarily, a manager receives 15% of their client's income and this, given that
there will also be agency fees, limits the number of entertainment personalities
who can afford a manager. Mark Morrissey's rule of thumb is that a client needs to be
earning in excess of $100,000 before they can afford management services. As a
result, while the agency arm of his firm has around 150 clients, the management side
has between five and ten clients at any one time. Only one of his staff is employed
exclusively as a manager, while the others divide their time between agent business
and management work. Morrissey himself manages only three clients: Steve Bastoni,
Alex Dimitriades and Bill Hunter. Others in his firm are involved in the management of some of the young soap stars of *Home and Away*, *Neighbours* and *Heartbreak
High*.

Frequently, in the Australian context, where the management contract emerges
from an agency contract many agencies have used this as an opportunity to expand
into management. Hilary Linstead and Associates, like Morrissey's company, has a
management arm where clients such as Tim Ferguson, Magda Szubanski and Wendy
Harmer are handled with greater attention and personal involvement. Ferguson's
long-term contract with Seven and his writing and performing credits, for instance,
demand a more engaged, career-building managerial role. Having an agency with a
stable of talent provides the foundation for building a management business from

the break-out successes of early career performers. This is clearly a process the agencies wish to encourage. Morrissey's agency offers a cut-price deal when managing becomes part of the service: instead of 15% commission for management, plus 10% for agent work, he renegotiates a reduced total commission and thereby holds on to the dual role.

Like Morrissey, Peter Rix, who has been managing entertainment personalities since 1974, has maintained an extremely limited client list. Although he engages in other activities and has been involved in a great number of Australian musicians' careers (he has been the producer of the annual award show of the Australian Record Industry Association, the ARIAs, since its inception in 1986), Rix has managed Marcia Hines, Deni Hines and Jon English for many years. All of them produce the consistent earnings that he requires. But the relationship is more than a financial one; he thinks of his role as integral to the production of their performances and their music.

Rix's take on the role of the manager is a consequence of a hands-on relationship with production that dates back to his original management of the 1970s pop band, Hush. His involvement with Hush is typical of management relationships in Australian popular music, in that it developed incrementally and relatively organically out of the individual's interest in the band:

PETER RIX: Every Friday night I ran a club in Sydney. I was hired as the manager of a club in Sydney, a gay club in the Cross, and Hush was one of the bands I used to book and they would turn up. I lived in Paddington: they needed a place to rehearse so they used to use my garage. Some record company turned up and said, 'We want to sign you [Hush]', so they turned up at my house again and said, 'Look, you're at university doing a law degree. Can you have a look at this contract for us?' and I thought God this is a dreadful contract and so I helped them with that. And then they needed someone to drive the truck another night, their little van, so I drove that one night and then . . .

Rix began handling more and more aspects of the business and production side of the band as it garnered greater success. He would spend ten months on the road, handling eighty or ninety shows a year, when Hush, along with Sherbet, was one of the top two teen pop bands in Australia.

After years of hotel living, Rix today is able to settle into managing some of the most successful Australian performers from his Sydney offices. Nevertheless, the experience of managing every aspect of a pop band has made him the quintessential 'classic' manager. As he explains, the manager of a personality/performer is involved in directing sales, keeping the accounts, marketing the artist, working on research and future developments of the product, and working on the image. To further complicate the job, these various tasks are not done 'in isolation – clearly a lot of it's done very much hand-in-hand with the band or artist that you work for; but someone has to be the legs and arms of those decisions'.

The classic manager is clearly different from the agent (even the new-wave agent); Rix maintains that the agent plays their part only 'after the real work' (presumably, of creative development) is done. There is a degree of sector specificity about his account, though, as the music industry is something of a special case. The infrastructure requirements for performing and touring bands demand some form of (at least) road manager, and this function can easily expand into a more entrepreneurial and developmental role. In most other areas of the entertainment industry, managers are rarely part of the early career of a performer. They only become an essential element of success as the performer's career produces a proliferation of offers and possibilities. The manager grows with the client.

At the time of our interview, Morrissey was literally packing to head off with Alex Dimitriades to Cannes Film Festival. Dimitriades was starring in the 1998 film *Head On* which was part of the Directors' Fortnight screenings of the festival. Morrissey makes it clear that there were times after Dimitriades' film debut in *The Heartbreak Kid* when his transition into adult roles had to be carefully managed (a transition ultimately completed with the role in the ABC series *Wildside*). But Morrissey believed that the *acclaim for* Dimitriades' performance in *Head On* provided an opportunity that had to be exploited to the full. Through his description of what he was about to do for his client, we can see the intense kind of investment that is part of the manager–client relationship at such moments:

MARK MORRISSEY: What I will do is promote and fend off for Alex. Whatever group of offers come up, I will help determine what might be good for him. I also plan to go to Los Angeles following Cannes and meet with American agents and managers to stitch up potential deals there. Alex will hold a press conference the morning of the opening of the film and I hope to be culling out offers, once his commitments to *Wildside* are over.

Morrissey was capitalising on what Rix would call the promotion of an artist's product. The critical acclaim that Morrissey foresaw accurately in Cannes becomes the moment where a manager can make the international transition for a client.

Where managers have emerged from agencies, one sees another phenomenon developing which, on a minor level, echoes a forty-year trend in Hollywood: managers are involved in 'packaging' to get a production off the ground. Morrissey considers that holding on to the traditional roles of agents and managers does not make sense for the Australian industry. Like the Michael Ovitzes and Stan Kamens of the Hollywood film industry, the ultimate power of the manager/agent is the ability to link talent with talent. This requires powerful agent/managers who are servicing different parts of the entertainment industry.

Thus, Hilary Linstead's business, which began, as Viccy Harper explained, by representing the interests of creative people who are not on the stage or in front of the camera, has been ideally suited to managing the development of a production. Their work in theatrical productions and stage shows demanded the linking together of writers, set designers, directors, and others. Occasionally, this expanded into Linstead's taking on the role of producer. With Linstead's representing key creative talents such as Jane Campion and Gillian Armstrong from a very early stage in their careers (immediately post-film school), one can see how the manager/agent nexus facilitates the orchestration of an ensemble of talent (and occasionally money) for the industry. Indeed, although Rix did not use the term 'packaging', by his wide range of activities and his close connection to talent he has been invaluable in staging a variety of productions that have been the mainstays of the Australian music industry. Probably the most successful producer/manager of them all, Harry M. Miller, spent much of his career packaging his own projects: producing, publicising and managing large-scale musicals or promoting concert tours by major American stars. In cases such as Miller's, the line between the producer, the manager and the packager is thin.

The role-specific manager: managing speakers

> If you ring Ita Buttrose she would send you to us.
>
> Winston Broadbent

Every single day in Australia, there is some kind of conference or convention running somewhere. In fact, every city sees it as a necessity to have a modern convention centre to handle this part of the tourist business, and every house is partly organised around facilities that appeal to corporate conferences. Conference organisation is a very big business. But every conference needs a keynote speaker, some individual who has a high public profile and the ability to convey a message that is both entertaining and useful. A support industry has grown around this need and manages the provision of their speakers at conferences.

Speaker managers, such as the Saxton Speakers Bureau, Celebrity Speakers and Speakers Network among others, are a very specific element of the celebrity industry. They do not develop the talent or the performance of traditional manager might do; they cultivate already existing public personalities and then seek to make speaking engagements a regular source of their income. Their specific skill is developing the value of the 'touch' to proximity of a celebrity. One of the 110 speakers that Saxton's manages is Max Walker, the former Test cricketer who has made a lucrative second career as a sports commentator for the Nine Network and who, by their estimates has been the most in-demand speaker for the last fifteen years. Walker created an intimate 'touch' environment for his corporate clients:

WINSTON BROADBENT: As he walks into a room to speak everybody knows Max Walker and he'll potter round the tables and chat to people individually. No airs and graces, very down to earth. By the time he stands up to speak, everybody loves him. So the user-friendly bit is a big part of the issue – so he stands up to speak and he creates these wonderful word pictures of anything from his cricketing days to his Channel 9 travelogue days to his South American trips for speaking to whatever and he just manages to create these wonderful, as I say, word-pictures.

Even though Broadbent emphasised that their speakers were principally hired for their record of achievement, and were not typically the material for women's magazines' celebrity reports, he did underline that his business is still in the domain of providing access to these public personalities:

WINSTON BROADBENT: [People] seem to love to have touched a star. Two months ago, we had an event here where we invited 200 people from the media industry and we brought in 35 personalities . . . They were just chatting to all these people that they only saw pictures of – it's a wonderful sensation. And then they go away and they talk about it for ever.

The particular craft of speaker management is to determine how a particular celebrity/personality can be marketed to the corporate world. The principal tactic is to translate the success these speakers have achieved in their various pursuits into a generic formula that can be offered to individuals within a corporate structure. Thus, the mountain climber Peter Hillary can be transformed into a speaker who talks about corporate teamwork or about reaching for transformed goals:

WINSTON BROADBENT: Peter Hillary was doing Toyota and they'd just fallen from being number one in Australia to number two – Ford had taken over the lead. And so Peter Hillary came up with this comment of the lost summit: once you climb Mt Everest something has gone out of your life – just as once you've become the top car producer you've lost something. So you've always got to be looking for new summits if you like to climb. It's a lovely twist in what he normally does, which is climbing your own Everest, but an ability to be able to tailor is critical for a speaker to be successful.

Business celebrities who populate the business sections of newspapers are some of the most natural candidates for the speaker circuit and are actively cultivated. James Strong, of Qantas and Australian Airlines fame, is in great demand because he can talk about mergers. Others who can form their message around hi-tech or the future are also popular. Corporations are willing to pay for personalities in order to have close access to the kind of exclusive information and background knowledge that cannot be given through television or open public appearances:

WINSTON BROADBENT: Obviously our fees are not cheap by comparison. Having said that, there's a number of ways of looking [at it] . . . When you start talking fees for 1000 people and say you talk $4000–1000 people at $4 a head – they spend more than that on the cappuccino that comes after the event. So for somebody with enormous expertise you often are getting 40 years of experience in 40 minutes and it's the essence of success that you're actually buying in the speech and so dollar for dollar you're getting an exceptional deal. You'd expect me to say that but that's the rationale behind the whole process.

The management role in this part of the celebrity industry can encompass a great deal. Broadbent indicates that they are responsible for press releases, a degree of publicity for their speakers, and focused work on matching corporate clients to individual speakers. They are also responsible for handling the celebrity – that is, the delivery of the speaker to the event, the establishment of the itinerary and the time commitment involved – as well as for coordinating relationships with the conference organisers. The fee for their service is 25% of the speaker's fee and Broadbent explained the odd reality that is so different from other managers: there is no written contract with any of their speakers and they all work under the handshake agreement system.

Speaker agencies' close connection to the corporate world can generate other kinds of spokesperson roles for their clients. For instance, Steve Bisley's recent work as spokesperson for Telstra's Big Pond advertising campaign was orchestrated by Saxton's. Broadbent described the essential work of such a campaign as a form of personality branding, aimed at a marriage between the personality and the company. In a similar vein, Saxton's provided Ita Buttrose for a Meat and Livestock Corporation promotion: the specific focus was the value of meat in combating iron deficiency in women and the corporation wanted a high-profile and credible spokesperson to represent it in a prominent and multimedia campaign.

The management of speakers, although not entailing complete personality management, is a very lucrative part of the Australian celebrity industry. Speaker management agents identify how celebrity status can be converted into other services, other forms of information and other products, thus playing an important part in the capitalisation and proliferation of such status. Finally, celebrity speakers and company spokespersons connect corporate Australia to the celebrity industry.

The impresario manager: 'Just talk to Harry'

> Yes, an impresario; but really an entertainment producer because we produce television as well. It's not my day job. My day job is running a business of celebrity management.
>
> Harry M. Miller

There is a third kind of manager operating in the Australian celebrity industry that does not necessarily emerge from a specific form of cultural production nor from a history of being an agent. Unlike Peter Rix, this kind of manager revels in the public sphere itself and, as part of the business, takes publicity beyond the entertainment industry and into the broadest public domain. Very few of us have heard of Winston Broadbent or Rebecca Williamson; however, if the names were Harry M. Miller or Max Markson, there is a high probability that we would be aware of their activities. Miller is certainly a celebrity figure in his own right and Markson seems bent on tracing out a similar trajectory through the promotion of his own media presence as well as that of his clients.

We have set up a category of the 'impresario manager', but, despite Markson's increasing media visibility, it is a category with only one member at the moment. The term 'impresario' does usefully connect Miller with a long line of theatrical entrepreneurs, skilled at reading public desires and presenting events and shows which capture that desire for paying audiences. P.T. Barnum, the nineteenth century master and manager of ceremonies, was precisely this kind of figure: intuitively gauging popular sentiment, he managed the curiosities and personalities of the world and displayed them for entertainment in the form of a 'museum' or a circus. The contemporary Australian impresario manager works the same public terrain, although there have been major changes in the locations where the celebrity spectacle takes place.

Harry M. Miller has built a number of careers from producing entertainments and promotional events, and has over time moved into managing key public personalities. His background as a sales representative in New Zealand in the 1950s and early 1960s, arranging a series of 'contra-deals' to link his products (mundane items such as socks, underwear and electric cookers) with other events and other products, stood him in good stead when he began to move into show business. After managing a New Zealand singing group, the Howard Morrison Quartet, he first came to public attention in Australia as the promoter of high-profile concert tours by well-known American and British performers, including the first Rolling Stones tour, Judy Garland's only appearances in Australia, and Sammy Davis Jr. He moved on to package larger and more complex shows; he developed and promoted Australian productions of the key international musicals of the late 1960s and early 1970s: *Hair, Jesus Christ Superstar, The Rocky Horror Show*, and *Boys in the Band*. Such was his prominence after the success of these productions that Miller could claim in our interview (with appropriate chutzpah) that he 'was, still am really, the most famous producer Australia ever produced and I was born in New Zealand'.

His move into celebrity management has been gradual and has only dominated his activities relatively late in his career. It has also tended to be at the request of others, seeking the kind of support and advice they saw Miller as uniquely able to provide. The element which seems to have made him an attractive manager for public figures such as Graham Kennedy, Maggie Tabberer and others is his apparent ease at working out how to do a deal with the media by understanding the nature of the media's commercial interest in a personality or information, and then manipulating that interest. Experience in promotion, production and management gives him an extremely broad understanding of the entertainment business. These days, Miller also possesses what he describes as 'leverage' in the media and business marketplace. Significantly, he is probably more well known than some of his clients. His own celebrity both precedes and facilitates his work for clients by providing the necessary access to influential people. In describing how a deal was worked out between Collette Dinnigan and Audi, he relates how his name on a fax produced an immediate reaction from Audi's marketing director to help set up a coordinated promotional deal:

HARRY M. MILLER: Fax from Harry M. Miller about a really famous person – you know she is going to ring [back] . . . So we're very good at leveraging that sort of stuff and that's part of our fame and when we don't know people – which is occasionally, not very often – but when we don't know people we just rely on our brand name [which] opens a lot of doors.

Consequently, the famous come to him to work out how they will be represented to the public. His first client, Graham Kerr, of *Galloping Gourmet* fame, wanted to make his unique cooking style and personality a fixture on television, radio and newspapers and Miller helped Kerr to achieve this.[2] Some of the more interesting clients have not emerged from the entertainment industry directly but have sought assistance when they have become the unwilling object of media attention. This is a relatively new category of celebrity, in fact, a consequence of changes in news values in the print and electronic media, and the intense competition between television networks since the end of the 1980s. While there are a number of other managers bidding for this kind of business — Max Markson and Leo Karis, for example — Miller's market dominance is significant. It is a market he is serious about serving. Unlike most other agents and managers, he admits to very little interest in representing actors or directors as an ongoing activity: 'I'd rather use them for something than be their agent'. Throughout his career, it is the deal which seems to attract Miller, and handling the accidental celebrities who are routinely thrown up by events, disasters or controversies provides plenty of opportunities for doing the deal. Not that he is entirely uninterested in packaging ideas for the entertainment industry. In our interview, though, we saw how he liked to synergise his varied interests, say, in a production deal that allows him to link personalities and figures to a given project that may have emerged from one of his clients. He described his plans for a further development out of the story of James Scott, whom he represents:

HARRY M. MILLER: I have no interest in reading some of these scripts and saying, 'Baby, this is a great idea for you'. We are more likely to take a script to somebody and ask them. Like this James Scott book. The film is about his sister — that's what it's about — how she persevered and finally they found him. The person to play that role is Nicole Kidman. It's a killer of a role for her, killer, and there are very few roles that are good for women. So we're saying to the guys that are developing it, 'Keep Nicole Kidman in mind when you're writing it'. And I am saying to Nicole's agent, 'Just down the road, it'll be there soon'. That's all we're doing, just keeping everybody on the case.

Far from the grassroots developmental process described by Peter Rix, all Miller's clients these days come with value and are therefore already a desirable product: what his firm does for them is 'enhance product'. Miller explains that only about 4% of his business comes from 'crisis management control': dealing with formerly 'ordinary' people who have become the focus of media attention, where his role is to control media access and to effectively organise singular deals with particular media sources. His own background has given him a heightened sensitivity to the media circus that can develop and he is ruthless in his control once a Stuart Diver or a James Scott is in his stable.

In his more regular client pool, Miller works towards what he labels a 'seamless outcome' between his client and a particular product. Deborah Hutton's recent spokesperson/promotional campaign with the mid-range and compact Holden cars is exemplary of that approach, as was her former role as Myers Department Store representative. Similarly, Maggie Tabberer, whom Miller describes as an 'icon' and someone who is 'very careful' with her image, was working with him at the time of our interview on coordinating her endorsement of Sydney's Stamford-on-Kent apartments so that they matched her public profile of elegance and concern for design.

Although there are entrepreneurial aspects contained in the development of the other managers studied, Miller is distinctive in that he considers each individual's media moment as an enterprise that requires its own form of management, its placement and (significantly) its development of ongoing desire. According to published accounts,[3] Max Markson seems to approach his management of sports personalities and other newly public figures in similar ways, in that he clearly sees the moment of media presentation of a personality as something that needs to be professionally produced. However, at this point in his career, he lacks the leverage which comes from the establishment of an identifiable public persona, an authority and celebrity that challenges those the media can invent for itself. Miller's frequent play in the scrum of the media frenzy is self-consciously designed to create the impression that he is more knowledgeable of its workings, its desires, its motives and its directions than anyone else. His interest in regulating media attention raises more than issues around publicity or promotion, however.

The publicist

Sandwiched somewhere between the managers, producers and agents, on the one side, and the media outlets on the other, are the publicists. As a group, they have certain clear characteristics: they are overwhelmingly female (70–80%, by one estimate); they are exceedingly accessible; they have often worked as journalists; and they are intimately connected to the network of interests that produce the Australian fame game. Listening to the publicists, you begin to see the interconnectedness of the celebrity industry. Tracey Mair employed an assistant who worked regularly for Markson; Kerry O'Brien's experience in promotion brought her into a working relationship with Miller; Georgie Brown was employed by the publicist *par excellence*, Patti Mostyn, who in turn used to work as publicist for Miller. Other professions are often associated with what we are grouping in the publicist category. The use of the description 'public relations' by freelance publicists seemed to be a strategy to connect them to potential corporate work. Generally, however, the category of publicist applied to those working in the entertainment industry; as the sphere of activity moved away from that, other terms – such as marketer or public relations expert – were employed by our interviewees.

A defining feature of the Australian publicist is that almost all contracts or positions are related to products first and personalities second, even though the personality may be the principal means of selling the product. Unlike Hollywood, where even supporting stars on a television sitcom (Cathy Negemi, for instance, from *Veronica's Closet*) might retain a personal publicist, Australian entertainment publicists rarely work for an individual. The promotion of Australian personalities and the handling of overseas personalities while touring Australia are dealt with in two quite distinct ways: either they are managed internally by the television network or the production company that is staging the show or producing/distributing the film; or they are piloted by freelance publicists who are called in to help orchestrate media coverage. Our analysis of the work that is done by publicists is divided along these lines: the freelance publicist and the media corporation publicist. Our conclusion highlights the varied roles of the entertainment industry publicist as well as their convergence with the strategies usually identified with public relations. Because the product is so central to the publicist's contract, corporate positioning is always somehow implicated in the use made of Australian and overseas personalities.

The freelance publicist

> They also know that when you're trying to find people, who's the one person who is going to have their mobile phone on until midnight seven days a week? – it's the publicist.
>
> Tracey Mair

To work independently as a successful publicist requires industry connections of the highest order. Although a great deal of publicity is handled by freelance companies, most have some form of background that helps to establish them in a certain range of activities. Rea Francis' career with the Australian Film Commission not only connected her to the entire Australian film revival, and the variety of producers, directors, stars and distributors that were implicated in the renaissance, but also enabled her to develop international connections through the promotion of Australian film via film festivals such as Cannes. When she set up her own firm in 1981, she retained the Australian Film Commission as a client. Similarly, Brown, another Sydney freelancer, has had substantial periods of employment with Channel 7. O'Brien worked in promotions for Sony Music to help bolster her independent status in publicity campaigns for tours and shows in Melbourne. So it is rare to find a publicist who has not worked at some time for a major media corporation; their freelance status may continue to be dependent on their former corporate connections.

The unit publicist: giving the media a 'handle'

In Australia, much of the entertainment industry is organised around the individual production. Thus, one of the key contract jobs is as a unit publicist for a film or television production. This entails any publicity that can be achieved while the film is in production and is financed by the production company. The collection of behind-the-scenes footage, on-the-set interviews, and the distribution of stills from the film to newspapers are fundamental parts of the job. Because of the size of the industry and the intermittent patterns of film and television production, unit publicists on local films are sometimes engaged for the complete campaign: from production to distribution and even orchestrating the promotions for exhibition. Mair, who says 80% of her work is on film and telefilm/series publicity, demonstrates the level of involvement that a publicist can have in the promotion of a particular film:

TRACEY MAIR: I was the unit publicist on *Shine* in the winter of 1995 and then I began working on the release publicity for it in Australia when it premiered at the Sundance Film Festival in January 96. And then it was released in Australia in August 1996. So I followed that whole process through and in fact my work wasn't complete until after the Academy Awards in 97. So that was a very long process. It was unusual to be in a position to do unit publicity and then follow through to release. I try to do it when I can and it depends who the distributor of the film is in Australia.

The ultimate product of unit publicity is the press kit, the guide that is distributed to newspaper columnists, magazine and feature editors, and film and television critics. To coordinate with the international distribution of material on film and television, Francis has developed a second business to service the film industry: the electronic press kit, which is distributed to television networks and syndicated programs that focus on entertainment. Here television program editors can find a video interview and then intercut their local host into the footage of the interview to lay claim to what looks like an exclusive.

Publicity, whether for film or other events, has basic objectives: it must appear to be newsworthy, it must be placed appropriately and it must be timed to coordinate with the product's release. As Mair, Brown and Francis underlined, the lead actor is the natural vehicle for the representation of a particular product as new, exciting and therefore worthy of coverage – after all, they present the public face of the film or television program. Placement of film publicity depends on how its appeal is constructed and the publicist actively works on surrounding a particular product with cross-media attractiveness. With the film industry, as opposed to television, operating with very few stars who have value for magazines and newspapers, a publicist has to create clear 'events' that highlight the film's content. Mair's success in promoting *Crackers* relied on working through both the themes of the film and the awkwardness of its shooting schedule to provide a 'handle':

TRACEY MAIR: A lot of my job is my phone conversation with the journalist, my pitch to the journalist and I'm always looking for the angle to pitch at journalists. On *Crackers* – its Melbourne stand-up comedians spent seven years bringing this script to the screen and, my God, look at the public reaction to it – they just adore it. How does someone hold onto that kind of dream for seven years? Filming in a Melbourne winter, it's a family Christmas nightmare kind of comedy. How do these actors survive sitting in bikinis in a Melbourne suburban backyard in the middle of July? You know, those kind of things that give a hook to it: What I'm trying to do is provide an excuse for a journalist to write about something, make their job easy for them, give them a handle on what the story might be.

Each media form was targeted with different interviews and different angles. Serious interviews with the director appeared in the major dailies, while Mair was able to construct an on-air Christmas lunch with the director, three of the actors and Kerri-Anne Kennerley for the *Midday* promotion. The theme: everyone would 'talk about their worst family holiday experiences'.

The importance of publicity for independent film and television producers is intensified in the Australian entertainment industry. Although unit publicists want their campaigns to be coordinated with an advertising onslaught, local films' promotional budgets are very limited. Gaining editorial coverage of a particular film or television series is therefore critical for the successful film run. A full campaign coordinates with media buys and efforts in publicity that provides appropriate background features for a given film. Publicists in these larger campaigns are liaising with the advertising agency to ensure their 'free' media coverage resonates both temporally and in terms of placement with these commercials.

Event publicists: electric dreams

Constructed events are the territory of all publicists. The unit publicist tries to construct events that are worthy of coverage beyond that of a critical review; however, other freelance publicists specialise in the orchestration of public events as a form of marketing. Each event has a target audience that the publicist is trying to attract and interest. At the Cannes Film Festival in the late 1970s, Francis lobbied to get Australian films into competition and then staged events that attracted international attention and critical appraisal. Because 'in those days a lot of Australian films were not pre-purchased . . . they needed a run press-wise internationally', so Francis cultivated as a core audience 'all the top film critics worldwide': 'I made it my business to become great friends with them and we indeed did'. An Australian barbecue on the beach at Cannes, supplying Australian directors, stars, fashion, wine, meat and cheese, became a Francis trademark.

Francis' expertise is in establishing the territory for networking. Describing herself as 'a very successful hostess', she attributes her sense of the value of this kind of interconnection to the English film producer Verity Lambert:

REA FRANCIS: Verity is very fond of saying there are only 300 people in the world and it's not a matter of the size of this. Camaraderie has nothing to do with the size of this country's industry – it's exactly the same in New York, its's the same in England. I know most of the English-speaking players in PR and in media round the world [and] it's the same small pond in each city.

Part of the objective of glitzy premieres and grand openings is to service this network, but it is also to construct the kind of event that attracts media coverage. Promoting the opening of a new Club Med resort in the Pacific region, Francis took a group of journalists there; not only travel journalists, though, but also those writing for sports, news, and a wider feature market. She called this strategy 'widening the press net'.

Event publicity has three objectives: making a media scene, satisfying the needs of the personality or personalities involved, and selling the show. For the publicist, it is crucial that this is achieved, as much as possible, with free advertising or editorial content. Publicists like O'Brien determine their success in terms of page-one newspaper placements and similarly high-profile magazine covers; if she achieved blanket coverage in the morning papers, she might have a celebratory lunch 'and take the rest of the day off'. All saw their function as excitement generators, translating hype into media presence and, finally, sales.

Louise Carroll had a virtual monopoly on publicity for international popular music tours of Queensland for a period of twelve years. She outlined the four phase of publicising a concert through the example of the successful Dolly Parton and Kenny Rogers 1989 tour:

- Phase One – The announcement. The promoters announced the tour two weeks before the tickets went on sale and the publicists had a whole team working on the moment, capitalising on the impact of the press release. Radio and newspaper features were part of that strategy.

- Phase Two – Over-the-counter sales. The day tickets go on sale has the potential to be a media event. One of the ticket offices in the Queen Street Mall in Brisbane had queues on a scale that had never been seen before and by 11 o'clock the concert was sold out. The speed of the sellout gave Carroll's team 'ample opportunities there to work with your media in a publicity sense of the emotion'. The result was that by the afternoon a second added show had been sold out. Maintaining a certain 'emotional' momentum led to the addition of further shows and the sale of a total of 53,000 tickets.

- Phase Three – Pre-show publicity and promotion. Even when a show is sold out, there is an effort to maintain 'general public awareness' in the three-month gap between the ticket sales and the concerts. Promotions, interviews and competitions through CD and ticket giveaways (now no longer necessarily given away but usually coordinated with advertising time for the concert) become critical as the relationship to radio stations and their audience is maintained. Part of this promotion is to give further cultural value to the tickets and the performance. The point of this is a more long-term benefit. A concert is a particular moment for the personality/star to connect to an audience and to establish their continuing presence as a performer of significance. Ticket sales are the first priority, but for the record company the CD sales that can result from this extended publicity campaign are often even more lucrative.

- Phase Four – Bringing it home. The final phase involves ensuring coverage of the actual concert itself. Live crosses from a radio station to the concert could be employed; getting journalists to review the concert with an appropriate press package is also part of the final strategy.

Publicity for concerts and touring shows may be handled by a variety of freelance publicists, but most of them depend on a close and continuing relationship with the small group of local concert promoters in order to contract the assignment. Success for the publicist in this field depends on the frequency of concerts. According to Carroll, there have been fewer international acts touring in recent years. This is in contrast to 1994 when, during a one-month period, she managed the publicity for forty shows. An independent publicist has to be flexible in responding to such a demand with an expanded team and office, before trimming back to the leaner operation that Carroll's office was in 1998.

In general, we observed that most freelance publicists seemed to have very few permanent staff, preferring to employ a regular group of support staff on a contract-by-contract basis. The reputation of the service was directly connected to the name of the principal, and this may explain why all of these publicists traded under their names and not through some authoritative or generic description of the service they provided. The freelance publicity business is as much about trading in names and networks as the celebrity industry itself.

Media corporation publicist

The hub of the Australian celebrity industry is in the publicity departments of major media corporations. Television networks have, as Carroll indicated, expanded from the single-person operations of the early 1980s to whole 'departments' with support staff dedicated to the task of making their personalities circulate prominently in other media. At the time of our interviews, the publicity department for Channel 9 in Sydney had a director, five full-time publicists, a part-time sports publicist and two assistants. Likewise, in film, Village Roadshow Distributors had three distinct departments (publicity, promotion and public relations) dedicated to advancing the profile of their films both nationally and internationally. Suzie MacLeod, publicity manager for Roadshow's distribution interests in Greece, Singapore and New Zealand, as well as film publicist for any Australian film produced and distributed by Roadshow, organises a continuous stream of international stars on promotional tours, introducing key figures from Australian films for press interviews and providing 'colour' images and stories for newspapers, magazines and television. Once you see the inner workings of the publicity departments of these major corporations, it is easy to recognise how much material they provide for the other media.

The everyday: the media feeding the media

Heidi Virtue, who was working for the Nine Network at the time of our interviews, embodies a great deal of what is needed to be a good network publicist: taking care of your 'talent' and ensuring regular editorial coverage for your particular programs. Because of the sheer size of the Nine Network, programs are divided up among the publicity staff; Virtue's portfolio, when we conducted the interview, included *Midday* and Kerri-Anne Kennerley, the stars of *Murder Call*, journalists from *60 Minutes*, and the host of *Australia's Funniest Home Video Show*, Kim Kilbey. But what makes her job a daily source of content for newspapers and magazines is that she is also responsible for all of Nine's international programs:

HEIDI VIRTUE: I am the sort of point of contact for the publicists in all the other states plus all the media. Whenever they want to do a story about *Friends* or *Veronica's Closet* or *Drew Carey* or *ER*, I've got all the contacts they require – the synopsis and all that sort of stuff. Then I liaise with our publicity/liaison person in our bureau in Los Angeles and he and I will come up with sorts of strategies of what we're going to place, and where, etc.

These strategies will be varied and contingent. For instance, because *Friends* had previously been screened by Channel 7, its move to the Nine Network in 1997 required a different kind of campaign than the promotion of a totally new series like *Veronica's Closet*. With *Friends*, audience familiarity with the cast and the leakage of knowledge about the stars through the United States meant that Virtue had to work on different angles and, in particular, to find a repertoire of photographs different from those provided (presumably, in the first instance, to Channel 7) by the Los Angeles distributor. Her task, then, would have involved trawling for photographs or 'trannies' (transparencies) which might be new and interesting for newspaper features. Publicity 'head shots' may end up being used for the regular television listings that appear in the Sunday paper previews, but they are not acceptable for illustrating a full-page feature about a particular show or star. Virtue would have sought more individual and less generic photographs of the *Friends* stars from such large American magazines as *TV Guide*. These shots would then have been purchased for $500 or $600 by the publicity department for free distribution to support such features. *Veronica's Closet* was publicised through a series of interviews with the cast members which emphasised its relative success in the United States. With the network publicist providing a lot of the written material used in the short features in newspaper supplements, it is clear that Virtue and her counterparts at other networks do a great deal of the work in setting up the content, style and image – and even the agenda – of the media treatment of television programs.

Interestingly, although network publicists do provide some of their 'colour', Virtue indicated that mass-market women's magazines usually do their own trawling for and purchasing of international star images. The key factor here is that a magazine's interest in gossip is not necessarily in accord with the commercial purpose of a network's publicity. Consequently, a network's energy tends to be concentrated on providing free images to newspapers, rather than to magazines, because they can be relied upon to treat the program and the stars somewhat differently in their entertainment pages:

HEIDI VIRTUE: Those magazines are after personal life and, you know, boyfriends, girlfriends, lovers and all that stuff. Whereas newspapers will talk to them about their career, about the show they're working on, the character they're working on, you know – there might be a little bit about their personal life, but they're not after that sort of angle.

Publicity for Australian-made programs on network television parallels some of these strategies but with much greater intensity. There are regular features about someone like John Wood of *Blue Heelers*, provided by Seven publicists who will also have arranged a series of interviews. Likewise, Virtue coordinates interviews with *Murder Call* stars for background features. Some consultation occurs with the producers of the particular program, but generally the network publicist organises the publicity shoots as if the network publicist were effectively the unit publicist for the Australian market and the producers. Part of any contract signed with a television producer (usually in very close association with the network that is buying the series) is a 'publicity clause' which stipulates that the star is available for publicity; their appearances fulfil that element of the contract and no further money changes hands. The Nine Network is particularly committed to using its performers and personalities for various forms of network and program publicity. Indeed, it prides itself on being the 'network of the stars'; CEO David Leckie is reputed to like referring to Nine as 'Australia's Hollywood'.

The networks: Australia's Hollywood

> The people driving television in this country are doing it for commercial gain, ratings and revenue . . . The byproduct of television is that publicists get to work and because of those objectives they drive the household names from those soap operas into becoming magazine covers, newspaper covers, television stars, in order to fulfil the brief by television management, and that has created a very different industry here in Australia . . . The networks are control freaks about publicity and the network publicists insist on controlling the publicity for the stars on the shows.
>
> Brian Walsh

The Hollywood reference is not inappropriate. In its attempt to develop stars and through them the profile and audience appeal of network programs, network publicity departments constitute the Australian incarnation of the old Hollywood studio system. Virtue describes Kerri-Anne Kennerley as a 'company woman', a star who understands the interdependencies which mean that it is in her long-term interests to loyally serve the Nine Network. History has proved that those who work within the system, including cooperating with publicity, will be rewarded with future assignments. According to Virtue, Kim Kilbey is also developing as a Nine girl, with appropriate forays into publicity ('in six months she's appeared in all the women's magazines') and an understanding of the pragmatics of network loyalty. By way of contrast, Virtue observes that some new hosts do not understand their dependence on the network for their professional profile.

Perhaps the most recent and surprising example of a (much older) personality who appears to be learning that lesson is Ray Martin. For years Martin represented the pinnacle of the studio/network system: he was Nine's brightest star and anchored its image nationally. His public comments about network decisions in 1999 (comments obviously not orchestrated through the publicity department), his complaints about the invasion of his privacy by John Safran and Shane Paxton (complaints which struck everyone as pretty rich coming from the former host of *A Current Affair*), and his ill-considered stint as the anchor for the World Cup cricket coverage show how easily a public reputation can unravel if it is not centrally managed. He was conspicuously absent from the presenting team for Nine's mega-broadcast, *Millennium Live*, on New Year's Eve, 1999.

Because of their concentration on the promotion of personalities, the network publicist is by far the most powerful single factor in shaping the celebrity industry. The Nine Network is particularly vigilant and focused on advancing its stars (presenters, journalists, and actors from high-rating drama series such as *Water Rats*) in other media, thus exploiting the cross-promotion possibilities of the Australian Consolidated Press (ACP) magazines. But it also foregrounds them through such events as its annual pre-season promotional campaign which depends solely upon images of its personalities (rather than on its programs). The Seven Network is more dependent upon actors from its successful local drama series and so promotes itself through John Wood and Lisa McCune of *Blue Heelers* and through teen/young adult stars such as Belinda Emmett of *Home and Away*. The Ten Network relies on its high-profile, mostly American programs for its targeted young adult demographic. Nevertheless, a benefit of Ten's recent raiding of the ABC's battery of youth-oriented comedy programs has been the development of a stable of stars with great appeal to its audience: the teams of young comics and personalities from *The Panel* and *Good News Week* which have become synonymous with Australian youth culture.

Other media forms, perhaps as a result of the networks' establishment of an expectation of personality promotion, have likewise developed publicity that is focused on the personality or the individual celebrity. Book publishing has become more and more concerned about the nature of the author's image/identity and how it might assist sales. Andrew Freeman, senior publicist of a team of five at Random House, explains that it is much easier to promote non-fiction than fiction authors because they generally come with a ready-made public profile. Established journalists, for instance, attract good publicity. Sydney columnist Paul Sheehan's *Among the Barbarians* was an immediate success, selling more than 40,000 copies in three weeks.[4] While the book was easily promotable because of its controversial opposition to political correctness, Sheehan's success, Freeman admitted, owed a certain amount to the fact that journalists are already part of the media and personality system, and the strength of the 'journalist network' means that they tend to be 'very good to their own' in terms of coverage.

The negotiations around the Ian Roberts biography provide a further indication of how celebrity percolates through the Australian media.[5] Once Random House had won the contract (which included an advance of $150,000) for Roberts' account of his life as the first openly gay rugby league player, Freeman sent advance manuscripts to newspapers to produce a bidding war for extracts. News Limited paid $30,000 for the exclusive rights to publish excerpts, coordinated with the publication date of the book. The three-month campaign was at its most intense over the three weeks surrounding the publication date. During that period, Random House arranged displays in all bookshops – these included a full-size cardboard cutout photo image of Roberts (which still decorates Freeman's office), book signings/autograph sessions, and prominently featured piles of books – as well as ensuring general reviewing in the major newspapers by both sports columnists and book reviewers. Because of the unique spin of sportsman and sexuality, the book had a high-enough profile that it led to features in newspapers that might not have carried the exclusive extract and, more importantly, it led to another battle over exclusivity for a television profile of Roberts. Freeman indicated that the favoured television program for author interviews would almost always be *60 Minutes*; however, in this case, Channel 7's *Witness* flew a crew up to interview Roberts in his hometown of Townsville and thereby eliminated any interest from other networks that might have provided prominent coverage as well.

Random House also organised a series of radio interviews with Roberts, designed so that they did not conflict with his playing commitments and training. In all, the publicity generated a level of media saturation that allowed Freeman to claim a publicist's success: a massive amount of editorial coverage of the book and sales in excess of 30,000.

The circulation of personalities through the celebrity industry is equally part of the business of running a large television production and distribution house. In the case of the Southern Star series *Water Rats*, for example, Lesna Thomas, from Southern Star, and the publicists at Nine work very closely to coordinate their strategies. If the series' stars are reticent about appearing on *TV Week* covers or inside posters, Thomas and her staff will try to facilitate the outcome desired by the network. Like all the other publicists, though, her general publicity goal is to move stories out of the television sections and into other areas of the newspaper and into magazines because 'this is the only way to make your audience grow'. And as was the case with Brian Walsh's mid-1980s massage of *Neighbours* into a youth program [. . .], Thomas identifies casting and script strategies aimed at drawing younger audiences. *Water Rats'* 1999 acquisition of young Aboriginal star Aaron Pederson was part of that strategy; a more concerted effort of refocusing a series on youth can be seen in the addition of Damian Walshe-Howling to the cast of *Blue Heelers* for 1998 and 1999.

One of Thomas' principal tasks is promoting and positioning Southern Star's dramatic programs internationally, and here again the marketing of the stars is important.[6] For the launch of the second season of *Water Rats*, she toured the major European buyers' markets (MIP-TV, MIP-Comm) so that star Colin Friels could talk to all of the major buyers. They followed up with a series of interviews with the principal entertainment magazines in Germany and London. Other stars used to promote local product overseas include Bryan Brown (*Twisted Tales*), Lisa McCune (*Blue Heelers*) and Gary Sweet (*Big Sky*). In a rather odd but almost universal pattern, Australian dramatic actors are more willing to expose themselves to international publicity circuits than domestically:

LESNA THOMAS: You find the sort of productions that we do, which are primetime quality drama, you're not going to get a star going on domestic networks saying, 'Hi, I'm so and so — you can catch me on Nine'; but I can get them to do it for overseas brochures because it's not their domestic market. If you're a star in Australia . . . you don't want necessarily to have [your] face out there talking to a camera telling people to watch you . . . and you won't get a Jerry Seinfeld doing that [in his home American market] either.

The various media corporations, with their permanent publicity staff, are able to construct a celebrity world for the Australian media from a blend of national and international personalities. Walsh, who is now director of programming, publicity and promotion for the pay television company Foxtel, has resurrected the large-scale promotional strategies that used to be more commonplace in Australian networks: bringing out the big American television star. For the launch of the stripped series of the *X-Files* on one of Foxtel's channels in 1997, he toured its star, Gillian Anderson:

BRIAN WALSH: I gave her a week at the Four Seasons in Bali — because half of these Americans have got no idea, they come down here and they think they can do Ayers Rock and the Barrier Reef in one day. So they come down here — and I did with Gillian Anderson what I did with Kylie and Jason. I took her to Westfield Shoppingtown Centres, and it was mayhem . . . And she couldn't believe it. She had never seen anything like it in her life, and we got unbelievable coverage from that tour . . . Now, you tell me what other company in broadcasting has 30,000 subscribers and gets front-page coverage like that? . . . Actually . . . what is the front page of the *Sunday Telegraph* worth? It's — you know, it all reinforces Foxtel as the brand leader . . . I have an entire dedicated LA office that just generates stories for me out of LA that I can then give my publicists here to resubmit to the Australian media.

The tour cost Foxtel $100,000, as did a similar tour by *Melrose Place* star Andrew Shue.

The international publicity tour is the staple activity for those involved in distributing Hollywood films. Suzie MacLeod regularly coordinates such tours for Hollywood stars and thereby provides a massive amount of editorial content for the Australian media. Tours coincide with the release dates of the films involved and combine planned public appearances with media interviews. MacLeod's job is to organise the itinerary, provide the images necessary for pre-publicity and then accompany the star throughout all of the activities. Stars are discharging their contractual obligations to provide publicity and are thus only paid daily rates ($150) — nevertheless, they are completely taken care of during their visits. Interviews are scheduled with journalists and a list of guidelines is handed to each interviewer, covering 'things like you can't ask for personal autographs' or possibly a range of personal questions that the star does not want to answer. The pattern of interview staging is all too familiar for major stars: the 'landing/arrival' press conference, followed by a day of hotel suite interviews — sometimes using two suites in order to keep to the fifteen-minute time frame for each interview. The publicist works to maintain this schedule so that the greatest number of media hits is made, and made effectively. Because the star is out of their usual territory, special rules do develop when they are promoting a film in Australia. Overseas stars, such as Matt Le Blanc who toured in support of *Lost in Space*, often have their own publicist with them. This risks potential conflicts over the presentation of the personality. The distribution publicist is concerned about using the star as the bait for general media coverage; the personal publicist is working towards managing the star's presentation as a distinct commodity that just happens at this moment to be connected to a particular film.

Column inches: Public relations and value

Publicity, while being at the very centre of the celebrity industry in Australia, suffers from the fact that its value is never entirely concrete. Because publicity, by definition, always appears to be something else (a news item or a feature story, for instance), and because it is therefore, again by definition, 'free', publicists are always looking for ways to identify and quantify the benefit of their work to the industry. One of the common ways of evaluating it is to calculate the dollar value of the coverage generated from the dollar value of an equivalent amount of purchased advertising space (column inches of newsprint) or time (seconds/minutes on air). MacLeod and Walsh regularly assess the value of their newspaper coverage in terms of column inches; hence, MacLeod could claim that a particular tour had produced over a million dollars' worth of coverage. Dollar value of exposure, however, still begs the question of effect or influence on the market; the advertising industry is notorious for not always knowing what works (in terms of generating sales) and what doesn't.

There is another way in which the publicist's function can be understood, though, a way that is more structural than commercial: they constitute a vital link in the chain of connections which enables the media to deal with the entertainment industry. All of the publicists we interviewed expressed the opinion that the media was 'very' or 'highly' or 'incredibly' dependent on their work. Georgie Brown, for instance, found that her material went so seamlessly into mass-market women's magazines that she started doing freelance writing for them. Suzie MacLeod explained that, whenever there is a media release publicising a tour, it is routinely swallowed and regurgitated by radio, with at least 'a couple of columns . . . always in the newspaper'. Heidi Virtue said that, although journalists will absolutely never admit it, entertainment writers and editors simply depend on her supply of content. The distribution of free images, declining staff numbers on newspapers, the 'non-news' or 'soft news' character of today's feature, lifestyle and entertainment sections, all contribute to press dependence on publicists for copy. Given the regularity of contact between editors and publicists, and the occasional junket that journalists receive through that contact, a convergence of industrial and commercial interests must develop.

Publicity has built the celebrity industry. Although the client of Australian publicists is only rarely the individual (generally, the producer is paying), the channel taken by publicists to represent the 'emotion' of the cultural product is invariably through particular personalities. Celebrities are all spokespersons in one form or another for some further commodity than themselves (think of how Southern Star has used its 'stars' to position its product internationally). The result of the increasing intensity of the competing and overlapping publicity campaigns selling various cultural and media products has been an emerging Australian star system. A register of the industrial significance of this system is the fact that, in many instances, the selling of specific newspapers, magazines and television programs is now dependent upon their deployment of these personalities as images, voices and quotes. In the media marketplace today, in a wide range of contexts, the publicity practitioners are the facilitators – the go-betweens – of product positioning and media coverage; their main tools are celebrities.

Notes

1   10BA was the clause in the tax Act that related to the tax concessions used to encourage investment in the Australian film industry from 1981. It was gradually wound down as its costs increased over the 1980s, leading to the establishment of the Film Finance Corporation in 1988–89.

2   Harry M. Miller and Denis O'Brien, *Harry M. Miller, My Story*, South Melbourne, Macmillan, 1983, pp. 147–54.

3   See Louise Evans, 'Max Markson's ring of confidence', *Sydney Morning Herald Good Weekend*, 14 July 1990, pp. 30–1, 33–4.

4   P. Sheehan, *Among the Barbarians: The Dividing of Australia*, Sydney, Random House, 1998.

5   I. Roberts, *Finding Out*, Sydney, Random House, 1998.

6   That said, it is not all a matter of celebrity promotion, as Thomas reveals: 'We have a very close relationship with the Nine Network [it is in fact a co-production] . . . but . . . *Water Rats* has sold to 168 countries and Australia is only one of them and what we need to meet their requirements and promotion can be very different from overseas . . . Overseas they love the shots of the Harbour Bridge and the Opera House every five minutes.'

Conclusion

T HERE IS SOMETHING INCONCLUSIVE about celebrity culture. Despite the cartographic work completed in this book – after all, I have with my contributors laid claim to celebrity's connection to modernity, to a notion of democracy, to a changed public sphere, to an understanding of a newly mediated cultural economy, and to a complex representation of individuality – celebrity culture is a discursive satellite of other constitutions of cultural activity. The linking of any practice to the notion of culture has become incredibly common and popular. Thus, in popular culture studies and in journalistic exposés, there are new forms of culture: NASCAR (National Association for Stock-Car Auto Racing) culture becomes an intellectual shorthand to comprehend the change in pleasure and practices of predominantly white middle/working-class America; street culture in a city might refer to the cosmopolitan grouping of restaurants and boutiques in a given section of the city and the patronization of these precincts by contemporary *flâneurs*, or it might be how the homeless in an area collectively navigate their lives; beach culture might refer to the codes, practices and hierarchies that occur on a Saturday at a beach; and so on. Attaching the word "culture" to an activity is in some senses a way to recognize its importance and significance and to imply that an anthropological investigation – a deep description perhaps – is what is needed to unpack the various and often complex patterns of signification, expressions of power and influence, and the organization of groups and their interactions.

As I indicated in the book's introduction, celebrity culture produces both surface and depth in its connection to wider cultural practices. Its ubiquity means that it is hard to avoid as a phenomenon, but this ever-presence does not imply that it is something that everyone treats with the same level of seriousness. Like popular culture itself, there is often a difference between its apparent lack of seriousness and its capacity to reverberate loudly through the entire culture. Celebrity as a cultural phenomenon has become a component of many other activities. Politics, with all its rhetoric of seriousness, is often enveloped in a celebrity culture that massages the populace into determining its affective investment in particular representatives. Reputations in the medical establishment are partially inflected by a kind of cult of personality that slides comfortably into another component of celebrity culture. Even the bizarre world of serial killers can be and has been integrated into a parallel dimension of fascination and celebration that resembles how other celebrities are viewed. The comfortable home of celebrity, the expansive world of the entertainment industries, in itself produces a rich variety of celebrities which express an equally rich landscape of public personas that are used by their audiences.

Defining celebrity culture as a discursive satellite of other cultural activities identifies the engagement and the distance that are simultaneously produced by celebrity culture. Because celebrity is an elaborate representation of individuality, it is enacted at various degrees of separation from audiences and users. The representative quality of celebrity produces a proxy effect in the public sphere. Celebrities act out in all the senses of the word, and we as audiences interpret the performances. Celebrity performances are not the same as a performance in a play or a film or even as a music performance: They become expressions of individuality in a playing field that is constructed as "real" and specifically beyond those "texts" (although very much influenced by those texts) that we normally think of as performance. Their representations in the public world are the material for our conversations, interpretations, and often our judgments. There is a large support industry of magazines, television talk shows, and online sites that both feed and guide our interpretations of celebrities and operate as a commodified discursive layer that resembles the wider populace's discussion of celebrity.

Let's take the metaphor of satellite further here in order to investigate the cultural implications of celebrity. Planets and satellites have mutual effects on each other. The moon, for instance, is at least partially influential in the Earth's oceans' tides. Likewise, the Earth produces a gravitational pull on the moon which helps generate its orbit and its own 1/6 gravity. What can be said about this relationship is that the effects are regular and experienced every day.

In a similar way, celebrity culture has been constructed as this separate world – a satellite – that influences various cultures, where culture is defined as a comprehensive field of a way of life, regularly. Celebrity culture is a certain representation of individuality, and this kind of individuality plays differently in different cultural configurations. In my own writing I have linked celebrity culture with the emergence of consumer capitalism: That is, it is a representative world/satellite that supports the kind of individuality, that is essential to the operation of consumer capitalism. I have also tied celebrity with the emergence of democracy: That is, celebrity culture is a representative system that expresses the agency that is essential for the operation of democratic systems in their connection to their people. And finally, as representations that intersect with the everyday from a distance – an unreal real – celebrity culture serves via its celebrity representations as a way to channel a variety of political, social and cultural issues into wider debate.

It is this uncanny quality of celebrity culture, where it is very much disconnected from the everyday and yet through its mediation is implicated as an unreal-real component of our everyday lives, which makes it both empty and rich, disposable and yet a source for comprehending key components of our culture and way of life. Celebrity culture's ethereal and representative quality has also allowed it to migrate transculturally and produce a similar discursive field in these different cultural spaces.

This reader on celebrity culture has been decidedly focused on Western if not specifically Anglo-American configurations of celebrity culture. And what needs further exploration and compilation is the work by other scholars who have investigated celebrity in specific cultural milieux. Some of this research is already well developed, although not necessarily translated completely – and here I am thinking of Saeko Ishita's important writing on fame in Japan. It is also equally important for research to explore the interactions between celebrity culture and a variety of other "cultures." Here I am thinking of how globalization and celebrity intersect as well as how issues around identity and something such as multiculturalism is refracted through the representations of individuality that the discourse of celebrity culture produces for even further discussion and debate in the populace. Two other areas are also deserving of further exploration. There is still not enough written about the body and celebrity, as much as there have been critiques about how celebrity/model body images have had a deleterious effect on identity formation in youth. And finally, there needs to be much further research on the changing subjectivity that new media has engendered and how that is shifting our representational/presentational regimes of meaning.

Ultimately, I hope this reader has been useful in compiling some of the key research and writing about celebrity and celebrity culture and will serve those who want to investigate these different directions in their own research. A project like this one is always incomplete and I encourage others to work towards these new areas in both using and understanding celebrity culture.

References

Introduction

Bourdieu, P. (1984) *Distinction: The Social Critique of the Judgment of Taste*, Cambridge, MA: Harvard University Press.

Carlyle, T. (1969: 1839) *On Heroes, Hero-Worship and the Heroic in History*, New York: Ams.

Creamer, M. and Ives, N. (2005) "Risky Business," *Advertising Age*, July 18.

Dyer, R. (1979) *Stars*, London: BFI.

Dyer, R. (2005) *New York Times*, March 11: 1.

Habermas, J. (1991) *The Structural Transformation of the Public Sphere: An Inquiry into a Category of Bourgeois Society*, Cambridge, MA: MIT Press.

Heinemann, A. (2005) 'In Search of the Right Dead Celebrity,' *Adage Online.com Online Edition*, www.adage.com, July 18.

Jenkins, H. (1992) *Textual Poachers: Television Fans and Participatory Culture*, London: Routledge.

Marshall, P.D. (1997) *Celebrity and Power*, Minneapolis: University of Minnesota Press.

Taylor, C. (1989) *Sources of the Self*, Cambridge: Harvard University Press.

Williams, R. (1965) *The Long Revolution*, Harmondsworth: Penguin.

1 Man as actor

Berman, M. (1970) *The Politics of Authenticity*, New York: Atheneum.

Cassirer, E. (1954) *The Questions of Jean Jacques Rousseau*, New York: Columbia University Press.

Cole T., Chinoy, H. (1970) *Actors on Acting*, New York: Crown.

Fielding, H. (1749) *Tom Jones*, London: Penguin.

Huizinga, J. (1955) *Homo Ludens*, Boston: Beacon.

Mantzius, K. (1903) *A History of Theatrical Art in Ancient and Modern Times*, London: Duckworth and Co.

Rousseau, J. (1968) *Politics and the Arts: The Letter to M. d'Alembert*, trans. A. Bloom, Ithaca; Cornell University Press,

Strasberg, L. (1957) *An Introduction to Diderot: The Paradox of Acting*, New York: Hill & Wang.

Trilling, L. (1972) *Sincerity and Authenticity*, Cambridge, Mass: Harvard University Press.

Vexler, F. (1922) *Studies in Diderot's Esthetic Naturalism*, New York: Ph.D. thesis, Columbia University.

Wilson, A. (1972) *Diderot*, New York: Oxford University Press.

2 The longing of Alexander

Despite the more than twenty contemporaries who wrote about Alexander, our own most direct sources were written in the first and second centuries A.D., some four or five hundred years after he lived, by weaving together the now lost primary sources and adding traditional tales and local details as they came to hand. Hamilton's commentary on Plutarch's biography of Alexander spends a good deal of time construing the text but also conveys a valuable picture of how Plutarch may have sifted his sources and what they were. The two-volume Loeb edition of Arrian's *History of Alexander and Indica* as well as the Penguin volume, *The Campaigns of Alexander*, make the most extensive surviving account of Alexander's career easily available. For an analysis of the sources on which Arrian and other historians drew, see Pearson, *The Lost Histories of Alexander the Great*. Of the recent biographies written about Alexander for a popular audience, Hamilton's reflects the approach of a sceptical historian, intent on pruning the elements of "romance" from the record, while Fox's has a welcome sensitivity to interpretive issues that go beyond the establishment of a narrow accuracy. Fox's notes also give a very full picture of the sources for the reader interested in following the thread of Alexander's career through the labyrinth of controversy. Bamm's biography has many acute remarks, as does Green's, along with some outstanding illustrations.

Arrian (1971) *The Campaigns of Alexander*, tr. Aubrey de Sélincourt. Penguin.
Arrian (1976–1978) *History of Alexander and Indica*, vol. 1, tr. P.A. Brunt; vol. 2, tr. E. Iliff Robinson. Loeb.
Bamm, P. (1968) *Alexander the Great*. New York.
Fox, R. L. (1973) *Alexander the Great*. London.
Green, P. (1970) *Alexander the Great*. London.
Guthrie, W.K.C. (1950) *The Greeks and Their Gods*. Boston.
Hamilton, J.R. (1969) *Plutarch: Alexander, a Commentary*. Oxford.
Hobbes, T. (1968) *Leviathan* [1651], ed. C. B. Macpherson. Penguin.
Homer (1974) *The Iliad*, tr. Robert Fitzgerald. Garden City, N.Y.
Homer (1961) The Odyssey, tr. Robert Fitzgerald. Garden City, N.Y.
Pearson, L. (1960) *The Lost Histories of Alexander the Great*. American Philological Association Monograph 20.
Plutarch (1973) *The Age of Alexander*, tr. Ian Scott-Kilvert. Penguin.
Plutarch (1941) *Lives of the Noble Greeks and Romans*, tr. Sir Thomas North. New York.
Seneca (1972) *Naturales Quaestiones, The Works of Seneca*, vol. 10, tr. Thomas Corcoran. Loeb.
Snell, B. (1953) *The Discovery of Mind*, tr. T.G. Rosenmeyer. Oxford.
Thoreau, H.D.(1971) *Walden*, ed. J. Lyndon Shanley. Princeton.
Vermeule, E. (1976) *Aspects of Death in Early Greek Art and Poetry*. Berkeley.
Zimmer, H. (1955) *The Art of Asian India*, 2 vols, ed. Joseph Campbell. New York.

4 From hero to celebrity

Amory, C. and Blackwell, E. (1959) *Celebrity Register*.
Emerson, R.W. (1850) *Representative Man*. Oxford University Press.

5 The discourse on acting

Allen, R.C. (1980) *Vaudeville and Film 1895–1915: A Study in Media Interaction*, New York: Arno Press.

Barthes, R. (1981) *Camera Lucida*, trans. Richard Howard, New York: Hill and Wang.

Bordwell, D., Staiger, J. and Thompson, K. (1985) *The Classical Hollywood Cinema: Film Style and Mode of Production to 1960*, New York: Columbia University Press.

Carroll, D. (1972) *The Matinee Idols*, London: Peter Owen.

Eaton, W.P. (1909) "The Canned Drama," *American Magazine* (Sept).

The Edison Kinetogram.

Gunning, T. (1991) *D.W. Griffith and the Origins of American Narrative Film: The Early Years at Biograph*, Urbana: University of Illinois Press.

"How the Cinematographer Works," *Moving Picture World*, May 18, 1907, p. 166. *Variety.*

McArthur, B. (1984) *Actors and American Culture, 1880–1920*, Philadelphia: Temple University Press.

Moving Picture World.

Musser, C. (1984) "Another Look at the 'Chaser Theory'," *Studies in Visual Communication*, 10, no. 4 (Fall): 24–44.

Musser, C. (1983) "The Nickelodeon Era Begins: Establishing the Framework for Hollywood's Mode of Representation," *Framework* 22–23 (Autumn): 4.

New York Dramatic Mirror.

Smoodin, E. (1979) "Attitudes of the American Printed Medium toward the Cinema: 1894–1908," unpublished paper, University of California, Los Angeles.

Souriau, E. (1953) *L'univers filmique*, Paris: Flammarion.

6 The powerless "elite"

Alberoni, F. (1960) *Contributo all' Integrazione sociale dell' Immigrato*, Milano, Vita e Pensiero.

Alberoni, F. (1961) 'Saggio critico delle differenze socioculturali tra due region meridionali,' *Internat. Soc. Science Rev.*, vols. 1 and 2.

Banfield, E. (1961) *Una Communita del Mezzogiorno*, Bologna, Il Mulino.

Panzini, A. (1963) *Modern Dictionary of Words which are not Found in Ordinary Dictionaries*, Milano, Hoepli.

Parsons, T. (1949) *The Social System*, Free Press.

Weber, M. (1968) *Economy and Society*, Bedminster Press.

8 Stars as images

Babuscio, Jack, "Screen Gays", *Gay News* nos. 73 ("Camp women"), 75 ("Images of masculinity"), 92 (Sissies'), 93 ("Tomboys").

Boorstin, Daniel, *The Image*. Weidenfeld & Nicholson, London, 1962; Penguin, 1963.

Harris, Thomas B., "The Building of Popular Images: Grace Kelly and Marilyn Monroe", *Studies in Public Communication*, 1, 1957, pp. 45–8.

Haskell, Molly, *From Reverence to Rape*, Holt, Rinehart and Winston, New York, 1974; Penguin, London.

Hess, Thomas B., "Pinup and Icon", in Hess, Thomas B., and Nochlin, Linda (eds), *Woman as Sex Object*, Newsweek, New York, 1972, pp.223–237.

King, Barry, "The Social Significance of Stardom," unpublished manuscript, 1974.

Klapp, Orrin E., *Heroes, Villians and Fools*, Prentice-Hall, Englewood Cliffs, 1962.

Lowenthal, Leo, *Literature and the Image of Man*, Beacon Press, Boston, 1957.

Lowenthal, Leo, "The Triumph of Mass Idols", in *Literature, Popular Culture and Society*, Prentice-Hall, Englewood Cliffs, 1961, pp. 109–140.

Lucas, Bob, *Naked in Hollywood*, Lancer Books, New York, 1962.

Meyer, Janet, "Dyke goes to the Movies," *Dyke* (New York), Spring 1976.

McGilligan, Patrick, *Cagney: The Actor as Auteur*, A.S. Barnes, South Brunswick, Tantivy, London, 1975.

McLean, Albert F. Jnr, *American Vaudeville as Ritual*, University of Kentucky Press, 1965.

Mills, C. Wright, *The Power Elite*, Oxford University Press, New York, 1956.

Morin, Edgar, *Les Stars*, Seuil, Paris, 1957; reprinted (trans. Richard Howard), Grove Press, New York, 1960.

Mulvey, Laura, "Visual Pleasure and Narrative Cinema", *Screen*, vol. 16, no. 3, Autumn 1975, pp. 6–18.

Rosen, Marjorie, *Popcorn Venus*, Coward, McCann & Geoghegan, New York, 1973; Avon Books, 1974.

Veblen, Thorstein, *Theory of the Leisure Class*, Macmillan, New York, 1899; Mentor, 1953; George Allen and Unwin, London, 1925; 1970 (paperback).

Walker, Alexander, *The Celluloid Sacrifice*, Michael Joseph, London, 1966; reprinted (new title, *Sex in the Movies*), Penguin, London, 1968. *Stardom, the Hollywood Phenomenon*, Michael Joseph, London, 1970; Penguin, London, 1974.

9 Television's "personality system"

Barthes, R. (1973) *Mythologies*, St Albans, Paladin.

Brunsdon, C. and Morley, D. (1978) *Everyday Television: "Nationwide"*, BFI Televison Monograph, 10.

Buscombe, E. (ed.) (1976) *Football on Televison*, BFI Television Monograph, 4.

Chibnall, S. (1977) *Law and Order News*, London, Tavistock Publications.

Danziger, K. (1976) *Interpersonal Communication*, Oxford, Pergamon Press.

Dyer, R. (1979) *Stars*, London, BFI.

Eaton, M. (1978/79) Television situation comedy, *Screen*, vol. 19, no. 4, Winter.

Epstein, E. J. (1973) *News for Nowhere*, New York, Vintage Books.

Hall, S. (1976) Television and culture, *Sight and Sound*, Autumn.

Hall, S. (1977) Culture, the media, and the ideological effect, in Curran, J. *et al.* (eds), *Mass Communication and Society*, London, Edward Arnold.

Heath, S. and Skirrow, G. (1977) Television, a world in action, *Screen*, vol. 18, no. 2, Summer.

Lowenthal, L. (1961) *Literature, Popular Culture and Society*, Palo Alto, Pacific Books.

McArthur, C. (1978) *Television and History*, London, BFI Television Monograph, 8.

Mills, I. (1980) Pulpit drama, the mythic form of T.V. news programmes, in Edgar, P. (ed.), *The News In Focus*, London, Macmillan.

Monaco, J. (1978) *Celebrity: The Media as Image Makers*, New York, Delta Books.

Schiller, H. I. (1969) *Mass Communication and American Empire*, Fairfield, Kelley.

Sennett. R. (1974) *The Fall of Public Man*, New York Vintage Books.

Tunstall, J. (1977) *The Media are American*, London, Constable.

11 Is straight the new queer?

Cashmore, E. *Beckham*. 2nd ed. Oxford: Polity Press, 2004.

Cashmore, E. and A. Parker. "One David Beckham? Celebrity, Masculinity and the Soccerati." *Sociology of Sport Journal* 20.3 (2003): 214–31.

Dyer, R. *Stars*. 2nd ed. London: BFI, 1998.

Hall, S. "Encoding/Decoding." Reprinted from original 1977 publication at Birmingham Centre for Contemporary Cultural Studies. *Culture, Media, Language*. Ed. S. Hall. London: Unwin Hyman, 1990.

Marshall, P.D. *Celebrity and Power: Fame in Contemporary Culture*. London: University of Minneapolis Press, 1997.

Mort, F. "Boy's Own? Masculinity, Style and Popular Culture." *Male Order. Unwrapping Masculinity*. Ed. J. Chapman and J. Rutherford. London: Lawrence and Wishart, 1998. 193–224.

Nixon, S. *Hard Looks: Masculinities, Spectatorship and Contemporary Consumption*. London: UCL Press, 1996.

Rahman, M. "David Beckham as a Historical Moment in the Representation of Masculinity." *Labour History Review* 69.2 (Aug. 2004): 219–34.

Turner, G. *Understanding Celebrity*. London: Sage, 2004.

Whannel, G. *Media Sport Stars: Masculinities and Moralities*. London: Routledge, 2002.

13 Feminine fascinations

Benjamin, J. (1990) *The Bonds of Love: Psychoanalysis, Feminism and the Problem of Domination*, London: Virago.

Cowie, E. (1984) "Fantasia", *m/f* 9: 71–104.

Friedberg, A. (1982) "Identification and the star: a refusal of difference", in *Star Signs: Papers from a Weekend Workshop*, London: British Film Institute.

Freud, S. (1920) "The psychogenesis of a case of homosexuality in a woman", in *Standard Edition* 18, London, Hogarth Press.

Greig, D. (1987) "The sexual differentiation of the Hitchcock text", *Screen* 28, 1, Winter: 28–48.

Handel, L. (1950) *Hollywood Looks at its Audience*, Urbana, IL: University of Illinois Press.

Laplanche, J. and Pontalis, J. (1968) "Fantasy and the origins of sexuality", reprinted in Burgin, Victor, Donald, Kaplan, Cora (eds) (1986) *Formations of Fantasy*, London: Methuen.

Merck, M. (1987) "Introduction: difference and its discontents", *Screen* 28, 1, Winter: 2–10.

Metz, C. (1974) *Film Language: A Semiotics of the Cinema* (trans. By Michael Taylor), New York: Oxford University Press.

Penley, C. (1984) paper given at *m/f* Conference, London.

Perkins, V. (1972) *Film as Film: Understanding and Judging Movies*, Harmondsworth: Penguin.

Rose, J. (1989) untitled entry, *Camera Obscura* 20/21: 274–9.

Stacey, J. (1990) "Romance", in Kuhn, Annette (ed.) with Radstone, Susannah, *The Women's Companion to International Film*, London: Virago.

Storr, M. (1992) "Psychoanalysis and lesbian desire: The trouble with female homosexuals", paper at the Activating Theory Conference, York University, in Bristow, Joe and Wilson, Angie (eds).

Studlar, G. (1989) untitled entry, *Camera Obscura* 20/21: 300–4.

Tudor, A. (1974) *Image and Influence: Studies in the Sociology of Film*, London: George Allen & Unwin.

Williams, L. (1989) untitled entry, *Camera Obscura* 20/21: 332–6.

Wright, E. (1984) *Psychoanalytic Criticism: Theory in Practice*, London: Methuen.

14 *Australian Idol* and the attention economy

"Australian Idol." Ten Network, Sydney, 14 July 2004.

"Australian Idol: The Winner's Story." Ten Network, Sydney, 21 November 2003.

Australian Idol: The Greatest Moments. Fremantle Media Operations, 2004.

Brody, E.W. "The 'Attention' Economy." *Public Relations Quarterly* 46.3 (2001): 18–21.

Davenport, T. and J. Beck. "The Strategy and Structure of Firms in the Attention Economy." *Ivey Business Journal* 66.4 (2002): 49–55.

Elliott, R. and N. Jankel-Elliott. "Using Ethnography in Strategic Consumer Research." *Qualitative Market Research* 6.4 (2003): 215–23.

Frank, Thomas. *The Conquest of Cool: Business Culture, Counterculture, and the Rise of Hip Consumerism*. Chicago: University of Chicago Press, 1997.

Gladwell, Malcolm. *The Tipping Point: How Little Things Can Make a Big Difference*. Boston: Back Bay Books, 2002.

Godin, Seth. *Unleashing the Ideavirus*. New York: Hyperion, 2001.

Henry, Amy. "How Buzz Marketing Works for Teens." *Advertising and Marketing to Children* April–June (2003): 3–10.

Lee, Julian. "Stealth Marketers Ready to Railroad the Unsuspecting." *Sydney Morning Herald* 24–5 July 2004: 3.

Maxwell, Ian. "True to the Music: Authenticity, Articulation and Authorship in Sydney Hip-Hop Culture." *Social Semiotics* 4.1–2 (1994): 117–37.

Negus, Keith. *Music Genres and Corporate Cultures*. London: Routledge, 1999.

Negus, Keith. *Producing Pop: Culture and Conflict in the Popular Music Industry*. London: Edward Arnold, 1992.

Rosen, Emanuel. *The Anatomy of Buzz: How to Create Word of Mouth Marketing*. London: Harper Collins, 2000.

Stahl, Matthew. "A Moment Like This: American Idol and Narratives of Meritocracy." *Bad Music: Music We Love to Hate*. Eds C Washburne and M. Derno. New York: Routledge, 2004. 212–32.

"Sydney Auditions: Conditions of Participation in the Australian Idol Audition." *Australian Idol* Website 10 June 2004. http://australianidol.com.au.

Turner, G., F. Bonner, and P.D. Marshall. *Fame Games: The Production of Celebrity in Australia*. Cambridge: Cambridge University Press, 2000.

15 Reading gossip magazines

Anderson, Benedict 1983: *Imagined communities*. London: Verso.

Bardoel, Jo and Peter Vasterman 1977: 'Sterren worden mensen, mensen worden sterren': de nieuwe aanval op het 'gat' in de markt ('Stars become ordinary people, ordinary people become stars': the new assault on the 'gap' in the market). *Groene Amsterdammer* (23 March).

Boodt, Joppe 1992: Mannen over vrouwenbladen (Men on women's magazines). *Inscriptie*, 1 (2), 4–15.

Bourdieu, Pierre 1980: The aristocracy of culture. Translated by Richard Nice. *Media Culture Society*, (2), 225–54.

Gray, Ann 1992: *Video playtime: the gendering of a leisure technology*. London and New York: Comedia/Routledge.

Gross, Larry 1989: Out of the mainstream: sexual minorities and the mass media. In Ellen Seiter, Hans Borchers, Gabrielle Kreutzner and Eva-Maria Warth (eds), *Remote control: television, audiences and cultural power*, London and New York: Routledge, 130–49.

Kobre, Sidney 1964: *The yellow press and gilded age journalism*. Tallahassee: Florida State University.

Meyer Spacks, Patricia 1986: *Gossip*. Chicago and London: University of Chicago Press.

Modleski, Tania 1984: *Loving with a vengeance: mass-produced fantasies for women*. New York and London: Methuen.

O'Sullivan, Tim, John Hartley, Danny Saunders and John Fiske 1983: *Key concepts in communication*. London and New York: Routledge.

Reesink, Maarten 1990: De waarheid, de hele waarheid en meer dan de waarheid: over de fascinerende *Privé*-grenzen tussen feiten en fictie, een verkenning van het leesplezier in het boulevardblad (The truth, the whole truth and more than the truth: on *Privé*'s fascinating borders between fact and fiction, an exploration of reading pleasure and the tabloid press). MA thesis, University of Amsterdam.

Ross, Andrew 1989: *No respect: intellectuals and popular culture*. New York and London: Routledge.

Schrøder, Kim Christian 1988: The pleasure of *Dynasty*: the weekly reconstruction of self-confidence. In Philip Drummond and Richard Paterson (eds), *Television and its audience*, London: British Film Institute, 61–82.

Sontag, Susan [1964] 1982: Notes on camp. In *A Susan Sontag reader*, London: Penguin, 105–19.

Introduction to Part Three

Schmidt, David (2005) *Natural Born Celebrities: Serial Killers in American Culture*. Chicago: University of Chicago Press.

16 Intimately intertwined in the most public way

Baum, G. (2004) A Celebrity Profile Formula. Online at http://aphrodigitaliac.com/mm/archive/celebprofile/, accessed, 8 March 2004.

Blakely, J. (compiler) (2004) Two or Three things I know about Celebrity Journalism. Seminar at USC Norman Lear Center, USC Annenberg School for Communication, 27 September 2002. Online at http://learcenter.org/pdf/powers_notes.pdf, accessed 10 March 2004.

Bumiller, E. (2004) Stolid Rumsfeld Soldiers on, but Weighs Ability to Serve, *New York Times*, 13 May, pp. A13.

Connell, I. (1992) Personalities in the Popular Media, in P. Dahlgren and C. Sparks (eds) *Journalism and Popular Culture*. London: Sage.

Durkheim, E. (1964) *The Division of Labor in Society*. Trans. George Simpson, New York: Free Press.

Dyer, R. (1979) *Stars*. London: BFI.

Keeps, D., Melcher, C., Virga, V. and Coz, S. (2002) *National Enquirer: Thirty Years of Unforgettable Images*. New York: Hyperion/Miramax.

Marshall, P.D. (1997) *Celebrity and Power: Fame in Contemporary Culture*. Minneapolis: University of Minnesota Press.

Mole, T. (2004) Romanticism and Celebrity. Paper presented at the Cultural Studies Association (US) Conference, Persona Series, Northeastern University, Boston, 5–9 May.

Ponce de Leon, C.S. (2002) *Self-Exposure: Human Interest Journalism and the Emergence of Celebrity in America, 1890–1940*. Chapel Hill, NC: University of North Carolina Press.

Reisman, D. (1950) *The Lonely Crowd*. New Haven: Yale University Press.

Rojek, C. (2001) *Celebrity*. London: Reaktion.

Turner, G. (2004) *Understanding Celebrity*. London: Sage.

Turner, G., Bonner, F. and Marshall, P.D. (2000) *Fame Games: The Production of Celebrity in Australia*. Cambridge: Cambridge University Press.

18 America's new son

Allen, K. (1996) "Advertising blitz to introduce Woods to the world at large." *USA Today*, August 29, p. 11C.

Andrews, D.L. (1996) "The fact(s) of Michael Jordan's blackness: excavating a floating racial signifier." *Sociology of Sport Journal* 13(2): 125–58.

Berlant, L. (1996) "The face of America and the state of emergency." In C. Nelson and D.P. Gaonkar (eds), *Disciplinarity and Dissent in Cultural Studies* (pp. 397–439). New York: Routledge.

Butler, J. (1998) "An affirmative view." In R. Post and M. Rogin (eds), *Race and Representation: Affirmative Action*. New York: ZONE Books.

Cole, C.L. (1996) "American Jordan: P.L.A.Y., consensus, and punishment." *Sociology of Sport Journal* 13(4): 366–97.

Cole, C.L. and Andrews, D.L. (2000) "America's new son: Tiger Woods and America's multiculturalism." In N.K. Denzin (ed.), *Cultural Studies: A Research Volume* (Vol. 5, pp. 109–24). Stamford, CT: JAI Press.

Crain, R. (1997) "Swoosh! There it goes: after much debate, Nike pulls controversial Woods spot from TV circulation." *Houston Chronicle*, October 6, p. 27.

Gabriel, J. (1998) *Whitewash: Racialized Politics in the Media*. London: Routledge.

Higginbotham, A.L., Francois, A.B., and Yueh, L.Y. (1997) "The O.J. Simpson trial: who was 'improperly playing the race card'?" In T. Morrison and C.B. Lacour (eds), *Birth of a Nation'hood: Gaze, Script, and Spectacle in the O.J. Simpson Case*. New York: Pantheon Books.

Jeffords, S. (1993) *Hard Bodies: Hollywood Masculinity in the Reagan Era*. New Brunswick: Rutgers University Press.

Kelley, R.D.G. (1997) *Yo' Mama's Disfunktional!: Fighting the Culture Wars in Urban America*. Boston: Beacon Press.

Knott, T. (1996) "Hello, Nike, and many thanks for telling Tiger's tale to America." *The Washington Times*, September 11, p. B1.

Lipsitz, G. (1998) *The Possessive Investment in Whiteness: How White People Profit from Identity Politics*. Philadelphia: Temple University Press.

Lipsyte, R. (1996) "Woods suits golf's needs perfectly." *New York Times*, September 8, p. 11.

Meyers, B. (1998) "Nike tees up to try again. Woods brand gets new look." *USA Today*, September 18, pp. 1B–2B.

Page, C. (1996) *Showing My Color: Impolite Essays on Race and Identity*. New York: HarperCollins.

Potter, J. (1997) "Woods widens game's appeal: role model encourages minorities." *USA Today*, January 15, p. 3C.

Ratnesar, R. (2000) "Changing stripes: Just as with his golf game, Tiger has had to adjust his life to meet the demands of celebrity." *Time*, August 14, pp. 62–6.

Reeves, J.L. and Campbell, R. (1994) *Cracked Coverage: Television News, the Anticocaine Crusade, and the Reagan Legacy*. Durham, NC: Duke University Press.

Scott, D.M. (1997) *Contempt and Pity: Social Policy ad the Image of the Damaged Black Psyche 1880–1996*. Chapel Hill: The University of North Carolina Press.

Smith, A.M. (1994) *New Right Discourse on Race and Sexuality: Britain, 1968–1990*. Cambridge: Cambridge University Press.

Spousta, T. (1996) "Ready for Tiger, not Nike." *Sarasota Heralt-Tribune*, September 11, p. 1C.

Stevens, K. and Winheld, M. (1996) "Fans flocking to catch Tiger at brink of fame." *USA Today*, September 19, p. D10.

Wernick, A. (1991) *Promotional Culture: Advertising, Ideology and Symbolic Expression*. London: Sage.

West, C. (1988) *The American Evasion of Philosophy: A Genealogy of Pragmatism*. Madison, WI: University of Wisconsin Press.

Williams, S. (1996) "Tiger a ratings master, too: his Grand Slam triumph is most-watched TV golf ever." *Daily News*. April 15, p. 87.

Wilson, W.J. (1997) *When Work Disappears: The World of the New Urban Poor*. New York: Vintage Books.

Yu, H. (1996) "Perspective on ethnicity: how Tiger Woods lost his stripes." *Los Angeles Times*, December 2, p. 4M.

19 The celebrity politician

Ankersmit, F.R. (1996) *Aesthetic Politics*, Stanford, Cal: Stanford University Press.

Braverman, H. (1974) *Labor and Monopoly Capital*, New York: Monthly Review Press.

Crewe, I. and Sarlvik, B. (1983) *The Decade of Dealignment*, Cambridge: Cambridge University Press.

Downs, A. (1957) *An Economic Theory of Democracy*, New York: Harper and Row.

Eyerman, R. and Jamison, A. (1998) *Music and Social Movements: Mobilizing Traditions in the Twentieth Century*, Cambridge: Cambridge University Press.

Falasca-Zamponi, S. (1997) *Fascist Spectacle: The Aesthetics of Power in Mussolini's Italy*, Berkeley: University of California Press.

Fay, B. (1975) *Social Theory and Political Practice*, London: Allen and Unwin.

Franklin, B. (1994) *Packaging Politics: Political Communications in Britain's Media Democracy*, London: Edward Arnold.

Gelder, K. and Thornton, S. (1989) *The Subcultures Reader*, London: Routledge.

Giorgetti, C. (2001) "Dress, Politics and Fashion, 1960–80", pp. 278–85 in L. Cheles and L. Sponza (eds) *The Art of Persuasion: Political Communication in Italy from 1945 to the 1990s*, Manchester: Manchester University Press.

Habermas, J. (1971) *Towards a Rational Society*, London: Heinemann.

Hargreaves-Heap, S. (1989) *Rationality in Economics*, Oxford: Basil Blackwell.

Hart, R. (1999) *Seducing America: How Television Charms the Modern Voter*, Oxford: Oxford University Press.

Heath, A., Curtice, J., Jowell, R., Evans, G., Field, J. and Witherspoon, S. (1991) *Understanding Political Change*, Oxford: Pergamon.

Hesmondhalgh, D. (2002) *The Culture Industries*, London: Sage.

Lees-Marshment, J. (2001) "The Marriage of Politics and Marketing", *Political Studies*, 49(4), pp. 692–713.

McLean, I. (1987) *Public Choice*, Oxford: Basil Blackwell.

Marshall, P.D. (1997) *Celebrity and Power: Fame in Contemporary Culture*, Minneapolis and London: University of Minnesota Press.

Pountain, D. and Robins, D. (2000) *Cool Rules: Anatomy of an Attitude*, London: Reaktion.

Pozzato, M.P. (2001) "Fashion and Political Communication in the 1980s and 1990s", pp. 286–98 in L. Cheles and L. Sponza (eds) *The Art of Persuasion: Political Communication in Italy from 1945 to the 1990s*, Manchester: Manchester University Press.

Sandel, M. (1996) *Democracy's Discontent*, Cambridge, Mass: Harvard University Press.

Scammell, M. (1999) 'Political Marketing: Lessons for Political Science', *Political Studies*, 47(4), pp. 718–39.

Schumpeter, J. (1976) *Capitalism, Socialism and Democracy*, London: George Allen & Unwin.

Weber, M. (1991) "Politics as a Vocation", pp. 77–128 in H.H. Gerth and C. Wright Mills (eds) *From Max Weber: Essays in Sociology*, London: Routledge.

20 Academostars

Arnowitz, Stanley. "Critic as Star." *Dead Artists, Live Theories and Other Cultural Problems*. New York: Routledge, 1994. 44–95.

Braudy, Leo. *The Frenzy of Renown: Fame and Its History*. 1986. New York: Vintage, 1997.

Brooks, Peter. "Aesthetics and Ideology: What Happened to Poetics?" *Critical Inquiry* 20 (1994): 509–23.

Butler, Judith. *Gender Trouble: Feminism and the Subversion of Identity*. 2nd ed. New York: Routledge, 1999.

Campbell, Colin. "The Tyranny of Yale Critics." *New York Times Magazine* 9 Feb. 1986: 20+.

Chomsky, Noam, et al. *The Cold War and the University: Toward an Intellectual History of the Cold War Years*. New York: New Press, 1997.

Davis, Lennard J. *My Sense of Silence: Memoirs of a Childhood with Deafness*. Urbana: University of Illinois Press, 1990.

deCordova, Richard. *Picture Personalities: The Emergence of the Star System in America*. Urbana: University of Illinois Press, 1990.

de Man, Paul. "Semiology and Rhetoric." 1973. *Allegories of Reading: Figural Language in Rousseau, Nietzsche, Rilke, and Proust*. New Haven: Yale University Press, 1979. 3–19.

––––– "The Resistance to Theory." *The Resistance to Theory*. Minneapolis: University of Minnesota Press, 1986. 3–20.

––––– "The Return to Philology." *The Resistance to Theory*. 21–26.

Dyer, Richard. *Stars*. London: BFI, 1979.

Fish, Stanley. "Stanley Agonistes." With Jeffrey J. Williams. *The Minnesota review* 52–4 (2000): 115–26.

Gamson, Joshua. *Claims to Fame: Celebrity in Contemporary America*. 1994. Berkeley: University of California Press, 1994.

Geiger, Roger L. *Research and Relevant Knowledge: American Research Universities since World War II*. New York: Oxford University Press, 1993.

Goldman, Charles A., Susan M. Gates, and Dominic J. Brewer. *In Pursuit of Prestige: Strategy and Competition in U.S. Higher Education*. New Brunswick: Transaction, 2001.

Graff, Gerald. *Professing Literature: An Institutional History*. Chicago: University of Chicago Press, 1987.

Grafton, Anthony. *The Footnote: A Curious History*. Cambridge, MA: Harvard University Press, 1997.

Guillory, John. *Cultural Capital: The Problem of Literary Canon Formation*. Chicago: University of Chicago Press, 1993.

Jencks, Christopher, and David Riesman. *The Academic Revolution*. New York: Doubleday, 1968.

Langbauer, Laurie. "The Celebrity Economy of Cultural Studies." *Victorian Studies*. 36.4 (1993): 466–72.

Lentricchia, Frank. *After the New Criticism*. Chicago: University of Chicago Press, 1980.

"The Lesson of Paul de Man." *Yale French Studies* 69 (1985).

Lewontin, R.C. "The Cold War and the Transformation of the Academy." Chomsky et al. 1–34.

Lowen, Rebecca S. *Creating the Cold War University: The Transformation of Stanford*. Berkeley: University of California Press, 1997.

MacFarquhar, Larissa. "Putting the Camp Back into Campus." *Lingua franca* Nov./Dec. 1993: 6–7.

Marshall, P. David. *Celebrity and Power: Fame in Contemporary Culture*. Minneapolis: University of Minnesota Press, 1997.

Menand, Louis. "The Demise of Disciplinary Authority." *What's Happened to the Humanities?* Ed. Alvin Kernan. Princeton: Princeton University Press, 1997. 201–19.

––––– "New New York Intellectual: An Interview with Louis Menand." With Jeffrey J. Williams. *The Minnesota Review* 52–4 (2000): 141–58.

Nelson, Cary. "Superstars." *Academe*. (Jan.–Feb. 1997): 38–54.

Opland, Jeff. *Anglo-Saxon Oral Poetry: A Study of the Tradition*. New Haven: Yale University Press, 1980.

Robbins, Bruce. "Celeb-Reliance: Intellectuals, Celebrity, and Upward Mobility." *Postmodern Culture* 9.2 (1999): <muse.jhu.edu/journals/postmodern_culture>.

Ross, Andrew. "Undisciplined: An Interview with Andrew Ross." With Jeffrey Williams and Mike Hill. *The Minnesota Review* 45–6 (1996): 77–94.

Scott, Janny. "Scholars Fear 'Star' System May Undermine their Mission." *The New York Times* 20 Dec. 1997: A1, B9.

Shumway, David R. "The Star System in Literary Studies." PMLA 112 (1997): 85–100. With postscript. *The Institution of Literature*. Ed. Jeffrey J. Williams. Albany: SUNY Press, 2001.

Spurgin, Timothy. "The *Times Magazine* and Academic Megastars." *The Minnesota Review* 52–4 (2000): 225–38.

Tompkins, Jane. "Me and My Shadow." *Gender and Theory: Dialogues on Feminist Criticism*. Ed. Linda Kauffman. Oxford: Basil Blackwell, 1989. 121–39.

Veysey, Lawrence. "Stability and Experiment in the American Undergraduate Curriculum." *Contents and Context: Essays in College Education*. Carnegie Committee on Higher Education Report. New York: McGrawhill, 1973. 1–63.

Waters, Lindsay and Wlad Godzich, eds. *Reading de Man Reading*. Minneapolis: University of Minnesota Press, 1989.

Webster, Grant. *The Republic of Letters: A History of Postwar American Literary Opinion*. Baltimore: Johns Hopkins University Press, 1979.

Wicke, Jennifer. "Celebrity Material: Materialist Feminism and the Culture of Celebrity." *South Atlantic Quarterly* 93 (1994): 751–78.

Williams, Jeffrey. "The Posttheory Generation." *Day Late, Dollar Short: The Next Generation and the New Academy*. Ed. Peter C. Herman. Albany: SUNY Press, 2000. 25–44.

23 Investigating the serial killer

Abbot, Jack Henry. *In the Belly of the Beast*. New York: Vintage Books, 1991.

Altman, Dennis. *The Homosexualization of America, the Americanization of Homosexuality*. New York: St. Martin's Press, 1982.

Beauvoir, Simone de. "Must We Burn Sade?" In *Selections from his Writings and a Study by Simone de Beauvoir*, Marquis de Sade. New York: Grove Press, 1953.

Bellah, Robert N., et al. *Habits of the Heart*. New York: Harper and Row, 1986.

Capote, Truman. *In Cold Blood: A True Account of Multiple Murder and its Consequences*. London: Hamish Hamilton, 1966.

Dahmer, Lionel. *A Father's Story*. New York: William Morrow, 1994.

Davis, Don. *The Milwaukee Murders*. New York: St. Martin's Press, 1991.

Deleuze, Gilles, and Felix Guattari. *Anti-Oedipus: Capitalism and Schizophrenia*. Preface by Michel Foucault. Introduction by Mark Seem. Trans. Roberty Hurley, Mark Seem, and Helen R. Lane. New York: Viking, 1977.

Dvorchak, Robert J., and Lisa Holewa. *Milwaukee Massacre*. New York: Dell, 1991.

Foucault, Michel. "About the Concept of the 'Dangerous Individual' in Nineteenth-Century Legal Psychiatry." Trans. Alain Baudot and Jane Couchman. *International Journal of the Law and Psychiatry* 1(1978): 1–18.

Foucault, Michel. *Discipline and Punish*. Trans. Alan Sheridan. New York: Vintage Books, 1979.

Freud, Sigmund. "The Uncanny," in *Standard Edition of the Complete Psychologistical Works*. Trans. under the general editorship of James Strachey, in collaboration with Anna

Freud, assisted by Alex Strachey and Alan Tyson. Vol. 17. London: Hogarth Press, 1953a.

Freud, Sigmund. *Civilization and Its Discontents*. Trans. J. Riviere. London: Hogarth Press, 1953b.

Halberstam, Judith. "Skinflick: Posthuman Gender in Jonathan Demme's *The Silence of the Lambs*." *Camera Obscura* 27 (Sept. 1991): 37–52.

House of Representatives Hearings before a Subcommittee of the Committee on Government Operations. *The Federal Role in Investigation of Serial Violent Crime*. 99th Cong., 2nd sess. April 9 and May 21, 1986.

Jenkins, Philip. *Using Murder: The Social Construction of Serial Homicide*. New York: Aldine de Gruyter, 1994.

Jenkins, Philip. "Sharing Murder: Understanding Group Serial Homicide." *Journal of Crime and Justice* 13, no. 2 (1990): 125–47.

Leyton, Elliott. *Compulsive Killers: The Story of Modern Multiple Murder*. New York: New York University Press, 1986.

Masters, Brian. "Dahmer's Inferno." *Vanity Fair* (November 1991): 183–269.

Masters, Brian. *The Shrine of Jeffrey Dahmer*. London: Coronet Books, 1993.

Norris, Joel. *Jeffrey Dahmer*. New York: Pinnacle Books, 1992.

Pfohl, Stephen J. "Ethnomethodology and Criminology: The Social Production of Crime and the Criminal." In *The Mad, the Bad, and the Different*, eds. Israel L. Barak-Glantz, and C. Ronald Huffs. Lexington, Mass.: Lexington Books, 1981.

Schwartz, Anne E. *The Man Who Could Not Kill Enough*. New York: Birch Lane Press, 1992.

Stallybrass, Peter, and Allon White. *The Politics and Poetics of Transgression*. London: Methuen, 1986.

Wilson, Colin, and Donald Seaman. *The Serial Killers*. London: W.H. Allen, 1990.

Young, Elizabeth. "*The Silence of the Lambs* and the Flaying of Feminist Theory." *Camera Obscura* 27 (September 1991): 5–35.

Murder by Number. Cable News Network, Inc., January 3, 1993.

Geraldo. Investigative News Group, Inc.

The Oprah Winfrey Show. Harpo Productions, Inc.

Larry King Live. Cable News Network, Inc.

Sonya Live. Cable News Network, Inc.

Day One. American Broadcasting Companies, Inc.

24 (Don't) leave me alone

A Current Affair. (1993a). Broadcast date, September 3.

A Current Affair. (1993b). Broadcast date, December 23.

Arrington, C. (1984). Hands up for all those who think Michael Jackson's glove is a many splendored thing. *People Weekly*, March 19: 98–9.

Bird, S.E. (1992). *For Enquiring Minds: A Cultural Study of Supermarket Tabloids*. Knoxville, TN: University of Tennessee Press.

Bowser, E. (1994). *The Transformation of the American Cinema: 1907–1915*. Berkely, CA: University of California Press.

Connell, I. (1992). Personalities in the popular media. In P. Dahlgren and C. Sparks (eds), *Journalism and Popular Culture*. London: Sage, 64–83.

Corliss, R. (1993). Peter Pan speaks. *Newsweek*, February 22: 66–7.

Durkee, C. (1987). Unlike anyone, even himself. *People Weekly*, September 14: 88–99.

Dyer, R. (1979). *Stars*. London: BFI Publishing.

Dyer, R. (1986). *Heavenly Bodies: Film Stars and Society*. New York: St Martins Press.

Frontline. (1994). Broadcast date, February 15.

Gold, T. (1988). On tour, he's still "Michael!" But his charity work has won him a new title: Dr. Jackson. *People Weekly*, March 28:–36–7.

Good news, bad news. (1987). *Rolling Stone*, August 13: 11.

Goodwin, A. (1992). *Dancing in the Distraction Factory: Music Television and Popular Culture*. Minneapolis: University of Minnesota Press.

Hamilton, P. (1992). The enlightenment and the birth of social science. In S. Hall and B. Gieben (eds), *Formations of Modernity*. London: Open University Press, 18–59.

Hard Copy. (1993a). Broadcast date, December 14.

Hard Copy. (1993b). Broadcast date, December 15.

Hershey, G. (1983). Michael Jackson: Life in the magical kingdom. *Rolling Stone*, February 7: 10–11, 17.

How Michael Jackson plotted for 2 months to pay off teen accuser (1994). *Star*, February 8: 5.

Lull, J. (1995). *Media, Communication, Culture: A Global Approach*. Cambridge: Polity Press; New York: Columbia University Press.

Mercer, K. (1993). Monster metaphors: Notes on Michael Jackson's Thriller. In S. Frith, A. Goodwin, and L. Grossberg (eds), *Sound and Vision: The Music Video Reader*. New York: Routledge, 93–108.

Michael Jackson's weekend with boys in secret playroom. (1993). *National Enquirer*, December 14: 26.

Michael's fatal attraction for little boys. (1993). *Globe*, September 14: 2–4.

Miller, J. (1983). The Peter Pan of pop. *Newsweek*, January 10: 52–4.

Robinson, L. (1970). The Jackson five. *Ebony*, September: 150–4.

Rubenstein, C. (1984). The Michael Jackson syndrome. *Discover*, September: 68–70.

Sigerson, D. (1987). Michael grows up. *Rolling Stone*, October 22: 87–8.

Tragic youngster trapped in Jackson sex scandal. (1993). *Globe*, September 7: 8.

Weller, S. (1984). The magic of Michael Jackson. *McCalls*, May: 38–40, 43–4.

Why I prefer kids to grown-ups. (1993) *Globe*, September 7: 9.

Why Michael hid out in a White House men's room, and other tales of the day power played host to fame. (1984). *People Weekly*, May 28: 74.

25 The quest for fame

Asimov, I. *The War of the Worlds*.

Braudy, L. *The Frenzy of Renown : Fame and Its History*.

Capote, T. *In Cold Blood*.

Chapman, R. W. *Life of Johnson*.

Chaucer *Works of Geoffrey Chaucer*.

Condry, J.C. *Psychology of Television*.

Foucault, M. *The History of Sexuality: The Care of the Self*.

Gamson, J. *Claims to Fame: Celebrity in Contemporary America*.

Hardy, T. *Jude the Obscure*.

Kelly, G.A. *Psychology of Personal Constructs*.

Kotre, J.N. *Outliving the Self: How We Live on in Future Generations*.
Livingston, S. *Talk On Television: Audience Participation and Public Debate*.
Marshall, P.D. *Celebrity and Power: Fame in Contemporary Culture*.
Pearson, J. *The Profession of Violence: The Rise and Fall of the Kray Twins*.

26 Celebrity, the tabloid and the democratic public sphere

Bonner, F. (2003) *Ordinary Television: Analyzing Popular TV*, London: Sage.
Carey, J.W. (2002) 'American journalism on, before, and after September 11', in B. Zelitzer and S. Allan (eds) *Journalism after September 11*, London and New York: Routledge, pp. 71–90.
Conboy, M. (2002) *The Press and Popular Culture*. London: Sage.
Connell, I. (1992) 'Personalities in the Popular Media', in P. Dahlgren and C. Sparks (eds) *Journalism and Popular Culture*, London: Sage, pp. 64–85.
Couldry, N. (2003) *Media Rituals: A Critical Approach*, London and New York: Routledge.
Dovey, J. (2002) 'Confession and the unbearable lightness of factual television', *Media International Australia Incorporating Culture and Policy*, No. 104, pp. 10–18.
Gough-Yates, A. (2003) *Understanding Women's Magazines: Publishing, Markets and Readerships*, London and New York: Routledge.
Hartley, J. (1996) *Popular Reality: Journalism, Modernity, Popular Culture*, London: Edward Arnold.
Hermes, J. (1995) *Reading Women's Magazines: An Analysis of Everyday Media Use*, Cambridge, Polity.
Horrie, C. and Nathan, A. (1999) *Live TV: Tellybrats and Topless Darts: The Uncut Story of Tabloid Television*, London: Pocket.
Lumby, C. (1997) *Bad Girls: The Media, Sex and Feminism in the 90s*, Sydney: Allen and Unwin.
Masciarotte, G.-J. (1991) 'C'mon girl: Oprah Winfrey and the discourse of feminine talk', *Genders*, 11, pp. 81–110.
Saltzman, J. (1999) 'Celebrity Journalism, the Public and Princess Diana' in B. Levy and D.M. Bonilla (eds) *The Power of the Press*, New York and Dublin: H.W. Wilson, pp. 73–75.
Schickel, R. (1985) *Intimate Strangers: The Culture of Celebrity in America*, Chicago: Ivan R. Dee.
Shattuc, J.M. (1997) *The Talking Cure: TV Talk Shows and Women*, New York and London: Routledge.

27 The celebrity legacy of the Beatles

Burrows, Terry (1996) *The Beatles: The Complete Illustrated Story*. London: Carlton.
Chambers, Iain (1985) *Urban Rhythms*. London: Macmillan.
Frith, Simon (1983) *Sound Effects*. London: Constable.
Hebdige, Dick (1988) *Hiding in the Light: On Images and Things*. London: Comedia/ Routledge.
Huyssen, Andreas (1986) *After the Great Divide: Modernism, Mass Culture, Postmodernism*. Bloomington: Indiana University Press.

Kroker, Arthur (1984) *Technology and the Canadian Imagination*. Montreal: New World Perspectives.

Le Bon, Gustave (1960) *The Crowd: A Study of the Popular Mind*. New York: Viking.

Marshall, P. David (1997) *Celebrity and Power: Fame in Contemporary Culture*. Minneapolis: University of Minnesota Press.

Weber, Max (1968) *Economy and Society*, Volume 3. New York: Bedminster.

28 Exemplary differences

Anderson, Benedict (1983) *Imagined Communities: Reflections on the Origins and Spread of Nationalism*, London and New York: Verso.

Benjamin, Jessica (1990) *The Bonds of Love: Psychoanalysis, Feminism and the Problem of Domination*, London: Virago.

Burchill, Julie (1998) *Diana*, London: Weidenfeld and Nicolson.

Bhabha, Homi K. (1994) *The Location of Culture*, London: Routledge.

Campbell, Beatrix (1998) *Diana, Princess of Wales: How Sexual Politics Shook the Monarchy*, London: Women's Press.

Coward, Rosalind (1984) *Female Desire: Women's Sexuality Today*: London: Paladin.

Deutsch, K.W. (1966) *Nationalism and Social Communication*, 2nd edition, Cambridge, Mass., and London: MIT Press.

'Dianarama' (1998) *De Volksrant* (Amsterdam), no. 60, 16 June.

Dollimore, Jonathan (1991) *Sexual Dissidence*, Oxford: Clarendon Press.

Epstein, Debbie and Johnson, Richard (1998) *Schooling Sexualities*, Buckinham: Open University Press.

Flett, Kathryn (1998) "Hurtling Towards Chaos", *Observer Newspaper Life Magazine*, 23 August.

Gay Times (1997) "Signs of the Times: The Revolution of the Flowers: Diana, A Tribute" (October), 50–4.

Gellner, Ernest (1983) *Nations and Nationalism*, Oxford: Blackwell.

Hall, Stuart (ed.) (1997) *Cultural Representations and Signifying Practices*, London: Sage.

MacArthur, Brian (ed.) (1997) *Requiem: Diana, Princess of Wales 1961–1997: Memories and Tributes*, London: Pavilion Books.

McGuigan, Jim (1992) *Cultural Populism*, London: Routledge.

Mackenzie, W.J.M. (1978) *Political Identity*, Manchester: Manchester University Press.

Merck, Mandy (ed.) (1998) *After Diana: Irreverent Elegies*, London: Verso.

Mitchell, Juliet (ed.) (1986) *The Selected Melanie Klein* Harmondsworth: Penguin.

Morton, Andrew (1997) *Diana: Her True Story – In Her Own Words 1961–1997*, London and New York: Michael O'Mara Books and Simon and Schuster.

Pilger, John (1998) "The Anniversary of Princess Diana's Death is a Reminder of the Hijacking of Feminist Journalism by Agony Aunts", *New Statesman*, 26 June 19.

Said, Edward (1978) *Orientalism*, London: Routledge and Kegan Paul.

Screen (1998) "Special Debate: Flowers and Tears: the Death of Diana Princess of Wales", vol. 39, no. 1 (spring): 67–84.

Sedgwick, Eve K. (1994) *Tendencies*, London: Routledge.

Smith, A.D. (1971) *Theories of Nationalism*, London: Duckworth.

Smith, A.D. (1979) *Nationalism in the Twentieth Century*, Oxford: Oxford University Press.

Stallybrass, Peter and White, Allon (1986) *The Politics and Poetics of Transgression*, London: Methuen.

Steinberg, Deborah, Epstein, Debbie and Johnson, Richard (eds) (1997) *Border Patrols: Policing the Boundaries of Heterosexuality*, London: Cassell.

Wilson, Elizabeth (1997) "The Unbearable Lightness of Diana", *New Left Review*, no. 226: 136–45.

Žižek, Slavoj (1991) *For They Know Not What They Do: Enjoyment as a Political Factor*, London: Verso.

29 Vanishing point

Amis, Martin. "The Mirror of Ourselves." *Time*, 15 September 1997: 57.

Carlton, Mike. "Diana: Media's sickening U-turn." *The Sydney Morning Herald*, 6 September 1997: 34.

Dyer, R. *Heavenly Bodies: Film Stars and Society*. London: British Film Institute, 1986.

Gilling, T. "How To Knit Yourself A Brand New Diana." *TheAustralian*, 1 October 1997: 13.

Marshall, D. *Celebrity and Power: Fame in Contemporary Culture*. Minneapolis and London: University of Minnesota Press, 1997.

Porter, H. "Her Last Summer." *VanityFair*, October 1997: 168–172.

Shawcross, W. "Patron Saint of the Global Village." *The Sydney Morning Herald*, 6 September 1997: 32.

Wilson, E. *Adorned in Dreams: Fashion and Modernity*. Berkeley: University of California Press, 1997.

30 I don't have a great body, but I play one on TV

Bringle, M.L. (1989). Confessions of a glutton. *The Christian Century*, 106, 955–58.

Cher, with R. Haas. (1991). *Forever fit: The lifetime plan for health, fitness, and beauty*. New York: Bantam.

Evans. L. (1983). *Linda Evans' beauty and exercise book: Inner and outer beauty*. New York: Simon and Schuster.

Faludi, S. (1991). *Backlash: The undeclared war against American women*. New York: Crown.

Finkelstein, J. (1991). *The fashioned self*. Philadelphia: Temple University Press.

Fonda, J. (1986). *Jane Fonda's new workout and weight-loss program*. New York: Simon & Schuster.

Kissling, E.A. (1991). One size does not fit all, or how I learned to stop dieting and love the body. *Quest*, 43, 135–147.

Kramarae, C., and Treichler, P., with A. Russo. (1985). *A feminist dictionary*. Boston: Pandora.

Miller, L., and Penz, O. (1991). Talking bodies: Female bodybuilders colonize a male preserve. *Quest*, 43, 148–163.

Orbach, S. (1986). *Hunger strike: The anorectic's stuggle as a metaphor of our age*. New York: Norton.

Penelope, J. (1990). *Speaking freely: Unlearning the lies of the fathers' tongues*. New York: Pergamon.

Principal, V. (1983). *The body principal*. New York: Simon & Schuster.

Principal, V. (1987). *The body principal*. New York: Simon & Schuster.

Seid, R. (1989). *Never too thin*. New York: Prentice-Hall.

Shields, B. (1985). *On your own*. New York: Villard.

Spender, D. (1985). *Man made language* (2nd ed.). London: Routledge & Kegan Paul.

Spitzack, C. (1987). Confessions and signification: The systematic inscription of body consciousness. *The Journal of Medicine and Philohophy*, 12, 357–369.

Taylor, E. (1987). *Elizabeth takes off: On weight gain, weight loss, self-image, and self-esteem*. New York: G.P. Putnam.

Welch, R. (1984). *Raquel: The Raquel Welch total beauty and fitness program*. New York: Holt, Rinehart & Winston.

Wolf, N. (1991). *The beauty myth: How images of beauty are used against women*. New York: Morrow.

31 Beauty and the female body

Banner, Lois W. 1983. *American Beauty*. New York: Alfred A. Knopf.

Barthes, Roland. 1985. *The Grain of the Voice, Interviews 1962–1980*. New York: Hill and Wang.

Baudrillard, Jean. 1988. *Selected Writings*. M. Poster (ed.), Stanford: Stanford University Press.

Berscheid, E., Dion, K., Walster, W., & Walster, G. 1971. "Physical Attractiveness and Dating Choice: A Test of the Matching Hypothesis." *Journal of Experimental Social Psychology* 7:173–189.

Bowlby, Rachel, 1987. "Modes of Modern Shopping: Mallarmé at the Bon Marché." In Nancy Armstrong and Leonard Tennenhouse (eds.), *The Ideology of Conduct*. New York: Methuen. 185–205.

Broverman, I.K., Broverman, D.M., Clarkson, F.E., Rosenkrantz, P.S. and Vogel, S.R. 1970. "Sex Role Stereotypes and Clinical Judgements of Mental Health." *Journal of Consulting and Clinical Psychology* 4: 1–7.

Brownmiller, Susan. 1985. *Femininity*. New York: Fawcett Columbine.

Chernin, Kim. 1981. *The Obsession: Reflections on the Tyranny of Slenderness*. New York: Harper and Row.

Collins, Patricia Hill. 1990. *Black Feminist Thought: Knowledge, Consciousness, and the Politics of Empowerment*. New York: Routledge.

Deleuze, Gilles and Guattari, Félix. 1983. *Anti-Oedipus: Capitalism and Schizophrenia*. New York: Viking.

Deutsch, Helene. 1930. "Significance of Masochism in the Mental Life of Women." *International Journal of Psychoanalysis* 11:48–60.

Douglas, Mary. 1966. *Purity and Danger: An Analysis of Concepts of Pollution and Taboo*. London: Routledge & Kegan Paul.

Featherstone, Mike. 1990. "Perspectives on Consumer Culture." *Sociology* 24 (1):5–22.

Featherstone, Mike. 1992. "The Heroic Life and Everyday Life." *Theory Culture & Society* 9:159–182.

Finkelstein, Joanne. 1991. *The Fashioned Self*. Cambridge: Polity Press.

Firestone, Shulamith. 1970. *The Dialectic of Sex*. New York: Bantam Books.

Frank, Arthur W. 1990. "Bringing Bodies Back In: A Decade Review." *Theory Culture & Society* 7:131–162.

Freud, Sigmund, 1957. "On Narcissim: An Introduction." In *General Selection from the Works of Sigmund Freud*. New York: Doubleday/Anchor.

Freedman, Rita. 1986. *Beauty Bound: Why Women Strive For Physical Perfection*. London: Columbus Books.

Garry, Ann. 1982. "Narcissism and Vanity." *Social Theory and Practice* 8(2):145–154.

Giddens, Anthony. 1991. *Modernity and Self-Identity: Self and Society in the Late Modern Age*. Cambridge: Polity Press.

Goffman, Erving. 1959. *The Presentation of Self in Everyday Life*. New York: Doubleday Anchor.

Hatfield, Elaine and Sprecher, Susan. 1986. *Mirror, Mirror: The Importance of Look in Everyday Life*. Albany: State University of New York Press.

Henley, Nancy M. 1977. *Body Politics*. Engelwood Cliffs, N.J.: Prentice Hall.

Kohut, Heinz. 1977. *The Restoration of Self.* New York: International Universities Press.

Kunzle, David. 1982. *Fashion and Fetishism: A Social History of the Corset, Tight-lacing and Other Forms of Body-Sculpture in the West*. Totowa, N.J.: Rowman and Littlefield.

Lacan, Jacques. 1977. *Écrits: A Selection*. New York: Norton.

Lakoff, Robin Tolmach and Scherr, Raquel L. 1984. *Face Value. The Politics of Beauty*. Boston: Routledge & Kegan Paul.

Laqueur, Thomas. 1990. *Making Sex: Body and Gender from the Greeks to Freud*. Cambridge: Harvard University Press.

Marwick, Arthur. 1988. *Beauty in History: Society, Politics and Personal Appearance c. 1500 to the Present*. Gloucester: Thames and Hudson, Hucclecote.

Millman, Marcia. 1980. *Such a Pretty Face*. New York: Berkeley Books.

Miller, T., Coffman, J., and Linke, R. 1980. "A Survey of Body Image, Weight, and Diet of College Students." *Journal of the American Dietetic Association* 17: 561–566.

O'Neill, John. 1985. *Five Bodies*. Ithaca, N.Y.: Cornell University Press.

Perrot, Philippe. 1984. *Le travail des apparences: Ou les transformations du corps féminin XVIIIe–XIXe siècle*. Paris: Éditions du Seuil. (Dutch translation: 1987. *Werken aan de schijn. Veranderingen van het vrouwelijk lichaam*. Nijmegen: SUN.).

Sanford, L. and Donovan, M. 1984. *Women & Self-Esteem*. Garden City, N.Y.: Anchor Press/Doubleday.

Scott, Sue and Morgan, David (eds.). 1993. *Body Matters: Essays on the Sociology of the Body*. London: The Falmer Press.

Shilling, Chris. 1993. *The Body and Social Theory*. London: Sage Publications.

Smith, Dorothy. 1990a. *The Conceptual Practices of Power: A Feminist Sociology of Knowledge*. Boston: Northeastern University Press.

Smith, Dorothy. 1990b. *Texts, Facts and Femininity: Exploring the Relations of Ruling*. New York: Routledge.

Smith, Dorothy and David, Sara (eds.). 1975. *Women Look at Psychiatry*. Vancouver: Press Gang Publishing Co.

Suleiman, Susan R. (ed.). 1985. *The Female Body in Western Culture*. Cambridge: Harvard University Press.

Turner, Bryan S. 1984. *The Body & Society*. Oxford: Basil Blackwell.

Wilson, Elizabeth. 1985. *Adorned in Dreams*. London: Virago.

33 'I'll be here with you'

Bizjack, Tony. 1987. Worshippers Are Keeping the Memory Alive. *The San Francisco Chronicle*, 10 August, 42.

Connell, Myra, Tricia Davis, Sue McIntosh and Mandy Root. 1981. Romance and Sexuality: Between the Devil and the Deep Blue Sea. In *Feminism for Girls: An Adventure Story*, eds Angela McRobbie and Trish McCabe. London: Routledge & Kegan Paul.

Coward, Rosalind. 1985. *Female Desires*. New York: Grove Press.

De Barbin, Lucy and Dary Matera. 1987. *Are You Lonesome Tonight?* New York: Villard Books.

Deen, Jeannie. 1979. A Young Girl's Fancy . . . In *Elvis: Images and Fancies*, ed. Jac L. Tharpe. Jackson: University of Mississippi Press.

Dyer, Richard. 1986. *Heavenly Bodies: Film Stars and Society*. New York: St Martin's Press.

Eagleton, Terry. 1983. *Literary Theory: An Introduction*. Minneapolis: University of Minnesota Press.

Freud, Sigmund. 1928. *Beyond the Pleasure Principle*. Translated by James Strachey. New York: Bantam Books.

Heath, Stephen. 1977/78. Notes on Suture. *Screen* 18(4): 48–76.

Hecht, Julie. 1978. I Want You, I Need You, I Love You. *Harpers* 256, 59–67.

Holzer, Hans. 1978. *Elvis Presley Speaks*. New York: Manor Books.

Kaplan, Cora. 1986. The Thorn Birds: Fiction, Fantasy, Femininity. In *Formations of Fantasy*, ed. Victor Burgin, James Donald and Cora Kaplan. New York: Methuen.

Kristeva, Julia. 1987. *Tales of Love*. Translated by Leon S. Roudiez. New York: Columbia University Press.

Lacan, Jacques. 1977. *Ecrits*. Translated by Alan Sheridan. New York: W.W. Norton.

Laplanche, Jean and Jean-Bertrand Pontalis. 1964/1987. Fantasy and the Origins of Sexuality. In *Formations of Fantasy*, eds Victor Burgin, James Donald and Cora Kaplan. New York: Methuen.

Laplanche, Jean and Jean-Bertrand Pontalis. 1973. *The Language of Psycho-analysis*. Translated by David Nicholson-Smith. New York: W.W. Norton.

Lasker, Patsy. 1979. Wife Was A Four Letter Word. In *Elvis: Portrait of a Friend*, eds Marty Lasker, Patsy Lasker and Leslie S. Smith. Memphis: Wimmer Brothers Books.

Miller, Jacques-Alain. 1977/78. Suture. *Screen* 18(4): 24–34.

Mitchell, Juliet. 1984. *Women: The Longest Revolution*. New York: Pantheon Books.

Modleski, Tania. 1982. *Loving With a Vengeance: Mass Produced Fantasies for Women*. New York: Methuen.

Modleski, Tania. 1986. Femininity as a Mas(s)querade: A Feminist Approach to Mass Culture. In *High Theory/LowCulture: Analyzing Popular Television and Film*, ed. Colin MacCabe. New York: St Martin's Press.

Moody, Raymond. 1987. *Elvis After Life*. Atlanta: Peachtree Press.

Oudart, Jean-Pierre. 1977/78. Cinema and Suture. *Screen* 18(4): 35–47.

Radway, Janet. 1984. *Reading the Romance*. Chapel Hill: The University of North Carolina Press.

San Francisco Chronicle. 5 November 1987: A10.

Vermorel, Fred and Judy. 1985. *Starlust: The Secret Fantasies of Fans*. London: W.H. Allen.

34 The psychology of achieved celebrity

Freedland, M. (1997) *All the Way: A Biography of Frank Sinatra*. London: Orion.

Friedwald, W. (1996) *Sinatra: The Song is You*. New York: Scribner.

Gray, J. (2002) Fame is the Filthy Lucre of a Celebrity Economy. *Sunday Times News Review*, Oct. 28.

Kelley, K. (1986) *My Way: The Unauthorized Biography of Frank Sinatra*. New York: Bantam Books.

Levy, S. (1998) *Rat Pack Confidential*. New York: Doubleday.

Mead, G.H. (1934) *Mind, Self and Society*. Chicago: University of Chicago Press.

Quirk, L.J. and Schoell, W. (1998) *The Rat Pack*. Dallas: Taylor.

Zehme, B. (1997) *The Way You Wear Your Hat: Frank Sinatra and the Lost Art of Livin'*. New York: HarperCollins.

35 "John, a 20-year-old Boston native with a great sense of humor"

Andrejevic, Mark (2004). *Reality TV: The Work of Being Watched*. New York: Rowan and Littlefield.

Anon. *Where Are they Now? Omarosa Manigault-Stallworth*. NBC.com. Online. Available http: <http://www.nbc.com/nbc/The_Apprentice_2/where/omarosa.shtml> (accessed June 23, 2005).

Armstrong, Craig, Cramsey, D., and Forman, T. (producers) (2004–) *Extreme Makeover: Home Edition* (television series). Los Angeles: American Broadcasting System.

Associated Press (November 9 2004). *Business Schools use tips from "Apprentice"*, MSNBC. Online. Available HTTP: <http://www.salon.com/ent/wire/2004/11/09/trump_tips/index_np.html> (accessed April 23, 2005).

Baudrillard, J. (1996). Disneyworld Company. *Liberation*, March 4 1996. Online. Available HTTP: <www.uta.edu/english/apt/collab/texts/disneyworld.html (accessed April 23, 2005).

Boorstin, Daniel (1961). *The Image*. London: Weidenfeld and Nicolson.

Burman, Al, Trump, D., and Burnett, M. (producers) (2004–). *The Apprentice*, Los Angeles: National Broadcasting System.

Burnett, Mark (producer) (2000–). *Survivor* (television series). Los Angeles: Columbia Broadcasting System.

Burnett, Mark (2001). *Survivor 2: The Field Guide*. New York: TV Books Inc.

Burnett, Mark, Katzenberg, J., and Stallone, S. (producers) (2005). *The Contender* (television series). Los Angeles: National Broadcasting Corporation.

Carter, Bill (January 17 2005) *Tough Odds as NBC Takes Reality TV into the Ring*. New York Times. Online. Available HTTP: <http://www.nytimes.com/2005/01/17/business/media/17nbc.html> (accessed April 23, 2005).

Cohen-Dickler, Susan, Cramsey, D., Dickler, J., Murray, R., Schwartz, S., Haslam, D. B., and Lundren, R. R. (producers) (2000–). *Trading Spaces* (television series). New York: The Learning Channel.

Craig, Mark (August 14, 2002). "Tiger Woods: Beyond a Shadow of a Doubt," *Star Tribune*. Online. Available HTTP: <http://www.startribune.com/stories/692/3155087.html> (accessed April 23, 2005).

Debord, Guy (1994). *The Society of the Spectacle*, trans. D. Nicholson-Smith, New York: Zone Books.

Deery, June (2004). "Reality TV as Advertainment," *Popular Communication*, 2(1):, 1–20.

du Gay, Paul (2000). "Markets and Meanings: Re-imagining Organizational Life," in Schultz, Hatch, Larson (eds). *The Expressive Organization*. Oxford: Oxford University Press.

Dyer-Witheford, Nick (1999). *Cyber-Marx, Cyber Marx: Cycles and Circuits of Struggle in High-Technology Capitalism*. Urbana and Chicago: University of Illinois Press.

Frot-Coutaz, Cecile, Warwick, K., Lythgoe, N. and Fuller, S. (producers) (2002–) *American Idol* (television series). Los Angeles: FOX Broadcasting Company.

Goffman, Erving (1967). *Interaction Ritual*. Garden City, New York: Doubleday and Company.

Gordon, C. (1991). "Governmental Rationality: An Introduction," in G. Burchell, C. Gordon and P. Miller (eds), *The Foucault Effect*. London: Allen and Unwin.

Hardt, Michael and Negri, Antonio (2000). *Empire*. Cambridge, MA: Harvard University Press.

Harvey, Abigial (producer) (2003–). *What Not to Wear* (television series). New York: The Learning Channel.

Jacoby, Melissa and Zimmerman, D.L. (2002). "Foreclosing on Fame: Exploring the Uncharted Boundaries of the Right of Publicity," *N.Y.U. Law Review*, 77: 1322–1368.

Kadlec, Daniel (2004). *Banking on the Stars*, Time.Com. Online. Available HTTP: <http://www.time.com/time/innovators/business/profile_pullman.html> (accessed April 23, 2005).

Koehn, Daryl (2001). "Ethical Issues Connected with Multi-level Marketing Schemes," *Journal of Business Ethics*, (29 1–2): 153–160.

Lasswell, Mark (August 23, 2004). *Brand Me Baby!* Broadcasting and Cable. Online. Available HTTP: <http://www.broadcastingcable.com/article/CA446675.html> (accessed April 23, 2005).

Lazzarato, Maurizio (2005) "Immaterial Labor." Trans. Collili and Emory. Online. Available HTTP: <http://www.ecn.org/valkohaalarit/english/lazz.htm> (accessed April 23 2005).

Lewicki, Roy (1981). "Organizational Seduction: Building Commitment to Organizations," *Organizational Dynamics*, 10: 5–21.

Magder, Ted (2004). "The End of TV 101," in Murray and Ouelette (eds), *Reality TV: Remaking Television Culture*. New York: New York University Press.

Mandese, Joe (January 17, 2005) *NATPE: Branded Entertainment is Topic A*. Broadcasting and Cable. Online. Available HTTP: <http://www.broadcastingcable.com/article/CA496808.html> (accessed April 25, 2005).

Mok, Ken (producer) (2001) *Tough Enough* (television series), Los Angeles: MTV.

Mok, Ken and Banks, T. (producers) (2003). *America's Next Top Model* (television series). Los Angeles: UPN.

Negri, A. (1989). *The Politics of Subversion: A Manifesto of the Twenty-First Century*. Cambridge: Polity.

Olsen, Eric (September 18, 2002). *Slaves of Celebrity*. Salon. Online. Available HTTP: <http://salon.com/ent/feature/2002/09/18/idol_contract/index.html> (accessed April 23, 2005).

Petersen, Andrea (November 8, 1996) "Metaphor of a Corporate Display: 'You Work and then you Die.' "*Wall Street Journal*, B1.

Pratt, Michael (2000). "The Good, The Bad and the Ambivalent: Managing Identification Among Amway Distributors," *Administrative Science Quarterly*, 45: 456–493.

Pratt, Michael and Rosa, Antonio (2003). "Transforming Work–Family Conflict into Commitment in Network Marketing Organizations," *Academy of Management Journal*, 46(4): 395–418.

Ross, Anthony, Stanley, D., Wernick, P., Reese, R., and Stone, S. (producers) (2003). *Joe Schmo* (television series). Los Angeles: SPIKE Television.

Schiller, Gail (February 10, 2005). *"Contender" could score financial KO. The Hollywood Reporter*. Online. Available HTTP: <http://www.hollywoodreporter.com/thr/search/article_display.jsp?vnu_content_id=1000797803> (accessed April 23, 2005).

Schiller, Gail (March 30, 2005). *Product Placement in TV, Films, Soar, Study Finds*, Reuters.com. Online. Available HTTP: <http://www.reuters.com/newsArticle.jhtml?type=industryNews&storyID=8031889> (accessed April 15 2005).

Singer, Jonathan and Mok, K. (producers) (2000). *Making the Band* (television series). Los Angeles: MTV.

Sirulnick, Dave and Lazin, L. (producers), (2004). *I Want a Famous Face* (television series). Los Angeles: MTV.

Smythe, Dallas (1977). "Communications: Blindspot of Western Marxism," *Canadian Journal of Political and Social Theory*, 1(3): 1–27.

Sternberg, Ernest. (1998). "Phantasmagoric Labor: The New Economics of Self-Presentation," *Futures*, 30(1): 3–21.

Vander Nat, Peter J. and Keep, William (2002). "Marketing Fraud: An Approach for Differentiating Multilevel Marketing from Pyramid Schemes," *Journal of Public Policy and Marketing*, 21(1): 139–151.

Van Maanen, John (1978). "People Processing," *Organizational Dynamics*, summer: 19–36.

Virno, Paolo (1996). "Notes on the 'General Intellect'," in *Theory Out Of Bounds*, Minnesota: University of Minnesota Press.

Virno, Paolo (2004). *A Grammar of the Multitude*. New York: Semiotexte.

Weed, Ken, Galan, N., and Smith, A. (producers) (2004–). *The Swan* (television series). Los Angeles: Fox Broadcasting Network.

Wernick, Andrew (1991). *Promotional Culture: Advertising, Ideology and Symbolic Expression*. Sage: London.

36 New media – new self

Burnett, R. and Marshall, P.D. *Web Theory: An Introduction*, London: Routledge.

Bruns, A. (2005) *Gatewatching: Collaborative online news production*, New York: Peter Lang.

Ifilm.com (2005) "Tom Cruise Kills Oprah" video, accessed Jan 2 2005. Oneline. <http://www.ifilm.com/ifilmdetail/2674673>.

Ifilm.com (2003) 'Arnold Schwarzenegger raver'. Online. Accessed January 2006 at <http://www.ifilm.com/viralvideo>.

Jaworoski, K. (2006) "Saturday Interview – with Michael Campbell" March 11: C3.

Kitzmann, A. (2004) *Saved from Oblivion: Documenting the Daily from Diaries to Web Cams* New York: Peter Lang.

Klaassen, Amy (2006) "Marketers lose Confidence in TV Advertising", *Adage.com*, March 22.

Liquidgeneration (2005) "Candyshop(with Tom Cruise and Katie Holmes)" animation. Online. Accessed Jan. 2006 at <http://www.liquidgeneration.com/content/a55hat.aspx?cid=1404>.

McKay, George (1998) *DIY Culture: Party and Protest in Nineties Britain*. London: Verso.

Marshall, P. David (1997) *Celebrity and Power: Fame in Contemporary Culture*, Minneapolis, MI: University of Minnesota Press.

Marshall, P.D. (2004) *New Media Cultures* London: Hodder Arnold.

Mole, T. (Nov. 2004) "Hypertrophic Celebrity," *M/C Journal*, 7(5). Online. Accessed 05 Apr. 2006 at <http://journal.media-culture.org.au/0411/08-mole.php>.

New York Times, June 21 2005 A1.

Soderberg, J. "Bush/Blair Endless Love" video. Online. Accessed January 2006 at <http://www.atmo.se>.

Taylor, Charles (1989) *Sources of the Self: The Making of Modem Identity*, Cambridge, MA: Harvard University Press.

Toffler, Alvin (1980) *The Third Wave*, New York: Morrow.

Waxman, Sharon (2005) "How Personal is Too Personal? Tom Cruise's Effusive 'Oprah' Appearance Raises Hollywood Eyebrows" *New York Times*, June 2: B1, 7.

Zalis, E. (2003) 'At Home in Cyberspace: Staging Autobiographical Scenes' *Biography*, 26(1): 84–119

38 Walter Winchell

Allen, Mearl. *Welcome to the Stork Club*. San Diego: A.S. Barnes, 1980.

Bishop, Jim. *The Mark Hellinger Story*. New York: Appleton-Century-Croft, 1952.

Bowles, Jerry G. *A Thousand Sundays: The Story of the Ed Sullivan Show*. New York: Putnam, 1980.

Broun, Heywood. "The Inside Story of Lepke and Mr. Walter Winchell." *Broun's Nutmeg* (September 2, 1939).

Carlisle, Rodney P. *Hearst and the New Deal: The Progressive as Reactionary*. New York: Garland Publishing, 1979.

Coblentz, Edmond D. *William Randolph Hearst: A Portrait in His Own Words*. New York: Simon & Schuster, 1952.

Cuneo, Ernest. *Life with Fiorello*. New York: Macmillan, 1955.

Eells, George. *Hedda and Louella: A Dual Biography of Hedda Hopper and Louella Parsons*. New York: Putnam, 1972.

Fisher, Charles. *The Columnists*. New York: Howell, Sockin, 1944.

Gauvreau, Emile. *Hot News*. New York: Macaulay Co., 1931.

Gauvreau, Emile. *My Last Million Readers*. New York: E.P. Dutton, 1941.

Gauvreau, Emile. *The Scandal Monger*. New York: Macaulay Co., 1932.

Gentry, Curt. *J. Edgar Hoover: The Man and the Secrets*. New York: Norton, 1991.

Goldman, Eric F. *The Crucial Decade — And After: America, 1945–1960*.

Hearst, William Radolph, Jr., with Jack Casserly. *The Hearsts: Father and Son*. Niwot, Colo.: Roberts Rinehart, 1991.

Hoffman, Irving. "Things You Never Knew till Now About Walter Winchell." *Radio Guide* (May 1, 1937).

Hopper, Hedda, and James Brough. *The Whole Truth and Nothing But*. New York: Pyramid Books, 1963.

Hopper, Hedda. *From Under My Hat*. Garden City, N.Y.: Doubleday, 1952.

Israel, Lee. *Kilgallen*. New York: Delacorte, 1979; paperback repring, New York: Dell, 1980.

Klurfeld, Herman. *Winchell: His Life and Times*. New York: Praeger, 1976.

Lewis, Marlo, and Mina Bess Lewis. *Prime Time*. Los Angeles: J.P. Tarcher, Inc., 1976.

Maloney, Russell. "Profile [of Leonard Lyons]." *The New Yorker* (April 7, 1945).

McEvoy, J.P. "He Snoops to Conquer." *Saturday Evening Post* (August 13, 1938).

McKelway, St. Clair. *Gossip: The Life and Times of Walter Winchell*. New York: Viking Press, 1940.

Morrell, Parker. "Mr. and Mrs. Walter Winchell." *Ladies' Home Journal* (June 1940).

Odets, Clifford. *The Time Is Ripe: The 1940 Journal of Clifford Odets*. New York: Grove Press, 1988.

Parsons, Louella O. *Tell It to Louella*. New York: Putnam, 1961.

Parsons, Louella O. *The Gay Illiterate*. Garden City, N.Y.: Doubleday, 1944.

Pringle, Henry F. "Portrait of Walter Winchell." *American Mercury* (February 1937).

Reichenbach, Harry, as told to David Freedman. *Phantom Fame: The Anatomy of Ballyhoo*. Introduction by Walter Winchell. New York: Simon & Schuster, 1931.

Reynolds, Quentin. "Have You a Reservation?" *Collier's* (October 1, 1938).

Sobel, Bernard. *Broadway Heartbeat: Memoirs of a Press Agent*. New York: Hermitage House, 1953.

Sobol, Louis. *The Longest Street: A Memoir*. New York: Crown, 1968.

Stack, Philip. *Love in Manhattan*. Introduction by Walter Winchell. New York: Liveright, 1932.

Sylvester, Robert. *In Pursuit of Gotham: Culture and Commerce in New York*. New York: Oxford University Press, 1992.

Sylvester, Robert. *No Cover Charge: A Backward Look at the Night Clubs*. New York: Dial, 1956.

Sylvester, Robert. *Notes of a Guilty Bystander*. Englewood Cliffs, N.J.: Prentice-Hall, 1970.

Tebbel, John. *The Life and Times of William Randolph Hearst*. New York: E.P. Dutton, 1952.

Thomas, Bob. *Winchell*. Garden City, N.Y.: Doubleday, 1971.

Tully, Jim. *A Dozen and One*. Hollywood: Murray & Gee, 1943.

Turkus, Burton, and Sid Feder. *Murder Inc.: The Story of "The Syndicate."* New York: Farrar, Straus and Young, 1951.

Walker, Danton. *Danton's Inferno: The Story of a Columnist and How He Grew*. New York: Hastings House, 1955.

Walker, Stanley. *City Editor*. New York: Frederick A. Stokes, 1934.

Walker, Stanley. *Mrs. Astor's Horse*. New York: Frederick A. Stokes, 1935.

Walker, Stanley. *The Night Club Era*. New York: Frederick A. Stokes, 1933.

Weiner, Ed. *The Damon Runyon Story*. New York: Longmans Green, 1948.

Whelan, Russell. "Inside the Stork Club." *American Mercury* (September 1944).

Woollcott, Alexander. "The Little Man with the Big Voice." *Hearst's International Cosmopolitan Magazine* (May 1933).

Zerbe, Jerome, and Brendan Gill. *Happy Times*. New York: Harcourt, Brace, Jovanovich, 1973.

39 The negotiated celebration

Cieply, M. (1988). "Hollywood's High-Powered Image Machine." *Los Angeles Times Magazine*, July 10, 1988.

Elliott, P. (1977) "Media Organization and Occupations: An Overview." *Mass Communication and Society*. Sage Publications.

Freidson, E. (1984) "The Changing Nature of Professional Control." *Annual Review of Sociology*. p. 1–20.

Gaines, J. (1991) *Contested Culture: The Image, the Voice, and the Law*. Chapel Hill: University of North Carolina Press.

Gandy, O. (1982) *Beyond Agenda Setting*. Norwood, N.J.: Ablex Publishing.

Hirsch, P. (1972) "Processing Fads and Fashions: An Organization-Set Analysis of Cultural Industry Systems." *American Journal of Sociology*. 77, 639–59.

Koch, N. (1991) "The Hollywood Treatment." *Columbia Journalism Review*. January/ February, 25–31.

Yoffe, E. (1991). "E! Is for Entertainment – Twenty-Four Hours a Day." *Newsweek*, August 12, p. 58.

Index

NOTE: Page numbers in **bold** indicate a chapter by an author.

Related titles from Routledge

The Actress:
Hollywood Acting and the Female Star
Karen Hollinger

The Actress: Hollywood Acting and the Female Star investigates the contemporary film actress both as an artist and as an ideological construct. Divided into two sections, *The Actress* first examines the major issues in studying film acting, stardom, and the Hollywood actress. Part Two examines five case studies: Meryl Streep, Susan Sarandon, Jodie Foster, Angela Bassett, and Gwyneth Paltrow, each of whose careers exemplify key issues in the creation of film stardom, the function of acting style, and the creation of celebrity.

Combining theories of screen acting and of film stardom, The Actress presents a synthesis of methodologies and offers the student and scholar a new approach to these two subjects of study. Throughout the book, Hollinger emphasizes the craft of acting, a dimension of the subject often given less attention than other elements in the study of female stardom.

ISBN 13: 978–0–415–97791–3 (hbk)
ISBN 13: 978–0–415–97792–0 (pbk)

Available at all good bookshops
For ordering and further information please visit:
www.routledge.com

Related titles from Routledge

Hitch Your Antenna To The Stars!
Early Television and Broadcast Stardom
Susan Murray

'*Hitch your Antenna to the Stars* is a tour de force. In tracing the centrality of TV stars for the economic and aesthetic development of the early medium, Susan Murray breaks important new ground for media studies. Masterfully researched and written in a lucid, intelligent style, this book is required reading for media scholars, cultural historians, and anyone interested in understanding the origins of today's celebrity culture.' – *Anna McCarthy, New York University*

'Susan Murray's path-breaking history of early television in the USA should be a must- read for anyone interested in media studies. She skillfully integrates analysis of broadcast networks, sponsors, advertising agencies, talent unions, talent agencies, and the audience to help us fully understand the meanings generated in 1950s broadcast stardom. I learned something new from every page.' – *Douglas Gomery, University of Maryland*

'*Hitch Your Antenna to the Stars* makes a significant contribution to our understanding of the era of network television in the United States. Susan Murray's carefully researched and engagingly written examination of the early history of TV stardom brings together issues of industry form, media audiences, and social context in original and highly productive ways.' – *William Boddy, City University of New York*

Hitch Your Antenna to the Stars! is the first cultural and industrial history of early television stardom. Susan Murray argues that television stars were central to the growth and development of American broadcasting and were used not only to promote programs and the sale of television sets and advertised consumer goods, but also to established network identities.

Through profiles of well-known performers including Milton Berle, Sid Caesar, Jackie Gleason, and Lucille Ball, she shows how the television industry gave birth to the idea of TV stars and established a system of star production and management notably different from the Hollywood star system of the studio era.

ISBN 13: 978–0–415–97130–0 (hbk)
ISBN 13: 978–0–415–97131–7 (pbk)

Available at all good bookshops
For ordering and further information please visit:
www.routledge.com

Related titles from Routledge

Introduction to the Theories of Popular Culture
Second Edition
Dominic Strinati

Praise for the first edition:
'An excellent introduction to popular culture. Complex theories are presented in a clear and concise manner' – *Stephen Dawkins, Park Lane College*

An Introduction to Theories of Popular Culture is a clear and comprehensive guide to the major theories of popular culture. Dominic Strinati provides a critical assessment of the ways in which these theories have tried to understand and evaluate popular culture in modern societies.

Among the theories and ideas the book introduces are mass culture, the Frankfurt School and the culture industry, semiology and structuralism, Marxism, feminism, postmodernism and cultural populism. Strinati explains how theorists such as Adorno, Barthes, Althusser and Hebdige have grappled with the many forms of popular culture, from jazz to the Americanization of British popular culture, from Hollywood cinema to popular television series, and from teen magazines to the spy novel.
Each chapter includes a guide to key texts for further reading and there is also a comprehensive bibliography. This new edition has been fully revised and updated.

ISBN 13: 978–0–415–23499–3 (hbk)
ISBN 13: 978–0–415–23500–6 (pbk)

Available at all good bookshops
For ordering and further information please visit:
www.routledge.com

Related titles from Routledge

Framing Celebrity

Su Holmes and Sean Redmond

'This important new book stakes out the breadth of current work on the attractions and obsessions of celebrity culture. Fame, power, adoration, idolization, gossip, madness, and death are all here. *Framing Celebrity* poses significant questions about the mediation of public identities and the popular figures who undeniably exert such influence in our lives.' – *Dr Paul McDonald, Reader in Film Studies & Director of the Centre for Research in Film and Audiovisual Cultures, Roehampton University*

Celebrity culture has a pervasive presence in our everyday lives – perhaps more so than ever before. It shapes not simply the production and consumption of media content but also the social values through which we experience the world. This collection analyses this phenomenon, bringing together essays which explore celebrity across a range of media, cultural and political contexts.

The authors investigate topics such as the intimacy of fame, political celebrity, stardom in American 'quality' television (Sarah Jessica Parker), celebrity 'reality' TV (*I'm a Celebrity ... Get Me Out of Here!*), the circulation of the porn star, the gallery film (*David*/David Beckham), the concept of cartoon celebrity (*The Simpsons*), fandom and celebrity (k.d. lang, *NSYNC), celebrity in the tabloid press, celebrity magazines (*heat*, *Celebrity Skins*), the fame of the serial killer and narratives of mental illness in celebrity culture.

The collection is organized into four themed sections:

- Fame Now broadly examines the contemporary contours of fame as they course through new media sites (such as 'reality' TV and the internet) and different social, cultural and political spaces.
- Fame Body attempts to situate the star or celebrity body at the centre of the production, circulation and consumption of contemporary fame.
- Fame Simulation considers the increasingly strained relationship between celebrity and artifice and 'authenticity'.
- Fame Damage looks at the way the representation of fame is bound up with auto-destructive tendencies or dissolution.

ISBN 13: 978–0–415–37709–6 (hbk)
ISBN 13: 978–0–415–37710–2 (pbk)

Available at all good bookshops
For ordering and further information please visit:

www.routledge.com